Strategy and Policy
Concepts and Cases

Strategy and Policy

Concepts and Cases

ARTHUR A. THOMPSON, JR.

A. J. STRICKLAND, III

both of
The University of Alabama

1978

BUSINESS PUBLICATIONS, INC.   Dallas, Texas   75243
Irwin-Dorsey Limited   Georgetown, Ontario   L7G 4B3

ISBN 0-256-02083-3
Library of Congress Catalog Card No. 77–085780

Printed in the United States of America

3 4 5 6 7 8 9 0 MP 5 4 3 2 1 0 9

PREFACE

THIS BOOK is intended for use in the capstone course in "business policy" customarily required of all business degree students. It offers both a thoroughgoing survey of strategy/policy concepts and a wide selection of cases suitable for acquainting business students with the manager's role in directing the total enterprise. We have incorporated four differentiating features that we think are noteworthy:

1. Six chapters of text are devoted to a wide-ranging, up-to-date synthesis of the growing body of literature about corporate strategy and policy administration. The conceptual treatments expose students to a systematic review of the prevailing views and ideas about the manager as an architect and implementer of strategy. The focus throughout is on strategic management— the process of choosing and defining purposes and objectives, formulating and implementing a viable strategy, and monitoring strategic performance and results. We have endeavored to present a complete picture of management's functions and responsibilities in charting the course of a business and to indicate the central significance of strategy and policy in managing organizations effectively. Terms and concepts are thoroughly explored. So also are the kinds of problems and issues that bear directly on an organization's ultimate success. The orientation is consistently pragmatic and managerial—our main objective being to give students the raw material needed to understand and apply the subject matter of strategy and policy in characteristic kinds of management situations.

2. Special pains have been taken to illustrate the use of strategy/policy concepts in actual practice. All six chapters of text are laced with concrete examples of the triumphs and failures of companies and their managements— what has worked, what hasn't, and why. However, since the ways in which managers and companies rely upon strategy/policy concepts cannot always be meaningfully presented in a passing sentence, footnote, or brief paragraph, we have included a series of in-depth *illustration capsules* offering extended insights into how strategy/policy concepts underlie management actions. These capsules, boxed off so as not to interrupt the discussion, keep the bridge between concept and application always open to the reader. None are

v

"trumped-up" or "one-of-a-kind attention grabbers"; rather, they are no-nonsense, practical applications that students will find worthwhile, enjoyable, and informative. Most involve companies or people that the student will have heard of previously and several are suitable for use as case incidents.

3. A full chapter is devoted to (1) giving students positive direction in how to size up and evaluate a company and (2) orienting them to the pedagogy of the case method. In our experience, many students are unsure about how to conduct a full-blown analysis of a company from a strategic management and policy point of view. This chapter, intended to lessen their uncertainties, includes a suggested approach for evaluating a company, a thorough checklist of areas to probe in sizing up a company's strategic position and identifying specific strengths and weaknesses, and a brief review on how to calculate and interpret key financial ratios. Also included is a discussion of the nature of cases and the case method, pointers on how to learn from cases, how to prepare a case for class discussion, and guidelines for written case analyses.

4. The 33 cases (5 of which have multiple parts), along with an industry note, offer a deliberately planned and balanced mix of organizational situations and circumstances for student analysis. The cases, prepared not just by the authors but also by seasoned case researchers all across the country and generously contributed to this volume, represent what we feel is a very attractive package, especially for senior-level students. There are short cases, long cases, multiple-part cases, "two-day" cases, cases about big companies and cases about small companies, cases about not-for-profit organizations, cases that students will closely identify with, "change of pace" cases, and two pairs of cases that allow intraindustry comparison. Although the cases are arranged in a logical sequence keyed to the text discussion, the arrangement is flexible; changes can readily be made to suit particular teaching preferences and techniques. (The *Instructor's Manual* contains several topical outlines and sequences for teaching the cases, as well as offering comprehensive teaching notes and suggestions on how each case may be used.)

A brief word about the philosophical underpinning of the book is in order. The entire text is predicated on the thesis that the role of the policy course in the business school curriculum, in addition to offering an integrating experience, is to develop an ability to see the enterprise as a whole and to understand how and why the various functions of the business are interdependent and need to be coordinated if the organization is to perform effectively and achieve the desired results. Strategy/policy concepts, even when synthesized and integrated, do not constitute a "theory" attended by elegant logic and analytical rigor in the traditional sense. But they very definitely do represent a "way of thinking," an approach, and a perspective that goes to the heart of what a business is about and how managerial effectiveness and organizational performance might be improved.

Decisions as to strategy and policy determine the nature of the business a company is to engage in, its character, and the direction it is heading. These are important matters, and affect managers and employees at every level. Thus, although many business school graduates may never reach positions of *top* management or have general management responsibilities, they still need a solid understanding of the overall company point of view—or what is often referred to as a business policy perspective. Hence, the thrust of the text material and the cases selected is the organization in its totality—the environment in which it operates, its corporate strategy, and its internal administrative activities. The emphasis, specifically, is on the kinds of problems and issues that affect the success of the entire organization.

The posture which we hope the reader will adopt is twofold: (1) that of generalist rather than specialist and (2) that of practicing manager rather than curious observer or impartial researcher. Such a stance not only is conducive to the study of business policy but it also contributes to the future development of students as managers. In our view, the business policy course is strategically positioned in the curriculum to build student self-confidence in what has been learned from previous courses and to "put it all together" (probably for the first time). The study of business policy concepts and cases should, ideally, serve to get students thinking seriously about their own management styles and approaches to running a business and to instill a sense of professionalism and pride that will launch them on their careers with a positive note.

Appropriately, though, in a competitive enterprise economy it is up to "the market" to decide how well our overall purpose has been executed and whether we have adequately met the needs for a book that is effective in conveying the essence and significance of the business policy discipline. We invite and welcome your remarks.

Acknowledgments

Our intellectual debt to the writers and academicians upon whose concepts and contributions we have leaned heavily will be obvious to any reader familiar with the literature of strategy and policy. So also is our debt to the case researchers whose efforts appear herein and to the companies and organizations whose experiences and situations comprise the case studies.

To the case contributors, especially, go our thanks and appreciation. The importance of good, comprehensive business policy cases in contributing to a worthwhile study of strategy and policy cannot be overestimated. This is so because research into strategy and policy matters has yet to produce a sizable body of general statements and principles upon which either academicians or practitioners can rely. The literature, although considerable and growing, includes mainly reported experience, sage advice based on this experience, and just the first fruits of empirical research. These are of course important, but the most useful strategy/policy literature for pedagogical purposes is still case studies. Without good cases that present the vehicles for diagnosing and evaluating strategic situations, for applying and testing strategy/policy concepts, and for drawing limited generalizations, the teaching of business policy would indeed be in sad disorder. We trust, therefore, that writing business policy cases will be a "growth industry" and that appropriate recognition will continue to be given to such efforts.

The following reviewers offered insightful comments and helpful suggestions for improving earlier drafts of the manuscript: W. Harvey Hegarty, Indiana University; Roger Evered, Pennsylvania State University; Charles B. Saunders, The University of Kansas; Rhae M. Swisher, Troy State University; and Claude I. Shell, Eastern Michigan University. Many of their valued recommendations have been incorporated.

Sincere gratitude goes to our several typists and to Kate Barnes, staff assistant, all of whom toiled many long hours under insistent prodding but still retained their patience and good humor. To our wives, Hasseline and Kitty, who have understandingly tolerated our diversions of time and energy and our absences from family activities, we happily announce our intentions to reform—at least for a while—and redress the imbalance.

Naturally, as custom properly dictates, we accept responsibility for whatever errors of fact, deficiencies in logic or in exposition, and oversights that may remain.

January 1978   ARTHUR A. THOMPSON, JR.
                                  A. J. STRICKLAND III

CONTENTS

List of Case Contributors   ix

**Part I
INTRODUCTION**

1. **Strategy and Policy: A General Management Overview**   3

Key Concepts and Terminology. The Interrelationships among Purpose, Objectives, Goals, Strategy, and Policy. Who is Responsible for Strategy and Policy? The Roles of Management. The Manager as Organization Strategist. The Manager as Organization Builder. The Manager as Personal and Organizational Leader. Is the General Manager's Job Too Demanding? How Policy Fits into the Management Picture. Strategy, Policy, and the Management Process.

**Part II
FORMULATING ORGANIZATIONAL STRATEGY**

2. **Concepts of Organizational Strategy**   29

The Need to Consciously Design Strategy. Where Strategy Formulation Begins—with a Concept. Arriving at a Definition of "What Is Our Business and What Should It Be?" The Common Thread—Is It Necessary? The Levels of Strategy. The Determinants of Strategy: *Product-Market Opportunities. Organizational Competence and Resources. Environmental Threats. Personal Values and Aspirations. Societal Constraints and Social Responsibility. Strategy and Organizational "Personality."* The Complete Strategy.

3. **Identifying Strategic Alternatives**   60

The Basic Strategic Alternatives: *Concentration on a Single Business. Horizontal Integration. Vertical Integration. Diversification Alternatives. Joint Ventures. Innovation Strategies. Retrenchment Strategies. Divestiture Strategies. Liquidation Strategies.* Combination Strategies. When Some Strategies Are More Logical than Others.

ix

4.   Strategic Evaluation and Strategic Choice   91

Developing a Strategic Profile. Auditing the Competitive Environment. The Role of Competition in Strategy Evaluation. Gearing Strategy to the Economic Environment. Narrowing Down the List of Alternatives. Aspects of Strategic Evaluation. Making the Strategic Choice. A Perspective View of the Strategy Formulation Process.

Part III
ORGANIZATION AND POLICY ADMINISTRATION

5.   Structuring a Strategically Effective Organization   115

Strategy and Organization. Stages of Organizational Development. Testing Organizational Adequacy. Approaches to Organizational Diagnosis. Making Use of Organizational Principles. Organizational Choices. *The Functional Organization Structure. Geographic Departmentation. Process, Market, Channel, or Customer Departmentation. Divisional and Product Group Organization. Newer Forms of Organization.* Perspectives on Organization Choice.

6.   Managing Organizational Processes   147

Motivational Considerations. Instilling a Spirit of Performance. Leadership. Instituting Management Controls. Communication and Management Control. Problem Areas in Managing People. Playing "the Power Game."

Part IV
ANALYZING ACTUAL MANAGEMENT PROBLEMS

7.   From Concepts to Cases: Practicing at Being a Manager   169

Practicing Management via Case Analysis. Why Use Cases to Practice Management? Objectives of the Case Method. Preparing a Case for Class Discussion. The Classroom Experience. Preparing a Written Case Analysis. Keeping Tabs on Your Performance.

Part V
CASES

A.   The General Manager: Tasks, Functions, Responsibilities   191

1.   Hewlett-Packard Company—A Time for Strategy
       Reappraisal? 191
2.   United Products, Inc., 209
3.1   The University of Arkansas Athletic Department (A), 224
3.2   The University of Arkansas Athletic Department (B), 230
4.   Riverview Apartments, 237
5.   Fourwinds Marina, 250
6.   Steadman Realty Company, 264

B.   Strategy: Evaluation and Alternatives   **281**

7.   Bright Coop Company, Inc., 281
8.   Wall Drug Store, 303
9.1   Ivie Electronics, Inc. (A), 322
9.2   Ivie Electronics, Inc. (B), 331
10.   Cottage Gardens, Inc., 340
11.   Jackson Brewing Company (C), 362

C.   Strategy Implementation and Policy Administration   **403**

12.   Alpha Electronic Systems Corporation, 403
13.   Narragansett Bay Shipbuilding and Drydock Company (A), 414
14.   Village Inn, 426
15.   The Spring Thing, 440
16.   Morgan Hospital, 453
17.1   Small City (B), 472
17.2   Small City (D), 485
17.3   Small City (E), 501
18.   Kramer Carton Company, 510
19.1   Public Assistance (A), 530
19.2   Public Assistance (B), 552
20.1   Citizens State Bank and Trust Company (A), 575
20.2   Citizens State Bank and Trust Company (B), 587
21.   Coral Industries, Inc., 599
22.   Better Burgers, Inc., 616

D.   Strategy Review and Reappraisal   **641**

23.   The Devil's Own Wine Shoppe, 641
24.   Triangle Construction Company, 657
25.   Northern Scrap Processors, Inc. (A), 668
26.   A Note on the Petroleum Industry, 686
27.   Exxon Corporation, 722
28.   Mobil Corporation, 770
29.   Alabama Power Company, 809

E.   Relating Corporate Strategy and Policy to the External Environment   **857**

30.   Consolidated Edison Company, 857
31.   Champions of Competition versus the Breakfast of Champions: The Case of Ready-to-Eat Cereals, 885
32.   A. H. Robins Company, 915
33.   *The Wall Street Journal* versus Combustion Engineering, 931

Index of Cases   **947**
Subject Index   **949**

LIST OF CASE CONTRIBUTORS

Case:

1. Roger M. Atherton and Dennis M. Crites
2. Jeffrey C. Shuman
3.1 Robert D. Hay and Frank Broyles
3.2 Robert D. Hay, Lon Farrell, Ed Fedosky, and Frank Broyles
4. Leon Joseph Rosenberg
5. W. Harvey Hegarty and Harry Kelsey
6. Richard I. Levin and Ian Cooper
7. B. G. Bizzell and Ed. D. Roach
8. James D. Taylor, Robert L. Johnson, and Gene B. Iverson
9.1 Melvin J. Stanford
9.2 Melvin J. Stanford
10. Bruce P. Coleman
11. Jeffrey A. Barach with Rodney A. Eggen, John Dausman, Michael Gerringer, William Paul, and Thomas Peterson
12. William R. Lockridge
13. Louis K. Bragaw and William R. Allen with Daniel J. McCarthy and Robert Ames
14. Diana Johnston, Russ King, and Jay T. Knippen
15. Bruce H. Fairchild and Mike E. Miles
16. Richard A. Elnicki
17.1 George G. Eddy and Burnard H. Sord
17.2 George G. Eddy and Burnard H. Sord
17.3 George G. Eddy
18. Richard E. Hill
19.1 John R. Russell
19.2 John R. Russell
20.1 Robert K. Landrum and Charles S. Sherwood
20.2 Robert K. Landrum and Charles S. Sherwood
21. Charles R. Scott, Jr.
22. J. Owen Weber and Kenneth R. Van Voorhis
23. Eleanor Casebier and Manning Hanline
24. Melvin J. Stanford
25. Richard S. Harrigan and Burnard H. Sord
26. Arthur A. Thompson, Jr., and Victor Gray
27. Arthur A. Thompson, Jr., and Victor Gray
28. Victor Gray and Arthur A. Thompson, Jr.
29. Arthur A. Thompson, Jr.
30. Robert J. Litschert and Arthur A. Thompson, Jr.
31. Anthony Hourihan with Jesse W. Markham
32. Robert J. Litschert
33. Arthur A. Thompson, Jr., and A. J. Strickland, III

PART I

Introduction

Chapter 1
Strategy and Policy: A General Management Overview

STRATEGY AND POLICY: A GENERAL MANAGEMENT OVERVIEW

*"Cheshire Puss," she [Alice] began . . . "would you
please tell me which way I ought to go from here?"
"That depends on where you want to get to," said the
cat.*

Lewis Carroll

EFFECTIVE organization strategies and policies are key ingredients of successful enterprise. The caliber of an organization's product-market strategy and how well it is executed is what separates the high performers from the low performers. Differences in market share, in technological accomplishments, in customer loyalty, in product innovation, in quality of manufacture, in sales growth, in aftertax profit, in return on investment, and in reputation and image all tend to derive, in whole or in large part, from an astute and timely organizational *strategy* that has been implemented through unified *policy* actions.

Just why strategy and policy are dominant contributors to organizational success is rooted in the familiar expression "if you don't know where you are going, any road will take you there." For an organization to avert aimless drift and mediocre performance, it should have a well-defined purpose which sets forth, either explicitly or implicitly, the mission of the organization and the services it intends to render to society. Its managers should reach a workable consensus on the gut issue of "what is our business, what will it be, and what should it be?" Lacking this, an organization's resources risk being drained by false starts and misdirected efforts. In addition, every organization needs a good concept of how it will produce and distribute its product offering; this means putting together a *comprehensive* strategic plan whose parts fit together like the pieces of a puzzle. It must assemble the resources needed for effective strategy execution and, in particular, build an organization with some distinctive competencies in its product line and/or in its methods of production and distribution (lest it fall victim to inefficiency and an inability to attract a clientele). Moreover, an organization must establish and maintain viable relationships with its many constituencies—suppliers, customers, employees, stockholders, creditors, and so on. It must have the staying power to win out over product-market uncertainties, the rigors of change, growth, and, in the case of profit-seeking enterprises, competition.

An organization's overall master plan for dealing with these real-life aspects of its existence is the core of what managerial strategy and policy is all about.[1] In general, then, *strategy and policy embrace the managerial activities associated with defining a purpose and mission, working out a comprehensive master plan for the organization, marshaling the resources requisite for strategic accomplishment, and directing pursuit of chosen goals and objectives.* Together, a well-conceived strategy/policy framework offers a solid conceptual basis for the direction of the total enterprise. It provides a perspective for evaluating the whole company from a general management point of view.

If it is not already obvious, it follows that the managerial tasks comprising the strategy-policy nexus are vital to all types of organizations, large or small, profit or not for profit. Thus, the study of managerial strategy and policy is fundamentally as applicable to a local real estate firm, a small manufacturer of chemicals, a chain of drugstores, or the Pittsburgh Steelers as to IBM or U.S. Steel. It speaks to the problems of managing hospitals, educational institutions, a local YMCA, the National Organization for Women, a state department of public safety, the Ford Foundation, Sigma Chi Fraternity, the Roman Catholic Church, and the U.S. Postal Service just as much as to privately owned, profit-motivated enterprises. In succeeding pages a serious attempt will be made to elaborate on the *general* applicability of the strategy-policy discipline to all sizes and types of organizations, although the major emphasis will, quite frankly, focus on profit-oriented enterprises operating in a competitive environment.

KEY CONCEPTS AND TERMINOLOGY

It will prove useful if, at the outset, we get a firmer grip on some of the key concepts and terminology that serve as the foundation for this text. This is especially important because throughout the literature of management such terms as purpose, objectives, goals, strategy, and policy are each subject to a variety of subtle meanings and interpretations.

Purpose.   At the heart of every organization is its *purpose* (or mission). Simply stated, *purpose* consists of a long-term vision of what the organization seeks to do and the reasons why it exists. Purpose specifies, in concrete and operational terms, not platitudes, exactly what activities the organization performs or intends to perform and the kind of organization it is or

---

[1] William H. Newman, "Shaping the Master Strategy of Your Firm," *California Management Review*, vol. 9, no. 3 (Spring 1967), pp. 77–88.

intends to be.[2] Put another way, purpose is an organization's concept of itself and its service mission to customers and to society, expressed in terms that give the organization meaning and legitimacy. In this sense, purpose delineates the theoretical and conceptual foundation upon which the organization rests and the nature of the business (or businesses) in which it intends to engage.

Rogers cites Westinghouse Electric Corp. in 1969 as having the following purpose and mission statement:

> It is the basic purpose of Westinghouse, in all of its decisions and actions, to attain and maintain the following:
>
> 1. A continuous high level of profits which places it in the top bracket of industry in its rate of return on invested capital.
> 2. Steady growth in profits, sales volume and high turnover investment at rates exceeding those of the national economy as a whole.
> 3. Equitable distribution of the fruits of continuously increasing productivity of management, capital and labor among stockholders, employees and the public.
> 4. Design, production and marketing, on a worldwide basis, of products and services which are useful and beneficial to its customers, to society and to mankind.
> 5. Continuous responsiveness to the needs of its customers and of the public, creating a current product line which is First in Performance and a steady flow of product improvements, new products and new services which increase customer satisfaction.
> 6. A vital, dynamic product line by continuous addition of new products and businesses and prompt termination of old products and businesses when their economic worth, as measured by their profit performance, becomes substandard.
> 7. The highest ethical standards in the conduct of all its affairs.
> 8. An environment in which all employees are enabled, encouraged and stimulated to perform continuously at their highest potential of output and creativity and to attain the highest possible level of job satisfaction in the spirit of the Westinghouse Creed.
>
> These eight points are indivisible. Together, as a unit, they state the fundamental management philosophy of the Westinghouse Electric Corporation.[3]

Professor George A. Steiner has reported that the purposes of Lockheed Aircraft during the late 1960s were:

> 1. To be the major company satisfying in the highest technical sense the national security needs of the United States and its allies in space, air, land, and sea.

---

[2] C. Roland Christensen, Kenneth R. Andrews, and Joseph L. Bower, *Business Policy: Text and Cases*, 3d ed. (Homewood, Ill.: Richard D. Irwin, Inc., 1973), p. 107.

[3] Westinghouse Electric Corporation, *Guide to Business Planning* (Pittsburgh, 1969), p. 1, as cited and quoted in David C. D. Rogers, *Business Policy and Planning: Text and Cases* (Englewood Cliffs, N.J.: Prentice-Hall, Inc., 1977), p. 84.

2. To employ technical resources in meeting the nondefense needs of governments and the requirements of commercial markets.
3. To achieve continuous growth of profits at a rate needed to attract and retain stockholder investment.
4. To recognize and appropriately discharge our responsibilities for the welfare of our employees, the communities in which we do business, and society as a whole.
5. To maintain a large proportion of sales in advanced technical products bearing the Lockheed name.
6. To maintain continuity of the enterprise by holding relatively low rates of change of ownership, management, and employees.[4]

Some organizations endeavor to conceal their "true purpose" in obscure and all-inclusive terminology. An umbrellalike statement that "our purpose is to serve the food needs of the nation" can mean anything from farming in Nebraska to operating a vegetable cannery to delivering bread to manufacturing farm machinery to running a Kentucky Fried Chicken franchise. Such statements of purpose are little more than noble rhetoric and are certainly too broad to guide management action. Generally speaking, sweeping statements of mission and purpose are inappropriate and wrongheaded. In the first place, a stated purpose is never "carved in stone," so the only danger of an organization "locking itself in" is contrived rather than real. The concept of purpose is properly dynamic not static and many, if not most, organizations should and do find it desirable to modify or fine tune their purposes from time to time. This is particularly true of firms which choose to diversify into activities that extend well beyond the original business (as when a sugar refining company diversifies into bananas). And even without diversification, a well-conceived purpose will seldom stay current for more than a decade or two.

Second, without a clear definition of purpose it is impossible to design sharply focused, results-oriented objectives, strategies, and policies. Purpose is the starting point for rational managerial action and for the design of organization structure, processes, and procedures. Put simply, managerial effectiveness tends to begin with clarity of purpose—with a clear-cut concept of the business.

A key feature of purpose is that its focus should be external rather than internal. Purpose is defined by the want a customer satisfies when he or she obtains the organization's product or service. In this regard, Peter Drucker maintains:

> To know what a business is we have to start with its *purpose*. Its purpose must lie outside of the business itself. In fact, it must lie in society since business enterprise is an organ of society. There is only one valid definition of business purpose: *to create a customer.*[5]

---

[4] George A. Steiner, *Top Management Planning* (New York: the Macmillan Company, 1969), p. 146.

[5] Peter Drucker, *Management: Tasks, Responsibilities, Practices* (New York: Harper & Row Publishers, 1974), p. 61.

Drucker's view, which in effect makes profit necessary but not sufficient as the underlying purpose and motive of enterprise, correctly emphasizes that unless an organization performs a function that is deemed legitimate and useful by a sufficiently large number of customers (and that is also within the law), it is destined to wither and die. The customer is the foundation of an organization and keeps it in existence.[6] Moreover, every organization, profit-seeking or not for profit, has an implied contract with society that calls not only for the organization's purpose to be ratified by its customers but also for the organization's activities to be consistent with the expectation of society at large. Society has, after all, entrusted a portion of its pool of scarce, productive resources to the organization and thus has the right to require they not be misused. For this reason, failure to act in socially responsible ways or to perform socially useful functions quite properly tends to trigger serious societal scrutiny of an organization's activities and, usually, a reevaluation by the organization of its purpose and behavior.

Organization Objectives. *Objectives* specify the end points of an organization's purpose and the results sought through the ongoing, long-run operations of the organization. These outcomes may consist not only of the desired results insofar as the organization's customer is concerned but also of what the organization perceives as the long-range results it intends to achieve internally.

Objectives are neither abstractions nor mere good intentions; on the contrary, if properly formulated they are the concrete, measurable *action commitments* by which the purpose of the organization is to be achieved.[7] To have meaningful impact, objectives must be *operational;* that is, they must be capable of being converted into specific targets and specific actions. They must give direction. They must set forth long-run organizational priorities. They must become the basis for work and for achievement. They must serve as the standards against which performance is to be measured.

Since the role of objectives is to guide the concentration of resources and efforts toward the desired ends, objectives should be selective as opposed to all-encompassing. Nonetheless, it is rarely possible to rely upon only a single objective. In general, objectives are needed in *all areas* on which the long-term *survival* and *success* of the organization depend.[8] More specifically, an organization has need for:

1. *Marketing objectives*—so as to create a viable, sustainable customer base and market for its products/services.
2. *Technology-innovation objectives*—so as to keep products/services up to date and competitive (thereby avoiding obsolescence).
3. *Profitability objectives*—so as to cover the risks of economic activity, to test the validity of the organization's contributions, and to generate the

[6] Ibid.

[7] Ibid., pp. 99–102.

[8] Ibid., p. 100. See, also, Charles H. Granger, "The Hierarchy of Objectives," *Harvard Business Review,* vol. 42, no. 3 (May–June 1963), pp. 63–74.

financial capital requisite for preserving (and enhancing if necessary) the organization's productive capability.

4. *Efficiency objectives*—so as to remain cost competitive and to make judicious use of the economic resources entrusted by society to its care.

5. *Resource supply objectives*—so as to help ensure the availability of human, capital, and natural resources needed for continuing to supply customers (society) with the organization's products/services.

6. *Social responsibility objectives*—so as to keep a watchful eye on whether and how the organization is discharging its obligations to society and to be in a position to take full responsibility for the impact which its activities have on the environment at large.

The foregoing list is, of course, by no means exhaustive. An organization may wish to have objectives relating to future growth, its position in the industry, its overall size and degree of diversity, recognition as a leader, technological prowess, the financial payoffs it seeks to provide stockholders (dividends, capital gains, earnings per share, price-earnings ratios, and so on), competitive strength, and posture toward risk.

In establishing its objectives, an organization should, again, take care not to resort to high-sounding rhetoric and should avoid objectives which are in a

Illustration Capsule 1

Examples of "Good" and "Bad" Organizational Objectives

Examples of "Good" (Clearly Defined) Objectives	*Remarks*
1. "We plan to make Product X the number one selling brand in its field in terms of units sold."	Leaves little doubt as to the intended sales objective and market standing.
2. "We strive to be a leader, not a follower, in introducing new products and in implementing new technologies by spending no less than 5 percent of sales revenue for R&D."	Indicates an attempt to remain on or near technological frontiers and says how this attempt is to be financed.
3. "Our profit objective is to increase earnings per share by a minimum of 8 percent annually and to earn at least a 20 percent after-tax return on net worth."	Clear, concrete, and readily measured.
4. "We seek to produce the most durable, maintenance-free product that money can buy."	An obvious focus on being the leader with respect to high quality.
5. "It is our objective to help assure that the wood products needs of this country are met by planting two seedlings for every tree we cut and by following exemplary forest management practices."	A specific commitment.

Illustration Capsule 1 (continued)

Examples of "Bad" (Poorly Phrased) Objectives	*Remarks*
1. "Our objective is to maximize sales revenue and unit volume."	Not subject to measurement. What dollar figure constitutes maximum sales? Also, may be inconsistent; the price and output which generate the greatest dollar revenue is almost certainly not the same as the combination which will yield the largest possible unit volume.
2. "No new idea is too extreme and we will go to great lengths to develop it."	Too broad. No firm has the money or capability to investigate any and every idea that it comes across. To even try is to march in all directions at once.
3. "We seek to be the most profitable company in our industry."	Vague. By what measures of profit—total dollars? earnings per share? return on sales? return on equity investment? all of these?
4. "In producing our products we strive to minimize costs and maximize efficiency."	What are the standards by which costs will be said to be minimum and efficiency maximum? How will management know when the objective has been achieved?
5. "We intend to meet our responsibilities to stockholders, customers, employers, and the public."	In what respects? As determined by whom? More a platitude than an action commitment.

conflicting or trade-off position with one another. Objectives which are ambiguous or which involve compromise with one another are of no help as a managerial guide. The role of objectives is, first and foremost, to serve as the guideposts by which to translate concept into direction and commitment into action. They are intended to pave the way for an organization to bridge the gap between the theory of its business (organization purpose and mission) and making the theory a workable reality. But as with organization purpose, objectives should not be viewed as a straitjacket; they should and must undergo revision to meet changing circumstances.

Illustration Capsule 1 contains a number of possible organizational objectives, some clearly defined and some poorly phrased, so as to better reveal the nature and features of objectives.

Organization Goals. The *goals* of an organization are the intermediate quantitative and qualitative "performance targets" which management seeks to attain in moving toward organizational objectives. Thus, whereas *objectives are long range* in nature, *goals are short range*. They serve to indicate the speed and momentum which management seeks to maintain in accomplishing the organization's objectives and purpose. They direct the attention of both management and employees toward the desired standards of performance and behavior in the near term.

The following statements illustrate what is meant by goals:

1. Our growth goal is to double sales revenues and earnings per share during the next year.
2. We have set our sights on a target market share of 15 percent this year and 17.5 percent next year.
3. We plan to increase the size of our engineering staff by 200 people over the next two years so as to develop the technical capability to secure an additional $35 million in aerospace contracts.
4. Our goal every year is the same—to win the national championship.
5. The company's goal is to open up at least two new sales territories each year for the next five years to boost our market coverage to eight states.
6. Our immediate goal is to modernize our plant facilities and achieve a more competitive degree of efficiency.
7. We intend to reduce new store openings by 10 percent this year.
8. Our immediate target is to increase donations and contributions by 20 percent.
9. Our aim is to cutback manpower requirements by 5 percent each of the next three years.
10. We seek to gain enough new accounts this year to reach our interim goal of $50 million in deposits.
11. We aim to reduce infant mortality rates to less than 1 per 1,000 births within 12 months.
12. The plant's annual production goal is an output rate close to 95 percent of rated capacity.
13. The goal of this year's rush is to get 20 new pledges.
14. Our goal is to fill every incoming order within four days.
15. One of our annual financial goals is to maintain the lowest prudent average daily cash balance so as to free excess cash for short-term investment.

Observe that the goal statements all reflect a short-range target level of achievement. Contrast this with the longer term focus of the stated objectives in Illustration Capsule 1.

Goals can be used as rallying points for coordinating the activities of organizational subunits and as a basis for establishing common purpose in the performance of diverse tasks. Acceptance of organizational goals and objectives by the people concerned promotes teamwork and a united approach to achieving the organization's purpose and mission. Where goals are stated in quantitative terms, they an serve as criteria for measuring and evaluating performance of (1) the organization as a whole, (2) organizational subunits, and (3) the individual managers. Illustration Capsule 2 provides an inside look at the managerial role and function of organizational goals.

Illustration Capsule 2

The Role and Function of Goals

The following remarks of a vice president of marketing for a small candy manufacturer illustrates the internal role and function of goals. (Observe that the manager uses goals and objectives interchangeably whereas we distinguish between goals as short range and objectives as long range.)

Basically I'm trying to operate so my people will grow along with the company. I set high standards. I know they won't all be met, but at least people will know what I'm looking for. I expect a subordinate to have ideas and to have plans on what he wants to do and how. I may differ with him, and I'll explain why I think another way is better, but I don't penalize people for doing things their own way. What I want is results, and if a man has his own way, that's O.K.

Our regional men and brokers have quotas and also specific goals to reach in each market. I ask them to set a quota for themselves, partly to get their appraisal of a market and partly so I can appraise their motivation and judgment. I don't want them to promise pie in the sky, but neither do I want to see them aiming low to be sure of hitting it and getting a bonus.

We give each regional manager a discretionary fund to spend as he pleases. It's only $5,000, but it is important in a couple of ways. For one thing the way a man uses it helps me appraise his judgment. Second, it makes him a much more important part of the organization. The brokers look to him to use some of the money for promotions in their territory—so it helps the regional man get the broker's cooperation. And don't forget that it's the strength of our distribution that has let us grow rapidly on so little money.

All this field work is done within the general framework of corporate marketing objectives. We write these up and send them out to each broker and regional man. Each month we send him a rundown on how he is doing compared to the objectives (based on information from the IBM reports). At the end of the year we go over the plan and each unfulfilled objective with every man. We try to determine if we were unrealistic, if it was unavoidable, or if it was a lack of something on his part. It isn't done to crucify someone; we want our objectives and quotas to be realistic or they are worse than useless. We want each man to believe he can hit them, so it's important that we all understand *why* they weren't reached.*

* As quoted in George A. Smith, Jr., C. Roland Christensen, Norman A. Berg, and Malcolm S. Salter, *Policy Formulation and Administration*, 6th ed. (Homewood, Ill.: Richard D. Irwin, Inc., 1972), pp. 363–64.

Organization Strategy. *Strategy* is a comprehensive description of an organization's master plan for achieving its goals, objectives, and purposes—in that order. In almost every case, an organization will have several options for going about what it is trying to accomplish; the role of strategy is to solve the problem of alternative means by laying out the organization's blueprint for action. Thus, *strategy indicates how the organization plans to get where it wants to go*. It guides the enterprise's development over both the short term and the long term toward what it seeks to do and to accomplish. By providing the organization with its directional signals, strategy shapes those decisions and actions which must be initiated to move the organization toward its goals and objectives.

To illustrate the significance of strategy to an organization, consider the case of Beatrice Foods' transformation from a local dairy operation into a $5 billion company:

> Beginning as a local butter and egg company in Beatrice, Nebraska, the company began an effort to diversify its product line and reduce its dependence on local conditions. It started by acquiring a string of small dairies. From the outset, Beatrice followed two key principles—diversification and decentralization. Only firms headed by independent-minded entrepreneurs were brought into the fold. Although Beatrice found that the dairy business had the disadvantage of low profit margins, it had the advantage of generating a lot of excess cash (mainly because inventories of milk are provided by nature and do not require endless financing). Thus, having acquired dairies coast to coast and grown into a $200 million dairy company, Beatrice began to invest some of its cash in higher-margin food companies. La Choy Food Products was the first acquisition and, when it worked out well, Beatrice began to push into other food lines at an accelerating rate. In the 1960s Beatrice acquired some nonfood firms and by the 1970s owned several different kinds of manufacturing operations, a warehousing division, and an insurance company. Among its products are such brands as Samsonite, Meadow Gold, Martha White (flour), Dannon (yogurt), Clark (candy bars), Eckrich (meats), Gebhardt's (chili and tamales), and LaChoy (Chinese foods).
>
> Beatrice's acquisition strategy followed some strict guidelines. Commodity-oriented firms were excluded because of the unpredictable price swings. Companies in head-on competition with such powerhouses as Kellogg's and Campbell Soups were avoided. In the non-food areas, Beatrice shied away from labor-intensive companies because of the risks of inflation of labor costs. Industries like steel and chemicals were avoided because of their heavy capital demands.
>
> The basic acquisition strategy was to go after companies with at least five years of sales and profit increases, and to eliminate from consideration any firm so large that failure could seriously damage Beatrice's overall profitability. Between 1952 and 1962 most of the acquired firms had sales of about $2 million. While Beatrice sought companies with a growth rate higher than its own, it insisted on a purchase price keyed to a price-earnings multiple about one-third below Beatrice's own current price-earnings ratio. Beatrice was generally suc-

cessful in buying firms it wanted at a ''discount'' because the Beatrice stock it was offering in return had performed so very well over the years.[9]

In 1977, Beatrice Foods overtook Kraft and Esmark to become the nation's largest food processor.

Organization Policy. Whereas strategy depicts *how* the organization's purpose is to be accomplished, it is the role of *policy* to guide and control strategy implementation and to indicate how internal organization processes will function and be administered. Thus *policy* refers to the organizational methods, procedures, and practices associated with implementing and executing strategy. Plainly, then, policy is subordinate to and supportive of purpose and strategy; policy is the result of operationalizing and institutionalizing the chosen strategy. Examples of policies which an organization might adopt in support of its overall purpose and strategy include:

1. A retail grocery chain giving store managers authority to buy fresh produce locally rather than ordering from the regional warehouse whenever they can get a better buy.
2. An oil company's deciding to lease properties and buildings for its service station operations so as to minimize long-term capital requirements.
3. A graduate school of business deciding not to admit to its MBA program any applicant who did not have at least two years of business experience as well as a B average on all undergraduate course work.
4. A firm's practice of requiring each of its product divisions and profit centers to file weekly sales and profit reports with headquarters as a means of monitoring and evaluating progress toward corporate goals.
5. A hospital's requiring all patients to make a $100 cash deposit upon being admitted, as part of its plan for maintaining financial solvency.

The foregoing examples should suggest that policy is a sort of ''decision rule'' in the sense that it signals what should and should not be done in order to further the achievement of strategy and purpose. Policy may take the form of written statements, or it may consist of unwritten understandings of past actions (which may or may not be intended to establish precedent or frames of reference for future action).

The need for both major and minor policy guides exists at all levels in the management structure. Thus, the scope of policy statements may range widely from such lofty principles as ''It is company policy to give our customers complete satisfaction or their money back'' and ''We are an equal opportunity employer'' down to more mundane matters as ''It is company policy not to accept personal checks for more than the amount of purchase''

---

[9] For a more complete discussion of Beatrice's strategy and operating philosophy, see Linda Grant Martin, ''How Beatrice Foods Sneaked up on $5 Billion,'' *Fortune*, April 1976, pp. 118–29.

and "It is the policy of this organization to pay one-half of the tuition fees of employees who wish to further their education."

Some policies concern operating procedures and amount to little more than work rules, as in the case of statements specifying the length of coffee breaks and the methods for obtaining reimbursement for travel expenses. Yet, others may provide vital support to an organization's strategic plan—for example, General Motor's policy of trying to standardize as many parts as possible in producing its many different models of Chevrolets, Pontiacs, Buicks, Oldsmobiles, and Cadillacs was aimed at achieving greater mass-production economies and minimizing the working capital tied up in parts inventories.

THE INTERRELATIONSHIPS AMONG PURPOSE, OBJECTIVES, GOALS, STRATEGY, AND POLICY

Taken together, an organization's purpose, objectives, and goals set forth *exactly what the organization intends to do and to accomplish*—in both the short run and long run. Purpose delineates the organization's service mission to customers and to society; objectives and goals serve to indicate the organization's priorities and commitments to specific actions and specific results. Strategy, then, addresses the issue of precisely how the desired results are to be accomplished; it is the means to the end; the game plan; the outline of how things are to be done. Policy refers to strategy implementation—the organizational procedures, practices, and structure associated with administering and operating the organization on a day-to-day basis. In conjunction, organizational purpose, objectives, goals, strategy, and policy define the

FIGURE 1–1
A Schematic of the Relationships among Purpose, Objectives, Goals, Strategy, and Policy

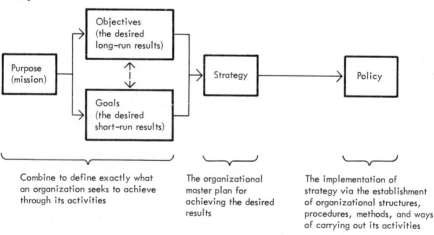

overall plan for the organization and the guidelines and principles by which it is to be managed. Figure 1–1 depicts these relationships.

Inevitably, of course, times and circumstances will change. Complications may arise. The outlook for the organization will be affected by the economy, population shifts, life-styles, technological advances, competitive pressures, and so forth. These will, in all probability, prompt the organization to modify (or radically change) its purpose, objectives, goals, strategy, or policies. The managerial task of developing a timely consistency and compatibility among organizational purpose, objectives, goals, strategy, and policy, then, is a continuous one.

It should be apparent from the foregoing discussion that *strategy is predicated upon and intertwined with an organization's purpose, objectives, and goals.* Thus, to consider purpose, objectives, and goals as an interconnected part of strategy (or the overall strategic plan) accurately lumps together the direction-setting components of organizational activities. In ensuing discussions, we shall therefore use the term strategy broadly to embrace and include the organization's purpose, objectives, goals, and plans for accomplishing them. This broad view of the nature and meaning of strategy is probably more consistent with the use of the term in actual practice.

Definition of Terms

Purpose denotes what the organization should be doing and why it exists. Purpose specifies exactly what the organization's business is or is to be and the kind of organization it is or is to be.

Objectives specify the action commitments being made to achieve an organization's purpose and the long-range results the organization seeks to bring about through its activities.

Goals are the near-term organizational performance targets which an organization desires to attain in progressing toward its objectives.

Strategy refers to a comprehensive description of an organization's master plan for achieving its goals, objectives, and purpose.

Policy concerns the organizational methods, procedures, and practices associated with implementing and executing strategy. Policy serves to signal *how* the organization will be administered and operated.

WHO IS RESPONSIBLE FOR STRATEGY AND POLICY?

Traditionally, responsibility for (1) assembling a master plan consonant with the organization's purpose and mission (strategy formulation) and (2) managing the accomplishment of purpose and strategy (strategy implementation, organization, and policy administration) has been viewed as falling more or less entirely within the province of top management. Virtually all small businessmen have major strategy-policy responsibilities, since in a small firm the owner-entrepreneur is clearly the organization's guiding light and dominant decision maker. The top executives of larger organizations, of course, have strategy-policy responsibilities and, in fact, spend much of their time on these very things. Yet, increasingly, large organizations, and especially giant corporations, are creating positions deeper down in the managerial hierarchy which entail wide-ranging strategy-policy responsibilities. This rise in the number of "general" management positions encompassing multiple functions and responsibilities is a direct outgrowth of the corporate movement toward divisional forms of organization where one person is held accountable for the overall performance of an operating subunit. Often, the process of divisionalization is carried beyond just the operating division concept to include several suborganizational units, each requiring a *general manager*. Thus, many large- and medium-sized organizations now have general management positions at the group level, the division level, and the departmental level.

Even so, the tasks of strategy and policy reach beyond the purview of top-level managers and the general managers of operating subunits. Almost every management job of any consequence entails actions which have implications for strategy and/or policy. In theory, an organization's blueprint for action is a product of definitive statements handed down from top-management levels. In practice, however, such statements are seldom definitive enough to provide unambiguous guidance through the maze of uncertainty and one-of-a-kind situations that constantly crop up. At the very least, lower level managers are expected to interpret, clarify, and fine tune the organizational master plan to meet the circumstances of daily operations. This means that a significant amount of managerial discretion resides below the top-management or chief executive levels. Consequently, whether in a line or a staff position, lower and middle managers influence the strategy-policy process through their everyday activities, despite a lack of formal responsibility for strategy-policy decisions. Furthermore, dealing with the problems posed by day-to-day operations contributes to the clarification of policies and a keener definition of strategy.

All this, perhaps, is a long-winded way of saying that all managers need to be acquainted with strategy-policy problems and how to deal with them—if, for no other reason, than they go to the heart of the management function and pertain directly to organization success or failure.

Admittedly, though, while every manager to some extent has a hand in strategy formulation and policymaking, there is no doubt that the higher up a person is in the managerial hierarchy, the more time he spends with the issues of strategy and policy and the greater is his influence upon them.

Let us turn now and get a bird's-eye view of the strategy-policy roles of the general manager. A more complete discussion of these will follow in succeeding chapters.

THE ROLES OF MANAGEMENT

There are two chief managerial roles to be performed in every organization.[10] The first is that of *entrepreneurship;* that is, focusing on opportunities to create markets, to develop new and improved products or services, to find better ways to meet customer needs, and to help raise the quality of life. The thrust of the entrepreneurship function is (or should be) to make the organization *effective*. Effectiveness means coming out with the right product at the right time so as to produce extraordinary *results* and to bring superior *performance* to the organization. It means keeping the organization responsive and capable of performance, growth, and change in the future. It means being a market *leader* and *pacesetter* in supplying products/services that match what customers need and expect. It means being shrewd and perceptive enough to establish the right kinds of priorities and to fund their pursuit.

The second management role is *to administer*—to manage and improve what is in place. The focus of administration is to optimize the yield from existing organization resources and to find better ways of doing what is already being done. The administration function of management is central to what economists mean when they speak of *efficiency*. To seek to administer efficiently is to be concerned with doing things right—with maximizing the output from a given input.

Of the two roles, entrepreneurship is the more important managerial task. The most efficient organization cannot survive, much less succeed, if it is efficient in doing the wrong things. Efficiency may keep a marginal organization alive for a while, but it takes effectiveness to generate long-term results and performance and to sustain a dependable base of customers.

THE MANAGER AS ORGANIZATION STRATEGIST

In fulfilling entrepreneurial responsibilities, the general manager quickly confronts the broad issue of strategy. Among other things, he or she must establish or preside over the setting of goals and objectives, identify strategic alternatives, assemble a strategic master plan, clarify and defend organizational goals against external attack or internal erosion, install purpose in place of improvisation, and substitute planned progress for organization drift.[11] Of these, perhaps the most crucial, insofar as long-term entrepreneurial performance is concerned, is that of searching out new strategic opportunities made valid by changing market outlooks, emerging societal wants and needs, and organizational capabilities. A constant probing for fresh strategies nurtures the firm's entrepreneurial spirit and capacity for successful

---

[10] Drucker, *Management,* pp. 45–48; Chester I. Barnard, *The Functions of the Executive* (Cambridge, Mass.: Harvard University Press, 1938), pp. 26–32, 55–61.

[11] Christensen, Andrews, and Bower, *Business Policy,* p. 17; Kenneth Andrews, *The Concept of Corporate Strategy* (Homewood, Ill.: Dow Jones-Irwin, Inc., 1971), chap. 1.

response. In other words, by keeping the potential of product-market changes high on the organization agenda, the strategist increases the likelihood of remaining alert and well-positioned to capitalize upon new opportunities.

In close conjunction with the task of new strategy identification, however, the general manager has to undertake an insightful, unbiased assessment of the pros and cons of strategic options. A carefully reasoned analysis of organizational capabilities is essential to sensible strategy design for the simple reason that without the necessary skills and resources the most appealing strategy cannot be executed effectively.

One of the hardest-to-come-by skills useful to the managerial strategist is that of investing the organization's strategy with a magnetic and cohesive quality. The value of an inspiring strategy (and the unity and commitment which results) becomes clear when pressures and temptations to deviate from it set in—as surely they will. Internal conflicts over goals, strategy, and values are certain to occur and it is the general manager's responsibility to see that they are resolved. Moreover, from time to time external developments will send signals that trigger attempts to modify the root strategy and master plan. It is no small job for the managerial strategist to know when to defend a properly focused strategy against superficially attractive alternatives (faster growth, diversification) and when emerging factors have rendered a once successful strategy obsolete, thereby making strategy reformulation propitious. This is why *continuous monitoring of strategies and policies is the only prudent procedure* for the strategist to follow. And it accounts for why the *process of strategy formulation is never-ending*—like death and taxes, change is certain and changing circumstances, in turn, will prompt the course of strategy to turn not only in new directions but also at new speeds.

THE MANAGER AS ORGANIZATION BUILDER

Once the creative and analytical aspects of strategy formulation are complete, the next step is to convert the strategic master plan into something operationally effective. Indeed, a strategy is never complete, even as a formulation, until it gains a commitment of the organization's resources and meets the tests of practical implementation.[12] Hence, as a second priority, the general manager's task is to bring into being and put into motion an organization which is capable of executing the chosen strategy—and with acceptable results.

The job of organization, broadly conceived, implies a variety of functions and activities. The technical tasks of research and development, production, finance, marketing, control, and personnel must be seen to and coordinated.

---

[12] Christensen, Andrews, and Bower, *Business Policy*, p. 673.

Line and staff activities have to be harmonized and integrated. People must be motivated and their performance evaluated (two facets of management, by the way, which can work against one another). Information systems and controls must be put into place. Competing demands for scarce organizational resources must be weighed against the primacy of organization goals and the validity of individual and departmental goals. Conflict must be mediated.

In deciding the organization structure, managers necessarily address themselves to the problem of how *best* to design and control organizational processes. Of course, so long as an organization is small enough for a single person to plan and direct all operations personally, questions of structure are superfluous. But when the magnitude of operations exceeds one-person proportions, organizational design options emerge and the difficulty of choosing among them becomes commensurate with the size and diversity of an organization's activities. The problem is compounded by a lack of universally accepted and proven criteria against which to judge alternative organizational models; in fact, most managers find themselves unable to subscribe wholeheartedly to any one organizational model or school of thought concerning organization design and structure.

By and large, strategy should dictate the design of organization structure and processes.[13] That is to say, the overriding criterion for evaluating alternative organization forms and administrative processes should be the relative extent to which each will contribute to an effective strategy implementation. Clearly, successful implementation of a strategy requires that an organization's structure be *supportive* of strategy and *serve* its peculiar needs. Unless the general manager judiciously shapes the formal organization scheme, its informal relationships, and the task-reward structure to the specific requirements of the organization's strategic plan, then the chances for internal wheelspinning and erosion of purpose become decidedly greater. And as soon as departmental and/or individual goals begin to usurp those of the total organization, then cohesion is jeopardized and the organization's ability to respond consistently as an entity is impaired. Conflicting and haphazard responses may be particularly damaging when organizational resources are strained or when external developments are threatening.

---

[13] The strength of the case for strategy being the controlling factor in designing organizational structure and administrative processes is partly indicated by examining some of the factors which in the past have shaped an organization's design. In some organizations the chief determinant of design appears to have been chance occurrences or historical accidents occasioned by the particular experiences and personalities of the organization's leaders, the position of a company in its industry, and the economic circumstances surrounding an organization's development (war, depression, sudden technological change). In other instances, organization design seems to have been influenced mainly by a conviction that one form of organization is intrinsically better than another, or by the recommendations of consultants, or by alleged principles of organization as depicted in textbooks on the subject. None of these, as a general rule, seem overly compelling as a guide to organization when compared to the needs of strategy. See Alfred D. Chandler, *Strategy and Structure* (Cambridge, Mass.: The M.I.T. Press, 1962); and Christensen, Andrews, and Bower, *Business Policy*, p. 675.

Managing Transition and Organizational Change.   Although the manager's role as organization builder is fairly simple in concept, it is complex in application. The dynamics of change produce, as a matter of course, an ongoing need to adjust the organization's structure and design. New facilities may have to be added and old facilities modernized or closed. New positions will have to be created and old positions phased out. Tasks will have to be redesigned and the work divided up differently. Both jobs and people will change and so will their interrelationships. The organizational challenge of making an intellectual strategy operational in the face of constant flux can be likened to the difficulties of building a road over shifting sands.

The ability of an organization to make a successful transition to new organization forms cannot be taken for granted, nor can the general manager's capacity to guide the transition. Change in established patterns of behavior is upsetting and frequently stirs resistance. This is especially true when it takes place against a background of success and when the purpose of organizational change is not so much to correct malfunctions as to promote continued success. Often, organizational changes are perceived as an ill-advised move to break up a winning combination rather than a response to strategic fine-tuning and anticipated developments. Such problems are one reason why the manager as organization builder has to be sensitive to the power structure existing in the organization and to relate strategic plans to the human side of organization. It does not take long to learn that the organization and the people who comprise it are, at once, the major constraint to strategy implementation and the vehicle through which the strategy must be made successful. Thus, a good general manager must be adept in figuring out how hard to push the organization and just what it is capable of doing and not doing.

In sum, the general manager (in fulfilling the role of organization builder) is confronted with (1) designing and adapting the organization to fit strategic plans, (2) making allowances for the constraints which organization places on strategy, and (3) resolving the conflicts between organization subunits or their members and organization strategy.

THE MANAGER AS PERSONAL AND ORGANIZATIONAL LEADER

In the role of organization leader, the general manager has, as foremost on a list of functions, the responsibility for organizational performance as measured against the targets of progress specified in the strategic plan. Achieving acceptable results requires the general manager to be informed and ready to intervene when performances fall short of expectations. Particularly there is a need to be resourceful in responding to crises, emergencies, and the demands of on-the-spot decisions.

In addition to the roles of taskmaster and crisis-solver, another leadership priority is securing the commitment of subordinates and members of organizational subunits to established goals and objectives. In getting organizational members to accept the priorities of strategy, the general manager must be a visible and effective communicator. Besides being familiar with varied viewpoints, a general manager will need the skills to persuade, to inspire confidence, to propose, to explain, to project empathy, to remain poised under fire, and to stay in command of difficult situations. Also needed will be a good sense of timing. Not infrequently, the manager will have to be tough in a showdown and an astute practitioner of organizational politics. A successful leader must be able to play the power game effectively.

The functions that attach to the communication of strategy and policy give the general manager an opportunity to infuse flair and distinction into the organization and its activities.[14] It also provides a chance to influence the organization with one's own ideas. But there will only be a limited number of a person's ideas that can be adopted. So to be an effective leader, the general manager will have to know how to stimulate the organization through idea people in other parts of the organization and how to encourage a flow of good proposals. Then comes the task of being skillful in arousing enough support for those ideas and proposals that are deemed worthy.

Also, it should be pointed out that whether a general manager's leadership style is visionary, charismatic, or lackluster, his energy, personality, and integrity will rub off on the organization and help set the tone of enthusiasm and motivation that go into making up an organization's personality. Thus, a general manager's own character and example keynotes the moral, ethical, and personal behavior that is expected of others.

IS THE GENERAL MANAGER'S JOB TOO DEMANDING?

Our sketch of the general manager as strategist, organization builder, and leader may seem to require more of a person than is humanly possible. Admittedly, the job of a general manager is complex but it is not an impossible job, nor does it require Herculean qualities. One reason is that the general manager is not forced to perform each of the roles and functions outlined

---

[14] Machiavelli in his famous classic *The Prince* offers a number of guidelines as to how a manager should conduct himself so as to acquire a reputation and to be a distinctive leader. Although Machiavelli's advice was to heads of state (or princes as he referred to them), it is readily evident that his suggestions apply to managers of any kind of organization:

> ". . . a wise man should ever follow the ways of great men and endeavor to imitate only such as have been most eminent; so that even if his merits do not quite equal theirs, yet that they may in some measure reflect greatness. . . . Nothing makes a prince so much esteemed as the undertaking of great enterprises and the setting of a noble example in his own person. . . . It is also important for a prince to give striking examples of his interior administration . . . when an occasion presents itself to reward or punish any one . . . so that it may be much talked about. But, above all, a prince should endeavor to invest all his actions with a character of grandeur and excellence."

See N. Machiavelli, *The Prince* (New York: Washington Square Press, 1963), pp. 20, 98–99.

above on a daily basis. Good managers know how to conserve time and energy for those few particular issues, decisions, and problems where personal attention is absolutely required. An astute general manager knows the distinctions between staying fully informed and being drawn into participating in lower level decisions or, even worse, making them. Hence, there is no need to be thrust into the position of constantly having to be all things to all people on all issues. Second, many managerial matters can be effectively handled by policy, thereby freeing managers to deal personally only with the exceptions rather than the rule and to devote most of their time to those areas having the greatest long-term impact on the organization.

HOW POLICY FITS INTO THE MANAGEMENT PICTURE

Policies are not only necessary for efficiently managing an organization but they also make the job easier. Day-to-day operations can be managed largely by policy and most routine problems solved by reference to "standard operating procedures." Indeed, such an outcome is the cardinal intent of policy. The managerial functions of policy can be summarized as follows:

1. Policy promotes *uniform handling of similar activities*—a uniformity which facilitates better coordination of work tasks and helps reduce friction arising from favoritism, discrimination, and disparate handling of common functions.
2. Policy introduces *continuity of action and decisions* throughout an organization, thereby minimizing zig-zag behavior and conflicting actions and establishing some degree of order, regularity, stability, and dependability in both the organization's internal and external dealings.
3. Policy acts as *an automatic decision maker* by formalizing organization-wide answers to previously made management decisions about how particular questions and problems should be resolved; policy thus becomes a guide for handling future such problems or issues as they recur without them being passed up through higher management echelons again and again.[15]
4. Policy offers a *predetermined answer to routine problems* and gives key decision makers more time to cope with nonroutine matters; in this way decisions pertaining to both ordinary and extraordinary problems are

---

[15] It goes almost without saying that the automatic decision-making function of policy should not be interpreted as either requiring or advocating all matters be settled by searching through an omnibus policy manual for the proper policy to apply to a situation, and if a suitable one is not found then forcing the application of something close. Policies are not designed to be rigidly applied without the exercise of judgment; exceptions and situations with unique twists always arise and all who apply policies are expected to recognize when a policy should be bent to fit the circumstances.

See also the views of H. Edward Wrapp, "Good Managers Don't Make Policy Decisions," *Harvard Business Review*, vol. 45, no. 5 (September–October 1967), p. 95.

greatly expedited—the former by referring to established policy and the latter by drawing upon a portion of the decision maker's current time.

5. Existing policies afford managers *a mechanism for insulating* themselves from hasty and ill-considered requests for a policy change. The prevailing policy can always be used as a reason (or excuse) for not yielding to emotion-based, expedient or temporarily valid arguments for policy revision.[16]

6. Policy serves as a *major communication link* to an organization's several constituents. External policy statements aid outsiders in appraising organization behavior and performance; internal policy pronouncements not only illustrate to employees what sort of actions and decisions are appropriate but they also assist in casting the organization's character and personality.

Ideally, policies flow from an organization's strategy; they can relate either to administrative matters or to operating procedures. Policies can be written or oral, stated or unstated, implicit or explicit, open or covert, firm or flexible, well-defined or deliberately vague. Whichever, the managerial thrust of policy is to set organizational mechanisms in place that will support strategic success.

More specifically, the strategy-implementing features of policy include setting goals for various functional departments and product lines and developing the methods and procedures to support their achievement. They include counteracting any tendency for parts of the organization to resist or reject goals and policies with an effective system of rewards and penalties. A network of management controls with clear reporting channels and ample information feedback will almost certainly have to be designed and installed so that compliance can be monitored. Reviewing current performance and reassessing operating goals and policies both require a flow of timely, reliable information and it is the general manager's responsibility to see that such information exists and to keep in touch with what is happening. Thus, keeping a close check on how well established policies are working is a key aspect of the general manager's operating concerns.

---

[16] The value of a healthy skepticism of policy change unless and until sufficient evidence in support of revision has been accumulated is illustrated by the experience of the manufacturers of Florsheim shoes. According to a top executive for Florsheim:

> "When Dupont was introducing Corfam, its marketing organization placed extreme pressure on quality shoe manufacturers, such as us, to incorporate the plastic material into our lines. This was a key factor in marketing strategy for Corfam: Get the material associated with quality before trading down to popular priced lines. All types of pressure and persuasion were employed to try to get us [Florsheim] to make some Corfam shoes. But our policy to make only quality leather shoes automatically made our decision for us in spite of the heavy pressure on us to change it. In this case we are quite glad to note that we escaped the problems that our competitors encountered with the material."

This quotation is reported in Richard H. Buskirk, *Business and Administrative Policy* (New York: John Wiley & Sons, Inc., 1971), pp. 147–48.

STRATEGY, POLICY, AND THE MANAGEMENT PROCESS

The closely coupled strategy-policy functions of managers form a problem-decision-action pattern which transcends the entire management process. Table 1–1 depicts the problems, decisions, and key decision characteristics which typify the managerial strategy and policy area. Note that the policy function can be divided into two distinct facets—administrative and operating. The administrative policy phase of management embraces the multifaceted task of organization building, whereas operating policies are concerned with selecting levels and volumes of activity deemed most conducive to optimal achievement of the organization's purpose and objectives.

Observe, also, the contrasting features of strategy and policy decisions shown in Table 1–1. Strategy formulation involves *centralized* decision making, the analytical assessment of *nonrecurring* environmental situations, and an *incomplete* and *imperfect* data base. At the other extreme, operating policy decisions are made under *decentralized* decision-making conditions, they are *repetitive,* and they are both *numerous* and *frequent.*

Each of three classes of problem-decision-action areas is related to the other two. Strategy, administrative policy, and operating policy must all be coordinated and integrated if an organization is to function smoothly. Yet, in many ways strategy is the major key to organization success, for even a brilliant organization design or an extremely efficient control of operations can leave an organization far short of its goals and objectives. One might therefore expect managers to be especially attentive to issues of strategy even though all three areas require top management time and attention.

Studies suggest, however, that managers attend to strategic problems periodically, not continually, and that a number of managements exhibit a "lag response" in recognizing environmental changes which call for strategy modification.[17] According to these studies of corporate enterprises, when changing conditions begin to undermine a firm's strategy and profit declines or losses appear, there is a tendency for managements to respond first by modifying operating policies and levels of activity; second, by initiating reorganizations and reviewing administrative policies; and last, by focusing on strategy.

One explanation for this response sequence derives from the difficulty of recognizing and quantifying the impact of environmental changes before these changes appear and before their consequences begin to be felt. Often, the relevance of specific environmental changes is not perceived unless and until they impact the organization. And even then the impact customarily shows up first in operating performance, thus naturally causing management to look first for operating deficiencies as the root cause of the problem and then for organizational inadequacies. A second reason for the response sequence is the normal priority accorded operating problems. Decisions relat-

---

[17] Chandler, *Strategy and Structure,* pp. 13–16; and R. A. Smith, *Corporations in Crisis* (Garden City, N.Y.: Doubleday and Company, 1963).

	Strategy	Administrative Policy	Operating Policy
Problem	To devise a comprehensive strategic plan which will lead to achievement of the organization's purpose and objectives.	To structure the organization's resources for strategic accomplishment and optimum performance and results.	To optimize realization of organization goals and objectives.
Nature of problem	How best to allocate organization resources among product-market alternatives and opportunities; how to position the organization in the external environment.	How to design the organization structure. Acquiring and developing organization resources. What kind of administrative policies and procedures to establish.	How to budget resources among functional areas and tasks. How to maximize efficiency and minimize costs. Selecting appropriate controls and review of operating procedures.
Key decisions and areas of concern ...	Objectives and goals. Product-markets. Expansion strategy. Growth method. Timing of growth. Marketing strategy. Finance strategy. Production strategy. Administrative strategy. Diversification strategy. R&D strategy.	Form of organization. Lines of authority and responsibility. Information flows. Type of production system. Setting up distribution channels. Facilities location. Financing arrangements. Acquisition of facilities and capital equipment, personnel, and raw materials.	Setting of operating objectives and goals. Price and output levels. Production schedules, inventory levels, purchasing, warehousing, shipping. Marketing tactics. Advertising and promotion. Research and development. Progress review and appraisal.
Special decision characteristics	Centralized decision making. Imperfect information. Nonrepetitive decisions.	Much time is spent arbitrating conflicts between strategy and operations and between organizational and sub-organizational objectives. Many decisions are triggered by fine tuning of strategy, unexpected operating problems, policy obsolescence, and policy inadequacy.	Decentralized decision making. Large volume of or repetitive decisions.

Source: Adapted from H. Igor Ansoff, *Corporate Strategy* (New York: McGraw-Hill Book Company, 1965), p. 8.

ing to operating policy are not easily postponed; moreover, general managers find them familiar and easier to deal with by virtue of their previous training at lower levels in the organization where operating decisions are the sole management responsibility.

The length of the lag response in reviewing strategy is subject to considerable variation, though. A history of unprofitable operations, persistent gaps between goals and performance, aggressive competitive moves by rival organizations, and a turbulent or unstable social-economic-market environment, either separately or in combination, act to trigger management sensitivity to strategy and produce a short or even nonexistent lag response to the question of strategic change. The point here is that care should be taken to design the decision-making process in ways which provide management ample time to attend to strategy issues without being overly encumbered by policy problems of either an administrative or operating nature.

SUGGESTED READINGS

Andrews, Kenneth. *The Concept of Corporate Strategy.* Homewood, Ill.: Dow Jones-Irwin, Inc., 1971, chap. 1.

Barnard, Chester I. *The Functions of the Executive.* Cambridge, Mass.: Harvard University Press, 1938, chaps. 15, 16, and 17.

Boettinger, Henry M. "Is Management Really an Art?" *Harvard Business Review,* vol. 53, no. 1 (January–February 1975), pp. 54–64.

Drucker, Peter F. *Management: Tasks, Responsibilities, Practices.* New York: Harper & Row, Publishers, 1974, chaps. 2, 4, 30, 31, and 50.

Granger, Charles H. "The Hierarchy of Objectives." *Harvard Business Review,* vol. 42, no. 3 (May–June 1964), pp. 63–74.

Katz, Robert L. "Skills of an Effective Administrator." *Harvard Business Review,* vol. 33, no. 1 (January–February 1955), pp. 33–42.

Koontz, Harold. "Making Strategic Planning Work." *Business Horizons,* vol. 19, no. 2 (April 1976), pp. 37–47.

Livingston, J. Sterling. "Myth of the Well-Educated Manager." *Harvard Business Review,* vol. 49, no. 1 (January–February 1971), pp. 79–87.

Machiavelli, N. *The Prince.* New York: Washington Square Press, 1963.

Mintzberg, Henry. "The Manager's Job: Folklore and Fact." *Harvard Business Review,* vol. 53, no. 4 (July–August 1975), pp. 49–61.

Ross, Joel, and Kami, Michael. *Corporate Management in Crisis: Why the Mighty Fall.* Englewood Cliffs, N.J.: Prentice-Hall, Inc., 1973.

Tilles, Seymour. "The Manager's Job: A Systems Approach." *Harvard Business Review,* vol. 41, no. 1 (January–February 1963), pp. 73–81.

Wrapp, H. Edward. "Good Managers Don't Make Policy Decisions." *Harvard Business Review,* vol. 45, no. 5 (September–October 1967), pp. 91–99.

PART II

Formulating Organizational Strategy

Chapter 2
Concepts of Organizational Strategy

Chapter 3
Identifying Strategic Alternatives

Chapter 4
Strategic Evaluation and Strategic Choice

CONCEPTS OF ORGANIZATIONAL STRATEGY

> *. . . a business enterprise guided by a clear sense of purpose rationally arrived at and emotionally ratified by commitment is more likely to have a successful outcome, in terms of profit and social good, than a company whose future is left to guesswork and chance.*
>
> Kenneth R. Andrews

> *Without a strategy the organization is like a ship without a rudder, going around in circles. It's like a tramp; it has no place to go.*
>
> Joel Ross and Michael Kami

FROM a conceptual standpoint it is a matter of indifference whether strategy is defined as (1) an organizational master plan, (2) a set of directional signals, (3) a blueprint for where an organization is trying to go and how it is going to get there, or (4) a coherent pattern of purposes, goals, objectives, and plans describing what "business" an organization is in or is to be in and the kind of organization it is or is to be. Each of these definitions conveys a compatible notion of strategy and does so in language which should make the basic meaning of strategy easy enough to grasp.

But it is one thing to understand the concept of strategy in its most elemental form and another thing to understand fully what is required to forge a full-blown strategic plan of action. This chapter explores the many-sided facets of a comprehensive concept of strategy in an effort to make the substance and scope of strategy formulation operationally useful.

THE NEED TO CONSCIOUSLY DESIGN STRATEGY

Every organization has a strategy however imperfect or unconscious it may be. Its strategy may be explicit or it may have to be deduced from its actions and operating patterns. The strategy may have been carefully calculated and regularly assessed from every angle or it may have emerged haphazardly and be mainly a product of chance and circumstance. Or, again, it may have evolved gradually over time standing as a result of trial and error and market feedback regarding what worked and what didn't.

Obviously, though, a good strategy needs to be carefully thought through; it needs to be consciously designed rather than just evolving from drift and day-to-day activities. The advantages of an organization having a consciously considered strategy concern: (1) the inadequacy of relying solely upon statements of purpose, objectives, and goals to answer specific questions of *how* they are to be achieved and whether any restraints are to be observed in the quest; (2) the necessity of planning ahead for the firm's total development and for activities with long lead times; and (3) the desirability of trying to *influence* rather than merely *respond* to product-market-technological-environmental change.[1] The third advantage is of acute importance. A well-managed enterprise will seek to *impact* the market with a well-conceived strategy. Indeed, the whole thrust of corporate strategy revolves around how to *initiate* and *influence* rather than just *respond* and *react*—though, obviously, it may occasionally be wise to employ defensive strategies as well as offensive strategies. Still, *the acid test of whether a strategy is well conceived is the extent to which it successfully impacts markets, buyers, rival firms, and the directions of product-market-technological change;* the desired outcome is one where the firm's products/services become differentiated and buyer preferences for them are created.

Moreover, making the organization's strategy *explicit* is nearly always a step forward.[2] Once strategy is made explicit, either orally or in writing, then there exists some basis for evaluating it or improving it. But if strategy remains intuitive and no effort is made to explain and clarify its features, there is ample room for the strategy to be misunderstood or at cross-purposes with some (or many) of the organization's activities. This is especially true in organizations large enough to have many points of strategic initiative. In recent years, a number of firms have begun to make some elements of their corporate strategy public, partly to attract investor attention and partly to build a corporate image—see Illustration Capsule 3.

Strategic success depends partly on people working together so that their efforts are mutually reinforcing. In the absence of an explicit concept of strategy it is easy for functional perspectives to blur strategic priorities. For example, one company trying hard to build up a new customer base for industrial castings found that work orders for castings were given the lowest priority in the milling and shipping departments because they were a new

---

[1] Kenneth R. Andrews, *The Concept of Corporate Strategy* (Homewood, Ill.: Dow Jones-Irwin, Inc., 1971), pp. 36, 41–44.

[2] Seymour Tilles, "How to Evaluate Corporate Strategy," *Harvard Business Review*, vol. 41, no. 4 (July–August 1963), p. 116.

item and required different handling procedures; the strategic importance of the castings had simply not found its way to these two functional subunits. The instances are legion where organizational subunits and their members have been frustrated by a lack of clear understanding of strategy and purpose and, in turn, have inadvertently thwarted strategic implementation.

In addition, many organizations, even "successful" ones, are not fully conscious of the strategic features underlying their own success. Evidence for this comes in the form of the miserable failures which have befallen established companies when they hastily assessed or else ignored the strategic implications of launching out in new directions. A case in point was Heublein's acquisition of Hamm's Brewing Company in 1965. Heublein, well-known for its Smirnoff vodka, Harvey's sherry, Lancer's wine, Black Velvet Canadian whiskey, A-1 steak sauce, and a variety of other specialty food and beverage products (and later the acquirer of Kentucky Fried Chicken) in 1965 had a strategy of marketing high-margin, high-quality consumer products aimed at the relatively prosperous, young adult market segment.[3] Heublein relied heavily on brand promotion, wide distribution, product representation in several price categories, and extensive offbeat advertising aimed directly at the young adult audience to gain acceptance for its products. The company aspired to make Smirnoff the number one liquor brand worldwide, to maintain a 10 percent sales growth annually via internal growth or acquisition or both, and to earn an after-tax return on equity of 15 percent or more. Heublein sought to secure strong distributor support through concern for the distributor's profit from Heublein products and through advertising.

In 1966, Heublein decided to take advantage of an "opportunity" to acquire the Theo. Hamm Brewing Company. Even though Hamm's market share and return on sales were on the decline, it apparently was Heublein's belief that its own expertise and market access could effect a turnaround in the Hamm's beer brand and that such a diversification move represented a logical extension of its alcoholic beverage line. But Heublein quickly discovered that its experience and capabilities were of less value in the beer business than had been anticipated; competition among rival beer breweries was not only vigorous but it also took different avenues than did those of Heublein's other products. Heublein's strong distributor relationships turned out to be of little value because many of Heublein's distributors did not carry beer or else were unenthusiastic about Hamm's brand image and sales volume. At the same time, Heublein's management proved to be unprepared for dealing with the technology and peculiarities of brewing beer. After several years of trying to make a go of it, Heublein gave up and in 1974 sold Hamm's at a substantial loss ($40 million).

From Heublein's strategy miscalculation one might conclude, with good

---

[3] E. P. Learned, C. Roland Christensen, Kenneth R. Andrews, and William D. Guth, *Business Policy: Text and Cases,* rev. ed. (Homewood, Ill.: Richard D. Irwin, Inc., 1969), p. 221.

reason, that while an organization may be successful without necessarily being fully cognizant of the success-causing features of its strategy, the chances of strategic failure become significantly higher when it tries to branch out into new ventures without having a deep understanding of their strategic implications and significance.

Another justification for making strategy explicit is the contribution it makes to effective managerial coordination. Management is a team activity and managers at all levels are in a position to affect an organization's success. An explicit strategy provides each manager with a more sharply focused understanding of the organizational role and the contribution he or she is expected to make to organizational goals and objectives. This becomes particularly important as organizations become larger and strategy-policy decisions are delegated to lower level general managers who act on their own assumptions about the degree of top-level commitment and the availability of organizational resources.

Ultimately, of course, the justification for making strategy explicit is not to produce a document which everyone understands but to improve organizational performance. Whether or not this happens hinges upon how much is learned from the process of developing a strategy statement, the quality of the strategy, and the skill with which it is implemented. By itself, a strategy statement is little more than a useful prelude to action.

WHERE STRATEGY FORMULATION BEGINS— WITH A CONCEPT

The necessary and logical starting point of strategy formulation is with the organization's purpose and mission. A number of basic questions have to be posed and answered: What should the concept of our business be—now and in the future? What products or services do we want to provide? What functions will they serve and are these functions worthwhile? Who will our

Illustration Capsule 3

Boise Cascade's Public Statement of Its Strategy

In 1975 and 1976, Boise Cascade ran a number of advertisements in such publications as *Business Week, Fortune,* and the *Wall Street Journal* stating what the strategy of its business was to be over the next several years. The ads stated that Boise Cascade could be a successful company ("money will grow on our trees if . . .") if it was able to cope with (1) the demand-oriented ups and downs of the building materials business, and (2) the supply-oriented fluctuations of the paper business. The company's announced strategies for accomplishing this were as follows (compiled and quoted verbatim from the company's two page ads in the November 3, 1975 issue of *Business Week* and the May 1976 issue of *Fortune*):

Illustration Capsule 3 (continued)

STRATEGY NUMBER 1

Maintain our relatively equal balance between our building materials and paper businesses by investing approximately equal shares of our 5-year (1974–1978,) $1.1 billion capital program in each, while staying within a 0.6:1 debt-to-equity ratio.

We plan to generate an average annual return on total investment of *at least 12 percent after taxes* on each project within the $850 million we're using to improve and expand our businesses. (The remaining $250 million are being used to keep our facilities well maintained, safe and environmentally sound.)

Rationale

1. This balance gives us a source of strength under almost all conditions because historically at least, the building materials and paper businesses have seldom lagged at the same time. Either both are strong, or one is.

2. Demand for paper products increases quite consistently with the growth of the general economy. It's excess supply that depresses earning power, and there's no near term prospect for that because the paper industry can't add capacity fast enough to meet demand.

3. Demand for building materials, while volatile because homebuilding activity is subject to the cost and supply of mortgage money, can be expected to increase long term because of the nation's growing need for housing.

4. Both businesses depend on a renewable resource that we have in good supply. Including joint ventures, we own 2 million acres of timberland and have long term harvesting rights on 5 million more.

5. Both are businesses we know well. We've been in them profitably since Boise Cascade was first formed back in 1957.

STRATEGY NUMBER 2

We plan to invest about one-third of our capital dollars in our converting and distributing operations in order to maximize the earning power of our forest-originated products.

Rationale

1. Converting and distributing operations offer very attractive returns on investments. (By converting operations, we mean businesses like manufactured housing and composite cans that *convert* lumber into single-and multi-family homes and paper into packaging.)

2. Converting / distributing businesses are relatively less susceptible to market fluctuations, owing to the range of products and the diversity of demand.

3. Our converting and distributing operations enable us to add to the value of many of our forest products after they leave our mills.

For example, when one of our mills sells lumber to one of our builder service centers so it can make and sell roof trusses to builders, we provide an additional service and earn an additional profit.

4. Our converting operations have a ready source of supply—our primary manufacturing operations.

5. While our converting and distributing operations are among the leaders in their respective businesses, their individual market shares are small so they have ample room to grow.

As these strategies suggest, we think the key to coping with "cyclicality" is balance—between building materials and paper products on the one hand, between primary manufacturing and converting/distributing on the other. The fact that we're already well-balanced on both counts means we start from a good position.

customers be? Why should they buy our product? How will we compete? How does our intended purpose mesh with competitive and market realities? What should we continue to do and what should we plan to abandon? And, in the case of diversified firms, should our several lines of business have a common thread? Not infrequently, the answers are far from clear-cut—even for well-entrenched enterprises. Nor are the answers ever final—changing circumstances can and do cause firms to redefine their business and to reorient organization purpose.

Indeed, organizations are confronted with a variety of plausible approaches for deciding "what is our business, what will it be, and what should it be?" Some organizations build the concept of their businesses around the dominant characteristics of their products or services. Thus, a trucking company may think of itself as being in the trucking business, a chemical company as in the chemicals business, and a shoe manufacturer as being in the shoe business. Similarly, in the nonprofit sector there are churches (whose product is "religion"), universities (whose business is "higher education"), the agricultural extension service (whose business is agriculture-related technical assistance and information) and the local fire department (whose business is fire fighting and fire prevention). Other organizations describe their business by the principal ingredient in their products, as with steel companies, aluminum companies, and paper companies. The "common thread" in still other enterprises is technology, an example being General Electric, whose thousands of products are related in varying degrees to the technology of electricity.

Still other organizations prefer a concept based on a *broad* view of the customers or markets they serve. Thus, rural electric cooperatives may construe their business as one of supplying electrical service to residents of less-populated rural areas. A community college may view its mission as one of furnishing two-year college programs to graduates of high schools within a 50-mile radius of its campus. An agricultural machinery manufacturer may define its business as supplying farm equipment to farmers. The business of home appliance manufacturers may be thought of as one of offering effort-saving and timesaving devices for household use.

Yet another alternative is for a firm to define its business in terms of a product aimed at a specific *market segment* or distinguishable group of customers having some common (and strategically relevant) characteristic—location, usage of product, timing of purchase, volume bought, service requirements, and so forth. For instance, typewriters sold as office equipment define a buyer segment quite distinct from portable typewriters sold to individuals through retail channels. Likewise the clientele of a major state university is fundamentally different from that of a small private liberal arts college. And the business of a neighborhood convenience food mart is different from that of a large supermarket. It can make sense, therefore, for an organization's concept of its business to combine a definition of its product with a definition of the class of customer or market segment to which that product is sold. This approach to defining the business seeks a strategic match between a particular product (or service) and the more narrowly focused target market for which it is primarily intended.

Finally, an enterprise may have a concept of itself that is predicated on the scope of its operations. For a small company, just part of an industry may constitute its sole field of endeavor; such would be the case of a firm whose business consists, say, of drilling offshore oil wells. This type of firm is often labeled as "specialized" and such a firm may well perceive its economic mission as none other than a specialty-type enterprise performing a limited service. Larger firms may, for reasons of scale economies, be active in several phases of getting a product to the final consumer and are thus said to be "integrated." This would be the case, for example, with an oil company which drills its own oil wells, pipes crude oil to its own refineries, and sells gasoline through its own network of branded distributors and service station outlets. Still other firms, large or small, are said to be "diversified" because their operations extend into several distinct industries—either related or unrelated.

Strictly speaking, most organizations are in a variety of distinct businesses. Either they sell the same product to different types of customers in distinctly different ways, or they utilize a number of different distribution channels in gaining access to customers and markets, or they have a diversified product line. Consequently, to gain a complete picture of the *total* organization's concept of its mission, it is necessary to consider the purposeful elements inherent in each one of its lines of business. Only then can an *overall* concept of purpose and master strategy (if one exists for the *total* organization) be delineated and understood at the most meaningful level of generalization—whether it be tied to specific products or product groups, markets or market segments, technology, end-uses and needs, scope of activity in an industry, narrow or broad diversification. However, in the case of true conglomerate organizations which, by design, are in a number of *unrelated* businesses, the overall purpose of the organization may relate more to issues of risk, financial objectives of the owners, growth, and management guidelines than to an integrated fit among its several product-market-technology activities.[4]

ARRIVING AT A DEFINITION OF "WHAT IS OUR BUSINESS AND WHAT SHOULD IT BE?"

For many years the most noted and perceptive authority on the whys and hows of an organization clearly defining its mission and purpose has been Peter Drucker. He argues quite forcefully that the theory of an organization's business should be thought through and spelled out clearly, for otherwise the organization lacks a solid foundation for establishing realistic objec-

---

[4] See, for example, Richard F. Vancil and Peter Lorange, "Strategic Planning in Diversified Companies," *Harvard Business Review*, vol. 53, no. 1 (January–February 1975), pp. 81–90.

Illustration Capsule 4

Strategic Miscalculation at W. T. Grant: Part of the Story behind Its Bankruptcy

In the mid-1960s, W. T. Grant, like a number of other retailers, began to undertake a large-scale capital expansion program. From 1963 to 1973, Grant opened 612 new stores and expanded 91 others, with the bulk of the increases starting in 1968. Most of the stores were large—the combined square footage of the new stores being opened averaged 6 million to 7 million square feet per year. However, Grant's expansion of its management organization did not match the pace of store expansion. According to a former operations executive: "Our training program couldn't keep up with the explosion of stores, and it didn't take long for the mediocrity to begin to show."

More importantly, though, Grant's top management could not agree on what kind of store it wanted to have. The gut strategic issue was whether to go the K-Mart route or attack Ward's and Penney's position. Grant's president had one view and the board chairman held the other. The outcome was a decision to take "a position between the two and that consequently stood for nothing."

To complement its program of larger stores, strategy called for a major broadening of its merchandise selection. However, store buyers, unaccustomed to stocking stores much bigger than the normal Grant outlet, bought such large quantities of merchandise that seasons, styles, and customer tastes were changing before they could be moved off the shelves. Although Grant's inventory control problems quickly became acute, corporate officials were reluctant to move in and take the necessary steps to balance inventory by the use of markdowns—for fear of wiping out profit margins. The net result was that much of the merchandise in the new stores soon became stale and Grant had so much tied up in inventory that it could not free up enough dollars to do a good seasonal merchandising job.

If this was not enough, Grant also opted for a merchandising strategy of emphasizing big-ticket items such as TVs, major appliances, and power tools sold under its own label—a label which had a poor consumer recognition level in product markets where brand image was very important. In an effort to move these items, Grant turned to a heavy credit promotion, but so few credit restrictions were placed on customers that within a short time Grant found itself with a disastrous bad debt ratio and a large writeoff of sales it could not collect.

In retrospect, Grant's bankruptcy was prompted by a number of strategic miscalculations:

1. The rapid pace of new store openings was not coordinated with generating a supply of qualified and able store managers.
2. The company did not carve out a distinctive market for itself, nor was its merchandising strategy matched carefully with its market positioning and market identity. Or, to put it another way, Grant failed to make clear to potential customers just what kind of store Grant's was and what kinds of goods could be bought there—possibly because Grant itself was not clear as to what the concept of its business was.
3. Grant did not have adequate purchasing and inventory controls to support its merchandising strategy of carrying a larger variety of items.
4. Grant tried to sell the wrong kinds of items under its own label.

Sources: "How W. T. Grant Lost $175 Million Last Year," *Business Week,* February 24, 1975, pp. 74–76; and Rush Loving, Jr., "W. T. Grant's Last Days—As Seen from Store 1192," *Fortune,* April 1976, pp. 108–14.

tives and goals, strategies, plans, and work assignments.[5] According to Drucker, while nothing may seem simpler or more obvious than "What is our business?" a neglect of this question is the most important single cause of organization frustration and failure—for an example, see Illustration Capsule 4 which indicates the strategic errors inducing W. T. Grant's bankruptcy. One reason is that managements shy away from addressing the issue head on. To raise the question always reveals fundamental cleavages and disagreement, even within top management. Drucker suggests that bringing these dissents out into the open is a big step toward management effectiveness since it enables the top-management group to work together better precisely because each member, being cognizant of the controversy, is more likely to understand his colleague's motivation and behavior.

But more importantly, Drucker offers a method for defining "what our business is." He argues:

> A business is not defined by the company's name, statutes, or articles of incorporation. It is defined by the want the customer satisfies when he buys a product or a service. To satisfy the customer is the mission and purpose of every business. The question "What is our business?" can, therefore, be answered only by looking at the business from the outside, from the point of view of customer and market. What the customer sees, thinks, believes, and wants, at any given time, must be accepted by management as an objective fact. . . .
>
> . . . [T]o the customer, no product or service, and certainly no company, is of much importance. . . . The customer only wants to know what the product or service will do for him tomorrow. All he is interested in are his own values, his own wants, his own reality. For this reason alone, any serious attempt to state "what our business is" must start with the customer, his realities, his situation, his behavior, his expectations, and his values.[6]

Following up on this rationale, Drucker advocates a searching inquiry into such questions as: Who is our customer and what are his needs? Where is the customer? What does the customer buy? Is it status? Comfort? Satisfaction of a physical need? An ego need? Security? What is value to the customer? Is it price? Function? Quality? Service? Economy of use? Durability? Styling? Convenience?

These questions plainly need to be posed and answered at the inception of a business and whenever it gets in trouble. But every so often a successful operation should also ask them.[7] Sooner or later, even the most successful response to "What is our business?" becomes obsolete. Therefore, in periodically addressing the question of "What is our business?" management is well-advised to add "and what will it be?"[8] This latter question forces the organization to look ahead and try to anticipate the impact of

---

[5] Peter F. Drucker, *Management: Tasks, Responsibilities, Practices* (New York: Harper & Row, Publishers, 1974), pp. 77–79.

[6] Ibid., pp. 79–80.

[7] Ibid., pp. 87–88.

[8] Ibid., p. 88–89.

environmental changes on the organization's purpose, objectives, products, markets, technologies, and so on. It lays the basis for conscious redirection of the organization. It reduces the chances of becoming smug and complacent. Answering it also means doing some serious thinking about "What are the customer's *unsatisfied* wants?"—the response to which may suggest the direction of changes in products, markets, and technologies. The clues thus uncovered should help in modifying, extending, and developing the organization's existing business concept.

Finally, it is pertinent to inquire "What *should* our business be?"[9] How can innovations be converted into new businesses? What other opportunities are opening up or can be created that offer attractive prospects for transforming the organization into a *different* (and more desirable) business? Should, for example, Exxon consider itself as primarily an oil company or an energy company? Should IBM's concept of its business be computers or information processing? Should the business of hospitals remain one of curing those persons who are sick enough to be patients or should they seek to become comprehensive centers for all types of medical and health care? Which things should the organization continue doing and which should it plan to abandon?

By and large, if an organization follows Drucker's prescribed methodology for periodically thinking through its definition of purpose and mission, the outcome will be a clearer and more perceptive understanding of how the enterprise should be managed.

THE COMMON THREAD—IS IT NECESSARY?

In defining its purpose or mission, an organization should be alert to the problems of arriving at a concept of its business which is too broad to be operationally useful.[10] While the widespread tendency of organizations to diversify has perhaps rendered the traditional identification of firms with particular industries obsolete and overly narrow, there is equal danger in establishing a "common thread" concept that is so encompassing as to obscure where the organization is heading and how it should proceed. For example, a hospital may perceive its mission broadly as one of "providing comprehensive health care to the residents of the surrounding community." But is this to include filling cavities and pulling teeth, examinations for eyeglasses, nursing of the aged, annual checkups, and rehabilitation services for the handicapped—all of which are often performed by medical professionals outside hospitals? A state university is unquestionably in the business of "higher education," but does this mean it should offer the *full* range of programs in "higher education"—including technical training, associate

---

[9] Ibid., p. 82.

[10] H. Igor Ansoff, *Corporate Strategy* (New York: McGraw-Hill Book Company, 1965), pp. 105–8.

degrees similar to those of junior colleges, adult and continuing education, as well as undergraduate and graduate programs in *all* disciplines and professions? A railroad company may decide to view itself as a "transportation company," but does this mean it should get into long-haul trucking or airfreight services or fleet car leasing or intercity busing or rapid transit? The Environmental Protection Agency is quite properly concerned with reducing air and water pollution to tolerable levels but does this mean that its mission should be broadened to promote the creation of a totally aesthetic environment that is free of all types of "pollution"—noise, slums, billboards, unsightly vacant lots, or whatever?

Generally speaking, an organization's concept of its business should: (1) avoid the ambiguity of purpose and strategy that comes with an overly broad concept, (2) give *specific guidance* as to strategy, goals, and objectives, and (3) not be so confining as to foreclose growth and adaptation to environmental change. There is some dispute, however, over whether an organization's concept of itself should provide a "common thread" for its several activities.

The prevailing view seems to be that it is desirable for an organization's activities, however diversified, to contain a common thread or else to possess some form of strategic fit. *Strategic fit* is a measure of the joint effects, or of the mutually reinforcing impacts, that engaging in different activities have on an organization's overall effectiveness and efficiency.[11] Or, to put it most simply, strategic fit is a $2 + 2 = 5$ phenomenon. The fit can take several forms. *Product-market fit* exists when different products follow common distribution channels, utilize the same sales promotion techniques, are bought by the same customers, and/or can be sold by the same sales force. *Operating fit* results from purchasing and warehousing economies, joint utilization of plant and equipment, overlaps in technology and engineering design, carryover of R&D activities, and/or common labor force requirements. *Management fit* emerges when different kinds of activities present managers with comparable or similar types of technical, administrative, or operating problems, thereby allowing the accumulated managerial know-how associated with one line of business to spill over and be useful in managing another of the organization's activities. The value of having a common thread and/or strategic fit in a diversified organization is the unifying focus and rationale it gives to management in planning and administering the organization's activities.

On the other hand, the conglomerate movement is by design characterized by lack of product-market-technology fit and a common thread concept. Textron, for example, has built a successful sales-profit record with activities as diverse as Bell helicopters, Gorham silver, Homelite saws, Sheaffer pens, Fafnir bearings, Speidel watchbands, Polaris snowmobiles, Sprague gas meters and fittings, Bostitch staplers, air cushion vehicles, iron castings, milling

---

[11] David T. Kollat, Roger D. Blackwell, and James F. Robeson, *Strategic Marketing* (New York: Holt, Rinehart & Winston, Inc., 1972), pp. 23–24.

machines, rolling mills, industrial fasteners, insurance, and missile and spacecraft propulsion systems—among others. In its *1976 Annual Report,* Textron outlined its business concept and objectives as follows:

> Textron is founded on the principle of balanced diversification, designed on the one hand to afford protection against economic cycles and product obsolescence and on the other to provide a means for participating in new markets and new technologies. The key elements are balance and flexibility in a rapidly changing world.
>
> Textron seeks to be distinctive in its products and services—distinctive as to technology, design, service and value. Superior performance will be achieved by way of excellence and quality.
>
> Textron operations are conducted through a number of divisions in five groups—Aerospace, Consumer, Industrial, Metal Product, and Creative Capital. Each division carries on its business under its own name and with its own organization. Textron's management philosophy is based on decentralization of day-to-day operations, coupled with centralized coordination and control to assure overall standards and performance.
>
> There are three priorities: People development. Internal profit growth. New initiatives.
>
> During the period of recovery from recession, continued emphasis has been placed on internal growth and refinement of operations.
>
> In 1972 Textron set objectives for the ten-year period from 1972 to 1982. The specific targets for average annual compound rates of growth are:

> Sales: 8 percent, to $3.5 billion in 1982.
> Progress, 1972 to date: 12 percent, to $2.6 billion in 1976.
>
> Net income: 10 percent, to $200 million in 1982.
> Progress, 1972 to date: 10 percent, to $121 million in 1976.
>
> Net income per common share: 10 percent, to $6.00 in 1982.
> Progress, 1972 to date: 9 percent, to $3.23 in 1976.

Using an aggressive acquisition-merger strategy quarterbacked by Harold Geneen, International Telephone and Telegraph (ITT) in the short span of 15 years grew from a medium-sized telecommunications company in 1959 into the nation's 11th largest industrial corporation with annual sales exceeding $11 billion in 1976. A congressional committee hearing in 1969 revealed that ITT's aggressive acquisition-merger strategy made "the world of ITT" a conglomerate structure of some 350 companies having an additional 700-plus, lower tier subsidiaries of their own. ITT products and companies run the gamut, including telephone equipment, Sheraton hotels, Wonder Bread, Avis Rent-a-Car, Smithfield Hams, Bobbs-Merrill Publishing Co., Hartford Insurance Co., Aetna Finance Co., Jabsco Pump Co., Gotham Lighting Co., Speedwriting Inc., Transportation Displays, Inc., Rayonier chemical cellulose, Bramwell Business School, South Bend Window Cleaning Co., and Scott lawn care products.

Textron and ITT, along with several other conglomerates, have been successful enough to cast doubt upon the *necessity* of a "common thread" concept or of strategic fit. But the final verdict is not in yet.[12] As acquisition-minded conglomerate enterprises neared the end of their merger spree in the late 1960s and early 1970s and either tried or were forced to concentrate on becoming "operating companies," significant numbers encountered serious difficulty. Managing widely diverse subsidiaries proved more complex than had been thought and profits started to suffer. Litton Industries, the kingpin of the glamour conglomerates, in 1968 was among the first to encounter harder times; Litton's top management found itself short on the experience and specific product-market knowledge requisite for providing guidance on the enormous number of unrelated problems being encountered at the operating level. Profits began to nose-dive (from a high of $2.13 per share in 1967 down to a loss of $0.14 per share in 1972) and so did the price of Litton's stock (from an all-time high of $101 in 1967 to $4 at year-end 1974). The problems which Singer had with diversification are presented in Illustration Capsule 5. On a broader front, during the 1967–71 period the profits of only 14 of 39 of the "leading" conglomerates were above the average annual rate of return on stockholders' equity for as many as four of the five years.[13]

Illustration Capsule 5

What Went Wrong with Singer's Diversification Program?

During most of its history Singer has been a profitable company. It was one of the first multinational corporations, and up until the late 1940s it produced two out of every three sewing machines sold in the world. In the late 1950s, however, Singer showed some telltale signs of decay and complacency. The company was still selling some machines designed in the 19th century. Its plants were outmoded and inefficiently utilized. Its management was lethargic, and profits were on a downslide. Japanese sewing machine producers were flooding the world with machines that sold at prices below Singer's cost of production. Singer's market share had fallen from a high of approximately 65 percent down to about 30 percent in the United States and to about 35 percent in most foreign markets.

To do something about the deteriorating situation Singer's board of directors brought in Donald Kircher as Singer's new president. Kircher's program to revive Singer consisted of two main objectives. The first was to get the sewing-machine business moving again and the second was to guide Singer into new fields of endeavor.

To take advantage of lower labor costs abroad Kircher directed that imports from Singer's foreign plants be increased and the cost savings used to bring prices down closer to those of the Japanese machines. Subsequently, one Singer model

---

[12] For an interesting discussion of some of the issues involved, see Lewis Meman, "What We Learned from the Great Merger Frenzy," *Fortune,* April 1973, pp. 70–73, 144–50.

[13] Federal Trade Commission, "Rates of Return in Selected Manufacturing Industries, 1962–1971" (Washington, D.C.: U.S. Government Printing Office, 1973), pp. 50–56.

Illustration Capsule 5 (continued)

was priced at $49.50—about half the former minimum. The company began an advertising campaign promoting the theme that home sewing was not something poor people do of necessity but, rather, a fashionable leisure-time activity. Singer moved many of its stores from downtown sections out to shopping malls and added smart, colorful fabrics to its materials line. Sewing machines were redesigned and came in many different colors. The result was a new image that not only expanded the market for sewing machines but also enabled Singer to sell a higher proportion of more expensive and more profitable models. Singer's market share in the United States edged up to 40 percent and in the world market the company was far outselling its nearest rival.

In seeking to diversify Singer's business, Kircher set forth several criteria for determining what kinds of companies and businesses should be considered. Kircher intended that Singer remain an operating company, not become a conglomerate holding company. Hence, the first criterion specified that diversification should take advantage of Singer's strengths, specifically Singer's skills in manufacturing small precision machines. At the time, Singer prided itself on producing such high-quality sewing machines in its 15 worldwide plants that it guaranteed them for 30 years. Singer also made the Craftsman line of power tools for Sears and manufactured small motors and blowers for vacuum cleaners.

In addition, Kircher felt that Singer's acquisitions should be in businesses that could use Singer's know-how in demonstrating products to customers and in providing expert mechanical service. In making foreign acquisitions, Kircher decided that there was less risk of Singer getting into industries that were technologically less advanced, because foreign markets for unsophisticated products were not yet saturated. But in its U.S. diversification program Kircher reasoned that Singer should seek out only companies and industries characterized by a very high rate of technological progress.

Singer's first major diversification move took place in 1963 when it acquired Friden, Inc., for $182 million in stock. Friden had a good reputation in electromechanical calculators and accounting machines used in banking and other businesses. Its products, like Singer's, required sales and maintenance forces skilled in demonstration and service. Furthermore, Friden was endeavoring to develop one of the first electronic calculators.

In 1968, Singer acquired General Precision Equipment Corp., at a cost of $450 million in Singer stock. General Precision had a profitable business and produced washing machines, automobile air conditioners, military computers, inertial navigation systems, missile guidance systems, and flight simulators. Kircher reasoned that General Precision would give Singer a very substantial advanced technology capability—something which he believed that a large company in the consumer products area needed in order to be really successful.

Next, Singer expanded into home and office furniture, encouraged mainly by the excellent profits it made on the wooden cabinets it sold along with its sewing machines. Since Singer was selling appliances through its European sewing-machines stores, the decision was made to acquire an Italian manufacturer of refrigerators and washing machines. In West Germany, Singer bought a mail-order house. None of these acquisitions stirred any serious debate within Singer's board of directors.

However, the unanimity of the board came to a rather sudden end in early 1971 with the acquisition of the Besco Group, a cluster of small home-building companies in northern California. The board could see no discernable relationship of

Illustration Capsule 5 (continued)

home building to the guidelines Kircher had set forth. Several board members vigorously opposed the acquisition but the majority went along with Kircher and approved the acquisition. Kircher explained the move into the home-building market in Singer's 1971 *Annual Report* as part of a "continuing process of aligning the company's principal fields of activity and investments with current and anticipated social and economic trends." (As things turned out, Singer's home-building business proved profitable even during the 1973–75 period when times were very lean for the residential construction industry. But Kircher himself conceded that the "question of its fit with the balance of the company—in philosophical terms—still exists.")

In 1973, Singer's profits climbed to record highs—$94.5 million on sales of $2.5 billion. Nonetheless, serious problems were developing at Friden where the revolution in solid-state electronics was rapidly obsoleting the electromechanical calculator, Friden's basic product. Moving to defend its position, Friden (and Singer) poured several million dollars into the development of new electronic calculators. Friden also developed minicomputer systems to replace its electromechanical billing and accounting machines. But the methods required to sell these new systems turned out to be quite different from the methods used to sell its older machines, and Friden's sales force never seemed to get the hang of the new techniques. In addition, Friden began developing too many different devices and applications for its sales force to handle adequately. Kircher also pushed Friden's executives against their will into developing point-of-sale terminals (or electronic cash registers)—a move which in time proved very costly. Friden (its name then changed to Singer Business Machines) went on to become first in the field with its electronic cash registers, obtaining over $350 million in orders from Sears, J. C. Penney, and others for 65,000-plus units. Nonetheless, Friden was an unprofitable leader—between 1970 and 1975 the division as a whole lost some $60 million. (More recently, NCR made rapid inroads and moved ahead of Singer.)

In 1974, Singer had to borrow $150 million, mainly to finance its business machines operations; the loans pushed the company's total debt over the billion-dollar mark. Also, in 1974, a decision was made to close out the electromechanical side of Friden, including the factory in the Netherlands that was producing essentially obsolete billing and accounting machines; the loss write-offs of this move amounted to $30 million (after taxes).

Singer eventually reported a net loss of $10 million for 1974 from its combined operations, the first year the company had not made a profit since 1917 (when the loss related to properties that were confiscated during the Russian Revolution).

In late 1975, Singer's board of directors decided that a new man was needed to bail Singer out of its growing multitude of problems. Donald Kircher was asked to resign. His replacement was an outsider, Joseph Flavin, who was enticed by Singer's board away from his job of executive vice president of Xerox.

Within one month of his arrival, Flavin announced that Singer was withdrawing from its highly troubled business machines operations and would write off $400 million in 1975's last quarter. The nearly record loss write-off, coupled with a $26 million write-off in the third quarter, brought Singer's losses for 1975 to $451.9 million. It also reduced Singer's stockholder equity by more than 50 percent and virtually assured that no common stock dividends would be paid by Singer in 1976 and 1977. Moreover, dividends on Singer's four series of preferred stock issues were cut 80 percent in order to meet a $545 million revolving credit agreement negotiated in July 1975.

Illustration Capsule 5 (concluded)

To raise cash after a reduction in its credit rating, Singer was forced to sell its consumer products receivables to General Electric Credit Corp. for $88 million. Shortly thereafter, the company announced closings of its graphic systems and telecommunications operations, its Italian appliance plant, several furniture factories, and an industrial sewing-machine plant, as well as the sale of its German mail-order house and its water resources business. The proceeds allowed Singer to pay back $40 million of its outstanding loan obligations.

In sum, most of Singer's problems stemmed from an acquisition program unsupported by adequate strategic guidelines and analysis. But the difficulties with Friden (which, both in the beginning and later on, seemed like a "perfect fit") came from a series of unsuccessful attempts to coordinate and solve the marketing and engineering problems associated with converting electromechanical calculating equipment to solid-state electronics.

As of early 1976, the only remaining pieces of Singer's attempt at strategic diversification were its traditional sewing-machine business, its aerospace operations, and its nonconsolidated housing subsidiary—none of which were deemed growth businesses at that time.

Sources: "How the Directors Kept Singer Stitched Together," *Fortune,* December 1975, pp. 100 ff.; and "Singer Performs Some Costly Surgery," *Business Week,* January 12, 1976, p. 30.

Furthermore, because broad diversification often defies the establishment of a common purpose among a conglomerate's several businesses, there is some question about a conglomerate's ability to establish a strong identity and market image. The confusion and uncertainty over corporate purpose, corporate objectives, and corporate strategy that is engendered by conglomerate diversification is evidenced by the number of firms which now designate themselves by initials—LTV, FMC, ACF Industries, SCM, NLT, MCA, AMAX, CPC International, AMP, A-T-O, TRW, GAF, NVF, DHJ Industries, UMC Industries, SCOA Industries, RLC, and NL Industries.

In conclusion, then, while it is not *absolutely essential* for a common thread or strategic fit to run through each of an organization's several activities, experience seems to indicate that few organizations have managed to build a successful organization concept and strategy without finding a common denominator for at least most of its business. The reason, simply enough, is that from the standpoint of managerial know-how the problems of managing diversification tend to get out of hand when an organization's range of operation spans many unrelated product markets and technologies.[14] The conglomerate's penchant for rate of return criteria as *the* decisive strategic guide thus runs the risk of deteriorating into mediocre long-run performance unless a conglomerate's managers are exceptionally good at using "management by the numbers" as a substitute for firsthand knowledge of the business.

---

[14] As an illustration of some of the difficulties a conglomerate company may encounter, see Dan Cordtz, "What Does U.S.I. Do? Why, Almost Everything," *Fortune,* February 1973, pp. 73–77.

THE LEVELS OF STRATEGY

Once an organization has gotten a firm grip on its concept of itself and what business it seeks to be in, attention must then focus more sharply on developing a strategic plan. The whole of an organization's strategy is always a compound of many distinct actions and decisions, rather than a single point of attack. A complete strategy consists of a hierarchical network of root strategies, supporting functional area strategies, and operating strategies. A *root strategy* (or *overall corporate strategy*) sets forth the main theme of an organization's strategic plan and also serves as the basis for designing whatever functional area support strategies are required to give the plan substance, completeness, and operational meaning. An organization's overall corporate or root strategy acts as an umbrella linking the several functional area support strategies; it provides guidance for making the support strategies in marketing, production, finance, and so on consistent with the overall strategic plan. The principal distinction between *supporting strategies* and *operating strategies* is that the former are "major" functional corollaries of the root strategy and thus are made in the higher echelons of the management structure, while the latter refer to specific means of carrying out the various facets of functional strategies (and fall within the purview of operating-level managers). Operating strategies define the *specific actions* which the enterprise intends to take in the marketplace in producing its products, in financing its activities, in securing needed resources, in structuring its organization, and in carrying out other day-to-day activities. Beyond this, the differences between functional area strategies and operating strategies reduce to matters of scope and of sequence within the management process. Needless to say, if the strategic plan is to be well-conceived, the overall corporate or root strategy, the several supporting functional area strategies, and the operating-level strategies will all need to be in harmony with one another and thus mutually reinforcing. In other words, the separate pieces of an enterprise's overall strategic plan must interlock and interface smoothly—like the pieces of a puzzle. It is obviously self-defeating when one or more strategic elements are in conflict and working at cross purposes.

Figure 2–1 depicts a hypothetical composite strategy and the several levels of directional actions and decisions requisite for making it operationally complete. Observe the logical flow from root strategy to supporting functional strategies to operating strategies. It should be evident from an examination of this figure why an organization's strategic plan is the sum total of the directional actions and decisions it must make in trying to accomplish its purpose and economic mission: *without supporting functional strategies and operating strategies, the statement of the root strategy lacks the completeness and operational specificity needed to give concrete guidance to organizational subunits and their members*. Moreover, it should be noted that while each of the strategy elements in Figure 2–1 has its own separate and distinct characteristics (and can thus be assessed or modified individually),

FIGURE 2–1
The Levels of Strategy for a Hypothetical Petroleum Company

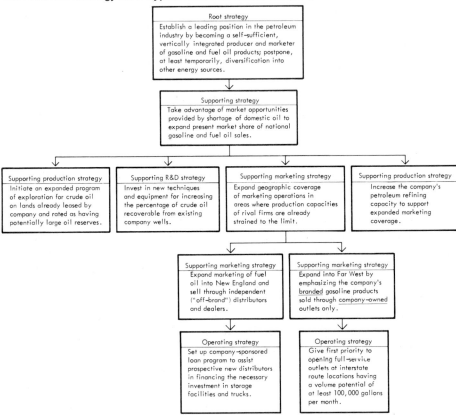

at some point they must be looked at *as a whole* to see if they form a *consistent* strategic design. In other words, it is important that each successive level of strategy be logically derived from and consistent with the preceding level and, further, that there be logical fit between the various strategic elements at each level.

THE DETERMINANTS OF STRATEGY

Formulating a suitable strategic plan involves matching an organization's internal capabilities with its external opportunities, subject to an acceptable degree of risk. The analytical process whereby this is done brings a number of the determinants of strategy to the forefront.

Product-Market Opportunities

Opportunity is always a factor in determining strategy.[15] Much of the time it is a *pivotal strategic consideration,* for unless one perceives (rightly or wrongly) that an opportunity exists there is little point in proceeding. But, on occasions, opportunity is just a necessary presence. For instance, when demand for one of a company's existing products is growing rapidly, it is virtually certain that strategy will quickly follow in one way or another the opportunity for increased sales and profits; the gut issue here is how to differentiate one's strategy from that of rival organizations.

In viewing the role of opportunity in the strategy formulation process, it is important to distinguish between *environmental opportunities* and *company opportunities.*[16] It is fair to say that there are always environmental opportunities in an economy as long as there are unsatisfied needs and wants backed up by adequate purchasing power. But none of these necessarily represent opportunities for a specific company. New forms of health care delivery are probably not an opportunity for Texaco, nor is a growing popularity of tennis necessarily an opportunity for manufacturers of pipe fittings and valves. The environmental opportunities that are most likely to be relevant to a particular company are those where the company in question will be able to enjoy a strategic or differential advantage.

A number of companies have been observed to pursue product-market opportunities in a particular strategic sequence. Starting from a single-product, limited-market base, a firm first seeks to increase its sales volume,

---

[15] As pointed out and neatly summarized by Philip Kotler, there is a difference of opinion in the literature of management regarding whether the strategy formulation process should begin with the identification of opportunities or with the defining of purpose, objectives, and goals. Those who say the first step should be to identify opportunities argue that (1) many organizations have gotten their start because they recognized the existence of a major opportunity (Xerox, Polaroid, Holiday Inns, IBM, and Coca-Cola, among others); (2) many organizations which lack sharply defined objectives and are unable to articulate what they are really trying to do have nonetheless compiled a good record of seizing opportunities; and (3) a number of organizations have changed their objectives when their opportunities changed (as did the March of Dimes in shifting to the problem of birth defects when the Salk vaccine virtually eliminated polio).

Those who argue that the setting of purpose, objectives, and goals should logically precede a search for opportunity point out that (1) a number of organizations have been observed to look for opportunities that will allow them to achieve sales, profit, and growth objectives, (2) the environment is simply too full of opportunities for companies to look merely for opportunities without a guiding purpose and set of goals and objectives; and (3) organizations can and do, from time to time, change their objectives—an event which, subsequently, leads them to search for new and different opportunities.

Both viewpoints have merit in theory and in practice. Quite clearly there is a close two-way link between an organization's search for opportunity and its definition of purpose, objectives, and goals. As long as this is recognized, there is little need to become embroiled in a "chicken or egg—which came first" type of controversy.

See Philip Kotler, *Marketing Management: Analysis, Planning and Control,* 3d ed. (Englewood Cliffs, N.J.: Prentice-Hall, Inc., 1976), p. 46.

[16] Ibid., p. 47.

improve its market share, and build customer loyalty. In essence, this phase represents a more intensive implementation of the existing strategy. Policies regarding price, quality, service, and promotion are fine tuned to respond more precisely to a detailed market need, often including the introduction of a bigger product line to meet minor variations in customer tastes and preferences. As this strategy approaches its full exploitation, a growth-minded company will next begin to assess the opportunities for geographical market expansion. Normally, the strategy of wider geographical coverage proceeds from local to regional to national to international markets, though the degree of penetration may be uneven from area to area because of varying profit potentials and may, of course, stop well short of global or even national proportions. When the opportunities for profitable market area expansion start to peter out, the organization's strategy typically shifts to opportunities for vertical integration—either backward to sources of supply or forward to the ultimate consumer. For some companies this is a natural strategic move, owing to the close relationships to the organization's main product line and to the potential for realizing economies of scale.

Once a firm has reached the limits of geographical market expansion for its original product line and has also come to terms with the possibilities of forward and backward integration, the strategic options are either to continue in the same lines of business and attempt a more intensive implementation or to shift the focus to diversification opportunities. Theoretically, sustained diversification could eventually cause an organization's strategy to span the full range of products and markets were it not for an inability to manage increasingly larger and more diverse organizations in an effective and efficient fashion.

Organizational Competence and Resources

No matter how appealing or how abundant product-market opportunities may be, the strategist is forced to validate the viability of each "opportunity" by inquiring into whether the organization has the means to capitalize upon it, given the opposing forces of competition or organizational circumstance. Opportunity without the competence to capture it is an illusion. An organization's strengths (demonstrated and potential) may make it particularly suited to seize some opportunities; likewise, its weaknesses may make the pursuit of other sorts of opportunities excessively risky or else disqualify it entirely. The strategist is thus well advised to seek out a match between opportunity and competence which exploits or extends organizational strengths and which contains or minimizes dependence upon its weaknesses.

An organization's skills and strengths derive primarily from gradually accumulated experience and sustained success in its business. Unique and occasional flashes of skill or strength are rarely as dependable as are those built up over a period of time and subjected to the tests of competitive pressure. It takes more than a year or two of experience and success to develop a level of expertise in which much confidence can be placed.

In practice, one finds that the strengths and capabilities of organizations vary significantly. Even organizations in the same industry will be found to have different financial resources, different marketing skills, different degrees of technical know-how, different costs, different morale, different images and market standing, different managerial depth—in short, different skills and degrees of expertise. Whether the differences prove to be strengths or weaknesses depends upon how they relate to the chosen strategy. But, clearly, significant differences between one organization and its major rivals may have the potential for being the cornerstone of strategy.

Hence in formulating its strategy, it is always worthwhile for an organization to ponder what distinctive skills and capabilities it can bring to bear that will allow it to draw business away from rival organizations. Some organizations excel in manufacturing a "quality product," others in creative approaches to marketing, and still others in innovation and new product development. An organization's *distinctive competence* is thus more than just what it can do—it is what it can do especially well as compared to rival enterprises.[17] In a competitive enterprise system some sort of distinctive competence is often necessary for long-term success or even survival and this may mean more that just having a "good" product or being "sharp" managers.

Typically, a key element in successful strategy formulation is the ability to build into the strategic plan a set of differences that will set the organization apart from others and give it some kind of strategic advantage. Generally, this means (1) following a different course from rival firms, (2) conceiving of a plan which will have quite different (and more favorable consequences) for one's own organization than for competitors, and (3) making it hard for other organizations to imitate your strategy should it succeed.[18] Obviously enough, these guidelines are easier to follow when an organization has some kind of distinctive competence around which to build its strategy. It is always easier to develop strategic advantage in a market where the success requirements correspond to the organization's distinctive competence, where other organizations do not have these competences, and where potential rivals are not able to attain these competences except at high cost and/or over an extended period of time.[19] But if an organization has no particular distinctive competence upon which to try to capitalize, the next best bet is to focus on ways to exploit existing differences between the organization and those of its competitors.

---

[17] Philip Selznick, *Leadership in Administration* (Evanston, Ill.: Row, Peterson & Company, 1957), p. 42.

[18] Bruce D. Henderson, "Construction of a Business Strategy," reprinted in Daniel J. McCarthy, Robert J. Minichiello, and Joseph R. Curran, *Business Policy and Strategy: Concepts and Readings* (Homewood, Ill.: Richard D. Irwin, Inc., 1975), p. 290.

[19] Kollat, Blackwell, and Robeson, *Strategic Marketing*, p. 24.

Environmental Threats

Very often, certain factors in the environment (existing or potential) present *threats* to an organization's (current or contemplated) strategy. These environment-related threats may concern possible technological or markets developments, the advent of new products or competition, recession, inflation, government action, changing consumer values and life-styles, projections of natural resource depletion, unfavorable demographic shifts, or the like. Such threats can be a major determinant in shaping organizational strategy and a wise strategist is as much alert to the threats of environmental change as to the opportunities that it presents.

Consider, for example, the technological threat (described in Illustration Capsule 6) which solid-state digital watches presented to Timex. Other examples of environmental threats which have produced major strategic implications include:

The possibility of nationalization and government takeover which transnational corporations face if they locate facilities in less-developed nations where there is a record of political instability.

The competitive threat which disposable diapers posed to local diaper service companies.

The rapidly developing technology of copying equipment which soon led to the use of plain paper and thereby ruined the business of the coated paper manufacturers.

The emergence of auto emission controls precluding the use of leaded gasoline and lead additives for reducing engine knock.

The scientific discovery that various fluorocarbons in aerosol sprays damage the ozone layers in the earth's atmosphere and the likelihood of future government bans on their use in aerosols which caused both the aerosol chemical manufacturers and the manufacturers of items sold in aerosol cans to initiate a high-priority search for substitute forms of product packaging.

Illustration Capsule 6

Strategic Implications of the Solid-State Technology Threat to Timex

In 1975, Timex ranked as the world's largest maker of finished watches. Its sales of some 40 million watches a year gave it a commanding 50 percent of the U.S. mechanical watch market and 70 percent of the electric watch market. The core of Timex's strategy was (1) to mass-produce a simple pin-levered movement watch in highly efficient plant facilities, and (2) to market them at rock-bottom prices through some 150,000 outlets—drugstores, variety stores, department stores, and even auto supply dealers. With eye-catching point-of-sale displays and skillful television adver-

Illustration Capsule 6 (continued)

tising (the "torture test ads" narrated by John Cameron Swazy) to go with its low prices, Timex watches made steady market inroads to become the leading brand.

But, unexpectedly in 1975, Timex found itself confronted with a major technological challenge to its market position: how to develop a strategic response to the digital watch and the technology of solid-state electronics—a technology that was on the verge of sweeping the watch industry and undermining the cost advantage Timex enjoyed with its simple pin-levered mechanical watches. To complicate matters, Timex had little, if any, digital technology capability of its own.

The solid-state revolution in digital display watches was spearheaded not by established watch companies (Timex, Bulova, Benrus, Gruen, and others), but by semiconductor companies, including Texas Instruments, National Semiconductor, Litronix, Hughes Aircraft, and Fairchild Camera & Instrument. These firms, although newcomers to the watch industry, moved aggressively to dominate the market. Accustomed to competing in an industry where technological breakthroughs change things almost overnight, they quickly began to ignore traditional watch business practices (such as financing the watch inventories of retail jewelers and considering a 50 percent margin of selling price over cost as standard). They initiated bold price cuts even though demand seemed to be outstripping supply. Whereas the strategy of several semiconductor firms was, originally, to seek to enter into joint ventures with the traditional watchmakers, when the latter reacted so slowly, the strategy was changed to one of beating them head-on in the marketplace. Developments were so fast-paced that by mid-1975 jewelers were worried about the digital watch killing their watch business—not only because of the sharply lower profit margins but also because the semiconductor companies planned to furnish what little service or repair was needed on digitals from the factory, rather than at the point of sale.

Digital watch technology represented a radical departure from the Timex pin-levered watch. The digital watch had no moving parts to wear out and was far more accurate (within a minute per year) than even the most expensive mechanical watch. It operates with just four components: a battery, quartz crystal, an integrated circuit, and a digital display. The battery causes the quartz crystal to vibrate at 32,768 cycles per second (in most watches). The integrated circuit divides the vibrations into one pulse per second, accumulates the pulses to compute minutes, hours, days, and months, and transmits signals to the display to illuminate the digits showing the time and date.

When the first digital watches appeared in 1972, Timex was not unduly alarmed. It, together with most other watch manufacturers, viewed digitals as a fad or at most a specialty watch. Moreover, the first digitals were poorly designed, big and ugly, and experienced 60 percent defective returns. The biggest problem was in the digital time displays which were unreliable and often unreadable. Within three years, however, the semiconductor firms had made rapid progress in making the displays dependable and easy to read; styling was much sharper; and components had been made much smaller. Then in a move reminiscent of their strategy in the calculator business, the semiconductor firms in early 1975 slashed the prices of components in half—to as low as $20 per watch. Lower digital watch prices quickly followed (about half of what prices were in 1974). The move caught Timex and other traditional watch manufacturers offguard. The apparent pricing strategy of the semiconductor firms was based on the "cost learning curve" whereby the prices of watches and component modules were to be lowered as production efficiency increased. But, at the same time, the digital watch firms were finding ways to reduce

Illustration Capsule 6 (concluded)

the number of parts in the module, ways to squeeze more of the electronic circuitry onto the main circuit, and ways to cut assembly costs. These savings permitted large price cuts to be made even sooner than planned.

As late as 1975, Timex had done little more than dip its toe into the digital market, with mediocre results. Solid-state technology was new to Timex. The company had no in-house capacity to produce such components as integrated circuits and digital displays, although it had introduced a digital watch line back in 1972.

Previously, Timex had rejected several contractual offers from semiconductor firms to supply it with digital-watch components. Hughes Aircraft Company, for example, which produced integrated circuits for Timex analog quartz watches, offered in 1971 to build a digital watch to sell under the Timex label if Timex would guarantee a minimum production run of 1 million units. The Hughes offer was for watches with light-emitting diode readouts which have to be turned on by pushing a button. Timex rejected the offer. Meanwhile, Timex's own efforts to develop in-house electronic watch capability progressed slowly. The head of its program to develop both digital and analog quartz watches left in 1973 to become director of watch operations at Rockwell International Corporation; his departure reportedly was due to Timex's failure to move rapidly in building up a digital capability.

The solid-state technology threat thus raised several strategy issues of vital concern to Timex's future:

1. Was the digital watch just a fad or was solid-state circuitry the wave of the future in watchmaking technology? (In 1974, digital watch sales totaled 650,000; some forecasts called for digital sales of 2.5 million units in 1975, and as much as 10 million in 1976.)
2. How quickly and to what extent would the rapidly falling prices of digital watches begin to create strong competitive pressures for Timex? (The prices of digital watches fell from $125 in 1974 to $50 in 1975, and to as low as $20 in early 1976.)
3. When and to what extent should Timex begin to push its own line of digital watches?
4. Should it purchase digital watch components from suppliers or should it develop its own digital component manufacturing capability? If the latter, then should the capability be developed internally or should Timex seek to acquire a firm with the technological know-how and experience?

In the minds of many observers, there was little doubt that Timex would soon have to offer a wide range of digital watches and, because of its carefully nurtured image as a producer of economy-priced watches, that the new digital watches would also have to be low priced. Otherwise, its market position would be in serious jeopardy.

Based upon information in "The Electronics Threat to Timex," *Business Week*, August 18, 1975, pp. 42 ff; "Digital Watches: Bringing Watchmaking Back to the U.S.," *Business Week*, October 27, 1975, pp. 78 ff; "Timex Corporation" in H. Uyterhoeven, R. W. Ackerman, and J. W. Rosenblum, *Strategy and Organization: Text and Cases in General Management* (Homewood, Ill.: Richard D. Irwin, Inc., 1973), pp. 309–20; and "The $20 Digital Watch Arrives a Year Early," *Business Week*, January 26, 1976, pp. 27–28.

For the most part, organizations appear to *react* to environmental threats rather than to plan for or to anticipate them. Actually, this is not a strong criticism of their managers; a great portion of the environmental changes having major strategic implications do not, even with hindsight, appear readily subject to prediction. Many occur without warning and with few, if any, advance clues. How, for example, would one have predicted the Arab oil boycott of the United States in 1973–74 and the success of the OPEC (Organization of Petroleum Exporting Countries) oil cartel in tripling the price of crude oil? Moreover, even when threatening signals are detected early, it is not always easy to assess the extent of their strategic significance. Trying to forecast those future events which have strategic significance is scarcely an exact science. But, this is not sufficient to provide excuses or alibis; it is management's function and responsibility to stay keenly tuned to the possibilities of environmental change and to have strategic plans for any contingencies.

Personal Values and Aspirations

Strategy formulation is rarely so objective an analytical process that the personal values and aspirations of managers are excluded. On the contrary, both casual observation and systematic studies of top management indicate that personal values are important determinants of strategy.[20]

Most managers have personal concepts of what their organization's strategy is or ought to be. These concepts are certain to reflect, in part, a manager's own set of personal values and aspirations. There is a natural tendency for all managers to behave in accordance with their own view of strategy and, in turn, their own values and preferences when choosing among alternative strategies and when interpreting the strategic plan. After all, a person's values and aspirations are such an intrinsic part of his life and behavior that he necessarily relies upon them as criteria for making decisions. On occasions this reliance is conscious and deliberate, at other times it is unconscious.

Consider the following examples of how personal values and aspirations influence strategy:

A minister aspires to be the pastor of the largest congregation in town so he launches a well-organized campaign to attract new members and, in turn, a fund-raising drive to build the biggest church in the area.

A corporate president has unswerving bias against dealing with unions, so he deliberately insists on locating plant facilities in geographical areas where workers have traditionally been indisposed toward unionism. In

---

[20] See, for instance, William D. Guth and Renato Tagiuri, "Personal Values and Corporate Strategy," *Harvard Business Review*, vol. 43, no. 5 (September–October 1965), pp. 123–32; also Andrews, *The Concept of Corporate Strategy*, chap. 4.

turn, he uses the ability to pay subunion wages as a tactic for gaining a competitive edge on costs and selling price.

A local chapter of the American Medical Association is composed of doctors who adamantly oppose any steps toward national health insurance and "socialized medicine," so they agree to encourage all members to charge fees no higher than Blue Cross-Blue Shield guidelines for reimbursements of policyholders in an effort to reduce public pressure for government-sponsored insurance plans.

A chief executive officer of a large corporation wishes to make his company "number one in sales in the industry" so he pushes for a marketing strategy that calls for increasing volume and sales revenue even at the expense of slightly smaller (though acceptable) profit margins and returns on investment.

Societal Constraints and Social Responsibility

The ethical, political, social, and economic aspects of the external environment obviously enter into strategy formulation. Actually, the interaction between strategy and societal factors is a two-way street—they influence each other. However, here, we wish to focus on how societal values influence strategic flexibility. Some illustrations of the strategic constraints and revisions which external forces can produce include:

The emergence of the energy shortage in 1973–74 forced oil companies and electric utilities to shift their marketing strategies abruptly from one of encouraging greater energy consumption to one of actively promoting energy conservation. Both industries ceased all publicly visible promotional activities and ran media ads advising consumers of ways not to be "fuelish."

Rising public consciousness of product safety and pollution problems caused many companies to revamp their products, alter plant facilities, move to new plant locations, and change production technologies so as to comply with state and federal regulations. (At the same time, the scramble to meet production control standards afforded firms with distinctive competencies in manufacturing pollution control devices with vastly expanded strategic and market opportunities.)

In 1972–73, when several consumerist groups focused attention on the nutritional content of breakfast cereals and on the subtle influence of the Saturday morning cereal commercials the breakfast cereal manufacturers responded by radically upgrading the nutrient value of their products and by revamping their TV ads so as to avoid suggestive implications that children should "Eat Winkies because they will help you become an All-American."

Federal rules and regulations regarding equal employment opportunities for minorities and women forced colleges and universities to reconsider strategies and practices for recruiting faculty and students.

The discovery that substantial numbers of large corporations made illegal financial contributions to political campaigns and regularly made illegal payoffs to officials of foreign governments to gain contracts not only raised serious questions about how to impose stiffer safeguards regarding corporate influence-peddling but it also prompted many companies to develop strong guidelines specifying the kind of ethical behavior expected of management officials. Particularly were firms doing business in foreign countries where bribes and payoffs were "normal" and "customary" forced to rethink and revise their approach to the market.

The strategic issues posed by consumerism, ecology, truth-in-packaging, equal employment, antitrust regulation, occupational health and safety, open housing, product safety, shifts in foreign policy, import quotas and tariffs, changes in national economic policy, tax reform, ethics and moral values, and other societal-based factors can scarcely be ignored by any organization. Many managements, since they exercise little control over external developments, view the political, social, and economic dimension of strategy formulation as a constraint and sometimes as a threat. This view is not without some justification; external changes can indeed be potentially threatening to an organization's strategy—as is indicated by Mobil Oil's public appeal to moderate the ecological regulations on offshore oil exploration in Illustration Capsule 7.

But, at the same time, external developments can bode good as well as ill for an organization. Although dwindling crude oil supplies pose obvious strategic threats to the oil companies and to industrial energy users, the effect is also to create major new market opportunities for organizations with expertise in energy research and for the manufacturers of oil drilling equipment, strip mining, insulation materials, and energy-saving devices of all kinds.

Irrespective of whether socioeconomic and political change destroys or creates strategic opportunities, constant monitoring of environmental developments is an essential ingredient of strategy formulation. Indeed the desirability (if not the imperative) of relating the organization to the needs and expectations of society has come to be a standard feature of strategy formulation and strategy implementation, falling under the heading of *social responsibility*. The concept of social responsibility, as it affects strategy and policy, entails (1) adapting the organization to the changing requirements of society; (2) endeavoring to keep organizational activities in tune with what is generally perceived as the public interest; (3) responding positively to emerging societal priorities; (4) demonstrating a willingness to take needed action ahead of confrontation; and (5) balancing stockholder interests against the larger interest of society as a whole. Being "socially responsible" has both carrot and stick aspects. There is the positive appeal for an organization to pursue strategies and policies that will enhance its opportunities to prosper—opportunities which are inexorably tied to the healthy well-being

Illustration Capsule 7

Mobil Oil Company's View of the Ecological Constraints Placed upon Offshore Oil Exploration

A Fable For Now:

The Procrastinating Lion

In the jungle of Yusa, where the lion reigned as king, the other animals came to him when decisions had to be made for the welfare of all. The lion, although strong and brave and certainly of more than average intelligence, did not just make decisions willy-nilly. He listened to the other animals before saying "yes" or "no" or "maybe" or even "let's wait a while."

The animals of Yusa depended on the fruit of the bugaboo tree to exist. Bugaboo trees were not easy to find. But their fruit, squeezed into juice, provided energy in large quantities to all the animals. The gazelles ran faster on it; the water buffalo worked harder; even the monkeys, who from their lofty perches kept watchful eyes on all that went on in the jungle, got their climbing power from the fruit of the bugaboo tree.

All went well in Yusa until one day an ox cart laden with bugaboo juice overturned, spilling the thick liquid on the jungle floor. The monkeys, from their tall trees, saw what happened and immediately went to the lion. "Stop giving permits to producers of bugaboo juice," they demanded. "Bugaboo juice is fouling the jungle."

The juice producers, on the other hand, when summoned by the king of beasts, pointed out that although accidents did happen, they were relatively rare occurrences. Besides, they said, "We cleaned it up in a hurry and no damage was done."

But the monkeys made so much noise that the lion, while he wouldn't say "no," wouldn't say "yes," either. As a result, no permits were issued, no new supplies of bugaboo were found, and the Yusa animals began dipping into storage or buying some from other jungles, where supplies were plentiful.

One day, the other jungles decided not to send any more bugaboo to Yusa. The lion's roar could be heard throughout the jungle. "Where," he said, "has all our bugaboo gone? Bring the producers to me."

"The bugaboo has not gone, your worship," the producers said. "It's there, but you won't let us look for it. Although you didn't say 'no,' you didn't say 'yes,' either. We think we can find it without hurting the jungle. We've done it 20,000 times and the jungle's still here. As a matter of fact, about five times more bugaboo juice lands on the jungle floor from natural causes than we spill."

"Too messy, too messy, too messy," the monkeys chattered. Loudly. And the lion demurred once more. The other animals wanted the bugaboo juice. But the monkeys had their way, because they made the most noise.

And, because the lion listened only to those who made the most noise, the jungle of Yusa continued to pay exorbitant prices to other jungles for their bugaboo juice—whenever they could get it.

Moral: Don't let exaggerated fears make a monkey out of you.

Some people, for example, make a real bugaboo about offshore drilling for oil and gas. Actually, there have been only four major spills out of approximately 20,000 wells drilled in U.S. waters, and even those were promptly cleaned up, without any long-term ecological damage. If America is to relieve its dependence on foreign petroleum, our country cannot afford further procrastination in opening new offshore areas, where there is significant potential for finding oil and gas. And that's no fable.

Mobil

of society. And there is the negative burden of public criticism and onerous regulation if it comes up short.

There is, however, no inherent conflict between the pursuit of organizational objectives and the pursuit of societal objectives. From the standpoint of entrepreneurial enterprises, the greatest success comes from satisfying the wants of individuals and society which otherwise are likely to go unfulfilled. From the standpoint of society, social objectives can be achieved quicker and more efficiently by enlisting the productive power of private enterprises through the opportunity for profit and by imposing harsh penalties for those business activities deemed socially harmful. Thus, social responsibility considerations should not be viewed as necessarily requiring fundamental reorientation of what an organization would otherwise select as its preferred strategy-policy set; it is better to look upon social responsibility as a constraint upon behavior. In fact, it may well be that socially responsible behavior is simply part and parcel of an objective of long-run survival and, in the case of profit-seeking enterprises, long-run profit maximization.

Strategy and Organizational "Personality"

Every organization has a personality and mode of behavior which is somewhat unique to itself. Some organizations are noted for being aggressive and exhibiting leadership; others are clearly more complacent and slow-moving, often quite content to assume a follow-the-leader role. A few older, long-established, family-dominated firms display the characteristics of paternalism toward employees or customers of long-standing. Companies may be variously noted for their conservatism, or their pervasive preoccupation with technological virtuosity, or their financial wheeling and dealing, or their hard-hitting competitive style, or their emphasis on growth, or their social consciousness, or their innovative management techniques, or their desire to avoid risk.

Very often, these traits have a direct bearing on an organization's strategy. For instance, a company whose management is hell-bent on a program of making the firm a world leader in the production of synthetic fibers is not likely to be distracted by low fiber prices, recession, and cutthroat competition in some of its markets or by acquiring an office equipment manufacturing firm in Italy even though the prospects of an attractive yield on invested capital is good. The influence of a company's values and personality on strategy is aptly illustrated in the following statement:

> We are a career company dedicated to coal, and we have some very definite ideas about growth and expansion within the industry. We're not thinking of buying a cotton mill and starting to make shirts.[21]

---

[21] Statement by James L. Hamilton, president of Island Creek Coal Company in *The Wall Street Journal,* September 11, 1962, p. 30.

THE COMPLETE STRATEGY

For a strategy to be truly complete, it should outline a full-blown action plan capable of offering specific guidance all the way down to the operating level. One test of a strategy's completeness is whether it provides full-fledged answers to the questions of *what, how, why, who, where,* and *when*.[22]

The *what* questions concern what business the organization seeks to be in, what its products or services will be, and what markets or market segments it will serve. By forcing itself to address the issues posed by the *what* questions, an enterprise gains a more precise grasp of the concept of its business, who its customers are, why they buy the company's products or services, and the product-market-technology aspects of its strategic plan. And if the *what* questions are pursued to their logical end, then the outcome is a clearer picture of the root strategy and what must be done to make it succeed.

The question of *how* relates to the means for undertaking the *what* aspects of strategy and for assuring that strategic objectives will materialize. In particular, how will the product flow through the various channels of distribution to reach the target market? How is the marketing mix of price, promotion, sales effort, and product development to be aligned with the *what* strategies? How is the process of developing the market (or customer base) for the organization's range of products and services to be handled? How is the strategic plan to be financed and administered? The *how* aspects of strategy, therefore, call the signals for the manner in which the organization is to implement and execute strategy.

The questions of *why* explore the justification and rationale for the *what* and *how* strategies. The issues of *why* look to the intended results of strategy to see if the organization's purpose and objectives are compatible with the imperatives and constraints of profitability, contribution to society, national security, national economic priorities (full employment, growth, price stability, energy conservation, preservation of the environment), international economic development, and social values. As mentioned earlier, every organization must pass the test of legitimacy and usefulness to society if it is to survive.

The *who, where,* and *when* aspects of strategy all touch upon the policy function of management and, in fact, act as check points for close coordination of strategy and policy. Specifically, the *who* questions pertain to issues of organization and commitment: Who is to be responsible for the implementation of strategy? Will implementation be assigned to established organizational units or will new units have to be created? Will established organizational modus operandi have to be changed? Who will assign an appropriate amount of resources to the tasks of strategy? Who will track progress and evaluate performance?

---

[22] This concept of a complete strategy is based on J. Thomas Cannon, *Business Strategy and Policy* (New York: Harcourt, Brace, & World, Inc., 1968), pp. xx–xxv.

Where concerns the physical location of the organization's operations (manufacturing, warehousing, sales), as determined by competitive influences, by the geographic locations of customers and suppliers, and by the answers to the *what, how, who* questions. *When* relates to the timing of strategy implementation. When will implementation begin? At what points in time will the various elements of the strategic plan be phased in (and phased out)? Is the timing of any of the implementation phases critical to strategic success?

In summary, then, a complete concept of strategy says a great deal about the organization involved—its present and future character. First, it defines the organization's business in terms of products, markets, and geographic coverage. These definitions are clear-cut enough to pinpoint product functions and uses as well as the precise customer classes for which these customers will be reached. Second, strategy provides direction and guidance for administrative processes and policies. It suggests, explicitly or implicitly, the requisite organizational design and the future character of the organization. It provides the basis for determining the amount and kinds of resources which will be necessary for implementation. Finally, the complete strategy points toward the criteria for establishing operating policies.

SUGGESTED READINGS

Andrews, Kenneth R. *The Concept of Corporate Strategy.* Homewood, Ill.: Dow Jones-Irwin, Inc., 1971), chaps. 2, 3, 4, and 5.

Ansoff, H. Igor. *Corporate Strategy.* New York: McGraw-Hill Book Company, 1965, chap. 6.

Cannon, J. Thomas. *Business Strategy and Policy.* New York: Harcourt, Brace, & World, Inc. 1968, chaps. 1 and 2.

Drucker, Peter F. *Management: Tasks, Responsibilities, Practices.* New York: Harper & Row, Publishers, 1974, chaps. 6 and 7.

Hall, William K. "Strategy Planning, Product Innovation, and the Theory of the Firm," *Journal of Business Policy,* vol. 3, no. 3 (Spring 1973), pp. 19–27.

Hanan, Mack. "Reorganize Your Company around Its Markets," *Harvard Business Review,* vol. 52, no. 6 (November–December 1974), pp. 63–74.

Levitt, Theodore. "Marketing Myopia," *Harvard Business Review,* vol. 38, no. 4 (July–August 1960), pp. 45–56.

Newman, William H. "Shaping the Master Strategy of Your Firm," *California Management Review,* vol. 9, no. 3 (Spring 1967), pp. 77–88.

Tilles, Seymour. "Making Strategy Explicit," *Business Strategy,* ed. H. Igor Ansoff (New York: Penguin Books, 1970), pp. 180–209.

Vance, Jack O. "The Anatomy of a Corporate Strategy," *California Management Review,* vol. 13, no. 1 (Fall 1970), pp. 5–12.

Vancil Richard F., and Lorange, Peter. "Strategic Planning in Diversified Companies," *Harvard Business Review,* vol. 53 no. 1 (January–February 1975), pp. 81–90.

3

IDENTIFYING STRATEGIC ALTERNATIVES

Markets are not created by God, nature, or economic forces but by businessmen.

Peter F. Drucker

IN the role as chief strategist, the general manager is the person most responsible for coming up with an effective strategic plan. The task requires courage as well as ingenuity. At the outset, taking a "creative" approach to the generation of strategic alternatives raises the possibility that the existing strategy will be sloughed aside, thereby threatening those in the organization who have vested interests in the current strategic plan. Second, imaginative strategy formulation never precludes serious consideration of options detrimental to the existing strategy, irrespective of the internal conflict and unrest it may generate or the hastened demise it may bring to the existing strategy. Nostalgic and inopportune adherence to one's own strategy merely opens the door for outsiders who, lacking strong attachment to strategies of the past or present, will surely be less reluctant to seize upon a fresh strategy if they view the entrenched strategies as vulnerable to attack.

To urge the strategist to leave no stone unturned in the search for alternatives is not, however, to imply that the incumbent strategic plan must always give way to creative alternatives each time the issue of strategy arises. Although every strategy will sooner or later need a major overhaul or even radical surgery, on most occasions reevaluation reveals the general thrust of strategy is appropriate. Usually, fine-tuning will suffice. Nonetheless, it is all too easy to let strategic reevaluation become no more than a time for finding clever variations to the familiar theme. The true purpose of identifying and developing strategic alternatives is to help the strategist avoid the complacency of viewing the prevailing strategy as too much of a given rather than as only one among many possibilities. Therefore, staying committed to an objective assessment of alternative strategies is a powerful guarantee against an organization becoming a prisoner of its own existing strategy.

THE BASIC STRATEGIC ALTERNATIVES

In trying to decide upon strategy to accomplish its chosen purpose, objectives, and goals, an organization has essentially nine different options to select from:

1. Concentration on a single business.
2. Horizontal integration.
3. Vertical integration.
4. Diversification.
5. Joint ventures.
6. Innovation.
7. Retrenchment.
8. Divestiture.
9. Liquidation.

Each of these options merit discussion.

Concentration on a Single Business

The number of organizations which have made their mark parlaying a single product, single-market, or single-technology strategy is exceedingly long. The power and achievement which attaches to concentrating on the right business at the right time is demonstrated by the remarkable performance of such companies as McDonald's, Holiday Inn, BIC Pen Corp., Campbell Soup Co., Gerber, and Polaroid. In the nonprofit sector the specialist strategy has proved successful for the Boston Pops Orchestra, the Peace Corps, the Girl Scouts, Phi Beta Kappa, and the American Civil Liberties Union.

The advantages of a single-pronged purpose and concentrated strategy derive from an ability:

1. To focus on doing *one* thing *very well,* thereby building a distinctive competence.
2. To zero in on specific markets and market segments, thus gaining greater market visibility and even a leadership position.
3. To make full utilization of limited organizational resources.
4. To detect structural changes in customer purchasing behavior and market conditions at an early stage, and to respond quickly to them.
5. To achieve a high degree of efficiency in meeting stiffer competition and in reacting to new market opportunities.
6. To create a differential strategic advantage via the reputation and market image that comes from having a distinctive competence.

At the same time, a specialized business is more manageable. Simplicity breeds clarity and unity of purpose. With the efforts of the total organization aimed at successfully catering to the needs and wants of a clearly identified consumer group, objectives can be made precise and results appraised more easily. Communication is direct. Managers have grass roots knowledge of the business, the organization, its customers, its technology, and its environment. As a consequence, the organization's productivity and overall efficiency tend to be above average, if not superior. The outcome can be an organization that is highly effective in the marketplace.

In fact, the managers of large, diversified companies often view their strongest competitors as being the small, specialized enterprise with concentrated, in-depth expertise rather than large companies to whom a particular product is only one among many of their interests. Such appraisals testify to the competitive strength of a specialized or concentrated strategy.

The listing below identifies some specific variations of the concentration strategy theme:

A. Seek Greater Market Penetration
   1. Increase current customers usage of the product.
      a. Increase the size of units offered for sale.
      b. Incorporate more features into the basic unit.
      c. Create and promote more uses for the product.
      d. Use innovation to shorten the time span for the product to become obsolete.
      e. Give price discounts for increased use.
   2. Attract customers away from rival firms.
      a. Increase advertising and promotional efforts.
      b. Establish sharper product differentiation and brand identification.
      c. Initiate price cuts.
   3. Attract nonusers to buy the products.
      a. Induce trial use through free samples, cents-off coupons, and low introductory price offers to trial users.
      b. Advertise new or different product uses and features.
      c. Reprice the product—up or down.
B. Move into New Markets
   1. Expand into additional geographical markets—regional, national, or international.
   2. Broaden the product's appeal to new market segments.
      a. Introduce new versions of the product aimed at more classes of buyers.
      b. Distribute the product through other channels.
      c. Advertise in different kinds of media.
C. Develop New or Better Products for Present Markets
   1. Focus on developing new features.
      a. Make shorter, lighter, smaller, stronger, thicker, longer, or add extra value.
      b. Change color, shape, odor, taste, sound, ingredients, components, layout, packaging.

2. Improve quality, service, convenience of use.
3. Offer additional models and sizes.

Nonetheless, the strategy of concentrating on a single business poses a major risk. By specializing, an enterprise puts all of its eggs in one basket. If the market for the enterprise's product or service declines, so does the enterprise's business. Changing customer needs, technological innovation, or new products can undermine or virtually wipe out a highly specialized, single-business firm in short order. One has only to recall what television did to the profitability and markets of the once-powerful Hollywood movie producers and what IBM electric typewriters did to the manual typewriter business formerly dominated by Royal-McBee, Underwood, and Smith Corona. And if the product/service is particularly vulnerable to recessionary influence in the economy, then the enterprise's fortunes are subject to wide swings and, consequently, a normally lower stock market appraisal. Illustration Capsule 8 indicates how inflation-recession and changes in the labor force participation rates of women combined to adversely affect Avon's strategy.

Illustration Capsule 8

The Need for Strategy Change at Avon?

As one analyst recently put it, "Avon may be one of the big casualties of how America has changed in the past few years."

The reasoning behind this statement stems from the observation that in the mid-1970s, Avon appeared to be losing access to a growing number of women. Its door-to-door marketing strategy worked brilliantly in the 1960s, but with two out of five American women holding jobs (and the percentage expected to increase), more and more of Avon's customers are not at home when the Avon lady comes calling. Moreover, during the 1970–75 period, inflation and recession combined to put a financial squeeze on many buyers of Avon products—the bulk of whom are blue-collar families; one result was that Avon's sales of items packaged in fancy decanters, vases, and candy dishes fell drastically—the very items where Avon's profit margins were greatest. As a consequence, Avon's market share slipped in a number of lines. The company's profits dropped in 1974 and rebounded in 1975 only after draconian cost controls were imposed.

In 1975, Avon spent only 2 percent of its revenue on advertising, compared with Revlon's 8 percent. Some analysts asserted that part of the slack in sales was due to a lack of "sex appeal" in Avon's products. For example, Avon's new teenage fragrance, "Sweet Honesty," competed with Pfizer's "Skinny Dip."

Avon's basic answer to the changing work habits and economic climate was to reformulate and fine tune its approach to the market. The company introduced variable commissions to encourage saleswomen to push more profitable items. Efforts were made to compile computerized lists of customers—information that had never been tracked before. A number of the products which came packaged in more expensive decanters were dropped. And finally, Avon stepped up its advertising.

According to Avon's president, David Mitchell, the primary strategic objective of these moves was to get Avon back into the sales and profit patterns of the 1960s.

Furthermore, by concentrating its expertise in a narrow area, an organization may find itself without the competence and know-how to break out of its shell and develop alternatives if and when the time arrives to cast off a fast-obsolescing strategic plan. Every product, every service, every technology eventually loses its market grip.[1] Sales volume may still be there, but profitability and growth opportunities shrivel. If the specialist firm is to escape stagnation, it must keep some fresh options open. And like any habit, doing something new and different must be kept sharp by practice. Otherwise the capacity for shifting to new strategies and new businesses is never developed or else withers away.

Horizontal Integration

A *horizontal integration* strategy consists of a firm seeking ownership (or increased control) of some of its competitors. Purchasing one's competitors can be accomplished by buying their common stock, by purchasing their assets, or by a pooling of interests. Horizontal integration is a form of growth by acquisition and, actually, is an offshoot or derivative form of a concentration strategy since the acquiring firm remains in much the same business (unless the competitor it acquires has other business interests as well). The chief constraint in employing a horizontal integration strategy is staying clear of Section 7 of the Clayton Act which forbids acquisition of competitors where the effect "may be substantially to lessen competition, or to tend to create a monopoly."

Vertical Integration

Two factors tend to trigger serious consideration of a vertical integration strategy: (1) diminishing profit prospects associated with further expansion of the main product line into new geographic markets, and (2) being the wrong size to realize scale economies and performance potentials.[2] Market saturation and the impracticalities of an oversize market coverage give rise to the first factor cited. A variety of causes underlie being the wrong size but the symptom is easy enough to spot: one (or a few) of the organization's production or distribution activities are out of proportion to the remainder, thereby making it difficult for the organization to support the volume, the product line, or the market standing requisite for economical operations and long-run competitive survival.[3]

---

[1] It has been estimated that 80 percent of today's products will have disappeared from the market ten years from now and that 80 percent of the products which will be sold in the next decade are as yet unknown. See E. E. Scheuing, *New Product Management* (Hinsdale, Ill.: The Dryden Press, 1974), p. 1.

[2] This section draws heavily from Arthur A. Thompson, *Economics of the Firm: Theory and Practice*, 2d ed. (Englewood Cliffs, N.J.: Prentice Hall, Inc., 1977), chap. 2.

[3] Peter F. Drucker, *Management: Tasks, Responsibilities, Practices* (New York: Harper & Row, Publishers, 1974), pp. 666–67.

Vertical integration has much to recommend itself as a strategy for dealing with these two factors. Consider first the benefits of integrating backward. To begin with, backward integration offers the potential for converting a cost center into a profit producer. This potential may be very attractive when suppliers have wide profit margins. Moreover, integrating backward allows a firm to supercede market uncertainties associated with supplies of raw materials. Where a firm is dependent on a particular raw material or service furnished by other enterprises, the door is always open for requisite supplies to be disrupted by strikes, bad weather, production breakdowns, or delays in scheduled deliveries. Furthermore, the cost structure is vulnerable to untimely increases in the prices of critical component materials. Stockpiling, fixed-price contracts, or the use of substitute inputs may not be feasible ways for dealing with such market uncertainties. When this is the case, bringing supplies and costs under its own wings may be an organization's most profitable option for securing *reliable deliveries* of essential inputs at *reliable prices*. In short, sparing itself the uncertainties of being dependent upon suppliers permits an organization to coordinate and routinize its operating cycle, thereby (1) avoiding the transient, but upsetting, influences of unreliable suppliers and wide swings in supply prices, (2) realizing the cost efficiencies of a stable operating pattern, and (3) insulating itself from the tactical maneuvers of other firms regarding raw material sources. In so doing, an organization can become more a master of its own destiny than a slave to fortuitous market circumstances beyond its control.

While backward integration may be justified by an economic need to assure sources of supply, it may also be the best and most practical way to obtain a workable degree of commitment from suppliers. The case of Sears offers a prime example.[4] A large portion of the merchandise which Sears sells is made by manufacturers in which Sears has an ownership interest. While this may be due to Sears' desire to ''control'' its suppliers, it is as probable that Sears found it could not get reputable suppliers to commit themselves to making goods especially for Sears unless assured of a long-term relationship. The reason is simple: for a firm to become the chief supplier of one of Sears' big-ticket or volume items is likely to make Sears the supplier's main customer and major channel to the market—maybe even its *only* customer and channel of distribution. For a supplier to allow itself to become a ''captive company'' of Sears without some sort of guarantee that the relationship would be a continuing one would be foolhardy and unduly risky. Thus for Sears to get major suppliers to forego their independence and agree to orient most or all of their business to manufacturing products to Sears' specifications to be sold under Sears' brand names and to be delivered according to Sears' demands very likely meant in some cases that Sears had to go beyond the offering of a ''long-term'' contract. Without ties as permanent as those of ownership, some key suppliers would surely have balked

---

[4] Ibid., p. 686.

and Sears would have found itself with unwanted gaps in its product line. Given Sears' merchandising strategy, being the "wrong size" to assure itself of ample suppliers at constant quality and reasonable cost would have been a serious strategic flaw.

The strategic impetus for forward integration has much the same roots. Undependable sales and distribution channels can give rise to costly inventory pileups and frequent production shutdowns, thereby undermining the economies of stable production operations. Loss of these economies may make it imperative for an organization to gain stronger market access in order to remain competitive. Sometimes even a few percentage point increases in the average rate of capacity utilization can make a substantial difference in price and profitability.

For a raw materials producer, integrating forward into manufacturing may help achieve greater product differentiation and thus allow for increased profit margins. In the early phases of the vertical product flow, intermediate goods are "commodities," that is, they have essentially identical technical specifications irrespective of producer (wheat, coal, sheet steel, cement, sulfuric acid, newsprint); competition therefore is extremely price oriented. Yet, the closer the production stage is to the ultimate consumer, the greater are the opportunities for a firm to differentiate its end product via design, service, quality features, packaging, promotion, and so on. Marketing activities become more critical and the importance of price shrinks in comparison to other competitive variables.

For a manufacturer, integrating forward may take the form of building a chain of closely supervised dealer franchises or it may mean establishing company-owned and company-operated retail outlets. Alternatively, it could entail simply staffing regional and district sales offices instead of selling through manufacturer's agents or independent distributors. Whatever its specific format, forward integration is usually motivated by a desire to realize the higher profits that come with stable production, large-scale distribution, and product differentiation or to enjoy the security that comes with having one's own capability for accessing markets and customers.

There is, however, one other aspect of vertical integration which warrants mention. The large size that accompanies full integration puts a firm in a position to exert a measure of monopolistic control over its costs, its selling prices, its production technology, and its customers' buying propensities and attitudes. Size breeds power, and power gives management latitude in making decisions and setting policies. For instance, to the degree that an integrated firm is self-sufficient at each of the intermediate stages of the production process, it is also partially insulated from the impacts of competition and short-run, price-quantity adjustments in the intermediate goods markets. Such freedom is not without design or social import. Max Weber, years ago, observed how complex organizations, moved by an instinct for self-protection and risk avoidance, acted to construct devices that would shield them from unwanted change while, at the same time, promoting a degree of order and stability conducive to achieving peak efficiency and profitability.

Aside from the obvious social disadvantages that *may* accrue from extensive vertical integration, there are internal organizational shortcomings as well. The large capital requirements of vertical integration may place a heavy strain on an organization's financial resources. Second, integration introduces more complexity into the management process. It requires new skills and the assumption of additional risks since the effect is to extend the enterprise's scope of operations. It means bearing the burdens of learning a new business and coping with the problems of a larger organization. While this may all be justified if it remedies a disparity between costs and profits, it can so increase a firm's vested interests in its technology and production facilities that it becomes reluctant to abandon its heavy fixed investments.[5] Because of this inflexibility a fully integrated firm is vulnerable to new technologies and new products. Either it has to write off large portions of its fixed investments or else it must endure a competitive disadvantage with innovative enterprises having no proprietary interests to protect.

Moreover, integration can pose problems of balancing capacity at each production stage. The most efficient sizes at each phase of the vertical product flow can be at substantial variance. This can mean exact self-sufficiency at each interface is the exception not the rule. Where internal capacity is deficient to supply the next stage, the difference will have to be bought externally. Where internal capacity is excessive, customers will need to be found for the surplus. And if by-products are generated they will require arrangements for disposal.

All in all, therefore, a vertical integration strategy has both important strengths and important weaknesses. Which direction the scales tip on integration depends upon (1) how compatible it is with organization purpose and strategy, (2) whether it strengthens an organization's position in its primary market, and (3) whether it permits fuller exploitation of an organization's technical talents. Unless these issues are answered in the affirmative, vertical integration is likely to weaken organizational performance.

Diversification Alternatives

A number of factors, singly or in combination, underlie the appeal of a diversification strategy:[6]

1. An organization may consider diversification because market saturation, competitive pressures, product line obsolescence, declining demand, or

---

[5] One suspects that General Motors' long-standing reluctance to discard its market emphasis on "full-sized" cars is at least partially rooted in its heavy fixed investment in big car-producing facilities and big-car-oriented dealerships.

[6] H. Igor Ansoff, *Corporate Strategy* (New York: McGraw-Hill Book Co., 1965), pp. 129–30; Peter Drucker, *Management*, p. 684; George A. Steiner, "Why and How to Diversify," *California Management Review*, vol. 6, no. 4 (Summer 1964), pp. 11–17; J. F. Weston and S. F. Mansinghka, "Tests of the Efficiency Performance of Conglomerate Firms," *Journal of Finance*, vol. 26, no. 4 (September 1971), pp. 919–36; and Ronald W. Melicher and David F. Rush, "Evidence on the Acquisition-Related Performance of Conglomerate Firms," *Journal of Finance*, vol. 29, no. 1 (March 1974), pp. 141–49.

fear of antitrust action no longer allow performance goals to be met solely through an expansion of its current product-market activities.

2. Even if appealing expansion opportunities still exist in its current business, an organization may diversify because its free cash flow exceeds expansion needs.

3. An organization's diversification opportunities may have a greater expected profitability than that of expanding its present business.

4. An organization may consider diversification because of a desire to spread risk and increase the flexibility of its operations. This desire may stem from uneasiness about "overspecialization" in particular products or technologies, the risks of having a disproportionately large fraction of sales to a single customer, dwindling supplies of a key raw material, or the threat of new technologies.

5. A firm may diversify because of a perceived financial serendipity associated with certain kinds of acquisitions. This search for financial-related advantages is said to account for attempts by firms with depressed earnings to diversify into areas of higher profitability so as to show a higher average earnings performance level, the pursuit of "instantaneous profits" whereby an acquiring firm buys out firms having a lower pre-merger price-earnings ratio in an attempt to immediately realize a higher stock price and earnings per share, and the attempt to increase one's borrowing capacity by acquiring enterprises with low debt to equity ratios. In such instances, the market and technology aspects of an acquisition are secondary to the financial considerations.

6. An organization may pursue diversification to prevent subunits from getting bored with doing the same things over and over. (This is not altogether frivolous. The psychology of something new, something different, something fresh and innovative has a way of keeping an organization alert and capable of successful change.)

One viewpoint even goes so far as to make diversification a condition of survival— "in the long run an organization must diversify or die."[7] The argument here is that a specialist strategy easily falls victim to the new obsoleting the old. Be that as it may, the wealth of organizational experiences with diversification strategies clearly demonstrates that there is *right* diversification and *wrong* diversification.[8] Drucker's analogy to the musician illustrates the point well:

> An accomplished and well-established concert pianist will, as a matter of course, add one new major piece to his repertoire each year. Every few years he will pick for his new piece something quite different from the repertoire through which he has made his name. This forces him to learn again, to hear

---

[7] Steiner, "Why and How To Diversify," p. 12.

[8] Drucker, *Management,* p. 692.

new things in old and familiar pieces, and to become a better pianist altogether. At the same time, concert pianists have long known that they slough off an old piece as they add on one new major one. The total size of the repertoire remains the same. There are only so many pieces of music even the greatest pianist can play with excellence.[9]

In short, then, the question of *what kind of diversification* (how exactly to apply the musician's rule) is a gut strategic issue. In general there are two basic kinds of diversification: *concentric* and *conglomerate.* A concentric diversification strategy is one where the firm seeks to move into activities which mesh to some degree with the present product line, technological expertise, customer base, or distribution channels; it is, in other words, diversification keyed to some common thread or strategic fit element. In contrast, conglomerate diversification, by definition, has no common thread nor does it possess, by conscious design, any features of logical fit.

Concentric Diversification. Concentric diversification has much to recommend as a strategy. Obviously, it allows an enterprise to preserve a common core of unity in its business activities while at the same time spreading the risks out over a broader product base. But more importantly, perhaps, concentric diversification has the advantage of allowing an organization to make the most out of its distinctive competence in related areas.

Specific types of concentric diversification include:

1. Moving into closely related products (a bread bakery getting into saltine crackers).
2. Building upon company technology or know-how (a synthetic fibers manufacturer diversifying into the production of carpets).
3. Seeking to increase plant utilization (a coarse paper bag manufacturer decides to utilize excess paper-making capacity by adding corrugated paperboard boxes to its product line).
4. Utilizing company sources of raw materials (a lumber products firm elects to devote some of its timberland to plywood production).
5. Making fuller utilization of the firm's sales force (a wholesaler of electrical supplies adds electric heating and cooling equipment to its line of products).
6. Building upon the organization's brand name and goodwill (a successful coffee firm diversifies into tea).

Numerous actual examples abound. Procter and Gamble has been eminently successful in building a diversified product line (Crest toothpaste, Ivory Snow, Tide, Duncan Hines cake mixes, Folger's coffee, Pringles potato chips, Head and Shoulders shampoo, Crisco shortening, Comet cleaner, Charmin toilet tissue—to mention a few) around its expertise in marketing household products through supermarket channels. Pepsi-Cola

---

[9] Ibid., p. 685.

practiced concentric diversification when it bought Frito-Lay, as did Coca-Cola in purchasing Minute Maid orange juice and Lockheed in encircling the needs of the Department of Defense with its product line of airframes, rocket engines, missiles, electronics, defense research and development, and ship-building. Sears learned that the absence of similarities between TV sets, auto repair centers, men's suits, draperies, refrigerators, paint, and homeowner's insurance posed no difficulty to its business strategy because the same customer buys them, in very much the same way, and with the same value expectations, thereby providing the essential link for its version of customer-based concentric diversification.

Technology-based concentric diversification has proved successful in process industries (steel, aluminum, paper, and glass) where a single processing technique spawns a multitude of related products. The same paper machines which produce newsprint are equally adept at turning out stationery, notebook paper, and specialty printing paper for books and magazines. The line of products emerging from a single steel mill can easily include sheet steel, steel rails, reinforcing rods, I-beams, metal door frames, and wire products.

Other firms (in chemicals and electronics particularly) have pursued a technology-linked diversification strategy because their expertise in a given scientific area led to the discovery of new technological branches having practical market application. Often, in the early stages of a major technology, it is not feasible to exploit an innovation fully by concentrating on just one or a few product markets. Simultaneous, or else closely sequenced, R&D efforts into several product areas may be optimal. Yet, beyond some stage the progressive branching out of a common technology spreads an enterprise so thin and pushes it in so many different directions that further diversification is counterproductive.

According to Peter Drucker, it may well be that extended technological diversification is becoming outmoded as a viable strategy precisely because the prolific branching out of technology eventually dilutes what once was clear advantage:

> That this might be the case is indicated by the fact that most of these giant extended technological families have a few areas in which they have strength and maintain their leadership position: GE and Westinghouse in heavy electrical apparatus, Philips in consumer electronics, Union Carbide in metallurgical chemistry, Du Pont in textile fibers and so on. In these areas they also maintain their innovative capacity. The reason for the relative sluggishness and vulnerability of these companies is not "poor management" but "spotty management." It is not that they are in too few "good" businesses but that they are in too many that do not "fit."[10]

In contrast, the specialist firms in the electronics industry (such as Sony and Texas Instruments) have sought to make a small corner of the fast-branching

---

[10] Ibid., p. 705.

electronics field their province rather than diversifying into all businesses where electronics plays a role. The success of the specialist approach may explain why in the late 1960s and early 1970s, GE and Westinghouse dropped out of a number of consumer and industrial products in which electricity was an incidental, rather than an essential, factor. As indicated in Illustration Capsule 9, a number of other firms have exhibited a preference for concentric diversification.

Illustration Capsule 9

Examples of Firms That Have Diversified by Building upon Their Distinctive Competence in Their "Original" Line of Business

Companies which have followed a concentric diversification strategy keyed to their product-market-technology know-how or other organizational skills and resources include:

American Biltrite Rubber. Rubber shoe heels and soles, rubber floor tiles, carpets, rubber chemicals, rubber industrial products, synthetic rubber.

Becton, Dickinson. Thermometers, syringes, bandages, other medical supplies, rubber gloves, surgical instruments, reagents, electronic components, laboratory equipment, biochemicals, medical electronic devices, science education aids, laboratory environmental controls, hospital computer systems, navigational instruments, aircraft fabrics, packaging machinery.

Bucyrus-Erie. Power cranes, excavators, drilling machines and tools, tractor equipment, conveyors and conveyor systems, industrial packaging machinery.

Dow Chemical. Industrial chemicals, agricultural chemicals, plastic chemicals and film, pharmaceutical intermediaries, styrofoam, acrylic fiber, coated paper, ethical drugs, animal health products, packaging machinery, medical diagnostic instruments and services, plastic building products.

Eastman Kodak. Films, cameras, projectors, plates and paper, motion-picture films, chemicals, yarns, plastic molding compounds, organic and commercial chemicals, military optical and other precision equipment, vacuum equipment, microfilm and equipment, vitamins, light chemicals, office copiers, plastic parts and tubing, microfilm EDP (electronic data processing).

General Motors. Cars, trucks, buses, motor homes, diesel locomotives, marine diesel engines, urban and public mass transportation systems.

B. F. Goodrich. Tires and tubes, industrial goods, synthetic rubber, druggists' goods, shoes, latex, rubber chemicals, other chemicals, tire fabrics, organic colors, wheels and brakes for aircraft, vinyl plastic, auto wheels and brakes, imitation leather, floor and wall coverings, petrochemicals, synthetic fiber.

Johnson & Johnson. Bandages, bandaids, surgical supplies, baby care products, sanitary paper products, tooth and hair brushes, nonprescription pharmaceuticals, adhesives, molded plastic medical equipment, ethical drugs, chemicals for textile manufacture, medical and surgical instruments, elastic fabric.

Minnesota Mining and Manufacturing. Pressure sensitive electrical and magnetic tape, adhesives, abrasives, gummed paper, heavy chemical by-products, office copiers, microfilm equipment, photo offset plates, electric ceramics, re-

Illustration Capsule 9 (continued)

> fractories, concrete, stone, coated paper, plastic insulators, ribbon, RFP sheet and pipe, varnish, resins, floor covering, synthetic rubber, cameras, projectors, broadcasting, cable, EDP microfilm.
>
> *National Biscuit.* Baked goods, snack foods, cereals, dog food, cake mixes, other grocery products, candy, frozen baked goods, institutional food service.
>
> *North American Phillips.* Phonographs, tape recorders, cassettes, AKG microphones and headphones, projection lamps for movies and slides, color TV studio equipment, closed circuit television systems, video cassette recorders, FM wireless systems, audiovisual systems, TVs, stereos, receivers, musical instruments.
>
> *Owens-Illinois.* Glass containers, closures, glass insulators, blocks, glass laboratory equipment, glass TV tubes, glass tableware, paper containers, plywood and veneer, plastic molding machines, plastic containers, paperboard, paper bags, plastic tableware, precision glass electronic components, fiber cans, plywood, glass resins, glass for fiber optics, optical systems, gyro test systems, engineering for aerospace, paper cups and plates.
>
> *St. Regis Paper.* Paper bags, ground wood paper, kraft pulp, paper and paperboard, plastic/paper laminates, bag-making and filling machines, paper containers, waxed paper, printing paper, lumber, plywood, polyethylene film and bags, injection molded plastics, stationery, school supplies, dairy products processing and handling equipment, special industrial equipment.
>
> *United States Steel.* Sheet, strip, other mill products, wire, pipe, tube, building materials, prefabricated buildings, coke oven chemicals, construction of buildings, bridges, oil well equipment, cement, titanium, titanium semifabricated products, aluminum building products, engineering consulting service, industrial and agricultural chemicals, plasticizers, chemical coatings, plastic parts, lumber, real estate development.
>
> *Weyerhaeuser.* Lumber, pulp, plywood, miscellaneous wood products, paperboard, particle board, cartons, coated paper, wood building products, chemical by-products, fine paper, home building.
>
> Sources: Richard P. Rumelt, *Strategy, Structure, and Economic Performance* (Cambridge, Mass.: Harvard University Press, 1974); and *Moody's Industrial Manual* (New York: Moody's Investors Service, Inc., 1975).

Conglomerate Diversification.   While one might expect an overwhelming majority of organizations to favor concentric diversification because of the greater likelihood of good strategic fit, the conglomerate strategy has nonetheless attracted some important companies. A simple criterion of "will it meet our minimum standard for expected profitability?" is enough to describe the strategy of such firms as Textron, Whittaker, ITT, Litton, Gulf and Western, and U.S. Industries.

However, other organizations have opted for the conglomerate approach because their distinctive competence either was so narrow as to have little in common with other businesses or was so lacking in depth that any diversification move was inherently conglomerate in nature. And still others have viewed a conglomerate approach as the optimal way of escaping a declining industry or overdependence on a single product-market area. Possible options for conglomerate diversification strategies include:

1. Seeking a match between a cash-rich, opportunity-poor company and an opportunity-rich, cash-poor firm.
2. Diversifying into areas with a counterseasonal or countercyclical sales pattern so as to smooth out sales and profit fluctuations.
3. Attempting to merge an opportunity-poor, skill-rich company with an opportunity-rich, skill-poor enterprise.
4. Seeking out a marriage of a highly leveraged firm and a debt-free firm so as to balance the capital structure of the former and increase its borrowing capacity.
5. Gaining entry into new product markets via licensing agreements or purchase of manufacturing or distribution rights.
6. Acquiring any firm in any line of business so long as the projected profit opportunities equal or exceed minimum criteria.

Aside from the pros and cons of being in businesses not having either a common thread or strategic fit, a purely conglomerate diversification strategy has several other advantages and limitations which should be set forth. First, a conglomerate strategy can lead to *improved* sales, profits, and growth when an organization diversifies into industries where the economic potential is stronger than its existing businesses. However, an organization should beware of being blinded by promising opportunities. Sooner or later every business gets into trouble. Thus, whenever management contemplates either acquisition or grass-roots diversification it should pause long enough to consider carefully whether "if this new business got into trouble, would we know how to bail it out?" If the answer is no, it is surely diversification of the wrong kind even though the lure of above-average profitability seems to exist.[11]

Second, despite the fact that its consolidated performance may improve, the price which a conglomerate pays to buy its way into a growth industry may impair stockholder earnings. This holds whether diversification takes place from within or through acquisition since in either case the absence of any $2 + 2 = 5$ effects stemming from common thread elements frequently results in conglomerate firms' paying a somewhat larger premium for future earnings. The above-market prices which they paid for their acquisitions, as well as the millions of dollars of purchased "goodwill" which appear on their financial statements, are ample evidence of the added costs of "buying in." Third, unless some kind of $2 + 2 = 5$ benefits can be developed, the consolidated performance of a conglomerate enterprise will tend to be no better than if its divisions were independent firms and it may be worse to the extent that centralized management policies hamstring the operating divisions. This implies that the best which conglomerates can generally expect is to be at no cost-efficiency disadvantage in trying to compete against nonconglomer-

---

[11] Of course, management may be willing to assume the risk that trouble will not strike before it has had time to learn the business well enough to bail it out of most any difficulty. See Drucker, *Management*, p. 709.

ates.[12] Fourth, although in theory a conglomerate strategy would seem to offer the potential of greater sales-profit stability over the course of the business cycle, in practice the attempts at countercyclical diversification appear to have fallen short of the mark. Conglomerate profits have evidenced no propensity to suffer milder reversals in periods of recession and economic stress.[13] In fact, during times of adversity, the staying power of conglomerates appears to be weaker than that of concentrically diversified firms.[14] Finally, the "financial synergism" of trying to marry businesses with a high-cash throw-off to businesses with a large cash appetite is more often than not an illusion. For a conglomerate strategy to be truly successful, a great deal more "fit" is needed than money alone.[15]

The investor disfavor which conglomerates have acquired, the poor performance of several prominent conglomerates, and the serious issue of how to manage a diverse number of businesses effectively have caused many highly diversified firms to avoid or discard the conglomerate label by developing "corporate unity themes." Multiproduct firms have come up with broad labels like leisure-time, high technology, consumer products, materials processors, communication systems, and total service to mask the variety of distinct businesses they operate. The idea seems to be to convey the image of being diversified around a concept ("a conceptually oriented conglomerate) rather than the image of a "free-form conglomerate."

A Perspective View.   In sum, diversification—whether of a concentric or conglomerate variety—can be neither recommended or condemned as such. The pros and cons of what kind and how much diversification an organization needs to get the best results from its distinctive competence weigh differently from case to case. A logical place for an organization's management to begin its evaluation is with a consideration of "what is the least diversification we need to attain our goals, accomplish our mission, and still remain competitive and prosperous?" At the other extreme, though, management is equally obliged to examine the question of "what is the most diversification we can manage, given the complexity it adds to our organization?"[16] In all likelihood, the optimal answer lies in between. And after deciding what to include and what to exclude, the next step is to make the

---

[12] Evidence to this effect is given in Stanley E. Boyle, *Economic Report on Conglomerate Merger Performance: An Empirical Analysis of Nine Corporations,* Staff Report to the Federal Trade Commission, reprinted in *Mergers and Acquisitions,* vol. 8, no. 1 (Spring 1973), pp. 5–41; Ronald W. Melicher and David F. Ruch, "The Performance of Conglomerate Firms: Recent Risk and Return Experience," *Journal of Finance,* vol. 28, no. 2 (May 1973), pp. 381–88; and Robert L. Coun, "The Performance of Conglomerate Firms: Comment," *Journal of Finance,* vol. 28, no. 3 (June 1973), pp. 754–58.

[13] Drucker, *Management,* p. 767.

[14] See H. I. Ansoff and J. F. Weston, "Merger Objectives and Organization Structure," *Quarterly Review of Economics and Business,* vol. 2, no. 3 (August 1962), pp. 49–58.

[15] Drucker, *Management,* pp. 707–8.

[16] Ibid., p. 692–93.

diversification strategy specific enough to define the role of each line of business within the total organization. The reverse approach of letting the composite strategy be merely the aggregation of each line of business strategy is a mistake—it can quickly deteriorate into marching in all directions at once. Illustration Capsule 10 indicates how Cooper Industries has put together its multiindustry strategy.

Illustration Capsule 10

Strategic Realignment at Cooper Industries

Until 1967, Cooper Industries was basically a one-product, one-market company making engines and compressors for energy-producing companies. Its business was very cyclical and Cooper's economic forecast indicated that the next downward cycle would be especially steep. As a consequence, Cooper's management decided to put some of the company's eggs into a second basket in an effort to help smooth out the cyclical fluctuations in its main business.

Cooper decided on hand tools as its first diversification move, reasoning that all kinds of people use hand tools—wrenches, pliers, files—year in and year out so that the demand is steady and not very sensitive to major ups and downs of the company. The first hand tool company Cooper acquired was the Lufkin Rule Company, a leading maker of measuring tapes and rules. Interestingly, Lufkin's own strategic plan was to build one strong hand tool company from several smaller, complementary companies. The new company would offer hardware dealers a variety of tools from a single source.

When Cooper acquired Lufkin, two more criteria were set up as a basis for building a well-rounded tool company. In addition to helping Cooper smooth out its earning cycle, any candidates for acquisition would have to:

1. Have a quality image and a first-class brand name, and
2. Be just as interested in joining Cooper as Cooper was in acquiring them.

In going multiindustry, it was Cooper's plan to continue to be an operating company, not just a holding company.

Within a very short time, the Cooper group of tool companies grew to include Lufkin; Crescent wrenches, pliers, and screw drivers; Weller soldering equipment; Nicholson files and saws; and Xcelite Electronics Tools. The sales strategy for Cooper's tool groups became "a single source for five great brands." By 1975 the Cooper tool division was an established leader in the hand tool industry with sales of $164 million.

Not long after the Nicholson File became a division of Cooper Industries the decision was made by Nicholson to drop 90 percent of its files from its product line. The reason? As long as Nicholson depended solely on files for its business, it felt it had to offer customers every kind of file imaginable; the strategy was "we've got 'em all." But when Nicholson joined forces with Cooper and became part of a group of companies boasting several top brand names in hand tools, the strategy of carrying every file under the sun became obsolete. Nicholson continues to manufacture almost 2,000 different types of files, including many specialty items. And despite dropping 90 percent of its files, Nicholson's sales and profits increased.

Illustration Capsule 10 (continued)

The same principle was applied to all the Cooper Industries tool companies. Low-margin and low-turnover items were dropped, averaging a 50 percent cut. All the emphasis went behind the bread and butter of the line; sales rose to new heights. Profits also went up for dealers and distributors, owing to a higher turnover of fewer items. At the same time, sales force economies were taken advantage of; five independent hand tool companies needed five salesmen to call on one customer. But when the five companies were put together, only one salesman per customer was required, thereby lowering the cost of selling. Besides combining sales forces, Cooper also combined warehousing, distribution, advertising, merchandising, and paperwork flows. Customers also benefited because they found it more convenient and less expensive to deal with one supplier instead of five.

In addition to the selling advantage of five companies in one, the tool companies benefited from becoming part of a multiindustry organization. For instance, the Energy Services Division of Cooper provided the tool companies with more than $50 million for modernization. Then, in 1975–76, the tool companies returned the favor, providing cash to take advantage of a sharp upswing in the markets for Cooper's energy products.

1971 was a bad year for Cooper's energy divisions and prompted a hard look at each product and each market to make sure it was worth staying in them. One of the decisions Cooper faced was especially tough: whether to keep making centrifugal compressors for certain process industries—mainly ammonia, ethylene, and methanol plants—or to drop out of that market and concentrate on natural gas compression. There were strong arguments on both sides. On the one hand, process industries were growing; to drop out would be to leave an expanding market. In addition, Cooper was a recognized quality leader in the market and Cooper felt that this gave prestige to the Cooper Industries name and professional pride to its engineers.

On the other hand, compressors for these plants required almost total custom design which meant high engineering costs. It also meant that Cooper found it hard to hold down costs by building several identical units, the way they did for the natural gas compression units. Moreover, Cooper Industries did not have as dominant a position in the process market as it had in natural gas compression. So when sales slacked off in the process market, Cooper was among the first companies to feel the squeeze. After a lot of soul-searching, Cooper decided to pull out of its business of making centrifugal compressors for the process industries. It was a controversial decision, but Cooper felt its commitment had to be to the long-term profitability of the company.

The earnings of its energy division went up in 1972 despite the fact that sales fell even lower because of the decision to get out of centrifugal compressors. In 1976, Cooper boasted that the changes that were made in 1971 were really beginning to pay off. In 1976, almost 40 percent of the centrifugal horsepower used in natural gas was built by Cooper-Bessemer—worldwide. In addition, the company found that the excess capacity created by pulling out of the weak markets in 1971 was being gradually brought back into production as market penetration in natural gas energy services increased. This meant that Cooper Industries did not have to invest heavily in new facilities to keep pace with mushrooming energy demand.

The company's strategy also included one of emphasizing products that generated follow-on sales. More than one third of its energy-related revenue in 1976 was estimated to come from parts and services, steadier revenue sources than the sale of original equipment.

Illustration Capsule 10 (concluded)

In 1976, Cooper Industries was touting itself as a "very well-balanced company with leadership positions in three different markets: hand tools, aircraft services, and energy services. This combination will help us ride out the economic ups and downs."

By business category the Cooper Industries companies as of 1976 were:

1. In hand tools—The Cooper Group (Lufkin, Crescent, Weller, Nicholson, Xcelite, Rotor tool).
2. In aircraft services—Cooper Airmotive.
3. In energy services—Cooper Energy Services (Cooper-Bessemer, Ajax, Penn Pump).

Sources: Cooper Industries *Annual Reports* and full page advertisements placed by Cooper Industries in *The Wall Street Journal,* February 12, 1976, p. 17; March 11, 1976, p. 15; and March 24, 1976, p. 15.

Finally, if and when diversification becomes a "go" proposition, an organization must decide whether to diversify via acquisition or to attempt its own internal grass-roots development of the chosen lines of business. The factors involved are those implicit in any "buy or build" situation, but often the most important considerations are time and money. Acquiring existing organizations, products, technologies, facilities, or talent and labor force has the strong advantage of much quicker entry into the target market while, at the same time, detouring such barriers to entry as patents, technological inexperience, lack of raw material supplies, substantial economies of scale, costly promotional expenses requisite for gaining market visibility and brand recognition, and establishment of distribution channels. Internally developing the knowledge, resources, and reputation necessary to become an effective competitor can take a year or more and entails all the problems of start-up.

Yet, acquisition is not without its drawbacks. Finding the right kind of company to acquire can sometimes present a problem. For instance, the acquiring firm faces the dilemma of buying a successful company at a high price or a struggling company at a low price. In the first case, the seller is in a position to demand a generous compensation for the risks that have been faced and for the effort expended in putting together a successful product, technology, market, organization or whatever is being acquired. If the buying firm has very little knowledge about the industry it is seeking to enter but has ample capital, then it may be better off acquiring a capable firm— irrespective of the higher price. Usually, though, it is more profitable to acquire a struggling firm at a bargain price provided the new parent sees promising ways for transforming the weak firm into a strong one and has the money and know-how to back up its turnaround strategy. In any event, evaluating the pros and cons of how the various acquisition alternatives stack up against internalized growth becomes an integral part of any diversification move.

Joint Ventures

The joint venture is an appealing strategy in several types of situations.[17] It is, first, a device for doing something which an organization is not capable of doing alone. Entering into a "consortium" kind of arrangement is a means of making a workable whole out of otherwise undersized levels of activity. In such cases, the whole is greater than the sum of its parts because alone each part is smaller than the threshold size of effectiveness. The Alaskan pipeline, for instance, is a joint venture in raw material supply which not only is beyond the financial strength of any one oil giant but which also is, in its most economic size, designed to carry more crude oil than one company is in a position to use. For each oil company owning oil reserves on the Alaskan North Slope to build its own pipeline geared to the size of its own production capability would make little business or environmental sense. But for them all to contribute to a jointly financed and jointly operated pipeline allows the group to make economic fits out of misfits and thereby realize a profit on their Alaskan oil reserves. At the same time, the strategy of joint venturing carries the advantage that risk is shared, and therefore reduced for each of the participating firms. This is no small matter in a relatively large undertaking.

A second type of joint venture emerges when the distinctive competence of two or more independent organizations is brought together to form a jointly owned business. In this joint venture format each company brings to the deal special talents which, when pooled, give rise to a new enterprise with features quite apart from the parents. The complementarity of two or more distinctive competences can create a degree of synergy that spells the differences between success and near success. For example, when in the 1920s, General Motors developed tetraethyl lead to cure engine knocking problems, it decided not to start its own gasoline production and distribution business to exploit the advantages of tetraethyl lead but, instead, it chose to enter into a joint venture with Standard Oil of New Jersey (now Exxon) which already knew the gasoline business and had the missing expertise. Thus was born Ethyl Corporation which grew into a worldwide supplier of tetraethyl lead for all the large gasoline marketers. With its joint venture strategy GM, in effect, made money on every gallon of tetraethyl lead gasoline sold—an undoubtedly more profitable approach than that of trying to compete directly against the oil companies.[18]

---

[17] Drucker, *Management,* pp. 720–24. Information regarding the joint venture activities of firms can be found in *Mergers and Acquisitions: The Journal of Corporate Venture,* published quarterly.

[18] General Motors and Standard Oil, N.J., sold Ethyl Corporation in the 1950s largely because Ethyl had become too big and too successful to be continued as a joint venture. Likewise, when Sears decided it was time for Whirlpool not only to supply Sears but also to sell appliances under the Whirlpool brand, Sears took the company public while retaining a controlling majority interest; gradually, then, Sears sold its holdings of Whirlpool shares as the company began to make it on its own. Such a spinning off of joint ventures into independent companies is not uncommon—either with or without the parent companies retaining an ownership interest.

To extend the life of a successful joint venture beyond some point in its development can

Lastly, there are joint ventures created chiefly to surmount political and cultural roadblocks.[19] The political realities of nationalism often require a foreign company to team up with a domestic company if it is to gain needed government approval for its activities. At the same time, there are added pressures for a foreign company to seek out a domestic partner to help it overcome language and cultural barriers. So powerful are nationalistic interests that in the smaller developing nations such as Brazil, Chile, Peru, and India it is not unusual for foreign companies to find themselves restricted to a minority ownership position. Indeed, local businesses in Brazil and India, even though deeply engaged in joint ventures with multinational corporations based in the United States and in Europe, have been quite vocal in demanding protection from multinational domination, advocating not just majority or at least controlling ownership but the closing off of whole economic sectors to multinationals as well.

Innovation Strategies

The essence of an innovation strategy is something *new* and something *different*. It is predicated on the assumption that existing products, markets, channels, and technology are vulnerable to the forces of change and that profitable opportunities exist to exploit this vulnerability. The posture of an organization which adapts an innovation strategy is one of a planned-for sloughing off of what is fading so as to free resources for working on things whose time has come.[20] The underlying premise is that the key to survival and long-term growth lies in the continuous development of new and improved goods and services.

An innovative strategy therefore does not concentrate on defending current positions. Instead, attention is aimed squarely at creating distinguishably new concepts of value and thereby generating a significant impact on the environment. To put it another way, innovation is concerned with satisfying a want or performing a function in a manner that sets it apart from

---

have the effect of stunting its growth. Moreover, conflicts begin to arise between objectives of the parent company and the mission of the joint venture. Hence, at some point it becomes propitious for a successful joint venture to begin to develop its own mission, objectives, strategy, and policies and for its management to become truly autonomous.

Alternatively, the joint venture can be liquidated with the parents splitting up the business and absorbing it into their own operations. This was the fate of Standard Vacuum, a joint venture of Standard Oil, N.J., and Mobil Oil begun in the World War I era to produce, refine, and market petroleum products in the Far East. In the 1950s Standard Vacuum's petroleum business in the Far East had expanded to a size where it was more desirable for each of the parents to proceed on their own rather than to continue a joint venture where their strategies and objectives were beginning to clash.

See Drucker, *Management,* pp. 722–24.

[19] Philip Kotler, *Marketing Management: Analysis, Planning and Control,* 3d ed. (Englewood Cliffs, N.J.: Prentice-Hall, Inc., 1976), pp. 472–74.

[20] Drucker, *Management,* p. 791. See also, E. E. Scheuing, *New Product Management* (Hinsdale, Ill.: The Dryden Press, 1974), chaps. 1 and 2.

existing products or technologies. Accordingly, a product innovation strategy seeks to develop products that feature a new (and lower) price—solid-state, pocket-sized calculators; new convenience in use—the electric razor; new performance—the Polaroid SX-70 camera; new durability—steel belted radial tires; a new function—quick copying machines; or a radically new technique for performing an old function—digital watches and microwave ovens. Creating novelty, altering appearance, or adding new variations to existing products do not really qualify as innovation.

In the case of a technologically oriented innovation strategy, the task is one of finding technological processes that create new product characteristics rather than just uncovering ways to improve existing methods. Channel-based innovation involves new techniques for accessing markets, as opposed to finding variations on prevailing techniques. In this regard, though, it is important to recognize that successful innovation is normally market-focused, not product- or technology-focused. A great many innovations could be classified as "miracle products" or "miracles of technology" but nonetheless turn out as only "near successes" because they missed the market or the market potential was misconstrued. Hence, the key to successful innovation is, first and foremost, to market new ideas and concepts; once these have gained acceptance, the rest is routine.

Needless to say, the mortality rate on innovation attempts is high. Booz, Allen, and Hamilton studied the "decay curve" of new product ideas for 51 companies.[21] They found that of every 58 ideas less than one fourth (about 13) pass initial exploration and screening tests showing them to merit further study and to be consistent with preliminary company criteria and resource availability. Of these 13, only 7 are able to survive a thorough evaluation of their profit potential and to evolve into a concrete go-ahead recommendation. Of these, about three get past the product development stage, two survive the test-marketing phase, and only one is launched commercially into full-scale production and sale.

Even then debugging a new product or technology can be costly, organizationally painful, and time-consuming.[22] Initial results may be meager. A long gestation may be encountered before "takeoff," if indeed there ever is a takeoff. Furthermore, timing is of the essence; an innovation can fail simply because it comes at the wrong time to make a significant difference. In sum, the various pitfalls and the inevitable unforeseen hurdles make an innovation strategy a high-risk option. But in a fast-moving, technologically progressive economy, it may be even more risky not to innovate.

---

[21] *Management of New Products,* 4th ed. (New York: Booz, Allen & Hamilton, Inc., 1968), p. 9.

[22] See Scheuing, *New Product Management,* chaps. 3–6; and Kotler, *Marketing Management,* chap. 10.

Retrenchment Strategies

The thrust of a retrenchment strategy is to fall back and regroup. It is a common short-run strategy for firms during times of economic recession, competitive adversity, or financial strain. Retrenchment can assume either of two variations: reductions in current operating expenses and levels of activity or a narrower scope of operations. In the first instance, a firm which finds itself in a defensive or overextended position basically elects to hold onto most or all of its business and weather the storm with various economy measures, including the following:

1. Cutting back on hiring new personnel.
2. Trimming the size of staff activities.
3. Encouraging early retirement.
4. Replacing high-salaried employees with low-salaried ones.
5. Curtailing marketing expenditures, especially sales promotion and advertising costs.
6. Stretching out the use of equipment and delaying replacement purchases.
7. Reducing inventory levels.
8. Leasing equipment instead of buying it or resorting to sell-and-lease-back methods for the financing of current fixed assets.
9. Implementing organizationwide budget cuts together with directives for new measures to improve productivity and cut costs.

The second variation of retrenchment is more drastic and may include pruning the product line of marginally profitable items, closing down outlying sales units and abandoning distant customers to save on transportation and direct sales costs, withdrawing entirely from geographical areas where sales volumes are low, or closing down older, less efficient plants.

Retrenchment is a typical reaction to adversity, though it usually is a temporary strategy for waiting out the return of growth and expansion opportunities. However, retrenchment may prove permanent in those instances where the industry is in a state of long-term decline or where rival firms have such a stranglehold on the market that no other strategy is workable.

Divestiture Strategies

Even a shrewd diversification strategy will result in a couple of acquisitions that just do not work out. Misfits or only "partial" fits cannot be completely avoided, if only because it is impossible to predict precisely how getting into a new line of business will actually work out. Moreover, market potentials change with the times and what once was a good diversification move may later turn sour. Subpar performance by some operating units is bound to occur, thereby raising questions of whether to continue. Other operating units may simply not mesh as well with the rest of the organization as was originally thought.

Sometimes, a diversification move which originally appeared to make good sense from the standpoint of common markets, technologies, or channels turns out to lack the compatibility of values essential to a "temperamental fit."[23] The pharmaceutical companies had just this experience. When several tried to diversify into cosmetics and perfume they discovered that their personnel had little respect for the "frivolous" nature of such products as compared to the far nobler task of developing miracle drugs to cure the ill. The absence of "temperamental unity" between the chemical and compounding expertise of the pharmaceutical companies and the fashion-marketing orientation of the cosmetics business was the undoing of the pharmaceutical's diversification move into what otherwise seemed to be a related technology and product area.

One would venture to predict a similar temperamental conflict would quickly arise if major state universities tried to diversify into the sorts of programs customarily offered by junior colleges and vocational and technical schools; many faculty members would be up in arms about a perceived lowering of course rigor, academic standards, and student quality and the resulting implications for blurring the university's reputation as a top-flight academic institution. The disdain which many professors would have for such "low-level" programs would easily rival the intensity of "personality conflict" the pharmaceutical companies encountered.

And there are bound to be occasional partial misfits where certain elements for eventual success are clearly present but where nevertheless an organization's ability to manage or its resources to do what is needed are being overtaxed. In still other cases, the market changes slowly but surely to where the consumer begins to define the value of the product differently from the seller, thereby breaking up what once was a good fit with the seller's other products. Likewise, technological branching can progress to the bounds where pruning becomes a wise course of action if not a necessary one.

When diversification moves turn sour (for any of the preceding reasons), divestiture may be the most attractive strategy. By and large, unsuccessful or marginally successful lines of business should be divested as fast as is practical. To drag things out in hopes of a breakthrough or a turnaround is liable to be futile and risks draining away valuable organization resources. This explains why every diversified organization needs a systematic "planned abandonment" policy for divesting itself of poor performers, losers, and misfits. Interestingly enough, though, until recently diversified firms used divestiture very sparingly. One study of ten conglomerates in 1969 showed that only two, Textron and Ling-Temco-Vought (LTV), were in-

---

[23] Drucker, *Management,* p. 709.

clined toward divestiture.[24] Since 1974, however, divestiture has become fairly common.

Divestiture can take several forms. Successful misfits may be spun off into financially and managerially independent companies, with the parent company electing to maintain either a majority or minority ownership.[25] On the other hand, a business may not be able to survive as an independent operation, in which case a buyer needs to be found. This is a "marketing" rather than a "selling" problem.[26] Generally, one should avoid approaching divestment with a view of "Who can we pawn this venture off onto and how much can we get for it?" Instead, it is stronger to undertake divestiture on the basis "For what sort of organization would this be a good fit and under what conditions would it be viewed as a sound bet?" In identifying organizations for whom the business is a "perfect fit," one also finds the buyers who will pay the highest price.

Liquidation Strategies

Of all the strategic alternatives, liquidation is the most unpleasant and painful, especially for a single-product enterprise where it means terminating the organization's existence. For a multiproduct firm to liquidate one of its lines is much less traumatic; the hardships of suffering through layoffs, plant closings, and so on, while not to be minimized, still leaves an ongoing organization and perhaps one that eventually will turn out to be healthier after its pruning than before.

In the case of either single- or multiple-product organizations, circumstances may make liquidation the best alternative. In hopeless situations, an early liquidation effort often serves owner-stockholder interests better than an inevitable bankruptcy. Prolonging the pursuit of a lost cause merely exhausts an organization's resources and leaves less to liquidate; it can also mar reputations and ruin management careers.

Unfortunately, of course, it is seldom simple for management to differentiate between when a cause is lost and when a turnaround is achievable. This is particularly true when emotions and pride get mixed in with sound managerial judgment—as often they do.

---

[24] See Robert S. Attiyeh, "Where Next for Conglomerates," *Business Horizons,* vol. 12, no. 6 (December 1969), pp. 39–44.

[25] One of the more unique approaches to divestiture involved Ling-Temco-Vought's reorganization of the Wilson Company in 1967. Shortly after it acquired Wilson, LTV split Wilson into three separate corporations: Wilson and Company, (meats and food products), Wilson Sporting Goods, and Wilson Pharmaceutical and Chemical Company. LTV then sold off a substantial minority portion of the stock of each of the three new companies at price-earnings ratios higher than it initially paid for the total Wilson operation. LTV was attracted to this approach because it allowed LTV to improve its return from the Wilson acquisition by recovering part of its initial investment, while retaining control over all three of the new Wilson companies. For a more complete discussion, see Attiyeh, "Where Next for Conglomerates," p. 42.

[26] Drucker, *Management,* p. 719.

COMBINATION STRATEGIES

The nine strategic alternatives above are not mutually exclusive. They can be used in combination, either in whole or in part, and they can be chained together in whatever sequences may be appropriate for adjusting to changing market circumstances. Moreover, there are endless variations of each of the nine "pure" alternatives themselves. Table 3–1 highlights some of these variations; these strategies, some of which are "winners" and some of which are "losers," are further indication of the ample room which exists for organizations to create their own individualized blend of product or service features, market segment emphasis, innovative posture, and degree of diversification. As a consequence, the difficulty of the problem confronting the strategist concerns not so much figuring out what options are open as evaluating the various viable alternatives.

TABLE 3–1

A Catalog of Specific Strategy Options: Some Winners and Some Losers

Strategies for Underdog or Trailing Firms
1. *Vacant niche strategy.* Search out and cultivate profitable *segments* of the market that larger firms are not catering to or are ignoring.
2. *"Ours-is-better-than-theirs" strategy.* Try to capitalize on opportunities to improve upon the products of the dominant firms and develop an appeal to the quality-conscious, performance-oriented buyer. (Example: Zenith's attempt to overtake RCA with its "the quality goes in, before the name goes on" theme.)
3. *Channel innovation strategy.* Find a new way to distribute goods that offers substantial savings or that reaches particular group of buyers more efficiently. (Examples include Avon's door-to-door selling of cosmetics and Timex's use of drugstores and discount stores as outlets for its watches.)
4. *Distinctive image strategy.* Seek to achieve a differential advantage via some distinctive and unique appeal—Dr. Pepper's taste, the VW beetle, Avis' "We're No. 2, We Try Harder" campaign.

Strategies for Dominant Firms
1. *Seize-the-offensive strategy.* Refuse to be content with just being a leader. Seek to continue to outperform the industry by breaking records the firm itself has already set. Become firmly established as *the* source of new product ideas, cost-cutting discoveries, innovative customer services, and better means of distribution. In general, exercise initiative, set the pace, and exploit the weaknesses of rival firms.
2. *Fortification strategy.* Surround the chief products with patents; foreclose the attractiveness of entry by introducing more of the company's own brands to compete with those already successful company brands; introduce additional items under current brand names.
3. *Confrontation strategy.* Defend the company's market base by being quick to launch massive promotional wars which underdog firms cannot hope to match; promptly meet all competitive price cuts of lesser sized firms to neutralize any benefits to would-be price-cutters; make it hard for aggressive-minded smaller firms to grow by selling at prices so low that smaller firms are denied the profit margins and total earnings needed to make further expansion attractive.

TABLE 3-1 (continued)

Strategies to Be Leery of

1. *"Me too" or "Copy-cat" strategy.*   Imitating the strategy of leading or success-ful enterprises; trying to play catch-up by beating the leaders at their own game. Weakness: Ignores development of firm's own personality, image, strategy, and policies.

2. *Take-away strategy.*   Trying to achieve greater market share and market pene-tration by attacking other firms head-on and luring away their customers via a lower price, more advertising, and other attention-getting gimmicks. Weakness: Invites retaliation and risks precipitating a fierce and costly battle for market share in which no one wins—including the firm trying to play take-away.

3. *Glamour strategy.*   When a firm gets seduced by the prospects of a new idea for a product or technology which it thinks will sweep the market. Weakness: The best laid plans. . . .

4. *Test-the-water strategy.*   Often arises when an enterprise is engaged in develop-ing new opportunities or is reacting to market-technological-environmental changes which call for a fundamental reformulation or redesign of the basic corporate strategy. In such cases, firms may "test-the-water" in venturing out into new fields of endeavor. Weakness: A half-way effort or "sideline stepchild" seldom succeeds for lack of adequate corporate commitment; it's usually best to either get in or stay out entirely.

5. *Hit another home-run strategy.*   This strategy is typified by a firm which has hit one "home run" (pioneering a very successful product and strategy) but which is now looking for ways to hit a second home run (by getting into a second line of business either related or unrelated to its first home run), so as to continue to grow and prosper at its former rate. Seeking out a second home-run strategy may be necessary because growth of the initial business is rapidly slowing down and becoming more competitive. Weakness: It may be questionable whether the distinctive competence gained from the first home run is transfer-able to other products, markets, and technologies and whether the firm has the know-how to make an effective transfer.

6. *Arm's race strategy.*   May emerge when firms of relatively equal size enter into a spirited battle for increased market share. Commonly, such battles are waged with increased promotional and advertising expenditures and/or increased R&D and new product development budgets and/or aggressive price cuts and/or extra services to customers. As one firm pours more money into its efforts, other firms feel forced to do likewise for defensive reasons. The result is escalating costs, producing a situation much like an arm's race. Weakness: Seldom do such battles produce a substantial change in market shares, yet they almost certainly raise costs—costs which must either be absorbed in the form of lower profit margins or else passed on to customers via higher prices.

Strategies to Avoid

1. *Drift strategy.*   When strategy is not consciously designed and coordinated but rather just evolves out of day-to-day decisions and actions at the operating level.

2. *Hope for a better day strategy.*   Emerges from managerial inertia and tradition and is exemplified by firms which blame their subpar sales-profits-market share performance on bad luck, the economy, unexpected problems, and other cir-cumstances "beyond their control." Such "entrepreneurial coasting" until good times arrive is a sure sign of a dim future and managerial ineptness.

3. *Downhill strategy.*   Arises in companies where a once successful (and perhaps spectacularly so) strategy is fading and no longer viable. Nonetheless, man-agement, blinded by the success-breeds-success syndrome, continues to be reluctant to begin to reformulate its strategy, preferring instead to try to rekin-

TABLE 3–1 *(concluded)*

dle the old spark with cosmetic changes—in hopes of reversing the downhill slide.

4. *Popgun strategy.* Seeking to go into head-to-head competition with proven leaders when the firm has neither a differential competitive advantage nor adequate financial strength with which to do battle.

Source: Adapted and compiled from a variety of sources including Joel E. Ross and Michael K. Kami, *Corporate Management in Crisis: Why the Mighty Fall* (Englewood Cliffs, N.J.: Prentice-Hall, Inc. 1973); and Philip Kotler, *Marketing Management: Analysis, Planning, and Control* (Englewood Cliffs, N.J.: Prentice-Hall Inc., 1972), chap. 8.

WHEN SOME STRATEGIES ARE MORE LOGICAL THAN OTHERS

The market circumstances of firms are often enough alike to justify grouping them into strategic clusters; these clusters serve as a useful framework for identifying whether some strategic alternatives offer a stronger logical fit than do others.[27] Consider, for instance, Figure 3–1 where a firm's competitive position is plotted against the rate of market growth to create four discernible strategic clusters. Firms which fall into quadrant I (rapid market growth and strong competitive position) are clearly in an excellent strategic position. In such circumstances a concentration strategy makes good sense and one can logically expect quadrant I firms to push hard to maintain and increase their market shares, to develop further their distinctive competences, and to make whatever capital investments may be necessary to continue in a leadership position. In addition, though, a quadrant I company may find it desirable to consider vertical integration as a strategy for undergirding its market standing and protecting its profit margins; this is especially true if the firm has financial and organizational resources to spare and if the manufacturer of its product is process oriented. Its distinctive competence may also make it opportune for an organization to look into concentric diversification as a means of spreading its risks while its star is still on the rise.

Firms falling into the quadrant II cluster should, first of all, direct their attention to a concentration strategy (given the high rate of market growth) addressing, in particular, the question of (1) why their current approach to the market has resulted in a weak competitive position, and (2) what it will take to become an effective competitor. With the market expanding rapidly,

---

[27] The notion of strategic clusters was pioneered and publicized by the Boston Consulting Group, using the two variables of market share and the rate of growth of a company's market to classify companies and define the clusters. However, strategic clusters can also be predicated on other variables—competitive power, number of available growth opportunities, technological or marketing prowess, financial resources, and so on. See C. Roland Christensen, Norman A. Berg, and Malcolm S. Salter, *Policy Formulation and Administration* 7th ed. (Homewood, Ill.: Richard D. Irwin, Inc., 1976), pp. 16–18.

FIGURE 3-1
Identifying Strategic Clusters

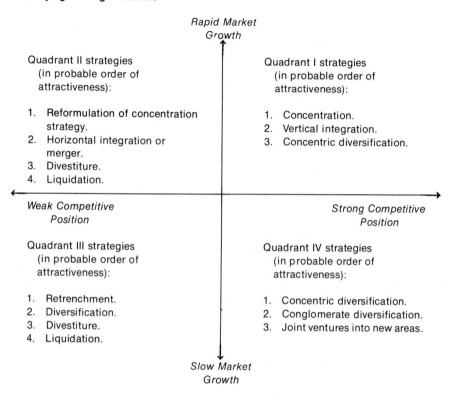

*Rapid Market
Growth*

Quadrant II strategies
(in probable order of
attractiveness):

1. Reformulation of concentration
   strategy.
2. Horizontal integration or
   merger.
3. Divestiture.
4. Liquidation.

Quadrant I strategies
(in probable order of
attractiveness):

1. Concentration.
2. Vertical integration.
3. Concentric diversification.

*Weak Competitive
Position*

*Strong Competitive
Position*

Quadrant III strategies
(in probable order of
attractiveness):

1. Retrenchment.
2. Diversification.
3. Divestiture.
4. Liquidation.

Quadrant IV strategies
(in probable order of
attractiveness):

1. Concentric diversification.
2. Conglomerate diversification.
3. Joint ventures into new areas.

*Slow Market
Growth*

there should be ample opportunity for even a weak firm to carve out a viable market niche, provided strategic and organizational shortcomings can be overcome and the needed resource base developed. Certainly, a young, developing company has a better chance for survival in a growing market where there is plenty of new business than it does in a stable or declining industry. However, if a quadrant IV firm lacks one or more key ingredients for a successful concentration strategy, then either horizontal integration (merger) with another company in the industry that has the missing pieces or else merger with an outsider having the cash and resources to support the organization's development may be the best strategic alternative. Failing this, the most logical strategies would entail getting out of the industry: divestiture in the case of a multiproduct firm or liquidation in the case of a single-product firm. While getting out may seem extreme, it is well to remember that a company which is unable to make a profit in a booming market probably does not have the ability to make a profit at all and has little prospect of survival—particularly if a recession hits or when competition stiffens.

Quadrant III companies with their weak competitive position in a more or less stagnant market would do well to consider: (1) retrenchment—so as to free up unproductive resources for possible redeployment; (2) diversification—either concentric or conglomerate, depending on existing opportunities elsewhere; (3) getting out of the industry (divestiture of this line of business); or even (4) liquidation—if profit prospects are nonexistent and other opportunities fail to materialize.

Quadrant IV organizations, given their dim growth prospects, may well wish to use the excess cash flow from their existing business to begin a program of diversification. A concentric approach keyed to the distinctive competence that gave it its dominant position is an obvious option, but conglomerate diversification should be considered if concentric opportunities do not appear especially attractive. Joint ventures with other organizations into new fields of endeavor are another logical possibility. Whichever, the firm will likely wish to minimize new investments in its present facilities (to do little more than preserve the status quo), thereby freeing the maximum amount of funds for new endeavors.

The significance of the strategic cluster concept lies in its ability to indicate why companies (even those in the same industry) may have good reason to pursue different corporate strategies. The nature of a firm's market standing, its competitive capabilities, its cash flow, its capital investment requirements, its ability to respond to emerging market opportunities, its distinctive competences, and so on all combine to shape its strategic requirements and strategic position. Sometimes a company's position is such that a radical change in strategy is called for; at other times, though, maintaining the status quo or just fine-tuning will suffice.

Continuing with the Current Strategy.   Continuing the existing strategy is simple and tempting—which is all the more reason for the strategist to pose some searching questions in conducting an evaluation of this alternative. Precisely what does the current strategy have going for it? Why is it better than other alternatives? Is reaffirmation of the status quo strategy the result of a hard-nose review or laziness? Is it justified on the basis of risk preference or is it just convenient? Is "more of the same" predicated on a timely "wait and see" attitude or on a desire to escape the unpleasantries of change?

The issue of whether to change strategies can go either way, of course. But a decision to retain the current strategic plan is obviously more meaningful when made in full view of the alternatives. The reasoning is straightforward. Every successful strategy helps sow the seeds of its own obsolescence through the new realities and new problems it brings; moreover, markets change and so do customer needs. So, sooner or later, every organization will confront the need for strategic changes. Still, as long as a full review of strategy continues to point solidly at maintaining the current strategy, then it can be continued with some confidence that the end of its life cycle has not yet been reached.

"Fine-tuning" the Existing Strategy.   Making minor modifications in the existing strategy is far and away the most frequently considered strategic alternative and also the most frequently adopted course of action. Wholesale shifts or revisions in strategy are triggered chiefly by major events outside the organization. Since these occur at irregular intervals, it follows that the majority of the time strategic realignment takes the form of "fine-tuning" or, to put it another way, of "continuing to do what we are doing, but trying to do it better."

Indeed, in between major strategic changes, competitive pressures and the push for improved organizational performance make continuous fine-tuning a built-in aspect of strategy formulation. Most firms appear fairly attentive to the needs of keeping lower level support strategies and tactics keyed in closely with ongoing product-market developments. Broadening the organization's line of products or services, changing the promotional mix, adding variations of existing products to zero in on specific customer needs more accurately, building a stronger market base and sales territory coverage (via either internal growth or horizontal merger and acquisition), and working out the kinks in production and distribution systems are all routine ways of extending the prevailing strategic plan.

And while fine-tuning need not go beyond changing certain of the organization's competitive tactics or perhaps slightly revising one or more first-level support strategies, even these adjustments can, over a period of time, add up to a significant strategic adjustment. Hence, it is fair to say that for most organizations the strategic plan is seldom static but evolves, however slowly, as day-to-day events unfold. Needless to say, the strategist is obliged to review the fine-tuning aspects of strategic realignment often enough to see that any changes are being thought through by lower level managers and are still in line with the primary elements of the overall grand design of strategy.

SUGGESTED READINGS

Ansoff, H. Igor. *Corporate Strategy.* New York: McGraw-Hill Book Co., 1965, chap. 7.

Ansoff, H. Igor, and Stewart, John M. "Strategies for a Technology-Based Business," *Harvard Business Review,* vol. 45, no. 6 (November–December 1967), pp. 71–83.

Bettauer, Arthur. "Strategy for Divestments," *Harvard Business Review,* vol. 45, no. 2 (March–April 1967), pp. 116–24.

Bloom, Paul N., and Kotler, Philip. "Strategies for High Market Share Companies," *Harvard Business Review,* vol. 53, no. 6 (November–December 1975), pp. 63–72.

Bright, Willard M. "Alternative Strategies for Diversification," *Research Management,* vol. 12, no. 4 (July 1969), pp. 247–53.

Cooper, Arnold C., and Schendel, Dan. "Strategic Responses to Technological Threats," *Business Horizons,* vol. 19, no. 1 (February 1976), pp. 61–69.

Doutt, J. T. "Product Innovation in Small Business," *Business Topics,* vol. 8, no. 3 (Summer 1960), pp. 58–62.

Drucker, Peter. *Management: Tasks, Responsibilities, Practices.* New York: Harper & Row, Publishers, 1974), chaps. 55, 56, 57, 58, 60, and 61.

Hanan, Mack. "Corporate Growth through Internal Spinouts," *Harvard Business Review,* vol. 47, no. 6 (November–December 1969), pp. 55–66.

Mason, R. S. "Product Diversification and the Small Firm," *Journal of Business Policy,* vol. 3, no. 3 (Spring 1973), pp. 28–39.

Schendel, Dan; Patton, G. R.; and Riggs, James. "Corporate Turnaround Strategies," *Journal of General Management,* vol. 3, no. 3 (Spring 1976), pp. 3–11.

Steiner, George A. *Top Management Planning.* New York: Macmillan Company, 1969, especially the chapter on "Diversification Planning."

Steiner, George A. "Why and How to Diversify," *California Management Review,* vol. 6, no. 4 (Summer 1964), pp. 11–17.

Vancil, Richard F., and Lorange, Peter. "Strategic Planning in Diversified Companies," *Harvard Business Review,* vol. 53, no. 1 (January–February 1975), pp. 81–90.

Webster, Frederick A. "A Model of Vertical Integration Strategy," *California Management Review,* vol. 10, no. 2 (Winter 1967), pp. 49–58.

Woodward, Herbert N. "Management Strategies for Small Companies," *Harvard Business Review,* vol. 54, no. 1 (January–February 1976), pp. 113–21.

4

STRATEGIC EVALUATION AND STRATEGIC CHOICE

Never follow the crowd.
Bernard M. Baruch

THE PRECEDING CHAPTER surveyed ins and outs of the major strategic alternatives. The task here is to examine some of the analytic considerations which go into the strategy evaluation process and the final selection of a strategy. Specifically, we will delve into such questions as what are the relevant industry factors to consider in making a strategic evaluation? How should future trends and economic conditions be incorporated into the strategic analysis? What are the key success variables in the product markets under consideration and what are their implications for strategy? What criteria should be used to separate the strong strategic candidates from the weak ones? What issues weigh most heavily in the strategy selection process? How does one finally decide upon a choice of strategy?

DEVELOPING A STRATEGIC PROFILE

Perhaps the most important phase of strategy evaluation is that of analyzing industry potential and the position an organization occupies (or is considering occupying) in that industry. The purpose of developing a strategic profile of an industry is twofold: (1) to evaluate specific knowledge about the opportunities open to an enterprise willing and able to try to mount a successful effort, and (2) to provide benchmarks for appraising the several strategic alternatives which may exist in that industry. To put it another way, the role of a strategic profile is to take what seems like a promising strategic alternative and gather the information requisite for making an adequate assessment of its overall desirability.

Often, there is a temptation to short-circuit this phase of strategy evaluation, especially when the strategic alternatives being considered each involve staying within familiar industry bounds or when the pressures of time and circumstance close in. The managements of some organizations may feel that their longtime industry experiences have programmed all of the key factors into their thinking. Supposedly, the reasoning goes, their administrative experiences have schooled them well in the whys and hows of being systematic in their evaluation of pertinent industry information. But experience can also boomerang. Prior knowledge and a stubborn defensive pride in its own way of doing things may blind management to change; a management may assume it knows things about the industry or the overall environment that are no longer accurate. Therefore, a periodic strategic profile analysis in which "the facts" are updated is well worth doing and it is certainly worth doing when entry into a new industry or product market or geographic area is being contemplated.

Table 4–1 contains a checklist of questions which are part and parcel of a thorough strategic profile. All of the topics and questions may not be pivotal in each and every situation, but the list does suggest the range of factors to be considered. Clearly, when an organization is contemplating alternatives encompassing several industries, separate analyses should be made for each.

Most of the items on the checklist in Table 4–1 are self-explanatory and warrant no further discussion. However, the item pertaining to the strategic forecast (G-2) merits elaboration.

TABLE 4–1
Checklist for Developing a Strategic Profile of an Industry

A. Product-Market Structure
1. Identify the industry's products, their characteristics, and position in the product life cycle.
2. How big is the market? What are the locations of greatest market concentration? Are there major geographic differences in saturation intensity?
3. Who are the customers and why do they buy the product? What is the degree of market penetration in terms of per capita usage or in terms of the target market (households, age categories, etc.)? What are customers really getting in terms of cost savings and/or better performance? Are there meaningful differences between types of customers?
4. What are the basic determinants of demand? What is the pattern of repeat business? What new product uses could be promoted to broaden the demand base?
5. Assess the significant market trends. What is the growth profile of the market? Is the market becoming more specialized? More application-oriented? More diverse in terms of customers or products?
6. What is the relationship between industry demand and general economic conditions?
7. Is demand sensitive to price changes? Changes in income?
B. History of the Industry
1. What is the industry's growth and profitability record?
2. At what stage is the industry in its life cycle—infancy? Growth? Maturity? Steady-state? Decline?

TABLE 4–1 *(continued)*

3. Has the industry been plagued by excess capacity? Have there been severe competitive shakeouts during periods of oversupply?
4. What are the industry's prospects for the future?

C. Technology and Cost
1. Identify the technologies by which the product is made and ascertain the cost structure of each. If there are wide divergencies in production methods and costs, then why do they continue to coexist?
2. What is the history of innovation in the industry? Which firms are generally recognized as the leaders in innovation? Has innovation produced major changes in costs and prices?
3. Are there any technological threats or opportunities on the horizon?
4. How crucial is technological proficiency to success? Are patents a significant factor? What is the nature and depth of the R&D effort in the industry?
5. How significant are economies of scale and what is the minimum entry size? How has the size of firms in the industry been changing and what are the underlying causes?
6. What are the key cost variables and cost trends? Have costs been rising or falling? Why? How have these changes affected price?

D. Financial and Operating Considerations
1. What sort of capital investment is required for entry? Are there any major barriers to entry and exit?
2. What is the expected life of plant and equipment? What is the chance that manufacturing facilities will be made obsolete by technological change or new forms of competition? How adaptable are manufacturing facilities to other uses?
3. What are the typical financial features in terms of debt versus equity, working capital requirements, investment payback, cash flow, inventory turnover, liquidity ratios, debt ratios, bond and interest coverages, and so on?
4. How is the industry viewed by the banking industry and by Wall Street?
5. What is the financial condition of firms in the industry?
6. What is the relationship between capacity utilization and profit margins?
7. Evaluate labor supply and raw material supply conditions. What is the union situation and the history of union-management relations in the industry?
8. How are raw materials and finished goods warehoused and shipped? Given service and cost considerations, how adequate are the available modes of transportation?

E. Marketing
1. What are the means and methods of marketing the product? Are market channels well-organized or underdeveloped? Do existing channels need shortening, lengthening, or a revised emphasis?
2. What makes a product competitive in the industry? Has the industry evidenced a capacity for exploiting new products and developing new markets?
3. What is necessary in terms of advertising, sales promotion, technical support for sales staff, and sales force organization?
4. What is the role of marketing research? Is R&D based on needs defined by market research and is it an integral part of new product development?
5. What sort of marketing mix typifies firms in the industry? What proportion of total costs are marketing and distribution expenses? What are the expenses of adding new customers?

TABLE 4–1 *(concluded)*

6. How significant is new product R&D? Brand consciousness? Trademarks and copyrights? Reputation? The degree of product differentiation? Product customization? Customer loyalty? Obsolescence factors? Customer turnover?

F. Competition
1. Draw up a profile of rival firms in terms of products, market shares, market coverage, growth, and competitive strategies. What are the *trends* in market standing among the various firms and how do these vary by area, customer type, and product application? Which firms are considered the industry leaders in price and in the introduction of new products and technologies?
2. What features distinguish the poorly performing firms from the outstanding performers?
3. Are there good substitute products and are they price competitive? For what reasons might customers turn to substitutes?
4. How strong are competitive pressures in the industry and what form do they take? Are these pressures equally strong in the target market niche being examined?
5. How secure are established firms from entry by new firms?
6. Are there geographic limits to competition? Is the focus of competition local, regional, national, or international? Are there any gaps in geographic coverage?
7. How active are trade associations in promoting or containing increased competition?

G. Key Success Factors and Strategic Forecasts
1. *What are the keys to being successful in this industry;* that is, *what does a firm have to be sure of doing right in order to succeed?* What particular distinctive competences does it need? Are there different requirements for success from one type of customer to another?
2. Make a strategic forecast; i.e., assess the overall shape of future economic, political, market, technological, and competitive conditions so as to provide a backdrop for viewing the total picture.
3. What conclusions can be drawn from the above with respect to strategy? What is the range of viable strategic options? How strong are the constraints on strategic flexibility?

The Strategic Forecast.   It has been noted on several previous occasions that the general manager in conducting a strategic analysis is obliged to assess both present and expected future conditions within and without the industry. Indeed, the nature of tomorrow's environment is of more overriding import than today's. Strategic forecasting, as we shall use the term, refers to the judgmental process of predicting the future course of relevant economic, political, market, technological, and competitive changes in an industry.[1] Strategic forecasting is not to be confused with simply extrapolat-

---

[1] For a more thorough discussion of strategic forecasting and its role in strategy formulation, see Hugo Uyterhoeven, Robert Ackerman, and John Rosenblum, *Strategy and Organization: Text and Cases in General Management,* rev. ed. (Homewood, Ill.: Richard D. Irwin, Inc., 1977), chap. 5; Francis Aguilar, *Scanning the Business Environment* (New York: The Macmillan Company, 1967).

ing past trends into the future. There is more to forecasting than just protecting trends, namely, the predicting of turning points and major structural changes—neither of which are deducible from trend analysis.

Trend projections are inherently rooted in the past and the past is seldom a perfect preview of coming events. Hence, while trends have a valid place in the making of an operational forecast, by themselves they are not a valid basis for predicting the future.

Although the specifics of a strategic forecast are understandably a function of each organization's own industry and market situation, the thrust of the general issues to be explored does not vary greatly. Table 4–2 is illustrative of the kinds of questions which tend to be part and parcel of a strategic forecast.

Obviously, though, strategic forecasting is laden with pitfalls and uncertainty. Different people may view the same set of ''facts'' and reach significantly different conclusions about the course of future events.

TABLE 4–2
Elements of a Strategic Forecast

1. *Technology.* What sorts of pertinent new products/services are likely to become technically feasible to produce in the foreseeable future. Will it be economically feasible to sell them at a competitively attractive price?
2. *Customer Needs.* Which customer needs are presently *not* being met by existing products? Why? Are R&D activities under way to develop means for fulfilling these needs? What is their status?
3. *Market Change.* What demographic and population-based changes can be anticipated and what do they portend for the size of the market and sales potentials?
4. *Competition.* How likely are important new competitive pressures to arise from substitute products? Entry of new firms? Strategic moves by existing rivals?
5. *Costs and Supply.* What is the likelihood of incurring major cost increases because of a dwindling supply of natural resource-based raw materials? Will sources of supply be reliable? Are there any other reasons to expect major changes in costs?
6. *The Economy.* What is the probable future course of the economy with regard to rates of inflation, unemployment, economic growth, money supply expansion and capital availability, increases in consumer purchasing power, and so on? Which economic variables have the greatest impact on the organization's business?
7. *Government Policy.* What changes in government policy can be expected regarding environmental controls, product safety, consumer protection, antitrust, foreign trade regulations (tariffs, quotas, trade agreements), tax policy, wage-price controls, energy conservation, transportation, and other pertinent regulations? What course will monetary and fiscal policies take in response to economic change?

What uses can be made of such forecasting techniques as intuitive methods of experts (e.g., the Delphi technique), trend extrapolation, regression and correlation analysis, econometrics, and dynamic predictive models (e.g., simulation) to arrive at quantitative estimates of how the above factors might combine to affect overall market and strategic opportunity?

Nonetheless, forecasting errors are more tolerable than flying blind with little or no notion of what lies ahead. At the very least, the areas of forecasting uncertainty and judgment can be made explicit and explored fully for their possible error content. Moreover, a set of forecasts can be prepared to test the sensitivity of the predictions to changes in the underlying assumptions; this makes contingency planning for forecasting errors much easier. Consequently, a serious attempt at strategic forecasting is better than no attempt. It beats guesswork despite the inaccuracies involved.

As an illustration of the usefulness of strategic forecasts, consider the strategic issues raised by dwindling world oil supplies. How long will oil users continue to rely on oil as a major energy source? When will high oil prices and short supplies force a switch to other forms of energy? Will radically innovative energy sources be developed with cost and supply advantages superior to those of currently known energy alternatives? Will the established oil companies have access to these new energy technologies or will antitrust factors make them the exclusive province of new companies? What competitive advantage will the new technology have over rival energy forms? How easy will it be for energy users to integrate backward and supply their own energy needs? Predictive answers to these questions have obvious strategic value to energy suppliers and major energy users and can scarcely fail to weigh heavily in their strategic investment decisions.

Table 4–3 provides a rundown of major sources of information for making strategic analyses and strategic forecasts and for evaluating a company's position.

TABLE 4–3
Sources of Information for Conducting a Strategic Analysis and Evaluating Companies

A. Population, the Economy, and Current Business Conditions
   1. U.S. Department of Commerce, Bureau of the Census, *Census of Population, Census of Housing, County Business Patterns, Census of Governments*—for periodic, but comprehensive and detailed, data on population characteristics, housing conditions, and various business and governmental statistics.
   2. U.S. Department of Commerce, *Survey of Current Business* (monthly), *Business Conditions Digest* (monthly), *U.S. Industrial Outlook, Statistical Abstract of the United States* (annually)—for current and historical statistics on the economy and business conditions.
   3. Council of Economic Advisors, *Economic Report of the President* (published annually)—contains a good variety of statistics relating to GNP, income, employment, prices, money supply, and governmental finance.
   4. United Nations, *Statistical Yearbook*—for various economic statistics of foreign countries.
   5. OECD, *Economic Outlook and Main Economic Indicators*—for international economic data.
   6. Board of Governors of Federal Reserve System, *Federal Reserve Bulletin* (monthly)—for data on banking, money supply conditions, interest rates, and credit conditions.

TABLE 4–3 *(continued)*

7. U.S. Department of Labor, Bureau of Labor Statistics, *Monthly Labor Review* (monthly), *Employment and Earnings* (monthly), *Handbook of Labor Statistics* (annually)—for data on employment, hours worked and earnings, productivity, wholesale and consumer prices, labor turnover, and area unemployment characteristics.

8. Editor and Publisher, *Market Guide* (annually)—contains rankings of cities, counties, and SMSA areas based on individual income, population, total retail sales, and food sales as well as pertinent local area information.

9. *Sales Management* magazine's "Annual Survey of Buying Power"—for rankings on the amount spent for selected products/services by geographical location.

B. Industry Information

1. U.S. Department of Commerce, Bureau of the Census, *Census of Manufactures, Annual Survey of Manufacturing, Census of Business, Census of Transportation*—for statistics relating to the volume of manufacturing activity, size and structure of firms, retail and wholesale trade, and transportation.

2. Federal Trade Commission, *Quarterly Financial Report for Manufacturing, Mining, and Trade Corporations* (quarterly)—for sales, profit, balance sheet, and income statement statistics by industry division and size of firm.

3. U.S. Department of the Treasury, Internal Revenue Service, *Business Income Tax Returns* (annually) and *Corporate Income Tax Returns* (annually)—for breakdowns on revenues, operating expenses, and profits by type of business organization and industry division.

4. National Industrial Conference Board: research and statistical reports issued periodically and the *Conference Board Record* (monthly).

5. Securities and Exchange Commission: quarterly reports of finance and capital expenditures.

6. Trade association and industry publications such as *Commercial and Financial Chronicle, Banking, Advertising Age, Automotive News, Public Utilities Fortnightly, Engineering News Record, Best's Insurance Review, Progressive Grocer*, and *Electronic News*.

C. Company-Oriented Information

1. Annual reports of companies.

2. Investment services and directories: Standard and Poor's, Moody's, *Value Line*.

3. Financial ratios: Dun & Bradstreet Annual Surveys, Robert Morris Associates *Annual Statement Studies*.

4. Securities and Exchange Commission, Form 10–K reports.

5. Periodicals: *Fortune, Barron's, Forbes, Wall Street Transcript, Dun's Review, Business Week, Financial World, Over-the-Counter Securities Review.*

For an additional classification and survey of information sources, see C. R. Goeldner and Laura M. Dirks, "Business Facts: Where to Find Them," *Business Topics*, vol. 24, no. 3 (Summer 1976), pp. 23–36.

AUDITING THE COMPETITIVE ENVIRONMENT

Once the industry profile is complete, the next step is to conduct a thorough audit of the competitive environment with specific reference to the reasons underlying the enterprise's own market standing or, in the case of markets where entry is being contemplated, to requirements for competitive success. The following questions suggest the major points to be considered:

How firmly does the company stand with its customers? What do customers think of the company and its product line? How does this compare with what they think of rival firms? What is the company's trend in market standing; e.g., is it moving up or falling behind? Is the company's reputation improving or not?

What is the image of each major competitor from the viewpoint of the consumer? What are the distinguishing features of each major competitor's strategy? Why and how are they approaching the market differently? What evaluation should be placed on the competitive programs, policies, and strategy execution of the major rivals? How do their strategies compare with the company being studied?

What benefits do customers get by buying from this company? Does it offer more or less value than the competition? What are the pivotal product features that prompt a buyer to purchase from one seller and not another? Does the company's product have these features and how successful has it been at promoting them?

What are the firm's biggest competitive weaknesses? What is it doing and what can it do about them in terms of competitive programs and policies or their execution?

In what segments of the market is the company strongest? Weakest? What potential customers is it missing? What is its record on expanding its customer base and what are the reasons for this record?

Is the firm's market posture innovative or responsive? Is this confirmed by its customer's perceptions? When customers have a problem do they look to this company or to its rivals for help?

Where does the company rank in the industry on overall competitive effectiveness? How strong is this ranking and how can it be strengthened?

In most cases, the preceding set of questions, if objectively probed, should pinpoint what it takes to compete successfully (the strategic advantage factors), thereby revealing why and how firms in the industry occupy their relative competitive positions. But in instances where the product line, the competition, or the market is unduly complex, it may be necessary to do a separate analysis of each product, each rival firm, and each identifiable market segment. This means conducting a detailed examination of what the specific dimensions of competition are for the distinguishable products and customer categories, followed up by an analysis of why and how rival firms vary in their emphasis on different product-customer categories. Determining what variations in competitive programs and policies, or their execution, underlie the market strategies of major firms goes a long way toward accounting for differentials in performance. It also facilitates drawing up a profile of the strategies of the major firms and evaluating their strengths and weaknesses.[2]

Once the competitive audit is complete, an enterprise is ready to decide what its own most advantageous strategy might be for this industry and how its market approach should be segmented to allow for differences based upon product applications, geographical territory, customer category, channels of distribution, or other relevant factors.

Just as in the case of the industry profile, a separate competitive audit is required for each different market environment in which the enterprise is considering strategic alternatives.

THE ROLE OF COMPETITION IN STRATEGY EVALUATION

The audit of the competitive environment sets the stage for thoroughly analyzing the impact of competition on an organization's choice of strategy. Whenever two or more enterprises sell in the same market, their partially conflicting economic interests become manifested in business rivalry. Each firm is motivated to try to outdo the other so as to gain a stronger foothold with buyers and thereby reap the rewards of market success. Out of this motivation, together with an awareness of the interactions of their approaches to the market, emerges an ongoing series of competitive strategies and counterstrategies, some offensive and some defensive, on the part of each seller in the market.

Each firm's competitive moves and countermoves are likely to be related to its overall corporate strategy for developing a viable business organization and for achieving a degree of success sufficient to sustain operations over the long run. With the passage of time, a firm's overall corporate strategy and/or its market-specific strategies will tend either to be fine-tuned or to undergo major overhaul, according to the firm's market successes (or failures) and the durability of its chosen competitive strategies in withstanding competitive challenges from rival firms.

When a firm makes a successful competitive move, it can expect increased rewards, largely at the expense of either rivals' market shares or their rates of sales growth. The speed and extent of the competitive encroachment varies with whether the product is standardized or differentiated, the initiator's competence and resources to capitalize on the advantage the strategy has produced, how difficult it is to shift buyer loyalties, and the ease with which the strategy can be copied. The pressures on rivals to respond vary with all these factors, together with whether the initiator is (1) a major firm with considerable market visibility, (2) a fringe firm whose efforts can be ignored for some time, or (3) a firm in financial distress and thus whose strategy is predicated on desperation.

---

[2] See Jerry Wall, "What the Competition Is Doing: Your Need to Know," *Harvard Business Review*, vol. 52, no. 6 (November–December 1974), pp. 22 ff.

For instance, if a firm's strategic offensive is keyed to a low price aimed at quick penetration but with a substantial risk that full costs will not be recovered, rivals may judge that the strategy will be short-lived; they may choose to respond or not, depending on their estimates of whether it will be better to meet the low price on a temporary basis or to ride out whatever buyer resistance may be encountered. If the initiating firm finds its move neutralized by rivals' countermoves, then it is challenged to seek out a better strategy not as easily defeated or else remain content with the stalemate it has encountered.

The ease with which a firm's alternative strategies can be neutralized is a major criterion of strategy selection; firms will gravitate strongly toward strategies which either are not easily imitated or are not easily defeated. Such considerations should strongly incline a firm to try to develop a distinctive competence whereby it can differentiate its product in ways not susceptible to successful imitation; acquiring a reputation and image on some facet or facets of its product offering will set the firm's product above and apart from that of other firms.

A variety of competitive outcomes may flow from the strategies of rival firms. The pattern of strategic behavior may range from one of cooperation or collusion to one of highly combative rivalry. Because what is the best strategy for firm A depends on firm B's choice, and because B in turn must choose its strategy in light of the options open to A, what is optimal fades into a fog of interacting uncertainties. And, except in the case of distressed firms in dire straits, no strategic choice is ever final. The sequence of move and countermove is never-ending.

It may be that only a few firms (large or small) will tend to initiate fresh strategic moves, and they may not do it often, but to the extent that they set the pace for the others, the give-and-take of move and response spreads and continues. An initiatory move may come from a firm with ambitious growth objectives, from a firm with excess capacity, or from a firm under pressure to gain added business. More generally, though, the important offensive strategies tend to be made by firms that see market opportunities and a chance to improve their standing. Such firms tend to be aware that they are starting a chain of moves and countermoves (if, in fact, it has not already been triggered by other firms) and they have confidence, (1) that they are shrewd enough to keep ahead of the game and (2) that they will be better off than they would be by holding back and letting others take the lead. Often, new marketing moves are undertaken by sales force organizations under pressure from top management to increase market penetration and/or otherwise improve performance, the thesis being that an organization which stands still soon stagnates. The more aggressive firms may well *create* competitive pressures that are sufficiently strong to *compel* responses from other firms and that also bankrupt the inefficient and ineffective firms (i.e., those which have been unable to build an organization with the distinctive competence to attract buyers and to carve out a market niche for their product).

Although initiatory moves may come from a variety of firms and for a variety of reasons, it is not likely that all, or even most, firms will take a turn at starting a fresh round of moves. It is to be expected that some firms will be bolder and more aggressive than others in trying to make an impact with their strategies. The defensive responses which follow will not only reflect time lags and uncertainties but their character will also tend to differ according to whether the new offensive consists of a new promotional campaign, introduction of a new product or product variation, a new channel of distribution, or an expansive move toward a new form of horizontal or vertical integration. Furthermore, the strategic process will not generally be so active that the market becomes unstable and chaotic. Short intervals of stabilized product offerings may surface so as to permit firms to better gauge trends and opportunities. In fact, a rapid-fire pattern of fresh moves may turn out to be counterproductive for all concerned because of the confusion and uncertainty which it generates among customers, suppliers, and rival firms.

However, any stalemates or pauses in moves and countermoves tend to be temporary because of the continuous stream of strategic opportunities and threats which emerge from the possibilities for product variation, cost-related technological changes, new buyer tastes and preferences, changing demographics and life-styles, shifts in buying power, new product availability, and so on. Apart from these market-related variables, ongoing changes can also be expected in the host of complex institutional factors that mold a firm's strategy choices from the outside and the intrafirm considerations which shape strategy from the inside. All of these aspects, together with the time sequence of strategic moves and the information base underlying them, act to shape the evaluation of strategic alternatives and the final choice of a strategy.

GEARING STRATEGY TO THE ECONOMIC ENVIRONMENT

Once a competitive assessment of the strategic alternatives has been made, a second area for analysis is to make sure that the strategic alternatives under consideration are each capable of succeeding in a variety of market situations. To opt for a strategy which is heavily dependent on general economic prosperity and a "seller's market" is to tempt fate; inevitably, periods of market slack will create excess capacity problems. When oversupply conditions are compounded by a high ratio of fixed costs to total costs, the outcome is a certain profit squeeze. Furthermore, during a recession competitive pressures intensify as firms scramble to maintain or build volume back up. The paper industry provides an excellent example of what can happen when strategy is not closely allied with the realities of the business cycle. Time and again, the paper producers have been lulled into overexpanding when demand was strong only to have their profit margins evaporate at the next cyclical downturn. While this occurred partly because additional papermaking capacity comes "on-stream" in big increments, it also was a result of individual firms acting without reference to their rivals' expansion plans and the implications these had for supply-demand equilibrium.

On the other hand, to adopt a cautious, defensive posture that minimizes downside risks may put a company in poor position to ride the waves of a booming market. Getting caught short on capacity means a potential loss of market share and a perhaps weaker competitive edge because production facilities, being relatively older, are less cost effective. Overcoming these disadvantages and trying to make up lost ground can be an expensive and time-consuming task. International Nickel Co. (Inco) found this out after complacently standing by while its share of the free world's nickel market dropped from 85 percent in the 1950s to 40 percent in 1974.[3] Late in responding to challenges from competitors, Inco found itself straining when nickel demand began a steep rise in 1963. A $1.1 billion expansion program was launched in 1966 to increase capacity by 30 percent. But by waiting three years to begin, Inco gave rival producers a golden opportunity. It takes a long time to expand nickel sulfide mines (Inco's principal source of ore) and in the meantime Inco's smaller rivals turned up offering a cheap and available source of low-grade nickel source called Lateritic ore from which ferro nickel could easily be made. Inco's market share deteriorated rapidly and then in 1971 just when Inco's new capacity was blossoming, market demand fell by 17 percent. Inco, whose market projections for 1971 had been very bullish, found itself stuck with huge inventories and inventory-maintenance charges. These charges came due precisely when the debt payments on the 1966 expansion program were peaking; during part of 1971 one Inco executive recalled "we were spending $1 million a day more than we were bringing in."[4] Not until 1974 did a new management team, which took over in 1972, shore up Inco's fundamental market position.

The Inco example is not unique.[5] As a general proposition, the more volatile a firm's markets are, the more flexible the firm's strategy needs to be for it to be effective. Moreover, the likely prospect of changing market conditions speaks to the desirability of having not only flexible strategies but also contingency strategies. *Business Week* in 1975 reported that the top managements of more and more companies were readying a "whole battery of contingency plans and alternate scenarios." According to *Business Week,* companies were reviewing and revising strategic plans more frequently so as to stay abreast of changing conditions; quarterly or even monthly updates are not as unusual as they once were.

---

[3] See Lansing Lamont, "Inco: A Giant Learns to Compete," *Fortune* (January 1975), pp. 104–16.

[4] Ibid., p. 110.

[5] See, for instance, Eleanor J. Tracey, "How A&P Got Creamed," *Fortune* (January 1973), pp. 103–14.

NARROWING DOWN THE LIST OF ALTERNATIVES

Once management has settled on a list of viable strategic alternatives and the information necessary to evaluate them has been gathered in the form of an industry profile and a competitive audit, then it is time to begin the process of narrowing down the list of candidate strategies. Although there is no set procedure for approaching this phase of a strategic analysis, inquiring into each of the following is likely to be a fruitful way of screening out weaker alternatives:

Which, if any, of the strategic alternatives call for greater competence and/or resources than the organization can muster?

Are any of the candidate strategies less attractive from the standpoint of profit outlook or return on investment criteria even though they meet minimum standards?

Do any of the alternatives fall short of adequately exploiting the organization's distinctive competence?

Are market conditions and competitive conditions relative to each of the candidates such that the best strategic advantage is to be had by challenging rival firms where they are strong? Or where they are weak?

How do the alternatives rank in terms of offering the best or strongest competitive advantage?

Which alternatives are most vulnerable to an effective strategic counterattack from rivals?

How vulnerable are each of the candidate strategies to environmental threats now existing or on the horizon? How flexible are the alternatives in terms of allowing for responses to unforeseeable events?

Should any of the candidates be ruled out because of a conflict with management's sense of social responsibilities or an incompatibility with personal values?

On the basis of the answers to the foregoing questions, which alternatives seem to be inferior?

In all likelihood, a penetrating investigation of the questions posed above will result in several of the strategic alternatives being discarded—or at least relegated to a long-shot position.

ASPECTS OF STRATEGIC EVALUATION

At this juncture, the strategist's task becomes one of reconciling the pros and cons of the remaining alternatives. Ideally, one would like to assemble a strategic plan where all or most of the vital considerations were simultaneously optimized. In practice, this objective proves much too utopian. Trade-offs are inevitably necessary. Trying to minimize risk exposure, for example, nearly always entails a sacrifice of potential profits. Likewise, strategic attempts to exploit every opportunity to its fullest can mean concomitant increases in the number of failures; the criterion of maximizing organizational strengths can be incompatible with minimizing organizational weaknesses. In addition, compromises are necessary in order to fashion a strategy which meets the needs of various coalition groups in the management hierarchy (marketing, manufacturing, finance) and which also is consonant with the interest of exogeneous groups (stockholders, labor, consumers, government, the general public). Also, the many-faceted aspects of a strategic evaluation often point to conflicting conclusions. Normally, therefore, the best one can do is to search out the alternative offering the most satisfactory blend of advantages and disadvantages. Toward this end, the strategist is forced to scrutinize the set of leading candidates from several angles:

Which strategic alternative offers the best match with the organization's competence and financial resources?

Which strategy promises to make the greatest contribution to overall organizational performance?

Which candidate offers the most dominant competitive edge and how vulnerable is it to a strategic counterattack from rival enterprises?

Which alternative minimizes the creation of new (and perhaps thorny) operating or administrative problems?

Which alternative has the best combination of high expected profitability and low-risk exposure?

Which alternative offers the most favorable trade-off between maximizing opportunities and minimizing weaknesses?

Which strategy appears best suited to management's know-how, philosophy, personality, and sense of social responsibilities?

Which of the leading candidate strategies appears most propitious from the standpoint of timing? Is now the opportune time to be bold or cautious, a leader or a follower? Which strategy offers the best trade-off among near-term, long-term, and flexibility objectives?

Which strategy, if successful, would provide the best platform for taking advantage of other opportunities that might present themselves?

Chances are, of course, that the answers to these questions will not all point to the same strategic alternative. This raises the further issue of how to reconcile the conflicts and inconsistencies. When an alternative scores well on some factors but negatively on others, the net effect is not simply a function of whether there are more pluses than minuses or vice versa. Some factors are more critical than others. And since the weight of a factor's importance varies from case to case, making an overall assessment inherently requires more than following some kind of quantitative decision procedure or depending on logical deduction.

Illustration Capsule 11

The Whys and Hows of GE's Strategic Divestment of Its Computer Business

In 1970, General Electric in a surprise move announced the sale of its computer manufacturing assets to Honeywell, Inc. The rationale underlying GE's divestiture of its computer operations recently came to light when highly confidential documents about GE's appraisal of its computer business were introduced as evidence by the Justice Department in its antitrust suit against IBM (alleging that IBM has monopoly power over the U.S. computer-systems market).

Although IBM considered GE as its strongest competitor in the mid-1960s, by 1970 the technical capabilities of GE's computer products were falling behind those of other firms and the company's competitive strength had deteriorated markedly. From 1957–70, GE sustained net losses from its computer operations of $162.7 million. Meanwhile, having just weathered a costly strike and with the nation in a slight recession, GE was under financial strains from short-run losses in two of its biggest product lines—nuclear power plants and jet aircraft engines. Both were deemed vital to GE's overall business in electrical products and were expected to turn profitable in the near future; as a consequence, GE's management felt these two lines had to be supplied with whatever cash was needed.

In contrast, the computer business had never been considered vital to GE and many of GE's top-management group were of the opinion that if the company was to salvage anything financially from its venture into computers, it would have to be the first of "the seven dwarfs" (as IBM's main competitors were known) to drop out of the market.

It was, then, in this environment that GE's computer division proposed to corporate headquarters to undertake the manufacture of a broad, new computer line that would have 20 percent–40 percent better performance than IBM computers, yet sell at about the same price. According to the plan, the new computer line would generate revenue of $8.2 billion and profit before taxes of $2.34 billion in the 13 years of 1969–81. However, the program was projected to incur losses through 1973 of $538 million. Profits would begin in 1974, but the cumulative losses would not be offset until 1977. GE's computer heads forecast a net cash drain of $685 million through 1974—a drain which would require GE to borrow at least $500 million to undertake the plan. If the plan succeeded, GE was projected to become a clear second to IBM, with an 8 percent market share by 1975, rising to 10 percent soon thereafter. This compared favorably with the current 4 percent to 5 percent share and was felt to be adequate to keep the division profitable.

However, the plan incorporated some shaky assumptions: (1) that GE could take customers from IBM; (2) that IBM would tolerate a sizable loss in market share without retaliating; (3) that GE could achieve key inventions on schedule and meet developmental deadlines; and (4) that IBM and other computer manufacturers would not leapfrog GE by bringing out still better computer products.

Aside from the fact that the assumptions were questionable and "fraught with risk," it was GE's assessment that IBM would continue to dominate the computer business, owing to its superior sales coverage, low manufacturing costs, and large base of customers—estimated at 72 percent of the market. IBM had steadily improving profit margins, strength in all aspects of computer technology, and overwhelming programming resources (software) to go with its computers. Although IBM was confronted with antitrust suits, some loss of skilled personnel to other companies, increasing specialization by competitors, and some gradual loss of its position in software and peripheral equipment technology, IBM's competitors still were earning only meager profits and were nowhere near as able as IBM to respond to the rapid

Illustration Capsule 11 (continued)

market growth, rapid technological change, and rapid developments in the uses of computers.

Whereas some computer companies were managing to compete on the basis of specialization in certain products for uses, GE was a generalist, attempting to compete across the board with IBM. In the view of GE's top executives, GE did not have a strong basis for specializing. Its major computer products were not as up to date and GE was weak in peripheral, mass-storage, and terminal devices—all of which were viewed as key products of the future. GE had limited technical strength in many areas of computer technology and its customer loyalty was reputed to be the lowest of any firm in the market.

Whereas IBM had 210 sales offices in the United States and 17,000 salesmen and systems analysts, GE had 38 offices with a staff of 600. To reach its 1975 market share objective, GE would have to increase sales force sizes by 60 to 70 percent per year and, at the same time, develop salesmen who were twice as productive as IBM's. Whereas GE's manufacturing costs were 47 percent of its computer revenue, IBM's were estimated at 20 percent. GE's assessments of other firms in the computer market included the following:

> Control Data Corporation. 4.2 percent of worldwide computer installations; growing faster than the market; specialists in large computer systems and government applications; technically strong but weak in business applications.
>
> Burroughs Corporation. 2.4 percent of the market; growing substantially faster than other firms; specialists in banking and some other uses; technically strong.
>
> National Cash Register Corporation. 2.2 percent of the market; specialists in smaller systems, banking and first-time users; weak in peripherals and software; unprofitable.
>
> Sperry Rand (UNIVAC). 6.8 percent of the market but losing ground; technically strong except for large-system software but had never fully used its strength; a generalist firm with weak marketing organization.
>
> Honeywell. 3.9 percent of the market; growing slower than the market; technically good but with an incomplete and somewhat out-of-date product line; a generalist firm which had seriously delayed product development in order to be profitable.
>
> RCA Corporation. 2.9 percent of the market and losing ground; a generalist firm with no identifiable customer segment; technically poor except in communications; aging and incomplete product line; no real strength; unprofitable.

Finally, GE's management viewed the industry as being on the threshold of a major merger movement. No one of the small-share firms was in a position to seriously challenge IBM or make a lasting impact on the market.

Given these considerations, beset with mounting pressures for immediate profit increases, and facing stringent financial demands from its nuclear power and jet engine businesses, General Electric decided to "disengage" from the industry and sell its computer business. Moving quickly, GE officials approached Control Data, Xerox, and Honeywell about "the structure of the industry" and the hazards posed by "the continuing dominance of IBM"—but without revealing its intention to get out.

Meanwhile, GE explored how well its own operations would mesh with the business of each of its competitors in the event a sale could be worked out and concluded: Honeywell and Burroughs, good; Sperry Rand and NCR, fair; Control Data and RCA, poor; Xerox, unrated. As for their financial capabilities of purchasing GE's computer operations (which had a $176 million depreciated net book value on an original investment of $472 million), GE's assessment was: Xerox, high; Honeywell, RCA, Burroughs, and NCR, medium; UNIVAC, low-plus; Control Data, poor.

GE found Honeywell to be most receptive to taking over GE's computer operations. Honeywell, stronger in the United States, and GE, stronger in Europe, would together be an undisputed "Number 2" with assets of $1.24 billion, combined 1972 revenues of $932 million, and 12,500 marketing and service employees worldwide. With the elimination of duplicate activities and the adoption of Honeywell's "more liberal" accounting policies, it was estimated that acquisition by Honeywell could produce a pretax profit of $66 million. According to a top GE vice president, such a deal seemed to be "an optimum fit with a well-managed and successful growth company."

At GE's urging, negotiations began at once (to minimize the chances of leaks) and within two months of its decision to get out of the industry, GE and Honeywell announced an agreement to combine their computer businesses and create a new company controlled and managed by Honeywell. In return for turning over its computer business assets to the new company, GE received $110 million in Honeywell notes, Honeywell stock valued at $124.5 million, and an 18.5 percent interest in the new company. GE kept its time-sharing service (which allows simultaneous operation of a computer by many users) and its process-control computers for industry, though in 1974 the process-control line was also sold to Honeywell.

Although GE was the first dwarf to get out, about a year later RCA announced it was abandoning its computer business at a net loss of $210 million. Sperry Rand bought some of the RCA assets. In 1975, Xerox also dropped out of the computer industry, taking a loss of $84.4 million and turning over some of its activities to Honeywell.

Source: *The Wall Street Journal,* January 12, 1976, p. 26.

Nevertheless, several quantitative approaches may prove helpful. For instance, if the various factors can be ranked in order of priority or relative importance, then the rankings can be used as "weights" to compute an overall weighted scale for each of the strategic alternatives. The problem here is that different weighting techniques and different numerical weights may result in different strategies being identified as superior or dominant. This can be partly overcome by using several weighting schemes and subjecting them to various tests for consistency. Comparing their results then gives a systematic basis for judging how the pros and cons of a strategy add up.[6]

The important thing is for the analyst to be on guard that the expected benefits of a strategic alternative represent *solid* prospects and not superficial promise. Thus, no matter how attractive an alternative may seem, it is essen-

---

[6] For a discussion of how various quantitative decision rules might be helpful in making a strategic choice, see H. Igor Ansoff, *Corporate Strategy* (New York: McGraw-Hill Book Co., 1965), pp. 182–88.

tial to dig into its operational and managerial consequences before an irrevocable choice is made. One of the legacies of the diversification/merger movement of the 1960s was the large number of corporate "marriages" that did not "take" because of an incomplete and faulty strategic evaluation.

MAKING THE STRATEGIC CHOICE

In the final analysis, strategic decisions boil down to a matter of judgment and choice. Even after a lengthy and exhaustive strategic evaluation, the general manager will probably be confronted with making some tough strategic decisions rather than merely confirming a clear-cut choice. Very rarely is the issue of what to do so cut and dried as to eliminate the judgment/choice problem. Facts and analysis by themselves usually do not resolve the problem of conflicts and inconsistencies. For this reason, intuition, personal experience, judgment, qualitative trade-offs, value preferences, intangible situational factors, and compromise of opinion become an integral part of the process of making a strategic commitment. And no formula or how-to-do-it description is ever likely to take their place.

Three elements of the strategic choice problem frequently assume a pivotal import in reaching a decision on strategy:

1. The risk/reward trade-off.
2. Timing the strategic move.
3. The vulnerability to strategic counterattack.

Risk/Reward Considerations. The first of these has been alluded to previously. It essentially involves the willingness of an organization to assume risk. Risk-averters will be inclined toward "safe" strategies where external threats appear minimal, profits adequate but not spectacular, and in-house resources ample to meet the task ahead. "Conservative" firms will prefer a low debt-to-equity financial structure to a more highly leveraged approach. They will probably opt to defer major financial commitments as long as possible or until the effects of uncertainty are deemed minimal. They may view pioneering-type innovations as "too chancy" relative to proven, well-established techniques; or else they may prefer to be followers rather than leaders. Often, the risk-averter places a high premium on strategies which shore up organizational weaknesses.

On the other hand, eager risk-takers lean more toward opportunistic strategies where the payoffs are greater, the challenges more exciting, and the glamour more appealing—despite the pitfalls which may exist. Innovation is preferred to imitation. Aggressive action ranks ahead of defensive conservatism. A confident optimism overrules pessimism. The organization's strengths, not its weaknesses, serve as a chief criterion for matching strategy and organizational capability.

Timing Considerations. An organization's risk/reward posture also spills over into the way it decides to time its strategic move. Where uncertainty is high, the risk-averter's tendency is to proceed with extreme caution or to stall. A defensive stance is likely to emerge. In contrast, the risk-taker is willing to move early and assume a trail-blazing role. Yet, the timing dilemma goes deeper than the risk/reward trade-off and a preference for an active or reactive style. It also relates to whether market conditions are ripe for the strategies being contemplated. A "good" strategy undertaken at the wrong time can spell failure. Chrysler Corp. had this experience in 1974–75 when it decided to put more emphasis on full-size, family cars and compete head-on with General Motor's Chevrolet Impala and full-sized Pontiacs, Buicks, and Oldsmobiles. Chrysler redesigned its Plymouth, Dodge, and Chrysler cars along the styling lines of GM's medium-priced models but, unfortunately for Chrysler, they had barely hit the market when the Arab oil boycott and the subsequent steep climb in gasoline prices made consumers wary of "big" cars. Chrysler found itself not only stuck with the high costs of having restyled its line of cars but also without an appealing selection of small cars to offer the growing number of small-car buyers.

In addition, there are several other timing-related issues which bear on strategy selection.[7] One pertains to the lead time between action and result and any difficulties which may ensue if this time is "too long" or "too short." In a closely related vein, whether management's primary concern of the moment is for the short run or the long run can prompt the selection of a strategy which promises to yield the desired results in the desired time interval. Still another involves whether the magnitude and rate of investment funding required to support a given strategy fits in with the organization's overall financial structure and cash flow requirements. Inasmuch as strategic investments commonly entail a stream of expenditures rather than a single lump-sum expenditure, the timing of the components may favor the selection of one strategy over another, especially if other factors are not decisive.

Competitive Reactions. Frequently, the problem of strategic choice originates as either a challenge or a response to competitors' actions. It is incumbent upon an organization therefore to take into account the potential reactions of competitors to one's own strategic moves. Particularly it is pertinent to investigate what sort of counterattack may be expected from rivals and how this will affect the likely success of contemplated strategies. Plainly, a strategy is more attractive (1) the less vulnerable it is to the moves and countermoves of rivals, and (2) the greater the chance that it will put an enterprise in a superior or at least equal competitive position vis-à-vis the strategies it confronts.

In weighing the competitive interplay of strategic moves and countermoves, several salient points merit consideration. To begin with, the posture of one's own proposed strategy has a bearing on the counterresponses of competitors. Attacking the competition squarely will elicit an almost sure response—and maybe a vigorous one at that, unless the attack is deemed feeble or doomed to failure. But, to choose a strategy that sidesteps direct

---

[7] Seymour Tilles, "Making Strategy Explicit," in H. Igor Ansoff, *Business Strategy* (Baltimore: Penguin Books, 1970), p. 197.

confrontation stands a fair chance of going ignored for a time period long enough to establish a lead over rivals. The comparative benefits of attacking competitors' strengths or weaknesses warrant careful assessment. Challenging rivals where they are strongest carries a higher risk of failure though, also, a greater payoff if the strategy succeeds. On the other hand, to attack weakness brings modest rewards unless competitive weakness is associated with strong market potential—as sometimes it is.

   Strategic Commitment.   The final component of strategic choice is the commitment decision. In fact, a strategic choice cannot be said to have been made until a clear commitment has been made. The act of commitment is what takes the issue of the strategic decision out of the category of an alternative and activates the chosen strategy to official organizational status. Commitment entails (1) directing some part of the organization to undertake the strategy selected, (2) assigning responsibility for implementing the strategic plan to the appropriate personnel, (3) allocating the resources necessary for implementation, (4) clarifying exactly where and under what circumstances implementation is to be undertaken, and (5) specifying the time interval for implementation. In effect, then, strategic commitment supplies answers to the questions of *who, where,* and *when* (posed in Chapter 2) and thus completes the *what, how, why, who, where, when* sequence that goes into formulating a complete strategy.

A PERSPECTIVE VIEW OF THE STRATEGY FORMULATION PROCESS

   The strategy formulation process has run its course. The chain of steps we have followed in arriving at a managerial methodology for strategic choice is summarized in Figure 4–1. The sequence begins when events trigger a strategic review because of adverse impacts on the organization's mission, objectives, and goals. The strategy formulation process starts in earnest with an external appraisal of market and competitive conditions, together with an internal appraisal of organizational capabilities and resources. The external appraisal seeks to determine, in preliminary fashion, the field of industries and product groupings where unexploited potential may exist; this appraisal thus extends beyond the organization's present activities and line of endeavor. The internal appraisal seeks to ascertain the growth and expansion opportunities within the current product/market scope and also to pinpoint organizational strengths and weaknesses. One outcome of the internal appraisal should be a sharper specification of the organization's performance objectives, both immediate and long term, as well as a fresh look at the organization's purpose and mission.

   If these two appraisals, viewed in the light of the organization's perceived purpose, mission, objectives, and goals, reveal a deficiency in the current strategy, then emphasis shifts at once to a search for attractive strategic alternatives and modifications and development of a preliminary strategic

FIGURE 4–1
The Strategy Formulation Process

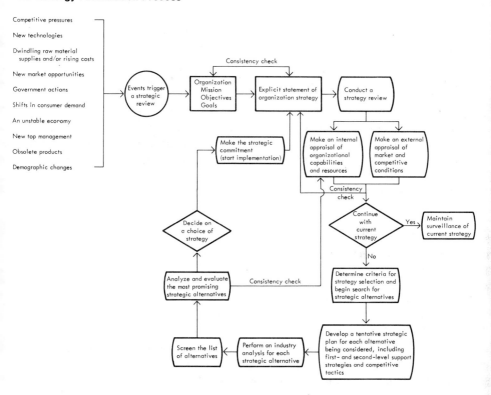

plan for each. Following this, a preliminary screening of the viable alternatives is conducted to eliminate those which are obviously unsuitable. Next, the feasibility of each of the remaining candidate strategies is explored by means of an industry analysis, after which comes a comparative assessment of the alternatives and a pruning of the list down to those candidates deemed as having the most potential. Those remaining alternatives are subjected to a thorough analysis relative to their respective abilities to satisfy all of the various search criteria. The resulting assemblage of information regarding the *what, how, why* questions provide the basis for the final evaluation and the choice of a new strategy.

This view of the strategy formulation process correctly suggests that the purpose of organizational strategy is to move the organization from its present position to a position closer to that described by its purpose and mission (as revised or updated), subject to the constraints of the organization's capabilities and the available opportunities. In this sense, the issue of strategy is one of whether and how the corporate identity will be redefined. At stake are the answers to the questions of "What are we?" and "What do we want to become?"

It should be noted, however, that the process of strategy formulation we have schematically outlined in Figure 4–1 is not without elements of ambiguity. At each point in the strategic decision-making sequence, there exist no clear-cut, infallible rules or procedures which, if followed to the letter, will lead to the "right" strategy choice. Strategy selection cannot be reduced to a precise, formulalike, analytic process. Intangible situational factors and preferences must be judiciously interwoven with the quantifiable and more concrete criteria for strategy selection. Thus, there is no substitute for the exercise of judgment and, consequently, no way of posing a strategy formulation methodology that will "guarantee" an optimal strategic choice. In other words, strategy formulation is a responsibility, not a technique; the process is not susceptible to a step-by-step "how to" description. One can, at most, offer some guidelines, indicate the pitfalls, and pose some of the right kinds of questions to ask.

SUGGESTED READINGS

Aguilar, Francis. *Scanning the Business Environment*. New York: Macmillan Co., 1967.

Buchele, Robert B. "How to Evaluate a Firm," *California Management Review*, vol. 4, no. 1 (Fall 1962), pp. 5–17.

Cannon, J. Thomas. *Business Strategy and Policy*. New York: Harcourt, Brace, & World, 1968), pp. 84–102.

Cohen K. J., and Cyert, R. M. "Strategy: Formulation, Implementation, and Monitoring," *Journal of Business*, vol. 46, no. 3 (July 1973), pp. 349–67.

Gilmore, Frank. "Formulating Strategy in Smaller Companies," *Harvard Business Review*, vol. 49, no. 3 (May–June 1971), pp. 71–81.

Hussey, David E. "The Corporate Appraisal: Assessing Company Strengths and Weaknesses," *Long-Range Planning*, vol. 1, no. 2 (December 1968), pp. 19–25.

Lunneman Robert E., and Kennell, John D. "Short-Sleeve Approach to Long-Range Plans," *Harvard Business Review*, vol. 55, no. 2 (March–April, 1977), pp. 141–50.

Mason, R. Hal; Harris, Jerome; and McLoughlin, John. "Corporate Strategy: A Point of View," *California Management Review*, vol. 13, no. 3 (Spring 1971), pp. 5–12.

Vancil, Richard F. "Strategy Formulation in Complex Organizations," *Sloan Management Review*, vol. 17, no. 2 (Winter 1976), pp. 1–8.

Wall, Jerry. "What the Competition Is Doing: Your Need to Know," *Harvard Business Review*, vol. 52, no. 6 (November–December 1974), pp. 22 ff.

PART III

Organization and Policy Administration

Chapter 5
Structuring a Strategically Effective Organization

Chapter 6
Managing Organizational Processes

STRUCTURING A STRATEGICALLY EFFECTIVE ORGANIZATION

. . . the purpose of formal organizations is to provide a framework for cooperation and to fix responsibilities, delineate authority, and provide for accountability. . . .

Edmund P. Learned

STRATEGY implementation is fundamentally different from strategy formulation. The latter is largely intellectual and requires the abilities to conceptualize, analyze, and evaluate; it requires shrewd judgment as to what constitutes an entrepreneurially effective strategy and what does not. But the general manager has to be much more than a good paper strategist. He must be able to convert plans into effective action. He must be good at building an organization and picking the right people to head up key activities. He must be skilled in the full range of managerial duties—planning, organizing, communicating, staffing, supervising, and evaluating—all of which weigh upon effective implementation of the strategic plan. It is, in fact, on matters of strategy implementation that a manager spends most of his or her time and energy.

Strategy implementation brings to the forefront the whole gamut of policy issues as to exactly *how* the chosen strategy will be carried out. Ongoing enterprises will have to determine whether they have the right organization to implement the chosen strategy and, if not, what changes need to be made. A new organization will have to decide how to build from the ground up. Next, internal operating policies will have to be developed to guide strategy implementation and these will need to be workable, practical, consistent, and efficient. Whether a few policies or a voluminous policy manual is needed varies with the size and complexity of the organization and its strategy. Later, management will have to assess the progress being made in the implementation process and how well the strategy is working out. This chapter and the next focus on these aspects of the general manager's job.

STRATEGY AND ORGANIZATION

It goes almost without saying that one of the highest priorities of strategy implementation is organization building. Accomplishing the strategic mission requires that organization be consciously planned rather than left to chance, historical accident, or industry custom. An effective organization structure does not automatically evolve. As Drucker says, "the only things that evolve in an organization are disorder, friction, malperformance."[1]

A number of distinct subactivities are involved in conceiving and putting in motion an organization capable of seeing the chosen strategy through to a successful conclusion. The key tasks to be performed (that is, those activities that have to be done right and on time if the strategy is to succeed) must be identified and responsibility for them assigned to individuals or groups having the appropriately specialized skills. A review of the formal organization structure, together with its informal relationships, will be needed to assure coordinated integration of separately performed functions; this entails not only assessing various supervisory and line-staff relationships but also making use of project staffs, task forces, teams, committees, and other ad hoc units. Ways must be found to communicate and instill the established goals and objectives in all organizational subunits, while at the same time allowing room for the satisfaction of individual aspirations. An information system must be made operational to keep each subunit posted on what it must know about other subunits and to let those in positions of authority know what is going on so that the task sequence can proceed without delay. Insofar as practical, efforts must be made to contain interdepartmental rivalries, interpersonal conflicts, and the maneuvers of subunits with vested interests to protect, lest too much energy be spent on internal politics and playing the power game.

There are no hard and fast rules on how to build a strategically effective organization. However, a strong case can be made that the pivotal consideration for all decisions on organizational structure and processes should be the extent to which each organizational alternative contributes to the accomplishment of strategic purpose and mission. In other words, *strategy should dictate the design of organizational structure and processes*. The logic behind the view that structure follows strategy is relatively simple: organization is (or should be) a means to an end—not an end in itself. The most appropriate end is the purpose for which the organization exists in the first place, as revealed by its strategy. Without coordination between strategy and structure, the most likely by-products are confusion, misdirection, and splintered efforts within the organization. Hence the task of organization building is most properly conceived as one of figuring out *strategically effective ways* of structuring the total work effort.

---

[1] Peter Drucker, *Management: Tasks, Responsibilities, Practices* (New York: Harper & Row, Publishers, 1974), p. 523.

Du Pont's experience offers a classic example of the rationale for strategy determining structure. In *Strategy and Structure,* Alfred Chandler writes:

> The strategy of diversification quickly demanded a refashioning of the company's administrative structure if its resources, old and new, were to be used efficiently and therefore profitably; for diversification greatly intensified the administrative load carried by the functional departments and the central office. Once the functional needs and the activities of several rather than one product line had to be coordinated, once the work of several very different lines of businesses had to be appraised, once the policies and procedures had to be formulated for divisions handling a wide variety of products, and, finally, once the central office had to make critical decisions about what new lines of business to develop, then the old structure quickly showed signs of strain. To meet the new needs, the new organizational design provided several central offices, each responsible for one line of products. At the new general office, the Executive Committee and staff specialists concentrated on the over-all administration of what had become a multi-industry enterprise. And in transforming the highly centralized, functionally departmentalized structure into a "decentralized," multi-divisional one, the major achievement had been the creation of the new divisions.[2]

A keen understanding of how organization, as a management tool, can be used to facilitate strategic accomplishment is thus imperative. In the remaining sections of this chapter we will explore aspects of structuring a strategically effective organization.

STAGES OF ORGANIZATIONAL DEVELOPMENT

In a number of respects, the strategist's approach to organization building is governed by the size and growth stage of the enterprise, together with the key characteristics of the organization's business. For instance, the type of organization structure that suits a small specialty steel firm is not likely to be suitable for a large, vertically integrated steel producer. The organization form that works best in a multiplant, multiproduct corporation with several divisions, subsidiaries, and profit centers is understandably, likely to be different yet again. Differences in the sizes and diversity of organizations have prompted several attempts to formulate a model of the stages of organizational development.[3]

The underpinning of the stages concept is that enterprises can be arrayed along a continuum running from very simple to very complex organizational forms and that there is a tendency for an organization to move along this continuum toward more complex forms as it grows in size, market coverage,

---

[2] Alfred D. Chandler, *Strategy and Structure* (Cambridge: The M.I.T. Press, 1962), p. 113.

[3] See, for example, Malcolm S. Salter, "Stages of Corporate Development," *Journal of Business Policy,* vol. 1, no. 1 (Spring 1970), pp. 23–27; Donald H. Thain, "Stages of Corporate Development." *The Business Quarterly,* (Winter 1969), pp. 32–45; Bruce R. Scott, "The Industrial State: Old Myths and New Realities," *Harvard Business Review,* vol. 51, no. 2 (March–April 1973), pp. 133–48; and Chandler, *Strategy and Structure,* Chapter 1.

and product line scope and as its technology-product-market relationships become more intricate. Four distinct stages of organization development have been singled out.

Stage I.   A Stage I organization is typified by one-person management; the owner-entrepreneur-manager has close daily contact with each employee and each phase of operations. Most employees report directly to the owner, who makes all the pertinent decisions as to finance, marketing, manufacturing, and so on. As a consequence, the organization's strengths, vulnerabilities, and resources are closely allied with the entrepreneur's personality, management ability and style, and personal financial situation. Not only is a Stage I enterprise an extension of the interests, abilities, and limitations of its owner-entrepreneur but also its activities often are concentrated in just one line of business that emphasizes one processing level (say, manufacturing or distribution) more than others. For the most part, today's Stage I enterprise is epitomized by small firms run by "independent business executives" who are "their own bosses" and having a strategy focused on a single product, market, technology, or channel of distribution.

Stage II.   Stage II organizations differ from Stage I enterprises in one essential respect: an increased scale and scope of operations create a pervasive need for management specialization and force a transition from one-person management to group management. However, a Stage II enterprise, although run by a team of managers with functionally specialized responsibilities, remains fundamentally a one-unit operation dealing in a limited line of technologically related products sold through one major distribution channel to one end market. This is not to imply, though, that the categories of management specializations are uniform among Stage II enterprises. In practice, there is wide variation. Some Stage II organizations prefer to divide responsibilities along classic lines—marketing, production, finance, personnel, control, engineering, public relations, procurement, planning, and so on. Of course, in infant Stage II companies several of these functions may be assigned to a single person. But in the largest Stage II enterprises, most notably big banks and certain of the oil, steel, aluminum, tire, and farm implement corporations, functional responsibilities are highly developed and specialized, even to the point of having numerous functional subunits. The marketing department of a major tire manufacturer, for example, might well be large enough to include subunits for sales, dealer relations, advertising, product development, market research, and product management.

In other Stage II companies functional specialization is keyed to the particular operating problems of the business; for example, the organizational building blocks of a vertically integrated oil company may consist of exploration, drilling, pipelines, refining, and marketing. Although the functional units of a Stage II company so organized may represent distinct processing units with their own specialities and competencies, their activities for the most part aim at synchronizing production with the next unit in sequence, as opposed to engaging independently in buying and/or selling in the open market. External market transactions are by no means precluded but, normally, in Stage II companies transactions between internal operating units dominate each sequence of the manufacturing process.

Alfred Chandler cites the experience of Goodyear and Firestone as examples of how vertical integration tends to lead to a process-oriented form of organization in companies concentrating on a single-product line. According to Chandler:

> Where Goodrich and United States Rubber considered all areas of rubber and rubber chemistry as their domain, Goodyear and Firestone until the 1930s focused the attention of their whole organization in a single line of products for the volume market. They integrated vertically more than either of their major competitors. Besides the extensive rubber fields, both had their own cotton plantations as well as textile mills for their tire cord and fabricating mills for their rims. Both gave much more attention to creating their own retail outlets. This concentration made development of new and diversified lines much more difficult. The two had had their chemical laboratories and development departments almost from the very beginning, but their efforts were devoted almost entirely to designing better tires and finding more efficient ways to make them.[4]

Stage III.   Stage III includes those organizations whose operations, though concentrated in a single field or product line, are large enough and scattered over a wide geographical area to justify having geographically decentralized operating units. These units all report to corporate headquarters and conform to corporate policies but they still have the freedom to develop their own channels of distribution and to buy and sell on their own behalf on the open market. Each of the semiautonomous operating units of a Stage III organization tends to be structured along the lines of functionally oriented Stage II companies or, more rarely, like Stage I enterprises (when the independent units are small and take on an entrepreneurial character). The key difference between Stage II and Stage III, however, is that while the functional units of a Stage II organization stand or fall together (in that they are built around one business and one end market), the operating units of a Stage III firm can stand alone (or nearly so) in the sense that the operations in each geographic unit are not rigidly tied to or dependent on those in other areas. Characteristic firms in this category would be breweries, cement companies, and steel mills having production capacity and sales organizations in several geographically separate market areas. Corey and Star cite Pfizer International as being a good example of a company whose business in 1964 made geographic decentralization propitious:

> With sales of $223 million in 1964, Pfizer International operated plants in 27 countries and marketed in more than 100 countries. Its product lines included pharmaceuticals (antibiotics and other ethical prescription drugs), agriculture

[4] Alfred D. Chandler, "Development, Diversification and Decentralization," in R. E. Freeman, ed., *Postwar Economic Trends in the United States* (New York: Harper & Brothers, 1960), p. 263.

and veterinary products (such as animal feed supplements and vaccines, and pesticides), chemicals (fine chemicals, bulk pharmaceuticals, petrochemicals and plastics), and consumer products (cosmetics and toiletries).

Ten geographic Area Managers reported directly to the President of Pfizer International and exercised line supervision over Country Managers. According to a company position description, it was "the responsibility of each Area Manager to plan, develop, and carry out Pfizer International's business in the assigned foreign area in keeping with company policies and goals.

Country Managers had profit responsibility. In most cases a single Country Manager managed all Pfizer activities in his country. In some of the larger, well-developed countries of Europe there were separate Country Managers for pharmaceutical and agricultural products and for consumer lines.

Except for the fact that New York headquarters exercised control over the to-the-market prices of certain products, especially prices of widely used pharmaceuticals, Area and Country Managers had considerable autonomy in planning and managing the Pfizer International business in their respective geographic areas. This was appropriate because each area, and some countries within areas, provided unique market and regulatory environments. In the case of pharmaceuticals and agriculture and veterinary products (Pfizer International's most important lines) national laws affected formulations, dosages, labeling, distribution, and often price. Trade restrictions affected the flow of bulk pharmaceuticals and chemicals and packages products, and might in effect require the establishment of manufacturing plants to supply local markets. Competition, too, varied significantly from area to area.[5]

Stage IV.   Stage IV is typified by large, multiproduct, multiunit, multimarket enterprises decentralized along product lines. As with Stage III companies, the semiautonomous operating units report to a corporate headquarters and conform to certain firmwide policies, but the operating units customarily produce different products using more or less different technologies; their products are marketed through distinctly separate channels and are sold to distinguishably different classes of customers. More importantly, each unit is run by a general manager who has profit and loss responsibility and oversees the entire unit with all its functions except, perhaps, accounting and capital budgeting (which traditionally are corporate functions). By and large, therefore, only a small amount of buying and selling goes on internally between divisions as opposed to the amount on the open market; in other words, the external market transactions of the several operating units dominate their activities. The operating units themselves may be structured along the lines of Stage I, II, or III types of organizations. Characteristic Stage IV companies include General Electric, ITT, Exxon, Uniroyal, Textron, and Du Pont. In the case of Uniroyal (formerly United States Rubber), Chandler observed:

---

[5] E. Raymond Corey and Steven H. Star, *Organization Strategy: A Marketing Approach* (Boston: Division of Research, Harvard University Graduate School of Business Administration, 1971), pp. 23–24.

As it began to diversify its product line . . . the United States Rubber Company gave more attention than most companies to its organizational structure. By 1917 President Samuel B. Colt, on the recommendation of Raymond Price's development department, separated the company's operating activities into four divisions (tire, general, industrial footwear, and clothing), a chemical subsidiary, and an overseas department to handle plantations and foreign sales. Except for the last, each unit handled its own manufacturing and sales, for coordination of manufacturing and sales of products for such different markets had been the company's biggest management problem. At headquarters the development, legal, and financial departments continued much as before.[6]

Movement through the Stages.   The stages model illustrates well how structure follows strategy and why there is a tendency of organization structure to change in accordance with product-market-technology relationships. However, it is to be emphasized that it is by no means imperative that all organizations begin at Stage I and then move sequentially toward Stage IV.[7] As Chandler noted, U.S. Rubber moved from a Stage II organization to a Stage IV form without ever passing through Stage III. Nor is there any compelling reason why some organizations might not exhibit characteristics of two or more stages simultaneously. Sears, at one time, was decentralized geographically for store operations, personnel, sales promotion, banking, inventory and warehousing, and maintenance, yet centralized for manufacturing and procurement of goods, thus overlapping the organization structures of Stages II and III. Furthermore, some companies have found it desirable to retreat into prior stages after entering a particular stage. For example, the Du Pont textile fibers department originated out of five separate, decentralized, fully integrated fiber businesses—rayon, acetate, nylon, "Orlon," and "Dacron."[8] Many weavers and other industrial users bought one or more of these fibers and used them in significantly different ways that also required different application technologies. According to Corey and Star:

> Customers objected to being solicited by five Du Pont salesmen each promoting a different type of synthetic fiber and each competing with the others. Users of synthetic fibers wanted sales representatives from Du Pont who understood their product lines and production processes and who could serve as a source of useful technical ideas.[9]

As a consequence, Du Pont consolidated all five units into a textile fibers department in an effort to deal more effectively with these customers. The new department established a single multifiber field sales force and set up market programs for four broad market segments—men's wear, women's

---

[6] Chandler, "Development, Diversification, and Decentralization," p. 261.

[7] For a more thorough discussion of this point see Salter, "Stages of Corporate Development," pp. 34–35.

[8] Corey and Star, *Organization Strategy*, p. 14.

[9] Ibid.

wear, home furnishings, and industrial products, each of which had a potential demand for all five fibers. In a similar vein, Socony Mobil in 1959, prompted by a marked lack of coordination in marketing and product supply activities among its three geographically decentralized units reverted to a new single, functionally organized operating company with direct control over crude oil supply, refining, and transportation operations in the United States and Canada.[10]

In general, then, because of the several ways which product-market relationships and strategy may turn, the paths along which an organization's structure may develop are more complex and variable than suggested by the stages model. Still, it does appear that as firms move from small, single-product businesses to large, single-product companies and then on to concentric or conglomerate diversification, their organizational structure evolves, in turn, from one-person management to large group functional management to decentralized, divisional management. This is substantiated by the fact that about 90 percent of the *Fortune 500* firms (nearly all of which are to some degree diversified) have a divisionalized organizational structure.

TESTING ORGANIZATIONAL ADEQUACY

In deciding whether an organization's structure is adequate, the general manager has a number of points to consider. First and foremost, of course, is the issue of whether the enterprise is organized and staffed to meet the needs of its strategy. Two questions should be posed: "What functions and activities must be performed excellently for the organization's strategy to succeed?" and "In what areas would malperformance seriously endanger or undermine strategy success?"[11] The answers to these two questions should point squarely at the basic functions essential to strategic success. In general, an activity's contribution to strategy should determine its rank and placement in the organizational hierarchy. Key activities should never be subordinated to non-key activities. Revenue-producing or results-producing activities should never be subordinated to support activities. By making success-causing factors the major building blocks for organizational structure, the chances are greatly improved that strategy will be effectively executed. Toward this end, a reassessment of organization structure is always useful whenever strategy is changed.[12] A new strategy is likely to entail modifications in key activities, which if not formally recognized and properly restructured, could leave the strategy unnecessarily short of its potential.

[10] Ibid., p. 12.

[11] Drucker, *Management*, p. 530, 535.

[12] For an excellent documenation of how a number of well-known corporations revised their organization structure to meet the needs of strategy changes and specific product-market developments, see Corey and Star, *Organization Strategy*, chap. 3.

A second test of organizational adequacy concerns the ability of the organization to react to and cope with new external developments of either a threatening or opportunistic nature. Is the organization structure adaptable to the pressures of a recession? Stiffer competitive forces? Rapid expansion? Is the organization's structure appropriate for dealing with future challenges and developments as revealed in the strategic forecast? Do the predictions contained in the strategic forecast imply that the organization structure will be outgrown in the near-term?

A third area of inquiry pertains to whether the organization structure is efficient. Do decisions often have "to go looking for a home" or do people know where within the organization the decision belongs? Does the organization structure put the attention of key people on the right things—major decisions, coordination of essential activities, performance, and results? Are the inherent and inevitable conflicts among: (1) the production manager for lower manufacturing costs; (2) the product engineer for designing a product that meets the engineering standards of simplicity and economy; (3) the inventory manager with holding down carrying costs; (4) the credit officer with minimizing bad debts; and (5) the marketing manager with improving quality, adding sales features, eliminating stockouts, and adding more customers all resolved in a timely and effective fashion? Are the firm's R&D activities attuned with the marketplace and with customer needs? Are the various dimensions of supplier-customer relationships (such as technical assistance, product service, delivery, allocation in periods of short supply, negotiation on price and other conditions of sale) being handled consistently among geographic territories? Are there too many people not doing enough things? Are there too many meetings attended by too many people?

APPROACHES TO ORGANIZATIONAL DIAGNOSIS

Several diagnostic approaches have evolved regarding the determination of organizational adequacy. The three which will be described briefly here are: (1) the problem approach, (2) the process approach, and (3) the results approach. [13]

The Problem Approach. The problem approach to organization diagnosis and organization building is basically that used in many management consultant studies which start by defining the problems of the business, identifying their causes, appraising the various alternatives for problem solution, and recommending a course of action and an implementation plan. The problems examined thus include, but by no means are limited to, those of organization structure. The whole enterprise is checked out much like a doctor giving a patient a thorough annual physical examination. Hence changes in organization structure may turn out to be a part of the overall recommendations and

---

[13] The following is drawn from J. Thomas Cannon, *Business Strategy and Policy* (New York: Harcourt, Brace, & World, 1968), pp. 314–17.

implementation plan or they may be diagnosed as not needed at all. This puts organization structure into its proper perspective of being one of a number of things to consider in evaluating an organization's situation. It also has the advantage of endeavoring "to fix first things first." The problem approach works less effectively when the needed emphasis is not so much on solving problems as on integrating organization functions and on bettering performance.

The Process Approach. The process approach to appraising organizational adequacy focuses on improving the coordination of functions that cut across departmental lines and areas of responsibility. It looks at whether the overall tone and conduct of activities is as sharp as it should be—irrespective of an apparent lack of organizational problems. In this sense its thrust is expeditive rather than curative and the objectives are simplification, efficiency, economy, and integration into a unified whole. A principal strength of the process approach is the contribution it makes to understanding the operating sequences and dynamics of the organization. This, in turn, makes it easier to design structural modifications aimed at reducing coordination problems, streamlining the layers of management, facilitating communication flows, and deciding where to delegate authority (or withhold it) in order to strengthen organization cohesion and unification.

The Results Approach. The unique feature of the results approach is not so much technique of diagnosis as a more concentrated emphasis on the ultimate objective—the accomplishment of strategy. It picks up on "the structure follows strategy thesis" and advocates an organizing-for-results approach keyed directly to the product-market-customer needs aspects of strategy. Thus the results approach suggests five steps in addressing what structure is best suited to the achievement of strategy:[14]

1. Delineate as precisely and clearly as possible the relationships of customer needs and product-market aspects to the organization's strategy, objectives, and goals.
2. Identify the key activities and functional skills requisite for strategic success.
3. Classify each of the key activities and skills according to (a) whether they are unique to the product-market being considered or analogous to those needed for other of the organization's product/markets and (b) their priority of contribution to strategic success.
4. Determine the degrees of authority and responsibility required to manage both the new functions and the priority function, keeping in mind two factors: (a) economy and (b) the degree of decentralization of decision making best suited to each.
5. Design organizational ties around these principal building blocks so as to ensure adequate coordination and integration.

---

[14] Ibid., p. 316.

Step 4 is a crucial one. The economy factor is the basis for deciding whether to provide a major product-market subunit with the services it needs from other existing functional units or letting it be self-sufficient and thereby install its own duplicate set of functions. The decentralization factor, while partly economic, is mainly a matter of providing appropriate checks and balances on the principal decisions that will confront the product-market subunit. Once steps 1–4 have been completed, the framework of a results-oriented structure should be in focus and organizing around key building blocks can proceed accordingly.

MAKING USE OF ORGANIZATIONAL PRINCIPLES

In pondering and finalizing the structural scheme there always arises the issue of whether and how to conform to the so-called classical principles of organization.[15] The principles listed in Table 5–1 are typical of those often said to exemplify "sound practice."

Although most of the "principles" in Table 5–1 speak for themselves and have proven their merit in many situations, they can be difficult to implement and keep implemented in the aggregate. In the first place, none is completely unambiguous in its application; there are any number of specific organizational forms that are consistent with each "principle," thus leaving unanswered the issue of which organizational form to employ. Second, the uniqueness of each organization's situation invariably creates circumstances where it is appropriate to "violate" one or another of the principles.[16] For instance, several large retail chains successfully "disobeyed" the span of control principle (item 12, Table 5–1) by having anywhere from 20 to 100 or more store managers reporting to a single higher level executive; at the same time, a great many organizations have only one or two vice presidents reporting to the president. As another case in point, a number of enterprises have detoured the "one boss" principle (item 11, Table 5–1) using matrix organizational forms whereby functional activities are departmentalized, but managerial authority is shared between functional heads and project managers.[17] Furthermore, a good argument can be made in some situations for

---

[15] Most prominent among the works of the classical management theorists are Henri Fayol, *General and Industrial Administration* (London: Sir Issac Pitman & Sons, 1949); Frederick W. Taylor, *The Principles of Scientific Management* (New York: Harper & Brothers, 1911); Chester I. Barnard, *The Functions of the Executive* (Cambridge, Mass.: Harvard University Press, 1938); H. S. Dennison, *Organization Engineering* (New York: McGraw-Hill Book Co., 1931); J. D. Mooney and A. C. Reilley, *Onward Industry* (New York: Harper & Brothers, 1931); O. Sheldon, *The Philosophy of Management* (London: Sir Issac Pitman & Sons, 1923); and L. Urwick, *The Elements of Administration* (New York: Harper & Row, Publishers, 1944).

[16] For a full discussion of how and why it is difficult for managers to apply "principles" in a consistent manner, see Abbott L. Lowell, *Conflicts of Principles,* rev. ed. (Cambridge, Mass.: Harvard University Press, 1956).

[17] See Jay R. Galbraith, "Matrix Organizational Designs," *Business Horizons,* vol. 14, no. 1 (February 1971), pp. 29–40; Corey and Star, *Organization Strategy,* chaps. 3, 4, and 5.

TABLE 5–1
Selected Principles of Organization

1. The organization should have clearly defined objectives and each position in the organization should be logically related to these objectives.
2. Design the organization around the key activities of the business, making an effort to keep structure impersonal and task focused.
3. Group-related activities and functions; separate those that are unrelated.
4. Avoid duplicate functions.
5. Assign each necessary function; limit the functions per person; and make sure the assignment fits both the person and the needs of the situation.
6. Define responsibilities clearly and make authority commensurate with responsibility.
7. Delegate decision making to the lowest competent level; i.e., as close to the scene of action as possible.
8. Keep the levels of management to a minimum and keep the chain of command short.
9. Clarify reporting channels; avoid confusing lines of communication with lines of authority.
10. Strive for organizational simplicity and minimize the number of structural changes.
11. Preserve unity of command by making each person accountable to only one superior.
12. Avoid an overly broad or overly narrow span of control.
13. Provide a means of coordinating the separated functions in support of organizational objectives.
14. Ensure there is reasonable balance *(a)* in the size of various departments, *(b)* between centralization and decentralization, and *(c)* between standardization of procedures and flexibility.

assigning an individual multiple functions rather than just one or two (item 5, Table 5–1) as a means of accelerating a manager's seasoning, forcing delegation, improving economy, and achieving a results-orientation.

Still, the checklist in Table 5–1 is a useful guide for organization design and structure, if for no other reason than it reminds the organization builder of the classic principles and may prod him into thinking through the justification of any exceptions and deviations which are being contemplated.

ORGANIZATIONAL CHOICES

The organization builder has a number of viable organizational forms to choose from in deciding how to structure operations. The basic choices include organizing by *(a)* functional specialities, *(b)* geographic location, *(c)* process of production, market channel, or customer class, and *(d)* semi-independent product divisions or product groups. These basic forms can, in turn, be combined in varying proportions and formats to generate an almost endless variety of mixed organization structures. The rationale and features of both basic and mixed organization forms warrant brief examination.

The Functional Organization Structure

Dividing key activities according to functional specialization takes as its premise the value of combining related effort and segregating unrelated effort. The resultingly deeper specialization and focused concentration on functional problems can then enhance both efficiency and the development of distinctive competence. Generally speaking, organizing by function promotes full utilization of the most up-to-date technical skills and makes it more possible to capitalize on the efficiency gains to be had from using specialized know-how, facilities, and equipment. Organizations that depend upon a single-product line and/or are vertically integrated tend to be organized in a centralized, functionally departmentalized structure.

However, the way an organization chooses to segment its major functions depends upon its strategy and the nature of the work activities involved. Thus, a large, technically oriented manufacturing firm may be organized around research and development, engineering, materials management, production, quality control, marketing, personnel, finance and accounting, and public relations; further, some of the departments may be line and others staff—as shown in Figure 5–1. A municipal government may, on the other hand, be departmentalized according to purposeful function—fire, public safety, health services, water and sewer, streets, parks and recreation, and education. A university may divide its organizational units up into academic affairs, student services, alumni relations, athletics, buildings and grounds, institutional services, and budget control.

The Achilles heel of a functional structure is proper coordination of the separated functional units. Functional specialists, partly because of their training and the technical nature of their jobs, tend to develop characteristic patterns of behavior and goal-orientation. The more that functional specialists differ in their patterns of behavior and their approach to task accomplishment, the more difficult it becomes to achieve effective coordination between them. They neither "talk the same language" nor have an adequate understanding and appreciation for one another's problems and approaches. As a consequence, while there may be a free flow of communication and ideas up and down within functional units, there often emerges a strong built-in bias against horizontal movements—a bias which plainly can not only impede coordination but also engender conflict and rivalry. This, in turn, can create an excessive decision-making burden at the top of the management hierarchy where much time is spent resolving cross-functional differences, enforcing joint cooperation, and opening lines of communication.

Geographic Departmentation

Organizing according to geographic areas or territories is a rather common structural form for physically dispersed enterprises. The thesis here is that performance in a given territory, branch, district, or region is significantly

FIGURE 5–1
A Functional Organization Structure (manufacturing company)

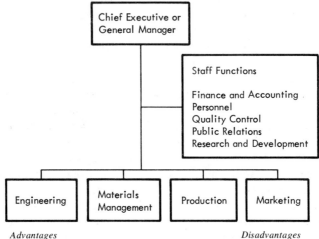

Advantages	*Disadvantages*
Produces excellent results where tasks are routine and repetitive.	Poses problems of functional coordination.
Preserves centralized control.	Can lead to interfunctional rivalry and conflict.
Allows benefits of specialization to be fully exploited.	May promote overspecialization and narrow management viewpoints.
Simplifies training of management specialists.	Limits development of general managers.
Promotes high emphasis on craftsmanship and professional standards.	Forces profit responsibility to the top.
	Not well-suited to situations requiring cross-functional problem solving.
	Conducive to empire building.
	More difficult for functional subunits to relate their tasks to the task of the whole.

improved by grouping all activities under the responsibility of a general manager. A geographic organization is especially attractive to enterprises whose operations are essentially similar from area to area since this facilitates holding general managers accountable for results in their assigned territories. In the private sector, a territorial structure is typically utilized by chain store retailers, cement firms, railroads, airlines, the larger paper box and carton manufacturers, and large bakeries and dairy products enterprises; the member companies of American Telephone and Telegraph which make up the Bell Telephone System all represent geographically decentralized units. In the public sector, such organizations and agencies as the Internal Revenue Service, the Small Business Administration, the federal courts, the U.S. Postal Service, the state troopers, the Red Cross, and religious denominations have adopted territorial departmentation in their efforts to provide like services to geographically dispersed clienteles. Figure 5–2 illustrates geographic departmentalization.

FIGURE 5–2
A Geographic Organizational Structure

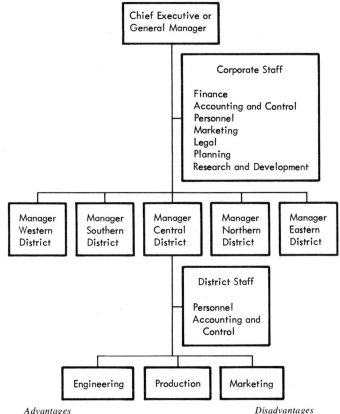

Advantages	*Disadvantages*
Allows more aggressive development of area markets.	Greater difficulty in maintaining consistent and uniform companywide practices.
Delegates profit/loss responsibility to lowest competent level.	Requires a larger management staff, especially general managers.
Improves functional coordination within the area.	Leads to duplication of staff services.
Takes advantage of economies of local operations.	Poses a problem of headquarters control over local operations.
Allows closer adjustment to specific needs of local markets and customers.	
Area units make an excellent training ground for general managers.	

Process, Market, Channel, or Customer Departmentation

Grouping an enterprise's activities around its several production stages, market channels, or customer groups is often employed where there are important manufacturing or market advantages to be gained from a specialized approach. A metal parts manufacturer may find it operationally effective to subdivide in series, thus having foundry, forging, machining, finishing, assembly, and painting departments. A large office may be departmentalized into batteries of machines doing similar work: typing, duplicating, card punching, accounting, labeling, and collating. Firms selling an essentially uniform product to widely diverse customer groups may orient their marketing activities so as to cater to the requirements of each buyer segment. For example, some years ago Purex Corp. decided that neither product nor territorial departmentation was as well-suited to its operations as was a market channel departmentation which allowed it to focus separately on selling to supermarket chains and drug chains. Local United Fund drives are typically organized into a number of individual solicitation units with each assigned to canvas a particular segment of the community—commercial establishments, industrial plants, unions, local schools, county government, city government, hospitals, and agriculture. There are various departments of the federal government set up expressly for veterans, senior citizens, the unemployed, small business executives, widows and dependent children, the poor, and others. Figure 5–3 illustrates departmentation by process, by market channel, and by customer category.

Divisional and Product Group Organization

Grouping activities along product lines has been a clear-cut trend among diversified enterprises for the past half-century, beginning with the pioneering efforts of Du Pont in the 1920s. Product line organizations emerged because diversification made a functionally specialized manager's job incredibly complex. Even with many immediate subordinates, a production executive could not effectively oversee the production of a large number of different items being produced at many different plant locations; for similar reasons, the jobs of engineering, sales, and R&D executives were also unwieldy. Product decentralization thus aimed at creating *manageable* organizational subunits that were responsive to customer needs, competitive behavior, and emerging market opportunities. As a case in point, in 1967 Monsanto reorganized its Organic Chemicals Division into six subunits. According to an internal memorandum describing the new organization and its rationales:

> Up to now the Organic Division has been organized as though it were one business—organic chemicals. The line departments have been in the traditional functional pattern of Manufacturing, Marketing Research, Development, and the various administrative functions. As the size of the Division increased, product directors were introduced to assist the General Manager on a staff basis to coordinate the functional groups with respect to an emerging number of different customer groups or "businesses."
>
> The Division has been quite successful in continuing its total growth as well as growth in its several businesses. In addition, new and different businesses have been developed within the Division charter.

FIGURE 5–3

A. Process departmentation

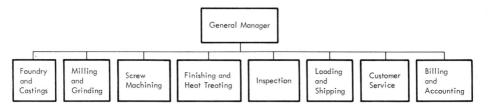

B. Market channel departmentation

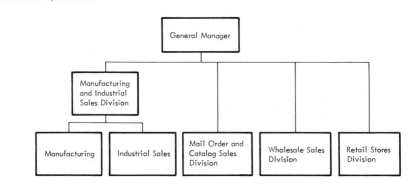

C. Customer departmentation

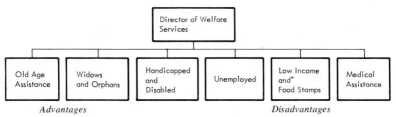

Advantages	*Disadvantages*
Structure is tied to performance of key activities.	Encourages pressure for special treatment.
Facilitates achievement of operating economies derived from use of specialized facilities and labor force.	Poses problems of how to coordinate inter-departmental activities.
May allow more opportunity for deeper market penetration.	May lead to uneconomically small units or underemployment of specialized facilities and manpower as nature of demand from unit-to-unit changes.

The general management burden has been further aggravated by the stepped-up rate of developing new products and obsoleting old products and the related changes in manufacturing processes in each of the several businesses. With this situation in mind, the Division conducted an intensive study of its functions, markets, and system of operation with particular emphasis on its methods of planning and executing the wide variety of programs called for.

Furthermore, by orienting itself to market requirements, a much wider vista for future growth opens up. Under this concept, for example, future products may not necessarily be limited to chemicals. In turn, this may lead to better earnings on investment than is possible in the capital-intensive general chemical manufacturing.[18]

Illustration Capsule 12

The Organizational Structure of the Post Division of General Foods Corporation

In 1966, General Foods Corporation was the largest manufacturer of packaged food products in the United States. The company ranked 32d on *Fortune's 500* listing. General Foods' product line included Maxwell House, Yuban, Sanka, and Maxim coffees, Jell-O, Birds Eye frozen foods, Gaines dog foods, Baker's chocolate products, Calumet baking powder, Swans Down cake flour and cake mixes, Minute tapioca, Dream Whip, Post cereals, Kool-Aid, Log Cabin syrup, Minute Rice, Tang, Toast'em Pop-ups, and S.O.S. soap pads, among others. Each of the company's products was assigned to one of five operating divisions: Maxwell House, Jell-O, Kool-Aid, Birds Eye, and Post.

The Post Division had traditionally been responsible for Post cereals and Postum beverages. In the late 1950s, Gaines dog foods and Swans Down cake flour products were assigned to the division. As of 1966, the Post Division handled 36 products of which 18 had been developed since 1958. An organization chart of the Post Division as of August 1966 is shown in Exhibit 1.

Exhibit 2 provides a more detailed look at the Post Division marketing organization as of August 1966. A brief discussion of each of these organizational units follows.

The National Sales Organization

The Post Division's field sales force consisted of 26 district managers and more than 400 sales supervisors, account managers, and salespeople. The field sales force called on about 2,000 direct accounts, including wholesalers, small chains, and branches of the large national and regional chains. Of these 2,000 direct accounts, 430 key accounts represented 70 percent of the total national food retail volume.

An account manager was responsible for sales to two or three key accounts; he kept in regular contact with the lowest multistore buying unit in his accounts and called upon a number of the assigned chain's retail outlets. A salesman was typically responsible for one or two smaller direct accounts and, in addition, called on some of the smaller retail outlets of key accounts.

The national accounts manager dealt directly with the national headquarters of three large food chains. While most actual buying decisions were made at the division and branch levels of these chains, the national accounts manager attempted to presell key promotions and new product introductions at the corporate level. The regional sales managers were responsible for contacts with the corporate headquarters of major multibranch chains not otherwise covered by the national accounts manager.

The sales development department prepared sales plans for implementation at the district level, including sales goals for each product, local advertising schedules, promotion schedules, and new product introduction schedules. Each of these were tailored to local marketing requirements. At the same time, it represented the sales

---

[17] Corey and Star, *Organization Strategy*, pp. 14–15.

EXHIBIT 1
Organization Structure of the Post Division of General Foods Corporation (August 1966)

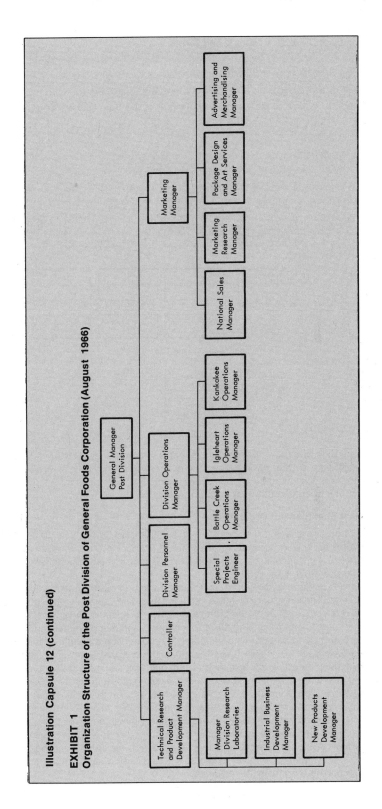

Illustration Capsule 12 (continued)

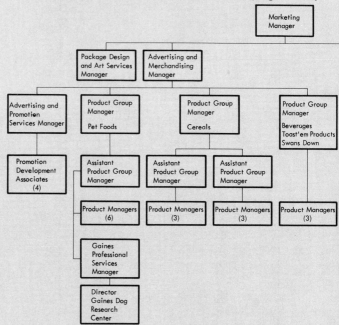

EXHIBIT 2
Organization Structure of Marketing Department of the Post Division (August 1966)

force in meetings with individual product managers in order to assure that the sales support called for in the market plans for each of the 36 products was in fact feasible, that product manager's goals were compatible with sales goals, and that no sales conflicts existed between the various market plans.

The Product Management Organization

The function of managing the Post Division's 36 product brands was carried out by an advertising and merchandising manager, 3 product group managers, three assistant product group managers, 15 product managers, and a number of associate and assistant product managers.

Each product manager prepared an annual marketing plan for each of his assigned brands. These marketing plans included quarterly sales volume goals, a marketing strategy, analysis of competitive activity, and specific plans for advertising, promotion, packaging, pricing, product changes, and marketing research. The marketing plan had to be approved ultimately by the general manager of the Post Division, after a series of reviews and recommendations by the lower level managers. Once the plan was approved, the product manager was responsible for overseeing and coordinating its implementation by working closely with the advertising agencies and various Post Division staff departments. For example, the product manager presented his marketing strategy to the division's advertising agency and asked it to prepare advertising copy and media plans. He then reviewed this material carefully and decided whether to recommend its approval by higher management. If his recommendation was approved, he then worked with the agency to execute the plan. The product managers relied upon other Post Division staff departments for technical expertise in virtually the same way.

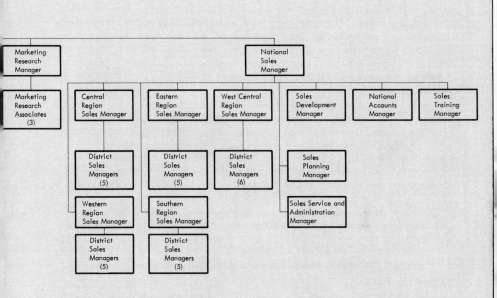

The Marketing Research Department

Marketing research personnel were assigned to individual brands. A marketing research project was generally proposed by the product manager for a particular brand. He and his marketing research counterpart then prepared a plan for carrying out the proposed research. In most cases outside research organizations did the actual work and tabulated the results. All marketing research plans were approved by the marketing research manager.

The Art Services Department

This department, staffed with eight commercial artists, was responsible for creating designs for Post packages and commercial materials. Members of the department worked with individual product managers and promotions specialists. Once the designs were approved, the final art work was generally subcontracted to outside firms.

The Advertising and Promotion Department

The division's advertising and promotion department was organized on a product group basis, with several promotion specialists assigned to each product group. In general, a product manager would ask the promotion department to design a promotion to achieve a given objective at a given cost. The recommended promotion might be a trade deal, an instore display, or cents-off coupons. The promotion staff had assembled extensive data concerning the results of different kinds of promotions and, consequently, was able to predict with a very small margin of error what the results of a particular promotion would be.

Illustration Capsule 12 (continued)

The Marketing Accounting Services Department

The role of marketing accounting services was to provide statistical support and detailed calculations for product and sales managers. For example, a product manager would give marketing accounting services his total sales goal for the year and information concerning variations in local marketing situations or marketing plans, and would receive back a sales breakdown by quarter and district. Similarly, the department furnished district sales managers with a weekly report of actual performance as measured against target performance.

The Marketing Plan

The marketing plans prepared by the product managers differed significantly in the degree to which they were integrated into an overall product group plan. The cereals' marketing plan was a composite of all of the marketing plans of each of the cereal brands and required a cereal brand product manager to coordinate his plans with that of his colleagues. The Tang product manager, on the other hand, was responsible for a product that was not closely related to any other Post product and, consequently, was relatively free to write his own plan with only a minimum amount of attention to coordination with other product managers.

Once the marketing plan for a brand was approved, a "plans letter" was then prepared to communicate elements of the plan to the various departments responsible for implementing it. A typical plans letter described what had to be done and by whom to achieve the given goals and objectives, in many cases setting forth time schedules and authorizing the commitment of resources.

Sales Planning

Market plans were tied in with the activities of the field sales force in a variety of ways. The marketing accounting services department broke down the quarterly sales goals into regional and district goals. The sales development department consolidated the brand sales goals for each district and established district sales budgets or quotas.

To some extent the sales budget itself established sales force priorities, since it was broken down on a brand basis. A district manager who was below budget on a brand would naturally give priority to raising its sales. Moreover, some goals, by their nature, received priority. New product introduction was scheduled for national or regional introduction on a specific date which meant the sales force had to devote its efforts to achieving distribution during a relatively short time period. Similarly, certain trade promotions pertained to specific calendar dates, which meant the sales force had to take advantage of them at that time.

Formal Communications and Reports

The national sales manager held a formal meeting with the regional sales managers several weeks prior to the beginning of each quarter. During these meetings, booklets containing promotion, advertising, and new product introduction schedules for the following quarter were passed out and discussed. In some cases, product managers were present at these meetings to describe their plans for the coming quarter. Shortly after the national sales manager's staff meeting, each regional manager held a meeting with his district managers. The quarterly schedules were passed out and discussed at these meetings in much the same way as at the national meetings.

Upon his return from the regional staff meeting, the district manager held a meeting of his sales personnel at which he presented promotion and new product introduction schedules and materials tailored to his district, and discussed his plan

Illustration Capsule 12 (continued)

for accomplishing the district goals and quotas. District sales managers received sales bulletins affirming each promotion or new product introduction several weeks before the sales effort was to begin and describing the activity, objectives, merchandising aids prepared by the division, calendar dates, and any special reporting procedures to be used.

District managers gave their sales personnel new assignments every four weeks keyed to the districtwide list of goals to be accomplished during that period. The salesmen and account managers submitted a sales planning report to their supervisor each Friday listing all of the accounts and their territories, the goals for each account, the accounts to be called on during the following week, and the goals to be accomplished on each call.

Marketing—Manufacturing Relationships

Although relations between manufacturing and marketing were generally good, there were periodic "communication" breakdowns. On occasions, product managers would ask manufacturing for cost estimates at a given level of production; the plant might then spend three man-days preparing detailed cost studies only to discover that the product manager needed only a rough estimate to test the profitability of his marketing plan. On other occasions, product managers did not fully assess the implications of their promotional plans for the operations department. For example, if a special label promotion was to begin at a time when the plant still had old label inventory, the plant had to hold the old label inventory until the promotion was over. This meant that after the end of a six week promotion, the plant might be shipping product eight or nine weeks old. Manufacturing felt this was easily avoided by staggering the date the promotion was to start in different areas, thereby creating outlets for the old label inventory.

Product Development

The technical research and product development department was responsible for all Post product development activities. The technical research staff developed all new products and designed the manufacturing processes to be used in making these products. The new product development staff, which was essentially a marketing research organization, limited its efforts to new products prior to the time when they were turned over to the product management organization. Approximately 90 percent of the ideas for new products originated in the technical research department from its efforts to find applications for advances in food technology. However, the new product development staff did suggest new products based on apparent consumer needs.

When a new product was judged ready for test marketing, it was presented to the Post Division general manager who decided whether it should be turned over to a product manager for test marketing. There was some disagreement concerning the state the new product should be in at the time of "turnover." The new product development staff often desired to turn over product with the name, package, and advertising strategy—in effect, an entire marketing plan. The product management staff, on the other hand, preferred to receive just the product and then develop its own marketing plan.

Comments

As the product line of General Foods' Post Division grew from Postum and several brands of cereal in the early 1950s to 36 different brands and products by 1966, the product management organization became more structured and pyrami-

Illustration Capsule 12 (concluded)

dal. Many of the Post brands were defined as segments of broader product group-ings which meant that product managers had to be team players, keying the strat-egy for an assigned brand to the broader strategy framework of the product group, while at the same time addressing the unique features of the market segment at which that brand was aimed. There was a formal process for making product plans consistent with overall division objectives and for translating strategies into action schedules for implementation.

As the number of Post products grew, a limited supply of broadly skilled product managers prompted the formation of technical support departments in market re-search, advertising and promotion, art, and accounting services. These department relieved the product managers of the necessity of being "jacks-of-all-trades" and allowed them to concentrate on the main thrust of strategy formulation and im-plementation. It also allowed for greater efficiency and effectiveness in performing the specialized tasks, owing to the fact that the division's products were enough alike in terms of marketing approach and manufacturing process to allow product managers to draw on common resources for support types of skills.

Source: Adapted and rewritten in summary form from E. Raymond Corey and Steven H. Star, *Organization Strategy: A Marketing Approach* (Boston: Division of Research, Graduate School of Business Administration, Harvard University, 1971), pp. 201–30.

Reorganizing on a divisional or product group basis permits top manage-ment to delegate to a single executive extensive authority over key operating and staff functions for specific products or product families. New semiautonomous divisions can then be created for each substantially different product-market grouping. By and large, the general managers of these divi-sions are given profit responsibility (which explains why such units are often called "profit centers") and are held accountable for short-run results and long-run market development. They determine the appropriate trade-offs in allocating resources between current operations and efforts for future growth. Within limits, they develop their own divisional staffs. The effect is to make the division general manager more like a semi-independent entrepreneur.

Figure 5–4 illustrates a typical divisionalized organization structure. One of the most well-known product organization structures is that of the Chev-rolet, Oldsmobile, Cadillac, and other divisions of General Motors. Other examples of product departmentation would include a toy manufacturer or-ganized into departments based on different kinds of toys (dolls, games, musical instruments, mechanical toys, stuffed animals, novelties); large de-partment stores; hospitals departmentalized on the basis of surgery, inten-sive care, maternity, pediatrics, emergency room, outpatient services, and so on; and banks with their trust departments, personal loan departments, commercial loan departments, real estate departments, and credit card departments.

Sometimes the number of divisions (or departments) becomes so numer-ous and so diverse that the span of control is too wide for a single chief executive. Then it may be useful to group those which are related and assign

FIGURE 5–4
A Typical Divisionalized Organization Structure

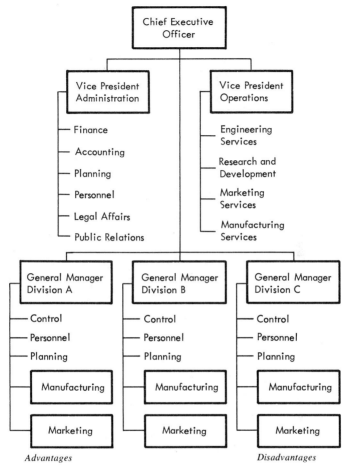

Advantages	*Disadvantages*
Offers a logical and workable means of decentralizing responsibility and delegating authority in diversified organizations.	Leads to proliferation of staff functions, policy inconsistencies between divisions, and problems of coordination of divisional operations.
Reduces layering of management.	Poses a problem of how much authority to centralize and how much to decentralize.
Improves coordination of functional activities for a specific product or product family.	
Allows better measurement of specific product performance.	

responsibility for them to a group vice president. While this imposes another layer of management between the divisional (or departmental) general manager and the chief executive, it may nonetheless improve top-management coordination of different activities. This explains the popularity of the group vice president concept among the so-called conglomerates. Figure 5–5 illustrates the product group concept of organization; the advantages and disadvantages parallel those for the divisional form of organization.

FIGURE 5–5
A Product Group Concept of Organization

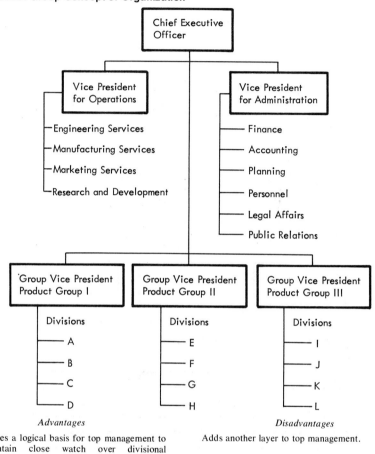

Advantages

Provides a logical basis for top management to maintain close watch over divisional operations.

Improves coordination between similar divisions.

Disadvantages

Adds another layer to top management.

Newer Forms of Organization

The foregoing structural designs have not proved adequate to meet the diversity of situations and activities confronting contemporary organizations. Many enterprises have responded not only by mixing the basic forms in varying combinations but also by introducing some novel features that effect interesting compromises between the pros and cons of the four basic designs. Among these are:

1. The *project manager* or *project staff* concept, whereby a separate, largely self-sufficient subunit is created to oversee the completion of a new

activity (setting up a new technological process, bringing out a new product, starting up a new venture, consummating a merger with another company, seeing through the completion of a government contract, supervising the construction of a new plant).[19] Project management has become a relatively popular means of handling "one-of-a-kind" situations having a finite life expectancy and where the normal organization is deemed unable or ill-equipped to achieve the same results in addition to regular duties. On occasions, however, "temporary" projects have proved worthy of being made "ongoing," thus resulting in either the elevation of the project unit to "permanent" status or a parceling out of the project's functions to units of the regular organization.

2. The creation of *cross-functional teams* or *task forces* to work on unusual assignments of a problem-solving or innovative nature where there is a need for a pooling of talent and tight integration among specialists. Special task forces provide increased opportunity for creativity, open communication across lines of authority, expeditious conflict resolution, and common identification for coping with the problem at hand, while at the same time facilitating intensified access to the requisite expertise. However, according to Drucker, team organization is more than a temporary expedient for dealing with nonrecurring special problems; he argues that the team is a genuine design principle of organization and is especially good for such permanent organizing tasks as top-management work and innovating work.[20]

3. The *matrix or grid organization* whereby the product and functional organizational forms are overlaid and the authority over the people involved is shared (see Figure 5–6).[21] In a matrix structure, the persons working have a continuing dual assignment: to the project and to their base department. Though creating problems of dual command and jurisdictional clarity, matrix management is attractive because of the opportunity it offers for capturing the advantages of *both* functional and product departmentation. To be successful, however, management must be sure that individual roles are clearly defined and, in particular, that the decision-making authority of the product manager is differentiated from

---

[19] For a more complete treatment of project management, see C. J. Middleton, "How to Set up a Project Organization," *Harvard Business Review*, vol. 45, no. 2 (March–April 1967), pp. 73–82; George A. Steiner and William G. Ryan, *Industrial Project Management* (New York: The Macmillan Company, 1968); Ivar Avots, "Why Does Project Management Fail," *California Management Review*, vol. 12, no. (Fall 1969), pp. 77–82; C. Reeser, "Human Problems of the Project Form of Organization," *Academy of Management Journal*, vol. 12, no. 4 (December 1969), pp. 459–67; R. A. Goodman, "Ambiguous Authority Definition in Project Management," *Academy of Management Journal*, vol. 10, no. 4 (December 1967), pp. 395–407; D. L. Wilemon and J. P. Cicero, "The Project Manager–Anomalies and Ambiguities," *Academy of Management Journal*, vol. 13, no. 3 (September 1970), pp. 269–82.

[20] Drucker, *Management*, pp. 564–71.

[21] A more complete discussion of matrix organization is contained in Jay R. Galbraith. "Matrix Organizational Designs," pp. 29–40; and John F. Mee, "Matrix Organization," *Business Horizons*, vol. 7, no. 2 (Summer 1964), pp. 70–72.

FIGURE 5–6
Matrix Organization Structures

A. A defense contractor

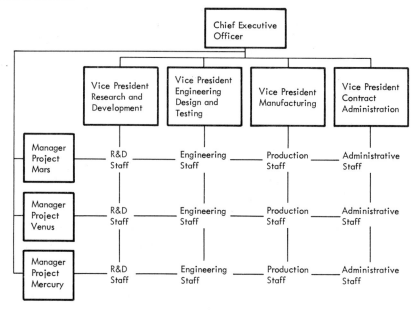

B. A college of business administration

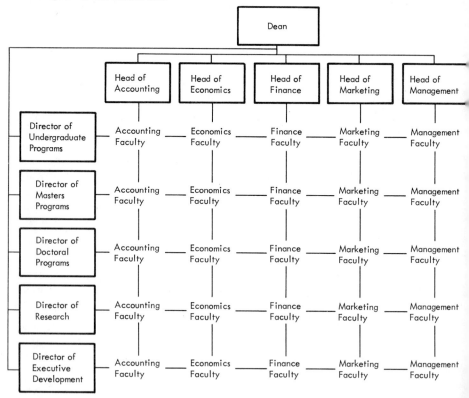

that of the functional manager.[22] An example of matrix organization is found in Du Pont's textile fibers department where there are product managers for acetate, nylon, "Orlon," and "Dacron" whose lines of responsibility cross those of the market managers for men's wear, women's wear, and home furnishings.[23]

4. The *venture team* concept whereby a group is brought together specifically to bring a specific product to market or a specific new business into being. Dow, General Mills, Westinghouse, and Monsanto have used the venture team approach as a regenesis of the entrepreneurial spirit. One difficulty with venture teams is if and when to transfer control of the project back to the regular organization and the problems of discontinuity and shifting purpose which result.[24]

PERSPECTIVES ON ORGANIZATION CHOICE

Organization theorists are agreed on two points: (1) there is no such thing as a perfect or ideal organization design and (2) there are no universally applicable panaceas for structuring an organization. Studies of organizations confirm that the same structural design which functions well in one organization can prove disastrous for another. What suits one type of strategy can be totally wrong for another. Structures that worked well in the past may not be as suitable for the future. Indeed, firms have a habit of regularly outgrowing their existing organizational form—either an internal shake-up is deemed periodically desirable or else changes in the size and scope of product-market-technology relationships make the firm's structure strategically obsolete. An organization's structure thus is dynamic; changes are not only inevitable but proper.

There is less agreement on whether organization design should commence with a conceptual framework or with a pragmatic consideration of the realities of the situation at hand—the special needs, the constraints imposed by the personalities involved and the way things have been done before. By and large, agonizing over which approach is best is counterproductive; both approaches should be used in parallel. A conceptual framework is essential if structure is to be firmly rooted in the organization's mission, objectives, strategy, and activities. But it must be adapted to the circumstances of the situation.

Yet, there is no one indisputably *best* structure or overriding principle of

---

[22] For a detailed study of how several large corporations have adopted product/market and functional organizational units to changing market environments, see Corey and Star, *Organization Strategy,* chaps. 3 and 4.

[23] Ibid., p. 18. Having both product and market management units is workable when the markets for a product are quite diverse and when end-use technology varies markedly from customer type to customer type.

[24] Philip Kotler, *Marketing Management: Analysis, Planning, and Control,* 3d ed. (Englewood Cliffs, N.J.: Prentice-Hall, Inc., 1976), pp. 200–1.

design—even for a particular organization at a single moment of time. All of the basic organizational forms have their strengths and weaknesses. Moreover, use of one form of departmentation does not preclude simultaneous use of the others. Many organizations are large enough and diverse enough to employ departmentalization by functional specialty, by geographical area, by process sequence, by market channel, by customer type, and by product group at the same time. Therefore, there can be ample rhyme and reason in organization building to depart from a slavish adherence to a basic conceptual framework and, thus, accommodate tailoring to the inevitable internal/external exceptions and special situations. Depending on an organization's strategy and stage of development, the general manager is confronted with different sorts of organizational problems and with a need to design a different sort of organizational structure. The critical element of organization building is figuring out how to translate the master strategy into an organization structure that is workable, efficient, pragmatic, and not just "theoretically sound" in terms of its strategy-supporting features.

There are, in effect, three philosophically different approaches that can be taken in constructing an effective organization. One is the "tight-ship" approach which entails a "run-it-by-the-book" bureaucracy and a more or less traditional organization form.[25] Here, the prescription is for an organization design with narrowly specialized jobs, small spans of control, clear authority relationships via a plainly hierarchical superior-subordinate pyramid, elaborate sets of rules and procedures, rigid interpretation and strict adherence to policies, tight budgetary controls, limited discretionary authority of lower and middle managers, and centralized decision making by top management. This type of organization is especially conducive to a functionally specialized management and seems to work best where the organization's tasks are largely routine and repetitive and jobs require little interdependence among specialists.[26]

The polar extreme of the "tight-ship" is the "free-form" approach to organization building. The free-form approach is predicated on the concepts of job enlargement, job enrichment, loose authority relationships, wide spans of control, a collegial or team-oriented relationship between subordinates and superiors, a minimal emphasis on hierarchical channels of decision making, self-discipline, individualized and self-generated controls, and broad participation in decision making and planning.[27] The idea behind the free-form philosophy is that an individual's motivation, creativity, and problem-

---

[25] The tight ship approach embraces the views of Max Weber, the Theory X style of management, and the true believers in *traditional principles* of management as exemplified in the writings of such classicists as Fayol, Taylor, Gulick, Urwick, Mooney, and their colleagues and successors.

[26] See Jay W. Lorsch and Arthur H. Walker, "Organizational Choice: Product vs. Function," *Harvard Business Review,* vol. 46, no. 6 (November–December 1968), pp. 129–38.

[27] The free-form approach encompasses the views on organization expressed by the Theory Y, System 4 school that includes McGregor, Likert, Argyris, and others.

solving ability is significantly enhanced in an environment where he or she is encouraged to become more involved and to play a major role in defining one's contribution to the organization's tasks. Advocates of the free-form approach claim that it leads to better results in situations where organizational tasks are less predictable and require innovative problem solving by teams of specialists whose work must be closely coordinated.

The third position on organization building is referred to as the contingency approach.[28] It is essentially an "it-all-depends" approach to organization and is predicated on the thesis that proper organization hinges more on effectively dealing with key situational and environmental factors (technology, competition, buyer behavior and needs, government regulation, social) than on choosing between the merits of the tight-ship and free-form philosophies or variations thereof. For instance, if an organization uses a continuous process or assembly-line type of technology, then the contingency approach would suggest a larger dose of the more traditional tight-ship principles of organization since common standards of performance as well as tightly sequenced integration is crucial. To use a more free-form organization style where highly interdependent subunits are individualized in their approaches to task accomplishment can make it more difficult to achieve a desirable degree of coordination and integration. Similarly, close and strict government regulation may prompt use of a more mechanistic organization structure, since there necessarily are more rules and procedures which must be observed and, consequently, less room for individualized discretion. On the other hand, if the firm's products are mostly custom-made, there is wide variety in the day-to-day work routine, or the production process is almost completely automated, then a heavier mix of free-form techniques can be more advantageous. From another view, the more uncertain and diverse the organization's product-market environment the more likely will a firm utilize a free-form approach, the logic being that it is more conducive to adapting organizational subunits to the unique features of their respective subenvironments.[29]

Drucker has summed up the intricacies of organization building well. He states:

> The simplest organization structure that will do the job is the best one. What makes an organization structure "good" are the problems it does not create. The simpler the structure, the less that can go wrong.
>
> Some design principles are more difficult and problematic than others. But none is without difficulties and problems. None is primarily people-focused rather than task-focused; none is more "creative," "free," or "more democratic." Design principles are tools; and tools are neither good nor bad in

---

[28] The contingency approach to organization building has been pioneered by Jay Lorsch and Paul Lawrence of the Harvard Business School. See, for example, P. R. Lawrence and J. W. Lorsch, *Organization and Environment: Managing Differentiation and Integration* (Boston: Division of Research, Harvard University Graduate School of Business Administration, 1967).

[29] Gene W. Dalton, Paul L. Lawrence, and Jay W. Lorsch, eds., *Organization Structure and Design* (Homewood, Ill.: Irwin-Dorsey, 1970, p. 6).

themselves. They can be used properly or improperly; and that is all. To obtain both the greatest possible simplicity and the greatest "fit," organization design has to start out with a clear focus on *key activities* needed to produce *key results*. They have to be structured and positioned in the simplest possible design. Above all, the architect of organization needs to keep in mind the purpose of the structure he is designing.[30]

In the final analysis, the test of an effective organization is not beauty of design, clarity of structure, or dedication to ideals but rather performance.

SUGGESTED READINGS

Ansoff, H. Igor, and Brandenberg, Richard.   "A Language for Organizational Design: Part II," *Management Science,* vol. 17, no. 12 (August 1971), pp. B-717-B-731.

Chandler, Alfred D.   *Strategy and Structure.* Cambridge, Mass.: The M.I.T. Press, 1962.

Corey, E. Raymond, and Star, Steven H.   *Organization Strategy: A Marketing Approach.* Boston: Division of Research, Harvard University Graduate School of Business Administration, 1971, chaps. 2, 3, 4, and 5.

Drucker, Peter.   *Management: Tasks, Responsibilities, Practices.* New York: Harper & Row, Publishers, 1974, chaps. 41-48.

Lawrence, Paul R., and Lorsch, Jay W.   *Organization and Environment: Managing Differentiation and Integration.* Boston: Division of Research, Harvard University Graduate School of Business Administration, 1967.

Lorsch, Jay W., and Walker, Arthur H.   "Organizational Choice: Product vs. Function," *Harvard Business Review,* vol. 46, no. 6 (November-December 1968), pp. 129-38.

Rumelt, Richard.   *Strategy, Structure, and Economic Performance.* Cambridge, Mass.: Harvard University Press, 1974.

Salter, Malcolm S.   "Stages of Corporate Development," *Journal of Business Policy,* vol. 1, no. 1 (Spring, 1970), pp. 23-37.

Scott, Bruce R.   "The Industrial State: Old Myths and New Realities," *Harvard Business Review,* vol. 51, no. 2 (March-April 1973), pp. 133-48.

Daniel, D. Ronald.   "Reorganizing for Results," *Harvard Business Review,* vol. 44, no. 6 (November-December 1966), pp. 96-104.

---

[30] Drucker, *Management,* pp. 601-02.

6

MANAGING ORGANIZATIONAL PROCESSES

Nothing makes a prince so much esteemed as the undertaking of great enterprises and the setting of a noble example in his own person.

N. Machiavelli

GIVEN that the organization's structure is suitably keyed to the needs of strategy, the general manager's priorities tend to focus on seeing that prescribed activities and processes are effectively carried out. This means motivating people, overseeing and coordinating day-to-day tasks, creating a timely flow of the right information to the right people, instituting controls to contain deviations from plan, and exercising appropriate leadership and communication skills. All of these functions are important and pose tests of the manager's basic administrative abilities. This chapter highlights how managerial performance of these functions relates to successful strategy formulation and implementation.

MOTIVATIONAL CONSIDERATIONS

Motivation is a key ingredient of strategy implementation. Obviously, it is important for organizational subunits and individuals to have a reasonably strong commitment to the achievement of the enterprise's goals, objectives, and overall strategy. Motivation is brought about most fundamentally by the organization's reward-punishment structure—salary raises, bonuses, stock options, fringe benefits, promotions (or fear of demotions), assurance of not being "sidelined" and ignored, praise, recognition, criticism, tension, fear, more (or less) responsibility, increased (or decreased) job control or autonomy, the promise of attractive locational assignments, and the bonds of group acceptance. As the foregoing suggests, motivational incentives can be positive or negative in nature. They may also be intrinsic, as in the case of the increased self-respect and gratification which comes with achieving a goal or solving a tough problem.

The prevailing view is that a good motivational system allows for blended fulfillment of both organizational goals and personal goals. No doubt this is a useful guideline. But, in practice, it is a ticklish task to gear the size of an individual's rewards to a corresponding contribution to organization objectives; rewards may be excessive, target achievement levels set too low, or contributions unrecognized and mismeasured. More often, though, the opposite is true, as suggested by the way Harold Geneen, former president and chief executive officer of ITT, allegedly motivated his subordinates through the combined use of money, tension, and fear:

> Geneen provides his managers with enough incentives to make them tolerate the system. Salaries all the way through ITT are higher than average—Geneen reckons 10 percent higher—so that few people can leave without taking a drop. As one employee put it: "We're all paid just a bit more than we think we're worth." At the very top, where the demands are greatest, the salaries and stock options are sufficient to compensate for the rigors. As someone said, "He's got them by their limousines."
>
> Having bound his men to him with chains of gold, Geneen can induce the tension that drives the machine. "The key to the system," one of his men explained, "is the profit forecast. Once the forecast has been gone over, revised and agreed on, the managing director has a personal commitment to Geneen to carry it out. That's how he produces the tension on which the success depends." The tension goes through the company, inducing ambition, perhaps exhilaration, but always with some sense of fear: what happens if the target is missed?
>
> The price in human terms is very high. "Geneen wants us all to be as gung-ho as he is," one manager said, "but somehow it isn't as much fun for the rest of us." The sense of strain is very noticeable in the Park Avenue skyscraper: not only the tension of worry and work, but the lack of the satisfaction of personal achievement.[1]

It goes without saying that if and when an organization's structure of rewards and punishments induces too much tension, anxiety, and job insecurity that the results can be counterproductive. Yet, it is doubtful whether it is ever useful to completely eliminate tension, fear, anxiety, and insecurity from the motivational system; there is, for example, no evidence that "the quiet life" is highly correlated with superior performance. On the contrary, high-performing organizations usually require an endowment of ambitious people who relish the opportunity to climb the ladder of success, who have a need for stimulation (or who want to avoid boredom), and who thus find some degree of position anxiety useful in order to satisfy their own drives for personal recognition, accomplishment, and self-satisfaction.

---

[1] Anthony Sampson, *The Sovereign State of ITT* (New York: Stein and Day, Publishers, 1973), p. 132.

Illustration Capsule 13

The Mysteries of Motivation

The eminently successful Paul W. Bryant, head football coach at the University of Alabama, tells of the time he unwittingly motivated a team just prior to game time:

When I was at Kentucky I got booed one night by a group of students who came to the train to see us off for a game with Cincinnati. I had fired some of our star players and they didn't like that. And we'd lost three of our first five games and they didn't like that either, which I can understand. I didn't like it myself. In fact, I hated it. For a young coach—which I was then—so keyed up I couldn't get to work in the morning without vomiting along the way, it was not exactly heaven on earth. The Cincinnati game took on added importance.

Cincinnati had fine teams then, coached by Sid Gillman, who has been a big name in the pros and is with the Houston Oilers now. What I'm about to say should not be taken as a lack of respect for Sid. You have to appreciate that my collar was tighter than it is now.

We got to the stadium at Cincinnati and I sensed something was wrong. When we went out to warm up for the game there was nobody in the stands. Just a few handfuls scattered around. I thought for a minute I was in the wrong place. When we finished our warm-up and the Cincinnati team still hadn't made an appearance, I said to Carney Laslie, one of my original assistant coaches, "What's that no-good conniving smart-aleck"—meaning the eminent Coach Gillman—"up to now? What the hell is that damn thief trying to pull?"

Carney just shook his head. He was as dumbfounded as I was.

I ordered the team back into the locker room—and then it dawned on me. I'd screwed up the schedule. We were an hour early.

I was too embarrassed to tell what I knew. I just walked around, up and down the aisles where the players sat waiting, my big old farmer's boots making the only noise in there. I couldn't think of anything to say, so I didn't say a word. For an hour I clomped up and down. Finally, when I'd used up enough time I delivered a one-sentence pep talk, the only thing I could think to say:

"Let's go."

They almost tore the door down getting out. Cincinnati was favored that day, but it was no contest. We won, 27–7.

Bryant tells of a second instance when coaching at Texas A&M where an approach he tried worked on one occasion but apparently failed when someone else tried it.

They'd been dead all week in practice before the SMU game, and I wondered, what could we do? What was left to try? I'd run out of ways to motivate them. Elmer Smith, one of my assistants, said he remembered one time when he was playing for Ivan Grove at Hendrix College. Grove woke him up at midnight and read him something about how a mustard seed could move a mountain if you believed in it, something Norman Vincent Peale, or somebody, had taken from the Bible and written in a little pamphlet. It impressed me.

I didn't tell a soul. At 12 o'clock on Thursday night I called everyone on my staff and told them to meet me at the dormitory at 1 o'clock. When they got there, I said, OK, go get the players real quick, and they went around shaking them, and the boys came stumbling in there, rubbing their eyes, thinking I'd

Illustration Capsule 13 (continued)

finally lost my mind. And I read 'em that little thing about the mustard seed—just three sentences—turned around, and walked out.

Well, you never know if you are doing right or wrong, but we went out and played the best game we'd played all year. SMU should have beaten us by 40 points, but they were lucky to win, 6–3. In the last minute of play we had a receiver wide open inside their 20-yard line, but our passer didn't see him.

Several years after that, Darrell Royal called me from Texas. He was undefeated, going to play Rice and worried to death. He said he'd never been in that position before, undefeated and all, and his boys were lazy and fatheaded, and he wanted to know what to do about it.

I said, "Well, Darrell, there's no set way to motivate a team, and the way I do it may be opposite to your way but I can tell you a story." And I gave him that thing about the mustard seed. He said, by golly, he'd try it.

Well, I don't know whether he did or not, but I remember the first thing I wanted to do Sunday morning was get that paper and see how Texas made out. Rice won, 34–7.

Source: Paul W. Bryant and John Underwood, *Bear: The Hard Life and Good Times of Alabama's Coach Bryant* (Boston: Little, Brown and Company, 1974), pp. 3–4, 6–7.

INSTILLING A SPIRIT OF PERFORMANCE

One test of administrative effectiveness lies in management's ability to perceive what each employee can do well and what he or she cannot. A good manager works at developing employees' strengths, neutralizing their respective weaknesses, and building upon and blending the individual skills of employees in ways that cause employees to perform consistently at or near peak capability. When successfully done, the outcome is a spirit of high performance and an emphasis on excellence and achievement.

Such a spirit of performance, sometimes referred to as "morale," should not be confused with whether employees are "happy" or "satisfied" or whether they "get along well together." An organization whose approach to "human relations" and "dealing with people" is not grounded in high standards of performance actually has poor human relations and a management that is liable to produce a mean spirit.[2] Certainly, there is no greater indictment of an organization than that of allowing or fostering an atmosphere in which the outstanding performances of a few people become a threat to the whole group and a source of controversy, backstabbing, and attempts to enforce safe mediocrity.

For an organization to be instilled with and sustain a spirit of performance, it must maintain a focus on achievement and on excellence. It must strive at developing a consistent ability to produce results over prolonged periods of time. It must be alert to opportunities and seek to capitalize upon them. It must succeed in utilizing the full range of rewards and punishment

---

[2] Peter F. Drucker, *Management: Tasks, Responsibilities, Practices,* (New York: Harper & Row, Publishers, 1974), p. 455.

(pay, promotion, assignments, tension, pressure, job security, and so on) to establish and enforce standards of excellence.

Particularly must management have the courage and willingness to remove people who consistently render poor or mediocre performance. Such people should, if for no other reason, be removed for their own good since people who find themselves in a job they cannot handle are usually frustrated, anxiety-ridden, harassed, and unhappy.[3] One does not do a person a favor by keeping him in a job he is not equal to. Moreover, subordinates have a right to be managed with competence, dedication, and achievement; unless their boss performs well, they themselves cannot perform well.[4] In general, then, an organization should not have to tolerate managers who fail to perform; they should be "sidetracked," or in extreme cases dismissed, so as not to undercut either the implementation of strategy or the careers of subordinates. One well-known proponent of this approach was General George C. Marshall, chief of staff of the U.S. Army in World War II.[5] Marshall reportedly said, "I have a duty to the soldiers, their parents, and the country, to remove immediately any commander who does not satisfy the highest performance standards." He repeatedly upheld this duty, actually removing a number of commanders from assignments. But when he did, he followed it up with the recognition that, "It was my mistake to have put this or that man in a command that was not the right command for him. It is therefore *my* job to think through where he belongs."

The toughest cases, of course, concern the need to reassign people who have given long and loyal service to the organization but who are past their prime and unable to deal effectively with demanding situations. The decision in such cases should be objectively based upon what is best for the company—which usually means removing the person from his or her job. Yet, it can be done in a compassionate and human fashion. When Henry Ford II was trying to revive Ford Motor Company after World War II, he felt that none of the nine top-management people in one key division were competent enough to handle new jobs created by reorganization.[6] Not one was appointed to the newly created positions. But while their incompetence was undisputed and it would have been easy to fire them, the fact remained that they had served loyally through trying periods. Ford took the position that while no one should be allowed to hold a job he or she could not perform in superior fashion, neither should anyone be penalized for the mistakes of the previous regime. So, the nine men were assigned as experienced technicians and experts to jobs they could be expected to do well. As things turned out, seven of the men did well in their new assignments—one so well that he was later promoted into a more important job than originally held. The other two failed; the older one was given early retirement and the younger one was

---

[3] Ibid., p. 457.

[4] Ibid.

[5] As cited by Drucker, *Management*, p. 459.

[6] This example is drawn from Drucker, *Management*, 459.

dismissed. A management that is concerned with building excellent organizational spirit takes the cases of loyal nonperformers seriously because, while they are (or should be) few in number, they have a major impact on morale and how their cases are handled tells others in the organization much about management's character and respect for its employees.

Two additional considerations weigh heavily on whether an organization attains a high spirit of performance in implementing the chosen strategy.[7] The first concerns the extent to which an organization is pointed toward capitalizing on opportunity as opposed to solving existing problems. An organization is prone to have higher morale and an acceptance of challenge when top priority is given to converting opportunities into results. Concentrating on solving problems tends to detract from an organization's momentum and to put it on "hold" until the problems at hand are solved or else brought under control. In contrast, an attitude of "damn the torpedoes, full steam ahead" works to keep the attention of the organization focused on generating the greatest impact on results and performance—an orientation which, in many circumstances, acts to enhance strategy implementation.

The second consideration which affects an organization's spirit of performance is the reward-punishment structure. Decisions on pay, on assignments, and on promotion are management's *foremost* "control" device. These decisions signal who is getting ahead and who is not, who is climbing up the ladder fastest, and who is perceived as doing a good job. They signal what sort of behavior and performance management wants, values, and rewards. Such decisions seldom escape the closest scrutiny of every member of the organization. If anything, an organization will overreact to these kinds of management decisions. What management may view as an innocuous move to solve an interpersonal conflict or to bypass an organizational obstacle may be interpreted as a sign that management wants one kind of behavior while preaching another. Hence, a good manager must be ever alert to his or her decisions on placement, pay, and promotion. They should be based on a factual record of performance as measured against explicit standards—never on "potential" or friendship or expediency or casual opinions. They should reflect careful thinking, clear policy and procedures, and high standards of fairness and equity.

Drucker offers a number of personal characteristics in a manager which can undermine a spirit of high performance:

> A lack of integrity.
> A lack of character.
> Cynicism.
> Emphasizing the negative aspect of what subordinates cannot do (their weaknesses) rather than the positive aspects of what they can do (their strengths).

---

[7] Ibid., pp. 460–61.

Being more interested in "who is right?" than "what is right?"

Being afraid of strong (high-performing) subordinates.

Not setting high standards for one's own work.

Valuing intelligence more highly than integrity.[8]

Obviously a management interested in nurturing a spirit of high performance and accomplishment should endeavor to weed out managers and candidate managers who display such characteristics.

LEADERSHIP

According to an old proverb, "Trees die from the top"—the implication being that there is no substitute for leadership. The litany of good leadership is simple enough: plan, decide, organize, direct, control, *win!*[9] Obviously, any organization benefits from having people who are able to "take charge" and serve as both "spark plug" and "ramrod" in implementing strategy. Leadership is exemplified by those who are known as "the movers" and "the shakers" in the organization. But at the same time, the ability to exercise extraordinary leadership is rare; not many managers are skilled in the art of inducing subordinates to accomplish their assignments with eagerness, enthusiasm, and to the maximum of their ability. Moreover, an effective leadership style in one setting may be ineffective in another.

To lead is to initiate, guide, direct, facilitate, change, and inspire; it entails lifting aspirations, raising performance to higher levels, and developing people to their fullest. It may involve great personal or career risk. The leader is part of the group, yet distinct from it. His skills revolve mostly around the art of inventing and using motivators to effect high performance. His role exists because of the need of people for someone to follow. Indeed, one of the most fundamental tenets of leadership concerns the tendency of people to follow those in whom they see a means of satisfying their own personal goals; hence *the more a manager understands what motivates his subordinates and the more he uses these motivations in carrying out his managerial activities, the more effective as a leader he is likely to be.*[10]

It is equally important to understand what leadership is not. It is not *necessarily* having a magnetic personality or charisma. It is not winning friends and influencing people. It is not being likable, loved, and well thought of. On the contrary, history describes a number of renowned leaders as demanding, arrogant, obstreperous, or hard to get along with—Napoleon, Patton, and Queen Elizabeth I serve as examples. A study of noted business

---

[8] Ibid., p. 462.

[9] Jay Hall, "To Achieve or Not: The Manager's Choice," *California Management Review,* vol. 18, no. 4 (Summer 1976), p. 5.

[10] Harold Koontz and Cyril O'Donnell, *Principles of Management: An Analysis of Managerial Functions,* (New York: McGraw-Hill Book Company, 1972), p. 559.

leaders would, no doubt, yield similar conclusions. The key to understanding leadership seems to hinge more on what leaders do rather than on their personal traits.

In general, four leadership patterns stand out: autocratic, participative, instrumental, and "great person." The autocratic leader tends to command, to be dogmatic, positive, and confident, and to rely upon authority and discipline; he leads through his control over rewards and punishment. The participative leader believes that people will work hard and accomplish their assignments best when supervised in a manner that lets them use their own initiative, be independent, contribute their ideas, and participate in decisions; participative leaders act as "coordinators" instead of bosses and endeavor to treat subordinates as "self-starters." The instrumental type leader is perceived as a manager who must plan, organize, direct, and control in whatever way best gets the job done; the instrumental leader may use autocratic or participative approaches but the emphasis is on the central task of allocating human and organizational resources in the most effective, efficient manner. The instrumental leader is skillful in arousing support and developing a consensus, in working with people, in achieving objectives and results on schedule, and in making the right things happen. The essence of the instrumental approach is that those who manage well are also effective as leaders. The "great person" concept of leadership is a combination instrumental-participative pattern whereby the leader exhibits balanced concern both for people and for production, but does so in ways which exemplify vision, a grand design, and innovative plans calling for major changes and progress. The great person pattern is a heroic leadership style and suggests that such persons are "natural" or "born" leaders who most likely will be successful leaders in any situation.

Although the historical position of most behavioral scientists has been anti-authoritarian and pro-participative management, the increasingly widespread view is that for managers, as leaders, to be effective they should utilize whatever leadership posture or style is best for them in that situation, quite irrespective of whether it is strongly authoritarian or strongly participative or somewhere in between.[11] More specifically, it is held that effective managers will tend to vary their leadership techniques as people, tasks, organization environment, and the requirements of strategy vary. This "contingency approach" to leadership is based on growing research evidence (as well as intuitive management opinion) that different kinds of organization groups, given their different tasks and staffing "personalities," function best

---

[11] Drucker, for one, has launched a powerful attack on some of the psychological aspects underlying participative management styles (represented most prominently by McGregor's Theory Y) and suggests that managers are correct in being leery of it. Drucker describes Theory Y management as "enlightened psychological despotism" and a "repugnant form of tyranny." According to Drucker,

"Most, if not all, of the recent writers on industrial psychology profess allegiance to Theory Y. They use terms like 'self-fulfillment,' 'creativity,' and 'the whole man.' But

when they are structured and managed and led in quite different and distinct ways.[12] For example, it makes sense that a manager's leadership behavior in implementing organization strategy will be influenced according to whether:

He feels strongly that individuals should have a voice in making decisions which affect them.

He has confidence in subordinates' qualifications to handle the problem/issue on their own.

He feels more comfortable functioning in a directive role or in a team role.

Subordinates exhibit relatively high needs for independence.

Subordinates are experienced enough to make responsible decisions.

Subordinates prefer to be given clear-cut directives or whether they wish to have wider areas of freedom.

Subordinates are interested in the problem and wish to have a voice in solving it.

Subordinates expect to share in decision making.

Subordinates work together as a unit effectively.

There is severe time pressure for immediate action.

The size of organizational subunits, their geographical distribution, and the degree of intraorganizational cooperation required to attain goals and objectives are such as to preclude use of authoritarian (or participative) practices.

There is a need for confidentiality.

---

what they talk and write about is control through psychological manipulation. They are led to this by their basic assumptions, which are precisely the Theory X assumptions: man is weak, sick and incapable of looking after himself. He is full of fears, anxieties, neuroses, inhibitions. Essentially he does not want to achieve but wants to fail. He therefore wants to be controlled. Indeed, for his own good he needs to be controlled—not by fear and incentive of material rewards but through his fear of psychological alienation and the incentive of 'psychological security.'

''. . . The manager, if one listens to the psychologists, will have to have insight into all kinds of people. He will have to be in command of all kinds of psychological techniques. He will have to have empathy for all his subordinates. He will have to understand an infinity of individual personality structures, individual psychological needs, and individual psychological problems.''

Such an approach, Drucker alleges, supposedly makes psychological control by the manager ''unselfish'' and in the worker's own interest but, more importantly, by becoming his workers' psychological servant the manager retains control as their boss. The effect, says Drucker, is to substitute persuasion for command, psychological manipulation for the carrot of financial rewards, and empathy for the fear of being punished.

Drucker maintains that such an approach is not only contemptuous but also will cause the manager-psychologist to undermine his own authority. Why? Because the integrity of the manager stems from his commitment to the work of the organization and any manager who pretends that the personal needs of subordinates, rather the objective needs of the task, determine what should be done is apt not to be believed and, therefore, risks losing his integrity and his subordinates' respect. See Drucker, *Management,* pp. 243–45.

[12] E. P. Learned and A. T. Sproat, *Organization Theory and Policy* (Homewood, Ill.: Richard D. Irwin, Inc., 1966), p. 61.

The organizational climate is flexible enough to allow for deviation from what higher-ups have established as approved behavior.[13]

In deciding what kind of leadership pattern to employ in strategy implementation, the manager may find it useful to ask two questions of himself: (1) Have I gotten the ideas and suggestions of everyone who has the necessary knowledge to make a significant contribution to the solution of the problem? and (2) What can the organization do and what can I do to help my subordinates the most in doing a superior job? He may also find it useful to ask subordinates what *they* can do to help him, as their manager, do the best job for the organization.

INSTITUTING MANAGEMENT CONTROLS

The role of management controls is to provide systematic verification of whether strategy implementation is proceeding in accordance with plan. Is the strategy being put in place on schedule? Are goals and objectives being met? Are the established policies being followed and are they effective? Have appropriate standards of performance been set? What sorts of deviations from these standards are being experienced? Is the strategy (and its accompanying set of policies) working?

The purpose of management controls is to provide feedback on the accomplishment of strategy; this includes pointing out weaknesses in standards (whether they are clear and realistic), uncovering and correcting negative deviations from agreed-upon standards, and preventing their recurrence. The desired effect is to carry out organizational activities smoothly, properly, and according to high standards. The whole concept of management control is therefore normative and concerned with what ought to be.

Controls are necessary because the structure of an organization, by itself, is never "tight" enough to ensure the proper commitment to and execution of organization strategy and policy. Organizational subunits have their own substrategies which are at least slightly deflected from the overall organizational strategy. Moreover, individuals have their own career goals and needs, as well as their own perceptions of strategy. Internal politics and rivalry among subunits and professional groups introduce still other possibilities for misdirection. Such happenings and considerations are all quite normal—even in high-performing organizations manned by people of competence and goodwill who are informed as to strategy and policy. As a consequence, the performance of individuals and subunits cannot be left to chance. And, understandably, the thrust of the control process is on goal-setting, standard-setting, measuring, comparing, and taking corrective action.

In designing a set of control devices, the manager should keep one princi-

---

[13] Robert Tannenbaum and Warren H. Schmidt, "How to Choose a Leadership Pattern," *Harvard Business Review,* vol. 36, no. 2 (March–April 1958), pp. 98–100.

ple firmly in mind—*controls follow strategy.* Unless controls are means to strategy accomplishment, there is undue risk of wrong action and "miscontrol." In addition, controls should satisfy seven other specifications:[14]

1. Controls should be economical and involve only the *minimum* amount of information needed to give a reliable picture of what is going on. In general, the less effort and fewer control devices which have to be created to maintain the desired standards, the better and more effective the control design; too many controls create confusion.
2. Controls should seek to measure only meaningful events (sales volume, product mix, market standing, productivity rates) or symptoms of potentially significant developments (lower profit margins, higher rates of turnover, and absenteeism). Controls should relate to key objectives, key activities, and priority considerations rather that the mass of trivia and events which are marginal to strategic performance and results.
3. Controls should report the variables being measured in ways which reveal the real structure of the situation and which are grounds for action. For example, reporting the *number* of grievances per thousand employees does not indicate the *importance* of the grievances in terms of the impacts on morale and performance.
4. Controls should be geared to provide information on a timely basis—not too late to take corrective action nor so often as to confuse and overburden.
5. Controls should be kept simple. Voluminous control manuals and complicated reports are likely to misdirect and obscure because of the attention that has to be paid to mechanics, procedures, and interpretive guidelines instead of to what is being measured. Moreover, the measures reported should be in a form that is suitable for the recipient and tailored to his needs.
6. Controls should be oriented toward taking corrective action rather than just providing interesting information. It is debatable whether reports or studies should receive wide distribution ("for your information"), but they should without fail reach the persons who can take action by virtue of their position in the decision structure.
7. Controls should, for the most part, aim at pinpointing the "exceptions"; this allows management to zero in on the significant departures from norm.

When corrective action is required, care should be taken to act in ways which do not dampen initiative and spirit of performance. For a manager to dwell on finding errors and mistakes in subordinates' work encourages them to play it safe, "cover up" difficulties, and use political tactics to stay on the

---

[14] Drucker, *Management,* pp. 498–504; Harold Koontz, "Management Control: A Suggested Formulation of Principles," *California Management Review,* vol. 2, no. 2 (Winter 1959), pp. 50–55; William H. Sihler, "Toward Better Management Control Systems," *California Management Review,* vol. 14, no. 2 (Winter 1971), pp. 33–39.

boss's good side. Attention shifts from doing things better to avoiding doing things wrong. One approach to get around this pitfall is to give as much attention to favorable variances as to unfavorable variances in control reviews. In other words, positive reinforcement, incentives, and rewards for performance above standards may in some situations be as effective in reducing negative deviations as are various forms of criticism, punishment, and disciplinary action. This gets back to the most fundamental control device of all—management's use of the reward-punishment structure.

Illustration Capsule 14

United Airline's System of Management Controls

As early as the mid-1950s, United Airlines had a computer-assisted system of reporting and controls which resulted not only in the chief executive officer having a profit and loss statement every 24 hours but also provided operating heads with up-to-the-hour information on how to respond to weather and passenger load patterns. According to an article in *Nation's Business* by Philip Gustafson:

The statement has its birth every day in the statistical production room at United's Denver operating base. Passenger and cargo volumes, collected from each flight, are combined at the end of the day. The results are wired to United's Chicago offices ready for processing at 8:30 A.M. Economic research employees apply revenue rates predetermined by experience and expense rates based on current operating budget requirements to the previous day's volume appearing on the wire. Within an hour, an operating profit or loss is estimated and passed on to top management.

The daily report shows the day's operating profit or loss along with a month and year to date accumulation. Also, daily revenue passenger-miles and the passenger load factor are given. Data are broken down in such a way as to give the passenger department information on which to decide whether to put more planes on the Chicago to San Francisco run or advertise to get additional passengers.

An intrinsic part of United's reporting system is what company executives like to call "the room with the 14,000-mile view." This is an information and planning center at Denver which is the business world's equivalent of the military briefing room. Facts funneled daily into this center present a clear picture of operations throughout United's 80-city system.

In keeping with the idea of expansive vision, the room has glass walls on one side. Modern white plastic chairs are grouped before a map of the United States, 8 feet high and 20 feet wide, on which United's routes are outlined. Colored lights (red for weather, green for maintenance, and white for passengers) at major terminals show current operating conditions. If the red light glows steadily, for example, it means adverse weather; if it is flashing, the weather is marginal. Electric clocks above the map show the time in each zone through which United operates.

The room is designed to provide management with operational facts in the most convenient form. Data, such as mileage flown, delays at terminals by type of plane and total number of departures, are posted on lucite panels, flanking the map. Dozens of supplementary charts deal with payload volumes and load factors, weather, actual performance as compared with schedule and related information.

Illustration Capsule 14 (continued)

Daily at 8:30 A.M., MST, United's operations executives meet in the room for a 14,000-mile view. Four briefing specialists review operations of the past 24 hours and outline what the next 24 are expected to bring. The opening summary is presented by a meteorologist who analyzes the decisive factors in yesterday's weather conditions from the Atlantic seaboard to the Hawaiian Islands. He then gives his forecast for the next 24 hours, accenting developments which may affect operations.

A mechanical specialist follows with information on the status of the company's fleet. He reports the number and types of aircraft withdrawn from service for overhaul and comments on the progress of various engineering projects at the San Francisco base.

A traffic specialist then gives a resumé of the previous day's performance in terms of any customer service problems which arose. Approximately 750 plane departures are scheduled daily. Those which deviate from schedule are spotlighted for management study to prevent possible recurrence.

The remaining gaps in the 14,000-mile view are filled in by a flight operations specialist who discusses the availability of equipment, and weather outlook on the line. The session then adjourns. Immediately afterwards, some department chiefs may call their staffs together to act on particular facets of the day's operating plan.

Source: Philip Gustafson, "Business Reports: How to Get Facts You Need," *Nation's Business,* vol. 44, no. 8 (August 1956), pp. 78–82.

COMMUNICATION AND MANAGEMENT CONTROL

It is management's job, of course, to communicate the organization's strategy and the plans and policies for implementing it to all members of the organization. That this must be done and done effectively requires no further elaboration. But it is worth noting that the control process provides a way of thinking about and approaching the task of informing members of the organization of the goals to be achieved, how these goals relate to overall objectives and strategy, and the relative priorities that various tasks should have. Control devices should clearly signal the kinds of results and behavior expected. And periodic reviews of the organizational unit's performance, together with the manager's periodic reviews of individual job performance with his or her subordinates, offer a golden opportunity to *(a)* evaluate standards of performance with employees, *(b)* review results on the job, *(c)* analyze the reasons for these results, *(d)* discuss plans for increasing on-the-job effectiveness, *(e)* consider each job incumbent's potential for advancement, *(f)* prepare plans, programs, and budgets for the coming year, and *(g)* agree on specific standards, goals, and objectives for periods ahead.

PROBLEM AREAS IN MANAGING PEOPLE

How well, or how poorly a manager manages people, is a major factor in the implementation of strategy and, ultimately, in the strategy's success.

Unfortunately, there is no neat formula of "five steps to follow" in managing people. Proper motivation and effective leadership, as discussed above, are plainly important. But during the course of strategy implementation there are also a number of questions relating to organization personnel and management which need to be asked regularly and the current practices reevaluated:

1. What type and quality of personnel does the organization now have and how does this compare with what it will need in the future? Is management competent to meet the challenges ahead? What are management's strengths and weaknesses? What are the ages of key executives and personnel? Will there be adequate replacements at retirement?

2. How and from where will the organization recruit new personnel? Is the organization attracting the right kinds of people to fill entry level positions? Is the organization attracting and keeping qualified personnel? Is there a high turnover rate among good employees at lower levels? To what extent should the organization promote from within or recruit from the outside?

3. Does the organization have a "key executive" problem—i.e., an executive without a replacement? To what extent would operations be impaired if something happened to the key executive?

4. Are the organization's personnel adequately trained? Is formal on-the-job training needed? Do new employees have trouble understanding what is expected of them?

5. How well are employees, including managers, performing? Does the appraisal system really measure performance or is it simply an exercise which management goes through to comply with organization procedures? Are promotable persons being identified through the appraisal system? Are those who need more training or better training being identified?

6. In what ways should people be compensated? Is the compensation structure adequate? Are compensation rewards correctly geared to the sought-for results and performance? Are those employees (and managers) perceived as "high-performing" or as "key executives" better compensated than other employees at their level? Are material rewards relied upon too heavily as the main (or only) positive motivator?

7. How should the performance of managers be evaluated? (This is not a small matter when one considers that the manager's job description includes such phrases as "maintaining relationships with," "supervising the operation of," "having responsibility for," and such activities as coordinating, problem solving, and administering—all of which lack concreteness and ready measurement.) To what extent should complexity of the work, general education and technical training required, the scope of responsibility for people and property, and the effect of the manager's decisions and activities upon profits (or other desired outcomes) be balanced against performance in determining the manager's compensation package? What relationship should the compensation of

managers and executives have with the monetary reward paid to others in the organization?

8. To what extent should the general manager manage his subordinates through personal contact and direct intervention, offering his own ideas and inputs and getting involved in day-to-day matters? Or, should he reject the "playing coach" approach and place greater reliance on instituting the necessary guidelines via formal planning, budgeting, control, and compensation systems? How far should he go in staying out of daily operating activities by delegating authority to subordinates?

PLAYING "THE POWER GAME"

All organizations are political. The drives and ambitions to climb the ladder of career achievement and success, the conflicts and coalitions that evolve in translating goals into action and on into results, and the hierarchical divisions of responsibility and authority combine to guarantee the existence of a political atmosphere. Positions of power and weakness are inevitable and the people involved are neither likely to be indifferent to power relationships nor passive in their own maneuvering and use of power. Jockeying for position is a normal activity. After all, careers, prestige, and egos are at stake, not to mention material rewards.

On occasions, therefore, ambition, personal biases, and favoritism may overrule "objective" analysis; conceivably, unscrupulous actions and unethical behavior may arise, together with selfish attempts to "feather one's own nest." One cannot assume that virtue guarantees rewards nor that doing a good job suffices for promotion. This is not to say that organizations are a political jungle with much effort put into political maneuvering and thinking up new power plays. Such can occur, but it is the exception not the rule. Usually, organizational politics is kept within bounds and does not deteriorate into wholesale plotting and schemes, backstabbing, and dissension. Yet, it would be naïve to presume that a manager can be effective and get ahead without being perceptive about internal politics and being adept at playing the power game. Like it or not, managers need to be sensitive to the political environment in the organization.

Middle-level managers are particularly susceptible to political considerations. Higher level executives measure success in terms of results; they tend to be less interested in how the results are produced. The middle manager's performance thus often hinges on how well the results of his or her actions match the general directives from above to get the job done.[15] But in

---

[15] Middle managers are seldom told how to get their jobs done in specific terms. The guidelines they receive from higher-ups regarding increasing sales or profits, carving out a bigger market share, or getting by on a smaller budget are mostly general and, so long as organizational policies are observed, the boss's attitude is most likely to be "I don't care how you do it, just get it done—and on time." In other words, the specifics are delegated to the next level down and it ends up the middle manager's job to figure out how what plans and concrete actions will be needed to generate the desired results. It is the middle manager, more than anyone else, who translates financial, sales, production, and strategic goals and objectives into a day-to-day operating plan and, then, communicates it in functional-specialist language to the technical, detail-oriented, first-line supervisors.

the course of translating these general directives into concrete action to be followed by first-level managers and technical unit heads, middle managers are vulnerable to heavy flak from both sides. They are caught between pressure from above for results to make their bosses look good and the need for the goodwill and cooperation of their own subordinates (plus other organizational subunits on which they must rely for support) to carry out their assignments. It is difficult for middle managers to shift blame or make excuses when things do not work out well. Hence, they are thrust into walking a political tight-rope, seeking compromise and workability between the goals of subordinates (whose cooperation is required) and the goals of superiors (whose approval is needed to get ahead). If they want to maintain the loyalty and respect of subordinates, middle managers must represent their interests and be willing "to go to bat" for them when the occasion demands. Middle managers must understand the organization's power structure and be sensitive to the direction of political winds. They need to ask themselves a series of questions: Who are my friends and who are my enemies? Who can I count on in a showdown or when the going gets tough? Whose opinions really count and whose can be ignored? Which department and division heads have the most influence and the most clout in shaping decisions? With whom should I develop strong alliances? On what issues do I need to take a stand and be willing "to rock the boat" if necessary and on what should I accept the status quo? Given the way the system works, am I better off with a job assignment in a nonkey activity where I can be a "star performer" (perhaps outshining a weak boss) or with a job assignment in an area "where the action is" (perhaps working directly for someone who is reliably reported to be "on their way up")?[16] To what extent should I strive for positions with high visibility and exposure to higher level executives?

Illustration Capsule 15

Playing the Power Game the Machiavellian Way

Niccolo Machiavelli, in his classic *The Prince,* presented a manual of methods and tactics in the acquisition and use of power. *The Prince* is full of straightforward, bitter truths about the drive for power and the realities of human motivation. Some say that *The Prince* is diabolical; others call it insightful and utterly realistic in its portrayal of human nature. Whatever adjectives one chooses to apply, there is no denying it as one of the most influential books ever written.

Although Machiavelli's study of power politics was addressed specifically to

---

[16] For a discussion of how to climb to higher ranks in an organization, see Ross A. Webber, "Career Problems of Young Managers," *California Management Review,* vol. 18, no. 4 (Summer 1976), pp. 19–33.

Illustration Capsule 15 (continued)

political rulers, the lessons apply equally well to management. Indeed, if in reading the excerpts below one will simply substitute "manager" for "prince" (or its equivalent), then the relevance of Machiavelli to modern management can be readily approached:

. . . men must either be cajoled or crushed; for they will revenge themselves for slight wrongs, while for grave ones they cannot. The injury therefore that you do to a man should be such that you need not fear his revenge.

. . . in taking possession of a state the conqueror should well reflect as to the harsh measures that may be necessary, and then execute them at a single blow, so as not to be obliged to renew them every day; and by thus not repeating them, to assure himself of the support of the inhabitants, and win them over to himself by benefits bestowed. . . . Cruelties should be committed all at once, as in that way each separate one is less felt, and gives less offence; benefits, on the other hand, should be conferred one at a time, for in that way they will be more appreciated.

. . . he who, contrary to the will of the people, has become prince by favor of the nobles, should at once and before everything else strive to win the good will of the people, which will be easy for him, by taking them under his protection.

. . . it is much more safe to be feared than to be loved, when you have to choose between the two.

. . . there are two ways of carrying on a contest; the one by law, and the other by force. The first is practiced by men, and the other by animals; and as the first is often insufficient, it becomes necessary to resort to the second. . . . It being necessary then for a prince to know well how to employ the nature of the beasts, he should be able to assume both that of the fox and that of the lion; for while the latter cannot escape the traps laid for him, the former cannot defend himself against the wolves. A prince should be a fox, to know the traps and snares; and a lion, to be able to frighten the wolves; for those who simply hold to the nature of the lion do not understand their business.

. . . a prince should seem to be merciful, faithful, humane, religious, and upright, and should even be so in reality; but he should have his mind so trained that, when occasion requires it, he may know how to change to the opposite.

. . . For the manner in which men live is so different from the way in which they ought to live, that he who leaves the common course for that which he ought to follow will find that it leads him to ruin rather than to safety. For a man who, in all respects, will carry out only his professions of good, will be apt to be ruined among so many who are evil. A prince therefore who desires to maintain himself must learn to be not always good, but to be so or not as necessity may require. . . . For all things considered, it will be found that some things that seem like virtue will lead you to ruin if you follow them; while others, that apparently are vices, will, if followed, result in your safety and well-being.

. . . the dispositions of peoples are variable; it is easy to persuade them to anything, but difficult to confirm them in that belief. And therefore a prophet should be prepared, in case the people will not believe any more, to be able by force to compel them to that belief.

Illustration Capsule 15 (concluded)

. . . The worst that a prince may expect of a people who are unfriendly to him is that they will desert him; but the hostile nobles he has to fear, not only lest they abandon him, but also because they will turn against him. For they, being more farsighted and astute, always save themselves in advance, and seek to secure the favor of him whom they hope may be successful.

We must bear in mind . . . that there is nothing more difficult and dangerous, or more doubtful of success, than an attempt to introduce a new order of things in any state. For the innovator has for enemies all those who derived advantages from the old order of things while those who expect to be benefited by the new institutions will be but lukewarm defenders. This indifference arises in part from fear of their adversaries who were favored by the existing laws, and partly from the incredulity of men who have no faith in anything new that is not the result of well-established experience. Hence it is that, whenever the opponents of the new order of things have the opportunity to attack it, they will do it with the zeal of partisans, while the others defend it but feebly, so that it is dangerous to rely upon the latter.

. . . a prince cannot depend upon what he observes in ordinary quiet times, when the citizens have need of his authority; for then everybody runs at his bidding, everybody promises, and everybody is willing to die for him, when death is very remote. But in adverse times, when the government has need of the citizens, then but few will be found to stand by the prince. And this experience is the more dangerous as it can only be made once.

A wise prince, therefore, will steadily pursue such a course that the citizens of his state will always and under all circumstances feel the need of his authority, and will therefore always prove faithful to him.

A prince . . . should always take counsel, but only when he wants it, and not when others wish to thrust it upon him; in fact, he should rather discourage persons from tendering him advice unsolicited by him. But he should be an extensive questioner, and a patient listener to the truth respecting the things inquired about, and should even show his anger in case any one should, for some reason, not tell him the truth.

It is obvious from the above quotations that a practicing Machiavellian divorces morals from power politics; indeed, moral considerations have no place in the Machiavellian system of power politics except where an evil reputation would be a political detriment. To many people, this is shocking if not abhorrent. But even if your own moral code totally rejects a Machiavellian use of power, the issue still remains what to do in your dealings with people who are Machiavellian in their attempts to acquire and use power. How would you deal with such a person? Do you not, in fact, know people who in your own experience are Machiavellians? What would your strategy be if you were one of the intended "victims?"

CONCLUSION

To sum up, making work productive and the worker achieving is a major dimension of strategy implementation. Personal satisfaction of the worker without productive work is failure. But, then, so is productive work that undercut's individual achievement. The former blocks strategic success and latter destroys morale and a high spirit of performance. Neither is tenable for very long.

Hence, in translating strategy into action it is extremely important that management strive to develop administrative policies that on the one hand are conducive to strategic success and that on the other hand allow workers to achieve and to realize appropriate nonmaterial satisfaction from their work. This means, in part, identifying all operations that are necessary to strategic achievement, rationally organizing the sequence of these operations to reflect a smooth, economical flow of work, and integrating these operations into individual jobs in ways that will ensure high organizational performance and individual opportunities for creativity, personal development, and meaningful work.

SUGGESTED READINGS

Adizes, Ichak. "Mismanagement Styles," *California Management Review*, vol. 19, no. 2 (Winter 1976), pp. 5–20.

Drucker, Peter F. *Management: Tasks, Responsibilities, Practices* New York: Harper & Row, Publishers, 1974, chaps. 16–19 and 33–39.

Fiedler, Fred E. "The Contingency Model—New Directions for Leadership Utilization," *Journal of Contemporary Business*, vol. 3, no. 4 (Autumn 1974), pp. 65–80.

Hall, Jay. "To Achieve or Not: The Manager's Choice," *California Management Review*, vol. 18, no. 4 (Summer 1976), pp. 5–18.

Herzberg, Frederick. "One More Time: How Do You Motivate Employees," *Harvard Business Review*, vol. 51, no. 3 (May–June 1973), pp. 162–80.

Koontz, Harold. "Management Control: A Suggested Formulation of Principles," *California Management Review*, vol. 2, no. 2 (Winter 1959), pp. 50–55.

Machiavelli, N. *The Prince*. New York: Washington Square Press, 1963.

McClelland, David C., and Burnham, David H. "Power Is the Great Motivator," *Harvard Business Review*, vol. 54, no. 2 (March–April 1976), pp. 100–10.

Morse, John J., and Lorsch, Jay W. "Beyond Theory Y," *Harvard Business Review*, vol. 48, no. 3 (May–June 1970), pp. 61–68.

Robbins, Stephen P. "Reconciling Management Theory with Management Practice," *Business Horizons*, vol. 20, no. 1 (February 1977), pp. 38–47.

Roche, W. J., and MacKinnon, N. L. "Motivating People with Meaningful Work," *Harvard Business Review*, vol. 48, no. 3 (May–June 1970), pp. 97–110.

Tannenbaum, Robert, and Schmidt, Warren H. "How to Choose a Leadership Pattern," *Harvard Business Review*, vol. 51, no. 3 (May–June 1973), pp. 162–80.

Tosi, Henry L.; Rizzo, John R.; and Carroll, Stephen J. "Setting Goals in Management by Objective," *California Management Review*, vol. 12, no. 4 (Summer 1970), pp. 70–78.

Webber, Ross A. "Career Problems of Young Managers," *California Management Review*, vol. 18, no. 4 (Summer 1976), pp. 19–33.

Zalenik, Abraham. "Power and Politics in Organizational Life," *Harvard Business Review*, vol. 48, no. 3 (May–June 1970), pp. 47–60.

PART IV

Analyzing Actual Management Problems

Chapter 7
From Concepts to Cases: Practicing at Being a Manager

7

FROM CONCEPTS TO CASES: PRACTICING AT BEING A MANAGER

> *I keep six honest serving men*
> *(They taught me all I knew);*
> *Their names are What and Why and When*
> *And How and Where and Who.*
>
> Rudyard Kipling

ASSUME for a moment that you have just decided to learn to play golf—and to play it seriously, not necessarily as a professional but not casually either. Excited by the idea, you immediately go to the nearest bookstore and purchase several paperbacks written by Jack Nicklaus, Arnold Palmer, Gary Player, Johnny Miller, or other golf experts. You read them carefully and make judicious, thoughtful notes on their recommendations as to the proper things to do and not do. You re-read the books from cover to cover, until you are satisfied you can deal with each of the various situations and predicaments you might find yourself in. You grow confident you have mastered all of the pointers on how to swing the clubs and how to correct problems in your swing should they arise. Are you now ready to think of yourself as a good golfer? Of course not! We both know that no one can qualify as a good golfer without ever having a swung a club, hit a golf ball, or played untold rounds on a number of difficult courses with scores at least in the low 80s. Book knowledge about golf, by itself, does not make one a good golfer.

It is the same with management. Management, too, is an action-oriented activity. It requires *doing* to achieve proficiency. Managers succeed or fail not so much because of what they know as because of what they do. A person cannot expect to succeed as a manager and become a "professional" simply by studying excellent books on management—no matter how thoroughly the text material is mastered and no matter how many As are earned at exam time. Moreover, just like a golfer needs to practice at being a better golfer, a person who aspires to become a manager can benefit from practicing at being a manager.

PRACTICING MANAGEMENT VIA CASE ANALYSIS

In academic programs of management education, students practice at being managers via case analysis. A *case* sets forth, in a factual manner, the conditions and circumstances surrounding a particular managerial situation or series of events in an organization. It may include descriptions of the industry and its competitive conditions, the organization's background, its products and markets, the attitudes and personalities of the key people involved, production facilities, the work climate, the organizational structure, marketing methods, and the external environment, together with whatever pertinent financial, production, accounting, sales, and market information upon which management had to depend. It may concern any kind of organization—a profit-seeking business, or a public service institution.

A good case offers about as live and effective a practice situation as can be achieved short of "the real thing." It puts the readers at the scene of the action and familiarizes them with the situation as it prevailed. As such, it is well suited as a pedagogical device for students' practicing what they, as managers, would do if confronted with the same circumstances—and to do so without having to worry about inexperience and making amateurish or costly mistakes.

The essence of the student's role in the case method is to diagnose and size up the organization's situation and to think through what, if anything, should be done. The purpose is for the student, as analyst, to develop answers to a number of questions, the gist of which include: What factors have contributed to the organization's success (or failure)? What problems are evident? How would I handle them? What managerial skills are needed to deal effectively with the situation? How should they be applied? What actions need to be taken?

In some cases the managerial issue or problem is readily apparent and the thrust of the case is to develop the analysis and propose a plan of action. In others, however, the point of the case is to sift through clues, symptoms, and conflicting opinions to figure out what the root problems are, as well as to conceive workable solutions.

The subject matter of cases is as varied as the uncertainties and problems confronting managers. Cases may concern areas as diverse as (1) starting a new venture, (2) implementing management by objectives, (3) evaluating corporate strategy, (4) establishing new financial policies, (5) revamping the product line and the marketing mix, (6) shifting to a divisionalized organization structure, (7) setting up employer stock options and bonus plans, (8) entering the market for a new product, (9) determining performance standards and control procedures, (10) evaluating personnel practices, (11) improving employee motivation and morale, (12) assessing the adequacy of distribution channels, (13) revising depreciation and inventory valuation practices, or (14) replacing key management personnel. A case may encompass one or a series of problems—either related or unrelated.

Some cases consist of only a brief one to three page description that is sharply focused upon a specific event or problem. Other case descriptions are more detailed and some are very detailed, offering a wealth of information about the organization and its situation. The short cases, however, are not necessarily the easiest to analyze nor are longer cases indicative of complexity. On occasions, the situation described in the case is disguised to preserve a firm's anonymity or to avoid disclosing competitively sensitive information. This is usually accomplished by using fictitious names for the companies and people involved, changing locations or products, and altering the nature of quantitative data. Nonetheless, any modifications in a disguised case can be counted upon to preserve key relationships and be true to life in its essentials.

It should be emphasized that most cases are *not* intended to be examples of right and wrong, or good and bad management. The organizations concerned are selected neither because they are the best or the worst in their industry nor because they are average or typical. The important thing about a case is that it represents an actual situation where managers were obligated to recognize and cope with the problems as they were.

WHY USE CASES TO PRACTICE MANAGEMENT?

> A student of business with tact
> Absorbed many answers he lacked.
> But acquiring a job,
> He said with a sob,
> "How *does* one fit answer to fact?"

The foregoing limerick was offered some years ago by Charles I. Gragg in a classic article, "Because Wisdom Can't Be Told," to illustrate what might happen to students of management without the benefit of cases.[1] Gragg observed that the mere act of listening to wise statements and sound advice about management does little for anyone's management skills. He contended it was unlikely that accumulated managerial experience and wisdom could effectively be passed on by lectures and readings alone. Gragg suggested that if anything has been learned about the practice of management, it is that a storehouse of ready-made answers does not exist. Each managerial situation has unique aspects, requiring its own diagnosis and understanding as a prelude to judgment and action. In Gragg's view and in the view of other case method advocates, cases provide aspiring managers with an important and valid kind of daily practice in wrestling with management problems.

The case method is, indeed, *learning by doing*. The pedagogy of the case method of instruction is predicated on the benefits of acquiring managerial "experience" by means of simulated management exercises (cases). The

---

[1] Charles I. Gragg, "Because Wisdom Can't Be Told," in M. P. McNair, ed., *The Case Method at the Harvard Business School* (New York: McGraw-Hill Book Company, 1954), p. 11.

biggest justification for cases is that few, if any, students during the course of their college education have an opportunity to come into direct personal contact with different kinds of companies and real-life managerial situations. Cases offer a viable substitute by bringing a variety of organizations and management problems into the classroom and permitting students to assume the manager's role. Management cases therefore provide students with a kind of experiential exercise in which to test their ability to apply their textbook knowledge about management.

OBJECTIVES OF THE CASE METHOD

As the foregoing discussion suggests, the use of cases as an instructional technique embraces four chief objectives:[2]

1. Helping you to acquire the skills of putting textbook knowledge about management into practice.
2. Getting you out of the habit of being a receiver of facts, concepts, and techniques and into the habit of diagnosing problems, analyzing and evaluating alternatives, and formulating workable plans of action.
3. Training you to work out answers and solutions for yourself, as opposed to relying upon the authoritative crutch of the professor or a textbook.
4. Providing you with exposure to a range of firms and managerial situations (which might take a lifetime to experience personally), thus offering you a basis for comparison when you begin your own management career.

If you understand that these are the objectives of the case method of instruction, then you are less likely to be bothered by something that puzzles some students: "What is the answer to the case?" Being accustomed to textbook statements of fact and supposedly definitive lecture notes, students often find that discussions and analyses of managerial cases do not produce any "answer." Instead, issues in the case are discussed pro and con. Various alternatives and relevant aspects of the situation are evaluated. Usually, a good argument can be made for one decision or another, or one plan of action or another. When the class discussion concludes without a clear consensus, some students may, at first, feel cheated or dissatisfied because they are not told "what the answer is" or "what the company actually did."

However, case descriptions of managerial situations where answers are not clear-cut are quite realistic. Organizational problems whose analysis leads to a definite, single-pronged solution are likely to be so oversimplified and rare as to be trivial or devoid of practical value. In reality, several feasible courses of action may exist for dealing with the same set of circum-

---

[2] Ibid., p. 12–14; and D. R. Schoen and Philip A. Sprague, "What Is the Case Method?" in M. P. McNair, ed., *The Case Method at the Harvard Business School* (New York: McGraw-Hill Book Company, 1954), pp. 78–79.

stances. Moreover, in real-life management situations when one makes a decision or elects a particular course of action, there is no peeking at the back of a book to see if you have chosen the best thing to do. No book of provably correct answers exists; in fact, the first test of management action is *results*. If the results turn out to be "good," the decision may be presumed "right"; if not, then, it was "wrong." Hence, the important thing for the student to understand in a case course is that it is the exercise of managerial analysis and decision making that counts rather than discovering "the right answer" or finding out what actually happened.

To put it another way, *the purpose of management cases is not to learn authoritative answers to specific managerial problems but to become skilled in the process of designing a workable (and, hopefully, effective) plan of action through evaluation of the prevailing circumstances.* The aim of case analysis is not for you to try to guess what the instructor is thinking or what his solution is. Rather, it is to see whether you can support your views against the counterviews of others in the group or, failing to do so, whether you can accept the merits of the reasoning underlying the approaches of others. Therefore, *in case analysis you are expected to bear the strains of thinking actively, of making managerial assessments which may be vigorously challenged, and of defending your analysis and plan of action.* Only in this way can case analysis provide you with any meaningful practice at being a manager.

In sum, the purpose of the case method is to initiate you and encourage you in the ways of thinking "managerially" and exercising responsible judgment. At the same time, you should use the cases that follow to test the rigor and effectiveness of your own theories about the practice of management and to begin to evolve your own management philosophy and management style.

PREPARING A CASE FOR CLASS DISCUSSION

Given that cases rest on the principle of learning by doing, their effectiveness hinges upon *you* making *your* analysis and reaching *your* own decisions and then in the classroom participating in a collective analysis and decision-making process. If this is your first experience with the case method, you may have to reorient your study habits. Since a case assignment emphasizes student participation, it is obvious that the effectiveness of the class discussion depends upon each student having studied the case *beforehand.* Consequently, unlike lecture courses where there is no imperative of specific preparation before each class and where assigned readings and reviews of lecture notes may be done at irregular intervals, *a case assignment requires conscientious preparation before class.* You cannot, after all, expect to get much out of practicing managing in a situation with which you are totally unfamiliar.

Unfortunately, though, there is no nice, proven procedure for studying cases which can be recommended to you. There is no formula, no fail-safe step-by-step technique that we can recommend. Each case is a new situation and you will need to adjust accordingly. Moreover, you will, after a time, discover an approach which suits you best. Thus, the following suggestions are offered simply to get you started.

A first step in understanding how the case method of teaching/learning works is to recognize that it represents a radical departure from the lecture/discussion/problem classroom technique. To begin with, members of the class do most of the talking. The instructor's role is to solicit student participation and guide the discussion. Expect the instructor to begin the class with such questions as: What is the organization's strategy? What do you consider to be the real problem confronting the company? What factors have contributed most to the organization's successes? Its failures? Which manager is doing a good job? Are the organization's goals and strategies compatible with its skills and resources? Typically, members of the class will evaluate and test their opinions as much in discussions with each other as with the instructor. But irrespective of whether the discussion emphasis is instructor-student or student-student, members of the class carry the burden for analyzing the situation and for being prepared to present and defend their analysis in the classroom. Thus, you should expect an absence of professorial "here's how to do it," "right answers," and "hard knowledge for your notebook"; instead, be prepared for a discussion involving what do *you* think, what would *you* do, and what do *you* feel is important.[3]

Begin your analysis by reading the case once for familiarity. An initial reading should give you the general flavor of the situation and make possible preliminary identification of issues. On the second reading, attempt to gain full command of the facts. You may wish to make notes about apparent organizational goals, objectives, strategies, policies, symptoms of problems, problems, root causes of problems, unresolved issues, and roles of key individuals. Be alert for issues or problems which are not necessarily made explicit but which nevertheless are lurking beneath the surface. Read between the lines and do not hesitate to do some detective work on your own. For instance, the apparent issue in the case might be whether a product has ample market potential at the current selling price while the root problem is that the method being used to compensate salespeople fails to generate adequate incentive for achieving greater unit volume. Needless to say, a sharp, clear-cut "size-up" of the company and its problems is an essential function of management; one cannot devise sensible solutions to an organization's troubles until the troubles have first been correctly identified. In short, before a company's problems can be solved, they must be understood; they must be analyzed; they must be evaluated; and they must be placed in proper perspective.

To help gain this perspective, put yourself in the position of some manager

---

[3] Schoen and Sprague, "What Is the Case Method?" p. 80.

or managerial group portrayed in the case and get attuned to the organizational environment within which the manager or management group must make decisions. Try to get a good feel for the "personality" of the company, the management, and the organizational climate. This is essential if you are to come up with solutions which will be both workable and acceptable in light of the prevailing environmental constraints and realities. Do not be dismayed if you find it impractical to isolate the problems and issues in the case into distinct categories which can be treated separately. Very few and significant real-world management problems can be neatly sorted into mutually exclusive areas of concern.

Most important of all, you must arrive at a solid evaluation of the company, based on the information in the case. Developing an ability to evaluate companies and size up their situations is *the key* to case analysis. How do you evaluate a company? There is no pat answer. But there are some guidelines—as specifically outlined in Table 7–1. In general, the financial position of the firm must be scrutinized closely, the firm's external opportunities and internal resources compared and evaluated, and an assessment of its future potential made. Decide how urgent the organization's difficulties are and weigh the probable impacts upon performance and capability. Pinpoint the key factors which are crucial to success or failure. Uppermost in your efforts, strive for defensible arguments and positions. Do not rely upon just your opinion; support any judgments or conclusions with evidence! Use the available data to make whatever relevant accounting, financial, marketing, or operations analysis calculations are necessary to support your assessment of the situation.

TABLE 7–1
Checklist for Evaluating a Company's Present Position and Future Potential

A. Product Lines and Competitive Position
   1. How do the firm's products (or services) stack up against those of rival firms? Has the firm been successful in differentiating its products from those of its rivals and in carving out a viable market niche for itself? Does the firm enjoy a position of market advantage and, if so, what is the basis for this advantage?
   2. How do customers and potential customers regard the company's products? What market shares does it have and how firmly does it hold them? Have market shares been increasing or decreasing? Is the company dependent on a few large customers for the bulk of its sales?
   3. What are the firm's profit margins? Have these been increasing or decreasing? Are the firm's margins above or below those of the industry? Is the firm in a position to be competitive on price?
   4. Where do the company's chief products stand in the life cycle? Is the industry young or mature? Are the markets for the firm's products expanding or contracting, and at what rates? How is the company's business affected by upswings and downswings in the economy? Is the firm's target market big enough to generate the revenues needed to be profitable?

TABLE 7-1 *(continued)*

5. Is the company confronted with increasing competition? What is the nature of this competition and how vulnerable is the firm's strategy to new competition? Is entry into the industry easy or hard? Has the firm demonstrated an ability to compete effectively?

6. Is the company a leader in its market area? Is the company being forced into head-to-head competition with proven leaders? If so, does the company have the competitive artillery it needs or is it trying to go to war with a popgun? Is the firm relying on a "me too" or "copycat" strategy?

7. What are the strengths and weaknesses of the company's marketing strategy? How well do its marketing efforts compare with those of rival firms? Is there a capability for exploiting new products and developing new markets? Does it have the necessary distribution channels or the ability to develop them?

8. If the firm is diversified, then are its product lines compatible? Is there evidence of strategic fit? Is the diversification plan well thought-out or has the company been seduced by the illusions of glamour products and glamour technology?

What is your summary evaluation of the firm's product line and competition position? What are its particular strengths and weaknesses and how important are these to the firm's ultimate success or failure?

B. Profitability and Financial Condition

1. What is the trend in the firm's profitability as concerns total profits, earnings per share, return on sales, return on assets, return on total capital investment, and return on equity investment? How does the firm's profitability compare with that of other firms in the industry? What is the "quality" of the firm's earnings?

2. How is the company viewed by investors? What is the trend in the company's stock price, its price-earnings ratio, dividend payout, and dividend yield on common stock?

3. Is the firm liquid and able to meet its maturing obligations? What trends are evident in the firm's current ratio and quick (or acid test) ratio? (See Table 7-2 for a summary of how these ratios are calculated and what they indicate.)

4. To what extent is the firm leveraged? What are the trends in the firm's debt ratios, its times-interest-earned coverages, and its fixed charge coverages? (See Table 7-2 for a summary of how these ratios are calculated and what they indicate.) Has the firm exhausted its debt capacity? Does it have the ability to raise new equity capital?

5. How effectively is the firm employing the resources at its command? What problems are revealed by such ratios as inventory turnover, accounts receivable turnover, fixed asset turnover, total asset turnover, and average collection period? (See Table 7-2 for a summary of how these ratios are calculated and what they indicate.)

6. Is cash flow adequate to supply the company with working capital? Is the company (or some of its businesses) a "cash hog" or a "cash cow?" (A "cash hog" business uses more cash than it generates, whereas a "cash cow" business generates more cash than is required to finance working capital and expansion needs.)

7. Is the company well-managed from a financial standpoint? Does it have adequate financial controls and careful cash planning? Have capital investment decisions been based on thorough calculations?

TABLE 7–1 (continued)

What strengths and weaknesses are evident in the firm's overall financial condition? How do these relate to the company's present competitive situation and strategy?

C. Operations and Internal Organization
1. How well do the firm's resources and capability match its strategy in the marketplace? Does the firm have the talent, the know-how, and the financial strength to succeed in executing its strategy? Does the company have the resources to make a commitment to see its strategy through to a successful implementation?
2. To what extent is the firm's manufacturing strategy, marketing strategy, R&D strategy, and financial strategy integrated, coordinated, and compatible? Are the organization's goals, objectives, and strategies suited to its skills and resources?
3. Is the firm threatened by new technological developments? Does it have enough R&D capability? What is its track record in innovation?
4. Is the firm large enough to take advantage of economies of scale? Is it efficient in its manufacturing and production activities? Are its equipment and facilities modern? Have capital expenditures been either inadequate or excessive with regard to ensuring future operating efficiency?
5. How vulnerable is the company to adverse shifts in raw material supply and labor supply conditions? Is there a major problem with unions or a history of poor union-management relations?
6. Is the firm developing the kinds of information it needs to solve its problems? Do operating-level managers have solid, pertinent, and timely data on the status of current operations? Is too much reliance placed on unsupported opinion or management hunch or seat-of-the-pants guestimates?
7. Does the firm have adequate knowledge about costs? Do its costs appear to be in line with other comparable firms? Is it generating the right kind of cost information?
8. How strong is the company's financial management? Are its inventory controls adequate? Are its purchasing procedures adequate?
9. Is the organization adequately staffed? Do key personnel appear knowledgeable and capable in performing their jobs?
10. Are the firm's pay scales and overall reward structure adequate? Is motivation a problem? Is there ample opportunity to promote good people? Are performance appraisals made on a regular basis? Does the company appear to treat employees fairly?

What distinctive competence(s) has the firm developed? How important has this been in accounting for the firm's success (or failure)? What distinctive competence(s) is it missing?

D. Management Capability
1. Is the firm well-organized? Is the organization structure supportive of strategy?
2. Does the firm's present management have a good track record? How well has it handled past problems and crises? Have previously set goals and objectives been achieved on schedule?
3. How capable are each of the firm's key management personnel? Do they have the necessary qualifications and experience? Do they appear to know their jobs well and are the areas for which they are responsible functioning smoothly?

TABLE 7-1 (concluded)

4. Are policies and control procedures in the various departments adequate? Is the organization efficient? Does it take too long for key decisions to be made?
5. Is the organization overly dependent on one person? Is there enough management depth for the type of business being run?
6. How good a job has top management done in selecting, training, and developing lower level management personnel? Have the right kinds of people been selected to fill new or vacant positions?
7. Is top management's leadership style adequate for the firm's situation and needs? Do the firm's managers know how to manage people? Do the managers have the respect of the people they supervise?
8. Does the extent to which the firm has diversified present undue problems of coordination and control to the present management?
9. Has management given evidence of an ability to adapt the firm and the organization structure to meet changing needs, priorities, and competitive conditions?
10. Does management have the respect of the financial community?

What is your summary evaluation of the company's management? What are its strengths and weaknesses and how do these weigh upon the firm's performance?

E. Prospects for the Future
1. Has the firm developed (or is it in a position to acquire) the technological proficiency it needs to remain competitive over the long run?
2. If the firm's competitive position is weak or is slipping, is it in a position to "play catch-up"? What are the chances that it can make up lost ground?
3. What is the future market potential for the firm's chief products? Will it need to diversify in the near future and, if so, does it have the financial and organizational strength to make new acquisitions or to build new businesses from the ground up?
4. What are the basic "facts of life" about product-market-technology and competitive trends in the firm's industry over the next decade? Will the company need to make fundamental revisions in its strategy in the near future?
5. What do the trends in the firm's profitability and overall financial condition suggest regarding the firm's prospects for growth and success? Does the firm have adequate long-range financial plans?
6. How adequate is management for coping with the challenges of the future?
7. Which factors have contributed most to the organization's successes? Its failures? How will these factors affect the firm in the future?
8. In view of the firm's overall strengths and weaknesses, and the challenges it faces, what are the odds that it will survive? At what level of success? Will it have to succeed by diversifying out of its present lines of business?

Source: Adapted with major revisions and additions by the authors from Robert B. Buchele, "How to Evaluate a Firm," *California Management Review*, vol. 5, no. 1 (Fall 1962), pp. 5–17.

Lastly, be wary of accepting *everything* stated in the case as "fact." Sometimes, information or data in the case will be conflicting and/or opinions contradictory. For example, one manager may say that the firm's organizational structure is functioning quite effectively, whereas another may say it is not. It is your task to decide whose view is more valid and why. Forcing you to make judgments about the validity of the data and information presented in the case is both deliberate and realistic. It is deliberate because one function of the case method is to help you develop your powers of judgment and inference. It is realistic because a great many managerial situations entail conflicting points of view.

Once you have thoroughly diagnosed the company's situation and weighed the pros and cons of various alternative courses of action, the final step of case analysis is to decide what you think the company needs to do to improve its performance and to set forth a workable plan of action. This is a crucial part of the process of case analysis since diagnosis divorced from corrective action is sterile; but bear in mind that making a decision and jumping to a conclusion are not the same thing. One is well-advised to avoid the infamous decision-making pattern: "Don't confuse me with the facts. I've made up my mind."

On a few occasions, some desirable information may not be included in the case. In such instances you may be inclined to complain about the lack of "facts." A manager, however, uses more than facts upon which to base his or her decisions. Moreover, it may be possible to make a number of inferences from the facts you do have. So, be wary of rushing to include as part of your recommendations "the need to get more information." From time to time, of course, a search for additional facts or information may be entirely appropriate but you must also recognize that the organization's managers may not have had any more information available than that presented in the case. Before recommending that a final decision be postponed until additional facts are uncovered, be sure that you think it will be worth while to get them and that the organization could afford to wait. In general, though, try to assess situations based upon the evidence you have at hand.

Again, remember that rarely is there a "right" decision or just one "optimal" plan of action or an "approved" solution. Your goal should be to find a practical and workable course of action which is based upon a serious analysis of the situation and which appears to you to be right in view of your assessment and weighing of the facts. Admittedly, someone else may evaluate the same facts in another way and thus have a different "right" solution, but since several good plans of action can normally be conceived, you should not be afraid to pursue your own intuition and judgment. One can make a strong argument for the view that the "right" answer for a manager is the one which he or she can propose, explain, defend, and make work when it is implemented.

THE CLASSROOM EXPERIENCE

In experiencing class discussions of management cases, you will, in all probability, notice very quickly that you will not have thought of everything in the case that your fellow students think of. While you will see things others did not, they will see things you did not. Do not be dismayed or alarmed by this. It is normal. As the old adage goes, "two heads are better than one." So, it is to be expected that the class as a whole will do a more penetrating and searching job of case analysis than will any one person working alone. This is the power of group effort and one of its virtues is that it will give you more insight into how others view situations and how to cope with differences of opinion. Second, you will see better why sometimes it is not managerially wise to assume a rigid position on an issue until a full range of views and information has been assembled. And, undoubtedly, some-where along the way you will begin to recognize that neither the instructor nor other students in the class have all the answers, and even if they think they do, you are still free to present and hold to your own views. The truth in the saying that "there's more than one way to skin a cat" will be seen to apply nicely to most management situations.

For class discussion of cases to be useful and stimulating you need to keep the following points in mind:

1. The case method enlists a maximum of individual participation in class discussion. It is not enough to be present as a silent observer; if every student took this approach, then there would be no discussion. (Thus, do not be surprised if a portion of your grade is based on your participa-tion in case discussions.)

2. Although you should do your own independent work and independent thinking, don't hesitate to discuss the case with other students. Man-agers often discuss their problems with other key people.

3. During case discussions, expect and tolerate challenges to the views expressed. Be willing to submit your conclusions for scrutiny and re-buttal. State your views without fear of disapproval and overcome the hesitation of speaking out.

4. In orally presenting and defending your ideas, keep in mind the im-portance of good communication. It is up to you to be convincing and persuasive in expressing your ideas.

5. Expect the instructor to assume the role of discussion leader; only when the discussion content is technique-oriented is it likely that your instructor will maintain direct control over the discussion.

6. Although discussion of a case is a group process, this does not imply conformity to group opinion. Learning respect for the views and ap-proaches of others is an integral part of case analysis exercises. But be willing to "swim against the tide" of majority opinion. In the practice of management, there is always room for originality, unorthodoxy, and unique personality.

7. In participating in the discussion, make a conscious effort to *contribute* rather than just talk. There *is* a difference.

8. Effective case discussions can occur only if participants have "the facts" of the case well in hand; rehashing information in the case

should be held to a minimum except as it provides documentation, comparisons, or support for your position.

9. During the discussion, new insights provided by the group's efforts are likely to emerge, thereby opening up "the facts" to reinterpretation and perhaps causing one's analysis of the situation to be modified.

10. Although there will always be situations in which more technical information is imperative to the making of an intelligent decision, try not to shirk from making decisions in the face of incomplete information. Wrestling with imperfect information is a normal condition managers face and is something you should get used to.

11. Ordinarily, there are several acceptable solutions which can be proposed for dealing with the issues in a case. Definitive, provably correct answers rarely, if ever, exist in managerial situations.

12. In the final analysis, learning about management via the case method is up to you; just as with other learning techniques, the rewards are dependent upon the effort you put in to it.

PREPARING A WRITTEN CASE ANALYSIS

From time to time, your instructor may ask you to prepare a written analysis of the case assignment. Preparing a written case analysis is much like preparing a case for class discussion, except that your analysis, when completed, must be reduced to writing. Just as there was no set pattern or formula for preparing a case for oral discussion, there is no ironclad procedure for preparing a written case analysis. With a bit of experience you will arrive at your own preferred method of attack in writing up a case and you will learn to adjust your approach to the unique aspects that each case presents.

Your instructor may assign you a specific topic around which to prepare your written report. Common assignments include (1) identify and evaluate company X's corporate strategy; (2) in view of the opportunities and risks you see in the industry, what is your assessment of the company's position and plan? (3) how would you size up the strategic situation of company Y? (4) what recommendations would you make to company Z's top management? and (5) what specific functions and activities does the company have to perform especially well in order for its strategy to succeed?

Alternatively, you may be asked to do a "comprehensive written case analysis." It is typical for a comprehensive written case analysis to emphasize:

1. Identification of key issues and problems confronting management,
2. A thorough analysis and evaluation of these issues and problems,
3. An assessment of action alternatives, and
4. Presentation of a plan of action.

You may wish to consider the following pointers in preparing a comprehensive written case analysis.[4]

Issues and Problems. As the checklist in Table 7–1 suggests, there are five vital areas in an organization which form an integral part of any comprehensive analysis: (1) its product line and basic competitive position, (2) its profitability and financial conditions, (3) its operations—production, personnel, organization structure, controls, and so on, (4) the caliber of top management, including not only management's past record but also its adequacy to cope with what lies ahead, and (5) the company's prospects for the future. A comprehensive analysis must survey all five of these areas, with a view toward identifying the key issues and problems which confront the organization. It is essential that your paper reflect a sharply focused diagnosis of these key issues and problems and, further, that you demonstrate good business judgment in sizing up the company's present situation. Make sure you understand and can identify the firm's corporate strategy. You would probably be well advised to begin your paper by sizing up the company's situation, its strategy, and the significant problems and issues which confront management. State the problems/issues as clearly and precisely as you can. Unless it is necessary to do so for emphasis, avoid recounting facts and history about the company (assume your professor has read the case and is familiar with the organization!). Consider when and why each problem arose, who is involved, and how critical the situation is. Indicate, where appropriate, the interrelationships between problems/issues. Be careful to distinguish between symptoms and root causes.

Analysis and Evaluation. Very likely you will find this section the hardest part of the report. Analysis is hard work! Study the tables, exhibits, and financial statements carefully. Check out the firm's financial ratios, its profit margins and rates of return, its capital structure and decide how strong the firm is financially. (Table 7–2 contains a summary of the various financial ratios and how they are calculated.) Similarly, look at marketing, production, managerial competences, and so on, and evaluate the organization's strengths and weaknesses in each of the major functional areas. Identify the factors underlying the organization's successes and failures. Decide whether it has a distinctive competence and, if so, whether it is capitalizing upon it. Is the firm's strategy working? Why or why not? Assess opportunities and threats, both internally and externally. Determine whether goals, objectives, strategies, and policies are realistic in light of prevailing constraints. Look at how the organization is hedging its risks. Evaluate the firm's competitive position. Establish a hard-nosed perspective view of each problem-issue and indicate problem linkages and interrelationships. Formulate a judgment as to the organization's future prospects. (Review the checklist in Table 7–1 to see if you have overlooked something.)

---

[4] For some additional ideas and viewpoints, you may wish to consult Thomas J. Raymond, "Written Analysis of Cases," in M. P. McNair, ed., *The Case Method at the Harvard Business School* (New York: McGraw-Hill Book Company, 1954), pp. 139–63. In Raymond's article is an actual case, a sample analysis of the case, and a sample of a student's written report on the case.

TABLE 7–2
A Summary of Key Financial Ratios, How They Are Calculated, and What They Show

Ratio	How Calculated	What It Shows
Profitability ratios:		
1. Gross profit margin	$\dfrac{\text{Sales} - \text{Cost of goods sold}}{\text{Sales}}$	An indication of the total margin available to cover operating expenses and yield a profit.
2. Operating profit margin	$\dfrac{\text{Profits before taxes and before interest}}{\text{Sales}}$	An indication of the firm's profitability from current operations without regard to the interest charges accruing from the capital structure.
3. Net profit margin (or return on sales)	$\dfrac{\text{Profits after taxes}}{\text{Sales}}$	Shows aftertax profits per dollar of sales. Subpar-profit margins indicate that the firm's sales prices are relatively low or that its costs are relatively high or both.
4. Return on total assets	$\dfrac{\text{Profits after taxes}}{\text{Total assets}}$ or $\dfrac{\text{Profits after taxes} + \text{interest}}{\text{Total assets}}$	A measure of the return on total investment in the enterprise. It is sometimes desirable to add interest to aftertax profits to form the numerator of the ratio since total assets are financed by creditors as well as by stockholders; hence it is accurate to measure the productivity of assets by the returns provided to both classes of investors.
5. Return on stockholders' equity (or return on net worth)	$\dfrac{\text{Profits after taxes}}{\text{Total stockholders' equity}}$	A measure of the rate of return on stockholders' investment in the enterprise.
6. Return on common equity	$\dfrac{\text{Profits after taxes} - \text{preferred stock dividends}}{\text{Total stockholders' equity} - \text{par value of preferred stock}}$	A measure of the rate of return on the investment which the owners of common stock have made in the enterprise.
7. Earnings per share	$\dfrac{\text{Profits after taxes} - \text{preferred stock dividends}}{\text{Number of shares of common stock outstanding}}$	Shows the earnings available to the owners of common stock.

TABLE 7–2 (continued)

Ratio	How Calculated	What It Shows
Liquidity ratios:		
1. Current ratio	$\dfrac{\text{Current assets}}{\text{Current liabilities}}$	Indicates the extent to which the claims of short-term creditors are covered by assets that are expected to be converted to cash in a period roughly corresponding to the maturity of the liabilities.
2. Quick ratio (or acid test ratio)	$\dfrac{\text{Current assets} - \text{inventory}}{\text{Current liabilities}}$	A measure of the firm's ability to pay off short-term obligations without relying upon the sale of its inventories.
3. Inventory to net working capital	$\dfrac{\text{Inventory}}{\text{Current assets} - \text{current liabilities}}$	A measure of the extent to which the firm's working capital is tied up in inventory.
Leverage ratios:		
1. Debt to assets ratio	$\dfrac{\text{Total debt}}{\text{Total assets}}$	Measures the extent to which borrowed funds have been used to finance the firm's operations.
2. Debt to equity ratio	$\dfrac{\text{Total debt}}{\text{Total stockholders' equity}}$	Provides another measure of the funds provided by creditors versus the funds provided by owners.
3. Long-term debt to equity ratio	$\dfrac{\text{Long-term debt}}{\text{Total stockholders' equity}}$	A widely used measure of the balance between debt and equity in the firm's overall capital structure.
4. Times-interest-earned (or coverage ratios)	$\dfrac{\text{Profits before interest and taxes}}{\text{Total interest charges}}$	Measures the extent to which earnings can decline without the firm becoming unable to meet its annual interest costs.
5. Fixed charge coverage	$\dfrac{\text{Profits before taxes and interest} + \text{lease obligations}}{\text{Total interest charges} + \text{lease obligations}}$	A more inclusive indication of the firm's ability to meet all of its fixed charge obligations.
Activity ratios:		
1. Inventory turnover	$\dfrac{\text{Sales}}{\text{Inventory}}$	When compared to industry averages, it provides an indication of whether a company has excessive inventory or perhaps inadequate inventory.

TABLE 7–2 *(concluded)*

Ratio	How Calculated	What It Shows
2. Fixed assets turn-over	$\dfrac{\text{Sales}}{\text{Fixed assets}}$	A measure of the sales productivity and utilization of plant and equipment.
3. Total assets turn-over	$\dfrac{\text{Sales}}{\text{Total assets}}$	A measure of the utilization of all the firm's assets; a ratio below the industry average indicates the company is not generating a sufficient volume of business given the size of its asset investment.
4. Accounts receivable turnover	$\dfrac{\text{Annual credit sales}}{\text{Accounts receivable}}$	A measure of the average length of time it takes the firm to collect the sales made on credit.
5. Average collection period	$\dfrac{\text{Accounts receivable}}{\text{Total sales} \div 365}$ or $\dfrac{\text{Accounts receivable}}{\text{Average daily sales}}$	Indicates the average length of time the firm must wait after making a sale before it receives payment.

Other ratios:

Ratio	How Calculated	What It Shows
1. Dividend yield on common stock	$\dfrac{\text{Annual dividends per share}}{\text{Current market price per share}}$	A measure of the return to owners received in the form of dividends.
2. Price-earnings ratio	$\dfrac{\text{Current market price per share}}{\text{Aftertax earnings per share}}$	Faster growing or less risky firms *tend* to have higher price-earnings ratios than slower growing or more risky firms.
3. Dividend payout ratio	$\dfrac{\text{Annual dividends per share}}{\text{Aftertax earnings per share}}$	Indicates the percentage of profits paid out as dividends.
4. Cash flow per share	$\dfrac{\text{Aftertax profits} + \text{depreciation}}{\text{Number of common shares outstanding}}$	A measure of the discretionary funds over and above expenses available for use by the firm.

Note: Industry-average ratios against which a particular company's ratios may be judged are available in *Modern Industry* and *Dun's Reviews* published by Dun & Bradstreet (14 ratios for 125 lines of business activity), Robert Morris Associates' *Annual Statement Studies* (11 ratios for 156 lines of business), and the FTC-SEC's *Quarterly Financial Report* for manufacturing corporations.

In writing up your analysis and evaluation, bear in mind that:

1. You are obliged to offer supporting evidence for your views and judgments. Do not rely upon unsupported opinions, overgeneralizations, and platitudes as a substitute for tight, logical argument backed up with facts and figures.
2. You should indicate the key factors which are crucial to the organization's success or failure; i.e., what must it concentrate on and be sure to do right in order to be a high performer. Is manufacturing efficiency the key to profitability? Or is it high sales volume? Or convincing customers that the product is of high "quality?" Or is it rendering good service? Or what?
3. While some information in the case is established fact, other evidence may be in the form of opinions, judgments, and beliefs, some of which may be contradictory or inaccurate. You are thus obliged to assess the validity of such information. Do not hesitate to question what seems to be "fact."
4. You should demonstrate that your interpretation of the evidence is both reasonable and objective. Be wary of preparing an analysis which omits all arguments not favorable to your position. Likewise, try not to exaggerate, prejudge, or overdramatize. Endeavor to inject balance into your analysis. Strive to display good business judgment.

Assessing Alternatives.   In dealing with this facet of the written report, you may wish to start with a brief account of the areas or categories where action needs to be initiated. Then, you will need to consider the various ways of undertaking each of the *action priorities.* Be sure to keep the focus on what can and should be done to solve the organization's problems. Decide what is feasible in light of the constraints involved. Weigh the risks that attach to each alternative, as well as the pros and cons. If there are important compromises or trade-offs, identify them.

The Plan of Action.   The final section of the written case analysis should consist of a plan of action (or alternative plans, if contingencies may arise). The action plan should follow directly from the analysis. If it comes as a surprise, because it is logically inconsistent with or not related to the analysis, the effect of the discussion is weakened. Obviously, any recommendations for action should offer a reasonable prospect of success. *Be sure that the company is financially able to carry out what you recommend;* also your recommendations need to be workable in terms of acceptance by the persons involved, the organization's competence to implement them, and prevailing market and environmental constraints. Unless you feel justifiably compelled to do so, do not qualify, hedge, or weasel on the actions that you believe should be taken. Furthermore, state your recommendations in sufficient detail to be meaningful. Avoid using panaceas or platitudes such as "the organization should implement modern planning techniques" or "the company should be more aggressive in marketing its product." State *specifically* what should be done and *make sure your recommendations are operational.* For instance, do not stop with saying "the firm should improve its market position," continue on with exactly *how* you think this should be done. And, finally, you should indicate how your plan should be implemented. Here, you may wish to give some attention to leadership styles, psychological approaches, motivational aspects, and incentives that may be helpful. You might also stipulate a timetable for initiating actions, indicate priorities, and suggest who should be responsible for doing what. For example, "Have the manager take the following steps: (1) _____ , (2) _____ , (3) _____ , (4) _____ .

In preparing your plan of action, remember that there is a great deal of difference between being responsible, on the one hand, for a decision which may be costly if it proves in error and, on the other hand, expressing a casual opinion as to some of the courses of action which might be taken when you do not have to bear the responsibility for any of the consequences. A good rule to follow in designing your plan of action is to *avoid recommending anything you would not yourself be willing to do if you were in management's shoes.* The importance of learning to develop good judgment in a managerial situation is indicated by the fact that while the same information and operating data may be available to every manager or executive in an organization, it *does* make a difference to the organization which person makes the final decision.[5]

It should go without saying that your report should be organized and written in a manner that communicates well and is persuasive. Great ideas amount to little unless others can be convinced of their merit—this takes effective communication.

KEEPING TABS ON YOUR PERFORMANCE

Every instructor has his or her own procedure for evaluating student performance so, with one exception, it is not possible to generalize about grades and the grading of case analyses. The one exception is that grades on case analyses (written or oral) almost never depend entirely on how you propose to solve the organization's difficulties. The important elements in evaluating student performance on case analyses consist of *(a)* the care with which facts and background knowledge are used, *(b)* demonstration of the ability to state problems and issues clearly, *(c)* the use of appropriate analytical techniques, *(d)* evidence of sound logic and argument, *(e)* consistency between analysis and recommendations, and *(f)* the ability to formulate reasonable and feasible recommendations for action. Remember, a hard-hitting, incisive, logical approach will almost always triumph over seat-of-the-pants opinions, emotional rhetoric, and platitudes.

One final point. You may find it hard to keep a finger on the pulse of how

---

[5] Gragg, "Because Wisdom Can't Be Told," p. 10.

much you are learning from cases. This contrasts with lecture/problem/ discussion courses where experience has given you an intuitive feeling for how well you are acquiring substantive knowledge of theoretical concepts, problem-solving techniques, and institutional practices. But in a case course, where analytical ability and the skill of making sound judgments are less apparent, you may lack a sense of solid accomplishment, at least at first. Admittedly, additions to one's managerial skills and powers of diagnosis are not as noticeable or as tangible as a loose-leaf binder full of lecture notes. But this does not mean they are any less real or that you are making any less progress in learning how to be a manager.

To begin with, in the process of hunting around for solutions, very likely you will find that a considerable knowledge about types of organizations, the nature of various businesses, the range of management practices, and so on has rubbed off. Moreover, you will be gaining a better grasp of how to evaluate risks and cope with the uncertainties of enterprise. Likewise, you will develop a sharper appreciation of both the common and the unique aspects of managerial encounters. You will become more comfortable with the processes whereby goals are set, strategies are initiated, organizations are designed, methods of control are implemented and evaluated, performance is reappraised, and improvements are sought. Such processes are the essence of management and learning more about them through the case method is no less an achievement just because there is a dearth of finely calibrated measuring devices and authoritative crutches on which to lean.

PART V

Cases

A. The General Manager: Tasks, Functions, Responsibilities

1. Hewlett-Packard Company—A Time for Strategy Reappraisal?*

IN 1972 AND 1973, Hewlett-Packard Company (H-P), a leading producer of electronic instruments and a major contender in minicomputers and calculators, found that its growth strategy was creating some significant problems. Although the company's objectives for expanding sales and market share were being met more or less successfully, Hewlett-Packard found itself (1) lowering prices to increase the competitiveness of its product lines, (2) reducing the percentage of sales revenue devoted to research and development so as to bolster profitability, and (3) easing credit and payment policies in an effort to attract more new customers. Despite substantial increases in sales and profits in both 1972 and 1973 (see Exhibit 1), the company was confronted with what it considered to be large increases in inventory, products put into production before they were fully developed, prices set too low to generate sufficient returns, and increased short-term borrowings. For the first time in company history, management considered converting some of its short-term debt into long-term debt. Chairman David Packard and President William R. Hewlett, who together had founded the company in 1939, decided improvements were needed in strategy, structure, and tactics.

THE INDUSTRY

Accelerating rates of technical change, increased competition, and economic uncertainty made long-range planning and strategic decision making increasingly complex for companies in the high-technology electronics industry. The world economic boom of 1972–73, followed almost immediately by depressed economic conditions, created operating pressures that demanded action. Recession conditions caused large financial dislocations for many companies accustomed to rapid growth. Some companies decided to reduce expenses by cutting product development. Others increased their research spending in order to be ready for the price cuts and new products that they expected to characterize the next upturn. Although the electronics

---

* Prepared by Professors Roger M. Atherton and Dennis M. Crites, the University of Oklahoma.

EXHIBIT 1
Five-Year Consolidated Earnings Summary (in thousands)

	1974	1973	1972	1971	1970
Net sales	$884,053	$661,290	$479,077	$375,088	$363,593
Other income, net	8,732	12,108	3,570	4,202	2,802
Total revenues	$892,785	$673,398	$482,647	$379,290	$366,395
Costs and expenses:					
Cost of goods sold	$422,104	$312,972	$223,690	$184,507	$173,731
Research and development	70,685	57,798	44,163	39,426	37,212
Marketing, administrative and general	247,232	202,999	138,716	107,822	105,587
Interest	8,502	5,057	1,764	1,239	2,212
Total costs and expenses	$748,523	$578,826	$408,333	$332,994	$318,742
Earnings before taxes on income	$144,262	$ 94,572	$ 74,314	$ 46,296	$ 47,653
Taxes on income	60,240	43,823	37,064	22,415	24,146
Earnings before accounting change	$ 84,022	$ 50,749	$ 37,250	$ 23,881	$ 23,507
Accounting change*	—	—	1,211	—	—
Net earnings	$ 84,022	$ 50,749	$ 38,461	$ 23,881	$ 23,507
Per share†					
Earnings before accounting change	$ 3.08	$ 1.89	$ 1.40	$ 0.92	$ 0.92
Accounting change	—	—	0.05	—	—
Net earnings	$ 3.08	$ 1.89	$ 1.45	$ 0.92	$ 0.92
Common shares outstanding at year end	27,298	26,816	26,450	26,038	25,649

* Cumulative effect on prior years (to October 31, 1971) of change in accounting method used for computing miscellaneous material and labor in inventories. The effect on net earnings and per share amounts in each year prior to 1972, assuming the change in accounting method had been applied retroactively, is insignificant.

† Based on the shares of common stock outstanding at the end of each year, giving retroactive effect for the 2 for 1 stock split in February, 1970.

Source: 1974 *Annual Report*.

industry was not capital intensive, a major determinant of growth was the ability to develop new products, particularly those which could not be quickly imitated. This forced the managements of high-technology companies to make some tough decisions about the probable impact of price changes on sales and profits, and the probable effects of research expenditures on growth and short-run and long-run profitability.

As *Business Week* reported, the management of technology—not only in electronics but also in pharmaceuticals, chemicals, and other specialties—is no longer an art but a discipline that is becoming better understood by a growing number of companies.[1] The narrow product specialization that once separated an instrument maker from a computer company or a component supplier has largely disappeared, as semiconductor devices have taken on new complexity and as instruments have been combined with calculators and computers to form new and extensive arrays of functionally oriented systems. Semiconductor companies have integrated forward into end products, and instrument makers have started making their own data-processing equipment. As a result, a large number of potential competitors exists for almost every conceivable product-market segment and niche of high-technology electronics.

An increasingly common tactic used by electronics companies to achieve market dominance is to price new products in relation to manufacturing costs they anticipate will be attained when the product has matured and when economies of scale have been achieved. This puts a premium on obtaining market share early in order to recover development and initial production costs, and to quickly attain sufficient volume to justify the predetermined price. As a result, many of the companies in the electronics industry vigorously pursue strategies designed to achieve both technical and market dominance. This puts a heavy emphasis on innovation and creativity, sensitivity to market and customer needs, skills in finding useful applications of developing technology, and marketing and distribution capabilities to exploit new opportunities and to obtain a dominant market share rapidly.

A representative sample of companies competing in this industry, together with their sales growth, profit margins, and earnings on net worth, are shown in Exhibit 2.

HEWLETT-PACKARD: ITS BACKGROUND AND HISTORY

Innovative products have been the cornerstone of Hewlett-Packard's growth since 1939, when Bill Hewlett engineered a new type of audio oscillator and, with David Packard, created the company in Packard's garage. Hewlett's audio oscillator was cheaper and easier to use than competitive products, and it was quickly followed by a family of test instruments based on the same design principles. By the 1950s, Hewlett-Packard was turning out two dozen new products every year. As of 1975, Hewlett-Packard was one of the giants of the high-technology electronics industry. Annual sales were climbing rapidly toward $1 billion; approximately one-half of the company's sales were made to international customers. The company's 29,000 employees were involved in designing, manufacturing, and marketing more than 3,300 products—including electronic test and measuring instruments

---

[1] "Hewlett-Packard: Where Slower Growth Is Smarter Management," *Business Week,* June 9, 1975, pp. 50–58.

EXHIBIT 2
Selected Performance Data on Certain Firms in the Electronic Instruments Industry, 1971–1975

	Sales Growth (percent of change)			
	*1974–75**	*1973–74*	*1972–73*	*1971–72*
Beckham Instruments	7%	21%	10%	8%
Fairchild Camera	−23	10	57	16
General Instrument	−6	−1	34	16
Hewlett-Packard	9	34	38	28
National Semiconductor.......	11	115	65	58
Raytheon.....................	16	21	9	12
Texas Instruments	−12	22	36	24
Textronix....................	24	37	21	12
Varian Associates	6	22	18	9

	Profit Margin (percent)				
	*1975**	*1974*	*1973*	*1972*	*1971*
Beckham Instruments	4%	4%	4%	3%	3%
Fairchild Camera...............	4	7	8	4	†
General Instrument.............	2	3	3	3	2
Hewlett-Packard	9	10	8	8	6
National Semiconductor	7	8	4	3	3
Raytheon	3	3	3	3	3
Texas Instruments	5	6	7	5	4
Textronix	8	8	8	7	6
Varian Associates	3	3	3	2	†

	Earnings on Net Worth (percent)				
	*1975**	*1974*	*1973*	*1972*	*1971*
Beckham Instruments	10%	8%	7%	6%	5%
Fairchild Camera	8	17	20	9	†
General Instrument	5	7	9	7	4
Hewlett-Packard	16	18	15	13	10
National Semiconductor	25	35	14	16	12
Raytheon	16	14	13	12	12
Texas Instruments.............	11	17	18	13	10
Textronix	13	12	11	8	8
Varian Associates	5	5	6	3	†

* Estimated by *Value Line*.
† = deficit.
Source: *Value Line Investment Survey* and casewriters' calculations.

and systems; electronic calculators, computers, and computer systems; medical electronic products (entered largely through acquisition); electronic instrumentation for chemical analysis; and solid-state components.

According to company sources, Hewlett-Packard has strived to remain a "people-oriented" company, with management policies that encourage individual creativity, initiative, and contribution throughout the organization. It has also tried to retain the openness, informality, and unstructured operating procedures that marked the company in its early years. Each individual has a certain freedom and the flexibility to implement work methods and ideas to achieve both personal and company objectives and goals.

CORPORATE OBJECTIVES

When Hewlett-Packard was first formed, Bill Hewlett and David Packard formulated a number of management concepts upon which to build and organize their company. As a result of their decision to have a decentralized organization, they tried to assemble a set of corporate objectives that would tie the organization more closely together and also ensure that the company as a whole was headed in a common direction. These objectives were first put into writing in 1957. They have been modified occasionally since then to reflect the changing nature of the company's business and environment. The intent and wording of the objectives in 1975 were, according to the founders, remarkably similar to the original versions. The introduction to the Hewlett-Packard Statement of Corporate Objectives states:

> The achievements of an organization are the result of the combined efforts of each individual in the organization working toward common objectives. These objectives should be realistic, should be clearly understood by everyone in the organization, and should reflect the organization's basic character and personality.

Exhibit 3 presents a brief listing of the Hewlett-Packard objectives as of 1974. Both Hewlett and Packard have indicated these objectives have served the company well in shaping the company, guiding its growth, and providing the foundation for the company's contribution to technological progress and the betterment of society.

EXHIBIT 3
Statement of Objectives

1. PROFIT

OBJECTIVE: *To achieve sufficient profit to finance our company growth and to provide the resources we need to achieve our other corporate objectives.*

In our economic system, the profit we generate from our operations is the ultimate source of the funds we need to prosper and grow. It is the one absolutely essential measure of our corporate performance over the long term. Only if we continue to meet our profit objective can we achieve our other corporate objectives.

Our long-standing policy has been to reinvest most of our profits and to depend on this reinvestment, plus funds from employee stock purchases and other cash flow items, to finance our growth. This can be achieved if our return on net worth is roughly equal to our sales growth rate. We must strive to reach this goal every year without limiting our efforts to attain our other objectives.

Profits vary from year to year, reflecting changing economic conditions and varying demands for our products. Our needs for capital also vary, and we depend

EXHIBIT 3 *(continued)*

on short-term bank loans to meet those needs when profits or other cash sources are inadequate. However, loans are costly and must be repaid; thus, our objective is to rely on reinvested profits as our main source of capital.

Meeting our profit objective requires that we design and develop each and every product so that it is considered a good value by our customers, yet is priced to include an adequate profit. Maintaining this competitiveness in the marketplace also requires that we perform our manufacturing, marketing, and administrative functions as economically as possible.

Profit is not something that can be put off until tomorrow; it must be achieved today. It means that myriad jobs be done correctly and efficiently. The day-to-day performance of each individual adds to—or subtracts from—our profit. Profit is the responsibility of all.

2. CUSTOMERS

OBJECTIVE: *To provide products and services of the greatest possible value to our customers, thereby gaining and holding their respect and loyalty.*

The success and prosperity of our company will be assured only if we offer our customers superior products that fill real needs and provide lasting value, and that are supported by a wide variety of useful services, both before and after sale.

Our responsibility to the customer begins with product development. Products must be designed to provide superior performance and long, troublefree service. Once in production, these products must be manufactured at a reasonable cost and with superior workmanship.

A prime objective of our marketing department is to see that the finished product is backed by prompt, efficient service. Moreover, good communication should be maintained with the customer and among various H-P sales teams.

Because of our broad and growing line of products, very often several sales teams will be working with a single customer. Each of these teams has a high degree of technical knowledge and sales skill. There must be considerable cooperation among teams to assure that the products recommended best fulfill the customer's overall, long-term needs.

H-P customers must feel that they are dealing with one company with common policies and services, and that our company is genuinely interested in arriving at proper, effective solutions to their problems. Confusion and competition among sales teams must be avoided by a clear assignment of sales responsibilities, plus sound judgment by H-P sales people in understanding customer needs and H-P objectives.

3. FIELDS OF INTEREST

OBJECTIVE: *To enter new fields only when the ideas we have, together with our technical, manufacturing, and marketing skills, assure that we can make a needed and profitable contribution to the field.*

The original Hewlett-Packard products were electronic measuring instruments. Today our product line has expanded to include instruments for chemical and biomedical measurement and analysis, computers to automate measurement and to process the data, as well as electronic calculators and complete computer systems. Thus our growth has led to a continuing expansion of our fields of interest. To a large extent, diversification has come from applying our resources and skills to fields technically related to our traditional ones.

The key to H-P's prospective involvement in new fields is contribution. This means providing customers with something new and needed, not just another brand of something they can already buy. To meet this objective we must continually generate new ideas for better kinds of products. It is essential that before a final

EXHIBIT 3 *(continued)*

decision is made to enter a new field, full consideration be given to the associated problems of manufacturing and marketing these products.

4. GROWTH

OBJECTIVE: *To let our growth be limited only by our profits and our ability to develop and produce technical products that satisfy real customer needs.*

How large should a company become? Some people feel that when it has reached a certain size there is no point in letting it grow further. Others feel that bigness is an objective in itself. We do not believe that large size is important for its own sake; however, for at least two basic reasons, continuous growth is essential for us to achieve our other objectives.

In the first place, we serve a rapidly growing and expanding segment of our technological society. To remain static would be to lose ground. We cannot maintain a position of strength and leadership in our field without growth.

In the second place, growth is important in order to attract and hold high caliber people. These individuals will align their future only with a company that offers them considerable opportunity for personal progress. Opportunities are greater and more challenging in a growing company.

5. OUR PEOPLE

OBJECTIVE: *To help H-P people share in the company's success, which they make possible; to provide job security based on their performance; to recognize their individual achievements; and to insure the personal satisfaction that comes from a sense of accomplishment in their work.*

We are proud of the people we have in our organization, their performance, and their attitude toward their jobs and toward the company. The company has been built around the individual, the personal dignity of each, and the recognition of personal achievements.

We feel that general policies and the attitude of managers toward their people are more important than specific details of the personnel program. Personnel relations will be good only if people have faith in the motives and integrity of their supervisors and of the company. Personnel relations will be poor if they do not.

The opportunity to share in the success of the company is evidenced by our above-average wage and salary level, our profit sharing and stock purchase plan, and by other company benefits.

The objective of job security is illustrated by our policy of avoiding large ups and downs in our production schedules, which would require hiring people for a short period of time and laying them off later. We are interested that each employee carry a full load and be eager to remain with and grow with the company. This does not mean we are committed to an absolute tenure status, nor do we recognize seniority except where other factors are reasonably comparable.

In a growing company there are apt to be more opportunities for advancement than there are qualified people to fill them. This is true at Hewlett-Packard; opportunities are plentiful and it is up to the individual, through personal growth and development, to take advantage of them.

We want people to enjoy their work at HP, and to be proud of their accomplishments. This means we must make sure that each person receives the recognition he or she needs and deserves. In the final analysis, people at all levels determine the character and strength of our company.

6. MANAGEMENT

OBJECTIVE: *To foster initiative and creativity by allowing the individual great freedom of action in attaining well-defined objectives.*

EXHIBIT 3 *(concluded)*

In discussing H-P operating policies, we often refer to the concept of "management by objective." By this we mean that insofar as possible each individual at each level in the organization should make his or her own plans to achieve company objectives and goals. After receiving supervisory approval, each individual should be given a wide degree of freedom to work within the limitations imposed by these plans, and by our general corporate policies. Finally, each person's performance should be judged on the basis of how well these individually established goals have been achieved.

The successful practice of "management by objective" is a two-way street. Management must be sure that each individual understands the immediate objective, as well as corporate goals and policies. Thus a primary H-P management responsibility is communication and mutual understanding. Conversely, employees must take sufficient interest in their work to want to plan it, to propose new solutions to old problems, to stick their necks out when they have something to contribute. "Management by objective," as opposed to management by directive, offers opportunity for individual freedom and contribution; it also imposes an obligation for everyone to exercise initiative and enthusiasm.

In this atmosphere it is particularly important that the strength of the whole company is kept in mind and that cooperation between individuals and between operating units is vital to our profitable growth.

It is important for everyone to realize there are some policies which must be established and strictly maintained on a corporate-wide basis. We welcome recommendations on these corporate-wide policies from all levels but we expect adherence to them at all times.

7.   CITIZENSHIP

OBJECTIVE: *To honor our obligations to society by being an economic, intellectual, and social asset to each nation and each community in which we operate.*

All of us should strive to improve the environment in which we live. As a corporation operating in many different communities throughout the world, we must assure ourselves that each of these communities is better for our presence. This means building plants and offices that are attractive and in harmony with the community; it means solving instead of contributing to the problems of traffic and pollution; it means contributing both money and time to community projects.

Each community has its particular set of social problems. Our company must help to solve these problems. As a major step in this direction, we must strive to provide worthwhile employment opportunities for people of widely different backgrounds. Among other things, this requires positive action to seek out and employ members of disadvantaged groups; and to encourage and guide their progress toward full participation at all position levels.

As citizens of their community, there is much that H-P people can and should do to improve it—either working as individuals or through such groups as churches, schools, civic or charitable organizations. At a national level, it is essential that the company be a good corporate citizen of each country in which it operates. Moreover our employees, as individuals, should be encouraged to contribute their support to the solution of national problems.

The betterment of our society is not a job to be left to a few; it is a responsibility to be shared by all.

Source: Hewlett-Packard Co., "Statement of Objectives," 1974.

CORPORATE STRATEGIES AND RELATED POLICIES

Hewlett-Packard's product-market strategy has concentrated on developing quality products which make unique technological contributions and which are so far advanced that customers are willing to pay premium prices. The company's product line has been limited to the area of electronic test and measurement and to technologically related fields.

Customer service, both before and after the sale, is given strong primary emphasis. The company's growth strategy has been to attain a position of technological strength and leadership by continually developing innovative products and by attracting high caliber and creative people.

Hewlett-Packard's financial strategy has been to use profits, employee stock purchases, and other internally generated funds to finance growth. It has avoided long-term debt and has resorted to short-term debt only when sales growth exceeded the return on net worth. Its motivational strategy has consisted of providing employees with the opportunity to share in the success of the company through high wages, profit sharing, and stock-purchase plans. H-P has also sought to provide job security by keeping fluctuations in production schedules to a minimum, by avoiding consumer-type products, and by not making any products exclusively for the government. One of H-P's managerial techniques was to practice "management by objective" rather than management by directive; the statement of corporate objectives was used to provide unity of purpose and as a basis for giving employees the freedom to work toward these goals in ways they determined best for their own areas of responsibility. At the same time, the company has, in its view, endeavored to exercise social responsibility by building plants and offices that are attractive and in harmony with the community, by helping to solve community problems, and by contributing both money and time to community projects.

THE UPS AND DOWNS OF THE 1970s

Hewlett-Packard considered itself fortunate to have entered the electronics industry early, before the rapid growth and expansion had started. Not only did its early start permit the company to share in the prosperity that the industry enjoyed generally, but its leadership also helped pave the way for successful diversification into computers, calculators, and components. Nonetheless, the first half of the 1970s was not smooth sailing.

Sales increased 30 percent in fiscal 1972 and almost 40 percent in 1973. At first, this rapid growth was pursued vigorously because the company had been adversely affected by the computer and aerospace downturns in 1970—earnings had declined slightly in fiscal 1971, despite austere cost control measures, including reduced workweeks for everyone and a resulting decline in companywide payroll outlays. But, in 1972–73, the sharp surge in sales growth brought problems of a different kind. Inventories and accounts receivable increased substantially. There was an unusually large influx of new employees who needed to be trained and absorbed into the company's widely dispersed and decentralized operations. A number of new products were put into production before they were fully tested. Prices were pegged too low to generate what the company considered to be an adequate return on investment. The subsequent financial strains necessitated a higher level of short-term borrowings which, by the end of 1973, amounted to $118 million. Although management considered converting some of the short-term debt to longer term debt, uncertain economic conditions created a reluctance to do so. Since the company had policies of keeping employment steady and operating on a pay-as-you-go basis, both Hewlett and Packard believed the company would be better off keeping its debt position as clear as possible, especially given the prospects of the weakening U.S. economy.

In 1973–74, H-P's top management thus decided to avoid adding long-term debt and to reduce short-term debt by controlling costs, managing assets, and improving profit margins. As Packard made clear to the management at all levels, the company had somehow been diverted into seeking market share as an objective. Both Packard and Hewlett began a year-long campaign of touring the divisions to reemphasize the principles they had developed when they began their unique partnership years previous. With many of H-P's competitors then pushing hard for increased market share, Hewlett-Packard's decision to refocus on profitability rather than market share presented certain risks. However, according to *Business Week,* neither Hewlett nor Packard saw themselves as risk takers and their approach was logical for a company that had consistently come up with truly innovative products.[2]

Meanwhile, Hewlett-Packard made a bold strategic move. As other companies dropped prices to boost sales and cut research spending to improve earnings, Hewlett-Packard did just the opposite. It raised prices by an average of 10 percent over the previous year, and it increased spending on research and development by 20 percent, to an $80 million annual rate. The aim was to improve company profitability and to slow down, quite deliberately, the rate of growth that caused the company's sales to more than double over the past three years.

The improvements in 1974 performance compared with 1973 were quite dramatic. During fiscal 1974, inventories and receivables increased about 3 percent while sales grew 34 percent to $884 million. The effect of this better asset control, combined with improved earnings, resulted in a drop in short-term debt of approximately $77 million. Earnings were up 66 percent to $84 million and were equal to $3.08 per share compared to $1.89 per share in 1973. Only 1,000 employees were added, compared to 7,000 in the previous year. The improvement continued in the first half of fiscal 1975; sales for the first six months were up 14 percent to $460 million, while profits increased 21 percent to $42 million. However, *Value Line Investment Survey* estimated that on a full-year basis annual sales for 1975 would be up 9 percent to $960 million while profit would increase about 2 percent to $85 million (see Exhibit 4).

Despite the improvements, both Hewlett and Packard were dismayed that

---

[2] Ibid.

EXHIBIT 4
Contributions to Sales and Pretax Profit Margin by Product Groups, 1971–1975

	1975*	1974	1973	1972	1971
Sales (millions of dollars)					
Test, measuring and related items	$460.0	$442.9	$362.3	$309.8	$264.8
Electronic data products	360.0	325.7	215.2	108.0	63.1
Medical electronic equipment	95.0	76.1	56.6	40.7	30.8
Analytical instrumentation	45.0	39.4	27.2	20.6	16.4
Total	$960.0	$884.1	$661.3	$479.1	$375.1
Pretax Profit Margin (percent)					
Test, measuring and related items	14.5%	15.1%	13.3%	14.5%	14.3%
Electronic data products	18.3	20.7	17.4	19.8	3.3
Medical electronic equipment	11.5	10.0	11.1	14.3	9.7
Analytical instrumentation	8.0	6.1	9.9	10.2	8.5
Total	15.1%	16.3%	14.3%	15.5%	12.3%

* Estimated by Value Line in *Value Line Investment Survey,* 1975.
Source: *Value Line Investment Survey.*

they had been forced to initiate and personally lead the efforts to get the company back on the track. It was particularly disconcerting to them because they believed the issues were fundamental to the basic strategy of the company. They had also had to intervene directly in day-to-day operational management, which was counter to their basic philosophy of a decentralized, product-oriented, and divisionalized organization structure.

ORGANIZATION STRUCTURE AND CHANGE

Both Bill Hewlett and David Packard recognized that their retirements could likely have a substantial impact on the company's management structure and future success. Packard would be 65 years old in 1977 and Hewlett would be 65 in 1978. Although the two owned about one half of the company's stock and could undoubtedly postpone retirement, they nonetheless took steps in 1974 to prepare the organization for an orderly succession. They also wanted to develop an organization structure which could respond more effectively to growth and diversification and would also provide more effective management of day-to-day operations. To accomplish these ends, several organizational changes were initiated shortly before the end of the 1974 fiscal year.

EXHIBIT 5
Hewlett-Packard Corporate Organization Prior to April 1975

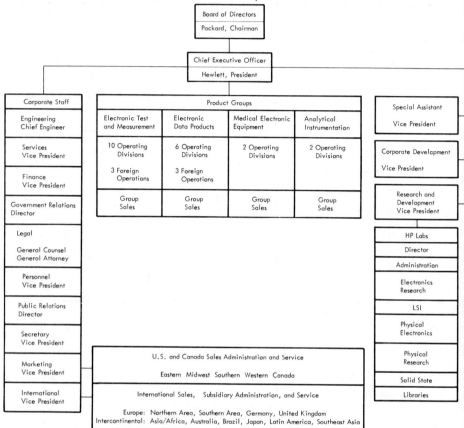

Source: Developed by casewriters from information provided by Hewlett-Packard Company.

Exhibits 5 and 6 show the company's management structure before and after the changes. The basic product groups were realigned from four to six. The purpose was to establish a more logical grouping of products and technologies, while creating group organizations of more manageable size and structure. Hewlett and Packard also established a new level of management to oversee day-to-day operations of the company. This consisted of two new executive vice presidents, jointly responsible for operations, and a new vice president for corporate administration. One of the executive VPs, John A. Young, 43 and a 1958 graduate of Stanford's MBA program, had been vice president of the electrical group since 1968 and before that was general manager of the microwave division. Ralph E. Lee had been an executive vice president and director of the company since 1969. His re-

XHIBIT 6
ewlett-Packard Corporate Organization, April 1975

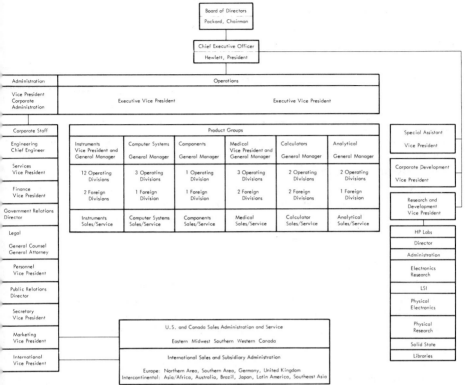

sponsibilities were expanded in this new position. Both men had engineering backgrounds and had come up through the H-P ranks. *Business Week* reported that both ''project the same relaxed self-assurance that characterizes the founders.'' Young, described as more outgoing, was predicted to take the high-visibility role played in recent years by Hewlett; Lee, who had a reputation as a troubleshooter, was expected to concentrate on internal problems. The third executive was Robert L. Boniface, 50, who had served as vice president of marketing since 1970. He was promoted to vice president for corporate administration, with responsibility for corporate staff functions.

These three executives, along with Hewlett and Packard, were set up as an Executive Committee to meet weekly in order to coordinate all phases of the company's operations. This was intended to bring new people into the upper levels of management to build the long-term strength of the company. The new structure was also expected to allow both Hewlett and Packard to devote more time to matters of policy and planning the company's future.

In the new organization, the six product groups each had a general manager, who had responsibility for both domestic and foreign product divisions. The change left intact Hewlett-Packard's basic strategy of approaching established markets through relatively autonomous product-oriented divisions. Because high-technology companies often have a problem keeping new-product development focused on the needs of the market rather than on pure research and technological improvements with little market potential, Hewlett-Packard tried to do most of its research and development at the division level. Of the $70.7 million spent on research and development in 1974, one sixth was allocated to corporate R&D and five sixths was spent by the divisions. Divisions were intentionally kept small to foster open communications and quick responsiveness to their individual market segments. Each product group, in addition to the group general manager, had a sales-service organization serving all the product divisions in the product group. Each product division had its own engineering, manufacturing, personnel, quality control, and marketing functions, although some of the smaller divisions in the same locations shared a functional department between them.

While H-P's divisions had considerable latitude in developing product strategies, they were not allowed to go outside their assigned markets or to borrow money. Even within the limits set by top management, new-product proposals were carefully reviewed at the preliminary investigation stage. The company considered itself conservative in funding projects and expected at least 80 percent of funded projects to be successful. Once development of a new product had been funded, the goal was to get it to the market in a hurry. The company believed that sales lost during development time could not be recovered since, if the technology were available to fill a market need, others could also conceive a product. As a result, both timing and the flexibility to exploit opportunities quickly were considered important reasons for having a multiple-product division structure.

The product-division marketing departments were responsible for order processing and shipping, sales-engineering and contract-administration, service-engineering, technical-writing, publications, and advertising and sales promotion. They also provided sales forecasts and were responsible for recommending and reviewing prices. The initial pricing of new products involved a major analysis of the marketplace, competition, profitability, and overall product strategy. The actual selling and customer servicing were handled by the six group organizations. Each division competed for the time of the group's field sales force. In order to attract the attention of the field sales engineers, the divisions had to offer extensive marketing support and new product training to these "customers." The broad, growing, and often interacting lines of products frequently resulted in several group sales teams working with one customer. The centralized sales organization was intended to assure that cooperation and communication between sales teams were maintained; Hewlett-Packard wanted customers to feel they were dealing with one company with common policies and services. Confusion and competition were avoided by a clear assignment of sales responsibilities and by organizing the sales force in a way that put primary emphasis on functional rather than product responsibility.

As shown in Exhibit 6, both Corporate Research and Development and Corporate Development reported directly to Hewlett. Also, one or both of the founders continued to sit in on annual review sessions for each division. As the 1974 *Annual Report* pointed out, the restructuring represented an evolutionary step in Hewlett-Packard's continuing growth and diversification, but there had been no changes in basic operating philosophy.

OPERATING POLICIES

In addition to the aforementioned strategic and structural changes, the company had certain operating policies which undergirded its business concept. The company's basic operating policy was often referred to by Hewlett-Packard people as "management by objective." Instead of leading and coordinating the organization primarily by factors such as hierarchical authority relationships, detailed rules and regulations, and a tight military-type organization, Hewlett-Packard chose to use clearly stated and agreed-upon objectives. Each individual at every level in the organization was expected to make plans to achieve the company's broader goals and objectives. After receiving supervisory approval, each individual was given a wide degree of freedom to work within the limitations imposed by his own plans and by general corporate policies. The purpose was to offer the greatest possible freedom for individual initiative and contribution. Top management indicated that this policy had been a major factor in Hewlett-Packard's ability to provide innovative, useful products of high quality and to develop people capable of accepting additional responsibility as the company has grown.

As *Business Week* has suggested, one of the keys to the success of Hewlett-Packard could rest with the unusual spirit of corporate loyalty that has seemed to permeate its work force, particularly the 1,900 R&D personnel. The company has distributed $64 million in cash profit sharing bonuses in the previous five years, and about half the employees were participating in a stock-purchase program. Rather than run the risk of "big" layoffs, Hewlett-Packard had a policy of not bidding on short-run government contracts. It also avoided getting into product lines where there were wide fluctuations in sales volume, such as in many consumer products. When faced with lean times, inventories were increased and everyone from Packard on down worked a reduced workweek. This had the effect of dividing the available jobs among all the employees, in contrast to termination or temporarily laying off somewhere between 1,000 and 2,000 people. As a result, Hewlett-Packard has seldom been afflicted with the migrations of people and ideas that many high-technology companies have experienced.

These general policies and the supportive attitudes of managers toward their subordinates were believed to be more important than specific details of the personnel programs. Personnel relations at Hewlett-Packard were considered "good" only when people demonstrated faith in the motives and integrity of their supervisors and of the company. One example of the company's faith in its employees was the program of flexible working hours. Under "flexi-time," most people at Hewlett-Packard were allowed to work and leave within two-hour "windows"—that is, employees could arrive anytime within a two-hour period at the beginning of the day and could leave after completing eight hours of work. In addition, individuals could vary their reporting times from day to day. Hewlett-Packard has not had time clocks for many years. The company's trust in the individual was believed to be the key to the program's success. As David Packard frequently said, "Motivation is the difference between a championship ball team and an ordinary ball team." Still, a number of observers wondered whether H-P's players would stay motivated when their two coaches were no longer with the team.

EXHIBIT 7
Comparison of 1974 and 1973 Consolidated Financial Positions (in $000s)

	1974	1973
Assets		
Current assets:		
Cash and marketable securities	$ 13,828	$ 8,925
Notes and accounts receivable	193,735	187,472
Inventories		
Finished goods	51,627	51,652
Work in process	82,410	84,687
Raw materials	61,177	52,307
Deposits and prepaid expenses	13,791	10,147
	416,568	395,190
Property, plant and equipment		
Land	26,566	23,940
Buildings and improvements	128,274	87,961
Machinery and equipment	109,342	94,210
Other	26,846	21,992
Leaseholds and improvements	10,002	7,056
Construction in progress	41,541	32,493
	342,571	267,652
Accumulated depreciation	117,709	93,882
	224,862	173,770
Other assets and deferred charges		
Investment in unconsolidated Japanese Affiliate	4,391	3,668
Patents and other intangibles	2,243	2,798
Other	6,317	4,240
	12,951	10,706
	$654,381	$579,666
Liabilities and Stockholders' Equity		
Current liabilities:		
Notes payable	$ 43,527	$ 94,749
Commercial paper	—	25,750
Accounts payable	26,491	36,072
Accrued expenses	74,778	51,471
Income taxes	34,476	12,745
	179,272	220,787
Long-term debt	2,899	2,182
Deferred federal income taxes	14,531	7,500
Shareholders' equity		
Common stock, par value $1	27,298	26,816
Capital in excess of par	112,157	82,763
Retained earnings	318,224	239,618
	457,679	349,197
	$654.381	$579,666

Source: 1974 *Annual Report*.

EXHIBIT 8
Consolidated Statement of Changes in 1974 and 1973 Financial Position (in $000s)

	1974	1973
Working capital provided		
Net earnings...	$ 84,022	$ 50,749
Add charges not affecting working capital		
Depreciation and amortization	31,519	22,917
Deferred federal taxes on income	7,031	5,412
Stock purchase and award plans	5,625	4,169
Other	4,549	522
Working capital provided from operations	132,746	83,769
Proceeds from sale of common stock	23,746	15,483
Proceeds of additional long-term debt	1,277	1,823
Total working capital provided.......................	157,769	101,075
Working capital used		
Investment in property, plant and equipment	86,327	81,162
Dividends to shareowners	5,416	5,332
Reduction in long-term debt...........................	560	1,558
Increase in equity in unconsolidated Japanese affiliate	723	1,054
Other, net	1,850	4,319
Total working capital used	94,876	93,425
Increase in working capital	62,893	7,650
Working capital at beginning of year	174,403	166,753
Working capital at end of year	$237,296	$174,403
Increase in working capital consisted of		
Increase (decrease) in current assets		
Cash and marketable securities	$ 4,903	$(10,723)
Notes and accounts receivable	6,263	69,057
Inventories	6,568	70,083
Deposits and prepaid expenses	3,644	4,256
	21,378	132,673
Decrease (increase) in current liabilities		
Notes payable and commercial paper	76,972	(103,201)
Accounts payable and accrued expenses	(13,726)	(26,837)
Federal, foreign and state taxes on income	(21,731)	5,015
	41,515	(125,023)
Increase in working capital	$ 62,893	$ 7,650

Source: 1974 *Annual Report*.

2. United Products, Inc.*

HAVING just returned from lunch, Mr. George Brown, president of United Products, Inc., was sitting in his office thinking about his upcoming winter vacation—in a few days he and his family would be leaving from Boston to spend three weeks skiing on Europe's finest slopes. His daydreaming was interrupted by a telephone call from Mr. Hank Stevens, UPI's general manager. Mr. Stevens wanted to know if their two o'clock meeting was still on. The meeting had been scheduled to review actions UPI could take in light of the company's sluggish sales and the currently depressed national economy. In addition, Brown and Stevens were to go over the financial results for the company's recently completed fiscal year—they had just been received from UPI's auditors. Although it had not been a bad year, results were not as good as expected and this, in conjunction with the economic situation, had prompted Mr. Brown to reappraise the plans he had for the company during the upcoming year.

COMPANY HISTORY

United Products, Inc., established in 1941, was engaged in the sales and service of basic supply items for shipping and receiving, production and packaging, research and development, and office and warehouse departments. Mr. Brown's father, the founder of the company, recognized the tax advantages in establishing separate businesses rather than trying to consolidate all of his operations in one large organization. Accordingly, over the years the elder Mr. Brown had created new companies and either closed down or sold off older companies as business conditions seemed to warrant. As of the mid-1960s, his holdings consisted of a chain of four related sales-distribution companies covering the geographic area from Chicago eastward.

In 1967, feeling it was time to step aside and turn over active control of the business to his sons, the elder Mr. Brown recapitalized and restructured his companies, merging some and disposing of others. When the restructuring process was completed, he had set up two major companies. United Products, Inc., was to be run by his youngest son, George Brown, with its

---

* Prepared by Professor Jeffrey C. Shuman, Babson College.

headquarters in Massachusetts, while his other son, Richard Brown, was to operate United Products Southeast, Inc., headquartered in Florida.

Although the Brown brothers occasionally worked together and were on each other's board of directors, the two companies operated on their own. As Mr. George Brown explained, "Since we are brothers, we often get together and discuss business, but the two are separate companies and each files its own tax return."

During 1972, United Products moved into new facilities in Woburn, Massachusetts. From this location it was thought that the company would be able to serve its entire New England market area effectively. "Our abilities and our desires to expand and improve our overall operation will be enhanced in the new specially designed structure containing our offices, repair facilities, and warehouse," is how George Brown viewed the role of the new facilities. Concurrent with the move, the company segmented the more than 3,500 different items it carried into eight major product categories;

1. *Stapling Machines.* Manual and powered wire stitchers, carton stitchers, nailers, hammers, and tackers.
2. *Staples.* All sizes and types (steel, bronze, monel, stainless steel, aluminum, brass, etc.) to fit almost all makes of equipment.
3. *Stenciling Equipment and Supplies.* Featuring Marsh hand and electric machines, stencil brushes, boards, and inks.
4. *Gummed Tape Machines.* Hand and electric, featuring Marsh, Derby, and Counterboy equipment.
5. *Industrial Tapes.* Specializing in strapping, masking, cellophane, electrical, cloth, nylon, waterproof tapes made by 3M, Mystik, Behr Manning, and Dymo.
6. *Gluing Machines.* Hand and electric.
7. *Work Gloves.* All sizes and types (cotton, leather, neoprene, nylon, rubber, asbestos, and so on).
8. *Marking and Labeling Equipment.*

In a flyer mailed to United Products' 6,000 accounts announcing the move to its new facilities, the company talked about its growth in this fashion:

> Here we grow again—thanks to you—our many long-time valued customers . . .
>
> Time and Circumstances have decreed another United Products transPLANT—this time, to an unpolluted garden-type industrial area, ideally located for an ever-increasing list of our customers.
>
> Now, in the new 28,000-sq.ft. plant with enlarged offices and warehouse, we at UNITED PRODUCTS reach the peak of efficiency in offering our customers the combined benefits of maximum inventories, accelerated deliveries, and better repair services.

By 1974, the company had grown to a point where sales were $3.5 million (double that of four years earlier) and 34 people were employed. Results for

EXHIBIT 1
Selected Financial Information, United Products, Inc.

	11-30-1971	11-30-1972	11-30-1973
Current assets	$ 862,783	$689,024	$ 937,793
Other assets	204,566	774,571	750,646
Current liabilities	381,465	223,004	342,939
Net worth	685,884	750,446	873,954
Sales...........................	n.a.*	n.a.*	3,450,000

Statement of financial
condition, November 30, 1973:

Cash on hand	$46,961	Accounts payable	$ 321,885
Accounts receivable	535,714	Notes payable	20,993
Merchandise in inventory........	352,136		
Prepaid insurance, interest,			
taxes........................	2,980		
Current Assets	$ 937,791	Current Liabilities	$ 342,878
Fixtures and equipment	$ 42,891	Retained earnings	$ 471,655
Motor vehicles..................	49,037	Capital stock	519,800
Land and buildings	658,768	Surplus	354,154
Total Assets	$1,688,487	Total Liabilities	$1,688,487

* n.a.: Not available.

1973 compared to 1972 showed a sales increase of 22 percent and a 40 percent gain in profits. Exhibit 1 contains selected financial figures for 1971, 1972, and 1973, in addition to the fiscal 1973 balance sheet.

COMPETITION

Mr. George Brown indicated that UPI does not have clearly defined rivals against whom it competes head-on with respect to all of its 3,500-plus items:

> It is hard to get figures on competition since we compete with no one company directly. Different distributors carry lines which compete with various of our product lines, but there is no one company which competes against us across our full range of products.

On a regular basis, Mr. Brown receives Dun & Bradstreet's *Business Information Reports* on specific firms with which he competes. Mr. Brown feels that since the rival firms are, like his own firm, privately held, the financial figures reported are easily manipulated and, therefore, are not a sound basis on which to devise strategies and plans. Exhibit 2 contains comparative financial figures for two competing companies, and Exhibit 3 contains D&B's description of their operations, along with D&B's comments about two other firms operating in UPI's New England market area.

EXHIBIT 2
Financial Information on Rival Firms

East Coast Supply Co., Inc.—Sales $1 million:

	Fiscal December 31, 1971	Fiscal December 31, 1972	Fiscal December 3 1973
Current assets	$88,555	$132,354	$163,953
Other assets	16,082	18,045	27,422
Current liabilities	41,472	47,606	74,582
Net worth	63,165	102,793	116,793

Statement of financial condition, December 31, 1973:

Cash	$ 42,948	Accounts payable	$ 39,19
Accounts receivable	86,123	Notes payable	27,58
Merchandise in inventory	34,882	Taxes	7,79
Current Assets	$163,953	Current Liabilities	$ 74,58
Fixtures and equipment	$ 15,211	Capital stock	$ 10,00
Deposits	12,211	Retained earnings	106,79
		Total Liabilities	
Total Assets	$191,375	and Net Worth	$191,37

Atlantic Paper Products, Inc.—Sales $6 million:

	June 30, 1970	June 30, 1971	June 30, 197
Current assets	$884,746	$1,243,259	$1,484,450
Other assets	93,755	101,974	107,001
Current liabilities	574,855	520,572	1,120,036
Net worth	403,646	439,677	471,415
Long-term debt	0	384,984	

MANAGEMENT PHILOSOPHY

When Mr. Brown took over UPI in 1967 at the age of 24, he set a personal goal of becoming financially secure and developing a highly profitable business. With the rapid growth of the company, he soon realized his goal of financial independence and in so doing began to lose interest in the company. "I became a rich person at age 28 and had few friends with equal wealth that were my age. The business no longer presented a challenge and I was unhappy with the way things were going."

After taking a ten-month "mental vacation" from the business, George Brown felt he was ready to return to work. He had concluded that one way of proving himself to himself and satisfying his ego would be to make the company as profitable as possible. However, according to Mr. Brown, "The company can only grow at approximately 20 percent per year, since this is the amount of energy I am willing to commit to the business."

In 1974, at age 31, Mr. Brown described his philosophical outlook as "very conservative" and surmised that he ran UPI in much the same way as

EXHIBIT 3
Descriptions of Major Competitors

East Coast Supply Co, Inc.

Manufacturers and distributes pressure sensitive tapes to industrial users throughout New England area on 1/10 net 30-day terms. Thirty-four employed including the officers, 33 here. Location: Rents 15,000 square feet on first floor of two-story brick building in good repair. Premises are orderly. Nonseasonal business. Branches are located at 80 Olife Street, New Haven, Connecticut and 86 Weybosset Street, Providence, Rhode Island.

Atlantic Paper Products, Inc.

Wholesales paper products, pressure sensitive tapes, paper specialties, twines and other merchandise of this type. Sales to industrial accounts and commercial users on 1/10 net 30-day terms. There are about 1,000 accounts in eastern Massachusetts and sales are fairly steady throughout the year. Employs 60, including officers. Location: Rents 130,000 square feet of floor space in a six-story brick, mill-type building in a commercial area on a principal street. Premises orderly.

The Johnson Sales Co.

Wholesales shipping room supplies, including staplings and packing devices, marking and stencil equipment. Sells to industrial and commercial accounts throughout the New England area. Seasons are steady. Terms are 1/10 net 30 days. Number of accounts not learned, 15 are employed including the owner. Location: Rents the first floor of a two-story yellow brick building in good condition. Housekeeping is good.

Big City Staple Corp.

Wholesales industrial staples, with sales to 2,000 industrial and commercial firms, sold on 1/10 net 30-day terms. Territory mainly New Jersey. Employs ten including the officers. Seasons steady and competition active. Location: Rents 5,000 square feet in one-story cinder block and brick structure in good condition, premises in neat order. Located on well-traveled street in a commercial area.

---

his 65-year-old father would. In describing his managerial philosophy and some of the operating policies he had established, he said:

> I am very concerned about making UPI a nice place to work. I have to enjoy what I'm doing and have fun at it at the same time. I cannot make any more money, since I'm putting away as much money as I can. The government won't allow me to make more money, since I already take the maximum amount.
>
> I like to feel comfortable, and if we grew too quickly it could get out of hand. I realize the business doesn't grow to its potential but why should I put more into it. . . . The company could grow, but why grow? Why is progress good? You have to pay for everything in life and I'm not willing to work harder. . . .
>
> Another thing. I am a scrupulously honest businessman and it is very hard to grow large if you're honest. There are many deals that I could get into that would make UPI a lot of money, but I'm too moral of a person to get involved. . . .
>
> To me, happiness is being satisfied with what you have. I've got my wife, children and health; why risk these for something I don't need? I don't have the desire to make money because I didn't come from a poor family; I'm not hungry.

I have never liked the feeling of owing anything to anyone. If you can't afford to buy something, then don't. I don't like to borrow any money and I don't like the company to borrow any. All of our bills are paid within 15 days. I suppose I've constrained the business as a result of this feeling, but it's my business. The company can only afford to pay for a 20 percent growth rate so that's all we'll grow.

ORGANIZATIONAL STRUCTURE

Upon returning to the company from his "mental vacation" in 1971 George Brown realigned UPI's organizational structure as shown in Exhibit 4 (the company does not have a formal organizational chart; this one is

EXHIBIT 4
Organization Chart—December 1974

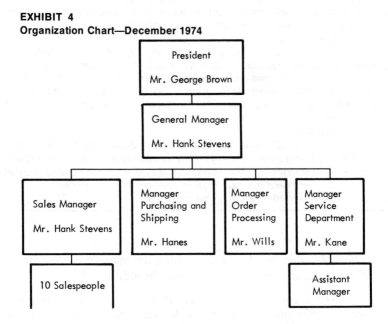

drawn from the case researcher's notes). With respect to the way his company was organized, he remarked:

> We have to have it on a functional basis now. We are also trying something new for us by moving to the general manager concept. In the past when I was away, there was no one with complete authority; now my general manager is in charge in my absence.

In discussing the new structuring of the organization, Mr. Brown was quick to point out that the company has not established formalized job descriptions. "Job descriptions are not worth anything. My people wear too many hats, and besides, we're too small to put it in writing." At present the company employs 34 people, including Mr. Brown.

Mr. Brown is quick to point out that he has never had a personnel problem. "All my people enjoy working here." He believes that "nobody should work for nothing" and has, therefore, established a personal goal of seeing to it that no one employed by UPI makes less than $10,000 per year. Mr. Brown commented on his attitude toward his employees as follows:

> The men might complain about the amount of responsibility placed on them, but I think it's good for them. It helps them develop to their potential. I'm a nice guy who is interested in all of my people. I feel a strong social obligation to my employees and have developed very close relationships with all of them. My door is always open to them no matter what the problem may be.
>
> I make it a policy never to yell at anyone in public; it's not good for morale. Maybe it's part of my conservative philosophy but I want everyone to call me Mr. Brown, not George. I think it's good for people to have a Mr. Brown. Although I want to run a nice friendly business, I have learned that it's hard to be real friends with an employee. You can only go so far. Employers and employees cannot mix socially; it just doesn't work out over the long run.
>
> This is not your normal business. I am very approachable; I don't demand much and I allow an easy open dialogue with my employees. Seldom do I take any punitive action. I'm just not a hard driving, tough guy . . . I'm an easygoing guy.
>
> It would take much of the enjoyment out of the business for me to come in here and run this place like a machine.[1]
>
> I find it hard to motivate the company's salesmen. Since we have so much trouble finding good capable men, I'm not likely to fire any that I have. This situation makes it hard for me to put pressure on them to produce.
>
> The bonus system, if you want to call it that, is I guess what you'd call very arbitrary. I have not set up specific sales quotas, or targeted goals for my inside people so, as a result, I base my bonus decisions on my assessment of how well I feel an employee performed during the past year.
>
> Recently, I've given some thought to selling the company. I could probably get around $3 to $4 million for it. If I did that, I'm not sure what I would do with my time. Besides my family and UPI there is not much that I am interested in. A couple of years ago when I took my extended vacation I got bored and couldn't wait to get back to the company.

UPI's PLANNING PROCESS

George Brown claims to be a firm believer in planning. "I find myself spending more and more time planning for the company. Currently, I'm averaging about 50 percent of my time and I see this increasing." As he described it, the planning process at United Products is really a very loose system:

> We have no set way as to how we do the planning. Basically, the process is directed at ways of increasing the profitability of the company. I look at the

---

[1] When the case researcher arrived at the plant one afternoon, he observed Mr. Brown running around the office deeply involved in a water fight with one of his office girls. By the way, he lost.

salesmen's performance on a weekly and monthly basis, and use this information in the development of the plans.

Since we have a very informal planning process, we only forecast out one year at most. The company's plans are reevaluated each month and, if necessary, new plans are set. Only on rare occasions have we ever planned beyond one year. However, I think the current economic and political situation may force us into developing plans that cover a two-year period.

I am familiar with commonly accepted theory about planning systems, but I do not feel it is necessary for UPI to institute, in a formal manner, any of those I've read about. We perform many of the activities advocated in the planning models, but we do them in a relaxed, casual fashion. For example, I am a member of many organizations connected with my business and receive industry newsletters on a regular basis. In addition, I receive input from friends and business associates both inside and outside my line of business. Since we do not have a formal process, planning tends to be a continuous process at UPI.

Although goals are not formally developed and written down, Mr. Brown said he established targets for the company to achieve in the areas of sales, profits, and organizational climate:

1. Increase sales volume of business by 20 percent per year.
2. Increase gross profit margin 0.5 to 1 percent per year.
3. Make UPI a friendly place to work.

Mr. Brown feels that the company has been able to grow at about 20 percent a year in the past and should be able to realize that level in the future. In addition, he believes that sales growth is a necessary evil: "Those companies that don't grow are swallowed up by the competition, and besides, given the level of energy I'm willing to exert, I think 20 percent is a reasonable level of growth."

In the area of profits, the company actually sets no specific targeted figures other than simply an increase in the gross profit margin (as stated above). Mr. Brown observed:

We do not set a goal because we would not have a way of measuring it. I have no way of knowing how much money I am making until the end of the year, without considerable time and effort.

When asked about UPI's strengths and weaknesses, Mr. Brown indicated that the company had four areas of strength:

1. The number of different products carried.
2. The quality of its employees, particularly salesmen.
3. The absence of any debt.
4. Purchasing capabilities.

The major weakness he viewed as an inability to get and train new personnel—primarily in the area of sales.

SALES FORCE

UPI's salesmen are not assigned a sales quota for the year, but rather are evaluated based on Mr. Brown's assessment of the particular salesman's territory and initiative. He feels his salesmen make more than the salesmen of his competitors. Several of UPI's ten salesmen have earned as much as $40,000 in a single year. All salesmen are compensated on a straight, sliding-scale commission basis calculated as follows:

8 percent for first $180,000 in sales.

7 percent for next $60,000.

6 percent for next $60,000.

5 percent for all sales over $300,000.

Mr. Brown is pleased with the sales success of his company and feels that United Products' greatest strength is its ability to "sell anything to anybody." Still, he perceives UPI's main problem as finding good salesmen. "There just aren't any good salesmen around and this is a problem because salesmen are the lifeblood of our business."

UPI's MANAGEMENT TEAM

At the time of the company's reorganization, Mr. Hank Stevens was brought in as general manager and assistant to the president. Over the past several years, Mr. Stevens' areas of responsibility have grown to an extent where they now comprise approximately 80 percent of the activities that were formerly done by Mr. Brown. As a result of this, George Brown sometimes finds himself with little to do and often works only five hours per day. As he described it:

> Hank's management discretionary power has increased steadily since he has been here—partly as a result of the extent of responsibility I've placed on him and partly due to his aggressiveness. As it now stands, he makes almost all of the daily operating decisions for the company, leaving me with only the top management decisions. Let's be realistic, there just aren't that many top-management decisions that have to be made here in the course of a day. A lot of the time, I walk around the plant checking on what other people are doing and, I guess, acting as a morale booster.

When asked about the management capabilities of Hank Stevens, Mr. Brown responded by saying, "Hank probably feels that he is working at a very fast pace, but when you evaluate the effectiveness of his actions, he is actually moving forward at what I would consider to be a very slow pace. However, everything else considered, Hank is the best of what is around. I guess if I could find a really good sales manager, I would add him to the company and relieve Hank of that area of responsibility."

Mr. Hank Stevens

Mr. Hank Stevens, 32, joined UPI at the time of the reorganization in 1970 after having graduated from a local university with a B.S. in economics. As general manager, Mr. Stevens' responsibilities included planning, purchasing, and sales management, as well as involvement in other decisions that affected UPI's policies. Mr. Stevens feels that he has been fortunate in that "Ever since I came to UPI, I've reported to the president and in essence have had everyone else reporting to me."

When asked about the goals of UPI, Mr. Stevens responded that, "As I see it, we have goals in three major areas: profitability, sales level and personal relationships." In discussing his own personal goals, Hank explained that he hoped that the organization would grow and as a result he would be able to grow along with it. Since Mr. Stevens works so closely with Mr. Brown, he has given considerable thought to his boss's business philosophy:

> I feel that George's business philosophy is unique. I guess the best way to describe it is to say that above all he is a businessman. Also, he has very high moral values and as a result of that he is extremely honest and would never cheat anybody. Actually, the company would probably look better financially if it was run by someone who didn't operate with the same values as George.

When asked about the sales force at UPI, Mr. Stevens commented that "when a new salesman starts with the company, he does so with full salary. After a period of about two years, we change him over to a commission basis." As has always been the case, UPI concentrated its sales efforts on large customers. Mr. Stevens noted that "on the average the company processes approximately 105 orders per day, with an average dollar value per order of roughly $132. It's not that we won't write small orders, we just don't solicit business from small accounts. It just makes more sense to concentrate on the larger accounts."

Mr. Jim Hanes

Jim Hanes, 24, has been with UPI for over six years and during that time has worked his way up from assistant service manager to his current position as the number-three man in the company—manager of purchasing and shipping. Jim is responsible for the front office, repair work, and the warehouse. He feels that his reporting responsibility is approximately 60 percent to Mr. Stevens and 40 percent to Mr. Brown. "Since I have responsibility for all merchandise entering and leaving the company, I get involved with both Hank and George, and, therefore, I guess I report to both of them."

In talking about where he would go from his present position, he explained that:

> I guess the next step is for me to become a salesman so that I can broaden my background and move up in the company. However, I am a little worried; I

don't think the salesmen in our company are given the right sales training. As the system works now, a new man is assigned to work with an experienced salesman for about six weeks—after which time he is given his own territory. Perhaps if our sales manager had more experience as a salesman, then he would handle the training differently.

In commenting on his understanding of Mr. Brown's philosophy, Jim summed up his position thusly, "George is a very open person. I think he is too honest for a businessman. He certainly gives his people responsibility. He gives you the ball and lets you run with it. I don't think enough planning is done at UPI. At most, it appears that we look ahead one year, and even then what plans are developed are kept very flexible."

UPI's CORPORATE STRATEGY

When asked about UPI's current strategy, Mr. Brown responded that "the company is presently a distributor in the industrial packaging equipment, shipping supplies, and heavy duty stapling equipment business. In the past when we've wanted to grow, we have done one or both of the following: either add new lines of merchandise or additional salesmen. For example, this past year I got the idea of what I call a contract sales department. It is a simple concept. I took one man, put him in an office with a telephone and a listing of the *Fortune* top 1,000 companies, and told him to call and get new business. You would be surprised at how easy it was to pick up new accounts."

Mr. Stevens looks at UPI as being in the distribution and shipping of packaging supplies business. "In order for UPI to reach the goals that have been set we have to sell more products. That is, we can grow by adding new salesmen, adding more product lines, purchasing more effectively, and undertaking more aggressive sales promotion."

Mr. Brown believes that UPI should try to maximize the profit on every item sold. To do this the company tries to set its prices at a level which is approximately 10 percent above the competition. Mr. Brown explained his pricing philosophy:

> I don't understand why people are afraid to raise prices. If you increase the price, you will pick up more business and make more money. That allows you to keep the volume low and still make more money. In addition, although the customer may pay more, he gets more. The higher price allows me to provide top notch service to all my customers.

In his view, UPI is an innovative company. "Until very recently we were always innovating with new products and new applications. Now I think it's again time that we started to look for additional new and exciting products."

Brown was aware that UPI's strategic emphasis on service, together with his business philosophy, had resulted in UPI's organization being larger than it had to be, given the level of business. Mr. Brown explained the reasoning behind this condition, "I know the organization is bigger than it has to be. We could probably handle three times the present volume of business with our present staff and facility. I think it's because of my conservative attitude; I've always wanted the organization to stay a step ahead of what is really needed. I feel comfortable with a built-in backup system and, therefore, I am willing to pay for it."

In December 1974, Mr. Brown talked optimistically about the future. He felt that sales should reach the $6–7 million range by 1978. "Looked at in another way, we should be able to grow at 20–25 percent per year without any particular effort." He went on to say:

> I want to grow and, therefore, I am making a concerted effort. I am constantly looking for possible merger avenues or expansion possibilities. I do not want to expand geographically. I would rather control that market area we are now in.
>
> I recently sent a letter to all competitors in New England offering to buy them out. Believe it or not, no one responded.
>
> I do not see any problems in the future. The history has been good, therefore, why won't it continue to happen?
>
> Growth is easy. All I have to do is pick up a new line and I've automatically increased sales and profits. Basically we are distributors, and we operate as middle-men between the manufacturers and users.
>
> In light of what has been happening in the market, I feel that supply and demand will continue to be a problem. Therefore, I am giving serious thought to integrating vertically and becoming a manufacturer. This will guarantee our supply.[2]
>
> Actually, I don't want to do the manufacturing. I think it would be better if I bought the manufacturing equipment and then had someone else use it to make my products.

THE FUTURE

Nevertheless, after reviewing with his accountant the results for the just-completed fiscal year, Mr. Brown was concerned about UPI's future course. "I know changes have to be made for next year as a result of this year, but I'm not sure what they should be." Mr. Brown continued:

> I think this next year is going to be a real bad year. Prices will probably fall like a rock from the levels they reached during 1974 and as a result those items that would have been profitable for the company aren't going to be, and we have much too large of an inventory as it is. It isn't easy to take away customers from the competition. As a result of this, I feel we have to step up our efforts to get new lines and new accounts. Recently, I've given some thought to laying off one or two people for economic reasons, but I'm not sure. I will probably give

---

[2] Refer to Exhibit 5 which contains minutes of a United Products sales meeting held at the end of 1973.

raises to all employees even though it's not a good business decision, but it's an ingrained part of my business philosophy.

When asked if he had informed his employees of his concern about the future, Mr. Brown referred to the minutes of a sales meeting that had been held in November 1974:

> . . . Mr. Brown then presided at the meeting, and announced that Al King had won the coveted award of "Salesman of the Month." This was a "first" for our Al, and well deserved for his outstanding sales results in October. Congratulations and applause were extended him by all present. The balance of the meeting was then spent in a lengthy, detailed discussion, led by Mr. George Brown, of the general, overall picture of what the future portends in the sales area as a result of the current inflationary, recessionary, and complex competitive conditions prevailing in the economy.

> The gist of the entire discussion can be best summarized as follows:

> 1. Everyone present must recognize the very real difficulties that lie ahead in these precarious economic times.
> 2. The only steps available to the salesmen and to the company for survival during the rough period ahead are as follows:
>   A. Minimize the contacts with existing accounts.
>   B. Spend the *majority* of time *developing new accounts* on the less competitive products; and *selling new products to established accounts*.
> 3. *Concentrate on and promote our new items.*
> 4. Mr. Brown and inside management are making and will continue to make every, concentrated effort to find new products and new lines for the coming year.

In preparation for his meeting with Hank Stevens, Mr. Brown had drawn up a list of activities to which Hank should address himself while running UPI during George's upcoming vacation. Mr. Brown believed that upon his return from Europe his activities at UPI would be increasing as a result of the problems caused by the uncertain economic conditions. The first item on the list was a possible redefinition of UPI's marketing strategy. Mr. Brown now believed that UPI would have to be much more liberal with respect to new products considered for sale. "I'm not saying we are going to get into the consumer goods business, but I think we need to give consideration to handling consumer products which require no service and which carry a high-profit-margin factor for the company."

As he sat at his desk thinking about possible changes which he could make in UPI's planning process, Mr. Brown was convinced that if he hadn't done some planning in the past, the situation would be more drastic than it was. Yet at the same time, he wasn't sure that a more structured and formalized planning process would put UPI in any better position to face the more difficult times that he saw ahead.

EXHIBIT 5
Minutes of UPI's Sales Meeting, December 5, 1973

Mr. Brown presided at the meeting. His opening remarks highlighted the ex-traordinary times our country and our company are going through as far as the general economy and the energy crisis are concerned, and the extraordinary effects of these unusual crises on people and businesses, including our company and our sources of supply.

He thanked all present for the many thoughtful, considered and excellent suggestions which they had offered in writing as to how best the salesmen and their company might handle the gasoline crisis without incurring an undue loss of sales and profits, and still maintaining the high standards of service to which UNITED PRODUCTS' thousands of satisfied customers are accustomed.

The whole situation, according to Mr. Brown, boils down to a question of supply and prices. Mr. Brown reported that on his recent trip to the Orient, there were very few companies who wanted to sell their merchandise to us—rather, THEY WANTED TO BUY FROM US MANY OF THE ITEMS WE NORMALLY BUY FROM FOREIGN COMPANIES, i.e., carton-closing staples, tape, gloves, et cetera . . . and at inflated prices!!! The Tokyo, Japan market is so great that they are using up everything they can produce—and the steel companies would rather make flat steel than the steel rods which are used for making staples. A very serious problem exists, as a result, in the carton-closing staple field not only in Japan, but also in Europe and America.

Mr. Brown advised that every year the company's costs of operating increase just as each individual's cost of living goes up and up yearly. Additional personnel, increased group and auto insurance premiums, increased Social Security pay-ments, new office equipment and supplies, new catalogues, "Beeper system" for more salesmen—all of these costs accumulate and result in large expenditures of money. Manufacturers cover their increased operating costs by pricing their products higher—but to date, UNITED PRODUCTS has never put into their prices the increased costs resulting from increased operating expenses. Last year, the 3 percent increase which the company needed then was put into effect by many of you. HOWEVER, in order for the company to realize that additional profit, this 3 percent price increase had to be put into effect ACROSS THE BOARD . . . all customers . . . all items!

THAT DID NOT HAPPEN!!!

Mr. Brown advised that UNITED PRODUCTS got LAMBASTED when all of the sources of supply started to increase their prices. When SPOTNAILS, for example, went up 10 percent, the salesmen only increased their prices 7 percent, et cetera. We did *not get the 3 percent price increase above the manufacturers' price increase*—and we needed it then and need it even more NOW.

Eliminating the possibility of cutting commissions, there are three possible so-lutions for the problem of how to get this much needed and ABSOLUTELY IMPERA-TIVE additional 3 percent PRICE INCREASE ACROSS THE BOARD to cover the constantly growing operating costs for running a successful, progressive-minded and growing business whose high standards of service and performance are highly regarded by customers and sources of supply alike, namely:

a.   A 3 percent increase on all items to all customers across the board.
b.   A surcharge on all invoices or decrease in discounts allowed off LIST.
c.   A G.C.I. charge (government cost increase) on all invoices.

Considerable discussion regarding these three possibilities resulted in the fol-lowing conclusions concerning the best method for obtaining this special 3 percent ACROSS THE BOARD PRICE INCREASE, as follows:

a.   A new PRICE BOOK should be issued with all new prices to reflect not only

EXHIBIT 5 (continued)

the manufacturers' new increased prices, but in addition the 3 percent UNITED PRODUCTS PRICE INCREASE. All of the salesmen agreed that it would be easier to effect the additional 3 percent price increase if the 3 percent was "Built in" on their price book sheets.

b. This new PRICE BOOK will be set up in such a way that prices will be stipulated according to quantity of item purchased . . . with no variances allowed. WITH NO EXCEPTIONS, the Price of any item will depend on the quantity a customer buys.

c. Some items will continue to be handled on a discount basis—but lower discounts in order to ascertain that UNITED PRODUCTS is getting its 3 percent price increase.

d. Until these new PRICE BOOKS are issued, all salesmen were instructed to proceed IMMEDIATELY to effect these 3 percent price increases.

TEN NEW ACCOUNTS CONTEST

Seven of our ten salesmen won a calculator as a result of opening up 10 new accounts each . . . a total of 70 NEW ACCOUNTS for our company!!! However, both Mr. Brown and Mr. Stevens confessed that the dollar volume amount stipulated in the contest had been set ridiculously low, as a "feeler" to determine the success and effectiveness of such a contest. All the salesmen voiced their approval of all of the contests offered to them—and agreed that they had enjoyed many excellent opportunities of increasing their personal exchecquers.

NEW CUSTOMER LETTERS

Mr. Brown again reminded all present that we have an excellent printed letter, which is available for sending to every new customer—and urged all to take advantage of this service by the office personnel by clearly indicating on their sales and order slips "NEW CUSTOMER." This procedure is but another step towards our goal of becoming more and more professional in our approach with our customers.

NEW CATALOGS

Mr. Brown advised that by the first of the new year, hopefully, all our hard-cover catalogs with their new divider breakdowns will be ready for hand-delivering to large accounts. These catalogs cost the company over $5 and should only be distributed by hand to those customers who can and will make intelligent and effective use of them.

EXCESSIVE ISSUANCE OF CREDITS

As a result of a detailed study made by Mr. Brown of the nature and reasons for the ever-increasing number of credits being issued, he instructed all of the salesmen to follow these procedures when requesting the issuing of CREDITS:

a. Issue the CREDIT at the right time.
b. Do not spell an item where it is not needed.
c. NEVER PUT "NO COMMENT" for the reason why merchandise is being returned. EVERY CREDIT MUST HAVE A REASON FOR ITS ISSUANCE.

The ever-increasing number of CREDITS being issued is extremely costly to the company: (1) new merchandise comes back 90-plus days after it has been billed, and frequently, if not always, is returned by the customer FREIGHT COLLECT; (2) CREDIT 9-part forms, postage for mailing, and extra work for both the Bookkeeping and Billing and Order Processing Departments mean higher expenses for the Company. More intelligent, considered and selective selling, plus greater care on the part of the Order Processing personnel, according to Mr. Brown, could easily eliminate a large percentage of these CREDITS.

3.1. The University of Arkansas Athletic Department (A)*

THE LATE John Barnhill, athletic director for the University of Arkansas Razorbacks (1945–68), had a philosophy that a "winning tradition" could overcome all obstacles. He did not believe in winning at all costs, but he did believe that a winning tradition would attract football players, aspiring coaches, fan support, alumni contributions, and security for coaches—all vital resources for a successful football program. "Winning is not everything but it surely beats second best," he used to say. "And a winning tradition is what we are shooting for. I don't like to be associated with a loser. What really counts for a football coach and his personnel is his win-loss record. Thirty days after a season is over, the win-loss record is what remains."

BARNHILL'S SCHEDULING STRATEGY

Barnie, as his associates called him, had another philosophy which became a part of his strategy of scheduling football games for the Razorbacks. Barnhill's thinking was embodied in such comments as "Don't overschedule your potential," and "Don't mismatch your resources." His conservative approach to scheduling of football games was seen in his scheduling strategy particularly for nonconference games. For conference games, however, it was standard for Arkansas to play each of the other members of the conference on a rotating home and away basis.

The University of Arkansas is a member of the Southwest Conference (SWC). Other schools included the University of Texas Longhorns (traditionally the power of the conference), the Texas A&M Aggies, the Texas Tech Red Raiders, the Southern Methodist Mustangs, the Rice Owls, the Baylor Bears, and the Texas Christian Horned Frogs. The University of Arkansas was the only conference member outside the state of Texas.

---

* Prepared by Robert D. Hay and Frank Broyles, the University of Arkansas at Fayetteville.

Barnhill inherited a losing tradition when he came to the University of Arkansas in 1945. One thing he noticed in reviewing the schedules of past seasons was that the Razorbacks rarely won a football game on Texas soil during September and October. He attributed this to the fact that Arkansas' players, used to the cooler mountain temperatures of northwest Arkansas, were unduly fatigued by the daytime heat in Texas. Beginning in 1948, Barnhill endeavored to schedule all of the conference away games in September and October at night. From then on, the Razorbacks won a larger percentage of the early fall conference games played against TCU, Baylor, and Texas—which typically were the first three SWC opponents each year.

John Barnhill's winning tradition and his scheduling strategy were made more specific in his scheduling of three nonconference games. Following his philosophy of not overscheduling the team's potential, he tried to make sure that the first two games, preceding the conference opener with TCU, were scheduled against teams where there was a reasonable chance to win. As it happened, those two teams were traditional rivals of the Razorbacks—the Oklahoma State Cowboys and the Tulsa Hurricane. Both of these schools had successful teams in the 1940s, but both had fallen upon hard times and were having difficulty in attracting crowds for home games in the 1950s and 1960s. Barnie prevailed upon both schools to play Arkansas in Little Rock or Fayetteville for 15 straight years, because both OSU and Tulsa could make more money playing away from home in Arkansas where football crowds on Saturdays in September would be anywhere from 20,000 to 40,000 people—many more than either school was currently averaging at home.

Barnhill figured that if the Razorbacks could win those first two games, the team would have a winning momentum when Arkansas played its first SWC opener with TCU, under the lights in Texas or in cooler weather in Arkansas when played at home. The strategy worked; during the decade of 1959–69 Arkansas beat Oklahoma State and Tulsa combined 19 times, with only 2 losses.

Another of Barnhill's scheduling strategies was to play a ''breather'' game half way through the football schedule. This allowed the Razorbacks a chance to regroup their forces if necessary, to lick their wounds, to allow time for injured players to recover, and to give second-stringers a chance to play and gain some experience down the homestretch of conference play against Texas A&M, Rice, SMU, and Texas Tech, the traditional November opponents. This breather game was always scheduled at home, usually against such lesser known schools as Hardin-Simmons, Wichita State, Kansas State, North Texas State, and others. The Razorbacks did not lose a breather game during the 1960s.

John Barnhill's philosophy and scheduling strategies, along with the leadership of head football coach Frank Broyles, helped the Razorbacks gain football respectability during the 1960s. For the 11-year period 1959 through 1969, the Razorback's win-loss record was:

	Wins	Losses	Ties	
1959	9	2		
1960	8	3		
1961	8	3		
1962	9	2		
1963	5	5		
1964	11	0		(National Champion)
1965	10	1		
1966	8	2		
1967	4	5	1	
1968	10	1		
1969	9	2		

A SHIFT IN STRATEGY

When John Barnhill retired at age 65 as athletic director in 1968, George Cole became athletic director. However, the scheduling function with its corresponding responsibilities, authority, and accountability was delegated to Frank Broyles, the head football coach.

In December 1969, the Razorbacks played the University of Texas (the "Big Shootout I") on national television, with President Nixon attending the game in Fayetteville. The latest AP poll had Texas ranked No. 1 and Arkansas No. 2. At the time, both Texas' Darrell Royal and Arkansas' Frank Broyles had identical conference coaching records (62–18–1). Texas won 15–14.

In January 1970, the NCAA, in an effort to counteract the financial deficits being experienced by a growing number of athletic departments, approved an 11-game football schedule. Frank Broyles had to make a decision of whether to go to an 11-game schedule and if so, whom to schedule. Overall, his teams of the 1960s had been successful. The 1969 team lost only to Texas, and Arkansas still had the makings of an excellent team in 1970. Broyles had recruited Joe Ferguson, a highly touted passer from Shreveport, and was confident that Arkansas would have a good team.

Criticism had arisen, however, of Barnhill's scheduling strategy. There were always those fans and sports writers who complained about the schedule of the Razorbacks—easy first two games and the breather game. Broyles had received numerous letters which were critical of the Razorback's schedule and called for Arkansas to play national powers instead of Tulsa, Oklahoma State, and Wichita State. Broyles was mindful of these letters since he had always answered each one personally.

The financial resources of the athletic department were adequate enough to stay in the black. However, there was the constant pressure of other sports—basketball, golf, baseball, track, and others—to get more financial resources which the football team could and did generate for the athletic department. All sports were financially supported by football revenues; very little came from state of Arkansas tax support.

There was a need to pay for the Astro-turf on the home field and in Little Rock and for additional funds to fulfill a dream of improving the athletic facilities at the university. Frank did not consult his players, but there seemed to be overwhelming support from the fans and alumni for an 11th game.

Pacific Eight football teams had a certain glamour to Frank Broyles. Besides, he was sure that the coaches and players would enjoy a trip to California to play Stanford, California, or Southern California. All three teams had good records in football over the years and Southern California, especially, was recognized as a perennial national powerhouse in football. And national, rather than regional, exposure was a significant factor in Frank's thinking. However, there were other alternative teams in the wings—Notre Dame, Oklahoma, Tennessee, Utah State, New Mexico State, and Colorado State.

Frank Broyles consulted John Barnhill about the 11th game and about possible contenders. Barnie told Frank that he (Barnie) was against playing those West Coast teams. However, he said, "Frank, you have the scheduling authority. Do what you think is right."

THE OUTCOME

Frank Broyles made the decision to go to an 11-game schedule and negotiated opening games with Stanford and California, both in Little Rock for 1970–71. He also arranged a home, away from home, and home game with Southern California for 1972, 1973, and 1974. In 1975, the first game was to be with the Air Force Academy. These opening games were scheduled in direct opposition to John Barnhill's scheduling strategy of playing opening games with teams where there was a reasonable chance to win and where some momentum could be gained in winning before the conference schedule began in October of each year.

In the fall of 1970, Frank arranged with ABC to televise a national TV opener with Stanford. To do so it was necessary to raise $500,000 for Astro-turf and lights for color TV, a feat performed by Little Rock supporters of the Razorbacks. The game matched two of several Heisman Trophy candidates, Jim Plunkett of Stanford and Bill Montgomery of Arkansas. The Razorbacks lost that game 34–28. However, they regrouped and finished the season with a 9–2 record, losing to Texas in the last game of the season ("Big Shootout II").

In 1971, the Razorbacks won their opener against the California Golden Bears, followed by a victory against Oklahoma State, but then they were upset by Tulsa, 21–20. The season record was 8–3–1, with Joe Ferguson providing a passing attack for the Razorbacks.

In 1972, Frank Broyles knew that USC would be a national football power. Both Frank Broyles and John McKay, head coach of the Trojans, surmised that the winner of the Arkansas–USC game would probably be No. 1 in the polls. USC romped over the Razorbacks 31–10, and wound up No. 1 for the rest of the season. Arkansas' record was 6–5.

Barnie told Frank, "You ruined a good coaching job." Frank lamented, "We'll never know how much losing to USC took away from us. I'll bet we lost $50,000 in revenues in future games that year because of our loss to USC." The opening game with USC in 1973 was another loss, 17–0, for the Razorbacks. It was followed by a second loss to Oklahoma State. The season record was 5–5–1.

STRATEGY CHANGE ONCE AGAIN?

During 1973, Frank Broyles was again faced with a scheduling problem. The University of Houston had been admitted to the Southwest Conference, and was to play Arkansas on a home and away basis on the date of the normal breather game in October. John Barnhill's scheduling philosophy again was being challenged. It was also during 1973 that Frank was deciding about his opening games for 1976, 1977, and 1978. He was considering New Mexico State, Utah State, and Colorado State, along with Notre Dame, Tennessee, and Oklahoma.

EXHIBIT 1
Selected Financial Information of the University of Arkansas Athletic Department*

Year	Balance 7/1	Income	Expend- itures	Trans- fers	Balance 6/30	Cash	Deferred Income
1955	$ 2,434	$ 747,835	$ 627,315	$ (29,934)	$ 94,200		
1956	94,200	709,918	610,792	(94,200)	106,384		
1957	106,384	683,116	610,792	(112,839)	66,318		
1958		670,709	633,390	37,318		$ 205,151	$ 205,151
1959		501,068	558,666	(90,931)	33,333	258,078	(224,746
1960	33,333	622,751	580,848	(7,502)	82,739	367,716	(284,977
1961	82,739	662,237	664,890	(19,022)	99,107	424,705	(325,597
1962	99,107	732,066	665,084	(13,176)	179,265	480,209	(300,944
1963	179,265	720,912	722,176	(13,670)	191,670	726,053	(534,384
1964	191,670	698,872	691,565	(3,575)	195,403	662,687	(467,284
1965	195,403	920,839	917,238	41,585	240,589	1,006,638	(766,049
1966	240,589	1,463,480	1,325,693	(118,817)	259,559	709,034	(449,475
1967	259,559	1,151,112	1,092,739	6,841	324,772	768,793	(444,021
1968	324,772	1,203,543	1,371,016	33,039	192,138	827,267	(635,129
1969	192,138	1,203,679	1,665,126	13,330	234,021	1,099,366	(865,345
1970	234,021	3,145,455	3,109,145	267,664	2,668	954,359	(951,691
1971	2,667	2,435,275	2,462,531	30,500	4,812	1,055,956	(1,051,144
1972	4,812	1,748,328	1,758,601	18,304	12,844	1,394,305	(1,381,461

* Figures for each year do not balance or reconcile because of other accounting entries not shown. A full schedule income and expenditures (for 1975) is shown in Exhibit 2 of the (B) case which follows (see p. 236).

EXHIBIT 2
University of Arkansas Football Attendance (home games)

Year	Attendance	No. of Games at Little Rock and Fayetteville	Average per Game
1965	293,850	7	41,978
1966	257,950	6	42,975
1967	309,587	7	44,225
1968	275,179	6	45,863
1969	302,072	7	43,153
1970	317,000	7	45,285
1971	381,221	8	47,652
1972	329,117	7	47,016
1973	299,981	7	42,854
1974	320,809	7	45,829

EXHIBIT 3
1974 Schedules of Other Teams Said To Be Using "the Barnhill Strategy"

Alabama*	Tennessee*	Penn State†
Maryland	UCLA	Stanford
Southern Mississippi	Kansas	Navy
Vanderbilt	Auburn	Iowa
Mississippi	Tulsa	Army
Florida State	LSU	Wake Forest
Tennessee	Alabama	Syracuse
TCU	Clemson	W. Virginia
Miss. State	Memphis State	Maryland
LSU	Mississippi	N. C. State
Miami, Fla.	Kentucky	Ohio U.
Auburn	Vanderbilt	Pittsburgh

Oklahoma‡	Texas§	Notre Dame†
Baylor	Boston College	Georgia Tech
Utah State	Wyoming	Northwestern
Wake Forest	Texas Tech	Purdue
Texas	Washington	Michigan State
Colorado	Oklahoma	Rice
Kansas State	Arkansas	Army
Iowa State	Rice	Miami, Fla.
Missouri	SMU	Navy
Kansas	Baylor	Pittsburgh
Nebraska	TCU	Air Force
Oklahoma State	Texas A&M	Southern Cal.

* Southeastern Conference.
† Independent.
‡ Big Eight Conference.
§ Southwest Conference.

3.2. The University of Arkansas Athletic Department (B)*

THE SOUTHWEST CONFERENCE (SWC) annual swimming and diving competition was held in Razorback pool in March 1975. All member schools in the Southwest Conference entered except for Baylor. As expected, Southern Methodist swept practically all the events, winning the meet by an overwhelming margin. For some 17 years SMU had dominated the conference and 1975 was no exception.

The Arkansas Razorbacks won fourth place, winning only one event—the 50-yard freestyle. However, another swimmer did come in second, just behind a Texas Longhorn swimmer who held a nationally ranked time in the 200-yard breast stroke event. Three members of the Razorback diving team who had met the national qualification standards while competing in the regular season finished sixth, eighth, and tenth in the diving competition. SMU divers won the first five places.

Since the three Razorback divers had met the NCAA qualifying standards, despite their poor showing in the Southwest Conference meet, the Arkansas swimming coach, Ed Fedosky, submitted a travel request of approximately $3,500 for the three divers, two swimmers, and two coaches to attend the NCAA Swimming and Diving Championship at Long Beach, California. The request first went to the assistant athletic director, Lon Farrell, to whom the swimming coach reported on administrative matters in the athletic department. Lon immediately raised the question of whether the department could afford to spend $3,500 to send five athletes and two coaches to the NCAA event—particularly in light of the poor showing of the three divers in the Southwest Conference meet. Lon approached Frank Broyles, the athletic director, to register his objection to the request to send all seven people to the NCAA meet. Broyles was left with deciding what course of action to follow.

HISTORY AND BACKGROUND

Two years ago, the Razorback swimming coach had requested to take nine qualifiers, but he was allowed to take only four to the national event.

---

* Prepared by Robert D. Hay, Lon Farrell, Ed Fedosky, and Frank Broyles, all of the University of Arkansas at Fayetteville.

230

Last year, two divers who had qualified attended the NCAA championship event. The swimming coach stated, "Fulfillment of national qualifying standards, with permission from the coach of the respective sport (such as swimming, golf, track, and tennis), and first place conference finishes have both been previously used in assessing qualifiers for attending NCAA meets."

He continued, "We never really had an established policy, and it really never entered our minds that we would need one. This year I submitted a request to take five athletes—two swimmers and three divers—and two coaches—John Phillips, our diving coach, and me. I thought that the athletic department would have enough money to honor my request, although I knew that our swimming budget of $38,000 did not include any provision to attend the NCAA meet."

Ed Fedosky continued, "Our swimming program is geared toward qualifying for the nationals. We try to do our best in the Southwest Conference meet, but SMU and Texas have so many guys already qualified for the nationals prior to the conference meet."

Lon Farrell, however, raised the question of whether sending the three divers and diving coach would accomplish anything for the Razorback swimming program. The budget was very tight and Farrell was of the opinion that perhaps the money could be spent in a better fashion next year for improving the swimming program. "Why waste our limited financial resources on sending three divers and a coach to an NCAA meet when there isn't a chance that they will come anywhere close to winning?" He further knew that last year, when two divers were sent to the NCAA meet, they scored 56th and 64th (on three dives) out of 69 contestants. In another diving event, one of the two divers scored 57th out of 59. Two years ago, a Razorback swimmer placed 32nd out of 37 in the 100-yard breast stroke and 25th out of 31 in the 200-yard breast stroke. Another swimmer placed 44th out of 50 in the 100-yard butterfly, and 39th out of 40 in the 200-yard butterfly.

REVIEW BY THE ATHLETIC DIRECTOR

Frank Broyles, upon hearing the pleas of Lon Farrell and Ed Fedosky, instructed Farrell to call the University of Oklahoma to find out what their policy was in regard to sending individual athletes to NCAA events. Oklahoma reported that the Big Eight school followed the practice of sending only conference winners to national meets. Broyles knew that the Southeastern Conference (SEC) schools generally, but not always, followed the same policy.

Further investigation revealed that SMU's budget for swimming was $26,000, not counting support from outside benefactors, while the Texas Longhorns spent more than the $38,000 budget of the Razorbacks. SMU followed the practice of sending only selected swimmers and divers to the national meet, regardless of whether they had qualifying scores (although everyone who went to the NCAA meet had qualified). Lon Farrell further rationalized that since SMU with its smaller budget did not send all of its qualifiers, why should the Razorbacks be different from SMU, the conference powerhouse in swimming.

Lon Farrell also knew that during the past year Frank Broyles had increased the swimming budget, as well as the budgets for all nonrevenue sports. He also had approved a capital expenditure of $10,000 for a timing device for the swimming pool. Lon stated, "We are worried about the effect of the energy crisis on football gate receipts. Football receipts, as we all know, provide the revenue for all sports. Basketball, the Razorbacks only other revenue sports program, lost $100,000 during the past year."

He added, "We are operating under financial handicaps that we've never had before. We estimate that next year's receipts will cover our expenses but there are so many variables. A lot of things are changing, and we have to be prepared for them."

Frank Broyles stated, "I feel that we must establish a qualification standard that will be fair to the coaches, the athletes, and still be within the financial limits of the athletic department as to individual competition in national meets."

Broyles also remarked, "I am interested in developing strong teams with sufficient numbers to win dual and triangular meets and the Southwest Conference championship. Perhaps any money saved can be wisely used to improve the overall swimming program." He further wondered about what policy he would recommend to the Faculty Athletic Committee as he temporarily decided to send only conference champs to national meets and so notified the swimming coach.

Several days thereafter, the assistant diving coach was interviewed by a regional TV sports director. The coach, along with the three divers, commented, "It would have made a big difference to us if such a policy had been established before the season started. We divers stayed at the University during spring break to practice. Then we found out that we could not go to the nationals. We had trained all year for this meet."

POLICIES AT OTHER SCHOOLS

About two weeks later, the results of an informal survey which Lon Farrell made of other schools became known. He had written to a large number of schools trying to determine what criteria athletic directors in the Big Ten, Big Eight, Southwest, and Southeastern conferences used in determining which individuals were sent to the NCAA championships in swimming, track, golf, and tennis. The following universities responded to Farrell's inquiry:

1. University of Nebraska (Big Eight)
2. University of Illinois (Big Ten)
3. University of Tennessee (SEC)

4. University of Houston (SWC)
5. Southern Methodist University (SWC)
6. University of Kentucky (SEC)
7. University of Alabama (SEC)
8. Kansas State University (Big Eight)
9. University of Colorado (Big Eight)
10. Michigan State University (Big Ten)
11. Louisiana State University (SEC)
12. University of Florida (SEC)
13. University of Wisconsin (Big Ten)
14. Iowa State University (Big Eight)
15. Oklahoma State University (Big Eight)
16. Purdue University (Big Ten)
17. University of Michigan (Big Ten)
18. Ohio State University (Big Ten)
19. Indiana University (Big Ten)
20. Rice University (SWC)
21. University of Arkansas (SWC)

The survey results are presented in Exhibit 1.

EXHIBIT 1
Criteria Different Universities Use in Their Selection of Individuals to Participate in NCAA Championships in Swimming, Track and Field, Golf, and Tennis

Criteria Used*	Swimming	Track and Field	Golf	Tennis
Merely meet NCAA standards	1	1	0	0
Meet NCAA standards and in estimation of coach and athletic director have chance to score points in Nationals	6	6	5	5
Place first in Conference meet or tournament	5	7	7	7
Place first or second in Conference meet or tournament and meet NCAA standards	5	4	3	6
Place first, second, or third in Conference meet or tournament and meet NCAA standards	4	5	4	4
Send entire team if they win conference championship	1	0	1	1
Have a time or rating in the top ten in the nation	1	1	1	1
Selected by District Committee	0	0	3	0
Strictly up to coach but must come out of his budget	1	1	1	1

* Some colleges reported more than one criterion.

ATTEMPTS TO RESOLVE THE POLICY DISPUTE

Three weeks later the swimming coach, the assistant athletic director, and the athletic director met to discuss the situation. The swimming coach made the following statements:

1. Farrell's survey *does not* include the following teams that contribute to the quality of the meet:

South Carolina	Air Force
North Carolina State	University of the Pacific
Miami of Florida	Long Beach State
(NCAA Individual Championship)	Kent State
Miami of Ohio	Texas at Arlington
Southern Illinois	Florida State
Tulane	

2. Our program at Arkansas is geared to the NCAA qualifying times. This is what we strive for and is a main factor when trying to recruit the better athletes.

3. The NAIA's swimming championship was a "bust" this year because of the stringent restrictions placed on the teams for entering the meet. The number of heats for each event was held down to three or four; fewer participants were in attendance during the meet; enthusiasm was very low and the final outcome was rather obvious from the beginning. The meet was very dull.

4. Tough conferences would eliminate most of the swimmers from the meet if only the first and second place finishers attended. Roughly 75 percent of the swimmers would know from the first day of practice that they would not be going to the NCAA championships and the greatest motivator would be lost. Such teams as SMU, Indiana, Tennessee, and USC would be the only teams at the meet.

5. The reasons why there are a great many entries in the NCAA championships who have not placed first or second in their respective conferences are:

   a. Some swimmers are very versatile and qualify in several events during the season but are limited to only three events in their conference championships.

   b. Very few of our top teams ever "peak" *during* the season *or* for conference meets.

   c. The major tapering, peaking, psyching-up (including shavings) *must come only at one time* during the season. It is extremely difficult to "peak" a second time during one season. (Oregon had a fantastic conference meet and did not score one point at the NCAA meet—they missed their "peak" or hit it early against SMU. Only one swimmer from the Big Eight scored.) Some individuals consider the NAAU's as the big meet of the year and only shoot for that meet, which comes two weeks after the NCAA championships.

   d. Diving is something else. It is all subjective opinion by the judges. On any given day even the No. 1 diver in the country will miss only *one* dive and not get into the finals. This happened to a diver from Ohio State this year. Last year he won both the 1 meter and 3 meter events. There are to be 94 entries in diving this year. Each diver will perform three dives and then the total will be "cut" to 32 divers. Those divers will do five more dives and the list will be cut to 12 who do three more dives in the finals. There is an attempt being made to allow those divers who meet the qualifying standards to perform all 11 dives before the "first cut." Time is a great factor in this situation.

6. I would like to make the following recommendations for future attendance at NCAA events:

    a. $3,000 be added to the swimming budget for use only for the NCAA meet. (The farther the distance from Fayetteville, the fewer participants in attendance.)

    b. All swimmers and divers who meet the NCAA qualifying standards to be eligible.

    c. The decision be left to the coach in determining those swimmers or divers who deserve the opportunity to represent the University of Arkansas at the NCAA championships.

EXHIBIT 2
Schedule of Revenues and Expenditures for the University of Arkansas Athletic Department, Year Ended June 30, 1975

Revenues:
Sports*

Football	$1,087,898.50
Basketball	35,702.27
Other sports	1,482.04
Southwest Conference—Pool Division	180,000.00
Radio and Television	109,456.74
Programs and concessions	77,305.40
Parking lot	2,483.75
Gifts and donations†	120,000.00
Other revenue items	133,215.65
Total Revenues	$1,747,544.35

Expenditures:

Administration and general	309,697.44
Buildings and grounds	65,195.77
Training room and publicity	25,474.33
Football	1,005,092.07
Baseball	52,920.73
Basketball	143,197.63
Track	75,794.98
Golf	21,604.14
Swimming	38,047.51
Tennis	23,841.51
Band	1,710.16
Radio and television	36,753.14
Concessions	39,507.82
Scholarships (total expenditures of $403,233.70 included with sports)	
Total Expenditures	$1,838,837.23

Transfers—additions (deductions):

Student fee allocation	166,500.00
Plant additions and improvements	(797.76)
Debt service	(37,689.29)
Band scholarships	(5,000.00)
Other nonrecurring transfers	(1,685.60)
Recovery of indirect costs	59,500.00
Total Transfers	$ 180,827.35
Change in fund balance	$ 89,534.47
Balance—July 1, 1974	5,905.11
Balance—June 30, 1975	$ 95,439.58

* Revenues are *net* after guarantees and options.
† For educational scholarships.

4. Riverview Apartments*

RIVERVIEW APARTMENTS, consisting of five buildings of 18–24 apartments each, were built during 1970–71 in Academe, home of State University, in response to continued demand for off-campus housing. Student enrollment at the university had increased almost 120 percent between 1960 and 1970.

LOCATION AND CONSTRUCTION

The apartment site is located three blocks from the university. Sidewalks exist for two of the three blocks. Since Academe had no bus service, there was a parking problem in the university area. Riverview Apartment residents, however, could walk to the campus.

The apartments are one-bedroom units, with living room, kitchen area, and bath. They have all modern features except dishwashers, including central heat and air conditioning, carpets, and drapes. Ninety-eight units are furnished; 80 with twin beds and 18 with double beds. The manager's apartment includes a double bed, and one unit was designated as a storage area. Coin-operated washers, dryers, and vending machines are located in a service building. A large swimming pool is the central recreation theme.

The first buildings were available for occupancy in September 1970, one week after university registration began. The managing realtor attempted to mollify future tenants because of the postregistration availability, and in several instances arranged motel accommodations for students who were unable to stay for several days with friends until the buildings were completed. The second building was ready for occupancy one week later. Despite the problems attendant with the completion date of the first two buildings, all 46 units were occupied by October 15, 1970. Seventy-four paved parking spaces were available.

Work continued on the third, fourth, and fifth buildings during winter, spring, and summer 1971. Owing to other construction activities, the swimming pool could not be completed until August 1971; no landscaping was done, and inspection of building features was hampered because tenants were waiting to occupy each unit as soon as it was completed.

The university changed its registration date in fall 1971, so that the fall

* Prepared by Leon Joseph Rosenberg, the University of Arkansas at Fayetteville.

semester would be completed prior to the Christmas holidays. Classes began on August 25, three weeks earlier than previous years. Final exams ended on December 22 and registration for the spring semester began on January 10. This change resulted in a three and one-half week winter vacation instead of the former two weeks.

The third, fourth, and part of the fifth Riverview buildings were completed in October 1971, five weeks after the fall semester began. Despite their late completion, 36 units were rented in October. The remaining units were finally finished late in February 1972, almost 18 months after the first apartment unit was completed.

MANAGEMENT AND OPERATIONS

The corporation that owned the apartments was headquartered in Capitol City, 175 miles from Academe. The managing realtors, who had a sizable position in the owning corporation, were also located in Capitol City. Further, the prime contractor, similarly located in Capitol City, was a principal investor in the ownership corporation. The prime contractor used the services of a number of subcontractors, several of whom were located in Academe.

Riverview's management policy called for the complex to be managed by a married graduate student couple. The managers were given an apartment and a salary of $200 per month. This was above the compensation level provided managers of other student apartment complexes in Academe. An extended recruiting and selection process resulted in the hiring of Jack Brite, a public administration student and his wife, Peggy, to manage the complex during the academic year 1970–71. Jack was a full-time graduate student; Peggy took one course each semester.

The managing couple was totally responsible for the Academe operation, including renting, advertising, and inside and outside housekeeping. Plumbers, electricians, and heating and air conditioning service companies were called when necessary. However, as long as construction continued, the prime contractors, having an ownership interest, provided necessary mechanical maintenance.

Owing to onsite construction activities, the swimming pool was not completed until the end of the summer of 1971. Despite Riverview's lower summer rental rate, a number of tenants moved to apartments with completed pools. The number of students attending the university during the summer was traditionally lower than during the regular academic year, so finding an available apartment presented no problem to the 1971 summer school students.

Jack and Peggy Brite received little guidance from the Capitol City property management office. The divisional manager of apartment residences was responsible for the operation of 25 complexes in Capitol City plus 3 located in towns near his headquarters office.

The successor management couple to Jack and Peggy were selected after numerous interviews, with Jack and Peggy participating in the selection. Bill Roberts, a pre-law senior undergraduate, and his wife, Ann, were employed. None of the other applicants for the position seemed to be as fully qualified for the managerial position. Jack and Peggy were continued on the payroll, and in an apartment, for four weeks to help train the new managers. Ann and Bill were both enrolled as full-time students.

The supervisor from Capitol City headquarters visited Academe after Bill and Ann were hired. A number of Riverview's tenants moved out at the end of the 1971 summer session. Bill and Ann rented many of the vacant units, but in October an additional 36 units became available—at just about mid-semester. Thirty-three units were rented, but the vacancy ratio of 12 percent in mid-October increased to 23 percent in mid-December (see Exhibit 1).

XHIBIT 1
ccupancy Record

	Units*	Vacancy†	Percent Vacancy		Units*	Vacancy†	Percent Vacancy
?70				**1972**			
September	22	1	4%	January	91	18	20%
October	46	0	0	February	97	22	23
November	46	0	0	March	97	25	26
December	46	2	4	April	97	24	25
				May	97	6	6
?71				June	97	1	1
January	46	0	0	July	97	2	2
February	46	0	0	August	97	1	1
March	46	0	0	September	97	1	1
April	46	1	2	October	97	4	4
May	46	0	0	November	97	5	5
June	46	5	11	December	97	11	11
July	46	2	4				
August	46	10	22	**1973**			
September	46	5	11	January	97	22	23
October	82	10	12	February	97	22	23
November	82	12	15	March	97	27	28
December	83	19	23	April	97	27	28
				May	97	33	34
				June	97	0	0
				July	97	1	1

* Riverview's first two buildings (24 units each) were opened during September 1970; more buildings were completed ween October 1971 and March 1972.

† Monthly vacancy rates for 1970 and 1971 are based on an analysis of monthly statements; 1972 and 1973 data are taken m weekly occupancy reports, at mid-month.

Although weather slowed construction in December 1971, and January 1972, the last nine units were completed. Meanwhile, since the new academic schedule resulted in a winter holiday break of three and one-half weeks between semesters, a number of tenants forfeited their damage deposit ($50 per apartment), moved out and either returned one month later, or moved into competitive apartment units.

When the total Riverview complex, consisting of 98 units plus the managers' apartment, and an apartment for storage or an assistant manager, was completed, there was a minimum of onsite inspection by the owning corporation representatives. Due to the weather, no action was taken on landscaping. Approximately 110 parking places were provided for the 100 apartment units, which had an average occupancy of 1.8 tenants per unit. No street parking was permitted by the city. At that time a maintenance manager, who was given no salary but was provided a rent-free apartment, was added to Riverview's managerial staff.

RENTAL RATES

Most of the occupants were students; they were asked to sign a nine-month lease at $155 per apartment, due on the first day of each month, during the fall and spring semesters. If they signed a 12-month lease, and remained during the summer, they were billed at $100 per month during June, July, and August. Although a number of students moved out during summer 1971, some of the vacancies were rented at $155 per month to students who lived in dorms, fraternities, sororities or other units during the regular academic year. Nonetheless, failure to complete the proposed swimming pool seemed to be the prime reason why 10 of the 46 units then available were vacant in August 1971 (see Exhibit 1).

The vacancy rate for the 1972 spring semester was 20 percent in January, 23 percent in February, and 26 percent in March. The managing realtor decided to replace the manager and his wife, Bill and Ann Roberts, since it was felt they were not working hard enough to keep the complex fully rented. The supervisor flew from Capitol City, fired the managing couple (who then decided to rent an apartment in the complex) and hired a young man who had registered with the State Employment Service. The terminated managers were given a month's severance salary. The new manager moved into the complex, and the supervisor flew back to Capitol City the following day. A new salary of $250 per month, plus apartment, was established.

The vacancy rate of 26 percent in March 1972 fell to just 25 percent in April. At that time it was discovered that the personal activities of the new manager were unsatisfactory, so Bill and Ann Roberts were rehired.

In an effort to fill the vacant apartment, a summer rate of $100 per unit was established. The vacancy rate dropped to 6 percent in May and averaged only 1 percent during the summer months.

The Roberts graduated in August 1972, and two male students, John Hall and Frank O'Brian, the former of whom was known by the Capitol City management realtor, were employed as co-managers. University enrollment declined slightly in fall 1972—to 23,804, down from 24,131 the previous fall.

The vacancy rate in fall 1972, averaged 4 percent, until mid-December when the long holiday vacation began. The vacancy rate jumped to 11 percent in December, 23 percent in January, 28 percent in April, and dropped to 0 percent in mid-June, when a 1973 summer rate of $110 was established.

EXHIBIT 2
Student Enrollments, Dormitory Construction, and Multiresidence Building Permits

	Student Enrollment (fall semester)	Dormitory Construction	Multiresidence Building Permits	
			Value	Number
1960	10,862		$ 90,000	5
1961	12,388	2	40,000	2
1962	12,867	2	150,000	4
1963	14,326	3	330,000	9
1964	14,912	4	1,209,000	40
1965	18,268	2	167,000	8
1966	18,973		694,000	18
1967	20,423	2	1,265,000	15
1968	20,549		2,289,330	45
1969	22,081		6,311,832	25
1970	23,709		5,697,472*	48
1971	24,131		6,004,756†	99
1972	23,804		7,855,400	109

* Includes first Riverview buildings.
† Includes fourth and fifth Riverview buildings.

At that time, one co-manager graduated and the other, Frank O'Brian, got married. The O'Brians stayed on as managers of Riverview, but Frank took a full-time job and attended some classes; Frank's wife was a part-time student. The Capitol City realtor supervisor was agreeable to the arrangement which was worked out in a long-distance phone call. However, subsequent efforts to talk with the new managerial couple by phone were largely unsuccessful. They were usually unavailable. Further, they went on trips almost every weekend. On some occasions the maintenance manager was available to handle problems, but he did not show apartments to prospective tenants during the 1973 fall semester.

ADVERTISING

An ongoing advertising program was maintained, at an annual cost of about 3 percent of rentals. This was comparable with similar apartments, according to the Capitol City realtor. The local newspaper, two student newspapers, and three local radio stations were utilized. Most students and townspeople knew about the Riverview Apartments.

INVESTMENT

The owner's total capital investment in Riverview Apartments approximated $800,000 and required about $90,000 annually in debt retirement payments. Studies made by the Capitol City supervisor indicated that over 90 percent of the Riverview Apartment expenses were fixed; only a few items were dependent upon the occupancy ratio. Gas and electric usage varied more with temperature than with the number of occupied units. The expense of water was also dependent upon the occupancy rate, but the large items, such as real estate taxes, management fee, and debt retirement, were fixed.

An operating statement summary for the period May 1972, through April 1973 showed that the complex incurred an annual loss in excess of $9,000 (see Exhibit 3). The corporation's treasurer prepared a break-even analysis during the spring of 1973, using an academic year rent of $155 and a summer rent of $110. He determined a 90 percent occupancy rate would result in a break-even operation.

EXHIBIT 3
Operating Statement Summary, May 1972—April 1973

Month	Receipts	Disbursements	Profit or (Loss)
1972			
May	$ 9,801	$ 10,890	$(1,089)
June	8,148	10,994	(2,846)
July	10,597	10,911	(314)
August	7,241	13,891	(6,650)
September....................	12,748	18,208	(5,460)
October	14,811	10,131	4,680
November	12,489	10,154	2,335
December	14,523	10,639	3,884
1973			
January	10,210	10,568	(358)
February	10,900	11,146	(246)
March	9,880	10,996	(1,116)
April	9,587	11,532	(1,945)
Total	$130,935	$140,060	$(9,125)

ATTEMPTS TO FIND THE PROBLEM

The spring semester final exam period ended May 14, 1973. Many students left the campus, including a number who planned to attend summer school. There was a three and one-half week vacation between the end of the regular academic year and summer school. A number of tenants forfeited their $50 damage deposit, and broke their leases by not returning after the holiday. Since summer occupancy had averaged about 97 percent during the previous two summers, the special summer rate was increased to $110 from $100 during the preceding summers.

In June 1973, the chief executive officer of the real estate firm and the senior vice president, Mr. Ernest Jones, determined that an intensive analysis should be conducted of the marketing program and general operation of Riverview Apartments. Though the apartments were incurring a significant dollar loss, their time was taken with other investment negotiations and a consultant was hired to conduct the necessary research and prepare a set of recommendations.

The consultant undertook a number of actions. Competitive apartments that appealed to the student market were visited, pictures taken of each, and rental schedules were secured (see Exhibit 4). Locations of the various apartments were plotted on a map of the city. None of the apartments were in excess of two miles from the campus, though most students who lived over six blocks from the campus preferred driving to the campus and searching for one of the inadequate number of parking spaces. There appeared to be no relationship between monthly rental and distance of the various apartments from the campus.

EXHIBIT 4
Rental Schedule Comparison

Apartment	Fall/Spring	Summer	Remarks
Riverview	$155	$110	Includes all utilities.
Howe Hill	135	135	(Only several one bedroom units.) Plus utilities.
Sherman Woods	185	135	Plus utilities.
Francis Jett	155 (monthly basis) 149 (9-month lease) 140 (12-month lease)	143	Plus electricity. Gas air conditioning.
University Terrace	110	110	Plus utilities.
Glover Creek	135	110	Plus electricity. Gas air conditioning.
Contemporary Arms	140 (9-month lease)	143	Plus electricity (six weeks $200). Gas air conditioning.
	150 (12-month lease)	143	Includes dishwasher and shag carpets. If 12-month lease signed prior to September 1, $20 per month *less*.
Hale	140	143	Plus electricity (six weeks $200). Gas air conditioning.
Hale II	150	143	Same as Hale. Both Hale and Hale II, 12-month lease $20 per month *less*.
Lee Gardens	160	120	Plus electricity. Gas air conditioning.
Silvia	150	150	Plus electricity. Gas air conditioning. If 12-month lease, last month reduced by $60, or equivalent to *$145 month*.
Joe-Ann	142 (monthly basis) 136 (9-month lease) 122 (12-month lease)	136	Plus electricity. Gas air conditioning.

Occupancy figures of the other apartment complexes were unavailable. While completing the rental survey of competitive apartment complexes (Exhibit 4), visual inspection of the various apartments led to the conclusion that most were more attractive, better landscaped, and had more parking per unit than did Riverview. Further, housekeeping standards of Riverview's grounds and parking areas were unsatisfactory. When a representative from Capitol City made several attempts to mention this to the managers of Riverview, neither the manager nor his wife were available. On each occasion, nontenant children who lived in the neighborhood were swimming in the pool, beverage cans were on the ground, and dog deposits were much in evidence.

Newspaper advertisements of Riverview and of its competitive apartments were reviewed as to content, size, and frequency. No significant differences were apparent.

Two questionnaires were designed to obtain present and past tenant input. The first set of questionnaires (Exhibit 5), each accompanied by a business reply envelope addressed to the residential property manager in Capitol City, was given to the manager to distribute to tenants who were living in Riverview at the time. Though several demanding phone calls were required before he distributed the questionnaires, the assignment was accomplished and replies were received from 48 percent of the tenants living in the various units of Riverview Apartments.

The consultant realized that a certain favorable bias might characterize the responses to the survey. The manager had copies of the questionnaire and could have urged friends to reply favorably, and might have failed to deliver a copy to a tenant whom he thought was dissatisfied with the managers. Nevertheless, in the interest of speed and cost, it was decided to take the risk since replies went to the Capitol City office.

EXHIBIT 5
Riverview Apartments: Questionnaire Results, Present Residents

We would appreciate you answering a few questions which will enable us to do a better job managing Riverview Apartments to your satisfaction. Your name is not necessary since we will tabulate and analyze the answers. Most questions just ask that you check the appropriate blank.

1. Please rate the following items:

	GOOD	AVERAGE	POOR
Cleanliness	17	23	3
Parking	1	10	29
Pool	13	21	9
Laundry	18	21	5
Grounds	12	24	9

EXHIBIT 5 (*continued*)

Furniture	29	13	2
Carpet.............................	23	15	4
Management.......................	7	21	6
Stove..............................	19	13	8
Refrigerator	15	10	11

2. What do you dislike about the Riverview Apartments? 16 Inadequate parking
   15 Maintenance
   8 Plumbing

3. What do you like about the Riverview Apartments? 29 Location
   14 Summer rental rate
   11 Pool
   7 Furnishings

4. Did you live in the Riverview Apartments in Spring 1973?

   Yes 14   No 29

5. Do you plan to live in Riverview Apartments during the academic year of

   1973–1974?   Yes 14   No 25   Undecided 6

   If not, why not? 8 Rent too high
   7 Leaving Academe
   4 Moving back to sorority or fraternity house
   4 Moving back to dormitory

6. What can we do to make living in the Riverview Apartments more fun for you?
   11 More parking
   8 Have game room, shuffleboard, parties around pool, college
   atmosphere
   7 Improve and speed up maintenance
   5 Prevent non-tenant children, dogs and cats around pool
   4 Nicer landscaping
   3 New diving board, lawn chairs beside pool, basketball goal

7. How many people occupy your apartment?

   One 11   Two 62   Three 9   (45 apts. completed
   questionnaires)

8. Are you, or all of you: (82 individuals live
   in the 45 apts.)
   Married 18   Single 64

9. Occupants in your apartment.

   Couple 20   One Man 6   Three Women 6

   Two Men 18   One Woman 5   Two Parents & Child

   Two Women 24   Three Men 3   One Parent & Child

EXHIBIT 5 *(continued)*

10. Age of Occupants:

Age	M	W
17		1
18	2	2
19	7	8
20	5	12
21	12	9
22	2	6
23	3	6
24		
25	1	
26	2	
27	1	
28		
29		
30		1
32	2	
Totals	37	45

11. (a) Are occupants in your apartment:

12	Nonstudents	2	Student and Husband
11	One Student	6	Student and Wife
42	Two Students	9	Other (please specify) (3 students)

(b) If students, are you:

4	Freshman	6	Graduate
8	Sophomore	1	Law
20	Junior		Medical
31	Senior		Special

(c) Expected date to receive degree?

Number	Date
4	Aug. 73
11	Dec. 73
21	May 74
15	Dec. 74

EXHIBIT 5 *(concluded)*

11	May 75
5	May 76

Thank you for completing this questionnaire. Please return it to us in the attached envelope.

Residential Property Manager
Beasley, Gibson, Inc.
111 Marion Avenue
Capitol City, Blank

A second questionnaire was prepared and sent to the hometown address of 45 tenants who had lived in the apartments until the end of spring 1973. Replies were received from 25 percent of the former tenants (Exhibit 6).

The consultant prepared an analysis of the 1972–73 annual rental rate of $1,725 and its relationship to the break-even occupancy rate, coming up with the following:

Annual Rental Rate	Break-Even Occupancy Percentage
$1,620	95
1,695	90

EXHIBIT 6
Riverview Apartments: Questionnaire Results, Past Residents

June 4, 1973

Dear _____

We are very interested in the service you received while a resident of Riverview Apartments in Academe. You can help us do a better job next fall by answering a few questions and returning in the enclosed postpaid envelope.

1. Please rate the following items:

	GOOD	AVERAGE	POOR
Cleanliness	5	6	
Parking.............................	8	1	2
Pool.................................	10	1	
Laundry	9	2	
Grounds............................	6	5	
Furniture	7	4	
Carpet..............................	5	5	1

EXHIBIT 6 (*continued*)

Manager............................ 7	4	
Stove.............................. 6	4	1
Refrigerator 4	3	4

2. What did you dislike about the Riverview Apartments?　3 Parking
　2 Refrigerators

3. What did you like about the Riverview Apartments?　8 Location
　4 Manager
　3 Size

4. What was the reason you moved?　8 Home for summer
　2 Lower rent

5. Do you plan to live in the Riverview Apartments during the academic year of 1973–1974?　Yes _____　No 9 　Undecided 2 _____

If not, why not?　2 Winter rent too high
　2 Not returning to Academe
　2 Too small for three people

7. (a) Were occupants:

1 Non-students		_____ Student and Husband
1 One Student		1 Student and Wife
5 Two Students		_____ Other (Please specify)
3 Three Students		

(b) If students, were you:

3 Freshman	_____ Graduate
6 Sophomore	_____ Law
_____ Junior	_____ Medical
1 Senior	_____ Special

Sincerely,

Beasley, Gibson, Inc.
Bill Cook
Property Manager

During the almost two years the apartments had been occupied, the owners had been adding additional funds to cover the negative cash flow of funds.

Color pictures of Riverview Apartments and competitive apartments were taken and sent to the realty firm in Capitol City. For information purposes, a number of the replies to the different sets of questionnaires were routed across the desk of the realty firm's senior vice president. He continued to be involved in a major negotiation and could not take time to visit the apartments in Academe. He requested that the consultant furnish a completed report, with substantiated recommendations, to him and the chief executive officer of the realty firm. He said they wanted an actionable report that would permit them to make recommendations to the officers of the corporation that owned the apartment complex.

5. Fourwinds Marina*

JACK KELTNER had just completed his first day as general manager of the Fourwinds Marina. It was mid-August and although the marina's slip rentals ran until October 30, business took a dramatic downturn after Labor Day. Jack knew that it would be unwise to change the way current operations were being run in the three weeks remaining in the season, but he also knew that before the following spring he would have to move decisively to implement some of the changes which he had been considering. Major changes would be required if Fourwinds Marina was to survive.

In his previous job as Fourwinds' controller, Keltner had been intimately involved in the operation of Fourwinds Marina. He believed, at a minimum, that the following changes should be made over the next 12-month period:

1. Add 80 slips on E, F, and G docks and put in underwater supports on these docks to deter breakage from storms. Cost: $250,000–300,000. Annual profits if all slips are rented: $74,000+.
2. Add a second girl to assist the present secretary-receptionist-bookkeeper. Savings: $300+ per month, provided the Indianapolis office is closed.
3. Reorganize the parts department and put in a new inventory system. Cost: $30,000. Savings: $2,500–$3,000 per year.
4. Keep the boat and motor inventory low. Boat inventory as of mid-August was approximately $125,000. It had been over $300,000.
5. Reduce the work force through attrition if a vacated job can be assumed by someone remaining on the staff.
6. Outfit E, F, and G docks for winter storage using an improved and more extensive bubbling system. Profits to be generated: uncertain and difficult to estimate.
7. Light and heat the storage building so that repair work can be done at night and in the winter. Cost: $12,000, which can probably be paid for from the profits in two winters of operation.

Keltner had no experience in marina management, but was considered a hard worker willing to take on tremendous challenges. He had joined the

---

* Prepared by W. Harvey Hegarty and Harry Kelsey, Indiana University.

Taggart Corporation after four years as a CPA at Ernst and Ernst, one of the "Big Eight" accounting firms. Functioning as controller of Taggart Corporation, which owned Fourwinds Marina and Inn of the Fourwinds on Lake Monroe, he found that a tremendous volume of work was demanded, necessitating late hours at the office and a briefcase full of work to take home with him most evenings. Keltner lived in a small community near Fourwinds Marina and had to commute frequently to the home office of the Taggart Corporation in Indianapolis, an hour and a half drive from Lake Monroe. Keltner stated that he hoped to shift all of his work to Lake Monroe, site of the marina and inn as soon as possible. In his view, handling the accounting for the marina, the inn, and other Taggart Corporation interests could be done just as effectively at the Marina. The inn and the marina comprised 90 percent of the business of the corporation.

Much of the explanation for Keltner's heavy work load lay in the fact that there had been virtually no accounting system when he first joined Taggart. He had, however, set up six profit centers for the marina and was now generating monthly accounting reports.

Keltner believed each of the seven changes he had in mind would add to the effectiveness and profitability of the marina operation and that was his prime concern. The operation of the inn was under control of another general manager and, further, was operated as a separate corporate entity. Keltner was responsible only for the accounting procedures of the Inn of the Fourwinds.

As he turned over the structure, background, and development of the inn and the marina, Keltner realized that his new role as general manager of Fourwinds Marina, when added on to his job as controller of the Taggart Corporation, presented an imposing challenge. Managing the marina was a full-time, seven-day-a-week job, particularly during the season. The questions uppermost in his mind were: (1) What would be the full plan he would present to Taggart to turn the operation around and make it profitable? and (2) How would the plan be funded? The financial statements of the marina presented a glum picture (see Exhibits 1 and 2), but Keltner had good data available to analyze revenue and costs on almost every segment of Fourwinds' operations. Moreover, there was the knowledge he had gleaned working with the past general managers and observing the operation of the marina.

THE PREVIOUS GENERAL MANAGER

The day the previous general manager resigned, Jack Keltner was called in by Sandy Taggart, president of the Taggart Corporation. Keltner was informed that Leon McLaughlin had just submitted his resignation as general manager of the marina—apparently because McLaughlin and Taggart had disagreed on some compensation McLaughlin felt was due him. Part of the disagreement concerned McLaughlin's wife who had

EXHIBIT 1

FOURWINDS MARINA
Income Statement
Fiscal Year Ending March 31, 1974

Revenue:

Sale of new boats	$774,352	
Sale of used boats	179,645	
Sale of rental boats	17,051	
Total Sales		$971,048

Other income:

Service and repair	$128,687	
Gasoline and oil	81,329	
Ship store	91,214	
Slip rental	174,808	
Winter storage	32,177	
Boat rental	99,895	
Other Income		608,110
Total Income		$1,579,158

Expenses:

Fixed Costs:

Cost of boats	$798,123	
Cost of repair equipment	56,698	
Ship store costs	64,405	
Cost of gasoline	51,882	
Boat rental costs	8,951	
Total Fixed Costs		980,059

Operating Expenses:

Wages and salaries	$228,154	
Taxes	23,725	
Building rent	58,116	
Equipment rent	8,975	
Utilities	18,716	
Insurance	25,000	
Interest on loans	209,310	
Advertising	30,150	
Legal expense	19,450	
Bad debt expense	8,731	
Miscellaneous	39,994	
Total Operating Expenses		670,321
Total Costs		1,650,380
Operating Loss		$ 71,222
Depreciation		122,340
Total Loss*		$ 193,562

* This represents the total operating loss of the Fourwinds Marina in the fiscal year ending March 31, 1974. Fourwinds sold a subsidiary in 1973—a boat sales firm in Indianapolis—on which a loss of $275,580 was written off.

XHIBIT 2

FOURWINDS MARINA
Balance Sheet
March 31, 1974

Assets				Liabilities	
Current Assets:				Current Liabilities:	
Cash	31,858			Accounts payable	89,433
Accounts receivable	70,632			Intercompany payables	467,091
New boats	199,029			Accrued salary expense	8,905
Used boats	60,747			Accrued interest expense	20,383
Parts	53,295			Accrued tax expense	43,719
Ship store	2,741			Accrued lease expense	36,190
Gas/oil	2,626			Prepaid dock rental	178,466
				Boat deposits	4,288
Total Current Assets	$ 420,928			Current bank notes	177,600
				Mortgage (current)	982,900
				Note payable to floor plan	225,550
Fixed Assets:		Less Depr.		Note on rental houseboats	71,625
Buoys and docks	984,265	315,450		Notes to stockholders	515,150
Permanent buildings	201,975	17,882		Dealer reserve liability	13,925
Office furniture	3,260	704		Total Current Liabilities	$2,835,225
Houseboats	139,135	15,631			
Work boats	40,805	7,987		Long-term note on houseboats	117,675
Equipment	72,420	38,742			
	$1,441,860	$396,396		Common stock—1,000 shares at par value $1 per share	1,000
Net Fixed Assets	$1,045,464			Retained earnings deficit	(990,105)
Other Assets:				Loss during year ending March 31, 1974*	(469,142)
Prepaid expense	2,940				
Deferred interest expense	25,321			Total Liabilities and Net Worth	$1,494,653
	$ 28,261				
Total Assets	$1,494,653				

* Loss during year ending March 31, 1974 is composed of an operating loss of $71,222 plus depreciation of $122,340, and a write-off loss of a sold subsidiary of $275,580.

been hired to work in the parts department and had spent little time there due to an illness. Taggart had wasted no time in hiring Keltner as McLaughlin's replacement.

McLaughlin had been the fifth general manager in the five years that the marina had been in operation. He had had 15 years of marine experience before being hired to manage the Fourwinds Marina. His experience, however, consisted of selling and servicing boats and motors in Evansville, Indiana, and was not in marina management. McLaughlin had taken pride in running a "tight ship" and had often said that the marina had an excllent chance in turning around after some lean times. McLaughlin had found it fairly easy to keep Fourwinds staffed because the resort atmosphere was so attractive, and his goal had been to have the majority of the staff employed on a full-time, year-round basis. Even though the marina was closed from November until April there was a considerable amount of repair work on boats needed during those months. McLaughlin was told when hired that he had a blank check to get Fourwinds shaped up and profitable; this promise, however, was later rescinded.

McLaughlin and his wife had a mobile home near the marina, but had maintained a permanent residence in Evansville. For the most part, McLaughlin had put in six full days a week, but he had usually not worked at all on Sundays, believing that he was entitled to one day per week off. In general, McLaughlin had proved to be an effective organizer; his biggest managerial weakness was in the area of employee and customer relations.

TAGGART CORPORATION

The other principal investors involved in the Taggart Corporation besides A. L. "Sandy" Taggart, III were William Brennan, president of one of the states' largest commercial and industrial real estate firms and Richard De-Mars, president of Guepel-DeMars, Inc., the firm that designed both the marina and the inn.

Sandy Taggart was a well-known Indianapolis businessman and chairman of the board of Colonial Baking Company. Colonial was one of the larger bakeries serving the Indianapolis metropolitan area and surrounding counties. He did his undergraduate work at Princeton and completed Harvard's Advanced Management Program in 1967. He was an easy-going man and did not appear to be upset by problems. He maintained his office at the Taggart Corporation in Indianapolis but tried to get to Fourwinds at least once every week. He kept in daily contact with Leon McLaughlin and continued to do the same with Keltner. He enjoyed being a part of the daily decision making and problem solving that went on at the marina and felt that he needed to be aware of all decisions, due to the corporation's weak financial position. Taggart believed that Fourwinds' current problems stemmed from a lack of knowledge of the marina business and a lack of experienced general managers when operations were begun some six years ago. Taggart acknowledged that a lack of expertise in maintaining accurate cost data and in cost control had plagued Fourwinds Marina, but he was pleased with Keltner's progress in correcting these problems.

LOCATION AND SETTING

The Fourwinds Marina and the Inn of the Fourwinds were located on Lake Monroe, the largest lake in Indiana. The lake is a 10,700-acre manmade reservoir developed by the US Army Corps of Engineers in conjunction with and under the jurisdiction of the Indiana Department of Natural Resources. With the surrounding public lands (accounting for some 80 percent of the

150-mile shoreline) the total acreage is 26,000. It is a multipurpose project designed to provide flood control, recreation, water supply, and flow augmentation benefits to the people of Indiana. Lake Monroe is located in the southwestern quadrant of the state, about nine miles or a 15-minute drive southwest of Bloomington, Indiana, home of Indiana University, and a 90-minute drive from Indianapolis (see Exhibit 3). The Indianapolis metropolitan area had a 1974 population of over 1 million people; estimated spendable income was about $3.5 billion annually. A recent *Fortune* survey indicated that the Indianapolis area was considered a desirable site for future expansion by many of the nation's top industrial leaders.

Indianapolis is located at a crossroads of the national interstate highway system; more interstate highways converge at Indianapolis than any other point in the United States. Its recently enlarged airport could accommodate any of the jet aircraft currently in operation; the city was served by most of the major airlines. In 1973, the per capita effective buying income in Indianapolis was $4,264, which contrasted with $3,779 for the United States as a whole; almost half of the Indianapolis area households had annual incomes of $10,000 and above. While approximately 75 percent of the customers of Fourwinds Marina came from the Indianapolis area, it was estimated that a total potential market of some 2.9 million inhabitants resided within a 100-mile radius of Lake Monroe.

Although both Fourwinds Marina and the Inn of the Fourwinds were owned by Taggart Corporation, they were operated as distinct entities. Being adjacent to one another on Lake Monroe, they cooperated in promoting business for each other. The inn occupied some 71,000 square feet on 30 acres of land. It was designed to blend into a beautifully wooded landscape and was constructed of rustic and natural building materials. The inn catered to a broad segment of the population, with double-occupancy rooms ranging in price from $21 to $33. The inn had 150 guest rooms (singles, doubles, and suites), together with meeting rooms for convention and sales meetings. The largest meeting room could seat 300 for dining and 350 for conferences. Recreation facilities included an indoor-outdoor swimming pool, tennis courts, sauna, whirlpool bath, and a recreation room with pool tables and other games. The inn had two dining rooms and a cocktail lounge. Although the inn was open year-round, its business was heavily concentrated in the summer months.

The Inn of the Fourwinds was the first lodge of its nature built on state property by private funds. By virtue of the size of its food service facilities (in excess of $100,000 per annum), it qualified under Indiana State Law for a license to serve alcoholic beverages on Sunday. The Indiana Department of Natural Resources exercised control over the room rates charged at the inn; this was part of the agreement between the state of Indiana and Taggart Corporation.

The Pointe, located three miles from the marina on 348 acres of lakefront property, was a luxury condominum development designed to meet the

EXHIBIT 3

Map of Indiana Showing Location of Lake Monroe (Fourwinds Marina) in Monroe County

Metropolitan Area	County	Population	Miles from Lake Monroe
Indianapolis	Marion	1,144,000	70
Terre Haute	Vigo	173,000	80
Louisville, Ky.	below Floyd	893,000	115
Evansville	Posey	289,000	127

housing needs of both primary and secondary home buyers. Seventy units were under construction. Twenty of these had already been sold and down payments had been received on 80 more. These condominiums ranged in price from $25,000 to $90,000, with an average price of $60,000. Approval had been secured for the construction of 1,900 living units over a seven-year period. The development had a completed 18-hole golf course. Swimming pools and tennis courts were under construction. The Pointe was a multimillion dollar development by Indun Realty, Inc., Lake Monroe Corporation, and Reywood, Inc.; Indun Realty was a wholly owned subsidiary of Indiana National Corp., parent firm of Indiana National Bank, the state's largest fiduciary institution.

FACILITIES AT FOURWINDS MARINA

The Fourwinds Marina occupied four acres of land and was one of the most extensive and complete marinas of its type in the United States. Its facilities consisted of boat docks, a salesroom for boats and marine equipment, an indoor boat storage facility, and a marine repair shop.

As shown in Exhibit 4, the marina had seven docks projecting out from a main connecting dock that ran parallel to the shore line. The seven parallel docks extended out from 330 to 600 feet into the lake at right angles to the connecting dock. The center dock housed a large building containing a grocery store, snack bar, and rest rooms, together with a section of docks used as mooring for rental boats. At the end of the dock was an office for boat rental, five gasoline pumps, and pumping facilities for removing waste from the houseboats and larger cruisers.

The three docks to the right of the center dock (facing toward the lake) were designated as docks A, B, and C and were designed for mooring smaller boats—runabouts, fishing boats, and small sailboats. A bait shop was on A dock. A, B, and C slips were not always fully rented. The three docks to the left were the prime slips (docks E, F, G); these were designed for berthing houseboats and larger cruisers. Docks E, F, and G were the marina's most profitable slips and stayed fully rented; as of mid-August there was a waiting list to get into these slips.

Fourwinds Marina had a total of 460 rentable slips priced from $205–$775 for uncovered slips and $295–$1,125 for covered slips per season (April

EXHIBIT 4
Physical Layout Fourwinds Marina

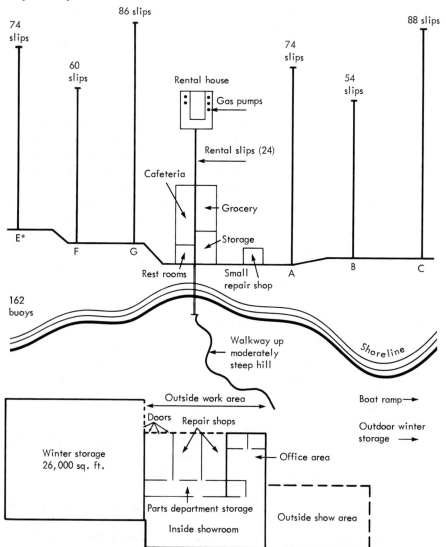

* E, F, and G range from 15 × 34 feet to 18 × 50 feet. About two thirds of these slips are covered.
† A, B, and C slips range from 9 × 18 feet to 12 × 32 feet. Over 80 percent of these slips are covered.

1–October 30). Seventy-five percent of all the slips were under roof and being in the more desirable location tended to be rented first. Electric service was provided to all slips, and the slips on E and F docks had water and trash removal provided at no extra cost. To the left of the prime slips were 162 buoys, renting for $150 per season. This rental included shuttle boat service to and from the moored craft. The rental buoys were not considered to be very profitable. Not only did the buoys shift and break loose occasionally but the dock staff went to considerable time and trouble to retrieve boats that broke loose at night or during storms.

TERMS OF THE LEASE WITH THE STATE OF INDIANA

The 34 acres of land on which the Fourwinds complex was located was leased to Taggart Corporation by the state of Indiana. In 1968, a prospectus was distributed by the Indiana Department of Natural Resources asking for bids on a motel and marina on the selected site. Only one other bidder qualified of the eight to ten bids submitted. The proposal submitted by Taggart Corporation was accepted primarily because of the economic strength of the individuals who composed the group and secondarily because of the favorable content of the bid.

The prospectus specified a minimum rental for the land of $10,000. Taggart Corporation offered in its bid a guarantee of $2,000 against the first $100,000 in marina sales and income and 4 percent of all income over that amount. For the inn, Taggart guaranteed $8,000 against the first $400,000 of income plus 4 percent of all room sales and 2 percent of all food and beverage sales over that amount. It was stipulated that the Indiana Department of Natural Resources would exercise control over the prices of room rates at the Inn of the Fourwinds and slip rentals at the marina; Taggart Corporation was free to price the other services and products as it saw fit.

An initial lease of 37 years was granted to Taggart with two options of 30 years each. At the termination of the contract, all physical property reverted to the state of Indiana and the personal property went to Taggart. The entire dock structure was floating and was considered under the personal property category.

Prior to tendering a bid, members of Taggart Corporation visited similar facilities at Lake of the Ozarks, Lake Hamilton in Hot Springs, and the Kentucky Lakes operations. They received a considerable amount of information from the Kentucky Lakes management.

Construction of the initial phase of the marina began in May 1969 and the first 100 slips were opened in August under a speeded up construction schedule. The inn had its formal opening in November 1972.

MARINA OPERATIONS

Slip Rental. Reservations for slips had to be made by November 15 of each year or else the slip was subject to rental on a first come basis. Ordinarily all slips were rented for the year. The rental period ran from April 1 through October 30. Rental varied from $205 to $1,125, depending on the size of the slip and whether it was covered. Because the marina was located on state property, the Indiana Department of Natural Resources had the right of final approval over the rates which Fourwinds charged on slip rental.

Buoy Rental. One hundred and sixty-two buoys were rented for the same April 1–October 30 season at a rate of $150. Shuttle boat service for transporting boat owners to and from their craft moored at the buoy area was operative 24 hours a day. It was not a scheduled service, but operated as the demand occurred. This required the primary use of a runabout and driver. The charge for the service was included in the buoy rental fee for the season. As long as the buoy field was in existence, it was felt that the shuttle service had to be operated on a 24-hour basis during the season.

Boat Storage—Winter. Experience at Fourwinds showed that it was more expensive to remove a boat from the water and store it than to allow it to remain moored at the dock all winter. The main inside storage building was not heated or lighted; this precluded doing repair work in this building. An investment of about $12,000 would cover the cost of lighting and spot heating to overcome this drawback. When boats were stored, they were not queued according to those needing repair and those not needing service. As a result, time was lost in rearranging boats to get to those on which work was to be performed. The storage facility was not utilized in the summer months. Keltner was considering whether to install lights in the winter storage facility so as to give the marina an inside display area for the used boats which it sold; the used boats currently were stored and displayed on a lot outside the main display area for new boats.

Presently the rates for winter storage were:

100 percent of base rate .... Inside storage.
 70 percent of base rate ......-.... Bubbled area of covered slips.
 60 percent of base rate .... Bubbled area of open slips.
 50 percent of base rate .... Open storage areas out of water.

The base rate for storing a boat depended on its size. Boats 6-feet wide were stored at a charge of $7 per foot of length; an 8-foot wide boat carried a charge of $10 per running foot. Hence, a boat 6-feet wide and 15-feet long would have a base rate of $90; a boat 8-feet wide and 20-feet long would carry a base rate of $200. The base rate did not include charges (approximately $75) for removing the boat from the water and moving it to either inside or outside storage areas.

Last winter, the inside storage facility was filled to capacity. One hundred boats were stored at an average base rate charge of $150 to $165. The marina had experienced some problems with vandalism on boats stored in the more remote areas of the uncovered, out-of-water storage area; however, the marina claimed no responsibility for loss, theft, or damage.

Boat and Motor Rental. The marina's rental equipment was up to date and well maintained; it consisted of:

15 houseboats—rental Monday to Friday $300
Friday to Monday $300

10 pontoon boats—hourly rental $20 for 3 hours
$35 for 6 hours
6 runabouts for skiing—$15–20 per hour
12 fishing boats—$12 for 6 hours
$18 for 12 hours

Maximum hourly rental was 13 hours per day during the week and 15 hours per day on Saturday and Sunday (the rental rate did not include gasoline).

It was not uncommon to have all 15 houseboats fully rented from Memorial Day weekend through Labor Day weekend. Pontoons were about 50 percent rented during the week. Utilization of runabouts was 50 percent, while fishing boats were rented approximately 40 percent of the available time. The man who operated the boat and motor rental for Fourwinds had a one-third interest in all of the boat rental equipment; the Marina owned the balance. Funds for the purchase of the equipment were contributed on the same one-third to two-thirds ratio. Net profits after payment of expenses, maintenance, depreciation, and so on were split according to the ownership ratio. The area utilized by the rental area could be converted to slips in the $500 range as a possible alternate use for the dock space. Rental income after expenses, but before interest and depreciation, had been slightly less than $20,000 the preceding season.

Small Boat Repair Shop.   A small boat repair shop was located between C and D docks. It was well outfitted with mechanical equipment and had a small hoist for removing small boats from the water for repair at the docks. However, the shop was currently closed because a qualified mechanic could not be found to operate the facility on a seasonal basis.

Grocery Store.   The grocery store at the marina was subleased to another party at $500 per month. The leasee was doing a profitable business and charged prices similar to those which might be expected at a seasonal recreation facility.

Snack Bar.   The snack bar was operated by the Inn of the Fourwinds and returned a 5 percent commission to the marina on food sales. Currently, Keltner felt that the manager of the snack bar was not doing a reliable job in operating the unit. Keltner had found the snack bar closed on several occasions for no apparent reason. Food offered for sale included hot sandwiches, pizza, snack food, soft drinks, milk, and coffee. The snack bar's prices were at the high end of the range for such items but Fourwinds' customers had expressed satisfaction with the quality.

Gasoline Sales.   Five gasoline pumps were located around the perimeter of the end of the center dock. They were manned 13 hours per day, from 7 A.M. to 8 P.M., seven days a week. The pumps for the removal of waste from the houseboats and other large craft were located in this same area. It took an average of five minutes to pump out the waste and the marina made no charge for this service. The marina's gasoline pumps were the only ones available on Lake Monroe.

Boat and Boat Accessory Salesroom.   A glass enclosed showroom occupying approximately 1,500 square feet of floor space was located at the main entrance to the marina property. Major boat lines such as Trojan Yacht, Kingscraft, Burnscraft, Harris Flote Bote, and Signa, as well as Evinrude motors, were offered for sale. In addition, quality lines of marine accessories were available. The salesroom building also housed the executive offices of the marina and the repair and maintenance shops. Attached to the building was the indoor winter storage area for boats. Last year, total boat sales were approximately $971,048. The marina's boat inventory had been reduced from last year's $300,000; recently, some boat lines had been dropped so that more emphasis could be placed on those which offered higher profit on sales.

Fourwinds Marina was the only sales outlet in Indiana that stocked larger boats. They were also the only facility in Indiana with large slips to accommodate these boats. With E, F, and G docks filled and a waiting list to get in, selling the larger, more profitable boats had become nearly impossible.

ASPECTS OF THE MARINA'S DOCK OPERATIONS

Dock Construction.   The entire dock section at Fourwinds was of modular floating construction and had an expected life of 20–30 years, if properly maintained. Built in smaller sections that could be bolted together, the construction featured a steel framework, with poured concrete surfaces for walking upon and Styrofoam panels in the side for buoyancy. In the event of damage to a section, a side could be replaced easily, eliminating repair of the entire segment of dock. Electrical conduits and water pipes were inside the actual dock units. The major damage to the Styrofoam dock segments came from ducks chewing out pieces of the foam to make nests and from gasoline spillage that literally "ate" the Styrofoam. An antigas coating was used to minimize the damage from gasoline spillage. Damage from boats to the dock was minimal. A maze of cables underneath the dock sections had to be kept at the proper tension to prevent the dock from buckling and breaking up. Three people were involved in dock maintenance. Original cost of the entire dock and buoy system was $984,265.

Winter Storage.   Winter storage tends to be a problem at a marina which is located in an area where a freeze-over of the water occurs. Nonetheless, it is generally better for the boat if it can remain in the water. Water affords better and more even support to the hull. By leaving the craft in the water, possible damage from hoists used to lift boats and move them to dry storage is avoided. These factors, however, are not common knowledge to boat owners and require an educational program.

To protect boats left in the water during the winter season, Fourwinds Marina had installed a bubbling system. The system, simple in concept, consisted of hoses that were weighted and dropped to the bottom of the lake around the individual docks and along a perimeter line surrounding the entire dock area. Fractional horsepower motors operated compressors that pumped air into the submerged hose. The air escaping through tiny holes in the hose forced warmer water at the bottom of the lake up to the top, preventing the surface from freezing and melting any ice that might have formed before the compressors were started. The lines inside the dock areas protected the boats from being damaged by ice formations, while the perimeter line prevented major damage to the entire dock area from a pressure ridge that might build up and be jammed against the dock and boats in high wind.

A policy of the marina prohibited any employee from driving any of the customer's boats. Maintaining a duplicate set of keys for each boat and the cost of the insurance to cover the employee were the prime reasons for this policy. This meant, however, that when boats were moved in the absence of their owners they had to be towed, thereby creating some possibility of damage to the boats during towing. Towing of boats occurred mainly during the off-season period for reasons of dock repair, storms, or cold weather conditions.

EXHIBIT 5
Organization Chart

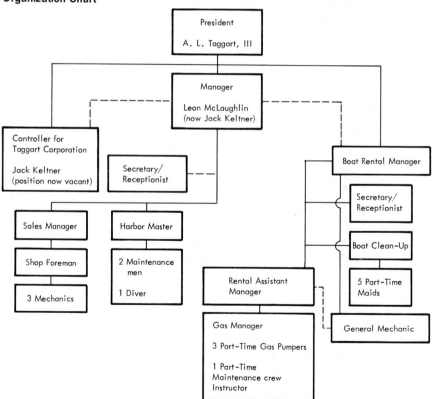

6.   Steadman Realty Company*

> I think that there are certain fundamental principles involved in all forms of
> selling, and they apply especially to selling homes. You must develop a reputa-
> tion for dependability and trustworthiness, and in the long run this can only be
> achieved by being dependable and trustworthy. In the end the willingness to
> provide the degree of service and attention to detail which this involves will
> determine the success or failure of a realtor.

So stated Henry Steadman, a successful realtor located in the town of
Hendrix. Using this philosophy he had, in ten years of doing business, built
Steadman Realty into one of Hendrix's leading real estate enterprises. Now,
in late 1974, he had reached a critical stage in the growth of his firm and was
considering what steps to take to ensure its continued profitable growth.

THE REAL ESTATE INDUSTRY

The typical real estate firm offers a variety of services involving detailed
knowledge of the real estate market. By far the main activity of small real
estate firms is assisting families in buying and selling residential properties.
Other segments of the real estate market include property management, sale
of commercial real estate, operation of a rental agency, and syndication of
real estate transactions. In general, the larger a firm is, the more of these
activities it will undertake.

The demand for the services of realtors is affected by the rate of turnover
in the occupancy and ownership of residential dwellings and by the rate at
which the local economy is growing. These in turn are influenced by population, occupations within the community, general credit conditions, income
levels, changing land use patterns, industrial growth rates, attractiveness of
the area to tourists, availability of recreation facilities, and so on. On a
nationwide basis, the dollar volume of real estate transactions has grown at
annual rates averaging 8 percent for the past decade.

Industry Structure.   The predominant form of business organization in the
real estate industry is the small proprietorship having fewer than ten sales
associates. Most recently, though, corporate organizational forms have be-

* Prepared by Richard I. Levin and Ian Cooper, Graduate School of Business Administration, the University of North Carolina at Chapel Hill.

come more numerous, especially in the case of enterprises doing large volumes of business and offering a full range of real estate services. In between these two organizational forms in both size and number are partnerships.

The strongest constraint of the growth of the individual firms has, in the past, been geographical. The vast majority of firms operate in a single community, out of one office or a small number of branch offices. Since the lifeblood of a realtor's business tends to be reputation and contacts within the community, this mitigates against large, multiunit, multilocational firms. With increasing transiency and impersonality, however, there is now more opportunity for large firms to exist, and affiliation with national chains like Century 21 and Gallery of Homes has recently become more popular in some areas of the country.

Entry into the Industry. A realtor must be licensed by the state as a real estate broker. This requires passing an examination which tests knowledge of many aspects of real estate, including construction, financing, appraisal, and law. Realtors usually are members of local boards of realtors, which, in turn, are affiliated with the National Association of Realtors; the latter association often requires additional training to meet higher standards than those required by the state licensing agency. The real estate salesperson must also be licensed by the state, but the requirements are less stringent than those for the broker.

The financial costs to enter the real estate field are fairly low, involving only sufficient funds to carry the expenses of maintaining an office and covering expenses for advertising, signs, and incidentals. As sales volume builds up, these expenses tend to be readily covered by the broker's sales commissions. The National Association of Realtors tries to maintain professional standards in the industry, but the ease of entry and exit means that there are many ''marginal'' firms doing business in the industry.

Marketing. The service of the realtor is bought by the prospective seller who ''lists'' his or her property with the firm. Upon sale of the property he pays to the broker a commission, calculated as a percentage of the sale price. Listings are generally secured as a result of personal contacts, advertising, contacting owners who are trying to sell their homes without the services of a realtor, and recommendations from satisfied clients. One of the most important elements in securing listings is reputation. The successful realtor endeavors to build a reputation for being able to sell his listings, for providing a high level of service, and for reliability. Ideally, such an image should be held by both buyers and sellers of homes, so marketing efforts tend to be aimed at both of these groups.

Competition. Most realtors share listings with others, either through a formal multiple listing service or on an informal basis. If a property is listed by one realtor and sold by another, they split the commission. Therefore, a high degree of cooperation and interchange often exists between firms doing business in the same location. Commission percentages do not usually vary between realtors, so the main competitive element is the degree of service offered. Since service is largely a subjective concept, there can be considerable diversity in the ways in which individual realtors operate their organizations.

Income.   The total commission on a transaction is usually about 6 percent of the selling price on improved property, 10 percent on unimproved land, and often negotiated on large commercial transactions. The individual who secures the listing, whether it be the broker or a salesperson, receives a listing fee. Normally this is between 10 percent and 20 percent of the total commission (between 0.6 percent and 1.2 percent of the selling price of the house). The rest of the commission is then customarily split about equally between the broker and the salesperson who sold the property. Various other systems of salesperson compensation involving such schemes as quotas and bonuses also exist. In the case of co-brokering (the situation where a property listed by one firm is sold by another), the two firms generally each take half of the commission. The selling realtor then splits his half with the salesperson who sold the property, and the listing realtor pays the lister his listing commission and keeps the rest. In the case where he obtains the listing himself, the listing realtor keeps the entire 3 percent. The realtor's commission income is highly dependent on changes in the housing market, financial conditions, and the skill of the broker and his salespersons in securing listings and selling property.

Costs.   All personal expenses involved in selling (car, entertainment) are borne by the individual salesperson, whose pay is often entirely in the form of commissions. The broker himself bears the cost of maintaining the office: rent, secretarial and clerical staff, advertising, utilities, telephone, and so on. The income of the broker comes from his share of the commissions net of these office costs. Since the office maintenance costs are relatively fixed, the broker's net income can be subject to considerable variation as the firm's volume varies.

Typical income and cost figures for a small realtor office might be:

Total commissions.	100%
Salespersons' share of commission............	50
Income to broker's office.	50
Costs as percentage of income to office	
Legal and professional	3
Telephone	6
Salaries:	
Clerical	15
Managerial	10
Promotion, entertainment, travel	5
Rent and utilities	6
Car and depreciation	5
Supplies and maintenance	5
Advertising	15
Other	5
Net profit.	25

The figures above are adapted from a realtor periodical, *Real Estate Today,* and apply to an office with one broker and about a dozen salespersons. The profit figure is, of course, the income to the broker.

Organization. The typical proprietorship has at least a secretary and a bookkeeper, as well as the broker and the salespeople. Larger firms have a sales manager and other staff to take care of customer service and areas of business other than residential sales. The hours which sales personnel work tend to be irregular, and evening and weekend work is common. The payment of sales personnel purely by commissions, the fact that real estate selling is a part-time position for many of them, and the growing number of women in sales generates a high rate of turnover among salespeople. This situation is exacerbated because entry to the profession does not have the heavy formal requirements of many other professions.

Key Trends. Just as in other industries, local realtors find that the nature of the business is changing somewhat. Decreasing personal contact and increasing transiency are lowering former barriers to size. The average size of real estate firms is increasing, and the corporate form of organization is becoming more common. With these changes is coming a desire by realtors to be recognized as a profession and to regulate standards of business practice within the industry.

To retain more professional personnel and to increase their control over the sales force, some brokers are beginning to pay their sales staff partially by salary. This also permits more formalized organizational structures, further enabling the growth of these firms.

There is increasing government involvement in the financing, construction, and planning of real estate. Large corporations from other industries are also moving into the field, and the future of realtors may lie in increased size, professionalism, more effective service, and ability to compete. Nonetheless, there are no strong signs, as yet, that the small local real estate firm is an endangered species.

HISTORY AND BACKGROUND OF STEADMAN REALTY

Mr. Steadman had moved to Hendrix in the early 1960s to work in an industry closely allied to real estate. In the course of his work he discovered that the realtors engaged in selling houses in Hendrix were generally content with the status quo and not innovative in the services that they offered. Such complacency in the face of steadily growing demand for realtor services led Mr. Steadman to believe that there was a good opportunity for a new realtor in the town.

In August of 1963, Mr. Steadman rented an office in Hendrix and opened Steadman Realty. His initial investment consisted of a few hundred dollars for supplies and furnishings and enough money to carry the modest operating expenses of the office until it could become self-supporting. The risk of the decision was considerable, however, since it involved giving up his job and being prepared to support himself and his family for the six months he estimated it would require for the business to become profitable.

From the start Mr. Steadman decided to specialize in helping families sell their individual homes. In 1974, 90 percent of the income of the firm still came from commissions on residential sales. At first business was slow, but as the town expanded and the reputation of the firm grew, the volume of transactions at Steadman Realty steadily increased. In 1967, the general economic recession hit the Hendrix real estate market rather hard, and Mr. Steadman was forced to retrench—a move which, in part, led to the dismissal of two salespersons out of the total of five who had joined the firm as it expanded.

From 1967 on, the business grew rapidly, except for a dip in activity caused by another economic recession in 1970. Operating statistics for the years 1970 to 1974 are given in Exhibit 1. By 1974, the commission income of

EXHIBIT 1
Operating Statistics, 1970–1974

	Years Ending August 31				
	1970	*1971*	*1972*	*1973*	*1974*
Total commission income.......	$140,000	$149,000	$204,000	$296,000	$316,000
Costs as a percentage of total commission income:					
Sales commissions	43.4%	34.0%	39.2%	46.5%	47.3%
Office salaries	6.1	6.7	6.0	7.0	9.6
Advertising	8.0	6.0	4.6	4.2	5.8
Telephone..............	2.5	2.7	2.3	2.1	2.3
Insurance	0.6	0.9	0.6	0.7	0.7
Rent	2.3	2.2	1.9	2.0	2.2
Customer service	2.9	4.6	3.2	2.1	1.4
Office supplies	1.1	0.6	1.4	1.5	1.3
Miscellaneous	6.2	6.0	6.5	5.7	6.1
Percentage total	73.1%	63.7%	65.7%	71.8%	76.7%
Percentage profit and salary to owner	26.9	36.3	34.3	28.2	23.3

the firm had grown to $316,000, and the number of salespeople to eight. This fast growth had been achieved by gaining an increasing share of an expanding market, and in 1974, Mr. Steadman estimated that he had a market share between 20 and 30 percent of the total residential home sales in Hendrix in which realtors were involved. This represented a substantial share since there were 20 real estate firms in Hendrix.

The office staff of the firm had grown along with the sales personnel. Mr. Steadman had begun with a single employee acting as a combination secretary and bookkeeper. As business had grown, these responsibilities were split between two employees. Three further staff members had been added at various times. The latest addition to the staff had been in 1973, when a young woman was hired to take over advertising and certain customer service responsibilities.

THE TOWN OF HENDRIX

In 1974, Hendrix was a town of 40,000 people; the major employers were several large research facilities that either were part of or did work for medical organizations, technical firms, and the government. The population of the town was diverse in geographic origin, well educated, and predominantly white collar. Income levels were high, but the career demands on the skilled research workers often meant that they would not stay permanently in the town. Most of the people buying houses in Hendrix could be expected to stay between 4 and 12 years in those houses.

As more research facilities located in Hendrix during the 1960s, the population grew at an average annual rate of 7 percent. To accommodate this growth there had been a boom in building activity in the town, and this had continued into the early 70s. Despite the new homes coming onto the market, vacancy rates were extremely low, and property values remained high. In addition to single-family homes, there were many apartments in the town, and in recent years apartments and condominiums had formed an increasing proportion of total dwelling units. Some statistics on the population and housing characteristics of the town are given in Exhibit 2.

EXHIBIT 2
Market Profile of Town of Hendrix, 1973

1973 population	37,900
Annual population growth rate (1963–74)	7%
Number of households	9,500
Annual growth rate of households (1963–73)	7%
Number of houses	5,900
Number of apartments	3,600
Number of residential homes sold 1973	610
Annual growth in number of homes sold (1963–73)	10%

COMPETITION AND LOCAL REALTOR PRACTICES

In 1974, there were about 20 realtors in Hendrix who acted as agents for the sale of individual homes. Few concentrated on this one activity as exclusively as Mr. Steadman, and other common areas of involvement were commercial real estate, insurance, property management, and large subdivision developments of new homes. The number of houses sold in Hendrix grew at an average annual rate of 10 percent from 1964 to 1974, and the price of homes had risen at about 8 percent annually throughout the period. In 1974, the tight money situation had caused a decline in the number of houses sold, but housing prices nonetheless rose almost 15 percent in 1974 alone—to about $45,000. In 1973, just over 600 houses changed hands in Hendrix; probably 10 percent to 15 percent of these transactions were carried out without the aid of a realtor.

All realtors in Hendrix charged a 6 percent commission on their sales. Traditionally there had been little competition in the degree of service which they offered. This, Mr. Steadman felt, was still true of many of the realtors in Hendrix. As an example, he cited the lack of care taken by some of the realtor firms to ensure that all details of the transaction (deeds, contracts, inspections, financing, homeowner's insurance, etc.) were completed before the final "closing" of the sale. He considered such attention to detail essential, and took great care to ensure that his sales personnel went to their closings with all these details finalized. Steadman also insisted that his sales-people prepare their clients for the closing with pre-closing statements and conferences.

Prospects for buying homes came from several sources, including the various research institutes. Often when a prospective employee would come to Hendrix on a job interview, the employer would make arrangements with one of the real estate firms in Hendrix for the visitor to be toured through the town and its residential areas. Many of these visits would not result in a sale for the realtor, and sometimes the newcomer would not even take the job in Hendrix, but nevertheless, this was the largest single source of contacts with prospective buyers of homes in the community. Mr. Steadman always tried to accommodate such requests, and arrange motel reservations if necessary, so that he could maintain the good relationship of his firm with the employers in the town.

The realtors in Hendrix did have a local board of realtors, but this tended to be a loose federation with little impact. It made no attempt to collect and distribute data, or to influence the conduct of any individual firm, nor did it undertake any institutional advertising to increase the proportion of house sellers employing the services of professional real estate firms.

STEADMAN REALTY'S PHYSICAL FACILITIES

The offices of Steadman Realty were located close to downtown Hendrix in an area predominantly occupied by small professional businesses. Each of the eight salespersons occupied a desk in one of four offices, two to an office. The secretary, the bookkeeper, and the three staff assistants each worked in separate offices, the secretary's area also being the reception area outside Mr. Steadman's office. There were other rooms in the same building which were available to Mr. Steadman if he wanted more space.

ORGANIZATION AND STAFFING

In 1974, there were 13 people employed by Steadman Realty, excluding Mr. Steadman. Eight of these were salespersons, compensated entirely by commissions. The other five included a secretary, a bookkeeper, a young woman responsible for advertising and post-sale customer service, and two young men. The two men were beginning to develop areas of business new to the firm. The most promising of these was the growing opportunity for putting together limited partnerships for various real estate investment purposes. Although this operation was not currently covering its costs, Mr. Steadman was confident that it would make a profit for the firm in 1975.

The other young man was acting as a property manager for a number of single-family homes and for a new housing project currently being rented. Mr. Steadman did not think that the income to his firm from the housing project service would warrant the time and effort put into it. Nevertheless, he was committed to staying with the program due to promises which he had felt obliged to make, and was prepared to carry the operation until other arrangements could be made.

All staff reported directly to Mr. Steadman, and relations within the office were very informal. He kept closely in touch with the work of the staff, and sometimes became involved in minor details. This enabled him to make sure that the concern for quality in the work of the firm was maintained, but Mr. Steadman realized that it was holding him back from other things that he should be spending time on. Although each employee was becoming more capable with experience, Mr. Steadman did not think that he could relax this close supervision. The basic problem in this respect was that, although the staff was well motivated, they sometimes lacked a business perspective on problems. For instance, when the advertising employee needed certain office supplies, she went to a retail office supply outlet rather than to one of Hendrix's wholesale supply firms. This fact came to Mr. Steadman's attention during a discussion with her of details of a project on which she was working, and enabled him to alter office purchasing procedure to solve the problem.

SALES PERSONNEL

The sales associates operated more independently than the office staff, but Mr. Steadman still monitored the details of their work. He did not think that they resented his supervision of their activities:

> I might walk past someone's desk and see a pile of papers, so I will just ask what they are. There is probably no reason for me to know, but I can't help being interested in the things that are happening in the office, and they understand that. Many an important detail has been brought to light by such casual observation. That doesn't speak well for my management style, but that's the way it is. The employee may not think it is important, but I often see something I might never have known about otherwise and, recognizing its importance, can do something about it before it is too late.

The sales associates were all women and had been with the firm for periods varying up to six years. Most were former homemakers who had come to Steadman Realty from another firm in Hendrix. The eight salespeople varied in both age and personality, and differences in individual productivities could not be accounted for by any readily identifiable personal characteristics. Mr. Steadman hired people whose personalities he felt would fit in with the philosophy of the firm, and who, he felt, would be compatible with the other employees. In one case of a bad personality clash between two of the saleswomen, he had thought it necessary to discharge one to preserve the harmony of the group. In this particular case Mr. Steadman, himself, had no difficulty getting along with either of the two people involved.

The saleswomen recognized the ability of Mr. Steadman to cope with difficult situations, and often came to him when they had a problem which they could not resolve. For instance, an overlooked detail might necessitate asking a favor of a lawyer involved in a sale; a buyer might have difficulty with financing and need to come to a special arrangement with the seller; or an obstinate seller might refuse a good offer for the sake of a few hundred dollars. In some cases the problems could be very personal and require a high level of diplomacy and understanding, qualities which had contributed considerably to Mr. Steadman's personal success as a realtor.

Some realtors in the town were interested in hiring away successful salespeople from the other firms. This was not a problem, however, for Steadman Realty, since the close personal relationships encouraged loyalty. On a purely business level, Mr. Steadman thought that his employees considered Steadman Realty to be the best in town to work for and wanted to be identified with it.

Prospective purchasers referred to him by personal contacts were each interviewed by Mr. Steadman. He would talk with them for about a quarter of an hour to discover general background information such as family size and financial means. From his assessment of the prospect's situation and needs, together with his knowledge of the number of clients and work load of each saleswoman, Mr. Steadman would then match the client with the saleswoman he thought most suitable. He had discussed with the sales staff whether it would be fairer to allocate prospective purchasers to them on a purely arbitrary rotational basis, but they had agreed that they preferred the present system.

The saleswoman to whom the customer was allocated would then work with him to crystallize his needs and financial ability, and select properties which were on the market and might be suitable. Over a period of time, often limited by the amount of time that the client would be in town, the saleswoman would then show the properties to the customer. This would often involve evening or weekend work for the saleswoman. Most of Steadman's saleswomen tried to take an active interest in each customer's situation and to develop a sense of rapport. Sometimes, however, a saleswoman would fail to follow up adequately a lead which she thought would not produce a sale, and Mr. Steadman tried to stay on top of each situation so he would know when to step in and make sure that sufficient care was being taken to ensure that a qualified buyer was not neglected.

Each week there was an hour-long sales meeting during which Mr. Steadman would inform all the staff of new listings, problems with clients, changes in policy, and any new developments in the firm. It was difficult to get all the sales staff to attend, since some would have appointments at the time of the meeting. Mr. Steadman had never made a big issue of these absences, however, since the saleswomen had to tailor their schedules around the availability of their clients. Feedback from the staff at these meetings was generally good, and most of the staff were quick to raise objections to anything with which they disagreed. A few of the saleswomen, though, did not consider the meetings very important, and Mr. Steadman was seeking ways to increase their enthusiasm and involvement.

MARKETING

A reputation for good service was the firm's most important marketing tool. Satisfied buyers, new to Hendrix, often talked to others about their experiences in buying their home, and the personal recommendations of satisfied buyers was, according to Mr. Steadman, strong encouragement for other prospective buyers to want to deal with the Steadman firm. Moreover, satisfied buyers who had dealt with Steadman were more likely to list their property with Mr. Steadman when the time eventually would come for them to sell. For these reasons, Mr. Steadman stressed the importance of taking care of all details of a sale, even if it involved spending part of the commission to improve minor defects in the property before the new owners moved in.

The saleswomen seemed to appreciate such details, but sometimes did not follow up the sale in the way Mr. Steadman considered necessary:

> We give a small gift to each purchaser after they move in, as a gesture of welcome. The saleswomen were not getting these delivered quickly after the sale, so I made it a firm policy that they would not get their commission check until the gift was out. Now we have no problem.

Some of the duties of maintaining post-sale contacts with home buyers had recently been taken over by the new female employee Steadman had hired to make follow-up contacts with clients, help with customer service, and oversee the firm's advertising program. Mr. Steadman considered that keeping in touch with previous buyers was one of the most important elements in the continuing growth of the firm and in developing a competitive edge over the other realty firms in Hendrix.

Mr. Steadman was very active in civic affairs in Hendrix, and had good relationships with both community groups and major employers in the town. Steadman felt obliged to maintain a visible civic profile because none of his other employees seemed inclined to assume this role. In Steadman's view, consistent public exposure, combined with a good selling reputation, was what drew most listings to the firm. When sellers called to inquire about listing their property, they would usually ask to speak to Mr. Steadman, who would then personally conduct the appraisal and discuss with the seller the specific features affecting the potential sale of the property.

Steadman Realty marketed its services in traditional ways. Generally, all listed properties were advertised in the local paper; this not only brought properties to the attention of potential buyers but it also made sellers feel that they were getting market exposure. It was Steadman's policy to take out ads in any local publication in which the majority of the realtors in Hendrix advertised—so as to neutralize any competitive advantage they might otherwise gain. One area of advertising where the firm did differ from others in the town was its heavier use of radio spots. Escalating rates were beginning to make this expensive, but Mr. Steadman believed radio was an effective medium to help convey the personalized service approach he was trying to achieve. To help reinforce that image, the firm did its own radio spots rather than using local announcers.

COSTS AND FINANCIAL DATA

Steadman Realty was organized as a corporation partly as a device for reducing Mr. Steadman's personal income tax on the profits he was reinvesting in the business and partly to give Mr. Steadman some flexibility in controlling the tax bracket of the firm through adjustments in the amount of salary that he drew. Exhibit 3 presents a percentage breakdown of the firm's costs for fiscal 1974 and shows how Steadman's percentages compared with similar operating percentages for a large, successful, multioffice realtor firm with over 50 sales associates. The proportion of the total commissions earned by Steadman Realty which was paid to the saleswomen tended to be lower than

EXHIBIT 3
Comparison of Operating Statistics of Steadman Realty for 1974 and a Large Successful Realtor Firm

Operating Statistics	Steadman Realty	Large Firm
Total commissions:	100.0%	100.0%
Sales staff share	47.3	51.5
Income to realtor's office	52.7	48.5
Costs as a percentage of commission income:		
Advertising	11.0	12.0
Office staff	18.5	15.9
Sales management	0.0	21.3
Telephone	4.4	5.2
Rent	4.2	4.9
Supplies	2.5	2.6
Customer service	2.7	2.5
Other	12.8	13.7
Total Percentage	56.1	78.1
Net income to broker	43.9	21.9

Source: Statistics reported in *Real Estate Today*.

for other firms since Mr. Steadman did most of the listing, and the listing fee thus accrued directly to the firm. In 1973 and 1974, the proportion of commissions paid to saleswomen was higher than for previous years because a larger fraction of Steadman's sales had involved other realtors' listings.

Steadman's salespeople earned gross commissions of between $10,000 and $25,000 each year, but there was only limited consistency in the level of earnings of each sales associate from year to year. The top salesperson one year could be number three or four the next year because of fluctuations in the percentage of clients who would actually buy a house—fluctuations which were not always within the salesperson's ability to control.

Staff costs comprised the largest category of overhead expense. Before Mr. Steadman hired a new staff member, he tried to make sure he had a large enough commission revenue to support the permanently increased level of overhead. Uncertainty about what kind of year 1975 would be made him wary of taking on more staff, but he knew that if he did so it would have to be during the slack period from November to January, so that he would have time to spare to train the person.

The selling costs Steadman Realty incurred in advertising, promotional efforts, and telephone costs were not always closely tied to the firm's sales volume. For instance, in slack years selling costs might actually be increased (as well as rising percentagewise) in an attempt to stimulate sales and try to keep commission income high enough to cover office overhead and salaries.

CONTROLS

No formal budget or sales goals were set by Mr. Steadman. Recording and filing systems had been developed as the firm grew, and were modified or expanded as new needs for information arose. The bookkeeper prepared monthly financial statistics, and Mr. Steadman studied these regularly to see how well costs were being kept in line. The number of closings planned, and the average price of these transactions, provided Mr. Steadman with a good indicator of how well the firm's income was being maintained. Annual comparative figures of monthly sales were of limited value, however, since the timing of sales activity in the market was likely to vary from year to year.

Mr. Steadman insisted that fairly comprehensive records be kept on prospective buyers and sellers; for example, the sales associates were expected to maintain a "client prospect card" on each buyer they were handling. From time to time, Mr. Steadman would go through these cards with his salespeople and check their progress with each customer he had assigned to them. Since the saleswomen were "independent contractors" and were compensated entirely by commissions, Mr. Steadman found that it was sometimes difficult to get them to adhere to his policy of keeping good records and updating files; some complained that they did not see these "duties" as being directly related to their job of selling or as being worth the time and effort it took. In responding to these complaints, it was usually sufficient for Mr. Steadman to emphasize that record-keeping and buyer follow-up were integral parts of the personalized and professional touch he was trying to create and that he wished them to adhere to policy. Chronic cases of nonadherence presented Mr. Steadman with a difficult choice as to whether to press the issue. Sometimes he did and sometimes he did not. On the issue of getting the gifts to the buyers promptly he had drawn a hard line but so far he had not thought it worthwhile to press the issues of slackness in recording customer data following closings and nonattendance of sales meetings.

The atmosphere in the office was generally relaxed, and the saleswomen seemed to enjoy working for the firm. On one occasion, though, a sales-woman remarked to Mr. Steadman that he criticized her faults but did not praise her good work. Mr. Steadman's response was "If you couldn't do your work I would take you aside and show you how. But you can do it, and are very good at it, so when you make a mistake you deserve criticism and constructive suggestions."

Managing the nonselling staff employees was easier; they were all salaried employees and reported directly to Mr. Steadman. He tended to supervise their work closely in an effort to get them used to paying attention to detail. Although Mr. Steadman felt that his office staff at times lacked commitment and initiative, the staff's conversations with the casewriter indicated that this might be due to the tight rein which Mr. Steadman tried to maintain over their work assignments. When informed of these views, Mr. Steadman commented to the effect that he did not think he could afford to give office staff enough responsibility to learn by making mistakes, since this would damage the image of the firm which had taken him so much time to build.

STEADMAN'S WORK LOAD AND TIME ALLOCATION

Mr. Steadman estimated that 20 percent of his time was spent working with sales associates, helping them with problems, giving them information, or discussing their work. As much, if not more, time was spent with the office staff dealing with day-to-day operations of the firm and supervising the special projects that each employee was assigned.

Another time-consuming activity was securing listings. Mr. Steadman personally obtained about 80 percent of the listings of the firm, because of his extensive contacts in the community and because the saleswomen were not either motivated or aggressively inclined to go out and secure listings on their own initiative. This was the case even though the salesperson received the listing fee when she got a seller to list property with Steadman Realty. Originally, Mr. Steadman had taken no listing fee out of the commission for the listings he secured and, in return, the sales associates had performed extra duties such as appraisals which were not directly part of their obliga-tion. Eventually, he had decided that the money he was losing by not taking the listing fee himself was not sufficiently compensated by these extra services. He had, in the face of opposition from the sales staff, started to retain a 10 percent listing fee on the listings he secured. Even so, he still did not think that this was sufficient, and hoped eventually to raise it to 20 percent. He was cautious of this change, however, since he knew it would provoke strong opposition from the sales staff.

Mr. Steadman had several reasons why he did not want to give up the responsibility for dealing with prospects seeking to list their homes with Steadman Realty. He was convinced that many of the sellers who listed with the firm did so because of his own reputation for handling listings personally and because of the fine record of the firm in being able to sell its listings. Second, Mr. Steadman believed that the time he spent working with charities and community groups brought him into contact with potential buyers and sellers and gave the firm needed public exposure. His community involvement was a key factor in distinguishing between his role in the firm and that of the sales associates. He considered civic activities to be an essential function of anyone who would take over some of his responsibilities, and did not think that it was possessed by any of his current staff or saleswomen. Mr. Steadman saw a major difference between the way he was committed to the firm and the way his sales staff was committed:

> The sales staff are dedicated, but not in the same way as I am. Right now one of them is out scraping down shelves in a house into which the new owners are moving tomorrow. She couldn't find the workmen to do it, so she is doing it herself. But if she wanted to go to the beach this weekend, she would just take off. I can understand that, since she has to fit in with her husband's schedule, but if a problem comes up someone must be here, and I'm the one who does that.

A third reason why Mr. Steadman continued to do the listing himself was the income it brought in to the firm rather than being paid out to the sales associates. If he assigned the seller to one of the saleswomen to perform the appraisal and take the listing, the listing fee would go to the salesperson instead of the firm. These fees formed a large part of the salary of the person hired to supervise advertising and to develop new business through customer follow-up.

A final reason that Mr. Steadman wanted to continue taking listings personally was that he enjoyed the process of talking to the sellers and discussing with them the best way to market their house. Moreover, tactful and sophisticated sales strategies often had to be used to convince potential sellers that he, as a realtor, was genuinely seeking to market their house in an effective, professional manner and that he was not merely after the financial gain. This same enjoyment of dealing with people was a reason why Mr. Steadman also took time to talk to prospective buyers before passing them on to the sales staff. Mr. Steadman remarked that he derived a great deal of nonfinancial satisfaction from helping people who were in the market of buying or selling a home fulfill their housing needs and solve problems related to something as important to them as their home.

Another indication of the involvement of Mr. Steadman in his profession was his policy of continuing to maintain a business phone in his home. He explained the reason for this:

> If that phone rings on the weekend it might mean a listing or a sale. It was put in when I couldn't afford to let opportunities like that go by. Now I keep it because I don't want to disappoint people by them not being able to reach someone on the weekend. My secretary has offered to have a phone put in her home for the weekend calls, and I might do that, since it would help her to feel important to the firm.

GROWING PRESSURES ON MR. STEADMAN'S TIME

Mr. Steadman viewed his main problem during the summer of 1974 as an increasingly severe pressure on his own time. The height of the selling season extended from March to September, and during this period he put in extremely long hours. He knew that if the local real estate market was very active in 1975 that his personal work load would be unduly heavy. Several alternatives for action seemed possible, but all had their drawbacks.

An obvious possibility was to hire a manager to take over either the sales management or the office management function. Mr. Steadman had, in the past, considered this step and had even checked into the backgrounds of some people who might be suitable. He had concluded, however, that the closeness of the working relationship and the considerable amount of time he would have to invest in training the person made it unwise to employ anyone about whom he had the slightest reservations. Since he had not found anyone suitable, he had never made a serious move to try to hire a sales or office manager. The characteristics which he required above all were that the person be committed to a real estate career, responsible, and a firm believer in the same professional and personal approach to real estate sales which he himself had. Mr. Steadman was not sure that he could identify the right kind of person for the job without first getting to know him (or her) very well, and, there again, the time involved was a major problem. He knew of people working for other realtors in the town who might meet the qualifications he had in mind, but it was his long-standing practice not to attempt to hire employees away from rival firms.

Another difficulty with employing a good managerial assistant was the high salary required and the added burden to overhead which this would entail; more overhead, felt Steadman, made the firm's profits more vulnerable to a market slump and he was not sure that such risk exposure was warranted. A final repercussion of hiring a manager related to the effect it would have on the firm's personnel. The two young men on the office staff might feel that it demonstrated a lack of confidence in them, and this could have serious consequences for their attitudes toward their jobs. Mr. Steadman thought that the sales staff might also react negatively:

If I do take on someone with whom I can work, I may lose a couple of sales associates who cannot work with him. What do I get in return for that loss?— time, peace of mind, and the opportunity to pursue other work I have to do. That's the choice I am faced with.

A second alternative to relieve the pressure on his time was for Mr. Steadman to delegate some of his responsibilities to the existing personnel. Yet, Steadman knew that he did not want to stop handling listings personally and that his commitment to quality service meant that he could not relax his close supervision of the work of his employees. While he could, perhaps, reduce the amount of time he spent with prospective buyers, Mr. Steadman did not think that this would be a significant saving, owing to the importance he attached to maintaining close personal involvement with as many customers as possible.

Nor did Steadman believe that the alternative of turning away potential business made good sense. Refusing listings or a deliberate lack of interest in clients would, Steadman felt, undermine the image and growth of the firm— and, eventually, would erode Steadman Realty's strong market position.

In the long run, Steadman saw a need for the firm to get more involved in land developments and speculative homebuilding; while he had a growing interest in pursuing these activities, he did not foresee his having the time it would take unless he made some managerial changes. The pressures of day-to-day operations had, in addition, kept Mr. Steadman from making progress on some internal projects which he had in mind. For instance, he wanted to investigate and possibly institute the use of a policy manual, but he had never found enough free time to devote to this project.

A more immediate and potentially troublesome problem was that one or two of his sales personnel were consistently below par in either their sales performance or their adherence to the firm's selling philosophy. Although circumstances were not so serious that Mr. Steadman felt forced to discharge them, he was alert to the major task he would face in finding better replacements:

> If my secretary or bookkeeper leaves her job, then the firm cannot function until I find a replacement. So I make time and get it done. But if there is a deficiency in the sales force and it is not sufficiently pressing to make a big difference in performance, I will not force myself to free the time to find a new employee.

A major difficulty Steadman encountered in planning the growth of the firm was the unpredictability of the real estate market. He had not found any practical way to predict from year to year what course it would take, and thus forecasting or projecting commission revenues was not very productive. Mr. Steadman did not make any formal business plan, and felt that even if he did it would turn out to be of marginal value in planning the growth of the sales staff:

If I want to hire a new saleswoman and I take her on before the work is there for her to do, the others will complain that I am taking work away from them. So I just have to wait until they are all working at capacity, and then they can see the need as well.

FUTURE OUTLOOK

Despite his large share of the residential real estate market in Hendrix, Mr. Steadman thought that there was still room for his firm to increase commission revenues from residential sales. Even when his market penetration in Hendrix topped out, he thought that the firm could still expand by entering the markets in nearby towns. One town, about half the size of Hendrix and located 20 miles away, looked particularly promising. Mr. Steadman was confident that if he opened an office there, it would be making money within a few years.

One of the most rapidly expanding segments of the real estate market in Hendrix was apartments. However, meeting the needs of landlords and apartment tenants required as much time and energy as for single-family homes, and under the pressure of time from other activities, Mr. Steadman had elected not to focus very heavily on property management. For similar reasons, he had also decided to stay out of the insurance field.

Commercial real estate sales lacked the personal involvement of residential sales and had, therefore, never appealed much to Mr. Steadman. The most interesting and potentially promising field of new involvement was, in Steadman's view, acting as a selling agent for local contractors and speculative homebuilders. He had been approached several times about entering into such a relationship but had turned them down because he was not sure that this was the best use of his time.

Mr. Steadman had sufficient contacts in all these fields to ensure him a good volume of business if he ever wholeheartedly took the plunge toward any of them. It was, again, lack of time which held him back from doing so, although he admitted that if a very lucrative offer came along he would have to think very hard before turning it down. Nonetheless, he was still not sure how best to proceed. Each course of action had sufficient drawbacks to prevent him from committing himself, but he knew that the problem was not one which would work itself out unless he took positive action. As a first step, he had studied his organization and reviewed how he used his time, endeavoring to correct inefficiencies in the way he operated personally in the office. Yet, he knew this was only a delaying action and would not solve the long-run problem. The ultimate solution was undoubtedly in making more fundamental kinds of changes.

B. Strategy: Evaluation and Alternatives

7. Bright Coop Company, Inc.*

WHEN A NUMBER of East Texas farmers got into the business of raising chickens on a mass production basis in the early 1950s, Charles Bright and his brother N. G. Bright, quite by accident, stumbled upon an opportunity to supply low-cost coops for transporting the birds to market. Prior to 1951, live poultry transporters used custom-built coops that required two men to load onto trucks; the coops were rented from coop builders rather than being owned outright by the truckers. The Bright brothers, upon discovering that there was a sizable market for a low-priced wooden poultry coop, wasted little time in setting up Bright Coop Company as a manufacturer of wooden coops, with operations in Nacogdoches, Texas.

From 1952 to 1975, Charles, 48, and N. G., 59, periodically expanded their factory to the point where the Nacogdoches firm was producing an average of 2,000 coops per day. In 1975, Bright Coop was the largest wooden coop manufacturer in the United States; its coops were shipped all over the United States and into Mexico and Canada as well. Many of Bright Coop Company's customers were of the opinion that no other coop producer matched Bright on the combined features of competitive price, quality, and service.

HISTORY AND BACKGROUND

Prior to forming Bright Coop Company, the Bright brothers owned a grocery store and had a sideline business making wooden chairs in Nacogdoches. In April 1951, a load of building materials for the construction of 500 chair parts overturned and a local live poultry hauler asked the Brights to construct chicken coops out of the ruined material. The Brights agreed and spent much of their time from November 1951 to the end of January 1952 completing the project. They received $2.25 each for 168 coops. Even though the Bright brothers ended up losing money on that first project because they underestimated the amount of manual labor that it would take to make the coops, they felt there was good business potential in constructing coops for sale to poultry haulers. The East Texas broiler industry was begin-

---

* Prepared by Professors B. G. Bizzell and Ed D. Roach, of Stephen F. Austin State University.

ning to grow rapidly and when the word spread in the poultry community that the Brights were producing coops, additional orders came in unsolicited.

Although, at first, the Bright brothers had a very limited knowledge of the woodworking business, they learned quickly and in 1953 began to make tools that would allow them to increase coop production more efficiently. At the time, coop-building tools and machinery were nonexistent. The Brights were clever enough to design and assemble most of the equipment they needed. They were also innovators in the design of their product. The Bright Coop Company introduced the first "one-man" coop which cut the loading and unloading costs of poultry haulers in half. Haulers liked the Bright's innovative coop design (aside from the laborsaving feature it had over the standard "two-man" coops) and orders increased steadily. As fast as they were able, the Brights moved to a more automated production of coops, thereby saving substantially on labor costs per coop and, at the same time, increasing the daily production rate.

In 1959, the Brights diversified into wooden turkey coops and metal racks. This required a different coop design because whereas chicken coops were stacked on flatbed trailers for shipping, the greater size and weight of turkeys required a larger coop, together with metal racks for support. In 1963, the production of wooden turkey coops was curtailed in favor of producing just metal racks.

In the mid-1960s, the lumber market changed drastically and the company had difficulty in finding acceptable quality hardwood for its coops. Supplies were so tight that the two brothers accepted odd-lot shipments of hardwood lumber of different grades; large amounts of these shipments proved unsuitable for coop production. In an effort to find some use for the leftover lumber, the Brights began constructing wooden pallets for sale to chemical and shipping firms. Soon this business, too, prospered and pallet construction was continued as a regularly offered product.

In 1966, the company moved another step toward completely fulfilling its motto, "Complete Poultry Truck Outfitters," by commencing the production of trailers capable of hauling coops and related equipment. Shortly thereafter, they expanded into all kinds of accessories for transporting coops including straps, loaders, pallets, and chains. These last additions made Bright a full-line producer of items needed by haulers of live poultry.

THE MARKET FOR COOPS

From the time the company was started in 1952, Bright Coop's sales grew every year until late 1974. During the last five months of 1974, Bright Coop found itself caught in the midst of the bust phase of the poultry cycle, an economic recession, and an emerging demand for plastic coops as a substitute for wooden coops. Brights' sales fell from nearly 2,000 coops daily to 450 per day. Almost 40 percent of Bright's work force had to be laid off. Whereas Bright had used 40,000 board feet of lumber a day during the peak sales periods of early 1974, its lumber usage fell to less than 20,000 board feet during the first half of 1975. Most of the lumber was purchased from lumber mills in the Nacogdoches area.

Studies of ups and downs in the poultry business indicate an approximate five-year "boom to bust to boom" cycle—especially as concerns the broiler, roaster, egg, turkey, and rock cornish hen segments of the poultry industry. The most recent appearance of the bust phase began in the third quarter of 1972 and was accelerated by historically high broiler production, coincident with high beef production. The competition between beef and poultry for the consumer's meat dollar resulted in a 12 percent to 15 percent contraction in poultry sales, with the broiler and turkey market segments being hit hardest.

These events resulted in a sharp downswing in Brights' sales of coops. Processors who had a large inventory of coops to draw down stopped ordering new coops for several months. Others simply cut back on the size of their coop orders. As an illustrative example of how changes in the demand for poultry can affect the sales of coops over the course of the poultry cycle, suppose that a processor uses 100,000 coops in his operation during average production periods. Further suppose that 1,000 coops wear out each week and are replaced by ordering 1,000 new coops per week from Bright. Then if the processor's production rate falls by 20 percent such that only 80,000 coops are needed, the processor has a 20–week coop inventory on hand and will not need to order any more coops for 20 weeks. On the other hand, if and when the processor increases production back to normal, he will need to order 20,000 coops on a one-time basis and then cut back to the normal 1,000 replacement amount. Such boom-to-bust swings in coop orders prompted Bright to try to respond quickly to such market shifts and was also a motivating factor in Bright's earlier diversification moves.

While the boom-to-bust cycle was taking its toll on Bright, two other factors were also at work. One was the appearance of the severe economic recession in late 1974 which further undermined the poultry industry in general and coops sales in particular. The second was a surge of enthusiasm for plastic coops as a substitute for wooden coops. A number of haulers were persuaded by the plastic coop manufacturers to give plastic coops a try. The combination of these three factors was believed by the Brights to account for why the bottom literally fell out of the company's coop sales in late 1974. However, in the spring of 1975, the poultry market began a recovery and, according to prognosticators, the long-run outlook for coop sales was for a gradual expansion during the next five years.

PRODUCT LINE

In 1975, Bright Coop introduced a new wood-plastic combination coop to compete with the increasingly popular plastic coop. According to the company's promotional brochures, the new coop represented a "perfect marriage of wood and plastic." See the illustration in Exhibit 1 (page 288).

Other Bright products as of 1975 included the Bright pullet and poultry harvester, the live turkey harvester, the specially designed drop-frame poultry trailer in two styles, and hen floors. These items are displayed in Exhibits 2, 3, 4, and 5 (pages 289–301).

PRODUCTION FACILITIES

All of Bright Coop's production facilities were located in Nacogdoches, Texas. The facilities included a coop manufacturing plant, a pallet manufacturing plant, and a building for assembling harvesters and trailers. The trailers were not manufactured by Bright; rather, they were built to specification by a trailer manufacturer and then outfitted by Bright in Nacogdoches.

MARKETING AND SALES

Bright's marketing efforts were concentrated in 11 poultry-producing states: Texas, South Carolina, Florida, Tennessee, Alabama, Mississippi, Georgia, Arkansas, Kentucky, North Carolina, and California. In addition, coops were exported to Canada and Mexico. The company estimated that it had a market share of about 40 percent in the wooden coop market segment as of 1974 and that there were roughly 1.5 million wooden coops in use. In general, a wooden coop had a life of about one year before it had to be replaced; however this varied with how many times a coop was used, the climate, and the care with which it was handled.

Although the company had only a one-man sales force, both the salesman and the Bright brothers maintained extensive personal contacts with customers via telephone, periodic trips to customer facilities, and at conventions. The Bright brothers were both personally acquainted with nearly 90 percent of the poultry haulers and processors in the United States, having built up their associations over 24 years. The company had exhibits for its products at three different national conventions and advertised regularly in a national poultry magazine.

From July 1, 1974 through June 30, 1975 (the latest full fiscal year), the company's sales breakdown by product line was as follows:

Sales of coops	$1,400,000
Sales of crates, pallets, and hen floors	1,221,000
Turkey-related items	349,000
Trailer sales (6 units)	650,000
Total sales	$3,620,000

The company made sales forecasts for six months in advance for planning purposes.

COMPETITION

When the Brights first entered the coop business in 1952 there were 26 other wooden coop manufacturers. As of 1975, there were only five; of these, Bright was the largest and the company did not encounter intense competition from any of the other four firms. Bright's strongest competition came from the 11 plastic coop manufacturers. Plastic coops first appeared in 1966 but had not made major inroads until the 1972–74 period when significant market gains were made. The plastic coop producers touted their product as lasting for three years, although this had not been substantiated in actual use situations. The main benefit of plastic coops was a reduced airflow as compared to wooden coops.

The plastic coop had undergone many modifications in its short existence, owing to a series of different problems relating to strength, rigidity, and design. One problem in particular was that when plastic coops were stacked on top of each other, they had a tendency to shift and slide. In some instances, this shifting had caused trucks in transit to overturn. Inability of the plastic coop manufacturers to solve the various structural problems was creating some customer dissatisfaction and in 1975 Bright Coop regained some of its former business lost to plastic coop firms.

Bright had been contacted by plastic coop manufacturers to take on a plastic coop line. However, with all the problems attending plastic coops, Bright elected to wait and see if the problems with plastic coops could be ironed out. Actually, both Bright brothers felt that the plastic coop would "fade out" in the future.

FINANCIAL INFORMATION

The Bright's organized their operations into three distinct companies: Bright Coop Co. stood as one entity; the trailer business was set up as Bright Sales Company; and a third company owned the land where all the plant facilities were located. Excluding the land and buildings, the total book value of the entire business was in the range of $150,000 to $200,000 (as of 1975).

The two brothers did not operate on the basis of a budget but they had plans to do a budget later in 1975. "We just spend what we need and then some," said one of the managers. To judge how well they were doing, the brothers compared their sales standing for the current year to date with that of comparable periods in years past.

To meet the rising volume of government regulations, the company had had to spend a combined total of about $300,000 over the past several years. Weekly payroll costs amounted to $10,000. Bright's bad debt ratio averaged about 0.5 percent of sales. A condensed income statement is presented below:

	Fiscal Year		
	1974	*1973*	*1972*
Sales	$2,635,927	$2,974,892	$3,034,049
Costs of goods sold	2,096,482	2,379,737	2,419,556
Gross profit	$ 539,445	$ 595,155	$ 614,493
Operating expenses	334,634	335,648	350,258
Net Income (excluding officers' salaries, income taxes, and depreciation)	$ 204,811	$ 259,507	$ 264,235

An estimated balance sheet is presented in Exhibit 6 on page 302.

ORGANIZATION

Charles and N. G. assume most of the company's management responsibilities. They are assisted in day-to-day operations by Joe Biggerstaff, the plant supervisor. Doug Swearingen, who is the Bright's brother-in-law, is in charge of sales. An organization chart is shown in Exhibit 7 (page 302). The Bright brothers do not view the organization of the company as being tightly structured; those with line authority are left relatively free to manage in their own ways and to carry out their own ideas.

EMPLOYEE RELATIONS

Bright Coop was proud of the relationship it had with employees. Many of the employees had been with the company since its inception and Charles Bright took special care to get to know each employee personally. In 1975, Bright had 125 employees; eight months previous the work force totaled 160 persons, but the sharp downturn in sales in late 1974 forced layoffs of 35 persons. Both Charles and N. G. felt badly about having to lay off workers because they felt a strong sense of obligation and responsibility to the community for providing job opportunities.

It was company policy to employ handicapped persons whenever a suitable job was available. Bright Coop had three blind workers on its payroll in 1975. At the same time, the company endeavored not to force a worker to retire. Rather a job was found or created for older employees who wanted or needed to continue work. Two of Bright's employees were 86 and 90 years old, respectively.

There was no union representation at Bright Coop Company. There had been previous attempts to unionize Bright's employees but each attempt had failed.

Workers were paid by the hour or by piece rate. Hourly wages ranged from $2.30 to $3. Personnel charts were kept on each employee, including information on number of days absent and production performance. A "merit system" keyed to absences and production performance was used as the basis for calling back employees who had been laid off.

FUTURE PLANS AND OUTLOOK

Although coop sales had been slack for the last six months, sales of pallets had increased to the point where plans were being developed to move the pallet plant to a new location having more operating space. The Bright brothers were also looking into several other expansion possibilities. There were plans to improve the broiler and turkey coops. Consideration was being given to adding a mulcher to the company's woodcutting process if and when coop sales increased to prior levels; a mulcher would enable the company to use 100 percent of its wood purchases, since scrap pieces could then be mulched and sold to poultry farmers as litter or desicants. Some thought had been given to producing wooden picnic tables, even though other picnic table producers had just recently managed to earn a profit. The Bright brothers were undecided about entering the plastic coop market because of the cost of tooling up for plastic coop production and because of the problems haulers were encountering with plastic coops.

But despite Bright Coop's being a leader in the poultry outfitting industry and the dominant producer of wooden coops, the Bright brothers were unsure how to go about improving and strengthening the company's position in the months and years ahead. Some of the major uncertainties bothering the two brothers were summed up by Charles Bright:

> I don't know what direction the company should take. I don't feel that plastics give the service offered by wood and the cost to produce is much higher. On the other hand, environmental requirements may make the wood coops obsolete— they may be difficult to clean. Yet, I am not sure I want to invest the capital required to tool up for a plastic product.

EXHIBIT 1

The Perfect Marriage of

Wood and Plastic

Reduce Coop Repair

Longer Life

17 Gauge Galvanized Wire Reinforced

Twelve PVC-Hardwood Core Dowels

Positive Action Door

1975 MODEL BRIGHT WOOD/PVC POULTRY COOP

With the use of mechanical devices such as "squeeze lift" and "fork lifts" throughout the poultry industry, we have been exploring new ways to lengthen the life of our coop. The answer: a new PVC-Hardwood Dowel Core which has more flexibility and sheer resistance.

Today we offer you the wire-reinforced wood poultry coop with twelve (12) Outdoor Rigid Polyvinyl Chloride (PVC) Jackets with a 7/16" diameter Hardwood Dowel Core. Two (2) PVC-Hardwood Dowel Cores on each corner, with one in center of end and side frame.

Call us for a load of the BRIGHT WOOD WIRE REINFORCED POULTRY COOP WITH PVC-HARDWOOD DOWEL CORES — today.

BRIGHT COOP COMPANY
803 West Seale   ·   713/564-8378
Nacogdoches, Texas 75961

EXHIBIT 2

BRIGHT'S
LIVE POULTRY BATTERIES

The birth of the East Texas Broiler industry in 1951 produced the need for a ready and economical supply of poultry coops for transporting birds to market. Responding to this need, the Bright brothers of Nacogdoches, N. G. and Charles; established a modest factory here, which has expanded yearly to the point that today coops are shipped to every corner of the nation and several foreign countries.

To earn the name "Complete Poultry Truck Outfitters," the first Bright Live Poultry Batteries were manufactured here in 1955, and since that time, have proven their ability to reduce live bird transportation cost. Over millions of birds hauled, millions of miles traveled, they have to be second to none in live poultry transportation!

Through the years of experience, and with constant improvements on our poultry batteries, our new designed models offer you these features. They cut labor cost, easier and faster washing and cleaning, reduce downgrades with less bruises, increased payloads with less weight. The Bright Batteries give you better ventilation and cooling ability, rugged construction with longer life and less general maintenance - - - -They can take it!

"BE BRIGHT BUY RIGHT BUY BRIGHT'S" has always been more than just a slogan.

BRIGHT COOP COMPANY
Complete Poultry Truck Outfitters
803 WEST SEALE ST. / DAY OR NIGHT PHONE (713) 564-8378 / NACOGDOCHES, TEXAS 75961

EXHIBIT 2 *(continued)*

Main frame is constructed of welded 1x1x.095 (thick wall) tube, base frame and all corner uprights are 1x2x.120 tube. All metal is cleaned, and primed with red oxide rust preventive paint, then another finish coat is applied after unit is completed, with bottoms and doors installed.

If repairs become necessary, bottoms can be easily replaced by sliding another sheet of plywood, under welded keepers, on outside edge of floor joists.   All bottoms are 3/8" exterior plywood, oiled treated and edges sealed to prevent moisture buildup, reducing overall weight.

All end and center partitions are fabricated of 1/8" x 1/2" flat steel, (unless wood is specified).   Each metal partition acts as a truss, strengthening the unit against road and load strain. All units are designed with the ease of washing and cleaning in mind. All partitions are raised off the floor, to prevent waste and feathers from catching on them. In the center of all standard units, there is a 1" crack in all floors, to allow waste to fall through to the floor beneath, making washing much quicker and easier.

Our original wooden dowel pin, overhead type door is standard on all units. Its operating action eliminates the necessity for any type hinge, fasteners or latches. It assures positive action in severe weather, and is designed to ride flush with the floor, preventing damages to wings and legs. Each door tract acts as a sway brace, reinforcing the frame and also strengthening same. Through experience we have found that the recessing inside type door, has many advantages over all types of outside doors when loading with a mechanical loader.

All four bottom corners are strengthened with triangle gussets. This also supplies one method for attaching the unit to a trailer. The slots in the triangles allows the trailer to move under load strains and road conditions, without damage to the unit, by giving it a slight sliding action. They also provide a means for casters to be attached to the unit.

This type door allows all compartments to be opened at one time, or left in an open position after unloading, to ease the washing and cleaning problem. They also can be left in an open position to help dry the unit out on the way back to the farm.

BE BRIGHT

BUY

EXHIBIT 2 *(continued)*

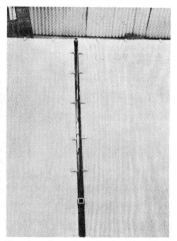

Top view of our standard unit with a 1" air space. This feature gives the unit added cooling ability, plus making the job of cleaning much easier. The use of bottom clips eliminates the necessity of screws to secure the bottoms, which eventually rust out.

Any width air spacing, in the center of the units are available, if desired at additional cost. Our standard air space model has a 6" isle. This feature adds additional weight, due to the extra center partitions and uprights.

Our standard steel end and center partitions can be replaced with our wooden dowel rod type partitions. This feature adds no extra weight, however, the unit has to be "X" braced, across the end and in the center.

All metal "Swing Out" type doors are optional features. The outside door has a lifting action, clearing the top "U" type keepers, then swings down on the outside of the coop. It is impossible to have all doors open at one time in order to let the air blow through the unit and help clean same.

EXHIBIT 2 *(concluded)*

Hanging brackets for loading platform are very light and simple to attach to the side of unit. This type bracket eliminates any type chain, latches, etc. It enables you to set up loading boards at any height you desire, without opening the door of the compartment.

Side view of a 40' unit, consisting of five 8' standard units, totaling 120 compartments. This is a very popular and well accepted way of spacing between each unit, give it better cooling ability and ventilation, by exposing each coop to the air. This type arrangement also eases the washing of the unit, allowing the feathers and waste to fall out between the units, as well as on the side.

This picture also shows a BRIGHT LIVE TURKEY HARVESTER AND POWER-PAK, in a loading position.

DIMENSIONS AND SPECIFICATIONS

	8 Foot Standard	4 Foot Standard	8 Foot Air Spaced	4 Foot Air Spaced
OVERALL (OUTSIDE)				
Height	98"	98"	98"	98"
Width	93½"	93½"	93½"	93½"
Length	94"	47"	94"	47"
INSIDE COMPARTMENT				
Height	15½"	15½"	15½"	15½"
Depth	45"	45"	42"	42"
Length	46¼"	46¼"	46¼"	46¼"
COMPARTMENT CAPACITY (Depending on Size & Weather)				
Toms	10	10	8-10	8-10
Hens	16-18	16-18	14-16	14-16
TOTAL COMPARTMENTS	24	12	24	12
OUTSIDE DOOR OPENINGS	43¼" x 14½"	43¼" x 14½"	43¼" x 14½"	43¼" x 14½"
WEIGHT	1580 lbs.	810 lbs.	1590 lbs.	815 lbs.

Should your live hauling operation require a different type or some special designed equipment, we at BRIGHT COOP COMPANY welcome the opportunity to make recommendations and to quote you on your requirements.

We also offer the well accepted BRIGHT Live Poultry Truck Trailers, designed and built with the live hauler in mind.

EXHIBIT 3

BRIGHT'S
Live Turkey Harvester

You, Mr. Turkeyman.... should be given full credit for the origination of the BRIGHT LIVE TURKEY HARVESTER. It was your continued constructive criticism, and suggestions, on how the present day loaders could be and should be built, to enable you to reduce your live loading cost in the field. We at BRIGHT COOP COMPANY want to thank you, and express our appreciation to all the industrymen who helped us design, build and field test our Turkey Harvester. With your help and our knowledge of building machinery for endurance, and workability, we have produced a loader we both can be proud of.

"BE BRIGHT   BUY RIGHT   BUY BRIGHT'S" has always been more than just a slogan.

BRIGHT COOP COMPANY
Complete Poultry Truck Outfitters

803 WEST SEALE ST. / DAY OR NIGHT PHONE (713) 564-8378 / NACOGDOCHES, TEXAS 75961

EXHIBIT 3 *(continued)*

The Bright Harvester is FABRICATED in our own shop, under close supervision of our own machinists, to give you maximum in quality and workmanship. Main frame is constructed of only heavy duty structural channel, cross braced with 2" pipe. Above picture shows roller conveyor underneath the woven wire belt friction free, reducing wear to belt, and power required to operate the machine. Entire machine is cleaned, primed with Red oxide primer, and two coats of automotive enamel.

Main conveyor belt moving birds to the coopers, is a galvanized woven wire belt, 11 ga. 1/4" mesh. Attached to each side is 2060 roller chain with oversized rollers to reduce friction and wear on the belt. The chains are attached to the mesh belt with rods space on 4½" centers passing through the mesh belt.

The wire belt enables more birds to be conveyed per square foot of belt, cleaner, easier to disinfect and prevents feathers from collecting inside machine.

The Harvester is equipped with drop type, torsion springs, assuring a level ride, easier pulling in transit. All wiring is in plastic conduits. All necessary lights, turn signals, reflectors, required by ICC. Electric brakes on front axle.

Machine is equipped with a "swing-A-way" tongue, allowing the entrance to be nearer the ground, while in a loading position hose connections are in a high position to protect the hydraulic system from dirt.

EXHIBIT 3 *(continued)*

Pickup conveyor folds down when in a loading position. Rubber belts are molded, with chains inside, allowing the use of sprockets for the drive, insuring a positive drive with no slippage, due to weather build up or extreme weather conditions. The pickup conveyor reduces bruises and downgrades to the birds, by eliminating the necessity to kick or shove the birds onto the conveyor belt.

BRIGHT'S LIVE POULTRY TRAILERS....

The rugged and sturdy construction gives the coopers a safer footing, reducing their fatigue while loading. The main conveyor belt is pulled by a compact hydraulic motor. Note: Feathers being carried out of the machine by the wire conveyor belt.

BRIGHT'S LIVE POULTRY BATTERIES!

THE PERFECT COMBINATION....

The two lifting cylinders are equipped with a fluid flow divider, assuring a level loading position for the coopers at all times, regardless of weight distribution of birds or operators. Proper level position of men prevents damage to birds while cooping them and makes a hard job easier. All hose connections are the reusable type, allowing repair in the field.

BRIGHT'S LIVE POULTRY HARVESTER....

The Bright's Live Turkey Harvester is a self-contained unit, carrying all equipment necessary to load birds, including corral boards, stake rods, loading platform. This feature frees the towing vehicle to transport personnel or anything desired.

EXHIBIT 3 *(concluded)*

This picture shows a hydraulic pumping unit, equipped on a pick-up truck. It is necessary to have a four speed transmission with a power-take off, in order to use this type power supply. It is also recommended to have a large heavy duty radiator, and extra blades on fan. Another source of power is a farm tractor equipped with a hydraulic pumping unit. Working pressure required to operate the machine efficiently is 1200 lbs., with 15 gals. per minute capacity.

Bright's "Power-Pak" is a compact, power unit, which also supplies lights for loading at night. It consists of a 12 H.P. engine reducing gears, pump, tank, filter, gauges, etc. It is electric starting, and has a generator unit. It can supply an output of 300 watt lighting while loading at night. This unit has been well accepted and has proven to be very economical to operate. One important feature about this unit is that it eliminates having to have a special equipped vehicle to operate machine.

GENERAL INFORMATION ON BRIGHT'S LIVE TURKEY HARVESTER

This unit can be set up and ready to load turkeys by two men, in less than fifteen minutes under normal conditions.

THE BRIGHT HARVESTER is designed with many factors in mind. First of all, it makes a very difficult and disagreeable job easier on the men loading the birds. It also makes labor easier to employ and keep happier for this type work in the field. Many users report that they can use younger men, such as school boys for this operation. With a new concept in handling the birds from the loader to the coops on the truck, it reduces bruises and downgrades. It eliminates the backbreaking way of catching and handling the birds up to the coopers by the legs, and allowing the birds to fight and flop. It saves D.O.A.'s and shrinkage by loading trucks faster, allowing the truck to be on its way faster.

If you desire to move young turkeys to the range, or larger turkeys from a truck, you can reverse the BRIGHT HARVESTER and unload birds from the opposite end of the machine. This has been very satisfactory for many users, because it enables you to place birds on the range without damaging and bruising the young birds.

Regardless of the type design doors your coops have, the loader will operate to a great advantage for your operation. However, we have found that, the type door design that the BRIGHT'S LIVE TURKEY BATTERIES have, is best suitable for a loader. The recessing door design which is completely out of the coopers way, is inside the coops, eliminates the loader from having to be too far away from the coops.

The BRIGHT LIVE TURKEY HARVESTER is a machine that you can be proud of and have a sense of pride in owning the best in the industry. It is simply a means of putting automation in your operation, by doing your loading with less effort and at a lower cost. As you know as well as we do, lower costs, means more PROFIT!

WHEN YOU SAY ....

Can't afford a BRIGHT HARVESTER
You are really saying
You can't afford to save money

You can't afford to reduce cost
You can't afford to increase profits
ALL of which means - You can't afford to stay in business.

BE BRIGHT   BUY RIGHT   BUY BRIGHT'S

EXHIBIT 4

BRIGHT'S SPECIALLY DESIGNED LIVE POULTRY

TRAILERS hitch you to GREATER PROFITS

BRIGHT'S HI·TENSILE DROP·FRAME FLOAT

WHY?

Why is Bright Coop Company in the trailer business?. . . . Everyday at Bright Coop Company, we load our customers' trailers from all over the country. After studying these trailers we have designed a trailer with many "built in" features designed for the hauling of live poultry. We have improved the stability of our trailer. To solve the top heavy load problem in hauling live poultry we have placed the center I-Beams wider than usual, this gives more rigidity against twisting. This is also aided by the pipe braces from the center I-Beams to the cross members near the side rail.

See the other features that have been incorporated into these live haul trailers.

BRIGHT COOP COMPANY
COMPLETE POULTRY TRUCK OUTFITTERS
803 West Seale Street
Day or Night Phone 7I3/564-8378
NACOGDOCHES , TEXAS 7596I

EXHIBIT 4 *(continued)*

BRIGHT'S Drop-frame Poultry Special

Here you see pictured the Bright drop-frame poultry special which can be built to your specifications from 36' to 45'. We presently have hundreds of these trailers in operation throughout all poultry areas, hauling the finest live poultry in these United States.

It is possible to get 600 - 10" coops on a 44', and have adequate air spacing between coops.

Deck drops can be 10", 11", 12" (20" wheels) or 20", 21", 22" (15" wheels). The capacity of this trailer is 50,000 lbs. over 15' span; 70,000 lbs. over 42'. Weight 10,500 lbs. - 40'.

We can deliver to your door a live haul trailer equipped with coops, chains, binders, tarps-ready to go to the field without servicing on your part.

CENTER FRAME	SIDE RAILS	LANDING GEAR
18-inch I-beam center frame of high tensile mill-rolled steel with 6 x 7/16-inch flanges and 5/16-inch webb. I beam centers are on 38-inch with pipe braces to side rails to prevent side sway. 3/8 x 4-inch sway braces of high tensile steel under each center rail to prevent sag.	8-inch structural channel side rails of high tensile steel. (High tensile steel has twice the rust resistance of mild steel and about twice the strength. This results in longer trailer life, plus added strength to haul the heavy payload).	2-speed Homan HH 500 heavy duty landing gear with sand shoes. **KING PIN PLATE** Quarter-inch king pin plate with reinforced king pin box section. **FLOOR** 15/8-inch tongue-and-groove yellow pine flooring.

BRIGHT'S Standard Platform Trailer

The above pictured trailer can be built to your specifications. We realize that your operation may require specialized equipment. A few of our many options are: full eight foot width, sliding tandems, air ride suspensions, extra lighting, tool boxes, choice of color, oil seals on all axles, spread axles, landing gears, and other various equipment that makes your trailers more suited to your particular operation. Our plant is flexible enough to meet demands of our customers.

When you buy a Bright Live Haul Trailer you assure yourself of the finest and most economical poultry trailer available any where.

OIL SEALS
Stemco wheel oilers; the superior oil seal.

AXLES
0,000-pound capacity standard orge axles; 5-inch tubular.

PAINT
ainting: acid cleaned, primed, ainted to customer's choice.

CROSS MEMBERS
6-inch I beam cross members pierced through center rails. Set on 16-inch centers.

SUSPENSION
44,000-pound capacity stacked springs or 50,000-pound capacity air springs.

LIGHTS
I.C.C. lighting system that is sealed in moisture-proof loom and two junction boxes easily accessible for maintenance.

WHEELS
3-spoke cool-flow wheels with heavy duty brake drums. This results in longer bearing life.

EXHIBIT 4 *(concluded)*

BRIGHT'S OPTIONAL LIVE-HAUL FEATURES

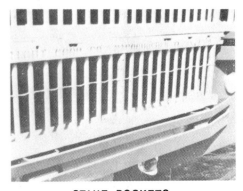

STAKE POCKETS

Stake pockets are full 2" x 4"′, level at top, and mounted flush with top of trailer deck, unless specified different. A one inch bar at top of our pockets helps support the outer coop rail, serving the same purpose as a full 8′ width deck, and keeps trailer conventional with stake pockets. Lower bar is for tie chain and binder.

SMOOTH SIDES

We recommend smooth sides, full width on trailer when used for turkey racks or coops. Gives more loading capacity, saves labor when working racks, and eliminates feather buildup in pockets and on rubrail. 1″ pipe underneath for chains and binders.

TOW HOOKS

The two heavy duty tow hooks on rear of trailer prevents damage to equipment when being winched by other vehicle.

FLOOR

Slatted or solid I 5/8 tongue and groove yellow pine treated flooring. The slatted floor stays dryer, last longer and safer for loaders. (Optional)

More Payload Capacity   Lower Operation Cost
Long Life

EXHIBIT 5

Ex 5

TAKE A LOOK At The . . .
BRIGHT HEN FLOOR

Today, more than ever before, you need a healthy, consistently productive, high performance breeder to put your operations in the money and keep them there. We at **BRIGHT COOP COMPANY** believe that this floor will do just that.

LESS SHAVINGS

DECREASE LABOR

HAPPIER HENS

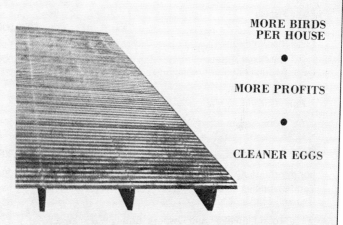

MORE BIRDS PER HOUSE

MORE PROFITS

CLEANER EGGS

CONSTRUCTION:

Support Beams are constructed of graded 5/4" pine lumber 6" wide, surfaced with top edge beveled to a 90° angle, machine notched with a special milled pattern knife that cuts uniform slots across the beveled edge. This gives a recessed floor enabling the debris and droppings to fall through and not build up. This also makes walking easier for bird and attendant.

Deck Slats are 15/16" precision pine squares fastened in uniform slots with galvanized, power driven staples, giving added strength.

SIZE	**WEIGHT**
Standard Width - 4 feet	Approximately 15 pounds per running foot.
Length - 4 feet to 12 feet	

OUR CUSTOMERS SAY

Cover 2/3 of floor space in houses - either along edges or middle.
Slats will allow one man to tend to 20-30% more birds at one time.
Hen floors will bring about a 5% increase in hatchable eggs.
One Poultryman Reported That He Paid For Bright Hen Floors On Two (2) Cycles Of Birds

BRIGHT COOP COMPANY

COMPLETE POULTRY TRUCK OUTFITTERS
803 West Seale
Phone 713/564-8378
Nacogdoches, Texas

EXHIBIT 6

COMBINED BRIGHT COOP AND BRIGHT SALES COMPANIES
Estimated Balance Sheet
(extrapolated from interviews with Charles and N. G. Bright)

Current Assets:

Inventory (includes material work-in-process and finished goods)	$431,000	
Accounts receivable	217,000	
Cash	12,000	
Total Current Assets	$660,000	

Fixed Assets:

Trucks	$272,000	
Plant and equipment	256,000	
Total Fixed Assets	$528,000	
Less: Accumulated depreciation	358,000	
Net Fixed Assets		$170,000
Plus: Current Assets		660,000
Total Assets		$830,000

Current Liabilities:	$ 81,000	
Long-term debt:	256,000	
Total Liabilities		$337,000
Owners' Equity		493,000
Total Liabilities and Owners' Equity		$830,000

EXHIBIT 7
Bright Coop Company Organization

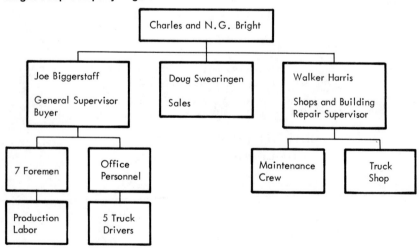

8. Wall Drug Store*

TED AND BILL HUSTEAD, primary owners and managers of Wall Drug Store, found themselves confronted with several key strategic issues in the winter of 1973. Should they invest aggressively in inventory for the tourist season of 1974, anticipating an increase in business, or should they buy conservatively? Should they continue to expand Wall Drug in the future or should they seek out new business alternatives? Although Wall Drug had been an unqualified success for the last 27 years and had been written up in newspapers and magazines on numerous occasions, times suddenly seemed more precarious. Rising gasoline prices, the prospect of a long-term fuel crisis, confrontation with the American Indian Movement (AIM) at Wounded Knee, and the highway beautification laws governing the location of Wall Drug's famous roadside signs all combined to pose new threats to tourist travel in South Dakota and to Wall Drug in particular.

COMPANY BACKGROUND

Ted Hustead majored in pharmacy at the University of Nebraska and graduated in 1929 at the age of 27. Less than three years later, in December 1931, Ted and his wife Dorothy (who grew up in Colman, South Dakota) bought the drugstore in Wall, South Dakota for $2,500. Dorothy and Ted, and their four-year-old son Bill, lived in the back 20 feet of the store for six years during the height of the Great Depression. Business was not good (the first month's gross revenue was $350) and Ted was not able to maintain a separate home and still keep the store going.

One writer described Wall in 1931 as follows:

> Wall, then: a huddle of poor wooden buildings, many unpainted, housing some 300 desperate souls; a 19th century depot and wooden water tank; dirt (or mud) streets; few trees; a stop on the railroad, it wasn't even that on the highway. US 16 and 14 went right on by, as did the tourists speeding between the Badlands and the Black Hills. There was nothing in Wall to stop for.[1]

---

* Prepared by Professors James D. Taylor, Robert L. Johnson, and Gene B. Iverson of the University of South Dakota.

[1] Dana Close Jennings, *Free Ice Water: The Story of the Wall Drug* (Aberdeen, S.D.: North Plains Press, 1969), p. 26.

Neither the drugstore nor the town of Wall prospered until Dorothy Hustead conceived the idea of placing a sign beside the highway promising free ice water to anyone who would stop at their store. The sign read "Get a soda/Get a beer/Turn next corner/Just as near/To Highway 16 and 14/Free ice water/Wall Drug." Ted put the sign up on a blazing hot Sunday afternoon in the summer of 1936 and no sooner had he done so than the first cars started turning off the highway to go to Wall Drug. This seemingly simple advertising effort marked a turning point in the Wall Drug's business strategy—and in the success of the enterprise as well.

With the value of highway advertising thus made dramatically apparent, Ted began erecting novel signs along all the highways leading to Wall. One sign read "Slow down the old hack/Wall Drug Corner/Just across the railroad track." The distinctive, attention-catching signs were a boon to Wall Drug's business and the town of Wall prospered, too. In an article in *Good Housekeeping* in 1951, the Hustead's signs were called "the most ingenious and irresistible system of signs ever devised."[2]

Just after World War II, a friend traveling across Europe for the Red Cross got the notion of putting up Wall Drug signs overseas. The idea caught on and small Wall Drug plaques were subsequently carried all over the world by South Dakota GIs who were familiar with the store's advertising techniques. A number of servicemen even wrote the store requesting signs. One sign in Paris announced "Wall Drug Store 4,278 miles (6,951 kilometers)." Wall Drug signs have appeared in Shanghai, Amsterdam, the Paris and London subways, the 38th Parallel in Korea, the North and South Pole areas, and on Vietnam jungle trails. The Husteads sent more than 200 signs to servicemen in Vietnam. The worldwide distribution of Wall Drug signs led to news stories and publicity which further nurtured the unique image and reputation of the store.

In the late 1950s, *Redbook Magazine* carried a story about Wall Drug which was later picked up and condensed in *Reader's Digest*. Since then, the newspapers and magazines carrying feature stories or referring to Wall Drug have included:

National Enquirer, November 11, 1973.

Grit, October 28, 1973.

Las Vegas Review—Journal, September 22, 1973.

Senior Scholastic Magazine, October 4, 1973, p. 11.

Congressional Record, September 11, 1973, Si6269.

The Wall Street Journal, September 5, 1973.

Omaha World-Herald, May 15, 1972.

Elsevier (Dutch magazine), February 12, 1972.

Rapid City Journal, April 12, 1970.

---

[2] Ibid., p. 42.

A Cleveland daily paper, May 16, 1971.

The New York Times, Sunday, January 31, 1971.

Oshkosh, Wisconsin, *Daily Northwestern*, August 2, 1969.

Sunday Picture Magazine, Minneapolis Tribune, September 21, 1969.

America Illustrated, U.S. Information Agency in Poland and Russia, June 1969.

Ojai Valley News and Oaks Gazette, August 14, 1968.

Chicago Tribune, Norman Vincent Peale's syndicated column, "Confident Living," October 8, 1966.

Norman Vincent Peale's book, *You Can If You Think You Can*, p. 34.

San Francisco Examiner, February 12, 1966.

Women's Wear Daily, September 16, 1966.

Coronet Magazine, April, 1964.

Cleveland, Ohio, *The Plain Dealer*, date not known.

The June 1969 issue of *America Illustrated*, a U.S. Information Agency publication distributed in the Soviet Union and Poland, featured a story entitled "The Lure and Fascination of Seven Fabulous Stores," by Mal Oettinger. The seven stores were Macy's, Wall Drug Store, Rich's, L. L. Bean, Inc., Neiman-Marcus, Gump's, and Brentano's.

GROWTH AND DEVELOPMENT OF WALL DRUG

The sales and square footage of Wall Drug have grown steadily since the 1940s. From 1931 until 1941, Wall Drug was located in a 24- by 40-foot rented building on the west side of Main Street. In 1941, an old lodge hall, which acted as the gymnasium in Wasta (15 miles west of Wall), was bought and moved to the east side of Main Street across from the original store. It then became the site of Wall Drug; the store now occupies over an acre, taking up the better part of one side of Wall's block-long business district.

When World War II ended, tourist travel to the Badlands and Black Hills picked up considerably and Wall Drug's highway signs attracted so many people to the store that the Husteads claim they were embarrassed because the facilities were not large enough. There were no modern rest rooms even. Sales in the late 1940s ranged from $150,000 to $200,000 per year.

In 1951, the Hustead's son Bill graduated from South Dakota State College at Brookings with a major in pharmacy and returned to Wall to join his father in managing Wall Drug. Ted and Bill proceeded to initiate a series of expansions of the business. In 1953, a storeroom on the south end of the building (see Exhibit 1) was remodeled and became the Western Clothing Room. The next year, a new area adjacent to the Western Clothing Room was added. Sales increased about 30 percent to around $300,000 per year as a result of these two expansions to the store. In 1956, a self-service cafe was

EXHIBIT 1
Layout of Wall Drug

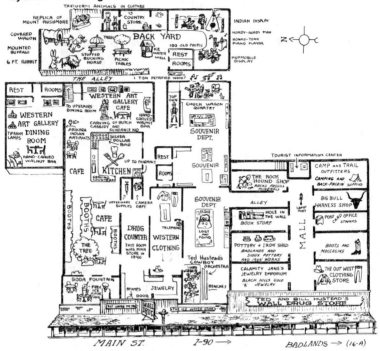

installed on the north side of the premises. By the early 1960s, sales had climbed to $500,000.

In the early 1960s, Ted and his son Bill began seriously thinking of moving Wall Drug out to the highway. The original Highway 16 ran by the north side of Wall, about two blocks from the store. But later Highway 16 was rerouted to the south side of Wall, though still only two blocks away from the drugstore. In the late 1950s and early 1960s, a new highway was built running by the south side of Wall paralleling the revised route. Ted and Bill Hustead were considering building an all new Wall Drug, along with a gasoline filling station, adjacent to the new highway just where the intersection to Wall was located.

They decided to build the gasoline station first, and did so, calling it Wall Auto Livery. But when the station was finished, they decided against moving the drugstore and, instead, elected to continue expanding the old store in downtown Wall. This proved fortunate, since soon after that a new interstate highway (I-90) replaced the new Highway 16 route and the new I-90 interchange ran right through the site of the proposed new Wall Drug.

Once the Husteads decided to keep the store in downtown Wall, expansion was continued. In 1963, a new fireproof construction coffee shop was installed where the present soda fountain is—see the store layout in Exhibit

1. In 1964, a new kitchen, again of fireproof construction, was added in back of the cafe and main store. In 1964 and 1965, offices and the new pharmacy were opened on the second floor over the kitchen. In 1968, the back dining room and backyard across the alley were added. This was followed in 1971 with the Western Art Gallery Dining Room. These expansions helped push annual sales volume to $1 million.

In 1971, the Husteads bought the theater that bordered Wall Drug on the south and continued to operate it as a theater through 1972. In early 1973, they closed the theater and began to convert the location into a new addition called the "Mall." By the summer of 1973, the north part of the Mall was open for business. The south side was unfinished. That year, Wall Drug grossed $1,600,000—an increase of about 20 percent over 1972. Bill attributed the increase to the new Mall addition. Currently, Wall Drug covers almost 32,000 square feet and is air-conditioned; the facility also contains 960 square feet of office space, and almost 12,000 square feet of storage space.

THE MALL

For about five years prior to starting construction, Bill Hustead thought about and planned the concept of the Mall. The Mall was conceived as a town within a large room. The strolling mall was designed as a main street with two-story frontier Western stores on either side—in the fashion of a recreated Western town. The shop fronts were reproductions of building fronts found in old photos of western towns in the 1880s. On the inside, the stores were paneled with such woods as pine from Custer, South Dakota, American black walnut, gumwood, hackberry, cedar, maple, and oak. Many photos, paintings, and prints lined the walls. The shops stocked products that were more expensive than the souvenir merchandise carried in other parts of Wall Drug and, in many respects, were like Western boutiques. The northern half of the Mall opened for business in July 1973. But Bill was uncertain as to whether to go ahead with construction of the south side.

The construction of the Mall prompted a distinct change in the financing strategy of Wall Drug. All previous expansions had been funded out of retained earnings or with short-term loans. But the Husteads built the Mall by borrowing approximately $250,000 for ten years. Part of this money was also used to erect 20 large new signs standing 660 feet from the interstate highway.

THE DRAWING POWER OF WALL DRUG

The Husteads operated Wall Drug and Wall Auto Livery as two separate corporations. Both businesses were heavily dependent on tourist travel and in 1973 the sales of each was at an all-time high. The economic base of Wall (1970 population, 786) consisted of 11 motels and a number of service stations—all keyed to the tourist traffic drawn by Wall Drug. The town's business district was one block long. Nearly a third of the labor force worked at Wall Drug. The president of the Chamber of Commerce once observed that without Wall Drug the town would dry up and blow away.

Wall is situated right on the edge of the Badlands (see Exhibit 2) and is 52

EXHIBIT 2

South Dakota: Location of Wall in Relation to the Black Hills, Badlands, Interstate 90, Rapid City, and Sioux Falls

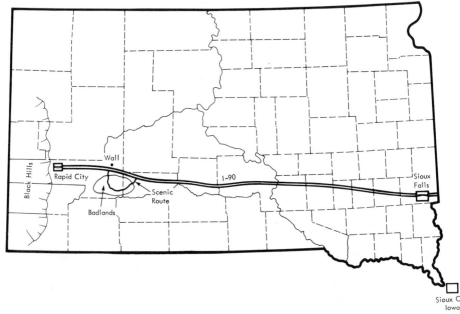

miles east of Rapid City, South Dakota's second largest city (1970 population, 43,836). For miles in either direction, travelers are teased and tantalized by Wall Drug signs. Along one 45-mile stretch of interstate highway leading to Wall, travelers encounter 53 Wall Drug signs. As tourists approach the town (those westbound usually after driving 40 miles or more through the Badlands), they are greeted by a large Wall Drug sign on the interchange and an 80-foot high, 50-ton statue of a dinosaur (see Exhibit 3).

As many as 10,000 people might stream through Wall Drug on a busy day. In the summer of 1963, a traffic count made on the highway going by Wall showed that 46 percent of the cars were eastbound and 54 percent were westbound. Of the eastbound traffic, 43 percent turned off at Wall. Of the westbound traffic, 44 percent turned off at Wall. On another occasion, a survey of state licenses of autos and campers parked in front of Wall Drug and in the camper and trailer park one block from Wall Drug between 8 A.M. and 10 A.M. on Wednesday, June 4 resulted in the following percentages:

EXHIBIT 3
The Wall Drug Dinosaur

Neighboring states and South Dakota (nonlocal) 37%
South Dakota, local county   32
Balance of states and Canada   31

THE MAIN ATTRACTION

The Husteads have made Wall Drug a place of amusement and family entertainment, a gallery of the West, a cultural display of South Dakota history, and a reflection of the heritage of the West. Some even say Wall Drug has become a South Dakota institution. Nostalgia addicts have a "field day" in the store and children delight in animated, life-size singing cowboys, a tableau of an Indian camp, a stuffed bucking horse, a six-foot rabbit, a stuffed buffalo, old 10-cent slot machines that pay out a souvenir coin, statues of cowboys, a coin-operated, quick-draw game, and souvenirs by the roomful.

Free ice water is still one of Wall Drug's biggest attractions. Ted Hustead, in his 70s but still on the job every day, estimated that the store gives out 5,000 glasses of water a day, plus filling and icing water jugs free of charge. The store has $30,000 worth of ice-making equipment with a capacity of one and one-half tons of ice per day—a far cry from earlier years when Ted cut winter ice from nearby farm ponds and stored it for summer use. Another of the store's traditions is a nickel cup of coffee and a breakfast of two eggs and a slice of toast for 25 cents. However, rising costs have since upped the price of the breakfast to 49 cents (as of 1973). On a busy day, patrons consume 250 dozen eggs and 6,000 homemade donuts.

The dining rooms are decorated with wood paneling and paintings of Western art; diners are entertained with Western music. Patrons can select from a moderately priced menu that includes buffalo burgers, roast beef, steak, and select wine, beer or a "Jack Daniels" at a rustic, American walnut bar. The original soda fountain has been expanded into a 475-seat cafe built around a huge cottonwood tree growing up through the roof.

STORE OPERATIONS

Wall Drug does most of its business during the summer months. In 1973, sales for June were $258,000; July, $423,000; and August, $414,500. April sales totaled about $40,000 and in May were $100,000. Late tourists and hunters traveling through typically generate a modest volume of business in September and October. About one fourth of Wall Drug's sales consist of food; beverages and soda fountain sales account for another 5 percent to 10 percent (although these percentages do vary with the weather). The remaining portion of sales revenue is distributed among jewelry items (10–15 percent), clothing and hats (15 percent), souvenirs (35–40 percent), and drug sundries and prescriptions (5–10 percent). Both Ted and Bill are registered pharmacists and they fill at least 20 prescriptions a day.

During the summer the store is staffed by a crew of about 150 people, working seven days a week in two shifts from 5 A.M. to 10 P.M. About 40 to 50 percent of the employees are college students recruited especially for the summer months. The students are housed in ten homes that over the years have been bought and converted into dormitory apartments. The students pay $8 per week rent, but if they stay through Labor Day, they get a $5 per week refund as an incentive to stay the full summer. There is a modern swimming pool for their use. The Husteads set curfews of 11 : 30 P.M. on weekdays and 1 : 30 A.M. on weekends for their student residents; according to Bill, now the general manager, "It's hard work, and we feel they need a full night's sleep to do a good job. Besides, auto accidents can happen late at night and we want to send our kids back home in one piece."[3] About half of the student workers return each year for another season.

When the student employees arrive at the beginning of a new summer season, they are given a cram course in the history of the Badlands and the Black Hills and are told to memorize the mileage from Wall Drug to other tourist attractions such as Mount Rushmore. Then, to make sure the information has been learned, the students are given a quiz. According to Ted Hustead such procedures are used because "If tourists remember Wall Drug, it won't be because we have such a great store but because of the people who waited on them. We want them to be cheerful and helpful."[4]

MERCHANDISE ORDERING

The inventory in Wall Drug varies from around $300,000 in the summer to a low of around $80,000 in the off-season. Ordering for the following summer season begins the preceding fall. Orders begin arriving in December, but most of the merchandise arrives in January, February, March, and April. Many large souvenir companies postdate their invoices until July and August. Each year brings new offerings from souvenir companies and other suppliers. Wall Drug generally buys its souvenir merchandise directly from the producers or importers. The same is true of photo supplies and clothing. Most of the purchasing is done by Bill and Ted, who admit they rely on trusted salesmen of their suppliers to advise them on merchandise purchases. Many of these companies have supplied Wall Drug for 20 years or so. In addition, the Husteads rely on their department managers for buying help. The manager of jewelry, for instance, will recommend on the basis of last year's orders and experience with customer reaction how much to order for the next season. All ordering is approved by Bill and Ted.

Years ago, much of what Wall Drug bought and sold was imported or made by manufacturers in the eastern United States. In recent years much

---

[3] As quoted in *The Wall Street Journal*, September 5, 1973, p. 12.
[4] Ibid.

more of the merchandise has been made locally and regionally. Nearby Indian reservations now have small production firms and individuals that supply handcrafted items to Wall Drug. For example, Wall Drug stocked items made by Sioux Pottery, Sioux Moccasin, and Milk Camp Industries.

The merchandise carried ranges from the usual drugstore items to steer skulls, cowboy boots, snakebite serum, lariats, Levis, leather chaps, as well as tourist souvenirs. One of the best selling items was a snake ashtray made from plaster of paris and painted to resemble a rattlesnake; these were obtained from a resident of the Black Hills who used live rattlers to make the molds for casting the ashtrays. Another feature item was jack-a-lopes (stuffed jackrabbits sporting antelope horns), made by a local taxidermist.

PROMOTION

As indicated earlier, Wall Drug relied heavily on roadside signs to bring people to the store. By 1968, there were about 3,000 signs displayed along highways and roads in all 50 states. The company utilized a truck and two men working nine months a year to maintain the store's signs in South Dakota and adjoining states; however, many signs were put up by volunteers. The store gives away approximately 14,000, 6 by 8 inch signs and 3,000, 8 by 22 inch signs a year to people who request them. The signs are plastic and weather resistant. Many people have sent in photographs and snapshots showing a Wall Drug sign displayed in some unusual place; these are prominently posted in the store for visitors to see. Making new signs keeps two professional sign painters busy; in 1973 Wall Drug had a $100,000 budget for new signs.

In the mid–1960s, the Highway Beautification Act was passed by Congress and signed into law by President Johnson. The act regulated the use of outdoor billboards along interstate highways and posed a threat to the Hustead's continued reliance upon extensive highway advertising. However, Bill and Ted believed that the media publicity about Wall Drug, together with their sign giveaway program, would help offset the possible reduction in highway signs. Nonetheless, the Husteads felt that it was very important for Wall Drug to gain as much attention and publicity as possible. Subsequently, small ads were placed in New York City's Greenwich Village publication *The Village Voice* advertising 5 cent coffee, 49 cent breakfasts, and animal health remedies at Wall Drug. These ads resulted in a telephone call, several letter inquiries, an article about Wall Drug in *The Village Voice,* and some attention from other media sources. An article in the *New York Times* and some other publicity led to Bill Hustead's appearance on Garry Moore's television program "To Tell the Truth." Wall Drug's posters in the London subway produced a 20-minute, taped telephone interview with Ted by the British Broadcasting Company. Shortly thereafter, several British newspapers carried stories about Wall Drug because of the signs on the London Underground trains. Posters and signs were also erected in the Paris Metro subway (in the

English language) and on the dock in Amsterdam in full view of people boarding sight-seeing boats.

Recently, the Husteads began printing two brochures: (1) *Motel Guide for South Dakota,* and (2) *South Dakota Campground Directory of Privately Owned and Operated Campgrounds and Trailer Parks.* Over 200,000 of these guides were given away to Wall Drug visitors each summer. The Husteads hoped that each of the motels and campgrounds in the brochure would reciprocate by displaying a Wall Drug sign on their premises, if asked to do so. This "we'll promote you if you promote us" approach, however, was in the initial stages and its success undetermined. Bill and Ted had plans for erecting Wall Drug signs which could be seen when travelers turned off the interstate at exits on either side of Wall; such signs on roads leading off the interstate, if appropriately located, were not under jurisdiction of the Highway Beautification Act.

FINANCE

Until December 1973, all of Wall Drug's expansion programs were financed with internally generated funds, supplemented with short-term borrowing. In effect, each addition was paid for as it was built (or soon thereafter). However, to fund construction of the Mall, a ten-year, $250,000 loan in the form of a real estate mortgage was negotiated. Payments on this loan, including 8 percent interest, were $34,000 in 1974 and $37,000 annually from 1975 through 1983.

The company generally financed inventory purchases for the upcoming season with short-term loans if internal funds were inadequate. However, seasonal billings by a number of suppliers obviated the need for heavy financing of inventories. Of course, the company was vulnerable to a cash squeeze if a large inventory was left unsold at the end of any tourist season. This potentiality was aggravated by the fixed annual repayments on the long-term loan.

Exhibits 4 through 10 present the financial condition of both Wall Drug and Wall Auto Livery.

EXHIBIT 4

WALL DRUG STORE, INC.
Balance Sheet
As of December 31

	1973	1972
Assets		
Current Assets:		
Cash on hand	$ 1,037	$ 946
Cash in bank	2,450	138
Investment in commercial paper, at cost	70,000	—
Accounts receivable—trade	12,121	7,183
Accounts receivable—officers and employees	4,300	3,323
Accounts receivable—income tax refund	—	19,824
Inventories	144,013	86,890
Accrued interest receivable	463	—
Prepaid insurance	9,455	9,068
Total Current Assets	$ 243,839	$127,372
Investment and Other Assets:		
Bonds, at cost	$1,675	$1,675
Organization cost, at cost	972	972
Total Investments and Other Assets	$ 2,647	$ 2,647
Property, Plant and Equipment, at Cost:		
Land	$ 70,454	$ 50,079
Buildings, building improvements, and parking lot improvements	692,488	527,456
Equipment, furniture, and fixtures	366,651	303,108
	$1,129,593	$880,643
Less-accumulated depreciation	427,866	369,743
Depreciated Cost of Fixed Assets	$ 701,727	$510,900
Goodwill, at cost:	$ 31,386	$ 31,386
Total Assets	$ 979,599	$672,305

Liabilities and Stockholders' Equity

	1973	1972
Current Liabilities:		
Notes payable—Wall Auto Livery, Inc.	$ 20,000	$ 50,000
Notes payable—bank	—	20,000
Current maturities of long-term debt	20,058	—
Accounts payable—trade	22,709	30,979
Income taxes payable	11,161	—
Accrued taxes payable	25,880	18,457
Profit sharing contribution payable	30,542	18,231
Accrued payroll and bonuses	40,073	28,559
Accrued interest payable	2,573	255
Total Current Liabilities	$ 172,996	$166,481

EXHIBIT 4 (*continued*)

Long-Term Debt:

Real estate mortgage payable	$ 232,742	—
Contract for deed payable	11,200	—
Total Long-Term Debt	$ 243,942	—

Stockholders' Equity:

Preferred stock, $100 par value, 4%, cumulative, nonvoting, 1,000 shares authorized, 300 shares outstanding	$ 30,000	$ 30,000
Common stock, $100 par value, Class A, 500 shares authorized, 480 shares outstanding	48,000	48,000
Common stock, $100 par value, Class B, nonvoting, 4,500 shares authorized, 400 shares outstanding	40,000	40,000
Retained earnings	444,661	387,824
Total Stockholders' Equity	$ 562,661	$505,824
Total Liabilities and Stockholders' Equity	$ 979,599	$672,305

The accompanying notes (Exhibit 7) are an integral part of these financial statements.

EXHIBIT 5

WALL DRUG STORE, INC.
Statements of Income and Retained Earnings
Years Ended December 31

	1973	1972
Net sales	$1,606,648	$1,335,932
Cost of goods sold	805,827	687,613
Gross profit	$ 800,821	$ 648,319
General and administrative expenses	690,461	577,767
Income from operations	$ 110,360	$ 70,552
Interest income	2,946	188
Rental income	3,647	4,248
Trailer park income	6,020	4,600
Theater income	—	5,197
Gain on sale of assets	176	4,286
Other income	747	902
	$ 123,896	$ 89,973
Other deductions:		
Interest	$ 19,735	$ 4,072
Theater expense	—	2,689
Trailer park expense	4,223	3,433
Loss on sale of assets	—	1,674
Loss on demolition of theater building	—	13,860
	$ 23,958	$ 25,728
Income before income taxes	$ 99,938	$ 64,245
Provision for income tax—current year	40,701	20,176
Net Income	$ 59,237	$ 44,069
Retained earnings:		
Beginning	387,824	343,755
	$ 447,061	$ 387,824
Dividends paid	2,400	—
Ending	$ 444,661	$ 387,824
Earnings per share	$ 65.95	$ 48.71

The accompanying notes (Exhibit 7) are an integral part of these financial statements.

EXHIBIT 6

WALL DRUG STORE, INC.
Statements of Changes in Financial Position
Years Ended December 31

	1973	1972
Financial resources were provided by:		
Net income	$ 59,237	$ 44,069
Add income charges not affecting working capital in the period:		
Depreciation	58,723	43,862
Demolition loss on theater building	—	13,860
Working capital provided by operations	$117,960	$ 101,791
Proceeds from borrowings	264,000	—
Basis of property and equipment sold	625	2,750
Total Resources Provided	$382,585	$ 104,541
Financial resources were used for:		
Acquisition of land	$ 21,000	$ 5,799
Acquisition of building	165,031	149,924
Acquisition of equipment and signs	64,144	50,636
Reduction in long-term debt	20,058	—
Dividends paid	2,400	—
Total Resources Used	$272,633	$ 206,359
Increase (decrease) in working capital	$109,952	$(101,818)
Working capital		
Beginning	(39,109)	62,709
Ending	$ 70,843	$ (39,109)
Increase (decrease) in components of working capital:		
Current assets:		
Cash	$ 2,403	$ (1,850)
Investment in commercial paper	70,000	—
Marketable securities	—	(59,375)
Accounts receivable—trade and other	(13,909)	684
Inventories	57,123	7,204
Other current assets—net	850	(3,650)
Total Assets	$116,467	$ (56,987)
Current liabilities:		
Note payable—banks and others	$ (50,000)	70,000
Current maturities of long-term debt	20,058	—
Accounts payable—trade	(8,270)	12,891
Income tax payable	11,161	(32,272)
Other current and accrued liabilities—net	33,566	(5,788)
Total Liabilities	$ 6,515	$ 44,831
Increase (decrease) in Working Capital	$109,952	$(101,818)

The accompanying notes (Exhibit 7) are an integral part of these financial statements.

EXHIBIT 7
Notes to Financial Statements

Note 1.   Summary of Accounting Policies

Accounting Method.   The corporation uses the accrual method of accounting for income tax and financial statement purposes.

Inventories.   Inventories are generally valued at the lower of cost or market on a first-in, first-out basis computed under retail method.

Fixed Assets.   Fixed assets are stated at cost. Depreciation is calculated under the straight-line method, 150 percent declining balance method and 200 percent declining balance method. The same depreciation methods are used for financial and tax purposes. The useful lives selected for the assets are as follows: Buildings and building improvements, 15 to 40 years; parking lot, 8 years; and furniture, fixtures and equipment, 5 to 10 years. The provision for depreciation for 1973 of $58,723 and 1972 of $43,862 was charged to operations.

Repairs and maintenance costs are generally charged to expense at the time the expenditure is incurred. When an asset is sold or retired, its cost and related depreciation are removed from the accounts and a gain or loss is recognized on the difference between the proceeds of disposition and the undepreciated cost as the case may be. When an asset is traded in a like exchange, the cost and related depreciation are removed from the accounts and the undepreciated cost is capitalized as a part of the cost of the asset acquired.

· Income Taxes.   The provision for income taxes is based on the elements of income and expense, as reported in the statement of income. Investment tax credits are accounted for on the "flow-through" method, which recognizes the benefits in the year in which the assets which give rise to the credit are placed in service.

Note 2.   Long-Term Debt

The real estate mortgage is an 8 percent mortgage dated December 3, 1973 and due October 1, 1983. The mortgage is to be paid in annual installments of principal and interest as follows:

10-1-74	$34,035.28
10-1-75 and thereafter	$37,257.50

The Drug Store in downtown Wall is pledged as security on this real estate mortgage.

The contract for deed payable is a 7 percent contract for deed, dated January 16, 1973 and is due January 16, 1978. The contract is to be paid in annual installments of $2,800 plus interest. This contract is for the purchase of approximately 202 acres of land which is the security for the contract for deed.

Note 3.   Profit Sharing Plan

The company has a profit sharing plan for all full-time employees who meet the qualification requirements. The company contributed $30,542 in 1973, and $18,231 in 1972 to the profit sharing trust.

EXHIBIT 8

WALL AUTO LIVERY, INC.
Balance Sheets
As of December 31

	1973	1972
Assets		
Current Assets:		
Cash on hand	$ 100	$ 100
Cash in bank	14,590	19,916
Marketable securities, at cost	58,715	—
Notes receivable—Wall Drug Store, Inc.	20,000	50,000
Accounts receivable—trade	1,967	8,205
Credit cards	2,010	—
Miscellaneous receivables	—	75
Inventory, at lower of cost (Fifo) or market	8,462	9,261
Prepaid insurance	1,557	1,469
Accrued interest receivable	729	247
Total Current Assets	$108,130	$89,273
Property and Equipment:		
Land	$ 7,367	$ 7,367
Buildings	103,133	103,133
Equipment	26,297	26,076
	$136,797	$136,576
Less—accumulated depreciation	57,685	52,548
Depreciation cost of fixed assets	$ 79,112	$ 84,028
Total Assets	$187,242	$173,301

Liabilities and Stockholders' Equity

	1973	1972
Current Liabilities:		
Current maturity of long-term debt	$ 5,000	$ 5,000
Accounts payable—trade	754	5,696
Income taxes payable	7,286	2,774
Accrued profit sharing contribution	2,666	2,446
Accrued payroll and sales taxes	840	756
Accrued interest payable	125	250
Total Current Liabilities	$ 16,671	$ 16,922
Long-Term Debt:		
Note payable noninterest bearing contract payable to F. M. Cheny maturing March 1, 1976	$ 5,000	$ 5,000
Note payable—6 percent to Perpetual National Life Insurance Company maturing in annual installments of $5,000 plus interest	—	5,000
Total Long-Term Debt	$ 5,000	$ 10,000
Stockholders' Equity:		
Common stock, $100 par value, 2,000 shares authorized, 444 shares outstanding	$ 44,400	$ 44,400
Retained earnings	121,171	101,979
Total Stockholders' Equity	$165,571	$146,379
Total Liabilities and Stockholders' Equity	$187,242	$173,301

The accompanying notes (Exhibit 7) are an integral part of these financial statements.

EXHIBIT 9

WALL AUTO LIVERY, INC.
Statements of Income and Retained Earnings
Years Ended December 31

	1973	1972
Net sales	$191,969	$172,195
Inventories—beginning of year	$ 9,261	$ 9,467
Purchases	132,698	124,399
Freight	35	—
	$141,994	$133,866
Inventories—end of year	8,462	9,261
Cost of goods sold	$133,532	$124,605
Gross profit	$ 58,437	$ 47,590
General and administrative expense	44,568	41,443
Income from operations	$ 13,869	$ 6,147
Interest income	5,441	2,436
Rental income	17,917	15,440
Miscellaneous income	—	1,434
	$ 37,227	$ 25,457
Other deductions:		
Interest expense	$ 510	$ 775
Rent expense—depreciation	3,005	3,128
	$ 3,515	$ 3,903
Income before federal income tax	$ 33,712	$ 21,554
Provision for income taxes	$ 14,520	$ 7,574
Net Income	$ 19,192	$ 13,980
Retained earnings:		
Beginning	101,979	87,999
Ending	$121,171	$101,979
Earnings per share	$ 43.23	$ 31.49

The accompanying notes (Exhibit 7) are an integral part of these financial statements.

EXHIBIT 10

WALL AUTO LIVERY, INC.
Statements of Changes in Financial Position
Years Ended December 31

	1973	1972
Financial Resources Were Provided by:		
Net income	$19,192	$13,980
Add income charges not affecting working capital in the period:		
Depreciation	5,137	5,390
Working capital provided by operations	$24,329	$19,370
Financial Resources Were Used for:		
Acquisition of equipment	$ 221	$ 3,310
Reduction of long-term debt	5,000	5,000
Total Resources Used	$ 5,221	$ 8,310
Increase in working capital	$19,108	$11,060
Working Capital:		
Beginning of year	72,352	61,292
End of year	$91,460	$72,352
Increase (decrease) in Components of Working Capital:		
Current assets:		
Cash	$ (5,326)	$15,394
Marketable securities	58,715	(58,087)
Notes receivable	(30,000)	50,000
Accounts receivable	(6,238)	3,371
Credit cards	2,010	—
Miscellaneous receivables	(75)	(57)
Inventory	(799)	(206)
Prepaid insurance	88	73
Accrued interest receivable	482	40
Total Assets....................................	$18,857	$10,528
Current Liabilities:		
Accounts payable—trade	$ (4,942)	$ 1,064
Income taxes payable	4,512	(1,925)
Other current and accrued liabilities	179	329
Total Liabilities.................................	$ (251)	$ (532)
Increase in working capital	$19,108	$11,060

The accompanying notes (Exhibit 7) are an integral part of these financial statements.

9.1. Ivie Electronics, Inc. (A)*

IN MARCH OF 1970, Ray Ivie was reflecting on the problems and accomplishments of the past five years and considering future directions for growth and progress of the company he had founded. He was concerned about making the kind of financing, manufacturing, and marketing arrangements which would help lead to rapid and widespread utilization of some unique new high-performance and low-cost communications equipment he had developed. Moreover, he wanted to proceed in a way that would not only be financially profitable for himself and the other stockholders of the company but also would provide the resources and time for him to develop to a workable stage a number of other radically new concepts in electronic communications equipment.

COMPANY BACKGROUND

Ivie Electronics was incorporated in Ogden, Utah, in January 1965 by Ray Ivie, H. Leon Ivie (Ray's father), and Robert A. Larsen, a friend. The company planned to engage in research and development work in electronics, and manufacture, distribute, sell, and service electronic and mechanical equipment. The specific project which led to the formation of the company was the development of an extremely compact and efficient solid-state communications transceiver. Ray Ivie had been working on the basic circuits and design of the transceiver for several years prior to organization of the company.

Ray Ivie had long been interested in electronics, obtaining his amateur radio operator's license in 1951 while still in high school. Several years later, while at college, he developed a five-watt transceiver. His paper on that transceiver won the 1962 IEEE student paper contest and a trip to the Seattle World's Fair.

In 1963, Mr. Ivie graduated from Brigham Young University with a bachelor's degree in engineering science. He then worked for the Boeing Company in Seattle and in Huntsville, Alabama, on the Saturn 5 space program. While at Huntsville, he designed and built one of the first 5,000

* Prepared by Professor Melvin J. Stanford, Brigham Young University. Copyright © 1974 by Brigham Young University. Reprinted by permission.

watt static power inverters ever made and which has since been in use as the emergency power source for research facilities at the Huntsville space flight center.

From the beginning of the company, Ray Ivie served as president and manager. His father, H. Leon Ivie, a retired government auditor and school-teacher, kept the books for the company and provided his garage for initial operations. In November 1967 Ivie Electronics moved to Orem, Utah, where development operations were carried on in an old house on five acres of land which the company had purchased on contract.

PRODUCTS

The Timp Transceiver, which Ray Ivie had developed from his first efforts on the five-watt transceiver, was believed to be unique in its field, with performance capabilities that far exceeded any equipment on the market. It was very small, just 1½ inches by 2½ inches by 4 inches, and weighed only 16 ounces. Despite its small size and weight, it boasted 28 watts of power, 24 channels, and a range of 15 to 20 miles. Transmissions between the transceiver and a larger base station unit could be heard loud and clear over much longer distances. Power for the transceiver could be provided in several ways, with detachable power sources for use in an automobile, for home or office, or for carrying on the person. The lightest personal power source was a series of small batteries, weighing 14 ounces, fastened into a light-weight vest which could also contain an antenna.

The Timp Transceiver contained 16 separate, highly compact, solid state electronic modules, all of which had been completed and were functional by 1970. Most of the mechanical tooling for making cases, channel select knobs, neoprene strain reliefs, extrusions and the like also had been completed. As of spring 1970, remaining work on the transceiver consisted largely of building test jigs for each module, combining the modules, and optimizing the component values through extensive field testing. Ray Ivie estimated that it would take about another 15 months to get the transceiver ready for a pilot production run of 100 units.

Other portable transceivers in the industry had power outputs of from 1.5 to 14 watts and sold in a price range of $600 to $2,400. No available equipment, however, was anywhere near as light and compact as the Timp Transceiver, and Ray Ivie did not think that anyone else even had workable designs which would compete on the basis of size and weight and the power and performance which the Timp Transceiver offered.

Mr. Ivie intended to file a patent application on the Timp Transceiver just prior to marketing it and then file periodic revisions to delay issuance of the patent (so the circuit diagrams could not be seen by competitors) until the company became firmly established in the market. In order to prevent someone from copying the actual transceiver, Mr. Ivie planned to encase the modules in an epoxy resin which would make it practically impossible to break down the module without damaging the component parts and circuitry beyond analysis. However, he felt that his best protection would be the continuous development of new technological elaborations and improvements, some of which he already had basic designs for. Ivie realized that owing to rapid progress in the field of electronics he would have to keep his innovations moving from concept through development to actual product with little delay, or someone else might come up with similar ideas. Some of these improvements were applied to the transceiver in the developmental stage. While this delayed the completion of the product, it made it even better. For example, Ray Ivie already had developed a way to fit a 100-watt, 100-channel transceiver into the same size package as the Timp Transceiver.

Another significant product of Ivie Electronics was a new type of audio amplifier system for home and commercial stereo systems. Ray had found a way to split the amplification of the audio frequency spectrum into three parts and to amplify each part separately. The result was far less distortion of sound than achieved by most of the equipment on the market. Moreover, using innovative circuitry techniques similar to those in the Timp Transceiver, it was possible to make all three amplifiers at a cost significantly less than the manufacturing cost of a single, average quality amplifier. Three amplifiers were combined with 12 speakers, all mounted in a large speaker box unit. A pair of these units could be built to sell at a price competitive with medium-priced units on the market, and yet the Ivie units, together with a preamplifier and a signal source (such as a radio tuner, turntable, or tape deck), could offer markedly superior performance. Several functioning prototypes of these units had been completed by late 1969, but Ray Ivie had not done anything further with them because of the urgency he felt to keep the work going on the Timp Transceiver. He did plan to apply for a patent on the audio circuits, and a patent search had been completed.

MARKETING OPPORTUNITIES

The Timp Transceiver had attracted considerable attention as word of its potential spread among some knowledgeable professionals in the field of electronics and communications. In 1967 and 1968, representatives from Litton Industries talked with Ray Ivie and offered him a job at Litton, at an attractive salary, to complete the development of the transceiver, using Litton's facilities. Litton further expressed an interest in obtaining a license to manufacture and sell the transceiver, as soon as it was completed, at a royalty to Ivie Electronics of 4 percent to 5 percent of gross sales. Litton spoke of an estimated first-year sales potential of from 10,000 to 20,000 units at $1,000 per unit, based in part on the strong interest the U.S. Army had shown toward the transceiver in discussing its performance with Litton. The transceiver was well-adapted to military needs and would outperform all other military portable transceivers with greater reliability and lower cost.

Patents in Ray Ivie's name would be obtained by Litton covering all of the patentable innovations in the Timp Transceiver. Mr. Ivie felt, however, that once Litton started manufacturing the transceiver there would be nothing to prevent the engineers of such a large company from developing similar designs for other products, which without patent infringement could still utilize enough of the technical concepts to pose a competitive threat to the unique innovative direction in which he seemed to be moving by himself. Largely because of his concern for this kind of threat, Ray Ivie did not go with Litton. He felt that he would have the transceiver completed on his own within 6 to 12 months and did not forsee any obstacles to so doing.

Subsequently, other companies in the electronics industry expressed an interest in manufacturing and/or marketing the transceiver when it was ready. Ray Ivie also received frequent telephone calls from potential users of the transceiver, such as the police chief of Birmingham, Alabama, who realized the value of the Timp Transceiver for police work and was eager to order a number of units. As of the spring of 1970, however, no marketing arrangements had been made by Ivie Electronics, and completion of the transceiver was still more than a year away. This was caused partly by the need for technical refinements that had come up from time to time as well as some delay resulting from the company's taking a contract to manufacture 10,000 circuit boards.

MANUFACTURING EXPERIENCE

In the fall of 1968, Ivie Electronics had obtained a $129,000 contract with JayArk Instrument Corporation for 10,000 AU-10, 10-watt audio circuit boards, which JayArk used in a portable audio-visual unit designed for sales presentations. Ray Ivie had hesitated to take the contract, because he knew it would delay the work on his transceiver. However, the contract was expected to yield a profit of more than $50,000, which was urgently needed, and it would enable Ivie Electronics to gain some valuable manufacturing experience. Accordingly, Mr. Ivie went ahead with the contract, hired several production workers, and began manufacturing the circuit boards.

The JayArk order was completed early in 1970, but as of March there remained an unpaid balance of $56,000 overdue from JayArk on the contract. Unfortunately, it appeared that JayArk was in financial difficulty and headed for bankruptcy.

FINANCES

From the first it had been a constant struggle for Ivie Electronics to keep enough money on hand to support the developmental work. Ray Ivie and his father had put what cash they could into the company, and most of those funds were spent for electronic equipment. Friends and relatives provided additional resources from time to time in order to help keep the work going. For his designs, services, and cash investment, Ray Ivie had been issued stock which, in March 1970, amounted to 59,330 shares of a total of 129,390 shares outstanding. H. Leon Ivie, then corporate treasurer, held 15,900 shares, and other friends and relatives owned the remainder of the stock. No individual stockholder other than Ray and Leon Ivie, however, held more than 10 percent of the stock outstanding. Total stock authorized was increased in February 1970 to 500,000 shares. At that same time a ten-for-one stock split had taken effect, resulting in an increase of the shares outstanding from 12,939 to 129,390 (see balance sheet, Exhibit 1, and addendum, Exhibit 2).

During the six months ended December 31, 1969, Ivie Electronics had earned a net income of $16,146 (see income statement, Exhibit 3). However, due to the developmental expenses of several prior years, the retained earnings account still showed a deficit of $21,146 at the end of 1969. With a low cash balance and the large receivable from JayArk in question, new funds were needed to continue the work on the transceiver and the audio system units. Prior to 1969 Ray Ivie had not received a regular salary. Since January 1969 he had been receiving a salary of $1,000 per month. He got married in February 1969.

Mr. Ivie had learned in early 1969 that there was a good possibility of obtaining $500,000 to $1,000,000 capital, through stock or debt, from some eastern financial sources. This amount of money would enable him to build a new research and manufacturing building and accelerate the development and completion of the transceiver. By taking such a course at that time, the company could move more rapidly toward providing local employment and economic growth, toward which Ray Ivie was dedicated. However, he wanted to maintain control of his company and avoid dilution for the stockholders. Moreover, he felt quite reluctant to borrow such a large amount of money from far-away sources and with any strings attached. Consequently, he did not investigate substantial financing further at that time.

Mr. Ivie figured that the company would need in excess of $90,000 to keep things going from March 1970 until sales revenues on the transceiver and other products started coming in by mid 1971. He listed those needs as follows:

Parts, material and labor—audio system units	$21,740
Working capital for completion of transceiver	15,000
Payments on land contracts	25,000
First wing of new plant building	30,000
Total	$91,740

To raise this amount, he was preparing an offering circular for a private placement of stock among a small group of local investors who knew of the unique quality of the company's products. He felt that he could get the

$91,740 by selling stock directly at $3 per share without paying any commissions and without any purchaser buying what would amount to more than 10 percent of the new number of shares outstanding.

Preliminary estimates by Mr. Ivie indicated that after the transceiver was completed, from $750,000 to $1,500,000 would be needed to build and equip manufacturing facilities and to market the product effectively. While such funds could probably be borrowed from eastern capital sources, Mr. Ivie felt inclined to consider a public stock issue in 1971 to raise the needed funds.

If Ivie Electronics manufactured the transceiver in its own plant, Mr. Ivie estimated the per unit cost of parts to be about $100, labor from $35 to $50, and overhead not more than $50, depending on volume of production. He planned that the unit would retail for about $800 initially. Normal markups from factory to dealer in the industry were in the range of 35 percent to 45 percent of retail on small quantity orders. Sales volume of the Timp Transceiver was estimated by Mr. Ivie at 10,000 to 20,000 units the first year, with an increase to 30,000 to 40,000 per year within three or four years. He based these estimates partly on information he had seen in some market surveys on portable communications transceivers and partly on his own appraisal of the performance features of equipment already on the market in comparison with what his transceiver could do.

Ray Ivie had not determined what the marketing costs might be for distribution by Ivie Electronics. If distribution were handled by an established company in the industry, Ivie Electronics would not be as directly concerned with marketing management and expense but would undoubtedly sell in larger quantities to the distributing company although at a greater discount than if to dealers.

FUTURE OUTLOOK

Ray Ivie realized that his best capabilities were highly technical and he preferred to spend most of his time in research and development. With limited management experience, he knew that the technical strength of his unique products had helped the company survive thus far. It was also quite clear that a sizable organization would have to be built and managed in order for the firm to manufacture and market the transceiver and other products. Mr. Ivie felt, however, that he would need to continue to spend a great deal of time developing his new concepts in order to keep on the leading edge of the state of the art.

Licensing opportunities were still available. Litton was still interested, along with several other well-known companies in the field, in discussing either a licensing or marketing arrangement. Mr. Ivie was confident that if he chose to license an established company such as Litton to manufacture and market the transceiver he could probably get better terms and higher royalties than had been discussed in the past, and he intended to negotiate for a royalty of 10 percent on retail selling price if he decided to grant a license at all. If the problem of other companies being in a position to learn perhaps too much about the basic circuit designs could be overcome, licensing could probably get the products to market more rapidly and at the same time provide substantial revenue to Ivie Electronics. This could be done without investment in manufacturing or marketing facilities, providing income to the stockholders and supporting new research and development.

In considering the various possibilities, Ray Ivie felt that it was important that a definite direction be established and specific plans made so that when the Timp Transceiver was fully completed and tested, Ivie Electronics would be ready to get it produced and marketed in a way befitting the high quality and advanced design of the product.

EXHIBIT 1

IVIE ELECTRONICS, INC.
Balance Sheet
December 31, 1969

Assets

Current Assets:

Cash	$ 1,211.53	
Accounts receivable—JayArk Instrument Corporation (part of this receivable has become past due and owing)	56,463.20	
Inventory—materials, work in process and finished goods, estimated (Note 1)	25,100.00	
Total Current Assets		$ 82,774.73
Property, plant and equipment:		
Land	$42,760.00	
Equipment (Note 2) $25,098.66		
Less accumulated depreciation 8,272.39	16,826.27	
Total Property, Plant and Equipment		59,586.27
Other Assets:		
Advances to suppliers		900.00
Transceiver circuits, designs and processes (Note 3)		51,147.00
Total Assets		$194,408.00

EXHIBIT 1 *(continued)*

Liabilities and Stockholders Equity

Current Liabilities:

Accounts payable	$19,709.17	
Notes payable—First Security Bank	10,000.00	
Land contract payable—Sanford Bingham (Note 4)	22,260.00	
Land contract payable—Ray Ivie (Note 4)	13,500.00	
Note payable—Ray Ivie	7,280.00	
Accrued payroll	112.00	
Accrued payroll taxes	738.08	
Total Current Liabilities		$ 73,599.25
Unearned revenue		800.00
Stockholders Equity:		
Capital stock, common, $1.00 par value		
12,939 shares issued and outstanding	12,939.00	
Paid in surplus	128,216.39	
Retained earnings	(21,146.64)	
Total Stockholders Equity		120,008.75
Total Liabilities and Stockholders Equity		$194,408.00

See accompanying notes (Exhibit 3) to financial statements.

EXHIBIT 2

IVIE ELECTRONICS, INC.
Addendum to Balance Sheet of December 31, 1969

The increase in authorized capital and ten-to-one stock split authorized by the shareholders on January 28, 1970, affect the capital section of the company's balance sheet as follows:

Stockholders' Equity:

Capital stock, common $1 par value, 129,390 shares issued and outstanding	$129,390.00
Paid in surplus	11,765.39
Retained earnings (as of balance sheet dated December 31, 1969)	(21,146.64)
Total Stockholders' Equity (as of 12/31/69)	$120,008.75

See accompanying notes (Exhibit 3) to financial statements.

EXHIBIT 3

IVIE ELECTRONICS, INC.
Statement of Income and Retained Earnings
Six Months Ended December 31, 1969

Sales		$ 68,461.10
Cost of sales (Note 5)		27,823.97
Gross profit		$ 40,637.13
Expenses:		
Salaries and wages	$17,643.19	
Payroll taxes	2,038.35	
Depreciation	2,944.15	
Amortization of incorporation expense	200.00	
Freight	252.95	
Office supplies and postage	90.83	
Utilities	480.17	
Repairs and maintenance	189.02	
Interest	157.50	
Travel	262.40	
Professional services	80.00	
Keyman term insurance	100.61	
Books and publications	3.65	
Donations	18.68	
Miscellaneous...................................	28.74	
Total Expenses		24,490.24
Net Income		$ 16,146.89
Retained earnings, June 30, 1969		(37,293.53)
Retained earnings, December 31, 1969		$(21,146.64)

Notes to Financial Statements

NOTE 1: The company has not taken a physical inventory of materials, goods in process, and finished goods. Inventory balances for June 30, 1969, and December 31, 1969, are estimates furnished by the corporation president, Ray Ivie. Net income for the period is directly dependent upon the accuracy of these estimates and can be relied upon only to the extent that said estimates may be relied upon.

NOTE 2: Includes tooling, test and office equipment depreciated over eight years on a straight-line basis.

NOTE 3: At the inception of the corporation, 5,683 shares of stock were issued to Ray Ivie which were recorded on the books of the corporation at $1 par value only, representing money and equipment put into the company by Ray Ivie. It was subsequently determined by the board of directors that the books did not accurately reflect the value of transceiver circuits, designs and processes obtained from Mr. Ivie at the time of incorporation. They were valued by the board at $51,147.00, representing the difference between par value and the selling price of the stock at the time of incorporation. Outside this original transaction, the corporation has issued no stock at a price under $10.00 per share.

NOTE 4: Sanford Bingham and Ray Ivie are stockholders and directors of the company. They originally acquired the purchasers' interest in three adjoining parcels of land abutting 1200 South and 400 West in Orem, Utah, in their names under contracts with the original owners. The company now has the purchasers' interest in these parcels under contracts with Sanford Bingham and Ray Ivie.

NOTE 5: Direct labor costs have been included in salaries and wages since the books and records of the company have not to date segregated manufacturing labor from administrative labor.

9.2. Ivie Electronics, Inc. (B)*

DURING THE TWO YEARS between March 1970 and the spring of 1972, Ivie Electronics, Inc., (IE) developed two new products and continued the development of its unique communications transceiver and stereo amplifier equipment. None of these products had yet been marketed in significant quantities. Ray Ivie and Robert Larsen were still managing the company as president and executive vice president, respectively.

With the assistance of some MBA students from a nearby university, the company prepared in May 1972 a three-year operating plan, which included details of marketing, production, finance, organization, and personnel. The summary of that plan is shown as Exhibit 1.

A balance sheet for the company as of December 31, 1971, is shown in Exhibit 2, and an income statement for the six months then ended is shown in Exhibit 3. The Cinegraphic account receivable was the balance of the uncollected amount due on the Jayark account. When Jayark went bankrupt, Ivie Electronics attached a Jayark receivable from Cinegraphics in an attempt to secure payment of what Jayark owed Ivie Electronics. A financial backer in Cinegraphics was considering making good all or a portion of its financial obligations including the amount payable to Ivie Electronics. The expected collection of this account had been included in IE's cash flow projections.

The cash balance of IE was $7,400 as of March 31, 1972. A line of credit was available at a local bank in the amount of $20,000, plus $10,000 more with additional collateral pledged. Guarantees for loans of up to $300,000 through the Small Business Administration had been arranged, and several investment bankers in Salt Lake City had indicated that they would like to underwrite a public stock offering for Ivie Electronics.

PRODUCTS AND MARKETS

The four unique products of Ivie Electronics were as follows:

1. Timp Transceiver—a powerful self-contained two-way radio using modular construction. The unit has its own test equipment built in and will have a 1,000 channel capability.

---

* Prepared by Professor Melvin J. Stanford, Brigham Young University. Copyright © 1974 by Brigham Young University. Reprinted by permission.

2. Triplex Stereo—a three amplifier sound system that provides quality sound reproduction at low cost.
3. Concoder II—an automatic control center capable of operating 16 different devices simultaneously. The unit is programmable.
4. Remote P.A. System—expensive sound system amplifiers than can be mounted in burglarproof and tamperproof areas of buildings. The entire system is fully controlled by a remote plug-in device which fits in the palm of the hand.

The total U.S. market potential for radio equipment in general was estimated from industry sources to exceed $500 million per year in the commercial section (see Exhibit 4). Transceivers sold separately were valued at about $85 million in 1970; this segment of the market included airborne, marine, and ground usage. Ray Ivie believed that the Timp Transceiver would be used mostly in the ground market, which showed a sales increase of 27 percent in 1969 and 9 percent in 1970 (a year of economic recession) to a 1970 level of $29 million.

It was intended that the Timp Transceiver be initially produced in a 28-watt model for the citizens band market, which included:

Reserve teams.	Power companies.
Physicians.	Telephone companies.
Construction.	Railroads.
Forest Service.	Taxicabs and limousines.
Oil companies.	

The U.S. market outlook for citizens band transceivers was estimated from published industry sources as follows:

1971	$ 9 million
1972	$11 million
1973	$14 million
1974	$12 million

The citizens band market was very competitive. Major producers with more than $100,000 annual sales decreased from nine in 1968 to six in 1969; in 1970 there were seven. The largest of these were Motorola and Bendix, whose 1970 total sales of $796 million and $1.44 billion, respectively, included a wide range of products.

The Timp Transceiver used a skillful engineering design that gave it both miniaturization and increased power output. For its size, it was a powerful transceiver, its outstanding characteristic. The advantages of the Timp Transceiver were:

1. Compact size.
2. Advanced design giving:
   a. A modular construction for ease of disassembly and repair.

b. A self-contained speaker and mike.

c. Increased power output and range.

d. Low input power requirements.

e. A rugged design that resists shock and corrosion of components.

3. Versatility—The Timp could be plugged into an antenna and power supply in a car, boat, plane; used as a base station in an office; or carried on one's person.

There were no other transceivers currently on the market that had all of the above characteristics. The price of the Timp, because of the above features, was quite high compared to other transceivers. The Timp would sell for $700 to $800 compared to $6.50 to $330 for other citizen band transceivers. Thus the Timp would appeal to a special segment of the citizen band market.

Ray Ivie predicted that the citizens band version of the Timp Transceiver would be ready for sale by the summer of 1973, with sales of 100 units the first year and 1 percent to 2 percent of that market in following years. Specific sales forecasts were:

	1973	1974	1975
In Dollars:			
Optimistic	80,000	236,000	254,000
Expected	40,000	118,000	127,000
Pessimistic	20,000	59,000	63,500
In Units:			
Optimistic	100	296	318
Expected	50	148	159
Pessimistic	20	74	78

Several contingencies were recognized. The Timp Transceiver was designed to have a power output of 28 watts. Some of the citizens band equipment was used by unlicensed operators and was restricted to five watts power output. If a large part of the Timp market segment as found to contain this class of users, then Ivie would want to switch over to development of the government model immediately. The government agencies are not limited to a five-watt output.

The possibility also existed that shortly after the transceiver was introduced, someone would duplicate it. If this occured, then Ivie intended to immediately license the production of the transceiver to a larger firm like Motorola, which would be able to market the transceiver on a nationwide basis through already established marketing organizations.

The government and military markets were much larger than the citizens band market. Prices were also higher: $1,200 to $2,200 for police and public safety transceivers, and $1,500 to $5,000 for army transceivers. Ray Ivie intended to do further research on government specifications and then begin development of a government-military transceiver, with up to 1,000 channels in January 1973. By March 1974, he planned to submit a model to the federal government so that testing could begin in July 1974. He hoped to begin production for government agencies in October 1975.

The stereo amplifier was also unique in its field. Ray Ivie had split the audio spectrum into three segments, with a separate amplifier for each segment. For stereo, the Ivie system had six separate amplifiers; the system did not need expensive loudspeakers to attain high quality output of 100 watts per channel. Ivie would price it at $200 wholesale and $300 retail. Competing amplifiers were the Maranz (140 watts per channel) and the MacIntosh (105 watts per channel), both of which sold for $495 retail and required expensive loudspeakers. Industry publications listed total U.S. sales of audio amplifiers as $23 million in 1968, $18 million in 1969, and $22 million in 1970.

The Concoder II was an encoder-decoder device used to control many other functions, such as dimming lights, turning on a projector, and starting a tape recorder. The Concoder II would be good for multimedia presentations needing to be carefully timed and controlled. Some of the organizations that could use the Concoder were:

a. Sales promotion organizations.
b. Sales convention facilities.
c. State, trade, and world fairs.
d. Visitor centers.
e. Tourist bureaus.
f. University and school auditoriums.
g. Theaters.

There was no other 16-channel concoder on the market. A competing eight-channel concoder sold for $3,200. Ivie's concoder could be sold with from 2 to 16 channels and was priced at $800, plus $50 per channel. A few Concoders had been sold by Ivie and were operating well. Production of additional units would be undertaken as orders were received. Without any market data to go on, future sales of the Concoder II were estimated by Ivie at:

Pessimistic	25 per year
Expected	50 per year
Optimistic	75 per year

Public address systems were usually purchased by sound contractors who installed them in churches, schools, clubs, live theaters, television studios, and conference rooms. Industry sources indicated $224 million in U.S. sales of commercial sound systems, with a forecast of $206 million for 1971. Ray Ivie planned to sell initially in the church market. He believed that the remote and self-adjusting freatures of his public address system would enable IE to build a sales volume rapidly. Market shares of competitors making conventional P.A. equipment were not known. Ray Ivie intended to complete and test the working model of his remote system so as to begin production in July 1972.

OBJECTIVES AND PHILOSOPHY

Ray Ivie's principal objective was to make IE profitable. He also wanted to achieve a tenfold increase in the price of IE stock within a five to ten-year period and eventually reach a multimillion-dollar level of sales. Moreover, Ray Ivie wanted to be able to employ 500 Utah people in the IE company. His research and development goals were toward unique, high performance products of high quality and reasonable cost. Ray Ivie did not wish to compete with big business in established markets.

Ivie Electronics, Inc., had a corporate philosophy strongly oriented toward social responsibility. As stated by Ray Ivie:

> In the midst of a technological expansion in this fast-moving world, Ivie Electronics is not content to keep abreast of current technology but is forging ahead as a leader in design of highly sophisticated miniature circuitry. Over the past eight years Ivie Electronics has developed some unique, highly efficient communications circuitry that promises to revolutionize the industry.
>
> The decision of Ivie Electronics to build its research and development facilities as well as its manufacturing plant in Utah Valley, near Brigham Young University and the Utah State Technical College, is the result of the basic philosophy that recognizes the mutual benefits and advantages accruing to the company and its employees and to the educational institutions and their students through the exchange of facilities and resources. In addition to the manpower resources of the students and faculty of a nationally prominent electrical engineering department at BYU, the Utah State Technical College will soon build its new facilities adjacent to the Ivie Electronics plant. This will provide qualified students of both the university and the trade tech an opportunity to bridge the gap between classroom theory and practical application. This action is in keeping with a significant industrial trend to locate near institutions of higher learning.
>
> Utah Valley is a fast growing and progressive area that still has a happy rural feeling. The family orientation in this area results in a highly educated and dependable labor force which is vital to the success of the company. The natural, cultural, and civic advantages which make this a desirable place to live will make it possible to attract and keep the highest type of qualified engineers.
>
> Continuous research and development in the electronics field coupled with close cooperation within the company of those charged with the physical and technical applications of production will result in the design, manufacture, and marketing of highly desirable quality products at realistic prices. Such production will provide management, capitalists, and employees with ample reward and will result in a significant economic benefit to all of Utah Valley.

EXHIBIT 1
Ivie Electronics Summary Sheet 1972–1974; Pessimistic, Expected and Optimistic Sales Levels

	Pessimistic Sales Levels			Expected Sales Levels			Optimistic Sales Levels		
	Year 1	Year 2	Year 3	Year 1	Year 2	Year 3	Year 1	Year 2	Year 3
Marketing (units):									
Timp Transceiver	00	1	19	00	13	46	00	46	103
Stereo amplifier	16	80	72	146	306	410	198	410	602
Chapel P.A. system	3	15	13	9	24	42	17	31	48
Concoder II	1	10	18	2	17	22	10	22	33
Income Statement:									
Sales	$ 58,825	$175,800	$326,550	$126,400	$404,700	$632,050	$250,725	$773,550	$1,141,725
Cost of goods sold	17,431	44,295	84,731	32,810	106,928	161,688	60,239	195,125	284,727
Operating expenses	81,907	94,993	95,979	81,907	97,715	105,882	81,907	109,443	133,873
Profits before tax	(40,513)	36,512	145,840	11,683	200,057	364,480	108,579	468,982	723,125
Balance sheet:									
Assets	$181,008	$184,520	$301,493	$210,892	$360,314	$551,871	$322,362	$568,970	$ 947,450
Liabilities	62,048	29,283	22,218	14,548	20,783	30,218	16,748	28,983	46,018
Capital	118,960	155,237	279,275	196,344	339,531	521,653	305,614	539,987	901,432
Cash Flows:									
Total receipts	$ 48,500	$170,125	$309,175	$133,963	$380,350	$614,300	$255,184	$646,300	$ 996,000
Total disbursements	101,726	133,519	194,660	123,463	139,311	437,676	163,957	524,245	760,428
Cumulative borrowings	48,100	12,100							
Financial Ratios:									
Break-even (dollars)	$111,747	$128,898	$140,872	$111,399	$147,420	$167,151	$112,632	$174,573	$ 225,333
ROI (percent)	(22.0)	30.5	79.9	6.2	72.9	53.6	55.8	76.7	66.9
Total Employment	8	8	12	9	13	15	11	16	20
Administration	2	2	2	2	2	2	2	2	2
Production	1	1	4	2	5	7	4	8	12
Marketing	3	3	4	3	4	4	3	4	4
R&D	2	2	2	2	2	2	2	2	2

EXHIBIT 2

IVIE ELECTRONICS, INC.
Balance Sheet
December 31, 1971

Assets

Current Assets:

Cash		$ 18,281.88
Accounts receivable, cinegraphics	$42,733.94	
Less allowance for doubtful accounts	17,546.29	25,187.65
Job orders receivable		31,642.00
Inventory		48,713.08
Total Current Assets		$123,824.61

Property, Plant, and Equipment:

Land		42,760.00
Equipment	$36,195.59	
Less accumulated depreciation	13,618.43	22,577.16
Total Property, Plant, and Equipment		$ 65,337.16

Other Assets:

Transceiver circuits, designs, and processes		51,164.75
Total Assets		$240,326.52

Liabilities and Stockholders' Equity

Current Liabilities:

Notes Payable		$ 800.50
Land contract payable, Sanford Bingham	$22,260.00	
Interest accrued	4,735.82	26,995.82
Land contract payable, Ray Ivie	$ 3,350.00	
Interest accrued	712.71	4,062.71
Accrued payroll		4,000.00
Taxes payable		590.51
Total Current Liabilities		$ 36,449.54
Warranty reserve, Temple project		3,000.00
Total Liabilities		$ 39,449.54

Stockholders' Equity:

Capital stock, common, $1 per value.

176,273 shares issued and outstanding		$176,273.00
Paid-in surplus		106,623.39
Retained earnings		(82,019.41)
Total Liabilities and Stockholders' Equity		$240,326.52

EXHIBIT 3

IVIE ELECTRONICS, INC.
Statement of Income and Retained Earnings
For the Six Months Ended December 31, 1971

Sales		$46,667.05
Cost of Goods Sold, per Job Orders:		
Warranty reserve	$ 3,000.00	
Direct materials and supplies	6,201.32	
Materials from stock	2,185.89	
Direct labor	13,683.89	
Application of overhead	7,933.11	33,004.21
Gross Profit		$13,662.84
Operating Expenses:		
Administrative labor and labor taxes	$ 1,846.11	
Depreciation expense	1,731.75	
Utilities	669.40	
Travel and transportation	912.16	
Repairs, maintenance, and small tools	1,487.59	
Rent on R&D shop	360.00	
Office and engineering supplies	266.34	
Taxes and licenses	226.96	
Professional services	465.90	
Westcon convention, seminar, trade books and		
magazines, and miscellaneous expenses	650.61	
Total overhead expenses	$ 8,616.82	
Applied to job orders	7,933.11	
Unapplied overhead		683.71
Net Profit on Operations		$12,979.13
Other Income and Expense:		
Interest expense	$ 5,697.56	
Less interest income	250.00	5,447.56
Net Profit		$ 7,531.57

EXHIBIT 4
Market for Radio Equipment 1969 to 1974 (in millions)

	1969	1970	1971	1972	1973	1974
Radio equipment (except microwave)	$ —	$ 21.6	$ 23.2	—	—	$ 37.7
Citizen band equipment	35.4	34.2	36.0	—	54.0	45.8
Land mobile radio equipment	212.0	216.1	225.4	—	—	256.0
Marine radio equipment	23.5	24.7	26.1	—	33.7	35.9
Airborne radio equipment	144.2	149.3	141.0	—	197.0	202.5
General radio equipment	548.7	559.3	569.3	—	76.6	745.9
Military communication equipment						
Army	603.0	315.0	273.0			
Navy	474.0	386.0	305.0			
Air Force	426.0	429.0	301.0			
Total	$1,503.0	$1,130.0	$879.0			

Source: Predicasts Annual Cumulative Edition. Published Quarterly by Predicast Inc., 10550 Park Lane, University Circle, Cleveland, Ohio 44106. Issues: No. 46, published Jan. 28, 1972. Cumulative 1971 published 1971. Cumulative 1970 published 1970.

10. Cottage Gardens, Inc.*

COTTAGE GARDENS, INC. is a wholesale grower and distributor of shade trees, evergreens, and shrubs. Headquartered in Lansing, Michigan, with farms in Ohio and Michigan, Cottage Gardens serves a primary market area ranging over five midwestern states. In 1971, the company showed a net profit of $14,503 on sales of $1,330,688. During the 1967–71 period, profit as a percent of sales ranged from 0.24 to 1.05. William Hicks, son of the president and currently shipping and office manager, summarized his feelings about the future of the company when he said in June 1972, "I know many things that need to be done, but I don't know where to start."

COMPANY BACKGROUND

Cottage Gardens was started in 1923 by Mr. Nick I. W. Kriek, a former Dutch-bulb broker. Kriek transformed Cottage Gardens from a neglected nursery into a viable business. At first he operated as a landscape nurseryman, but gradually propagation houses were constructed and the product line broadened to include plant liners as well as landscape material. As the firm developed, valuable expertise was gained in the propagation of evergreens; by the 1940s the company had acquired a reputation for quality nursery plants. It was among the first (if not the first) to introduce yews into Michigan landscapes. Its 1930 catalog listed: "New to trade; 'Kriek's Yews' one and one-half-foot plants at $8 each." Nick Kriek's basic policy was: "If you can make a profit on an item, sell. Don't hold it for a possible higher price. You may not get it."

In 1946, Mr. Harold Hicks, Nick Kriek's son-in-law, joined the firm. Under the influence of Harold Hicks, who was heavily sales and volume oriented, the firm gradually changed from a landscape business to a wholesale grower, or production agency nursery. It became Cottage Garden's policy to grow on its Michigan and Ohio farms only those species that could be produced economically in these two climates. Cottage Gardens relied upon plant growers in other sections of the nation to supply it with species not readily grown in Michigan and Ohio. Most of the plants sold by

* Prepared by Bruce P. Coleman, Graduate School of Business Administration, Michigan State University.

Cottage Gardens were put in containers and "jobbed" directly to large retail outlets. The company also supplied other landscape garden centers—both with plants it had grown itself and with plants bought and shipped from other areas of the country.

PRODUCT LINE

As of 1972, the company was one of the largest growers and buyers of shade trees in the United States and was among the larger growers and distributors of evergreens. In 1969, it added rhododendrons and azaleas to its list of species carried. Cottage Gardens' concept of service to its customers was to provide "the right plants, at the right time, in the right quantities, and at the right price."

The product line of Cottage Gardens consisted of liners and general nursery stock—shade and ornamental trees, evergreens, and shrubs. The 1972 Fall Wholesale Price List contained 135 different types and varieties of plants. The shade and ornamental trees consisted of maple, birch, crabapple, ash, cork, cherry, oak, and mountain ash. Evergreens and shrubs included juniper, yew, azalea, burning bush, and rhododendron.

PRODUCTION OPERATIONS

Plant material was both grown and purchased by Cottage Gardens as indicated below:

Type of Plant Material	Percent Grown	Percent Purchased
Shade trees	60%	40%
Evergreens (including azaleas, rhododendrons)	90	10
Shrubs	30	70
Liners	0	100

The company was moving toward growing all of the shade trees it sold. It had no tree propagation of its own, but did propagate its evergreens. Plant purchases included nursery stock bought and replanted for sale in future years as well as stock bought for resale the same season. Of the total, about 75 percent was for resale the same season.

In 1972, the company leased 580 acres of land from the owners as shown below:[1]

---

[1] The land in Ohio was owned by Harold and William Hicks, Jim Sabo, and his assistant. The Michigan land was owned by Hicks, Ted Meyers, and the field supervisor. (See organizational chart, Exhibit 2.)

Location	Acres Leased	Acres Cultivated	Percent Cultivated
Lansing, Michigan	80	80	100%
Okemos, Michigan	120	60	50
Copemish, Michigan	240	20	8
Perry, Ohio	140	130	93
Total	580	290	50%

Shade trees were grown on the Michigan farms and evergreens on the Ohio farm.

In addition, three other farms grew exclusively for Cottage Gardens:

Owner's Name	Location	Size of Farm (acres)	Acres Cultivated
Milarch	Copemish, Michigan	100	60
Petruska	Perry, Ohio	40	40
Youdath	Perry, Ohio	30	30

As with the leased land, shade trees were grown in Michigan and evergreens in Ohio. These latter three farms accounted for about 30 percent of sales. Prices for material grown were set by Cottage Gardens.

The amount of material planted was based on estimates of demand. These estimates included not only the type of plant material to be grown, but also the number of each for different size requirements. Thus the lead time for planting was one to seven or more years—on the low end of this range for evergreens and shrubs and on the high end for various sizes of trees.

Production operations consisted of planting, growing, and harvesting. The growing season was from April to October. Plants were harvested from late March to December, although harvesting could continue through to January. Plants, when harvested, were shipped in one of three forms—potted, bare root, or balled and burlapped. They were then transported by truck, often in truckload lots.

Weed and insect problems were well controlled through new technology. Two other problems associated with production operations persisted. The first was personnel requirements. Cottage Gardens had about 25 full-time employees but total employment increased to 150 in spring, 50 in summer, and 150 in fall to accommodate the harvest and shipping periods. The second problem was weather and its effect on harvesting. If there was too much snow, rain, or cold in the spring, harvesting was difficult or impossible. On the other hand, warm weather might come too quickly; some plants could not be dug after buds began to sprout leaves. About half of the production work force reported to Dick Hart, the Ohio field supervisor and half to Tony Pulido, the Michigan field supervisor.

SALES AND ADVERTISING

Although sales had expanded a total of 30 percent during the previous five years, and 1971 showed a 10 percent increase in sales over 1970, the growth trend was uneven. While 1971 sales were at a record high, the previous two years had showed a decline. (See Exhibit 4.)

Approximately 80 percent of total sales volume was in Michigan, with 10 percent in Ohio, 5 percent in Iowa, and the remainder in Indiana and Illinois and other locations throughout the United States. The three major types of customers were: (1) landscapers, constituting 35 percent of total sales, mainly trees; (2) garden centers (including chain stores), 40 percent of sales, mainly evergreens and shrubs; and (3) municipalities, 25 percent of sales, all shade trees.

Cottage Gardens had about 500 customers (700, if individual stores of chains were counted separately). Among its major customers were Frank's Nursery Sales, Inc. (Detroit), Richter's Gardens, Inc. (Lansing), K-Mart (Lansing), and Anderson's (Maumee, Ohio). The cities of Chicago and St. Paul were among the company's major municipal customers.

The company had three salesmen, five distributors, and four local representatives. Salesmen were paid on a commission basis. They took orders in five midwestern states but concentrated on Michigan. The three sales territories consisted of: (1) metropolitan Detroit, (2) half of Michigan, and Iowa, and (3) half of Michigan, Illinois, Indiana, and Ohio. The distributors were wholesalers who bought the company's plants at a discount (equal to salesmen's commissions) and held the plants for distribution in their respective areas. They also handled noncompeting lines of nursery stock. The local representatives were nurseries in the areas of Detroit, Flint, Saginaw-Bay City, Michigan, and Indianapolis. In addition, there were five house accounts.

The company also had a distribution function in Lansing. This consisted of a cash-and-carry arrangement for small orders—over the minimum order size of $300 but too small for shipment. Plants were kept on hand (in inventory) for local landscapers.

Cottage Gardens served as the Michigan representative for several other nurseries. They included Monrovia Nursery Company of Mazusa, California for container-grown plants; Bork Nurseries of Illinois for peat-balled plants; Rhode Island Nursery for yews (18 inches–24+ inches); and small specialized nurseries. As the representative, Cottage Gardens received a 10 percent commission; half was given to the salesman and half retained by the company.

Prices were set by adding to current year's prices whatever increase was believed needed to cover projected expenses and still be supported by the market. Cottage Gardens kept a close watch over competitors' prices. Prices were quoted f.o.b. Lansing, but savings were provided the customer for material ordered direct from sources. Quantity discounts were provided.

Municipal sales were made on a bid basis. In February 1972, a $50,000 shade tree order for Chicago was won.

Very little advertising was undertaken. Mailing fliers and advertisements in trade magazines constituted the total effort. A very small ad was placed in each issue of *American Nurserymen*. The ad contained the name of the company, address and telephone number, owners' names, and the words, "Shade and Ornamental Trees—Evergreens—Shrubs." A quarter-page ad in the *1972 Michigan Association of Nurserymen Year Book* contained most of the items which appeared in the smaller ad but also cited their 49 years of experience, the names of salesmen to contact, and the words, "Shade and Ornamental Trees—Evergreens—Rhododendrons—Azaleas—Shrubs." All advertisements contained the logo of a Dutch girl picking tulips, illustrated in Exhibit 1.

ORGANIZATION AND MANAGEMENT

The 1972 organization of Cottage Gardens, Inc. is illustrated in Exhibit 2. The company's chairman, Nick Kriek, though mostly retired, signed checks occasionally and took part in such major decisions as the acquisition of land.

Harold Hicks, the president, was primarily responsible for the growth of the company during the last 15 years. William Hicks said of his father:

> His philosophy has been to make a profit and keep up with the competition. Most of the time he has succeeded at both. But the problem is he has done this all himself. He has objectives, but they are only in his mind, not explicitly written down. He has just now started to delegate some of his work and responsibilities to his subordinates. He very much enjoys what he is doing but at the same time doesn't get carried away, so he has lots of time to enjoy his family. I think it is fair to say the same of every executive or supervisor working in the company.

The sales manager, Gene Ryan, had worked for the company for ten years. He had risen through the ranks to his present position and only recently had started having the true responsibilities of sales manager delegated to him.

The shade tree manager, Ted Meyers, and the evergreen manager, Jim Sabo, had worked for the company for seven years. William stated: "Both have done a good job of building the quantity and quality of products sold in an economical way." Jim Sabo, Ohio evergreen manager, was reputed to be one of the best evergreen propagation experts in the nation. He had developed new methods of propagation, new and hardier strains of evergreens, and new methods for growing and protecting plants.

William N. Hicks, presently shipping and office manager, received his B.S. degree in business administration from Michigan State University in 1972. William had started with the company at the age of six pulling weeds in the fields. He worked during weekends and vacations throughout his schooling and obtained a wide variety of experience in the operations of the firm. He also gained knowledge of the business by going on sales trips, attending association meetings, and visiting competitors. William said, "Even though I have yet to prove myself under year-round, everyday operations, I have done sufficiently well during the spring rush to be accepted as a fellow executive and future boss. I think the cooperation and coordination among the other executives and myself is very good and we all have a feeling of team effort to bring the company along."

ACCOUNTING AND FINANCE

A local CPA firm drew up financial statements for the company for income tax purposes. Exhibits 3 and 4 contain consolidated financial statements for the years 1967 through 1971 based upon a year-end date of March 31. Exhibits 5, 6, and 7 contain financial data for the period April 1, 1971 through January 31, 1972 to reflect the change of accounting year-end date in 1972.

Cottage Gardens was classified as an agricultural business. Accounting statements conformed to reporting requirements for firms so classified. While the agricultural classification had certain tax benefits for the company, it placed restrictions upon operations. One such requirement was that the company grow at least 50 percent of what it sold.

The company did not have a ready method for determining the inventory value of nursery stock on hand, either growing or in the warehouse ready for delivery. Those items were considered as a cost of sales or purchased at the time acquired or as a sale when delivered. The result of this practice was that the value of inventory was not included in any annual balance sheets. The inventory value of all nursery stock, at wholesale prices, was $1,212,290 as of March 31, 1971, and $1,928,728 as of January 31, 1972. This included salable and nonsalable stock at all farms.

Exhibits 8–12 are excerpts from an Operating Cost Study conducted by the Horticulture Research Institute. Exhibits 8–10 provide data for all 51 reporting wholesale nurseries. Of those companies, ten had sales of under $200,000; 19 had sales of $200,000 to $499,999; and 22 had sales of over $500,000. Exhibits 11 and 12 provide operating cost data reported by the larger firms. In Exhibits 9–12 the "lower, median, and higher cost" percentages are not averages; they are actual costs of a particular company in an array of the total. In other words, they define quartiles such that one fourth of the companies had costs below the lower cost figure, one fourth had costs above the higher cost figure, and so on. Furthermore, in utilizing the data for comparative analysis, costs must be compared on a line-by-line basis. Not every firm in the study reported all costs; thus each item was treated separately. Adding columns will not equal the total shown except by coincidence.

Ownership of the corporation in 1972 was held by three individuals: Harold Hicks (79 percent), Nick Kriek (20 percent), and Eugene Ryan (1 percent.)

ASSOCIATION ACTIVITIES

The company maintained memberships in the American Association of Nurserymen (AAN) and the Michigan Association of Nurserymen (MAN). The AAN is very active in lobbying, conducting research, sponsoring management seminars, monitoring legislation and other activities related to nursery operation, and in disseminating information through pamphlets, research reports, and its bimonthly publication, *American Nurseryman*. This latter publication contains a wealth of information related to association activities, research, marketing, advertising, pricing, and production.

Company personnel had been or were active in the MAN. For example, Nick Kriek was secretary-treasurer in 1932–33 and Harold Hicks was president in 1959. In 1972, Gene Ryan and Harold Hicks were on several MAN committees, Gene Ryan was a representative on the MAN board of directors, and Ted Meyers was secretary-treasurer of the Central Michigan Landscape & Nurseryman Association. The stated purpose of MAN was:

To unite the Nurserymen of the state of Michigan for mutual benefit, protection, and improvement in their business.

To encourage among the members a closer personal acquaintance and a friendly spirit of cooperation.

To gather, receive, and disseminate such information, with respect to the nursery and allied business, as may seem helpful to the members.

To forward and promote the general welfare and prosperity of the members, and to attain and maintain a high standard of business ethics in all dealings with the public.

To cooperate with all governmental agencies, both legislative and administrative, and to assist in the furtherance of all commendable horticultural developments.

COMPETITION

Competition in the nursery business was characterized by many small firms in a region and by a few large ones. William Hicks made this observation:

> We have four or five major competitors in the Midwest and thousands of minor competitors who raise plants for their local area. The competition is very keen among the major competitors and this keenness of competition has led to no cooperation among companies. There are no figures on total sales in the United States or any other figures to help the individual companies see where they stand.

Principal competitors identified by William were:

Name	Location	Product Line
Horton Nurseries	Madison, Ohio	Evergreens, shrubs
Cole Nurseries	Circleville, Ohio	Shade trees
Manbeck Nurseries	Dayton, Ohio	Shade trees
Wandell's Nurseries	Urbana, Illinois	Shade trees
Northland Evergreen Co.........	Monroe, Michigan	Evergreens, shrubs
Zelenka Nursery Co.	Grand Haven, Michigan	Evergreens, shrubs

INDUSTRY TRENDS

A number of trends in the American nursery industry were discussed in the 1971 issues of the *American Nurseryman*. In summary form, these included:

1. The landscaping business will continue to boom because of rising income levels.
2. Specialized landscaping will evolve because of the increase in town houses, apartments, mobile homes, and so on in such forms as roof gardens and container planted balconies.
3. The continued concern for the beautification of the environment will transfer the nursery industry's products from the luxury category to that of a basic commodity.
4. More and more cities are passing "landscape ordinances," which require that properties such as town houses, apartments, and business offices be landscaped.
5. Chain and department stores that sell plants and garden supplies only in the spring for promotion will, in the future, either discontinue those sales altogether or elevate the status of the garden department to a year-round operation.
6. The chain garden center, e.g., Franks, will become the major marketing vehicle for nursery products.
7. The share of the market long held by mail-order type nurseries is on the decline.
8. Assembly-line landscaping will be the mode of production in the future. Small growers will grow their specialties up to a certain size and ship them to regional interim growers who will assemble the entire range of plants suitable for an area. The interim growers will then grow the plants to a larger size and be geared to efficient distribution and installation.

THE FUTURE

William Hicks commented on several problems which he saw in the operations of the company:

> The present bookkeeping system puts out a statement for the entire company and leaves it at that. We have no idea which division is doing best or worst. We have an idea that the distribution area is losing money but we have

no way of knowing for sure. Therefore, a new accounting system (I hope to have it under way in a year or two) is needed that will break down the accounts according to divisions to give us much of the basic information we need to guide the company. The costs, sales, and contributions to profits of each division would aid us greatly in making many decisions. Along with the accounting system, some advice on our financing is badly needed. Not being a financing expert, I don't know what we could do, but I do know that we borrow several hundred thousand dollars each year from the bank. There is a good possibility of either cutting this sum down through good financial planning or obtaining loans somewhere else. This part of the business has never been touched upon because there are many other problems closer to the day-to-day operations that need attention.

A cost analysis system is needed to support a pricing policy. At present, price is obtained by adjusting our price to the prices in the general market. We make a small attempt to include costs but the real costs are so unknown that nothing that even approaches accuracy can be obtained. For this reason I have stressed getting a cost analysis system in use that is simple yet elaborate enough to give us some costs that are at least close to the real cost of the plant. A true cost would be very hard to obtain because of the thousands of variables that are in play when a plant takes five to ten years to grow. But I'm sure that some usable figures could be arrived at through careful and consistent analysis. These figures could then be applied toward a pricing policy that would be much more realistic in covering costs. It has been shown through simple cost analysis that large volumes of plants have been sold at a loss while it was believed a profit was being made.

A third area that needs investigating is sales. We presently sell to anyone who has good credit (or cash) and who wants to buy our products. I think an analysis of our customers should be made. We need to investigate the potential of each customer, especially the larger ones, to see if we can capitalize more on our opportunities. Also, we need to drop several small customers that cost us more than they are worth (or at least we should set up a special system or better operated division for them). I think a crucial decision must be reached in the near future on whether we are going to try to service the large retail chain stores or the landscapers and cities, or expand enough to supply both. The latter is what we are trying to do now, but we will have to grow at a much faster pace if we intend to keep up.

In commenting on the basic direction of the company, William made these observations:

> To start with we need to sit down and study where our competitive advantages lie. We have started in that direction by specializing in shade trees and evergreens, but a little more in-depth study may show a few surprises.
>
> Once we have decided where our emphasis will be, we must set some definite objectives—objectives that can and will be reviewed each year. These objectives should be things like a 10 percent increase in profits, or a 10 percent decrease in costs, and other attainable goals.
>
> Strategies need to be set. Questions should be asked like: Are we going to meet our competition head-on or should we take up the slack they leave? I think in our case we can beat them at head-on-head competition, so now we must decide how to do it. Our strategy or plan of attack should be mapped out

very carefully with every step and implementation of steps carefully thought out. Since nothing like this has ever been done before, I think our strategies should be built with extreme care yet must remain very flexible so that they can be changed to fit our needs. I don't want to get very specific about the strategies we should take because I think this is something we must all consider and meet about several times.

Finally, in reflecting on the organization and his future in the company, he commented:

The organization structure has just recently been changed to accommodate me and the new responsibilities that have been given to the other managers. I also expect it will keep changing rapidly in the future for two reasons. One is that because the company is so small, it is easy to change the structure without really affecting the variables involved too much. The other is to accommodate my (hopefully) rapid advancement up through the company. At first I thought my advancement would create many personnel conflicts and problems throughout the company, but so far this advancement has been expected by all. Two of my co-executives seem to be supporting me very strongly. They say they are very happy with their positions and the opportunities they see for themselves. I would like to think that they are encouraging me because I have proven myself with my present accomplishments, but this seems unbelievable to me. So while they are encouraging my rapid advancement, I am trying to slow things down so that I don't over extend myself and my experience. It becomes very confusing at times.

UNEXPECTED EVENTS

In September 1972, Gene Ryan, the sales manager, suddenly resigned after ten years with Cottage Gardens. Ryan joined an Ohio nursery as a partner—an opportunity which apparently enabled him to be more independent and help build his own business firm. Since only growing and propagation were undertaken, the Ohio firm was not in market competition with Cottage Gardens. Prior to leaving, Ryan had handled the large house accounts and, because no replacement for him was available, Harold and William Hicks split his job. Harold took over the accounts and William assumed the sales management duties.

In December 1972, the foreman who had been in charge of the distribution function in Lansing quit. Just a short time later, the man who performed all plant digging was killed when his machine overturned. Cottage Gardens had contracted with him for years and he had been a highly skilled, efficient operator in an area of critical importance to the nursery's operations.

In November, Mrs. Kriek, William's maternal grandmother, died. Following her death, Nick Kriek, chairman of the board, withdrew completely from the company. About the same time, Mrs. Hicks, William's paternal grandmother, was placed in a nursing home. During those difficult times and for a period of several months thereafter, Harold Hicks, the president, was away from the business. William was left to manage the company at the peak of the selling and harvesting season.

EXHIBIT 1
Cottage Gardens' Logo

EXHIBIT 2
Organization Chart, 1972

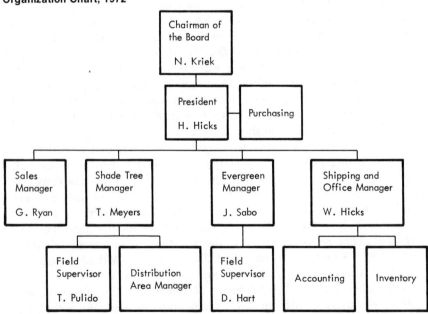

EXHIBIT 3

THE COTTAGE GARDENS, INC.
Consolidated Balance Sheets, 1968–1971
Years Ending March 31

Assets	1971	1970	1969	1968
Current Assets:				
Imprest cash	$ 700	$ 700	$ 700	$ 700
Cash in bank	7,223	7,864	12,448	782
Accounts receivable	203,983	163,109	207,040	169,816
Notes receivable	3,150			
Less allowance for doubtful accounts	(1,510)	(1,179)	(2,117)	(3,431)
Employee advances	918			421
Bid deposits	6,901	3,971	3,601	2,626
Inventory—supplies	6,920	3,513	4,557	9,451
Total Current Assets	$228,285	$177,978	$226,229	$180,365
Fixed Assets:				
Machinery and equipment	110,999	100,224	90,545	93,943
Furniture and fixtures	3,873	3,125	3,012	2,405
Autos and trucks	36,944	35,770	30,940	20,480
Yard improvements	473	473	473	473
Less: Allowance for depreciation	(103,785)	(92,795)	(76,283)	(67,206)
Total Fixed Assets	$ 48,504	$ 46,797	$ 48,687	$ 50,095
Other Assets:				
Lake Geneva lot (at cost)	1,823	1,823	1,823	1,823
Total Assets	$278,612	$226,598	$276,739	$232,283

Liabilities and Stockholders' Equity

	1971	1970	1969	1968
Current Liabilities:				
Accounts payable	$ 74,437	$ 13,781	$ 36,205	$ 63,846
Accounts receivable—credit balance			21,062	
Notes payable	147,450	147,182	161,681	112,885
Employee advances		67	40	
Employee savings	4,553	13,736	6,513	5,816
Employer insurance deductions	38	358	189	36
Accrued social security taxes	1,400	1,014	1,049	
Accrued interest payable	734	460		
Total Current Liabilities	$228,612	$176,598	$226,739	$182,583
Stockholders' Equity:				
Common stock—par value $10 per share authorized and issued 5,000 shares	50,000	50,000	50,000	50,000
Total Liabilities and Equity	$278,612	$226,598	$276,739	$232,583

Source: Company Annual Reports, 1968–71.

EXHIBIT 4

THE COTTAGE GARDENS, INC.
Income Statements 1967–1971
Years Ending March 31

	1971		1970		1969		1968		1967	
	Dollars	Percent	Dollars	Percent	Dollars	Percent	Dollars	Percent	Dollars	Percent
Sales of Nursery Stock:										
In Michigan	$ 988,524	74.3%	$ 941,077	78.0%	$ 956,800	76.1%	$1,045,869	79.5%	$ 848,426	83.5%
Outside Michigan	343,694	25.8	274,536	22.7	310,507	24.7	278,449	21.2	178,448	17.6
Total Sales	$1,332,218	100.1%	$1,215,613	100.7%	$1,267,307	100.8%	$1,324,318	100.7%	$1,026,874	101.1%
Less discounts allowed	1,530	0.1	8,939	0.7	9,977	0.8	9,316	0.7	10,812	1.1
Net Sales	$1,330,688	100.0%	$1,206,674	100.0%	$1,257,330	100.0%	$1,315,002	100.0%	$1,016,062	100.0%
Expenses:										
Purchases (net)	$ 717,336	53.9%	$ 644,420	53.4%	$ 697,051	55.4%	585,348	44.5%	466,653	46.0%
Salaries—administration	39,987	3.0	39,785	3.3	41,230	3.3	39,973	3.0	37,287	3.6
Salaries—office	26,925	2.0	27,591	2.3	26,980	2.1	25,641	1.9	18,296	1.8
Salaries and wages—operations	253,800	19.1	241,305	20.0	260,089	20.7	329,981	25.2	224,475	22.0
Commissions	29,691	2.2	29,729	2.5	17,491	1.4	24,752	1.9	11,720	1.2
Advertising	5,165	0.4	6,915	0.6	4,941	0.4	3,375	0.3	4,395	0.4
Bad debts	1,775	0.1	976	0.1	0	—	1,361	0.1	417	—
Depreciation	13,129	1.0	16,512	1.4	14,014	1.1	16,626	1.3	11,563	1.2
Donations	1,605	0.1	280	—	371	—	84	—	52	—
Dues and subscriptions	1,678	0.1	1,619	0.1	1,570	0.1	1,661	0.1	1,410	0.1
Electricity and water	2,237	0.2	1,767	0.1	1,577	0.1	1,826	0.1	1,256	0.1
Freight in	57,041	4.3	50,167	4.2	52,216	4.1	69,134	5.4	62,306	6.1
Freight out	9,121	0.7	10,866	0.9	(3,998)	(0.3)	26,654	2.0	23,851	2.4
Fuel heat	1,823	0.1	1,479	0.1	1,412	0.1	740	—	2,071	0.2
Insurance	4,920	0.4	8,063	0.7	9,562	0.8	14,795	1.1	10,434	1.0
Insurance—employee benefits	1,353	0.1	1,285	0.1	1,249	0.1	1,346	0.1	1,161	0.1

	(1)	%	(2)	%	(3)	%	(4)	%	(5)	%
Interest	6,745	0.5	4,103	0.3	6,218	0.5	1,641	0.1	2,693	0.3
Legal and audit	2,468	0.2	2,277	0.2	2,467	0.2	1,305	0.1	1,105	0.1
Rents	31,758	2.4	9,880	0.8	20,245	1.6	18,395	1.4	14,303	1.4
Maintenance and repair	34,223	2.7	36,213	3.0	40,282	3.3	63,349	4.8	41,238	4.1
Mileage and auto	5,007	0.4	4,992	0.4	5,774	0.5	4,454	0.3	3,048	0.3
Supplies—office	3,572	0.3	2,699	0.2	3,373	0.3	2,950	0.2	3,102	0.3
Supplies—operations	57,200	4.3	52,097	4.3	47,039	3.8	56,835	4.3	56,004	5.6
Small tools	1,330	0.1	1,064	0.1	1,442	0.1	1,888	0.1	1,551	0.1
Taxes	25,958	1.9	25,654	2.1	25,679	2.1	25,646	1.9	20,421	2.0
Telephone and telegraph	7,805	0.6	8,252	0.7	7,155	0.6	6,523	0.6	5,093	0.5
Travel	5,970	0.4	6,017	0.5	6,541	0.5	5,717	0.4	4,443	0.4
Miscellaneous	1,848	0.1	2,964	0.2	2,406	0.2	11,712	1.0	2,651	0.3
Customer relations	3,021	0.2	3,374	0.3	3,080	0.2	1,901	0.1	1,861	0.2
Collection costs	732	0.1	149	—	710	—	0	—	—	—
Labor not on payroll	11,536	0.9	1,587	0.1	—	—	—	—	—	—
Employees' retirement plan	7,801	0.6	8,374	0.7	—	—	—	—	—	—
Total Expenses	$1,374,560	103.4%	$1,252,455	103.7%	$1,298,166	103.3%	$1,345,613	102.3%	$1,034,860	101.8%
Excess of Net Sales over Expenses	$ (44,877)	(3.4)%	$ (45,781)	(3.8)%	$ (40,836)	(3.3)%	$ (30,611)	(2.3)%	$ (18,798)	(1.8)%
Other income:										
Interest income	5,445	0.4	4,155	0.3	2,500	0.2	2,803	0.2	10,500*	1.0
Miscellaneous	106	—	110	0.1	729	—	413	—	4,112	0.4
Over and short	(70)	—	(5)	—	—	—	10	—	96	—
Sales commissions	53,290	4.0	50,218	4.2	40,418	3.3	36,638	2.8	2	—
Rent received	600	0.1	610	0.1	430	—	190	—	15,895	1.6
Total Other Income	$ 59,371	4.5%	$ 57,085	4.7%	$ 43,794	3.5%	$ 40,049	3.0%	$ 29,603	2.9%
Net Income	$ 14,494	1.1%	$ 11,304	0.9%	$ 2,958	0.2%	$ 9,438	0.7%	$ 10,805	1.1%

* Damages—State Highway Department—$10,500.

Source: Company Annual Reports, 1967–71.

EXHIBIT 5

THE COTTAGE GARDENS, INC.
Balance Sheet
January 31, 1972

Assets

Current Assets:

Imprest cash			$ 700.00
Cash in bank			11,408.68
Accounts receivable—customer	$ 76,977.96		
Accounts receivable—employees	1,638.74		
Notes receivable	2,650.00	$81,266.70	
Less: Allowance for doubtful accounts		815.97	80,450.73
Land contract receivable (due within one year)			144.00
Bid deposits			3,383.50
Inventory—supplies			8,102.75
Prepayments			20,846.19
Total Current Assets			$125,035.85

Fixed Assets:	Cost	Accu-mulated Deprec.	Cost Less Deprec.	
Machinery and equipment	$110,715.22	$ 77,382.90	$33,332.32	
Furniture and fixtures	3,818.65	2,369.24	1,449.41	
Autos and trucks	36,794.28	28,279.14	8,515.14	
Yard improvements	473.50	188.72	284.78	
	$151,801.65	$108,220.00		43,581.65

Other Assets:

Land contract receivable (due after one year)	2,211.62
Total Assets	$170,829.12

Liabilities

Current Liabilities:

Accounts payable		$ 16,224.99
Notes payable:		
Michigan National Bank	$55,938.28	
N. I. W. Kriek	2,900.78	
H. E. Hicks	30,329.23	89,168.29
Employee savings		2,285.06
Accrued social security tax		875.46
Accrued interest		400.13
Employee insurance		504.37
Total Current Liabilities		$109,458.30

Stockholders' Equity:

Common stock—par value $10.00 per share authorized and issued 5,000 shares	$50,000.00	
Shareholders' undistributed taxable income	11,370.82	61,370.82
Total Liabilities and Stockholders' Equity		$170,829.12

Source: Company records.

EXHIBIT 6

THE COTTAGE GARDENS, INC.
Statement of Income
April 1, 1971 to January 31, 1972

	Michigan	Ohio	Total	Percentage of Sales
Sales:				
In Michigan	$657,580.64	$260,653.90	$ 918,234.54	80.9%
Outside of Michigan	217,320.65		217,320.65	19.2
Interdepartment	(37,722.50)	37,722.50	0	—
Total Sales	$837,178.79	$298,376.40	$1,135,555.19	100.1%
Less: Discounts allowed	1,031.14	0	1,031.14	0.1
Net Sales	$836,147.65	$298,376.40	$1,134,524.05	100.0%
Cost of sales (See Schedule)	757,037.50	272,106.02	1,029,143.52	90.7
Gross Profit on Sales	$ 79,110.15	$ 26,270.38	$ 105,380.53	9.3%
Commissions on direct shipments	47,994.53	0	47,994.53	4.2
Gross Income	$127,104.68	$ 26,270.38	$ 153,375.06	13.5%
General Expenses:				
Salaries—administrative	$ 24,062.98	$ 7,187.64*	31,250.62	2.8%
Salaries—office	21,890.87	6,538.83*	28,429.70	2.5
Commissions	26,995.72	8,063.66*	35,059.38	3.2
Advertising	2,602.12	777.26*	3,379.38	0.3
Bad debts	2,358.47		2,358.47	0.2
Depreciation	656.81		656.81	0.1
Donations	1,291.85		1,291.85	0.1
Dues and subscriptions	1,507.00	20.00	1,527.00	0.1
Electricity and water	148.24	41.74	189.98	—
Fuel	279.58	57.38	336.96	—
Insurance	538.79		538.79	—
Insurance—employee benefits	197.52	24.48	222.00	—
Interest	5,592.63	1,670.53*	7,263.16	0.6
Legal and auditing	2,280.00		2,280.00	0.2
Employee retirement plan	3,185.45	68.19	3,253.64	0.3
Rent	3,240.00		3,240.00	0.3
Mileage and auto expense	2,191.48		2,191.48	0.2
Office supplies	2,936.51		2,936.51	0.3
Taxes	5,599.37	15.52	5,614.89	0.5
Telephone	5,168.79	627.76	5,796.55	0.5
Travel expenses	2,808.93	196.98	3,005.91	0.3
Miscellaneous expense	1,297.38	624.78	1,922.16	0.2
Cash over and short	17.14		17.14	—
Customer relations	2,380.26	66.30	2,446.56	0.2
Collection expense	254.98		254.98	—
Total General Expenses	$119,482.85	$ 25,981.05	$ 145,463.90	12.8%
Net Operating Income	$ 7,621.83	$ 289.33	$ 7,911.16	0.7%
Other Income:				
Interest	$ 1,449.65		$ 1,449.65	0.1%
Miscellaneous	1,410.01		1,410.01	0.1
Rent	600.00		600.00	0.1
	$ 3,459.66		$ 3,459.66	0.3%
Net Income for the Period	$ 11,081.49	$ 289.33	$ 11,370.82	1.0%

* Expense allocated to Ohio on a sales ratio (23 percent).
Source: Company records.

EXHIBIT 7
Schedule of Cost of Sales, April 1, 1971 to January 31, 1972

	Michigan	Ohio	Total	Percentage of Sales
Purchases	$503,584.15	$ 89,186.72	$ 592,770.87	52.2%
Direct Expenses				
Salaries and wages—				
administrative	0	16,140.00	16,140.00	1.4
Salaries and wages	149,058.67	86,150.43	235,209.10	20.8
Contract work	478.15	1,290.00	1,768.15	0.2
Depreciation	7,265.21	3,579.58	10,844.79	1.0
Electricity and water	1,334.15	375.63	1,709.78	0.2
Freight in	17,143.20	4,194.10	21,337.30	1.9
Freight out	1,841.43		1,841.43	0.2
Fuel.............................		516.40	516.40	—
Insurance	4,849.15	1,373.78	6,222.93	0.5
Insurance—employee benefits	790.08	97.92	888.00	0.1
Employer retirement plan	351.89	57.30	409.19	—
Rent	3,960.00	2,760.00	6,720.00	0.6
Maintenance and repairs—				
building and grounds	608.27	1,695.84	2,304.11	0.2
Maintenance and repairs—				
machinery and equipment	30,130.09	4,853.21	34,983.30	3.1
Maintenance and repairs—				
trucks	8,301.94	2,015.20	10,317.14	0.9
Mileage and auto expense..........	2,604.16		2,604.16	0.2
Small tools	420.57	972.70	1,393.27	0.1
Supplies—operations	16,618.54	49,192.24	65,810.78	5.8
Taxes—social security	6,560.67	5,167.39	11,728.06	1.0
Travel expenses	1,137.18		1,137.18	0.1
Taxes—property		2,487.58	2,487.58	0.2
Total Cost of Sales...........	$757,037.50	$272,106.02	$1,029,143.52	90.7%

Source: Company records.

EXHIBIT 8
Annual Trends—Wholesale Nurseries (all data shown are median figures)*

	1967	1968	1969	1970	1971
Percentage of Annual Sales:					
January		3.4%	5.3%	4.4%	3.9%
February		6.4	6.7	6.6	6.0
March		16.0	12.8	17.0	14.9
April		26.3	24.8	23.4	26.0
May		13.9	14.5	13.0	13.0
June		5.2	4.7	5.1	5.4
July		3.7	3.6	3.4	3.0
August		4.1	4.2	3.8	3.7
September		5.7	6.0	5.4	6.3
October		6.2	6.2	7.2	6.4
November		6.0	6.8	6.6	7.2
December		3.1	4.4	4.2	4.2
Operating Cost Highlights (percentage):					
Total cost of goods sold	67.0%	64.7%	59.3%	67.5%	67.7%
Storage, maintenance, packaging, shipping costs	8.4	7.8	11.2	7.8	8.4
Selling expenses	3.7	3.9	3.4	2.8	3.7
Administrative expenses	14.2	13.4	13.0	12.3	14.3
Net profit before taxes	7.1	7.1	6.5	3.8	3.2
Comparative Highlights:					
Bad debt losses	0.6%	0.6%	0.7%	0.1%	1.0%
Pension and benefit costs	1.7%	2.0%	1.7%	2.0%	1.9%
Full-time employees	22	18	18	20	21
Sales per acre	$1,287	$2,059	$1,450	$1,691	$1,735
Sales per full time employee	$16,001	$19,554	$20,842	$18,276	$21,265
Net profit to total net worth	10.0%	10.7%	12.3%	17.4%	12.6%
Net profit to net working capital	21.4%	14.0%	21.0%	23.7%	15.4%
Net Profit Before Taxes (percent of volume):					
All companies	7.1%	7.1%	6.5%	3.8%	3.2%
Under $200,000	8.7	7.2	7.7	1.2	5.0
$200,000 to $499,999	7.2	6.0	12.4	2.6	2.8
Over $500,000	4.6	7.2	6.2	8.3	4.9

* Based on a study of 51 companies.
Source: Horticultural Research Institute, Inc., *Research Summary: Operating Cost Study* (Washington, D.C., 1972), p. 5.

EXHIBIT 9
Comparative Operating Cost Data—Wholesale Nurseries, All Sizes, 1971

	Percent of Total Sales		
	Lower Cost	*Median Cost*	*Higher Cost*
1. Sales			
Plant materials produced.	85.4%	98.0%	100.0%
Plant materials purchased and resold.	2.3	14.0	27.0
Hard goods.	0.2	0.7	1.0
Other.	1.4	3.0	6.2
2. Direct Costs			
Direct production labor.	24.1	32.1	39.8
Nursery stock.	5.7	8.5	12.0
Fertilizers, herbicides, etc.	1.3	1.9	3.5
Production equipment and supplies.	6.1	9.4	13.0
Production facilities.	4.4	6.5	11.2
Research and breeding.	0.2	0.5	0.9
Total Cost of Materials Produced.	49.6	58.5	70.8
Cost of plant material purchased for resale.	2.0	12.0	27.7
Cost of hard goods.	0.2	0.5	0.9
Cost of other sales	1.5	2.3	3.2
Total Cost of Goods Sold.	55.8	67.7	75.6
3. Gross Profits on Sales			
From plant materials produced.	40.0	30.4	21.2
From plants purchased and resold.	9.6	4.0	0.6
From hard goods.	0.3	0.2	0.2
From other.	4.0	1.4	0.5
Total Gross Profit on Sales.	44.2	31.7	24.3
4. Storage, Maintenance, Packaging, Shipping			
Direct labor—storing and maintaining.	0.7	2.6	5.8
Direct labor—packaging and shipping.	1.9	5.5	9.2
Total Direct Labor.	3.3	6.0	15.4
Packaging and shipping supplies.	0.8	2.1	4.0
Other costs.	1.3	2.4	5.6
Total Storage, Maintenance, Packaging, Shipping.	3.5	8.4	17.5
5. Selling Expenses			
Salesmen compensation and expenses.	0.9	2.5	4.6
Direct mail.	0.3	0.4	1.1
Space advertising.	0.2	0.5	1.2
Promotion.	0.3	0.5	1.2
Other.	0.4	0.8	1.6
Total Selling Expenses.	1.5	3.7	5.7
6. Administrative Expenses			
Managerial.	6.2	8.3	12.2
Office and administrative.	1.9	3.8	5.7
General.	0.7	1.4	4.8
Total Administrative Expenses.	10.2	14.3	18.4
7. Total Storage, Maintenance, Packaging, Shipping, Selling and Administrative Expenses	15.9	28.5	36.2
8. Net Profit on Wholesale Operations	9.7	3.8	(−0.9)
9. Other Wholesale Income	2.3	0.7	0.4
10. Other Wholesale Expense	1.1	2.4	3.5
11. Net Profit Before Taxes	8.9	3.2	(−1.2)

Source: Horticultural Research Institute, Inc., *Research Summary: Operating Cost Study* (Washington, D.C., 1972), p. 6.

EXHIBIT 10

Comparative Operating Cost Data—Wholesale Nurseries, All Sizes, 1971

	Lower Cost	Median Cost	Higher Cost
Bad debt losses	0.2%	1.0%	1.0%
Allowances for depreciation	1.8%	3.5%	4.6%
Pension and benefit costs	0.7%	1.9%	5.0%
Full-time employees	7	21	42
Part-time employees	1	6	17
Seasonal employees	11	30	70
Sales per full-time employee	$32,138	$21,265	$12,700
Sales per acre	$ 4,943	$ 1,735	$ 1,137
Net profit before taxes to total net worth	34.9%	12.6%	4.3%
Net sales to net worth	321.6 times	80.0 times	14.5 times
Net profit before taxes to net working capital	57.5%	15.4%	5.0%
Current ratio	125.2 to 1	38.6 to 1	2.0 to 1

Source: Horticultural Research Institute, Inc., *Research Summary: Operating Cost Study* (Washington, D.C., 1972), p. 7.

EXHIBIT 11

Comparative Operating Cost Data—Wholesale Nurseries, Sales over $500,000, 1971

		Percent of Total Sales		
		Lower Cost	Median Cost	Higher Cost
1.	Sales			
	a. Plant materials produced	95.3%	99.3%	100.0%
	b. Plant materials purchased and resold	0.6	2.0	27.0
	c. Hard goods	*	0.5	*
	d. Other...................................	*	*	*
2.	Direct Costs			
	a. Direct production labor...................	22.7	31.7	39.8
	b. Nursery stock	1.7	3.2	8.3
	c. Fertilizers, herbicides, etc.................	1.5	2.3	3.5
	d. Production equipment and supplies	4.8	8.9	11.5
	e. Production facilities	3.7	5.5	10.8
	f. Research and breeding	*	*	*
	g. Total Cost of Materials Produced	44.6	56.2	67.7
	h. Cost of plant material purchased			
	for resale	0.5	1.7	17.6
	i. Cost of hard goods	*	0.5	*
	j. Cost of other sales	*	*	*
	k. Total Cost of Goods Sold	49.4	62.6	73.0
3.	Gross Profits on Sales			
	a. From plant materials produced	49.6	35.1	23.4
	b. From plants purchased and resold	5.3	0.8	0.5
	c. From hard goods	*	*	*
	d. From other	*	*	*
	e. Total Gross Profit on Sales	50.6	37.4	27.0
4.	Storage, Maintenance, Packing, Shipping			
	a. Direct labor—storing and maintaining	1.4	2.7	4.6
	b. Direct labor—packaging and shipping	1.2	4.6	14.5
	c. Total Direct Labor....................	2.2	6.8	16.8
	d. Packaging and shipping supplies	0.6	1.7	2.8
	e. Other costs	0.4	2.4	6.8
	f. Total Storage, Maintenance,			
	Packaging, Shipping	3.3	14.4	22.2
5.	Selling Expenses			
	a. Salesmen compensation and			
	expenses	0.8	3.4	5.4
	b. Direct mail.............................	0.2	0.3	0.8
	c. Space advertising	0.2	0.4	0.9
	d. Promotion	0.2	0.6	0.9
	e. Other..................................	0.3	0.8	1.8
	f. Total Selling Expenses	1.0	4.9	6.6
6.	Administrative Expenses			
	a. Managerial	5.0	6.5	10.4
	b. Office and administrative	2.1	3.8	5.5
	c. General	0.6	1.2	5.9
7.	Total Storage, Maintenance, Packaging, Shipping, Selling and Administrative Expenses..................................	20.7	28.5	38.0
8.	Net Profit on Wholesale Operations	12.3	5.1	0.2
9.	Other Wholesale Income	4.8	1.3	0.6
10.	Other Wholesale Expense	0.6	2.6	4.8
11.	Net Profit Before Taxes	9.7	4.9	0.2

* Insufficient data.

Source: Horticultural Research Institute, Inc., *Research Summary: Operating Cost Study* (Washington, D.C., 1972), p. 12.

EXHIBIT 12
Comparative Operating Cost Data—Wholesale Nurseries, Sales over $500,000, 1971

	Lower Cost	Median Cost	Higher Cost
Bad debt losses	0.2%	0.8%	1.1%
Allowances for depreciation	1.4%	3.0%	3.9%
Pension and benefit costs	0.9%	1.8%	4.1%
Full-time employees	28	46	70
Part-time employees	2	8	25
Seasonal employees	50	67	100
Sales per full-time employee	$31,255	$18,230	$12,804
Sales per acre	$ 2,804	$ 1,632	$ 1,137
Net profit before taxes to total net worth	23.9%	9.5%	1.8%
Net sales to net worth	100.0 times	56.0 times	16.5 times
Net profit before taxes to net working capital	17.6%	8.5%	3.0%
Current ratio	68.5 to 1	19.3 to 1	2.5 to 1

Percentage of Annual Sales:

January	4.2%	July	2.9%
February	6.3	August	3.8
March	15.5	September	6.3
April	26.1	October	6.2
May	13.4	November	6.4
June	5.2	December	3.7

Source: Horticultural Research Institute, Inc., *Research Summary: Operating Cost Study* (Washington, D.C., 1972), p. 13.

11. Jackson Brewing Company (C)*

THE SEPTEMBER 1972 MEETING of the Marketing Committee of the Jackson Brewing Company (JBC) was to be devoted to an appraisal of Fabacher Brau, the company's new premium beer. Fabacher Brau had been introduced the previous summer to compete with the national premium beers which were becoming increasingly popular in the South Central portion of the United States. JBC had committed a large budget during this introductory period for the promotion of Fabacher Brau. The rationale for introducing Fabacher Brau was that the new beer could effectively compete with the major national premium brands because of the high-quality image derived by using imported hops in the brewing process, and that Fabacher Brau would compliment JBC's established Jax beer, which was considered to be a popular local brand.

In reviewing the volume and market share data for Fabacher Brau for the last 16 months, however, Mr. Dick Brown, JBC's marketing administration director, was uncertain as to the success of the brand. At the September meeting he would be required to give a detailed report concerning the future potential of Fabacher Brau, together with any possible changes in strategy which might increase sales volume.

INDUSTRY BACKGROUND

The earliest Babylonian clay document, c. 6000 B.C., depicts the brewing of beer. The Indians who greeted Columbus drank beer. One reason the Mayflower did not sail farther south was a pressing shortage of beer.

Although there was a commercial beer brewery in New Amsterdam before 1625, most beer brewed in America until the first half of the 19th century was brewed in households as a domestic art. The industrialization of beer brewing during the 19th century was accelerated by two key factors: the introduction of lager beer and the immigration to the United States of large numbers of Germans, many of whom had beer brewing skills.

* Prepared by Professor Jeffrey A. Barach, Tulane University, with the assistance of Rodman A. Eggen, research assistant, and John Dausman, Michael Gerringer, William Paul, Thomas Peterson, M.B.A. candidates, and the cooperation of Dick Brown, Charles Thomason, and Ben D. Sisson, of the Jackson Brewing Company. Copyright © 1974 by the Graduate School of Business Administration, Tulane University. Reproduced by permission.

By 1870, beer production was over 6.5 million barrels, equivalent to annual per capita consumption of 5.3 gallons. By 1900, sales approached 40 million barrels, at 16 gallons per capita, and by 1914 reached 66 million barrels and 21 gallons per capita. Consumption declined during the war, and almost ceased during prohibition (1920–33). From 1934 to 1970, production of beer grew steadily, reaching 134,653,181 barrels, with total tax paid withdrawals (beer for domestic consumption) of 122,550,191 barrels as of the fiscal year ending June 30, 1970. Per capita consumption during the period was less consistent, rising from 10.3 gallons in 1935 to 18.5 gallons in 1948, then declining to a low of 14.9 in 1961, and increasing thereafter to 18.7 gallons per year in 1970. Additional data on the brewing industry are presented in Exhibits 1 and 2.

Although there were breweries in 33 states as of 1970, the total number of breweries and brewers in the United States had been declining steadily—

EXHIBIT 1

Malt Beverage Sales by States—for Calendar Year 1970* (in barrels)

State	Number of Breweries Operated†	Taxpaid Packaged Sales	Taxpaid Keg Sales	Total Taxable Sales
California	11	6,486,989	1,405,788	7,892,777
Colorado	3	6,238,507	1,131,933	7,370,440
Florida	4	4,359,465	354,507	4,713,972
Illinois	5	4,188,025	323,878	4,511,903
Indiana	4	2,199,930	274,402	2,474,332
Louisiana	3	1,852,776	56,348	1,909,124
Maryland	5	2,770,616	415,352	3,185,968
Michigan	5	4,165,912	351,275	4,517,187
Minnesota	6	3,391,811	931,601	4,323,412
Missouri	5	8,832,817	1,022,441	9,855,258
New Jersey	6	8,832,884	1,460,489	10,293,373
New York	11	8,461,548	2,207,547	10,669,095
Ohio	8	3,992,981	1,031,041	5,024,022
Pennsylvania	20	5,046,044	1,504,178	6,550,222
Texas	7	7,572,377	508,511	8,080,888
Washington	4	4,213,624	791,613	5,005,237
Wisconsin	15	12,816,703	2,473,341	15,290,044
Arizona, Oregon, Hawaii	4	1,027,986	167,650	1,195,636
Georgia, Kentucky, North Carolina, Virginia, West Virginia	6	4,585,412	309,546	4,894,958
Iowa, Nebraska, Oklahoma	4	797,125	102,022	899,147
Connecticut, Massachusetts, Rhode Island, New Hampshire	7	2,786,451	415,888	3,202,339
Total	143	104,619,983	17,239,351	121,850,334

* Excludes breweries whose reports are delinquent.
† Represents number of breweries authorized to operate July 1, 1970.
Source: Compiled from reports of U.S. Treasury Department, Internal Revenue Service, Alcohol, Tobacco and Firearms Division; as found in U.S. Brewers Association, *Brewers Almanac 1971.*

EXHIBIT 2
Production, Draught and Packaged Sales, and Total Taxpaid Withdrawals of Malt Beverages, 1933–1970 (quantities in 31 gallon barrels)

Calendar Year	Production	Packaged Sales	Percent of Total	Draught Sales	Percent of Total	Total Taxpaid Withdrawals
1933*	24,501,678	6,467,400	31.6%	14,002,241	68.4%	20,469,641
1940	53,863,734	26,761,946	51.7	25,049,151	48.3	51,811,097
1945	88,205,537	52,664,148	64.3	29,177,247	35.7	81,841,395
1950	88,178,356	59,487,521	71.8	23,342,616	28.2	82,830,137
1955	90,285,488	66,179,019	77.9	18,798,255	22.1	84,977,274
1960	93,415,363	70,955,595	80.7	16,957,244	19.3	87,912,839
1965	108,221,725	82,624,078	82.3	17,796,839	17.7	100,420,917
1970	133,090,660	104,619,983	85.9	17,239,351	14.1	121,859,334

* April through December.
Source: U.S. Brewers Association; *Brewers Almanac 1971*.

EXHIBIT 3
25 Largest U.S. Brewers 1969–1970*

Brewer	1969 Sales (in barrels)	1970 Estimated National Market Share
1. Anheuser-Busch	18,712,432	18.5%
2. Schlitz	13,709,000	12.4
3. Pabst	10,225,000	8.8
4. Coors	6,351,466	6.0
5. Schaefer	5,432,524	4.8
6. Falstaff.............	6,700,000	4.4
7. Millers	5,100,000	4.3
8. Carling	5,440,000	4.1
9. Hamm	4,250,000	3.5
10. Associated	3,971,000	3.1
11. Rheingold	3,488,000	2.9
12. Olympia	3,375,000	2.8
13. Stroh	2,939,000	2.7
14. C. Schmidt	2,941,000	2.5
15. Heileman	2,298,000	2.5
16. National	2,218,000	1.9
17. Ballantine	2,000,000	1.6
18. Pearl	1,908,813	1.4
19. Meister Brau	1,000,000	1.3
20. Genesie	1,445,000	1.2
21. Grain Belt	1,250,000	1.0
22. Lucky	1,303,000	1.0
23. Long Star	1,167,189	0.9
24. Pittsburgh	1,055,352	0.9
25. Jackson	900,000	0.7
	109,179,776	95.2%

* Ranked by estimated 1970 sales.
Source: *Marketing/Communications*, January 1971.

Exhibit 3 lists the 25 largest U.S. brewers as of 1969–70, giving 1969 sales and 1970 estimated national market share.

In May 1971, *Forbes*[1] reported that while the U.S. beer industry had been characterized by hundreds of family-owned local brewers who distributed within very limited areas well into the 1930s, by 1961 there were only 171 brewers, and by 1971, only 80 brewing companies remained. Furthermore, according to *Fortune,*[2] the largest brewers (Anheuser-Busch, Schlitz, and Pabst) recently had experienced a growth rate more than twice the industry average rate of 4 percent. The nine largest regional brewers, on the other hand, had realized only a 1.4 percent gain, and several firms—Falstaff, Carling, and Associated—had lost ground badly.

According to *Fortune,* smaller brewers faced heavy odds, due to the nature of the industry. Beer had been hard to market profitably because the product was bulky, had a fairly short life span (three months was optimum), was costly to distribute, was heavily taxed, and had high labor costs (average hourly wages were exceeded only by the construction industry). Big brewers had been able to raise productivity through capital investment in new plants and equipment which smaller brewers could not afford. In 1970, to be very efficient, a brewery needed an annual capacity of 1.5 million barrels. Canning equipment which was considered high speed in 1965 filled 800 cans per minute, but by 1970 the best equipment ran at 1,200 cans per minute without increase in personnel. Similarly, bottle filling speeds rose from 500 to 900 per minute. Furthermore, some of the larger brewers had integrated vertically into malt houses and can making to reduce costs.

With such high labor costs, productivity per man-hour was crucial. Schlitz had two "beer factories," both of which had 4.4 million barrel capacity and employed only 483 production workers, while Falstaff had 1,800 workers in four of its plants with a combined capacity of 4.1 million barrels. The respective production per man-year was 9,110 barrels versus 2,277 barrels. One analyst estimated that beer from Falstaff's plants cost $4.39 per barrel compared to $1.08 for Schlitz. Rumor also was that Schlitz's new North Carolina plant could produce beer and ship it 500 miles to New York cheaper than the Schlitz New York plant could produce it.

A survey reported by *Business Week* (September 13, 1969) estimated that the "big-three" brewers earned net profits of $2 per barrel, but that many regional and local brewers made no more than $0.50 per barrel.

One of the most important advantages of big brewers (for example, Anheuser-Busch, Schlitz, and Miller, plus Coors) is the premium prices they can charge: these customarily run 10 to 20 cents per six pack above the so-called popular priced beers. The premium pricing system had its origins in the 1930s when some of the stronger brewers began shipping excess capacity

---

[1] "Those Vanishing Brews," *Forbes,* vol. 107, no. 26 (May 1, 1971), p. 26.
[2] Charles Burch, "While the Big Brewers Quaff, the Little Ones Thirst," *Fortune,* November 1972.

to distant areas. The extra charge was to cover freight, and was justified in terms of quality, which was often clearly higher than that of small local brewers. However, by the 1970s it was hard to find significant quality differences between premium priced and popular priced beers, and there was no real cost difference to produce them. *Fortune* reported, for example, that the difference in cost between premium priced Budweiser and the same firm's popular priced Busch Bavarian was less than one-half cent per bottle. Shipping costs no longer justified the difference in price any more, since the majors had plants in many parts of the country.

Still, consumers were willing to pay the difference in ever-increasing numbers. The extra money helped finance new plants and large marketing expenditures which have helped keep the premium mystique alive.

The trend toward nationally distributed beer started when Falstaff expanded from St. Louis to New Orleans and Omaha in the 1930s. Schlitz and Pabst followed in the 1940s, with Anheuser-Busch joining in 1951. According to *Fortune,* the national brands were not particularly successful with their expansion plants until Anheuser-Busch introduced the systematic testing of several marketing models to determine the effects of changes in price structure, advertising expenditures, and media mix on consumer preferences. As a result of these tests, a $7 million switch from outdoor advertising to television in 1963 enabled Anheuser-Busch to introduce their Busch Bavarian brand in market after market with spectacular success. This success was later repeated with Budweiser and by other national breweries.

One technique that evolved out of these introductions was the practice of temporarily cutting the price of the national brand to induce local drinkers to try it. It was discovered that when the price differential was restored, not all the "converts" returned to the local brands. The success of this technique was attributed to a shift in purchasing habits away from local taverns and toward liquor stores and supermarkets (where it was felt that national brand images carried more weight). The same tactic was not available to local and regional brands because price cuts had not proven particularly effective in luring premium drinkers away from their brands.

In order to cope with competition from the nationals, some breweries experimented with advertising, packaging, and new products. Some of the packaging changes were particularly successful—the keg-shaped bottle introduced by Carling in 1967, and the widemouth bottle. Several local breweries turned to new "pop-flavor" beers to boost sales, but their success was considered highly doubtful. The president of a New York regional brewing firm stated that "to the best of my knowledge no new (regional) brand has been introduced since the 1930s that has made money."

Another significant area of trends in beer sales concerned packages used in the distribution of beer. Nationally, packaged beers greatly outsold draft beers. The trend away from keg draft to packaged beer has been continuing for a long time. As of 1970, packaged beer constituted almost 86 percent of the total beer sold in the United States. Among packaged beer, cans have been gaining in popularity and were estimated by the United States Brewers Association, Inc. to account for over half of all packaged beer sales. Assuming a 12-ounce standard bottle and can, the quantity of beer shipped in cans rose from 1963 to 1970—from 28,504,000 to 54,818,000 barrels. The greatest percentage increase in package shipments over the same period was concentrated in the one-way bottle, which rose from 12,313,000 barrels in 1963 to 25,031,000 barrels in 1970, for an approximate 21 percent share of market. Returnable bottles had approximately 28 percent share of the market.

Twelve-ounce containers were the most popular size, amounting to 69 percent of the total packaged beer market. However, this represented a decrease from 77 percent in 1958. Quart bottles were also experiencing a decrease in market share, accounting for only 8 percent of total packages sold. Packages which were increasing in popularity were nonreturnable bottles less than 12 ounces and the 16-ounce can. Popularity was also rising for the 10-ounce and the 14-ounce cans in certain areas.

Packaged beer pricing was generally segmented throughout the country. Imported and top-of-the-line domestic beers (for example, Michelob) held the top price strata. National premium beers (Bud, Schlitz, Miller's) were priced beneath these, but above local popular priced beers. Local or regional beers were generally priced between 11 percent and 17 percent below premium beers. (Alternately stated, premium beers sold at 13 percent to 20 percent over local beers). In most markets national, regional, and/or private brand merchandisers offered price brands selling at approximately $1 per six pack. Periodically, price promotions of normally higher priced brands were at this level also.

CONSUMER CHARACTERISTICS

It was generally thought that about half of the adult population was beer drinkers, and that 60 percent of these adults were men. Furthermore, heavy users consumed most of the beer sold in the United States. In fact, best estimates indicated that 25 percent of the male beer drinkers consumed 80 to 90 percent of the beer sold in the United States.

JBC management felt that the highest per capita usage in its market was among males between 25 and 55 with high school or less education, most of whom held blue-collar jobs. A large percentage of these heavy beer drinkers was thought to be blacks.

A breakdown of consumer expenditures for beer and ale in the United States by demographic category is presented in Exhibit 4.

The East and West Central States (comprising most of the Jackson Brewing Company marketing area) had demonstrated, according to Bloom Advertising Agency studies made for the Jackson Brewing Company, significant growth during the decade of the 1960s, outpacing U.S. growth by 1 to 2 percent. Furthermore, per capita consumption in the West South Central area surpassed the national average. The East and West South Central areas

EXHIBIT 4
Consumer Expenditures for Beer and Ale: National Average Weekly Expenditures per Family

	Dollars	*Percent*
Age of head		
Under 25	$0.45	4.7%
25–34	0.51	19.3
35–44	0.60	22.9
45–54	0.52	19.4
55–64	0.38	15.4
65 and over	0.19	18.4
Total	0.45	100.1
Family income		
Under $2,999	0.15	21.3
$3,000–4,999	0.32	20.4
$5,000–7,499	0.52	26.8
$7,500–9,999	0.65	16.7
$10,000–14,999	0.77	11.2
$15,000 and over	0.56	3.7
Total	0.45	100.1
Occupation of head		
Professionals and technicians	0.47	11.3
Managers and officials	0.43	12.8
Clerical and sales	0.48	11.7
Foremen and craftsmen	0.70	16.2
Operatives........................	0.58	15.2
All other..........................	0.23	32.8
Total	0.45	100.0
Education of head		
Grade school or less	0.34	34.7
Some high school	0.56	18.6
High school graduate	0.50	25.6
Some college......................	0.51	9.6
College graduate or higher	0.46	11.5
Geographical region		
North-East........................	0.63	27.2
North-Central	0.47	27.6
South	0.25	28.9
West	0.46	16.3
Total	0.45	100.0
Population density		
Metropolitan areas		
Central cities	0.50	34.6
Urban fringe	0.58	26.9
Other	0.46	6.1
Nonmetropolitan areas		
Urban	0.36	15.7
Rural...........................	0.23	16.8
Total	0.45	100.1
Race		
White	0.46	89.1
Nonwhite	0.39	10.9

Source: *Expenditure Patterns of the American Family*, National Industrial Conference Board, sponsored by *Life* magazine, 1965.

posted 7 percent and 9 percent per capita consumption gains, respectively, according to the Bloom Agency. Per capita consumption data for the Jackson Brewing Company marketing area is given by states in Exhibit 5.

Data concerning the behavior of JBC competitors, however, revealed that national and seminational brands were posting greater gains than the national average even though full price differentials had generally been maintained between these brands and local brands. Exhibit 6 presents an example of relative retail pricing in 1972.

Exhibit 7 presents share of beer sales by price catagory in the top ten marketing areas (called ADIs, or areas of dominant influences, a television advertising term) in which Jax was sold for the first six months of 1970. Since

HIBIT 5
Capita Malt Beverage Consumption, JBC Market Area, by States, 1966–1970 (in gallons)

State/Area	Total Population					21 Years Old and over				
	1966	1967	1968	1969	1970	1966	1967	1968	1969	1970
bama	6.7	7.3	8.5	8.8	9.6	11.8	12.8	14.0	15.2	16.4
ansas	8.2	9.0	10.1	10.6	11.6	14.2	15.4	17.1	17.7	19.2
rida	15.2	16.3	16.7	17.7	18.4	24.9	26.8	26.9	28.7	28.8
uisiana	15.4	16.1	16.4	17.3	18.8	28.3	29.6	30.1	31.2	33.6
sissippi	7.9	9.0	10.0	11.5	12.9	14.8	16.7	18.1	20.7	23.0
v Mexico	14.6	15.2	16.3	17.7	18.4	28.9	30.0	30.9	34.2	33.7
ahoma	9.8	10.3	11.2	11.9	13.0	16.1	17.0	18.5	19.3	21.0
nessee	10.4	11.1	11.9	13.1	14.3	17.7	18.8	20.1	21.6	23.7
as	17.2	18.0	19.2	20.2	21.1	30.4	31.8	33.4	35.1	36.5
t South Central	—	—	—	—	13.0	—	—	—	—	22.1
st South Central	—	—	—	—	18.6	—	—	—	—	32.0
Total	16.4	16.7	17.2	17.8	18.6	27.9	28.4	28.9	29.7	30.8

urce: U.S. Brewers Association, Inc., *Brewers Almanac 1971*, pp. 57, 59.

EXHIBIT 6
Retail Pricing Six 12-Ounce Cans, September 1972, Selected Markets,
National Versus Local Versus "Price" Brands*

Market Area	National	Local	"Price" Brands
Corpus Christi	$1.45	$1.35	$0.89
Dallas	1.39	1.35	n.a.
Houston	1.29	1.23	0.89–0.99
Jackson	1.49	1.35	0.99–1.19
New Orleans	1.35–1.39	1.24–1.29	0.97–0.99
Baton Rouge	1.39–1.41	1.29–1.31	0.99
San Antonio	1.45	1.35	0.89

n.a. = not available.
* Ten-ounce national brands are sold at the same price as "local" 12-ounce brands; 14-ounce brands are generally sold at the 12-ounce "local" beer price.
Source: JBC Management.

EXHIBIT 7
Share of Beer Sales by Price Category, Top Ten JBC ADIs—
1st Six Months, 1970

	Market Share	
Area of Dominant Influence (ADI)	National Price Brands	Local Price Brands
Rio Grande Valley	16%	84%
San Antonio	23	77
Corpus Christi	25	75
New Orleans...............	38	62
Austin	41	59
Houston	42	58
Waco/Temple	50	50
Shreveport	62	38
Baton Rouge	63	37
Dallas	77	23
Jackson	82	18

Source: Bloom Advertising survey submitted to JBC.

then, there has been a small but steady gain in share for national price beers throughout every ADI.

It was apparent that national versus local brand performance varied greatly within the Texas-Louisiana-Mississippi marketing area. However, no complete marketing study was available for analyzing various segments. The exhibits which follow represent the best information (in bits and pieces) that could be used in 1972 to devise a marketing plan. The information ranges from highly reliable (1970 government census statistics) to sketchy data of uncertain validity (demography of Jax drinkers). Exhibit 8 deals with population demographics for Louisiana, Mississippi, and Texas. Exhibit 9 deals with local versus national brand performance for these key states. Exhibit 10 presents the results of a consumer preference survey of the brand of beer liked most in the New Orleans area in 1972, and Exhibit 11 presents estimates of demographics of beer drinkers in the Jax marketing area.

BEER CHARACTERISTICS—PRODUCT VERSUS IMAGE

In general, beer was considered to be a taste differentiable product by most consumers: that is to say, many beer drinkers had strong brand preferences. Brewmasters went to great length to secure proper hops, barley, rice, corn, and so on, and earned a reputation on their ability to produce the consistent taste for which their beer was known. At the same time, market research taste tests consistently demonstrated little if any ability on the consumer's part to differentiate beers. One such test reported by Ralph I. Allison and Kenneth P. Uhl concluded:

> Participants, in general, did not appear to be able to discern the taste differences among the various beer brands, but apparently labels, and their associa-

EXHIBIT 8

A. Population Demographics for Louisiana

Area	Total Population	Percent Nonwhite	Percent Under 18	Percent 18–64	Percent Over 65
			General Characteristics		
State	3,641,306	30.2%	38.1%	53.5%	8.4%
Urbanized areas	1,703,126	31.4	36.5	55.5	8.0
Central city	1,142,809	38.7	34.7	55.7	9.6
Urban fringe	560,317	16.4	40.2	55.0	4.8
Rural	1,235,156	28.7	41.0	50.3	8.7
Baton Rouge	285,167	29.0	36.9	57.0	6.0
New Orleans	1,045,809	31.4	36.6	55.1	8.3
Shreveport	294,703	33.2	37.3	53.4	9.4

Education (Percentage: Persons 25 Years or Older)

Color	No School	Elementary School 1–4 Years	Elementary School 5–8 Years	High School 1–4 Years	College 1–4 Years	College 5 or More Years
White	2.7%	5.8%	22.3%	38.1%	16.8%	4.3%
Nonwhite	7.3	18.8	34.4	32.1	6.0	1.5

Income	Total Percent	Percent White	Percent Nonwhite
		Family Income	
Less than $2,000	11.7%	7.5%	24.1%
$ 2,000–$ 3,999	14.2	10.1	25.7
4,000– 5,999	13.6	11.8	18.7
6,000– 7,999	13.8	14.3	12.6
8,000– 9,999	13.1	14.9	7.8
10,000– 14,999	20.8	25.3	8.1
15,000– 24,999	9.9	12.4	2.6
25,000 and over	2.9	3.8	0.5
Median income	$7,530	$8,820	$4,021

Source: *1970 Census of the Population*, U.S. Department of Commerce.

EXHIBIT 8 *(continued)*

B. Population Demographics for Mississippi

			General Characteristics		
Area	*Total Population*	*Percent Nonwhite*	*Percent Under 18*	*Percent 18–64*	*Percent Over 65*
State	2,216,912	37.2%	38.1%	51.9%	10.0%
Urbanized areas	320,592	28.0	36.5	56.6	6.8
Central city	243,245	31.2	34.4	57.8	7.8
Urban fringe	77,347	17.8	43.1	53.0	4.0
Rural	1,230,270	39.7	39.7	49.8	10.6
Biloxi-Gulfport	121,601	18.9	35.8	57.5	6.7
Jackson	258,906	37.4	37.0	55.1	7.9

Education (Percentage: Persons 25 Years or Older)

		Elementary School		High School	College	
Color	*No School*	*1–4 Years*	*·5–8 Years*	*1–4 Years*	*1–4 Years*	*5 or More Years*
White	1.2%	4.0%	20.4%	52.5%	18.5%	3.4%
Nonwhite	6.2	22.3	39.5	25.9	5.3	1.0

	Family Income		
Income	*Total Percent*	*Percent White*	*Percent Nonwhite*
Less than $2,000	16.6%	9.9%	32.3%
$ 2,000–$ 3,999	17.2	12.4	28.4
4,000– 5,999	15.7	14.8	17.9
6,000– 7,999	14.6	16.5	10.2
8,000– 9,999	11.3	13.9	5.2
10,000– 14,999	16.4	21.4	4.6
15,000– 24,999	6.4	8.8	1.0
25,000 and over	1.8	2.5	0.3
Median income	$6,071	$7,578	$3,209

Source: *1970 Census of the Population*, U.S. Department of Commerce.

EXHIBIT 8 (concluded)

C. Population Demographics of Texas

			General Characteristics		
Area	Total Population	Percent Nonwhite	Percent Under 18	Percent 18–64	Percent Over 65
State	11,196,730	13.2%	35.7%	55.4%	8.9%
Urbanized areas	6,917,345	14.4	36.4	56.6	7.0
Central city	5,386,628	17.4	35.8	56.5	7.8
Urban fringe	1,530,717	4.1	38.6	57.0	4.4
Rural	2,275,784	10.6	35.2	52.5	12.3
Dallas	1,555,950	16.7	35.6	57.2	7.2
Fort Worth	762,086	11.4	35.3	57.1	7.6
Houston	1,985,031	20.0	37.1	56.9	6.0
San Antonio	864,014	8.0	37.7	54.6	7.7

Education (Percentage: Persons 25 Years or Older)

		Elementary School		High School	College	
Color	No School	1–4 Years	5–8 Years	1–4 Years	1–4 Years	5 or More Years
White	3.0%	5.6%	20.0%	47.7%	19.0%	4.7%
Nonwhite	3.4	11.2	28.6	35.7	8.7	1.5

Family Income

Income	Total Percent	Percent White	Percent Nonwhite
Less than $2,000	7.4%	6.4%	15.8%
$ 2,000–$ 3,999	11.7	10.6	20.6
4,000– 5,999	13.1	12.3	19.4
6,000– 7,999	14.2	13.9	16.1
8,000– 9,999	13.8	13.7	11.5
10,000– 14,999	23.4	24.8	12.4
15,000– 24,999	12.7	13.9	3.6
25,000 and over	3.8	4.2	0.6
Median income	$8,490	$8,930	$5,392

Source: *1970 Census of the Population*, U.S. Department of Commerce.

EXHIBIT 9
Local Versus National Brand Performance Key States—1969 versus 1970 (8 Months)

	Barrels (000)		Percent Change	Share of Market		Percent Change
Major Brands	1969	1970		1969	1970	
Texas						
Budweiser	589	696	+18%	12.6%	14.3%	+14%
Coors	435	492	+13	9.3	10.1	+ 9
Miller	170	193	+15	3.6	4.0	+11
Schlitz	971	1,216	+25	20.7	25.0	+21
Jax	366	354	− 3	7.8	7.3	− 6
Falstaff	564	457	−19	12.0	9.4	−22
Lone Star	786	741	− 6	16.8	15.3	− 9
Pearl	802	707	−12	17.7	14.6	−18
Louisiana—7 months only						
Budweiser	214	242	+13%	17.7%	19.5%	+10%
Miller	47	68	+46	3.8	5.5	+45
Schlitz	366	376	+12	27.8	30.3	+ 9
Pabst	26	17	−35	2.1	1.3	−38
Jax	157	155	− 1	12.9	12.5	− 3
Dixie	132	135	+ 2	10.9	10.8	− 1
Falstaff	223	192	−14	18.4	15.5	−16
Old Milwaukee	7	11	+59	.6	.9	+50
Pearl	44	34	−22	3.6	2.8	−22
Mississippi						
Budweiser	162	196	+21%	29.4%	32.0%	+ 9%
Miller	24	21	−13	4.4	3.4	−23
Schlitz	183	230	+25	33.3	37.6	+13
Jax	29	25	−14	5.3	4.2	−21
Falstaff	60	43	−29	10.9	7.1	−35
Pabst	28	28	− 1	5.0	4.6	− 8
Pearl	25	23	−10	4.5	3.7	−18
Old Milwaukee	33	39	+18	5.9	6.3	+77

Source: Bloom Advertising study submitted to JBC.

EXHIBIT 10
Consumer Preference Survey of New Orleans Residents, 1972

Sample Characteristics

	White		Nonwhite		Total	
	No.	Percent	No.	Percent	No.	Percent
Race						
White	739	100.0%	—	—	739	73.9%
Nonwhite	—	—	261	100.0%	261	26.1
Total	739	100.0%	261	100.0%	1,000	100.0%
Age						
Under 40	344	46.6%	139	53.3%	483	48.3%
40 and over	395	53.4	122	46.7	517	51.7
Total	739	100.0%	261	100.0%	1,000	100.0%
Sex						
Male	106	14.3%	36	13.8%	142	14.2%
Female	633	85.7	225	86.2	858	85.8
Total	739	100.0%	261	100.0%	1,000	100.0%
Education						
High school or less ...	427	57.7%	217	83.1%	644	64.4%
More than high school	295	39.9	35	13.4	330	33.0
Other and no answer	17	2.4	9	3.5	26	2.6
Total	739	100.0%	261	100.0%	1,000	100.0%
Income (per year)						
Under $7,000	'239	32.4%	187	71.6%	426	42.6%
$7,000 and over	470	63.7	67	25.7	536	53.6
Other (retired and unemployed)	30	3.9	7	2.7	38	3.8
Total	739	100.0%	261	100.0%	1,000	100.0%

Usage (July 1972)

	No.	Percent
Families who buy beer	652	65.2%
Families who do not buy beer	348	34.8
Total	1,000	100.0%
Families who bought in the last seven days	441	67.6%
Families who use but did not buy in the last seven days	211	32.4
Total	652	100.0%

EXHIBIT 10 *(continued)*

Brand Share

Combined home share (July, 1972–New Orleans, Louisiana)

	1971		1972		
	July	*October*	*January*	*April*	*July*
Budweiser	10.8%	8.9%	10.2%	11.2%	10.9%
Ballantine..............	*	6.7	6.5	5.3	5.6
Pearl	1.1	0.3	0.3	0.3	0.3
Dixie	18.5	21.2	23.7	24.2	23.5
Falstaff	18.2	18.8	16.7	15.6	13.3
Jax and Jax Draft	14.4	14.6	10.0	12.8	12.5
Fabacher Brau	*	0.7	0.3	0.4	1.4
Miller	3.3	2.6	4.5	3.6	3.5
Old Milwaukee	*	2.6	4.2	3.4	7.8
Regal	1.4	1.1	0.4	0.3	0.3
Schlitz	13.5	16.7	15.7	16.7	13.7
Others and no answer ..	18.8	5.7	7.5	6.2	7.2
Total	100.0%	99.9%	100.0%	100.0%	100.0%
	N = 724	N = 718	N = 689	N = 756	N = 773

Home brand share by age: White

	Under 40†		Over 40‡		Total§	
	No.	*Percent*	*No.*	*Percent*	*No.*	*Percent*
Budweiser	50	16.8%	22	8.1%	72	12.7%
Ballantine	35	11.8	3	1.1	38	6.7
Dixie	78	26.3	87	32.2	165	29.1
Falstaff	21	7.1	33	12.2	54	9.4
Jax and Jax Draft	30	10.1	39	14.4	69	12.2
Fabacher Brau	4	1.3	6	2.2	10	1.8
Miller	5	1.7	14	5.3	19	3.4
Old Milwaukee	22	7.4	19	7.0	41	7.2
Schlitz	31	10.4	15	5.6	46	8.1
Others and no answer	21	7.1	32	11.9	53	9.4
Total	297	100.0%	270	100.0%	567	100.0%

EXHIBIT 10 *(continued)*

Home brand share by age: Nonwhite

	Under 40[II]		Over 40#		Total[¶]	
	No.	Percent	No.	Percent	No.	Percent
Budweiser	8	6.5%	4	4.8%	12	5.8%
Ballantine	5	4.1	1	1.2	6	2.9
Dixie	6	4.9	10	12.0	16	7.8
Falstaff	21	17.1	28	33.8	49	23.8
Jax and Jax Draft ...	18	14.6	9	10.8	27	13.1
Fabacher Brau	1	0.8	—	—	1	0.5
Miller	7	5.7	1	1.2	8	3.9
Old Milwaukee	10	8.1	9	10.8	19	9.2
Schlitz	43	35.0	18	21.8	61	29.6
Others and no answer	4	3.2	3	3.6	7	3.4
Total	123	100.0%	83	100.0%	206	100.0%

Brand share by income (percent)

	White		Nonwhite	
	Under $7,000	Over $7,000	Under $5,000	Over $5,000
Budweiser	15.4%	12.1%	4.5%	7.7%
Ballantine	6.3	6.9	1.8	4.5
Pearl	—	0.3	0.9	—
Dixie	26.6	29.9	6.4	10.0
Falstaff	14.7	7.6	26.4	18.9
Jax and Jax Draft	16.1	10.8	15.5	10.0
Fabacher Brau	0.7	1.9	—	1.1
Miller	4.9	2.9	3.6	4.5
Old Milwaukee	2.8	8.4	8.2	11.1
Regal	0.7	—	0.9	—
Schlitz	5.6	9.1	29.1	30.0
Others and no answer	6.2	10.1	2.7	2.2
Total	100.0%	100.0%	100.0%	100.0%
	N = 143	N = 407	N = 110	N = 90

EXHIBIT 10 *(concluded)*

Brand share by education (percent)

	White		Nonwhite	
	High School or Less	More than High School	Completed Grammar School	High School or More
Budweiser	13.6%	11.3%	6.4%	6.3%
Ballantine	6.8	6.8	2.1	3.9
Pearl	—	0.4	—	0.8
Dixie	27.2	32.7	10.6	6.3
Falstaff	12.6	6.1	31.9	20.5
Jax and Jax Draft	14.2	8.9	10.6	14.2
Fabacher Brau	1.3	2.3	—	0.8
Miller	2.6	4.0	—	4.7
Old Milwaukee	6.8	7.3	8.5	9.4
Regal	0.3	—	2.1	—
Schlitz	7.8	8.5	23.5	30.7
Others and don't know	6.8	11.7	4.3	2.4
Total	100.0%	100.0%	100.0%	100.0%
	N = 309	N = 248	N = 47	N = 127

Media Research

Beer commercials mentioned in response to:	*Frequency*

Do you have a favorite TV commercial or one
   that you particularly like?

Dixie	27
Budweiser	7
Falstaff	5
Jax	1
Old Milwaukee	1

Can you think of any TV commercial that you particularly
   dislike?

Jax, Fabacher	2
Falstaff	1

Source: Study conducted for JBC by Gordon L. Joseph and Associates.
* Included in others.
New Orleans SMSA population estimate 1970:
   † 485,000
   ‡ 244,000
   § 729,000
   ‖ 233,000
   # 75,000
   ¶ 308,000

EXHIBIT 11
Demographics of Beer Drinkers in JBC Marketing Area

Jax Drinkers (N = 97)	Percent	Other Adult Beer Drinkers (N = 92)	Percent
Age		Age	
21–29	26.8%	21–29	51.6%
30–39	34.0	30–39	30.1
40–49	12.4	40–49	17.2
50–59	6.2	50–59	1.1
60 and over	1.0	60 and over	—
No answer	19.6		
Weekly beer consumption (cans)		Weekly beer consumption (cans)	
1– 5	8.2%	1– 5	41.9%
6–10	14.4	6–10	25.8
11–15	16.5	11–15	9.7
16–20	14.4	16–20	9.7
Over 20	25.8	Over 20	12.9
No answer	20.7		
Favorite beer		Favorite beer	
Lone Star	24.7%	Budweiser	19.4%
Jax	20.6	Pearl	18.3
Schlitz	14.4	Falstaff	14.0
Pearl	8.2	Schlitz	11.8
Falstaff	7.2	Lone Star	11.8
Miller	3.1	Dixie	9.7
Other	2.1	Jax	2.1
No answer	19.7	Other	8.6
		No Answer	4.3

Source: Study submitted to JBC by Gordon L. Joseph and Associates.

tion, did influence their evaluations. In other words, product distinctions or differences, in the minds of the participants, arose primarily through their receptiveness to the various firms' marketing efforts rather than through perceived physical product differences. Such a finding suggested that the physical product differences had little to do with the various brands' relative success or failure in the market (assuming the various physical products had been relatively constant). Furthermore, this elimination of the product variable focused attention on the various firms' marketing efforts, and, more specifically on the resulting brand images.[3]

As of 1972, there still existed conflicting opinions as to abilities to differentiate different beers of various types.

ADVERTISING EXPENDITURES

Because image and the power of advertising to effect that image was considered important in the success of beer merchandising, advertising

---

[3] Ralph I. Allison and Kenneth P. Uhl, "Influence of Beer Brand Identification on Taste Perception," *Journal of Marketing Research,* August 1964.

played an important part in the brewer's marketing mix. Both the Joseph Schlitz Brewing Company and Anheuser-Busch, Inc. were among the top 100 national advertisers. *Advertising Age* estimates for selected major brewers' national sales, advertising, and advertising costs per barrel for 1965–71 are given in Exhibit 12. Exhibit 13 gives media expenditures by brand for the period July 1969 to June 1970 for selected major Jax marketing areas.

COMPANY BACKGROUND

The Jackson Brewing Company was incorporated in 1890 and began its operations in New Orleans, Louisiana. It is the only New Orleans brewery to

EXHIBIT 12
Advertising Costs by Brand

Brewer	1971	1970	1969	1968	1967	1966	1965
Anheuser-Busch							
Barrels sold in millions..	24.3	22.2	18.7	18.4	15.5	13.6	11.
Ad expenditure (000s) ...	$23,715	$18,687	$16,057	$14,610	$16,981	$13,367	$16,36
Ad cost per barrel	$ 0.98	$ 0.84	$ 0.86	$ 0.79	$ 1.10	$ 0.98	$ 1.3
Schlitz							
Barrels sold in millions .	16.7	15.1	13.7	11.6	10.2	9.5	8.
Ad expenditure (000s) ..	$17,166	$16,704	$16,424	$17,557	$16,311	$17,163	$15,57
Ad cost per barrel	$ 1.03	$ 1.11	$ 1.20	$ 1.51	$ 1.60	$ 1.81	$ 1.8
Coors							
Barrels sold in millions .	8.5	7.3	6.4	5.3	4.6	4.0	3.
Ad expenditure (000s) ..	$ 1,863	$ 1,762	$ 1,021	$ 786	$ 1,217	$ 727	$ 26
Ad cost per barrel	$ 0.22	$ 0.24	$ 0.16	$ 0.15	$ 0.26	$ 0.18	$ 0.0
Miller							
Barrels sold in millions .	5.2	5.2	5.2	4.9	4.6	4.2	3.
Ad expenditure (000s) ..	$13,468	$10,928	$ 9,483	$ 8,901	$ 8,829	$ 7,564	$ 5,84
Ad cost per barrel	$ 2.59	$ 2.10	$ 1.82	$ 1.83	$ 1.90	$ 1.82	$ 1.5
Falstaff							
Barrels sold in millions .	5.2	5.4	6.2	6.3	6.6	7.0	6.
Ad expenditure (000s) ..	$ 6,324	$ 8,137	$ 6,565	$ 8,467	$ 8,337	$11,769	$12,93
Ad cost per barrel	$ 1.22	$ 1.51	$ 1.06	$ 1.34	$ 1.26	$ 1.68	$ 2.0
Ballantine							
Barrels sold in millions .	2.2	2.2	2.9	3.1	3.6	3.8	4.
Ad expenditure (000s) ..	$ 3,168	$ 3,515	$ 2,317	$ 2,570	$ 5,146	$ 6,559	$ 6,32
Ad cost per barrel	$ 1.44	$ 1.60	$ 0.80	$ 0.83	$ 1.40	$ 1.73	$ 1.8
Pearl							
Barrels sold in millions .	1.7	1.7	1.9	1.8	1.8	1.8	1
Ad expenditure (000s) ..	$ 2,160	$ 2,671	$ 1,657	$ 2,766	$ 3,411	$ 3,010	$ 2,48
Ad cost per barrel	$ 1.27	$ 1.57	$ 0.87	$ 1.54	$ 1.90	$ 1.67	$ 1.4
Lone Star							
Barrels sold in millions .	1.1	1.1	1.2	1.2	1.2	1.3	1
Ad expenditure (000s) ..	$ 1,001	$ 624	$ 618	$ 414	$ 712	$ 1,129	$ 1,09
Ad cost per barrel	$ 0.91	$ 0.57	$ 0.52	$ 0.35	$ 0.59	$ 0.87	$ 0.9
Jackson Brewing (Jax)							
Barrels sold in millions .							1
Ad expenditure (000s) ..			(comparable figures not available)				$ 1,08
Ad cost per barrel							$ 0.9

Source: *Advertising Age*, October 30, 1972.

EXHIBIT 13
Media Expenditure by Brand by ADI, July 1969–June 1970 ($000s)

Area	Total All Brands	Schlitz	Budweiser	Jax	Falstaff	Pearl	Lone Star	Dixie
Alabama								
Mobile-Pensacola	$ 505	$ 89	$ 72	$ 67	$ 79	—	—	$ 7
Louisiana								
Baton Rouge	320	51	45	52	32	$ 16	—	37
Lafayette	253	46	37	57	26	16	$ 3	23
New Orleans..........	1,356	141	148	215	251	12	—	355
Shreveport	684	118	83	87	46	86	23	—
Other	439	46	66	75	34	42	12	—
Mississippi								
Gulfport-Biloxi	95	12	7	5	15	—	—	9
Hattiesburg	89	8	12	13	10	—	—	10
Jackson	318	51	63	56	24	5	—	—
Other	189	26	23	18	28	—	—	—
Oklahoma								
Ada-Ardmore	85	14	6	15	4	8	5	—
Oklahoma City	660	119	66	45	41	—	21	—
Texas								
Austin	496	59	62	54	39	85	75	—
Corpus Christi	351	44	29	55	40	50	58	—
Dallas-Ft. Worth	3,102	393	253	340	372	477	230	—
Houston	2,888	400	235	377	313	436	339	—
Rio Grande Valley	324	30	24	37	64	66	43	—
San Antonio	1,352	158	89	173	211	273	172	—
Other	2,023	324	213	223	204	268	130	—

Source: Company records.

operate continuously since that time. The prohibition era only saw the shifting of operations from beer to near beer and soft drinks, rather than the closing of the brewery.

In 1890, it employed 56 people, its plant covered 64,900 square feet, and it produced 50,000 barrels of beer. In 1972, it was still a one-plant operation, having an annual capacity of 1,350,000 barrels and employing over 500 people.[4]

Since the early 1900s, JBC had been a family financed and operated firm. After four generations, the Fabacher family sold the company on December 9, 1970, to JBC Corporation, a Delaware holding company whose majority stockholder, Mr. James Howard, was the president of Meister Brau in Chicago.[5] In 1972, the Miller Brewing Company showed an active interest in acquiring JBC and moving it to another state. However, in July 1972, Ben D. Sisson, chairman of the board of the Jackson Brewing Company, purchased all of the stock of the brewery and announced that he would keep it in metropolitan New Orleans.

---

[4] One barrel of beer contains 31 gallons, or approximately 13.78 cases of 24 12-ounce bottles.
[5] Meister Brau is a local beer sold in the Chicago area.

SALES TRENDS

Sales of Jax beer had been declining since 1965, with the exception of 1969, and the second quarter of 1972. Current sales levels were almost down to those of 20 years previously. On an index basis, for example, sales had peaked twice in 1957 and 1965 at about 115 percent of 1954 levels but were currently at only 78 percent of 1954 volume.

Recent trends were not encouraging in spite of the improved second quarter of 1972. Case volume for the 12 months ending August 1972 was down 9.7 percent from the corresponding period ending August 1971.

Exhibit 14 gives case sales of Jax by month, with totals from 1967–72. With some exceptions, the declining sales trend was occurring throughout the Jax marketing area. Exhibits 15 and 16 give a geographical breakdown of the most recent sales trends for Jax beer.

DISTRIBUTION

· The JBC marketing area comprised most of the South Central portion of the United States and included Alabama, Arkansas, Florida, Louisiana, Mississippi, New Mexico, Oklahoma, Tennessee, and Texas. The three-state area of Texas, Louisiana, and Mississippi accounted for over 95 percent of case sales in 1972.

Outlets for beer were grouped into two major catagories: (1) on-premise; and (2) off-premise. On-premise outlets included bars, restaurants, and nightclubs. Off-premise outlets consisted of supermarkets, convenience stores, and package stores.

EXHIBIT 14
Jax and Jax "Genuine Draft" Packaged Beer Case Sales Volume 1967–1972 (000s)

Month	1967	1968	1969	1970	1971	1972
January	989	856	809	770	726	629
February	934	940	823	801	801	756
March.....................	1,216	964	852	913	886	837
April	1,149	1,102	991	989	795	898
May	1,367	1,190	1,059	1,020	758	778
June	1,395	1,082	1,172	1,091	1,010	969
July	1,199	1,176	1,247	1,123	938	739
August	1,282	1,164	1,144	1,042	925	834
September	1,087	944	1,035	975	846	771
October	1,091	1,010	1,028	904	814	—
November	1,025	886	862	846	800	—
December	1,002	927	989	933	785	—
Total	13,736	12,241	12,011	11,407	10,084	—
January–September Total ...	10,618	9,418	9,132	8,724	7,685	7,211

Source: Company records.

EXHIBIT 15
JBC Geographical Sales Trends, January–August, 1969–1972*

	Case Sales (000s)			
Area	1969	1970	1971	1972
Alabama	131	107	84	89
Arkansas	58	47	40	32
Florida	23	20	22	23
Louisiana				
New Orleans.........	601	602	582	654
Rest of state	1,798	1,709	1,402	1,337
Mississippi	390	342	283	254
New Mexico	3	1	1	0
Oklahoma	176	131	81	53
Tennessee.............	0	0	0	19
Texas	4,919	4,790	4,503	4,339
Totals	8,099	7,749	6,998	6,800

* Includes Jax, Fabacher Brau, private labels, and small amounts of malt liquors.
and so on, distributed but not brewed by JBC.
Source: Company records.

EXHIBIT 16
Selected Jax Sales by Area of Dominant Influence

		Cases Sold, January–August	
State	Area of Dominant Influence	1970	1969
Alabama	Mobile-Pensacola	157,211	183,953
Louisiana	Baton Rouge	372,777	368,978
	Lafayette	224,553	247,024
	New Orleans	1,035,286	1,034,685
	Shreveport	368,262	426,565
Mississippi	Gulfport-Biloxi	76,261	85,144
	Hattiesburg	42,931	44,199
	Jackson	139,490	171,438
Oklahoma	Ada-Ardmore	26,621	32,246
	Oklahoma City	46,504	61,808
Texas	Austin	270,967	286,605
	Corpus Christi	616,964	617,658
	Dallas-Ft. Worth	446,861	507,856
	Houston	1,446,389	1,532,803
	Lower Rio Grande	203,843	168,555
	San Antonio	1,311,097	1,211,381

Note: Area of dominant influence was a term used to describe marketing areas covered by major television stations.
Source: Company records.

Sales of beer for on-premise consumption had been steadily declining during the past decade. It was estimated by company officials that sales for off-premise consumption would account for at least 70 percent of total sales during 1972.

Historically, Jax had enjoyed good distribution. In many instances it had better shelf availability than movement warranted. The 1970 Jax distribution penetration in its major marketing area is given in Exhibit 17.

EXHIBIT 17
Percent of Retail Accounts Serviced by Jax

State	Off-premise	On-premise
New Orleans............	100%	100%
Louisiana	100	100
Mississippi	88	81
Texas	99	95
Oklahoma	91	82
Alabama	77	71

Source: Company records.

PACKAGING

JBC packaged its beer in a variety of containers. Jax package trends are illustrated in Exhibit 18. Following the national trend toward off-premise consumption, sales had increased for six pack cans (12 ounce), one-way bottles (12 ounce), and 16-ounce cans. On-premise sixes such as the export bottle and partition cans continued to decline.[6]

EXHIBIT 18
Package Trends for Jax Beer*, January–May, 1969–1972 (in thousands of cases)

Package Type	1969	1970	1971	1972
24/12-ounce "Export" (returnable bottles).....	1,351	1,176	945	767
24/12-ounce can partitions (not six packs).....	508	453	363	257
4/6 cans, 12-ounce (six packs)	1,431	1,566	1,582	11,842
One-way 24/12-ounce bottles................	581	625	533	494
16-ounce cans	55	59	52	48
One-way quarts	365	387	331	326
All packaged "Genuine Draught".............	224	171	38	2

* Only Jax and Genuine Jax Draught Brands. Fabacher Brau, private labels, and keg draught excluded.
Source: Company records.

---

[6] An export bottle was a 12-ounce returnable container, and partition cans were cases of loose cans (not in six pack). Both packages were primarily sold to the trade for on-premise consumption.

In Louisiana there was a noticeable trend away from the conventional 12-ounce package. (See Exhibit 19.) Most national brands had experienced considerable success in promoting a 10-ounce size in Louisiana. The national brands generally sold a six pack of 10-ounce cans at the price of "popular" priced six packs of 12-ounce cans.

EXHIBIT 19
Share of Unit Sales (percent) by Size of Package, 1969 versus 1970

Size of Package	Texas		Louisiana		Mississippi	
	1969	1970	1969	1970	1969	1970
6- to 8-ounce......	—	—	5.6%	4.9%	0.8%	2.3%
10-ounce.........	—	—	35.8	39.7	3.9	5.9
12-ounce.........	98.0%	98.0%	51.4	47.5	63.4	59.7
14-ounce.........	—	—	0.3	.5	6.3	7.1
16-ounce.........	—	—	3.4	3.9	17.4	18.1
24-ounce.........	—	—	0.1	—	—	—
32-ounce.........	2.0	2.0	3.4	3.5	8.2	6.9
	100.0%	100.0%	100.0%	100.0%	100.0%	100.0%

Source: Company records.

In the Gulfport market, Old Milwaukee, Busch, and Falstaff marketed 14-ounce cans at the same price as competing 12-ounce cans. These brands were thought to have taken 40 percent of that market. In Texas, the situation was different because beer could only be sold in 12-ounce and 32-ounce sizes by law.

In general, there was little seasonal variation in the mix of Jax cans, one-way bottles, and quarts. Export bottle sales, however, varied very little from month to month. One exception was in south Texas where, during the harvest season, a marked increase in sales of the long-necked export bottles resulted from preferences of Mexican-American migrant workers for this type of container.

PRODUCT LINE

In addition to Jax beer (and recently Fabacher Brau), JBC had from time to time merchandised private brands or other labels. In 1965, they had introduced a packaged draught beer. While Jax Genuine Draught was apparently successful at the outset, the nationwide interest in packaged draught beers declined rapidly.

Jax keg draught beer was declining in popularity in line with nationwide trends. Because of shipping costs and other difficulties, kegs were not sold in any great number at long distances from the plant. For the first seven months of 1972, keg draught amounted to only 2 percent of JBC sales. In the New Orleans market, however, Jax keg draught amounted to 18 percent of Jax New Orleans sales. Management estimated that while Jax's share of market in New Orleans for packaged beers was approximately 10 percent, Jax had about 20 percent of the New Orleans keg draught business.

PRODUCTION COSTS

Generally, production costs were a very important aspect of breweries' competitiveness. It became a particularly difficult problem for local breweries because they lacked the efficiency of scale of the national brewers. These deficiencies were partially a function of the size of the brewery and partially a function of improved technology. The JBC plant was more efficient than some local breweries, but by no means the equal of the newer Schlitz or Budweiser breweries.

A typical cost structure for Jax 12-ounce cans is given in Exhibit 20.

EXHIBIT 20
Jax per Case Cost Structure: 4/12-ounce Can Packs

Item		Cost
Case price per 24/12-ounce cans to retailer..........		$4.65
Parish and city tax*		0.109
State tax		0.726
Federal tax		0.653
Distributor gross margin†		0.762
JBC net receipts†		$2.40
Packaging costs	$1.02	
Cans‡	$0.90	
Lids, conex, tray and miscellaneous	0.12	
Labor and processing costs§	0.15	
Beer§	0.30	
Warehousing expense...........................	0.03	
Total variable costs		$1.50
Contribution to overhead, marketing expense and profit...		$ .90

* In Louisiana, counties were called parishes.
† In New Orleans, JBC operated its own distribution system. Thus, JBC net receipts were $3.162 per case in New Orleans, $2.40 elsewhere. Costs of this distribution system are not reflected in the figures presented in this exhibit.
‡ The 1972 can contract had three categories of costs: (1) yearly fixed charge of $379,500 ($0.0876 per case at a 2 million can per week level); (2) direct charge of $33.85 per thousand cans ($0.8124 per case); (3) charge of $3 per thousand for all quantities over 2 million cans per week ($0.072 per case). The production cost of Jax cans was calculated as the sum of items (1) and (2), on a per case basis.
§ Includes all direct costs plus some semivariable processing labor and expenses.
Source: Company records.

One-way bottles cost between five and six cents less than cans, while export bottles cost more than cans, but because they were reused, on the average 20 times, the net cost to Jax was considerably below that of the cans or one-way bottles.

Out of the company's contribution margin, an average cost of 15 cents per case was spent on advertising. Also, from time to time JBC allowed its distributors temporary promotional discounts. These discounts could run up to as much as $1 per case, the burden of which was shared equally between the manufacturer and the wholesaler.

The philosophy behind discounting was to achieve increased market share, maintain production levels in slow periods, fight competitive moves, and hopefully to make profits through sufficiently increased volume to out-weigh the reduced gross margin. Exhibit 21 is a request for sales promotion allowance which was currently in use at JBC.

Starting in the summer of 1971, extensive discounting of Jax beer took place, with the deepest discounting occurring from January to June 1972. The sales manager had estimated sales in June 1972 of 1,300,000 cases at a discount of $1 per case. In return for the discount, supermarkets generally agreed to large aisle displays, point-of-purchase materials, and a price of $0.99 per six pack to consumers. Such merchandising often resulted in a tenfold increase in sales over a comparable nondiscount period. At the same time, smaller "ma-and-pa" stores and restaurants seldom passed on such discounts to the consumer. Also, sales normally declined sharply in the weeks following the discount due to loading by the retailers. Consequently, the net increase in sales was often no more than three times normal. In June 1972, rival firms also entered into extensive discounting. Consequently, Jax sales were disappointing, leading to significantly reduced contribution. In addition, due to stocking during the sale, July sales were adversely af-fected. These results are reflected in Exhibits 15 and 16.

JBC's contracts for private label beer usually produced a 25-cent per case margin. Dick Brown thought that there might be added margin and/or a reduced price level at which marginal revenue could be produced from pri-vate label contracts due to the peculiarities of the contract with JBC's can supplier.

The can contract combined fixed charges and direct costs, the treatment of which could vary the accounting cost of private label beer. As given in the notes to Exhibit 20, the contract provided a yearly fixed cost, plus a direct cost per thousand within a maximum limit of 2 million cans per week utiliza-tion. At more than 2 million cans per week, an extra charge per thousand cans was levied.

It had been proposed that the fixed cost of $379,500 per year be charged to Jax beer, under the rule of "direct cost" in accounting, since the charge would be encountered regardless of whether or not any private label prod-ucts were produced.

Mr. Brown thought that in order to be consistent, JBC must charge the extra $3 per thousand ($0.072 per case) to private label products.

The real unanswered question for Mr. Brown was how often JBC ex-pected to incur this charge. If JBC always purchased private label cans when Jax and Fabacher Brau requirements were below 2 million cans per week, JBC could conceivably reduce overall costs for private label merchandise by not only the per case equivalent of the yearly fixed charge but also the extra

EXHIBIT 21

Request for Sales Promotional Allowance to Meet a Temporary Competitive Situation

JBC / 18			Date	
	TO BE FILLED IN BY PERSONS RECOMMENDING PROMOTION			
Distributor				Code
State	Promotion Period Beginning		Promotion Period Ending	
Product	AMOUNT OF SPA PER CASE			
	Brewery's Share		$_____	
	Distributor's Share		$_____	

SALES DATA				ESTIMATED	ACTUAL
WITH PROMOTION	1	Sales During Promotion		_____	_____
	2	Sales for_____ *Period after Promotion	_____	_____	
WITHOUT PROMOTION	3	Normal Sales During Promotion Period		_____	_____
	4	Normal Sales for___*Period after Promotion	_____	_____	

		FOR BREWERY OR DISTRIBUTOR USE			
MARGIN	5	Per Case Brewery Margin		$_____	$_____
	6	Per Case Distributor Margin		$_____	$_____
CONTRIBUTION TO PROFIT	7	Total Margin $(1+2) \times (5)$ or (6)		$_____	$_____
	8	Total Cost of Promotion (No. of Cases sold at discount × amount of discount)		$_____	$_____
	9	Total Margin With Promotion $(7)-(8)$		$_____	$_____
	10	Total Margin Without Promotion $(3+4)$ $\times (5)$ or (6)		$_____	$_____
FEASIBILITY	11	Net Gain (Loss) $(9)-(10)$		$_____	$_____
	12	Net Increase (Decrease) in Sales $(1+2)-(3+4)$		$_____	$_____

RECOMMENDED BY:	
APPROVED BY:	
* Fill in estimated period in which sales will be affected	

Note: The brewery is NOT committed to pay any portion of the cost of a promotion until the request is approved by the brewery.

INSTRUCTIONS TO DISTRICT MANAGER:

After the promotion is over, use copy 2 to report actual sales to the brewery (Lines 1 and 2). Retain copy 3 for your files.

COPY 1—ORIGINAL

charge per can in excess 2 million per week. This could result in a direct cost of production savings of almost 9 cents per case. On the other hand, if JBC was always in an "additional charge" situation, it would be able to reduce overall costs by 1.56 cents per case.

Dick Brown also wondered to what extent such reasoning could be applied to special promotions and whether there were any strategic implications for Fabacher Brau.

JBC ADVERTISING

JBC conducted a number of different advertising campaigns during the years 1960–72 which led up to the introduction of Fabacher Brau. A brief description of each is given below.

1960–65. The advertising campaign that was begun in 1960 was a radical departure from previous campaigns. The purpose of this campaign was to convey a quality image while appealing to the heavy beer drinker in a friendly, warm, and highly memorable manner. It was based on the jingle, "Premium brewed from 100 percent natural ingredients for real beer taste." A series of animated cartoons with the voices of Elaine May and Mike Nichols were developed which eventually became extremely popular. In a survey of the JBC marketing area, approximately 82 percent of the people sampled expressed a liking for these cartoon commercials. Users as well as nonusers liked the campaign. However, this brought up the question of whether the campaign was actually increasing sales. After a long run, the campaign was terminated in 1965 partially because of technical difficulties involved with Nichols and May, the agency, and Jax management, and also because Jax management thought that although these cartoons were very popular, they lacked "hard sell" and were not clearly an effective means of significantly increasing sales.

1965. Package draft beer was introduced in 1965 and two different advertizing campaigns were being run concurrently: the "Round Beer" campaign for Jax, and the "Genuine Draft" campaign. The "round beer" campaign marked the development of a new Jax advertising theme: "Round Beer Flavor . . . today's Jax has it!" The campaign was designed as a "flavor" sell based upon a new musical theme used on radio and television. However, management was not impressed nor enthusiastic about the "Round Beer" idea, and its expectations about the success of the campaign proved to be true. It stayed on the air for only three months.

The "Genuine Draft" campaign employed extensive advertising consisting of 10- and 60-second TV commercials, radio spots, newspaper ads, and sheet posters. This campaign conveyed two specific messages: the innovativeness of Jax draft beer in bottles and the convenience of being able to buy "carry-home" Jax draft beer. However, within six months, the draft beer in bottles fad largely died out nationwide.

1966. In 1966, the "Good Natured" campaign was developed. Advertising for this campaign included a combination of music and skits where a "Good Natured Jax" jingle was played alternately by popular musicians. These included Pete Fountain, Godfrey Hirsch, Ronnie Cole, and the Ramsey Lewis Trio. The skits featured "Good Natured" people placed in unpleasant situations, and Jax was the means of reversing the unpleasantness. Although management expected good results, sales data were not encouraging. So in late 1966, JBC hired a new ad agency, Rockwell, Quinn, and Wall, Inc. composed of the originators of the Nichols and May campaign who had left DCSS to form RQW.

1967. The new agency decided that the packaged draught could represent a viable, high-volume market and consequently they developed a "Genuine Draft" campaign targeted at younger people. It consisted of two 60-second and 20-second color TV commercials which featured active people and "people who make things happen," and a 60-second radio commercial featuring modern, lively music.

A "Mellow Brew" campaign geared to a somewhat older audience was also·developed. JBC had used the word "mellow" many times in its advertising prior to the 1960s. Two types of commercials were used: (1) brewery scenes that focused on the production of "Mellow Jax," and (2) scenes showing happy, active people enjoying themselves while at a hayride or other social function. JBC management was enthusiastic about this new "Mellow Brew" campaign. It thought that both the "Mellow Jax" and "Jax Genuine Draft" jingles would be very effective in reaching their prospective target audiences.

During 1967, Jax also initiated a high-intensity campaign designed to concentrate on the New Orleans beer market. Jax had been losing a share of the market in its home city, and management felt that the New Orleans market was of vital importance to the overall success of Jax. To support this effort, JBC allocated part of its advertising budget to the sponsorship of the New Orleans Saints and Dallas Cowboys football games on regional television. Jax also sponsored the radio broadcasts of the local professional basketball team, the New Orleans Buccaneers. Sponsorship of local sports events continued through 1970.

1968. The idea of "mellowness" continued to be developed in Jax advertising copy. The advertising theme for 1968 was "Jax—mellow enough to go down easy—but a man knows it's a beer." Management wanted the campaign to appeal to men (it was thought that they made the purchase choice) without alienating women. The advertising aimed at the heavy, male beer drinker by emphasizing product quality. Later research indicated that the Jax ads registered with the heavy beer drinker at a level two times higher than the average beer commercial. However, JBC wanted a more subtle approach, while still increasing the consumer's brand awareness of Jax. The agency did not produce this to JBC's satisfaction.

1969–70. In early 1969, JBC hired a new ad agency. Because of stiff competition from national and regional brands which all had an established personality for their products, JBC was now trying to establish its own identity for Jax. In response, the new agency developed the character Andrew Fabacher and attempted to establish a link between him and Andrew Jackson; $6 million was spent to help build the Fabacher image, using the theme: "If they don't have Fabacher—ask for Jax."

According to the original Bloom Agency proposal: "The execution of this unique, great, creative proposition—that Andrew Jackson was really Andrew Fabacher—directly conveys the important selling propositions: . . . by providing top-of-mind awareness of Jax brand name . . . by establishing Jax as a beer which has been premium brewed for four generations by a family whose name implies the favorable Germanic brewing tradition . . . by providing a natural opportunity for numerous pouring sequences, frequent package identification, and considerable hard sell in the audio."

For the first year, five 60-second, two 30-second, and four 20-second commercials were planned. The agency suggested that Jax concentrate 93 percent of its 1969 budget (compared to 71 percent in 1968) in TV; 80.4 percent was to be spot television, and 12.6 percent was to go for sponsoring ads during NFL football games. Co-op advertising would be held at 3.5 percent of the budget and about 2 percent each would be used for outdoor and ethnic advertising. Hence, the major change for 1969 would be the elimination of radio completely (it had 23.3 percent of the 1968 budget). To increase the impact of the campaign, Jax was to advertise only in those markets where industry volume and Jax sales were high. Thus, Bloom proposed to concentrate on areas which accounted for only 72 percent of the households in Jax's total distribution area, but which represented 79 percent of industry sales and 93 percent of Jax sales. This meant that in some key areas, such as Houston, Jax would be able to dominate TV beer advertising. It was further recommended that Jax use heavy flights of commercials to make sure that the television viewer could not avoid being acutely aware of the Jax advertising message.

A variety of distributor, point of purchase, trade directed materials, and public relations efforts were planned for this novel campaign. Fabacher stickers were even distributed to bartenders to paste over the Jax label to heighten the interest in the campaign. In addition, the actor who played Andrew Fabacher made enthusiastic personal appearances at distributor meetings and at colleges in the area.

Management felt that the campaign had increased Jax's association with the image of New Orleans as a fun and romantic city. In addition, it was felt to be Jax's most memorable campaign since the Nichols and May commercials of the early '60s. The local gossip about whether Jax would change its name was evidence of the effectiveness of the campaign in generating interest in Jax.

Because of the memorability and humorous elements of the campaign, management and the agency were worried about the campaign going stale. Consequently, in late March and early April 1970, a new twist was added by creating the character of Wolfgang Fabacher who was supposed to be the new brewmaster. These commercials raised the question that better taste might be due to changes in the brew, but the question was teasingly unanswered by Wolfgang's winking.

At the same time, a new package label and can design was introduced. It had a more Germanic flair and the slogan "The Fabacher Family Brew" added to the label.

With the decision to introduce Fabacher Brau as a premium beer aimed at the younger, more affluent market being captured by Bud and Schlitz, it was felt that the confusion between Jax and Fabacher Brau had to be dispelled. A final series of commercials was created in late 1970 which used Andrew to introduce Jax as "The Great American Beer." At the same time, Wolfgang was used to introduce Fabacher Brau.

Problems with the agency-client relationship and the proposed new directions for the "Great American Beer" campaign led to the suspension of TV advertising in the fall of 1971.

Except for some print and a small amount of radio advertising around Thanksgiving and Christmas, no major advertising expenditures were incurred until late January of 1972, when radio advertising was resumed and mid-February when TV was resumed. The media strategy was to use flights or waves of advertising for a number of weeks, then ceasing advertising for a number of weeks, then resuming heavy advertising. Some studies had shown this to be more effective than a consistent average level of advertising throughout the year, and Jax management agreed with this notion. The 1972 advertising budget for Jax and Fabacher is presented in Exhibit 22. The last quarter of 1971 and early 1972 were filled with uncertainty as JBC had no more than an in-house agency and was looking for a new agency to take over their advertising. It was not until January that a new agency was retained.

The new agency, Ketchum, Macleod, and Grove, Inc., prepared a new campaign based on the traditional full, hearty, taste appeal of local, non-premium priced beers. Its theme was "The Taste You Can Hold Onto," along with the slogan "the flavor and fun of a couple of beers in one." A two-handled mug was to be createed to symbolize this taste appeal. The first two commercials for this campaign were filmed in New Orleans and were initially shown in late February 1972. In all, six Jax commercials were produced for the 1972 campaign at a cost of approximately $150,000. The agency's seven Fabacher Brau commercials cost nearly $50,000 to produce, but only one was ever used.

MARKET RESEARCH: JAX BEER

Over the years JBC had conducted a number of market research surveys; one of the most intensive was conducted in 1960 and focused on the image of

XHIBIT 22

anuary 17, 1972 Plan for Advertising Budget for All Media, February 1, 1972 through anuary 31, 1973

Budget Item	February–April	May–July	August–October	November–January	All	Cost per Case†
edia						
Jax	$344.0	$387.0	$381.0	$338.0	$1,450	$0.131
Fabacher Brau	52.8	64.8‡	64.8‡	57.6‡	240‡	0.400‡
Media	396.8	451.8	445.8	395.6	1,690	0.146
oduction of Ads	80.0	110.0	5.0	5.0	200	0.017
search for Ads	12.5	—	12.5	—	25	0.002
Total	$489.3	$561.8	$463.3	$400.6	$1,915	$0.165

Media Expenditures (in thousands of dollars)

Note 1: Two Jax "Taste You Can Hold On To" commercials filmed in New Orleans area were used. One Fabacher u commercial of horse and carriage in New Orleans City Park (theme "Fabacher Brau, What a Brew. . . ." to tune "Good Old Mountain Dew") was used while awaiting new Fabacher Brau commercials which were not run due management dissatisfaction with Fabacher Brau sales and execution of the commercials. The new Jax commercials e approved by management in August 1972, and were to be aired in the fall.

Note 2: Media plan called for "flights" or "waves" of TV advertising appearances. E.g., ads were to appear in starred (*) ks only during months indicated:

February 7, 14, 21*, 28*.
March 6*, 13*, 20*, 27*.
April 3*, 10, 17, 24.
May 1, 8*, 15*, 22*, 29*.
June 5, 12, 19*, 26*.
July 3*, 10, 17*, 24, 31.

† Based on estimated sales of 11 million Jax cases and 6 million Fabacher Brau cases.
‡ Dissatisfaction with commercials led to reduction and then by July 1972 complete suspension of all Fabacher advertising.

the brand. The results indicated that Jax had a very weak, diffuse image. Moreover, in the 1930s and early 40s Jax was the leading seller among blacks, but after World War II Jax lost its preeminence in the black community largely to Falstaff. But while Jax lost the sales, it did not lose its identification of being very popular among black beer drinkers. Furthermore, a large segment of the beer-drinking populace considered Jax as a low-quality beer.

"What quality means in a beer," Mr. Thomason, JBC's director of marketing research, pointed out, "is somewhat obscure. Quality statements are usually expressed in terms of taste, or being a low-class beer rather than as references to purity standards of manufacture, for example." However expressed, on a relative-feeling-about-brand scale, Budweiser, Schlitz, and Miller consistently rated at higher quality than regional and local beers in the research JBC had conducted over the years. While Jax rated above some local brews, such as Regal, it never enjoyed a high-quality image. Follow-up surveys during the period of 1960 and 1966 indicated that even during the highly successful Elaine May and Mike Nichols advertising campaign, when consumers' feelings about Jax's advertising was consistently rated very high, the image of the quality of Jax beer did not increase dramatically.

When the new agency (Rockwell, Quinn, and Wall, Inc.) took over the account in 1967, another study was conducted in order to measure top-of-mind brand awareness among beer drinkers. The results confirmed management's fears that Jax had a weak and diffused image. Brand awareness of Jax beer was much lower than was experienced during the Elaine May and Mike Nichols campaign era. This led to a growing sense that Jax needed not only well-executed and well-targeted advertising, but something extra, something to increase memorability of the advertising and increase the recall and awareness of the Jax name. In a sense, one of the prime benefits, in management's opinion, of the Andrew Fabacher campaign was the high awareness that it gave to Jax.

FABACHER BRAU

From 1966 to 1968, JBC's market share dropped an average of 15 percent each year. In 1969, the rate of decline dropped to 8 percent and management felt that this was due to the relative success of the Andrew Fabacher campaign that started in March of 1969. Feeling that this image campaign was working, and acting on the advice of the Bloom Advertising Agency, JBC decided to develop a new beer to be introduced in 1971.

The fundamental reason for the development of the new beer was to appeal to the youth market (18–34), which JBC had never successfully appealed to previously. Since this market was also the market to which the national premium beers were appealing, it meant that JBC was going to compete directly with the premium beers.

The Bloom Advertising Agency specifically suggested that JBC develop a premium priced beer for the 18–34 age market, that the beer have a German name like most other successful American beers, and that imported hops be used in the brewing process to differentiate it from Jax and all other American beers. JBC adopted all of these suggestions. The result was Fabacher Brau, a German-named beer that was aimed at the youth market and was brewed with imported hops. Additionally, it was to be of lighter body than Jax, again in order to tailor it to the taste of younger beer drinkers.

With new management taking over control of JBC in December 1970, a controversy arose as to whether Fabacher Brau should be marketed. Old management was for it and new management was against it. Finally Ben D. Sisson, the chairman of the board, decided to produce and market Fabacher Brau in a limited area starting in April 1971. Of the 29 metropolitan markets in which JBC had some strength and all of which JBC was considering, 5 were selected for initial entry. The remaining were entered in phases.

The introduction of Fabacher Brau to distributors centered on a packet called "The Fabacher Brau Advertising and Sales Bulletin." It contained a description of the free promotional materials available to the distributors along with certain cooperative materials that JBC would provide at or below cost. It also specified the content and scheduling of media advertising to be done in each of the distributors' areas. Information distinguishing Fabacher Brau from Jax and explaining the target markets Fabacher Brau was aimed at was also provided. Generally JBC stressed to the distributors that their efforts on behalf of Fabacher Brau would directly increase their profits and indirectly make Fabacher Brau easier to sell to their customers.

The mass media advertising was done in four phases. In the first two phases television spots (30 and 60 seconds) were purchased such that each television set in use during prime time would be exposed to two commercials per week for a period of four weeks. For the remaining 22 weeks of the introductory period, three more 4-week blocks were purchased with 2 weeks between each. Newspaper advertising was used daily for the first two weeks, then every other week for the next four weeks. Space was purchased in all of the major newspapers serving a particular ADI. Radio time was used over the first 14 weeks of the introduction. Radio time was purchased on those stations that primarily appealed to Fabacher Brau's target markets.

In most areas where more than one radio station aimed at young adults (18–34), advertising was staggered so that at least one station per week was servicing the target market. The stations alternated every week. When a station that catered especially to the black population could be identified, advertising time was purchased on a less frequent basis since the new beer was intended for market segments where Jax was not already strong. However, the advertising was the same on all stations. In the third and fourth phases of the introductory campaigns, advertising on television was discontinued while the other media advertising mix remained the same.

The advertising itself accentuated the difference between Jax and Fabacher Brau. Its primary goal was to increase consumer awareness and desire for Fabacher Brau. This sharply contrasted with the traditional Jax advertising, which essentially sold the Fabacher and New Orleans traditions. Actual media expenditures were approximately as planned through August 1971.

Fabacher Brau's introduction and subsequent marketing encountered many problems. The first problem concerned the bottles. Originally Fabacher Brau was to be sold in dark green bottles to further differentiate it from Jax and to follow the European tradition of marketing expensive beers in green bottles. The manufacturer of the dark green bottles was unable to produce them properly. JBC had to decide whether to accept the improperly manufactured bottles and risk possible "light" damage to the beer, or to wait three months for the right bottles and ruin the timing of their promotional efforts. JBC decided to accept the bottles as they were and the worst possible thing happened. The beer was not properly protected from light and much of it spoiled on the shelves. Eventually most of this beer had to be recalled at a loss.

A second problem arose in relation to can size. Since the national brewers all marketed their beer in ten-ounce cans in Louisiana, Fabacher Brau was also planned to be sold this way in Louisiana. Outside Louisiana, Fabacher Brau was sold in 12-ounce cans. In fact, Texas required this by law. Unfortunately, delivery of the 10-ounce cans was held up. The pressure caused by their promotion in the surrounding ADI's where they were already selling Fabacher Brau in 12-ounce cans, forced them to market a 12-ounce can in Louisiana. This resulted in the pricing of a six-pack of Fabacher Brau between $1.35 and $1.40. Although, the price per ounce was competitive with the nationals, consumers refused to pay the $1.35 per six pack when they could get 10-ounce national brands for $1.23 per six pack.

Another problem was caused by the difficulty that JBC had in differentiating Fabacher Brau from Jax. Due to the Andrew Fabacher campaign to promote Jax, consumers became confused when Fabacher Brau was introduced. Instead of thinking Fabacher Brau was a new beer, many felt that Jax had just changed its name.

Fabacher Brau had another setback due to the declining sales of Jax. JBC had decided to drop the Bloom Advertising Agency because JBC management was extremely disappointed with the agency's new commercials. This meant that the agency's Fabacher Brau introductory campaign, then in process, was halted as of August 1971. All advertising for Fabacher Brau scheduled for the fall of 1971 was stopped. JBC had to form its own in-house agency until a new agency could be found. By the end of the summer of 1972, six, ten-second spot commercials for Fabacher Brau had been produced at an average cost of between $3,500 and $4,000 each. In addition, a 30-second marching band Fabacher Brau commercial had been produced at a cost of $27,000. Except for one commercial filmed in New Orleans City Park and the marching band commercial, management had strongly differing opinions of the commercials. None of these commercials had been aired as of August 1972 except for a modest showing of the City Park commercial during the first and second quarter of 1972. Hence the 1972 media plan was only partially carried out (see Exhibit 22).

FABACHER BRAU SALES HISTORY

Sales of Fabacher Brau was much lower than anticipated. Exhibit 23 gives the sales of Fabacher Brau by month and Exhibit 24 summarizes JBC's disappointment with the introduction by graphically representing projected and actual sales.

There were no direct records of percent on-premise and off-premise distribution of Fabacher Brau during its introduction. Information was gathered from distributors as to the degree of coverage. These reports continued only for the first six weeks because of the extensive paper work involved. From these reports, management estimated that Fabacher Brau achieved 75 percent distribution overall during its first month of introduction in those areas where the beer was introduced.

Because of the problem with the defective bottles, only cans were available at first. This meant considerable resistance from on-premise retailers (who mainly served bottles). Therefore, Mr. Thomason, director of marketing research, estimated that Fabacher Brau was really achieving 80 percent distribution off-premise but only 50 percent distribution on-premise. It was not known how these estimates varied among sales areas. While there were no quantitative figures, subjectively management felt there were some variations. Dallas, in particular, never reached any of these levels. Although the distributors' reports stopped shortly after introduction, management felt that by the summer of 1972 Fabacher Brau retained only 50 percent off-premise distribution and even less distribution in on-premise outlets (even after the bottles were available). Interest in the beer was declining and Fabacher Brau had been withdrawn from some markets. Even in the areas where it was still sold, some distributors were refusing to carry it.

Fabacher Brau was marketed in only three containers: 12-ounce bottles, 12-ounce cans and 10-ounce cans. Due to problems with the bottles and the unavailability of 10-ounce cans in 1971, 91 percent of sales were 12-ounce cans; 9 percent were bottles. In 1972, however, of all 12-ounce containers sold, two-thirds were cans; one-third were bottles. In areas where the nationals sold 10-ounce cans, Fabacher Brau was sold only in 10-ounce cans in 1972.

Three full color TV sommercials and five radio commercials were evaluated by 37 beer users selected to approximate the target audience for Fabacher Brau. Individual responses and group discussions were used. Reactions to the technical presentation, acting, and so on of the commercials were generally negative. Respondents felt some of the themes were trite, not related to the product, and in one case possibly verging on bad taste. Some respondents felt the commercials did not give enough product information, nor gave any reason to buy the product. Brand identification was weak, and attempts at humor were mostly seen as unbelievable or silly. There was, furthermore, an indication of confusion with the Andrew Fabacher commercials.

THE FUTURE

In the fall of 1972, Dick Brown, JBC's marketing administration director, had to make his recommendations. He knew that whatever the proposal, he would be faced with a variety of executive opinions. Those in favor of continuing support for Fabacher Brau argued that it represented the best way to fight the nationally distributed brands, and that with proper advertising, perhaps a following like that accorded Coors could be developed. They felt that the problems encountered during the introductions so far did not preclude the possible success of Fabacher Brau, particularly if efforts were concentrated on fewer key market areas. With this approach, a more effective allocation of promotional funds and efforts to obtain off-premise distribution could be made.

Some of those against spending additional promotional dollars on

EXHIBIT 23
Fabacher Brau Sales by Market, April 1971–August 1972, in 24/12-ounce Case Equivalents

Market	Retailers		1971						
	Off	On	April	May	June	July	August	September	October
Louisiana									
Alexandria	173	456	0	0	0	0	0	0	
Baton Rouge	436	1,160	4,259	4,333	3,440	2,380	2,259	1,618	1,0
Lafayette	971	1,006	0	0	131	157	107	69	
Lake Charles	301	437	1,667	937	611	338	278	228	1
Monroe	318	421	0	0	0	0	3,201	1,750	9
New Orleans*....	1,658	3,564	94	189	284	354	8,142	5,780	4,4
Shreveport	730	634	0	0	0	0	0	259	3,9
Texas									
Austin	329	1,045	4,036	3,381	2,978	2,491	1,910	1,656	1,0
Beaumont	530	595	0	0	0	0	0	241	5
Corpus Christi* ..	567	1,021	6,740	5,274	4,783	7,245	2,943	2,424	2,2
Dallas	1,599	2,071	0	0	0	13	10,039	6,368	6,7
Houston	2,902	4,936	16,483	15,479	14,928	12,851	9,879	7,709	6,3
McAllen	482	670	0	0	75	0	0	0	3
San Antonio	1,455	3,015	219	122	118	63	50	215	5,2
Laredo	109	125	0	0	0	0	0	0	
Trinity	54	65	0	0	0	0	0	114	4
Waco	466	890	0	0	0	0	0	175	1,6
Wichita Falls ...	307	286	0	0	0	0	0	42	
Other									
Greenwood	n.a.	n.a.	0	0	0	0	0	0	
Gulfport	291	705	0	0	0	0	1,124	1,194	7
Hattiesburg	n.a.	n.a.	0	0	0	0	0	0	3
Jackson	627	1,309	0	0	0	311	538	247	1
Meridian	96	203	0	0	0	0	0	0	
Little Rock	n.a.	n.a.	0	0	0	0	0	0	
Mobile	899	743	0	0	0	0	0	37	1,0
Total			33,498	29,715	27,348	26,203	40,470	30,126	37,6

n.a. = not available.
* March 1971 sales were 1,216 cases, of which 714 were in New Orleans, 502 in Corpus Christi.
Source: Company records.

Fabacher Brau argued that the existence of Fabacher Brau necessitated abandoning whatever image Andrew Fabacher had created for Jax. Since Jax was by far the main source of revenue, it was argued that the very existence of Fabacher Brau might be hurting the image of Jax and this could be disastrous.

The new agency did not particularly like the prospect of living with the Andrew Fabacher campaign, and had launched its "The Taste You Can Hold On To" campaign, which it considered more fundamentally sound because it stressed qualities which were deemed more appropriate for the local beer drinker.

While the new Jax campaign did not confuse Jax and Fabacher Brau, it

| 1971 | | 1972 | | | | | | | | |
No-vember	De-cember	Jan-uary	Feb-ruary	March	April	May	June	July	August	Total
1,143	964	454	340	341	267	292	424	221	223	4,669
921	879	515	433	501	519	589	598	545	748	25,620
1,032	771	281	305	175	225	160	129	421	178	4,191
155	204	178	152	56	83	50	37	90	67	5,279
871	635	885	754	249	215	297	173	136	1,338	11,470
3,360	2,135	3,054	1,857	1,953	1,870	4,388	2,310	8,545	6,738	55,470
1,685	1,143	675	847	669	600	590	372	290	314	11,363
883	767	577	989	662	644	523	501	362	282	23,688
265	172	103	136	72	60	57	49	40	27	1,787
3,951	1,512	1,161	2,066	1,286	884	1,272	1,333	1,523	5,213	51,813
5,051	4,420	2,283	2,449	2,530	2,081	3,829	1,974	1,707	1,950	51,394
7,216	5,533	4,089	3,174	3,290	4,231	3,795	3,535	3,127	2,405	124,067
1,196	565	268	407	520	397	493	176	111	97	4,633
3,025	2,375	8,243	1,346	1,221	886	774	846	792	2,047	27,578
321	185	156	174	104	73	74	60	61	55	1,263
257	260	202	176	195	177	167	197	118	125	2,469
1,065	788	478	620	553	361	449	436	299	228	7,122
37	8	8	7	7	186	0	0	0	0	346
0	0	0	0	0	18	0	12	9	0	39
550	441	239	232	248	225	219	189	168	118	5,732
762	441	229	188	174	146	139	218	103	39	2,824
122	425	238	142	122	75	40	45	36	6	2,526
0	0	0	0	0	12	4	2	1	1	20
0	0	0	0	0	16	72	53	54	105	300
535	335	235	207	194	143	173	181	81	123	3,299
,403	24,958	24,551	17,001	15,122	14,394	18,446	13,850	18,840	22,427	428,962

was not going to be easy to argue for an extensive advertising budget for Fabacher Brau on any terms, given the poor sales record of Fabacher Brau, and the growing feeling at JBC that a small regional brewery could not successfully launch a premium priced brand.

At the same time, Mr. Sisson, the chairman of the board and sole owner of the company, was concerned that traditional appeals to the older, male, heavy drinkers might deprive Jax of its future market. Consequently, Mr. Sisson was concerned about the place of women (influence on purchase choice) and youth (future heavy beer drinkers) in JBC's overall marketing strategy.

At the moment, Dick Brown was pondering whether JBC should drop the

EXHIBIT 24
Projected and Actual Sales of Fabacher Brau

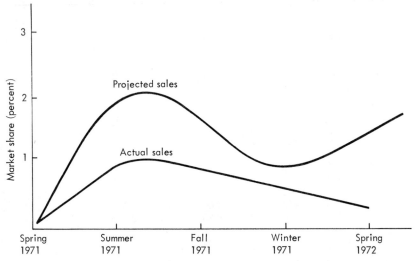

advertising of Fabacher Brau and let the brand die, or whether JBC should continue an ad campaign hoping that Fabacher Brau would finally catch on, or whether some other strategy could be employed.

Mr. Charles Thomason, director of marketing research, summarized his perspective on the problem as follows:

> Major national brewers are moving into our markets rapidly. They are taking share from everyone (except Coors, of course, and that is a special situation I wish we were in). It used to be the local brewers could beat the nationals on a price basis. Frankly, today it would be the other way around. We can't match their advertising impact, their distribution facilities are first rate, and this is an age when major brands are gaining over minor ones. What's worse is that Bud and Schlitz are making their greatest inroads with the younger drinkers who will be tomorrow's market.
>
> The Bloom agency believed that the only way to fight them was on a premium beer level. In fact, they wanted Fabacher Brau to sell at a higher price than Bud and Schlitz! We had to do that for a while at the outset in Louisiana because we only had 12-ounce cans. Even though we were priced on an equal price per ounce with Bud and Schlitz, it was a disaster.
>
> In a sense it seemed presumptuous for a little, Deep South brewery to try to compete with Bud and Schlitz at a premium beer level, and the sales figures appear to have borne me out.
>
> On the other hand, there is no question that the introduction of Fabacher Brau had real problems. We had the confusion of Fabacher and Jax, the problem with the bottles, and even with the introductory commercials. The agency went to Germany to film them, and some of the accents were so heavy that parts of them were impossible to understand.

Furthermore, as you know, we did not do a very good job getting on premise distribution with Fabacher Brau. That may have had an influence too. Given that on-premise sales are less important than off-premise sales, you still can make an argument that in order to put a new beer brand across—particularly a premium beer—sampling at a tavern or a restaurant might be important. What is more, the heavy beer drinker or the college crowd might be influenced to try the beer and have a positive impression of it if urged to buy from the bartender or even bought a round by the bartender. There is no question that we did not employ an effective strategy to promote on-premise trial by the consumer. We tried to make it available, but we didn't succeed in getting a bartender and waitresses to push it. How important that is, I don't know.

Some of our management believes that if we regroup and make a thorough effort with even heavier media penetration using commercials we really like and concentrating in only a few key markets, so that we could afford to devote that kind of energy without hurting our efforts for Jax, which is our bread and butter, Fabacher Brau might possibly have a chance to launch itself as a fighting brand against Bud and Schlitz. It certainly hasn't got a chance the way things are right now. And it isn't clear to me, given the image problems we had in the past, that it makes strategic sense to destroy all of the image building we have done for Andrew Fabacher. The very presence of Fabacher Brau means we have to separate its image from our main source of revenue, Jax. We've got to the point now where we are deliberately trying to undo everything that the Andrew Fabacher campaign did for us.

Dick Brown had talked at length with Charlie Thomason and the other members of the Jax management group both in meetings and privately. He knew the KM and G agency's feelings that the Andrew Fabacher campaign, no matter how catchy, cute, and memorable, could not be carried out indefinitely. In fact, management had agreed that the latter part of the Andrew Fabacher campaign, starting with the introduction of the character of Wolfgang Fabacher were weaker than the earlier ones. He also knew that the agency felt that a regional beer should appeal to the traditional beer drinking segment of the market and that the Andrew Fabacher campaign, in spite of its memorability, had not done this very well, certainly not as well as the agency's own—"The Taste You Can Hold On To"—campaign.

There had been a number of personnel changes since Mr. Sisson took over the brewery. More changes were likely in the future. Dick Brown knew that if he could show his ability through his recommendations at the next meeting, it might have a great deal to do with his potential to rise rapidly to a position of increased responsibility in the Jackson Brewing Company.

C. Strategy Implementation and Policy Administration

12. Alpha Electronic Systems Corporation*

ALPHA ELECTRONIC SYSTEMS CORPORATION is an engineering and production company. It enjoys a reputation among government and corporate customers as a leader in advanced electronic systems and techniques. Its present capabilities cover a wide spectrum of electronic applications and skills, ranging from satellite systems to electronic warfare. Alpha has continued to distinguish itself for advances in the state of the art and for superior quality on numerous prototype and initial operational equipment developed for U.S. government agencies. Fully 95 percent of its business is on government R&D contracts, either directly or for prime government contractors.

Alpha's success is largely due to the competence, dedication and stability of its staff. Of its 3,328 employees, over half have engineering or scientific degrees. Approximately 15 percent of these have M.S., Ph.D., or M.B.A. degrees or are working toward them. The primary resource of the company is the brain power of these men who are professional specialists in diverse fields.

The company is organized into nine engineering divisions, each oriented to a related group of technical disciplines. Each division is subdivided into departments which concentrate on a particular discipline or technique. Another division does all of the manufacturing for the engineering groups. The divisions are permitted to run their operations on a semiautonomous basis, using certain central staff services for support.

LAW AND REGULATIONS

In July 1940, the federal government initiated a series of measures aimed at integrating minority groups into the war effort. These were mostly informal requirements, but as time went on they were made more stringent by executive orders and, subsequently, by legislation and regulations. The Civil Rights Act of 1964 is the basis for the current policy and actions.

Title VII of the Civil Rights Act of 1964 prohibits employment discrimination on the basis of race, color, religion, sex, or national origin, by employers, unions, and employment agencies, with rare exceptions. State legis-

---

* Prepared by the late William R. Lockridge, formerly of Long Island University. Used with permission of Mrs. Lockridge.

lation, in some cases, added age as a discrimination factor. In 1965, the president issued Executive Order 11246, assigning enforcement on government contractors to the Secretary of Labor.

The order vests responsibility in the secretary for the adoption and issuance of rules and regulations necessary and appropriate to achieve the purposes of the act. It also provides that each government contracting agency is primarily responsible for obtaining compliance with the secretary's rules, regulations, and orders with respect to contracts entered into by that agency or its contractors. These government contracting agencies are directed to appoint compliance officers, whose jobs are to seek compliance with the order by "conference, conciliation, mediation, or persuasion."

Executive Order 11246 also provides a variety of sanctions and penalties that can be used by the secretary of labor or the contracting agency in the event that other means of obtaining compliance fail. These include the right to recommend to the Department of Justice that criminal proceedings be brought, and the right to *cancel, terminate, or suspend government contracts* for failure to comply. They also provide that *a contractor may be declared ineligible* to receive future government contracts.

In September 1968, the Secretary of Labor issued rules and regulations replacing temporary regulations adopted earlier, outlining the obligations of contractors and subcontractors. These included a requirement for an "affirmative action program" (see following). These rules and regulations now have a profound effect upon the equal employment plans and programs of Alpha and its subcontractors.

AFFIRMATIVE ACTION PROGRAM

The Department of Labor, through its Office of Federal Contract Compliance, has directed government contracting agencies to include in their agreements with their contractors numerous items relating to equal employment. A portion of the nondiscrimination clause included in Alpha's contracts reads as follows:

> The contractor will take affirmative action to ensure that applicants are employed, and that employees are treated during employment, without regard to their race, color, religion, sex or national origin.

The words "affirmative action" appearing in the preceding quotation are further defined in the rules and regulations which specify that a contractor is required to develop a *written affirmative action compliance program* for each of its establishments.

ALPHA'S EMPLOYMENT POLICY

Alpha's policy has always been to practice nondiscrimination in employment. On openings for outside recruitment, it considers all applicants and endeavors to make a selection on the basis of education and experience related to the job, without regard to color, religion, age, sex or ethnic background. On inside promotions, everyone is periodically reviewed by his supervisor and by the wage and salary committee, and advancements are made purely on merit and available openings.

But because of the high technical skill required of most of its employees, Alpha receives few applications for employment from "minority group" individuals. It has some incumbents in unskilled and semiskilled jobs, but the overall ratio is very low.

COMPLIANCE REVIEW

On July 15, 1968, two inspectors from the Defense Contracts Administration Section called upon Alpha by appointment to review its compliance with Title VII of the Civil Rights Act and Executive Order 11246. They sought to obtain specific information on the number of employees who were from "minority groups" as compared to the total. This was difficult to ascertain because Alpha kept no record on the ethnic background of its employees. However, through visual inspection and by conferring with supervisors, the company came up with the figures shown in Table 1.

"This isn't good enough," commented Herb Walker, the senior compliance officer, "You'll have to do better."

"But we've tried," responded Joe Solomon, Alpha's personnel manager. "We just can't find the qualified people."

In the discussion that followed, it developed that Walker felt the company had only been passively offering jobs to minority group personnel, but had

TABLE 1
Personnel Mix

Category	Total Personnel	Minority Personnel	Percentage
Skilled:			
Officials and managers	107	2	1.8%
Professionals	977	19	1.9
Technicians	657	32	4.9
Office and clerical	643	27	4.2
Craftsmen skilled	691	41	5.9
Subtotals (skilled)	3,075	121	3.9%
Semiskilled and unskilled:			
Operatives semiskilled	157	27	17.2%
Laborers unskilled	27	4	14.8
Service workers	69	34	49.2
Subtotals (semi and unskilled)	253	65	25.7%
Grand Total	3,328	186	5.6%

not been doing any aggressive recruiting among them and had no special training programs for upgrading them after they were brought in.

"The government's no longer willing to go along with this attitude," Walker remarked. "You've got to come up with a program of affirmative action."

He went on to explain that this meant a documented plan covering all aspects of the situation—company policy, recruiting, interviewing, training, testing, and the opening up of the channels of promotion to professional, administrative, and executive positions. He further pointed out that Alpha must establish numerical goals for future minority group employment. The company would also be required to indoctrinate and train its management and supervisory personnel in the concepts and techniques of the EEO program, set up a procedure for hearing complaints, validate the employment tests, and increase participation in outside community relations activities.

"I want to make it crystal clear," he continued, "that you'll not get by with mere 'window dressing.' This program must have real teeth in it. It must be staffed with people who have definite assignments and responsibilities. We'll want documented progress reports from time to time, and we'll conduct periodic inspections. The government will approve this activity as an allowable cost under your contracts, but it wants results, not promises."

"That's a big order," Solomon replied, "but I assure you we'll do our best. When'll you want our plan?"

"By November first—that is, for preliminary approval," Walker answered. "But we'll expect you to have your final plan in operation by the first of the year."

DEVELOPING THE AFFIRMATIVE ACTION PROGRAM

John Monroe, vice president for administration, discussed the problem with Horton Woolsey, president. "I'm afraid we can't assign this job to Joe Solomon, he's got too much to do now," he commented.

"I agree," Woolsey replied, "and we don't have anyone else we can put on it. Also, I don't think we can handle this through our regular personnel organization. It'll take full-time attention. The only way it'll work is to appoint a czar and put him in complete charge."

"Are you saying that we should go outside and recruit someone with know-how in this area?" Monroe asked.

"Yes, and I think he should be from a minority group and should report directly to me," Woolsey answered. "That'll give the position status. It'll offset any claim that it isn't impartial, and it should please the government. Moreover, he'll have an understanding of minority group problems both at the plant and community levels. We haven't anyone with that experience in our organization now."

EQUAL EMPLOYMENT OPPORTUNITY OFFICER

After considerable search and screening. Alpha hired Raymond Allison as its equal employment opportunity officer. Allison was a black, had a baccalaureate degree from one university and had done graduate work at several others. He had been deputy director of several law enforcement agencies in the equal employment opportunity field and had served as a consultant in antipoverty and nondiscrimination work in several cities.

Allison was given the assignment to develop an affirmative action program for Alpha and to implement it into action.

ALPHA'S NONDISCRIMINATION POLICY

In a meeting with Walker, Allison showed him the Alpha policy manual, which read as follows:

Nondiscrimination Policy

It is, and always has been, the policy of Alpha that employment, promotion, layoff, and salary increases are based solely on merit, ability, and seniority without regard to race, color, creed, national origin, or age of the individual.

"That's too much like 'God and mother'," Walker commented. "You've got to make specific reference to the statutes, make your affirmative action plan part of the policy, and pin down responsibility for implementing its performance."

RECRUITING ACTIVITY

When Allison reviewed Alpha's recruiting activity, he found that the company placed advertisements in the general newspapers in its employment area and sometimes in *The New York Times*. But he could find no newspapers published in the ghetto areas near the plants, and he was advised that many people in these areas did not read the general newspapers. Radio appeals had produced practically no results.

Alpha also sent bulletins to colleges throughout the country and had a professional recruiter who set up interviews on their campuses, including some predominantly black or "minority" colleges. But these were for professional-level employees and did not tap the vast number of unskilled or low-skilled minority group personnel. (Table 2)

"You've got to send someone into the pool rooms and bars and talk the language they understand, if you want them to come to you," a social worker advised. "The churches and social clubs aren't enough. The problem is to get across the message that you're really offering them something better than relief."

TABLE 2
Recruitment

"Minority" Colleges.*
    Number of minority colleges visited   6
      Howard University
      Southern University
      Tuskegee University
      Hampton Institute
      North Carolina A&T
      Tennessee A&T
    Number of campus interviews.
                                          31
    Number of prospects invited to the plant   8
    Number of offers made   6
    Number of offers accepted   0
"Regular" Colleges.*
    Number of regular colleges visited   35
    Number of campus interviews.
      (total—35 schools) . . . . (approx) 800
    Number of prospects invited to the plant . . . . (approx) 150
    Number of offers made   72
    Number of offers accepted.   18

     * Recruitment was for engineering and computer science grads.

Allison also contacted each employment agency that Alpha used and made them certify that they were interviewing and considering people from minority groups for the available jobs. "You've got to watch those agencies," Walker had warned. "They'll take the easy way out to earn their fee. Make them give you some figures and continue to monitor what they're doing."

INDOCTRINATION OF MANAGEMENT PERSONNEL

In going about the company, Allison found that most managerial and supervisory personnel knew little about the equal employment opportunity statutes and regulations. They were concerned with their regular operational assignments and gave this subject little attention. He was pleased to find that there was no outright prejudice against minority group personnel, but on the other hand, he found no particular effort to help them advance their potential. Nearly all of the supervisor positions were held by whites.

It was obvious that if the affirmative action program was ever to succeed, supervisors would have to be indoctrinated and motivated. But here he was faced with a plethora of communications media—policy manuals, the house organ, supervisors' fact sheets, special bulletins, standard procedures, seminars, discussion groups. To make any of these effective, he had to have the material well organized for consumption and use. What should he use—written communications, training sessions, or both?

COMPLAINT PROCEDURE

Alpha had no formal grievance committee or procedure. An employee had three channels through which he could appeal. The first was his own supervisor. But many preferred to avoid this route, particularly if the grievance involved the supervisor. Also, since there were no criteria, different supervisors handled similar cases differently.

The second was the suggestion-box channel. An employee could drop his gripe in the box, signed or unsigned, and it would be reviewed by a committee. But this system was primarily designed for suggestions on cost improvement and various innovations, and the committee ducked handling personal grievances so far as possible.

The third channel was the "open door" to any executive or officer of the company. In theory, any employee could walk in to the president and sound off. But the president was busy with many other things and this required an appointment. Furthermore, it irritated supervisors because an employee could go over their heads and involve them without their knowledge or any chance to defend themselves until later. Also, while it sounded good in theory, many employees just did not have the courage to go in to see a company officer about a personal matter.

If the nondiscrimination policy was going to work in Alpha, some form of procedure would have to be established to hear and resolve complaints.

NUMERICAL GOALS

As part of the program of affirmative action, Allison had to come up with some numerical goals for minority groups within the company. This created a problem because the overall level of employment fluctuated with the volume of government contracts. If he established a fixed number, the percentage ratio would go up as the total employment went down.

Allison groped for some criteria to help him fix a quota. He looked at the percentage figures of the communities in the Alpha employment area. The composite overall percentage for minority groups was 7.4 percent. He considered whether he should establish a flat figure company-wide, or whether he could make variances among the various levels of jobs. It appeared under the regulations that he could establish goals by plant location, by organizational unit (operating division), by category of skill or level of position, or by apprenticeship or trainee programs.

But he was faced with complaints that his was "reverse discrimination" against whites. As one supervisor put it, "If you've a job open and both a white man and a black man apply, with nearly equal qualifications, you'll take the black man because you have a quota to meet on him."

TESTING PROCEDURE

Alpha had no company-wide formalized testing procedure. It went on the theory that each supervisor knew best what he wanted in his men and that it was up to him to give them such tests as he deemed appropriate. Some of the tests used were generally current in the industry, but none of them had ever been "validated" as required by the order of the secretary of labor, dated September 9, 1968.

From research into the regulations, Allison determined the following guidelines applying to employment tests:

a. Title VII of the Civil Rights Act of 1964 provides that an employer may give and act upon the results of "any professionally developed ability test provided that such test . . . is not designed, intended or used to discriminate because of race."
b. A professionally developed ability test means a test which fairly measures the knowledge or skills required by the particular job or class of jobs which the applicant seeks, or which fairly affords the employer a chance to measure the applicant's ability to perform a particular job or class of jobs.
c. The fact that a test was prepared by an individual or organization claiming expertise in test preparation does not, without more, justify its use within the meaning of Title VII.
d. The sample population (norms) used in validating the tests should include representative members of the minority groups to which the tests will be applied.
e. Only a test which has been validated for minorities can be assumed to be free of inadvertent bias.

From an examination of the tests used at Alpha, Allison discovered that some had inherent defects that had never been recognized. Most were designed to test the capability of a middle-class, white employee and did not take into account the different background of a minority group employee. For example, in a college-generated test used by one department, he found the question: "What color wine do you serve with a fish dinner?"

"Don't you realize," he commented to the supervisor, "that a guy from a minority group can't afford to serve wine with any meal? And, furthermore, what has this got to do with testing his proficiency for the job?"

TRAINING PROGRAM

Aside from a "tuition refund" program which Alpha offered to all employees who desired to take outside courses on their own time to improve their skills, Alpha did little to train its employees. Few minority group employees took advantage of these courses because they were at the college level and were oriented to technical skills.

The only in-plant training was what the employee learned on his job under supervision. Allison felt that he had to come up with a definite training program for minority group apprentices. The government would pay for it, if he produced a definite program. But he could see that this would cause resentment among present employees. Why were these "outsiders" given training to upgrade their skills, when company employees were offered no similar help?

Then there was the problem of what to teach. Most of those eligible for the instruction would not have completed high school and were devoid of employment skills. Should he start with the rudiments of manufacturing activities? Could any parallel be developed for those who showed some potential for going up the office or administrative channel?

UNION PROBLEMS

"We've only one union in the company and that's with the truck drivers," Allison told President Woolsey. "It's an old contract and it doesn't have a nondiscrimination clause."

"Well, can't you get a letter or something from them saying that they won't discriminate, and that'll probably do until the contract comes up for renewal?" Woolsey replied. "After all, they're subject to the civil rights law the same as we are. We should make it part of our written policy that we'll endeavor to obtain a nondiscrimination provision in any union contract we negotiate in the future."

GUARD PROBLEM

In one of Allison's periodic meetings with the compliance officer, Walker commented, "You've got 12 security guards and all of them are white. Why don't you have anyone from a minority group? After all, these aren't skilled jobs."

Allison explained that the company policy was to hire mature men with experience. "You can't put a youngster on this job," he said. The staff was composed of retired policemen and retired private security guards. Very few minority group applicants had this kind of background, and younger men who were qualified wouldn't take the job at the pay offered.

"I still think you could get at least one minority group employee in this area if you really tried," Walker said as he departed.

ALLEGED AGE DISCRIMINATION

Harry Eggmond was an administrator in the microwave department. He was 60 and had been with the company eight years. His records were well kept, his reports were complete and on time, he kept things flowing through the department in an orderly manner, and, in general, his work was satisfactory and above average.

"I think they're discriminating against me because of my age," he complained to Allison. "I haven't had a raise in five years, yet they keep complimenting me on the fine job I'm doing and they've never once criticized anything I did. But I see all these young fellows coming in to other departments, and they all get promotions and raises while I get nothing."

"As near as I can figure," he continued, "the company knows I can't go elsewhere and get a similar job at my age. And even if I did, I don't have enough working years left to qualify for a pension. So they've got me over a barrel and I can't afford to quit. That's why they pass me up on every rate review. They've gotten their value out of me and now they just want me to die on the vine or quietly go away."

PROBLEMS WITH SEX NONDISCRIMINATION

Joe Solomon, the personnel manager, was discussing EEO problems with Ray Allison. "I'm damned if I can figure out what I'm supposed to do under this sex provision," he said. "Does it mean that I have to go to Vassar to recruit engineers, or should I be seeking male secretaries instead of the miniskirted variety? We've mostly women in the fine precision assembly areas and muscular giants of men in the sheet metal department. But what do I do if one of these Goliaths wants to apply for a delicate precision job? I can't find any regulations or ground rules on this."

"There aren't any," Allison replied.

EMPLOYEE ATTITUDES

Allison tried to get close to some of the rank-and-file employees to learn their attitudes toward nondiscrimination. It was obvious that if they didn't understand, no program he could develop would fully succeed.

The comment of Hank Barslove, a white "bull-of-the-woods" shop foreman, was typical of how some of them felt:

"This business of equal opportunity is for the birds," Hank said. "All men aren't born equal. Some have more native ability than others."

"I say a supervisor should have the right to pick who'll work for him and who won't. It's a personal relationship. If he likes the guy, they'll get along well. If he doesn't, there'll be trouble and the work will suffer."

Joe Anderson, a buyer in the purchasing department said:

> What's wrong in discriminating among people according to their skills? If you put me in a jungle, I'd probably perish in a couple of days. I've no skill on survival in primitive conditions. So what right would I have to walk in and demand a job as a safari leader?
>
> Yet all these minority group people are demanding jobs in industry here. We're an industrialized nation. They come from farming or primitive backgrounds. And in one or two generations they expect to be the equal of those who have lived for thousands of years in sophisticated society.
>
> I admit that I can't do many of the things they can. Why are they given the right to demand that we go out of our way to make a place for them? God knows, it's hard enough for a qualified white man to find a job in many places.

Andy Brown, a black stock handler, expressed his view as follows:

> The guys who work with me treat me like anyone else. We eat lunch together and I'm on their bowling team. I get raises like everyone else. But when it comes to moving up the supervisory ladder, I feel there's discrimination. The management's afraid it will upset things if it promotes a black too far. They think that the whites won't buy him as their supervisor.

Jose Rodriquez, a Puerto Rican technician, commented, "I find it in overtime. Whenever they need someone, they tap somebody else, not me. They always have some lame excuse."

"I've a discrimination complaint in my assembly department." Tony Anselmo, a shop superintendent, told Allison. "Mario Filino claims he's discriminated against because he's Italian. He says he hasn't got raises as fast as the others.

"I've looked at his record, and, in addition to being late, he's been absent three times in the last quarter without phoning in. Worse yet, inspection has rejected 5 percent of his assemblies whereas the average for his group is 2 percent.

"There are seven men in his department—four Italians and three non-Italians. Mario is above the average for the group and three of the Italians are ahead of the others. He's griping because he hasn't received a merit raise, which he doesn't deserve."

"I know. You've got to watch these cases," Allison commented. "You've got to protect yourself by keeping accurate records and being able to justify what you do. Did his foreman explain to him why he didn't get a raise on the last review?"

"Well, that's part of the problem," Anderson replied. "That damn fool foreman told him bluntly that he was no good, and that hurt his pride."

COMMUNITY RELATIONS ACTIVITIES

Allison realized that to attract minority group personnel, Alpha would have to create a favorable image in the surrounding communities. It was cooperating in the apprentice training programs, counseling services, and industry-education cooperation programs of local industry associations. But he felt that it needed to do something more direct and personal. But what— plant tours, speakers for meetings, participation in civil rights organizations? How far should the company go? Some of these were dangerous and could backfire.

13. Narragansett Bay Shipbuilding and Drydock Company (A)*

IT was a typically cold, wet, and windy New England day as Jim Butons reclined in his chair and looked out the window at the bay and the cluster of shops, dry docks and building bays near the water's edge. He well remembered those days before he became general manager, when he fought the wet, bitter cold as a young engineer on the waterfront. As he reflected on those days, it brought back pleasant memories of the camaraderie that existed in the shipyard as they built and delivered the "90-day wonder" ships during the war.

Pat Woods, his secretary, interrupted, "Bob Doyle is returning your call."

"Yes, Bob," Jim said, as he snapped back to reality. "I've been looking over the new design package with some of my management engineering people and I think we ought to have a staff meeting to discuss our strategy as it will apply to this effort. I want you there as engineering director. I would also like you to bring the managers of your design departments so we can get their feelings on reorganizing to meet this new effort. As you know, we're going to attempt to break from the traditional design approach and try what we're calling the Seaborne method. I think this presents quite a challenge, but with proper organization we should be able to handle it."

"I agree Jim, but don't you think Bill Moore should also attend to represent the shipyard, since he is director of operations?"

"You're right, Bob, especially since our ultimate product will be production-oriented drawings rather than the traditional system-oriented drawings.[1] Let's see if we can get together next Wednesday and try and brainstorm some alternatives for organizing the design effort."

"Sounds good to me, Jim. We'll do some preliminary work here and get a

---

* Prepared by Professors Louis K. Bragaw, United States Coast Guard Academy, and William R. Allen, University of Rhode Island, in collaboration with Daniel J. McCarthy and Robert Ames.

The name of the company is disguised.

[1] Production-oriented drawings sought to facilitate land-based prefabrication of entire ship sections whereas traditional system-oriented drawings emphasized the working system around which the ship would be built.

good handle on what it will take to get production-oriented results. See you Wednesday.''

COMPANY BACKGROUND

Narragansett Bay Shipbuilding and Drydock Company (NBSD) was established around the turn of the century. Although some of its first work was commercially oriented, it soon developed a close association with the Department of Defense, and the Navy in particular. Navy contracts continue to be the company's primary source of business.

The company was particularly proud of its contribution in developing ships as a major weapons system. NBSD, in fact, participated with the Navy as lead design shipyard on many ship designs. During the rapid development of nuclear ships during the 1950s and 1960s, the company had participated in a number of different innovations relating to the Navy's search for such things as optimal speeds, more effective offensive and defensive weapons systems, quietness, and other operating improvements. Out of this participation NBSD developed an extensive engineering design department that operated under the general manager almost completely independent of the rest of the shipyard.

During the mid-1960s, NBSD was invited by the Institute for Defense Analysis to participate in a program to develop a new missile system for the 1980s. This program was to be unlike anything previous, and the Institute for Defense Analysis wanted to spur competition between the Army, Air Force, and Navy for the best system. This led to a challenging and active period for NBSD's advanced engineering department as it departed from conventional approaches and tried to blaze new trails for the future. Every time NBSD conceived of a novel idea it was then dissected thoroughly by the Institute's design, economic, and threat divisions.[2] Over a period of several years numerous concepts were analyzed, including truck borne missiles proposed by the Army, airborne or flying platforms by the Air Force, and stationary undersea platforms on the Continental Shelf by Navy sources. However, in the late 1960s, NBSD was successful in winning the competition with a ship-type launch platform.

The design contract was long term and would likely provide NBSD with stable work, including construction, through the 1970s and into the 1980s. However, it was also at this time that both the Department of Defense and Congress were seeking more participation in design by contractors, with the government maintaining an overview position. This was a departure from tradition (see Exhibits 1 and 2) and was the reason that NBSD was faced with its present problem of accommodating the government's wishes and at the same time designing and constructing one of the most sophisticated ships ever built.

---

[2] The threat division would try to show how vulnerable or threatening to the safety of the United States the concept could be.

EXHIBIT 1
Traditional Ship Design Evolution

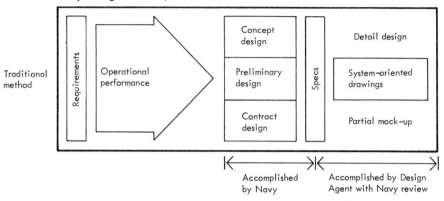

EXHIBIT 2
The Seaborne Design Method

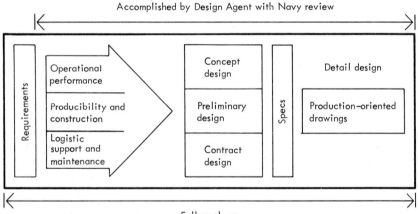

ORGANIZATIONAL PROBLEMS POSED BY THE NEW CONTRACT

In the week since Jim Butons and Bob Doyle had talked, the weather had been typically New England—unpredictable. While spirits had risen with the prediction of a clear day, it had been snowing since late Tuesday night. Jim Butons thought how lucky he had been to schedule the meeting for midmorning since this would give everyone a chance to fight the snow and get to work.

Dan Hall, manager of advanced engineering, met Jim on the way to the conference. "What a day, Jim! The weather sure changes fast here on the Bay!"

"It's liable to do most anything," responded Jim, "and even after 30 years here, I'm still not used to it!"

As they entered the conference room, Jim scanned the table hoping that everyone was present. Bob Doyle was at one side flanked by his staff managers: John Wilson of marine engineering, Carl Anderson of electrical engineering, Joe Harrington of naval architecture, and Tom Parker of arrangements.[3] Bill Moore was in deep conversation with Paul Michaud of industrial relations (which Jim surmised related to union problems); George Blanchard of management engineering was seated drawing block diagrams—as he always seemed to be doing.[4]

Jim took his place at the head of the table and began immediately. "Good morning, gentlemen! I trust you have all been informed as to why we are here. Basically, we're here to discuss our ability to respond effectively to our new ship design contract for the Seaborne project. As you know, we're calling this the Seaborne method. Seaborne is going to be our bread and butter for the next 10 to 15 years, and I want to ensure that we don't underestimate the scope of the job or overestimate our ability to perform."

John Wilson interrupted, "I don't see any big problem here, Jim. We've been designing ships here for years. Why, I can remember that as we struggled with our first nuclear design we had plenty of problems, but each engineering discipline responded and the problems were solved without too much difficulty."

"I agree!" interjected Joe Harrington. "Our department has always been responsive and, to my recollection, there have never been any design problems we couldn't solve."

As the others were talking, Dan Hall started giving each person at the table a schematic arrangement of the traditional and Seaborne methods of design evolution (see Exhibits 1 and 2).

"I'm not sure you're seeing the problem, gentlemen," Jim responded. "I'm not trying to belittle the ability of your organizations or their historical contribution to the company.[5] What I'm trying to evaluate is their effectiveness in the present situation. Perhaps Dan, who has been working on the Seaborne concept since the competition phase, can shed some light on what I'm driving at."

"Right, Jim," said Dan, as he completed passing the schematic arrangements around the table. "Traditionally, the Navy would state its requirements and operational performance objectives to its own team within the civilian department of the Navy. This portion of the Navy organization would

---

[3] The arrangements staff was charged with locating various equipment and other items within the vessel so as to enhance convenience and functional effectiveness.

[4] Management engineering participated in all organizational changes in an effort to smooth the transition and provide advice on how to improve the engineering department's management structure.

[5] See Exhibits 3, 4, 5, 6, and 7 for the design engineering functional organizations.

EXHIBIT 3
Management Organization Chart

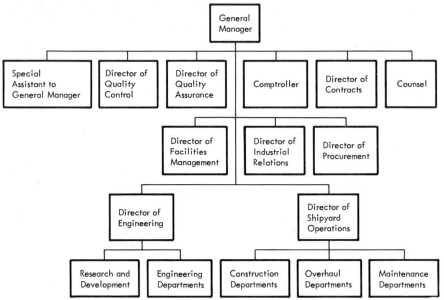

work on the concept design, preliminary design, and contract design, with the end product being a set of ship's specifications."

"Sure, Dan," interrupted Bob Doyle, "but my people also participated."

"Agreed, Bob, but generally on a very small scale. The Navy would call and say they would like, let's say 20 designers, for the contract design phase and you would pick as required from your organization. But let me emphasize that up to the ship's specification stage our participation was minimal."

"I see your point," Bob responded.

"After the ship's specifications were written," Dan continued, "the Navy would award the detail design contract and the design agent, typically ourselves, would be off and running. We would then allocate to our functional design departments that part of the ship design which fell within their responsibility and they would ultimately produce ship's drawing."

"And that's one of my problems," Bill Moore of operations interjected. "Nowhere in this scheme has a serious attempt been made to consider our construction problems. The first time my organization is considered is when the plans are delivered to the shipyard."

"Well, I think with the Seaborne system we can alleviate some of those problems," Dan continued. "As you can see in the Seaborne method we, as the design agent having won the competition, will participate from the inception, with the Navy playing a minimal role as a review activity. We will integrate the Navy requirements and operational performance objectives,

EXHIBIT 4
Marine Engineering Organization Chart

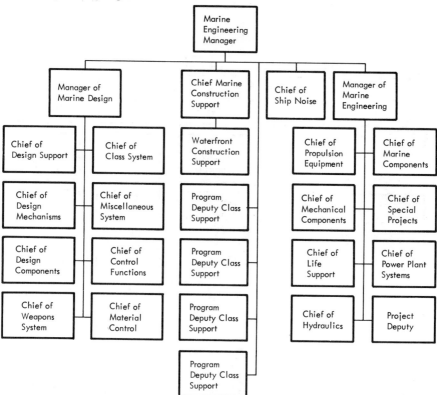

logistic support, and maintenance objectives before we begin concept design.[6] We will then enter the concept design, preliminary design, and contract design phases, ultimately writing the ship's specifications. The end product of this method should be a set of production-oriented drawings, which is what I think you're after, Bill. Right?"

"Yes, Dan, it certainly sounds like it would help our end of the operation," Bill replied.

"Thank you, Dan," said Jim Butons as he stood up. "As you can see we can expect total involvement in this Seaborne method, but I'm not sure we're organizationally geared up for it. I don't think we can expect our functional engineering organization to handle this task effectively as independent units. In my mind I envision a restructuring of our engineering effort to be more responsive to this new method. What I'd like is for you fellows to

---

[6] After a certain period of deployment at sea, it was customary for ships to return to a shipyard for upkeep, logistics support, and maintenance. Maintenance was considered in the design stage in an effort to minimize the time that ships would have to be "off station."

EXHIBIT 5
Electrical Engineering Organization Chart

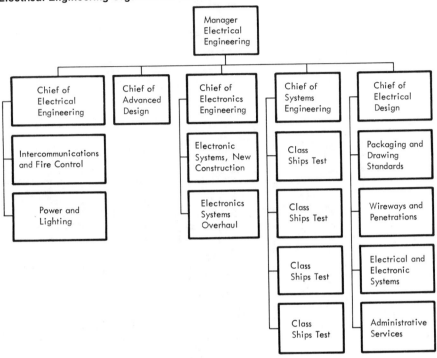

go back, think about what we have to accomplish, and talk among yourselves about viable alternatives. I know this may be pushing but I'd like to
reconvene in one week."

INTERIM MEETING

Recognizing the necessity to act with some degree of haste, Bob Doyle
called a meeting of his staff managers shortly after Jim Buton's meeting.

"Gentlemen," Bob began, "I'd like to start by reassuring you that the
problem at hand is in no way a reflection on yourselves or on the way in
which your organizations have performed. You've performed satisfactorily
in the past, as I would expect you to do in the future. I only mention this
because we need some fresh thinking here, and I don't want our discussions
influenced by attempts to unnecessarily fight change to protect existing organizations."

"Does this mean that we've already ruled out handling Seaborne with out
present structure," Carl Anderson interrupted.

"I didn't say that, Carl," Bob responded. "I just don't want to get bogged
down defending our existing structure."

EXHIBIT 6
Naval Architecture Organization Chart

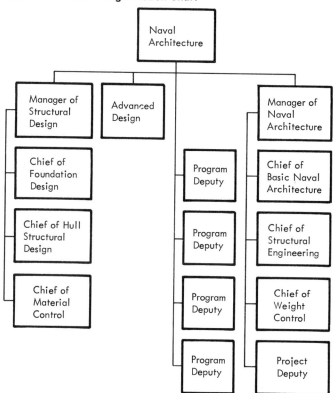

"Let's see where we stand today," John Wilson began, as he leaned forward in his chair and put his pipe down next to the yellow pad he had been staring at. "I think we are all in agreement that we have the in-house technical expertise to handle the design phase of this project."

The others at the table nodded agreement.

"I also think we have competent management people within the company to handle the administrative end," John continued. "The problem would appear to be how to more effectively utilize this talent."

"Our present experience up to the awarding of the detail design phase of the contract has been minimal," Tom Parker interjected. "It would seem to me that this would be our weakest area."

"I agree, Tom," Bob replied, "and I think this is the area we should concentrate on. When we get to the detail design phase I'm confident we can perform adequately, but getting to that point may prove somewhat of a problem."

Joe Harrington cleared his throat and stood up, "I don't think our indi-

EXHIBIT 7
Engineering Services Organization Chart

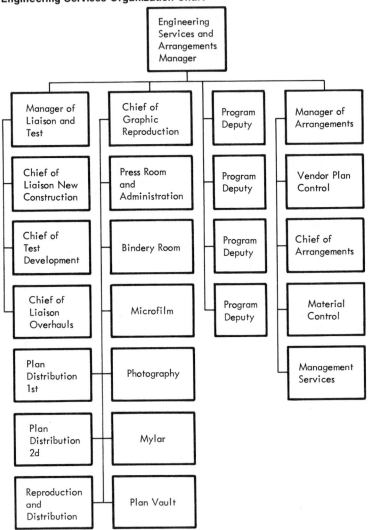

vidual organizations would be responsive to a total involvement approach—independently—without a significant potential for duplication of effort."

"I think you're right, Joe," Bob interjected.

Joe continued. "What I can envision is the need for a project office which would act as a point of contact with the Navy and direct our effort here."

"Yes, Joe," Carl interrupted, "but you know the difficulty we have pulling people from the functional organizations for project-type organizations. When the project ends they are usually on their own and find their positions within the original organizations filled. This has traditionally made it hard to get top-notch people for project-type organizations. If we want top-notch people for this effort, we may have a problem unless we also consider what will happen as the project dissolves, if we go that way."

"You've got a good point, Carl," Joe replied as he sat down.

"Well, gentlemen, I think the single point of contact is a good idea, and I think the project approach, in some form, is the way we should point this effort," said Bob Doyle as he stood and paced the floor. "I also think we will have to face the traditional problem with staffing a project organization. One way to circumvent this problem would be to establish a small project on the general manager staff level which would pool from the existing functional areas as required on a temporary basis."

"Would this retain the present functional organizations?" Carl Anderson asked.

"Yes, Carl," Bob responded. "Another approach would be to break off and establish a new organization to exclusively handle the project up to the detail design phase, at which time we would dissolve it and continue the design essentially as we do now. This project would be the single point of contact with the Navy and have total responsibility for this effort."

"I can see that if we draw this organization from the existing functional organizations it might also be a good time to reorganize their efforts in preparation for the detail design phase," Tom Parker interjected.

"Good point, Tom," Bob replied. "Any more ideas?" Bob scanned the table and there were no replies. "Okay, let me work up these ideas for a presentation at Jim Buton's next meeting. Thank you for your help," said Bob, as he gathered his notes and started to leave the conference room.

THE ALTERNATIVES

The weather had stayed cold and the snow was still on the ground as Jim Butons reconvened the meeting.

"Well, gentlemen, let's get down to business," Jim began. "I trust you've all had an opportunity to think the situation over and come up with some viable alternatives."

"I think I can best speak for the group," Bob Doyle interjected.

"Fine, Bob, let's see what you've got," Jim replied.

"First, let me say that it hasn't been easy to analyze this situation objectively," Bob began. "As the name implies, our traditional design approach has in its course caused functionally oriented departments to emerge which are justly proud of their accomplishments and skills. As such, the thought of change is not easy to swallow. However, after much discussion I think we all realize our approach should change as the design approach changes. Once we agreed on this we were able to narrow our viable options to the following.

"One option would take someone from Dan Hall's advanced engineering group who has been familiar with the Seaborne program, and, with a small

EXHIBIT 8
First Option

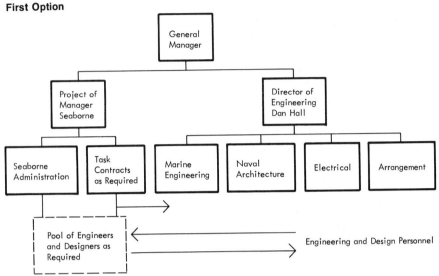

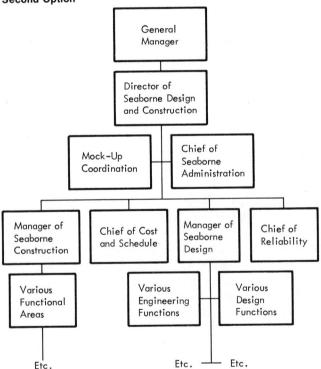

EXHIBIT 9
Second Option

group of subordinates, coordinate the Seaborne method within the existing functional design departments. He would have the right to pool talent as required or delegate task-type contracts to the functional organizations.[7] He would report directly to the general manager and be the sole point of contact with the government. This option would cause a minimum reorganization and would give a single controlling position (see Exhibit 8).

"Another option would entail the creation of an entirely new department. The project would be headed by a director of Seaborne design and construction. He would pull the cream of the crop from the existing functional departments to form his own organization (see Exhibit 9). This department would handle the design phase up to and through the ship's specification phase, at which point the detail design would revert to the functional organization. In that this option would draw from the functional organizations it would also be a good time to reorganize the functional departments and eliminate duplication of effort as they prepare for the detail design.

"It's our opinion, Jim, that these are the only real viable alternatives. We must choose one of these if we are to handle the Seaborne design contract effectively."

---

[7] A task-type contract is one where services for one specific task (or job) are requested from the technical departments.

14. Village Inn*

THE VILLAGE INN, located on Bermuda Boulevard in San Diego, was only a few blocks away from San Diego State University and was within several miles of some of California's largest tourist attractions. Visiting lecturers, speakers, professors interviewing for jobs, and people attending conferences at the university resulted in a considerable amount of business for Village Inn.

The Inn was also near a concentrated area of light and heavy industry. The largest shopping mall in San Diego was under construction across the street from the Inn. A relatively new VA hospital and the University Community Hospital were both located within one mile. The Inn's very favorable locational features, together with the fact that it was a franchise of a major national noted chain, had made it a profitable investment. During the past 12 months, the Inn had an average occupancy rate of between 65 and 70 percent, some 15 or more percentage points above the break-even occupancy rate of 50 percent.

Although the Village Inn had only modest competition from other hotel or motel facilities in the immediate vicinity, a new Travelodge Inn was under construction next door. The other closest competitors were nearly three miles away at the intersection of Bermuda Blvd. and Interstate 8. Village Inn offered a full range of services to its guests, including a restaurant and bar. The new Travelodge next door was going to have just a coffee shop. Insofar as its restaurant/bar business was concerned, the Village Inn's strongest competitor was the popular priced University Restaurant, two blocks away. Village Inn did not consider its own food service operations to be in close competition with the area's fast-food franchises or with higher priced restaurants.

OWNERSHIP OF VILLAGE INN

Mr. Johnson, a native of Oregon, opened the first Village Inn in San Diego in 1958. Since that time, he had shared ownership in 15 other Village Inns, several which were in the San Diego area. He opened the Bermuda Blvd. Inn

---

* Prepared by Diana Johnston, Russ King, and Professor Jay T. Knippen, the University of South Florida.

in October 1966. Prior to his focusing on the motel and restaurant business, Mr. Johnson had owned and operated a furniture store and a casket manufacturing plant. A suggestion from a business associate in Oregon influenced his decision to seek out Village Inn franchises and get into the motel business. In some of his Village Inn locations, Mr. Johnson leased out the restaurant operations; however, the restaurant and bar at the Bermuda Blvd. Village Inn was not leased out. Mr. Johnson felt that because the occupancy rate at this location was so favorable it was more profitable to own and operate these facilities himself.

MANAGEMENT OF THE INN

Mr. Johnson had employed Mrs. Deeks as the innkeeper and manager of the entire operation. She had worked in Village Inns for the past seven and one-half years. Previously, Mrs. Deeks had done administrative work for Davis General Hospital and before that had been employed as a photo lab technician for two years. Her experience in the motel/restaurant business included working for several restaurants and lounges for five years as a cocktail waitress just prior to joining Village Inns.

Mrs. Deeks stated that her main reason for going to work for Village Inns was because she felt there was more money to be made as a waitress than anything else she had tried. Her formal education for her present position of innkeeper consisted of a three-week training course at the Home Office Training Center, in Louisville, Kentucky, and one-week refresher courses each year at the Training Center.

Recently, the assistant innkeeper had been promoted and transferred to another location. Both Mr. Johnson and Mrs. Deeks agreed that there was a pressing need to fill the vacancy quickly. It was the assistant innkeeper's function to supervise the restaurant/bar area and this was the area which always presented the toughest problems to management. Unless the food was well prepared and the service was prompt, guests were quick to complain. Poor food service caused many of the frequent visitors to the area to prefer to stay at other motels. Moreover, it was hard to attract and maintain a sizable lunchtime clientele without having well-run restaurant facilities. With so many restaurant employees to supervise, menus to prepare, and food supplies to order, it was a constant day-to-day struggle to keep the restaurant operating smoothly and, equally important, to see that it made a profit. Mrs. Deeks, with all of her other duties and responsibilities, simply did not have adequate time to give the restaurant/bar enough close supervision by herself.

While searching for a replacement, Mr. Johnson by chance happened to see a feature article in the *Village Inn Magazine,* a monthly publication of the Village Inns of America chain—copies of which were placed in all of the guest rooms of the Inns, describing the operation of a successful Village Inn in nearby San Bernardino. The article caught Mr. Johnson's attention because it described how the Inn at San Bernardino had gained popularity and acclaim from guests because of the good food and fast service provided by the head chef of the restaurant operations. After showing the article to Mrs. Deeks, Mr. Johnson wasted no time in getting in touch with the head chef of that Inn, Mr. Bernie, and persuading him to assume the new role of restaurant/bar manager for the Bermuda Blvd. Village Inn in San Diego.

FOOD SERVICE FACILITIES AND LAYOUT

Exhibit 1 depicts the arrangement of the lobby area and food service facilities at the Inn. A brief description of the restaurant/bar area follows.

EXHIBIT 1

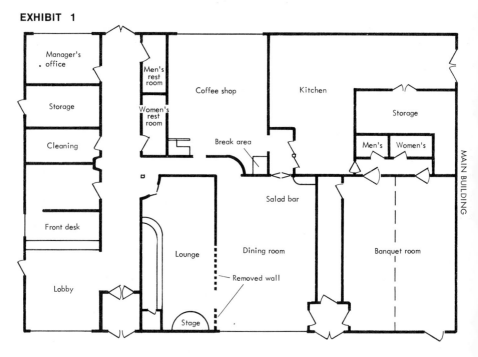

Restaurant.   The restaurant itself consists of a dining room which seated 74 people, a coffee shop which seated 62 persons, and a bar which seated 35 people. The Inn's banquet facilities were just behind the main dining room and could seat 125 people.

The essential role of the restaurant and bar area was to provide pleasant and convenient facilities for the Inn's guests. The contractual franchise agreements with the national chain required all owners to provide these services in conjunction with the overnite accommodations. There were periodic inspections of the facilities by a representative from Village Inn's corporate officer. Village Inn required each franchisee to comply with minimum standards for its food service facilities in an effort to promote comparability and ensure attractiveness. Restaurant services were to be available to guests from 6:30 A.M. until 11:00 P.M.

Coffee Shop. The coffee shop was open from 6:30 A.M. to 11:00 A.M. to serve breakfast to motel guests. At 11:00 A.M. these facilities were closed and the main dining area was opened. The coffee shop was occasionally used beyond scheduled hours to serve customers for lunch and dinner when there was an overflow from the dining area. Tables in both the coffee shop and the dining room were decorated and set uniformly.

Dining Room. The dining area was open from 11:00 A.M. until 11:00 P.M. It was located next to the lounge and was physically separated from the coffee shop by a wall. The lunch and dinner offerings featured a salad bar along with menu items which were somewhat uniform with other Village Inns and which were prescribed by the franchise agreement. However, menu deviations were allowed if approved by corporate representatives from Village Inn's central office.

Bar. The bar, separated from the dining room by a partition, was open for business from 10:00 A.M. until 1:00 A.M. It had tables and booths and customers who preferred to do so could have their food served to them in the bar area. A small dance floor was located in front of the entertainer stage near the front window; a juke box furnished music when there was no live entertainment. A small bar stockroom was located at one end of the bar counter. The cash register area was centrally located to receive payments from customers in all three areas—dining room, coffee shop, and bar.

Kitchen. The kitchen facilities, located beside the coffee shop and dining room, had a stainless steel counter at the entrance door from the restaurant area. It was here that waitresses turned orders in to the cooks and that the cooks served the orders up to the waitresses. The cooking area was located in the center of the room and sinks were located along the sides of the kitchen.

RESTAURANT OPERATIONS

As was to be expected, customers' activity in the restaurant area fluctuated widely. Busy periods were generally at the traditional meal hours, but the peak load at any given mealtime period often varied by as much as an hour from one day to the next. At lunchtime, for example, customers sometimes seemed to come all at once, while on other days the arrival times were more evenly distributed throughout the 11:30 A.M. to 1:30 P.M. interval. Experience had shown that these peaks were hard to anticipate and that the staff had to be prepared for whatever occurred. Moreover, on Monday, Tuesday, Wednesday, and Thursday evenings, the customers were mostly business people, sales representatives, and university visitors, whereas on weekends there were more family travelers. Because of the Inn's location, its clientele consisted somewhat more of the former than the latter.

The Inn's restaurant business was also subject to some seasonal fluctuations. There were always a certain number of people who spent the winter in Southern California to escape the harsh northern and Canadian winters; these included not only winter tourists but also the "Canadian Snow Birds" who came to Southern California to work in the late fall and returned to Canada in March or April. In addition, the Inn's business picked up noticeably during the June graduation exercises at San Diego State University and during the week when the fall term opened. By and large, the daily fluctuations were harder to predict than the seasonal fluctuations.

RESTAURANT STAFFING

Because of the alternating between peak periods and slack periods, the employees in the food service area tended to work together, take breaks together, and eat their meals together. In commenting on the kind of people who tended to work in hotel-motel operations, Mrs. Deeks indicated that employees were typically gregarious and were there because they wanted to be. They had to contend with an uneven work pace, a low-wage scale (often no more than the minimum wage), and irregular working hours. Since waitresses often earned only a token wage ($0.75 to $1 per hour) and relied mainly on tips for their income, they could not afford many "slow days" or "bad days" at work. Their livelihood and degree of service was dependent upon how well they greeted customers, a friendly smile, prompt service, and, in general, an ability to make customers feel satisfied with the attention they received. When the food was cold or ill-prepared or the service less than expected, customers left smaller tips and the waitresses' disgruntlement carried over to the kitchen staff, the hostess, and the busboys. But even more disruptive than the loss of tips were the customers who complained directly to the Inn's management; if this occurred frequently, then the pressure and anxiety felt by the restaurant staff increased noticeably. Mrs. Deeks noted that people who could not adjust to the tempo and temperament of the restaurant business usually did not stay in it long. She noted further that it was extremely difficult to "standardize" the human service aspects of the restaurant business and that trying to attract and keep a good, experienced food service staff was a challenging task.

Mrs. Deeks supplied the following job descriptions of the restaurant staff; these descriptions, however, came from her thoughts and perceptions and had never been formally set forth in writing to the Inn's employees:

Bartender.   Cut up fruit for drinks, wash glasses, serve counter drinks, clean behind bar, stock liquor and mixes, stock beer, fill room service orders, ring up checks, balance register, and help with inventory.

Hostess/Cashier.   Take room service orders, seat guests, deliver menu, direct seating, supervise waitresses and busboys, perform any functions within their prescribed area that speeds service, check out customers from dining area, check out register, file cash register receipts, and assign stations.

Waitresses.   Take food orders, deliver order to kitchen, pick up and serve orders, serve food and beverages, and perform any function that speeds service as directed by the hostess.

Busboys. Bus tables, put clean place settings on tables, clean dining rooms, stock supplies, take ice to all areas, get supplies for cooks, help set up banquets, deliver room service orders, help with maintenance, and perform any function that will speed service as directed by the hostess and manager.

Dishwasher. Wash dishes, pots and pans, sweep and mop floors.

Cook. Prepare meals, schedule meals for prep cook, assist management in stock orders, receive food supplies, supervise and direct kitchen help, and assist management in menu changes. Report to management any changes or problems that occur.

Prep Cook. Prepare all food that the cook needs for the dinner and evening meals. Assist cook in any meal preparation that is necessary to expedite service to guests. Inform cook of any problems that need attention and help cook see that facilities are clean at all times.

Breakfast Cook. Open the kitchen in the A.M. Prepare breakfast food for motel guests. Provide information necessary to maintain in-stock supplies.

MR. BERNIE

When Mr. Bernie arrived to assume his new duties as restaurant/bar manager, he wasted no time in demanding and receiving total obedience from the personnel under his direction. He made it clear that he would not tolerate insubordination and that the consequence would be immediate discharge. Although Mr. Bernie stayed in his new job less than three months (from January to March), he nonetheless created an almost instantaneous climate of ill will and hatred with his subordinates. The intense dislike for Mr. Bernie was voiced by nearly every employee. One example of this was a statement by Elaine, the day hostess/cashier who had been employed in this capacity for the past two and one-half years: "I enjoy my job because I like people. But Mr. Bernie was something else! I generally do not use this term in my vocabulary, but Mr. Bernie was a bastard from the day he arrived until the day he left."

Mr. Bernie's unpopularity was further brought out by a busboy's impromptu comment. Elaine was trying to possibly justify Mr. Bernie's temperament by pointing out that he was not of American nationality. Unable to recall his nationality she inquired of a nearby busboy if he could remember. The busboy immediately and sincerely replied, "He crawled out from under a rock."

Mr. Bernie spent considerable time trying to impress upon his staff the "right way" (his way) of accomplishing tasks (see Exhibits 2 and 3). Most of the employees resented Mr. Bernie's close supervision. Ann, a veteran employee and waitress, describing her resentment, said, "No one really needs to supervise us, especially the way Mr. Bernie stood over us. Usually the

EXHIBIT 2
Memo No. 1 from Mr. Bernie to Food Service Staff

People,
    Please help keep the floor clean.
    If you drop something, pick it up.
    Wipe table off in a trash can.
    If you spill something the mops and brooms are outside.
    It's no fun scrubbing the floor Saturday, and if you don't believe it, be here Saturday night at 11:00 P.M.

Mr. "B"

EXHIBIT 3
Memo No. 2 from Mr. Bernie to Food Service Staff

March 11

TO ALL FOOD AND BEVERAGE EMPLOYEES:

    I wish to thank each and every one of you for the very good job you have done in the past two weeks. The service has greatly improved on both shifts. There has been a better customer/employee relationship, but there is a long way to go yet. We are nearing the end of our winter season so it is most important to all of us that we concentrate on more service in order to obtain a local year-round business. Appearance, neatness, and good conduct on the floor will obtain this, along with good food.

    A waitress and busboy are like salesmen. The hostess/cashier can determine the quality of service in this organization.

    I expect my waitresses while on duty to be on the dining room cafe floor at all times. I should find waitresses and busboys at the cashier stand only when getting a ticket or paying a check.

    I smoke myself—probably more than the rest of you put together. Your service area is beginning to look like a cigarette factory. I do not expect people to give up their smoking habit, but I do expect them to curtail to the rules and regulations of Village Inn, Inc., and those of the health department, "No Smoking on Premises." I would not like to enforce this law.

    In the last two weeks I have walked into the operation after a busy breakfast or dinner and found everyone sitting around the first three booths of the cafe. I do not say it cannot be used, but when I find no waitresses on either floor day or night and customers have to call for service because waitresses are off the floor I believe each waitress and busboy on all shifts should ask themselves one thing; what kind of service would I like if I were a guest? There is only one thing I know, in this part of California when the tourist is gone, half of the employees are worked on a part-time basis, which is not good on anyone's pocketbook. Therefore, I say let's not be second best but let's be first.

    With regard to employees taking their meal breaks, I do not wish to schedule them but I cannot have everyone eating at once. Busboys will eat one at a time.

    Thank you once again for your good performance.

Mr. "B"

hostess is the supervisor, but all the old girls know what they are doing and everyone does their job."

Although an intense dislike for Mr. Bernie was foremost in the minds of the employees, he did manage to make a number of improvements and innovations. Physical changes became obvious within all departments under his authority. In the kitchen a general cleanup campaign was instituted, an order spindle was added, and new oven equipment installed. In the coffee shop and restaurant, new silverware, china, and glasses were purchased, and the menu was improved and complemented by the use of a salad bar. *Explicit* work duties were written and verbally defined to all employees under Mr. Bernie.

Mr. Bernie separated the cashier/hostess function into two distinct jobs. The cashier was confined to the cash register station and given instructions as to the duties she was to perform in that area. The hostess was given instructions to greet people, seat them, and supply menus. When Mr. Bernie was absent, he instructed the hostess to see that the waitresses and busboys carried out their jobs efficiently and effectively. According to Gay, one of the two-day hostesses:

> When Mr. Bernie was here I never had any employee problems. Waitresses and busboys did what I asked. But now if we have a busboy absent or we are crowded, some of the waitresses inform me they will not bus tables. Today there's no one in charge of anything. We need more employees here. It is always better to have more help than not enough. That's one thing Mr. Bernie did, he doubled the help the day he came.

The changes which Mr. Bernie instituted regarding the waitresses were significant in several aspects. All waitresses were required to wear fitted uniforms. This necessitated them driving across town for a uniform fitting. Mr. Bernie's detailed scrutinizing consisted of specific instructions on how to serve customers and which station locations each waitress would serve. He even went as far as to show them how to wrap the silverware and the napkins, and gave explicit instructions to veteran waitresses on how to fill out the order tickets.

Mr. Bernie had the wall between the dining room and bar taken down. He then brought in an entertainer who supplied dinner music for both the restaurant and bar guests. Today, the waitresses are getting some dysfunctional effects from this innovation; according to one:

> Mr. Bernie brought in an organ player, while this was conducive to a more pleasant dining atmosphere, the organist was not good enough to keep the people beyond their meal. But now that Mr. Bernie is gone, our new entertainer is causing some serious problems. For example, last night I had a family of five sit at a table in my station for two and a half hours after their dinner. If people won't leave and they won't buy drinks, I can't make tips.

Mr. Bernie instilled an atmosphere of insecurity and day-to-day doubt in the minds of the employees as to how long they could weather the barrage of innovation and directives. To some, just remaining on the job became a challenge in itself. Elaine (the day hostess) phrased it in this manner:

> I have been employed with the Village Inn for almost two and one-half years. I have worked most of my life and have never felt insecure in any of my jobs. The last job I held was a swimming instructor for ten years with the Academy of Holy Names in San Diego. The reason I had to leave there was because of the change in the educational background requirement which called for a college degree.
>
> My children are all college graduates with highly responsible positions. They achieved this by hard work. I instilled this in their minds because I am a hard worker. But when Mr. Bernie was here, I experienced for the first time in my life the feeling of not knowing from one day to the next if my job would be there when I came to work. What few personnel he failed to drive away, he fired.

Linda, who was a bartender in the lounge area, commented further on Mr. Bernie's supervisory tactics:

> Bernie was a rover. When he walked into an area, including my area, the bar, he could not stand to see someone not involved with busy work. He even made me clean under the bar on the customers' side. I'm not a maid and I often wanted to tell him so. But the way he was hiring and firing employees, I just kept my mouth closed and did as he told me. My experiences with Mr. Bernie were nothing compared to the relationship he had with the busboys. From the bar he would sneak around and watch them in the dining area. If they did anything the least bit out of line, he would call them aside and give them lectures that could last for half an hour. He really treated the busboys like the scum of the earth. When the boys did get a break, they would come over to the bar and get a coke and ice. You know, he even started charging them 25 cents for that!

Sam, a cook hired by Mr. Bernie, offered a slightly different perspective view of Mr. Bernie:

> My wife was working here as a hostess and I used to bring her to work everyday. One day I came in with her and for some reason they were short of help in the kitchen. They needed a dishwasher. I was sitting in the coffee shop and Mr. Bernie walked over and asked me if I could use a job. I had been interested in cooking ever since I was in the Navy. There are two things you can do in your spare time in the Navy . . . drink and chase women, or find a hobby. I found a hobby, which was cooking. On my two days off I used to go down to the galley and help the cooks. There I learned everything I know today. When I got out of the service I worked as a prep cook in a restaurant in Pennsylvania for a year or so. My real specialty is soups, though. Anyway, I had been a dishwasher here for about two days when the cook walked off the job after three years of service here. Mr. Bernie came in and asked how I'd like to be the new cook and here I am today. Mr. Bernie really taught me a lot. He taught me that a restaurant has three things it must give a customer: service, good food, and a pleasing environment to dine. If you have these three, customers will return.

I've spent most of my working career in the automotive business doing such things as driving trucks. But I'm really into this cooking thing. Mr. Bernie taught me that about 50 percent of the customers who come in and order from the menu have no idea what they are ordering. The menu is too complicated. The customer doesn't know what he thinks he ordered and what you think he ordered. Another thing that fascinates me is trying to think like the customer. His definition of rare, medium, and well done is altogether different from my idea of how it should be. One addition by Mr. Bernie was the salad bar. This is a tremendous help to my job. If the waitress can get to the customer before they go to the salad bar and take their order, this gives me plenty of lead time to be sure the meal will be cooked right and served in the attractive manner that Mr. Bernie was so particular about. This lead time is especially important on those days that we are unusually busy. For example, I have prepared as many as 250 meals on some days and as few as 40 on others.

The employees who left or were dismissed by Mr. Bernie included two hostesses, two waitresses (one had an employment record at the Inn that dated back five years), and two busboys. Two of the personnel that Mr. Bernie fired have since returned to their old jobs. One of the waitresses that subsequently was rehired described her reason for leaving as follows:

I really enjoy being a waitress and have been here for about five years. The work isn't really too hard and the pay is good. I took all the "directives" I could take from Mr. Bernie! A week before he left, I gave my resignation and took a vacation. When I returned, I learned of his departure and here I am again. I'm really glad things have worked out as they did.

Mrs. Deeks' opinion of Mr. Bernie's performance was one of general dissatisfaction with the way he handled his dealings with employees:

Mr. Bernie was highly trained, but he was an introvert who stood over his subordinates and supervised everything they did. Cooks are a rare breed of people all to themselves. The help situation has changed greatly in the past few years. It used to be that you could give orders and tell people what they were supposed to do. Now, you have to treat them with "kid gloves" or they'll just quit and get a job down the street. This problem is particularly true with cooks. They are very tempermental and introverted and they expect to be treated like "prima donnas."

Mr. Johnson and I really tried to work with Mr. Bernie during his 90-day trial period. We knew that terminating him without a replacement would be hard on us, but we had no choice. We are now without a restaurant/bar manager of assistant innkeeper. We have been looking for a replacement, but finding a person that is knowledgeable in both the hotel and restaurant management is something of a chore.

CONDITIONS AFTER MR. BERNIE'S DEPARTURE

Since Mr. Bernie had departed, the restaurant personnel were in general agreement that their operation was understaffed. Often guests were seated in both the dining area and coffee shop waiting to be served; even though the waitresses were apparently busy, many customers experienced waits of 20 to 30 minutes. Elaine, one of the two hostesses, explained the lack of prompt service as follows:

> The coffee shop is supposed to take care of the guests until 11 A.M. and then the restaurant part is to be opened. Mr. Bernie handled the situation differently than we do now. When he was here he would not open the dining hall in the morning no matter how crowded the coffee shop was. I can remember mornings when people were lined into the hallway and all the way outside the front door. I guess he knew two girls and two busboys could not handle two rooms.
>
> But today we handle the situations differently. If the coffee shop gets crowded or we have many dirty tables we open up both rooms. This really makes it hard on the girls trying to serve both rooms. What we generally have when this happens is poor service to all concerned and consequently some guests leave unhappy and without tipping the waitresses.

Ralph, a busboy, indicated the problem was not exclusively felt in the restaurant only. He seemed to feel the lack or absence of a manager was the primary problem:

> Mrs. Deeks just can't run this operation by herself. It is physically impossible for her to be here seven days a week from 6:30 A.M. until 11:00 P.M. and manage the kitchen, restaurant, bar, coffee shop, front desk, maid service, and maintenance crew all at the same time.

Some of the employees perceived their duties and functions differently. For instance, the restaurant's two-day hostesses alternated work shifts. Elaine would seat customers, give them their menu, take beverages to customers to help out the waitresses, help out busing tables when it was very busy and had very little to say in supervising the waitresses and busboys. On the other hand, the other day hostess, Gay, would seat customers and give them menus but would not do what she perceived to be the duties of waitresses and busboys. Instead, she exercised supervisory authority over these personnel and when they were not able to get everything done, she would try to find out why not, rather than doing them herself.

There were similar discrepancies in the ways the waitresses and busboys performed their duties. In some cases, waitresses would help busboys clear tables during overcrowded periods and busboys would also help out the waitresses by bringing water and coffee to the people who were waiting to be served. The other side of the coin occurred also. Some of the waitresses, particularly those who had been employed for some time, felt that it was the busboys' responsibility to clear tables and would not lift a finger to help them. In these instances the busboys did not go out of their way to help the waitresses.

Gene, the other bartender, offered yet another view of the Inn's problems:

> You know, I could tell management a few things about the restaurant business if they asked me. I knew from the first day Mr. Bernie arrived that he wouldn't work out. But Mr. Bernie is not the only problem they had. One of the biggest

problems they have with this restaurant is in the banquets they have. We have a luncheon here every week with such clubs as the Sertoma, Kiwanis, and the like. Their luncheons start at noon and last until one-thirty or so. Have you ever noticed how they park outside? Well, I'll tell you they park all over the front parking lot and when local people drive by they assume our restaurant is full and go on down the street. These businessmen tie up most of our help and yet the dining room may be empty. These banquet people people don't buy drinks with lunch like the local businessmen do who take clients out to lunch and often have a bigger bar bill than their restaurant checks. There's only one successful way to have a banquet business and that's not next to your dining room. If the banquet room was on the opposite side of the restaurant, then it would be okay.

EMPLOYEE TRAINING

The Village Inn provided a minimal amount of job training for employees with the exception of the management staff. The contractual agreement between franchise owners and Village Inns of America required all innkeepers, assistant innkeepers, and restaurant managers to attend the Home Office Training Center within a year of being hired. They also had to attend refresher courses on a yearly basis.

The restaurant personnel, in contrast, were given little job training. Instead, efforts were made to hire cooks, waitresses, and bartenders who had previous experience in the field. But in practice this policy was not always adhered to—as was exemplified by the way Linda became a bartender:

My training on the job was really short and sweet. Mr. Bernie came in one day and inquired, "How would you like to be a bartender?" At the same time he handed me a book on mixing drinks. I went home and studied it and "poof" I was a bartender.

Within a short time on the job I began getting a lot of help and advice from the waitresses who came over to the bar for drink orders. Sometimes when we do get a drink mixup they are very nice about it. I've even had people from other departments in the Inn to help me when the situation called for it. One night I had two ladies in here, one from the "crazy house" and the other her bodyguard. After a few "shooters" as they referred to the drinks, they asked for their check. They wanted to use a credit card instead of paying cash. This was not a problem but so I would get my tip I offered to carry the check and credit card to the front desk. Then they said I would cheat them on their bill once I was out of their sight. The front desk man heard the hassle and came in and escorted the ladies to the desk. This type of working together happens here all the time. Mrs. Deeks, my boss, is really a nice person to work for. She doesn't come around very much, except if she needs information or to advise me about something.

PAY SCALES

Management indicated that there was a shortage of good employees and that a low pay scale was characteristic of the restaurant business. Some of the employees expressed their awareness of this also.

(Bartender) Linda: The pay scale is really low compared to other areas. My first job as a cocktail waitress in San Diego was in a dive downtown. They paid us 50 cents an hour plus tips, but the tips were lousy. Here they're paying 80 cents an hour plus tips which is somewhat better, but it's still way below the wages elsewhere. I really don't feel like I'm suited for this work, but I make more money at the bar than I did as a cocktail waitress.

(Hostess) Gay: I make $2 an hour here. With all the responsibility and experience I've had, the pay scale here compared to other parts of the country is deplorable. The busboys make almost as much as I do. They make $1.45 an hour plus 15 percent of the waitress's tips. Even though the pay scale is low, there is always overtime available to most of all of the employees who want it. My husband who is a cook here has worked 145 hours so far in this two-week pay period and he still has five more days to go.

Barb, one of the waitresses, further substantiated the availability of overtime by saying she got at least one hour overtime each day. She attributed the extra hours of overtime to the fact that the Inn's restaurant staff always seemed to have at least one person unexpectedly absent each day.

The problem in the restaurant was apparently compounded by the fact that it was operating with a minimum number of employees. Timmy, a busboy, indicated the wide range of activities that were expected of him and the other busboys:

We do everything; I clean and bus tables, sweep floors, and do janitorial work. I don't mean in just my area either. If the front desk needs a porter or runner, or if some type of room service is needed, I do that too. Mr. Bernie was really hard to work under but he always confined us to restaurant duties. When he was here we didn't do all those jobs outside our area. Those duties were handled by a front desk porter. But, I'd still rather have to do things all over the place than have to put up with Mr. Bernie.

SEARCHING FOR MR. BERNIE'S REPLACEMENT

In outlining her thoughts on trying to replace Mr. Bernie, Mrs. Deeks stated:

I really had a good track record with personnel before Mr. Bernie came along. I strongly objected to his dictatorial supervision. In my experience I have learned employees perform their jobs better when left alone most of the time. I once tried to set up off-job activities for my employees. I reserved a room at the hotel for employees to meet together after working hours to play cards and drink coffee. Unfortunately the room was not used enough to merit keeping it on reserve. However, I still support functions that the employees suggest. We are presently sponsoring a bowling team that two of my waitresses belong to.

Most of the waitresses would rather work night shifts if they have their choice. Some of the girls have children and husbands that require them to be home at night. This balances the shifts real well. One reason I prefer to schedule the waitresses is because of peculiar problems which occur. For example, I have two extremely good waitresses that will not work on Saturdays and Sundays. The other waitresses do not know this and I feel if I were to allow the hostess to do the scheduling I would have some immediate personnel problems. To further complicate any benefits that might be derived by allowing the hostesses to make out schedules, it would be necessary to reveal my awareness of the slower waitresses we have which I schedule on Saturday and Sunday—our slower business days.

I am really more active in management and day-to-day problems than most of the employees realize. Any significant changes in rules or policies are usually passed in the form of a written memo. I prefer to handle communication in this way for two reasons: first, there is no room for distortion, and second, it does not give the employees a feeling that they are being closely supervised. However, I do need an assistant to help me manage this place. I have verbally put the word out to other Inns and motels. I'm really not concerned whether I get a restaurant manager or an assistant innkeeper so long as he has a knowledge of the food and beverage service. I'm really going to be cautious in the selection of this person as I don't want to jump out of the frying pan into the fire.

The absence of Mr. Bernie is now a well-known fact by all of the Inn's personnel. However, it was not known to everyone. One day, Mr. Trainor, a well-liked sales representative walked into the restaurant and inquired, "Where is Mr. Bernie today?" There was a hush of silence and then in answer to his own question he replied, "Why is everyone smiling?"

15. The Spring Thing*

IN THE FALL OF 1975, Layton Chambers was struck with the idea of organizing and promoting a rock concert to be held the following May. The event, to be called the Spring Thing, would be a one-day concert presenting several of the country's top rock groups. Chambers conceived of Spring Thing as a "festival" that would be void of the ills experienced at other concerts but which still would be a venture that would provide a handsome profit. In his view, he faced two major obstacles: (1) raising the capital necessary to finance a venture so risky as a rock concert, and (2) developing an effective set of plans, policies, and procedures that would help ensure both a profitable and a publicly acceptable concert.

THE STRATEGY AND THE PLAN

Chambers, a recent liberal arts graduate and in his early 30s, was relatively inexperienced in business affairs but very interested in concert promotion. Although his financial resources were fairly limited, he had managed to organize two moderately successful jazz and soul concerts at the local level. However, the attendance at these events had never exceeded 5,000. Chambers anticipated using the Spring Thing to establish himself on a larger scale as a creditable concert promoter with a reputation for quality production and financial success. To accomplish this goal, the planning for the Spring Thing was to include sufficient facilities to assure spectator comfort and avoid the criticisms that often follow such an event. Free amenities were to include ample parking, camping areas, water supplies, and portable toilets. Additionally, spectators would be permitted to bring their own food and beverages into the concert site, except for items in glass containers which were to be prohibited as a safety precaution. In short, Chambers envisioned a top-quality rock concert providing good entertainment in a "hassle-free" environment.

Chambers selected Springfield, Missouri, as the geographical area in which to have the concert because of its proximity to several large population centers and its scenic setting at the edge of the Ozark Mountains. With a

---

* Prepared by Bruce H. Fairchild, University of Colorado, and Mike E. Miles, University of North Carolina at Chapel Hill.

population of 140,000, Springfield is located 150 miles south of Kansas City, 220 miles southwest of St. Louis, 130 miles northeast of Tulsa, Oklahoma, and 210 miles north of Little Rock, Arkansas. The specific site of the concert was to be a 130-acre tract of undeveloped land situated at the intersection of Interstate Highway 44 and U.S. Highway 65 in the northeast part of the city. The land had been acquired by a St. Louis developer during the height of the late 60s development boom. Chambers considered the site ideal. The tract was a gently sloping field that provided a natural amphitheatre for viewing the entertainment. There were few trees and the plot was bounded on all four sides by improved roads which would permit vehicle access without entrance bottlenecks. In addition, the parcel was sufficiently large to accommodate the expected crowds. The owner of the land, Mark Stafford, agreed to let Chambers use the tract for the concert in exchange for the food and beverage concessions and 5 percent of ticket sales. Such a financial arrangement increased the site's attractiveness to Chambers as it substantially reduced the amount of required front-end capital. Furthermore, the concert would not be subject to the stringent provisions of a recently passed state law governing mass gatherings, as the site was inside Springfield's city limits and the city had no specific mass gathering ordinances. With this site, the location of the Spring Thing could be touted as the "Crossroads of the Midwest."

Garnering the approval of the local government was facilitated by the recent installation of a city council regarded as one of the most liberal in the Midwest. Because Springfield's city leaders had been elected by a coalition of university students, local liberals, and a combination of minority groups, the council's constituency was considered as amenable to a rock concert as was thought possible. Furthermore, Chambers had actively campaigned for one of the stronger members of the council in the last election; through their personal relationship, the two developed a strategy for gaining council support and approval of the concert. This program involved conducting a survey of the neighborhoods surrounding the concert site to indicate resident acceptance and submitting an organizational plan to various government units (traffic control; police, fire, and health departments; and the city manager's office) for their comments and approval. Armed with the results of the poll and the various official approvals, the proposed concert would be presented for full council consideration just prior to the event. This strategy was designed to avoid an open public hearing that might jeopardize the festival and would serve no useful purpose from the promoter's standpoint.

Chambers felt that extensive advertising and promotion were crucial to the success of the Spring Thing and anticipated heavy expenditures in this area. The public relations firm that had successfully handled the tour of an internationally famous rock group two years prior was to be engaged to direct the promotional effort. The principal in the public relations firm would be allowed a free rein in designing advertisements and in selecting and arranging contracts with the various media. Chambers did suggest that his name be included in all advertising in order to develop and solidify his reputation as a concert promoter.

FINANCING THE VENTURE

Having completed the preliminary planning for the concert and convinced that the Spring Thing concept was sound, Chambers next began figuring out where and how to acquire the capital to finance the project. Since he was not an established promoter, musicians and suppliers would not extend him credit, and substantial front money would be required to pay for all expenses incurred prior to the event. Chambers worked up a tentative budget, including an additional 10 percent for unexpected items, which indicated that almost $270,000 would be needed to cover anticipated costs (Exhibit 1). Although this was a sizable amount, the potential revenues from the concert were almost three times as great. Tickets would be sold in advance for $10 each and at the gate for $12. Chambers estimated that total receipts could be as much as $800,000, depending upon the turnout. Furthermore, he believed that concession sales could bring in an additional $50,000 in profits.

EXHIBIT 1
Tentative Expense Budget, November 15, 1975

Talent:		
Artists' fees	$100,000	
Limousines	2,880	
Catered food and drinks	1,100	$103,980
Admission tickets		943
Advertising (including production)		30,000
On-Site Preparation:		
Mowing	$ 5,000	
Stage and platform construction	6,300	
Fencing	28,102	
Portable toilets (including servicing)	7,000	
Barricades and construction materials	1,250	
Electrical labor and equipment	3,000	
Earth moving and grading	200	
Clean-up	650	51,502
Security (including armored car)		15,976
Stagehands		2,745
Sound system rental and setup		15,000
Liability insurance		7,000
Administrative Office Expense:		
Staff salaries	$ 13,300	
Office rent	1,000	
Telephone and supplies	600	14,900
Tent and tarpaulin rental		1,000
Legal fees		500
Miscellaneous		1,565
Contingency surplus (10% of above total)		24,501
Total Anticipated Expenses		$269,612

Chambers identified four potential sources for meeting the financing requirements for the Spring Thing. He could go to a commercial bank (as he had for both of his previous concerts). However, the banks had always required a cosigner and finding someone to guarantee a loan of the size required for the Spring Thing would be difficult. Chambers had heard about "venture capital" firms that made loans to new, high-risk enterprises. This idea appealed to him since his long-range plan was to establish a production company and a working relationship with a venture capital firm could be useful; nonetheless, he knew little about venture capital firms or their requirements. A local investment counselor had indicated to Chambers that he might be able to organize a syndicate to handle the financing, but there were legal problems if the number of participants in the group became too large. Finally, Chambers felt that one wealthy individual might be willing to underwrite the entire project. But, not being a member of the country club set, Chambers was not personally acquainted with individuals possessing such wealth.

Approaching these potential sources also created a problem since Chambers expected each source to view the risks and payoffs of the concert differently. A variety of factors affecting both revenues and expenses contributed to the uncertain profitability of the concert. Receipts would be influenced not only by the public's general acceptance of the Spring Thing concept but also by spectator enthusiasm, weather conditions, security measures, and possible political and legal actions. Specifically, preconcert excitement and buildup would greatly affect the number of advance tickets sold; a warm spring day would substantially increase spectator turnout while a rainy weekend could result in the concert being a bust; onsite security would determine the number of persons getting into the concert without purchasing a ticket; and local government or legal actions could limit attendance or completely halt the project. Production costs were similarly uncertain. Although Chambers' budget included a built-in cushion, the majority of the expense items were only estimates and did not represent firm agreements. There was always the possibility that additional costs would be incurred as a result of contract negotiations with rock groups, lawsuits, municipal stipulations, and so on.

Chambers realized that evaluating the uncertainties involved with the concert would be difficult, but he felt that he needed to demonstrate an acute awareness of the entrepreneurial risks inherent in the proposal. Chambers repeatedly had heard his business friends refer to distinctions between economic and financial risk, internal and external risk, and to the risks associated with operating and financial leverage. Chambers was unsure how to synthesize these various aspects of risk; yet, he was certain that a realistic risk-reward assessment should be an integral part of the presentation he would have to make to potential financing sources.

During the next four weeks, Chambers unsuccessfully promoted the Spring Thing to various banks, venture capital firms, professional money locators, and wealthy individuals. The banks felt that the project was too risky; the venture capital firms disliked the nature of the one-time event; the potential members of the syndicate were averse to the various legal implications of the deal; and most of the individuals contacted were not sufficiently liquid to provide the required cash. Finally, Chambers was introduced to Dave Ralston, a well-to-do Kansas City businessman who had substantial cash on hand and was known to occasionally accept a gamble. After several conversations with Chambers reviewing anticipated expenses and potential receipts, Ralston agreed to arrange for $220,000 front-end cash to fund the venture. The remaining $50,000 would not be needed until just prior to the concert, and it was planned that advance ticket sales receipts would be used to finance these costs.

MANAGING THE RISK-REWARD TRADE-OFFS

The inherent uncertainties of the proposed concert caused Ralston to consider various ways of structuring the project so as to reduce the entrepreneurial risks to which he would be exposed. He felt that certain actions on his part could substantially decrease or even eliminate revenue/cost uncertainties, while others could be spread among the remaining concert participants or transferred to outside parties.

Ralston's initial concern was how to amass enough cash to meet his commitment. Most of his liquid assets were currently in either marketable securities or tied-up in other business ventures. His banker was willing to make him a personal loan for $200,000 at 12 percent, but Ralston was hesitant to finance the Spring Thing with borrowed funds.

The primary source of risk, however, Ralston attributed to the extremely high operating leverage associated with this type of venture. Although the original budget was designed so that virtually all costs would be fixed and have to be paid regardless of the concert's outcome, Ralston thought that it might be desirable to contract as many of these expense items as possible on a percentage rather than flat fee basis. Such an arrangement would transfer some of the risks to the other concert participants and, as with the land agreement, reduce the amount of his original investment. The principal input suppliers—the musicians, concessionaires, promotional and media groups, site construction contractors, lawyers, accountants, local government officials, and Mr. Chambers and his staff—might be amenable to this type of arrangement. However, Ralston was not certain which groups would agree to a participating interest, how to set the terms of these agreements, or how to approach the potential partners with his proposal.

Ralston also thought about covering some of his risk exposure with insurance. Rain insurance against inclement weather and liability insurance against various legal actions were available, although costly. Rain insurance, for example, would cost $12 per $100 of coverage even though the probability of measurable precipitation (as defined by the Lloyds of London insurance policy) was less than 1 in 20 in Springfield during May. Liability insurance might be an essential expense, but Ralston had no idea of the amount needed. Unlike most ventures, the downside risk of the concert would not be limited to the original investment. The possibility of substantial lawsuits dramatically increased the project's vulnerability to losses. In both cases, insurance would have the adverse effect of increasing the operating leverage as additional fixed costs would be incurred. Because of the complexity and expense of these insurance alternatives, Ralston was having difficulty incorporating them into a risk-reward framework.

Ralston recognized that one way to reduce some of his risks was through a legal restructuring of the promoting organization. Presently the venture was set up as a sole proprietorship with Ralston as the owner and Chambers a manager receiving a salary and bonus. This arrangement not only made Ralston personally liable for any legal actions against the concert, but also subjected him to substantial income tax disadvantages. Chambers and Ralston had discussed incorporating the venture or organizing a limited partnership, but they were unsure of the exact benefits of either of these ownership forms and whether they would be worth the time, complications, and costs involved with arranging them.

As plans went ahead for the concert, both Ralston and Chambers came to recognize management problems associated with the operation of the concert. Such things as theft, musicians failing to perform, spectator riots, and medical emergencies would all be factors affecting the concert's profits. Although Ralston retained ultimate authority over the concert's operations, the primary responsibility for dealing with these problems was left with Chambers and his management.

DETERMINING WHAT MANAGEMENT CONTROLS WOULD BE NEEDED

In the first week of March, two months prior to the event, Chambers began considering ways of controlling the operating risks of the concert and deciding which areas should receive the highest priority in terms of time and money. He and his staff identified promotion and admissions, advance and on-site ticket sales, and concession sales as the factors that would most affect revenues. Similarly they determined that the major cost uncertainties would revolve around budget control over expenses of the rock musicians and spectator services, and the prevention of medical and security incidents that would result in post-concert litigation. Although each of these areas involved considerable uncertainty, handling them effectively would be critical to the concert's ultimate profitability. While some of the operating problems could be markedly contained by establishing strict internal controls, there would be substantial costs, both real and opportunity, associated with implementing tight controls.

As contract negotiation progressed and costs became more firm, the original budget proved to be less and less reliable. Although the November 15, budget had called for $30,000 in advertising, the public relations firm Chambers had contracted with indicated that the promotion effort should be substantially more extensive. In order to be relatively assured of drawing up to 75,000 spectators, the agency suggested that $72,500 be spent for promotion and submitted a proposed advertising campaign for Chambers' review (Exhibit 2). They maintained that this amount was consistent with the industry rule of thumb requiring a dollar of advertising per spectator. Chambers questioned whether the additional expense would be necessary, but realized that greater advertising expenditures would better serve his personal goal of self promotion.

Twelve outlets had been selected to sell advance tickets; 3 in both St. Louis and Springfield, and 2 each in Kansas City, Tulsa, and Little Rock. The outlets in Kansas City, St. Louis, and Tulsa were major department stores and ticket agencies; they received a 5 percent commission on sales and deposited all receipts in an escrow account until after the concert. The other advance ticket sales were handled gratis through record stores and "head shops" with the money they collected periodically remitted directly to Chambers. Although a ticket monitoring system was to be established, Chambers had no idea of how many tickets would be sold in advance. The public relations agency projected that 30,000–50,000 tickets would be sold prior to the concert and that approximately 60 percent to 70 percent of these

EXHIBIT 2
Proposed Advertising Campaign for the Spring Thing

Agency fee		$10,000
Media Expenses:		
Print media	$17,200	
Broadcast media	30,000	
Broadcast production	750	
Radio dubs	7,500	
Printing releases	100	55,550
Artwork and Photography:		
Artwork	$ 1,000	
Posters, flyers, press kits	4,300	
Productions, stats, velox	450	
Photo reprints	150	5,900
Miscellaneous:		
Mailing service	$ 100	
Bus	50	
Telephone expense	125	
Deliveries	100	
Travel	150	
Postage	125	650
Miscellaneous		400
Total Advertising Campaign Expenses		$72,500

would be through the major outlets with the remainder being sold through the local shops.

It was anticipated that one third of total sales would be made well in advance of the concert, another third in the three days preceding the event, and that the remaining third would be onsite sales. The onsite sales created a special problem due to the limited physical facilities available and the rowdy condition of the crowd. Not only was there uncertainty as to the number of tickets that would be sold on the day of the concert, and therefore as to the number of ticket sellers needed, but there was a chance that employee theft or an actual robbery might occur. Since Chambers felt that a "hassle-free" atmosphere would be imperative to attract spectators, blatant security measures could not be taken. However, from $125,000 to $250,000 in cash in small bills would be involved with the on-site ticket sales and some controls would be mandatory.

In conjunction with ticket sales, Chambers wanted to minimize the number of spectators getting into the concert or viewing the performance without purchasing a ticket. As illustrated in Exhibit 3, the concert area was to be located in the middle of the land tract and would be surrounded by the parking and camping areas. Nonpaying admissions could be gained either by unauthorized entrance through the gates or by spectators climbing over, under, or through restrictive barriers. Several alternatives were available to control this situation, the simplest being to construct a chain-link fence topped with barbed wire strands. Chambers' analysis indicated that such a fence would cost $10,800 and although it would be reasonably effective, some 4,000–6,000 spectators would probably still be able to circumvent this barrier. Another possibility, in addition to fencing, was to hire security personnel to constantly patrol the perimeter. Chambers estimated that this would result in increased wages of $4,500 while reducing nonpaying entries to 2,000–3,000 persons. A final alternative would be to install a double ring of perimeter fences with a "no man's land" between them to be patrolled by a few security guards and possibly watchdogs. Although the second fence would cost an additional $11,000 and the personnel and dogs $1,000, it would virtually eliminate any gate-crashing.

Under all of these options, Chambers still had to determine the number of entrance gates to install. Although a greater number of gates would reduce the possibility of an enthusiastic and impatient crowd from stampeding the fence, it would also require more facilities and personnel. This would result in increased fencing costs, additional wages of $200 per gate, and would permit more ticket takers' "friends" to enter without paying. Similarly an exit and entrance procedure would have to be established so that spectators could leave the concert and return later without being able to transfer their passes to others who had not purchased tickets.

All of Chamber's cost projections had been based on an attendance estimate of 75,000; the actual costs, of course, could be expected to vary, although not proportionately, with the size of the crowd. Also, while Cham-

EXHIBIT 3
Site Diagram

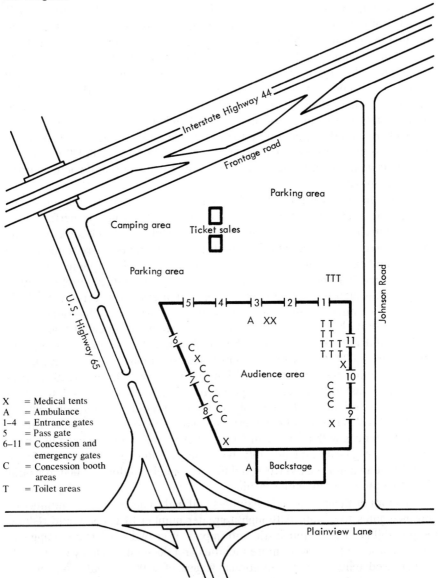

X   = Medical tents
A   = Ambulance
1–4 = Entrance gates
5   = Pass gate
6–11 = Concession and
        emergency gates
C   = Concession booth
        areas
T   = Toilet areas

bers was convinced that a relaxed and unstructured environment would help attract a large crowd, the financial impact of losing up to 6,000 ticket sales due to lax controls was quite disconcerting.

The sales of concessions was the other area that would significantly affect the concert's total revenues. Although the landowner, Mark Stafford, had been granted the food and beverage concessions, Chambers had retained a 25

EXHIBIT 4
On-Site Concessionaires

Food and Beverage Concessions:
Beer and wine .... Ron's Liquor Stores
Soft drinks .... M and B Catering
BBQ beef, hamburgers, hotdogs, etc. .... M and B Catering
BBQ chicken, nachos, corn on the cob, etc. .... Carol Warren
Ice cream .... Joan Marlin
Fruits and health foods .... Good Eats, Inc.
Watermelons .... Red's Fruit Stand
Clothing and Apparel:
Blouses, shirts, and jackets .... Exotic Imports
Al's cutoff jeans .... Al Davis
Belt buckles and jewelry .... The Posse
"Spring Thing" blankets .... Sam Johnson
Miscellaneous:
Suntan oil and jewelry .... Bob Conroe
Cigarettes .... The Tobacco Shoppes
Herbs and spices .... Living Good Together, Inc.

percent override on gross sales. In addition, he had contracted with independent nonfood and beverage concessionaires for a fee of 30 percent of their net income (Exhibit 4). Chambers did not know what to expect from concession sales as this would largely be a function of the crowd turnout, but he felt that revenues could range anywhere from $50,000 to $250,000. With this much cash involved, Chambers identified three factors which would influence his percentage of the concession take: (1) skimming by the concessionaires, (2) the types of inventory controls and reports imposed on the concessionaires, and (3) robberies. Since many of the concessionaires appeared to be of rather questionable character, it was estimated that up to 25 percent of receipts might not be reported. Furthermore, procedures had not been established to control the flow of inventory in and out of the concert area or for keeping strict account of sales revenues. Finally, the heavy traffic around the concession booths would make it relatively easy for a spectator to rob a concessionaire and disappear into the crowd.

Chambers studied several methods of alleviating these problems. Although the least expensive approach for determining concession sales would be to accept vendors' figures, auditors could be hired for $1,500 to spot-check sales and inventories. Alternatively, a required reporting system for the concessionaires could be set up to account for merchandise flows and cash receipts, but this system would be dependent upon vendor compliance and some on-site auditing would still be required. A final possibility would be for Chambers' people to be physically present at each concession booth and participate directly in cash register transactions of the vendors. Although this would cost around $3,000 and encounter some vendor opposition, it would eliminate the majority of the concessionaire skimming.

Chambers was also concerned about the safety of the cash that would be collected from both concessions and ticket sales. An on-site armored car, into which receipts could be periodically deposited, could be hired for $1,000; uniformed security guards would have to be paid $200 apiece.

However, the presence of too many of these uniformed security guards might give the adverse impression that the concert was a "rip-off" and being held solely for the financial benefit of the promoters. The only alternative to an armored car would be to make deposits directly to the Springfield National Bank by private car. This would be complicated by traffic congestion both on and off the concert site, the one to two hours it would take to make the deposits, and the lack of security during the trip.

Besides these problems affecting expected revenues, Chambers experienced difficulties keeping some costs in line with his original projections. Specifically, he was having troubles negotiating contracts with the musicians. In order to sign those rock groups that Chambers felt would draw crowds of 60,000–70,000, he would have to offer them $165,000. Although this was substantially above the $100,000 budget on November 15, if he were forced to stay within this original amount it was doubtful if the concert would attract more than 30,000 people. Most of the other concert costs had been fairly well budgeted, and while some were underestimated, others had been overestimated.

To limit the possibility of sizable losses due to post-concert legal suits arising from medical incidents, personal injuries, and/or property damage, Chambers had to decide what medical facilities were to be supplied, the amount of security to provide for spectators, musicians, and adjacent property owners, the extent of parking and traffic control, and the amount of liability insurance to purchase. An agreement was made with a community counseling and medical aid group to be at the concert to handle drug and minor injury problems. Chambers was unsure as to how much professional help would be needed to take care of the more serious cases. The cost of five doctors, ten nurses, and two ambulances totaled approximately $5,000 for the day.

According to Chambers's best estimates, a complete security program capable of handling most of the security problems which could arise would cost $15,000 *above* the necessary minimum of $6,695. This would include $2,000 for off-duty policemen to direct traffic, $5,000 for a group of professional bouncers to guard the musicians and stage area, $5,000 for untrained "field hippies" to handle parking, prevent vandalism, and aid spectators, and $3,000 for special agents to mingle with the crowd looking for weapons and to prevent fights or riots.

The cost of liability insurance varied, although not proportionately, with the amount of coverage. Contact with a local insurance broker indicated that a $1 million policy could be purchased for $7,000, while $5 million and $10 million coverage would cost $12,000 and $18,000, respectively.

FINALIZING MANAGEMENT PROCEDURES AND CONTROLS

Faced with all these wide-ranging problems of management and control, Chambers realized that numerous decisions would soon have to be made.

The strain of preparing for the concert was beginning to show on the staff, and Chambers had developed an ulcer. To complicate matters, a local citizens group had just announced their intention to seek a court injunction to halt the concert.

With only four weeks remaining before the concert was to be held, it became apparent that the original budget of November 15 was no longer valid. On April 1, a revised estimate of expenses was prepared under the assumption that only minimal steps would be taken to reduce the various operating risks (Exhibit 5). This new budget revealed that the concert would

EXHIBIT 5
Revised Expense Budget, April 1, 1976

Talent:			
Artists' fees		$165,000	
Limousines		2,400	
Catered food and drink		1,100	$168,500
Admission tickets			762
Advertising (including production)			72,500
On-site preparation:			
Phone connections		$ 11,484	
Stage and platform construction		5,300	
Fencing		10,800	
Portable toilets (including servicing)		7,000	
Barricades and construction materials		750	
Electrical labor and equipment		12,050	
Earth moving and grading		1,700	
Clean-up		650	49,734
Basic security			6,695
Stagehands			3,696
Sound system rental and setup			15,000
Liability insurance			7,000
Administrative Office Expense:			
Staff salaries		$ 15,346	
Office rent		10,000	
Telephone and supplies		1,500	26,846
Tent and tarpaulin rental			125
Legal fees			5,000
Miscellaneous			12,814
Total Revised Expenses			$368,672

require at a minimum $370,000 front-end financing, $100,000 more than originally anticipated.

Armed with this revised cost estimate, Chambers contacted Ralston to discuss the additional capital requirements and ascertain his ability to provide the necessary funds. Ralston indicated that he would have extreme difficulty arranging for the extra cash and that it would seriously threaten his personal solvency. Furthermore, Ralston said that he was becoming very uncomfortable with the risk elements inherent in the concert and questioned whether the potential returns were adequate compensation for the risks he was taking. Ralston asked Chambers to pinpoint the key risks, the potential cost overruns, and the effects on the concert's profits and to present him with alternative budgets reflecting these possibilities. Only then, said Ralston, would he consider committing any additional funds to finance the Spring Thing.

16. Morgan Hospital*

THE CONTROLLER OF MORGAN HOSPITAL completed the second of two irregular Monday morning conferences and walked to the employee cafeteria for lunch. The first conference was with the hospital's administrator and probable new chief of radiology. The hospital had been negotiating with the radiologist for the prior six months: he reaffirmed his stand that he and his prospective group would accept only a percentage of gross billings or direct billing as a payment method. Morgan Hospital was one of the last three hospitals in the region to have salaried radiologists. The second conference was with the administrator. After an exhaustive review of their last 12 months of problems with the radiology department, the administrator specified several possible alternatives and asked the controller to determine the costs to various persons and parties of the radiologist's request and to prepare recommendations on a course of action.

It was 12:45 P.M. and the employee cafeteria was closing—Jim Baker, the controller, had missed another luncheon with his wife. They were planning to leave that morning, and then that afternoon, for a week of skin diving at a resort far from Morgan Hospital. Jim had finished and sent to Blue Cross and the state his December 31, 19X9 audited cost study last Saturday morning. The radiology department problem required the cancellation of the planned week's vacation as had the opening of Morgan's new building in September, accreditation inspection in October, Blue Cross's auditors for Blue Cross in November, and the Blue Cross's auditors for Medicare in December. The hospital's experiences with, and interviews with, prospective radiologists left Jim Baker with no doubts that any qualified radiologist could check out of Morgan on Friday and have another position on his terms by the following Monday evening. Hence, the requests of the radiologist had to be considered immediately on a priority basis: he was due to start in about four weeks, March 1, 19Y0.

BACKGROUND

Morgan Hospital was a 223-bed voluntary, nonprofit full-service acute hospital in "Megapolis," the heavily populated coastal strip of the north-

* Prepared by Professor Richard A. Elnicki, the University of Florida. All data have been disguised.

eastern United States. It was located about six blocks from an interstate highway in a relatively small industrial town. About 12 miles southeast on the interstate system were two larger hospitals in the center of a standard metropolitan area; one was affiliated with a university medical school. About 35 miles to the west on the interstate system were two larger hospitals in the center of another standard metropolitan area. The town of Morgan was included in the former.

The hospital was in the process of completing another phase of its long-run community service facility improvement program. The hospital had been founded in 1911. The two oldest buildings had been built in 1928. They were currently under renovation. The buildings in use were started into construction in 19W2, 19X2, and 19X8, the latter being dedicated in September 19X9. Morgan Hospital's net plant, property, and equipment increased from about $3.5 million to $8.5 million as a result of the completion of the building. The hospital's resulting bed and room mix is shown in Table 1.

The opening of the new building gave the hospital 40 new and badly needed medical-surgical beds. But of more importance was the necessity for balancing the hospital's primary and domiciliary services. Additional space was necessary for the expansion and modernization of the hospital's pharmacy, morgue and autopsy rooms, physical medicine department, dietary service, housekeeping service, and maintenance department. Existing space was too small to hold needed new equipment, and locations required extensive transportation within the hospital. A primary reason for the undertaking was to enable the hospital to attract more physicians and qualified medical personnel. Almost all of the hospital's services would be relocated as a result of the current and next phase of the expansion program. The regional hospital planning agency considered Morgan's long-range master plan well-designed and described the current projects as the result of excellent planning processes. The agency suggested that the board of trustees' involvement in self-study and community needs be a possible prototype for similar programs by the governing boards of other hospitals.

TABLE 1
Bed and Room Mix, January 19Y0

	Rooms				Total	
	1 Bed	2 Bed	4 Bed	6 Bed	Rooms	Beds
Medical-surgical	11	75	—	—	86	161
Pediatrics	8	1	—	1	10	16
Intensive care	—	—	—	1	1	6
Self-care	11	—	—	—	11	11
Maternity	1	10	2	—	13	29
Totals	31	86	2	2	121	223
Bassinets						29
Incubators						10

ORGANIZATION

The hospital was governed by a board of 36 trustees. The full board met annually. An executive committee consisting of 12 board members, having at least 1 member from the town of Morgan, Northeaston, Northweston, and Southweston, appointed all committees. The administrator, William Caldwel, had held his position for the prior 16 years. He had an M.S. in hospital administration and was a lecturer at his alma mater and at the school of public health at the nearby university. The controller and chief financial officer, Jim Baker, was a CPA, a fellow of the Hospital Financial Management Association, and had been with the hospital for 15 years.

Morgan's medical staff consisted of five groups: active, courtesy (first-year status), consulting, honorary, and intern and resident. The active staff consisted of local physicians and was also broken into five groups: seniors (via the bylaws), attending (board certified diplomats), assistant attending (juniors to diplomats), associate (general practitioners) and junior associates. The hospital had six medical departments: medicine, obstetrics-gynecology, pediatrics, radiology, pathology, and surgery, the latter consisting of six divisions: anesthesiology, dentistry, ophthalmology, otolaryngology, orthopedics, and urology.

The executive committee appointed the hospital's medical board annually. The medical board was responsible for recommending to the executive committee names of physicians to be appointed or reappointed to the medical staff and for acting on the reports of its various committees (e.g., tissue, pharmacy, library). The medical board consisted of the department chiefs, general practice section chief, division chiefs as designated by the executive committee, and the president of the medical staff. The full medical staff (active) elected officers; excluding the president, offices could be held consecutively. The medical board elected the chief of staff annually from among its members.

The active staff consisted of 51 physicians (see Table 2). Nineteen were general practitioners assigned to various departments; the remainder were specialists. The distribution of these physicians among the local communities and various community admissions statistics are shown in Table 3.

The distribution of the above admissions, lengths of stay, and associated utilization data are shown in Exhibit 1. The percentage breakdowns were 74.4 percent medical-surgical, 1.9 percent intensive care, 9.8 percent pediatric, and 14.0 percent obstetrics-gynecology.

HOSPITAL SERVICE PATTERNS

Morgan Hospital was experiencing a shift in service patterns common in the region. Outpatient visits grew over four times faster than all inpatient days between 19X6 and 19X9 (see Exhibit 2). This was in part due to the hospital's long-run community service plan. A questionnaire distributed in

TABLE 2
Physician—Medical Department Distribution

		Number	Percent
Surgery			
Anesthesiologist	1		
Dentist	1		
General surgeons	6		
Neurosurgeon	1		
Ophthalmologists	3		
Orthopedic surgeons	2		
Urologist	1		
Otolaryngologist	1	16	31.4%
Medicine			
Internists	3		
Physiatrist	1		
Psychiatrist	1	5	9.8
Obstetrics-gynecology		5	9.8
Pediatricians		3	5.9
Pathologists		2	3.9
Radiologists		1	2.0
General Practitioners		19	37.2
Totals		51	100.0%

TABLE 3
Physicians and Admissions: Geographic Distributions, 19X8

	Distance from Morgan*	Physician Office Location	Percent of Admissions	Population Growth Per Year 19X0–X7	Population 19X8	Total Hospital Admissions	Admissions to Morgan Hospital No.	Admissions to Morgan Hospital Percent
Morgan	0.0	29	18.8%	0.6%	15,000	2,070	1,391	67.2%
Northeaston†	1.5	13	30.0	0.2	19,900	2,754	2,229	80.9
Northweston†	3.5	5	16.1	1.9	11,900	1,460	1,194	81.8
Southweston†	3.0	2	21.9	3.4	23,700	3,038	1,622	53.4
Upnorthton	8.5	—	4.3	3.5	4,500	484	317	65.5
Southeaston†	6.5	1	1.4	7.9	13,700	1,107	104	9.4
Urbanton	15.0	1	0.4	−0.4	172,000	20,218	29	0.2
Other	—	—	7.1	n.a.	n.a.	n.a.	400	n.a.
Totals	n.a.	51	100.0%	n.a.	n.a.	n.a.	7,286	n.a.
(Region)				2.1%				

n.a. = not available.
* Distance in miles from Morgan Hospital to the population centers of cities and towns.
† The names of these "towns and cities" show their locations on the borders of Morgan.

EXHIBIT 1
Selected Inpatient Statistics 19X5 to 19X8

	Medical-Surgical				Intensive Care			
	19X5	19X6	19X7	19X8	19X5	19X6	19X7	19X8
Beds	131	130	130	139	4	6	6	6
Discharges	4,561	*	4,974	5,425	162	*	—	128
Patient days	46,934	47,903	46,557	53,715	1,394	1,244	1,454	1,185
Occupancy rate.........	98.2	100.9	98.1	105.6	95.5	56.8	66.4	54.0
Average L.O.S.†	10.29	—	9.71	9.90	8.60	—	—	9.26
Beds per 1,000 population	0.23	0.23	0.23	0.24	0.01	0.01	0.01	0.01
Admissions per 1,000 population	8.12	—	8.30	9.44	0.29	—	—	0.22

	Pediatric				Obstetric-Gynecology			
Beds	18	22	22	22	31	29	29	20
Discharges	1,204	*	1,166	715	1,723	*	1,467	1,018
Patient days	4,885	4,879	4,855	4,219	5,557	5,596	6,787	3,748
Occupancy rate.........	74.4	60.8	59.2	52.4	49.1	52.9	64.1	51.2
Average L.O.S.†	4.06	—	4.08	5.90	3.23	—	4.63	3.68
Beds per 1,000 population	0.03	0.04	0.04	0.04	0.06	0.05	0.05	0.03
Admissions per 1,000 population	2.14	—	2.02	1.24	2.91	—	2.54	1.77

	Psychiatric				Total			
Beds	—	—	—	—	184	187	187	187
Discharges	—	—	—	—	7,650	7,607	7,286	7,286
Patient days	—	—	—	—	58,770	59,622	59,653	62,867
Occupancy rate.........	—	—	—	—	75.1	87.4	87.3	91.9
Average L.O.S.†	—	—	—	—	7.68	7.89	8.02	8.63
Beds per 1,000 population	—	—	—	—	0.33	0.33	0.32	0.33
Admissions per 1,000 population	—	—	—	—	13.61	13.21	12.86	12.68

* Failed to report discharges by services for 19X6.
† Length of stay.
Source: State Department of Health, Hill-Burton Annual Surveys.

Morgan's four primary towns indicated that a regularly staffed emergency room and ongoing psychiatric clinic were desired by a large proportion of the population.

Nonmaternity patient days were stable from 19X6 through 19X8 primarily because the hospital's effective capacity limits were reached. This was due to an insufficient supply of medical-surgical beds. The problem was eliminated in 19X9 when 40 beds were added to the medical-surgical units. Maternity and newborn days were dropping off, as was par for the region.

The number of equivalent full-time employees (total hours paid divided by 2,080 hours per year) by major categories grew disproportionately. As is shown in Exhibit 2, primary and professional service employees grew at the rate of 5.4 percent per year from 19X6 through 19X9: floor nursing employees, 2.6 percent; general and domiciliary, 15.9 percent; and total growth, 7.6

EXHIBIT 2
General Statistics, 19X6 to 19X9

	19X9	19X8	19X7	19X6
Nonmaternity patient days	63,064	55,767	55,473	55,159
Beds (average)	189.7	167.0	167.0	171
Occupancy rate	87.0	91.0	90.7	88.4
Discharges	6,791	6,268	6,320	6,499
Maternity patient days	3,478	3,748	4,080	4,242
Beds (average)	20.0	20.0	20.0	24.0
Occupancy rate	47.6	51.2	55.9	48.4
Discharges	964	1,018	1,107	1,128
Newborn patient days	3,862	4,278	4,646	4,685
Bassinets (average)	29.0	29.0	29.0	33.0
Occupancy rate	36.5	40.3	43.9	38.9
Discharges	910	936	1,017	1,044
Births	855	888	987	983
Employees*				
General and domiciliary	181.0	140.6	129.7	116.1
Floor nursing	157.3	148.7	147.1	145.7
Primary service and				
professional	177.1	162.3	153.0	151.3
Total	515.4	451.6	429.8	413.1
Interns, residents and				
physicians*	6.2	7.1	5.8	5.0
Outpatient visits				
Emergency room	20,197	15,948	14,682	16,120
Clinics†	5,331	1,651	2,070	2,507
Private referral for tests	29,233	28,813	22,907	17,947
Total	54,761	46,412	39,659	36,574
State rate days	3,737	2,089	1,807	3,053
Medicare days	31,402	19,403	19,626	n.a.
Blue Cross full service	14,058	—	—	—
Blue Cross room and				
board indemnity	8,472	—	—	—
All other	18,873	38,023	38,120	56,348
Total	76,542	59,515	59,533	59,401
Floor area (sq. ft.)	198,097	118,466	121,329	113,388
Depreciation age				
Buildings	7.4	8.4	7.9	11.1
Fixed equipment	5.0	14.4	20.1	13.0
Movable equipment	7.8	8.6	8.1	8.8

n.a. = not available.
* Full-time equivalents.
† Excludes psychiatric 19X6 to 19X8.

percent. This disproportionate growth was primarily due to the physical restructuring of the hospital, and a report from a nationally known industrial engineering organization stating that some departments were grossly under-staffed, for example, housekeeping. Exhibit 3 shows the staffing changes by department between 19X8 and 19X9. Associated activity bases of the de-partments are also shown, these bases being, with some exceptions, the

EXHIBIT 3
Equivalent Full-time Employees and Activity

	Employees			Activity		
	19X8	19X9	Percent Change	19X8	19X9	Percent Change
General Service Departments:						
Administration and general:						
Discharges	45.7	48.8	+7%	7,286	7,755	+6%
Dietary:						
Meals served	34.1	38.3	+12	223,066	243,773	+9
Housekeeping:						
Square feet serviced	23.8	44.2	+86	117,290	165,262	+41
Laundry:						
Pounds cleaned	13.8	17.1	+24	703,520	799,045	+14
Linen service:						
Pounds cleaned	3.6	4.1	+14	703,520	799,045	+14
Maintenance of personnel:						
Live-ins	0.7	0.8	+14	21.3	12.4	−42
Operation of plant:						
Square feet serviced	7.1	12.1	+72	110,369	163,261	+48
Repairs and maintenance:						
Square feet serviced	11.8	15.6	+32	107,518	175,258	+63
Professional Service Departments:						
Nursing service administration:						
Nurses administered	8.0	8.3	+4	204.2	201.2	−1
Interns, residents, and physicians:						
Patient days	7.1	6.2	−13	59,519	66,542	+12
Medical records and library:						
Pages	10.9	11.1	−1	1,397,449	1,601,852	+15
Social service:						
Visits	2.0	2.0	—	784	819	+4
Primary Service Departments:						
Operating rooms:						
Man-minutes	19.1	14.7	−23	398,240	440,802	+11
Postoperative room:						
Cases	2.3	2.2	−4	2,292	2,647	+15
Anesthesiology:						
Man-minutes	4.7	6.2	+32	182,490	201,642	+10
Delivery room:						
Births	5.7	5.8	+2	888	855	−4
Radiology:						
Standard unit values	18.6	23.1	+24	3,457,794	3,889,270	+12

EXHIBIT 3 *(continued)*

	Employees			Activity		
	19X8	*19X9*	*Percent Change*	*19X8*	*19X9*	*Percent Change*
Laboratory:						
Standard unit values	29.3	27.3	−7%	4,582,988	5,189,563	+13%
Electroencephalography:						
Examinations	1.0	1.0	—	317	454	+42
Electrocardiology:						
Examinations	2.0	2.0	—	341	369	+8
Physical therapy:						
Minutes	6.8	8.5	+25	351,652	412,072	+17
Central sterile supply:						
Dollar volume	9.3	19.8	+112	$ 39,543	$106,261	+169
Inhalation therapy:						
Charges	4.1	4.0	−2	$ 76,635	$ 87,892	+15
Intravenous therapy:						
Infusions	2.6	3.4	+31	10,772	14,247	+32
Pharmacy:						
Cost of drugs						
requisitioned	3.5	3.6	+3	$104,020	$109,230	+5
Emergency service:						
Visits....................	15.2	17.8	+17	17,880	22,506	+26
Isotope therapy:						
Procedures	0.3	0.5	+67	476	427	−10
Routine Service:						
Nonmaternity patient days:						
Medical-Surgical	103.6	113.1	+9	—	—	—
Pediatrics	11.9	13.7	+15	4,219	—	—
ICU	9.9	10.6	+7	1,185	—	—
SCU	4.7	3.3	−30	—	—	—
Total	130.1	140.7	+8%	55,767	63,064	+13%
Maternity patient days........	7.8	6.5	−17%	3,748	3,478	−7%
Newborn patient days	8.4	7.7	−8	4,278	3,862	−10
Outpatient clinics						
Visits....................	2.4	2.4	—	1,651	1,417	−14
Other						
Research	0.5	0.4	−20	—	—	—
Psychiatric clinic						
Visits....................	4.8	4.9	+2	2,678	3,914	+46
Health education	3.9	4.3	+10	—	—	—
Total	451.0	515.4	+14%	—	—	—

bases used to allocate costs among using departments and patient care
areas.[1]

---

[1] The cost allocation basis for administration and general is employees as opposed to discharges (dis.), as shown in Exhibit 3. Man-minutes (man-min.) consist of the sum of times paid hospital employees spend with a patient times the number of employees involved in the service: operating room and anesthesiology. Standard values (std. values) are determined for radiology (diagnostic) and laboratory based on schedules that equalize the resources entering into various tests.

FINANCIAL TRENDS

Morgan Hospital was recognized in the region as one with outstanding financial management for more than a decade. Its prices were traditionally low with respect to other hospitals in the region with comparable services, as were its costs. However, the results as of 19X9 showed some major changes in the hospital's financial condition. The level of general fund assets almost doubled between 19X6 and 19X9, while general fund liabilities more than tripled (see Exhibit 4). Endowment fund assets were cut almost in half. Net plant, property, and equipment more than doubled as did total plant fund assets. Plant fund liabilities increased almost eightfold, the latter being due to the hospital's first major long-term debt issue.

Morgan's operating results deteriorated badly in 19X9. An analysis of the hospital's revenues, expenses, and operating financial flows is shown in Exhibit 5. The hospital's gross margin, total charges less net total expenses, reached a new low in 19X9, namely, 12 percent. Total charges over the period grew at an annual rate of 21 percent; net total expenses grew at 22 percent. The hospital's total deductions decreased as a percentage of total charges, but total additions from unrestricted endowment earnings and miscellaneous activities decreased proportionately more. The net result was a 19X9 net accounting gain equal to 3.3 percent of total charges, significantly less than the prior three years' net gains of 6.4 percent, 7.1 percent, and 5.6 percent.

The addition to the net accounting gain gave the hospital's accounting operating margin: the 19X9 figure of $475,000 was 7.8 percent of total charges, an all-time low—30 percent below the average of the prior three years. Morgan's net receivables position changed drastically for the first time in four years. Net patient accounts receivable from patients and responsible third parties, primarily the state, Blue Cross, and Medicare, are offset by current financing (interest-free loans) for Blue Cross and Medicare to give this increase in net receivables. It took 30 percent of the accounting operating margin leaving 70 percent, $332,000, as the "real" cash flow from operations. This financial operating margin of $332,000 was 5.4 percent of total charges or a little over one-half of the prior three-year average of 9.5 percent.

Up to 19X9, Morgan had been able to generate cash from operations for its small debt service, to fund depreciation, and to make needed additions. However, in 19X9 the financial operating margin covered only three fourths of the new-debt service level. Changes would have to be made in the future if the hospital was merely to meet its debt obligations, much less put cash in depreciation funds and make necessary operating additions. The 19X9 debt service payments were 7.3 percent of total charges. The historical mode of Morgan—and almost all the hospitals of the region—was to generate the bulk of the gross margin in a few primary services, for example, radiology and laboratory, and on medical-surgical room and board prices, as shown in Exhibit 6.

EXHIBIT 4
Selected Fund Account (dollar figures in thousands)

	19X9	19X8	19X7	19X6
General Fund:				
Cash	$ 105	$ 133	$ 240	$ 98
Accounts receivable	974	806	773	670
Allowance for uncollectible accounts	(80)	(70)	(62)	(62)
Inventories	155	87	81	72
Deferred compensation reserve	205	70	15	—
Other	146	84	21	23
Total Assets	$1,505	$1,110	$1,068	$ 801
Accounts payable	$ 136	$ 96	$ 86	$ 83
Salaries, wages, FOAB taxes payable	123	89	60	54
Deferred compensation fund	205	70	15	—
Medicare and Blue Cross advances	146	131	90	—
Deferred Grant Inc.	134	111	89	52
Other liabilities	127	87	51	87
Total Liabilities	$ 871	$ 584	$ 391	$ 276
Endowment Fund:				
Cash	$ 24	$ 107	$ 175	$ 161
Stocks	329	262	211	201
Bonds	447	462	952	1,028
Due from general fund	25	25	21	13
Total Assets	$ 825	$ 856	$1,359	$1,403
Unexpended income	$ 62	—	$ 47	$ 43
Principal:				
General	510	$ 525	1,120	1,190
Restricted	253	331	192	170
Total Liabilities and Principal	$ 825	$ 856	$1,359	$1,403
Plant Fund:				
Plant property and equipment, net	$8,483	$3,536	$3,580	$3,667
Unamortized underwriting fees	86	104	—	—
Under construction	57	4,994	1,372	382
Cash and investments	797	353	156	136
Total Assets	$9,423	$8,987	$5,108	$4,185
Plant accounts payable	$ 12	$ 15	$ 28	$ 94
Bonds payable	2,459	2,706	—	—
Notes payable	154	186	216	247
Due to building fund	53	—	—	—
Total Liabilities	$2,678	$2,907	$ 244	$ 341
Pledges receivable (not confirmed)	$ 345	$ 468	$ 826	n.a.

n.a. = not available.

EXHIBIT 5
Revenues, Expenses and Operating Financial Flows (dollar figures in thousands)

	19X9	19X8	19X7	19X6
Inpatient charges:				
Primary services	$2,269	$1,817	$1,746	$1,464
Room, board, floor nursing	3,151	2,353	2,133	1,694
Outpatient charges:				
Primary services	368	313	258	189
Emergency room visits	325	144	133	109
Total Charges	$6,113	$4,627	$4,270	$3,456
Salaries and wages	$3,596	$2,778	$2,419	$2,082
Nonsalary expense......................	1,661	1,124	943	859
Depreciation (straight line)	271	167	164	137
Miscellaneous activity income	(161)	(126)	(9)	(96)
Net Expenses.....................	$5,367	$3,943	$3,517	$2,982
Gross margin	$ 746	$ 684	$ 753	$ 474
Less: Contract adjustments...............	$ 456	$ 359	$ 413	$ 265
Free beds	9	12	13	18
Employees and staff allowances	43	35	31	25
Bad debt: Provision	184	137	163	126
Recoveries	(74)	(58)	(48)	(34)
Total Deductions	$ 618	$ 485	$ 572	$ 400
Add: Unrestricted endowment earnings.....	$ 35	$ 45	$ 57	$ 59
Miscellaneous earnings and				
general gifts	41	52	67	59
Total Additions	$ 76	$ 97	$ 124	$ 118
Net Accounting Gain	$ 204	$ 296	$ 305	$ 192
Add: Depreciation	$ 271	$ 167	$ 164	$ 137
Accounting operating margin	$ 475	$ 463	$ 469	$ 329
Less: Net accounts receivables increase.....	$ 158	$ 25	$ 103	$ 74
(plus): Current finance charges	(15)	(41)	(90)	—
Net Receivables Charge	$ 143	$ (16)	$ 13	$ 74
Financial operating margin	$ 332	$ 479	$ 456	$ 255
Less: Debt service: Interest	165	8	8	5
Principal	279	30	31	18
	$ 444	$ 38	$ 39	$ 23
Available for funding, replacements, etc.....	$ (112)	$ 441	$ 417	$ 232

RADIOLOGY DEPARTMENT

Morgan's radiology department consisted of a diagnostic unit and an isotope therapy unit. Isotope therapy activity was negligible in terms of dollars and cents; the unit paid for itself since it was started (recognizing that the radiologists' salaries are allocations of amounts that would have to be otherwise covered in diagnostic radiology). The diagnostic activities were

EXHIBIT 6
Selected Revenue and Full Cost Data (in dollars), 19X9

	Inpatient			Outpatient			Total
	Non-maternity	Maternity	Newborn	Clinics	Private Referred	Emergency Room	
Routine services:							
Charges	$2,904,866	$137,322	$ 89,035	$ 28,051	—	$325,201	$3,484,475
Full costs	2,480,606	161,231	112,114	101,992	—	317,834	3,173,777
Gross Margin	$ 424,260	$ (23,909)	$ (23,079)	$ (73,941)	—	$ 7,367	$ 310,698
Laboratory:							
Charges	$ 516,238	$ 16,179	$ 2,926	—	$ 68,526	—	$ 603,869
Full costs	371,688	9,178	1,328	—	64,858	—	447,052
Gross Margin	$ 144,550	$ 7,001	$ 1,598	—	$ 3,668	—	$ 156,817
Radiology (diagnostic):							
Charges	$ 391,676	$ 5,508	$ 748	—	$180,777	—	$ 578,709
Full Costs	307,708	4,641	579	—	116,022	—	428,950
Gross Margin	$ 83,968	$ 867	$ 169	—	$ 64,755	—	$ 149,759
All other primary services:							
Charges	$1,220,564	$107,007	$ 8,485	$ 6,569	$ 87,302	$ 16,515	$1,446,442
Full Costs	986,944	142,191	6,604	4,184	111,051	12,647	1,263,621
Gross Margin	$ 233,620	$ (35,184)	$ 1,881	$ 2,385	$ (23,749)	$ 3,868	$ 182,821
Total primary services:							
Charges	$2,128,478	$128,694	$ 12,159	$ 6,569	$336,605	$ 16,515	$2,629,020
Full Costs	1,666,340	156,010	8,511	4,184	291,931	12,647	2,139,623
Gross Margin	$ 462,138	$ (27,316)	$ 3,648	$ 2,385	$ 44,674	$ 3,868	$ 489,397
Totals:							
Charges	$5,033,344	$266,016	$101,194	$ 34,620	$336,605	$341,716	$6,113,495
Full Costs	4,146,946	317,240	120,625	106,176	291,931	330,481	5,313,400
Gross Margin (loss)	$ 886,398	$ (51,225)	$ (19,431)	$ (71,556)	$ 44,674	$ 11,235	$ 800,095
Nonpatient care costs*							$ 52,954
Gross Margin							$ 747,141

central to the functioning of Morgan Hospital. Exhibit 7 shows the department's service distributions for the years 19X6–X9. The "units" for diagnostic radiology are standardized relative resource expenditure measures that are applied to each test. All outpatient diagnostic radiology tests are included in the "private referred" category in Exhibit 7.

EXHIBIT 7
Radiology Department Service Distribution, 19X6–19X9

	19X6	19X7	19X8	19X9
Diagnostic Radiology Units:				
Nonmaternity	2,369,364	2,403,181	2,459,985	2,789,937
Maternity	36,295	41,636	39,085	42,085
Newborn	6,455	6,230	7,345	5,265
Clinics	—	—	--	—
Private referred	796,250	872,011	951,379	1,051,983
Emergency room	—	—	—	—
Total	3,208,364	3,323,058	3,457,794	3,889,270
Isotope Therapy Procedures				
Nonmaternity	—	155	392	356
Maternity	—	—	63	1
Newborn	—	—	—	—
Clinics	—	—	—	—
Private referred	—	37	21	70
Emergency room	—	—	—	—
Total	—	192	476	427

The diagnostic unit contributed more to Morgan's gross margin than any service excluding nonmaternity room, board, and floor nursing. Diagnostic radiology contributed 20 percent of the hospital's gross margin in 19X9. This financial importance of diagnostic radiology was the common mode in almost all the region's hospitals.[2] In view of the change in the hospital's overall financial condition in 19X9, changes in the radiology department financial structure could have a major impact on the future financial health of the hospital.

Exhibit 8 shows the radiology department's charges and line item expenses for the years 19X7 through 19X9. The number of diagnostic units increased by 17 percent while the cost per unit increased 52 percent and the charge per unit increased 7 percent over the three years. Hence, the gross margin per unit decreased by 42 percent. The result of these changes in terms of the hospital's total gross margin was significant: in 19X7 diagnostic radiology accounted for almost 30 percent of the $753,000 total gross margin. The

---

[2] In 19X8, the hospitals in the region averaged 4,188,040 radiology diagnostic units, 280 beds, and 84,014 patient days. The average radiology diagnostic charge in the region (simple average) was $0.125; the average cost, $0.107. The unit margin $0.018, 14.4 percent, contributed an average of $75,384 to the average total gross margin of $362,000 (about 21 percent).

19X9 percentage was 20 percent as noted in the above paragraph. Hours per unit increased by 11.5 percent and the average wage per hour increased 19.2 percent; supplies per unit increased 78.3 percent; and allocated expenses increased by 62.9 percent per unit. Ten percent of one radiologist's time (of 2,080 hours) and salary was allocated to isotope therapy.

EXHIBIT 8
Radiology Department Charges and Line Item Expenses, 19X7–19X9

	Diagnostic Radiology			Isotope Therapy		
	19X7	*19X8*	*19X9*	*19X7*	*19X8*	*19X9*
Standard units per procedure	3,323,058	3,457,794	3,889,270	192	476	427
Charges	$463,938	$477,361	$578,709	$5,735	$15,240	$16,031
Charge per unit or procedure	$ 0.1396	$ 0.1381	$ 0.1488	$29.87	$ 32.02	$ 37.54
Hours paid:						
Radiologists	3,120	4,160	4,160	208	208	208
Technicians	27,456	28,496	37,648	416	416	416
Secretarial-clerical	6,240	6,032	6,240	—	—	—
Total	36,816	38,688	48,048	624	624	624
Salaries:						
Radiologists	$ 49,771	$ 49,811	$ 68,841	$1,850	$ 3,600	$ 4,000
Technicians	59,886	72,956	107,070	718	1,934	2,304
Secretarial-clerical	13,892	14,841	16,244	—	—	—
Total	$123,549	$137,608	$192,155	$2,568	$ 5,534	$ 6,304
Supplies:						
Films/Isotopes	$ 35,544	$ 39,080	$ 43,657	$2,055	$ 6,543	$ 6,514
Chemicals	2,800	2,708	3,239	—	—	—
Other.............................	8,747	10,814	48,838	—	—	—
Purchased services................	875	799	9,573	—	—	—
Repairs	3,545	4,894	7,099	—	—	—
Office supplies	2,669	828	590	—	—	—
Uniforms and gowns	185	75	462	—	—	—
Total	$ 54,365	$ 59,198	$113,458	$2,055	$ 6,543	$ 6,514
Depreciation:						
Major movable	$ 7,530	$ 9,472	$ 11,805	$ 660	$ 1,319	$ 1,319
Fixed equipment	755	728	2,256	22	21	51
Buildings	2,452	2,480	3,308	73	72	76
Total	$ 10,737	$ 12,680	$ 17,369	$ 755	$ 1,412	$ 1,446
Transfers and miscellaneous credit to expenses	$ (5,518)	$ (4,864)	$ (4,931)	$ (21)	$ (102)	—
Allocated:						
Administrative and general (employees)	$ 29,917	$ 36,962	$ 59,746	$ 542	$ 735	—
Housekeeping (square feet served)	4,644	5,862	13,655	150	189	—
Laundry and linen (pounds cleaned)	$ 1,409	$ 1,609	$ 1,986	—	—	—
Plant operation (square feet served)	6,908	5,231	11,602	$ 233	$ 169	—
Repairs and maintenance (square feet served)	5,657	6,134	8,138	182	198	—
Dietary (meals served)	2,690	3,316	4,003	46	55	—
Personnel maintenance (live-ins)	3,472	3,563	6,100	—	—	—
Interns, residents and physicians (hours)...............	2,185	2,364	2,372	—	—	2,280
Central sterile (dollar volume)	1,278	1,497	3,296	—	—	—
Total	$ 58,160	$ 66,538	$ 110,898	$1,153	$ 1,346	$ 2,280
Total	$ 241,293	$ 271,160	$ 428,949	$6,510	$14,733	$16,544
Cost per unit or procedure	$ 0.0726	$ 0.07842	$ 0.1103	$33.91	$ 30.95	$ 38.74
Margin per unit or procedure	$ 0.0670	$ 0.0587	$ 0.0385	$ (4.04)	$ 1.07	$ (1.20)

* Includes $20,901 equipment rental, $10,065 moving expense, and $17,872 in minor start-up and miscellaneous charges.

In February 19X9, Dr. Farley, the chief of radiology, asked administration to change the method by which he was paid. He said that his colleagues had been criticizing him for accepting a salary basis and asked administration to authorize either direct billing or a percentage of gross as the payment method. The administration stated that the change of payment method question must go to the executive committee. The committee turned down the request for a change of payment method. As a matter of philosophy, the hospital board would not accept percentage of gross or direct billing for any full-time physician. All full-time physicians had to remain on a salary basis. While the payment basis could not be discussed, the executive committee was willing to discuss the amount of salary.

A few months later, after he was told of the executive committee decision, Dr. Farley said he would think about the committee's decision. In May of 19X9, Dr. Farley submitted his resignation effective six months later (October 1). In June, Dr. Farley said he wanted to visit his uncle in a neighboring state. He said he would be back in a few days. But, ten days later no one at Morgan Hospital knew where Dr. Farley was located. A few days later a friend of Mr. Baker saw Dr. Farley in the private offices of a radiology group in a nearby state. Mr. Baker called Dr. Farley on the phone and Dr. Farley said he would be back in a few days. Dr. Farley returned in a few days and worked one week. On Friday of that week, he walked into the administration offices and said he was leaving the following Monday to work with the radiologist group in the nearby state. This radiology group was handling patients on an out- and inpatient basis, was billing separately, and had offices in the hospital it served.

In the meantime, Morgan Hospital still had its associate radiologist, Dr. Granger. In addition, Dr. Granger was assisted by resident radiologists from the hospital at the nearby university medical center. This coverage started late in June 19X9. Morgan Hospital began an extensive search in June 19X9 to find a replacement for Dr. Farley. The hospital had contacts with 15 radiologists and had discussions with 8 who made a trip to Morgan to discuss the hospital's needs. The hospital was initially optimistic about finding a new chief of service. This was because the radiology department had been moved in January and had, with the exception of a few pieces of equipment, completely new facilities.

Only 2 of the 15 radiologists contacted by the hospital would discuss a salary payment basis. Of those two, one asked for a starting salary of $55,000, to be increased to at least $75,000 within three years. The other jokingly suggested $100,000 if the department had two men, but would take $75,000 if the department had three men. The hospital had always had a two-man radiology department. But this thinking was rendered questionable by the uniform thinking of the 15 radiologists contacted by the hospital. They were all of the opinion that the hospital needed at least a three-man department.

The interviewees' attitudes toward payment were almost uniform. They expressed a desire for a percentage of gross in the area of about 40 percent. Only one would consider the professional component relative value (PCRV) basis for payment. This basis consists of a set of professional time standards for various tests established by the American College of Radiologists. All others considered the method too complicated.

Two nearby hospitals used the PCRVs to pay their radiologists on the basis of 70 cents and 75 cents per unit. The amounts so computed were adjusted for bad debts. These particular hospitals give the radiologists office space in the hospitals. In general, radiologists with private offices in the area charged about $1.40 per PCRV unit.

The one radiologist who would consider the PCRV unit system said he would accept it if he could find two other radiologists who would accept the system. After an amount of negotiation between administration and this radiologist, Dr. Hill, it was proposed that Morgan Hospital offer Dr. Hill the chief of radiology position given that he could get two radiologists. However, the negotiations fell through when two who had expressed an interest in working with Dr. Hill were not willing to discuss the PCRV unit system of payment.

There were more discussions with the prospective chief of radiology, Dr. Hill. He thought he could not get anyone to join him unless the hospital paid a percentage of gross or allowed the group to bill directly. However, the board did not want to consider and, therefore, be responsible for the increase in radiology costs that would result (they would have been higher by about $200,000 in 19X9), since the increases and future increases would be beyond their control. Negotiations continued, and it became clear that the hospital could attract radiologists only if it permitted direct billing or a percentage of gross. During this time there was extensive discussion between Dr. Hill and administration as to his relationship to the hospital. The radiologist would start on March 1, 19X0. No decision had been made on the payment basis, but administration knew that the salary basis would have to be eliminated.

Dr. Hill was from Europe where he had received his board certification in radiology. He was, at the time of the negotiations, an associate chief of radiology in one of the hospitals in the larger nearby metropolitan area. However, Morgan was not trying to "steal" a radiologist. Dr. Hill had made the first contact with Morgan. The associate radiologist, Dr. Granger, gave the hospital notification that he would leave at the time when the incoming group took over the service. He gave his wife's desire to return to their country of origin in South America as the reason for leaving, but there was gossip in the hospital that the new radiologists would not fully accept Dr. Granger in the group even though they offered him a position in their group.

At the time of the agreement, the associate position was under discussion with a radiologist in academia. The third spot was being discussed with a resident radiologist at the nearby university medical center. The hospital's board considered it a great concession to switch from a salary basis. They thought the hospital's new facility, the closeness to the university center, and a reasonably attractive living area would make it reasonably easy to attract a new radiologist. The new chief of radiology would have an academic position at the medical school in the nearby university medical center.

Morgan's bylaws include a statement that all readings of X rays are to be done by a board-certified or board-eligible radiologist. The Joint Commission on the Accreditation of Hospitals requires that X rays be interpreted by physicians that are ". . . competent in the field." The commission's explanatory supplement to the standards reads as follows:

> In the radiologic department, the need for qualified personnel is greatly stressed. Every hospital should have a qualified radiologist, either full time or part time on a consulting basis, both to supervise the department and to interpret films that require specialized knowledge for accurate reading. Hospitals without the services of a radiologist in any capacity, whose medical staffs read all films themselves, are not considered as rendering high quality care.

The public health code of the state was *somewhat* more specific in requirements:

> (D) there will be departments of medicine, pathology, pediatrics and radiology, each of which will be under the overall direction of a chief who will be responsible for supervising the quality of service given. Such a chief will be a physician qualified on the basis of postgraduate approved training or experience or a combination of both, ...

REQUESTED ANALYSIS

The radiology department payments in 19X9 included $68,841 in diagnostic radiologists' salaries, $4,000 in isotope therapy radiologists' salaries, $5,569 in intern salaries, and $9,573 in outside fees paid to the resident radiologists from the university medical center. The new chief of radiology requested a payment basis that would require cash payments to the three totaling $280,000 under percentage of gross. If the group went on direct billing, the three would still receive payments of $280,000 under the program proposed by the new chief. Since the radiologist would have to hire at least one secretary and to rent office space, under the direct billing program, the total billings to patients would have to be in the area of $300,000 for professional services under the direct billing program. The radiologists would practice exclusively in the hospital's radiology department under either payment method. All expenses of the hospital's radiology department, except radiologist salaries, but including the intern salary, would continue under the direct billing basis. Under the percentage of gross, radiologist salaries would have been $199,155 more than in 19X9 ($280,000 less the diagnostic radiologists' salaries, isotope therapy radiologists' salaries, and outside fees).

Mr. Caldwel asked Jim Baker to analyze the various alternatives they discussed. The analyses were to include the effects of each alternative, if any, on (1) the hospital's financial condition (2) the hospital's average per diem nonmaternity and outpatient visit average costs, (3) the hospital bills actually paid by various patients, (4) the total costs to the communities served, and (5) the total costs to the state and federal governments in 19X9 as compared to the actual outcomes. The alternatives were:

1. Include in all radiology charges the additional costs of $200,000. Isotope therapy would receive $9,333 in radiologists salaries (10 percent × $280,000 × ⅓). State, Blue Cross, and Medicare contracts would cover these costs automatically on a retroactive basis for patients supported by the three third parties. Charge-cost differences are contractual adjustments on the hospital's financial reports. Other patient charges would have to be greater than costs to cover the 8.03 percent bad debts associated with each privately billed dollar. There were 18,873 noncost contract patient days including maternity days. Newborn and all outpatient activities involve insignificant proportions of cost contract services.
2. Make no changes, that is, absorb the $200,000 cost increase in the hospital's existing financial flows. Do not change any prices to cover the higher payments to the radiologists.
3. Have the radiologists bill separately for their professional services, thereby taking the professional salaries off the hospital's books.

Special studies had shown that cost contract nonmaternity patients consumed the same average number of diagnostic radiology units as noncost contract nonmaternity patients.

The various alternatives had to be considered in the light of other problems. The board and community had accepted, but with a large amount of negative reaction, the last round of price increases. The average room, board, and floor nursing service per diem price, excluding ICU, SCU, and maternity, increased from $42.31 to $47.05, which was 11.2 percent, the largest increase in the hospital's history.

The largest contributor to the associated cost increases was salaries. The average salary increased from $6,151 in 19X8 to $6,977 in 19X9: 13.4 percent (albeit a much-repeated reason). The hospital would still have problems in the future hiring and retaining of nonprofessional and professional personnel. Unionization pressures among the nonprofessionals were increasing. Any price increase to be borne directly by community residents would not be popular.

The Medicare spending overruns were well known: the economy-related elimination of the "2 percent" factor had cost the hospital about $31,000 in a recent year. The state government appeared to be working its way into another major financial crisis: another major tax appeared likely in the near future. The Blue Cross Association serving the region was in serious financial and major political trouble: reserves after the last quarter hit a new, almost illegal low, and the association had "locked horns" with the state commissioner of insurance (who was leaving office along with his appointing governor).

Jim Baker was to recommend to Mr. Caldwel a course of action. It was the general philosophy of the Morgan board and administration that the general hospital and hospital-related needs of the local communities be met as efficiently as possible by the hospital. A healthy, viable financial condition was considered an integral policy of this philosophy.

17.1. Small City (B)*

"My God! I never expected anything like this!" exclaimed Mayor Edward Burns as he hung up the telephone following a vitriolic conversation with one of the town's most prominent citizens about the city's recently passed ordinance regulating the use of septic tank systems. Although the Small City Council had passed the ordinance without substantive public opposition, it now seemed as if his telephone would never cease ringing, as one irate resident after another called him to complain. Some of the complainers were fairly restrained (although obviously angry), but many were not even civil. One caller's language was so foul that the mayor, who was a relatively mild man, lost his own temper and shouted back before banging his telephone down. He began to wonder if the abuse would ever cease.

Opposition to the ordinance was plainly mounting. The mayor had just received a petition signed by more than 200 residents demanding that the ordinance be rescinded. There were even mutterings by some residents about suing the city to overturn the regulation. Mayor Burns was well aware that the next meeting of the city council—to be held in the elementary school auditorium—was likely to be the stormiest in his two years of office.

THE CITY COUNCIL MEETING

The mayor's expectation of a large turnout was accurate; the meeting attracted a full house of over 100 community dwellers. Almost before the mayor could gavel the meeting to order, Reginald Jackson was on his feet demanding to be heard for the purpose of presenting the city council with his latest petition against the ordinance and announcing the names of several prominent citizens who had signed it. The mayor deferred to his request, and when Mr. Jackson had finished with his enumeration, he proceeded to launch a highly emotional tirade impugning the competence and the motives of the mayor directly and the city council in general.

When Jackson finished, he turned to another man who was seated nearby and they spoke for a few moments. Turning back to the mayor and the council, who were seated at a long narrow table at the front of the audience, Jackson announced that he wished to introduce a Mr. Royce, a lawyer

---

* Prepared by George G. Eddy and Burnard H. Sord, the University of Texas at Austin.

retained by an unidentified group of protesting residents. Immediately, Royce began to dissect the ordinance in a manner that one council member later described as "aggressively hostile." This sparked a series of heated exchanges with several council members, including the mayor. In the background, private discussions sprang up throughout the auditorium, making it difficult to understand what the lawyer was stressing. He concluded abruptly with a threat of a lawsuit to overturn the ordinance, and almost as promptly another man began to speak.

At this point the mayor had to gavel for order, since neither he nor the council members could hear or learn the identity of the new speaker. After a moderate degree of decorum was obtained, the council discovered another lawyer was on the attack. He rambled on, frequently alluding to the unfortunate "necessity" to institute suit unless the council retracted the obviously "ill-conceived" and "illegal" statute. From time to time, the city attorney interjected comments but few seemed to heed him. Finally, after a blistering exchange between the second lawyer and a council member, the former sat down.

Obviously experiencing difficulty in remaining calm, the mayor stood up and began to address the group assembled. He reiterated his belief in the need for such an ordinance to protect and preserve the quality of the environment. He stressed the importance of Small City's taking the initiative and instituting appropriate controls on individual home septic systems before some state agency, particularly the Water Quality Control Board, interceded and imposed its own directives. Trying to summarize the events and conditions leading to the drafting and adoption of Small City's "Water Pollution Control and Abatement Ordinance," Mayor Burns emphasized the following points:

1. Small City relied entirely on private septic systems for the disposal of household waste.
2. Due to the failure of some homeowners in matters of care and maintenance of their private sewage disposal systems, Small City had been cited on several occasions in local newspapers as a source of water pollution.
3. The State Water Quality Acts of 1967 and 1969, with adoption of additional codes in 1971, provided for a fine of $1,000 per day for each instance in which the actions of industrial and municipal corporations, or individuals, resulted in the pollution of streams and lakes.
4. Approximately one third of Small City had been included in a special zone designated for attention by the Water Quality Control Board to insure that proper measures were being taken to prevent water pollution. This was because this portion of Small City's topography and soil characteristics, together with its proximity to Lake Blue, made it particularly susceptible as a water pollution contributor if septic tank systems were used.

5. The granting of septic tank system permits, along with the design and supervision of construction of septic systems in Small City, had for many years been handled by officials of the Health and Sanitation Department of Big City. In the past two years, the mayor, some council members, and some residents of Small City believed they had reason to question how effectively these functions were being performed by Big City owing to:

    a. Apparent indiscriminate issue of permits for septic systems on all lots on application by builders or owner, irrespective of the size, slope of the surface, soil thickness and relationships to ravines, and other critical criteria required to be analyzed by the codes established by the State Department of Health.

    b. Public utterances by employees and others associated with the Big City Health Department, indicting Small City for its sanitation problems—particularly the odor and visible seepages of effluent in numerous instances from septic systems previously approved by Big City officials.

6. Studies of the sanitation situation, problems, and possible alternative solutions commenced prior to the present term of the mayor. Such studies were under the supervision of a professionally qualified sanitation engineer who lived in Small City. Sample tests, taken on a randomly selected basis throughout the community, had confirmed the presence of a real pollution problem.

7. Nothing in the body of municipal law within the state, or rulings by the courts related directly or specifically to the regulation of existing septic systems. The state had, however, authorized cities to take appropriate and necessary measures to control pollution in pertinent acts passed by the state legislature in 1971. These acts also defined functions and authorities of the Water Quality Board. The legal basis for entry on private property for inspections in the face of opposition by the owner was contained in the 14th Amendment to the State Constitution. A warrant to permit such inspections could be issued on the basis of complaints by neighbors offended by unsanitary conditions.

8. Suggestions to the Municipal League, lawyers, and legislators that the authority for control of septic systems be definite and specifically spelled out in legislation had not been acted upon as yet.

The mayor, believing he had touched on all of the significant issues concluded by saying:

> I think everyone will agree that our terrain and soil characteristics make septic tanks, as a proper waste disposal method, highly suspect. Nevertheless, this is what we have, and as I've said previously, if we don't provide for proper controls the state will force our hand by requiring we install a central waste disposal collection system. I've tried to point out to our citizens that that could be prohibitively expensive. Additionally, since we live here on a layering series

of rock strata, the blasting and all that goes with construction would seriously and permanently disfigure our landscape. One of the main attractions of our community is just that landscape, and our underlying objectives always have been to preserve it in its natural state to the maximum extent feasible. I'm convinced that by instituting the measures embodied in our ordinance that we can forestall the need for a central collection system for many, many years to come. Really, I believe it is the only way. . . . Now I'd like to call on Mr. Henry Blackmore to comment on the objections many of you have raised concerning the manner in which his firm, Brownlee Engineering, has been conducting septic system inspections.

As Blackmore began to speak, the mayor realized with dismay that the engineer from Brownlee was not really going to allay the suspicions of the majority of those present who had been contending, among other things, that the Brownlee firm was not doing its inspections in a thoroughly professional manner. While the focal point of citizens' anger seemed clearly the $50 inspection fee ("It's just another damn tax on top of already damn taxes, and for what?"), the quality of these inspections was drawing extensive ire. Several in the audience began to shout out their feelings, completely drowning out Mr. Blackmore's rather feeble attempts to explain the firm's methods. Some especially irate residents made it clear that they would not tolerate "inspections" made by some "damned, college-kid hippie" who ambled haphazardly over their property, while "his flashy girl friend sat impatiently waiting for him in a small foreign car, occasionally tooting the horn while the radio blared on."

Stirring uneasily in the midst of such a hostile audience, Mayor Burns concluded that this just did not seem to be his night. As the interruptions to Blackmore gained momentum, the mayor wondered if he should call upon George Anderson at all. Anderson was a representative of the State Water Quality Control Board whom Burns had asked to attend for the purpose of reinforcing the city's position that it was well within its rights to regulate individual septic systems in the community. While Anderson had seemed to be a forthright and positive person during private discussions with the mayor, the board also was coming under increasing attacks in neighboring communities lately for its stringent water control rulings. Mayor Burns had not seen Mr. Anderson respond on his feet before an unfriendly group, and this meeting was getting out of hand. In a few moments the mayor knew he had to make a number of important decisions.

Suddenly there was an unexpected quiet in the auditorium. Everyone was eyeing Mayor Burns. Clearly, he was expected to speak.

SIZE AND STRUCTURE OF SMALL CITY'S GOVERNMENT

A small community of some 1,500 residents and 600 homes, Small City's area encompassed approximately 2,000 acres of wooded rolling hills. On one of Small City's borders was Big City, with a population of over 100,000 people. Small City received water and electricity from Big City utilities, and the majority of Small City homeowners worked in Big City. The dense vegetation, steep hillslopes, canyons, and numerous creeks in Small City provided a particularly scenic, rural environment.

For years Small City operated with a voluntary contribution program to pay city expenses. Although some residents contributed nothing, enough homeowners sent the city sufficient funds to provide for the very simplest demands for services. With the rapid growth of Big City nearby and the realization of the need for some modern city planning, the city council agreed that a tax program was needed to give Small City fiscal responsibility. In May of 1970, the council passed a tax program of 25 cents per $100 of valuation, the assessed valuation representing 75 percent of market value. The intent of such a program was to take care of road repairs and maintenance, and the modest salaries of paid officials (the secretary-treasurer, police chief, two policemen, and the city attorney) and Small City's share of developing a master plan in conjunction with Big City on a pro rata funding basis as sponsored and largely funded by the federal government. Exhibit 1 on page 480 shows the organization of Small City's government.

The city had no official office space or building of its own in which to conduct municipal business. The city council had informal "work sessions" in the mayor's home. Official city council meetings were convened once a month in the elementary school auditorium, where the public was invited to attend and participate as desired in the administration of city affairs. Opportunity was afforded the residents of Small City to address the council members and the mayor, individually or collectively, and to make suggestions for council action, to protest pending legislation, to request the status of any administrative matter, and so on. Usually only a handful of the residents ever bothered to attend the regular council meetings, and the city's business was concluded quietly, quickly and without lengthy debates or arguments. When controversial matters were posted on the agenda, however, more than 100 citizens might appear. On the other hand, the work sessions were not open to the public; however, no official city action could be taken at these gatherings. (The state subsequently passed an open-meetings law requiring these work sessions to be conducted in a public meeting place.)

PRESERVING SMALL CITY'S
ENVIRONMENTAL ATTRACTIVENESS

The major areas of concern, both to the residents and Small City's administrative body, were: (1) preservation of the environment; (2) control of population density; (3) protecting residential property from encroachment by commercial, industrial, and apartment intrusions by means of a zoning and planning commission; (4) establishing standards for the development of subdivisions; and (5) development of an appropriate master plan to help insure an orderly and systematic growth in keeping with the natural environment.

The city council, recognizing the value of Small City from an ecological and scenic point of view, had taken several actions to protect the quality of the environment:

1. A one-acre minimum lot size was established (*a*) to protect against a crowded developmental pattern which could mar and clutter the community's natural beauty, and (*b*) to prevent a proliferation of septic tanks, thereby reducing the possibility that the natural drainage and water runoff from Small City into Lake Blue would create a pollution hazard.

2. The city council applied for a federal 701 planning grant through the Governor's Planning Office, and was on the list for funds in 1972. Although no efforts had as yet been made to contact planning consultants, two highly reputable firms had already asked to be considered because of their interest in the exciting possibilities here for the new type of "open-space planning," which could make Small City an example for the entire state. It was hoped that land developers and real estate people would see the advantages of an area that had a protected environment and open-space, quality planning.

3. The city council passed an ordinance strictly controlling the size and location of all signs in Small City; neon flashers and other "offensive" type signs were expressly discouraged or forbidden.

4. An Architectural Advisory Committee was established under the Zoning and Planning Commission to offer free architectural advice to business enterprises interested in building in Small City.

5. Under study in the Zoning and Planning Commission were two ordinances aimed at increasing the aesthetics of the community:

   a. An off-street parking ordinance which, among other things, would require a landscaped strip between the road and parking lot.

   b. A cluster-enabling ordinance, which would permit houses in a subdivision to be grouped so as to economize on roads and utilities and yet, with an average of one house per acre, would provide land in the development for open spaces and green belts.

6. Realizing the importance of going all-out to protect the scenic environment, the city council in 1968 activated the Conservation Committee. In the chairman's words, "The Conservation Committee went to the citizens of Small City last year with a series of eight neighborhood meetings with 125 in attendance. There was an endorsement of the committee's plans to support the rural atmosphere of Small City and the encouragement of green belts through the one-acre minimum, conservation easements, and the establishment of green belts through a city plan."

THE PASSAGE OF ORDINANCE 34

It was in keeping with its understanding of the community's desire to preserve the environment and control water pollution that the council passed

Ordinance 34 to regulate septic systems. Pertinent extracts of the ordinance are shown in Exhibit 2 on page 48.

Believing the most economical and efficient manner for implementing this regulation was by means of a professional firm possessing expertise in sanitation engineering, the mayor and the council entered into a contract with Brownlee Engineering. The fee for an inspection by this firm was established at $50, a figure the mayor and the council considered to be reasonable. At the same time, they recognized that Big City had been providing inspection services for homeowners in Small City for about half that amount. The mayor, however, was dissatisfied with the quality of such inspections; he believed these inspections were largely perfunctory, and that the Big City inspectors were too easily influenced by large builders and real estate developers. His opinions subsequently were reinforced by the initial results of Brownlee's inspections: Some 15 percent of those septic tank systems inspected were classified as defective, and all these had been approved initially by Big City inspectors from the Health Department. Additionally, investigations by the Small City health officer disclosed that nearly 50 percent of the effluent from waste disposal systems was contaminated: moreover, the health officer had found contaminated effluent in ditches alongside city roads.

This new ordinance, which required each homeowner to apply for a license to operate his septic system, was passed by the council without any complaints of note by community residents. Within a month after the council action, Mayor Burns wrote each homeowner a personal letter, calling attention to the following:

> Your city council, after publishing notice in the official newspaper [*The Big City Daily News*] and after notice posted in public places of a public hearing on December 7th, adopted Ordinance No. 34. This ordinance deals with water pollution control and abatement within our city. It provides an organized approach to the task of obtaining compliance with the requirements of the Water Quality Board.
>
> Over 500 private sewage disposal systems are in operation within our area. This area is drained by streams that are tributary to Lake Blue. The probability of water contamination without strict regulation of the use of our disposal systems is high.

The mayor's letter went on to emphasize that the ordinance was passed only after careful and extensive consideration of the facts and alternatives, and that a reputable law firm had been employed to draft the ordinance to assure compliance with the requirements of the State Water Quality Board. Mayor Burn's letter stressed:

> Since the estimated cost of funding and construction of an organized collection system is out of our financial reach with our present tax base, and also for the near future, the only open course of action was to adopt our Ordinance No. 34. The ordinance provides for the payment of fees of $50 for inspection and

licensing of private disposal systems. The term of the license for a system will be for five years. This cost of $10 per annum may be compared with the alternative cost of an organized system which would have a minimum effect of quadrupling our present tax rate. Our estimates of the cost of an organized collection system takes into account the effects of federal grants of 55 percent of the cost of certain parts of the system.

Included in this same letter was notice that the firm of Brownlee Engineering had been engaged to assist in implementing the ordinance and, further, that Ordinance 34 authorized the formation of a Water Pollution Control and Abatement Division for Small City.

INITIAL ATTEMPTS TO IMPLEMENT ORDINANCE 34

Approximately a month after the distribution of the mayor's letter, each homeowner received a letter from Brownlee Engineering which contained an application form each property owner was requested to complete. (See Exhibit 3.) The letter also pointed out that:

. . . . due to the number of inspections to be made, it will be impossible to make every inspection in the presence of the property owner. . . after an inspection of your property has been made, an evaluation of the system will be made. This evaluation includes an analysis of the size and adequacy of the system to serve the apparent loading. Our findings and recommendations will then be given to your city council who will decide whether or not to issue a license. You will be notified of their decision by our firm.

Soon thereafter Brownlee Engineering's representatives began to make inspections. Within a very short time, the grumblings mounted, soon to take the form of bitter, complaining telephone calls to the mayor (and his wife if she happened to answer the telephone). When the mayor realized how extensive the dissatisfaction had become, and that only a relative handful of property owners had submitted applications for septic tank inspections, he called upon the council to (1) exclude inspections for those property owners whose septic tank systems were less than two years old, (2) reduce the inspection fee by $5, and (3) extend the deadline for submitting applications. In a series of public meetings commencing two months after Ordinance 34 was passed, the council passed such amendments.

Public furor did not subside. Complaints poured into the mayor's office about the "excessive" fee for the inspections and the "substandard" performance of Brownlee Engineering. Several citizens began to collect signatures on petitions demanding the repeal of Ordinance 34, although few people professed disagreement with the objective of controlling and abating potential water pollution attributable to septic tank systems.

Soon the rhetoric opposing the ordinance became charged with invective, with the principal target being the mayor. So pronounced did it become that Mayor Burns nearly decided not to run for reelection. Refusing to be intimidated, however, by what he considered to be a small clique of perpetual malcontents, the mayor decided to run again. Self-reliant and wealthy, the mayor had been in responsible positions for many years prior to his retirement as a professional man. Unusually energetic and responsive to challenge, Mayor Burns prided himself on his ability to identify a major problem, assess pertinent alternatives, promptly decide, and act decisively. He had moved to Small City about ten years ago, buying several large lots atop a prominent hill.

As soon as his desire to try for another term was public knowledge, his opponents—some of whom had lived in the community for over 20 years and were large property owners in and around Small City—undertook a strident campaign to defeat him. The central issue was Ordinance 34, its opponents contending it was both illegal and unnecessary. Regarding the latter claim, many agitated residents could not understand why Small City property owners could not continue to use the relatively inexpensive services of the Big City Health Department inspectors. Soon the mayor discovered that he was being accused of incompetence, stupidity, contempt for his fellow citizens, misuse of his office for alleged personal gain, and almost every other ulterior motive that could be conceived. Despite this well-organized attack,

EXHIBIT 1
Organization of the Small City Government

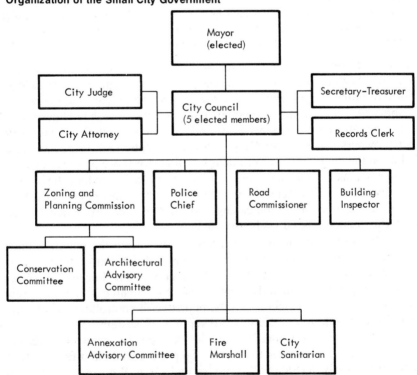

Mayor Burns won reelection—by a margin of less than 15 votes. Mayor Burns believed that the acrimonious atmosphere engendered by the bitter invective of his opponent for the office of mayor, Hank Greenwell, Jr., would probably take a prolonged period to subside.

It was shortly after his reelection that Mayor Burns encountered the largest gathering of community residents he had ever seen when he presided over the council to reexamine Ordinance 34.

EXHIBIT 2
Pertinent Extracts from Ordinance No. 34

SECTION 1. Definitions. For the purpose of this Ordinance, certain terms, words, and phrases are defined as follows:

1.4. *Septic tank* means a vented, watertight tank, which serves as a sedimentation and sludge digestion chamber, which is placed between the house sewer and the soil absorption field.

1.5. *Septic tank system* means a system for disposing of sewage through soil absorption and consisting of the following components, the house sewer, the septic tank, and the soil absorption field.

1.6. *Soil absorption field* is that part of a septic tank system consisting of drainage tiles and surrounding permeable soil used for the subsurface disposal of septic tank effluent.

1.7. *Private sewage facilities* means septic tanks, pit privies, cesspools, sewage holding tanks, injection wells used to dispose of sewage, treatment tanks, and all other facilities, systems, and methods used for the disposal of sewage.

* * * * *

SECTION 5. *Water Pollution Control and Abatement Division.* The Water Pollution Control and Abatement Division is hereby created to administer the licensing, investigative and administrative functions provided herein. Appeal of an action by this Division shall be to the City Council. The Mayor is authorized to appoint a person as the head of this Division and to provide such Staff as necessary to carry out its functions. The Mayor is authorized, with the consent of the City Council, to contract with private firms for administration of this Ordinance.

* * * * *

SECTION 6. *Schedule of Fees.* The following fee schedule is adopted for the inspection and licensing services of this Ordinance:

6.1. Septic Tank Systems
    a. Single Unit (family) Structure.
       (1) Existing Non-Licensed Systems
          $ 5.00—Application Fee
          $45.00—Inspection Fee
       (2) New Systems
          $ 5.00—Application Fee
          $75.00—Inspection Fee (includes one set of six percolation tests)
       (3) Transfer of License
          $ 5.00

EXHIBIT 2 *(concluded)*

SECTION 7.   *Rules Covering Licenses for Private Sewage Facilities*

7.1.   *Term of Licenses.*   Licenses for private sewage facilities issued under this Ordinance, other than temporary and conditional licenses issued pursuant to this Ordinance, shall be effective for a term of five (5) years. Licenses may be renewed for successive terms of five years if the City finds that the lot or tract in question may continue to be served by the private sewage facility without causing pollution or injuring public health. Any license issued under this Ordinance shall automatically terminate if there is a subdivision of the property served by the private sewage facility, if the property is used for a purpose other than described in the license, or if the loading of the system is significantly increased beyond that stated in the license. In addition, any license issued hereunder may be amended, revoked, or suspended for good cause.

*   *   *   *   *

SECTION 8.   *Private Sewage Facility Licence Procedure.*   The following procedures shall govern the issuance of licenses for private sewage facilities under this Ordinance:

8.3.   Within sixty (60) days after receipt of an application, the City will cause to be performed such inspections and tests as may be deemed necessary, which may include percolation tests as provided in *A Guide to the Disposal of Household Sewage* published by the State Department of Health, site inspection and other such tests and inspections as the City may consider appropriate. If the City approves the application, it shall so notify the applicant who may then proceed with the construction of the private sewage facility in accordance with the plans submitted with the application. If the application is disapproved as submitted, but the City is of the opinion that a private sewage facility of a different design may be constructed on the property, it shall advise the applicant in writing of the changes necessary to obtain a license.

*   *   *   *   *

SECTION 10.   *Existing Private Sewage Facilities*

10.1.   Private sewage facilities existing within the City as of the date of passage of this Ordinance are required to obtain a conditional license. Applications for such licenses shall be made within sixty (60) days after the effective date of this Ordinance. For good cause, the City may permit late filings of such application. However, the City reserves the right to invoke the penalties herein even if a late filing is permitted.

10.2.   Any license issued under the authority of this Section shall be temporary and conditional and shall be for a period not to exceed five (5) years.

10.3.   Any license issued under this provision shall automatically terminate if the system is changed, if the loading on the system is significantly increased from that existing at the date of issuance of the license, or if the property served by this system is subdivided or resubdivided.

*   *   *   *   *

SECTION 17.   *Penalties.*   Any person who violates any of the provisions of this Ordinance is guilty of a misdemeanor, and upon conviction shall be punished by a fine not exceeding $200.00 for each offense. Each day of violation constitutes a separate offense.

EXHIBIT 3

EXISTING SYSTEM APPLICATION FOR PRIVATE SEWAGE FACILITY LICENSE	APPLICATION NO. _____
$ _____ Fees Enclosed	Amount Enclosed $ _____
Application ( )	DO NOT WRITE IN THIS BLOCK
Inspection ( )	
Percolation Tests ( )	PLEASE DRAW A LAYOUT OF YOUR LOT AND SEWAGE SYSTEM ON THE BOTTOM OF THIS FORM

TO THE CITY: I hereby make application to operate a private sewage facility within the jurisdiction of the City as required by the City Ordinance No. 34 passed December 7, 1971.

(All information below must be completed)

Property Owner: _____ _____ _____
                      (Last)   (First)   (Middle)

Mailing Address: _____ _____
                 (Number)   (Street)

Telephone Number: _____

Subdivision: _____ _____ _____ _____
           (Name)   (Section)   (Block)   (Lot)

Type Dwelling: House ( )   Mobile Home ( )   Other ( )

Average Number Occupants: _____   Days per year used _____

ALL APPLICANTS please write TOTAL no. of items below & leave blank for "none."

1. Bedrooms	____	5. Showers	____	9. Auto. Dish	
2. Commodes	____	6. Bathtubs	____	Washer	____
3. Urinals	____	7. Kitchen Sinks	____	10. Garbage	
4. Lavatories	____	8. Clothes Washers	____	Disposals	____
				11. Grease Traps	____

(Sewage System Information)

APPLICANTS for EXISTING SYSTEM LICENSE ONLY please complete this block

Septic Tank Information:

1. No. of separate systems at this location: _____

NOTE: If more than 1 system, give same info. as below for tank & field on back of this form.

2. Nearest water well or cistern distance _____ ft.
3. Distance to organized sewer collection system line: _____ ft.
4. Tank capacity: _____ gal.   5. Yr. installed _____
6. No. of tank compartments: _____
7. Name the Installer: _____
8. Tank made of: ( ) prefab metal
   (check one)   ( ) prefab concrete
              ( ) concrete poured in place

EXHIBIT 3 *(continued)*

Absorption Field Information:
1. Type field: (   ) Trench or ditch system (   )
   Absorption Bed System a. Trench size:
   (Wd) ——————— in. X (Dp) ——————— inches X (Total Lg.) ——————— ft. (OR)
   b. Bed Bottom-Size: (WD) ——————— ft. X (Lg.) ——————— ft.
   c. Distribution Pipe Size: ——————— inches dia.
   d. Kind of Pipe: (   ) Vitrified Clay (   ) Concrete, (   ) Plastic
2. Distance from Field to Nearest Lake Shore: feet

Authorization is hereby given to the City, Water Quality Board, the State Department of Health, the engineers, Brownlee Engineering, and to their agents or designees, singularly or jointly, to enter upon the above described property during daylight hours for the purpose of making soil percolation tests, inspecting private sewage systems, or for any reason consistent with the water quality-program of the Water Quality Board, the State Dept. of Health, and the City.

SIGNATURE OF APPLICANT

Date: ——————————, 19————

LAYOUT SPACE—Property outline, size and location of improvements:
Please indicate: EXAMPLE:
1. Direction of north
   at property.
2. Direction and distance
   from field to nearest
   lake shoreline.

17.2. Small City (D)*

"Mr. Underwood, do you have your report ready for presentation?" the mayor inquired as he glanced toward the end of the narrow table used for all council meetings. The occasion was a regular monthly session of the council of Small City which the public was invited to attend; usually few visitors ever appeared at these meetings. As he waited for the response, the mayor quickly reflected on the difference between the current meeting and the one of some seven months before when near bedlam prevailed. The issue at that time was Ordinance 34 which the council had passed some four months earlier for the purpose of regulating privately owned septic systems for waste disposal. At that meeting more than 100 people were present; tonight less than 12 were in attendance.

Noting that Mr. Underwood was arranging a packet of papers in preparation for his speech, Mayor Burns hurriedly interjected another query: "How long do you think it will take?" Looking up from his papers, Mr. Underwood replied:

> I don't think it will take much more than ten minutes, Mayor. I have the memo that I would like to read, the document that officially transmits the work of the special sanitation committee which the Council appointed several months ago. It's been so long that I guess you had begun to wonder if we'd ever finish. . . . What we've done is to prepare for the consideration of the Council a re-draft of the original Ordinance 34 and its two amendments. Every member of the special committee has signed the memo of transmittal, but you will note there are certain caveats expressed. I believe that this re-draft reflects the opinions of the majority of our community with reasonable accuracy, and further than it does not "tie" the hands of the Council in the administration of its functions. It is important, however, to recognize the general consensus of the special committee on those certain matters considered to be of basic significance. . . . I hope I haven't confused you with this long preamble, and I'll now read the committee's memo.

> SUBJECT: Report of the Special Committee on Ordinance 34
> TO: The Mayor and City Council of Small City
> FROM: Special Committee Appointed to Review the Small City Sanitation Ordinance

---

* Prepared by George G. Eddy and Burnard H. Sord, the University of Texas at Austin.

The purpose of this document is to submit a redraft of Ordinance 34 and its two amendments for the consideration of the mayor and council of Small City. This work was accomplished in accordance with the expressed desires of the council to provide a means to reflect as broad a base of the opinions of our residents as reasonably possible concerning the regulation of waste disposal systems in our community. The committee has tried to meet this objective and believes the enclosed redraft of Ordinance 34 reflects this "charter" placed upon it.

With regard to this basic task, there are a number of specific matters that this committee wishes to bring to the attention of the mayor and the council for appropriate action. In brief, they are:

1.   Freedom of Choice.   Provision must be made to insure the opportunity of each citizen of Small City to select on his own initiative a qualified person or persons to accomplish necessary waste disposal system (WDS) inspections. This includes the individual selection of the firm or other agent to build the WDS in the first place, to service it as may be required, and its repair, modification, rehabilitation or the like.

2.   "Authorized" Inspectors.   Accordingly, the foregoing means the termination of the present contract with Brownlee Engineering for inspections and certifications of individual WDS at the earliest feasible date. Alternatives to this firm should include, primarily, the utilization of the Big City Health Department and/or the hiring or training of a qualified sanitary engineer (or equivalent) as an employee of Small City on some mutually satisfactory basis. In this regard, Messrs. Jackson, Ronald, and Litner object even to inclusion of the alternative of contracting with a private firm (Article 5.3). Finally, it seems reasonable to add this duty to those of the recently hired city administrative assistant.

3.   Fees.   The mayor and the council should exert every feasible effort to provide such required services contemplated by this ordinance at the lowest possible cost to the citizens, irrespective of the alternative ultimately chosen. This statement is made based on the concern of many citizens that the present fee of $45 for Ordinance 34 inspections is considered to be too high. Cognizance is taken that in the Mounton Lake Area, the Green River Authority is currently charging $60, whereas apparently similar services have been performed by the Big City Health Department for $8 for reinspections. This committee is not attempting to pass judgment on the relative competence of either agency for such functions, and does recognize that such fees always are subject to future revisions. In any event, the subject of costs to the citizens remains a basic matter to all. Finally, the committee believes that record-keeping of matters pertinent to WDS should be a function of the city, and that such records should be maintained in the designated city office by a city employee.

4.   Other Special Points.   With regard to Article or Section 9 of the redraft Ordinance 34, Messrs. Jackson, Ronald, Litner, and Johnson believe that servicing organizations should be bonded, but not licensed. With regard to Section 14, Messrs. Jackson, Ronald, Litner, and Johnson believe the word "approval" should replace the word "license" regarding the operation of existing WDS.

5. Public Notice. The council should provide the opportunity to the citizens of Small City to become acquainted with this redraft of Ordinance 34 and the special matters included in this document by conducting at least two public readings, together with the usual public notices, prior to the ultimate adoption of a revised ordinance.

S/Reginald Jackson   S/William Underwood

S/Henry Allen

S/Alex Ronald

S/Harry Litner

S/Anthony Willard

S/Peter Johnson

After reading the memo verbatim and noting the names of each person who signed it, Underwood remarked that he particularly appreciated the work done by Mr. Jackson, who had called him prior to the council meeting to state that he regretted that he could not attend, as much as he wished to do so.

Jackson had told Underwood that he did not want him to feel that his absence was due to lack of continued interest in the sanitation ordinance or the work of the committee. Jackson indicated that he had a prior engagement of great importance which he could not cancel, and that he hoped Underwood would understand. Underwood had been appointed to head the special sanitation committee in the first place because he had made a speech at one of the stormy council meetings lashing out at those who always seemed eager to focus on personalities instead of issues and those to whom court actions to "solve" problems appeared to hold a special appeal.

Underwood fully appreciated the power and community prestige of those who opposed the mayor; one of the principals in this regard was Jackson.

FORMATION OF THE COMMITTEE

Underwood readily recalled the termination of that wild council meeting some six months before when Mayor Burns seemed buried in an avalanche of criticism over Ordinance 34. At the height of the tension and hostility, the mayor seemed unusually well poised. Speaking calmly, he said that he believed that the only way to resolve the controversial aspects of the ordinance was to provide both opponents and proponents with an opportunity to express themselves further and to appoint a special review committee. Turning to the council members beside him, the mayor asked for such a motion. At once Councilman Andrews proposed the motion that the mayor had just outlined. Instantly seconded by Councilman Nash, the motion was approved unanimously and the meeting suddenly was over. Three "opponents" and three "proponents" of Ordinance 34 were to be selected, so that the special committee could get under way.

Underwood believed that he had been appointed to head the special committee because the mayor thought he fully supported the sanitation ordinance. Actually, Underwood had expressed his displeasure with several provisions of Ordinance 34, but his public comments were essentially supportive of the council, and he had urged Small City residents to restrain their emotions and address the issues calmly and rationally. A week later, after the stormy council meeting at the school auditorium, Mayor Burns called Underwood at home and asked him to serve as the chairman of the special committee to review Ordinance 34. A trifle dismayed because he had not wished to become so involved in community affairs so soon after moving to Small City, Underwood had eventually acquiesced with reservations. Brushing aside Underwood's doubts, the mayor finally convinced him he could accomplish something worthwhile. Mayor Burns pointed out that one of his biggest problems was to get competent individuals involved in community affairs in a meaningful way. "On the other hand," the mayor observed, "I've never had any trouble in getting plenty of free advice and loads of abuse."

About the same time that the Special Committee was appointed, Mayor Burns distributed throughout the community a resumé of the actions taken by the council to provide what he considered to be a proper perspective in judging Ordinance 34. He pointed out that advance public notice of the hearing on the proposed sanitation ordinance was provided and that when it was approved by the council "there was no opposition to the adoption of the ordinance among those present at the meeting." Mayor Burns also advised all residents that the fees were being reduced, the deadline for submitting applications for inspections was being extended, and that reports on inspections made by Brownlee of the first 48 systems showed 7 were deficient. Concerning comparative costs of a central collection system versus operations under Ordinance 34, the following figures were provided:

Cost of a Centralized Municipal Sewer System and Treatment (five years)

Debt service	$750,000
Treating cost	127,000
Total	$877,000

Cost of Operating under Ordinance 34 for Five Years

Fees at the $50 rate applied to 600 systems	$ 30,000
Administration and engineering	9,000
Total	$ 39,000

In conclusion, the mayor stated, "You are invited to consider the question of whether or not the negligence of 14 percent (based on 7 failures out of 48 inspections) of our people should require 86 percent of the people to participate in the costs of an organized collection system in the near future."

A SAMPLING OF PUBLIC COMMENTS

An editorial in *The Big City Daily News,* which appeared during the apex of the controversy over Ordinance 34, noted that "Community officials apparently have agreed to modify the restrictions, but opponents are calling for outright repeal. . .opponents in this case appear to be on a collision course with the state's water quality act. If the water supply that serves most people hereabouts is to be safeguarded, certain standards must be maintained."

A sanitation engineer who lived in Small City and who had assisted the mayor and the council with technical guidance during the drafting of Ordinance 34, urged Small City residents to support it in a personal letter he distributed to all property owners in the city. He claimed that:

> It should first be understood that Ordinance 34 is consistent with the Water Quality Act passed by the State Legislature in 1967, conforms to the overall recommendations submitted in an engineering report to the State Water Quality Board in 1971, and was drafted by an attorney who was extremely knowledgeable in the procedures, rules, authority, and objectives of the Board. . .this Ordinance [was] not drafted in the context of "ecological hysteria," but rather as a city law designed to provide for the most logical, practical, and economical solution for controlling water pollution and preserving the natural beauty in the residential portion of Small City for the next five to ten years. The Mayor has taken the first positive action toward preserving the water quality in our city that I have seen during my six years of residence here and I commend him for it.

THE FIRST MEETING OF THE SPECIAL COMMITTEE

When Mr. Underwood called the first meeting of the special committee together to discuss the provisions of Ordinance 34, it soon became clear that hardly anyone had read the ordinance completely or thoroughly. As soon as the meeting began, Mr. Jackson announced he wanted to submit a prepared statement that, he said, represented the views of hundreds of Small City residents. Without waiting for Underwood's reaction, Jackson distributed copies to the members of the committee (see below) and proceeded to read and expand on the statement.

Mr. Jackson's Prepared Statement
  I.   We are not opposed to a reasonable septic tank ordinance.
  II. We want immediate repeal of Ordinances Nos. 34, 34-A, 34-B. Also cancellation of existing contract with Brownlee Engineering.
  III. We would like to see percolation tests be made a part of the subdivision ordinance.

IV.   Specifications as to design and installation of septic systems be made a part of a building code. Also have rigid inspections as to new installations as well as the rebuilding or modifications of existing septic systems.

V.   All septic system installers or repairmen be bonded.

VI.   Builders or homeowners would have the choice of a registered, professional engineer or registered sanitarian to conduct the required percolation test or to inspect the installation of new septic systems or the repair and overhaul of existing systems.

VII. Complaint method for malfunctioning septic systems. Complainant would notify sanitation officer of a suspected system. Sanitation officer would make an on-premise inspection of suspected faulty system and advise offender of said complaint, and if said system is found to be faulty, offender would be given reasonable time to make such repairs or corrections as is required. If no repair or correction is made in a reasonable time, sanitation officer would take whatever legal steps that are necessary to see that offender complies with the sanitation ordinance.

VIII. A copy of a plat or drawing would be kept in city files, showing the approximate location of septic systems on each residence or commercial or public building.

IX.   The possibility of the city hiring an engineer to be building inspector, sanitation officer, road and bridge commissioner, etc.

Mr. Jackson interspersed his reading of the prepared statement with highly critical comments about the mayor and the council in general. The words "devious," "indifferent," "nonresponsive," "arbitrary," and others of a similar nature were frequently used. When he finished, Henry Allen, who was considered by the mayor as an opponent, quickly endorsed Jackson's views and added that he felt the $50 inspection fee was ridiculous.

Mr. Litner, who had "invited" himself to the meeting—he was not one of those specially appointed by the mayor—and was a vociferous opponent of the mayor, interjected his conviction that the whole affair was illegal and consequently the ordinance had to be repealed "or else." He rambled on, finally subsiding without conviction when Underwood reminded him that one of the first points made by Jackson was that "we" (meaning the opposition) were not opposed to the need for regulating septic systems. While Litner was fulminating against Ordinance 34, Underwood wondered whether he should ask him to either hold his tongue or leave, since Litner could be considered as an interloper by his unilateral appearance at the initial meeting of the special committee. He did not really know Litner, but he heard that Litner was a highly emotional person who easily lost his temper and usually expressed himself with curses no matter who was in range. Litner was a builder who had allied himself with Greenwell's candidacy for mayor against Edward Burns.

After Mr. Ronald, another "opposition" member, had delivered a diatribe against the mayor and the council, labeling their actions as "steamroller tactics" specifically designed to frighten community residents into silence and acquiescence by contending the ordinance was essential to meet "emergency" conditions, Underwood was both impressed and distraught at the extent of the hostility and actions taken to discredit city officials. (See Exhibit 1, p. 497.) He decided to tolerate Litner's presence and to permit him to make comments, although Underwood suspected he might regret it before the committee completed its work. With Litner, the "opposition" now totaled four, or one more than the three "proponents." Underwood was convinced also that the "opposition" had held its own special meeting prior to this one to agree on an organized position. He had not discussed Ordinance 34 with either Dr. Johnson or Mr. Willard (classified by the mayor as proponents or "friendlies"), and had never met either until this first official session of the special committee. He knew that Willard was a local attorney and that Johnson was a medical doctor specializing in obstetrics. That was the extent of his knowledge about Willard and Johnson, who were supposed to be on his side despite the fact that he had yet to specify his own views publicly.

So far during the meeting all that had been accomplished was to provide the opportunity for emotional outbursts, and as the meeting was being held in Underwood's home, he hoped that his wife had not overheard Litner's intemperate remarks. At this moment, Jackson declared emphatically that he was totally opposed to inspections of existing septic systems. When Ronald and Allen immediately agreed, Willard shouted that he was dumbfounded that such a position could be expressed, especially in view of Jackson's opening statement. Dr. Johnson said he felt that it would be impossible to regulate waste disposal in Small City under such terms, and that if this viewpoint prevailed there was no use in continuing further discussions. Ronald retorted that inspections of existing systems would be prohibitively expensive if really done professionally and thoroughly. Allen claimed that even if such inspections were conducted, the community would have no guarantee that the septic system would continue functioning properly over the next five years. [See Section 7.1 of Exhibit 2 in Small City (B).]

Jackson called attention to point VII of his prepared statement, contending that a malfunctioning septic tank system could be remedied primarily through the device of complaints levied against the system by neighbors. Dr. Johnson disagreed with Jackson, saying it would not work because of the inherent unwillingness of many persons to complain. He asserted that many would rather suffer in silence than get involved in any hassle with an adjacent homeowner—usually a most unpleasant experience.

Ronald interrupted with a remark that he was alarmed at the inordinate power placed in the hands of the mayor and the council to grind an "offender" down with successive $200 fines for alleged violations. He declared this "infernal" ordinance, as presently written, provided too great a temptation for irresponsible people to engage in personal vendettas against those who had angered them and were in no position to defend themselves.

Seeing that Underwood was becoming visibly appalled at the tone and tenor of the arguments being spurred by Jackson, Willard quickly interposed the suggestion that the meeting adjourn so that each member could study the ordinance in detail and come prepared at the next session with specific suggestions for revisions. Allen responded by indicating his concurrence and offered to be the next host. To Underwood's relief, everyone seemed to agree, and the first meeting was promptly concluded. It had lasted nearly four hours, and as Jackson departed he told Underwood privately that he, like Will Rogers, had never met a man he did not like.

Underwood responded, "That may be a fine philosophy, but you know there are some people I hate." Jackson laughed. Litner stood nearby with a wide grin on his face. In a few moments all committee members had departed.

THE COMMITTEE'S SECOND MEETING

Ten days later, the second meeting began with some opening remarks by Underwood. He said that he had briefly told the mayor what had transpired at the first session, that the council had voted to extend the deadline date for inspection applications again, and that no completion date for this committee's work had been established by the Small City Council. "I assume you are all ready," Underwood declared, "to tackle this Ordinance sentence by sentence and, if so, I suggest we begin."

There were no objections to the first two pages which dealt with definitions and descriptions. On page three, however, Allen stated that he did not believe the city could enforce the provisions of Ordinance 34 in the extraterritorial area contiguous to the southern boundary of Small City. It was a small residential area, about one-tenth the size of Small City, which had never been incorporated either by the nearby small community of Lakedale (about one-half as large as Small City and also sharing a boundary with Big City to the east) or into Small City. Underwood said that he would check this with the city attorney.

The original ordinance contained 14 pages, plus two amendments of 4 pages each, for a total of 22 pages. From page three on, there were objections or suggested changes proposed on nearly every page and section of the ordinance. Finally, after about four hours of struggle, the committee had reached page 11, which covered existing private sewage facilities. At this point, everyone agreed to adjourn and to continue this same sentence-by-sentence examination at the next meeting. Dr. Johnson agreed to host it approximately one month later.

The areas of concern primarily involved the means to regulate septic systems (Section 5), the fees (Section 6), rules covering licenses for private sewage facilities (Section 7), private sewage facility license procedure (Section 8), and conditional licensing of septic systems (Section 10). The discussions on Section 5 were particularly prolonged and somewhat heated. The "opposition" was unanimously and vehemently against the city being authorized to hire a private firm (like Brownlee) to implement the ordinance. They insisted the city should reinstate inspections previously performed by the Big City Health Department. Allen did suggest that the city hire a qualified person to perform such inspections, and Litner offered to contact someone he knew that might be interested in such a position with Small City. Willard and Underwood argued that all options of implementing the ordinance should be incorporated, even the authority to hire a private firm. While Dr. Johnson tended to support the viewpoint favoring the use of Big City inspectors, he did agree that the committee should focus on "issues and not personalities." Finally, it was decided that Willard would redraft Section 5, that Dr. Johnson would verify if Big City would be willing to resume septic system inspections for Small City residents, and Litner would see if his "friend" would be willing to perform such functions as a Small City employee.

Another section which received extensive debate was No. 7; the belief was expressed by several members that the manner in which it was currently written offered no assurance to Small City that homeowners, once in possession of a license (following a proper inspection), would be required to insure continued proper operation of their septic systems. "Hells bells," said Ronald in voicing this concern, "a septic system could cease functioning properly the next day after an inspection—especially by Brownlee—and the way I see this ordinance, this situation could go on for five years without proper correction or relief to the neighbors. We've got to do something about that."

THE COMMITTEE'S THIRD MEETING

When the third meeting convened at Dr. Johnson's home, Mr. Underwood told the members of his conversations with Mayor Burns since the last meeting. The mayor, he said, had talked with the attorney for the Water Quality Board about Small City's authority in the extraterritorial jurisdictional area. The city attorney stated that it was his opinion that the city had the necessary authority to enforce Ordinance 34. Additionally, the mayor declared the city had tried to find a person qualified to perform sanitation engineering-type inspections prior to contracting with Brownlee, but had not been able to find anyone. The mayor further remarked, Underwood reported, that the city would be willing to discontinue the present contract with Brownlee if Small City could find and hire a qualified individual to do the presently contested inspectional services. Litner then asked what would happen to those persons who already had paid the $50 inspection fee if the city hired someone to do this task. The council would have to make such a determination, responded Mr. Underwood.

Willard read the redraft of Section 5 and all members seemed to agree, although there was some grumbling about the mayor's authority to hire a private firm for performing inspections. After some discussion of other sections, the committee turned its attention to Section 17 on penalties. Most believed that the provisions were much too severe: $200 fine for a violation, and an additional $200 for each day thereafter if the violation persisted. Eventually, the committee concurred in modifying the language which made continuing fines discretionary where the offender showed evidence of good faith and efforts to correct cited deficiencies in his septic system. Final agreement also was achieved to amend the last section of the ordinance to omit the statement contained in the original Ordinance 34, "That an emergency being apparent for the preservation of the safety, health, and general welfare of the public, requires that the rule requiring the reading of ordinances on three (3) separate days be suspended and the same is hereby suspended. . . ."

This meeting was concluded with the understanding that Willard would have the re-draft typed and delivered to Underwood, who would distribute a copy to each member as soon as possible. Later another meeting would be called to obtain final approval of a revised ordinance. At that same meeting, each member would have the opportunity to examine a proposed memorandum to serve as the means for transmitting the re-drafted ordinance to the council and to emphasize any special matters the committee wished to stress. Underwood agreed to draft such a memorandum and send each member a copy soon.

INTERVENING EVENTS

Several months passed before the committee could meet again. In the meantime, Underwood distributed copies of the re-drafted ordinance and the proposed memorandum (see Exhibits 2 and 3, pp. 498–99).

The council again extended the deadline date for applications for inspections, and a few more residents had Brownlee perform them in line with the original provisions of Ordinance 34. The majority of Small City residents, however, refused to comply; the mayor estimated only one fourth of all septic systems had been inspected. A pathologist, who lived in Small City, continued to take samples of effluent from suspected septic systems and recorded test results. These tests indicated there were at least three principal areas in Small City where septic systems obviously were deficient. While the existence of water pollution seemed established, the city had yet to identify specifically which individual septic systems were the offenders, due to the clusters of homes on hilltops and slopes. The topography made it nearly impossible to pinpoint single homesites without additional tests (such as the use of colored dyes) which required the homeowner's permission to conduct.

THE COMMITTEE'S FOURTH AND FINAL MEETING

The final meeting was held, again in Mr. Underwood's home. All members were present except Mr. Willard (who, it later was discovered, forgot about it and went to a party where he could not be reached.) There were immediate objections to several points in the memorandum and in the re-drafted ordinance. When Dr. Johnson suggested they go over every section, sentence by sentence, again, Underwood became obviously agitated. The initial focus was Section 5, to which Mr. Litner voiced strong objection. After launching an attack on the provision which authorized the mayor to hire a private firm to do the septic system inspections, he suddenly produced an unsigned letter which contested the very authority of the city to license septic systems. The letter bore the heading of a local law firm, and the text covered the entire page. It was dated prior to the stormy council meeting when the council voted to create the special committee now in final session.

The normally calm and quiet Underwood exploded:

> If you want to institute suit against the city, Litner, to try and overturn Ordinance 34, go right ahead! I think you'll be a damned fool to do so, but go ahead if your mind is so set. I don't think you've got a chance of winning, but that's just my opinion. I really don't care what the hell you do. . . . And, furthermore, if you think I'm going to rehash Section 5 one more time, you're crazy as hell! We've been over it time and time again, and by God, it is written exactly as you all have wanted it! It has everything in it that you wanted—portions that I did not consider necessary, but nevertheless they're in that section. So, I'll be damned, damned, if I'll go over it again!"

He had risen from the head of the table as his agitation mounted, but he did resist the impulse to pound on the top as he realized it was made of glass. The other members looked at him with astonishment, and Litner sat still and did not reply.

Mr. Jackson quickly made a few placating remarks, the others stirred, and Underwood finally sat down. At this moment, Dr. Johnson suggested the proposed transmitting memorandum be examined, offering to jot down recommended revisions.

Immediately, Mr. Ronald declared aggressively he would not sign it as long as it inferred in any way the council had acted in good faith or with proper authority in adopting Ordinance 34 in the first place. Mr. Allen and Mr. Jackson "seconded" this position. They also demanded the insertion of additional qualifying remarks and reservations concerning the subject of fees and the use of private firms for inspectional purposes. Regarding the fees, Litner reiterated the proper comparison was not between $45 now being charged Small City residents and the $25 required by Big City inspectors for original inspections, but with the $8 Big City charged for re-inspections. The "opposition" also contended the city should not have the authority to charge and license septic system maintenance or servicing firms; requiring performance bonds was considered sufficient. They also objected to the use of the word "license" in connection with the authorization to operate a private waste disposal system (following a satisfactory inspection). Finally, one member of the committee insisted again that the primary inspecting agency be identified as the Big City Health Department.

Suddenly, Litner said he felt the only way the council could demonstrate genuine good faith in its relationships with this committee and Small City homeowners was to announce publicly the suspension of the original Ordinance 34 until final action was taken by the council on this committee's recommendations. "To do otherwise," he asserted, "is to continue to perpetrate a fraud on the community, because I don't believe the council will consider our work at all. It's been just a big deception by the mayor to kid us into thinking something different would come out of this grandstand stunt of appointing a 'bipartisan' group to remedy everything!" Echoing this stance, Ronald loudly proclaimed the mayor should make such an announcement himself immediately, and further that he should have done so months ago.

"I really thought he was going to do that right at the time he asked the council to vote on the establishment of our committee," added Jackson.

"You mean you want the mayor to tell everyone in Small City to disregard an ordinance that is on the books?" asked Underwood incredulously. "You cannot be serious."

"Well, maybe he could do it informally," offered Litner. "It certainly would help convince everyone worried about the abuse of his authority that he really was sincere in getting community participation in this matter."

"Those 300 or so property owners who signed the petition," interjected Ronald, "obviously recognized that their rights were being abrogated by the likes of Mayor Burns and his yes-men on the Council."

"My God, I don't understand you at all!" exclaimed Underwood, "I'm amazed that you believe an official could legally advise anyone to forget about obeying a law, whether he helped write it or not. That assuredly would be a basis for impeachment, if nothing else! And although I don't know the mayor very well, I can hardly see him doing anything on the subrosa basis you are suggesting. I'll tell you this: I'll never make such a recommendation to Mayor Burns, but if any of you want to, go ahead and try it."

Jackson made a motion to Litner who bent his head closer to Jackson and they held a short private conversation. Then they looked up but said nothing. Mr. Ronald seemed perplexed but likewise remained silent.

As there seemed to be no further desire to push this viewpoint, Underwood suggested a cup of coffee might be welcomed. In a few minutes each committee member was examining the contents of his cup intently. After a few sips, a calmer Underwood was agreeing to incorporate such qualifying statements in the transmittal memorandum as might be desired. He indicated he would identify specific reservations with the names of those who wished to be so associated. Asking Dr. Johnson for his notes, Underwood promised the committee he would have it ready for review and signature within one day. There seemed to be no additional matters for the committee to discuss, and the meeting ended abruptly.

The next day Underwood distributed copies of the revised memorandum. In one week everyone had signed it and it was back in his hands. No changes had been made to it or the redrafted ordinance. It appeared the committee's work was done. . . .

REPORTING BACK TO THE CITY COUNCIL

After reading the special committee's memorandum to the mayor and the council, Underwood concluded:

> And that's about it, Mayor Burns. The principal changes to the original Ordinance 34 are Sections 5 and 17, and the deletion entirely of Section 6 on fees. Fees are subject to change, and we felt they did not belong in the ordinance. . . . I want to thank all committee members publicly, especially Mr. Jackson, for the time and trouble spent on behalf of the community. I realize we haven't solved all the problems regarding the regulation of septic systems, and that there probably always will remain some areas of disagreement over specific provisions. I do think it is worth recognizing, however, that the work of this special committee on an all-volunteer basis has provided the opportunity for our residents to get involved—to really participate—in a matter of real importance to us all. Well, I guess that's all I have to say, except, Mr. Mayor and members of the council, it's back in your hands.

EXHIBIT 1
A Citizen's View of Mr. Ronald's Tactics

Mr. Alex Ronald recently called upon citizens in Small City asking for signatures on a petition to do away with the Sanitation Ordinance. As we talked to Mr. Ronald:

1. It became evident that he had not read the ordinance he was attempting to get repealed, and he admitted that he had not read it. This led to many misrepresentations and totally inaccurate statements as he attempted to recruit signatures to the petition:

   a. He thought the ordinance applied only to old systems already in operation and did not think that it set any standards for new construction. He declared he would like an ordinance to cover only new systems.
   b. He did not know the ordinance was already in effect and thought that the postponement by city council of the date for filing an application for inspection and payment of fee was in effect postponement of the date the ordinance would go into effect.

2. He declared the Sanitation Ordinance was illegal and would not stand up in court—threatening citizens with increased taxes to pay for a lawsuit he declared inevitable if the ordinance were not repealed. He based his declaration and assumptions upon the opinion of two lawyers hired by opponents of the ordinance. The fact that legal counsel for the city, who had reviewed the ordinance in detail and at length and was well qualified to render an opinion, stated it was legal in every respect did not impress him, nor did he give credence to the statement by the executive director of the Water Quality Control Board that the city had a right to pass such an ordinance, nor did he recognize that the mayor read to the meeting that portion of the Water Quality Act giving cities of less than 5,000 the authority to establish a water quality control program.

3. Mr. Ronald declared himself in favor of establishing a citywide sewage treatment system in lieu of septic tank controls and was under the illusion a treatment system could be started for the amount that would be collected for inspection fees—indicating an abysmal ignorance of the total problem. He cited the figure of $36,000 as income from the ordinance which could be utilized, ignoring the fact that the cost of sewage treatment facilities for the city has been researched by the committee which drew up the Sanitation Ordinance and which felt that such a

EXHIBIT 1 *(continued)*

system is out of reach of the present population. Mr. Ronald did not see the logic in preventing pollution from septic systems in order to give the city time to grow into a sewage treatment system, nor did he recognize the potential pollution problem from uncontrolled septic tanks affecting the quality of the lakes which supply drinking water to the whole region.

4. Mr. Ronald complained that the city "railroaded" the ordinance through by declaring it an emergency measure and giving it only one reading rather than three. He was unaware that a city the size of Small City does not have three readings on any ordinance and did not know that the Sanitation Ordinance had been under study and discussion for the past three years.

5. In response to the question put to him, Mr. Ronald stated that he would have no objection to the Sanitation Ordinance, and he did not think that most of the people who signed the petition would have any objection to it if the inspection were free.

EXHIBIT 2
Pertinent Extracts from Redraft of Ordinance No. 34

SECTION 5. *Water Pollution Control and Abatement Division.* The Water Pollution Control and Abatement Division is hereby created to administer the licensing, investigative, and administrative functions provided herein. Appeal of an action by this Division shall be to the City Council. In order to properly administer this ordinance, the Mayor is authorized, with the consent of the City Council, to take any one or more of the following steps:

5.1 To hire a duly qualified individual, or other entity, to carry out the tests and other duties required by this ordinance.
5.2 To establish a list of duly qualified, bonded contractors or individuals from which any citizen may choose to perform the tests required by this ordinance.
5.3 To contract with private firms for the administration of this ordinance.
5.4 To establish liaison with the Big City Health Department for performance of inspections and other duties for the administration of this ordinance.

SECTION 6. *Schedule of Fees.* (deleted)
SECTION 7. *Rules Covering Licenses for Private Sewage Facilities*
7.1 *Term of Licenses.* Licenses for private sewage facilities issued under this Ordinance, other than temporary and conditional licenses issued pursuant to this Ordinance, shall be effective for a term of five (5) years. Licenses may be renewed for successive terms of five years if the City finds that the lot or tract in question may continue to be served by the private sewage facility without causing pollution or injuring public health. Any license issued under this Ordinance shall automatically terminate if there is a subdivision of the property served by the private sewage facility, if the property is used for a purpose other than described in the license, or if the loading of the system is significantly increased beyond that stated in the license. In addition, any license issued hereunder may be amended, revoked, or suspended for good cause. It is the responsibility of the property owner to insure that his waste disposal system functions properly, and to take all necessary measures to correct any deficiencies that might develop to insure effective compliance with the intent and specific provisions of this Ordinance. The issue of a license or permit, irrespective of its duration, in no way relieves the affected property owner of his continuing responsibility to insure effective and safe operation of his waste disposal system.

EXHIBIT 2 *(continued)*

SECTION 17. *Penalties.* Any person who violates any of the provisions of this Ordinance is guilty of a misdemeanor, and upon conviction may be punished by a fine not exceeding $200.00 for each offense. Each day of violation constitutes a separate offense unless good faith efforts have been made and will be made to remedy the violation constituting the offense.

EXHIBIT 3
Initial Draft of Proposed Memo of Transmittal

SUBJECT: Report of Special Committee on Ordinance 34

The purpose of this paper is to submit a redraft of Ordinance 34 and its two amendments for the consideration of the Mayor and the Council of Small City. This work was accomplished in accordance with the expressed desires of the council to provide a means to reflect as broad a base of the opinions of our residents as possible concerning the regulation of waste disposal systems in our community. The committee has tried to meet this objective, and believes the enclosed redraft reflects this "charter" placed upon it.

With regard to this basic task, there are a number of specific matters that this committee wishes to bring to the attention of the mayor and the council for appropriate action. In brief, they are:

1. *Freedom of Choice.* Provision must be made to insure the opportunity of each citizen of Small City to select on his own initiative a qualified person or persons to accomplish necessary waste disposal system (WDS) inspections. This includes the individual selection of the firm or other agent to build in the first place, to service it as may be required, and its repair, modification, and rehabilitation or the like.

2. *"Authorized" Inspectors.* Accordingly, this means the termination of the present contract with the firm Brownlee Engineering for inspections and certifications of individual WDS at the earliest feasible date. Alternatives to this firm should be, at the least, utilization of the Big City Health Department, and/or the hiring of a qualified sanitary engineer as an employee of the city on some mutually satisfactory basis.

3. *Fees.* The mayor and the council should exert every possible effort to provide such required services at the lowest possible cost to the citizens, irrespective of the alternative ultimately chosen. This statement is made based on the concern of many citizens that the present fee of $50 for Ordinance 34 inspections is considered to be too high. Cognizance is taken that in the Mounton Lakes Area, the Green River Authority is currently charging $60, whereas apparently similar services have been performed by the Big City Health Department for $25.00. It is further recognized that these fees may be revised in the future. Nonetheless, the subject of costs to the citizens remains a basic matter to all.

4. *Public Notices.* The council should provide the opportunity to the citizens of Small City to become acquainted with this redraft of Ordinance 34 by conducting at least two public readings, together with the usual public notices of these occurrences prior to the ultimate adoption of a revised ordinance.

This committee recognizes that, despite the controversy over the provisions of the existing Ordinance 34 and amendments, the city must have proper regulations and their implementation regarding WDS to protect the health and well-being of our community. The committee is satisfied this is the view of the majority of the residents of Small City.

EXHIBIT 3 *(continued)*

This committee also recognizes—again despite the controversy the ordinance engendered—the authority of Small City to pass such an ordinance, and that considerable effort has been expended to research the matter of WDS generally and in particular for our community to provide the basis for such an official act.

This committee further recognizes that it is easy to criticize the actions of others, no matter how well-intentioned, but would hope that more—many more—of our citizens would apply the same kind of energy and zeal that has been largely devoted to follow-on criticisms to a more wholehearted participation in the *formative* stages of such significant measures.*

* Note: Before Underwood circulated this memorandum he discussed it with Dr. Johnson and Mr. Willard and decided to delete the last paragraph. He also added the following sentences to the next-to-last paragraph:

"The principal areas of community concern have involved the method of implementation and the fee schedule. The committee has tried to address these issues, and others, as realistically as possible in consonance with the health and sanitary requirements of our community."

17.3. Small City (E)*

"Why is it," Mayor Burns sighed, "that Don Flowers is always late?"

None of the council members responded, for it was true that Flowers rarely appeared on time for either regular council meetings or the informal work sessions that the mayor called whenever it seemed necessary for the members to study important actions together before voting on them during subsequent regular meetings.

"Well, I don't see why we have to wait to get on with the discussion of the revisions to the sanitation ordinance," declared Mike Redford, who always liked to get right to the point.

"I suppose you're right," agreed the mayor, who began to sort the papers that he had before him on the dining room table that served as the focal point for these deliberations.

"There's plenty of coffee here for everyone," Mayor Burns announced, as he poured a cup for himself. "Please don't hesitate to help yourselves."

William Underwood got up and filled his cup, reflecting on the strange situation in which events had unexpectedly placed him. Only a few months ago he was trying to maintain order as the chairman of a raucous citizens' committee to review Ordinance 34, and now here he was occupying a position as councilman and being called upon to pass on *his* committee's recommendations! Underwood was still unsure whether he should take a strong stand or keep relatively quiet during the discussions about to commence—discussions that he suspected might become rather spirited.

UNDERWOOD'S APPOINTMENT TO THE COUNCIL

During the time he was chairing the special citizen's committee appointed by the city council to reexamine Ordinance 34, council member Malcolm Hightower had informed Mayor Burns that his personal business demands were such that he no longer could continue to serve on the city council. Hightower told the mayor that he would not submit his resignation until a replacement was located, but that he could not defer this action very much longer. When Mayor Burns approached Mr. Underwood about taking on such a position, the latter wondered if he wanted to get so entangled in community

---

* Prepared by George G. Eddy, the University of Texas at Austin.

affairs—especially given all the animosities and acrid controversy surrounding Ordinance 34 and the mayor. It seemed to Underwood that there were two distinct factions in Small City: those who sided with the mayor, and those who were aligned with the Greenwells.

Underwood realized that by acceding to the mayor's urgent prodding to join the council he would be regarded instantly as a foe by the Greenwells. Although he barely knew them, Underwood thought he had some appreciation of their influence in the community. He was certain that his joining the council probably would be interpreted as an automatic and complete alignment with Mayor Burns. While Underwood was not pleased with the prospect of being referred to as "one of Burns's boys," or to be in Burns's "pocket," he was impressed with the mayor and his ideas of city government. However, Underwood did believe that he could assert his independence and that he could make this clear to the community at large. Nonetheless, the animosities that characterized the recently concluded city election for mayor, in which Mayor Burns's margin of victory was razor-thin, would arise, Underwood thought, whenever any controversial measure came before the council. With the sanitation ordinance still under attack, and the council having to act on the special committee's recommendations, Underwood knew that some further bitter confrontations might be in store for the council. Although Underwood had been hesitant to be drawn into such a power struggle, he finally agreed to allow his name to the put before the city council as a replacement for Hightower.

The mechanics of his appointment had been simple and quick. One of the present council members—it might have been Bill Cartright—proposed Underwood's name to fill Hightower's unexpired term of office which had nearly one year to run, and after considering another person nominated by Councilman Mike Redford, the council voted 3–1 for Underwood. As he happened to be at that particular council meeting (but unaware that his name would be considered so soon after his conversation with the mayor), Underwood immediately was asked by Mayor Burns to come forward to the council table and be sworn in. Surprised by the suddenness of these actions, Underwood nonetheless found a vacant chair at the table and sat down. Someone shoved a sheaf of papers his way, and he realized a vote was about to occur on a matter he knew nothing about. Shuffling hurriedly through the papers before him, (Exhibit 1) Underwood realized that he had a lot of catching up to do if he expected to function as a councilman for the city in a reasonably effective manner.

When he had moved to Small City about a year previously, Underwood thought that he might get involved later on in community affairs but at that time such considerations were vague and remote. After many years spent working abroad, where he held progressively more difficult and demanding administrative and executive positions, Underwood now was employed as a business consultant in a local firm. Accustomed to executive-level decision making, Underwood was familiar with the uncertainties associated with such posts. Furthermore, his background had, he believed, allowed him to develop an appreciation for the varied consequences that a decision usually entailed.

Still, he had not forgotten the explosive moment years ago when his sharply worded remarks nearly had triggered a brawl at a routine meeting to evaluate certain inconsistencies in the annual performance (efficiency) reports by one unit of the company he was working for. Impatient with what he termed the "bureaucratic mind," Underwood was satisfied that his outspoken comments had been logical and forthright. Later on, though, Underwood reflected dolefully that his tendency to say exactly what he thought was likely the cause of his being labeled anomalously as both a "wild liberal" and a "contentious hard-nose" by those that he apparently had antagonized.

THE COUNCIL MEMBERS

Awaiting Flowers' arrival for this working session, Underwood wondered how the council was going to resolve the "hot potato" characteristics that the sanitation ordinance seemed to have acquired. He began to consider the mayor and the council members, their personalities, their backgrounds, and their viewpoints. His assessment took form in the following vignettes:

Mayor Edward Burns, in his mid-60s, was a retired engineer, long used to prompt decision making under stress and in conditions of uncertainty; furthermore, his experiences caused him to rely on subordinates to implement the decisions he reached after a methodical assessment of alternatives and consequences. He became irate with those he believed were procrastinators or "water-muddiers" who obstructed or interfered (deliberately or inadvertently) with the implementation of actions which he perceived were needed. Yet, he did not pretend to knowledge that he did not possess, and actively sought advice from those he considered to be experts in their fields. Taking the welfare of the city seriously, he never hesitated to contribute from his personal resources those funds that he believed were essential to the continued operation of the city. Probably few residents ever would know how many thousands of dollars he had personally donated or encouraged others to join him in so doing to enable the city to pay for the legal fees in the defense of its charter.

Donald Flowers, in his mid-40s, was the wealthy vice president of a local enterprise, to which much of his own assets were dedicated, and he usually assumed a philosophical approach to city government. Married, with three children, he was ever-conscious of his businessman's image in the community. Generally, he tried to be conciliatory in dealing with controversial matters, and occasionally expressed himself to profound depths in council meetings when he felt it necessary to establish the basis for his position. Sometimes he did this to provide a "breather" when intemporate remarks from those in the audience were becoming unduly provocative. He deplored those occasions when a council member reacted heatedly to what the latter construed as hostile or offensive comments from the floor.

William Cartright, in his mid-30s, was a radiologist with a highly successful private practice in Big City. Cartright came from well-to-do parents, was married, and had two small children; he liked to hunt and fish, owned and piloted his own small airplane, and enjoyed driving foreign sports cars. He possessed an alert, inquiring mind, made decisions readily and easily, and brought to the council a satisfying and positive maturity that belied his relative youth. Impatient with any boorishness or posturing that he detected in others, he was quick and abrupt to squelch such displays.

Fred Matlock, in his early 30s, dedicated to church and community services, worked in a local family business, was married to an intensely religious woman, and they had one small child. Because of his standing in the community, the fine reputation his family enjoyed there, and his recognized concern with the "public interest," he was appointed by the council as the mayor pro tem. He conducted himself with great seriousness, always came prepared to council meetings, and was considered a steady, dependable, if phlegmatic, person.

Mike Redford, close to 50, was an aggressive and dramatic councilman, used to decisive stands probably acquired during many years of military service, wherein he believed that each issue was subject to a clear-cut distinction. Married, with two grown children, he was a long-time and well-known resident of the community, where he had spent his youth. He had returned to Small City to live following his military retirement. A harsh critic of incompetent or slothful performance, he was doing research on a book that he hoped to write on the subject of problem solving by administrators. He believed that the city was seriously deficient in the enforcement of its ordinances, and he kept pressing the mayor for remedial actions.

THE COUNCIL MEETING

With Underwood's thoughts starting to wander back to the issues at hand, Don Flowers walked in puffing on a large cigar. Careful to maneuver himself out of the range of Flower's cigar, Underwood announced:

"Now that you're here, Don, I'd like to make some comments about the recommendations of my special committee on the sanitation ordinance."

"Why, sure, go right ahead," Flowers agreed, now almost enveloped in clouds of cigar smoke that began to drift toward Underwood, uneasily stirring in his chair.

"It's pretty clear to me," interposed Redford, "that we'd better be damned careful how we go about selecting what changes to make. But, that's not the end of it, by no means, no sir. What bothers me is how we are going to get the inspections done . . ."

"Yes, how about that," interrupted Cartright. "How are we going to cancel the Brownlee contract without severe penalty to the city—and then, assuming we can do that, where do we go from there?''

"That's a good point, Bill,'' responded the mayor, as he turned to address Cartright directly. "I've talked to Sanford this past week about that, and he said his firm, Brownlee, would be willing to drop the whole thing. Well, pretty much that, anyway. Their septic tank system inspections have been costly to them, and the static they've built up from some of the angry homeowners has persuaded Brownlee that the firm's image is suffering out here so much that they'd be happy to consider an appropriate termination. Sanford conceded that the firm made some blunders in some of their inspections, but this is such an incidental part of their total engineering business that they don't want this sort of work to continue to entangle them in local controversies. It just isn't worth it.''

"Well, I suppose that's something,'' Flowers remarked.

"But that still leaves us with the problem of how to get these inspections done, doesn't it?'' queried Cartright.

"That's right, that's right!'' Redford exclaimed, and he stabbed the air with his forefinger, pointing toward Underwood, who had moved to another chair that he hoped was out of range of the smoke that Flowers' cigar was generating. Although he knew that it could not be so, it seemed to Underwood that the cigar looked even bigger than when Flowers had arrived.

"Could we get to the committee recommendations now?'' asked Underwood plaintively, and as he expected no answer, he continued, "Maybe it would help to summarize them briefly. One of the first points the committee stressed was freedom of choice, which is another way of saying that many Small City residents don't want to be dictated to in the choice of who makes the septic tank inspections. There's so much anger with Brownlee that I don't think that outfit ever will be acceptable anymore. They really blew it with their very first series of inspections by their selection of inspectors. No matter how you look at it, they provided the rope with which to hang themselves—maybe the council, too—so I don't think we can look to Brownlee for anything useful. This leads . . .''

"You mean it wouldn't work even if they brought lollipops for the kids and a bottle of perfume for the mother?'' Cartright interjected sardonically.

". . . to the next point: who can inspect? Your opposition, Mr. Mayor, is insisting that this be done by the Big City Health Department. Yes, I know your objections to them. You feel they are too subject to pressure from the big realty companies and contractors to be objective and stringent in their inspections. And Brownlee's inspections so far have uncovered enough deficiencies in existing septic tank systems that initially were checked by Big City men to make you wonder about the quality of their work.''

"The initial results of Brownlee's inspections revealed that some 14 percent were defective in one way or another,'' reminded the mayor.

"Yes, I recall that figure,'' Underwood concurred, "but you'll also recall that Jackson, Litner, and Ronald do not even want the city to have the authority to contract with *any* private firm for this purpose. Less objectionable to them was the provision for the city to hire a qualified man to inspect—but at no fee to the homeowner: no license fee, no inspection charge, either. But, finally, it was recognized that there would have to be some charge, but only a nominal one that currently is being levied by the Big City Health Department. Right now, I think that's about $8 for a reinspection. There were some other points, none of which I'd call major ones, except for holding at least two public hearings on the revisions to Ordinance 34.''

''A city of our size doesn't have to hold two hearings,'' declared Cartright, ''and God knows we've held enough of them already! We've been at this for more than two years. When will it ever end?''

''But, how in the world are we going to find someone who is competent to do these inspections?'' lamented Matlock. ''And if we try to put him on the city payroll, where will we get the money to pay his salary? We'd likely have to come up with at least $12,000, and I don't see any way that we can do that. Besides, what would he do when he wasn't out making septic tank inspections? We tried before and we could not locate a single, qualified person.''

''Brownlee has an outstanding reputation as an engineering firm, and their previous work for the Water Quality Board certainly shows their competence in this field. We had no choice but to go to them, and we were damned glad that they agreed! I realize that they fouled up when they got started here in Small City, but we couldn't wait any longer to get these defective septic tank systems identified and corrective measures under way. You all know that we've got contaminated effluent running in bar ditches alongside our roads, and if that isn't serious, I don't know what is! We've just got a major problem here with pollution and we'd truly be derelict in our duties to the community if we had dallied any longer. We can't play games while people's health is at stake.'' As he spoke, Mayor Burns looked about him, as if to see whether any council member would challenge his assertions. No one did.

''Yeah, we did have to act, alright,'' concurred Redford, ''and I agreed that Brownlee was our only option. But who could have dreamed we'd run into such a brick wall as we did! What a mess!''

''We did what we had to, and I have no regrets,'' Cartright affirmed.

''Well, I think that's the case, too,'' said Flowers, trying to keep his cigar going as he spoke. ''But, maybe somewhere along the line our judgment was clouded. I just have to agree that freedom of choice is a fundamental right that we have an obligation to preserve. I can understand that a lot of folks here want to make their own decisions on such matters, and I can sympathize with the importance of maintaining the privacy and integrity of one's property. By golly, I wouldn't want any stranger traipsing around in my yard, poking, and digging about, maybe stomping on my garden, without my knowledge or permission! And all in the name of the good of the community.

What is the good of the community? It seems to me that we've got a real touchy matter here, and . . ."

"What in the world are you talking about, Don?" Underwood was exasperated, noting that Flowers was succeeding in keeping his cigar lit. "I can't follow you at all. I think that we've got to try some more to find a person who's qualified to inspect our septic tank systems. I cannot believe that there's no one around who can't do this kind of work. Maybe someone will surface if we poke around enough."

"You're naïve, Bill," retorted Redford sharply, "We've tried already, and you know it."

Before Underwood could react to this verbal jab, the mayor's wife came into the room, holding a letter in her hand. "Excuse me for interrupting," she said, "but this just arrived in the mail, and I thought that it might be important. It's from Brownlee, and I knew that you all were going to be talking about septic tank inspections today." She handed the letter to the mayor, and he tore it open.

"Oh!" he exclaimed, "Oh, look at this!" Suddenly he waved it before them. "Brownlee is offering to perform these inspections for each individual that wants one for the same price as now—$50—providing we handle all the administrative chores and absorb whatever expenses are involved in processing the applications, the final license, and so forth. While this would be the individual homeowner's choice, that is to select Brownlee, they ask—that's Brownlee—that the city accumulate 25 to 50 applications or so as a block before Brownlee would come out and do the inspections. They couldn't afford to do it for this price, otherwise. So, what do you think about that?"

EXHIBIT 1
Treasurer's Report, August 197X

	August	Budget for Year	To Date	Balance
I. *General Fund*				
Income:				
Property tax	$ 383.43	$39,600.60	$ 558.34	$39,042.26
Franchise tax	267.24	737.93	267.24	470.69
Sales tax	0	6,562.04	0	6,562.04
Other tax	0	65.00	0	65.00
Royalties	0	150.00	0	150.00
Licenses and permits	0	100.00	0	100.00
Fines	1,279.00	4,505.84	2,404.50	2,101.34
Investments	0	500.00	0	500.00
Current Service[a]	430.00	5,886.74	860.00	5,026.74
	$2,359.67	$58,108.15 =	$4,090.08 +	$54,018.07
Expenditures:				
Legal services	0	6,000.00	0	6,000.00
Office rent[b]	0	1,440.00	0	1,440.00
Receptionist[c]	0	2,700.00	0	2,700.00
Engineering	0	700.00	0	700.00
Planning[d]	0	3,350.00	0	3,350.00
Public relations	28.00	500.00	28.00	472.00
Police salaries[e]	1,275.00	15,630.00	2,201.00	13,429.00
Police car[f]	0	1,800.00	0	1,800.00
Police car operation (gas)	170.36	1,300.00	257.12	1,042.28
Repair to car radio	220.60	325.00	220.60	104.40
Police supplies	22.10	1,000.00	85.35	914.65
Municipal court	20.40	160.00	101.20	58.80
Capital outlay (police)[g]	0	990.00	0	990.00
Street contractual services	327.88	12,468.40	333.88	12,134.52
Street materials	159.15	6,843.60	159.15	6,684.45
Street signs	0	492.00	0	492.00
Secretary/treasurer salary	250.00	3,000.00	500.00	2,500.00
Mailing/postage	0	80.00	8.00	72.00
Publication notices	0	800.00	0	800.00
City telephone	36.50	300.00	36.50	263.50
Office supplies	0	300.00	141.17	158.83
Election supplies	0	142.15	6.50	135.65
Tax office contract[h]	150.00	1,850.00	300.00	1,550.00
Annual audit of city books	0	750.00	0	750.00
Municipal membership	0	400.00	0	400.00
Insurance	365.43	750.00	542.43	207.57
Capital outlay[i]	0	1,212.00	0	1,212.00
	$3,025.42	$65,283.15 =	$4,920.90 +	$60,362.25

EXHIBIT 1 (concluded)

	August	Budget for Year	To Date	Balance
II. *Building Permit Fund* Income	$ 0	$ 2,700.00	$ · 0	$ 2,700.00
Expenditures	0	1,025.00	0	1,025.00
Sanitation Fund[j] Income	0	$12,000.00	$1,255.00	$10,745.00
Expenditures:				
Supplies	15.50	500.00	23.50	477.50
Contractual services	0	5,000.00	0	5,000.00
Capital outlay	0	1,000.00	0	1,000.00
	$ 15.50	$ 6,500.00	$ 23.50	$ 6,477.50

Recap: Budget for the Year

	Income	Expenditures
General fund	$58,108.15	$65,283.15
Building fund	2,700.00	1,025.00
Sanitation fund	12,000.00	6,500.00
	$72,808.15	$72,808.15

Small City checkbook balance	$10,653.92
Building permit fund	$ 147.99
Sanitation fund	$ 2,005.20
Certificates of deposit	$ 7,000.00

Notes:
General
1. Budget year July 1–June 30.
2. Tax rate is $0.25/$100 on 75 percent assessed valuation.
3. Building Fee is $0.02 per finished square foot and $0.01 per unfinished square foot. Building inspector receives $15 per permit issued.
4. Police force consists of one full-time chief, one full-time police officer, one part-time police officer. There is one police car.

Special
[a] Small City is reimbursed by nearby town of Clearmont on a pro rata basis for police services provided by Small City.
[b] Small City plans to rent office space in a new building beginning next January.
[c] When the city establishes its official office in January, it will be necessary to hire one full-time receptionist.
[d] The city plans to let a contract during the year to complete the first phase of a comprehensive city master plan. This amount is the city's share in the cost of a $10,000 planning grant from the federal government under Planning Grant No. 701.
[e] Salaries are as follows:

Chief	$7,350.00
Full-time officer	5,580.00
Part-time officer	1,800.00
Court Clerk	900.00

[f] This reflects the anticipated amount needed to augment revenue sharing funds ($3,200) to purchase one new police car.
[g] This is for additional radio and ancillary equipment for the police car.
[h] The city has a contract with the school district tax office to provide tax evaluation, assessment and collection services.
[i] This is for the purchase of reproduction equipment for the new city office.
[j] The income/expense amounts are predicated on expected financial aspects of implementing Ordinance 34. The capital outlay is for a water quality monitoring program.
Source: Small City treasurer.

18. Kramer Carton Company*

A. J. KRAMER, president of Kramer Carton Company, was born in 1897. From age 10 to 15, he lived on a farm in Ohio with his grandparents. He discontinued his formal education during the time he was in the eighth grade and, shortly thereafter, left Ohio to join his father who worked at Kalamazoo Vegetable Parchment Company in Kalamazoo, Michigan. His father was able to get him a job at the company wrapping bundles.

As it turned out, Kalamazoo Vegetable Parchment Co. enjoyed modest success; Mr. Kindleberger, the owner and chief salesman of the company, developed wax paper and also implemented a parchment paper process for packaging lard and butter. Young Kramer eventually became a sheeter operator and, soon, was promoted to printing press operator.

At the age of 18, Kramer took a chemistry course through International Correspondence School—his immediate goal for the future being to become a chemist. He set up a chemistry laboratory at home in the attic to experiment with his newfound interest.

When World War I began, Kramer enlisted and was placed in the Army Signal Corps. He was trained in radio/teletype communications through a special course at Indiana University. Upon termination of the war, he was released from the army and had to decide whether to remain at the university to complete his degree. This would have taken one year of additional study; however, due to his recent marriage and birth of a son, he found it necessary to leave school and obtain a job.

KRAMER'S CLIMB THROUGH THE RANKS

While Kramer was in the army, his father had quit his job at Kalamazoo Vegetable Parchment and had gone to work for Sutherland Paper Company. Kramer joined his father at Sutherland and became a foreman in the Parchment Division at the age of 22. He was in charge of the printing department and also ran a press. This division of the company was sold to Mr. Kindleberger of Kalamazoo Vegetable Parchment, and Kramer was transferred to the carton department.

During this period, Kramer worked under the plant manager for Suther-

---

* Prepared by Professor Richard E. Hill, California State University, Sacramento.

land, Mr. Brisbois. Brisbois went to California in 1925 to join National Paper Products Company (eventually to become Fibreboard Corp.). He offered Kramer a job as foreman of the carton department with National Paper Products. When Kramer came to California, he brought his cutting man and gluing man from the Sutherland plant. In addition, he brought his "little black book" containing all his knowledge and the rules of printing, cutting, and gluing he had learned up to this point.

Kramer was in charge of the carton plant in Stockton, California, and was earning $350 per month. When he took over the plant, he "closed it down by firing everybody who knew anything" and then reopened it with the people he had brought with him, training his own men. According to Kramer, "In those days you could do that, but now you can't due to the unions and so on." In Kramer's view, it was he who brought the know-how of the folding carton business to northern California: and while at Stockton, Kramer introduced cost reduction programs for three of National's plants in his capacity as efficiency man for the company.

Kramer rose to the position of assistant general manager of three plants and helped the company develop corrugated plants in Los Angeles and Antioch. While in this position, an instance arose that helps to characterize him. He tolerated the supposed inefficiency of a crippled foreman, but then decided that he had to fire him. This resulted in a strike by the 25 personnel who worked for the foreman. Kramer stated, "I got up on a table to try to convince them to stay, but about half of them left."

In 1923, Kramer decided there were virtually no more advancement opportunities in the National hierarchy. He answered an advertisement in a trade magazine and, subsequently, was hired as a plant manager of a cardboard box plant in Indiana. His annual salary was $10,000 plus 2 percent of the profit. After three months, he was making good progress:

> Firing like hell, as always, because I couldn't get many people to do what I wanted. I finally had to fire Joe, the Italian line foreman, but he went over my head to Mr. Kline, the company owner in Chicago. Mr. Kline came down to the factory one afternoon to inform me that he had rehired [his friend] Joe. I said, 'I'm running this business' and Kline answered, 'I own this business.' So I said, 'It's either Joe or me.' Kline told me, 'If you want to run a business you better own it.'

Kramer then returned to National to take over the Antioch Carton and Corrugated Plant, replacing the two men who ran it, at a monthly salary of $400. He observed that there were major problems in the Antioch plant and proceeded to reorganize the plant, rearranging the flow of work and firing everyone but 2 of a total of 30 people. He kept a "lazy" Texan machinist because he thought he had "imagination" and would devise the "easiest" way to do a job.

During the next 13 years (1929 to 1942) with Fibreboard, he became president of the Antioch Chamber of Commerce, and an active member of the Lion's Club, American Legion, and Boy Scouts of America. Mr. Kramer felt that he was a civic leader. He also took correspondence courses in foremanship and plant management at Alexander Hamilton. He invented a number of items used in the paper box industry and obtained patents on a milk carton, a fiber drum, an oil carton, an egg carton, and other containers.

In 1929, when he recognized that he could not advance with Fibreboard, Kramer decided that he would open his own business. In 1936, with $5,000 capital and his patents, he attempted to start a paper carton business. Being unfamiliar with all the items that he should accomplish for this venture, he obtained the services of an attorney and a promoter. The two spent his $5,000 to no avail and the venture terminated. Kramer remained at Fibreboard, but kept looking for an opportunity to go into business for himself.

HISTORY OF KRAMER CARTON COMPANY

In September 1941, Mr. Kramer approached several smaller cardboard plant owners to purchase their companies. The contacts did not result in acquisition because of his lack of capital. Later that year he was approached by Mr. Bockman, owner of Bockman Printer and Box Company, who had a terminal illness and wanted to sell his business to provide financial security for his family. Bockman offered to sell for $10,400. This time Kramer saw to it that he got better accounting, legal, and banking advice. To raise the money he needed, Kramer sold his home and used his $1,500 equity as a down payment.

On November 1, 1941, the sale was finalized; the sales agreement allowed for clear title to the property, thereby allowing Kramer to mortgage his equipment and obtain working capital of $4,000. When he took over the company, it had seven employees and annual sales of $24,000; some of the equipment in use was 30 years old. Initially, Mr. Kramer performed the dual functions of manager of operations and salesman. During the first full year of operations, which was the first year of World War II, sales were in excess of $48,000—doubling Bockman's 1941 sales volume.

While expanding in the next few years, Kramer ran into a major difficulty. Zellerback Paper Company, his primary paper supplier, stopped the line of credit to Kramer, thus forcing him to restrict production due to the lack of raw materials. Although Kramer was guaranteed eight tons per month allotment of paper by the federal government, it was still very difficult to arrange for a permanent supply. Mr. Kramer thought he could overcome this by increasing his quantity of output. In early 1943, he obtained a large order from J. C. Penney to furnish a carload of boxes. He didn't have enough supplies to meet this order, so he contacted Pacific Paperboard Company of Longview, Washington, with an offer to buy a full carload of paper if Pacific would continue to supply him on a regular basis. Since Mr. Flood of the Pacific Paperboard Company was just beginning his business, this arrangement was more than satisfactory. Kramer then filled J. C. Penney's order and eventually got all of Penney's West Coast carton business.

During World War II, Kramer began to produce paper coat hangers; their sales eventually mounted to 50 percent of Kramer's business.

He felt that he could have made a "million dollars" on these hangers had he been able to get enough paperboard. But, alas, after the war demand for wire hangers again replaced that for those made of paper. Also, during the war, he continued to do a limited amount of printing, using Bockman's old equipment.

From 1942 to 1949, Kramer's sales increased and the company expanded steadily. In 1949, he employed from 25 to 30 men and women, with sales in excess of $300,000 and a net worth that had grown from $1,500 in 1942 to in excess of $100,000.

In December 1949, there was a large setback. A major fire destroyed the original plant in downtown Sacramento. The company's offices were moved to the home of the president. Two buildings were rented for temporary operating space. Some used equipment was purchased and some was rented on a temporary basis. Kramer contacted competitors to help fill orders until he could purchase more equipment. In May 1950, the company moved to its present location.

PLANT FACILITIES

At the time of the fire, Kramer Carton Company had a signed contract for a 20,000-square foot plant which it was going to lease from the builder and owner, Mr. Harold. Although much of Kramer's operating capability was lost as a result of the fire, Mr. Harold went ahead with construction since the building could be used for other purposes if Kramer Company did not recover from its losses. The building was only a 100-foot by 200-foot shell and it was Mr. Kramer's responsibility to finish it by installing wiring and plumbing and providing building maintenance in accordance with the terms of the lease agreement. This building now serves as the basic production area and office area.

In 1952, another 20,000-square foot building was constructed. Approximately two thirds of the building is now used to store finished goods; the remainder contains production equipment. In 1957, a 20,000-square foot building was taken over from a neighboring lumber company that went out of business. It was used as storage for raw materials. An additional 8,000-square foot warehouse, also used for finished goods, was added in 1967.

The entire facilities provided Kramer with a total of 68,000 square feet, which in 1971, were leased from Mr. Harold for $2,750 per month. The lease has been in effect for 20 years. Kramer, originally, had wanted to purchase the land and buildings but did not feel he had sufficient capital to do so. In 1971, Mr. Kramer considered buying the property (land and buildings) for

$500,000; however, when his banker suggested that the monthly lease payments would probably be more economical than purchase, Kramer proceeded no further.

PRODUCTION PROCESS

In producing clothing boxes, meat boxes, ice cream boxes, and most other types of printed boxes, it is necessary to process many different types of raw materials. To make a finished product, three basic types of equipment are used: (1) printing machines which print labels on the boxes; (2) presses which cut and perforate the basic cardboard sheets; and (3) folding and gluing machines.

As shown in Exhibit 1, Kramer Carton Company uses the following machines for the operations indicated: (1) one Koenig & Baur, high-speed, dual-output printer; (2) two printing machines using the dry offset printing (without water) method; (3) two machines which have the capability of printing and cutting at the same time; (4) a dyeing machine used for background coloring of the boxes; (5) two machines which can fold and glue simultaneously; (6) one machine for folding only; and (7) one window machine that cuts and glues-in transparent windows and waxes. In addition to the ten major machines in use, Kramer utilized various smaller support machines as shown in Exhibit 1.

EXHIBIT 1
Factory Layout

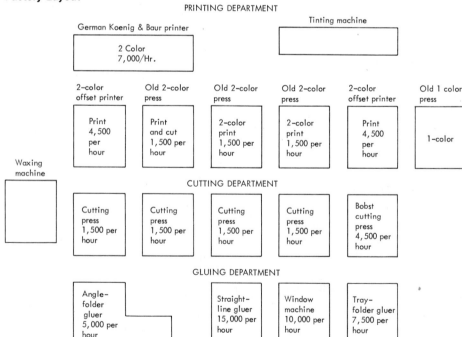

In 1968, Kramer visited Koenig & Baur's factory in Wurzburg, Germany, which produced heavy equipment for the paperboard container industry. He bought the Koenig & Baur printer now in use at a cost of $160,000; the new machine gave the company capability for the simultaneous printing of two colors; it operated at the rate of 7,000 units per hour and had a setup time for each new job of two to three hours. By comparison, the two-color 40-year-old letterpress printers operated at a rate of 1,500 units per hour, and required 10 to 12 hours of setup time. Mr. Kramer stated that now the old printers are only used on one shift; before, without the new machine, they were used on two shifts.

Two-color, offset printing will produce 4,500 units per hour. Although most large cardboard manufacturers used the wet, offset printing process, Mr. Kramer believed that the letterpress and dry offset gave more accurate registration and color distribution than the wet offset process. Hence, Mr. Kramer felt that he would not junk the old equipment, as it could be used on certain jobs economically and keep more people employed.

Mr. Kramer stated that he could purchase another German printer and eliminate all other printers. This would decrease the total amount of equipment required, reduce the floor space used, reduce maintenance, cut costs, and increase production. However, he has, as yet, not made such a purchase because of the heavy cash outlay.

The offset printing machines require two half-cylinder master plates. In order to obtain a new master plate, Kramer must send the design to a company in San Francisco for special fabrication. Plates for the new machine can be made in-house.

Kramer commented that the company used to manufacture laminated, aluminum paperboard but recently discovered that it could be bought cheaper from Kaiser Corporation because of the waste in his shop. Now he buys paper laminated with aluminum, prints it, cuts it, and glues it; the folder-gluer (and stacker) finishes the product. These aluminum boxes are principally used for packaging baking products.

The process for producing a paperboard box is basically composed of the following steps:

1. Designing the box to include size, shape, weight, and art scheme.
2. Preparing a master printing plate and a master cutting and folding plate.
3. Setting up the appropriate machines.
4. Operating the machines in the following sequence: printer, cutter, folder, gluer.
5. Shipping.

Kramer in 1925 designed a job scheduling board which is still used today. The order and its specifications are written on a card and the card placed on a rack opposite the name of the machine which is to be used on the job. The operator can quickly see on a given day what jobs must be done on what machines in what order. He takes the card for the job, does the job according to the instructions on the card, and returns the card to the proper place on the rack when the job is complete. Kramer, his son, and the estimator control the board and, according to Kramer, the system works very well.

INVENTORY

Kramer carries a raw materials inventory of many sizes and rolls of cardboard. Since the cutting machines cut the proper length, the only economies which can be achieved are to minimize the excess waste of the cut. Presently the company has a $380,000 inventory—50 percent raw materials and 50 percent finished goods. Inventory is controlled through a perpetual inventory system but supplemented with three or four annual checks. In the estimating procedure, there is a 3 percent average waste factor calculated which includes the amount recovered by reselling the scrap waste. Recovery costs range from $20 per ton for corrugated cardboard to $90 per ton for white paper.

Raw material inventory is of two types; rolled-paper cardboard and precut flat sheets. An assortment of widths, thicknesses, quality, and variety is kept, with the amount of each being a function of experience. Kramer may have on hand as many as 15 different widths of any one type of cardboard. It had been suggested that a standard width should be used to minimize inventory and reorder costs. Mr. Kramer rejected this idea based on his experience, although no quantitative analysis was performed. (A former employee tried to establish his own box company with a lower inventory, and eventually went out of business. Mr. Kramer claims the failure was a result of the lower inventory.)

The company spent $1.25 million on raw materials in 1970. Purchase terms are generally on a 1 percent/10/net 30. Mr. Kramer believed that if the company had its own paper mill, it could save $10 to $40 per ton. Kramer's major competitors were vertically integrated companies with their own paper mills; Kramer felt this enabled them to obtain paper at a lower price per ton. As a consequence, in 1960, he attempted to arrange for finances to buy a paper mill at a cost of $1 million to $1.5 million. Neither the Small Business Administration nor any banks would grant Kramer a loan for the needed amount; thus the idea was abandoned.

Presently, Kramer obtains its paper and cardboard supplies from firms located in Lewiston, Idaho; Tacoma, Washington; Los Angeles, California; Port Angeles, Washington; and other states on the Gulf of Mexico. Mr. Kramer stated that he did not have a complete breakdown of raw materials sources by location, quantity available, type, or unit price.

COST ESTIMATING

When an order for boxes is received in the factory from sales representatives, the estimator estimates all costs and establishes machine require-

EXHIBIT 2
Cost Estimation and Quotation Forms

	Per M	
Date ___		QUOTATION
Name and description ___		KRAMER CARTON CO.
Quantity ___		1800 61st Street Phone 457-5701 Sacramento, CA
Estimated by ___		
Caliper and grade of stock ___ Colors ___		

	Per M
Cost per ton ___	
Rate ___ Unit ___ Amount ___	
Stock ___	
Waste ___	___
Ink ___	
Wax ___	___
Glue ___	___
Containers or wrappers ___	
Electros ___	
Print M.R. ___	
Print run ___	
R.S.H. ___	
Composing--Lino. ___	
Die making ___	___
Cutting M.R. ___	
Cutting run ___	
Stripping ___	
Glueing ___	
Waxing ___	
Ream cutting ___	
Wrapping ___	
Freight ___	
Selling and O.H. ___	
Cost ___	
Profit ___	
Selling price ___ Total ___	

We are pleased to quote you a price of $ ___
for the following:

Our quotation covers only the work mentioned above. Any addition to or alteration of the work quoted on will be charged for at the regular rate per operation.

Kramer Carton Co.

Date ___ By ___

ments for production (see Exhibit 2). Net costs of the job are calculated through a proprietory empirical formula developed by Mr. Kramer. Mr. Kramer's view was that "We still do estimating the old-fashioned way, but it works pretty good."

Some of the factors considered in the formula are the freight costs of raw materials and finished products, wax, glue (amount per square inch), wrappers, dye, waste factors, the cost of the plate, the size of the run, the possibility of subsequent runs, direct labor, machine costs, and overhead. The waste factor used in the calculations varied between 2 percent and 5 percent depending upon the designer's layout. Probably labor costs could be estimated from previous or similar projects, since each employee filled out a time slip for each job. To the total cost estimate was added a $1 allowance for profit; if and when it was deemed advisable, the quoted price for a job reflected a subjective estimate of a potential competitor's bid. A typical example of the complexity of the estimating process was a job layout for the packaging of various kinds of ammunition. This job required ten different size boxes with 69 different size labels. Mr. Kramer acts as the senior estimator on key jobs and he exercises his final authority over the estimation of any job he chooses. He felt that any executive who did not understand his costs would not be successful.

MARKETING AND SALES

The company markets its products in seven western states and Hawaii. Total sales for various years are shown in Exhibit 6. Sales representatives are located in Los Angeles, Honolulu, and San Francisco. Robert Larson, Kramer's son-in-law handles the territory bounded by the Oregon border; Reno, Nevada; and Bakersfield, California; including Sacramento, California. There are also four jobbers who account for 10 percent of the total sales. The jobbers receive commissions from 2.5 percent to 10 percent, depending on the size of the order.

All sales are made to industries that use paperboard packaging for their products on the basis of 1 percent/10/net 30. Applications for credit by purchasers are all approved by Mr. Kramer. If he deems necessary, he will go to

EXHIBIT 3
Sample Ad of Kramer Carton Indicating Its
Product Line

KRAMER CARTON COMPANY

PAPER BOX MANUFACTURERS
Of Folding Cartons

We Manufacture

CAKE BOXES
Lock Corner and Automatic, Plain and Printed,
with or without windows applied

BAKERY SUPPLIES
U Boards and Automatic Trays
Machine Lock Trays
Glued, Tapered and Nested Trays

CLOTHING BOXES

Lock Corner and Automatic, Plain and Tinted
MILLINERY BOXES
SAUSAGE AND MEAT CARTONS
Automatic glued 1 pc and 2 pc

MEAT BOARDS
CHICKEN BOXES
ICE CREAM CARTONS
Stock and/or Special Print Designs
Special Made To Order Cartons Of All Kinds

WE SPECIALIZE IN
DEVELOPING NEW IDEAS
IN THE PACKAGING LINE

IF YOU HAVE A PACKAGING PROBLEM
WE CAN HELP YOU

the Sacramento Credit Managers' Association for further verification. Often, Mr. Kramer said, he has an intuitive feeling if an account will not pay.

Mr. Kramer feels that the company needs several large-volume sales orders with a low-profit margin/key account like Continental Baking Company, a cupcake maker. Such accounts ensure continuous utilization of employees and machines. About 30 percent of the business is large-volume, low-profit. The balance is in small- and medium-sized orders with better profit margins. Mr. Kramer believes such a product mix allows an economical production flow and ensures a profit.

Kramer Carton's toughest competition was from the very large cardboard box manufacturers such as Container Corporation. These firms not only were vertically integrated in terms of woodlands and paper mills but they also had a more diversified product line to offer packaging users than did Kramer. Exhibit 3 indicates the major items in Kramer's product line.

ORGANIZATION AND PERSONNEL

The organizational structure of the company is depicted in Exhibit 4. The informal organization is shown in Exhibit 5. In addition, there is an office staff headed by Mr. Fessia, the estimator, and lifelong friend of Donald Kramer, plus six other employees, one of whom is part-time. Functions performed by this staff are the planning and writing up of factory orders, billing and invoicing, sales record-keeping, payroll, personnel records, accounting, and correspondence. Mr. Kramer feels that one of his reasons for

EXHIBIT 4
Formal Organization, 1971

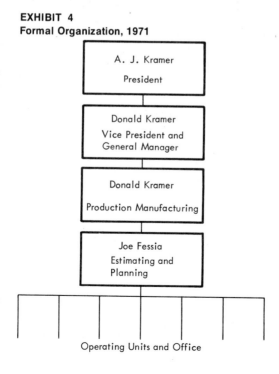

| A. J. Kramer |
| President |

| Donald Kramer |
| Vice President and General Manager |

| Donald Kramer |
| Production Manufacturing |

| Joe Fessia |
| Estimating and Planning |

Operating Units and Office

EXHIBIT 5
Informal Organization

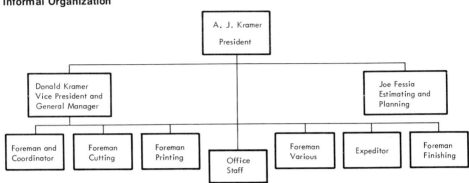

success is the low overhead resulting from his small office staff. In addition to these employees, he recently hired an individual to install a cost accounting system. The individual is not an accountant (because Mr. Kramer did not feel he could afford the salary required to attract a professional cost accountant), so he is being trained by Mr. Kramer to do the work.

The minimum female hourly wage is $2.76 per hour. The minimum male hourly wage is $3.04 per hour. Hourly employees are in a company union, and both employees and Kramer appear to be satisfied with pay rates. Although Kramer felt that the union constrained his management of the company, his dynamic personality effectively controlled the elected union representative. The union contract is negotiated annually, with a 6 percent per year cost of living increase in the contract. This increase has been passed on in increased prices to customers or else offset by reducing costs elsewhere. The company union maintains an affiliation with the National Printing Specialties and Paper Products Workers Local 460. One employee belongs to the Machinists' Union and two of them belong to the Photo-Engravers' Union.

A breakdown of the length of time Kramer's employees have been with the company is indicated below:

No. of Years Employed at Kramer	No. of People
0–5	17
5–10	23
10–15	14
15–20	14
20 and over	9
Management and Sales	18
Total	95

FINANCE

When the company was incorporated in 1961, it issued 22,000 shares of common stock at $10 per share. In 1971, the ownership of the company's common was:

	Shares
President, A. J. Kramer	16,782
Vice president, Donald Kramer (A. J. Kramer's son)	1,291
Secretary/treasurer, V. Larson (A. J. Kramer's daughter)	1,320
Three key employees	1,900
Total:	21,239

A profit sharing plan was also established in 1961. Ten key employees were given the option to purchase company stock at a par value of $10 per share. This was done through a payroll deduction plan in which employees could have up to 20 percent of their payroll directed to stock. The plan required employees to redeem or sell the stock back to the company at book value on the date of termination of work. As of November 30, 1970, the book value was $22 per share.

There have never been any dividends declared or paid on the stock; however, to compensate key employees who owned stock, the company has paid an average annual bonus of 6 percent on the book value. Kramer had always felt that profit sharing was the key to employee incentive; however, after he tried to use the system to finance expansion and boost incentive, he concluded the plan had limitations, particularly with respect to its ability to raise capital from company employees. Nonetheless Kramer did not try to go outside the company to get additional equity financing—even though as far back as 1960 he had had offers by investors to buy stock in the company. Kramer always rejected these offers because he wanted to keep his business family centered.

Various financial data for the company are shown in Exhibits 6 through 10.

Kramer commented that the company's city and county taxes, primarily on inventory, amounted to $14,000 per year. These, he indicated, were too high and had caused him to consider moving at least outside of the county and possibly to Reno. There he would buy land, erect a building, sell it, and lease it back. Kramer also noted that the company's present site was bounded by a public utility. Since the utility was boxed in on its other sides by a railroad and freeway, any further expansion by the utility at this site would have to be done by acquiring the property Kramer leased from Mr. Harold, under the right of eminent domain.

Kramer Carton has never employed anyone to oversee the company's finances. Mr. Kramer feels that there is no need for a financial management specialist and that he can handle this function himself.

PRODUCT DEVELOPMENT AND INNOVATION

In 1964, Mr. Kramer had an idea which he thought would help to smooth production and increase profits. He wanted to manufacture Styrofoam egg carton fillers as a substitute for the familiar cardboard-type egg carton. The project included designing the machine to produce the fillers. Develop-

EXHIBIT 6
Comparative Profit and Loss Statements, 1966–1970

	11-30-70	11-30-69	11-30-68	11-30-67	11-30-66
Sales	$2,721,126	$2,296,209	$2,239,291	$2,311,620	$2,197,165
Less: Cost of goods sold	2,172,214	1,839,494	1,831,318	1,847,453	1,823,140
Gross Profit	$ 548,912	$ 456,715	$ 407,973	$ 464,167	$ 374,025
Expenses:					
Freight out	118,231	101,210	98,563	100,098	102,417
Selling expense	117,802	121,475	103,251	101,258	104,366
General and administrative	187,501	165,474	166,701	143,297	142,157
Total Expenses	$ 423,534	$ 388,159	$ 368,515	$ 344,653	$ 348,940
Operating profit	125,378	68,556	39,458	119,514	25,085
Other Income:					
Interest earned	4,252	5,116	4,711	3,911	2,117
Discounts earned	3,889	3,117	3,001	3,329	3,276
Miscellaneous	240	—	—	—	—
Total Other Income ...	$ 8,381	$ 8,233	$ 7,712	$ 7,240	$ 5,393
Other Expenses:					
Discounts allowed	23,403	15,823	16,012	13,429	21,672
Interest expense	12,882	14,721	15,726	3,120	3,311
Donations	1,306	916	1,260	875	1,117
Officers' Life Insurance	3,624	3,624	3,624	3,624	3,624
Miscellaneous	7	—	—	—	—
Total Other Expenses	$ 41,222	$ 35,084	$ 36,622	$ 21,048	$ 29,724
Net profit before taxes	92,537	41,705	10,548	105,706	754
Taxes	45,332	16,682	2,844	51,796	233
Net Profit	$ 47,705	$ 25,023	$ 7,704	$ 53,910	$ 521

ment attempts spanned a period of one and a half years and $150,000 was expended before Mr. Kramer finally conceded that the high-waste factors would not permit efficient machining and, as he later admitted, since the filler could not be used by large chicken farmers who had automatic egg-packing equipment—something he did not discover until an egg packer tested the final version of the product.

In 1966, Kramer launched an in-house project to develop disposable Styrofoam plates which could be used on picnics or in ultrasonic ovens. Kramer thought Styrofoam plates with a plastic coating would also be useful for camping since they could be used several times. A distributor, Zellerback, had agreed to handle the products. Kramer figured that if he could make eight good plates every 30 seconds he could produce them for two cents each. The machine to manufacture the plates was estimated to cost $25,000 and would have a capability of forming five Styrofoam plates simultaneously. But, before the final design was completed, a total of $150,000

EXHIBIT 7
Comparative General and Administrative Expenses, 1966–1970

	11-30-70	11-30-69	11-30-68	11-30-67	11-30-66
Manager's salary	$ 48,500	$ 48,000	$ 42,000	$ 42,000	$ 36,000
Salaries	100,219	79,862	77,347	72,501	68,702
Payroll taxes	3,762	3,594	3,471	3,396	3,048
Telephone	9,322	11,601	13,972	7,651	5,948
Taxes and licenses	86	104	174	64	82
Office supplies and expense	6,019	4,712	7,132	3,595	6,310
Dues and subscriptions	1,503	1,921	1,417	962	2,350
Depreciation	1,747	1,747	1,221	942	942
Legal and accounting	2,750	2,500	5,300	2,000	2,000
Insurance	710	921	644	676	857
Pension	4,388	3,788	3,702	3,591	3,472
Bad debts	8,490	6,717	10,321	5,919	12,381
Miscellaneous	5	7	—	—	15
Total General and Administrative	$187,501	$165,474	$166,701	$143,297	$142,107

EXHIBIT 8
Comparative Selling Expenses, 1966–1970

	11-30-70	11-30-69	11-30-68	11-30-67	11-30-66
Salaries	$ 53,068	$ 61,017	$ 47,382	$ 45,001	$ 51,719
Commissions	12,432	10,321	10,279	10,444	9,911
Payroll taxes	1,625	1,540	1,471	1,457	1,291
Auto and travel	16,713	17,997	15,421	14,998	15,071
Promotion and entertainment	31,567	27,672	26,541	26,872	24,334
Advertising	1,614	2,112	1,417	1,721	1,253
Depreciation	630	630	630	570	570
Insurance	153	186	110	195	117
Total Selling Expense	$117,802	$121,475	$103,251	$101,258	$104,266

had been expended, only to discover that the Styrofoam plates could not compete in the principal market area with regular paper plates because of the inefficiency of the machine. The two abortive projects cost the company approximately $300,000 over a period of three years and prompted Kramer to remark that he would be more careful before going into a new venture in the future—especially if it was out of his line of business.

Over the past several years, Mr. Kramer thought he should consider automating some of the company functions for two basic reasons: first, it would give the company a stronger base for continuing operation upon his death, and second, it would reduce the number of clerical workers in the front

EXHIBIT 9
Comparative Cost of Goods Sold, 1966–1970

	11-30-70	11-30-69	11-30-68	11-30-67	11-30-66
Materials	$1,255,419	$1,013,040	$1,062,943	$1,159,201	$1,090,641
Wages	634,472	567,885	516,507	472,193	508,628
Payroll taxes	31,839	27,382	25,473	23,808	24,525
Supplies	44,692	39,871	41,712	34,510	39,717
Repairs and maintenance	47,118	41,910	53,229	44,801	50,096
Personal property tax	13,510	10,440	9,673	9,595	9,109
Depreciation	32,143	31,796	16,911	3,914	4,117
Rent	35,275	35,275	34,975	33,675	33,525
Insurance	21,016	18,742	18,004	16,981	16,442
Utilities	10,476	8,921	8,762	8,849	8,312
Services	212	521	1,217	54	15
Employees' pension and welfare	46,042	43,711	41,912	39,872	38,014
Total Cost of Goods Sold	$2,172,214	$1,839,494	$1,831,318	$1,847,453	$1,823,141

office. He had contacted several computer service bureaus but thought their prices were too high and they would be less responsive to his demands for completion of particular jobs, especially payroll and billing. In April 1971, IBM announced its IBM System 3, Model 6 computer line designed for use in small companies. To accompany the machine IBM had developed an impressive software package, with programs for each of the following activities:

Invoicing.
Invoice register.
Inventory management report.
Inventory sales analysis.
Sales analysis.
Trial balance.
Inventory analysis.
Accounts payable—Vendor
  analysis.
Accounts payable—Cost
  requirements.
Payroll register.

Labor distribution—Work in
  progress.
Labor distribution—Completed job
  summary.
Economic order quantity analysis.
Production waiting line problem
  (queueing).
Standard deviation and variance.
Graph and forecast display.
Manufacturing routing and cost
  estimating.
Forecasting and inventory.

The purchase price of the computer was $60,000 and all of the programs were available at a price of $10,000; or, both were available on a lease arrangement. Another $2,000 in initial training was required along with $2,500 in supplies and support equipment. Mr. Kramer was reasonably sure

EXHIBIT 10
Comparative Balance Sheets, 1966–1970

	11-30-70	11-30-69	11-30-68	11-30-67	11-30-66
Current Assets:					
Cash	$ 22,456	$ 13,721	$ 38,797	$ 60,193	$ 21,321
Accounts receivable (net)	230,223	166,214	152,321	161,723	176,389
Inventory	371,374	305,856	256,211	222,003	186,410
Advance to employees	1,326	26,321	22,821	8,321	1,673
Prepaid expense	36,094	51,714	29,711	41,037	39,711
Total Current Assets	$661,473	$563,826	$499,861	$493,277	$425,504
Machinery, Equipment and Leasehold (Net):					
Machinery and equipment	172,144	198,611	216,821	77,311	70,009
Leasehold improvements	147	2,156	4,217	4,562	4,651
Auto	2,807	4,667	6,427	1,716	2,912
Office furniture and fixtures	2,200	2,823	3,571	4,499	3,683
Total Machinery, Equipment and Leasehold	$177,298	$208,257	$231,036	$ 88,088	$ 81,255
Other Assets:					
Deposits	21,125	23,750	18,750	18,750	18,750
Surrender value—life insurance	20,105	17,250	15,010	13,240	11,725
Investment—country club	1,800	1,800	1,800	1,800	1,800
Total Other Assets	$ 43,030	$ 42,800	$ 35,560	$ 33,790	$ 32,275
Total Assets	$881,801	$814,883	$766,457	$615,155	$539,034
Current Liabilities:					
Notes payable	$ 27,000	$ 21,086	$ 24,327	$ 15,671	$ 14,912
Accounts payable	174,006	141,318	126,488	112,040	135,640
Contracts payable	32,297	37,187	15,495	—	—
Accrued expense	48,971	29,919	42,886	23,717	16,824
Taxes payable	35,048	19,721	5,744	47,910	3,133
Total Current Liabilities	$317,322	$249,231	$214,940	$199,338	$170,509
Long-Term Liabilities:					
Notes payable	14,895	14,895	5,086	5,086	5,086
Contracts payable	80,716	117,903	133,398	—	—
Total Long-Term Liabilities	$ 95,611	$132,798	$138,484	$ 5,086	$ 5,086
Total Liabilities	$412,933	$382,029	$353,424	$204,424	$175,595
Capital:					
Capital stock issued	221,110	221,110	221,110	221,110	221,110
Retained earnings	247,758	211,744	191,923	189,621	142,329
Total Capital	$468,868	$432,854	$413,033	$410,731	$363,439
Total Liabilities and Capital	881,801	814,883	766,457	615,155	539,034

this system would meet his objective but after losing so much in the new product development area he was not sure what he should do. He felt he could lease both the computer and the programs and break even in 40 months.

A NOTE ON THE PACKAGING INDUSTRY

Nature of the Market

For many years, expanding markets, new materials, and consumer preference for disposability have enabled the packaging industry to grow at a rate considerably faster than either the population or the paper products industry as a whole. This trend was expected to continue in the 1970s. Consumer preference for disposability was one of the keys to product marketability. This posed the technological problem of how to meet this preference with economical containers that could be readily disposed of without posing pollution problems.

In 1970, the market for packaging materials ranked as one of the largest sectors of the U.S. economy, with sales of about $20.6 billion versus $19.5 billion in 1969. The approximate sales breakdown was: paper and paperboard containers, 37 percent; metal containers, 20 percent; glass containers, 9 percent; flexible packaging materials, including wrapping paper, cellophane, and polyethylene, 8 percent; component materials, including adhesives, tapes, and labels, 5 percent; closures, 3 percent; wooden containers, 3 percent; aerosols, 2 percent; cargo or bulk containers, 1 percent; and miscellaneous, 9 percent. The sales breakdown, while not significantly different from that of the past ten years, did show relatively sharp gains for aerosols and plastics, whereas the market share of paper and paperboard containers had declined somewhat.

From 1968 through 1970, the dollar value of shipments within the paper and paperboard container segment posted the following percentage gains: grocery, variety, and miscellaneous bags, 54 percent; folding paper boxes and cartons, 63 percent; sanitary food containers, 104 percent; rigid paper boxes, 108 percent; and solid fiber and corrugated shipping containers, 109 percent. Shipments of items such as glassine, waxes, or parchment bags, and paper shipping sacks were relatively flat or lower over this period. The overall growth in shipments of paper and paperboard during this 12-year span was almost 87 percent.

By 1980, sales of the packaging industry were projected to grow to $30 billion, with the greatest percentage gains most likely in plastic packaging materials—especially if both major soft drink companies were to decide to use plastic bottles. Lightweight, flexibility in shape, and good protection against breakage favor plastics as a packaging material, sometimes at the expense of more established materials such as paper and paperboard. Aluminum, though still a relatively expensive packaging material, was in 1970 becoming an increasingly popular container for beer and soft drinks, primarily because of its lightweight.

Recently, companies in the three leading packaging segments—paper and paperboard, metal containers, and glass bottles—had experienced a squeeze on profit margins because of rising costs of wages, freight, and fuel (see Exhibit 11). However, the primary market influence, with long-range implica-

EXHIBIT 11
Profit Margins as a Percentage of Sales (percent)

| | Composite Data | | | Operating Income Paper Containers | | | | | | | |
	425 Industrials*	Paper Containers	Glass Containers	Brown	Diamond International	Federal Paper Board	Fibre-Board	Hoerner Waldorf	Inland Container	Maryland Cup	Stone Container
Operating Income:											
1969	15.4	12.5	13.8	6.3	16.0	10.9	12.3	18.2	9.0	18.7	9.0
1968	15.8	12.9	14.0	5.3	17.0	12.1	12.8	18.2	9.2	19.2	8.7
1967	15.5	12.8	13.4	7.1	16.6	11.8	11.3	17.8	10.1	18.3	10.3
1966	16.4	13.4	13.5	6.7	16.7	11.1	11.3	18.1	11.3	20.5	10.0
1965	16.3	12.8	13.5	6.9	17.1	11.0	11.1	19.1	12.0	19.8	8.7
1964	15.9	12.8	12.2	8.0	15.8	8.9	13.4	18.0	12.3	19.4	8.0
1963	15.7	13.1	12.1	8.6	14.3	10.8	13.1	17.2	13.1	18.4	10.8
1962	15.2	13.6	12.2	8.4	14.7	11.7	11.3	12.9	13.9	17.9	12.2
1961	14.7	13.5	12.2	10.8	14.8	11.6	11.1	11.0	12.8	18.0	12.5
1960	14.7	13.3	10.4	10.6	13.8	9.4	10.3	11.9	14.7	16.5	10.4
Net Income:											
1969	5.7	4.2	4.6	0.8	7.2	3.2	3.8	5.1	5.8	5.1	3.5
1968	6.1	3.4	4.9	def.	7.3	3.6	4.6	6.5	5.8	6.3	4.3
1967	6.1	4.2	5.0	0.4	7.3	3.9	2.5	6.4	6.4	7.0	4.3
1966	6.6	4.6	5.3	1.8	7.9	3.5	3.4	8.0	6.3	8.0	5.2
1965	6.8	4.2	5.1	2.6	7.6	3.4	3.1	7.7	6.2	8.1	5.0
1964	6.6	4.1	4.3	3.3	6.3	2.4	3.8	9.0	5.9	7.6	4.0
1963	6.2	3.8	3.8	3.5	5.7	2.9	3.3	7.7	6.6	6.8	3.5
1962	5.9	4.2	3.8	1.3	5.7	3.8	2.3	5.6	6.5	6.7	4.3
1961	5.7	4.2	3.7	2.6	5.5	3.9	2.0	3.9	6.9	6.9	4.3
1960	5.7	4.2	3.1	2.3	5.4	4.6	1.9	4.5	7.2	6.5	3.6

* Based on Standard & Poor's Industry Group Stock Price Indexes.

tions, was the spectre of strong pollution controls. While most companies in the packaging industry were not direct pollutants of the atmosphere or water, the disposal of packaging materials results in some form of solid waste pollution which, in turn, presents problems of effective municipal disposal. Legislation had already been passed in isolated cases, and was being proposed on a much greater scale, to cope with solid waste pollution. The proposals ranged from banishment to taxation to recycling. On the long-term horizon was the possibility that new packaging materials possessing shorter life spans in terms of biodegradability would have to be developed.

Currently, paper and paperboard products are the primary pollutants, and attempts are being made to alleviate this situation by increasing the recycling or use of waste paper. The present low price which consumers get for collecting and returning waste paper undermines recycling as a major solution. Over a period of time, however, a tight world supply situation for pulp could force prices of waste paper upward, thus enhancing the profitability of waste paper reclamation, as well as accelerating trends toward this adoption by paper manufacturers. A breakthrough on the brightness problem for recycled papers, one reason why much of waste paper goes into newsprint, could also expand markets.

Consumer Demand for Packaging Products

As just indicated, increased competition from alternative packaging materials, especially plastics, had recently slowed the rate of growth in demand for paper and paperboard. The year-to-year gain in value of shipments from 1968 to 1970 was no more than 3.5 percent (reflecting mainly higher prices, rather than greater output), which pointed to this segment's dependence for growth on general economic expansion. Growth rates in the future were expected to vary for different products, with that for corrugated shipping containers projected at 6 percent–7 percent annually, depending upon the extent of gains in economic activity and technological innovations. Folding cartons, on the other hand, were forecast to post smaller percentage gains, since increased inroads by plastics were expected. Fiber cans, a small factor in 1970, had some potential for strong growth, if bolstered by use for more products.

Historically, demand for cartons, boxes, and other paper and paperboard packaging materials has been closely geared to general business activity. Widening uses and applications during the postwar years, coupled with large-scale expansion of facilities and/or acquisition of smaller concerns, permitted the large firms to score sales increases even during recessionary periods. A nationwide economic slowdown reduced demand in 1970.

Plant and Equipment Outlays

Capital spending among companies in the paper container groups is cyclical in character, since the economics of the business require that additions to capacity be made in relatively large increments. Since it often takes several years to absorb the expanded capacity, a company's capital expenditures normally decline following a major expansion program, until demand once again catches up with supply capability. Moreover, because of the protracted rise in the per ton cost of new capacity, each expansion cycle has, in recent years, carried capital expenditures to new highs.

19.1. Public Assistance (A)*

As of 1971, nearly one third of all families living in New York City were eligible for some kind of public assistance. Of these, nearly 65 percent were receiving financial aid in some form in the summer of 1971. This meant a case load of over 475,000 families (1,200,000 persons), an increase of almost 300,000 families since 1966. During this same period (1966 to 1971), the amount distributed to recipients annually grew from $382 million to $1.2 billion. Responsibility for the management of this large and growing program rested with the city's Bureau of Public Assistance (BPA).

THE BUREAU OF PUBLIC ASSISTANCE

The Bureau of Public Assistance, in 1971, was one of six bureaus included in the Department of Social Services (DSS), itself an arm of one of the city's superagencies, the Human Resources Administration (HRA). (Exhibit 1 shows the HRA organization.) Of all the organizational units within HRA, BPA was by far the largest. Its annual budget of $1.3 billion for fiscal year 1970–71 was 69 percent of the DSS total. It employed over 16,000 of the 25,000 people working for DSS. Six basic categories of public assistance were under its jurisdiction:

1. *Aid to Dependent Children (ADC) and Aid to Dependent Children of Unemployed Parents (ADC-U).* ADC served minors deprived of parental support or care by death, incapacity, or absence of one or both parents. Grants were provided so the minor could be cared for in the home of his parent(s) or other relatives. ADC-U provided similar assistance where there was an employable but unemployed parent, provided the parent was registered with the New York State Employment Service and had not refused (without good cause) an offer of employment or training.
2. *Aid to the Blind (AB).* Provided grants to persons who were legally blind and in financial need.
3. *Aid to the Disabled (AD).* Provided assistance to persons in need who

---

* Prepared by Professor John R. Russell, formerly of Harvard Business School and currently at Boston University. Copyright © 1972 by the President and Fellows of Harvard College. Reproduced by permission.

EXHIBIT 1
Organization of the Human Resources Administration

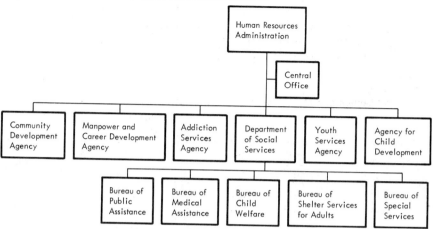

were permanently and totally disabled. The category included those who were mentally ill, alcoholic, or addicted to narcotics.

4. *Home Relief (HR).* State and locally supported assistance for persons who were in their own homes and who were unable to provide for themselves or to secure help from any other source including other public assistance categories.

5. *Old Age Assistance (OAA).* Assisted persons who were 65 or older who could not support themselves and were not in a hospital, public home, or state institution.

6. *Veterans Assistance (VA).* State and city aid supplied to needy veterans who did not qualify for federal programs.

The monthly grants under these programs averaged $200 per month per family but varied according to program and family size as shown in the table below.

Number in Family	Monthly Allowance as of April 1971	
	AB, AD, OAA	HR, VA, ADC, ADC-U
1	$ 84	$ 76
2	134	121
3	179	161
4	231	208
5	284	256
6	329	296
Each additional person	45	41

The amounts shown in the table are exclusive of additional amounts given for shelter, fuel, and several other items for which special allowances were available. In the case of shelter and heating fuel, these were based on the type and quality of housing as well as family size and ranged in amount from $100 to $300 per month. Information on the case load and growth rates for the six assistance categories are set forth in Exhibit 2. In July 1971, the growth rate in total case load was about 5,000 per month.

EXHIBIT 2
Case Load Growth and Mix by Public Assistance Category

Category	Case Load as of April (in thousands)					
	1966	1967	1968	1969	1970	1971
ADC and ADC-U	96.5	121.6	156.9	195.6	208.3	239.8
AB	2.1	2.0	2.2	2.4	2.4	2.6
AD	21.4	23.9	26.8	41.1	55.7	76.1
HR	35.2	48.6	72.2	80.4	69.7	73.7
ÓAA	33.5	43.1	49.4	57.1	65.2	75.2
Total	188.7	239.2	307.5	376.6	401.3	467.4

Category	Data for Fiscal Year 1970–1971				
	Average Number of People (000)	Average Number of Cases (000)	Percent of Total Cases	Funding (000,000)	Percent of Funding
ADC and ADC-U	818.9	215.8	50.8%	$ 755.4	69.0%
AB	2.4	2.4	0.6	4.1	0.4
AD	68.3	68.3	16.1	109.9	10.0
HR	138.8	66.0	15.5	117.9	10.8
OAA	69.1	69.1	16.2	101.3	9.2
VA	8.7	3.3	0.8	6.1	0.6
Total	1,106.2†	424.9*	100.0%	$1,094.7‡	100.0%

* Total number of cases as of July 1971 was 475,000.
† Total number of people as of July 1971 was 1,200,000.
‡ Yearly grant rate as of July 1971 was $1.2 billion.

For all grants except Home Relief and Veterans Assistance, the federal government reimbursed the city for 50 percent of the grant while the state paid 25 percent. For Home Relief and Veterans Assistance, the city and state each paid 50 percent. When these sharing formulas are applied across the six assistance categories in 1970–71, the city's share of the $1.2 billion paid was 28.5 percent ($340 million).

THE WELFARE CENTER

The delivery of both financial assistance and social services was carried out by BPA's 44 welfare centers—12 in Manhattan, 17 in Brooklyn, 12 in the Bronx, 2 in Queens, and 1 in Richmond. In the late 1960s, as the number of public assistance cases increased so did the number of welfare centers (from 26 in 1966 to 44 in 1970) and the number of people who staff these centers. In 1971, 12,000 of BPA's 16,000 employees worked in the centers while the remaining 4,000 were at the bureau's central office. The total cost to run BPA's operations exceeded $100 million per year.

Experience showed that a new center had to be opened for each additional 10,000 cases. An "average" center had a case load as shown below. (Individual centers varied substantially from this norm.)

Category*	Number of Cases	
HR	1,500	
ADC	5,000	
ADC-U	200	6,700†
OAA	1,650	
AB	50	
AD (Nonnarcotic addict)	1,200	
AD (Narcotic addict)	400	3,300
		10,000

* Veterans Assistance was handled by a single, specialized center.

† HR, ADC, and ADC-U cases combined were known as "family" cases.

The services provided by the welfare centers could be divided into two categories—income maintenance and social. The former included determining an applicant's eligibility for financial aid, establishing the size of regular and supplementary grants to which a recipient was entitled, and assuring that payments were actually made. The latter included a number of other services designed to help the recipient and his family in matters not directly related to income maintenance. Some of these social services were mandated by law and had to be accepted by anyone wishing to receive financial support. These required services were job counseling for those judged able to work, protective services for children where there was evidence of either neglect or abuse, access to family planning information, and a periodic assessment of the family's total social service needs. Voluntary services included help with housing, advice on housekeeping and budgeting, and others. A few social services were provided by referring clients to public or private agencies outside the welfare center. Most were given by the general caseworkers at the center or by the center's specialist group. Specialist groups were composed of:

A *homemaker/housekeeper* to secure homemaking and housekeeping services for qualified recipients.

A *home economist* to assist clients in learning to run a household and to help establish budget levels for recipients.

A *DAB[1] worker* who specialized in helping clients in the AD, OAA, and AB categories.

A *housing adviser* to help recipients locate housing, handle relocation problems, and solicit vacancies from real estate contacts.

An *employment specialist* to help clients find jobs.

Until 1969, the effective delivery of both income maintenance and social services depended heavily on a close relationship between the recipient of public assistance and a person designated as "his caseworker." The first floor of a typical center consisted of an intake area, a waiting room, and conference rooms. Caseworkers' offices were on the second floor. A new client or reapplicant was interviewed, in the intake area, by a caseworker who filled out the necessary application forms. During the next few days, another caseworker verified the statements made on the application to determine whether or not the client was, indeed, eligible under one of the public assistance programs. If the applicant was eligible, his case was permanently assigned to a single caseworker who filled out additional forms and determined the size of the new client's monthly grant. From that point on, whenever the recipient returned to the center with a problem, question, or change of status, the intake caseworker would notify the client's caseworker who would come downstairs and talk to the client in one of the conference rooms. If some specialized service was needed—such as housing assistance—the caseworker would consult a center specialist and pass the information on to the recipient. Clients also contacted their caseworkers frequently by mail and telephone.

The caseworker was required to make periodic field trips to a recipient's home to see for himself the conditions under which the client and his family were living. After the first six months, and yearly thereafter, each client's eligibility was reviewed by his caseworker to ensure that any change in status was properly reflected in the amount of the recurring grant.

The intent of this arrangement between caseworker and client was to develop a close and continuing relationship that would be of maximum benefit to those receiving public assistance. On the one hand, each client would have a single, familiar person to contact and consult at the center, thus increasing his willingness and ability to seek advice and counsel. On the other hand, the caseworker's ability to provide the services needed by a particular family would be enhanced because of his familiarity with its problems and progress over an extended period of time. Moreover, by involving the caseworker in the delivery of financial assistance as well as social services, there was assurance that every transaction between caseworker and client regarding income maintenance would provide an opportunity to reassess the need for services other than financial. Studies showed that most caseworkers spent between 75 percent and 90 percent of their time dealing

---

[1] OAA, AB, and AD cases combined were called "DAB" cases (Disabled, Aged, and Blind).

with income maintenance matters. These included not only the determination of initial grants but also changes in grant levels as recipients' circumstances changed, processing special grants, following up complaints that checks were not delivered, and making clerical changes.

To be eligible for a job as caseworker, an applicant was required to have a college degree, although the field of study was not considered critical. Thus, while many caseworkers held majors in sociology and psychology, many others had academic backgrounds in fields like political science and home economics. Few below the rank of supervisor had an advanced degree. In addition, during the past several years, the profile of the typical caseworker had been changing. There were still a number of the traditional "mother hen" type who had been caseworkers for many years but, more and more, the increasing demand for caseworkers had been filled by young people directly out of undergraduate school. Turnover, particularly among the new workers, was extremely high (over 100 per month).

The caseworkers were represented by the Social Service Employees Union (SSEU). This union had fought a bitter battle in the early 1960s to wrest control and bargaining rights from Local 371 of the American Federation of State, County, and Municipal Employees, AFL–CIO. Following its certification, the SSEU took a militant, hard-line approach to its dealings with the city regarding both wages and working conditions. In early 1968, a 28-day strike (the longest for public employees in the city's history) brought the caseworkers substantial pay raises and the right to make the number of cases assigned to each worker a bargainable issue. The new contract set this number at 60 per worker. The supervisory ratio, also part of the contract, was set at one-to-five through four levels of supervision; that is, one unit supervisor for five caseworkers, one case supervisor for five unit supervisors, and so forth.

In 1969, the number of cases per worker was increased to 67 in return for an across-the-board pay raise of $740 per year. In 1970, it was increased again, to 75, for a raise of $380. (By the middle of 1970, a number of factors—including the rapid growth of case load—had brought the apparent number of cases per worker to 93. There was evidence that some caseworkers were "dumping" everything over their quota of 75.)

Exhibit 3 shows the total staffing for a 10,000-case center based on the case load quota of 75, the five-to-one supervisory ratio, and a rule of thumb that one clerical person was required to support each two caseworkers. Information is also shown on salary levels and total direct labor costs.

THE SEPARATED CENTER

During the late 1960s, some of the assumptions underlying the operation of public assistance programs began to change. In particular, many people concluded that financial assistance should be considered more a right than a privilege and that eligibility should be established on the basis of the appli-

EXHIBIT 3
Pre-1969 Staffing for a Typical 10,000-Case Welfare Center

Title	Number of Employees	Average Annual Salary	Annual Direct Labor Cost (000s)
Professional Staff:			
Caseworkers (1/75 cases)	134	$ 9,800	$1,310
Specialists (5/center)	5	9,800	49
Supervisor I (1/5 caseworkers)	27	10,800	292
Supervisor II (1/5 supervisor I)	6	12,400	74
Supervisor III (1/5 supervisor II)	2	14,500	29
Assistant director (1/center)	1	16,300	16
Total	175		$1,770
Clerical Staff:			
Clerks (1/2 caseworkers)	67	6,800	455
Supervisory clerks (1/5 clerks)	14	8,800	123
Administrative assistants (1/5 supervisory clerks)	3	10,300	31
Senior administrative assistant (1/center)	1	12,200	12
Total	85		$ 621
Total for Center........................	260		$2,391

cant's work rather than an elaborate verification procedure. Second, they believed, now, that the need for monetary assistance did not necessarily imply a need for social services. Based on these conclusions, the city began in 1968, to restructure BPA and its 44 welfare centers so that income maintenance services would be *(a)* provided on the basis of a simple declaration of need by the applicant and *(b)* separated organizationally from the delivery of social services. One DSS manager referred to this "separation" program as "the most significant change in public welfare administration in the last three decades."

In 1969, the first step in the overall separation process was completed; income maintenance and social services delivery for DAB cases were separated in all welfare centers. Clerks[2] were hired to do the income maintenance work and the social workers thus freed were transferred to other centers and/or other duties in the system. In 1970, the separation effort was expanded to include the remaining public assistance categories—ADC, ADC-U, and HR. By March, three centers were completely separated. At each one, approximately 60 income maintenance clerks were hired and 65 caseworkers transferred to other centers. By February 1971, three more centers had been fully separated.

During the spring of 1971, the city's program to separate the remaining centers took on new urgency. Officials in Washington announced that on July

---

[2] These clerks were called "Income Maintenance Specialists" and were paid at the level of a supervisory clerk—$8,800 per year.

1, 1971 the formula for reimbursing the administrative cost of public assistance services would be changed. The federal government would reimburse only 50 percent of the costs of operating nonseparated systems.[3] For separated systems, it would continue, as in the past, to pay for 75 percent of the cost of social services and 50 percent of the cost of income maintenance services. The difference could mean almost $460,000 per month to the city. In order to minimize this loss of income, a crash program was undertaken to ensure the completion of separation by October in accordance with an interim plan. Under this plan, caseworkers would be used temporarily to fill income maintenance specialist and eligibility investigator positions.

A separated center operated as follows: Eligibility for monetary assistance was determined solely on the basis of a client's declaration of need. If his statement indicated that he met federal and state eligibility requirements (and a simple check showed that he had not defrauded the system in the past), he received aid without further investigation. Only the applications of addicts and a few other special categories were subject to complete verification by the center's staff of approximately 18 eligibility investigators. (A staff of special investigators, located at the DSS Central Office, performed a monthly quality control audit of a random sample of one half of 1 percent of all ADC and DAB cases. The audit verified eligibility and checked for errors in payment amounts.) With regard to social services, all (except those mandated by law) were completely voluntary; that is, the welfare client was made aware of the selection of social services that were available but it was up to him to request whatever services he wished. This was based on the premise that the client was the best judge of his own needs. In addition to making services voluntary, all (including the mandated ones) were delivered in what was termed a "goal-oriented/time-limited" fashion. In other words, before a service was given, the caseworker and client had to establish a specific goal toward which the service was directed and a date by which the goal was to be accomplished. This date could not be more than 90 days after delivery of the service started.

Income maintenance (IM) services were provided by IM specialists working in groups of five with one supervisor and the direct support of two clerks. Five IM groups were under the supervision of an assistant office manager. IM specialists were supported by a number of ancillary services including eligibility investigation, disbursements and collections, and a number of other routine office services. The groups were divided alphabetically within a center; when a client needed assistance regarding IM problems, he was helped by any specialist available within his alphabetical groups.

The staffing pattern for the delivery of social services was somewhat more complicated. Caseworkers were assigned to one of four new organizational groupings or to the specialist corps (now called the "Special Service Sec-

---

[3] This referred to the operating cost of the centers, not to the grants provided welfare recipients.

tion'') that existed in the nonseparated centers. The four new groups were Assessment, Counter, General, and Protective.

A. The Assessment Section. This section developed with the recipient of ADC or HR a plan for social services encompassing voluntary and mandated services. It served as the entry for newly accepted applicants of family cases to the social services system.

The assessment fulfilled the federal and state mandate that ''a plan and program of service'' be developed for each family and child who was accepted for public assistance and who required services.

The assessment was carried out through interviews with families and individuals and included the following activities:

1. Gathering facts about the current situation of the family or individual which bore on needs for social services.
2. Identifying problem areas and assessing needs for services to help solve the problems.
3. Formulating a social service plan with the family or individual.

B. The Counter Section. The Counter Section included all those services, largely of a concrete and environmental nature, that could be delivered with promptness and that did not require a sustained relationship with the deliverer of services. They included those services that could be delivered by a generalist as distinguished from the more specialized services.

Services given at the counter were:

Information-Giving. Listening to the request made by the potential user of a service, clarifying the request, and providing options from among which the user might choose.

Referral. Deciding which agency, division or section was appropriate to meet the request and explaining the intake procedure of the system to the potential user. The goal of referral was making the connection between the user and the resource's service.

Intercession. Reviewing the request of the user for assistance in negotiating with DSS or other agencies and honoring those requests with which DSS was capable of dealing for the purpose of obtaining delivery of requested services.

C. The General Service Section. This section had two broad objectives:

1. To provide a link to needed services for persons who, because of lack of knowledge, inexperience, fear, illness, or incapacity, were unable to find and use service facilities without active assistance and support. Examples might be young high school dropouts.
2. To provide sustaining services to families and individuals to help them improve or maintain current levels of functioning, or to prevent further breakdown.

General Service units acted as a backup and supplement to all other service sections, including Assessment, Counter, Protective, Special, and other social services.

Need for General Service might arise from many aspects of a person's life—general family functioning, problems of child rearing, home or money management, unmarried parenthood, and so forth.

Those served included:

1. Youths 16 to 21 who had dropped out of school and/or lacked marketable skills and needed counseling around preparation for employment, training, or education.
2. Pregnant adolescents needing assistance in planning for themselves and their babies.
3. Families with members who had physical, mental or emotional disorders and needed sustained assistance in coping with the problems that resulted from the disorder or illness (e.g., mentally retarded children or adults, child-caring persons suffering from incapacitating illnesses, and so forth).
4. Families experiencing problems in child rearing and supervision, marriage, and so forth, who requested help in identifying and working on these problems.

D. *Protective Service for Children Section.* [4] Protective Service was a specialized and distinctive service especially designed to protect the child whether the need for that protection manifested itself on the basis of neglect or abuse. The service was mandated. Referrals came from the Assessment Section or other sections or individuals within DSS who had reason to believe a child was neglected or abused. Also, there was prompt investigation of all community complaints of child abuse or neglect. The case load delivery system was utilized in this section. There was intensive effort to strengthen the role of the parent to assume his responsibilities, but at all times the protection of the child received first consideration.

The Special Service Section. [5] The Special Service Section, in addition to providing consultant services to staff, provided direct services to recipients and took a more active role with community groups in relation to their specialty.

The Special Service Section was staffed by personnel who had developed expertise in their particular specialty. The work of the specialist was focused on services that required a high degree of competence and expertise in particular fields.

As in all other sections, services were goal oriented and time limited. In contrast to past practice, the specialist worked directly with recipients either individually or in groups.

---

[4] Protective Services might be given to families not receiving public assistance as well as to those who were.

[5] The Special Service Section corresponded to the specialist group in a nonseparated center.

The specialist identified those areas of his specialty which lent themselves to direct service delivery both through the individual and group methods. One-to-one contact with the recipient was limited to those situations which were highly complex and made individual interpretation necessary.[6]

The benefits that DSS management expected from the separation of income maintenance and social services were substantial. In a speech before the New York Public Welfare Association, DSS Commissioner Winifred Lally commented:

> The restructuring process is an attempt to streamline and modernize the administration of Public Welfare so that those eligible for money payments receive assistance as a matter of right and that those eligible receive this assistance promptly and in an atmosphere that enhances their dignity and self-respect. On the other end, social services are being viewed on the basis of their own intrinsic value for those who need and desire services rather than as a prerequisite to financial assistance. Under the new system the effectiveness and validity of both programs can be considered, delivered, and evaluated on their own terms as they could not be in the past when they were considered and operationalized as interdependent.

THE OPERATIONS IMPROVEMENT STUDY

As the separation effort got under way, DSS management decided to undertake a broad-scale operations analysis of center operations to determine whether or not significant productivity improvements could be made as part of the separation process. Accordingly, arrangements were made to have the city's Project Management Staff carry out an operations improvement study in the spring and summer of 1971. During that time, a nine-man team gathered data by conducting personal interviews at 14 centers and making a detailed six-week study of one center that had been separated. The group focused on the measurement of direct labor work loads, the analysis of forms and procedures, center organization, the handling of narcotics addicts on public assistance, evaluating parts of the DSS EDP system, and analyzing total system capacity. The results of their studies in four of these areas are summarized below.

Check Issuance

Over 600,000 checks were issued by DSS every two weeks to satisfy the recurring and special needs of public assistance clients. Most checks were issued centrally by the EDP Bureau but some were prepared at the welfare centers. Several different payment "rolls" were used to meet a variety of regular and special needs: The Regular Roll, A-Roll, B-Roll, Daily Special Roll, and Emergency Roll.

---

[6] The description of Social Service Sections has been adapted from the Summer 1970, issue of *Welfarer*, the DSS house organ.

Most active public assistance cases received a biweekly grant under the *Regular Roll* covering rent, food, and other recurring expenses. Over 450,000 of these checks were issued automatically by EDP on the 1st and 16th of the month based on authorizations issued by IM groups at the centers. A reauthorization was required every 12 months or whenever a change in financial status required that a client's normal budget be amended. These amendments could be made up to 13 days before the date of check issuance. After that, the Regular Roll was closed and the rebudget could not be picked up until the following check cycle.

The *A-Roll* was used to process budget changes that could not be submitted prior to the 13-day closing deadline for the Regular Roll. To provide for proper cash assistance during the skipped cycle a special grant was processed under the A-Roll and issued concurrent with the Regular Roll checks. On the next and succeeding cycle, the A-Roll special grant was automatically made part of the client's Regular Roll check. About 20,000 A-Roll checks were issued each cycle. The A-Roll was active for a six-day period beginning when the Regular Roll closed. A-Roll checks were issued for both up and downbudgets and as the initial grant for new cases. For downbudgets, an A-Roll check was written for the full amount of the recipient's budget and the Regular Roll check was cancelled. For an upbudget, the A-Roll check could be issued either for the full budget amount or a supplementary amount.

The *B-Roll* was used for two purposes: To provide grants covering certain nonrecurring expenses (such as moving costs, day-care fees, and employment program expenses) and to cover budget changes that occurred after the A-Roll had closed. Approximately 18,500 B-Roll checks were issued biweekly for nonrecurring expenses and 6,500 for rebudgets. Rebudgets under the B-Roll could be handled up to three or four days before the date for issuance of Regular Roll checks. (A breakdown of the reasons for issuing A- and B-Roll checks is set forth in Exhibit 4.)

EXHIBIT 4
Comparison of A- and B-Rolls by Reason for Check Issuance

Reason for Check Issuance	A-Roll Checks		B-Roll Checks	
	Number Issued per Cycle	*Percent of Total*	*Number Issued per Cycle*	*Percent of Total*
Downbudget—Full amount	5,000	25%	1,240	5%
Upbudget—Full amount	1,540	8	380	2
Upbudget—Supplement	7,660	38	1,880	7
Initial grant—New cases	4,900	25	2,860	11
Transfers and errors in regular grants	900	4	220	1
Special grants— recurring and nonrecurring	0	0	18,420	74
Total	20,000	100%	25,000	100%

The *Daily Special Roll* was used to cover nonrecurring expenses that required more immediate assistance than was possible with the two-week interval of the B-Roll. Checks processed by EDP as part of the Daily Special Roll reached the client within two or three days following his request. Some of the reasons for issuing checks under the Daily Roll were large upbudgets, lost check replacements, and family disasters. Approximately 50,000 of these daily checks were written every two weeks.

The *Emergency Roll* was made up of those checks issued directly by the disbursement activities at the individual welfare centers. These grants, as their name implies, were made when a client's need was so immediate that he could not wait the two or three days that were required to process and deliver a check under the Daily Special Roll. Each day, 5,500 of these checks were issued by the 44 centers.

All checks printed by EDP were sent to the Check Release Section at the DSS central office. Here, they were prepared for mailing and mailed on the proper date. Whenever a client's budget was reduced or his case closed, the IM specialist working on the case would send a notice to the Release section who would pull the client's check before mailing and return it to EDP for cancellation.

The pulling operation required the full-time attention of five clerks, one senior clerk, and one supervising clerk. An additional staff of nine people during the day shift and eight at night worked part time on check pulling. Altogether, they pulled approximately 385,000 checks per year at a cost of $73,500 or $0.19 per check. This cost, together with others incurred in processing checks under the A-, B-, or Special Daily Rolls, is shown in Exhibit 5. Data regarding the dollar amounts of both rebudgets and special grants is shown in Exhibit 6.

EXHIBIT 5
Estimated Cost to Process an A- or B-Roll Check

Welfare Center Staff	Man Minutes per Check	Labor Cost per Check
IM specialist	40	$3.20
IM supervisor and other supervisors	10	.96
Clerks	30	2.08
	80	$6.24
EDP:		
Processing cost		0.31
Check Release:		
Check stopping	5	0.33
Check pulling	*	0.19
		$0.52
Total Cost		$7.07

* Cost based on average number of full- and part-time staff.

EXHIBIT 6
Distribution of Dollar Amounts of Rebudgets and Special Grants per Check Cycle

	Net Dollar Change*				
	$1 to $5	$6 to $10	$11 to $20	>$20	Total
Number of Rebudget Transactions:					
Upbudget................	3,850	1,930	2,640	15,640	24,060
Downbudget	2,750	915	1,570	7,865	13,100
Total	6,600	2,845	4,210	23,505	37,160
	Dollar Value of Grant†				
	$1 to $5	$6 to $10	$11 to $20	>$20	Total
Number of Special Grant Transactions:					
B-Roll	555	370	1,110	15,965	18,000
Daily Special Roll	2,500	2,500	5,500	39,500	50,000
Total	3,055	2,870	6,610	55,465	68,000

* The average upbudget is $43; the average downbudget, $29.
† The average B-Roll special grant is $63; the average Daily Special Roll grant, $59.

Staffing for Social Services

Before separation, the number of employees in each center was determined on the basis of only two considerations: First, the quota of cases that could be assigned to a caseworker; second, the number of supervisory and clerical personnel needed to support each caseworker. Both considerations were subject to contract provisions. As soon as the number of cases was known for a center, the size of the required staff to meet contractual obligations could be determined. No performance standards existed beyond the quota of 75 cases per worker, nor had any data been collected regarding the time that a worker spent servicing a welfare case.

To make staffing decisions for a separated center required considerably more information than the old quota per caseworker. First, it was necessary to have some understanding of the time it took to service clients in each of the social service sections (Counter, General, Special, and so forth). Second, it was important to know what the demand would be now that clients had the option of accepting only those services that they wanted. When the separation effort began in 1969, Larry Perlman and Al Pinchoff, two experienced social work supervisors now assigned to the DSS Office of Program Development (OPD), were asked to make reasonable estimates of both these quantities. Advised by the DSS labor relations specialist, that the SSEU would not allow "time studies" in any form to be taken, Perlman and Pinchoff made their estimates solely on the basis of their own experience in the social service system. They described the process as follows:

With regard to Counter Services, we decided that giving information or making a referral should take about 20 minutes. That figure was simply an estimate. We recognized that some referrals might take only a minute while others might require the better part of a day to make seven or eight phone calls and write a letter or two. The 20 minute estimate also assumed that the counter would have access to good, well-cataloged information about the kinds of social services that were available and where they were located.

On the demand side, we looked at client inflow in nonseparated centers and concluded that 20 percent of it was for social services and the rest for income maintenance. We assumed that it would remain about the same in volume under separation and that the total demand for Counter Services, including telephone calls and mail inquiries would be about four times as great as the demand from clients who came into the center.

General was real guesswork. We figured that no more than 5 percent of the case load would require General Services and that some portion of that 5 percent would be referred outside the center. We then estimated that two thirds of the cases would be handled through group work and the other one third on an individual basis. We also concluded that about one half of the cases would have a second family member that required services.

Then we estimated that an average group would contain 15 people, that group sessions would last for one hour, and that each one would require an hour's setup time by a caseworker. Cases being treated on an individual basis would require an average of one hour per week of direct contact and one and a half hours per week of other activity. A factor was also added to allow for the time to do field work with those cases that were handled one-to-one.

Similar estimating procedures were applied to the activities of the other social service sections to develop estimates of demand and standard times to perform typical services. These were combined and summarized into the following quotas:

Section	Services per Worker per Period	Quota
Counter	88 per week	1 Caseworker per 1,000 total cases
Assessment	68 per month	1 Caseworker per 750 family cases
General	8 per week	1 Caseworker per 500 family cases
Protective	5 per month	1 Caseworker per 800 family cases
DAB	n.a.	1 Caseworker per 800 DAB cases
Special	n.a.	n.a.

n.a. = not available.

(A quota of one IM specialist per 150 cases was also established.) Staffing for the first six centers to be separated was based on these standards and is summarized in Exhibit 7.

One of the tasks set for the operations improvement team was to check the operation and validity of these standards to see whether they were appropriate for the 38 additional centers currently undergoing separation. To do this, the team reviewed weekly reports submitted by caseworkers over a

47-week period (April 1970 to March 1971) at three of the separated centers—East End, Clinton, and Franklin. The results of this data gathering are shown in Exhibit 8. In addition to collecting the material shown in the exhibit, the analysts also examined the size of the backlog of uncompleted Protective and General Services cases in the three centers with the following results:

		Number of Active Cases	
Center		April 1970	March 1971
Protective Services:			
East End	....	69	52
Franklin	....	58	45
Clinton	....	220	173
General Services:			
East End	....	1,346	816
Franklin	....	274	302
Clinton	....	2,755	615

In the process of gathering this basic information, the operations improvement team made several other observations. First, they concluded that, for the most part, the original standards for the number of social services completed per worker per time period, as developed by Perlman and Pinchoff, were a reasonably accurate reflection of actual operations in the separated centers. Nevertheless, caseworkers at all three centers seemed to be idle a great deal of the time. The team thought that efficiency might be improved substantially if, for administrative purposes, the functions performed by Counter and Assessment were absorbed into the General section and General's quota modified to one caseworker per 445 family cases. The team also observed that the 90-day limit for the duration of Protective and General cases was frequently being circumvented. In the case of General Services, this was done by closing the case and then reopening it, ostensibly for another problem, but actually for treatment of the old one. In Protective, caseworkers were seeking frequent extensions of time, sometimes because court proceedings and/or child placement took longer than the 90-day limit, sometimes because they were reluctant to turn their cases over to the General section which they considered less skilled and less conscientious about handling cases of child neglect and abuse. Finally, it was noted, with some concern, that the typical narcotic case handled by the DAB section took six times as much of the caseworkers' time as the blind, aged, or other disabled.

Income Maintenance Staffing

The study of income maintenance staffing, as performed by the operations improvement group, had two purposes: To develop time standards for each element of an IM specialist's job and to measure the demand for these elements that was originated by recipients in each category of public assis-

EXHIBIT 7
Staffing Pattern for the First Six Separated Centers (assuming 10,000 cases per center)

Title	Nominal Employee Requirements	Number of Five-Person Groups Required	Actual Employees on Staff
Social Services Staff:			
Counter (10,000/1,000)*	10.0	2	10
Assessment (6,700/750)*	8.9	2	10
General (6,700/500)*	13.4	3	15
Protective (6,700/800)*	8.4	2	10
DAB (3,300/800)*	4.1	1	5
Special (5 workers per center)	5.0	1	5
Total		11	55
Supervisor I (1/Service unit)	—	—	11
Supervisor II (1/5 Supervisor I)	—	—	2
Supervisor III (1/5 Supervisor II)	—	—	1
Assistant director (1 per center)	—	—	1
Total			15
Income Maintenance Staff:			
IM Specialists (10,000/150)†	67.0	14	70
Eligibility investigators (18 per center)	18.0	—	18
Total			88
Administrative assistants (1 per IM group)	—	—	14
Clerical Staff:			
Clerks (40 per center plus 1 per IM group plus 1 per social services group)	—	—	62
Supervisory clerks (1/5 clerks)	—	—	13
Administrative assistants (1/5 supervisory clerks)	—	—	3
Senior administrative assistant (1 per center)	—	—	1
			79
Total for Center			251

* Based on the number of cases for a typical center.
† IM specialists were paid at the same rate as supervisory clerks.

tance. The study was conducted with the cooperation of the deputy director of DSS for Income Maintenance, the clerical workers' union, and the office managers of the six centers already separated. Four IM groups at each center, selected randomly, participated in the data gathering phase between April 12 and May 7, 1971. The specialist's job was broken down into 13 work categories[7] and the potential clientele into seven groups.[8] Each specialist

[7] The 13 work categories were: Budget change, reclassification, address change, change in case composition, application, closing, suspension, transfer in, transfer out, emergency grants, ID cards, information and referral, and miscellaneous.

[8] The seven-clientele groups were: Home Relief, Old Age Assistance, Aid to the Blind, ADC, ADC-U, Aid to the Disabled (nonnarcotic addicts), and Aid to the Disabled (narcotic addicts).

EXHIBIT 8
Data on the Delivery of Social Services at Three Separated Centers

	Case Load	OPD* Standard Quota Cases per Caseworker	Mean Number of Case-workers on Duty	Mean Number of of Actions per Worker	OPD* Standard Number of Actions per Worker per period
Assess (family):					
East End	5,400	750	8.5	44 per month	68 per month
Franklin	3,400	750	7.6	22	68 per month
Clinton	5,800	750	15.3	31	68 per month
Counter (all cases):					
East End	7,800	1,000	3.5	34 per week	88 per week
Franklin	4,300	1,000	3.1	32	88 per week
Clinton	9,000	1,000	8.7	24	88 per week
General (family):					
East End	5,400	500	16.2	5 per week	8 per week
Franklin	3,400	500	9.5	4	8 per week
Clinton	5,800	500	16.8	6	8 per week
Protective (family):					
East End	5,400	1,000	6.3	2.4 per month	5 per month
Franklin	3,400	1,000	3.0	3.3	5 per month
Clinton	5,800	1,000	11.0	1.9	5 per month

* Office of Program Development.

kept a running record of the kind of work he was doing, when he started the job, when he finished it, and the type of public assistance client being served.

From this data, time standards were developed for each work category by averaging the reported times to perform that kind of service. In addition, a record was developed of the rate at which each type of public assistance recipient would require each kind of IM service. The results of this analysis are shown in Exhibits 9 and 10. (In both exhibits, the data have been con-

EXHIBIT 9
Time Standards for Processing Income
Maintenance Transactions

Transactions	Mean Time (minutes)
Rebudget	34.7
Emergency grant	30.9
Information and referral	25.5
Application	56.1
I.D. card	13.8
Other*	31.4

* Includes reclassification, address change, change in case composition, closing, suspension, transfer in, transfer out, and miscellaneous.

EXHIBIT 10
Number of Income Maintenance Transactions Demanded Weekly for Each 1,000 Clients in Each Client Category

		Client Category		
Transaction Type	*HR*	*DAB (nonaddict)*	*DAB (addict)*	*ADC ADC-U*
Normal Week:				
Rebudget	29	21	24	38
Emergency grant	46	23	271	38
Information and referral	59	33	84	69
Application	18	8	30	12
I.D. card	20	16	33	20
Other*...........................	54	31	96	51
Total	226	132	538	228
Peak Period:				
Rebudget	54	28	19	53
Emergency grant	70	30	299	57
Information and referral	67	41	55	70
Application	13	7	24	17
I.D. card	31	26	39	30
Other*...........................	56	40	88	70
Total	291	172	524	297

* Includes reclassification, address change, change in case composition, closing, suspension, transfer in, transfer out, and miscellaneous.

densed substantially.) For purposes of applying the time standards, the group knew that IM specialists worked a 35-hour week of which 2.5 hours was scheduled for coffee breaks. Of the remaining time, it was believed that 20 percent would be nonproductive. (Twenty percent is a relatively standard figure for clerical work.) The group also noted that the demand for various kinds of service by different clientele groups showed a marked change between "normal" days of the check cycle and "peak" days (the two or three days immediately following issuance of checks). Exhibit 10 shows the demand characteristics normalized to a one-week period—for both the normal and peak demand times.

Processing Narcotics Addicts

In November 1969, DSS instituted a procedure for granting public assistance to narcotic addicts under the federal category of Aid to the Disabled. (This meant that the city's share of financial support would be 25 percent compared to 50 percent if the Home Relief category had been used.) By the late spring of 1971, the number of addicts receiving assistance had reached 23,000 and was growing at the rate of over 1,200 per month. Grants were running at more than $68.4 million annually. Both the growth rate and the addict population as a whole were very unevenly distributed throughout the city and, therefore, among welfare centers. The Queens center, with an addict population of 2,459, was adding about 200 per month, while Euclid with 101 addicts was adding only 3 per month. The distribution of addicts in the centers is shown below.

Number of Addict Clients	Number of Centers
Less than 200	7
200–500	23
501–1,000	10
1,001–2,000	3
More than 2,000	1
	44

To be eligible for public assistance, an addict had to meet two requirements: First, he had to provide medical verification of his addiction; second, he had to be a participant in an addiction treatment program or be on the waiting list for one. Only a few addicts were already receiving treatment when they applied for assistance. Most were not and, in a separated center, it was the DAB worker's job to enroll him in a program of his choosing or place him on the waiting list. The addict could remain on a waiting list for one month and still receive assistance. If no opening was available after this time, however, he had to begin treatment in any program where there was a vacancy. If he refused to enroll, assistance was terminated.

BPA attempted, with difficulty, to maintain an up-to-date catalog of reputable programs throughout the city. No standards existed for evaluating programs; most were small and frequently transient. Of over 180 programs listed by BPA in early 1971, only 23 had capacity for more than 100 addicts, and only 35 had 50 or more public assistance recipients enrolled. Nearly all (particularly those using methadone maintenance) had substantial waiting lists.

Once placed in a program, an addict had to attend regularly or his assistance was stopped. For the first few weeks of treatment and during the time that he was on a waiting list, he picked up his check at the welfare center. Once his attendance in the program was regular, the check was usually sent by mail. This process continued as long as his attendance, which was verified monthly by the DAB service worker, continued. If he dropped out of the program, assistance stopped.

Several centers departed from the basic procedures outlined above. One, for example, when it placed an addict on a recurring grant, had the checks mailed to him at the center rather than his home. This was especially true when the addict or the program in which he was enrolled was considered unreliable. Other centers tended to keep addicts on a single issue, emergency roll grant even after they were officially enrolled in a treatment program. In either case, the frequency with which addicts returned to the centers was greater than the standard procedure would have required. Indeed, the operations improvement team's survey of the six reorganized centers showed that over one half of the addict population returned to the centers to receive weekly special grant checks.

All of these procedures, both standard and nonstandard, reflected the need to control addict cases more carefully than others. Of all clients, addicts were most likely to attempt in some way to defraud the system, often through multiple registration, under different names at different centers. In addition, it was extremely difficult to monitor attendance at treatment programs effectively and accurately. If a program closed (which was not unusual) or an addict stopped attending, it was frequently a month or two before the center was able to verify the addict's change in status and discontinue assistance.

On the other hand, attempts to exert stronger control by increasing the number of times that addicts visited the centers posed other problems. To begin with, addicts were a security risk. With the advent of separation, clients (including addicts), had to move about the centers to transact their business. Reports indicated that "business," as far as addicts were concerned, often included theft, vandalism, and harassment of both staff and clients. Addicts had been known to make purchases of drugs on the premises and shoot-up in the rest rooms. There was evidence that pushers were accompanying addicts to the centers or waiting for them just outside. In fact, some staff members believed that pushers were notifying their customers of the availability of public assistance and "managing" their applications to be sure they were properly filled out.

Another consequence of the growing number of addicts visiting the centers was a deterioration of service to other DAB clients. DAB workers at the six separated centers were observed to spend three or four hours per day placing addicts in programs, checking attendance at these programs and authorizing special grant checks. The time left for servicing other disabled and the blind and aged was extremely limited. At the East End center, for example, where there were 580 narcotic and 2,420 other DAB cases, less than a third of the nonaddicts received any social services whatsoever during 1970, although there was a backlog of demand.

Several suggestions had been made for dealing with the addict problem at the centers. Two, that represented opposite points of view, were to (a) create special welfare centers that would handle only addicts and (b) outstation income maintenance specialists at selected narcotic treatment programs.

The first called for creation of four centers (one in each borough—except Staten Island) each handling 5,000 to 6,000 addicts and each capable of expansion to accommodate 10,000. The centers would be located in nonresidential fringe areas such as docks or industrial sites. They would be staffed much like a normal welfare center with a director, administrative staff, and income maintenance and social service personnel. The social workers would be responsible for maintaining close liaison with and placing addicts in the various narcotic treatment programs. Other social services, such as housing and employment, would be handled by specialists who would visit the addict centers periodically.

The second alternative involved distributing checks at the treatment program sites thereby increasing the probability that addicts, once enrolled, would continue to attend the programs regularly. An income maintenance specialist would be assigned to distribute special issue checks at those programs where the number of addicts receiving treatment was large enough to justify the time spent by the specialist and the administrative costs necessary to operate the system. The specialist would visit a few programs each day and return to each program semimonthly. If an addict missed the specialist, he could go to the welfare center to pick up his check. The centers would continue to be responsible for addict intake, eligibility determination, program placement, and other services.

A number of criteria seemed to the operations improvement group to be important in evaluating these two, or any other, alternative means of providing assistance to the addict population. They included: capacity to service a rapidly growing case load; start-up and operating costs; level of service to both addicts and other DAB clients; control of treatment program attendance and check issuance; security at the regular welfare centers; and probable community reaction. In addition to these considerations, there was some chance that pending federal legislation would remove DAB clients from the welfare system and place them under Social Security. Since federal officials believed that addicts would not qualify as "disabled" under this new legislation, it seemed important to prepare for a shift of addicts to the Home Relief category if the federal legislation were passed and the city decided to continue supporting its addicts despite the increased cost.

19.2. Public Assistance (B)*

In September 1971, Mayor Lindsay appointed Arthur Spiegel, age 32, to be executive director of DSS. Spiegel, a graduate of the Harvard Business School, had been director of plans and programs in the city's Housing and Development Administration and responsible for implementing the new rent control program. He had left the city government after this position and, until his appointment at DSS, had been selling second home real estate developments in Pennsylvania's Pocono Mountains. Spiegel reported directly to Jule Sugarman. Sugarman had been named to head the Human Resources Administration (HRA) in 1970 after a 20-year civil service career which included the successful implementation of the Head Start program.

A short time after his appointment, Spiegel was quoted in *The New York Times* as saying:

> In any large organization, you're bound to get some slop but what you have here is a walking disaster. The problem is that for years the department was run by social workers instead of administrators and its gotten so out of control that no one can get on top of it. You've got a $3 billion budget—you've got 30,000 people in the department and it's a mess which means that it's wide open. It's exciting in another respect which is that welfare politics are up for grabs today. There are no truths so in very broad terms, it's a good time to be in welfare.

Spiegel's first project was to recruit a support staff for himself—a group which could design and implement some of the policy and operational changes that he felt would be necessary. He obtained a $3 million authorization for 200 new administrative posts. His top three appointments were Kenneth Brody, a 41-year-old assistant vice president of the American Stock Exchange, to run the EDP operation; Kenneth Harris, 29 years old, who had headed the operations improvement team that had studied DSS, was put in charge of a project management group; and John Alexander, the 44-year-old director of corporate development at Allied Chemical, was selected to recruit and direct a management engineering department.

Harris was enthusiastic about the possibilities of his new job:

* Prepared by Professor John R. Russell, formerly of Harvard Business School and currently at Boston University. Copyright © 1973 by the President and Fellows of Harvard College. Reproduced by permission.

I really knew the workings of DSS after spending nine months there. It was a once-in-a-lifetime opportunity to have the authority and responsibility for implementing a consulting study. Professionally, it was an opportunity to see if I could really manage something large. I wanted to see how good I really was.

Alexander, after surveying the operations of DSS, remarked:

I visualize the department as a big paper factory. You put a client on the conveyor belt at the beginning and she gets off at the other end with a check or some other service. That's what is supposed to happen but too often she gets sidelined and this sideline becomes a second conveyor.

These men placed advertisements in the financial section of *The New York Times* addressed to "results-oriented MBAs and Engineers" which read: "We've been charged with turning around a $3 billion government agency and have two years to do it." Harris sent recruiting brochures to business schools with a lead statement as follows: "This is not a career opportunity. It is a once-in-a-lifetime chance to get in on the ground floor of a massive undertaking and experience the thrill of having your abilities and personality as the major constraints on achieving results. This is an opportunity to find out how good you really are."

Spiegel next moved to fill the post of director of BPA. (Mrs. Hilda Hollyer, an experienced social service worker who held the post of deputy director had been serving as acting director for almost a year.) It took time to find an appropriate person, but in April 1972, Charles Morris, age 32, was named to head the Bureau. [In the interim, BPA's name had been changed to the Bureau of Income Maintenance (BIM).] Morris an assistant director of the city's Bureau of the Budget (BOB) and formerly director of the New Jersey Office of Economic Opportunity, was the first person to head BPA without holding a Master's degree in Social Work. At BOB, he had been in charge of designing a budget reform system that decentralized decision-making authority by allowing individual agencies to make spending and personnel hiring decisions. His work at BOB proved Morris to be not only a creative planner but also a skilled negotiator and administrator. He earned the reputation of being someone who was as likely to illustrate a point by quoting a line of poetry as by citing a statistic.

BPA ORGANIZATION

Before separation BPA's top-level organization consisted of a director and three deputy directors (Exhibit 1). Two of the deputies had responsibility for social service activities and had 11 field directors reporting to them. Each field director, in turn, supervised four center directors and was concerned with the demand for social services, the initiation of new service activities, and the referral and progress of clients who used these services. The field directors, who visited each of their centers about twice a month, periodically prepared and submitted studies and surveys on these activities to their

EXHIBIT 1
Bureau of Public Assistance (BPA) Organization (preseparation)

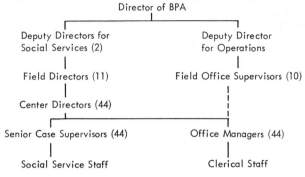

Director of BPA

Deputy Directors for Social Services (2)   Deputy Director for Operations

Field Directors (11)   Field Office Supervisors (10)

Center Directors (44)

Senior Case Supervisors (44)   Office Managers (44)

Social Service Staff   Clerical Staff

supervising deputy directors. The two deputy directors and all 11 field directors had graduate degrees in social work and had come up through the social service ranks: from caseworker, to senior caseworker, to senior case supervisor, to center director.

The third deputy director was in charge of clerical operations. He had responsibility for processing the paper work required to provide financial assistance, for developing statistical reports, and for ensuring that there was a large enough staff to perform other clerical support activities at the centers. He had ten field office supervisors reporting to him who acted as technical consultants to the office managers at the centers. The office managers were responsible to their center directors for clerical and administrative activities. The field office supervisors had about the same frequency of contact with office managers as field directors had with center directors but lacked any direct authority over center personnel. Field office supervisors had moved up through the clerical ranks of DSS having held positions as clerks, section heads, assistant office managers, and office managers in the centers.

Center directors supervised 300 to 350 people and were responsible for the entire operations of their centers. Their main tasks involved designing the implementation of policy changes dictated by the BPA central office; dealing with local representatives of the Social Services Employees Union (SSEU) and the Clerical Workers Union (CWU); deploying staff to meet increases in case load and changes in the composition of the case load; reviewing the productivity of different units; and keeping track of absenteeism and lateness through the center's timekeeper. Center directors had to contact the BPA central office for decisions on a number of matters concerning questions of client eligibility and extra allowances for such expenses as housing and educational expense for dependents. If a director simply needed advice, he could consult either his field director or one of several special units set up at BPA headquarters to answer questions about housing, DAB[2], employment,

---

[2] OAA, AB, and AD cases combined were known as DAB cases (Disabled, Aged, or Blind).

and so forth. Some center directors communicated with the BPA staff frequently, while others did so rarely, preferring to keep all decision making at the center, even to the point of making decisions which supposedly required BPA approval. A center director's relationship with his field director depended primarily on the personalities of the two individuals, with certain field directors visiting some of their centers constantly and actually taking part in the direction of daily operations.

Center directors, most of whom had at least 25 years service with DSS, were reluctant, by and large, to discuss very many of their problems with BPA staff. There was a strong feeling that the central office would not understand the particular conditions at the center which contributed to the problem. Center directors also believed that exposing problems could be taken as a sign of ineffective management by high level DSS officials and were unsure of the amount of protection and support they would receive from their field supervisors. Although, under civil service regulations, dismissal or demotion could come only as a result of gross incompetence or criminal activity, there were cases of center directors being transferred to obscure staff positions at BPA headquarters.

Reporting to each center director was a senior case supervisor and an officer manager who were responsible for social service and clerical activities, respectively. Center directors relied heavily upon the senior case supervisors, who also had graduate degrees in social work. About half the office managers had college degrees and all had more than 20 years of experience in DSS. The relationship between the office manager and his field office supervisor depended, to a great extent, on how the center director managed his center. In centers where the director avoided contact with the central office, office managers were inclined to communicate less with their field office supervisors. In other centers where there was greater interchange between the director and BPA management, there was likely to be frequent contact between office managers and field office supervisors.

Although separation required a great deal of organizational realignment at the centers (see Public Assistance [A]), only one significant change took place at levels above the center director: BPA's deputy director of clerical operations was put in charge of all income maintenance activities at the headquarters. (At the centers, these activities were now supervised by the office managers.) This was consistent with one of the basic reasons for separation—to make income maintenance into a relatively simple, straightforward clerical operation. It was anticipated that the change would compel both center directors and their office managers to work much more closely with the clerical field office supervisors than they had in the past.

In addition to this organizational change, BPA management also instituted new, separate reporting systems for income maintenance and social service activities. All actions that required a change in the type or amount of income maintenance authorized by a center were compiled by the center's statistical unit for inclusion in a daily report of action taken (DRAT). Multiple copies of

EXHIBIT 2
Income Maintenance Operations Activity Report

Page 1

Week Ending 6/16/72

Centers	Accept	NA'd	Closed	Total under Care Incl. Chelsea	Old Age Homes	Income Maint.	Family Cases	A.S.C. Cases
Total This Week	6,993	253	6,545	527,233*	9,787	213,074	295,801*	1,967
Total Last Week	5,930	220	6,107	526,845*	9,605	213,562	295,016	1,911
11— Low. Manhattan	244	0	280	11,307	202	4,559	6,748	24
13— Waverly	249	0	301	10,099	164	5,634	4,465	35
15— Gramercy	164	0	187	11,099	0	3,748	7,351	2
19— Yorkville	114	0	104	8,684	297	8,684	—	102
23— East End	111	0	92	7,059	0	7,059		
24— Amsterdam	161	5	145	8,474				
25— Franklin	69	0	57					

Page 2

Week Ending 6/16/72

	Pending Activity			
Centers	Balance Prev. Week	Balance This Week	Int. + PTI − PTO	Created
Total This Week	1,873	1,919	575	2,912
Total Last Week	1,841	1,861	419	2,292
11— Low. Manhattan	0	0	0	156
13— Waverly	0	0	0	144
15— Gramercy	0	0	0	79
19— Yorkville	0	0	0	3
23— East End	0	0	0	
24— Amsterdam	16			
25— Franklin				

* Includes 3,556 cases in transit.
Abbreviations:
    NA'd—Not accepted.
A.S.C.—Approved State Charges (for recipients whose support is fully paid by the state).
    Int.—Intake.
    PTI—Pending transfers in.
    PTO—Pending transfers out.

the DRAT were distributed each day to various offices at the center and to a central DSS statistical unit which used the information to develop a monthly book of statistics. This book became available approximately five months after the referenced month and was the agency's primary information document.

At the centers, the statistical units tabulated various categories of actions on the DRAT (case openings, closing, transfers in or out of center, change in the number of dependent children and so forth) into two weekly reports which were sent to a statistical group attached to the deputy director of BPA for IM operations. Here the data was condensed into the IM Activity Report (Exhibit 2) and the IM Specialist Report (Exhibit 3). Both were available the

EXHIBIT 3
Weekly Record of Activity of Income Maintenance Specialists

Week Ending:

	Intake	Mail	Tele-phone	Appl.	Under-care	Total Actions	Man-Days Worked	Average No. of Actions per Day per Spec	Group Back-log
Low. Man.									
Waverly									
Gramercy									
Yorkville									
East End									
Amsterdam									
Franklin									
St. Nicholas									

week after the data was submitted by the individual centers. These reports were utilized by BPA management to spot center-specific or citywide operational problems and trends. The centers also submitted a weekly personnel status report to BPA which compared the actual number of employees in various categories with the number authorized. This was used to analyze general staffing patterns and spot unfilled positions.

The different social service units at the center submitted reports on the number and type of services given, such as placements in educational and vocational training programs and health care assistance rendered. This data was condensed and forwarded on a weekly basis to the two deputy directors in charge of social service activities.

At the time separation was taking place, Mrs. Hollyer and several other top-level BPA managers had been skeptical about the ultimate benefits of reorganization and concerned about the pace at which change was taking place. She commented:

> There was a great deal of ambivalance among the operations people about the reorganization of public assistance. But when you're part of a bureaucracy—outside of writing a few memos—it is difficult to take too strong a position because if whatever you do fails it is believed that it failed because of your lack of enthusiasm.

CONDITIONS POSTSEPARATION

The basic unit in the separated center was the income maintenance group of five specialists, two clerks and a supervisor. The number of IM groups assigned to each center was determined using a formula developed by the operations improvement team during its study. The formula was based on empirical observations of (1) the average number of each different kind of income maintenance transaction required each week by clients in different categories of public assistance (ADC, OAA, and so forth) and (2) the mean time required to perform each kind of IM transaction. These two figures could be used to determine how many man-hours per week were required to process all the transactions for a recipient of, say, OAA or ADC and this standard, in turn, could be applied to the actual client mix at a center to determine the total number of specialists needed. (For a center with a typical case load, this process resulted in a quota of about 1,000 cases per IM group.)

Social service staffing patterns for the newly separated centers duplicated the staffing arrangements at the centers that had been separated earlier. These were arrived at by estimating client demand for social services—as separate from IM assistance—and calculating the amount of time a social service worker would need to provide these services. (For further information see Public Assistance [A].)

BPA obtained IM Specialists in two ways. Since the job was defined as "clerical," people were hired who could pass a third-level civil service clerk examination. These were mainly city employees who were high school graduates. The salary for an IM specialist ranged from $8,000 to $11,000 a year. New specialists were scheduled to have six weeks formal training with special emphasis on face-to-face interviewing but because of the pressing need for IM personnel immediately following separation, this formal training was cut to two weeks with the remainder scheduled to be given on-the-job.

DSS had also made a contractual arrangement with the SSEU to allow many of the 4,500 caseworkers, whose jobs were done away with by separation, to perform IM specialist roles until social service jobs were available. (Before separation, approximately 7,000 of BPA's 13,500 employees were social workers assigned, in the traditional way, to handle both the income maintenance and social service needs of individual public assistance cases.) Caseworkers with the lowest seniority were put into their own IM groups and ended up doing IM work in 34 of the 44 centers. Despite the fact that a number of social service workers transferred out of BPA or quit their jobs while separation was taking place, 75 percent of the 3,800 IM specialist jobs were filled initially by former caseworkers who earned from $9,500 to $14,000 annually. By April, when Morris entered office, 50 percent of the IM slots were still held by social workers.

During the months following separation, two trends became clearly evident at the centers. First, the amount of social services delivered to public assistance clients dropped to less than half the preseparation level. Now that most of these services were voluntary, clients simply were not asking for them. Second, the number of welfare recipients visiting the centers for one reason or another was growing dramatically. Part of this increase in traffic could be attributed to growth in the welfare population. The number of public assistance cases continued to rise at a rate of approximately 5,000 per month of which 1,900 were narcotics addicts. (As of the end of October, approximately 30,000 of all DAB cases were addicts.) Addicts were required to report to the centers either to pick up their checks or for mandatory interviews with social service workers regarding their enrollment and attendance in treatment programs. After separation, more and more of them could be found at the centers each week.

Changes in regulations regarding employable home relief (HR) recipients were also responsible for some of the increased traffic. A state law that went into effect on July 1, 1971, required these clients to pick up their checks at a New York State Employment Services (NYSES) office and to accept employment if a suitable job was available. The law also stipulated that if HR employables could not be placed in jobs by NYSES within 30 days, then DSS had to place them in city created public works projects where they could work off their welfare grants at $2 to $4 an hour depending on their skills and experience. In order to make the necessary determination of employability for the 60,000 HR cases and to process referrals to NYSES and public works projects the employment sections at the centers had been increased to between seven and ten specialists. (The IM sections were responsible for the actual transference of checks to NYSES, the closing or suspension of assistance due to no compliance, and the reclassification of HRs to the DAB roles in the event that medical unemployability was proven.)

Even these identifiable causes could not explain all of the increase in clients visiting the centers. Many were ADC mothers who seemed to be present in unprecedented numbers. They could often be found, accompanied by their families, wandering through the center searching for the correct person to answer a question or solve a problem. During the three-day period following the biweekly issuance of checks, it became routine to find as many as 500 persons waiting in line, before a center opened, to pick up a check or lodge a complaint about the amount of payment.

Physically the centers were ill-equipped to handle the increased work load. Many were former warehouses and it was not unusual to find falling plaster, cockroaches and empty beer bottles in the hallways. Steve Rosa, an industrial engineer who had been assigned to work with BPA commented:

> Most of the buildings were not designed as welfare centers. The Department of Real Estate got space anywhere because it was hard to find landlords who were willing to rent their buildings for use as welfare centers. The buildings were not prepared to hold the case load levels. There were dark hallways, crevices, addicts shooting up in the bathrooms, muggings on the stairwells. The centers had just about the most atrocious combination of factors which in some instances put them in violation of fire and building ordinances.

By the end of 1971, conditions had deteriorated seriously. Some centers were seeing as many as 900 persons a day. Violence was erupting with increasing frequency and SSEU was responding by calling two and three work stoppages per week. Following an incident, IM specialists and social service workers were staying off the job as long as three or four days. Those who took part in the stoppages lost their pay for the time they were absent, but this did not prevent the absences from aggravating the traffic situation and interrupting the completion of routine work.

In early 1972, the incidents continued. During January, 75 workers at two Bronx centers walked off the job demanding more security, after a staff member was assaulted by an irate applicant. At the time the incident occurred, three patrolmen and several unarmed guards in civilian clothes were in the center. The SSEU, which did not sanction this particular walkout, reported 45 instances of violence at centers from January to April with a number of major incidents taking place in March. On March 6, several hundred workers left two centers when lye was thrown in a supervisor's face by a client. In another center, 600 clients occupied the building when they did not receive their scheduled checks.

Two weeks later in a Queens center servicing 30,000 clients, 300 workers locked themselves in when a drug addict drew a gun and threatened to shoot workers unless he received a check. The following week, 500 staff members walked out when a Home Relief recipient in the employable category allegedly struck a supervisor when he could not find his check at the state employment office or at the welfare center. A BPA staff member remarked that these were only the overt instances of violence: "You don't read about the number of clients who sit down at the IM specialist's desk and pull out a knife, nail file, or letter opener which they put on the desk before they ask to go on welfare."

Patrolmen at the centers had job actions of their own in which they refused to patrol singly and demanded that they be assigned in pairs. An SSEU official was quoted as saying, "It has reached a point where workers, to protect their own health and safety, may have to discontinue reporting to centers."

In April, during a campaign to elect new union officers, a group challenging the incumbent SSEU leadership distributed a platform statement to all union members which included the following section:

> Income Maintenance has become the most unpopular assignment ever given to our members. In their rush toward "instant reorganization" the Department created this understaffed, chaotic and even dangerous mess and [the incumbent leadership] must bear the blame for allowing it to happen and for tolerating its continued existence. Perhaps the Department does not care when workers and clients are verbally and physically assaulted, but this union must respond. Despite the directive adopted at the Delegate Assembly in January, workers remain in IM, the physical plant remains unchanged, and workers still must lose pay for refusing to work in unsafe conditions. In short, [the incumbent] has produced nothing. Are we going to wait for someone to get killed before anything is done? [Our] slate will force the city to bring in enough staff to meet the needs of the clients; we will make them provide a physical setup conducive to the comfort and safety of both workers and clients. Most importantly, we will get our workers out of IM now on a large-scale basis before the federalization threat becomes a reality.

In addition to the problems of violence and disruption at the centers, a growing backlog of unprocessed work began to develop. By January 1972, this had risen to over 160,000 actions including 10,000 case closings and suspensions, 5,000 suspected fraud actions and 22,000 budget adjustments. Management Engineering was asked to initiate a plan for dealing with the situation. One ME staff member remarked:

> The average biweekly check was $100. Considering the number of unprocessed case closings we had a potential loss of $25 million a year from that alone. We went to the centers and found that there was no system for categorizing backlog. In one center there was a large wicker basket filled with unprocessed cases. The supervisor didn't know it was there much less how to handle it. You would see one IM group very busy while the next group was twiddling their thumbs doing nothing.

The ME plan, implemented by BPA management, called for the use of 52,000 hours of paid overtime, costing $335,000, at the 17 centers with the worst backlog problems. Two major features of the plan were the systematic separation of new input from backlog and the establishment of case closings and suspensions as priority actions to be taken.

Another problem area in the newly separated centers was the workings of the declaration system for determining client eligibility. Prior to separation each center had an intake section made up of caseworkers who interviewed all incoming applicants. Each applicant had to supply documents such as birth certificates, rent receipts, and certificates of unemployability in order to establish his need for public assistance. The concept of the declaration system was that eligibility should be based on the applicant's word rather than on corroborating evidence. After separation, therefore, a new application form and an interview by an IM specialist were used to determine eligibility.

The specialist was responsible for questioning the applicant on each of the major areas of the form (financial, housing, identifying information, and case composition) and ensuring that the applicant's answers had the internal consistency that a prudent person would demand. If the specialist concluded that the applicant's answers were acceptable, income maintenance assistance began immediately. Applicants were not asked to present any documented proof of need.

Mrs. Hollyer explained what took place after the introduction of the declaration procedure:

> The client was supposed to come in and give a story and we were supposed to believe it, much like an income tax return, and issue assistance on the spot. But it was really different than the income tax return. With income tax you have employee records, bank statements and so forth but you didn't have any of that here.

Before separation the citywide reject rate on new applications had been in the area of 30 percent. In the months following separation this rate dropped to less than half of what it had been formerly and at one center it remained in the neighborhood of 1 percent for a period of months. This phenomenon was not totally unexpected since the rejection rates at the six centers that had been separated earlier had declined dramatically after separation but then climbed back steadily to their original levels. (See Exhibit 4.)

EXHIBIT 4
Average Rejection Rates for Three Welfare Centers Separated in 1970*

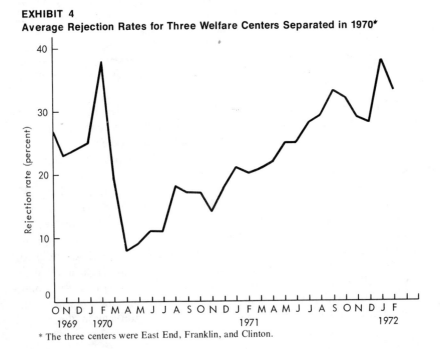

* The three centers were East End, Franklin, and Clinton.

The magnitude of the traffic, the unprocessed case action backlog, and rejection rate problems led both Management Engineering and the DSS Project Management Staff to begin a thorough examination of the operations at several centers. In one they found an average of 40 percent of the IM specialists absent daily. In another 31 of 49 IM specialists were late eight times or more during a 90-day period; most reported to work after 9 A.M.; and all IM supervisors and specialists took lunch from noon to 2 P.M. Conditions were by no means uniform across all centers, however. One center, typical of about one third of the total, had, from separation until April, continual incidents of violence, a growing backlog problem, numerous grievances registered by the unions, high absenteeism among all workers and a reject rate that had leveled off at about half of what it was before separation. Another center, representative of a much smaller group, had avoided disturbances by clients, cleaned up its backlog quickly, had good relations with the unions, pushed its reject rate up to preseparation levels and was beginning to show productivity gains under the new system. No center, however, was able to escape all of the problems following separation.

PRESSURE FROM THE STATE

One of the persistent questions regarding public assistance in New York City was the number of people receiving welfare who were actually ineligible. Many BPA people believed that the nature of the problem was systemic and this position was articulated by Mrs. Hollyer:

> It must be remembered that people who come for income maintenance come at a time of crisis in their lives and in most cases they are not able to explain themselves very well. The income maintenance specialist must know how to ask, how to listen—to hear what is being said. Can you imagine what it means to say "no" to a person coming in for public assistance? It's possible to say "no"—but to say it in such a way that you show empathy. You can make other referrals that are necessary. You can say "no" on a reasonable, human basis so that you don't degrade the other fellow. To say "no" without being God is a tremendously difficult thing to do. It brings out the worst in people and they say "no" when they shouldn't or it brings out the fear in people and they say "yes" when they shouldn't.

One SSEU member, doing income maintenance work, was quoted in *The New York Post* as saying:

> Client misrepresentation is a necessity because poor families will do anything not to go under. The welfare grant level is under the federal poverty level. If a family claims an extra child to increase their grant, it's reported as welfare cheating but such claims would be generally accepted by society if people knew the facts.

In August 1971, Governor Nelson Rockefeller named George Berlinger, a retired businessman, to the newly created post of welfare inspector general with the broad mandate to examine all phases of public assistance to insure proper expenditure of funds. Berlinger had the authority to issue subpeonas and conduct investigations in any manner that he saw fit. He made it clear that his major function would be "to restore public confidence in the welfare system."

Soon after his appointment Berlinger began investigations of new applications and recertifications of clients at individual New York City centers to determine ineligibility rates. In December, he announced to the press that ineligibility among new applicants accepted and clients recertified ranged from 16 percent to more than 30 percent in three centers that his staff had investigated. On the basis of these findings, Berlinger claimed that 6 percent of all families on public assistance were actually ineligible; 20 percent were overpaid; and 10 percent underpaid. He was quoted as saying that the basic reason for these errors was "loose administration at HRA and the absence of proper controls."

Berlinger's pronouncements on ineligibility contrasted sharply with DSS claims that total ineligibility among the city welfare population was about 3 percent. The DSS findings were derived from quarterly quality control investigations mandated by the federal government and from validation studies carried out by the state comptroller. The quality control reports were compiled by 200 civil service inspectors who reviewed a random sample of 0.5 percent of the city's ADC and DAB cases each quarter to assess both eligibility and payment errors. Federal guidelines set a 3 percent tolerance level on ineligibility and 5 percent on payment errors, which if not met could result in a discontinuance of federal funds. A summary of data from the quality control reports for the last three calendar quarters of 1971 is shown in Exhibit 5. The state validation covered both the ADC and HR categories. Based on samples of about 3,000 of these cases in nine centers in September 1971 and 3,000 cases in ten different centers in December, the state had concluded that

EXHIBIT 5
Summary of Federal Quality Control Reports for Last Three Quarters of Calendar Year 1971

	Federal Government Tolerance	National Average		Three-Quarter Average, NYC		
		AFDC	DAB	AFDC	DAB	Combined
Not eligible for assistance	3.0%	5.6%	4.9%	5.3%	1.2%	3.7%
Incorrect payments	5.0	—	—	27.1	30.2	28.7
Overpayment	5.0	14.6	7.9	18.1	22.4	—
Underpayment	5.0	9.7	4.9	9.0	7.8	—
Failed to cooperate	—	—	—	—	—	2.0
Could not be located	—	—	—	—	—	3.3
Miscellaneous	—	—	—	—	—	3.1
Total						40.8%

1.2 percent of the ADC cases and 5.2 percent of the HR cases were financially ineligible. (Cases in state's sample that were indeterminate were excluded from the results. An "indeterminate" case was one that the inspectors were unable to locate [UTL] or who failed to cooperate [FTC] with the inspectors.)

Jule Sugarman, the HRA administrator, stated that Berlinger had grossly misrepresented the facts and commented, "I think it is recognized that we are trying to do the best job that we can here. It is one thing to have the luxury of Mr. Berlinger to take pot shots but it is quite another to make the system work."

Berlinger responded with another study that involved the investigation of 45 cases at random out of 450 acceptances in one month at one center. At a second press conference he announced an ineligibility rate of 17 percent to 26 percent based on the sample and claimed ineligibility in the city was conservatively 10 percent to 15 percent with a potential loss of $120 million a year. Sugarman accused Berlinger of being "recklessly irresponsible" for basing his findings on 45 cases out of a citywide total of 500,000. He was quoted as saying that such a sample was subject to a probability error of better than 99.9 percent.

In an effort to resolve these conflicting views on the amount of ineligibility, Harris' DSS Project Management Staff undertook a thorough analysis of the issue early in 1972.[3] Harris assigned a team to look at 800 cases drawn from three centers. A major effort of the investigation was to track down those cases that the quality control and state validation reports excluded because the recipient would not cooperate with eligibility investigators or could not be located. Berlinger always cited two numbers in giving his estimates of ineligibility—one based on the assumption that all these eligibility indeterminates were in fact eligible and another based on the opposite premise. The quality control reports that DSS relied upon did not take these cases into account at all.

The PMS team was able to gather information on 93 percent of a sample group of 72 cases listed as FTC and located 96 percent of 101 cases which were in the UTL category. They concluded that 43 percent of the FTC group and 30 percent of the UTL group were ineligible. When added to the previously known ineligibles, this meant that 5.5 percent of the total case load was ineligible at a cost of $37.4 million per year. As to over- and underpayment of those who *were* eligible, PMS determined that 28.7 percent of the total case load was incorrectly paid at a net loss of $31.5 million per year. In addition, 2.2 percent of all cases were misclassified. Thus, there were errors of some kind in 36.4 percent of the case load at a minimum annual cost of $68.9 million. (Misclassifications, when corrected, would not mean a change in payment amount but only a move, say, from the ADC to the HR rolls.) PMS also studied the source of these errors and concluded that 61 percent ($42

---

[3] Harris' group now consisted of almost 50 MBAs, industrial engineers, and systems analysts plus a few young BPA staff members.

million per year) were the fault of the BPA system while the remainder were the result of client fraud. About one third of the BPA errors occurred at the point of initial client entry into the system and the remainder after a client was on the rolls. Exhibits 6 and 7 are a condensation of the PMS error analysis.

EXHIBIT 6
Responsibility for Identified Eligibility Errors

| | | Annual Cost of Errors (millions) | | | |
| | | Agency Errors | | Client Errors | |
Client Category	Total	Failure to Act	Incorrect Action	Uninten- tional*	Fraud
Totally ineligible	$23.7	$ 4.7	$ 4.6	$ 4.4	$10.0
Underpayment/overpayment.....	31.5	12.7	6.6	7.6	4.6
Unable to locate	7.0	—	1.4	—	5.6
Failed to cooperate	6.7	—	—	—	6.7
Total	$68.9	$17.4	$12.6	$12.0	$26.9

* PMS believed most unintentional client errors might really be due to agency neglect. The amount of $12 million, therefore, was added to agency error in the PMS summary statistic.

EXHIBIT 7
Distribution of the Cost of Agency and Client Errors

	Percentage of Total Cost
Agency Errors (Total cost = $42 million)	
Failure to Act:	
1. Failure to rebudget for known change	32.6%.
2. Failure to act on social security	15.9
3. Failure to act on return of spouse	15.2
Other Agency Error:	
4. Incorrect policy application	14.1
5. Misbudgeting	11.1
6. Incorrect budget computation	4.9
7. Other	6.2
Total	100.0%
Client Errors (Total cost = $26.9 million)	
1. Failure to acknowledge income/benefits/support	45.5%
2. Failure to report change in earning/income/benefits (social security)	22.8
3. Failure to notify of returned employed spouse	21.2
4. Dependent children leave home	4.8
5. Payment for person not in home	5.4
6. Other	0.3
	100.0%

Harris and his staff believed that several causes underlay the size of the ineligibility problem. These included 1,000 fewer center employees than specified by PMS standards, the impact of "instant" separation, the limited experience and training of center personnel, poor working conditions, the rapid growth of the addict population on welfare, increased client traffic at the centers, and the absence of a good management control system. By April, they had developed a nine-part corrective action plan. The plan emphasized the following programs:

New Application Process. A pilot study of applicants recently certified as eligible for public assistance at three welfare centers showed that 5.3 percent were ineligible based on the information that appeared on their applications; 5.3 percent were found to be ineligible when asked to supply corroborating documentation such as birth certificates or rent receipts; and 16.9 percent would not cooperate when asked to document the information submitted in their applications. PMS suggested that the "simple declaration of need" now used by the IM specialists to determine eligibility be modified to require a reasonable amount of client documentation and that a supervisory review be made of the specialists' actions before financial assistance could begin. Further, they recommended that field investigation units be reestablished in each center for the purpose of gathering data on specific questions about selected applicants (not for making full field investigations as was done before separation). And they suggested that one IM unit in each center should be responsible for all eligibility determinations. It was expected that these new procedures would increase the average rejection rate from its present level of 23 percent to over 30 percent, thereby saving about $30 million per year.

Face-to-Face Recertification. Under existing regulations, each client's eligibility had to be reconfirmed every six months. This was done by mailing recipients a questionnaire on which they could explain the nature of any change in status. If the client indicated there was no change, he was automatically recertified and assistance was continued at the previous level. Clients who did indicate a change were called in for interviews to redetermine their eligibility and the correct amount of support. During its three-center study of BPA operations, PMS had pilot tested a different approach to recertification—one in which everyone would be called in for an interview rather than sent a questionnaire. Of those called during the test, PMS found that 14.8 percent were being overpaid, 6.5 percent underpaid, 3.6 percent were totally ineligible, and 9.8 percent failed to report. PMS proposed, therefore, that a program be undertaken to provide at least a one-time, face-to-face recertification of *all* public assistance clients in order to purge the rolls of ineligibles and eliminate existing payment errors. These face-to-face interviews would include documentation checks (birth certificates for children, rent receipts, income statements, and social security cards); collateral verifications with employers, landlords, banks, and other sources; and referral, as appropriate, to employment, social service units, or law enforcement officials. PMS anticipated that net overpayments of $30 million per year could be eliminated during this one-time recertification and another $30 million per year saved through case closings. It was also recommended that the initial face-to-face recertification be followed by a continuing program of regular recertification interviews with the period between interviews and the depth of questioning tailored to the characteristics of different client groups. For example, addicts would be recertified by interview more frequently than recipients of Old Age Assistance.

An Error Accountability Program.   At present, no regular assessment was made of the error rate at individual centers. PMS proposed that it examine a sample of cases from each center each month and rank the centers by type, rate, and cost of eligibility, payment, and classification errors. The BPA central office would publish a monthly ranking report and an intensive review would be undertaken by PMS of cases in the five centers with the lowest ratings. This review would place responsibility for errors with individual IM groups and recommend, as well as implement, corrective action.

THE NEW MANAGEMENT CONTROL SYSTEM

While the Project Management Staff had been conducting its analyses of the eligibility problem, John Alexander and his staff of 55 at Management Engineering had been busy designing a new control system for BPA.[4] Their goal was a system that would lead eventually to the following innovations: work load forecasting; work standards; scheduling techniques; assignment procedures; work schedule control; and individual productivity measures.

One engineer who worked on the project stated:

> In the new system the first-level supervisors will hand out all work and will pick up incomplete work at the end of the day. They will check on group productivity and question why differences exist among groups. Each management level will review the preceding level and the center director will be held responsible for differences in output between IM groups.

The proposed management control package, which was ready for Morris when he arrived in April had four integrated procedures:

A backlog control form to be filled out daily by each IM specialist. This would enable individual center directors and BPA managers to monitor progress on the reduction of backlogs. The form would show the beginning work load and daily production for each specialist and would indicate the hours so that individual productivity could be calculated.

A Daily Record of Activity that would supersede the present weekly reports (Exhibits 2 and 3) and contain the same basic information.

A Director's Action Report that center directors would complete on a

---

[4] Most of the group were industrial engineers and systems analysts with at least ten years experience in business.

weekly basis. It would list major problems, corrective action planned, and follow-up action required. This would create a regular channel of communication between the directors and the central office and would allow BPA management to become more closely involved in center operations.

A Weekly Personnel Report that would give management an accurate picture of staff availability. The report would provide a count of center staff that could be matched against client demand. This would allow PBA management to evaluate long- and short-term staffing requirements and review measures of productivity.

BPA

BPA personnel, from Mrs. Hollyer (now the deputy director) on down were not very enthusiastic about the recommendations made either by PMS or by Management Engineering. They were particularly distressed when PMS suggested, in February, that the increased demands for income maintenance services created by steadily expanding rolls be met by hiring personnel in accordance with the formula of 1,000 cases per IM group. The resulting citywide quota of 524 groups they felt, was much too low, and could only hamper efforts to tighten eligibility procedures and reduce the backlog of unprocessed actions. Most center directors believed a more reasonable standard would be 750 cases per group and 600 to 700 groups in the system. In an effort to prove BPA's point, Mrs. Hollyer asked Steve Rosa, the industrial engineer, to reexamine the PMS standard. After interviewing several field office supervisors and center directors and observing the operations at a number of centers, Rosa concluded that most of the centers did, in fact, have to cope with one or more "special" conditions that required an upward adjustment in the number of IM specialists as determined by the PMS quota.

> We did things like calling in the Field Office Supervisors to find out if particular centers were the kind of neighborhood building where people just like to hang out. If they were, it meant more traffic for the specialists and more specialists needed to handle the same size case load. It also turned out to be important to know how many stories the building had because more stories meant more time in traveling from office to office to process a case. Alcoholics had to be figured in and were as bad a problem as addicts. Some centers had large transient case loads with people disappearing all the time. We devised 16 criteria [Exhibit 8] for adjusting the PMS quota. When we applied these adjustments systemwide, we came up with 686 groups—about 750 cases per group.

Also in February, BPA management had asked each center director to comment in writing on his major problems. The responses tended to confirm the differences of opinion regarding staffing levels and suggested, moreover, that there were a number of other issues on which BPA managers and

EXHIBIT 8
Criteria Developed by Steve Rosa for Adjusting a Center's Quota of Income Maintenance Specialists

Criterion	Additional IM Specialists
1. Abnormally high rate of new applications.	
450–550 applications per month	1 additional IM specialist.
550–650 applications per month	2 additional IM specialists.
650–800 applications per month	3 additional IM specialists.
800 and up applications per month	4 additional IM specialists.
2. Number of stories in building over three	1 specialist per additional story.
3. Abnormally high traffic because center is conveniently located in the neighborhood it serves	2 specialists.
4. Responsibility for special state or federal programs	1 IM specialist group.
5. Employment (adjust for every 10 percent of case load over 50 percent family cases)	1 specialist.
6. No on-line computer facilities for calculating clients' budgets	3 specialists.
7. Known disruptive client groups	2 specialists.
8. Known disruptive staff union groups	2 specialists.
9. Serious language problems (Spanish, Chinese, and others)	½ specialist per 2,000 clients.
10. Known excessive client mobility (transfers to and from other centers)	½ specialist per 2,000 clients.
11. Known areas of excessive housing costs	½ specialist per 2,000 clients.
12. Known unpopular center location (security problems created for center employees)	1 specialist for each 2,000 cases over 7,000.
13. Centers with large hotel populations	1 specialist.
14. Known high number of hospital discharges	½ specialist per 2,000 clients.
15. Absence of instructors for training specialists ...	2 specialists.
16. Special problems such as large numbers of alcoholics.	To be determined individually.

Spiegel's staff at DSS did not share the same priorities (see Exhibits 9 and 10). Said one official at BPA:

> We welcomed assistance in correcting operational problems and devising new systems. They jumped right in, but this was not a factory for bottling beer. Here, people handle people—alcoholics, broken homes, addicts. Our feeling was that in order to be able to understand these problems you have to have daily contact with the people. Business education, graphs, and numbers aren't the same thing. We told center people how these new people would be helpful, how they could improve center operations and assist us. We said, "Give them a chance." But the centers only saw useless studies and instant experts.

EXHIBIT 9

THE CITY OF NEW YORK
DEPARTMENT OF SOCIAL SERVICES

MEMORANDUM

DATE: 2/9/72

TO: Mr. John Stackhouse, Field Office Supervisor
Bureau of Public Assistance

FROM: Mr. William Johnson, Director, Willis Center (49)
Mrs. Constance Benson, Office Manager

SUBJECT: *NEEDS OF WILLIS CENTER*

STAFFING: Since Reorganization our case load has increased to 10,000 cases. Our quota is ten IM Groups. Each group has an average of 900 cases. As a result staff has not been able to handle the current work, nor attack the accumulated backlog, except through overtime work.

Willis at the current time does not have a person available to take the position of Homemaker-Housekeeper. Our D&C* staff is inadequately staffed to handle the normal flow of work and in addition, the installation of the plastic ID cards has created the need for at least two additional clerks.

Our Timekeeping Section is also in need of an additional clerk due to the tremendous volume of work. The assistant office managers, whose span of supervision is too great, is in need of additional supportive staff.

The Control Unit is also considered under-staffed due to the need to designate a person as the Duplications Control Clerk and also to handle the increased number of financial transactions which the enlarged caseload has brought about.

The staffing situation is especially crucial since there is no reserve to offset the increased absenteeism that we are experiencing.

The General Service staff cannot perform its mandated services due to their insufficient number. The Center is also handicapped by the inability to use staff selectively because of contractual agreements. It was not possible at the point of separation to utilize staff in the most effective manner because of the requirements of seniority and juniority provisions.

It is our considered opinion that we would require, on the basis of our current caseload, at least four additional groups. This lack of adequate staff to provide service to the client has aroused community resentment.

MORALE: The staffing condition as described above has led to a deterioration in staff morale. The inability to provide services has created hostility between the income maintenance specialists and the clients. This in turn has led to confrontations and a demand for greater security. Until recently Willis did not

EXHIBIT 9 *(continued)*

<table>
<tr><td></td><td>have adequate security patrolmen assigned to this Center. We feel that we need at least six patrolmen assigned to Willis alone, pending more suitable physical arrangements.</td></tr>
<tr><td>PHYSICAL STRUCTURE AND WORKING CONDITIONS:</td><td>The physical structure of Willis Social Service Center has certain difficulties. We share the building with the Bergen Social Service Center. The three elevators are not sufficient to handle the traffic, particularly in the morning rush. Due to the increased case load and the inability of clients to reach their caseworkers, the traffic in Willis has greatly increased, leading to overcrowding in every section of the office. There is an urgent need for additional chairs in our primary reception area. The D&C Unit must be either removed from its present location or physically rearranged in such a manner as to prevent them being overwhelmed by clients reaching for their checks. In addition Group 1, which services some 150 people on a check day (primarily narcotic users), must be relocated to a more protected area or there must be again some type of physical barriers erected. Without adequate security patrolmen it is impossible to attempt to handle the flow of clients. Willis normally serves on check days, 450 to 500 people. In addition we have had adverse experiences with clients seeking to use our telephones. We feel that there should be installed in this Center public telephones.

For six months the toilet facilities on our fourth floor has been out of order despite efforts made by our custodial staff to have the landlord make the necessary repairs. There is no valid reason why this condition should exist.</td></tr>
<tr><td>OTHER PROBLEMS:</td><td>Willis is an ABC† Center and is dependent upon the machines in our office as well as the Central EDP to process financial actions and reduce the flow of clients into our office. We reported on several occasions the fact that one of our machines is in a state of constant disrepair and the other in a state of almost constant breakdown. Central EDP with its failure to deliver checks to the proper place at the proper time, creates almost insurmountable problems in terms of handling the irate clients and disgruntled staff who must duplicate their work.

In summary, the needs of Willis Social Service Center can be summarized as follows: (1) inadequate staff; (2) inadequate physical facilities and layout; (3) poor working conditions.

One of our immediate and pressing needs is the erection of a partition to enclose Group 1 located on the first floor. This group services narcotics users and always have a large number of clients and applicants waiting to be seen. Because the group is located on the open floor, clients have access to records, supplies, etc. They constantly harrass the staff of this group to a point where the original group clerk would have to leave her desk at the point of tears and has since been replaced. The case</td></tr>
</table>

EXHIBIT 9 *(concluded)*

load for this group is rapidly increasing and we do not expect any improvement if the physical setup remains as is. This situation is critical and demands immediate attention.

WJ/dg

* Disbursing and Collecting (D&C).
† ABC was an on-line computer system that IMSs could use to determine the level of income maintenance to which a client was entitled. Not all centers were equipped with ABC.

EXHIBIT 10

THE CITY OF NEW YORK
DEPARTMENT OF SOCIAL SERVICES
MEMORANDUM

DATE: Feb. 22, 1972

TO: Mr. Irving Novin, Field Office Manager
9th Floor
C.O.

FROM: Isidore Gosian, Director
Greenwood Center

SUBJECT:

We are requesting additional IM groups inasmuch as the growth of the case load in this center, and various concomitant problems are making it rapidly impossible for us to function any further.

Our family IM groups range from 808 cases to 859 cases. Our narcotics groups have 651 cases, our DAB IM group from 1,495 to 1,705. It should also be born in mind that these figures are after our ATO cases have gone out and before our ATI cases have come in.

Since 10/1/71 we have 260 cases more in DAB, 538 cases more in the family groups; there appears to be no prospect whatsoever that the increase will not continue at the same or even a higher rate.

The various groups in this building are scattered over five floors. We have only two small elevators which are constantly crowded, making communication between floors very difficult. It is necessary to go to the first floor for emergency checks. It is necessary to go to the fourth floor to see the consultants. There is a great deal of leg work required because of this. In addition, although we have 16 groups, we have only 3 file clerks. This has put an extra burden on our group clerks to the extent that a number of them have requested to be transferred.

Further, our telephone situation has augmented the work to be done. For instance, we have three groups which have no telephone in the groups whatsoever; and several others which have only a single phone.

EXHIBIT 10 *(continued)*

Inasmuch as our experience has indicated that a family group cannot adequately handle more than 700 to 750 clients, we are requesting the addition of two family groups.

Although the increase in the DAB groups has not been as high, a problem has arisen in the handling of narcotics cases, increasing numbers of which (as they become reclassified from PAD* to AD) are being transferred from the drug unit to the various DAB units. For example, most of these become AD group 2 so that continuing work is necessary on them. In addition they present greater difficulty in handling by the DAB IM workers who, being all clerical, have had no experience in handling such persons. Some of the experiences that this clerical force has had with the narcotic cases have been so frightening that several of the IM workers are requesting demotions.

This rise in the case load (which in this office is now nearly 17,000 cases) in addition necessitates an increase in both the Control and Statistics quota. Much additional work has been added to the Control Section such as the 325Hs, checking on number of duplications, more two party checks for rent due to duplication. Due to vacations and heavy absences a realistic quota for this section can mean no less than 12 persons. Obviously in handling follow up 661s or special checks which do not go out on time, many extra hours are needed to undo and redo these checks for a later date or to process what would have been an unnecessary emergency check.

As for Statistics, our office, which in the last three months has reclassified PAD cases to the extent of 485 cases, in addition to all of the extra work occasioned by the case load increase cannot manage without at least one additional person added to the quota of that section.

There can be no question that the great backlog of control and movement of the IM work in both family groups and DAB falls on the shoulders of the assistant office managers. Not only to facilitate their work, but to enable them to do it at all, there must be at least one administrative assistant for each two assistant office managers, as well as a secretary. The time of the assistant office managers is being wasted on leg work and the handling of controls which should be handled by such administrative assistant and/or secretary.

Further, the great backlog of work concentrated with the office manager requires a second administrative assistant to her. It should be noted that this same work (with a lesser case load) when it was assigned to two senior case supervisors, had a quota of four administrative assistants to the two senior case supervisors.

It should additionally be recalled that the quotas for IM groups were set not at the point of separation but some time prior to that when our case load was even less so that the increase of 800 cases, as shown above, does not dearly present the increase as allied to the number of IM groups.

The gravity of this situation has now reached a point where we will soon not be able to guarantee an adequate control of whatever backlog is currently being accumulated, despite the fact that due to the heroic efforts of these staff members the old backlog (for which paid overtime has been made available) has been completed.

I am requesting immediate consideration of this problem and a very early reply as to what will be done about it.

IG:JB

* Provisionally accepted on the AD roles (PAD).

20.1. Citizens State Bank and Trust Company (A)*

ON MARCH 5, 19X5, Mr. Robert Lake, the president of Citizens State Bank and Trust Company of Louisville, Kentucky, mailed a letter to Mr. Ed Mays, a vice president and director of the bank. Lake had written the letter by hand in order to keep its contents concealed from anyone else, including his secretary and had marked the envelope "Personal and Confidential":

> Dear Mr. Mays,
>
> This letter will deal with the future . . . with the future relationship between you and me as banking associates.
>
> As I hope you understand, I have striven to do the best job at Citizens State Bank of which I am capable. I sincerely believe that I have cooperated with you and those persons whom you have referred to me. What I ask of you is to understand that I, as president, am responsible for all acts and all assets. I do not turn my back on this responsibility. And I shall not.
>
> Specifically, this letter is concerned with several borrowers that you have brought to Citizens State Bank since, or shortly before, my employment here. With many of them, there are questions—questions as to worthiness for the amount of credit extended, or questions as to the intent and ability to meet payment schedules; or questions as to proper documentation and authorization. In addition, there is a question as to the commitment of $2,000,000, or so, of our limited assets to such customers when Citizens State Bank—now with over 70 percent of available funds loaned, the highest percentage of any Louisville bank—can use these funds to attract customers who will become permanent and sizable depositors. Attached is a list dated today showing details on the larger of those particular borrowers who have received loans or loan commitments from Citizens State Bank. Please review the list. Thank you.
>
> In addition to the observations stated above about loan size and security and repayment plans, I wish to dwell on the loan concentration that concerns me most.
>
> My conclusion is that, henceforth, all borrowing arrangements on the attached list—and others—must rest upon sound, affirmative credit judgment. This applies to renewals as well as new loans.

---

* Prepared by Professors Robert K. Landrum and Charles S. Sherwood, Eastern Kentucky University. Reprinted by permission. All rights reserved by the authors of the case.
This case is disguised as to both time and place.

If we can have a complete meeting of minds on this subject, which I sincerely hope we can, I shall not bring it to our Board meeting on March 12th.

My proposal is that you renounce any loaning authority as an officer and as a director of Citizens State Bank. If not this, then any loan over a certain amount, say $25,000, must be approved in advance by the Board of Directors or Executive Committee. I strongly prefer the former, for the alternative would "tie the hands" of our business development efforts and our emphasis on speedy, "committeeless" decisions on credit applications.

Most sincerely yours,

Mr. Robert Lake, President
Citizens State Bank and Trust Co.
Louisville, Kentucky

Mays was not only a vice president and director of Citizens State Bank, but he was also a major stockholder in Peoples Holding Company that owned 80 percent of the bank's capital stock. Mays and his "partner" Mr. Johns held voting control of the holding company which, in turn, held the 80 percent control of Citizens State Bank, together with stock in several other subsidiary corporations. So Mays was not like any other vice president of the bank; he was a superior to Lake as well as being subordinate to Lake. (Query 1: What right had Mays to be a superior to Lake?)

HISTORY AND BACKGROUND

The Citizens State Bank and Trust Company of Louisville, Kentucky, was first organized in 1922 as the Blue Grass Savings Bank. It was chartered by the state of Kentucky. In April 19X4, two partners, Mr. Mays and Mr. Johns, purchased a majority interest (80 percent) in the Blue Grass Savings Bank at the seller's asking price of $3 million. At the time, the bank's assets were $14 million and, despite its small size relative to other Louisville banks, it was considered to be a sound financial institution.

To effect the purchase of the bank, Mays and Johns formed Peoples Holding Company, with the principal assets of the holding company consisting of the 80 percent interest in the bank and the chief liability of the holding company being a $3,825,000 loan. As part of their overall financial plan, Mays and Johns intended to offer a substantial number of shares of the holding company's stock to the public as soon as a prospectus could be prepared and the securities issue approved by state authorities. Part of the proceeds of the stock sale would then be applied toward the payment of the loan Mays and Johns had secured in making the purchase. Mays and Johns both felt that having the bank stock as the primary asset of the holding company would enhance the marketability of the holding company stock issue to the general public. In order to enhance this potential, Mays and Johns planned to:

1. Move the bank to a high-rise office building then under construction in downtown Louisville.
2. Change the bank's name from the Blue Grass Savings Bank to Citizens State Bank and Trust Company.
3. Hire a new, progressive president for the bank.
4. Adopt an aggressive credit-granting and deposit-acquiring program for growth and image-building.

THE BOARD OF DIRECTORS

The board of directors of the newly renamed Citizens State Bank and Trust Company consisted of seven members (one of whom soon resigned):

Mr. Mays and Mr. Johns—Held majority interest (80 percent) through the holding company. They were also active in the bank's operations, thus making them in effect "inside" directors. Mays was a vice president and possessed the power to approve loans. Mays, age 54, was an attorney and successful financier, while Johns, older by ten years, was an experienced corporate executive. Both men were reputed to be millionaires.

Mr. Robert Lake—President of the bank who had been hired in 19X4 to revamp the bank's operation. In February, Lake had acquired the minimum of 50 shares of bank stock (representing only 0.05 percent) which was required for him to be a director.

Mr. Dodd—An "outside director" and local attorney (age 60) who owned 18 percent of the shares. Dodd had attempted for ten years to gain a seat on Citizen's board of directors without success. When Peoples Holding Company acquired majority interest in the bank, Dodd co-signed the large note which Mays and Johns needed to make the purchase. With this additional leverage, Dodd managed to obtain his long sought after directorship.

Mr. Adkins and Mr. Ballard—The remaining two "outside" directors, each holding a very small number of shares.

Mr. Adams—Former vice president of Blue Grass Savings Bank who was elevated to acting president until Lake's arrival in September. Adams became chairman of the board when Lake took over as president. Adams resigned as chairman in March 19X5.

THE NEW PRESIDENT

When Lake was interviewed by Mays and Johns for the presidency of the bank in July 19X4, he learned none of the details of the holding company stock issue, as the particulars were not submitted to the Kentucky Division of Securities until August. Lake was informed, however, about Mr. Dodd's background and role in the bank and holding company. For ten years, Dodd had owned his 18 percent interest, but until Mays and Johns acquired the 80 percent interest earlier in 19X4, Dodd had not been voted to membership on the board of directors. Not only did Mays and Johns bring Dodd onto the board in April 19X4, but Dodd and his wife became co-makers on the holding company's $3,825,000 note at a large local bank. Dodd and the holding company put up their Citizens Bank stock as collateral. These three men, who voted 98 percent of the Citizens Bank stock, were in apparent harmony with each other and with the other three Citizens directors when Lake was interviewed in July. (Query 2: Should Lake have insisted on learning more about Peoples Holding Company?)

However, by the time Lake departed from the presidency of a bank in another state and became president of Citizens Bank on September 1, the relationship had altered between the three big stockholders. Unknown then to Lake—and to Lake until six months later—Dodd had refused to sign the renewal note for $3,825,000 in late August. Neither would Dodd's wife co-sign the large note of Peoples Holding Company. Dodd got back his collateral (Citizens Bank stock) that he had hypothecated for the benefit of the holding company. (Query 3: Should the lending bank have released the two co-signers and their collateral?)

Lake learned that it was not unusual for Dodd to be on the "outs" with people of his acquaintance. For instance, he was not on speaking terms with Lake's predecessor, Mr. Adams. Moreover, Dodd only entered the bank's premises to attend the monthly board meetings. This was partly a result of Dodd having sued the bank and its former owners more than once during the ten years following Dodd's purchase of his 18 percent stock interest.

In addition to Lake's being in the dark about the apparent rift between the 80 percent owners (Mays and Johns) and the 18 percent owner (Dodd) when he became president on September 1, he also felt betrayed by Mays and Johns. Mays told Lake the day before (August 31) that Adams, who had been a vice president of the bank when Mays and Johns bought the 80 percent in April and who had been elevated to acting president at that time, would move up to chairman of the board. This revelation startled Lake. He had been told by Mays and Johns in July, when they offered him the presidency, that Adams would revert to the rank of vice president. Adams had indicated to Lake that he expected to be demoted when a new and younger president was employed. Lake was not certain whether Adams or he was to have more authority. Lake thus began to have second thoughts about the trustworthiness of the promises made by Mays and Johns. However, Lake had "burned his bridges" with his former employer by this time and, therefore, decided to "hang in" at Citizens Bank—at least for a time. Lake figured he would soon be able to gauge his authority against that of the older Adams, as well as to determine if Mays and Johns would follow through on their other promises to support him in transforming Citizen's State Bank into one of the major banks in Louisville. The immediate plans for revamping the bank's image and market position called for:

1. Increasing the quantity and quality of board membership.
2. Opening a first and second branch office.
3. Moving the main office to a prestigous location with handsome, functional banking quarters.
4. Promoting growth in deposits and loans.

Lake had moved to Citizens State Bank for some of the same reasons that Mays and Johns acquired it as the main subsidiary corporation in the holding company. The bank had a big capital base; with $2 million in its capital structure, it could support up to $35 million of deposits. Deposits were only one third that amount in 19X4. Consequently, Lake viewed the bank as being in a financially stronger position relative to other banks in Louisville, because it could grow substantially in deposits (and in the leveraging of its income) without more capital being invested or profits retained to finance the growth. Also to the liking of Lake was the fact that the bank's bond portfolio was relatively large and of good quality; if need be, some of the bonds could be easily sold to provide the liquidity from which more loans could be made. Even though the bank was not as well known in the community as were the other banking institutions, it had a conservative image which, coupled with its obvious capital strength, put it in good position to gain new deposits and loans with the promotional and marketing efforts that Lake envisoned.

PEOPLES HOLDING COMPANY

Several weeks after he became Citizens' president, Lake acquired a copy of the holding company's new prospectus on the public sale of its Class A stock. He was shocked to learn for the first time that each Class A share was, in his view, "50 percent water." Yet, the People's stock offering had been approved by the Kentucky Division of Securities and, as of October 19X4, securities salesmen reported that sales of the stock "were going well."

According to the prospectus, there were a million shares in the Peoples Holding Company, 500,000 shares of Class A voting stock to be sold to the public for $12.50 per share to produce a net of $5,312,500 after salesmen's commissions of 15 percent. The other 500,000 shares were Class B and were issued half to Mays and half to Johns. Each of the two men put up $250 for his shares, and thus their total involvement in the one-bank holding company was only $500. Although Class B stock is often nonvoting stock, Mays and Johns had voting privileges and other privileges that the Class A owners had. However, Class B stock would not be sold to the public, and for this reason Mays and Johns were required to hold their stock until the time their shares could be converted one for one into Class A shares (and, then, if they wished into cash from the sales of Class A shares on the market). Class B stock could only be converted into Class A when the net annual earnings of the holding company increased 10 percent over the net earnings of the previous year.

As it turned out, Mays and Johns had in mind to lessen the dividends paid by Citizens State Bank to its stockholders in 19X5. By this means they could establish an unrealistically low earnings base for the holding company in 19X5 in order that 19X6 earnings could easily increase 10 percent over the net earnings of the previous year. (Query 4: Was this scheme fair to Dodd and the owners of the remaining 2 percent of Citizens stock? Why do you think Lake looked upon the holding company stock as "50 percent water"?)

While reading the prospectus in October, 19X4, Lake began to wonder if all those favorable reference opinions that he had received on both Mays and Johns were valid. He found himself wishing that he had not accepted the job as the bank's president. What Mays and Johns were doing was not illegal, but Lake felt there were ethical questions about the terms of the stock issue. True, the prospectus spelled the offering terms out in black and white, but Lake was of the opinion that Mays and Johns were simply counting on the abilities of the underwriter's salesmen to sell the holding company stock to the "unsuspecting" public. (Query 5: What should Lake tell people who asked him about the value of Peoples Holding Company's Class A shares?)

MR. DODD

Lake did not meet Dodd until his first directors meeting on September 18. Three days thereafter Dodd took Lake to lunch and told Lake how pleased he was that such a knowledgable and progressive president was now at the helm. Dodd said he was all in favor of the move to the new building, of making the new quarters elegant and functional, and of opening up on the new corner before a large competitor (Louisville National Bank) could move and open its new main office at the same intersection.

Lake and Dodd developed a good relationship in these first six months of Lake's tenure—a time when the bank was in the process of moving to its new quarters. Dodd took Lake to lunch on another occasion and, in January 19X5, had Lake and his wife to a dinner party with the Dodd family at a Louisville country club. Even though the two men had little in common outside talk of the bank and even though Dodd did quiz Lake on the activities of Mays and Johns, Dodd made it clear to Lake that he was particularly pleased about two things Lake had done. The first was in October when Lake went to the superintendent of the Division of Banks to plead for the alteration of two financial requirements of the bank which had been promulgated by the superintendent early in the summer. One was the requirement that annual rental payments in the new location not exceed $30,000 per year. On this requirement Lake got the ceiling raised to $40,000 by explaining what space would be occupied in the new building, terms of comparable leases in Louisville, projected increases in the bank's earnings, and so on. Alteration of the superintendent's other requirement was much dearer to Dodd. On this Lake persuaded the superintendent to drop altogether the requirement that $1 million more capital be invested in the bank by existing and/or new stockholders. This accomplishment by Lake was of more significant benefit to Dodd's interest than to that of the 80 percent owner, for it was outlined in the prospectus that $800,000 from the proceeds of the sales of Class A stock would be invested in the bank. As for Dodd, he would have had to put an additional $180,000 into the bank if he desired to retain his same proportionate interest of 18 percent. Dodd also told Lake that he was not in favor of any words or deeds by Lake in support of the holding company's stock issue. (Query 6: Should Lake have complied with Dodd's wishes in this instance?)

Another act by Lake that pleased Dodd took place in November and December. It began in Dodd's law office. Dodd had called Lake and asked him to come by to talk about a business matter. At the meeting, Dodd requested that Lake approve a $100,000 loan for him. After discussing the matter at a subsequent meeting of the two and after wrapping up particulars of the loan application, including Dodd's personal financial statement, Lake took the matter to Mays and Johns. ''Before I turn this loan down strictly on the basis of creditworthiness, I want to get the thinking of you two gentlemen because of who is the applicant,'' said Lake.

''I believe we should make it,'' replied Johns. ''We have kept relative peace with Mr. Dodd, and I think we should do all we can not to upset him.'' (Query 7: Might Johns's sanctioning of loans made by Mays have influenced Johns's decision on this loan to Dodd?)

Mays added, ''I agree and will recommend it at the next [December] board meeting.'' He did, and the loan was approved when Dodd was excused from a portion of the meeting.

MEETING OF THE BOARD OF DIRECTORS

Lake was very disappointed in the conduct, disclosure, and results of board meetings. There was no agenda. The only information supplied on new or renewed loans was the name of the borrower and the amount; not included were the name of the lending officer, interest rate, collateral, use of proceeds, repayment plan, amounts loaned to same borrower on other notes, or availability to the directors of the credit file containing financial statements, credit bureau inquiries, and so on. Minutes of each meeting were condensed down to one page or less. These and many other shortcomings in what the directors were told and the degree to which they participated at the monthly meetings prompted Lake, after attending his first two meetings as a nonmember in September and October, to make suggestions to Chairman Adams about improvements on how the board should be organized. One suggestion was to form, staff, and activate four standing committees—an Executive Committee, a Loan and Investment Committee, a Trust Committee, and a Committee of Examinations—together with three special committees on (1) marketing and business development, (2) obtaining more new directors, and (3) branch banking. Adams was agreeable and did so. In compliance with Lake's suggestions, Adams presented to the meeting in January 19X5 an authority chart listing each of the bank's officers and the various banking duties/tasks requiring authority, but Adams overlooked getting that approved by motion and vote of the directors. (Query 8: What was the legal effect of this action by Adams regarding the authority chart? What "banking duties/tasks" might require authority? What is *authority* in a corporation?)

Another disturbing aspect of Citizens' board meetings was Johns' insistence that Lake meet with him and Mays on the eve of each monthly meeting to go over what was to be brought before the board the following day. On the first occasion Lake asked if he should invite Adams to such pre-board meetings. Johns said, "No. Only the three of us will have these preparatory meetings, but we do want to know in advance whatever Adams plans to bring up." (Query 9: What did this response by Johns tell Lake? Should Lake have asked about inviting Dodd just as he asked about Adams?)

LOANS

Lake had talked to Mays and Johns during the employment interviews about which officers should have the authority to grant loans up to the statutory limit—in this case $200,000 to any one borrower (given CSB's size). Adams and Mays had been exercising such lending authority up until Lake's arrival on September 1, and the three of them did until Adams resigned six months later in March 19X5. In July 19X4, Lake was given a copy of the April 19X4, Federal Deposit Insurance Corporation (FDIC) examination report on Citizens State Bank to study before deciding on accepting the job offer. The report did not reveal several large loans that Mays (and, in a case or two, Johns) had authorized since the April report. Johns told Lake at their second interview meeting in July 19X4 that, "The Bank's loan portfolio is as good now as it was in late April when the FDIC made this favorable examination. Ed [Mays] has made some loans since then which have attracted business to the bank and which add to the quality of the loan portfolio." Lake asked no more hard questions about loans until more than a month after he began to perform in the role as president on September 1, 19X4.

Unknown to Lake until several weeks later, on September 1, 19X4 Mays made a $75,000 loan to an officer of the holding company (not Johns, but with Johns's approval). After Mays granted a $200,000 loan in September and a $125,000 loan in October 19X4, both of which Lake deemed questionable, Lake went to Johns in early November to question the lending authority that Mays was exercising and whether Mays should continue to make loans. Instead of receiving support from Johns in curtailing Mays's lending activities, Lake was told by Johns that Mays had become a millionaire at lending money in the home mortgage business and that he (Johns) was certainly not going to consider just these two loans in evaluating what Mays was doing to help build up Citizens State Bank and Trust Company. (Query 10: What more could Lake have done? What more should he have done?)

Nonetheless, Lake determined that the lending activities at Citizens State Bank had to be clarified and upgraded. For one thing, Lake felt that the bank's lending officers (excluding Mays) had to be switched from "conservative" to "progressive" attitudes. This and other changes Lake began to work on during the months prior to moving to the new building, even though it required the deferral of policy shifts needed in some other areas. Still, Lake concentrated the bulk of his time on planning the move to the new offices and he purposely attempted not to get deeply involved in lending policies until after the move (on March, 19X5). Lake knew that loans were time-consuming and, more importantly, loan applicants in Louisville were strangers to Lake whereas they were not to Mays and the other lending officers of Citizens State Bank. (Query 11: Was Lake consistent in setting high priority on improved lending and yet spending his time on the move rather than lending?)

After a number of meetings and interviews with his new fellow officers, Lake learned what lending experience each had and acquired some idea as to the potential for each to develop lending ability. By November, lending authority and limits were set; they were informally reviewed with the board in January 19X5. An officers' loan committee was formed and met each Tuesday and Friday morning for 30 minutes before the bank opened for business. In revamping the bank's lending policies and so as to be clear about the newly instituted practices thereunder, Lake wrote several memos establishing loan procedures and guidelines:

1. Lending officers were authorized to approve loans up to a specific dollar limit in each of several loan categories (cars, boats, home improvements, etc.) without first getting approval from the bank's loan committee. (Query 12: What do you think of this individual versus group decision making?)
2. Two authorized lending officers were required to turn down a loan, rather than just one officer, in order to avoid any prejudice of a single officer against the applicant and in order to have two opinions rather than just one.
3. If a loan was refused, then the loan officer had to explain in writing both why the application was declined and how the loan could have been made, for example, with co-signer, collateral, higher rate of interest, or decrease in dollar amount requested.
4. A credit file on every loan application was established—including those turned down, dropped, or withdrawn—with such files being located in a central, accessible place rather than in the office of the chairman of the board.

5. Loan officers were instructed to search out and concentrate on making high-yield installment loans (in order to meet the Mays' and Johns' objective of increased earnings after 19X5).

6. Outstanding lines of credit were to be reviewed annually whether in use partially, wholly, or not at all.

7. Loan officers were required to initial each new promissory note put into the loan portfolio so other personnel would know who was administering the borrowing arrangement.

8. Officers would oversee the collection of any delinquent loans they had granted, although in special cases two loan officers would swap assignments on troublesome borrowers in order to bring about or restore objectivity to the collection effort.

9. There would be periodic reviews of outstanding *(a)* demand loans, *(b)* problem or classified loans, and *(c)* charged-off loans.

10. Annual financial statements were required of businesses and persons to whom large loans were made.

11. Loans to officers and employees had to meet the same credit standards as did loans granted to other customers.

12. A quarterly schedule was set up to reevaluate all collateral held in the vault.

13. At the twice-weekly loan committee meetings, the loan officers were to review the particulars on note maturity notices to be mailed to borrowers.

SETTING OBJECTIVES FOR THE BANK

As part of his plan to get the bank moving in some new directions, Lake held a series of participative staff meetings to develop a set of objectives for the bank. After several rounds of meeting and sets of working drafts, Lake and the bank's officers and staff reached a consensus on ten objectives:

1. To be regarded by the residents of Louisville and Jefferson County as the bank at which PEOPLE ENJOY doing business.

2. To have our STAFF believe this bank to be the BEST BANK in town at which to work.

3. To assume the ready AVAILABILITY and COMPLETE SAFETY of the funds of our customers.

4. To provide ALL needed BANKING SERVICES to a broad base of customers of all ethnic and vocational groups.

5. To continually try to IMPROVE our corporate IMAGE and REPUTATION . . . by the personal conduct of our staff, in our promotional efforts, and through the proper rendering of bank services.

6. To COMMUNICATE REGULARLY with our customers and with the public.

7. To EXCEL in FAIR COMPETITION among financial institutions by

means of aggressive lending policies, active promotion, and superior servicing.

8. To provide, through our staff, an active contribution to those community affairs which promote the CULTURAL and CHARITABLE WELFARE of Louisville and Jefferson County.
9. To take LEADERSHIP in meeting the FINANCIAL NEEDS of the trade area we serve.
10. To follow a program of FUTURE PLANNING for new banking services, techniques, and facilities . . . toward the end that our bank may constantly IMPROVE its position of LEADERSHIP in a widening field of service.

THE BANK EXAMINERS' FEBRUARY AUDIT

When both the state and FDIC bank examining teams walked into the bank at closing time on February 1, 19X5, they could not have picked a busier time. It was a Monday. It was the first day of the month. It was exactly a month before the move, and the bank's entire staff was engrossed in planning and preparing for that. Lake and the other officers took time out to give the examiners a warm and hospitable reception. The examiners, in turn, were complimentary of the bank's condition and operational practices, for they listed no exceptions. Thus, as far as the examiners were concerned, Citizens State Bank had a clean bill of health since its takeover by the holding company. They did complain strongly, however, about Lake not having located and purchased 50 shares of the bank's stock out of the 100,000 shares outstanding, for Lake could not qualify as a director and take the oath until he acquired the 50 unencumbered shares in Citizens. Moreover, the president of a Kentucky-chartered bank was required to be a member of the board of directors. Lake had tried to buy 50 shares from Mays, Johns, and Dodd, but none of the three would sell.

When the examiners departed, Lake was told by a fellow officer that an examiner said that the bank would be receiving noncritical written reports from each of the two examining agencies. Lake wondered, "How could they have overlooked the large loans made by Mays?" (Query 13: Should Lake have volunteered to the bank examiners "what was wrong" at Citizens State Bank; or should he have remained silent because he was not specifically asked about loans made by Mays?)

Late in February, Mays made several loans which Lake considered as very questionable and out of line with the loan policies he had established a few months earlier. A second loan of $75,000 was made to that officer of the holding company. In addition, on March 1, Mays (with the concurrence of Johns) made an unsecured loan of the bank's maximum legal lending limit of $200,000 to the holding company despite the fact that the accompanying financial statement showed a negative net worth. Moreover, the loan was at a low interest rate. Finally, on March 3, Mays made unsecured loans to two of his business associates, also at low interest rates, for $125,000 and $200,000. It was this latest flurry of large loans which caused Lake to write the letter to Mays on March 5, 19X5 asking that he renounce his loaning authority. The bank examiners had overlooked the previous loans made by Mays, but Lake was very concerned over what their reaction would be to the newly granted loans. He wondered what reaction Mays would have to his letter and just how he was going to proceed.

20.2. Citizens State Bank and Trust Company (B)*

IN MID-MARCH 19X5, both teams of bank examiners returned for a second look at Citizens' financial position. The second visit by the examiners came as a surprise to Lake for two reasons. First, over a month had passed since their first visit indicating that no problem existed. Second, the oral report given in February by the captain of each examining team had been favorable. However, it was the large loans made by Mays, both before and since their February visits, that brought the examiners back.[1] After visitations by the two teams of examiners on two additional nights, Lake and his fellow officers knew that the forthcoming written examination reports would be highly critical.

APRIL 1, 19X5

On April 1, Lake was called to the office of the superintendent, Division of Banks. The chief examiner of the FDIC, who had requested this meeting, was also present. It was the examiner who did most of the talking since it was the FDIC investigators who had uncovered the several exceptions in March. For Lake it was a preview of the criticisms that would be included in the written report. Lake was requested to arrange for all members of the bank's board of directors to meet with the regulators before the end of the month. The date of April 16 was agreed upon, the day of the monthly board meeting at the bank. At President Lake's suggestion, the superintendent agreed to require a monthly letter indicating progress in alleviating the problems enumerated in the examiner's report. (Query 1: What might have motivated Lake to suggest that he be required to write these letters?)

---

* Prepared by Professors Robert K. Landrum and Charles S. Sherwood, Eastern Kentucky University. Reprinted by permission. All rights reserved by the authors of the case. This case is disguised as to both time and place.

[1] Examiners classify bank loans as "loss," "doubtful," or "substandard." Estimated losses are required to be charged off immediately. Doubtful loans are usually considered to require reserves of 50 percent. Substandard loans are defined as "containing more than normal banking risk" but not necessarily a loss potential.

APRIL 1 TO APRIL 16, 19X5

Prior to the April board meeting, examination reports were received from the two regulatory agencies. The "Conclusions and Recommendations" sections of both were long and critical. The large loans made by Vice President Mays to his interests and to the interests of his "partner" Johns constituted the bulk of the exceptions. In light of these reports, Lake decided to ask Mays to resign as vice president although he would remain as a member of the board of directors. In Lake's view, Mays's resignation as an officer of the bank was necessary to ensure that Mays terminate his lending practices and to satisfy the examiner's requirement of positive efforts at improvement. While Mays had relinquished his lending authority shortly after receiving Lake's handwritten letter, assurance had to be obtained that such practices did not resume. This could be permanently done, thought Lake, only by removing Mays from the officer ranks. (Query 2: Evaluate this tactic of Lake's.)

The two meetings took place on schedule on the 16th—the April board meeting and the summary call of directors to the superintendent's office. All parties remained cool and serious. During the first meeting, Lake asked Mays to resign and Mays complied without further comment. There was no excitement except in the eyes of Johns who appeared somewhat surprised at Lake's boldness. Later in the superintendent's office the bank regulators voiced strong criticism of the board and especially of Mays for the loans which were rated substandard or worse. Mays was given a time schedule to get the loans paid off, reduced substantially, or more fully secured. In addition, the deputy superintendent told the assemblage that the bank's president would be required to write a joint letter to the superintendent and to the FDIC office on or about the middle of each month. The purpose of the letter was to keep the regulators fully informed on any significant changes in the bank's structure or operations. Before the end of the meeting, Dodd spoke up to say that he could not understand why these examination reports should do anything to delay the bank's pending application for a branch operation. Dodd stated, "If we open a branch bank and it doesn't do as well as anticipated, it is the bank that is taking the risk, not you gentlemen or your agencies." (Query 3: What were the flaws in Dodd's pronouncement?)

THE EVENTS OF APRIL 16 THROUGH MAY 19X5

On April 19, Lake wrote a letter to Mays and one to Johns asking for a guarantee in writing of the loans each director had made to his interests. Neither complied, although both had agreed to do so at the meeting with the regulators on April 16. (Query 4: What could or should Lake have done to force compliance by the two men who hired him as president and who together owned over 50 percent of the voting stock in Peoples Holding Company?)

One of the loans made by Mays the previous October figured prominently in the controversy. The bank regulators insisted on April 16 that $117,000 of this $125,000 loan be charged off as uncollectable. This charge-off was made the following day. The loan had been made to one of Mays' partners to provide first installment funds for the two men to purchase a thoroughbred racetrack at Lexington. In late April, there was front page publicity about the racetrack sale and about Mays being the president of the new corporation formed to own the track. Citizens State Bank lost over $400,000 in deposits as a result. According to the president of a large Louisville bank that acquired the withdrawn funds, the two largest depositors switching to his bank from Citizens stated "Horse racing and sound banking don't mix." Other Citizens' depositors came into the bank lobby following the publicity and asked the tellers, "Where is the $5 window? Where can I buy a $6 combination ticket to win, place, or show?" Whether the remarks were in jest or an acrid expression of concern was unclear.

The events of April compelled Johns to go see the two "outside" directors Mr. Adkins and Mr. Ballard. These two men who had only a small ownership stake in Citizens State Bank were threatening to resign. One of them had spoken to several other Louisville bankers about the bad examination report. Both were disturbed by the implications of that report for their own reputations as well as the effect on the bank of the race track publicity. Johns persuaded the two directors to stay on during this crisis period and to assist in making progress to get the bank out of trouble. (Query 5: Would you have stayed? What are the responsibilities and potential liabilities of a bank director? Comment on the makeup of a bank board consisting of only six directors where: two of them are "outsiders" with minimal stockholdings; one is an "outsider" with 18 percent ownership; two who, together, controlled the ownership of 80 percent of the bank's shares; one "insider"—Lake—with minimal stockholdings, president, and a newcomer to the scene.)

One morning early in May, Dodd came to see Lake at the bank. He asked to see the $125,000 note which had been charged off. Dodd, who was an attorney and who at this time was visibly angry about the racetrack publicity, started to take the large note with him and leave the bank saying, "I am going to the courthouse with this note and seek judgment on it. Then we will have solved one of our bank's biggest problems." (Query 6: What other motivating reasons could Dodd have had for this behavior?)

Lake was stunned. Heretofore, Dodd had been strongly supportive of Lake and his leadership. In addition, Lake knew that a director could never act alone but could only vote on actions as a member of a group, the board of directors. Dodd had no authorization to remove this asset from the bank, much less take legal actions in regard to it. Lake did not want to have a confrontation with a tough-minded Dodd if such was avoidable. However, he insisted that the note remain at the bank and Dodd departed without it.

Dodd called Lake two days later, expressed his anger, and demanded that a special board meeting be called to decide on taking the $125,000 note to the courthouse. Lake told Dodd that he hoped to get $87,500 of the note paid off by mid-May and the balance in September. Since Dodd would not wait for Lake's strategy to run its course and persisted in his demand for a special board meeting, Lake called a meeting for May 10. All directors were notified of the meeting time and the purpose for which the special meeting was called. Lake called Dodd's office before the meeting began and was told that Dodd had gone to play golf. Those present unanimously approved Lake's plan to get $87,500 paid then and $37,500 in early autumn. Lake also got Mays to sign guarantees of his note, notes owed by his interests, and other notes Mays had acquired for the bank. The next day the expected $87,500 payment on the loan was made to the bank.

On May 15, Lake wrote his first monthly letter to the superintendent and the regional FDIC head. Progress was reported not only on the $125,000 note but on other loans and banking practices.

JUNE 1 TO JULY 9, 19X5

Dodd invited Lake to be his partner at his club's invitational golf tournament in early June. During the practice round and two tournament rounds Dodd "pumped" Lake about information on Mays, Johns, the bank's problem loans, and Peoples Holding Company. Lake told as little as he could and volunteered no unrequested information. On the last day of the tournament Dodd proposed to Lake, "If you will join forces with me against Johns and Mays, I will make it worth your while."

Lake responded directly to Dodd, "I can't side with you against anyone else on the board as long as I am president and a director of the bank."

"I wish you would think it over," said Dodd. Lake did not respond as he thought it best to say nothing further.

A few days later Dodd telephoned Lake. He again asked Lake to side with him. Lake replied, "I prefer not to side with any person or group or, in any way, contribute to factionalism on our board of directors. If I ever must side with a faction, it is only proper that that faction hold a majority vote on the board or represent a majority of the shares." (Query 7: Evaluate Lake's answer to Dodd and the tactics he used in turning Dodd down.)

Dodd replied, "I won't ask you again." And he did not ask again. In fact, from that time forward there was running conflict between Lake and Dodd.

At the board meeting in June 19X5, Dodd delivered an ultimatum that if the two large loans connected with the racetrack purchase were not paid by the date of the next board meeting (July 9) he intended to take legal action against the borrowers. In the three weeks between those two board meetings, Dodd sent an agent to the large Louisville bank that originally had loaned $3 million to the Peoples Holding Company to acquire the 80 percent stock interest in Citizens State Bank and Trust Company. Johns and Mays were co-signers of that note. The agent's mission was to persuade the bank to sell the loan collateral consisting of 80,000 shares in Citizens State Bank to a buying group headed by Dodd. The alternative was a lawsuit which would involve that bank as a defendant. Despite this threat, the bank refused to sell the shares to Dodd or anyone else.

Dodd was effectively stopped from starting legal proceedings on July 9, because that morning, just prior to the bank's monthly board meeting, the two large racetrack loans were paid off. This last-minute feat was accomplished by having Mays sell out his interest in the Lexington racetrack to a creditworthy purchaser from Paducah. Dodd was visibly angered at the July board meeting when the loan repayment was announced. (Query 8: Why would Dodd, who held an 18 percent interest in the bank, not be in favor of solving a major problem of that bank? Cite as many reasons as you think plausible.)

Dodd called Lake at home that evening: "You'll never embarrass me again like you did at that board meeting you little ———." Before Lake could respond, Dodd hung up the telephone.

JULY 10 TO SEPTEMBER 10, 19X5

The monthly letter of July communicated to the regulators that progress was being made on the problem loans. In spite of this, the superintendent declined in late July the bank's new branch application at a large regional shopping center. No reasons were given in the turndown letter. (Query 9: What reasons might have been discussed at a meeting of the superintendent with his advisory board?)

During July and August, Mays proceeded to liquidate some of his stocks and bond holdings to generate the cash needed to pay off both a loan he owed the Citizens State Bank and another loan owed by an official of Peoples Holding Company. Consequently, Lake's August letter to the regulators told of further progress in rectifying the problem loans.

During August, Dodd went to see the heads of two divisions in the Kentucky Department of Commerce. He told the superintendent of the Division of Banks that Citizens State Bank was in such poor condition that its majority owner (Peoples Holding Company) should not be permitted to continue to own the bank stock. Dodd told the superintendent of the Division of Securities that the problems of the bank were so great that the holding company should not be extended beyond its expiration date of August 31. Dodd, who was a close friend of the governor, prevailed upon the superintendent to have a public hearing on August 25 regarding the extension.

This public hearing had both Mays and Johns very upset. The holding company's stock sales had started the previous September 1, 19X4, and had almost netted enough in sales proceeds to release the first of two escrow accounts. The reason that Peoples Holding Company stock sales had not reached "first escrow size" by August was believed to be because of the racetrack publicity that hurt the reputation of both the bank and the holding company. Release of the first escrow would permit the holding company to make a payment on its $3.8 million note and pay off $200,000 owed to Citizens State Bank. This $200,000 loan was one that the bank regulators wanted to see retired, and Lake knew it to be the weakest credit in his bank's loan portfolio. Retirement of this loan would strengthen Mays' personal financial situation in that he had personally guaranteed its payment. In addition, this action would make Mays' other written guarantees to the bank more credible.

The public hearing was formally recorded by having a court reporter present and transcribing. Lake was one of the witnesses who testified under oath. He was asked numerous questions about the bank's troubles. Dodd did not appear, although he had promoted the very rare public meeting for extension of a stock offering. (Query 10: Why might Dodd have wanted the holding company's stock issue to fail? What explanation can you offer for not attending the hearing?)

Despite Dodd's attempts to the contrary, early in September the superintendent of the Division of Securities approved the extension for another year. The $200,000 note due Citizens State Bank was paid in full on September 10. As a consequence of this, Lake not only went to see the presidents of the three large national banks in Louisville to tell them of the progress made on problem loans since April 16, but Lake wrote a specific letter to both the regulatory agencies. Lake asked for a special examination before the end of the year in order to get official verification on Citizen's improved financial status. (Query 11: Appraise the steps taken by Lake on September 10 following payoff of the $200,000 loan.)

OCTOBER 18, 19X5 TO FEBRUARY 5, 19X6

The bank examiners did return before 19X5 ended. State and FDIC examining teams returned on October 18 to begin what proved to be a surprise to Lake. He was surprised because they were as critical as they had been at the examination begun in February and resumed in March. This unexpected criticism—rather than the expected pat on the back—deflated Lake. He attributed the more than thorough search for exception to the rivalry between these representatives of the two regulatory agencies. He suspected that the one with primary responsibility, the Kentucky Division of Banks, was chagrined that the FDIC had uncovered the questionable loans in March, so this time the Division of Banks' examiner changed yardsticks and took a hard-line approach. In turn, the FDIC sensed the competitiveness and attempted not to be outdone.

As a consequence of this "examiners' war," 15 percent of the loans were rated substandard. This was up from 11 percent in the February–March (19X5) examination report in spite of all the progress made since then. When the Citizens' board reviewed the examination reports at its December 19X5 and January (19X6) meetings, the members expressed an understanding of the situation, except for Dodd. In his first hostile and disruptive behavior since the summer of 19X5, Dodd concurred with what the examiners had reported and proclaimed to the assembled board members on January 26, 19X6, "This bank's loans are in worse shape than they were back in April." In addition, he demanded that all loans of directors and officers be paid off by the February board meeting, ten days later. Following these remarks he left the meeting early. Prior to leaving, Dodd had seconded and voted for the motion to reelect all the bank's officers for another year, including Lake.

At the annual stockholders meeting in January, all directors were reelected for another year.[2] In spite of contrary opinions expressed by the other directors, Johns was insistent that Dodd's name be included on the slate. (Query 12: What reasons might Johns have for wanting Dodd kept on the bank's board?)

FEBRUARY 19X6

On February 2, Dodd paid off a large unsecured loan at Citizens State Bank by borrowing from another bank where his stock in Citizens could be used as collateral. (Query 13: Why might this stock not have served as collateral at Citizens State Bank?) This cleared him from being in violation of the demand he made at the January 26 meeting regarding full payment of loans by officers and directors.

The following day, February 3, Dodd called Johns and Mays to his law office and told them that if they did not pay him $1 million for his 18 percent stock ownership in the bank by February 15, he would bring a lawsuit for $2 million against Mays. Dodd contended that the minutes of board meetings were incorrect and that he would demand Lake's resignation in the lawsuit because of his incompetence. Immediately following the meeting, Mays and Johns reported the episode to Lake. All three took the threat seriously because of Dodd's reputation and past performances. However, they did have difficulty understanding how Dodd could expect to receive $1 million for stock worth half that amount. Upon separation, the three men agreed to consider the proposition for a few days and discuss it again. Before Mays, Lake, and Johns could get together again, Dodd moved on another front.

At the February 5 board meeting, Dodd read a long letter whose contents were unknown to the listeners in advance. This letter to the board contained the following demands:

1. Lake who "had clearly demonstrated that he is incompetent . . ." be requested to resign "as president and director . . ." Dodd contended that Lake had engaged in ". . . numerous activities damaging to the

---

[2] In being reelected to membership, Dodd was assured of occupying the position of director for 12 more months. Consequently, he could engage in almost any form of behavior—short of flagrantly violating the statutes—and still have all the bank's records and meetings open to him.

Bank and its shareholders . . ." and that such activities were ". . . improper, illegal, and unjustified. . . ."

2. Johns, Dodd, and another specified director "function as an Operating Committee . . . until a new President is obtained. . . ."

3. "That all substandard loans be required to be paid in full on or before February 15, 19X6." (Query 14: Why might ten days not be enough time?)

4. "That you adopt a resolution designating me as a Director of the Bank and as an attorney-at-law to take appropriate action on behalf of the Bank to enforce payment of all the foregoing loans on or before February 15, 19X6, or as soon thereafter as judgments thereon can be obtained. (Query 15: Is it standard procedure for banks to take such heavy-handed action on substandard loans? If not, how do banks operate in this regard?)

5. "You are hereby notified that if you refuse or neglect to carry out the foregoing demands, or any of them, within the periods above stated or by March 1, 19X6, whichever is later, I intend to bring a derivative suit in my capacity as a shareholder for the benefit of the Bank and all other shareholders similarly situated."

The board members were stunned by the content of this letter. Following Dodd's departure, the consensus of the remaining directors was to sit tight, keep the subject confidential to avoid a "run on the bank," and be prepared for other surprises Dodd might unload at or before the next monthly meeting on March 5. (Query 16: How would you evaluate these demands and opinions expressed by Dodd? What would you, as a director present at this February 5, meeting, have advocated be done about this letter?)

Dodd kept up the attack. He wrote another letter on February 9 in which he again labeled Lake as incompetent and one who showed partiality to Mays. Then Dodd took the February 5 letter to the superintendent of the Division of Banks and to the two top officials of the national bank where Peoples Holding Company had their $3.8 million loan. (Query 17: What harm might have been done to (1) the Citizens State Bank, (2) Mays, and (3) Lake as a result of Dodd taking the February 5 letter to the superintendent? Taking it to the top officials of a competitor bank?)

MARCH 19X6

By the time of the March 5 board meeting, the directors had not decided on a course of action to deal with Dodd's aggressiveness, even though the heads of both bank regulatory agencies had urged the board members to do so. At that meeting Dodd read aloud a handwritten letter in which he accused Lake of ". . . misfeasance and malfeasance in office . . ." and of conspiring with Johns and Mays. (Query 18: If you were in Lake's position as chairman of the meeting, what would you have done when Dodd read aloud the accusations of this letter? What would you have done after Dodd left the meeting? What might you have done in the days following the meeting?)

Three days later Dodd wrote a six-page letter to the superintendent of the Division of Banks. In addition to reciting loan and other information about the bank that the regulators already knew, he requested that the superintendent pursue a particular banking statute which would permit removal of Mays and Lake as directors. There was repetition of the criticisms in prior letters about Mays and Lake.

On March 22, Dodd filed a lawsuit against Mays, Lake, Johns, and Citizens State Bank. It made double-banner headlines on the front page and across all eight columns of Louisville's evening newspaper. Ten loans were mentioned in the legal petition even though seven of the ten had already been paid in full or substantially reduced. (Query 19: If you were Lake, what action would you take to prevent or dampen a "run" on the bank? What would you have told your family and friends about the headlines if you, as Lake, had three-fourths-inch headlines above your picture announcing: THREE CITIZENS STATE BANK DIRECTORS FACE CONFLICT OF INTEREST CHARGE?)

In his derivative lawsuit (Query 20: What is that?) Dodd sought the judgment of the Kentucky court (1) against Mays for $400,000; (2) an accounting by the individual defendants; (3) for Mays to reduce the loans owed by him and his interests. While these were the only demands made by Dodd, the newspaper and TV publicity affected the defendants and the bank adversely. Total bank deposits went down over $600,000 due to the filing of this lawsuit. Moreover, FDIC personnel were in the bank during business hours every day for six weeks, and Lake received calls at home by purported customers who were critical of how he and others were treating the bank. (Query 21: What would you say to a complaining caller who said you have hurt his bank and that he had removed or would remove his account to another bank?)

None of the defendants commented to the press about Dodd's lawsuit, hoping that the matter would fade away. Dodd, however, proceeded to try to keep the issues alive and ongoing by writing more letters. One written March 31, accused Lake of perjury before the Division of Securities at that meeting in August 1965 which Dodd requested but did not attend.

At the suggestion of his attorney, Lake began looking elsewhere for employment. He communicated with banks all over the country and planned on leaving when he could find a suitable job in banking and after he was released by Dodd from the lawsuit. (Query 22: What problems do you see for Lake in obtaining a job elsewhere?)

APRIL 19X6

Dodd had a part in a second lawsuit brought against Mays and Citizens State Bank on April 14. The plaintiff, whose attorney was counselled by

Dodd, was a former partner of Mays in the racetrack deal. The filing of this petition with the court received publicity but not on the front page.

MAY 19X6

By early May, there was only one loan remaining of the ten substandard loans that Dodd had included in his first lawsuit filed on March 22. It was a loan of $118,000 to Mays who, in spite of his many personal and financial problems, had cooperated fully during the preceeding 12 months to get all the other classified loans paid off and this one reduced from $200,000. The $118,000 balance was secured by over $1 million of collateral and Mrs. Mays was a co-signer.

Despite this progress by Mays, Dodd continued his attacks against the holding company, Mays, and Johns. He encouraged and assisted a subscriber to holding company stock to sue the three parties on behalf of all public owners of this stock. The complaint which Dodd filed as the plaintiff's attorney on May 10 contended that Johns and Mays acquired 500,000 Class B voting shares for $500 and sold 500,000 Class A voting shares to the public for $6,250,000 which "amounted to an unjust enrichment to themselves and a detriment and fraud upon the corporation and future Class A shareholders. The complaint alleged that the scheme was perpetration of a fraud and demanded that Johns and Mays pay a sum of $6,250,000 less their $500 investment. Local newspapers carried stories announcing that a third lawsuit involving officials of Peoples Holding Company and Citizens State Bank had been filed. Although these stories were not front-page items, Johns seemed more concerned about this suit than the other two. (Query 23: Why was Johns so concerned about the charges in this particular lawsuit?)

But, still, no one would "step into the ring" with Dodd. One might have expected the filing of countersuits, libel charges, or dismissal of Dodd from the bank's board after the table pounding by him at bank board meetings, after the strong letters he wrote, and after the filing of three lawsuits. The defensive strategy which Johns engineered was to let Dodd "shadow box alone in the ring" rather than confront him on the part of any of the individual defendants, the bank's board, the local banking community, or the banking regulators.

JULY 19X6

At the bank's board meeting on July 22, Dodd attended for only a short while. All other directors were present and remained. When Dodd departed in a huff, he left threatening to put the bank into the hands of a court receiver before the August meeting of the board; his parting comment was "Unless something is done by the next meeting, someone else will be running this bank." The other directors discussed this new threat after Dodd left. The consensus was that practically all targets at the bank had been removed from

Dodd's aim and that there was no basis whatsoever for receivership action. The only loan remaining was Mays' $118,000 one, and Dodd had already forced Mays' resignation from the board of directors. In fact, Mays was out of contact with the bank altogether.

AUGUST 19X6

By early August, word was getting around the bank and Louisville that Dodd was drawing up the papers to have the court put Citizens State Bank into receivership. Dodd's law office associates confirmed this. Lake contacted the superintendent of the Division of Banks, the FDIC, and the president of the Louisville clearinghouse association asking for their help in moving Dodd off this incredible tangent.

On the eve of the bank's August board meeting, Lake received a call at home from the lawyer he had hired in late March. Lake's lawyer said, "Bob, you must resign at the board meeting tomorrow." (Query 24: If he does so, what should he ask for in a trade-off to benefit himself and his five dependents?) Lake was stunned. In reply he said, "You can't be serious! What happens if I don't resign?"

"Then you'll be fired at the board meeting tomorrow morning," the lawyer responded. "If you resign, you will get most of the main concessions you told me you wanted. The March 22 lawsuit is to be dismissed, and Dodd will give you a signed release promising no additional legal action. Directors of the bank will affirmatively recommend you, but they insist that you sell all the stock you own in the bank at what you paid for it. Also, the receivership action will not happen." This meant to Lake that (1) he would not get any termination pay to carry him until he found new employment; (2) he would not get releases from Citizens State Bank and its directors, from the Division of Banks, or from the FDIC; and (3) no assurance would be issued that this "deal" with Dodd would not be a "sell out" by Peoples Holding Company of its subsidiary, Citizens State Bank. (Query 25: What should Lake have done when he learned what he would get and what he would not get?)

"These terms were practically dictated to me late this afternoon," the lawyer stated. "You see, Bob, we want to get you out of this mess. And we are getting you out as whole and unscathed as we possibly can. You can leave Citizens with your head held high, for you did as good a job as anyone could have possibly done."

"Well, I did that," sighed Lake. "Never did I have a conflict of interest. Never did I let the bank and its objectives suffer at the expense of my own personal objectives. I suppose the way I can give the bank the most at my final hour is to resign, get what concessions I can get now that my bargaining position has disintegrated, not force the bank's directors to discharge me, and remove the bank from the turmoil it is in."

Lake was nevertheless surprised to learn that Johns and Dodd had entered into a written agreement prior to his ouster. In that agreement Dodd removed his last obstacle (Lake) to gaining a power base in the bank he had always desired. In return for dismissing the three lawsuits, Dodd received a lifetime guarantee of membership on the bank's board of directors. (Query 26: Have you ever heard of a lifetime director of a corporation? If yes, explain.) He also was made general counsel for the bank for a minimum of seven years at a minimum retainer of $1,000 per month. (Query 27: Would the bar association describe this as solicitation of business? Would you?) Finally, Dodd would have veto power on the naming of Lake's successor.

On the day following the phone call, Lake's resignation letter that his lawyer drafted for him was read at the bank board meeting. The resignation was accepted.

21. Coral Industries, Inc.*

Frank Pilsch, general manager of Coral Industries, was giving serious consideration to increasing the prices of the company's shower door line by 30 percent. At the same time, he was looking at various measures to increase production efficiency and whether to recommend combining some of the company's manufacturing operations with another subsidiary of Coral's parent firm—Midwest Fabricators, Inc. Pilsch felt a need to scrutinize operations carefully because Coral Industries was having a difficult time breaking even; four years ago, the company had been profitable at a sales volume of $30,000 per month and now it was operating in the red at a sales volume which recently had averaged $52,000 per month. True, some of Coral's troubles were due to the added cost burdens of having just relocated its plant facilities, but that was past and it was important to restore profitability as quickly as possible.

BACKGROUND

In August 1971, Midwest Fabricators purchased the Closure Company and immediately changed its name from Closure to Coral Industries. The purchase of Coral was only one of a number of companies which Midwest Fabricators had acquired over the past 15 years. In effect, Midwest Fabricators was a "miniconglomerate" which had been put together by two ambitious and able entrepreneurs; some of the subsidiary companies they had started from scratch, while others had been purchased.

Closure Company had a history of ups and downs when Midwest bought it in 1971. Closure had originally been formed by a Mr. Pasta in the late 1940s as a manufacturer of shower enclosures, with plant facilities in New York state. The company was successful enough to branch out into the manufacture and sale of patio doors and, at its peak, had achieved a sales volume of $250,000 per month. When Mr. Pasta died, the business was taken over by his two sons who elected to split the management of the company—one took charge of sales and the other headed up production operations. Soon the two brothers came to disagreement and the company went into bankruptcy.

* Prepared by Professor Charles R. Scott, Jr., The University of Alabama. The location of the company is disguised.

About 1960, Closure was acquired by a pipe company and its operations were moved to New Jersey; the pipe company selected one of Closure's managers who had had many years of experience in the industry to head up the division. At first, the company did not do well at all; sales slipped over a period of months to a low of about $5,000 per month, but then increased back up to the $30,000 per month range. Despite the fact that operations had become profitable, in 1971 the pipe company elected to sell Closure to Midwest Fabricators because it felt it had lost control over Closure's operations.

OPERATIONS AND MANAGEMENT

During the first two years after the acquisition, while it was learning the business, Midwest maintained the operations of Coral Industries in New Jersey in the same facilities. But, in 1974, actions were taken to move the company's manufacturing activities to a site location adjacent to Midwest Fabricator's main plant and headquarters' offices in St. Louis. Midwest had a building which was only partly in use and the empty portion was felt to be suitable for Coral's manufacturing operations. The move was completed in early 1975 and production was reasonably stabilized at the new site by June.

Shortly after Midwest acquired Closure and renamed it Coral Industries, Frank Pilsch, a son-in-law of the president of Midwest, was made general manager of Coral. Pilsch had been with Midwest Fabricators for nine years; he had worked part-time at Midwest while completing his college education in political science. Previously, Pilsch had managed two other Midwest subsidiaries—a warehouse and a small chemical company—and in each case had made the subsidiary profitable.

An organization chart for Coral Industries is shown in Exhibit 1. Coral receives a significant amount of administrative services and support from its parent, thereby eliminating a need for a full-blown managerial staff. The class proximity and relationship between the two companies allows Midwest to provide Coral with computerized accounting, budgetary, and operating information at an economical fixed fee.

PRODUCT LINE

Coral's product line included bathtub enclosures, shower doors, panels, and accessories. Exhibit 2 depicts one of Coral's bathtub enclosures and Exhibit 3 shows an instruction sheet for installers. The doors are made of glass or plastic panels surrounded by aluminum extrusions, with a rubber glazing between the panels and the aluminum. The enclosures also have frames so that the door(s) can slide on rollers to open and close. Bars, handles, and other accessories are included with each unit as standard equipment. The unit is shipped ready to install either by residential contractors or do-it-yourself homeowners.

Between 1959 and 1975, the prices of shower and tub enclosures did not

EXHIBIT 1
Organization Chart

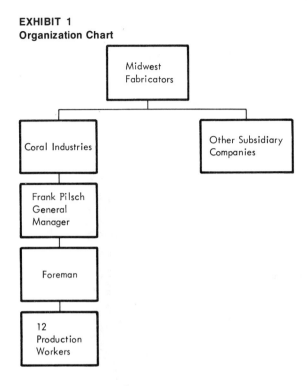

change appreciably. However, in 1975 shifts in market and cost conditions placed heavy pressure on the prevailing price structure. Safety glass, which is about three times as expensive as regular glass, began to be required in doors sold in many areas. Inflation was driving prices up sharply for various materials and components of tub and shower enclosures. At the same time, though, design changes in aluminum framing allowed lighter frames to be used with comparable enclosure performance, semitransparent plastic panels were being increasingly substituted for glass in the lower priced enclosures, and standardization of construction techniques was beginning to allow manufacturers to concentrate more on making standard stock sizes and models rather than custom-ordered units.

PRODUCTION PROCESS

The manufacturing process which Coral used was relatively simple: materials and parts were purchased; components were cut and processed; the pieces were assembled; and the finished product was boxed for shipment. Coral purchased most of its aluminum strips in lengths appropriate for each door size it makes; the ends of each strip were subsequently sawed at 45°-degree angles (leaving little waste), then punched for screws and moved to the assembly area. The first assembler obtained the correct type and size

EXHIBIT 2

Bath and Shower Enclosures

Tub Enclosures

Patrician

46P — 50P — 56P

A Luxury enclosure in the moderate price range. Gleaming smooth-faced extrusions which are bright-anodized with our own "evalume" process give this unit the appearance of luxury priced bath tub equipment.

Exclusive adjustable roller positions make this unit the ultimate in operating ease.

Special cut-to-size orders accepted in this model.

E-channel wall jambs add to its distinctive appearance.

Beautiful precision-fitted chrome handles make the Patrician towel bars an eye-catching feature of this tub enclosure.

Designs

Glass Doors in 5 stunning patterns, sand-etched for lasting beauty.

MERMAID   **SWAN**   **TROPICAL FISH**   **MONOGRAM**   **FLYING GEESE**

CORAL industries, Inc.

EXHIBIT 2 *(continued)*

Tub Enclosures

Contender

50C

Economy Bathtub Enclosure — made with bright ANODIZED aluminum extrusions — features three-hole adjustable roller suspension for ease of installation and operation — two towel bars.

Deluxe

46CD — 50CD — 56CD

Same as above.

Popular enclosure with sliding glass panels designed for all standard recessed tubs — Special cut-to-size orders accepted in this model. Decorator designed chrome brackets make this unit distinctive.

Tridoor

46R — 50R — 56R

For the housewife-mother who needs additional room for "bathing babies" — a sturdily-designed three-panel enclosure — bright anodization, 7/32" glass, ball-bearing rollers, towel bars.

Available in a number of standard sizes and also to specific measurements.

Two-thirds of the bathtub area is made available with this enclosure.

This Tridoor unit is available from 36" wide to 60" x 70" height for shower enclosures under designation Tridoor 25R.

EXHIBIT 3

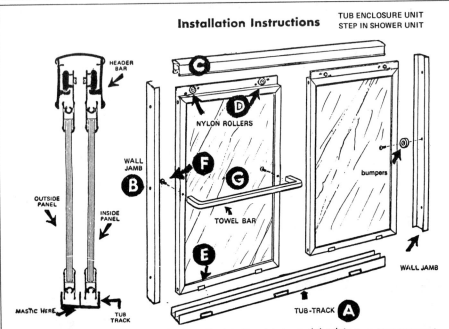

Installation Instructions

TUB ENCLOSURE UNIT
STEP IN SHOWER UNIT

1. Measure from wall to wall on tub rim and cut bottom tub track (A) 3/16" less than measured size. Lay a ribbon of tub mastic or caulk* on underside of track and across both ends. Press down on center of rim, making sure drain holes face inside of tub.

2. Put a bead of any commercial caulking* on back of wall jamb (B) and install on wall, pushing jamb down tight to tub rim and bottom track in corner. Drill a hole in tile thru center hole in jamb with 3/16" tile bit. Insert plastic plug in hole; attach bumper to 8x1" screw and insert screw in plastic plug, making sure jamb is plumb vertically. Repeat with other jamb.

3. Measure from wall to wall on top of wall jambs and cut header to size. Lay header (C) on top of wall jambs.

4. Install nylon rollers (D) in top holes of wide side of panels. Tap nylon silencers (E) on bottom of panels.

5. Lift each panel and install in top of header bar. Roll panels to test. Panels can be adjusted by shifting rollers to other holes if necessary. If panels roll easily drill the rest of the holes in tile. Insert plugs and screw in jambs and tighten.

6. Attach towel bars (G) to shower door panel frames by inserting self-tapping screw (F) through hole in glazing frame and into slot provided in towel bar end and tightening screw.†

   LET BOTTOM TRACK MASTIC DRY BEFORE USING WATER. Keep clean and bright with damp cloth. If bathtub is over 3/8" off level, a wedge filler may be used.

   TOOLS NEEDED: Ruler, screw driver, hacksaw, drill, 3/16" masonry drill bit and pencil.

* A tube of mastic or tub caulk and caulking compound may be purchased from your dealer.

†The shower door you purchase may have a slightly different towel bar and bracket assembly than shown in the diagram but installation is the same.

glass panel, placed a strip of rubber glaze around the edge of the glass, and moved the assembly to the next operation. The next assemblers placed the aluminum frame members around the glaze, and fastened the ends and sides together with screws to form a door. If the enclosures were to be shipped immediately to a customer, the assembled unit was packaged in a corrogated box with its accessories and carried by forklift truck to the shipping ramp. If the unit was for inventory, it was boxed and placed on a pallet to be moved to storage.

The sequence of assembly and approximate times for each operation are shown in Exhibit 4. The building layout is depicted in Exhibit 5 and the

EXHIBIT 4
Operations and Estimated Times to Produce Four Typical Enclosures

	Operations	No. of Parts (four enclosures)	Time (minutes) (four enclosures)
1.	Unwrap, saw sides, 3 at a time, move 16 to punch	16	6
2.	Unwrap, saw tops, 3 at a time, move 8 to punch	8	3
3.	Unwrap, saw bottoms, 3 at a time, move 8 to assembly area	8	3
4.	Punch tops, move 8 to assembly area	8	4
5.	Punch bottoms, move 8 to assembly area	8	2
6.	Glaze glasses, 1 at a time, move to assembly area	8	8
7.	Assemble doors, 1 at a time	2	16*
8.	Move doors to boxing area	2	1
9.	Unwrap, punch tub-track, 1 at a time	4	4
10.	Move 4 tub-track to wrapping table	4	¼
11.	Unwrap, punch jambs, 1 at a time	8	8
12.	Move 8 jambs to wrapping table	8	¼
13.	Unwrap, move 4 headers to wrapping table	4	1
14.	Unwrap, saw towel bars, 4 at a time	4	1
15.	Bend towel bars and move 8 to wrapping table	4	4
16.	Wrap tub-track, 2 jambs, header, and towel bar	4	20
17.	Place 4 sets in rack	4	¼
18.	Bag 4 miscellaneous parts bags, 1 at a time	4	16
19.	Move 4 parts bags to boxing area	4	¼
20.	Assemble in carton, staple carton, and place on fork lift truck		16*

Note: Material is moved to storage from Door 2 by forklift truck. Aluminum is moved sometimes by hand cart and sometimes by forklift truck to the first operations. About 10 to 100 pieces are moved at a time. One hundred panels of glass are moved by forklift truck to glazing.
* Requires two workers.

arrangement of the production and assembly areas is indicated in Exhibit 6. All material was received at door 2 and then moved to its designated area by forklift truck.

The finished units were shipped by Coral's trailer trucks to customers throughout the Northeast, the Midwest, and the lower Mississippi Valley states. A trailer load ranged from 350 to 450 units. Small orders (one–ten units) were shipped by common carrier.

EXHIBIT 5
Plant Layout

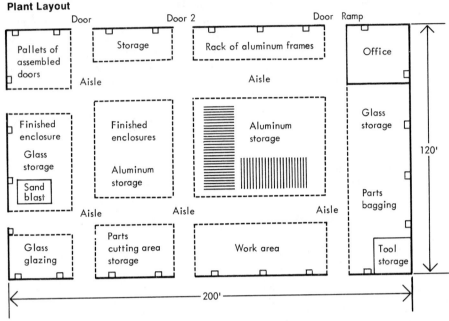

EXHIBIT 6
Layout of Production Area

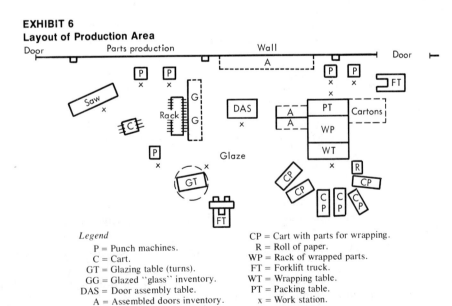

Legend

P = Punch machines.
C = Cart.
GT = Glazing table (turns).
GG = Glazed "glass" inventory.
DAS = Door assembly table.
A = Assembled doors inventory.

CP = Cart with parts for wrapping.
R = Roll of paper.
WP = Rack of wrapped parts.
FT = Forklift truck.
WT = Wrapping table.
PT = Packing table.
x = Work station.

During the transition of shifting Coral's base of operations from New Jersey to St. Louis, production activities were maintained at both locations. With a combined work force of 25 to 30 workers, Coral's production rates were such that sales efforts had to be stepped up sharply to avoid an excessive inventory buildup. Some regular customers were persuaded to buy more units primarily through price discounts, but Coral also used the extra production to furnish samples to new potential customers in the Midwest and lower Mississippi Valley states where it was trying to build a new clientele. When the New Jersey plant was closed and the move to St. Louis was completed, production rates and sales efforts returned to "normal." Twelve workers were engaged in producing 105 enclosures during an eight-hour shift; such production levels supported about $60,000 per month in sales. Mr. Pilsch indicated that Coral was striving to maintain an inventory backlog of about $30,000 in finished goods so as to stabilize production activities and keep order-to-shipment times down to two weeks.

Because of Coral's current lack of profitability, Pilsch was investigating the feasibility of combining Coral's production activities with the production efforts of Midwest's other subsidiary in the same building. This would allow workers to be transferred from line to line as sales fluctuated. Both operations employed unskilled workers, many of whom were hired "off the street" and "trained" in a day or two. In Pilsch's view, the ease with which Coral could hire employees allowed the company to expand or contract production rates with only a small loss of productivity. However, management's reliance on work force flexibility and overtime caused a high level of labor turnover. In turn, the high turnover led to increased breakage in the movement of glass by inexperienced forklift truck operators, together with a higher rate of defects in workmanship. However, these problems were not believed serious enough to warrant changes in Coral's work scheduling policies.

Coral paid its regular production employees a wage of $2.75 per hour. Workers were informed each morning of the types and amounts of each enclosure to be produced that day. Close supervisory practices were not followed and employees were told to shift from work station to work station as needed to keep production moving.

SALES

No sales personnel were employed by Coral; instead, the company relied upon 16 representatives and agents to generate sales from mail-order houses, discount houses and, in smaller amounts, to retail lumber dealers. These representatives were paid a 5 percent commission on their sales. However, Mr. Pilsch made sales calls—via a WATS line and on road trips—to some of the larger accounts.

Listed on the top of the next page are Coral's monthly sales from January 1974 through June 1975:

	Total Sales ($000s)		Total Sales ($000s)
1974		**1975**	
January	$50	January	$47
February	50	February	31
March	61	March	67
April	47	April	71
May	46	May	31
June	76	June	61
July	83		
August	83		
September	98		
October	58		
November	59		
December	66		

The "Open Orders" sheets for June (one page of nine pages of "Open Orders" is shown in Exhibit 7) contained a list of unshipped orders of almost $65,000 from about 60 customers. Seven customers accounted for 75 percent of the unfilled orders. Most of the parts on order were sold at retail prices to replace damaged parts of installed enclosures. Mr. Pilsch had recently obtained from a large mail-order house a "substantial" contract for orders to start in fall 1975.

Since its move from New Jersey, Coral had been increasingly troubled by requests from customers in the northeastern area. Whereas in the past the company often had orders for 100 units or more from each of several customers in the Northeast (with total sales in the Northeast of about $50,000 a month), sales to northeastern customers dropped to about $25,000 per month in 1975. More and more orders from these customers were just for one, two, or three odd-sized or customized units. Some wanted immediate delivery and others telephoned collect to change specifications or time of delivery. In one case, an order for 300 units was received, and was produced and loaded; just prior to shipment a phone call was received to delay delivery. The loaded trailer sat for almost a week at the siding awaiting shipping instructions. Mr. Pilsch attributed part of the drop in sales to customers in the Northeast to competition from former employees at the old New Jersey plant who had gone to work for other tub and shower door firms in the northeastern United States.

Because of these developments, Mr. Pilsch was considering eliminating any concessions to obtain business in the Northeast. Many of the small orders being received were for special-sized enclosures for old homes. This was in contrast to the high percentage of sales of "standard" units to Coral's customers in the South and Midwest where relatively more new homes were being built. In addition, Mr. Pilsch felt that changes might be needed in Coral's delivery policies on northeastern shipments. To charge Coral's full delivery costs on units shipped to customers in the Northeast would tend to

EXHIBIT 7
Open Orders as of 6/20/75

Customer Number	Order Number	Date Ordered	Quantity	Type	Unit Price	Amount Unshipped
1730	01199	6/16/75	2	66s30gtg	25.00	50.00
						11,875.45
1794	00831-7	5/27/75	1	50csampl	20.00	20.00
1794	00831-7	5/27/75	1	66ssampl	20.00	20.00
1794	00958-7	6/20/75	10	66s24tg	23.87	238.70
1794	00958-7	6/20/75	6	50k58tg	31.33	187.98
1794	00958-7	6/20/75	1	160PTG	101.97	101.97
						568.65
2025	Verbal	6/18/75	1	50ktgsam		
2025	Verbal	6/18/75	1	66stgsam		
2028	Verbal	3/05/75	6	Panels		
2028	Verbal	5/16/75	6	Parts	.75	4.50
2028	Verbal	5/16/75	100	Rollers	.30	30.00
2028	751	6/18/75	50	25ce46tg	28.65	1,432.50
2028	751	6/18/75	50	66sparts	.65	32.50
2028	751	6/18/75	44,693	Parts		
2028	751	6/18/75	44,693	Parts		
2028	751	6/18/75	6	T.Glass	7.82	46.92
						1,546.42
2031	Verbal	5/14/75	20	Parts		
2031	Verbal	5/14/75	20,063	Glazing		
2035	Verbal	6/03/75	24	Rollers		
2035	Verbal	6/03/75	2	66s33tg	21.55	43.10
2035	Verbal	6/03/75	3	25c42tg	31.11	93.33
2035	Verbal	6/03/75	4	25c42tg	31.11	124.44
2035	Verbal	6/03/75	10	50ctg	26.11	261.10
2035	Verbal	6/03/75	6	66S24tg	19.89	119.34
2035	Verbal	6/03/75	2	66S28tg	21.55	43.10
2035	Verbal	6/19/75	1	Parts	2.80	2.80
2035	Verbal	6/19/75	2	Parts	.75	1.50
						688.71
2060	Verbal	5/21/75	42	Parts	1.50	63.00
2060	Verbal	5/28/75	1	50cssm		
2060	Verbal	5/28/75	1	50cssm		
						63.00
2140	12029	3/06/75	18	50c	24.90	448.20
2140	Verbal	5/01/75	1	25cetg		
2140	Verbal	5/01/75	1	50cdtg		
						448.20

price the units out of the market. It was about an 950-mile trip one way to make deliveries and with the growing number of small orders, it took many more orders and careful scheduling to make it economically feasible for Coral to send one of its tractor trailers with a shipment to the Northeast. Coral had only five trailers and two tractors in its fleet and a trip to the

EXHIBIT 8

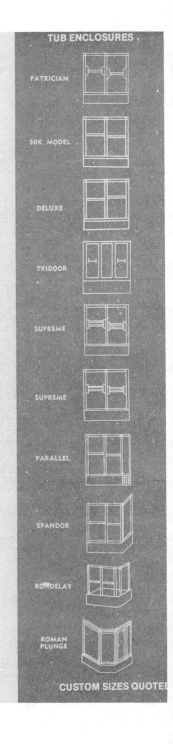

TUB ENCLOSURES

50P/46P/56P PATRICIAN and enclosure that features smooth-faced extrusions and gives this unit the Luxury Look. Three adjustable roller positions and 'E' channel wall jambs permit more effective installation.
46P, 50P $72.18   56P $82.17

50K MODEL An excellent value in an economy bath. Tub enclosure, bright anodized finish--smooth or rough semi-obscure tempered glass--overhead suspension--two towel bars standard equipment $52.22

50 CD/ 46CD/ 56CD Same as above. Popular enclosure with sliding glass panels designed for all standard recessed tubs. Decorator designed chrome brackets make this unit distinctive.
46CD/ 50CD $68.89   56CD $75.56

50R TRIDOOR For the housewife-mother who needs additional room for "bathing babies"--a sturdily-designed three-panel enclosure made with the same attention to construction as our other models--bright anodization, 7/32" glass, ball-bearing rollers, towel bars. Available in a number of standard sizes and also to specific measurements. Two-thirds of bathtub area is made available with this enclosure. $89.95

50X/ 46X/ 56X SUPREME A Bathtub Enclosure that is the ultimate in design and engineering, allowing each glass panel to be positioned in double overhead track with absolute ease. Extra heavy extrusions are "evalumed" by a process of high polishing and electrolytic anodizing, combined with bright dipping.
46X/ 50X $122.22   56X $144.44

50XA/ 46XA/ 56XA SUPREME Same as above except with patented two-part adjustable bottom track and two adjustable side jambs.
46XA/ 50XA $133.33   56XA $155.55

140P PARALLEL Two sliding doors operating on overhead suspension plus one adjacent stationary panel (at 180 degrees to sliding doors). Specify location of panel from point of view of facing tub. Used also to close in area when tile parapet is built at tub end. . ,. $119.95

150P SPANDOR Two sliding doors operating on overhead suspension with one stationary panel at right angle to sliding doors (90 degree angle). Designed for an open end tub with square corner. Specify location of shower head and whether end panel is to right or left of tub when facing it.
$139.95

160P RONDELAY Two sliding doors operating on overhead suspension with two stationary panels. Designed for open end tub with 135 degree angles. Specify location of shower head and whether panels are to right or left of tub when facing it. $169.95

170P ROMAN PLUNGE Designed to enclose the popular corner tub. Hinged door with three stationary panels.
$179.50

PATRICIAN

50K MODEL

DELUXE

TRIDOOR

SUPREME

SUPREME

PARALLEL

SPANDOR

RONDELAY

ROMAN PLUNGE

CUSTOM SIZES QUOTED

Northeast from St. Louis consumed three days, thereby delaying shipments of other orders. In comparison, Coral had one chainstore customer in Kentucky and another in Kansas City each of whom ordered a truckload a month and could be serviced in a day's time.

Between 60 percent and 65 percent of Coral's orders were for the 50C style of enclosure and another 20 to 25 percent were for the 25C style. Within each of these styles were variations of size and decoration. Exhibit 8 shows the design features and prices on one page of a four-page brochure, dated November 1, 1974, sent to potential customers. Coral had two flyers which it mailed out to potential customers. One, of eight pages, (Exhibit 2) displayed pictures with reading material about the enclosures and a diagram of the construction of Coral's enclosures. The other flyer (Exhibit 8) listed various models and included the price list.

Mr. Pilsch endeavored to make sales forecasts as a basis for future planning. He did not have great confidence in being able to make reliable forecasts because the company had been in business such a short time and because sales had varied so greatly from month to month. The surge in sales during the last four months of 1974 when both the St. Louis and New Jersey plants were in production created even more of a distortion. Nonetheless, Pilsch believed Coral Industries had a bright future. More new homes in the Midwest and South were being built with shower and tub enclosures. And while Coral faced stiff competition from several much larger producers, Pilsch believed that Coral's small size gave it more flexibility to act quickly in obtaining sales and new customers.

INVENTORY AND DATA PROCESSING

Midwest charged Coral Industries a fixed fee for data processing and the creation of management information systems. Midwest had had in-house computer capability since 1969 and, in April 1975, placed in operation a new IBM System 32 machine to replace a higher rent, less flexible computer which had previously been used to serve all of Midwest's companies and divisions.

Coral had a terminal which was used to input data into Midwest's IBM System 32 and which received some of the printouts. Most of the computer runs were printed out in Midwest's computer center and hand-carried to Coral—about one eighth of a mile. Regular records were kept for accounts receivable, accounts payable, inventory, open orders, and financial statement preparation. Coral received weekly printouts of open orders and inventory. Midwest had the programming capability to prepare computerized reports and information on almost any kind of item that may concern any of its division managers. When a division requested a new kind of computerized report, the necessary programming was done by Midwest; Midwest then checked with the division to make sure that all of the desired information was being developed and that the printout format was satisfactory.

Coral's parts inventory status report showed an item description, the beginning balance (number of units or pieces on hand), additions and deletions, the current balance, unit cost, and the dollar value of each item held in inventory. About 575 items were listed on the inventory report, although Coral did not always keep stocks of every item listed. Coral's April 30, 1975 inventory report showed an inventory for 360 of the 575 items listed; 170 items showed a transaction for the current week—all deletions. Coral had 25 items with an inventory value of $2,500 or more; these 25 items accounted for about $133,000 of the total inventory value of $325,000.

Additions to parts inventory were made to the inventory record from the receipt slip for material received. Deletions were made at the end of the period from production records of output. The computer received the coded identification of the items produced and the parts shipped, "exploded" the enclosures into the parts needed, added the separate parts shipped and computed the deletions from inventory for each part for the period.

The report formed the basis for purchases during the coming period. Upon receipt of the inventory listing, Mr. Pilsch checked to determine if any items need to be replenished. Then as orders were received, the inventory list was checked again to determine if the specific parts needed were in stock. If not, the existing inventory, the current order, and estimates of future orders were used to determine the size of purchase order to issue.

The largest volume and cost of items in inventory were in the aluminum framing and glass. Most of Coral's aluminum framing was purchased from a supplier in the St. Louis area which had the dies needed to extrude the strips. Coral was a relatively small customer of the aluminum framing supplier and, until recently, it took three to five months for Coral to get delivery on its orders; in early 1975 the supply situation had eased to the point where deliveries were received in two to three months. The glass items were obtained from several suppliers and the delivery lead time was about one to two months. Most of the small items such as screws were standard items obtainable quickly from several sources. Even though Coral was small, it had been able to obtain discounts for purchasing in truckload lots. On all items, it tried to obtain the best price.

Mr. Pilsch indicated that a substantial portion of Coral's inventory had been included as part of Midwest's purchase of Closure Co. Much of this inventory included small quantities of parts which did not fit the enclosures now made. Pilsch estimated that the total value of "obsolete" inventory on the books plus that of slow-moving items was between $75,000 and $100,000.

Incoming shipments of aluminum framing were received in bundles of about 500 pieces; the bundle contained six smaller, individually wrapped packages of aluminum strips. Glass for the enclosures came in bound in palletized wood crates of about 100 "lights"; the crates had paper between each glass panel, boards to protect the glass from breakage, and steel bands around each crate. A typical crate of glass panels weighed about 3,000 pounds.

COMPETITION AND PRICING

With the advent of discount stores and mail-order houses, the business of selling shower doors and tub enclosures became quite competitive. Many buyers, especially homebuilders, were very price conscious. According to Pilsch, most small contractors who build low- and medium-priced homes on a speculative basis (that is, homes not pre-sold prior to construction) are not concerned about the quality of the product. They want the lowest priced unit which looks good. Pilsch said that while there were a number of cost-saving ways for holding the price of tub and shower enclosures down, most of them also decreased the quality. Pilsch averred that he did not want to have Coral get a reputation for poor quality and, consequently, was seeking to maintain a level of production quality that he felt was "good." However, Pilsch admitted that Closure had had a poor reputation for quality with some of its past customers, and that it had been hard for Coral to get these customers back. Pilsch further observed that different sections of the country had different conceptions of what was good quality and what was poor quality. As general manager of Coral, Pilsch took the brunt of customer complaints about quality. In one instance, a customer called Coral, asked for Pilsch and said "you cut the bars too short." Pilsch remarked to the casewriter, "Of course, I did not but I am the goat. This is the problem of a small business. I am identified with the product of the company whereas a large company has people lower in the organization to handle the problems."

Exhibit 8 shows the suggested retail prices of a number of Coral's enclosures. Discounts were given to customers according to the schedule below:

Number of Units Ordered	Discount from Retail List Price
1–49	40% + buyer pays a shipping charge
50–100	50
over 100	55

Although material costs had averaged 35 percent of selling price when Closure owned the company, Mr. Pilsch noted that he was trying to keep material costs at or below 58 percent of selling price. He estimated that Coral's cost for a typical 50C enclosure was composed as follows:

Aluminum strips	$12.00
Glass	6.35
Other materials	3.00
Labor and overhead	6.50
Boxing for shipment	1.02
	$28.87

EXHIBIT 9
Income Statement June 30, 1975

Description	This Month To-Date	Last Month To-Date	Current Month
Sales and Cost of Goods Sold			
Sales	$ 423,368.97	$ 362,006.00	$ 61,362.97
Sales discounts	(3,094.67)	(2,847.98)	(246.69)
Sales scrap	5,240.00	5,240.00	—
Net Sales	425,514.30	364,398.02	61,116.28
Beginning inventory	481,742.89	481,742.89	
Materials purchased	222,812.48	203,316.10	19,496.33
Purchases discounts	(28.01)	(23.65)	(4.16)
Inter-dept charges	2,061.83	2,061.83	
Freight & cartage	8,445.71	7,806.95	638.76
Ending inventory	(360,197.12)	(379,471.01)	19,273.89
Net Materials	354,837.78	315,432.91	39,404.87
Shop wages	67,312.20	61,208.04	6,104.16
Plant management salaries	15,236.00	13,892.00	1,344.00
Shop supplies & expense	12,056.72	10,522.07	1,534.65
Shop equipment rental	2,364.00	2,144.00	220.00
Shop miscellaneous	233.00	163.10	69.90
Net Labor	97,201.92	87,929.21	9,272.71
Gross Profit	(26,525.40)	(38,964.10)	12,438.70
Operating Expense-Direct			
Building & equipment repair	3,183.72	3,183.72	
Depreciation	5,426.16	4,747.89	678.27
Hazard insurance..............................	6,498.00	6,498.00	
Licenses & taxes-business use tax, franchise	524.50	524.50	
Miscellaneous	818.00	818.00	
Payroll tax	5,451.55	4,740.99	710.56
Rent	20,800.00	18,200.00	2,600.00
Sales commissions	20,665.90	19,302.59	1,363.31
Telephone & telegraph	6,107.89	5,579.05	528.84
Truck & automobile expense	5,459.06	5,459.06	
Utilities	6,490.01	7,240.01	(750.00)
Total Operating Expense—Direct	81,424.79	76,293.81	5,130.98
Operating Expense-Indirect			
Salaries-other	6,027.89	5,467.89	560.00
Advertising	9,427.87	8,802.34	625.53
Group insurance premiums	433.74	414.30	19.44
Janitorial services	1,451.59	1,451.59	
Office equipment rental	512.78	405.32	107.46
Office supplies & expense.....................	1,685.53	1,513.47	172.06
Professional service-adult & tax	1,989.75	1,989.75	
Professional service-legal & administrative	(1,000.00)	(1,000.00)	
Travel & entertainment	5,450.85	5,063.29	387.56
Miscellaneous	150.39	150.39	
Rental automotive	4,748.15	4,557.15	191.00
Total Operating Expense—Indirect	30,878.54	28,815.49	2,063.05
Total Operating Expense	112,303.33	105,109.30	7,194.03
Net Profit or Loss	$(138,828.73)	$(144,073.40)	$ 5,244.67
Other Income			
Interest income................................	245.09	148.00	97.09
Miscellaneous	72.04	72.04	—
Bad debt recovery	879.70	879.70	—
	1,196.83	1,099.74	97.09
Other Deductions			
Bad debts.....................................	(329.92)	(329.92)	—
Contributions	(50.00)	(50.00)	—
Interest	(47,261.12)	(21,399.52)	(25,861.60)
	(47,641.04)	(21,779.44)	(25,861.60)
Net Income or (Loss)	$(185,272.94)	$(164,753.10)	$(20,519.84)

FINANCIAL STATISTICS

Exhibit 9 shows Coral's income statement for the months of May and June 1975 and for the first eight months of fiscal 1975. However, Mr. Pilsch indicated that these figures were not entirely representative, owing to some continuing holdover costs associated with moving from New Jersey to St. Louis. Rent of $2,000 per month on the New Jersey plant was still being paid because the lease did not expire until July 1975. Utility expenses would also drop by $600 per month when the New Jersey plant lease expired. Furthermore, said Pilsch, Coral would not have to incur any additional closing or start-up expenses such as been incurred in the January through May 1975 period. Nor would the company have to furnish as many more samples of its product line to potential customers in the Midwest and lower Mississippi Valley states in an effort to get itself established in its new market area. However, Coral's sizable interest expenses, which were mainly for the loan obtained to purchase the Closure Company, were expected to continue for the immediate future. Nonetheless, Mr. Pilsch was fairly confident that July 1975 would be profitable, given that both management and its employees had more experience in company operations. However, the casewriter was not so sure that July would be as profitable as Mr. Pilsch seemed to believe.

22. Better Burgers, Inc.*

THE Better Burgers, Inc., unit on East Boulevard in Sunshine City, Florida, was established nearly a decade ago, largely with the hope of capitalizing on the appetites of the numerous visitors patronizing a well-known tourist attraction located across the street. The East Boulevard unit was one of ten (plus two more under construction) Better Burgers outlets in and about Sunshine City, all owned by Mr. Alan Greene. These units together achieved sales of some $2.5 million last year. Mr. Greene's Better Burgers units represented only one small geographic segment of the international Better Burgers, Inc., franchised chain, consisting of approximately 2,200 outlets which last year surpassed $1 billion in total sales.

Although Alan Greene was, overall, quite well satisfied with the growth and success of his ten Better Burgers franchise units, he was currently reviewing the operations of several particular outlets in order to improve performance even more. Among these units was the East Boulevard location, and Greene had called in one of his four supervisors, Jim Pentland, to help interpret survey data recently obtained from customers patronizing this outlet. Along with information from standard Better Burgers, Inc., operations analysis forms and financial statements, the survey results indicated several areas in which steps could be taken in order to increase sales, customer satisfaction, and profits at the East Boulevard unit.

After a preliminary examination of all available written information, Mr. Greene planned to discuss past performance and future goals with Mr. Kerry Thomas, manager of the East Boulevard unit. Kerry had been one of the best performers in Greene's organization for almost ten years. Moreover, Greene had found that Kerry liked to "be his own boss," operating largely autonomously during the periods between these joint performance evaluation and goal-setting sessions—unless extremely unusual circumstances arose.

Ever since attending a recent Rotary Club dinner meeting where a professor from the nearby university presented a speech on the latest management concepts, Greene had been somewhat disturbed over whether his philosophy of highly centralized control was becoming obsolete. After a great deal of "soul-searching," Greene had decided to make the transformation to a more

---

* Prepared by Mr. J. Owen Weber and Professor Kenneth R. Van Voorhis of the University of South Florida. The name and location of the company are disguised.

"behaviorally oriented approach," giving his ten unit managers more freedom in running their operations.

THE FAST-FOOD FRANCHISING INDUSTRY

Few forms of business endeavor have enjoyed as rapid a rise in success and popularity as has the fast-foods franchising industry. From a virtually insignificant position in the restaurant industry 20 years ago, fast foods grew to account for annual sales of approximately $6.4 billion by 1972. Fast-foods franchising executives were quick to suggest that a number of factors augur well for a continued skyrocketing of fast-food sales. In addition to steadily increasing population numbers, rising incomes, more plentiful leisure time, and greater mobility, the ever-busy schedules of typical American families characterize a society which is continuously on the move—factors which dictate an ever-increasing demand for meals away from home, with a special emphasis on quick and reliable service.

Complementing the sharp rise in demand for fast-foods service and the improving technology which made possible the satisfaction of market demands was the increasing number of people who saw franchising as a means of starting their own businesses and becoming their own bosses. Over 500,000 franchised business outlets of various types now generate approximately $100 billion in annual sales. The staff of *Fortune* magazine recently estimated that nearly 90 percent of all existing franchise operations (not limited to fast-foods enterprises) have been started since 1954. A large segment of this "franchise boom," of course, is represented by the multitudes of fast-foods franchises.

Why has this form of business enterprise been so popular? The Bank of America has compiled a list of 17 benefits often cited by proponents:

1. Allows the investor to open a business without prior experience.
2. Less capital is needed by both parties.
3. Ease of access to financial assistance.
4. Consumer-accepted image of trademarks, brand names, etc.
5. Maintenance of quality standards.
6. Combined buying power.
7. Basic training provided, followed by continued assistance.
8. Location or site analysis.
9. Financial capability to buy choice sites.
10. Advantageous rental and leasing rates.
11. Well-designed facilities, fixtures, displays, and supplies.
12. Managerial and records assistance.
13. Sales, advertising, and marketing assistance.
14. National publicity, promotion, and recognition.
15. Higher income potential.
16. Lower risk of failure.
17. Continual research and development.

The most visible support provided by the major franchisor is the national advertising campaign. Better Burgers, Inc., and its major competitors in the fast-foods segment of the franchising industry, devote many millions of dollars of their annual budgets to this end. But even more vital to neophyte franchisees who have had little or no prior business experience are the operating system guidelines, the training, and the continued management assistance.

Fast-foods franchising entrepreneurs have been quick to capitalize upon consumer demand for inexpensive meals away from home which can be served rapidly and with consistent standards by opening up new units at locations all across the country as rapidly as possible. It is generally conceded in the industry that no firm has done so more successfully than Better Burgers.

BETTER BURGERS, INC., PARENT CORPORATION

Better Burgers, Inc. enjoys the distinction of being the largest single organization in the highly competitive fast-foods franchising industry. Battling over 300 franchising organizations with more than 30,000 combined units, Better Burgers' outlets managed to attract over one fifth of the industrywide sales of over $6 billion last year. While a number of firms in this volatile business have found the going extremely tough or have closed their doors permanently (with primary hopes for success based, perhaps, only on a celebrity's name), Better Burgers, Inc., has enjoyed sales increases on the order of 30 percent or better during the last several years.

A profile of the major characteristics of this organization is considered by many in the industry as the standard to emulate or to modify as specific circumstances dictate. A recent study of the Better Burgers organization conducted by the staff of *Fortune* magazine developed the following picture of its major attributes:

1. Nationwide operation.
2. Approximately 2,200 retail outlets.
3. Annual sales of over $1 billion.
4. Corporate training center for franchisees.
5. Franchise operator's manual 400 pages long.
6. Significant percentage of company-owned stores.
7. Team of field service managers who call on franchisees regularly.
8. Well-developed system of management controls.
9. Institutional advertising program conducted on a national basis.

Moreover, the "typical" retail outlet in this system is described as one which:

1. Requires an initial franchise fee of $100,000 or more paid to the franchisor (Better Burgers, Inc., parent corporation).

2. Has annual gross sales of over $450,000.
3. Employs 35 people.
4. Is open for business 84 hours per week.
5. Has "a battery of complex measuring and cooking machines."
6. Has "a huge turnover of fresh and frozen food inventory."
7. Earns annual profits of $50,000 to $75,000.

And, finally, the "average" Better Burgers owner-operator, as described recently by a high-level BBI corporate executive, is one who:

1. Is older than 35 years of age.
2. Has worked his way up in another business.
3. Has a tidy bank account.
4. Is "good with people."
5. Will follow the Better Burgers system.
6. Appears to have "potential for success."

Of these owner-operator characteristics, it may be the fifth one which is most important. In its initial discussions with a prospective franchisee, the parent corporation emphasizes that, "Better Burgers, Inc. isn't selling food so much as it is a system. The food just isn't that good!" The system, of course, offers a "total experience" to the (family) customer; and to the franchisee it provides the benefits cited previously if the franchise unit is well operated. But BBI executives insist that they follow their system more effectively than their competitors—even conducting special in-depth courses at their "Hamburger University" where every new outlet manager must acquire all the skills and knowledge necessary to earn a "Bachelor of Hamburgerology, with a minor in French Fries." Veteran owners and managers attend training sessions covering advanced operations. Continuing "consulting" services from the parent corporation help each franchisee or company operator to solve special problems encountered, in addition to helping maintain a high level of "QSC" (quality, service, and cleanliness) in all units.

Much of the credit for selling billions of hamburgers, say BBI executives, must be attributed to the careful development of an "image" and the appropriate advertising campaigns to maintain and exploit this image. Some $40 million was devoted to national advertising last year alone. This large advertising outlay was financed out of a monthly "service fee" which each owner-operator pays to the BBI parent corporation, as stipulated by the franchise agreements. The total service fee amounts to 11.5 percent of monthly sales.

Aside from anticipating a sizable profit on the initial BBI unit, those owner-operators who "follow the system" and perform well are usually rewarded by being offered opportunities to open additional Better Burgers outlets when new sites are secured by the parent corporation. Alan Greene regarded this clause in his franchise agreement as being one of the most important.

ALAN GREENE'S BETTER BURGERS UNITS

Before Better Burgers, Inc., started to franchise units, Alan Greene owned a clothing store located in a suburb of Chicago. Greene watched with considerable interest the opening and operation of one of the earliest Better Burgers units across the street from his own store. When personal health suggested the advisability of his moving to a warmer climate, he decided to look seriously into the possibility of obtaining a Better Burgers franchise rather than opening a new clothing store in a southern city.

In January, 16 years ago, Mr. Greene secured a franchise from Better Burgers, Inc., to open a new unit in Sunshine City, Florida. With Greene, his wife, sons, and daughter comprising the nucleus of the work force for this first location, business began to thrive. After two and half years of success at the initial Sunshine City unit, the acceptance of an offer for another location from BBI, and considerable negotiation with various bankers to arrange the necessary financing, Alan Greene's second unit was constructed and opened. Over the next two years, business continued to improve steadily. Again, Greene was offered another location opportunity by the BBI regional representative and formerly reluctant bank executives were this time eager to provide the necessary financing.

Alan Greene was convinced that a site location on East Boulevard, situated directly across the street from a new tourist attraction, was far superior to the one actually offered to him. But the BBI "system" was quite difficult to alter, and almost a year passed before approval to change the originally authorized site was secured, financing was arranged, and construction was completed.

In the nine years which followed the opening of the East Boulevard unit, Alan Greene's Better Burgers chain expanded to a total of ten operating outlets—all successful—with plans for the construction of two more units tentatively approved by the franchisor. (See Exhibit 1 for locations of these units.)

Generally adhering closely to the standard "BBI system," Alan Greene made a few modifications of his own which he felt improved the performance of most of his units—some consistently outperformed comparable Better Burgers units managed by other owner-operators across the country. Only once did Greene's decision to buck standard BBI policy really give him cause for concern, perhaps resulting in his losing "several very desirable new site acquisition opportunities" in the Sunshine City area to another BBI franchisee operating in a nearby town. This incident occurred several years ago when Greene refused to accept a new location which the parent corporation wanted to open, insisting that his personal studies indicated several other pieces of property offered greater potential. This disagreement with the research opinions of BBI's real estate appraisal staff, Greene believed, caused the other franchisee to gain the aforementioned new unit instead. Since then, however, Greene has had no major disagreement with BBI representatives or BBI policy.

EXHIBIT 1
Map of Sunshine City, Florida, Depicting Locations of Better Burgers Units

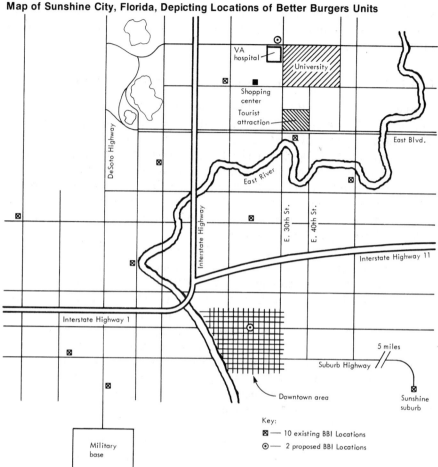

MANAGEMENT PHILOSOPHY

Mr. Greene felt that careful selection of unit managers who, in turn, hire their own employees according to preestablished guidelines was one of the real keys to success. He and Sam Hargrove, his administrative assistant whose talents were secured after Greene opened his second unit, were primarily involved in making policy decisions, arranging financing, contracting for the best possible sources of supply, and overseeing operations for all ten units in the Alan Greene Better Burgers group. In accord with Greene's new management philosophy in coordinating his ten units, each individual manager was encouraged to make as many operating decisions as possible, including the establishing of objectives for sales, unit costs, and profitability. Greene and Hargrove, after consulting with BBI field representatives, spend the bulk of their time finding solutions to special problems rather than maintaining a close scrutiny over day-to-day activities. However, Hargrove traveled around to the group of units regularly (visiting each location at least twice a month) in order to be sure that "lines of communication" remained open and active.

GREENE'S EAST BOULEVARD BETTER BURGERS UNIT

Alan Greene's East Boulevard Better Burgers unit opened its doors a little over nine years ago, and was his third BBI location. Mr. Greene had recognized the desirability of locating a new unit near Sunshine City's new tourist attraction because of its potential for bringing thousands of hungry visitors to a good, reliable, well-known, fast-foods franchise operation. He had secured an option to purchase the needed property long before discussing the possibility of opening a Better Burgers unit here with the BBI field representative, and was quite unyielding in insisting on this location when the franchiser offered a third expansion opportunity.

Just north of the tourist attraction was a small industrial park. The areas to the east, west, and south of the desired site location were largely residential in character. Having won his way with BBI, Mr. Greene had to convince the city council that appropriate rezoning of the chosen piece of property should be considered. Local residents were much opposed and many attended the public hearings on the rezoning request, but the council was "persuaded in a private session" and legal problems subsided. Although some of the immediate neighbors were perhaps angered temporarily by the construction of "another hamburger joint," Mr. Greene felt that most have now come to express a high regard for the appearance and character of the unit. Past surveys have indicated that many of these residents are among the unit's most satisfied customers.

From early sales volumes of about $200,000 annually, the East Boulevard unit has enjoyed rapid growth—spurred, as Mr. Greene had predicted, by the increasing popularity of the tourist attraction. However, the franchise has not totally escaped adversity. Three years ago, in an attempt to kill off what they considered "parasitic businesses," the management of the attraction decided to close its entrance/exit gates which were located directly across the street from the Better Burgers unit. Even though incurring a great deal of expense to their own organization, the tourist attraction relocated the gates on a perpendicular street adjacent to the edge of their property. (See Exhibit 2.) Nonetheless, after what could be considered a very mild slack period, the volume of tourist customers patronizing the East Boulevard unit resumed its upward climb.

Naturally, each of the units in Alan Greene's organization had its own special strong points and weaknesses. It was through such analyses as the one currently being conducted at the East Boulevard unit that these were identified, with the former subsequently being exploited and the latter, hopefully, being circumvented or overcome.

EXHIBIT 2
Site Location and Layout of East Boulevard Better Burgers Unit

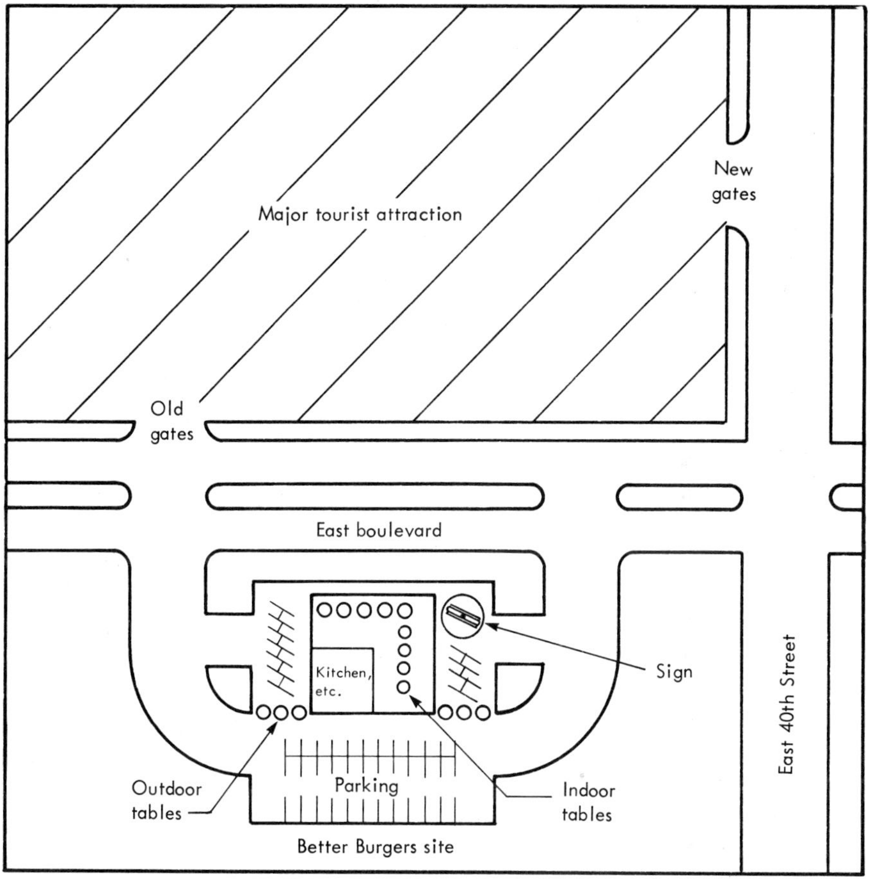

MARKETING

As was true for all Better Burgers units across the country, Alan Greene's East Boulevard unit relied heavily on national franchiser advertising to stimulate customer demand. Similarly, most of the marketing research was conducted by an experienced staff department in the franchiser's headquarters organization, although localized efforts were typically handled by local advertising agencies. Special locations in geographically separated areas of the country were usually selected for test marketing new products, slogans, and signs and also for experimenting with new operating policies and procedures.

However, within the limits prescribed by the franchise agreement, it was Alan Greene's policy to conduct studies and surveys on his own, making whatever changes were suggested by the findings. For instance, what had begun as a single-field survey project of a marketing student at the local university had been picked up and continued as part of Greene's regular periodic review of the operations of each unit. Among the survey questions asked of the customers patronizing a Better Burgers location on a particular day were:

1. Location from which you came to Better Burgers unit.
2. Destination upon leaving Better Burgers unit.
3. Frequency of eating at this Better Burgers unit.
4. Ratings of this Better Burgers unit regarding *(a)* quality, *(b)* service, *(c)* cleanliness.
5. Miscellaneous demographic data, including *(a)* age, *(b)* number in family, *(c)* distance of home from this Better Burgers unit, and *(d)* income range.
6. Familiarity with Better Burgers national advertising slogan and certain current promotional campaigns (when applicable).
7. Desirability of adding new items to usual menu; e.g. *(a)* breakfast, *(b)* fried chicken, or *(c)* roast beef.
8. General suggestions for improvement (open-end question).
9. Miscellaneous questions pertaining to other points of special interests, depending on circumstances of each unit.

The typical format used was a single-page, check-sheet questionnaire which customers could easily complete during the short time they were waiting for their orders to be filled.

Exhibit 3 presents in summary form some of the data gathered in the surveys conducted at the East Boulevard unit during February and July of this year. Both Mr. Greene and Mr. Hargrove were scheduled to go over the results with the unit manager, Mr. Kerry Thomas. The East Boulevard store's ratings on quality, service, and cleanliness were certain to be analyzed carefully in order to identify and explain reasons for changes at this unit over the five-month period.

Mr. Greene stated that the placement of the familiar Better Burgers franchise sign could have been more effective if the dimensions of the East Boulevard piece of property had been slightly different. Instead of being directly adjacent to the street in front of the store, the illuminated sign was at the edge of the parking lot next to the outdoor eating tables. (See Exhibit 2.) While this positioning had been acceptable for a number of years, recent growth of business establishments all along the same side of the street, many of which displayed their own large advertisements and signs, had gradually made the Better Burgers trademark less visible. Further a city ordinance now prohibited movement or elevation of the sign to a more prominent setting.

Mr. Greene's Better Burgers franchise operation spent time and money trying to be a good business citizen in the community, helping to sponsor the "Little League" baseball and Sertoma (Junior Chamber of Commerce) char-

EXHIBIT 3

Results of Consumer Questionnaire Surveys Conducted at East Boulevard Unit

	Quality		Service		Cleanliness		Overall	
	East Blvd.	All	East Blvd.	All	East Blvd.	All	East Blvd.	All
February Survey:								
Excellent	38.58%		61.60%		62.00%			
Good	42.86		32.32		32.30			
Fair	17.14		4.66		4.62			
Poor	1.42		1.42		1.08			
Total	100.00%		100.00%		100.00%			
July Survey:								
Excellent	44.28%	42.86%	64.28%	57.14%	44.28%	45.72%	48.57%	42.86%
Good	45.72	55.72	27.14	41.43	37.14	47.14	50.00	45.72
Fair	8.58	1.42	8.58	1.43	12.86	7.14	1.43	10.00
Poor	1.42	—	—	—	5.72	—	—	1.42
Total	100.00	100.00	100.00	100.00	100.00	100.00	100.00	100.00

ity programs. Mr. Greene believed that such activities helped to promote a good image for the BBI units. While these image-boosting efforts certainly were very limited in comparison to the national advertising campaigns conducted by the franchiser, Mr. Greene had concluded that his efforts to enhance his acceptability on the local level had been helpful.

Each unit manager was strongly urged to participate in suggesting ideas for innovative local marketing programs. Greene employed a local advertising agency to help develop and coordinate these plans with the efforts of the national franchiser organization.

Although general product pricing guidelines were established by the national franchise headquarters, each franchise owner had a certain latitude in raising or lowering specific prices in accordance with local conditions—particularly reflecting competitors' prices and operating costs. Over the past three years, prices at the East Boulevard Better Burgers' unit had been increased 20 percent. While only a few customers had actually complained or made negative comments, Mr. Greene tried to maintain "readings" on the market's reactions to price changes. Kerry Thomas, unit manager, stated that the units biggest competition was not so much from other franchises or independent operators as from two of Greene's other Better Burgers units, located approximately two miles to the northeast and southwest. (See map in Exhibit 1.)

Greene was of the opinion that point-of-purchase displays probably constituted the major supplement to nationally sponsored television and radio advertising. These displays called attention to particular products and were aimed at customers who had gained a general awareness of the Better Burgers image through other sources. Special programs promoting selected menu items were established at various times of the year, depending on current and projected sales trends. For example, the East Boulevard unit had promoted cheeseburgers during June and milk shakes during December of the year just ended. Furthermore, numerous point-of-purchase displays were used to announce the offering of any new additions to the menu. If customer response during these special campaigns did not produce relatively high-volume levels the new items were discontinued, while those which were successful became permanent menu features.

Other advertising efforts for Greene's Better Burgers units included occasional ads in student newspapers at the nearby university and local high schools and limited use of direct mail solicitations. Most popular of the direct mail efforts were coupons which could be redeemed for a free item from the menu. Survey results revealed that over 50 percent of the coupons redeemed were brought in by customers who had not been in the store during the previous three-month period.

Greene had a hunch that coupon advertising might be particularly useful at the East Boulevard unit where sales correlated highly with the tourist seasons. (See Exhibit 4.) At a recent managers' meeting, a great deal of concern was expressed over this pronounced seasonality and the unit's in-

EXHIBIT 4

Comparison of Monthly Sales Patterns for Latest Fiscal Year and Five-Year Average

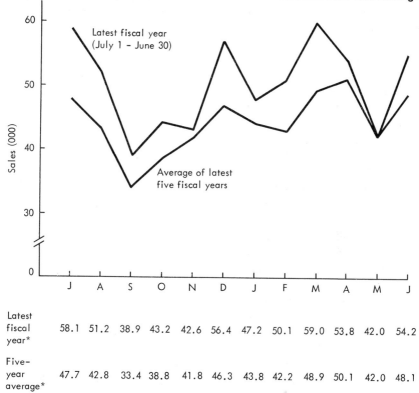

	J	A	S	O	N	D	J	F	M	A	M	J
Latest fiscal year*	58.1	51.2	38.9	43.2	42.6	56.4	47.2	50.1	59.0	53.8	42.0	54.2
Five-year average*	47.7	42.8	33.4	38.8	41.8	46.3	43.8	42.2	48.9	50.1	42.0	48.1

* Figures stated in thousands of dollars.

ability to penetrate significantly the surrounding residential areas. At the conclusion of the meeting, Mr. Greene offered a bonus to anyone who formulated a plan which would alleviate the store's dependence on tourists. So far, however, no plan had been forthcoming.

PROCUREMENT AND INVENTORY CONTROL

Better Burgers franchisees, by contractual agreement, purchase a number of standard supplies as well as virtually all equipment through the franchiser corporation. While the purchases of meats, breads, drinks, and other perishable items are negotiated privately between franchisees and local vendors, the BBI "field consultants" have as one of their primary concerns the maintaining of the national image of Better Burgers quality.

All of Alan Greene's units were supplied from the same sources, including a single commercial meat market and a single area bakery, except for minor "emergency" shortage replenishments. Although Mr. Greene wondered from time to time whether more dependable deliveries and more favorable purchase terms might be secured by utilizing multiple vendors, the Better Burgers, Inc., field consultant advised him to continue to deal with just one local source for each type of item needed. The consultant noted that single sourcing allowed for expert selection of ingredients from the manufacturers, provision of storage and transportation services, assumption of risks due to sudden price changes, damage, or spoilage, and more favorable credit arrangements.

Inventory control was considered extremely important in any successful fast-foods business, and Mr. Greene devoted more of his personal time to reviewing this aspect of his unit managers' operations than almost any other (since much of the advertising effort was handled by professional agencies locally and nationally). Although each store had its own unique pattern of sales, the East Boulevard unit typically exhibited more erratic and seasonal sales of certain items than did the others in the group because of the store's proximity to the tourist attraction. These variations, in turn, required a more concerted inventory control program at this location.

Kerry Thomas used a sophisticated series of specially designed forms to monitor the flows of foods, cash, and various supplies through the course of business conducted at his unit. Certain target standards expressed as ratios, multipliers, index factors, and so on had been carefully developed by the BBI headquarters staff and outside consultants in order to facilitate internal control measures. Although the specific standards were not disclosed outside the franchise system, several examples of "typical" blank and completed forms are reproduced in Exhibits 5, 6, and 7.

Alan Greene required each of his store managers personally to complete these forms, as well as several other statistical reports, rather than allowing delegation to assistant managers or other personnel. This, he felt, assured closer scrutiny and better control by the managers of the units in his chain. Typically, reordering was done when stock levels reached approximately those to be required during the replenishment periods. The inventory turnover cycles varied by item (for example, weekly for meats, twice a week for breads, and so on). Periodic physical "counts" of each item in stock complemented the statistical analyses and "paper records" to permit cross references between daily, weekly, and monthly reports generated.

Although occasional grumbling had been received from some unit managers who found the paperwork tiresome, most agreed that the planning and control benefits achieved outweighed the time and trouble involved. Among the advantages frequently cited were improved efforts in reducing excessive inventories and preventing shortages, precluding major pilferages of foods and other items by the numerous part-time employees, focusing on areas of inefficiency or waste, and implementing appropriate corrective measures.

EXHIBIT 5
Better Burgers Statistical Report for Month of May 19xx

BETTER BURGERS STATISTICAL REPORT

EAST BOULEVARD UNIT
BETTER BURGERS, INC.
STORE STAMP

MAY 19XX
Month & Year Reported — TV Market — Licensee No. or MCOPCO No.

ITEM	Open Inv.	Units Purch.	Closing Inv.	Units Used	Promo / Waste	Units Sold	X Factor	Computed Sales	% of Sales	% of Total Sandwiches
1. Hamburgers				(A) 21,895	25 / 47	21,823	.20	4,364.60	13.00	37.26
2. Cheeseburgers				(C) 10,041	5 / 14	10,022	.25	2,505.50	7.16	17.11
3. DBL. H.B. Boxes	6,684	2,600	6,543	(B) 2,747	9	2,738	.39	1,067.82	2.44	4.68
4. DBL. C.B. Boxes	2,061	13,000	8,429	(D) 6,632	8 / 12	6,612	.49	3,234.88	8.66	11.29
5. Fish Portions	352	7,020	1,112	(E) 6,260	7 / 16	6,237	.39	2,432.43	5.95	10.65
6. Big Mac Buns	530	11,310	234	(F) 11,606	13 / 4.48	11,122	.55	6,117.10	15.90	18.99
7.										
8.										
9. TRIPPLE RIPPLE	145	2,496	—	2,641	12 / 2	2,627	.20	525.40	1.25	4.49
				TOTAL SANDWICHES		59,103	100%			**% TO Total Sand.**
10. Fry Bags - Regular	37,843	39,000	46,935	31,758	31 / 1-16	31,710	.20	6,342.00	15.11	54.15
11. Fry Boxes - Large	7,900	5,850	7,168	6,582	3	6,578	.35	2,302.30	5.48	11.23
12. Pie Portions	172	4,056	346	3,882	10 / 94	3,778	.20	755.60	1.80	6.45
13. Shake Cups	7,170	14,415	9,612	11,973	3 / 4	11,966	.29	3,470.14	7.13	2.04
14. Cold Cups - Regular	11,736	16,250	10,258	17,728	20 / 22	17,686	.15	(P) 2,652.90	6.32	30.20
15. Cold Cups - Large	3,426	20,605	7,537	16,494	9 / 12	16,473	.20	(N) 3,294.60	7.85	28.13
16. Milk	92	664	42	714	1	713	.15	106.95	.34	1.22
17. CHERRY PIES	24	624	—	653	3 / 38	612	.20	122.40	.46	1.05
18. Hot Choc. Cups				(G)			.15			
19. Coffee Cups				(H) 2,016	16 / 8	1,992	.15	248.80	.71	3.40
				TOTAL ALL UNITS		153,238				

ITEM	Open Inv. +	Units Purch.	Closing Inv.	Promo / Waste	Units Used			
20. Hamburger Buns	2,262	48,828	1,825	1643	(J) 47,572	Computed Return a	39,598.42	
21. Cheese Buns	9,817	40,435	12,646	34	(K) 37,573	Recorded Employee Food Consumption b		
22. 8 oz. Hot Cup	2,557	1,300	1,872		2,015	Computed Sales c	39,598.42	GROSS SALES
23. Meat Patties (lbs.)	2,873	72,540	2,301	53	73,112	Net Sales d	39,538.61	SALES TAX
24. Hot Choc. Tins						Difference e	59.39	= NET SALES
						% Difference e/d =	.15	

48	236	78		
Number Inside Seats	Number Outside Seats	Number Parking Stalls	Transaction Count	☐ Check Box (✓) If Testing New Products

PATTIES VS. BUNS		CHEESEBURGERS USED		HAMBURGERS USED	
Buns Used (J)	47,572	Cheese Slices (K)	37,573	Buns Used (J)	47,572
− Fish Used (E)	6,260	− Big Mac Buns (F)	11,606	− Total Doubles Used	9,379
=	41,312	=	25,967	(B) + (D) =	38,193
+ Discarded Filet Portions (Uncpl. Sand.)	—	− Discarded Big Mac Buns (Uncompleted Sand.)	418	+ Discarded, Unused Dbl. Hb. & Dbl. C.B. Boxes (Waste Sh.)	—
= ADJUSTED BUNS	41,312	=	26,435	=	38,193
+ Total Dbl. Buns (B) + (D)	9,379	− 2 x Dbl. C.B. Boxes (D)	13,264	− Cheeseburgers Used (C)	10,038
=	50,691	=	13,171	=	28,155
− Discarded, Unused Dbl. H.B. & Dbl. C.B. Boxes	—	+ 2 x Discarded Empty Dbl. C.B. Boxes (Waste Sheet)	—	− Fish Portions (E)	6,260
=	50,691	=	13,171	=	21,895
+ 2 x Big Mac Buns (F)	23,212	− ½ Fish Portions (E)	3,130	+ Discarded Filet Prtns. (Uncompleted Sand.)	—
=	73,903	=	10,041	= Hamburgers Used (A)	21,895
− 2 x Discarded Big Mac Buns (Uncompleted Sand.)	936	+ ½ Discarded Filet Prtns. (Uncompleted Sand.)	—		
= Projected Patties	72,967	= Cheeseburgers Used (C)	10,041	HOT CHOCOLATE CUPS USED	
− Lbs. Meat Used x 10	73,112			(M) ___ x 21 (#2½ Tins) ___	
= Patties (Over/Short)	−145	NOTE		(M) ___ x 84 (#10 Tins) = ___ (G)	
If Lbs. Meat Used x 10 is more than Projected Patties, Patties are Over.		When Dbl. Sandwiches Are Discarded Or Consumed by Employees, the Dbl. Boxes Holding the Sandwiches Must Also Be Discarded.		COFFEE CUPS USED	
				(L) ___ − (G) ___ = ___ (H)	

EXHIBIT 5 *(continued)*

YIELDS

ITEM	Open Inv. +	Units Purch. −	Closing Inv. −	Promo & Waste =	Units Used
25. Potatoes	1,593	13,338	1,472	75	13,384
26. Mix	44	1,170	77		1,137
27. Van. Syrup	20	23	13		30
28. Choc. Syrup	34	55	17		72
29. Straw. Syrup	17	23	16		24
30. Coca Cola	163	423	182		404
31. Orange	35	55	51		39
32. Root Beer	51	55	47		59
33. Catsup	82	164	64		182
34. Mayonnaise	43	62	46		59
35. Vegetable Mix	9	23	13		19
36. Mustard	16	25	17		24
37. Pickles	55	195	47		203
38. Onions (Dehy.)	150	156	139		167
39. Coffee	183	499	81		601
40. Shortening	715	1,500	434		1,781
41. Salt Packets	9,100	78,000	57,200		29,900
42. Raw Onions					
43. Cream	10	31	13		28
44. Marshmallows					
45. Sugar Packets	5,200	7,800	7,150		5,850
46. Bulk Salt	33	260	130		163
47. CO₂	5	7	7		5
48. Pepper	3	0	1		2
49. Big Mac Sauce	54	102	47		109
50. Lettuce	22	520	65		477
51. Ketcup Packets	8,710	15,000	8,190		15,120
52.					
53.					
54.					
55.					

FRY YIELD

Fry bags regular + (fry boxes large used x 1.62) = a __60,334__

Discarded empty bags + (discarded empty boxes x 1.62) = b __40__

(a − b) X 100 ÷ lbs. potatoes used = __450__
Yield CWT

SHAKE YIELD

$\dfrac{\text{Shake Cups Used} - \text{Empty Cups}}{\text{Gals. Mix Used}} = \dfrac{16.2}{\text{Shakes/Gal.}}$
Discarded

BEVERAGE YIELD

$\dfrac{Ⓕ + ◯}{\text{Gals. Syrup Used}} = \dfrac{14.93}{\text{Yield/Gal.}}$

TARTAR SAUCE YIELD

$\dfrac{\text{Fish Portions Used} - \text{Filet Portions}}{\text{Tins Mayonnaise Used}} = \dfrac{165}{\text{Serv./Tin}}$
Discarded

CATSUP YIELD

$\dfrac{\text{Adjusted Buns}}{\text{Tins Catsup Used}} = \dfrac{322}{\text{Serv./Tin}}$

COFFEE YIELD

$\dfrac{\text{Cups of Coffee x .15}}{\text{Units of Coffee Used}} = \dfrac{1.03}{\text{Yield/Unit}}$

ONION YIELD (DEHYD.)

$\dfrac{\text{Adjusted Buns} + Ⓑ \frac{2 \text{ x Total Dbls.}}{+ Ⓓ} \frac{2 \text{ x Big}}{+ \text{Mac}} Ⓕ}{\text{Packages Onions Used}} = \dfrac{696}{\text{Serv./Pkg.}}$

MUSTARD YIELD

$\dfrac{\text{Adjusted Buns}}{\text{Gal. Mustard Used}} = \dfrac{2,374}{\text{Serv./Gal.}}$

BIG MAC SAUCE YIELD

$\dfrac{\text{Big Mac Buns Used} - \text{Big Mac Buns}}{\text{Tins Big Mac Sauce Used}} = \dfrac{138}{\text{Sand./Tin}}$
Discarded

LETTUCE YIELD

$\dfrac{\text{Big Mac Buns Used} - \text{Big Mac Buns}}{\text{Lbs. Lettuce Used}} = \dfrac{32}{\text{Serv./Lb.}}$
Discarded

Meat Price Per Lb. _____	Potato Price Per Lb. _____	
Mix Price Per Gal. _____	Lettuce Price Per Lb. _____	
Hamburger Bun Price Per Doz. _____	Big Mac Bun Price Per Doz. _____	

LABOR HOURS

Total Store Labor Hours (Including all management) _____ = __5,310.48__ Labor Hours Used

AVERAGE CREW HOURLY RATE

$\dfrac{\text{Total Store Labor Dollars} - \text{Mgr.(s) and Asst. Mgr.(s) Labor Dollars}}{\text{Total Store Labor Hours Used} - \text{Mgr.(s) and Asst. Mgr.(s) Labor Hours}} \left(\dfrac{\text{Total Crew Labor Dollars}}{\text{Total Crew Labor Hours}}\right) =$ $ __1.79__ Av. Crew Hourly Rate

SALES PER MAN HOUR

$\dfrac{\text{Net Sales}}{\text{Total Store Labor Hours}} =$ $ __11.04__ Sales Per Man Hour

LABOR DOLLARS

$\dfrac{\text{Total Store Labor Dollars (All Management Plus All Crew)}}{} =$ $ __10,634.34__ Labor Dollars

LABOR PERCENTAGE

$\dfrac{\text{Total Store Labor Dollars (All Management Plus All Crew)}}{\text{Net Sales}} =$ __18.20__ % Labor Percentage

Prepared by __Jerry Thomas__ Date __May 1981__   A Monthly Statistical Report is to be submitted with your P & L Statement.

EXHIBIT 6
Better Burgers Paper Inventory Blank Chart Format

BETTER BURGERS PAPER INVENTORY CHART

UNIT_____ NO. _____ MONTH ENDING_____ 19 _____

MAJOR 611 SOURCE	STOCKROOM						FRONT	SUB CODE	COMBINED TOTAL	x	(1) PRICE PER M	=	(2) AMOUNT
	CASES	PKG. PER CASE	TOTAL	# INNER PKGS	PKG. PER INNER	TOTAL	BROKEN LOT						
DBL. HB. BAGS		8000			1000			57					
DBL. CB. BAGS		8000			1000			58					
DBL. HB. BOXES		2000						57					
DBL. CB. BOXES		2000						58					
FRY BAGS		15000			1000			63					
SHAKE CUPS		1000			50			38					
16 OZ. COLD CUP		1000			50			48					
12 OZ. COLD CUP		2500			100			49					
DUNK KUPS		2500			50			75					
8 OZ. HOT CUPS		1000			50			51					
7 OZ. CUPS		2500			100			52					
LIDS–DUNK KUP		1000			100			29					
LIDS–16 OZ.		3000			100			26					
LIDS–12 OZ.		4000			100			27					
LIDS–8 OZ.		3000			100			28					
TRAYS–2 HOLE		500						81					
TRAYS–4 HOLE		400						82					
BAGS–4 LB.		4000			500			64					
BAGS–6 LB.		2000			500			65					
BAGS–10 LB.		2000			500			66					
BAGS–1/6 BBL.		250						67					
BAGS–PIE		5000			1000			62					
WRAP–BLUE		12000			1000			02					
WRAP–RED		12000			1000			03					
WRAP–GREEN		12000			1000			04					
WRAP–ROAST BEEF								05					
WRAP–BIG MAC		5000						97					
NAPKINS		6000			125			93					
STRAWS–BULK		10000			250			94					
STRAWS–WRAPPED		10000			500			95					
STIR–STIX		10000			1000			92					
MENU TICKETS		15000						91					
CARRY-OUT BOXES		50						96					

(1) INDICATE EACH PRICE TO FOUR DECIMAL POINTS

(2) MULTIPLY COMBINED TOTAL BY PRICE, MARK OFF SEVEN DECIMAL FIGURES AND ROUND OFF TO TWO DECIMAL POINTS

TOTAL _____

PREPARED BY_____ MGR. _____ ASST. _____

EXHIBIT 7
Better Burgers Daily Inventory and Cash Control Blank Chart Format

						UNIT OF INVENTORY:						MONTH:	
BEGINNING	+ RECEIVED	− ENDING	= USED	× RETURN FACTOR $	=COMPUTED SALES	DAY DATE	BEGINNING	+ RECEIVED	− ENDING	= USED	× RETURN FACTOR $	=COMPUTED SALES	
				$	$	1					$	$	
					$	2						$	
					$	3						$	
					$	4						$	
					$	5						$	
					$	6						$	
					$	7						$	
					$	8						$	
					$	9						$	
					$	10						$	
					$	11						$	
					$	12						$	
					$	13						$	
					$	14						$	
					$	15						$	
					$	16						$	
					$	17						$	
					$	18						$	
					$	19						$	
					$	20						$	
					$	21						$	
					$	22						$	
					$	23						$	
					$	24						$	
					$	25						$	
					$	26						$	
					$	27						$	
					$	28						$	
					$	29						$	
					$	30						$	
					$	31						$	

BETTER BURGERS

DAILY INVENTORY AND CASH CONTROL

	BEGINNING	RECEIVED	ENDING	USED			BEGINNING	RECEIVED	ENDING	USED
MONTHLY INVENTORY:	+	−	=				+	−	=	

PERSONNEL

The BBI franchiser corporation was quite meticulous in its selection and approval of franchisees, but it allowed unit managers to have wide latitude in hiring operating personnel. The BBI guidelines required that all employees "present a neat and clean appearance" and "render competent, sober, and courteous service to the patrons" of Better Burgers establishments. The manager of any BBI unit was specifically precluded from employing or seeking to employ people who were currently working at other BBI locations.

Alan Greene prided himself on his selection of unit managers and how they, in turn, had hired good people at the units. According to Mr. Greene, high turnover among part-time employees could lead to prohibitive training costs; hence prospective employees needed to be selected carefully. He consistently tried to provide "equal opportunities" for all, seeking and accepting qualified minority groups and women employees long before outside demands for such practices were common.

Most of the operating employees in Alan Greene's Better Burgers units worked on a part-time basis. High school and college students, as well as homemakers, made up the majority of the unit personnel. Local work study programs in which teenagers attended school in the mornings and worked during either afternoons or evenings accounted for the largest single group of these employees. Although some other local businessmen participating in the work study program paid lower wages, Mr. Greene had always paid at least the "regular adult minimum wage" specified by federal law.

UNIT SUPERVISORS

In addition to Sam Hargrove, his administrative assistant, Alan Greene's Sunshine City BBI organization included three unit supervisors. (See organization chart shown in Exhibit 8.) Each of these supervisors had responsibility for three BBI units. Mr. Greene saw these supervisors as a key ingredient in the smooth operation of the overall system because they reduced the number of direct subordinates with whom he needed to interact on a daily basis. These supervisors played a vital role in analyzing the longer term needs and problems of each of their BBI units and also served in an administrative/advisory capacity to the unit managers.

Sam Hargrove served as chief administrative assistant to Alan Greene and as supervisor of unit 1. As Greene's assistant, Hargrove acted as the primary liaison between Greene's BBI organization and the local advertising agency which handled this account; he coordinated the implementation of all local ad campaigns, making sure that they were carried out properly and punctually; and he was in charge of setting up and running various manager training programs.

The unit supervisor's position, in addition to insuring that all BBI units were operating within generally prescribed guidelines and helping to maintain harmony throughout the system, provided an avenue of promotion for a highly capable unit manager. Alan Greene had been particularly careful to evaluate each supervisor's abilities to motivate and work with people effectively and adapt to changing environments, before making promotions. It was anticipated that as Greene's franchise system expanded to include more Better Burgers units, additional supervisory positions would be created, thereby making it possible to promote several of the top unit managers. In fact, when the 11th and 12th BBI units opened, Sam Hargrove was scheduled to assume the role of operations manager, a line position directly below Alan Greene. One of the outstanding unit managers would then be promoted to a unit supervisor position, creating an organization with four such supervisors, each coordinating the activities of three Better Burgers Units.

UNIT MANAGERS

Alan Greene believed strongly in the philosophy of "promotion from within" where possible. Moreover, he believed that the best way to gain outstanding performance from an employee was to show that employees

EXHIBIT 8
Organization Chart for Alan Greene's Better Burgers. Inc., Franchise System

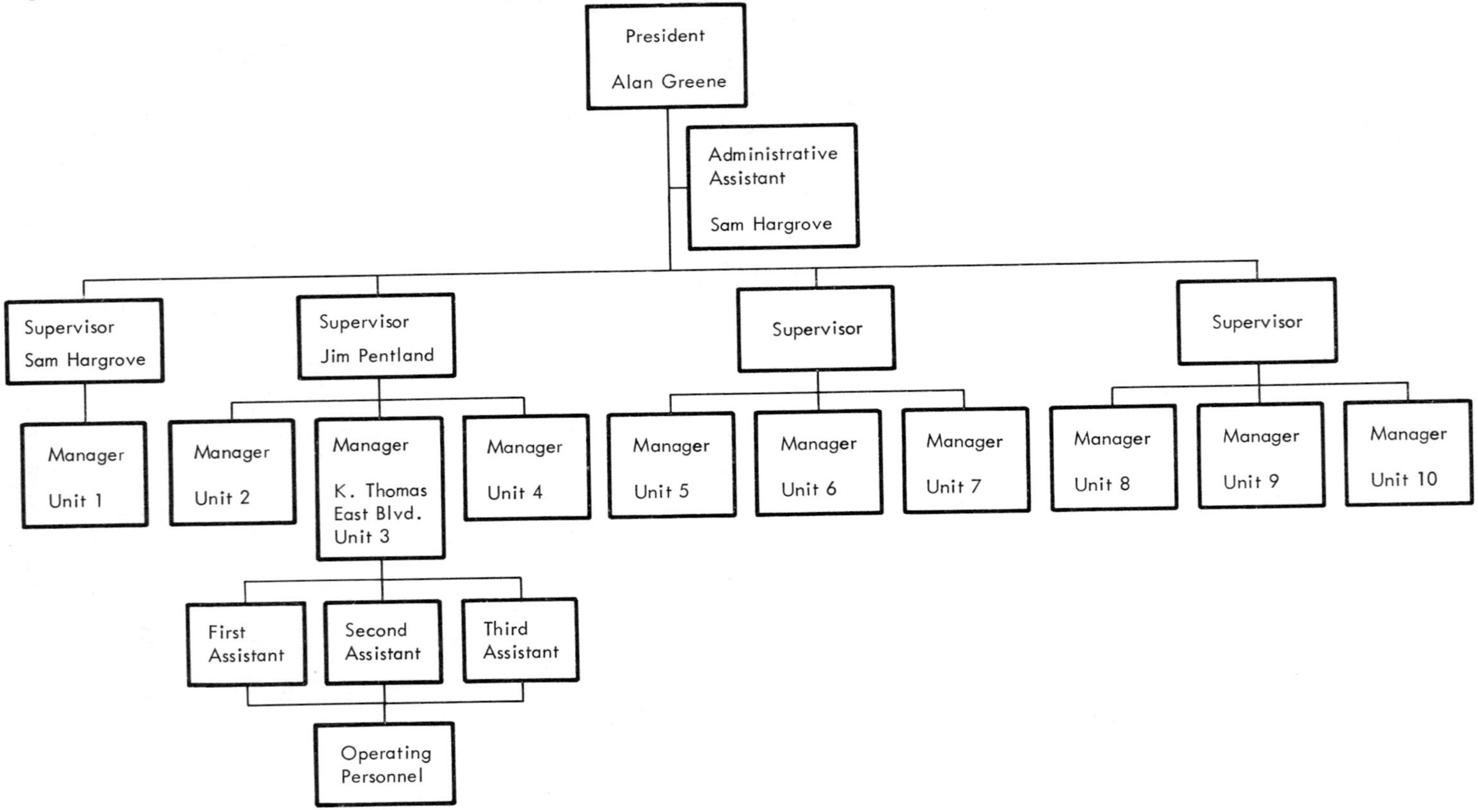

who did a good job could expect to be rewarded accordingly. Merit, then was a much more important factor than seniority in determining which employees became assistant managers or unit managers. Those who demonstrated initiative, integrity, and potential were invited to enter a mangement training program.

Mr. Greene declared that he imposed no set standard period of time for employees to develop the competency requisite for advancement, citing as examples: *(a)* a highly capable 20-year-old unit manager who had been with the organization only two years, and *(b)* several middle-aged assistant managers who had aspired for several years to become unit managers, but who "are not yet ready to accept the responsibilities entailed."

A unit manager's primary functions involve directing and supervising unit operations, maintaining and increasing sales volumes and profit levels, and developing a capable, motivated work force that will follow the general policies and procedures formulated by the franchiser and modified somewhat by Alan Greene. Although the organization chart suggests that unit managers report to unit supervisors, it would be more correct to say that they report directly to Alan Greene; the supervisors actually perform more advisory-related staff functions. Whenever a unit's performance falls below "standard," a unit manager discusses the underlying problems and develops solutions in "performance review sessions" conducted personally by Mr. Greene—with a BBI national field representative and the appropriate unit supervisor also presenting ideas and serving as advisers. Greene's unit supervisors do not delegate responsibilities to the unit managers; they usually consult with Alan Greene on a constant basis, attempting to design and execute corrective actions as soon as problems can be predicted or detected.

Naturally, each unit manager is directly responsible for supervising the assistant managers, "swing" manager (night manager), full-time, and part-time operating staff. The following listing is typical of the duties and responsibilities of a BBI unit manager:

1. Maintains and increases the volume level and profits of his assigned unit.
2. Develops and maintains controls to ensure the production of food meeting Better Burgers quality standards.
3. Maintains his assigned unit in a continual state of cleanliness and sanitation.
4. Directs his crew in the maintenance of perfect service to the customer.
5. Regularly reviews the performance of all subordinates according to a fixed schedule.
6. Trains and develops subordinates for present and possible future assignments.
7. Develops and maintains preventive maintenance programs for grounds, buildings, and equipment.
8. Secures prompt repair or replacement of faulty or inoperative equipment.

9. Determines staffing requirements at varying volume levels.
10. Directs training and orientation of all new employees.
11. Maintains competitive wage levels and rewards outstanding performance.
12. Maintains an awareness of competition within his neighborhood area.
13. Maintains accounting records in accordance with established procedures.
14. Procures materials from approved suppliers on a timely basis and receives, inspects, stores, and inventories them in accordance with established procedures.
15. Functions as a Better Burgers representative in the local community.
16. Coordinates with the local advertising, promotional and sales program.
17. Assists the unit supervisor or owner-operator in preparing an annual projection of the unit's profit plan and makes revisions on a quarterly basis.

Mr. Greene noted that the orientation and training of subordinate employees was a very important responsibility and could be overlooked by a unit manager preoccupied with matters such as sales volumes and cost standards. Typically, however, the unit manager was expected to spend at least a few hours personally getting new employees oriented before delegating primary responsibility to an experienced employee for subsequent on-the-job coaching. Frequently, training sessions using audiovisual aids such as films, cassette tapes, and reading material developed and provided by the national franchiser were used for supplementary off-the-job development.

Alan Greene supported monetary compensation as an extremely important vehicle for motivating employees to perform well and strive for promotions. He readily admitted that the salaries he paid were "probably higher than they need to be" in order to attract good employees but, on the other hand, suggested that on the average the benefits accruing from higher salaries outweighed the costs. The prevailing salary ranges in Greene's organization were:

Supervisor	$14,000–$25,000
Manager	10,000– 14,000
First assistant	8,000– 10,000
Second assistant	7,000– 8,000
Trainee	6,000– 7,000

Liberal "fringe benefits" including company cars, gasoline and other expense accounts, company-paid insurance, and retirement programs added to the attractiveness of these salaries. Special outstanding performance or suggestions were also rewarded with "appropriate bonuses."

FINANCE

In the broadest sense, Alan Greene's East Boulevard Better Burgers, Inc., unit constituted a leasehold franchise operation. The national franchiser owned the land which was used for Greene's franchise for a period of 20 years. When the current lease expired, Greene and the national BBI firm could opt to extend the lease for a series of subsequent five-year periods. The BBI national system included a large proportion of such leasehold operators, with the other Better Burgers units either owned by individual franchisees or owned by the BBI corporation itself.

Beginning a new franchise under the BBI system required a sizable amount of capital from the franchisee. The use of the Better Burgers, Inc., name for the conduct of a fast-foods establishment carried an initial fee of $10,000. The use of patented building and equipment designed and provided by BBI required an additional investment of approximately $100,000. Of this $110,000, the franchisee had to provide at least $65,000 in cash from his own personal sources. The remainder could be borrowed through a bank or other financial institution. According to BBI top executives, the "average" franchisee was able to erase this debt within five years of operation.

As was noted earlier, the franchisee (in the usual leasehold arrangement) paid a continuing franchise fee of 11.5 percent of sales, in addition to the initial investment. This continuing fee, remitted on a monthly basis, included payment of rent for the land owned by BBI, management services rendered by BBI headquarters and field consultants, and national advertising.

The income statements covering the East Boulevard Better Burgers unit for the most recent year and a "typical" month within this year reveal that food and labor costs constituted the unit's largest operating expenses—see Exhibits 9 and 10. BBI management services, rent, and advertising were also relatively large expense items, with paper inventories, depreciation and amortization being among the slightly lower major expenses.

The BBI franchiser carefully screened the financial backgrounds of all potential franchisees before licensing new Better Burgers operators. Further, to maintain the favorable credit rating and purchasing power of the national system, each unit was required to make prompt payments to suppliers (as well as to the franchiser) in accordance with the terms of the invoices or statements. Any failure on the part of the licensee to do so was considered a breach of the franchise agreement, and if serious enough, could warrant the termination of the franchise agreement.

The average $50,000–$75,000 net income said to be earned by the typical BBI establishment served as a very broad financial yardstick against which to measure the East Boulevard unit's success. The $62,490 earned by this store made it an about average unit at this time. Alan Greene believed the unit's potential for increasing financial returns was very bright due to rising tourism in the local area.

Net income which is not withdrawn either for Mr. Greene's personal

EXHIBIT 9

EAST BOULEVARD BETTER BURGERS UNIT
Income Statement
For the Month Ended June 30, 19XX

Net Sales			$42,092.32
Cost of Goods Sold:			
Food inventory—beginning	$ 1,554.55		
Plus purchases and payables	14,235.55		
Less: ending inventory	(2,219.67)		
Total Food Cost		$13,570.43	
Paper inventory—beginning	1,326.48		
Plus purchases and payables	2,066.23		
Less: ending inventory	(1,595.81)		
Total Paper Cost		1,796.90	
Total Cost of Sales			15,367.33
Gross Profit			$26,724.99
Operating Expenses—Manager Controllable:			
Labor	$ 8,299.21		
Payroll taxes	382.16		
Travel expenses	32.50		
Advertising	1,800.40		
Promotion.................................	24.83		
Outside services	276.06		
Linen	76.97		
Operating supplies	65.09		
Maintenance and repairs	970.76		
Utilities....................................	154.91		
Office expenses	80.74		
Cash over/short	—		
Miscellaneous	90.83		
		$12,254.46	
Other Operating Expenses:			
Rent	$ 3,054.86		
Services fees	923.17		
Legal and accounting	110.50		
Insurance	252.25		
Taxes and licenses..........................	390.00		
Depreciation and amortization	1,441.97		
Interest expense	165.71		
Miscellaneous expense/income	(70.94)		
Total Operating Expenses		6,267.52	
Total Expenses			18,521.98
Net Operating Income			$ 8,203.01
Other Costs:			
Management services	$ 4,551.30		
Owner's salary or draw	—		
Total Other Costs			4,551.30
Net Income			$ 3,651.71

EXHIBIT 10

EAST BOULEVARD BETTER BURGERS UNIT
Income Statement
For the 12-Month Period Ending June 30, 19XX

Net Sales			$542,645.56
Cost of Goods Sold:			
Food inventory-beginning	$ 2,721.37		
Plus purchases and payables	167,465.87		
Less: ending inventory	(2,219.67)		
Total Food Cost		$167,967.57	
Paper inventory-beginning	$ 2,166.62		
Plus purchases and payables	21,539.47		
Less: ending inventory	(1,595.81)		
Total Paper Cost		22,110.28	
Total Cost of Sales			190,077.85
Gross Profit			$352,567.71
Operating Expenses—Manager Controllable:			
Labor	$104,622.96		
Payroll taxes	5,360.41		
Travel expenses	394.22		
Advertising	20,064.21		
Promotion	393.91		
Outside services	3,036.60		
Linen	635.13		
Operating supplies	2,840.81		
Maintenance and repairs	7,194.36		
Utilities	9,170.69		
Office expenses	832.42		
Cash over/short	—		
Miscellaneous	1,601.22		
Total Controllable		$156,146.94	
Other Operating Expenses:			
Rent	$ 39,437.94		
Service fees	11,938.47		
Legal and accounting	3,867.50		
Insurance	2,945.86		
Taxes and licenses	4,453.15		
Depreciation and amortization	16,747.52		
Interest expense	1,929.42		
Miscellaneous expense/income	(807.40)		
Total Operating Expenses		80,512.46	
Total Expenses			236,659.40
Net Operating Income			$115,908.31
Other Costs:			
Management services	$ 53,418.30		
Owner's salary or draw	—		
Total Other Costs			53,418.30
Net Income			$ 62,490.01

account or to repay part of the debt capitalization went back into the business as retained earnings. This source of funds for future capital was occasionally tapped for a major improvement beyond the scope of normal maintenance and repairs. For example, at the time when the East Boulevard Better Burgers unit opened, the fast foods market was generally oriented toward drive-in facilities with limited outside seating and no inside seating capacity. Approximately $50,000 of internally generated capital was recently used for building and grounds improvements, including primarily the modification of the building to accommodate indoor seating and a parking lot expansion.

Even though Mr. Greene regards the financial potential for the East Boulevard unit as outstanding and the performance so far as quite acceptable, other units in his chain were realizing higher efficiency and profitability. Among the major topics to be discussed at the meeting soon to be held with the unit supervisor and the unit manager were the exploration of possible alternatives for enhancing this unit's financial posture and overall performance.

D. Strategy Review and Reappraisal

23. The Devil's Own Wine Shoppe*

BRUCE NELSON looked around the handsome wine store and remarked to his wife Mary Lee, "We may have given the old saying, 'in vino veritas,' a new and even more sardonic meaning. In the end, this wine shop may have provided us with an education in the ways of business but—oh my!—at a cost of $10,000." It was difficult for the Nelsons to think about the likelihood of such a loss, but events required that they face the possibility.

Just that morning, Bruce's boss, the sales manager of a large Chevrolet dealership, had called Bruce to his office for a talk. He explained to Bruce that he had a good deal of confidence in his ability as a salesman and felt that Bruce could become one of the agency's most productive salesmen if he would only give undivided attention to selling as his work. The sales manager knew that the Nelsons had opened a wine shop about nine months earlier and that Bruce was working at the wine shop when he did not have floor duty at the dealership. The sales manager believed that the extra time and worry of the wine shop was affecting Bruce's performance as a salesman and, not unpleasantly, suggested that a choice between working at the dealership or the wine shop ought to be faced by Bruce.

There were other reasons for deciding what to do about the wine shop quite soon. The Nelsons had a $15,000 bank loan and the bank was asking for repayment to begin and for agreement about a schedule of regular payments even though the wine shop was operating at a loss. In personal terms, the Nelsons had two small children and the present necessity for one of the Nelsons to be at the wine shop when it was open was disrupting their home life and, they felt, unfavorably affecting them as parents. Bruce himself had several classic symptoms of "nerves." At times he had a rash on his body and hands and found it difficult to relax or be at all still. He knew that he was tense; he was, in his own words, "obsessed with his problems."

PERSONAL BACKGROUND

"My dream—my goal—has been to have my own business," Bruce explained to a fellow car salesman who was sympathizing with him and trying

---

* Prepared by Professors Eleanor Casebier and Manning Hanline, the University of West Florida.

to understand how Bruce had gotten himself into his present difficult situation. "My father was an independent hardware store owner in Pontiac, Michigan, and, as I was growing up, I recognized that I wanted the kind of life that can come from having a successful, personal business." To Bruce that meant not only having a degree of independence but, frankly, it also meant being successful in economic terms. If he had not read tales of Horatio Alger, he nevertheless had acquired similar values and hopes from his home background.

Bruce was the oldest of three boys all of whom had grown up helping in the hardware store. "Why didn't you stay in Pontiac and continue in business with your father?" the car salesman asked. Bruce answered: "I might have except that the Vietnam War took me away from Pontiac and other events also occurred to keep me from returning permanently.

"I joined the Marines in 1964 and, after training, was sent to the Pensacola, Florida, Naval Air Station for duty. I met and married my wife while stationed at NAS. She was born and reared in Pensacola. After leaving the Marines, I went to work for the Gulf Power Company in Pensacola for a short period of time but returned to Pontiac to help my father who was critically ill.

"We stayed in Pontiac for two years and during that time my father died. I may as well be frank about my relations with my mother. She and my wife did not get along well. I offered to stay and help with the business but only if I could acquire part ownership. I would not work for my mother.

"As it turned out, my 'middle' brother stayed to help with the hardware store. However, he has left the business and is teaching school. My mother runs the business now and my younger brother is helping her.

"My wife and I came back to Pensacola and I began to work here selling cars. I really do like to sell and, in a way, I've always felt that I would have mastered a real challenge if I were to be a successful new-car salesman. It is so different from other work I've done and I've had no particular training for it as I find it being done here. Nevertheless, my dream of having a personal business led to our opening the wine shop last fall."

The fellow car salesman wondered, "If you wanted your own business, why didn't you open a hardware store? I can understand that you returned to Pensacola because it's your wife's hometown."

"It would take somewhere between $60,000 and $75,000 for inventory alone to open a good hardware store," Bruce observed. "There were also two other factors that I considered. The hardware business is a 'cut-rate or discount' business these days. It's extremely competitive. In addition, I know from hard experience that it can be a 'dirty' business. Customers expect you to take their greasy tools or what-have-you—or even their bathroom fixtures—and find parts for them. You might spend a half-hour finding one small ten-cent bolt for something-or-other."

"On the other hand, my wife and I became interested in wine: the subject appealed to us. It's certainly a 'clean' business and a first-rate wine store doesn't require nearly the inventory investment that a hardware store does.''

STORE LOCATION

A regional economic analysis for the Pensacola Standard Metropolitan Statistical Area (SMSA) was prepared by planning consultants aided by a federal grant in 1973. This study indicated that growth and change were to be expected in the Pensàcola area. The city had a population of about 80,000; the SMSA, about 245,000. Population was expected to grow at a faster rate than in the nation as a whole. According to the study, "The general area possesses a viable economy, an adequate natural resource base, and abundant geographical and climatic amenities." The Pensacola SMSA had made impressive gains in per capita income over the past ten years and had experienced, and was expected to continue to experience, a substantial growth rate in the higher income ranges.

The study stated that the economy of Pensacola SMSA was well balanced with activity including manufacturing, government (largely military, including substantial repair facilities), tourism, and some oil drilling and refining, in addition to a representative share of retail trade, construction, transportation, finance, insurance, and real estate. According to the analysis, the area had "the potential to be a primary tourist center."

The Devil's Own Wine Shoppe was located in a "mature" shopping center first opened in 1958. The center was "L-shaped" in design and was the type where storefronts were connected by an outside walkway with a roof overhead. There was a large parking area between the two legs of the "L."

The center had experienced a considerable turnover in stores and a noticeable reduction in customer traffic during the past two years—mainly because three larger, enclosed shopping malls and several other smaller shopping centers of the open type had recently opened in Pensacola. However, there was a branch store of a large, regional department store in the shopping center and a respectable variety of stores and shops in the center. The general look of the center was not one of prosperity, though, and Bruce knew that businesses in the center were having a difficult time. (It was satisfying to Bruce that other store owners and managers had come to accept him as a compeer in the nine months he had been in business and to confide their business concerns to him.)

A particular feature of the shopping center was that it included a five-story office building which housed various professional and service organizations. The office building was connected to the center by a patio-type roof. Attractive planters had been placed in the area between the center and the office building. The Devil's Own Wine Shoppe was situated in the shopping center at the point that it was connected to the office building (the front corner; at the end of the longer leg of the "L," in effect) and, therefore, overlooked both the planted patio area and the parking lot.

In making the decision to locate in the shopping center, Bruce relied upon the following factors:

1. The shopping center was near the "center of population" of the Pensacola area and located at one of the busiest intersections of the city.
2. Relative to possibilities in other shopping centers, lease costs were lower. One of the enclosed malls wanted $1,000 a month for a space just slightly bigger than the present location of The Devil's Own Wine Shoppe. Another wanted $750 a month and a percentage of sales plus requiring the payment of dues to an association of tenants and an amount for maintenance of the common area of the center. This same mall wanted $5,000 to prepare the site (for carpeting, doors, a sign, and so on).
3. He could locate no acceptable building with adequate parking that was not in a shopping center. Many retail businesses had moved out of downtown Pensacola; it had obviously been affected by the competition of the newer shopping malls and centers as the following local newspaper story illustrated:

Business Association Decides 'Down' Is Out And 'In' Is In

Downtown Pensacola is no longer "down" but "in" as members of the Intown Business Association (IBA) seek to change the downtown image to intown Pensacola.

The IBA, formerly the Downtown Development Association met Tuesday in the San Carlos Hotel to announce to merchant members that they are changing the name of the organization.

President (Bob Smith) says the new name is designed to keep downtown alive, because many of the nation's downtown areas are plagued with desertion, leaving the impression of being really "down."

The Nelsons had signed a three-year lease on August 3, 1974, to pay rent at $369 a month. Utilities were furnished by the leasee.

ECONOMIC CONDITIONS

The economic recession of the mid-1970s in the United States was a matter of record. The state of Florida developed a rate of unemployment 2 percent to 3 percent higher than the national average during this period. The Pensacola area felt the effects of recession more gradually than either the state or nation, but by the third quarter of 1974 had exceeded the national average rate for unemployment while remaining somewhat under the state average rate.

As reported by the Department of Commerce, state of Florida, in its "Pensacola SMSA Labor Market Trends," which included statistics for the surrounding two-county area, the unemployment rate was 10.1 percent as of June 1975.

Local economic optimism during this time centered on tourism. Tourist trade as reflected by such informal indexes as tourists' requests for help and motel occupancy rates continued strong. The main attraction in the Pensacola area was the beautiful, open beach along the Gulf of Mexico but historical attractions and museums were also emphasized and publicized.

COMPETITION

The Devil's Own Wine Shoppe was unique in Pensacola; that is, it was the only store offering wine and related products exclusively. All grades of wines from the least expensive to the very expensive were stocked. Both domestic and foreign wines were carried but the Nelsons attempted to promote and develop a clientele for California wine.

Outside of wine, a limited number of wine racks and wine glasses were carried. The initial wine inventory cost approximately $10,000; there had not been money for party or other complementary items, according to Bruce.

Wine was available in Pensacola, however, from a variety of sources: grocery stores, drugstores, and liquor, or package, stores. It was Bruce's understanding (gleaned from wholesaler salesmen) that three of the four largest wine accounts were grocery supermarket chains and the fourth, a drugstore chain. Their volume came from sales of less expensive domestic wine.

For this type of wine, retail price competition was strong. Wholesalers offered the same volume-discount pricing structure to all customers. The large-volume grocery and drug chains bought selected items at the lowest wholesale prices and marked them up little, if at all. Bruce was convinced that one drug store chain had begun a policy of selling its limited variety of domestic wine at wholesale cost simply to attract customers into its stores; subsequently, another local drug store had been spurred to discount its wine at prices equivalent to a 10 percent markup. These wine prices were regularly advertised in the local newspaper by both the grocery and drug outlets.

There was other competition, especially from a local liquor (package) chain which did extensive advertising in the newspaper and on radio. In one campaign, it labeled itself as "the ubiquitous package store" easily available to all; in another, it claimed to carry the "greatest selection of imported and domestic wines" in northwest Florida.

The Nelson's pricing policy was to mark up the relatively inexpensive, domestic wine by 20 percent–25 percent over wholesale cost; to mark up the middle range of wine by 40 percent; and the very best by 50 percent. Bruce estimated that his average gross profit was 28 percent.

Figuring out how to price against the discount wine stores was not the

Nelson's only dilemma. Bruce had come to believe that "advertising is fantastically expensive." He had signed a contract with an advertising agency prior to opening the wine shop and, in 1974 with the help of the agency in preparing copy and placing ads, spent almost $1,100 on advertising. He had purchased spot announcements on three AM radio stations and on two FM stations. He had advertised in the local newspaper. Copy featured The Devil's Own Wine Shoppe as a distinctive place to buy wine but also contained specials at competitive prices.

Bruce had not been able to measure directly the effect of this type of advertising on sales or to notice any accumulative positive effect. For these reasons, and because of its high cost, he had almost stopped advertising. On the advice of the advertising agency, he was evaluating the technique of direct-mail and had compiled a list of doctors, lawyers, and other professional persons by using the yellow pages of the telephone book. He was not convinced, however, that present circumstances justified expenditures for postal permits and mailing.

The advertising agency had charged The Devil's Own Wine Shoppe very little in fees; it hoped to develop the account into a larger one in the future. It had supplied Bruce with a copy of a research report on the wine industry. (See Exhibit 3 at end of the case.)

FINANCIAL CONSIDERATIONS

On their own, the Nelsons had invested $7,000 in The Devil's Own Wine Shoppe. To add to this, they had obtained a loan of $15,000 from a local bank with interest at 9.85 percent. At the time the Nelsons arranged the loan, the prime rate of interest was 12 percent, as Bruce recalled the circumstances. (Florida had a usury law which prohibited lending at over an annual percentage rate of 10 percent.)

The loan officer of the bank explained his reasons for granting the loan: "The decision to lend Bruce the money was based on several factors. He had reasonable capital in the form of family money, and had both the enthusiasm and training to be successful with what we felt, and still feel, was a unique idea. He had nearly completed an M.B.A. degree program and was reasonably skilled in bookkeeping and accounting." The loan officer might have added, but did not, that Bruce and the vice president in charge of the Loan Division of that bank were close acquaintances, having gotten to know one another as fellow students in the M.B.A. degree program.

The loan officer further explained that the wine inventory and store fixtures of The Devil's Own Wine Shoppe were required as collateral. "While loans of this type usually are made by the bank for a 90-day period," he said, "in this instance the loan was drawn so that it could extend up to five years." During the first 90 days, Bruce was to have decided what size payments he would make and in effect thereby determine the term of the loan. Actually, at the end of 90 days, Bruce asked for an extension and the loan officer agreed to it. Other 90-day extensions followed; however, the last extension carrying The Devil's Own Wine Shoppe through May 1975, was for 60 days.

He did not worry about losing money on the loan, the loan officer stated, because of the collateral but did recognize the high "mortality rate" among new, small businesses. "Only about 1 percent of the amount we lend goes to new businesses," he said. "Had Bruce requested $50,000, for example, the decision could very well have been different. We're aware of the disturbing statistics showing that, except for those with exclusive franchises, seven out of ten new businesses fail. Often, the symptoms of failure are apparent as early as, say, six months and most often are quite clear within two years."

Both the loan officer and the vice president of the Loan Division were pleased that Bruce had regularly and voluntarily stopped by the bank to discuss his situation. On these occasions, they expressed their confidence in his ultimate success.

They did not feel that his difficulties were due to location. They felt that Bruce's analysis of alternatives before choosing his site was sound and that relocation would be expensive and simply not solve what they felt was his problem. It was, they thought, the type of competition that the wine shop faced, especially for low-cost wines. They recommended that The Devil's Own Wine Shoppe should increasingly emphasize fine wines for which there was much less, in fact very little, competition.

The bankers made several allied suggestions to Bruce which would indicate that he should supplement both his present promotional and retail store activities. They suggested consideration of the following:

1. Arrange wine-tasting parties. Wholesalers would provide the wine; local country clubs might be willing to host such parties.
2. Begin to solicit business by telephone. Bruce and Mary Lee could utilize the time they are at the wine shop and not busy otherwise for this.
3. Convince banks and other business firms to give Christmas baskets filled with different types of wines, priced around $25. There was a large market for the Christmas business gift and wine might be considered to be more aristocratic than whiskey, the current vogue in commercial "giving."

The bankers claimed that data were available proving that sales of liquor stores had continued to be good, if in fact they had not increased, during the economic slump. "People drink when they are happy and when they are sad, it would seem," one said. In any event, they did not consider general economic conditions to be an important factor when considering the problems of The Devil's Own Wine Shoppe.

COSTS AND OPERATIONS

When planning the layout of The Devil's Own Wine Shoppe, Bruce designed a special rack to display the most expensive wines and a U-shaped counter not only for use in waiting on customers but also for storing supplies, records, display material, and so on. He had these built to order by a cabinetmaker. In addition, he purchased standard wall shelves, floor display racks, a cooler, and a cash register. All together, fixtures cost $4,415, as itemized below:

Cash register	$ 400
Custom fixtures	848
Wine island floor fixtures	1,026
Wall fixtures	458
Shelving fixtures	749
Finishing fixtures	153
Lumber for shelving	157
Cooler	624
	$4,415

Expenditures by the Nelsons for leasehold improvements, largely to carpet the store and to buy and have signs installed, included:

Carpeting	$ 743
Store sign.......................	650
Window signs	174
Parking lot sign	130
Lumber	46
	$1,743

In June 1974, the Nelsons purchased a Chevrolet van which was carried on the accounts of The Devil's Own Wine Shoppe. The down payment was $176; monthly payments were $97.

Wine purchases in 1974 totaled $15,316; to date in 1975, wine purchases amounted to $3,024. Miscellaneous purchases of merchandise for sale amounted to $1,323 in 1974, and to $26 so far in 1975. For daily sales from the time the store was opened in August 1974 to May 1975, see Tables 1 and 2.

Outlays of cash not provided for in the foregoing accounting data in 1974 totaled $8,011; in 1975, $4,319. These outlays are itemized below.

Other Outlays of Cash in 1974

Rent	$1,476	Telephone	$ 219
Chamber of Commerce dues	47	Labor	2,143
Licenses and taxes	265	Social Security	124
Supplies	164	Withholding tax	251
Utility deposits	60	Payroll tax	245
Freight	399	Florida sales tax	264
Postage	78	B. Nelson, drawing	350
Repairs and maintenance	29	Advertising	1,080
Bank charges	81	Accounting	60
Insurance	384	Donations	7
Interest on bank loan	285		$8,011

Other Outlays of Cash in 1975

Rent	$1,845	Telephone	$ 182	
Supplies	8	Labor	21	
Repairs and maintenance	17	Social Security	1	
Insurance	10	Payroll tax	24	
Interest on bank loan	682	Florida sales tax	366	
Janitorial service	40	Advertising	235	
Child care	888		$4,319	

TABLE 1
Sales in 1974*

Week Ending	Monday	Tuesday	Wednesday	Thursday	Friday	Saturday	Weekly Total
8/16 (Sunday)							$ 40.42
8/17	$ 58.22	$ 54.33	$ 18.86	$ 18.73	$ 60.44	$216.69	427.27
8/24	41.74	71.26	45.02	69.76	68.40	88.79	384.97
8/31	70.11	130.43	22.13	68.77	134.57	182.45	608.46
9/7	Holiday	74.86	41.66	26.40	81.99	58.67	283.58
9/14	64.70	63.19	35.65	48.31	68.97	50.61	331.43
9/21	38.06	38.20	50.73	48.06	73.35	160.82	409.22
9/28	149.90	11.87	38.33	52.87	156.02	303.67	712.66
10/5	10.29	70.02	58.44	52.67	73.32	75.47	340.21
10/12	20.05	8.01	15.66	36.63	279.48	72.54	432.37
10/19	187.04	60.42	55.92	55.39	49.23	73.55	481.55
10/26	85.67	238.54	73.95	66.59	95.37	53.59	613.71
11/2	141.40	45.17	61.58	43.39	61.72	55.03	408.29
11/9	21.62	47.69	23.66	28.33	136.44	24.21	281.95
11/16	39.82	10.81	24.41	67.99	97.49	121.91	362.43
11/23	91.66	32.60	67.65	31.76	74.60	82.87	381.14
11/30	119.63	62.69	245.44	Holiday	66.36	85.32	579.44
12/7	34.65	52.04	31.38	109.78	120.84	83.34	432.03
12/14	40.64	41.34	121.30	67.17	111.69	106.08	488.22
12/21	53.06	186.79	130.97	76.47	230.55	263.84	941.68
12/28	255.73	297.79	Holiday	47.27	70.09	42.12	713.00
12/31	79.63	128.61	Holiday				208.24

* Daily sales data include 4 percent Florida sales tax.

These cash outlays were ordinary, but the circumstances calling for several of them were singularly related to The Devil's Own Wine Shoppe.

The Nelsons had not intended that Mary Lee should work in the wine shop when they opened it. At the beginning, they hired a full-time clerk (a younger girl in her early 20s) at a salary of $500 a month. Bruce planned to be at the shop during lunch-hours and late in the afternoons. The girl was laid off in the middle of December 1974, and Mary Lee began to work regularly. From then on, she and Bruce shared being at the shop. They enrolled their preschool child in a nursery and hired a baby-sitter to watch over their other school-age child after school until Mary Lee could get home.

The Nelsons carried fire insurance on the contents of The Devil's Own

TABLE 2
Sales in 1975*

Week Ending	Monday	Tuesday	Wednesday	Thursday	Friday	Saturday	Weekly Total
1/4				$ 53.01	$ 31.38	$111.02	$195.41
1/11	$ 31.67	$ 75.68	$31.60	19.66	100.59	137.96	397.16
1/18	31.94	18.22	70.82	47.63	53.92	18.67	241.20
1/25	63.30	39.95	26.39	16.27	47.92	63.00	256.83
2/1	25.98	85.43	92.21	74.34	57.32	142.64	477.92
2/8	20.95	48.60	30.90	115.61	34.87	399.96	650.89
2/15	127.81	53.83	17.68	137.31	163.16	122.70	622.49
2/22	43.49	46.94	40.13	30.67	91.25	202.39	454.87
3/1	47.79	50.89	78.20	24.22	83.32	98.40	382.82
3/8	30.68	23.44	50.48	48.27	50.78	101.45	305.10
3/15	23.47	12.74	14.36	39.03	123.17	130.55	343.32
3/22	3.54	20.83	18.02	12.58	115.78	147.19	317.94
3/29	14.63	113.22	41.75	27.68	133.86	135.76	466.90
4/5	44.36	139.72	35.71	22.25	64.76	31.79	338.59
4/12	11.46	0	43.61	102.04	133.09	134.42	424.62
4/19	28.34	64.12	59.82	24.95	67.69	141.84	386.76
4/26	118.38	23.87	41.99	16.33	28.07	48.44	277.08
5/3	37.35	10.42	44.89	26.80	74.15	32.85	226.46
5/10	35.22	25.00	14.88	20.78	56.52	66.19	218.59
5/17	32.69	27.66	33.12	55.67	74.01	72.30	295.45
5/2	7.48	20.22					27.70

* Daily sales data include 4 percent Florida sales tax.

Wine Shoppe. They did not carry burglary insurance because, Bruce reasoned, the shopping center was well lit at night and guarded by armed security men and trained dogs. An inventory as of the end of 1974 showed the wholesale value of wine and other merchandise for sale on hand to be $8,038. Cash on hand was $102.

ASSESSING THE SITUATION

With his background, Bruce did not have difficulty thinking in a traditional way about the financial condition of The Devil's Own Wine Shoppe. He wondered, though, if the newer quantitative techniques which he had learned in operations research and management science would be helpful. He set out to try them with help from a mathematically skilled friend. In fact, his friend became so interested that he prepared the following report for Bruce:

An analysis of costs, volume, and profit relationships reveal that you have sound reasons for concern, Bruce.

In an effort to use the normal curve to make predictions, daily sales were plotted. There are 239 days for which data are available. The first six classes plot something like a normal curve. The frequency polygon shows extreme skewness with a few very good days causing a tailing out toward the right. (See Table 3 and Exhibit 1.)

TABLE 3
Frequency Classification of Daily Sales

Class	Frequency
$ 0 and under $20	24
20–40	54
40–60	51
60–80	43
80–100	14
100–120	12
120–140	19
140–160	6
160–260	11
260–360	4
360–460	1
	239

EXHIBIT 1
Frequency Polygon of Daily Sales

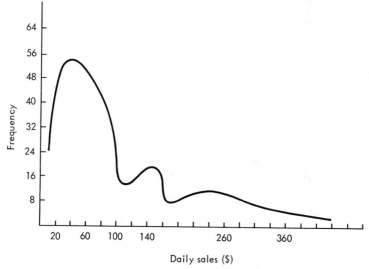

Daily sales ($)

It was assumed without rigorous statistical testing that additional data on daily sales would fully justify the assumption that the distribution could be described by a normal curve. The average monthly sales were $1,888 and the standard deviation was $394. With the mean, standard deviation, and an assumption about the distribution of the random variable (sales), it was possible to use normal curve areas and assess the probability of sales reaching certain desirable levels. (See Table 4.)

Costs per month were computed with and without a salary for you, Bruce. This made it possible to find a level of sales which would permit you to break even given the present arrangement, and also makes it possible to determine what volume would permit you to quit your job and devote full time to the

TABLE 4
Monthly Sales, August 16–May 15

Year	Month and Day	Sales
1974:	8/16–9/15	$ 2,076
	9/16–10/15	2,142
	10/16–11/15	1,779
	11/16–12/15	2,003
1975:	12/16–1/15	2,576
	1/16–2/15	2,128
	2/16–3/15	1,486
	3/16–4/15	1,641
	4/16–5/15	1,166
	Total	$16,997

Average monthly sales (rounded) = $1,888 = $\overline{X}$

Standard deviation of monthly sales (rounded) = $394 = \sigma$

Note: Sales data were available from August 16, 1974, to May 20, 1975. In order to use as much of the available data as possible, sales are shown from the middle of one month to the middle of the following month. Four days have been omitted at the end.

business. First without considering money withdrawn by yourself, expenses have averaged $1,330 a month. This figure was computed as follows: Total ordinary expenses were $12,330 for the nine months of operation. This amount was reduced by the amount shown in the drawing account ($350), and the total expenses used is $11,980 which amounts to approximately $1,330 a month for the nine months.

Markup on sales is estimated at 28 percent. This is an estimated overall markup consisting of a 20 percent–25 percent markup on low-priced items and higher markups on more expensive wines. Since sales of low-priced items have the greatest volume, an average markup seems to be justified. (You have estimated that the average price per item sold is $3.)

With a 28 percent markup on average monthly sales of $1,888, there is a $528 contribution available to cover costs. With ordinary cash outlays of $1,330 a month, the business has been losing money at the rate of about $802 a month. However federal income tax refunds—which you have gotten—based on losses amounted to about 25 percent, so these losses can be reduced by $200 to $602 a month.

However, it is obvious that the matter of the bank loan cannot be ignored indefinitely. Also, Bruce, you are overextending your energies, so that you either have to hire someone to operate the business or give up your job and devote all your attention to it. The maximum length of the loan was to have been five years. Repayment of principal, then, would amount to $250 monthly.

With a monthly expense of $1,580 which included payments on principal of $250, but no salary for you, a sales volume of $5,642 a month would be required to break even. This represents a 28 percent contribution and includes sufficient income to cover normal costs of operating the business as well as repayment on the principal of the loan. Your salary at the auto dealership averages $1,000 a month, you have said. If this is included in the calculation, the expenses go to $2,580, and a sales volume of $9,214 a month would be required to break even.

The original intent was to use the normal curve areas and assess the probability of breaking even or making a profit. This can be shown as the probability of $X > Q$, where X is monthly sales and Q is break-even point. As a picture, this is represented in Exhibit 2.

EXHIBIT 2
Normal Curve Showing Mean and Break-Even Point

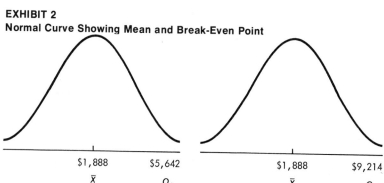

$1,888	$5,642		$1,888	$9,214
$\bar{X}$	Q_1		$\bar{X}$	Q_2

A Z value can be computed as follows:

$$Z = \frac{Q_1 - \bar{X}}{\alpha} = \frac{5,642 - 1,888}{394} = \frac{3,754}{394} = 9.52$$

Thus, there is almost no likelihood using normal curve areas and present data that the business will reach a break-even point sufficient to cover expenses excluding a salary for you. Obviously, there would be even less likelihood including that amount.

Data do not indicate that the outlook for the future of the wine shop is good, Bruce. A monthly trend line shows that sales are declining at the rate of $115 a month. Acknowledgement is made that trend analysis is designed for long-term annual data. Of course, such data are not available for the wine shop. Also, it is quite obvious that there is a strong seasonal influence on sales, with the peak occurring around the holidays at year's end. Since data are available for only nine months, they do not lend themselves to a statistical computation of seasonal influence. Recognizing all these factors a trend line was computed, and it is as follows:

$$Y' = 1,888 - 115X$$
Origin — 1/1/75
X in months
Y in sales dollars.

WHAT TO DO?

"It's decision time," Bruce said to Mary Lee, "things just aren't righting themselves." Mary Lee agreed. Even with agreement, they found decision making to be hard because in their case it involved dreams, economics, home life, and career: all in all, a way of life.

EXHIBIT 3
Profiles on Leading Categories of Business

Size of Business.   Consumer expenditures and gallonage for recent years:

	Expenditures (Supermarketing)	Gallons (Wine Institute)
1974	$2,200,000,000	370,000,000
1973	1,944,000,000	347,317,000
1972	1,700,050,000	336,985,000
1971	1,545,500,000	305,221,000

Types of Wine.   Of 1973 sales, 84.1 percent were domestic brands (69.6 percent California), and 15.9 percent imported. Of the imports, Italy supplied 26 percent, France 24.3 percent, Spain 17.2 percent, Portugal 14.9 percent, Germany 10.3 percent, all other countries 7.3 percent. Table wines were 55.1 percent of sales, followed by dessert wines (20 percent), flavored wines (17.2 percent), champagne and sparkling wines (6 percent), and vermouth (2.9 percent) (*Wines & Vines*, April 1974).

When Business Occurs.   Wine sales by months *(1973 Wine Marketing Handbook):*

January	7.0%	May	7.2%	September	7.1%
February	7.6	June	7.7	October	8.6
March	7.2	July	8.5	November	10.3
April	9.8	August	6.1	December	12.9

Where Sold.   Liquor stores 60 percent, food stores 33 percent, others 7 percent (*Supermarketing,* liquor store magazines). Average liquor store stocks 79 domestic and 151 imported types.

Place of Consumption.   A Trendex survey found 84.7 percent of wine drinkers last had wine at home, 8.1 percent in someone else's home, and 7.7 percent in a restaurant or bar. A 1972 *Food Service Magazine* survey found 55 percent of restaurants serving wine, but only 26 percent of adults ever order wine when dining out. By demographics:

Sex:	Men	26%	Income: $15,000+	38%
	Women	24	$10,000–14,999	28
			$ 7,000– 9,999	25
			$ 5,000– 6,999	15
			Under $5,000	16
Age:	18–34	32%	Region: Northeast	31%
	35–49	30	North Central	19
	50+	16	South	17
			West	40

Why People Drink Wine.   Like taste, 60 percent; be sociable, 45 percent; celebrate an occasion, 41 percent; stimulates appetite, 35 percent; helps one relax, 27 percent; habit, 17 percent; thirst-quenching, 5 percent (*Beverage Industry,* March 24, 1972).

Reason for Last Specific Purchase (Women).   Dinner, 26 percent; regular use, 18 percent; party or celebration, 15 percent; special dinner, 13 percent; gift, 11 percent; other, 17 percent (*Family Circle,* 1973). For buying specific brand; personal experience, 59 percent; husband's influence, 40 percent; friends/relatives influence, 29 percent; other, minor.

EXHIBIT 3 *(continued)*

Most Recent Usage. Newsweek survey asked last time wine was:

	Personally Consumed	Bought
Within past week	57.6%	32.1%
Within past four weeks	22.8	29.5
Within past six months	14.9	25.2
Longer ago, don't recall	4.7	13.2

Wine Drinking Occasions. The *Time* survey found 85 percent of wine users serving it during dinner, 50 percent before dinner, 31 percent after dinner, 10 percent other times. The *Newsweek* survey found 72 percent agreeing with the statement "meals generally taste better when accompanied by wine;" also 72 percent agreeing that "wine should be served whenever you have guests for dinner." 66 percent substituted wine for liquor on occasions (*Time*).

Buying Habits. A survey for the French government found 47.3 percent had discovered their favorite wine from a friend's suggestion, 31 percent from a wine-tasting session, and 10.7 percent from a waiter; 86.4 percent had decided to buy before entering a package store, and three out of four had already chosen the country of origin; 63.7 percent had decided on a specific brand or type; 13.8 percent considered vintage dates very important and 24.9 percent fairly important (*Wines & Vines,* September 1971). The *Time* survey found for home use, that men decide brands 51 percent of the time, women 22 percent, together or equally 38 percent. Men make the purchase 53 percent of the time, women 23 percent, together or equally 24 percent. The *Newsweek* survey found the decision on type to buy made before the shopping trip 66.1 percent of the time, in the store 26.6 percent; 53.7 percent decided brands before shopping and 35.6 percent in the store; 79 percent sometimes change brands, 8 percent never do, and 12 percent don't buy by brand name (*Time*). When women shop alone, 83 percent made final decision on type/brand (59 percent unaided, 24 percent somewhat influenced by others).

Gift Market. The *Time* survey found 55 percent having given wine as a gift within the past year, while 58 percent received wine as a gift; 11 percent of women had made their last purchase as a gift (*Family Circle*).

Prices. Forty-nine percent of brands are less than $1.25 a bottle, 43 percent between $1.25 and $3.50, and 8 percent more than $3.50 (*Ad Age,* October 23, 1972); 22 percent in the *Time* survey found price "very much" a factor, 50 percent said "somewhat," 28 percent "little importance."

Demographics. The 1972 *Time* survey (done in large markets only) found wine drinkers to have the following characteristics:

Sex:	Men	73%	Income:	Over $25,000	38%
	Women	27		$15,000–24,999	38
				$10,000–14,999	16
				Under $10,000	8
Age:	Under 25	3			
	25–34	16			
	35–49	39			
	Over 50	42			

EXHIBIT 3 *(concluded)*

> *Young Adult Market* is important for "pop wines . . . about 25 percent of today's sales; 70 percent consume wine, of which 61 percent drink wine at least once a week; 50 percent use table wines, 33 percent fruit wines, 17 percent "pop" wines. Most important purchase factors: type 43 percent, brand 33 percent, price 23 percent. Average weekly expenditure on wines is $4 (ABC-FM Stereo Rock Market Study, fall 1971). A *Redbook Magazine* survey found 83 percent serving wine at home; 39 percent use it for drinking, 6 percent for cooking, 55 percent both. The respondent (mostly women 18–34) buys the wine 67 percent of the time. Factors influencing brand choice include others suggestions (50 percent), advertising (36 percent), price (27 percent), and taste (17 percent). Occasions for guest use: dinners, 46 percent; when guests ask for it, 10 percent; before dinner, 7 percent; holidays, 7 percent. A National Educational Adv. Services survey found half of college students drink wine; one out of seven at least once a week.

They especially wondered about two questions. Would the market for wine in Pensacola support an all-out effort by them? Were they, themselves, committed enough to being in business to sacrifice what it would involve to make the all-out effort?

Bruce indicated that they had five options:

1. Sell the store.
2. Merge with a sandwich shop, or cheese store, to introduce wine to more people and to make it generally more available at more times.
3. Have Bruce quit his job and devote full-time to the wine shop, emphasizing the introduction of new promotion and selling activities.
4. Close the store and liquidate the assets.
5. Declare bankruptcy.

24. Triangle Construction Company*

ALF JACOBSON, the president of Triangle Construction Company, was born in Sweden and received a degree comparable to that of a bachelor of science in civil engineering in 1945 from the Stockholm Institute of Technology. His major was structural design, and after graduation he worked for five years as a consulting engineer in Stockholm where the main part of his work was in construction of large industrial plants.

Mr. Jacobson came to America in 1950 and stayed in Chicago for two years, working for one of the major building contractors as a chief engineer. His basic duty was surveying layout areas. In 1952, he returned to Sweden to his position as consulting engineer.

In 1953, Mr. Jacobson came back to the United States, settling in California. He obtained a job with Frederickson and Watson Construction Company, a large engineering and grading contractor. It was in California that he started working on highway construction; his work consisted of estimating and bidding jobs, managing work, and acting as superintendent of some of Fredickson and Watson's larger construction jobs.

Alf left Fredickson and Watson in 1962, and, together with two partners, formed the Triangle Construction Company, basing his operations in Tuscon, Arizona. "We started on a fairly small scale with capitalization of approximately $30,000. We had pretty good fortune. We kept going, and we increased our gross each year and also were able to purchase small amounts of machinery," Mr. Jacobson commented.

By buying out his two partners in 1965, Mr. Jacobson obtained a majority of the stock. At that time he brought in a new partner who was interested in the company only from a financial point of view, and Mr. Jacobson became president of the Triangle Construction Company.

COMPANY BACKGROUND

Historically speaking, the company's contracts had been 60 percent to 70 percent private work, mainly subdivision and land development for private

* Prepared by Professor Melvin J. Stanford, Brigham Young University. Copyright © 1974 by Brigham Young University. Reprinted by permission.

developers, and the remaining 30 percent to 40 percent had been public work. Both kinds of contracts, private and public, proved profitable. Most of the contracts were acquired through competitive bidding, with a small portion being negotiated.

The private work consisted of subdivisions and parking lots (basically the earth-moving portions), concrete block work, curb and gutters, drainage structures, drainage pipes, and asphalt pavings. In its public contracts, Triangle constructed bridges and larger concrete structures, although by 1968 Triangle was not doing any large structural work, electing normally to sublet this type of work out to specialty contractors.

Triangle had also diversified into construction equipment rentals and ran this subsidiary as a separate entity. The earnings and other financial data were consolidated into the Triangle Construction Company's financial statements (see Exhibits 1 through 4). Triangle had increased its sales volume from a modest $500,000 in 1962 to a gross of approximately $1.6 million a year in 1967–68 (Exhibit 3).

The largest contract Triangle had been involved in was a joint venture contract for interstate road construction near Flagstaff. The joint venture partners were Babel Sand and Gravel Company, Triangle Construction Company, and Barton Construction Company. Triangle had the engineering and administrative responsibilities, Babel was supplying the bonding capacity and equipment (rented to the joint venture), and Barton was participating with Triangle in administrative duties. Because of relative size and financial position, Babel had 50 percent interest in the contract, while Triangle and Barton shared equally the other 50 percent.

MARKET AND INDUSTRY CONDITIONS

The number of contracts for construction work had increased tremendously during the 1960s in Arizona. All surveys appeared to indicate a continued growth, even though not necessarily at a uniform rate. A heavy program of construction was expected to continue into the 1970s and even the 1980s. For the engineering contractor, the prospects for work looked good.

The population of Tucson in 1968 was estimated to be near 250,000, that of Phoenix was about 500,000, while the population of Pima and Maricopa counties combined was estimated to be near 1.2 million. Arizona was expected to have a continued influx of residents. More homes, schools, churches, and business establishments would have to be built. Road construction would be less affected by such influx, however, since the growth of road construction tended to be cyclical in nature, even though there was an overall upward trend. During the late 1960s, the roadbuilding industry had experienced a substantial decline in Arizona. The years of the early 1960s were probably the best in the area, coming to a peak in 1965.

Subdivision developers were finding it difficult to meet the current and future demands for construction since the sharp rise in expenditures for the war in Vietnam and the international monetary problems had made the money market extremely tight. Consequently, the cost of capital was going up and reached a point in 1968 where there was often no money available at any reasonable price. This caused subdividers to postpone their plans for expansion. The number of newly opened subdivisions in Tucson and Pima County during 1967 declined 50 percent from previous years. This downward trend in construction had made it difficult for individual engineering firms and caused price cutting and near-cost competitive bidding.

Management of labor and equipment was a problem, for if a contractor geared up for peak demand he would have a hard time trying to utilize the skilled manpower and equipment when work slackened. Reduction of manpower, machinery sitting idle, and postponed purchases of new equipment made it difficult to maintain orderly scheduling of work. Hence, in a construction business slowdown, a small contractor with limited equipment and a limited number of men tended to have an easier management task. On the other hand, because small contractors usually had small amounts of equity capital, during slack periods their typically higher leverage factor made them more vulnerable from a financial standpoint.

Another main difficulty of the smaller company was the lack of availability of raw materials for construction projects. The deposits that were suitable for production of crushed rock bases, asphalt, and concrete were well known, and had been under lease or ownership of larger companies that quite often combined their raw material production with contracting in their own names. The construction company that did not have its own aggregate sources was, as time went on, likely to find it increasingly hard to remain competitive. The purchasing of raw materials involved a profit by the producer, and the construction company that had to buy these materials from the extracting firm would place another profit on them. Because of various managerial, operating, and capital requirements economies, a construction firm having internal sources of raw materials supply could often underbid a small, nonintegrated contractor and still make a satisfactory profit; moreover, if it was badly in need of new work, an integrated firm was in a better position to shave its profit margins. On balance, the larger contractors seemed more able to survive, and in the late 1960s a trend for smaller firms to be absorbed by larger firms characterized much of the contract construction industry.

BABEL SAND AND ROCK COMPANY

The major partner in the Babel-Triangle-Barton joint venture was Babel Sand and Rock Company, with headquarters in Prescott. The president of Babel was Mike Hebert, a personal friend of Alf Jacobson. They had met several years previously and had business connections together during Mr. Jacobson's employment with Fredickson and Watson Construction Company. During the latter part of 1967, Mr. Hebert called on Mr. Jacobson and said he was contemplating bidding on a large project near Phoenix and wondered if Alf would like to go over the high points of the job with him. During their conversation, the idea of combining their two companies and bidding on the job as a joint venture was discussed.

The history of Babel went back a number of years to its original founder, who operated a small sand and rock business in Prescott. Fred Roberson took over sometime in the 1940s, built up the company, and apparently had a successful business venture. However, he died in 1964 and was succeeded as president by his oldest son, Tom Roberson. Apparently Tom wasn't particularly interested in remaining head of the corporation and was succeeded by Mike Hebert, who was married to Fred Roberson's oldest daughter.

Mr. Hebert was a certified public accountant and had a large public accounting office in Prescott. In addition, he had half a dozen other business enterprises in the geographical area surrounding Prescott. He admittedly was not an expert in construction, though he possessed a fair knowledge of the business.

Babel Sand and Rock Company was incorporated under the laws of Arizona on June 1, 1965, as successor to the business originally founded in the 1940s. The company's principal activities included (1) the processing and sale of basic construction materials such as rock mix (a portion of the basic materials processed was used in the company's own construction projects); (2) the performance of public and private construction contracts covering highways, streets, and bridges, on-site and off-site subdivision improvements, and water, sewage, and drainage projects; and (3) the rental of its construction equipment to other contractors.

Babel's products were sold throughout the Prescott area of Yavapai County, and construction contract work was generally limited to the same locality. That area, in terms of construction activity, represented about 25 percent of the total of such activity in the entire county of Yavapai.

Babel's general offices, maintenance facilities, and equipment storage yard were located in Prescott. In addition, Babel had permanent facilities located at:

Ash Fork—aggregate (rock and sand) plant, asphalt plant, and ready-mix concrete plant.

Prescott—aggregate plant, asphalt plant, and ready-mix concrete plant.
Cottonwood—aggregate plant and asphalt plant.

Each of these locations had its own source of raw materials at the plant site. All plant sites and raw material deposits were owned by Babel or its shareholders.

The Prescott area, having experienced sustained population growth since the early 1950s, was by 1968 one of the key centers of construction activity in Yavapai and Coconino counties, as can be seen in a breakdown of building permit valuations:

	Permit Valuation	Percent of Total
Flagstaff	$22,077,340	28%
Prescott	19,337,570	24
All other areas	37,842,700	48
Total	$79,257,610	100%

The population of each of the major communities in Coconino and Yavapai counties was as follows:

	1950	1960	1970
Yavapai County	24,991	22,912	37,005
Prescott	6,764	12,861	13,283
Cottonwood	1,626	1,861	2,815
Coconino County	23,910	41,857	48,326
Flagstaff	7,663	18,214	26,117
Williams	2,152	3,559	2,386

Flagstaff had long been noted as one of the nation's popular and growing resort areas. During the 1967–68 season, direct airline flights were begun to the city from Phoenix and Tuscon.

Building permits in the Prescott area increased in 1968 about 40 percent over the 1967 level. In view was a substantial, well-rounded program for the construction of industrial, commercial, and residential units, together with street improvements and additional interstate highway construction. Upcoming projects included:

Project	Budgeted Amount
Highway 89 to Ash Fork	$33,026,000
Highway 89A to Cottonwood	986,000
Interstate 17 near Flagstaff	11,012,000
Total	$45,024,000

These projects, all of which called for substantial amounts of basic construction materials, were due to be bid by the middle by 1969.

Since Babel's inception, each of its businesses had achieved and maintained a dominant market position. This was especially true with regard to the supply of basic construction materials. It was estimated that Babel provided approximately 75 percent of all of such materials used in its marketing area. Such materials were either put in place by Babel itself or were sold for placements by others.

Competition in contracting operations had been keen, especially in recent years, although there was only one other contractor based in the area who could be considered equal to Babel in ownership of equipment, bonding capacity, and construction experience.

As of 1968, the officers of Babel Sand and Rock Company included Mike Hebert, president; Thomas Roberson, secretary; and Daniel Roberson, treasurer. Other key personnel were:

Name	Title	Age	Years with Babel
Howard Watson	Chief engineer	49	14
Jack Gibson	Construction superintendent	47	22
Marvin Glenn	Maintenance superintendent	51	21
Harold Babcock	Plant production superintendent	44	21
John Adams	Chief accountant	37	9

As of July 31, 1967, Babel had an authorized 15,000 shares of capital stock ($100 par value); the ownership of those shares issued and outstanding was:

	Shares
Thomas Roberson	2,976
Daniel Roberson	2,976
Mike and Janet Hebert	5,952
Total	11,904

Because of personal federal income tax considerations, no dividends had ever been paid on the capital stock.

Year-end consolidated balance sheets as of July 31, 1966, 1967, and 1968, are shown in Exhibit 4. A summary of federal income tax returns covering the years 1947 through 1968 is given in Exhibit 5. Babel's tax returns had been audited and closed by the Internal Revenue Service through 1963.

In the years since Babel's inception, it had seen fit to conduct various phases of its business through subsidiary companies. Babel Investment Company controlled these subsidiaries, and its statements were consolidated with Babel Sand and Rock Company. All financial data contained in Exhibits 4 and 5 were consolidated in order to reflect the operations of Babel as one economic entity.

INITIAL JOINT VENTURE EFFORTS

The invitation to some sort of a joint venture between Babel and Triangle was born out of the fact that Alf Jacobson had an extensive background in the engineering and construction field, and Mike Hebert felt that Mr. Jacobson could supplement Mr. Hebert's own limited knowledge of construction.

The first project that they discussed in Phoenix was a large undertaking, and they felt that bidding it was premature. Subsequent to that project they discussed several other contracts and unsuccessfully bid on one or two projects. They were low bidders on the current job in Flagstaff and were awarded this contract in February of 1968.

THE POSSIBILITY OF MERGER

The idea of a closer tie between the two companies had come up for discussion and on September 1, 1968, was developing toward a possible merger of the two firms—Triangle Construction Company and Babel Sand and Rock Company. Alf Jacobson felt that it would be advantageous for Triangle to enter into a merger for the following reasons:

1. The natural resources of sand and rock and asphalt plants in possession of Babel would provide a suitable competitive background to get work in the Prescott and Flagstaff areas.
2. The competition for contracts of any size in the general area of Prescott was largely limited to one other company with similar raw materials, resources, men, and equipment.
3. The Babel Sand and Rock Company had considerable assets in equipment and capital that would help provide a basis for tackling larger jobs. The greater economic resources would allow bonding on a larger project that would otherwise be prohibitive for a smaller construction company.
4. The specialized financial knowledge that Mike Hebert possessed would help the combined company and would prove to be helpful in any future business decisions.

Mr. Jacobson felt that there were obviously some disadvantages in a merger. For example, the area of the main business of Babel Sand and Rock Company was isolated from major population centers. Prescott is surrounded by some small towns, but construction activities were not great in any one of them.

Babel's market area for sand, rock, and asphalt was basically concentrated in the Prescott-Flagstaff area. Along with these factors, Alf Jacobson was concerned about the loss of control of his own business. In preparation for further merger discussions with Mike Hebert, he began a thorough review of financial and other data to get a better idea of what the relative positions of the parties might be in a merged company.

EXHIBIT 1

TRIANGLE CONSTRUCTION COMPANY, INC.
Consolidated Statement of Financial Position
June 30, 1968

Assets

Current Assets:

Cash on hand and in banks		$ 22,463.13
Accounts receivable	$188,545.75	
Less allowance for doubtful accounts	(6,976.53)	181,569.22
Notes receivable		775.59
Due from Babel-Triangle-Barton		
joint venture		25,000.00
Cost of jobs in progress		4,855.54
Prepaid expenses		5,884.00
Total Current Assets		$240,547.48

Fixed Assets:

Cost	$220,553.50	
Accumulated depreciation	137,395.45	
Net Book Value		83,158.05

Other Assets:

Real estate—pledged	$ 17,884.30	
Due from Triangle-Barton joint venture	336.31	
Due from shareholder	8,100.00	
Deposits	2,484.90	
Organization expenses—net	59.76	
Total Other Assets		28,865.27
Total Assets		352,570.80

Liabilities and Capital

Current Liabilities:

Accounts payable	$121,765.21	
Note payable—due shareholder	15,000.00	
Contracts payable	27,425.75	
Less: Long-term portion	(4,059.25)	23,366.50
Mortgage payable—due shareholders	$ 12,065.73	
Less: Long-term portion	(10,349.73)	1,716.00
Payroll taxes withheld and accrued		4,738.84
Accrued federal income tax		4,474.04
Accrued expenses		14,073.96
Total Current Liabilities		$185,134.55

Long-term Liabilities:

Contracts payable	$ 4,059.23	
Mortgage payable	10,348.73	
Total Long-Term Liabilities		14,407.96

Capital:

Capital stock	$ 33,391.00	
Retained earnings	119,637.29	
Total Capital		153,028.29
Total Liabilities and Capital		352,570.80

EXHIBIT 2
Consolidated Statement of Retained Earnings, June 30, 1968

	Triangle Construction	Triangle Equipment	Total
Balances—June 1, 1968	$96,172.75	$49,198.25	$145,371.00
Adjustment of overaccrual of federal income taxes—year ended June 30, 1967	2,816.09	939.00	3,755.09
Refund due from internal revenue resulting from current year's loss carryback	2,008.99		2,008.99
Net income (loss)—year ended June 30, 1968 (Exhibit 3)	(47,648.17)	21,623.69	(26,024.48)
Net loss Alpha Division—year ended June 30, 1967	(999.27)		(999.27)
Provision for federal income taxes— year ended June 30, 1968		(4,474.04)	(4,474.04)
Balances—June 30, 1968	$52,350.39	$67,286.90	$119,637.29

EXHIBIT 3
Consolidated Statement of Net Income June 30, 1968

		Amount	Percent
Sales		$1,660,163.47	100.00%
Cost of Sales		1,594,755.58	96.06
Gross profit		65,397.89	3.94
Sales Expenses			
Sales salaries	$ 1,950.00		0.12
Travel and entertainment	3,070.87		0.18
Auto lease	5,322.69		0.32
Plans and specs	677.23		0.04
Advertising	141.00		0.01
Total Sales Expenses		11,161.79	0.67%
		$ 54,231.10	3.27%
Administrative Expenses			
Clerical salaries	$17,907.08		1.08
Officers salaries	25,925.00		1.56
Office supplies	2,256.56		0.14
Postage	225.99		0.01
Rent.................................	1,800.00		0.11
Dues and subscriptions	2,329.42		0.14
Legal and accounting	2,877.20		0.17
Telephone	6,019.79		0.36
Office maintenance	747.75		0.05
Bad debts	2,643.61		0.16
Group insurance	808.44		0.05
Equipment rental	1,870.00		0.11
Taxes and licenses	7,311.47		0.44
Insurance—general	494.33		0.03

EXHIBIT 3 *(continued)*

Amortization of organization expense	59.69		0.00
Utilities	988.72		0.06
Duplication—office equipment	260.67		0.02
Commission and bonus	1,103.76		0.07
Total Administrative Expenses		75,629.48	4.56%
		$(21,398.38)	(1.29)
Other Expenses—Net			
Purchase discounts	$(675.61)		(0.04)
Interest income	(1,168.51)		0.07)
Miscellaneous	(240.57)		(0.01)
Gain on sale of equipment	(428.53)		(0.03)
Interest expense	7,139.32		0.43
Other Expenses—net		4,626.10	0.28
Net Loss		$(26,024.48)	(1.57)

EXHIBIT 4

BABEL SAND AND ROCK CO. AND BABEL INVESTMENT CO.
Balance Sheets

Assets	June 30, 1966	June 30, 1967	June 30, 1968
Current Assets:			
Cash	$ 48,639.47	$ 33,520.56	$ 87,478.67
Notes and accounts receivable (net)	1,636,078.87	1,117,801.91	851,623.61
Inventories	62,495.71	171,434.15	196,737.96
Other current assets	31,505.15	17,058.34	58,842.86
Total Current Assets	$1,778,719.20	$1,339,814.96	$1,194,683.10
Less: Current Liabilities	826,167.58	749,573.29	438,199.56
Net working capital	$ 952,551.62	$ 590,241.67	$ 756,483.54
Fixed assets (less reserves for depreciation)	998,297.46	995,878.03	914,664.50
Other assets	109,700.78	103,694.68	100,676.24
Total Assets	$2,060,549.86	$1,689,814.38	$1,771,824.28
Liabilities and Capital			
Long-term liabilities	$ 301,228.59	$ 237,191.40	$ 263,024.98
Capital and surplus	1,759,321.27	1,452,622.98	1,508,799.30
Total Long-term Liabilities and Capital	$2,060,549.86	$1,689,814.38	$1,771,824.28

EXHIBIT 5

Babel Sand and Rock Co. and Babel Investment Co.—Summary of Federal Income Tax Returns Covering the Years 1949 through 1968 Year Ending June 30

	Total Income	Operating Expenses	Operating Profit*	Depreciation	Net Profit†
1949	$ 459,669.92	$ 361,828.96	$ 97,840.96	$ 42,938.40	$ 54,902.56
1950	546,053.67	433,796.57	112,257.10	52,052.89	60,204.21
1951	504,506.71	400,484.00	104,022.71	62,423.41	41,599.30
1952	481,244.83	363,383.84	117,860.99	58,991.51	58,869.48
1953	574,517.92	464,600.65	109,917.27	47,941.75	61,975.52
1954	602,949.76	487,678.27	115,271.49	52,972.57	62,298.92
1955	671,105.37	558,265.98	112,839.39	50,713.65	62,125.74
1956	794,259.24	664,381.14	129,878.10	71,879.79	57,998.31
1957	1,330,409.03	1,052,406.68	278,002.35	110,882.30	167,120.05
1958	1,936,064.27	1,526,219.22	409,845.05	118,503.31	291,341.74
1959	2,594,071.57	2,163,658.35	430.413.22	191,297.34	239,115.88
1960	4,093,417.54	3,370,244.48	723,173.06	297,376.34	425,796.72
1961	5,125,484.23	4,513,647.03	611,837.20	447,123.86	164,713.34
1962	4,133,843.37	3,618,857.02	514,986.35	442,697.60	72,288.75
1963	4,533,233.12	3,934,653.62	598,579.50	459,232.89	139,346.61
1964	5,474,852.70	4,966,560.14	508,292.56	426,026.74	82,265.82
1965	6,661,680.62	6,236,720.22	424,960.40	430,968.91	(6,008.51)
1966	4,600,140.61	4,267,845.60	332,295.01	266,193.22	66,101.79
1967	4,911,590.58	4,502,514.33	409,076.25	289,307.19	119,769.06
1968	6,981,321.27	6,581,418.84	399,902.43	310,203.99	89,698.44
Total	$57,010,416.33	$50,469,164.94	$6,541,251.39	$4,229,727.66	$2,311,523.73

Note: The above totals are for the 20-year period.

* Operating profit excludes depreciation.

† Net profit as indicated above is before percentage depletion allowance and federal income tax.

25.   Northern Scrap Processors, Inc. (A)*

IN JANUARY 1975, Mr. David Longer, owner and president of Northern Scrap Processors, Inc., learned that an outside firm had approached the local city government with a proposal to take over the municipal trash collecting operations. Although Mr. Longer's business was presently confined to processing scrap metals for recycling, he feared that the initial intrusion into the local waste removal business by this outside firm could eventually lead to an undue amount of competition in the local scrap market. Therefore, he was considering whether to make a counterproposal to the city, and if so, what the terms of such a counterproposal might be. At the same time, he had to consider the implications of this decision for his scrap business which was facing new competitive pressures from other important sources.

COMPANY BACKGROUND

Mr. Longer had bought Northern Scrap Processors in late 1969 and assumed control of operations on January 1, 1970. Northern Scrap, which served a growing northwestern city (population 50,000) and neighboring areas, was in the business of processing all common kinds of scrap metals. The company did not deal in nonmetallic materials. The main business of Northern Scrap was salvaging old automobiles, washing machines, and similar durable goods as well as industrial scrap. This raw scrap was separated into various categories and processed into different grades of reusable materials. Then, it was sold, generally through brokers, to various iron and metal manufacturers.

When Mr. Longer, a professional engineer with considerable experience in defense-related industries, took over the business in 1970, it was unprofitable and in a run-down state. (See Exhibit 1.) One of his early moves was to find a new site for his metals processing and storage operation in a different part of the city. The site he chose had a railroad siding and was large enough to provide for eventual expansion of the business. A metals house was erected on the site. This house served as secure storage for the more valuable metals

---

* Prepared by Richard S. Harrigan and Burnard H. Sord, the University of Texas at Austin. The firm's name and location are disguised.

(copper and brass) as well as office space. The layout of Northern Scrap's new site is shown in Exhibit 2.

In 1970, Northern Scrap had a dozen employees. Among these were a truck driver, a crane operator, several torch cutters, and a foreman. Problems with the foreman resulted in Mr. Longer doing a substantial amount of personal supervision. By mid-1972, Mr. Longer had found a competent and dependable foreman; as a consequence, he was able to spend more time in the office and less time in the yard.

By early 1975, Mr. Longer could look back over five years of steady growth. His sales for 1974 had been $1,556,453, his employees numbered 18

EXHIBIT 1

1969 Federal Income Tax Return Information for Northern Scrap Processors (year prior to purchase by Mr. Longer)

IMPORTANT—All applicable lines and schedules must be filled in. If the lines on the schedules are not sufficient, **see instruction M.**

GROSS INCOME	1 Gross receipts or gross sales .... Less: returns and allowances	152,321.18
	2 Less: cost of goods sold (Schedule A) and/or operations (attach schedule)	125,016.24
	3 Gross profit	
	4 (a) Domestic dividends	
	(b) Foreign dividends	
	5 Interest on obligations of the United States and U.S. instrumentalities	
	6 Other interest	
	7 Gross rents	
	8 Gross royalties	
	9 Gains and losses (separate Schedule D, Form 1120S)—	
	(a) Net short-term capital gain reduced by any net long-term capital loss . . .	
	(b) Net long-term capital gain reduced by any net short-term capital loss (if more than $25,000, see instructions)	
	(c) Net gain (loss) from sale or exchange of property other than capital assets	
	10 Other income (attach schedule)	
	11 Total income, lines 3 through 10	27,304.95
DEDUCTIONS	12 Compensation of officers (Schedule E)	
	13 Salaries and wages (not deducted elsewhere)	34,857.25
	14 Repairs (do not include capital expenditures)	5,620.51
	15 Bad debts (Schedule F if reserve method is used)	
	16 Rents	127.00
	17 Taxes (attach schedule)	6,092.86
	18 Interest	4,034.00
	19 Contributions (**not over 5% of line 28 adjusted per instructions**—attach schedule) . . .	
	20 Casualty or theft losses (attach schedule)	
	21 Amortization (attach schedule)	
	22 Depreciation (Schedule G)	1,581.05
	23 Depletion (attach schedule)	
	24 Advertising	455.39
	25 (a) Pension, profit-sharing, stock bonus, annuity plans (attach Form(s) 2950)	
	(b) Other employee benefit plans (see instructions)	
	26 Other deductions (attach schedule)	21,720.37
	27 Total deductions on lines 12 through 26	74,466.75
	28 Taxable income, line 11 less line 27	(47,161.90)
TAX	29 Income tax: (a) On capital gains (Schedule J)	
	(b) Surcharge—enter 10% of line 29(a) (Fiscal year corporations: see instructions for Schedule J)	-0-
	30 Credits: (a) Tax deposited—Form 7004 application for extension (attach copy) . . .	
	(b) Credit for U.S. tax on nonhighway gas and lube oil (attach Form 4136) .	
	31 TAX DUE (line 29 less line 30). See instruction G for Tax Deposit System . . . ➤	-0-
	32 OVERPAYMENT (line 30 less line 29) . . . . ➤	

EXHIBIT 1 *(continued)*

Schedule L—BALANCE SHEETS (See instructions)

ASSETS	Beginning of taxable year (A) Amount	(B) Total	End of taxable year (C) Amount	(D) Total
1 Cash		11,464.55	101.60	761.34
2 Trade notes and accounts receivable	11,415.73			
(a) Less allowance for bad debts		11,415.73		101.60
3 Inventories		14,187.02		15,000.00
4 Gov't obligations: (a) U.S. and instrumentalities . .				
(b) State, subdivisions thereof, etc.				
5 Other current assets (attach schedule)				
6 Loans to shareholders				
7 Mortgage and real estate loans				
8 Other investments (attach schedule)				
9 Buildings and other fixed depreciable assets . . .	128,213.42		96,236.79	
(a) Less accumulated depreciation	121,899.09	6,314.33	89,666.99	6,569.80
10 Depletable assets				
(a) Less accumulated depletion				
11 Land (net of any amortization)		3,850.00		1,200.00
12 Intangible assets (amortizable only)				
(a) Less accumulated amortization				
13 Other assets (attach schedule)		258.30		
14 . Total assets		24,560.83		23,632.74
LIABILITIES AND SHAREHOLDERS' EQUITY				
15 Accounts payable . (.payroll taxes).		414.96		513.89
16 Mtges., notes, bonds payable in less than 1 yr. . .		36,975.00		38,400.00
17 Other current liabilities (attach schedule)				
18 Loans from shareholders		315,170.36		370,153.70
19 Mtges., notes, bonds payable in 1 yr. or more . .		12,473.35		2,200.00
20 Other liabilities (attach schedule)				
21 Capital stock		10,000.00		10,000.00
22 Paid-in or capital surplus (attach reconciliation) .				
23 Retained earnings—appropriated (attach schedule) .				
24 Retained earnings—unappropriated		(350,472.84)		(397,634.85)
25 Shareholders' undistributed taxable income . . .				
26 Less cost of treasury stock	( )		( )	
27 Total liabilities and shareholders' equity . .		24,560.83		23,632.74

Schedule M-1—RECONCILIATION OF INCOME PER BOOKS WITH INCOME PER RETURN

1 Net income per books	(47,162.01)	7 Income recorded on books this year not included in this return (itemize)	
2 Federal income tax		(a) Tax-exempt interest. $...............	
3 Excess of capital losses over capital gains . .			
4 Taxable income not recorded on books this year (itemize)		8 Deductions in this tax return not charged against book income this year (itemize)	
5 Expenses recorded on books this year not deducted in this return (itemize)		9 Total of lines 7 and 8	
6 Total of lines 1 through 5 . . .	(47,162.01)	10 Income (line 28, page 1)—line 6 less line 9	(47,162.01)

Schedule M-2—ANALYSIS OF UNAPPROPRIATED RETAINED EARNINGS PER BOOKS (line 24 above)

1 Balance at beginning of year	(350,472.84)	5 Distributions out of current or accumulated earnings and profits: (a) Cash	
2 Net income per books	(47,162.01)	(b) Stock	
3 Other increases (itemize)		(c) Property . . .	
		6 Current year's undistributed taxable income or net operating loss (column 6, Schedule K) .	
		7 Other decreases (itemize)	
		8 Total of lines 5, 6, and 7	
4 Total of lines 1, 2, and 3	(397,634.85)	9 Balance at end of year (line 4 less line 8) . .	(397,634.85)

EXHIBIT 2
Layout of Facilities

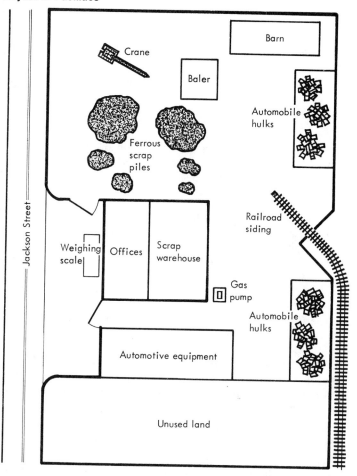

skilled people, his new site was operational, and his company was gaining stature in the community though, in his words, "it had a long way to go."

THE INDUSTRY

The environmentally fashionable industry of resource recovery actually had its origin in the much older business of waste processing. Waste processing embraces three relatively exclusive categories based on the physical state of the untreated waste when it is deposited into the environment: (1) gas, (2) liquid, and (3) solid. With the increase in the regulation of systems that inject "pollutants" into the environment, and a change in the economics of recovering resources rather than relying on virgin materials, distinct competitive markets developed around each of the three waste categories. The technology, type of competition, and the specific firms in each market vary widely.

The solid waste business involves both processing solid wastes such as trash and garbage for ultimate disposal, and reclaiming junked automobiles and other metal equipment (scrap processing).

One of Northern Scrap's competitors gave the following view of solid waste processing:

> The industry offers an unusual speculative opportunity to the investor willing to cope with a high-risk undertaking. If a firm can gain control of technology that would make its process more profitable than competitors', it could lead to substantial growth and provide the keystone to establishing a large, diverse corporate entity from humble beginnings. The elements of the speculation are as follows:
>
> 1. Energy costs will remain high.
> 2. The demand for the products extracted from today's waste will remain constant or increase.
> 3. The composition of solid waste will not change radically in the near future.
> 4. Legal and physical control can be obtained over processes, providing a clear advantage in separating and processing economically recoverable elements of solid waste.
> 5. The world economy will remain healthy enough to sustain basic material demands worldwide.

Social pressures for environmental policing and the perception of dwindling world reserves of raw materials, combined with an increasing materials usage, produced added pressure for sophisticated, efficient, and effective recycling programs. Post-consumer solid wastes amounted to 125 million tons, or 3,132 pounds per day per person in 1971. When firms package their wares using wasteful designs, such as individually wrapped portions, the cost of disposal soars. In 1966, for example, American consumers paid $25 billion for 52 million tons of packaging material, 90 percent of which was eventually discarded. Packaging wastes were 75 million tons in 1975, and were projected to increase to a level of 89 million tons by 1980.

The relative components of this national waste are given in Exhibit 3. Projected demand for key raw materials and related data can be found in Exhibit 4.

RAIL RATES

Mr. Longer indicated that the bulk of all of Northern's scrap shipments to steel mills or other users was made by rail. Barge transportation, being cheaper, was used by some scrap dealers in areas accessible by large rivers or lakes. Since Northern's market area was not adjacent to rivers or lakes,

EXHIBIT 3
The "National Garbage Can"

It takes a heap of garbage . . .

Type of waste	Percentages
Paper	31
Yard wastes	19
Food	18
Glass	10
Metals	10
Wood	4
Plastic	3
Rubber and leather	3
Textiles	1
Miscellaneous	1

Every American generates roughly 1,000 pounds of solid waste a year, according to the Environmental Protection Agency. The country's trash, as measured by weight, consists of the varied items listed above.

Mr. Longer considered the Interstate Commerce Commission's (ICC) regulation of rail freight rates for scrap steel to be critical to his business.

Rail rates for scrap steel were substantially higher than the corresponding rates for shipping iron ore, despite the fact that the pure iron recovered from a given quantity of scrap was substantially greater than the pure iron recovered from a corresponding quantity of iron ore. Moreover, rail freight rates for scrap steel had risen sharply over recent years. In 1969, the cost of shipping one gross ton from Mr. Longer's yard to one of his key customers was $4.25. In 1974, the rate was $8.97 per ton.

Northern Scrap belonged to the Institute of Scrap Iron and Steel, Inc., an association that was actively lobbying with the ICC and the railroads to get the rate differential between iron ore and scrap reduced. When asked whether he felt that the scrap industry was winning or losing the rate battle, Mr. Longer replied,

> We have won a few, but recently there have been a few decisions that indicate that we are not winning. Not long ago, one group of environmentalists instituted a suit to prevent the further increase of scrap steel rates. The basis for this suit was the tenet that scrap and iron ore are competitive—a fact which

EXHIBIT 4

Projected Usages of Key Materials and Estimated Scrap Recovery Rates

	1960	1980	1990	2000
Selected metals (comparative usage—1960 = 100)				
Aluminum	100	360		1000
Copper	100	198		390
Zinc	100	190		355
Steel	100	172		285
Lead	100	158		230
Tin	100	130		180
Aluminum (millions of tons)				
Projected consumption:				
Low		3.4	4.9	6.6
Medium		5.6		14.4
High		10.1	18.7	31.1
Relative consumption (percent of total metals):				
Low		10.9%	12.5%	16.8%
Medium		11.2	11.6	17.0
High		13.5	15.8	18.2
Projected secondary recovery from obsolete scrap:				
Low		0.48	1.02	1.68
Medium		0.61	1.50	2.94
High		0.94	2.55	4.94
Copper (millions of tons)				
Projected consumption:				
Low		2.2	2.5	2.8
Medium		3.6	5.2	6.8
High		5.2	9.6	14.0
Relative consumption:				
Low		2.1%	2.1%	2.2%
Medium		2.2	2.3	2.4
High		2.1	2.3	2.5
Projected secondary recovery:				
Low		1.3	1.3	1.4
Medium		1.4	1.6	2.0
High		1.5	2.0	2.9
Aluminum: projections (medium) of markets (millions of tons):				
Building and construction		1.60	2.49	4.25
Electric power construction		0.16	0.22	0.32
Consumer durables (except autos)		0.51	0.84	1.41
Product durables (except transport equipment)		0.55	0.84	1.32
Containers and packaging		0.70	0.97	1.22
Transportation equipment		2.04	3.71	6.07
Defense and miscellaneous		0.09	0.11	0.13
Net and end-use consumption		5.65	9.18	14.72
Steel: projections (medium) of markets (millions of tons):				
Heavy structural shapes	5.2	6.5		7.0
Oil-country goods	1.5	3.0		5.5
Nails and staples	0.2	0.2		0.2
Galvanized sheet	3.8	7.5		12.1
Railroads	8.7	13.8		20.2
Concrete reinforced bars	2.1	4.1		6.3
Line pipe	2.7	5.0		5.7
Total	24.2	40.1		57.0

to me seemed self-evident. The ICC came up with a study to support the position that they are not competitive. It seems just ridiculous. This ICC study was recently upheld by the courts, and scrap freight rates were raised by $1 per ton.

SOURCES OF SCRAP

Mr. Longer indicated that Northern dealt primarily with two types of scrap—industrial scrap (or by-product scrap) and obsolete scrap (old autos, washing machines, and so on). When Mr. Longer took over Northern Scrap in 1970, industrial scrap constituted about 10 percent of his incoming scrap. By 1974, that figure had increased to 25 percent. Mr. Longer attributed this increase primarily to an improved local market image of Northern Scrap and, to a lesser degree, to growth in the area's industrial base and the resulting larger amount of industrial scrap that stemmed from this growth. According to Longer, Northern's improved image was due to two things: "First, we now have reliable, efficient materials handling. Second, we have our containers at our customers' places of business."

Approximately 90 percent of the "obsolete scrap" which Northern obtained was brought to the yard by individuals seeking a small salvage value. Since Mr. Longer had one local competitor, the price he was willing to pay for scrap was quite important in determining the extent of his volume in the "obsolete" segment of the local scrap market. He used a pricing formula that was based on the prices being offered to him for processed scrap. Currently, he was buying ferrous scrap for $56 a gross ton. He estimated that on the average he was being paid $68 to $70 for a gross ton of processed scrap; such a spread, he felt, gave him a pretax profit margin of between 8 percent and 10 percent of sales.

COMPETITION

Northern's ability to attract scrap was also affected considerably by the actions of its competitors. In addition to one local competitor, Northern had to contend with a very aggressive competitor based in a city about 50 miles away—Yakima Scrap, Inc. Recently, Yakima had invested in a shredder—a sophisticated piece of scrap processing machinery that was designed primarily to process crushed cars at the rate of one car every 45 seconds. Scrap processed by a shredder was of purer quality and presently sold for about $88 a ton, as compared to Northern's baler processed scrap, which sold for about $68 a ton. This differential allowed Yakima Scrap to offer to pay more for old autos than Northern Scrap. After Yakima installed the shredder, Northern experienced a 40 percent decline in its volume of junked auto bodies. Moreover, because of the high cost of shredders (generally in excess of $1 million), Yakima had a strong incentive to utilize it as fully as possible. In an effort to build up the utilization of its shredder, Yakima Scrap invested in a car crusher unit costing about $60,000. (Northern currently owned neither a car crusher nor a shredder.) The car crusher unit consisted of a large front-loading device, a piece of machinery that flattened auto hulls, and a long platform truck on which the two were loaded. Essentially, the purpose of the car crusher unit was to compress old cars and make them economical to haul. Yakima had begun sending its car crusher into junkyards[1] in Northern's immediate market area for the purpose of crushing cars, and then hauling them away to its own shredder. This "invasion" caused Mr. Longer considerable consternation. "I know I will have to take some action to avoid having scrap bled away from me to a catastrophic degree," he said.

In 1972, Mr. Longer asked one of the large manufacturers of shredders to do a market survey in his locality in an effort to determine if there was sufficient scrap available to justify an investment in a shredder. At the same time, Mr. Longer did a survey of his own. Both surveys led to the same conclusion—there was not sufficient potential now or in the foreseeable future to justify the presence of a shredder in Mr. Longer's area.

Nevertheless, the shredder question continued to reassert itself. Shredders were being installed in an increasing number of scrap yards throughout the country. The number of shredders in the state in which Northern operated had increased by a factor of five over the past three years. The average shredder was capable of processing one car every 45 seconds. Longer was concerned whether his business could survive over the long term without a shredder.

Yakima Scrap was not the only organization encroaching on Northern Scrap's market area. Some steel mills made deliveries of finished goods in Northern's vicinity. Rather than having the delivery trucks return to the mill empty, the management of the mills decided that these trucks could pick up old autos from junkyards and haul these back to the mill. Over the past couple of years, an increasing number of small and intermediate size steel mills had begun to backhaul scrap, apparently because they viewed this to be a more economical source of supply. Mr. Longer knew of one steel mill located about 150 miles away which had invested in a shredder. He had driven by the mill several weeks earlier and said he had seen "acres and acres of cars" waiting to be processed.

The trucks that Mr. Longer currently owned were physically capable of hauling cars from a junkyard to his processing site. However, the cost of using these trucks to haul uncompressed cars was so high that, with few exceptions, Mr. Longer did not employ the trucks for that purpose. Consequently, 90 percent of the autos processed by Northern Scrap were brought to the yard by their owners.

Longer figured that if he purchased a car crusher, he could then haul cars more economically, being able to transport 16–20 cars on each trip as op-

---

[1] Junkyard as used here refers to an establishment that stores inoperative autos and sells parts and finally sells the hulk for salvage. Such junkyards do not process metal.

posed to 2 or 3 per trip using his present equipment. After crushing the cars which he could buy from junkyards at a price ranging from $30 to $35, he had two options. First, he could process them into steel bales at his own yard using his baler. Alternatively, he could sell the crushed cars directly to Yakima where they would be shredded. Yakima was currently offering $65 a ton for crushed cars because of its ability to sell shredded output at a considerable premium.

For Northern to realize full utilization of a car crusher, Longer judged that he would have to hire an additional truck driver (expected wage, $4.50 an hour) and two additional workers (expected wage, $3.50 an hour). Alternatively, he could rely on his present work force and simply use the crusher on a part-time basis.

SCRAP PROCESSING

For processing purposes, it was Northern's practice to divide its scrap supplies into two categories—nonferrous and ferrous. Nonferrous scrap, which consisted of copper, brass, aluminum, car radiators, and similar items, represented about 30 percent of Northern Scrap's total sales volume. Workers using small metal shears grade, sort, and cut these nonferrous materials into convenient sizes and shapes for shipping. Since this scrap was of considerable value on a per pound basis, the great majority of it was kept inside the metals house until time for shipping.

In processing ferrous metals, the "old standby" piece of equipment was the flame-cutting torch. The torch was used to separate certain nonmetallic parts from the metallic parts of purchased scrap as a prelude to further processing, as well as to separate various grades of ferrous material such as the body tin of an auto from the "dirty" cast of the engine. All workers at Northern Scrap were required to know how to use a torch. Mr. Longer said, "A good torch-man is worth considerable money because there is an art to rapid, yet efficient, torching."

Northern Scrap also had a hydraulic shear that could be used for shearing car bodies into "slabs." "From time to time, there is a market for this type of steel," Mr. Longer added.

"One of the key pieces of equipment in the scrap yard," Mr. Longer explained, "is the baler." Cars and other scrap were loaded into the baler by means of a crane. At that point, hydraulic mechanisms compressed the scrap into small bales which were usable by steel mills. Mr. Longer had the following comments about his baler:

> We will undoubtedly need to give some thought to getting a better baler one of these days. The baler we have now has had eight years of hard life. It was a marginal baler to begin with. If continuously fed, it can process one car body every six minutes. It is capable of processing 5 tons an hour, but the inability of feeding it continuously means that we can only get 25 tons a day maximum. It

has paid for itself a number of times over. If we want to have the widest possible market for our bales, we need a better quality baler.

Our current market is quite limited because of the marginal quality of our bales. Specifically, there are two problems with our current bales. First, the size of the bales put out by our machine tends to be large. Our smallest bales are 2 by 2 by 3 feet, but many of our bales are 3.5 to 5 feet long, which is awfully long. Second, the density of our bales is not what it should be. Steel mill specifications generally require a minimum density of 75 pounds per cubic foot. We are just barely capable of reaching that density, and there are many times that we don't reach it. A good baler operator can do much toward improving the size and the density of the bales.

The steel mills operate using a batch process. They have a pot of a given size, and, the greater the weight of scrap iron that they can put in that fixed pot size, the more efficient their operation is. When the steel industry is slack, they shun the poorer quality bales. In boom periods, they are interested in all qualities of bales.

. Mr. Longer added that there were balers on the market that would process 50 tons a day of consistently high-quality bales. The downtime on his present baler was still negligible. It was currently used about 50 percent of the time; of this, 30–50 percent was spent processing car bodies.

Mr. Longer explained that labor was the high-cost item in the scrap business. The skills needed were truck drivers, crane operators, torch cutters, men experienced in the sorting of nonferrous metals, men who could operate the baler or the shear, and a mechanic to help maintain the equipment. Men who had combined skills were, of course, more valuable. When a man was hired, considerable effort was made to broaden his skills. Because the work was dangerous, insurance costs ran about 16–18 percent of total labor costs.

Since the demand for scrap and the prices offered by the mill were currently reaching all-time highs and the unemployment rate in Mr. Longer's city was around 1 percent, he had difficulty in finding good employees. Mr. Longer said, "We have our share of unreliables." However, he felt many of his labor problems could be worked out with time.

PURCHASERS OF PROCESSED SCRAP STEEL

Northern Scrap sold ferrous scrap through brokers almost without exception. Dealing through brokers was typical in the scrap industry. The exceptions to this practice were a very few large scrap processors who sold directly to local mills. Mr. Longer dealt primarily with two brokers from a large, nearby metropolitan area and one other broker who specialized in sales to the Canadian market. His dealings with the brokers were explained as follows:

> At the beginning of a month, the major steel mills announce a price. This price, which can be found in various publications, is telephoned to me informally by my brokers. I then must tell them how much I want to sell. I am then

bound to make delivery on that amount by the end of the month. They, in consideration, are bound to the announced price.

If I were to decide later in the month that I want to sell more than the original amount, I don't know what price it can be sold for, or if it can be sold at all.

Northern Scrap was too small to exercise any leverage with steel mills on the matter of price. Mr. Longer pointed out that sometimes larger scrap processors did exercise some leverage with steel mills. These yards "secured a special deal for themselves," and it worked to the detriment of other scrap processors.

Mr. Longer was asked if he ever held on to inventories of scrap metals in anticipation of higher prices. He replied, "A couple of years ago, the answer was 'without qualification, we never do.' In 1974, the steel market was hectic. By that, I mean there were many peaks and valleys. Nevertheless, I felt the intrinsic value of scrap was on an upward trend, so I accumulated a large inventory of scrap and later sold it at a higher price.

"Lately our average inventory has been higher than it was in the more distant past. In earlier years, we simply didn't have the operating capital to allow us to hold an inventory."

Regarding whether scrap dealers' speculative holding of inventories affected the price at which steel mills would buy, Mr. Longer stated, "I don't think any one dealer is big enough to alter the price, except possibly in the special case where there is only one scrap dealer in a given area and also one steel mill, and there are no other dealers within a 200-mile radius. In my area, we have several aggressive, competitive dealers."

CITY TRASH COLLECTION CONTRACT

Prior to 1960, the city in which Northern Scrap was located conducted its trash collection through a contract with local businessmen. However, the reliability of the collection service deteriorated considerably over time. Consequently, the city passed an ordinance in 1960 prohibiting commercial trash collection by anyone except the city. For reasons unknown, the ordinance also stipulated that the rates charged by the city for trash collection could not exceed 75 percent of the cost of providing the service.

The rates were set by the superintendent of sanitation. Theoretically, the rates were supposed to vary as the amount of service required varied. A cursory check by Mr. Longer revealed that this was not the case. Some industrial and commercial establishments were having their trash hauled for $5 a month and certain other establishments were having their trash hauled for "literally zero." Mr. Longer attributed this deficit policy more to "lethargy and inertia" than to "politics."

In early 1972, Mr. Longer approached the city commission about the possibility of letting Northern Scrap get into the trash collection business. In contrast to the city operation which consisted of manually emptying trash cans into a dump truck, Mr. Longer proposed a service whereby he would install a more durable, sanitary container at the customer's place of business and would schedule pickups more in accordance with customer's needs. Using one of two large, roll-off trucks, which he had already bought for the purpose of serving his industrial scrap customers (see Exhibit 5), he would dispatch a driver to the customer's location where the driver would mount the large container onto the roll-off truck using hydraulic power, transport the container to a dumping site, empty it, and return the empty container to the customer's place of business.

EXHIBIT 5

In preparation for making his proposal to the city commission, Mr. Longer conducted a survey of local businessmen, and found some interest in having this more efficient roll-off service. The city took a cursory survey which drew a more pessimistic picture of the desire for roll-off service and decided to reject Longer's offer.

When, in late January 1975, Mr. Longer learned that an outside firm had proposed a trash collection contract to the city, he knew that he had to look into whether Northern Scrap should, once more, consider a trash collection contract with the city. Mr. Longer believed that if the other company was

EXHIBIT 5 (continued)

DETACHABLE CONTAINERS

The DEMPSTER-DINOSAUR is a new system of materials handling that employs small or large detachable containers ranging up to 40 cu. yd. capacity, with larger containers available for special situations. Only one man, the driver, operates the system which, in most situations, will do the work of several trucks. All operations are hydraulic and handled from simple controls in the cab. Over-the-road gross loads up to 30,000 lbs. may be handled. In off-the-road applications, weight and container size is limited only by the size of the truck. Uses of the DEMPSTER-DINOSAUR in the refuse collection, materials handling and scrap collections industries are almost endless.

HOW IT WORKS

The DINOSAUR is of extremely simple design, consisting of a tipping frame, two hydraulic raise-lower cylinders and a "U" shaped bail which is moved back and forth by a double-acting cylinder. Containers are mounted on a base which has a guide rail with recessed lifting hooks spaced from front to back at intervals to coincide with the length of the bail cylinder stroke. As illustrated in photos **70** through **73**, the bail enters and engages the first lifting hook. The cylinder pulls the container up on the tipping frame, then moves back to engage the bail in the second hook. This forward and backward ratcheting action is repeated and the frame is lowered until the container base is pulled into carrying position and locked. Progress of the bail is shown by white circles. To put container off on ground, dock or legs, the action is reversed with the bail pushing against the back of the lifting hooks. Photos below show pickup of an actual container.

awarded the contract and entered his locality to haul trash, then they might soon begin to haul scrap also. Other considerations shaped Mr. Longer's thinking as well. The scrap business, in his view, was a volatile business subject to periodic recessions. The trash business, on the other hand, was unlikely to exhibit these same mercurial shifts in volume and could thus serve as an economic base to buffer the company from the ups and downs of the scrap business.

Another factor Longer had to deal with was whether and how to increase the utilization of equipment that Northern already owned. In 1972, he had bought two large roll-off trucks and a number of containers in order to serve industrial scrap customers. In January 1975, Northern was only getting 30 percent utilization of this equipment.

REAPPRAISAL

Mr. Longer recognized that submitting a bid for the city trash collection contract meant confronting these and a number of other fundamental issues. One such issue concerned the minimum length of time for which the trash contract should run. Longer, of course, preferred any contract to span a time period long enough for him to recover whatever investment would have to be made in trash hauling equipment.

The issue of the time length of the contractual period led directly to a second issue—should Northern undertake to provide front-loader trash collection service? Front-loader service was considerably more efficient than roll-off service. Special front-loader trucks (see Exhibit 6) were dispatched

EXHIBIT 6

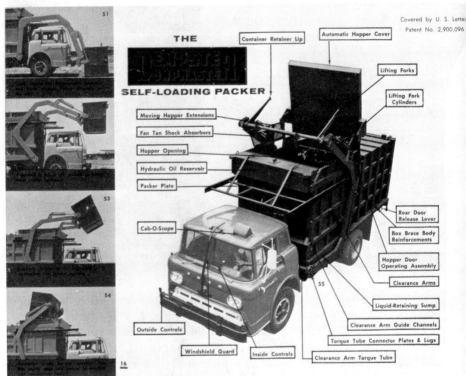

to the customer's place of business, where special garbage containers (provided to the customer as a part of front-loader service) were emptied into the front-loader truck by means of a hydraulic mechanism and then returned to their original position. Inside the truck, a compactor mechanism compressed the garbage in order to increase the truck's carrying capacity. The key advantage of front-loader service was that many customers could be serviced before the truck had to make a trip to the dumping site—as opposed to roll-off service which necessitated that each customer's container be brought to the dump individually and returned to its origin before another customer could be serviced.

If the front-loader option were chosen, Longer estimated that it would be necessary to buy at least two front-loader trucks in order to insure reliable service. New trucks retailed for about $30,000 apiece. Mr. Longer would have to hire one truck driver, in addition to those he currently employed. Wages for truck drivers of this type were generally $4–$5 an hour. The trucks would require liability insurance, registration fees, and collision insurance during their early life. Containers for customers would cost in the range of $200 to $400 apiece, depending on the size of the container and Northern's ability to order them in truck-load lots—the most economical order quantity. A truckload of containers consisted of 6 to 22 units, depending on the size of each unit.

In looking into the issue of front-loaders, Longer learned of a place where he could acquire two used front-loader trucks. The price for both trucks would have to be negotiated, but indications were that the total price would range between $18,000 and $25,000. These trucks were currently inoperable.

EXHIBIT 7
Estimated Monthly Service Rates for Containerized Waste Collection and Disposal Service

Commercial size (front-loader) containers:

Container Capacity			Monthly Rates for Basic Service* (pickups per week)						Per Additional Pickup
Cubic Yards	Gal- lons	No. of 20-Gallon Trash Cans	1	2	3	4	5	6	
3	480	24	$22	$35	$ 48	$ 61	$ 75	$ 88	$3.50
4	640	32	30	47	65	82	100	100	4.50
6	960	48	34	58	73	97	121	145	6.75
8	1280	64	44	77	103	130	150	176	9.00

Industrial size† (open top, roll-off) containers:

Container Capacity (cubic yards)	Monthly Rates for Basic Service* (pickups per month)				Per Additional Pickup
	1	2	3	4	
15 or 20	$ 66.50	$ 87.00	$107.50	$128.00	$20.50
25	78.00	104.50	131.00	157.50	26.50
30	89.50	122.00	154.50	187.00	32.50
40	101.00	144.50	188.00	231.50	43.50

* Basic service provides for:

Standard front-loader and open-top roll-off containers of selected size.
Pickup within three-mile radius of corner of Main Street and Central Avenue.
Commercial pickup during regular route runs.
Industrial pickup during regular working hours.
Waste to consist of benign materials, only; no free liquids.
Absence of unusual location conditions which increase cost of pickup.
Standard contract period (not temporary service).

The basic service rates are in compliance with city permit and ordinances. Rates are subject to changes as may be approved by the city.

† The rates for industrial size containers are exclusive of the city landfill dumping charge ($2.50 per load).

They could be towed to the Northern Scrap yard for a cost of $1,000. Mr. Longer estimated that there was a 50 percent chance that the repairs necessary to bring these trucks into operable condition would cost $10,000, a 25 percent chance they would cost $12,500, and a 25 percent chance they would cost $15,000. However, the useful life of these trucks should be at least three years and they could last up to ten years.

Based on conversations with prospective customers, city officials, and citizens of similar cities where a private trash collection program was currently in use, Longer developed a schedule of service charges which he believed would be acceptable to all of the parties concerned. This is shown in Exhibit 7.

Longer was aware that if Northern entered into a contract with the city to haul industrial and commercial trash, then the city might eventually want Northern to take over the hauling of trash from private residences. Longer viewed this possibility unenthusiastically, but it had to be weighed against having Northern Scrap undertake the task or allowing an outsider to do the job.

EXHIBIT 8

NORTHERN SCRAP PROCESSORS, INC. (A)
Income Statements, 1973 and 1974

	1974	1973
Sales of recyclable materials	$1,556,453	$719,568
Environmental protection revenue	65,892	699
	$1,622,345	$720,267
Cost of recyclable materials	1,015,406	418,136
Gross profit	$ 606,939	$302,131
Salaries and wages	$ 163,458	$ 69,068
Depreciation	39,365	13,892
Transportation expense	62,606	12,274
Maintenance	40,327	28,155
Insurance	12,334	10,975
Property and other taxes	19,929	9,364
Other expense	87,928	31,521
Total operating expense	$ 425,947	$175,249
Profit from operations	$ 180,992	$126,882
Interest expense, net	18,076	16,992
Profit before federal income tax	$ 162,916	$109,890
Federal income tax	57,367	0
Net income after tax	$ 105,549	$109,890
Retained earnings beginning of period	($ 271,622)	($381,512)
Net income per books	105,549	109,890
Federal income tax adjustment	(12)	—
Retained earnings at end of period	($ 166,085)	($271,622)

Finally, if Northern did enter into a contract with the city, there was the issue of how best (if at all) to promote this new service. Should Longer hire a PR man or contract with an ad agency? Should he rely completely on phone calls and personal selling? Should he mail brochures or use local radio and TV?

The city council was meeting in one week to consider, among other things, the issue of trash collection. Mr. Longer had to make his decision and, if the decision on trash collection was affirmative, then to submit a written proposal to the council. Yet, he knew that his decision on the trash collection issue must be coordinated with his decisions regarding investments in new equipment such as a car crusher, a new baler, or a shredder.

EXHIBIT 9

NORTHERN SCRAP PROCESSORS, INC. (A)
Balance Sheets, 1973 and 1974

	1974	1973
Current Assets:		
Cash	$ 78,803	$ 5,216
Accounts receivable	1,277	0
Inventory	28.554	89,417
Income tax deposits	85,000	—
Construction contract deposit	10,000	—
Other current assets	466	907
Total Current Assets	$204,100	$ 95,540
Land, buildings, and facilities	$421,547	$243,565
Reserve for depreciation	(76,067)	(38,461)
Fixed assets, net of depreciation	$345,480	$205,104
Total Assets	$549,580	$300,644
Current Liabilities:		
Federal income tax payable	$ 57,367	—
Other current liabilities	462	$ 1,213
Current portion of long-term notes payable	62,251	16,400
Total Current Liabilities	$120,080	$ 17,613
Long-term portion of notes payable	$200,131	$159,199
Common stock, $100 par value, 100 shares issued and outstanding	$ 10,000	$ 10,000
Additional paid-in capital	385,454	385,454
Retained earnings (or deficit)	(166,085)	(271,622)
Net equity	$229,369	$123,832
Total Liabilities and Equity	$549,580	$300,644
Working capital	$ 84,020	$ 77,927

26.   A Note on the Petroleum Industry*

In 1858, the Seneca Oil Company sent Col. E. L. Drake to Titusville, Pennsylvania, to explore for a commercially marketable supply of oil. Prior to that time, petroleum was skimmed from oil springs and creeks or obtained by throwing a flannel or woolen blanket on top of oil springs or creeks and letting it absorb the oil. In other instances it was produced incidentally in salt wells. None of these methods produced enough oil to market on an extensive scale. When Drake arrived in Titusville he began collecting oil from the springs on the Brewer, Watson & Company farm, started to *dig* a well, abandoned the idea because of water and cave-ins, and decided to *drill* for oil. He was successful and thus began the petroleum industry. The Drake well not only was the first oil well to be deliberately drilled but it also, and more importantly, pointed the way for obtaining petroleum in large enough quantities to make its production and sale commercially feasible.[1]

THE EMERGENCE AND GROWTH OF THE MAJOR OIL COMPANIES

The oil industry in the early post-Civil War years was structured and managed like most other industries at the time. It consisted principally of small firms specializing in one function. Gradually, however, firms became larger and some even began to integrate backward and forward from their original operation. Outstanding in both the size of its operations and its growth via horizontal and vertical integration was The Standard Oil Company, incorporated in 1870 by John D. Rockefeller, his brother William, and three other partners. From the outset, Rockefeller stressed the importance of large capacity and efficient operations as means of reducing costs and increasing profits. The company discovered, as early as 1884, that by concentrating 75 percent of its production in three big refineries that its average refining costs per barrel fell to 0.534 cents compared to 1.5 cents for the rest of the industry. Standard Oil's rise to a position of market dominance is business legend. So also is the Supreme Court's historic declaration that the

---

* Prepared by Professor Arthur A. Thompson, Jr., and Victor Gray, research assistant, The University of Alabama.

[1] Paul H. Giddens, "The Significance of the Drake Well," *Oil's First Century* (Boston: Harvard Graduate School of Business Administration, 1960), p. 23.

Standard Oil trust was an illegal monopoly under the Sherman Act of 1890 and, consequently, had to be dissolved.

The breakup of Standard Oil created 34 "new" companies. Exhibit 1 summarizes what has happened to the 34 descendants of the old Standard Oil Company. Interestingly enough, before the split-up in 1911, the net worth of the old Standard Oil Company was $660 million. In 1975, the net worth of each of the seven surviving descendants (Exhibit 1) was greater than that of the former parent, some of them many times greater. At least a dozen companies which were never part of the Standard Oil trust have also grown to be larger than the Standard Oil Company of 1911, including Royal Dutch/Shell, Texaco, and Gulf Oil.

From the time of the Standard Oil breakup until the present, seven companies have ranked among the leaders in supplying oil to world markets: Exxon, Royal Dutch/Shell, British Petroleum, Gulf, Texaco, Mobil, and Standard Oil of California or Socal (which markets under the Chevron brand name). These seven companies—five American, one British, and one Anglo-Dutch—were all major companies prior to the 1920s and, for a variety of reasons, are often referred to as "the Seven Sisters"—mainly because of their "cooperative" activities and "closeness." Some of the interlocks and ties among the Seven Sisters are suggested by Exhibits 2, 3, and 4. The Sister's cooperation and closeness are further illustrated by the following two events. In 1928, with some French interests, British Petroleum, Royal Dutch/Shell, Exxon, and Mobil entered into what became known as the "Red Line Agreement." The agreement provided for the four partners to share all oil discovered in the new, developing fields of the Middle East and included provisions which minimized any competition in production, refining, or securing concessions within the area. The effect was to monopolize the supply (according to oil industry critics) or to steady an unstable situation (according to the companies). A second 1928 agreement between the integrated majors:

> . . . called upon the major oil companies to accept and maintain their relative shares of world petroleum markets as of 1928; in other words, their position as is.
>
> The six remaining principles dealt with matters essential to maintaining effective international control through the pooling of company resources. These called upon the companies: (1) to mutually share among themselves on a preferential cost basis their existing facilities; (2) to avoid unnecessary duplication of new facilities; (3) to maintain for each geographic producing area its natural financial advantage with respect to its nearby geographic markets; (4) to draw supplies for a given market from the nearest producing area; (5) to avoid use of surplus crude production from any geographic area to upset the price structure in any other area; and (6) to eliminate measures that would materially increase costs and prices.[2]

---

[2] David I. Haberman, Hearings before the Senate Subcommittee on Multinational Corporations, 1974, Part VII, p. 14.

EXHIBIT 1
Tracing the 34 New Companies through History

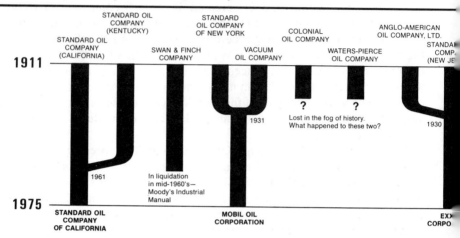

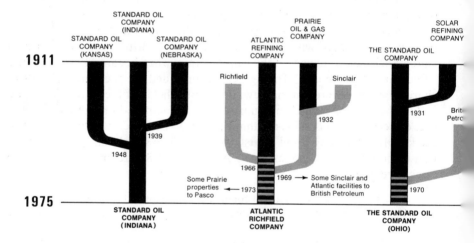

Note: Here's what has happened to the 34 descendants of the old Standard Oil Company, dissolved by a federal court order in 1911. This chart is not intended as an exact definition of corporate relationship. For example, a merged company is not wholly owned by the company shown as the survivor in all cases. Several of the merger dates are approximate, as some of the mergers were a gradual process.
Source: Standard Oil of California.

After the end of World War II, the companies expanded the number of interlocking jointly owned production companies and were combined with a system of long-term mutual supply contracts. Socal, Texaco, and Gulf joined the other four in their Middle East understandings.

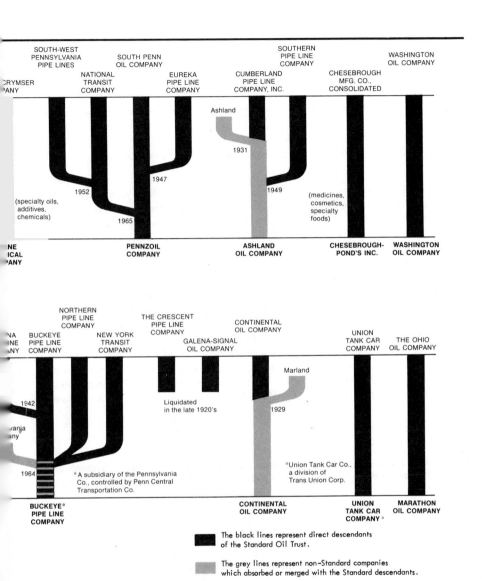

In 1952, a Federal Trade Commission study entitled *The International Petroleum Cartel* eventually led to an out-of-court consent decree whereby the Seven Sisters agreed to certain modifications in their practices. Irrespective, though, of the alleged cartel and monopoly activities among the Seven Sisters, many new oil companies became active and successful in international oil in the 1950s and 1960s:

	1950	1960	1970	1974
Largest international companies	7	7	7	7
U.S. independents	10	18	30	34
Foreign independents	2	4	31	41
Foreign government entities		2	13	17
Total	19	31	81	99

One critic has summarized and portrayed the Seven Sisters' behavior thusly:

In Pittsburgh the solid stone monument of Gulf, with a pyramid on the top, has dominated the city for forty years, still linked with the wealth of the first Pittsburgh family, the Mellons. In San Francisco the tower of the Standard Oil Company of California, or Socal, looms over the bay like a fortress, the richest company in the city. In New York two of the sisters face each other across 42nd Street, but with almost opposite viewpoints: Texaco, inside the Chrysler building, cultivates a reputation for meanness and secrecy, while Mobil over the road is the most loquacious and extrovert of them all, churning out explanations, complaints and counterattacks through the TV channels and newspapers. Across the Atlantic in London, the headquarters of BP rises up from its own piazza, announcing with its name Britannic House that here is an oil company that is part of the nation's patriotism, half-owned by the government.

Within these corporate citadels there was little doubt that they were competing ferociously with each other. Their inhabitants seem to belong not so much to the world of "oildom" as of Mobildom or Gulfdom, and with some coaxing

EXHIBIT 2
Ownership Links between the Major International Oil Companies (including Compagnie Française des Pétroles) and the Major Crude Oil Producing Companies in the Middle East

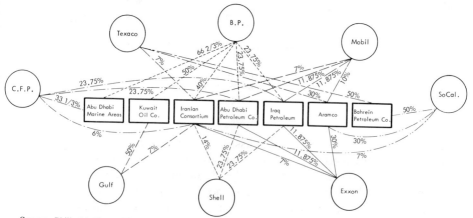

Source: Philip M. Stern, *The Rape of the Taxpayer* (New York: Random House, Inc. 1974).

EXHIBIT 3

Interlocking Directorates among International Oil Companies in the Middle East

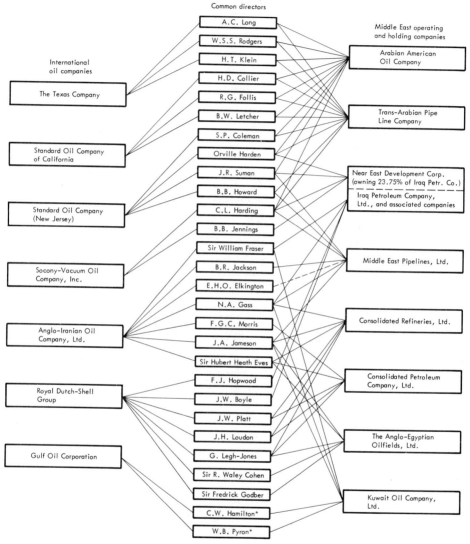

Broken line represents alternate directorships.

Note: This chart was prepared as of January 1, 1950, except for the following: A. C. Long was listed as a director of The Texas Company in the *Annual Report* for 1950 of the company, but the effective date of the appointment was not given; the directors of the Trans-Arabian Pipe Line Company are given as of January 18, 1949, the last date for which this information was available to the Commission.

* Vice Presidents for Foreign Operations.

Source: FTC, *The International Petroleum Cartel*, 1952.

EXHIBIT 4

Relationships between International Oil Companies and Major Domestic Oil Companies through Indirect Interlocking Directorates*

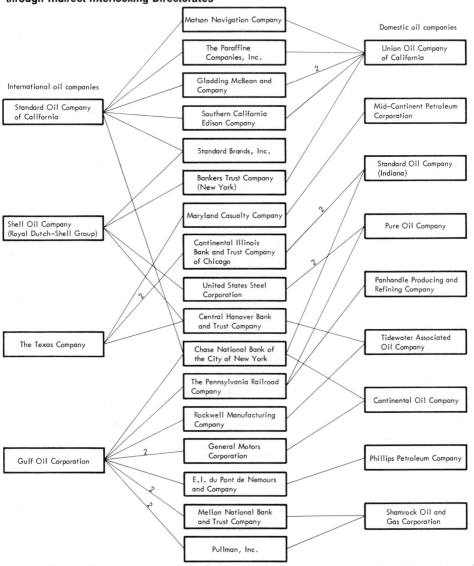

* As of January 1960.

Note: In cases where there are more than one interlocking directorate, the appropriate number is shown.

Interlocking directorates among major domestic oil companies not having important international interests are excluded from this chart. For examples of such interlocks, see the Federal Trade Commission, *Report on Interlocking Directorates*, 1951, chap. 12.

Source: FTC, *The International Petroleum Cartel*, 1952.

they could be persuaded, I found, to criticise each other. Yet each had been linked to all the others through a web of joint ventures and concessions across the globe, from Alaska to Kuwait: sharing now with one partner, now with another, in different permutations. It was this strange cavorting of the sisters, competing one moment and conniving the next, which had made them such an enduring subject of suspicion and investigation by politicians, economists and nationalist leaders.[3]

THE STRUCTURE OF THE INDUSTRY

The petroleum industry comprises a wide range of geographically separate and technically distinct activities relating to getting oil from the ground to the final user. The main stages in the process are (1) finding and producing the crude oil, (2) transporting it to the point of processing, (3) refining it into marketable products, (4) transporting the products to regions of use, and (5) distributing them at retail. However, in the search for oil, producing companies are inadvertently or contingently involved in the production, use, and sale of natural gas. Thus many of the major oil companies are also major suppliers of natural gas.

In the United States, over 10,000 companies are involved in oil and gas exploration and production. No one firm accounts for more than 11 percent of oil and gas production. Over 75 percent of total U.S. crude output comes from Texas, California, Louisiana, and Oklahoma, with almost 40 percent from Texas alone. It moves mainly through 74,000 miles of gathering lines and 79,000 miles of trunk pipelines, as well as on oceangoing tankers, river barges, railroad tank cars, and trucks, to some 260 operating refineries, with a total 1973 capacity of 14.2 million barrels per day. These refineries are operated by approximately 131 companies; in 1974, the top four companies accounted for 31 percent of refining capacity, and no one company had more than 9 percent. Ignoring differences in individual performance and minor year-by-year fluctuations and focusing only on principal petroleum products, a barrel of crude when refined breaks out roughly as 46 percent gasoline, 1.3 percent kerosene, 8.7 percent residual fuel oil, 3.7 percent asphalt, 6.8 percent jet fuel, and 33.5 percent gas, oil distillates, and miscellaneous products. In 1974, about 100 pipeline companies were engaged in transporting crude oil and refined products on an interstate basis; additional companies operated intrastate. The top four pipeline companies accounted for about 24 percent of total volume moved, with the largest having a share under 7 percent.

The greater proportion of these products move from the refinery to the final customer via one or more intermediate storage facilities. Although residual fuel oil, for example, may go to large utility and industrial customers directly from the refinery, most products go first to large terminals, located generally at the outlet of a pipeline, or on a river, lake, or coastal port, where they can take barge or tanker delivery. By far most of these terminals are

---

[3] Anthony Sampson, *The Seven Sisters* (New York: The Viking Press, 1975), p. 7.

owned by refiners, although independent wholesaler-owned terminals take a substantial portion of the distillate and residual oils. Most gasoline and home heating oils go next to still another storage facility, the so-called bulk plant—although some is sold directly to large commercial, industrial, and governmental users. The bulk plants are generally smaller than the terminals and are located near the final customers. From the bulk plants, the gasoline is transported to service stations and the heating oil to the storage tanks of homes and commercial establishments. However, in the case of gasoline it is not uncommon for terminal operators—mostly within the marketing departments of the refinery companies—to bypass bulk plants and ship directly to the service stations. This development was made possible by the construction of large-volume retail outlets and the use of increasingly efficient truck carriers.

In 1975, there were about 15,000 wholesale distributors, and about 190,000 service station retailers (down from a peak of 226,000 in 1972). These figures do not include an indeterminate number (more than 100,000) of other outlets such as convenience food stores, motels, and car washes that also retail gasoline as a secondary activity. The large oil companies own less than 10 percent of the retail outlets which they supply; most are owned (or leased) and operated by wholesalers and retail resellers who establish their own prices and operating practices.

The accompanying table summarizes the structure and extent of concentration in the industry as of 1974.

Concentration Ratios, 1974 (percent)

	Top 1	Top 4	Top 8
Production:			
Oil (net liquid hydrocarbons)	10.0%	31%	49%
Gas (net)	10.7	29	44
Refining capacity	8.4	31	55
Marketing:			
Retail branded gasoline sales	8.1	30	52
All petroleum products	10.7	31	52
Petroleum pipelines (interstate; by volume)	6.9	24	43
All U.S. manufacturing average		39%	60%

VERTICAL INTEGRATION IN THE OIL INDUSTRY

As early as 1900–11, vertical integration had become a part of the oil industry's way of life insofar as the large, successful companies were concerned. The dissolution of Standard Oil added impetus to vertical integration because a number of the newly created companies had major gaps in their business operations. Ohio Oil and Prairie Oil and Gas were chiefly producers and pipeline operators; Continental and Standard of Kentucky were purely marketing companies and Standard of New York was almost a pure marketing company; Standard Oil (N.J.) and Atlantic Refining Company were, for the most part, refiners, although both engaged to some extent in domestic marketing. Standard Oil of Ohio and Standard Oil of Indiana were refiner-marketers (the latter was prevented by its charter from engaging in crude oil production).

Over the next decade or so, with the demand for petroleum products increasing, with sales of automobiles beginning to mushroom, and with alternating periods of crude oil shortage and oversupply, nearly all of the major companies found it less risky (and sometimes essential for competitive survival) to integrate both vertically and geographically. In the case of a refiner-marketer, there was always the threat that the feast of new crude oil discoveries would be followed by famine if and when the fields ran dry or demand increased faster than supply. So, both to preserve their profitability in the case of mushrooming supplies and to guard against possible shortages, it was desirable to integrate backward, part or all the way. This meant cultivating the goodwill of producers and drillers and making continued exploratory efforts attractive by constructing gathering lines and storage facilities as rapidly as possible and in sufficient volume to handle whatever was offered. It also meant going into production whenever and wherever necessary.

Crude oil producers, in turn, could escape their feast or famine dilemma only by developing their own markets outlets, integrating forward into both refining and retail distribution. Without assured markets, producers were necessarily subject to the randomness of crude oil discovery and the ease of competitive entry in drilling and exploration. In both situations vertical integration contributed to the stability of the integrating company, first by providing some security against market fluctuation and instability and, second, through greater certainty of profit margins associated with a continuous utilization of producing capacity, pipelines, refinery facilities, and marketing outlets. In general, the oil companies which chose to integrate appeared to be seeking a degree of balance in their operations so as to protect them against what they perceived as an uncertain profit and competitive position associated with heavy fixed costs and with being heavily dependent on uncontrolled intermediate markets. By maintaining a balance in each of the stages in which they did business, the operations at each stage tended to become mutually reinforcing and, thus, a contributor to greater operating efficiency and stability.

According to the classic study of integration and competition in the petroleum industry by Professors Melvin de Chazeau and Alfred Kahn in 1959, the following composite paraphrase represents a rough consensus of how the executives of almost all the leading oil companies viewed the importance of integration:

> We certainly try, in general, to keep a balanced operation. We will not ordinarily make major investments in one level without seeing that we are pretty well covered at other levels. So we do not expect to make the same

return from our investments in production, refining and marketing. As a general rule we will not demand as high a return from prospective investments that put us in balance as from those that put us out of balance. We have a going organization, with substantial commitments at all levels; we cannot shift from one to the other with each short-term fluctuation of returns; we have to protect the positions we already have.[1]

Professors de Chazeau and Kahn also concluded as a result of their study that:

The only places where it seemed monopoly profits could still be locked in between, say, 1911 and 1935, were in pipeline transportation, where entry was not easy and an integrated company could at least for a time hold on to the difference between the pipeline costs and rail tariffs; in the adoption of thermal cracking, where patent control blocked access of independents; and possibly in undertaking distribution of one's own branded gasoline through the construction of one's own service stations. In each instance . . . the high promised returns materialized, but could not be preserved definitely. These areas become the new foci of integration and investment decisions because changing circumstances made these the operations a large company had to control for its own protection—if only temporary and partial—against the eroding influences of free markets.[5]

Of these three possibilities, pipeline transportation was the most attractive. A refiner who had control over the pipelines in a given oil field was in a good strategic position to convince producers that their most profitable alternative was to sell their oil at the wellhead. Smaller, nonintegrated refiners, who were unable to finance such pipelines, either had to locate their refineries in the field close to the wellhead or to pay the charges which pipeline owners insisted upon to carry their oil.

However, in 1935 when the states in which large crude oil supplies were being found began to exercise control over the amount of oil produced from each well each year (via a system called "prorationing"), production became the strategic area for almost the first time in the history of the U.S. oil industry. Control over production meant that the tyranny of a highly unstable and inelastic supply of crude oil could be curbed, allowing the crude market to be effectively stabilized and the profits of successful producers made less uncertain. Integration of marketing, refining, and pipelines alone no longer offered the only promise of market stability. Pipeline owners found it far more difficult to give preference to their own producing wells in periods of excess supply; and nonintegrated refiners and marketers were confronted with the somewhat uncomfortable situation of buying in a market where prices were relatively stable compared to the retail markets in which they sold. In such an environment, it was not surprising that the major companies,

---

[4] Melvin G. de Chazeau and Alfred E. Kahn, *Integration and Competition in the Petroleum Industry* (New Haven, Conn.: Yale University Press, 1959), p. 114.

[5] Ibid., pp. 116–17.

already committed to an appreciation of advantages of vertical integration, began to work hard at improving the balance between their producing and their downstream operations.

Currently, about 50 petroleum companies in the United States can be classified as vertically integrated in that they operate in at least three stages—production, refining, and marketing. However, since even the largest oil companies are not so integrated as to be self-sufficient in all stages of operation (see Exhibit 5), significant markets for crude and for refined

EXHIBIT 5
Worldwide Self-Sufficiency of the 17 Leading U.S. Refiners, 1969 and 1959

U.S. Rank in Crude Refining Capacity, 1969	Company	Self-sufficiency, 1969 (percent)	Self-sufficiency, 1959 (percent)
1	Standard (New Jersey)—now Exxon....	88.3%	77.1%
2	Standard (Indiana)	66.4	51.5
3	Texaco	106.7	92.4
4	Shell Group	72.5	74.2
5	Standard (California)	138.1	105.4
6	Mobil	75.5	69.5
7	Gulf	193.0	172.7
8	ARCO	96.7	64.6
9	Sun	87.4	55.7
10	Union	85.6	50.0
11	Standard (Ohio)*	28.9	28.1
12	Phillips	65.4	71.3
13	Ashland	13.9	8.8
14	Continental	158.4	104.0
15	Cities Service	89.5	44.6
16	Getty	241.1	71.8
17	Marathon	163.2	109.0
	Top 4	84.8	76.5†
	Top 8	96.2	84.2†
	All 17	97.1	96.8†
	Five largest United States international companies.‡	108.9	93.5†

* Does not include British Petroleum which had a self-sufficiency in 1959 and 1969 of 131.1 percent and 157.4 percent, respectively.
† Data for the same 4, 5, 8, and 17 leading companies in 1969.
‡ These are Standard Oil (New Jersey), Gulf, Texaco, Standard Oil (California), and Mobil.
Source: Ratios obtained from the *Oil and Gas Journal*, January 18, 1971, pp. 22–23. Multicompany measures were computed from production and capacity data contained in the same source.

products exist. Almost every oil company to one extent or another buys or sells crude and refined products to balance out its operations; this results in oil companies engaging in numerous transactions with one another.

These transactions (called exchange agreements) occur for several reasons:

1. To help lower transportation costs.
2. To give refiners greater flexibility in securing appropriate quality crude.

3. To help reduce inventory and operation costs and supply interruptions caused by temporary surplus/shortage situations at refineries or terminals.

For example, when a company's crude is of the desired type and is geographically close to its refinery, the company will arrange transportation from the oil field to the refinery. If the company owns more crude than it needs in its refinery, it will sell the volumes least attractive to it. If its crude is not the proper type or is remote from its refinery, the company can arrange to exchange with another refiner who can run this crude economically. Through exchanges and purchases and sales, companies are able to minimize transportation and refining costs, thus providing lower cost products to the consumer.

As another example, short-term disruptions may create a need for spot or emergency exchanges. Pipelines or refineries may be shut down for several days due to fires, mechanical failure, process upsets, and so on; tankers or barges may be delayed due to weather conditions, strikes, or operating problems. The short-term disruption can be solved if another company makes a spot or emergency exchange. For instance, Company A might lend 5,000 barrels of product to Company B whose shipments have been delayed. Then a few days later when its shipment arrives, Company B can return the barrels. An exchange of this nature may save many miles of costly trucking from a distant terminal and allow uninterrupted service to consumers.

Many oil industry critics, however, see vertical integration as a monopolistic element. To the extent that firms are integrated, they are insulated in part, from demand-supply changes at each of the processing stages; this, in turn, results in prices which may not be completely responsive to market conditions. Critics also allege that vertically integrated firms are able to put a squeeze on independents by shifting profits to their production operations, thereby keeping marketing and refining profits artificially low so as to discourage entry and further expansion of nonintegrated independent refiners and marketers. Allegedly, integrated majors can raise the crude price without raising refined product prices and make their profit primarily in production. Until the oil depletion allowance was eliminated, this was possible, in part, because of the tax break which producers received—see Exhibit 6. Insofar as exchange agreements are concerned, critics see these as being, on some occasions, a way to exchange information and promote relaxed competition and, on the other occasions, as being a vehicle for squeezing or punishing maverick firms—especially independents. Exhibit 7 shows how the 1975 assets of the U.S. sisters were distributed among the various vertical stages.

PIPELINE OPERATIONS

Most interstate pipelines in the United States are owned by more than one company. This stems from exceptionally large economies of scale (see Ex-

EXHIBIT 6

Example 1. Tax Results of Integrated Oil Firm Selling Its Crude Oil at Normal Prices	*Example 2.* Tax Results of Integrated Oil Firm Selling Its Crude Oil at Inflated Prices

Crude Oil Level:
Cost to recover crude oil . . . . $ 30
Gross income from sale of crude   30

Income before taxes . . . . $ 0

Refinery Level:
Cost of crude oil $30
Cost of refining   40

Total cost $70

Gross income $100
Cost of goods sold   70

Income before taxes . . . . $ 30

Tax Liability:
Oil depletion allowance (20% . . . . $ 6
  of wellhead gross income)
Taxable income   24
Corporate tax   12

Net profit after taxes . . . . $ 12

Real net profits after taxes . . . . . $ 18
  (allowance and profits)

Crude Oil Level:
Cost to recover crude oil . . . . $ 30
Gross income from sale of crude   60

Income before taxes . . . . $ 30

Refinery Level:
Cost of crude oil . . . . $ 60
Cost of refining   40

Total cost $100

Gross income $100
Cost of goods sold 100

Income before taxes . . . . $ 0

Tax Liability:
Oil depletion allowance (20% . . . $ 12
  of wellhead gross income)
Taxable income . . . . $ 18
Corporate tax   9

Net profit after taxes . . . . $ 9

Real net profits after taxes . . . . . $ 21
  (allowance and profits)

Source: James E. Inman, "A Contrived Oil Shortage," *Atlanta Economic Review,* November/December 1974, p. 21.

EXHIBIT 7
Distribution of Assets among the Various Vertical Stages, U.S. Sisters Only, 1975
(dollar figures in millions)

Company	Production		Transportation		Refining†		Marketing		Other		Total Assets
	Amount	Per-cent*	Amount	Per-cent	Amount	Per-cent	Amount	Per-cent	Amount	Per-cent	
Exxon	$8,487	33%	$4,275	16%	$7,693	29%	$4,374	17%	$1,263	5%	$26,092
Gulf	5,326	45	1,023	9	3,170	27	1,667	14	700	6	11,886
Mobil	4,524	38	1,371	12	3,287	28	2,426	21	187	2	11,795
Socal	4,925	48	1,032	10	2,713	27	1,406	14	161	2	10,237
Texaco	7,345	53	1,186	9	3,173	23	1,974	14	164	1	13,842

* May not add to 100 percent due to rounding.
† Refining includes chemical operations.
Source: U.S. Treasury Department, *Implications of Divestiture,* staff study (Washington, D.C., June 1976).

hibit 8) which extend the efficient volume of a pipeline beyond the level which a single company can utilize. Moreover, the risk capital required for a large pipeline project can be immense; for instance, the Trans-Alaska Pipeline system is the largest single capital project ever undertaken by private enterprise.

EXHIBIT 8
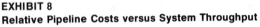
Relative Pipeline Costs versus System Throughput

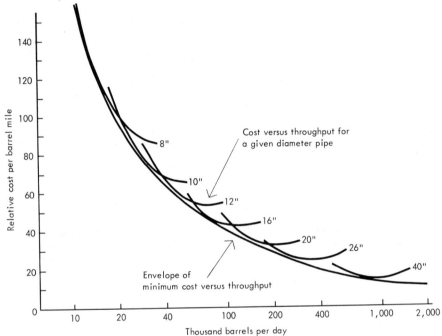

Source: Exxon Company, U.S.A.

Pipeline owners may require throughput guarantees or some other provision for the recovery of costs incurred before they will connect a new shipper to the system. The cost of a new connection may include laying a pipeline to the new shipper or installing new metering facilities to account for shipments or building additional working tankage. Throughput guarantees commit the shipper who is requesting the connection to either ship sufficient volumes or pay sufficient tariffs to provide some reasonable assurance that the added investment by the pipeline owner will be paid off. The ICC has authority to address any abuses, including the prevention of excessive throughput guarantees. Small nonowner firms are guaranteed access to pipelines on an equal basis with large owner-users and thus crude and product transportation is available to producers, refiners, and marketers alike.

Pipeline practices such as minimum tender requirements are dictated by considerations of efficiency. Crude oils vary greatly in quality, as do the different types of refined products. To minimize mixing and contamination at the interface between sequential batches of crude or product, the pipeline sets minimum batch sizes. When a full batch is accumulated, it is pumped through the pipeline.

Whenever common carrier pipeline capacity is inadequate to meet volumes tendered, government regulations require that available capacity be allocated equitably. Pipeline proration rules allocate capacity in proportion to recent shipments or current tenders of new shippers and historic shippers alike. Deviation from the pipeline's proration rules in favor of an owner company is a violation of the law. Under ICC regulations and the common carrier status of the interstate pipelines, users have the right to appeal for relief to the ICC if they feel they have been treated unfairly. The ICC has broad remedial powers in the event that a pipeline fails to conduct its operations as a true common carrier.

Pipeline tariffs are regulated by the ICC and have fallen steadily since the early 1950s, mainly because new technology has allowed larger and larger diameter pipelines with their resultant economies of scale and greatly reduced costs. According to ICC statistics, the average industry revenue per barrel moved 1,000 miles fell from 65 cents in 1955 to 50 cents in 1971. Pipeline tariffs tend to be competitive with alternative transportation modes, such as Gulf/East Coast tankers and Mississippi barges.

REFINING

Historically, the refining segment of the oil business seems to have been the least profitable (see Exhibit 9). Nonetheless, the refining capacity of the oil industry has continued to expand in step with market demands. At the same time, investment in refineries grew, owing to the implementation of

EXHIBIT 9
A. Rates of Return on Net Worth: Petroleum Industry and Other Manufacturing (in percent)

	Oil and Gas Producing Companies	Refining and Integrated Companies	Other Manufacturing Companies
1950–1954, average	17.2%	14.8%	13.4%
1955–1959, average	14.5	12.4	12.7
1960–1964, average	13.9	10.7	11.2
1965–1969, average	15.9	12.3	13.6
1970	13.3	10.9	9.8
1971	13.6	11.1	10.7
1972	14.0	10.6	12.5
1973	15.2	15.7	14.7
1974	21.0	19.9	14.0
1950–1974, average	15.4%	12.8%	12.6%

Source: Petroleum Department, First National City Bank, New York, N.Y., April 1975.

EXHIBIT 9 *(continued)*

B. Net Income after Taxes as a Percent of Stockholders, Equity for the Eight Largest Integrated Petroleum Firms, 1951–1971*

	1971	1970	1969	1968	1967	1966	1965	1964	1963	1962
Exxon	12.6	12.0	10.4	13.0	13.0	12.1	11.9	12.6	12.8	11.1
Mobil	11.2	10.6	10.1	10.5	10.0	9.7	9.2	8.8	8.6	8.2
Texaco	13.4	13.1	13.1	15.4	15.3	15.9	15.5	15.2	15.5	14.8
Gulf	10.2	10.4	12.1	13.2	13.1	12.3	11.2	11.0	10.9	10.6
Shell	8.7	8.7	10.9	12.3	13.8	13.4	13.4	12.3	12.0	11.2
Standard (Indiana)	9.6	9.3	10.0	10.1	9.5	9.1	8.1	7.5	7.3	6.6
ARCO	6.9	7.4	8.4	11.0	10.2	9.4	8.1	7.3	7.0	7.7
SOCAL	10.4	9.8	10.2	10.7	10.8	12.1	11.9	11.3	11.2	11.6
Weighted average	11.1	10.8	10.8	12.4	12.4	12.1	11.6	11.5	11.5	10.7
Return on equity in all manufacturing†	9.7	9.3	11.5	12.1	11.7	13.4	13.0	11.6	10.3	9.8
Net difference‡	1.4	1.5	−.7	.3	.7	−1.3	−1.4	−.1	1.2	.9

	1961	1960	1959	1958	1957	1956	1955	1954	1953	1952	1951
Exxon	10.4	10.1	9.4	8.7	14.0	15.8	15.2	13.6	16.2	16.6	18.4
Mobil	7.8	7.0	6.5	6.4	9.3	12.0	11.2	10.7	11.6	11.3	12.4
Texaco	14.4	14.3	14.1	13.6	16.2	16.3	15.7	14.8	13.7	13.6	14.6
Gulf	10.9	11.6	11.0	13.5	16.2	14.8	14.3	13.4	14.4	13.0	14.1
Shell	9.5	10.3	11.1	8.8	13.8	15.0	15.4	16.3	17.2	15.2	17.8
Standard (Indiana)	6.5	6.4	6.5	5.7	7.5	7.9	9.2	7.4	8.7	8.8	11.7
ARCO	8.1	8.6	5.8	6.8	7.4	10.1	9.0	9.6	12.2	10.7	12.6
SOCAL	11.7	11.8	12.0	13.0	15.5	15.8	15.1	15.3	15.0	15.0	16.2
Weighted average	10.4	10.2	9.8	9.6	13.1	14.1	13.7	12.8	13.9	13.6	15.3
Return on equity in all manufacturing†	8.9	9.2	10.4	8.6	10.9	12.3	12.6	9.9	10.5	10.3	12.1
Net difference‡	1.5	1.0	−.6	1.0	2.2	1.8	1.1	2.9	3.4	3.3	3.2

* Based on *Moody's Industrial Manual.*
† *"Economic Report of the President."* January 1973, p. 280.
‡ Weighted average return for the eight companies less that of all manufacturing.

more capital-intensive technologies. Between 1946 and 1955, the cost of building a new refinery increased from approximately $575 to $872 per daily barrel of crude oil capacity. As of the late 1970s the per barrel cost of new refinery capacity was approximately $2,000, up from about $1,000 per barrel in the late 1960s.

Oil company executives accounted for the growing investment in refinery facilities as necessary to maintain balanced operations, even though the return on new refinery investment was subpar. In their view, the requirements of their marketing divisions had to be met and the growth in the allowable crude oil production had to be matched. To do otherwise meant possible loss of market share. Moreover, firms that expected to remain competitive in selling their branded refined products had to invest in whatever refinery improvements and technological advances were available and to otherwise stay in the forefront of refinery know-how. Exhibit 10 shows how refinery margins have changed in the U.S. oil industry during the 1952–72

EXHIBIT 10
Refinery Gross Margins, 1952–1972

Year	(1) Average Product Price per Barrel	(2) Average Crude Petroleum Price per Barrel	(3) Refinery Gross Margin (1) − (2)
1952	$3.62	$2.526	$1.094
1953	3.76	2.684	1.076
1954	3.73	2.775	0.955
1955	3.81	2.765	1.045
1956	3.96	2.788	1.172
1957*	4.24	3.087	1.153
1958	3.89	3.013	0.877
1959†	3.87	2.903	0.967
1960	3.84	2.882	0.958
1961	3.87	2.886	0.984
1962	3.84	2.905	0.935
1963	3.79	2.894	0.896
1964	3.71	2.877	0.833
1965	3.83	2.864	0.966
1966	3.84	2.882	0.958
1967	3.92	2.915	1.005
1968	3.84	2.941	0.899
1969	3.89	3.092	0.789
1970	4.16	3.177	0.983
1971	4.43	3.385	1.045
1972	4.40	3.400	1.000

* A voluntary import quota program was initiated in 1957.
† A mandatory import quota program was initiated in 1959.
Source: "U.S. Wholesale Prices of Crude Petroleum and Principal Products." Independent Petroleum Association of America, 1973. Because invested capital grew rapidly over the period, margins as a percent of capital fell much more dramatically.

period. Refinery margins represent the difference between the value received for products refined and the total cost of crude and other raw materials; a refiner must pay all operating costs, cover depreciation, and earn a profit out of the refinery margin.

New technology has significantly improved refining efficiency. From 1950 to 1972, wage rates tripled, fuel costs doubled, and an increased proportion of higher quality products (higher octane gasoline, lower sulfur distillate fuels, better lubricants) demanded additional processing and higher costs. Nonetheless, the industry held its operating cost increases to about 2 percent per year and wholesale prices in real terms were kept almost constant, reflecting both technological improvements and competition. Probably the most dramatic technological advances in refining in the last 25 years have been the large-scale introductions of new processing facilities such as catalytic cracking and reforming, alkylation, and hydrocracking. These have allowed refinery yields and product qualities which would not otherwise have been possible or economically feasible. For example, without catalytic reforming, gasoline octanes would probably be lower than they are today, the compression ratios of internal combustion engines would be correspondingly lower, and automobiles would be less efficient.

The capital requirements to enter the refining business on an efficient scale are often larger than in production. From 1950 through 1973 about 80 refineries were built with a total capacity of about 3 million barrels per day; about one fourth of this new capacity was built by independent refiners. In 1951, the largest 20 refiners had 81 percent of total U.S. capacity; as of 1974, these same refiners had only 75 percent of capacity and the number of refiners with capacity of 50,000 barrels per day or more had grown from 20 percent in 1951 to 38 percent in 1974. U.S. oil companies expanded their refining capacity by 51 percent during the 1967–77 period; total operable capacity as of January 1977 was 16.1 million barrels per day, up from 10.7 million barrels in 1967 and 13.7 million barrels in 1973.

MARKETING

More than any other branch of the petroleum industry, the distribution and marketing of refined products is the domain of small enterprises. Over the years, of course, there has been tremendous change in the character, location, and operation of distribution and retail facilities (see Exhibit 11), but even more important, perhaps, there has been intense rivalry for consumer patronage. The major companies loom large in most of the markets in which they operate. Their brands command wide and reasonably loyal public acceptance. Usually, they are disposed to channel their competitive efforts

EXHIBIT 11
How U.S. Retail Marketing Is Changing

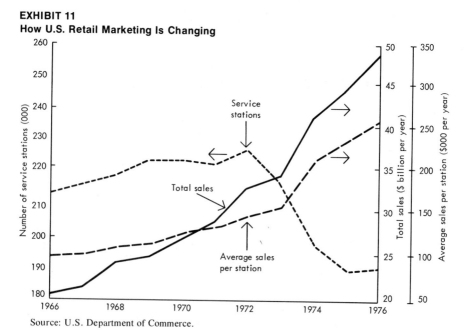

Source: U.S. Department of Commerce.

away from price and more toward quality of service, reliability, and dependability.

However, the independent refiner-marketer is typically more willing to use price as a competitive weapon, either when demand is slack or as a substitute for the full range of services and lack of a reputation and image. To some extent, the independents have evidenced a greater willingness to experiment and to innovate, in order to offset the strategic advantages and possible operating efficiency of the larger majors. Because the independents are "outsiders" and because their situation tends to be so different from the integrated majors, the presence of the independents, according to many observers and especially the critics of the large firms, makes it difficult for the 10 to 15 largest oil firms to "rig the market" to their own advantage and to otherwise collude on price. Industry analysts generally agree that the independents add an important competitive element to the retail marketing part of the oil business—primarily because they offer a different type of service to the consumer (called intratype competition, as opposed to intertype competition). The so-called independents or nonmajor brand marketers accounted for 30.1 percent of the market in 1974, compared to 22.8 percent in 1968.

Exhibits 12 and 13 summarize some statistics on the U.S. oil industry. Exhibit 14 presents the operating performances and other 1976 data for 20 of the world's largest oil companies, and Exhibit 15 depicts information relating to the stockholders of the major oil companies.

THE EMERGENCE OF OPEC

In August 1960, due to an oversupply of crude oil on the world market, Exxon announced a 10 cent per barrel reduction in its offer price for crude oil; this followed an 18 cent per barrel reduction the previous year. Other companies, though some did so reluctantly, followed Exxon's example and before long all the Seven Sisters were offering and paying the same lowered price for crude oil—an outcome which disgruntled the governments of the foreign oil-producing nations since it reduced the tax revenues which they received on each barrel of crude produced. Prior to this time, the major producing nations had met to consider uniting into some form of combined front against the Seven Sisters, but no action had resulted. However, the second reduction in the posted crude oil price catalyzed a further conference of the oil-producing countries, the objective of which appeared to be to form "a cartel to confront the cartel." Whether this was indeed the objective, the result nonetheless was exactly that and precipitated the formation of the Organization of Petroleum Exporting Countries (OPEC). OPEC's first resolution was to indicate clearly its stance as a foe to the Seven Sisters and their "kin."

Initially, the new organization had little effect, but as time passed it gained greater internal strength. By 1970–71, many of the religious and linguistic

EXHIBIT 12
U.S. Wholesale Prices of Crude Petroleum and Principal Products (refined products in eight refinery markets)

Year	Motor Gasoline (cents per gallon)	Kerosine (cents per gallon)	Light Fuel (cents per gallon)	Heavy Fuel (cents per gallon)	Average Four Products (cents per gallon)	(dollars per barrel)	Crude Petroleum (dollars per barrel)
1956	11.75	10.99	9.45	5.30	9.43	3.96	2.788
1957	12.34	11.54	10.05	6.15	10.10	4.24	3.087
1958	11.74	10.96	9.39	4.82	9.27	3.89	3.013
1959	11.64	11.26	9.31	4.79	9.22	3.87	2.903
1960	11.61	11.17	8.79	4.88	9.15	3.84	2.882
1961	11.62	11.49	9.10	4.85	9.21	3.87	2.886
1962	11.52	11.42	9.11	4.78	9.13	3.84	2.905
1963	11.35	11.51	9.18	4.61	9.01	3.79	2.894
1964	11.27	10.93	8.65	4.50	8.83	3.71	2.877
1965	11.52	11.28	9.04	4.81	9.12	3.83	2.864
1966	11.59	11.49	9.09	4.73	9.15	3.84	2.882
1967	11.84	11.96	9.71	4.53	9.33	3.92	2.915
1968	11.55	12.03	9.84	4.30	9.14	3.84	2.941
1969	11.80	11.98	10.06	4.20	9.27	3.89	3.092
1970	12.33	12.43	10.45	6.14	10.20	4.28	3.177
1971	12.70	12.90	10.75	7.76	10.94	4.59	3.385
1972	12.70	12.87	10.61	7.60	10.87	4.57	3.388
1973	14.72	14.08	12.61	8.45	12.49	5.25	3.885
1974	25.53	24.02	22.57	20.43	23.48	9.86	6.739
1975	30.27	27.41	26.09	22.03	27.03	11.35	7.560
1976	33.82	31.67	30.38	21.66	29.55	12.41	8.130
1977 (June)	37.63	36.11	34.71	25.36	33.44	14.04	8.500

Note: Refined product prices based on low quotations from Platt's Oilgram Price Service. Individual product prices weighted as follows: Oklahoma (16.8 percent), Midwestern Group 3 (20.8 percent), New York Harbor (11.2 percent), Philadelphia (4.0 percent), Savannah (2.4 percent), Boston (2.4 percent), Gulf Coast (22.4 percent), and Los Angeles (20.0 percent). Four Products Average weighted as follows: Gasoline 50 percent, kerosine 5 percent, distillate 15 percent, and residual fuel 30 percent. Annual Crude Price data from U.S. Bureau of Mines. Monthly Crude Price data estimated by IPAA, based on announced price adjustments, volumes affected, and data published by FEA.

This information reflects the trend in oil prices but not the actual sales realization for producers or refiners.

Source: Independent Petroleum Association of America.

barriers, conflicting political goals, and internal economic priorities had been settled to such an extent that OPEC began to be a factor with whom the major oil companies had to reckon. The 1971 Teheran Agreement, which involved the Seven Sisters and the major Middle East oil producers, outlined significant changes in the crude oil prices which producers would be paid by the oil companies.

As is well known, the strength of OPEC reached a new plateau in November 1973, when a complete embargo was undertaken of nations which were considered unfriendly to OPEC. The balance of power had shifted from the companies to the OPEC cartel. A number of nationalization moves by various OPEC members cut the Seven Sisters holdings in crude oil reserves. The ''new owners'' continued to deal with the major oil companies but with a new purpose. The oil companies' role was to supply the expertise in logistics and provide the essential refining-distribution-retailing network needed to support OPEC's crude oil production targets. The OPEC nations sought to limit production to match demand at the price they, the producers, set. OPEC's power in the new situation derived not from its newly asserted ability to control the major companies, but from the dependence of the consuming nations on OPEC oil. World demand for crude had grown to the point where the major consuming nations had to depend on imports as a source of supply—because domestic sources were no longer adequate. The growing worldwide importance of OPEC oil is suggested by Exhibits 16 and 17.

As of the mid-1970s, OPEC countries accounted for roughly 95 percent of the non-Communist country trade in international crude oil. The OPEC nations met regularly to determine the cartel's price of crude oil and, since they controlled over half of the free world's oil reserves (see Exhibit 16), there seemed little doubt over their continued ability to control the world market to their own advantage—barring major new discoveries outside their borders. Exhibits 18 and 19 provide further indication of the free world's increasing dependence on OPEC oil. In 1976, the members of OPEC accounted for 68 percent of the crude oil output in non-Communist nations.

THE U.S. ECONOMY AND ENERGY

As Exhibit 20 indicates, there has been a close historical relationship in the United States between increases in growth and increases in energy use. Equally significant is the fact that the United States, with only 6 percent of the world's population consumes about one third of the world's annual energy supplied and produces almost one third of the world's total output of goods and services. The energy consumption patterns among various nations are shown in Exhibits 21 and 22.

Exhibits 23 through 26 provide an indication of the relative importance of oil as an energy source in the United States, both now and as projected, along with the likely range of dependence of the United States on foreign oil imports to the year 1990. Exhibits 27 through 29 provide additional information about the oil and the energy industries.

In 1976, of the total wells drilled by oil and gas companies, approximately 41 percent produced oil, 22 percent natural gas, and 33 percent were dry. This included some 9,200 exploratory tests drilled in areas where no oil or gas had previously been discovered; 74 percent of these test wells were dry holes. Consumption of petroleum products in the United States reached an all-time high in 1976, averaging 17.4 million barrels daily, up 7 percent over the 1975 average of 16.3 million barrels daily, and exceeding the previous peak of 17.3 million barrels daily set in 1973. The greatest percentage increases in domestic consumption occurred in residual fuel oil, which was up 12.3 percent over 1975; and in distillate, up 9.2 percent on a year-to-year

EXHIBIT 13
Statistical Summary of the U.S. Petroleum Producing Industry, 1946–1976

Year	Production Crude Oil (1,000 B/D)	Production Natural Gas Liquids (1,000 B/D)	Production Total (1,000 B/D)	Imports Crude Oil (1,000 B/D)	Imports Refined Products (1,000 B/D)	Imports Total (1,000 B/D)	Other Supply*	Total Supply (1,000 B/D)	Petroleum Demand Domestic (1,000 B/D)	Petroleum Demand Export (1,000 B/D)	Petroleum Demand Total (1,000 B/D)	Crude Oil Value (million $)	Crude Oil Price ($ per bbl.)
1946	4,751	322	5,073	236	141	377	—	5,450	4,912	419	5,331	2,443	1.41
1950	5,407	499	5,906	487	363	850	2	6,758	6,509	305	6,814	4,963	2.51
1955	6,807	772	7,579	782	466	1,248	34	8,861	8,493	368	8,861	6,870	2.77
1960	7,035	930	7,965	1,015	799	1,814	146	9,926	9,807	202	10,009	7,420	2.88
1965	7,804	1,210	9,014	1,238	1,230	2,468	220	11,702	11,523	187	11,710	8,147	2.86
1966	8,295	1,284	9,579	1,225	1,348	2,573	245	12,397	12,095	198	12,293	8,727	2.88
1967	8,810	1,410	10,220	1,128	1,409	2,537	292	13,049	12,569	307	12,876	9,375	2.91
1968	9,096	1,503	10,599	1,290	1,550	2,840	348	13,787	13,404	231	13,635	9,795	2.94
1969	9,238	1,589	10,827	1,409	1,757	3,166	340	14,333	14,148	233	14,381	10,427	3.09
1970	9,637	1,660	11,297	1,324	2,094	3,418	355	15,071	14,709	259	14,968	11,174	3.18
1971	9,463	1,692	11,155	1,681	2,245	3,926	439	15,520	15,225	224	15,449	11,693	3.40
1972	9,441	1,744	11,185	2,216	2,525	4,741	444	16,370	16,379	223	16,602	11,707	3.39
1973	9,208	1,738	10,946	3,244	3,012	6,256	485	17,687	17,321	231	17,552	13,058	3.89
1974	8,774	1,688	10,462	3,477	2,635	6,112	491	17,065	16,666	220	16,886	21,581	6.74
1975	8,362	1,633	9,995	4,105	1,920	6,025	527	16,547	16,514	210	16,304	23,116	7.56
1976	8,125	1,605	9,730	5,265	1,985	7,250	n.a.	16,980	n.a.	n.a.	n.a.	24,187	8.13

Year	New Wells Drilled						Footage Drilled		Total Proved Reserves on Dec. 31† (Mil. Bbls.)	Total New Reserves Added† (Mil. Bbls.)	Average Hourly Earnings	
	Oil (No.)	Gas‡ (No.)	Dry (No.)	Service§ (No.)	Total (No.)	Percent Dry	Total (Mil. Ft.)	Per Well Drilled			Crude Oil ($ per Hour)	All Mfg. Industries ($ per Hour)
1946	15,851	3,090	8,051	2,237	29,229	27.5%	101.1	3,459	24,037	2,658	1.24	1.08
1950	24,430	2,843	14,757	1,249	43,279	34.1	159.3	3,681	29,536	3,329	1.72	1.44
1955	31,567	3,613	20,742	760	56,682	36.6	226.3	3,992	35,451	3,386	2.20	1.86
1960	21,186	5,258	17,574	2,733	46,751	37.6	190.7	4,079	38,429	3,090	2.69	2.26
1965	18,761	4,724	16,025	1,922	41,432	38.7	181.5	4,380	39,376	3,880	3.03	2.61
1966	16,780	4,377	15,227	1,497	37,881	40.2	166.0	4,383	39,781	3,858	3.13	2.72
1967	15,329	3,659	13,246	1,584	33,818	39.2	144.7	4,280	39,991	3,892	3.25	2.83
1968	14,331	3,456	12,812	2,315	32,914	38.9	149.3	4,536	39,305	3,141	3.38	2.94
1969	14,368	4,083	13,736	1,866	34,053	40.3	160.9	4,726	37,775	2,401	3.59	3.19
1970	13,020	3,840	11,260	1,347	29,467	38.2	142.4	4,834	37,104‖	3,397‖	3.83	3.36
1971	11,858	3,830	10,163	1,449	27,300	37.2	128.3	4,700	35,767‖	2,665‖	4.16	3.57
1972	11,306	4,928	11,057	1,464	28,755	38.5	138.4	4,809	33,536‖	1,796‖	4.46	3.81
1973	9,902	6,385	10,305	1,010	27,602	37.3	138.9	5,032	32,155‖	2,555‖	4.80	4.06
1974	12,784	7,240	11,674	1,195	32,893	35.5	153.8	4,676	31,000‖	2,614‖	5.33	4.40
1975	16,408	7,580	13,247	1,862	39,097	33.9	178.5	4,566	29,350‖	1,937	6.05	4.80
1976	16,996	9,045	13,690	1,690	41,421	33.1	185.2	4,471	n.a.	n.a.	n.a.	n.a.

n.a. = not available.

* Includes net processing gain, unaccounted for crude oil and other hydrocarbons.
† Includes natural gas liquids.
‡ Includes condensate wells since 1956.
§ Includes stratigraphic and core tests.
‖ Excludes Alaskan North Slope.

Source: Petroleum supply, demand, crude oil value and crude oil price from U.S. Bureau of Mines. Wells and footage drilled from *Oil and Gas Journal*, A.P.I. and A.A.P.G. reserves from American Petroleum Institute. Average hourly earnings from U.S. Bureau of Labor Statistics based on 1957 Standard Industrial Classification.

EXHIBIT 14
Comparative Statistics on Leading Oil Companies, 1976

Company	Sales*	Assets*	Income Equity*	Stock-holders' Equity*	Percentage Return on		Estimated		Number of Employees
					Stock-holders' Equity	Total Assets	Oil Reserves (million barrels)	Gas Reserves (cubic feet in trillions)	
Exxon	$48,630	$36,331	$2,640	$18,470	14.3%	7.3%	18,817	60.0	126,000
Royal Dutch/Shell	34,030	28,348†	2,214	11,683†	17.8	7.4†	2,385	25.8	161,000†
Texaco	26,452	18,194	869	9,002	9.7	4.8	7,188	21.8	72,766
Mobil Oil	26,062	18,767	942	7,651	12.3	5.0	2,310	7.4	199,500
Standard Oil (California)	19,434	13,765	880	7,007	12.6	6.4	1,210	16.4	38,397
British Petroleum	17,988	14,615†	306	5,414†	6.8†	2.5†	7,590	15.8	77,000†
Gulf Oil	16,451	13,449	816	6,942	11.8	6.1	1,375	8.4	53,300
Standard Oil (Indiana)	11,532	11,213	893	6,146	14.5	7.9	3,938‡	5.4	45,399
Atlantic Richfield	8,462	8,853	575	4,091	14.1	6.5	3,103	3.0	26,972
Tenneco	6,389	7,177	384	2,651	14.5	5.3	299	n.a.	82,074
Continental Oil	7,957	6,041	460	2,635	17.5	7.6	2,146	3.4	43,899
Phillips Petroleum	5,697	5,086	412	2,720	15.1	8.0	1,703	n.a.	27,797
Sun Oil Co.	5,387	4,835	356	2,555	13.9	7.3	924	2.1	32,499
Union Oil	5,350	4,227	269	2,103	12.8	6.3	948	5.6	15,725
Occidental Oil	5,525	3,904	184	1,305	14.1	4.7	1,142	8.3	33,600
Getty Oil	3,058	3,628	258	2,157	12.0	7.1	2,182‡	5.6	12,187
Cities Service	3,965	3,614	217	1,798	12.1	6.0	388	4.5	17,600
Marathon Oil	3,488	3,043	196	1,150	17.0	6.4	885	9.1	12,927
Amerada Hess	3,914	2,777	153	1,161	13.1	5.5	n.a.	n.a.	6,634
Cie Française des Pétroles	9,557	8,036†	(1.6)	1,812†	9.3†	2.0†	n.a.	n.a.	44,300†
ENI (Italy)	9,488	12,475†	(35)	1,937†	(6.9)†	(1.0)†	n.a.	n.a.	99,850†
ELF—Aguitane (France)	7,255	8,601†	327	2,095†	9.5†	2.3†	n.a.	n.a.	23,346†
Petrobras (Brazil)	6,516	6,770†	840	3,365†	20.9†	10.4†	n.a.	n.a.	51,044†
Idemitsu Kosan (Japan)	4,368†	4,143†	(11)†	44,168†	(0)†	(0.2)†	n.a.	n.a.	11,363†
Petrofina (Belgium)	4,374	3,906†	169	1,165†	13.9†	4.1†	n.a.	n.a.	20,800†

n.a. = not available.

* Dollar figures in millions.

† 1975 figures.

‡ Includes natural gas liquids.

Source: All data are from *Fortune* (May 1977), pp. 320–21, (August 1976), pp. 232–33, except for the information on oil and gas reserves which was compiled from information supplied courtesy of John S. Herold, Inc.

EXHIBIT 15
Who Owns Big Oil?

The American Petroleum Institute commissioned Toltec Associates in mid-1974 to study the shareowners of the six largest U.S. oil companies. The research department of the New York Stock Exchange acted as technical adviser for the study. The principal findings of the study follow.

The largest oil companies in the United States in terms of total assets, gross income, and net income that were studied are: Exxon, Gulf, Mobil, Standard of California, Standard of Indiana, and Texaco.

A. Total Individual Owners

Direct owners	2,300,000
Indirect owners	11,750,000
Total owners	14,050,000

B. Characteristics of Direct Owners

	The Retired Group	The Employed Group
Percent of total	46%	53%
Estimated number	1.06 million	1.24 million
Average age	70.6 years	52.2 years
Average household income	$14,000	$19,600
Education (average years of school)	14.7 years	16.7 years
Average value of all stocks held by household members	$25,000	$18,400
Years since first stock purchased	33 years	17 years

C. Geographic Location of Direct Shareowners

Region	Percent
New England	11%
Middle Atlantic	21
North Central	20
South Atlantic	15
South Central	15
Mountain	4
Pacific	14
Total	100%

D. Occupations of Direct Shareowners in the Employed Group

	Percent
Professional and technical	40%
Managers, officials, and proprietors	29
Other white collar	17
Craftsmen and foremen	7
Other	7
Total	100%

EXHIBIT 15 (continued)

E. Indirect Owners

Group	Estimated Number
Mutual fund owners	5,620,000
Pension and retirement plan, annuitants and participants	6,000,000
Shareowners, stock insurance companies	1,349,000
State employee retirement plans	810,000
State teacher retirement plans	248,000
Participants, insurance company, separate accounts	610,000
Shareowners and partners of brokers and securities dealers	113,000
Beneficiaries of common trust funds	139,000
Beneficiaries of estates and individual trustee accounts	66,000
	14,955,000
Reduced to eliminate duplication	3,189,000
	11,766,000

F. Other Important Owners

Mutual insurance companies	189
Colleges and universities	91
Charitable and educational foundations	1,000

Source: From a speech by Frank N. Ikard, president, American Petroleum Institute.

EXHIBIT 16
World Oil and Gas Reserves

	Oil (billion barrels)	Gas (trillion cubic feet)
World total	735	2,575
Middle East	401	673
Africa	68	147
Western Hemisphere (including United States)	97	402
Southeast Asia	20	61
North Sea–Western Europe	25	124
Subtotal	611	1,407
Other	124	1,168

Source: CIA Research Aid, *Major Oil and Gas Fields of the Free World*, 1976.

EXHIBIT 17
Daily World Crude Oil Production, 1960, 1970, and 1974

Area and Country	Thousand of Barrels			Percent Distribution*		
	1960	1970	1974	1960	1970	1974
Western Hemisphere	11,315	16,131	15,390	53.8%	36.0%	28.0%
United States	7,055	9,648	8,890	33.6	21.3	16.0
Canada	519	1,305	1,720	2.5	2.4	3.1
Venezuela	2,845	3,703	2,970	13.5	8.2	5.3
Others	896	1,475	1,810	4.3	3.3	3.2
Western Europe	289	375	390	1.4	0.8	0.7
Middle East	5,269	13,937	21,710	25.1	30.7	38.9
Saudi Arabia	1,319	3,798	8,480	6.3	8.4	15.2
Iran	1,057	3,831	6,040	5.0	8.4	10.8
Kuwait	1,696	2,983	2,550	8.1	6.6	4.6
Iraq	969	1,563	1,780	4.6	3.5	3.2
Abu Dhabi	0	691	1,410	—	2.0	2.5
Others	228	1,071	1,450	1.1	2.4	2.6
Africa	289	5,982	5,330	1.4	13.2	9.6
Libya	0	3,321	1,500	—	7.3	2.7
Nigeria	18	1,090	2,270	0.1	2.4	4.1
Algeria	185	976	940	0.9	2.2	1.7
Others	86	595	620	0.4	1.3	1.1
Asia-Pacific	554	1,340	2,300	2.6	3.0	4.1
Indonesia	419	855	1,360	2.0	1.9	2.4
Others	135	485	940	0.6	1.1	1.7
Communist Countries	3,310	7,610	10,650	15.7	16.8	19.1
Soviet Union	2,960	7,049	8,950	14.1	15.5	16.1
Eastern Europe, China	350	561	1,700	1.7	1.2	3.1
World Total	21,026	45,375	55,770	100.0	100.0	100.0

* Percent distribution do not total due to rounding.
Note: OPEC consists of 12 countries (in order of the size of their estimated oil reserves): Saudi Arabia, Kuwait, Iran, Iraq, Libya, United Arab Emirates (Abu Dhabi, Dubai, five others), Nigeria, Venezuela, Indonesia, Algeria, Qatar, and Ecuador.
Source: U.S. Council on International Economic Policy, *International Economic Report of the President* (Washington, D.C.: U.S. Government Printing Office, 1975).

basis. Motor gasoline consumption was nearly 7 million barrels daily, up 4.3 percent over 1975. Imports provided nearly 7.3 million barrels per day, or 42 percent, of 1976 U.S. oil consumption. Crude oil imports averaged nearly 5.3 million barrels daily, an increase of 28 percent over 1975, while imports of refined products rose about 2.5 percent to 2 million barrels daily.

Just how long the world's crude oil reserves will last is debatable. In 1977, the Carter administration presented studies that the world only had about 20 years of proven reserves and would run out of crude oil supplies by the year 2000. Other observers discounted the significance of the government study since it did not allow for new discoveries; some estimates of the remaining recoverable reserves indicated adequate supplies would be available for several centuries. One such estimate is presented in Exhibit 26.

EXHIBIT 18

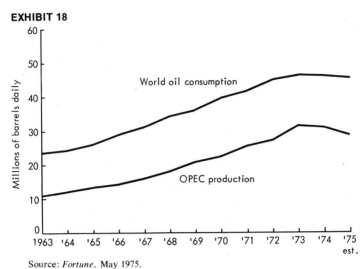

Source: *Fortune*, May 1975.

EXHIBIT 19
Major Worldwide Oil Flow, June 1977* (importing areas and volumes—barrels per day)

Exporting Areas →	United States	Canada	Western Europe	Far East	South America	South Africa
Middle East	2,670,000	570,000	9,260,000	5,670,000	1,600,000	500,000
North Africa..........	1,050,000		1,610,000	70,000	150,000	
South America	2,150,000	300,000	400,000	20,000	130,000	40,000
Eastern Europe	60,000		1,020,000	240,000	220,000	
West Africa	1,350,000	50,000	880,000	70,000	210,000	
Alaska	170,000					
Far East	700,000			1,010,000	80,000	10,000
Mexico	90,000					
Canada	570,000					

* Flow rates estimated based on actual 1976 data and projected to June 1977 based on increased shipments reported by API and CIA.
Source: *Oil and Gas Journal*, April 1977.

Professor Ross Wilhelm, a business economist at the University of Michigan, observed that:

> If you go back and study our history you will discover that in each year over the past 50 years we have had about 20 years of proven reserves of petroleum products on hand. Yet we did not run out of petroleum then and the evidence indicates we need not do without petroleum for the next 200 years, even if we do not undertake a preservation program.
>
> The energy crisis is not a crisis that arises from inadequate potential supplies of energy. The energy crisis for the American people is that they feel the prices of energy are too high and they would like to see them come down.

EXHIBIT 20

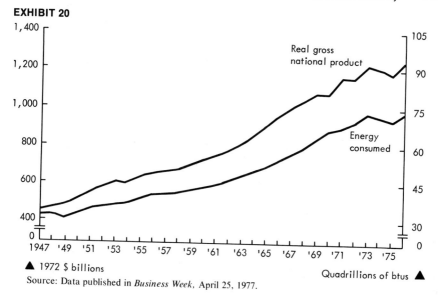

▲ 1972 $ billions

Quadrillions of btus ▲

Source: Data published in *Business Week*, April 25, 1977.

EXHIBIT 21
Energy Consumption per Capita, 1973 (barrels oil equivalent)

	Population (millions)	Total Energy Consumption (million barrels)	Energy Consumption per Capita (barrels per year)
United States	210.2	13,434	64
Canada	22.2	1,365	62
Sweden	8.14	359	44
Netherlands	13.48	535	40
Belgium/Luxembourg	10.09	391	39
Denmark	5.02	168	34
United Kingdom	56.01	1,787	32
West Germany	62.04	1,966	32
Australia	13.22	419	32
Switzerland	6.49	181	28
U.S.S.R.	249.93	6,584	26
France	52.19	1,323	25
Japan	108.35	2,676	25
Italy	54.78	1,122	21
Spain	34.83	399	12
Argentina	24.28	248	10
Saudi Arabia	7.5	62	8
Mexico	54.48	373	7
Iran	30.55	186	6
Brazil	101.69	348	3
Turkey	37.94	121	3
India	575.89	649	1

Source: Hearings before the Senate Subcommittee on Multinational Corporations, 1976.

EXHIBIT 22
World Primary Energy Consumption, 1974

Area and Country	Million Tons of Oil Equivalent						Percent of World Total
	Oil	Natural Gas	Solid Fuels	Water Power	Nuclear	Total	
Western Hemisphere	1,052.4	672.5	360.9	167.6	34.0	2,287.4	37.7
United States	785.4	560.4	331.9	76.9	28.8	1,783.4	29.4
Canada	88.1	64.1	15.0	59.4	4.9	231.5	3.8
Others	178.9	48.0	14.0	31.3	0.3	272.5	4.5
Western Europe	699.2	146.1	261.9	100.3	18.5	1,226.0	20.2
European Community of Six*	418.1	107.9	134.0	28.7	7.4	696.1	11.5
United Kingdom	105.8	30.8	68.9	1.3	7.3	214.1	3.5
Others	175.3	7.4	59.0	70.3	3.8	315.8	5.2
Eastern Hemisphere†	991.3	315.7	1,145.4	96.4	9.4	2,558.2	42.1
Japan	261.1	5.1	58.8	19.0	4.1	348.1	5.7
Australasia	33.9	4.1	26.1	2.4	—	66.5	1.1
Soviet Union, Eastern Europe, China‡	468.9	264.5	925.7	53.9	4.3	1,717.3	28.3
Others	227.4	42.0	134.8	21.1	1.0	426.3	7.0
World Total	2,742.9	1,134.3	1,768.2	364.3	61.9	6,071.6	100.0
Free World Total§	2,274.0	869.8	842.5	310.4	57.6	4,354.3	—

* Belgium, France, Italy, Luxembourg, Netherlands, and West Germany.
† Excluding Western Europe.
‡ Including Albania, North Korea, and North Vietnam.
§ World total excluding Eastern Europe, China, and Soviet Union.
Source: *Statistical Review of the World Oil Industry, 1974* (London: British Petroleum Company, 1975).

EXHIBIT 23
Percentage Share of U.S. Energy Market by Energy Source

Energy Source	1920	1973	1980	1990
Oil	18%	46%	41%	32%
Gas	18	31	28	22
Coal	78	18	20	19
Nuclear	—	1	7	22
Hydro and other	4	4	4	5
Total Energy	100	100	100	100

Source: Exxon Corp.

The only way to bring about lower prices over the long run is to begin to increase supplies now. President Carter's program does not adequately provide for increasing supplies now.[6]

---

[6] *Automotive News,* June 20, 1977, p. 15.

EXHIBIT 24
U.S. Energy Supply (million barrels per day oil equivalent)

	1960	1977	1980	1990	Growth Rates 1960–1973	Growth Rates 1973–1977	Growth Rates 1977–1990
Hydro, geothermal, and solar	0.8	1.5	1.6	1.6	4.6	2.4	0.4
Nuclear	—	1.3	2.0	6.2	40.8	31.7	13.0
Coal	5.0	7.0	8.0	13.7	4.3	(4.0)	(0.2)
Gas	6.6	9.8	8.7	9.5	1.8	2.5	5.3
Oil	9.8	18.1	20.5	23.3	4.4	1.2	1.9
Total	22.2	37.7	40.8	54.3	4.0	0.5	2.8

Source: Exxon Corp.

EXHIBIT 25
U.S. Energy Imports (post-1974 forecasts)

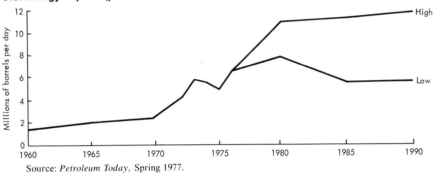

Source: *Petroleum Today*, Spring 1977.

Wilhelm argued that it was economically unsound for producers to search out and maintain more than about 20 years of proven reserves of crude oil. But irrespective of whomever's estimates one chose to believe, it was clear that all of the estimates depended on (1) the rapidity with which new sources of energy were developed and their relative costs, (2) discoveries of new reserve deposits, (3) OPEC's willingness to use up its oil reserves to meet world demand, (4) the rates of worldwide economic growth, (5) the success of conservation measures, and (6) governmental energy policies—to mention only the more important.

In 1977, several energy realities relating to the international energy problem were fairly clear:

The OPEC countries held more than 80 percent of proved oil reserves in the non-Communist world and accounted for almost 70 percent of current production.

Even with the development of the North Sea, two thirds of Europe's oil

EXHIBIT 26
U.S. Oil Demand and Producing Capacity (million barrels daily)

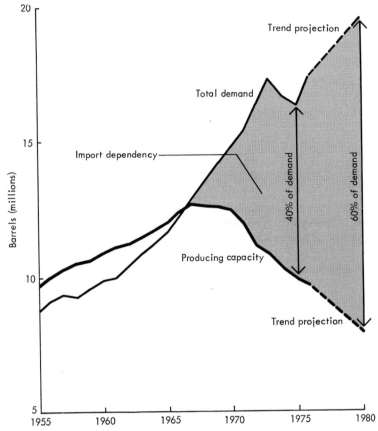

Sources: U.S. Bureau of Mines and Independent Petroleum Association of America.

consumption would likely come from OPEC sources by 1985. Japan would probably depend almost 100 percent on OPEC oil by that same time.

The United States, once self-sufficient, had been using six to ten times as much oil, and twice as much natural gas, as it had been discovering in recent years. By 1980, the United States could be importing more than one-half its oil.

While coal and nuclear energy would likely begin to cut into the rising demand for oil sometime in the 1980s, oil would likely still account for approximately one half of the world's energy consumption in the 1990s.

Anything which slowed down the displacement of oil by other fuels would increase the free world's reliance on OPEC oil.

EXHIBIT 27
U.S. Petroleum Resource Base

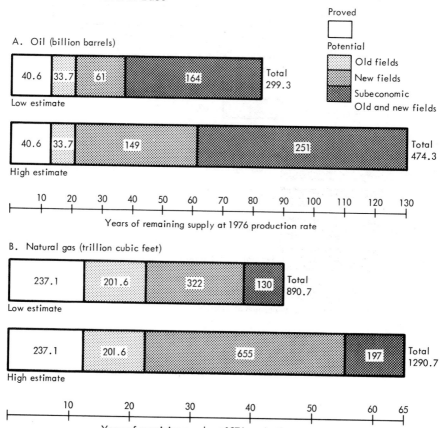

Source: U.S. Geological Survey (1975). These USGS estimates do not include potentially large supplies in tight sands, shales, or geopressured reservoirs or from water depths greater than 660 feet.

EXHIBIT 28
The U.S. Petroleum Industry, 1972 versus 1956

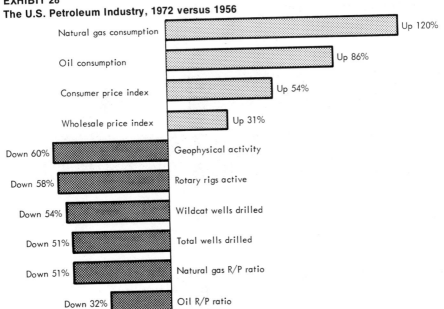

Source: Independent Petroleum Association of America.

EXHIBIT 29

Selected Developed Countries: Retail Petroleum Product Prices (U.S. cents per gallon)

	Regular Gasoline		Premium Gasoline		Diesel Fuel	
	Price*	Tax	Price*	Tax	Price*	Tax
United States:						
1973 October	$0.40	$0.12	$0.44	$0.12	$0.23	$0.12
1974 January	0.46	0.12	0.50	0.12	0.32	0.12
1975 January	0.53	0.12	0.57	0.12	0.50	0.12
1976 January	0.58	0.12	0.63	0.12	0.50	0.12
1977 January	0.60	0.12	0.65	0.12	0.54	0.12
Japan:						
1973 October	0.88	0.39	1.05	0.39	0.48	0.21
1974 January	1.15	0.39	1.33	0.39	0.54	0.21
1975 January	1.52	0.47	1.70	0.47	0.78	0.21
1976 January	1.56	0.47	1.74	0.47	0.86	0.21
1977 January	1.67	0.59	1.85	0.59	0.93	0.27
West Germany:						
1973 October	1.12	0.81	1.24	0.82	1.12	0.76
1974 January	1.37	0.83	1.49	0.84	1.39	0.79
1975 January	1.29	0.84	1.40	0.84	1.37	0.76
1976 January	1.41	0.84	1.51	0.85	1.41	0.79
France:†						
1973 October	0.95	0.65	1.03	0.69	0.66	0.39
1974 January	1.23	0.69	1.33	0.73	0.79	0.41
1975 January	1.29	0.73	1.39	0.77	0.88	0.38
1976 January	1.34	0.75	1.45	0.80	0.95	0.47
1977 January	1.59	0.97	1.71	1.03	0.99	0.48
United Kingdom:						
1973 October	0.51	0.32	0.53	0.32	0.51	0.32
1974 January	0.55	0.32	0.57	0.32	0.55	0.32
1975 January	1.00	0.39	1.04	0.39	0.79	0.39
1976 January	1.07	0.54	1.09	0.53	0.88	0.39
1977 January	1.07	0.55	1.10	0.55	1.02	0.50
Italy:†						
1973 October	0.75	0.56	0.79	0.58	0.41	0.26
1974 January	0.81	0.57	0.85	0.59	0.48	0.27
1975 January	1.22	0.69	1.28	0.87	0.58	0.27
1976 January	1.28	0.84	1.34	0.87	0.62	0.27
1977 January	2.05	1.47	2.13	1.53	0.72	0.29

Note: Converted at March 28, 1977 exchange rates.
* Including tax.
† Government price ceilings in effect.
Source: CIA Office of Economic Research, *International Oil Developments,* June 22, 1977.

27. Exxon Corporation*

IN 1976, Exxon Corporation ranked number one in sales, number one in assets, and number two in aftertax profits on *Fortune's* list of the 500 largest U.S. industrial corporations. Insofar as a worldwide ranking among all corporations of all types, Exxon was number one in sales, number two in assets, and number three in aftertax profits in 1976. The company's sales revenues were $51.6 billion, total assets were $36.3 billion, and aftertax profits were $2.6 billion. Although Exxon was clearly a giant corporation by any standard, its profitability rates were modest compared to other *Fortune 500* companies. The company's aftertax return on stockholder's equity was 14.3 percent in 1976, good enough only for a rank of 204 among the *Fortune 500;* its growth rate in earnings per share during 1966–76 period was 8.84 percent, which ranked just 201st out of 500; and the company's total return to investors (dividends plus capital gains) from 1966 through 1976 was 11.08 percent—which yielded a ranking of 140.

Exxon Corporation and its subsidiaries and affiliated companies operated in the United States and nearly 100 other countries; the firm was an acknowledged leader in the world petroleum industry. Exxon's principal businesses included exploring for and producing crude oil and natural gas, petroleum and chemical manufacturing, and transporting and selling crude oil, natural gas, and petroleum and chemical products. The company's *1976 Annual Report* proclaimed the following as "milestone" accomplishments:

Earnings up 5.5 percent to $2.6 billion.

Capital and exploration spending hits record $5.1 billion, $3.7 billion of it to find and develop energy resources.

Dividends increase 9 percent.

Stock split to broaden Exxon ownership.

Exxon leads all bidders in first federal lease sales off Atlantic Coast.

Trans-Alaska pipeline system over 90 percent completed.

First oil produced from Brent field, largest in The United Kingdom, North Sea.

---

* Prepared by Professor Arthur A. Thompson, Jr., and Victor Gray, research assistant, The University of Alabama.

Exxon completes first year in Venezuela in new role as crude buyer, service company (following nationalization of its Venezuelan affiliates' assets on December 31, 1975).

Exxon affiliate sets industry record by drilling in 3,461 feet of water.

Exxon discovers major deposit of zinc and copper ore in Wisconsin.

Offshore oil development resumes in Malaysia as production-sharing agreement is signed with government.

Industry's tallest production platform installed by Exxon in Santa Barbara Channel.

Construction resumes on Wyoming coal mine as Supreme Court clears way for surface mining operations.

Chemical revenues rise 23 percent to record $3.7 billion.

Exhibits 1, 2, and 3 provide additional financial and operating information about the company.

COMPANY HISTORY AND BACKGROUND

Exxon Corporation is the surviving parent company from the legendary breakup of the Standard Oil Company in 1911. The Standard Oil Company, of course, was headed by the man who dominated the oil industry in its early years and who became a symbol for both the sins and the virtues of capitalism—John D. Rockefeller. Rockefeller, his brother William, and three other partners formed the Standard Oil Company in January 1870; the company was capitalized at $1 million and John D. Rockefeller was elected the first president. By the early 1870s, Rockefeller's Standard Oil Company owned virtually every refinery in Cleveland, Ohio—then the leading refining city. By the end of that decade, Pittsburgh, Philadelphia, New York, and the particular regions where oil was being discovered came under Standard's domination as well. Many observers, especially Rockefeller's contemporary critics and competitors, believed that his negotiations of a lower transport fee with the railroads for his oil was the chief method by which he came to dominate the oil industry. The railroads, chiefly the Erie and the New York Central, justified the practice of giving lower prices to large shippers because of economies of scale. Such discounts allowed users to bring their products to market at significantly less cost than smaller competitors.

In the meantime, Rockefeller and his associates continued to buy up other oil companies—either for cash or in exchange for stock in Standard Oil. In 1899, all of these companies were reorganized under laws of the state of New Jersey and merged into the Standard Oil Company of New Jersey. In 1899, the company controlled 82 percent of all the refinery capacity in the United States; in 1906 it controlled 70 percent; and in 1911 the company controlled 64 percent. During the period 1906–11, Standard Oil enjoyed roughly a 75 percent market share in kerosine, a 66 percent share in gasoline, a 31 percent

EXHIBIT 1

EXXON CORPORATION
Consolidated Statement of Financial Position
December 31, 1976–1972

Assets	1976	1975	1974	1973	1972
Current Assets:					
Cash, including time deposits of $972,148,000 and $639,376,000	$ 1,278,578,000	$ 876,017,000	$ 938,997,000	$ 562,752,000	$ 482,443,000
Marketable securities, at cost, which approximates market	3,795,259,000	3,773,361,000	3,819,354,000	2,525,429,000	1,210,379,000
Notes and accounts receivable, less estimated doubtful amounts of $95,810,000 and $99,838,000	5,354,462,000	5,098,154,000	5,281,970,000	4,062,949,000	3,328,428,000
Inventories					
Crude oil, products and merchandise	3,794,454,000	3,596,672,000	3,768,653,000	2,020,013,000	1,546,213,000
Materials and supplies	439,833,000	399,086,000	375,104,000	205,809,000	199,228,000
Prepaid taxes and other expenses	389,361,000	261,544,000	602,932,000	416,561,000	331,888,000
Total Current Assets	$15,051,947,000	$14,004,834,000	$14,787,010,000	$ 9,793,513,000	$ 7,098,579,000
Investments and advances	1,563,211,000	1,515,203,000	948,703,000	1,349,876,000	1,299,509,000
Property, plant and equipment, at cost, less depreciation and depletion	18,671,208,000	16,152,137,000	14,837,521,000	13,461,516,000	12,644,745,000
Deferred charges and other assets	1,044,980,000	1,167,224,000	581,255,000	474,589,000	515,424,000
Total Assets	$36,331,346,000	$32,839,398,000	$31,154,489,000	$25,079,494,000	$21,558,257,000

Liabilities	1976	1975	1974	1973	1972
Current Liabilities:					
Notes and loans payable	$ 1,859,844,000	$ 1,598,099,000	$ 1,729,120,000	$ 1,126,667,000	$ 1,161,142,000
Accounts payable and accrued liabilities	7,714,068,000	6,486,280,000	5,903,470,000	3,994,166,000	2,734,133,000
Income taxes payable	947,529,000	1,260,640,000	1,913,446,000	1,187,055,000	811,834,000
Total Current Liabilities	$10,521,441,000	$ 9,345,019,000	$ 9,546,036,000	$ 6,307,888,000	$ 4,707,109,000
Long-term debt	3,696,798,000	3,451,146,000	3,051,672,000	2,670,863,000	2,616,946,000
Annuity and other reserves	646,668,000	609,313,000	640,338,000	624,670,000	572,848,000
Deferred income tax credits	2,149,931,000	1,621,369,000	1,528,650,000	1,076,369,000	750,200,000
Other deferred credits	71,630,000	77,878,000	83,028,000	90,871,000	105,270,000
Equity of minority shareholders in affiliated companies	774,526,000	710,262,000	671,022,000	591,142,000	536,415,000
Total Liabilities	$17,860,994,000	$15,814,987,000	$15,520,746,000	$11,361,803,000	$ 9,288,788,000
Shareholders' Equity:					
Capital	$ 2,608,591,000	$ 2,583,480,000	$ 2,577,551,000	$ 2,594,607,000	$ 2,637,212,000
Earnings reinvested	15,861,761,000	14,440,931,000	13,056,192,000	11,123,084,000	9,632,257,000
Total Shareholders' Equity	$18,470,352,000	$17,024,411,000	$15,633,743,000	$13,717,691,000	$12,269,469,000

Source: Annual Reports.

EXHIBIT 2

EXXON CORPORATION
Financial Summary
1976–1972

Consolidated Statement of Income	1976	1975	1974	1973	1972
Sales and other operating revenue:					
Petroleum and natural gas					
Petroleum products*	$36,867	$33,040	$31,597	$20,681	$16,072
Crude oil*	8,474	9,548	8,488	3,985	3,177
Natural gas*	1,509	1,262	903	748	646
Other*	1,260	1,114	1,099	924	788
Total*	$48,110	$44,964	$42,087	$26,338	$20,683
Chemical Products*	3,238	2,594	2,787	1,563	1,258
Other*	278	238	147	121	130
Total Sales and Other Operating Revenue*	$51,626	$47,796	$45,021	$28,022	$22,071
Dividends, interest and other revenue*	959	965	772	454	365
Total Revenue	$52,585	$48,761	$45,793	$28,476	$22,436
Costs and other deductions:					
Crude oil and product purchases*	$26,776	$21,702	$18,607	$ 7,456	$ 6,022
Operating expenses*	4,691	4,311	4,279	3,805	3,001
Selling, general and administrative expenses*	2,719	2,628	2,439	2,277	2,104
Depreciation and depletion*	1,448	1,524	1,265	1,136	1,059
Exploration expenses, including dry holes*	423	382	360	255	265
Income, excise and other taxes					
Income*	5,190	7,279	7,848	3,739	2,345
Excise, duties and other*	8,318	8,047	7,419	6,856	5,750
Debt-related costs*	265	262	420	374	248
Income applicable to minority interests*	114	123	126	127	83
Total Deductions*	$49,944	$46,258	$42,763	$26,025	$20,877
Net Income*	$ 2,641	$ 2,503	$ 3,030	$ 2,451	$ 1,559
Net income per share, after adjustment for stock split	$ 5.90	$ 5.60	$ 6.77	$ 5.47	$ 3.48
Cash dividends per share, after adjustment for stock split	$ 2.725	$ 2.50	$ 2.50	$ 2.125	$ 1.90
Earnings to average shareholders' equity (percent)	14.9%	15.3%	20.6%	18.8%	13.1%
Earnings to total revenue (percent)	5.0%	5.1%	6.6%	8.6%	6.9%
Property, plant and equipment, less reserves*	$18,671	$16,152	$14,838	$13,462	$12,645
Total additions to property, plant and equipment*	$ 4,098	$ 3,558	$ 2,910	$ 2,235	$ 1,984
Working capital*	$ 4,531	$ 4,660	$ 5,241	$ 3,534	$ 2,398
Ratio of current assets to current liabilities	1.43	1.50	1.55	1.56	1.51
Long-term debt*	$ 3,697	$ 3,451	$ 3,052	$ 2,671	$ 2,617
Shareholders' equity*	$18,470	$17,024	$15,634	$13,740	$12,284

EXHIBIT 2 (continued)

Shareholders' equity per share, after adjustment for stock split	$ 41.22	$ 38.05	$ 34.95	$ 30.69	$ 27.39
Average number of shares outstanding (thousands)	447,744	447,315	447,540	448,179	448,310
Number of shareholders at year-end (thousands)	684	689	707	720	755
Research and development expenditures*	$ 202	$ 187	$ 174	$ 124	$ 106
Wages, salaries, and employee benefits*	$ 2,661	$ 2,694	$ 2,232	$ 1,862	$ 1,679
Average number of employees (thousands)	126	137	133	137	141

　* in millions of $.
　Source: *1976 Annual Report*.

EXHIBIT 3
Operating Summary

	1976	1975	1974	1973	1972
Gross production of crude oil and natural gas liquids and petroleum supplies available under special arrangements (thousands of barrels daily).					
United States	927	970	1,019	1,084	1,114
Canada	236	265	337	345	262
Other Western Hemisphere	19	1,131	1,483	1,666	1,519
Europe	59	46	48	53	59
Middle East and Africa	1,205	1,041	1,169	2,153	2,590
Australia and Far East	237	231	215	224	190
	2,683	3,684	4,271	5,525	5,734
Petroleum supplies available under special arrangements.	2,893	1,727	2,096	1,193	411
Worldwide	5,576	5,411	6,367	6,718	6,145
Refinery crude oil runs (thousands of barrels daily).					
United States	1,277	1,182	1,123	1,202	1,029
Canada	412	394	437	441	395
Other Western Hemisphere	394	689	1,069	1,147	1,004
Europe	1,737	1,564	1,966	2,165	2,015
Middle East and Africa	125	110	162	237	196
Australia and Far East	414	392	426	569	507
Worldwide	4,359	4,331	5,183	5,761	5,146
Petroleum product sales (thousands of barrels daily).					
Aviation fuels	316	292	301	358	358
Gasolines, naphthas	1,457	1,421	1,463	1,587	1,442
Home heating oils, kerosene, diesel oils	1,470	1,319	1,372	1,594	1,475
Heavy fuels	1,523	1,389	1,778	1,998	1,836
Specialty products	587	569	591	641	590
Total	5,353	4,990	5,505	6,178	5,701

EXHIBIT 3 (continued)

United States	1,830	1,561	1,782	1,980	1,730
Canada	456	433	443	449	408
Other Western Hemisphere	473	580	624	625	613
Europe	1,943	1,812	2,008	2,279	2,185
Other Eastern Hemisphere	651	604	648	845	765
Worldwide	5,353	4,990	5,505	6,178	5,701
Natural gas sales (millions of cubic feet daily). 1975 and prior years restated for comparability.					
United States	4,673	4,937	5,312	5,758	5,952
Canada	376	410	419	477	423
Other Western Hemisphere	41	104	104	91	68
Europe	5,111	4,776	4,615	3,858	3,241
Other Eastern Hemisphere	477	418	342	333	239
Worldwide	10,678	10,645	10,792	10,517	9,923
Oceangoing tanker capacity, owned and chartered (thousands of deadweight tons, daily average).	27,005	24,400	26,420	23,804	19,880
Pipeline throughput (thousands of barrels daily).	5,836	6,491	7,575	8,098	7,569

Note: Operating statistics other than pipeline throughput include 100 percent of operations of majority-owned affiliates; for other companies, gas sales and crude production include Exxon's ownership percentage, and crude runs include quantities processed for Exxon. Pipeline throughput represents quantities delivered for Exxon by all companies in which a stock interest is held. Gross production includes royalties and oil payments due others but not quantities belonging to other joint owners or participants. Petroleum supplies available under special arrangements includes (1) offtake from Iran from March 21, 1973, under terms of the purchase-sale agreement with the National Iranian Oil Company, (2) buyback of part of the governments' share of production under terms of participation agreements effective January 1, 1973, and as amended thereafter, (3) major purchases from others under special arrangements and (4) crude oil and product purchases from the Venezuelan government company, Lagoven, effective January 1, 1976.

Source: *1976 Annual Report.*

market share in fuel oil, a 67 percent market share in waxes, and a 55 percent market share in lubricating products. The company's control over crude oil supplies ranged from 92 percent in 1880 to 70–80 percent of older fields and 10–30 percent in newer fields in the west in 1911. Standard Oil did not actually dominate production of crude oil; rather, because of its purchasing power and its ownership position in pipelines, it was able to set the price of the crude oil it purchased. Standard Oil had almost a total monopoly over pipeline transportation in 1911. Through its relationships first with railroads and then with the pipelines, Standard was able to transport crude oil at a lower cost than its competitors.

In 1900, John D. Rockefeller owned 42.9 percent of Standard Oil of New Jersey. Fifteen other individual stockholders accounted for an additional 39.5 percent. This meant that over 80 percent of the company which virtually dominated the petroleum industry was owned by only 16 individuals. In 1911, ten men still owned 37.7 percent of Standard Oil's stock, with 24.9 percent held by Rockefeller. At the time of its breakup in 1911, all of the stock of Standard Oil Company was held by only 6,000 stockholders. Economic historians have indicated that Standard Oil's profit rates were twice those of profit rates in general during the years leading up to 1911. Standard's profit as a percentage of net worth was 23.1 percent in 1906; 20.7 percent in 1904; 27.0 percent in 1902; 27.0 percent in 1900.

On May 15, 1911, the Supreme Court ruled that the Standard Oil Company of New Jersey constituted a monopoly in restraint of trade. Standard Oil was given six months to divest part of its business and create 33 new companies. The stocks of each of the 33 new companies were distributed on a pro rata basis to the 6,000 shareholders of Standard Oil. The effect of divestiture on the Standard Oil Company of New Jersey management was immediate. John D. Rockefeller resigned as president; William Rockefeller and his son William G. Rockefeller also stepped down from their positions in the company.

However, except for changes in officers and directors, for many years there was little indication that much had happened. Each company retained its original corporate name with the result that there were now eight "Standard" companies: Standard Oil Company (New Jersey)—now Exxon Corporation; Standard Oil Company (Indiana); Standard Oil Company (Kentucky); Standard Oil Company (New York); Standard Oil Company (California); Standard Oil Company (Kansas); Standard Oil Company (Nebraska); and Standard Oil Company (Ohio). The name "Standard" was so well known to consumers that these companies felt it unwise to change their names. For this reason, even though the companies were separate and independent, the general public often failed to make any distinction and many people continued to think of them as a single company.

In many respects this was accurate. The same seven individuals who had held a majority of stock in Standard of New Jersey held a majority of stock in each of the other 33 companies. Each of the marketing companies continued to market in the territory originally assigned to it, and for some years they did not actively compete with one another. Active competition did not immediately develop because there was no particular incentive to invade the marketing territory of another company, given the rapidly growing demand for petroleum products and the fact that each company had plenty of business available within its own territory. Equally as important, as long as the old Rockefeller men managed the various companies, there was a community of interest, a friendly feeling, and no overall benefits from invading one another's territory.

But with the passage of time, market circumstances prodded the Standard units into competition with one another. The primary reason for this was that most of the companies, not being integrated fully, were in a somewhat insecure position. Some had an immense investment in refining facilities but were without a crude oil supply or pipelines; others were large marketing companies without refineries or pipelines; and others had pipelines but no refineries or marketing organizations. The companies discovered, in time, that they had to integrate to survive and to make their investments secure.

For more than 50 years, the Humble Oil and Refining Company was the chief domestic operating unit of the Standard Oil Company (New Jersey); it engaged in producing, transporting, refining and marketing petroleum products in the United States. Its trademark, ESSO, was one of the best known in the world and was a recognized symbol. The company was originally organized in Texas in 1917 as a successor to the Humble Oil Company. In 1917, Humble was the fifth largest producer in Texas and also operated a small refinery and topping plant; in 1918, it began building a marketing division. Humble's producing prospects were promising, but the company was badly in need of working capital. Standard Oil (New Jersey), which had ample funds, an inadequate producing capacity, and an interest in securing a foothold in Texas, approached Humble about merger. On January 29, 1919, Humble signed an agreement calling for the sale of a 50 percent interest in the company to Standard Oil (New Jersey) for $17 million.

In 1960, Standard Oil (New Jersey) merged a number of its subsidiaries into Humble, placing the parent company in a position to market nationwide through Humble. With the merger, Humble adopted a uniform design for its service stations. Since the nationwide use of ESSO as a trademark had been ruled by the courts as inappropriate, owing to conflicts with other Standard Oil trademarks, Humble adopted the brand name ENCO (from ENergy COmpany). However, in the East the company continued to market its products under the ESSO brand; in the Southeast, depending on the state, both ESSO and ENCO were used; in Ohio the name HUMBLE was used. ENCO was used principally in the West and the Southwest. In 1960, Humble, as a result of other Standard Oil (New Jersey) subsidiaries having been merged into it, was marketing in 35 states. That same year, Humble announced its intention to market nationwide and to adopt a uniform design for its service stations. In 1972, after almost 35 frustrating years of trying to establish a single trademark under which to market and advertise nationwide, Standard Oil (New Jersey) and its domestic operating subsidiary, Humble Oil and Refining Oil Company, announced that they would, henceforth, use the name EXXON as their single primary trademark on a nationwide basis. Subsequently, Standard Oil (New Jersey) became known as Exxon Corporation, and Humble Oil and Refining Company became known as Exxon Company, U.S.A.

One other episode in Exxon's growth deserves mention because of the significance it has come to have presently—some have even referred to it as the most important strategic decision in the company's history. In 1960, when Monroe J. Rathbone started his five-year stint as Exxon's chief executive officer, both the industry and the company were enjoying ample supplies of cheap crude oil. Even if the markets for refined products were occasionally torn by price wars, Exxon with its cheap crude sources in Saudi Arabia and Venezuela was able to make up at the wellhead what it lost at the retail pumps. Nonetheless, Rathbone saw trouble ahead; he believed that the demand for oil, rising faster than new discoveries, would one day convert a glut to a scarcity and that the Middle East oil-producing countries would be able to charge much higher prices for their crude. Thus, even though Exxon then had more crude than its refined products markets could absorb, Rathbone persuaded the company's board to approve major outlays for a search for oil outside the Middle East. Rathbone set up a brand-new subsidiary called Esso Exploration and sent geologists and drilling crews into new areas of the world; Exxon's existing subsidiaries were ordered to begin combing their territories for more oil. In the period 1964–67 Exxon spent nearly $700 million on exploration, mostly in non-OPEC areas. Other major oil companies indicated their amusement at Exxon's move by declining to follow suit on any large scale. Mobil, for instance, with the greatest lack of crude oil reserves of any major U.S. company, spent just $267 million for exploration during the same period. Nonetheless, Exxon's decision paid off. As of 1977, Exxon had more proven oil reserves outside the Middle East than any other major company. For his role and foresight in engineering Exxon's move, *Fortune* in 1975 named Monroe J. Rathbone to its Business Hall of Fame—he was one of four living executives so chosen (together with 15 other deceased laureates among whom was John D. Rockefeller).

BOARD OF DIRECTORS

Until 1966, the Exxon board of directors was composed entirely of company officials. Over the next ten years, however, outside directors were added and, as of 1976, a majority of Exxon's board consisted of "outsiders." Exhibit 4 presents a synopsis of each member of Exxon's board elected in 1977. The board holds regular monthly meetings and generally considers dividend action at the January, April, July, and October meetings. In December, the board reviews Exxon's consolidated four-year investment plans and capital budget for the next year.

Exxon has had an audit committee since 1968; since 1973, this committee has been composed entirely of outside directors. The audit committee recommends the appointment of Exxon's independent auditor (although since Price Waterhouse has been the company's auditor since at least 1934, it is questionable just how influential the committee has been in the choice of an auditor). The audit committee also reviews the results and costs of Exxon's internal auditing system and reports its findings to the board. The committee has direct access to the corporation's general auditor and to the independent auditor.

At the company's annual meeting on May 19, 1977, one of Exxon's shareholder's presented the following resolution:

> *Resolved:* That the stockholders of Exxon hereby recommend to the Board of Directors that the necessary steps be taken to insure that future chairmen and presidents of Exxon will serve in their positions of chairmen or

presidents for a term of no longer than four years and that in addition future directors of Exxon shall not serve longer than for four consecutive years as directors of Exxon, with the express stipulation that this shall apply only to new directors, chairmen and presidents who have not previously served in these positions (prior to 1977).

Reasons: Younger men should be given an opportunity to serve the corporation, men with new and different ideas than the present ones so that the corporation will benefit from a continued flux of new and talented people and so that there will be a minimum of entrenched management.

The President of the United States, many Governors and other elected officials serve a fixed length of term, so should chairmen, presidents and directors of Exxon.

If you AGREE, please mark your proxy FOR this resolution, otherwise it is automatically cast against.

In its notice of the annual meeting and proxy statement, management recommended a vote against this resolution and stated:

Exxon's Board of Directors is currently comprised of seven employee and nine non-employee directors. All directors are elected annually by the shareholders of the Corporation and the Board of Directors in turn elects the Chairman and President for one year. Employee directors normally serve on the Board until about the time of their retirement as employees (not later than their 65th birthday). Under the present practice of the Board, non-employee directors who will reach their 70th birthday prior to the annual meeting do not stand for reelection at that meeting. Employee directors are drawn from senior executives who have demonstrated a high degree of competence during their careers with Exxon and its affiliates and have accumulated valuable experience by the time they are elected to the Board. That experience provides the Board with a core of directors who are highly knowledgeable about Exxon's complex business activities and can therefore make a particularly effective contribution to the Board's deliberations.

Non-employee directors have been selected from persons of outstanding ability and experience in the fields of industry, education and science. One or more serve on each of the Board's committees. Two of the Board's committees—Audit and Compensation—are comprised solely of non-employee directors. In the opinion of the Board, to lose the services of either employee or non-employee directors at a time when they have acquired the knowledge and experience to most effectively carry out their duties would not be in the best interests of the shareholders.

The Board believes that continuity of management at the Board level is essential to the operation of a corporation as large and diverse as Exxon. This proposal would impede such continuity. The Board further believes that a principal purpose of identifying and electing younger executives of outstanding ability to serve on the Board is to gain the benefit of an extended period of service by them as employee directors. To arbitrarily limit that benefit would be self-defeating.

The resolution was defeated at the annual meeting by a vote of 98.5 percent *against* and 1.5 percent *for*.

EXHIBIT 4
Exxon Corporation Board of Directors, 1977

THOMAS D. BARROW
Senior Vice President

Chairman—Investment Advisory
Committee

Director of Texas Commerce Bancshares Inc. and the New York Philharmonic Society. Trustee of the American Museum of Natural History. Member of the Geological Society of America, American Association of Petroleum Geologists and the National Academy of Engineering.

Director since 1972   Exxon shares owned 22,574

JACK F. BENNETT
Senior Vice President

Vice Chairman—Investment Advisory
Committee

Former Undersecretary of the Treasury for Monetary Affairs; Trustee of Committee for Economic Development. Director, Adela Investment Company, S.A. Member of Council on Foreign Relations, Inc. and Council of Harvard Graduate Society for Advanced Study and Research.

Director since 1975   Exxon shares owned 720

JACK G. CLARKE
Senior Vice President

Chairman—Petroleum Supply
Coordination Committee
Member—Board Advisory
Committee on Contributions

Director of Amstar Corporation. Member of the Board of Trustees of Hofstra University. Trustee and member of Executive Committee of the United States Council of the International Chamber of Commerce.

Director since 1975   Exxon shares owned 2,012

DONALD M. COX
Senior Vice President

Vice Chairman—Petroleum Supply
Coordination Committee

Director of the National Foreign Trade Council Inc. Trustee and member of the Executive Committee of the Council of Americas. Member of the Board of Trustees of Bluefield College. Member of the American Chemical Society.

Director since 1971   Exxon shares owned 10,926

SIR RICHARD DOBSON
Chairman of British Leyland Ltd.

Member—Audit Committee

Photo by Mark Gerson

President of B.A.T. Industries Ltd. Chairman of Tobacco Securities Trust Company, Limited. Director of Davy International Limited, Molins Limited and Foseco Minsep Ltd.

Director since 1975   Exxon shares owned 200

WILLIAM H. FRANKLIN
Director of Caterpillar Tractor Co.
(Retired Chairman and Chief Executive Officer)

Chairman—Audit Committee
Member—Board Compensation
Committee

Trustee and Chairman of the Committee for Economic Development.

Director since 1969   Exxon shares owned 408

CLIFTON C. GARVIN, JR.
Chairman and Chief Executive Officer

Chairman—Executive Committee

Photo by Karsh, Ottawa

Director of the American Petroleum Institute, PepsiCo, Inc., Citicorp, Citibank, N.A., United Way of America and Committee for Economic Development. Chairman, Council for Financial Aid to Education, Inc. Member of The Business Council and National Petroleum Council.

Director since 1968   Exxon shares owned 16,780

HARRY J. GRAY
Chairman, President and Chief
Executive Officer,
United Technologies Corporation

Joined United Technologies Corporation as President and Director in 1971, became Chief Executive Officer in 1972 and Chairman in 1974. Director of Citicorp, Citibank, N.A., and Aetna Life and Casualty Company, Hartford. Member of The Business Council and The Conference Board.

Director since 1977   Exxon shares owned 300

EXHIBIT 4 *(concluded)*

EDWARD G. HARNESS
Chairman and Chief Executive Officer
of The Procter & Gamble Company

Vice Chairman—Board Compensation
Committee

Chairman of the Board of Trustees of Marietta College.
Member of The Business Council, The Policy Committee of The Business Roundtable and The Conference Board.

Director since 1975   Exxon shares owned 200

J. KENNETH JAMIESON
Retired Chairman and Chief Executive
Officer of Exxon Corporation

Photo by Karsh, Ottawa

Director of The Equitable Life Assurance Society of the
United States, Mercantile Texas Corporation, Dallas,
and Chairman of the Board, Crutcher Resources Corp.,
Houston.

Director since 1964   Exxon shares owned 76,048

HOWARD C. KAUFFMANN
President

Vice Chairman—Executive Committee

Director of the American Petroleum Institute, the International Executive Service Corps, The Chase Manhattan
Corporation, The Chase Manhattan Bank, N.A., and
United Fund of Greater New York.

Director since 1974   Exxon shares owned 20,166

FRANKLIN A. LONG
Professor of Chemistry and Henry R.
Luce Professor of Science and Society
at Cornell University

Member—Board Compensation
Committee and Board Advisory
Committee on Contributions

Trustee of Associated Universities, Inc. Member of the
American Academy of Arts and Sciences, the American
Chemical Society and the National Academy of Sciences.

Director since 1969   Exxon shares owned 608

DONALD S. MACNAUGHTON
Chairman and Chief Executive Officer
of The Prudential Insurance Company
of America

Chairman—Board Compensation
Committee, Vice Chairman—Audit
Committee

Director of American Telephone & Telegraph Company.
Member of the New York Federal Reserve Money
Market General Committee. Member of The Business
Council and the Board of Overseers, Wharton School.

Director since 1970   Exxon shares owned 308

MARTHA PETERSON
President of Beloit College

Member—Board Compensation
Committee, Audit Committee and Board
Advisory Committee on Contributions

Director of The Metropolitan Life Insurance Company,
First Wisconsin Corporation, American Arbitration Association, United Bank of Illinois, N.A., and Council for
Financial Aid to Education, Inc. Member of the Board of
Trustees of Notre Dame University.

Director since 1974   Exxon shares owned 200

GEORGE T. PIERCY
Senior Vice President

Director of Aramco, Chemical Bank and Chemical New
York Corporation. Trustee of the Educational Broadcasting Corporation. Member of The American Institute of
Chemical Engineers, Council on Foreign Relations, Inc.
and the Board of Governors of Public Broadcasting Service

Director since 1966   Exxon shares owned 13,618

OTTO WOLFF VON AMERONGEN
Chairman of the Management Board
and Chief Executive Officer of
Otto Wolff AG, Cologne, West Germany

President of the Association of German Chambers of
Commerce and Industry.

Director since 1971   Exxon shares owned 3,200

ORGANIZATION AND MANAGEMENT

Exxon adopted the principle of decentralized management of its operations in the late 1920s. Since then its volume of business has grown some 20 times and its operations have become substantially more complex. Generally speaking, policy formulation, planning, and coordination were functions of Exxon Corporation's senior management and staff. Activities such as drilling wells, running refineries, and marketing products were delegated to local and division managements close to the scene of these activities. Management positions in Exxon's foreign affiliates and subsidiaries were, with few exceptions, almost entirely staffed by nationals of those countries.

Prior to 1966, some 40 affiliated companies were reporting directly to corporate headquarters in New York. Feeling that this system was becoming unwieldy and inefficient. Exxon reorganized its divisions and companies into a small number of regional and operating units. The top officials in each of these subunits were given broad responsibilities and their own staffs in an effort to permit quicker response to changing conditions and, further, to reduce the number of people reporting to corporate headquarters. Some of these subunits were given responsibilities for certain parts of the world, such as the United States, Europe and Africa, Latin America, and the Far East. Others had worldwide responsibilities for particular segments of Exxon's business, such as chemicals or research. As of 1977, there were 11 such subunits, each headed by a senior executive: Exxon Company, U.S.A., Esso Middle East, Exxon Chemical Company, Exxon International Company, Esso Eastern Inc., Esso Europe Inc., Esso Exploration Inc., Esso Inter-America Inc., Exxon Enterprises Inc., Exxon Research and Engineering Company, and Imperial Oil Limited (70 percent owned by Exxon).

In 1977, the principal link between the corporation and each regional or operating subunit was provided by one of seven senior management officials (either a senior vice president or the corporation president) who were on Exxon's board of directors. The officer-director was designated as the "contact executive" for at least one of the regional or operating subunits. The concept of "contact" responsibilities was, according to Exxon, a significant innovation when introduced in 1943. A contact executive's responsibilities were implicit rather than precisely defined, but his chief role was to provide policy guidance to the subunits for which he was responsible. When he did so, it was understood that he spoke for the chief executive officer. The contact executive endeavored to stay well informed about the plans of the regional or operating subunits and the problems they faced. They consulted him on any matter they expected to review with the corporation's management committee (composed of all seven officer-directors) or the compensation and executive development committee (known informally as the COED committee and having the same membership as the management committee). On many matters the contact executive had final review authority. From time to time, the contact assignments of the officer-directors were rotated so as to provide new viewpoints and broaden their own experience.

In 1977, Exxon's board chairman was Clifton C. Garvin; he had been board chairman since August 1975, and a director since 1968. Mr. Garvin began his career with Exxon some 30 years previous in 1947. A graduate of Virginia Polytechnic Institute, he joined Exxon as a process engineer at Exxon's Baton Rouge refinery and became operating superintendent in ten years. Later, he moved through a series of positions in Exxon Company, U.S.A., gaining experience in other major functions of the oil business. In 1964, he went to New York as executive assistant to Exxon's president. During the three years prior to his election as a director, he headed Exxon Chemical, U.S.A., and then Exxon's worldwide chemical organization. Mr. Garvin regularly consulted with the corporation's management committee composed of all seven employee directors; he was chairman of this committee and was also chairman of the COED committee which was primarily concerned with the continuity and quality of Exxon's management. The COED committee directly concerned itself with about 200 senior management positions around the world and indirectly kept an eye on another 400 top management jobs in affiliated companies and subsidiary operations. The COED committee met weekly.

Exxon's president was Howard C. Kauffmann; he served as vice chairman of both the management committee and the COED committee. Mr. Kauffmann started with Exxon as an engineer trainee in Oklahoma in 1946. He spent 11 years in Exxon's U.S. producing operations. During the next 11 years he held a series of positions concerned with Exxon's operations in Latin America, including assignments in Peru and Columbia. In 1966, he became president of Exxon's then newly established regional organization for Latin America. In 1968, he moved to the United Kingdom as executive vice president of the regional organization for Europe and became its president in 1971. He was elected a director of Exxon in 1974, and president in 1975.

Exhibit 5 shows the remuneration of Exxon's top management in 1976. Exhibit 6 presents a discussion of top management succession at Exxon as reported in *Forbes*. Anthony Sampson, in describing each of the Seven Sisters, said the following about Exxon and its management:

> In the middle of Manhattan, in the line of cliffs adjoining the Rockefeller Center, is the headquarters of the most famous and long-lived of them all: the company known in America as Exxon, and elsewhere as Esso, and for most of its 100 years' existence as Standard Oil of New Jersey or simply Standard Oil. It is a company which perhaps more than any other transformed the world in which we live. For much of its life it was automatically associated with the name of Rockefeller, and some links still remain. The family still own 2 percent of the stock; Nelson Rockefeller once worked for it in Venezuela; and the desk of the founder, John D. Rockefeller I, is still preserved as a showpiece at the

EXHIBIT 5
Compensation of Top Management, 1976

Name of Director	Capacity during 1976 in Addition to Serving as Director	Direct Remuneration*	Bonus Grants Made November 22, 1976			Employer Thrift Plan Contributions‡
			Cash/Stock Bonus Grants	Stock Appreciation Bonus Unit Grants†		
T. D. Barrow	Senior vice president	$ 222,917	$ 65,000	1,800		$ 13,575
J. F. Bennett	Senior vice president	170,417	55,000	1,500		10,225
N. J. Campbell, Jr.	Senior vice president (through November)	235,000	65,000	1,800		14,100
J. G. Clarke	Senior vice president	170,000	55,000	1,500		10,200
D. M. Cox	Senior vice president	220,833	65,000	1,800		13,250
C. C. Garvin, Jr.	Chairman	420,833	190,000	5,000		25,250
H. C. Kauffmann	President	287,500	115,000	3,000		17,250
G. T. Piercy	Senior vice president	252,500	70,000	2,000		15,150
M. A. Wright	Executive vice president (through March)	103,846	—	—		—
All directors and officers as a group (66 persons)		$7,497,892	$1,824,000	41,040		$458,000

* Includes, where applicable, payments under corporation's disability benefit program, and those required by law for periods of disability but excludes bonus grants and Employer Thrift Plan contributions shown in the last three columns.

† The stock appreciation bonus units shown are those with respect to 1976 earnings with a maximum appreciation factor of $25 per unit, realization of which is dependent upon dividends paid based on record dates after November 22, 1976, and appreciation above $50.25, the market value of one share of stock at time of grant, but do not include awards of stock appreciation bonus units granted in April 1976 in relation to 1975 earnings.

‡ In 1976, employer contributions were made to the Thrift Fund accounts of 57 employee directors and officers included in the group of 66 persons referred to above. Aggregate employer contributions to this group for the years 1961–76 were $3,428,720. Individual aggregate employer contributions since 1961 were as follows: Messrs. Barrow $89,131; Bennett $15,025; Campbell $130,403; Clarke $65,401; Cox $90,554; Garvin $155,023; Kauffmann $112,950; Piercy $115,866; Wright $177,061.

EXHIBIT 6
Exxon: Men within a System

Every five years or so, just like clockwork, the top job at Exxon Corp. changes hands. The incumbent chief executive officer, usually the board chairman, is required to depart at age 65. And a new man, invariably the former president, steps in at roughly age 60 for *his* brief stint at the helm—to live mainly with decisions made by his predecessors, to make new ones affecting his own successors more than himself.

What happened recently at rival Texaco—where Augustus C. Long finally retired after eight years as CEO, then came back six years later at age 65—could never happen at Exxon.

That's good for the younger executives at Exxon: All down through the ranks it causes new jobs to be constantly opening up. But is it good for the company to have its top brass coming and going so frequently? Surely it must be tempting for an Exxon CEO to concentrate on short-run decisions, to make his own brief record look good and retire a hero.

EXHIBIT 6 *(continued)*

Yet it doesn't seem to happen that way. The Exxon system produces solid, long-range decision-making at the top. Decisions like the one Monroe Rathbone made during the early 60s . . . where the payoffs are anything but short-range. How does Exxon defy the textbook notion that a man ought to be CEO long enough to have to live with his own decisions?

For one thing, his time at the top isn't as short as it appears. Before serving as CEO, a man is usually president for five years or so under the man he ultimately succeeds. And at Exxon the CEO and the president work in tandem. When Chairman J. Kenneth Jamieson, the present CEO, reaches 65 and retires in 1975, President Clifton C. Garvin will already have had almost six years of shaping top-level policies. The big decisions made during Jamieson's tenure, from 1969 through 1975, will in large part be Garvin's, too.

For another thing, neither Jamieson nor Garvin is really involved in shortrun decisions, the kind that might produce a sharp uptick in earnings for a few years. The day-to-day operating decisions are elaborately decentralized away from them and down through the organization. Jamieson's and Garvin's—as that of their predecessors—job is to concentrate on longer range strategy.

"We may ask about the cost of heating oil from time to time," says Garvin, "but Mike Wright [M.A. Wright, chairman of Exxon Co., USA], not Ken or me, is the man the board holds accountable for things like that."

There's another, more important reason why the Exxon system works. After several decades on the Exxon executive ladder, any top executive is a thoroughgoing company man.

"I think of it as a proprietary relationship," says Cliff Garvin. "Like running a company of which I am the owner. It is just my duty, but my deep personal desire is to keep it in the best shape possible for the men who will come after me. That will determine whether I was successful or not—not a sharp uptrend in profits while I was there."

How does a corporation go about breeding company men? At Exxon it begins with hiring the cream of the college crop. A young man joining the company will find among his peers mostly men who graduated in the top tenth of their classes. He knows right off he is a member of an elite group. As he moves up through the company, he finds he is amply rewarded, not just with money but with meaningful additional job responsibilities as well. With a $21-billion (gross assets) worldwide company, there is no shortage of opportunities and challenges.

Sometimes the pace of advancement is not fast enough for some young men. Mobil Oil Corp.'s 46-year-old Executive Vice President Richard F. Tucker was an Exxon man who got impatient. But most are patient, for they know the advancement pace, if not swift, is regular, that higher jobs are always opening up. They know, too, that no one is likely to be brought in from the outside to fill the job ahead of them.

All these things combine to produce tremendous loyalty and dedication to the company. Not a mindless sort of loyalty, but the loyalty of a man who knows that the system will serve his ambition and intelligence.

"You must be consumed by a tremendous ambition to make it to the top of a 150,000-employee company," says Garvin. The point is that *personal* ambition alone is not enough: You have to be ambitious for the long-term prospects of the company as well.

Reprinted with permission from *Forbes*, April 1, 1973, p. 32.

top of the building. But Exxon has long ago outgrown the control of a single family. It is, by assets, the biggest company in the world. It has 300,000 shareholders, its subsidiaries operate in 100 countries, and in 1973 its profits were a world record for any company in history—$2.5 billion.

The tranquil style of Exxon's international headquarters seems to have little in common with the passionate rhetoric of Arab politicians in Algiers. Beside a bubbling fountain and pool on Sixth Avenue, the fluted stone ribs soar up sheer for 53 stories, and inside the high entrance hall is hung with moons and stars. On the 24th floor is the mechanical brain of the company, where the movements of its vast cargoes are recorded. A row of TV screens are linked with two giant computers, and with other terminals in Houston, London, and Tokyo, in a system proudly named LOGICS (Logistics Information and Communications Systems). They record the movement of 500 Exxon ships from 115 loading ports to 270 destinations, carrying 160 different kinds of Exxon oil between 65 countries. It is an uncanny process to watch: a girl taps out a question on the keyboard, and the answer comes back on little green letters on the screen, with the names of ships, dates, and destinations across the world. From the peace of the 24th floor, it seems like playing God—a perfectly rational and omniscient god, surveying the world as a single market.

Up on the 51st floor, where the directors are found, the atmosphere is still more rarefied. The visitor enters a high two-story lobby with a balcony looking down on high tapestries; the wide corridors are decorated with Middle East artifacts, Persian carpets, palms, or a Coptic engraving. It is padded and silent except for a faint hum of air-conditioning, and the directors' offices are like fastidious drawing rooms, looking down on the vulgar bustle of Sixth Avenue. It all seems appropriate to Exxon's reputation as a "United Nations of Oil."

But in this elegant setting, the directors themselves are something of an anticlimax. They are clearly not diplomats, or strategists, or statesmen; they are chemical engineers from Texas, preoccupied with what they call "the Exxon incentive." Their route to the top has been through the "Texas pipeline"—up through the technical universities, the refineries and tank farms. The Exxon Academy, as they call it, is not a university or a business school, but the giant refinery at Baton Rouge, Louisiana. Watching the Exxon board at their annual meeting, I found it hard to imagine them as representatives of a world assembly. It was true that there were, in 1974, two foreign directors— Prince Colonna, the former commissioner of the Common Market, and Otto Wolff, the German industrialist; and there was also one director, Emilio Collado, with experience of government. But the core of the board was made up of the engineers, enclosed in their own specialized discipline.

Ken Jamieson, the chairman and chief executive, a tall cliff of a man with a wide deadpan mouth, was brought up a Canadian, in Medicine Hat, the son of a Mountie; but Texas has since become his adopted home, and he will soon retire there. Jim Garvin, the president, an engineer from Virginia, worked his way up through chemicals and Texas, insulated from the world outside oil: he is expected to be chief executive for eight years. Mike Wright, the Chief Executive of Exxon, U.S.A., began as a rough-neck in Oklahoma before he, too, went down to Texas, where he now lives: a wiry outspoken champion of the fight for free enterprise. Tom Barrow, a short, thick-set man, comes from an old Texan oil family with a shareholding in Exxon: he studied geology in Texas and

California, made his name in exploration, and came back to Texas as President of Exxon, U.S.A.; he is likely to be Garvin's successor. George Piercy, the Middle East negotiator, is the director who is most constantly concerned with diplomacy and foreign countries: he has a combative look, with a quiff of hair and a bulldog face, as if built to battle over barrels. He too came up through the pipeline: He became a chemical engineer in Minnesota, and graduated at the Bayway Refinery.

Within their own citadel these men seem confident enough, with some reason: they are directors of a company that has survived for a century, they have acquired great expertise, and they each earn over $200,000 a year. They move in a world enclosed by the rules of Exxon, which belongs to them. "I think of it as a proprietory relationship," said Garvin in 1973, "Like running a company of which I am the owner. It is not just my duty, but my deep personal desire, to keep it in the best shape possible for the men who will come after me." But once outside their own territory, their confidence easily evaporates. Confronting their shareholders they seem thoroughly nervous, sitting in a row, their fingers fidgeting and their cheekbones working, as they listen to questions about Exxon's African policy, Exxon's salary policy, Exxon's kidnap policy, Exxon's Middle East policy. They know well enough that their company, while one of the oldest, has also been the most hated.

It is in Texas, not New York, that the Exxon men feel more thoroughly at home, and it is the Exxon skyscraper in Houston, the headquarters of Exxon U.S.A., which seems to house the soul of the company. At the top is the Houston Petroleum Club, with two entire stories making up a single room, where the oilmen can lunch off steak and strawberries every day of the year. They like to show visitors the view, of which they are justly proud. The flatlands stretch in every direction, broken only by the jagged man-made objects: the domes and tower-blocks in place of cliffs and hills; the curving freeways instead of rivers; the giant road-sings instead of trees. The glaring gasoline signs stick up from the desolate landscape, like symbols leading to some distant shrine: Exxon, Texaco, Shell, Gulf, Exxon. The fluid which has wrought all these changes is concealed from the view: around Houston, there are only a few little pumps nodding in the fields, a few piles of pipelines, to indicate the underground riches. But no-one needs reminding: it was all done by oil.[1]

EXXON CORPORATION IN 1976: A REVIEW AND SUMMARY OF OPERATIONS

Exploration and Production. In 1976, Exxon's worldwide production of crude oil and natural gas liquids increased 3 percent over 1975 to a level of 5,576,000 barrels a day (one barrel = 42 gallons). Declining production in the United States and Canada, and smaller flow of petroleum supplies from Venezuelan sources were more than offset by increased Middle East production. The company's sales of natural gas in the United States declined by 5

---

[1] Anthony Sampson, *The Seven Sisters* (New York: The Viking Press, 1975), pp. 8–10. Quoted with permission.

percent to a level of 4.7 billion cubic feet a day. Total liquids production by Exxon Company, U.S.A., dropped by 4 percent. The lower production rates in both cases reflected declining capability of mature fields.

Exxon, U.S.A., participated in 75 exploratory wells in 1976, compared with 40 wells in 1975. The 1976 drilling activities resulted in 16 apparent discoveries, the most significant of which were on tracts in the Gulf of Mexico. From 1974 through 1976, Exxon's discoveries in the Gulf, if expectations were met, amounted to over 1 trillion cubic feet of gas and 100 million barrels of oil.

In an August 1976 auction of oil and gas leases held by the U.S. Department of the Interior for drilling rights in the Baltimore Canyon area 50 miles off New Jersey's shore, Exxon paid $343 million for rights on 171,000 acres, nearly one third of the acreage leased by the industry. In reporting on the bidding a *Business Week* reporter wrote:

> . . . Exxon repeatedly brought gasps with its enormous bids. "Clobbered," moaned one oil man, his companion nervously gulping Rolaids, as an Exxon bid was opened and read off by the auctioneer—$51.3 million, double the highest competing bid. On another tract, Exxon overwhelmed a $12.4 million bid with $86.4 million. "They left $74 million on the table on that one," Mobil's Hohler remarked wryly.
>
> All told, Exxon made bids totaling $730 million, nearly three times as much as Shell, the next highest bidder. And it won on $343 million in bids, almost four times the outlays of Mobil, the second biggest winner. Said a government staffer: "Exxon just hit everyone over the head with their money."[2]

The man in charge of the bids which Exxon made at such auctions as the Baltimore Canyon tract and who headed Exxon's search for oil and gas was John L. Loftis, Jr.—senior vice president of exploration and minerals for Exxon, U.S.A. Loftis has been described as a burly but soft-spoken Texan who might be taken for a suburban high school teacher around his hometown of Houston. A graduate of the University of Texas, he began at Exxon working with a seismographic crew as a wellside geologist; later he moved up to research. One top Exxon, U.S.A., official, newly retired, said of Loftis, "John is not interested in anything but geology. He's not a marketing or a refining man. But he has a real good record of discovering oil—and of judging how his competitors will behave at auctions."[3] In 1976, Loftis had a staff of 2,150 employees which he headed; he sat on Exxon, U.S.A.'s management committee, and he had direct responsibility for Exxon's pattern of bidding at every lease sale.

According to the president of another oil company, Loftis and Exxon were obliged to bid heavily at every lease sale "because any major oil company with a huge investment in refineries like Exxon can't afford not to

---

[2] "Exxon's High Roller in Oil Lease Sales," *Business Week*, September 20, 1976, p. 116.
[3] Ibid., p. 117.

have an oil supply."[4] Exxon viewed the market in the northeastern United States as important since it had a major refinery in New Jersey and could readily benefit from a major nearby discovery of crude oil. Loftis was considered as a superior bidder at leases because Exxon in recent years had a 20 percent success rate in finding oil and/or gas on new tracts where it had obtained drilling leases—compared to an industry average of 10 percent. Loftis indicated that there was no real alternative to anteing up and rolling the dice: "You have nightmares going into these things, but an exploration man has to learn early that it's better to try and fail than not to try and have nothing."[5]

To try to reduce the risk on tracts on which auctions were to be held, Exxon, like other oil companies, sent out seismographic teams to assess the probability of discovery. In the case of Baltimore Canyon, 31 companies banded together to drill a test hole to determine if the geological structure had the necessary porosity to qualify as a "reservoir" where oil might have collected with perhaps 70 percent probability. But the hole was too shallow to test for hydrocarbon source rocks—limestone and shell—at the depth required for oil or gas. And it was drilled adjacent to rather than on top of the area up for lease. In fact, the oil companies did not want to find oil prior to the auction because of the likely reluctance of Congress to let the tract go if any oil had been found before the auction. The U.S. Geological Survey used a complex computer program called the "Monte Carlo System" to estimate the average amount of oil and/or gas which each parcel up for auction might be expected to produce; their estimates for the Baltimore Canyon area ranged from 400 million to 1.4 billion barrels of crude oil and from 2.6 trillion to 9.4 trillion cubic feet of natural gas. But oilmen irreverently called this estimating approach the SWAG ("Scientific Wild Ass Guess") method.[6]

Shortly after the Baltimore Canyon lease sale took place, Suffolk County (New York) and others filed a suit challenging the environmental impact statement submitted by the U.S. Department of the Interior in conjunction with the lease sale. In February 1977, a U.S. District Court judge ruled against the secretary of the interior and declared the lease sale null and void. Although the secretary of the interior filed an appeal, he declared that no exploration would be permitted until the outcome of the appeal was determined.

Insofar as production and exploration activities elsewhere were concerned, Imperial Oil, Ltd., a Canadian company in which Exxon had a 70 percent interest, saw its production output decline 11 percent in 1976 as compared to 1975, owing to restrictions on petroleum exports imposed by the Canadian government. However, Imperial stepped up its exploration efforts in western Canada in response to improved gas prices and tax incentives enacted by the provincial governments of Alberta and British Columbia.

---

[4] Ibid., p. 120.
[5] Ibid.
[6] Ibid., p. 116.

In Alaska, construction and preparations continued on the Trans-Alaska Pipeline, expected to commence operations in June 1977. The pipeline had a capacity of 1.2 barrels per day of which Exxon's share was expected to be close to 240,000 barrels per day. Preparing for the opening of the Alaskan pipeline, in 1976 Exxon contracted for two 165,000-ton tankers to be used in transporting Alaskan oil from the company's pipeline terminal at Valdez to West Coast ports. The company was also modifying five smaller tankers for the same task, and was engaged in chartering other tonnage to meet projected needs. Since Exxon's Alaskan crude would make more oil available than the company's Benicia, California, refinery could use (or which could be readily sold to others on the West Coast), the company was providing for tankers to move some of its Alaskan oil to the Gulf of Mexico and possibly to East Coast markets where it would replace oil which otherwise would have to be imported.

The company's share of oil production from its North Sea holdings off the coast of Great Britain reached 40,000 barrels per day by year-end 1976. As of early 1977, Exxon had invested $1.2 billion in oil fields and related facilities in the North Sea area and expected its oil production to reach about 300,000 barrels per day by the 1980s. These fields were held jointly with Shell and the latter acted as the operator. Exxon also held a 9 percent interest in the Statfjord field off the coast of Norway—the North Sea's largest oil field— where production was scheduled to begin in early 1979.

In 1976, natural gas sales from Exxon's holdings and purchases in the Netherlands, Great Britain, and West Germany increased 7 percent to an average of just over 5.1 billion cubic feet per day. The company's European gas production was just over 4 billion cubic feet per day, a rate which was expected to be maintained over the next several years.

In the Middle East and Africa, Exxon obtained 3,103,000 barrels per day of crude oil and natural gas liquids, up 12 percent over 1975 amounts. Of this total, 2,248,000 barrels came from Saudi Arabia—a 21 percent increase over 1975. Oil supplies from Libya (another OPEC country) rose 33 percent and the company's Libyan gas plant achieved new annual production records of 297 million cubic feet per day of liquefied natural gas and 21,000 barrels of naphtha, all of which went to supply the company's European customers.

Exxon Production Research Company successfully completed the first year's test of a "guyed tower" installation in the Gulf of Mexico, demonstrating that the design offered potentially significant advantages over other systems for producing oil and gas in water depths between 600 and 2,000 feet. Installed in 300 feet of water off the Louisiana coast, the tower was a one-fifth scale model of a drilling and production platform designed to accommodate the drilling of 24 wells in 1,500 feet of water. It was secured by guy lines attached to anchors on the sea floor so as to reduce the requirements for heavy structural elements. Eleven other companies participated in the project operated by Exxon.

Refining and Transportation. In refining, Exxon was the world's largest, with a capacity of 6.6 million barrels per day—double the capacity of the next largest refiner, Texaco. In 1974, Exxon's refineries ran at only 77.6 percent of capacity overall and at 60 percent of capacity overseas. The oil embargo substantially reduced the availability of crude in the first part of 1974 and the recession softened demand later on. Between price controls and depressed demand, Exxon reportedly only broke even on its refining and marketing operations in 1974. Since then, things have improved somewhat.

Crude oil runs in Exxon refineries averaged 4,359,000 barrels a day in 1976, virtually unchanged from the previous year. However, the 1976 figure did not include the output of two Venezuelan refineries which were nationalized with other Exxon assets in that country at the end of 1975. Excluding Venezuela, the operating rate of the company's worldwide refining system increased by 10 percent in 1976.

Reflecting the increase in petroleum product demand in the United States, Exxon's five U.S. refineries operated near maximum capacity throughout 1976, with output up an average of 8 percent to 1,277,000 barrels per day. A 250,000 barrels per day expansion at Baytown, Texas, neared completion at a cost of approximately $500 million; start-up was scheduled for the second quarter of 1977. The U.S. economic recovery also resulted in a 32 percent higher output at Exxon's refinery on Aruba in the Caribbean.

Exxon's refineries in Europe realized output gains of 11 percent in 1976, but continued to operate with large excess capacity. As a consequence, some older units were temporarily shut down and work was begun on modifying other equipment to accommodate a shift from heavier to lighter refined products. A $280 million expansion and modernization was completed at the company's refinery in Antwerp, Belgium—a project that increased capacity to from 88,000 barrels to 250,000 barrels per day and that included installation of processing equipment for the manufacture of low-sulfur fuel oil.

The company's energy conservation efforts at its refineries, begun in 1974, had by year-end 1976 reduced energy consumption per barrel of product by 12 percent worldwide. At current fuel cost, this represented an annual savings of $140 million. In the same period, slow steaming and fleet restructuring reduced the annual fuel consumption of the company's tanker fleet by more than 20 percent. These efforts, together with related efficiencies, produced savings of some $60 million in 1976.

In 1976, work continued on Exxon's tanker fleet modernization program aimed at reducing transportation cost and adjusting to a world tanker surplus. The company sold or scrapped 19 older, less efficient vessels during the year and took delivery on 7 new vessels, including a 412,000-ton tanker and 4 other tankers of more than 270,000 tons. An additional nine tankers, including two 500,000-ton ships, were on order. The restructuring effort, scheduled to be completed by the end of 1978, aimed at giving Exxon a fleet of 158 oceangoing tankers having a total capacity of 18 million tons.

Marketing. Exxon's sales volume of petroleum products increased 7 percent to 5,353,000 barrels per day in 1976; the increased demand was attributed to the general recovery in the economy from depressed levels of 1974 and 1975. Gains in sales were most pronounced in the United States, where volume rose 17 percent over 1975; the biggest increases were in sales of heavy fuel oil and aviation and marine fuels. Exxon's market share of overall petroleum industry sales in 1976 was up slightly to a level around 10.5 percent.

The Federal Energy Administration removed the price controls on products accounting for about half of Exxon, U.S.A.'s sales volume, including fuel oil and home heating oil. Controls remained in effect on gasoline, kerosine-based jet fuel, propane, and butane.

A number of marketing changes occurred at the international level in 1976. Exxon sold its marketing and refining interest in Pakistan and its remaining interest in refining assets in India to the governments of those countries. It sold its marketing interest in Nigeria to that government, and agreed on terms for the sale of its interest in Morocco following a 1975 order by the Moroccan government which "requisitioned" those assets. The company's assets in Madagascar were nationalized, but no agreement on compensation had been reached. Exxon ceased its operations in Lebanon due to war conditions which made it impossible to ensure the safety of employees or conduct an orderly business. Total Exxon sales volume in these countries averaged less than 25,000 barrels per day. Negotiations were under way in Argentina, where the government had proposed reversing its action nationalizing Exxon's retail business in 1974. The loss of the internal Venezuelan market as a result of nationalization caused Exxon's worldwide sales volume to be approximately 2 percent less than otherwise would have been the case.

During 1976, the number of service stations selling Exxon brands decreased from 68,000 to 66,500 worldwide. In general, the company's affiliates continued divesting less efficient and low-volume outlets. Exxon, U.S.A., announced the testing of a discount-for-cash program at participating Exxon service stations in Abilene, Texas, and Charleston, South Carolina. Under this program, customers had the choice of using their Exxon credit cards or paying cash and saving up to 5 percent of their purchases. The tests sought to determine the reaction of service station dealers, customers, and the general public to the discount-for-cash concept.

Chemical Operations.   Total revenues of Exxon Chemical Company rose 23 percent to a record $3.7 billion—mainly because of the strong economic rebound throughout 1976. Improvement in sales volume extended to all product lines and to all regions except Canada, where reduced demand for agricultural chemicals offset other sales increases. Major capital projects completed during the year at a cost of $383 million included the expansion of olefins facilities at Cologne, West Germany, which would increase the company's ethylene capacity to 1 billion pounds per year and a low-density polyethylene plant at Meerhout, Belgium, with an annual capacity of over 500 million pounds. New solvents facilities commenced operations at Antwerp, Belgium; Fawley, England; Trecate, Italy; and Singapore. Construction work continued on the expansion of a low-density polyethylene plant at Baton Rouge (scheduled for completion by mid-1977) and a polypropylene expansion at Baytown, Texas. Site preparation began at Baytown for an olefins plant costing nearly $500 million—the biggest capital project ever undertaken by Exxon Chemical.

Exxon Chemical's ongoing effort to conserve energy reduced 1976 fuel consumption per unit of production 9.3 percent below 1973 levels, saving the equivalent of 3.6 million barrels of oil.

Minerals. The minerals exploration program of Exxon, U.S.A., resulted in the discovery of a large zinc-copper deposit near Crandon, Wisconsin. Geological data indicated a 75 million ton deposit averaging about 5 percent zinc and 1 percent copper, with substantially lesser values of silver, gold, and lead.

Operating Results and Performance. Exhibits 7, 8, and 9 provide further indication of Exxon's recent performance and how well its shareholders have fared.

Environmental Protection Efforts. Exxon spent $685 million (including capital and operating expenses) for environmental conservation measures in

EXHIBIT 7
Earnings Summary, by Line of Business

	Millions of Dollars	
	1976	1975
Energy operations		
Petroleum and natural gas		
United States		
Exploration and production	$ 977	$ 939
Refining and marketing	287	212
Foreign		
Exploration and production	1,046	1,074
Refining and marketing	231	324
International marine	92	(39)
Coal and nuclear	(43)	(34)
	2,590	2,476
Chemical operations		
United States	148	109
Foreign	86	86
Minerals	(8)	(6)
Other operations	(9)	(10)
Total Operations	2,807	2,655
Nonoperating items	71	72
Total before Financial Charges	2,878	2,727
Less: financial charges	(237)	(224)
Net Income	$2,641	$2,503

Source: *1976 Annual Report.*

EXHIBIT 8
Functional and Geographic Analysis of Results*

	Operating Earnings (millions of dollars)		Average Capital Employed (billions of dollars)	
	1976	1975	1976	1975
Energy operations				
Petroleum and natural gas				
United States				
Exploration and production	$ 977	$ 939	$ 4.6	$ 3.6
Refining and marketing	287	212	2.4	2.2
Foreign				
Exploration and production	1,046	1,074	3.0	2.3
Refining and marketing	231	324	5.2	5.7
International marine	92	(39)	1.6	1.6
Coal and nuclear	(43)	(34)	0.3	0.2
	$2,590	$2,476	$17.1	$15.6
Chemical operations				
United States	148	109	0.6	0.5
Foreign	86	86	1.0	0.9
Minerals.................................	(8)	(6)	—	—
Other operations.........................	(9)	(10)	0.3	0.3
Total Operations	$2,807	$2,655	$19.0	$17.3
Nonoperating items	71	72	4.8	4.6
Total Before Financial Charges	$2,878	$2,727	$23.8	$21.9
Less: financial charges	(237)	(224)		
Net Income	$2,641	$2,503		

* Capital employed consists of shareholders' equity, debt, and minority interests but does not include the value of underground reserves of oil, gas or minerals. Financial charges consist of interest expense (net of related income taxes), foreign currency translation gain/loss on debt and minority share of earnings. Transfers of crude oil or products between business activities are at estimated market prices. Results for the international marine activity are derived from revenues based on charges to other activities at a weighted average industry charter cost.
Source: *1976 Annual Report.*

1976, bringing total expenditures for this purpose over the past ten years to $3.5 billion. Wet gas scrubbers were installed in the company's refineries at Baton Rouge, Louisiana, and Linden, New Jersey. The scrubbers used a process developed by Exxon affiliates for removing fine particles and most of the sulfur oxides from the stack gases of fluid catalytic cracking units; the company was making the process available to other firms in the industry under licenses. A process developed by Exxon Research and Engineering Company for reducing nitrogen oxide emissions from large boilers was licensed and successfully used by a major Japanese chemical company.

Exxon continued a program started in 1975 to equip all company-owned tankers in excess of 120,000 tons with facilities for crude washing, a tank cleaning technique which significantly reduced the risk of pollution. This

EXHIBIT 9

Average Return from Holding Exxon Stock over Time (dividends and appreciation)

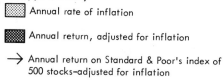

☐ Annual rate of inflation

■ Annual return, adjusted for inflation

→ Annual return on Standard & Poor's index of 500 stocks–adjusted for inflation

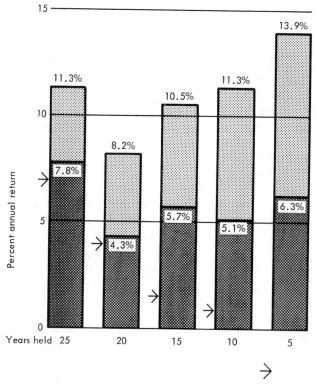

* Return calculated through year-end 1976 taking into account the time value of money.

Source: *1976 Annual Report.*

equipment was installed on 38 of 50 vessels by year-end. Exxon's reliance upon an internally developed program to screen vessels before chartering them resulted in a rejection of four tankers which were involved in major polluting incidents in the winter of 1976; Exxon rejected all four as a result of its standard review procedures to determine that prospective tankers had acceptable navigation aids, equipment, and crew.

Public Interest Activities. In 1976, Exxon's contributions to public interest activities in the United States totaled more than $20 million—a 20 percent increase over 1975. About half of this went to support education, including Exxon's contribution to the Exxon Education Foundation. This foundation made grants totaling almost $5 million to improve the quality of higher education, particularly innovations in teaching and administration. Exxon made grants to M.I.T., Cal Tech, Stanford, Chicago, and Texas under a five-year program to finance studies of energy policies and energy technology. Grants totaling $350,000 were made to support minority engineering studies at a number of colleges, and an additional $100,000 grant went to the National Fund for Minority Engineering to fund engineering scholarships.

The company provided more than $4 million for support of public television by underwriting drama, dance, and music programs in the "Great Performances" series as well as the "NOVA" series of science documentaries and "The MacNeil-Lehrer Report," a public issues discussion program. Another $400,000 went to support a bilingual education program for children. Exxon's contribution to the nation's bicentennial celebration included sponsorship of "The Eye of Thomas Jefferson," a six-month exhibit of Jefferson's art and architectural drawings at the National Gallery of Art in Washington, D.C., and a $200,000 grant to establish a park at South Street Seaport in New York City. Exxon, U.S.A., sponsored a series of 52 concerts in Washington's Kennedy Center by musical groups from all over the United States and from the armed forces. In collaboration with the national endowment for the humanities and New York's Metropolitan Museum of Art, Exxon underwrote a two-year, six-city tour of the "Treasures of Tutankhamun"—55 objects found with the body of the Egyptian boy-king when his ancient tomb was discovered in 1922. Outside the United States, Exxon affiliated companies contributed more than $5 million to a variety of activities in the countries in which they operated.

Equal Employment Opportunities. At year-end 1976, minorities accounted for 13.8 percent and women for 17.5 percent of Exxon's U.S. work force. More than one third of Exxon's U.S. employees were in managerial or professional jobs; of these, 3.9 percent were filled by minorities and 2.8 percent were filled by women. On the professional staff, 6.6 percent of the jobs were held by minorities, and 7.6 percent by women. Minorities represented 19.1 percent of the skilled and semiskilled employees at Exxon. Special efforts were made to recruit women for these jobs and at year-end 1976, 3.5 percent of Exxon's blue-collar jobs were held by women.

During 1976, 4,089 persons were hired into Exxon's U.S. work force. Of this total, 20.4 percent were minorities, and 33.2 percent were women. About three quarters of these new hires were for clerical and blue-collar jobs. Among the college graduates which Exxon recruited, minorities represented 9.3 percent of the new hires and women 19.3 percent.

In 1976, Exxon paid almost $2.7 billion in wages, salaries, and employee benefits to approximately 126,000 employees—an average of over $21,000 per employee. This compared with an average of roughly $11,900 in 1972 paid to some 141,000 employees.

EXXON'S PROJECTIONS OF U.S. ENERGY DEMAND

In 1975, Exxon projected that total U.S. energy demand would increase from an estimated 36.6 million barrels per day of oil equivalent in 1976, to about 54 million barrels per day in 1990—an average annual growth rate of just under 2.9 percent per year but significantly below the average growth of 4 percent during 1960–73 (prior to the Arab oil embargo). Exxon attributed the lower growth rate to changing consumption patterns and to a more efficient use of energy brought about by government initiatives and higher energy costs. Nonetheless the projected growth rate in demand represented a 50 percent increase in demand over the period and convinced Exxon of a genuine need to continue development of U.S. energy supplies.

Exxon forecasted that future discoveries of oil and gas would be barely sufficient to offset the decline in U.S. production from existing reserves for many years. For this reason, nuclear fission and coal and, eventually, synthetic fuels from oil shale and coal, solar, and nuclear fusion were viewed by the company as increasingly important energy sources needed to meet these projected energy demands. The exact distribution of these energy supplies was difficult to project and varied depending upon what economic, political, and environmental assumptions were made. The company was aware that its projections, while not necessarily exact, still demonstrated that production of energy sources other than oil and gas would need to increase.

Exxon estimated that in 1990, domestic coal output would approach 1.5 billion tons a year, more than double of the expected 1977 production. About 6 percent of coal production in 1990 was expected to be used to produce synthetic oil and gas. Synthetic oil from coal and oil shale was pegged at about 2 percent of total oil demand by 1990. Synthetic gas from coal was projected to be over 3 percent of total gas demand in that year. Nuclear energy sources were expected to increase almost fivefold between 1976 and 1990, a growth rate of 12 percent per year. The company believed that slower-than-forecast growth in domestic supplies of coal, nuclear, synthetic fuels, or any form of indigenous energy, unless accompanied by reductions in consumption, would translate directly into additional oil imports, which Exxon estimated would climb to 12 to 13 million barrels per day in the 1980s, or about half of expected total oil demand in the United States. The company believed that by 1985 imported oil could account for about 28 percent of total energy usage in the United States, compared with 17 percent in 1975.

In the company's view, the United States needed to develop all viable domestic energy sources to the fullest so as to limit growing reliance upon foreign oil supplies. In so doing, the vulnerability to future embargoes and to OPEC pricing decisions would be reduced, balance of payments strains would be mitigated, and the inevitable transition from oil and gas to other fuels would begin sooner. The company took the position that legislation which impeded energy development without generating compensating benefits would have significant adverse effects on the nation's future well-being.

Furthermore, studies made by the company indicated that from 1976 to 1990 cumulatively, in order to provide the domestic energy capabilities necessary to realize the projected outlook, the United States would need to add the equivalent of over 210 large coal mines (5 million tons per year each); 2,700 unit trains (100 cars each); 7 oil shale synthetic plants (50,000 barrels per day each); 7 coal gasification plants (250 million cubic feet per day each); 3 coal liquefication plants (50 thousand barrels per day each); and 30 uranium mining and milling complexes (2 million pounds per year each); all in addition to more than 450,000 new oil and gas wells and 31 new refineries (150 thousand barrels per day each). The capital requirements associated with these facilities amounted to an average of about $30 billion per year in constant 1976 dollars, compared with an average of less than $8 billion per year in capital expenditures for such facilities for the ten-year, pre-embargo period of 1963 through 1972. The Federal Energy Administration estimated that capital requirements, when chemical facilities and electric utility requirements were included, would average $58 billion per year (constant 1975 dollars) for the period 1975 through 1984.

THE STRATEGIC SHIFT TO BECOME AN ENERGY COMPANY

The foregoing trends and statistics were not new to Exxon's management. As far back as the 1960s the company had begun to sense that oil and gas reserves would be inadequate to meet the world's need for energy. It was with this in mind that Exxon started laying the groundwork for a major strategic shift from being just a petroleum company to becoming an energy company.

EXXON'S DIVERSIFICATION EFFORTS

Exxon's strategic move into alternate energy sources was motivated by two factors: (1) projections that all types of new and existing energy sources would be needed to meet a growing U.S. and world demand for energy and (2) the conviction that Exxon could meaningfully contribute to meeting these needs in a fashion that served both consumers and shareholders. Top management was convinced that the skills needed to develop these energy sources were similar to those Exxon had acquired in its existing business. Randall Meyer, president of Exxon Company, U.S.A. and vice president of Exxon Corporation, described Exxon's assessment of the desirability of diversifying thusly:

Over many years Exxon has regularly prepared energy supply/demand outlooks for both the United States and the world. In the early 1960s we were projecting that oil and gas demand would continue to grow at about the same rate as the total demand for energy; however, it was not clear just where in the long term these supplies would come from. It appeared to us at that time that domestic production of both oil and gas could peak during the 1970s. We were also aware that there were very substantial reserves of oil and gas located overseas; however, like others, we were becoming increasingly concerned over the national security aspects of increased imports. Thus, we concluded at this early date that there could be substantial future needs for synthetic oil and gas. It also appeared that, since coal reserves are so plentiful in this country, a high percentage of the synthetic fuels would be made from coal. . . .

Another important conclusion reached by our appraisals during this period was that use of electricity was going to grow about twice as fast as the demand for total energy. The high projected growth rate for electricity led to our interest in uranium. Looking ahead toward 1980, it appeared to us that nuclear power would play a significant and increasingly important role in meeting the electric utility demand growth. . . .

An important question which had to be answered before we made a decision to enter either the coal or uranium business was the availability of resources. . . . Our studies indicated that of this amount of potential reserves, approximately 65 percent were not owned or under lease by any company then producing coal. . . .

In the case of uranium, the reserves situation was quite different. Because uranium is difficult to find, it has a very high discovery value. This resource had been much more actively sought after than coal, and all known reserves were controlled by companies which were already active in the business. We believed, however, that the Company's accumulated oil and gas exploration skills would offer a good start toward discovering new reserves. . . . Most of the known uranium deposits in the United States occur in sedimentary rocks. Since oil and gas occur in a similar environment, we had a great deal of geological expertise which could be applied to uranium exploration. Also, Exxon, U.S.A. had an extensive library of geological and geophysical information that had not yet been examined with the objective of locating uranium deposits. Many of the areas of the United States containing known or potential uranium deposits had been explored in the course of our oil and gas exploration effort. It seemed possible that rock samples and detailed geological information could be reexamined for guides to locating uranium deposits. In addition, the Company held mineral leases which covered not only oil and gas but also other minerals, including uranium. For all these reasons, we believed we could contribute to uranium discovery.

In addition to our exploration capabilities, we had other strengths which could be effectively used in establishing a position in the nuclear fuel and coal businesses. For example, we had developed over the years considerable expertise in processing hydrocarbons in our refineries. We believed that much of the research and development work we had done in refining would prove useful in developing processes for converting coal to gas or liquids.

It was determined at an early date that, to be successful, the coal and nuclear fuel businesses would require sizable amounts of front-end capital.

Another important factor was that our Company had considerable experience in the area of high-risk capital-intensive, long-lead-time ventures. In short, we concluded that the needs to be met in these energy fuel areas were compatible with the capabilities of our Company.[7]

THE ALTERNATIVE OF DIVERSIFYING INTO COAL

Exxon's studies in the 1960s, which utilized reports published by the United States Geological Survey and the Bureau of Mines, estimated economically recoverable domestic coal reserves, at then current costs and technology, to be in the range of 200 billion tons. When compared to annual coal production at that time of about half a billion tons, these reserves represented more than a 400-year supply. Since coal was plentiful, it was expected to be a raw material for production of synthetic fuels. And, synthetics were believed to be a likely future raw material for Exxon's refineries and chemical plants, or to be substitutable as retail products.

Since coal was a fuel with ready marketability regardless of the success or failure of synthetic research, it offered an opportunity for Exxon to broaden its primary business of energy production and sale. When this was coupled with Exxon's considerable experience in such commercial undertakings as land and resource management, the wholesale marketing of fuels, and activities involving core or directional drilling, logging, fracturing, and transporting, Exxon's management concluded that the company had the internal capabilities required to compete effectively in the coal business.

EXXON'S ENTRY INTO COAL MINING

Exxon's coal activities became the responsibility of a subsidiary, the Carter Oil Company. The purchase of undeveloped coal reserves began in 1965. Once the general availability of leasable coal was established, the company still had to conduct a substantial amount of core hole drilling and testing to define the exact location, extent, and quality of these deposits. Considerable effort was spent assembling blocks of reserves of sufficient size to develop in order to compete effectively in coal markets.

Exxon's management maintained that large blocks of minable reserves were needed to realize economies of scale in coal mining and to be price competitive on coal supplied to large electric utilities. A large mine, for example, could produce sufficient quantities to justify assembling unit trains traveling *direct* from the mine to a utility's coal-fired generating plant; unit trains were a substantially more economical mode of transportation. Also, potential coal suppliers had to have adequately large coal reserves if they wished to compete for the long-term contracts desired by utilities; many utilities wanted assured coal supplies of known quality for a major portion of

---

[7] Testimony before Senate Committee on Interior and Insular Affairs, December 6, 1973.

the useful life of their new plants before committing the capital for such generating facilities. (For instance, a 1,000-megawatt coal-fired plant requires about 3 million tons of coal per year.)

Exxon has bituminous coal reserves in Illinois, West Virginia, and Wyoming, and lignite reserves in Arkansas, Montana, North Dakota, and Texas. At year-end 1976, Exxon had a total of about 8.4 billion tons of coal reserves, about 3.7 billion of this east of the Mississippi River, and 4.7 billion tons in the West. This represented about 3.5 percent of the 250 billion tons of the coal which Exxon estimated was economically recoverable in the United States as of 1976.

Since commercially viable coal synthetics operations were not projected to be developed for several years after initial purchase of coal reserves, Exxon's management felt it was logical to start mining and selling coal as a boiler fuel. This was done not only to generate income on the coal investments, but also to provide the necessary operating experience in coal mining that would be needed to support the raw material production for coal synthetics operations.

Exxon's coal marketing activities began in 1967. Initially, coal from the Illinois reserves offered the best prospects for marketing because of its proximity to major markets. In 1968, a sales contract was negotiated with Commonwealth Edison of Chicago, and Monterey Coal Company, a Carter subsidiary, was formed and began development of its first mine. Located in southern Illinois near Carlinville, this mine commenced production in mid-1970. As of 1976, the mine employed about 500 people, had a maximum capacity of about 3 million tons of coal per year, and was one of the largest and most modern underground mines in the country. Through the experience gained in this initial operation, Exxon was developing the organizational and operating capabilities to permit expanding coal operations.

In May 1974, the development of a second underground mine in Illinois was announced; construction began that fall and the mine was scheduled to open in 1977. Its design capacity was 3.6 million tons per year, and had a projected employment of 650 people when full capacity was reached in 1980. The Public Service Company of Indiana had contracted to buy the mine's coal output.

As of 1976, additional markets for Exxon's Illinois coal, which had a sulfur content of 3 to 4 percent, were limited by air pollution regulations. As commercial equipment became available for removing sulfur from coal, either directly during combustion, or from smokestacks after combustion, the prospects for marketing the company's Illinois coal were expected to improve greatly.

In May 1974, the Carter Oil Company signed an agreement with Columbia Coal Gasification Corporation exchanging a 50 percent interest in certain Illinois lands containing coal reserves for a 50 percent interest in a like amount of Columbia's West Virginia land. This agreement allowed development of the lower sulfur coal in West Virginia and committed some of Exxon's high-sulfur coal in Illinois to a possible gasification project when the economics and technology were commercially demonstrated. The Monterey Coal Company was to develop and operate two jointly owned underground West Virginia mines that were expected to produce over 4 million tons per year for 30 years at full capacity; each company was to market its own share of the coal. The mines would employ 1,500 people and the first mine was scheduled to open in 1978.

The Carter Mining Company, another subsidiary of the Carter Oil Company, was developing Exxon's coal reserves in the West. In January 1974, Carter announced the development of a surface mine in Wyoming (Rawhide Mine) originally scheduled to open in 1976, to employ 250 people, and to produce 12 million tons per year by 1980. Although Exxon maintained that land reclamation would assure negligible long-term environmental impact, and despite a favorable Final Environmental Impact Statement issued by the Department of the Interior in October 1974, progress on this mine (and on others in the area) was restricted in January 1975 as a result of a court injunction obtained by the Sierra Club and others against the Department of the Interior. The injunction prohibited the secretary of the interior from issuing mining permits and approving mining plans. The suit sought development of an extraordinary regional environmental impact statement. Ironically, the company's western coal reserves, development of which was held up by the environmental suit, had a lower sulfur content than Illinois coal and could more easily meet environmental regulations.

In February 1976, the U.S. Supreme Court removed the injunction under the Sierra Club litigation, and the Department of the Interior approved Carter's Rawhide mining plan. On June 28, 1976, the Supreme Court ruled in favor of the Department of the Interior in the Sierra Club case. Carter resumed full-scale construction at the Rawhide Mine on a schedule which would allow the production and shipping of coal in July 1977—over a year later than was originally scheduled.

Exxon's record in coal production was:

	1970	1971	1972	1973	1974	1975
Exxon's coal output (million tons)	0.3	1.2	2.0	2.7	2.5	2.9

Exxon's underground coal mine productivity in 1975 was 23 tons per man-day compared with 17 tons per man-day for all underground mines in Illinois (1974), and less than 10 tons per man-day for all U.S. underground mines (1975).

From 1967 to mid-1976, Exxon made over 600 sales contacts and 25 formal bid proposals, and currently had 4 long-term sales contracts. In addition, the company had one short-term agreement to sell coal. Exxon was striving to negotiate more sales contracts which could lead to the opening of additional mines.

Excluding synthetics, current company plans included appropriations for nine mines to be operating by 1985, with a total output exceeding 40 million tons per year. Yet, even this very high rate of growth in coal production was forecast to result in a market share of only about 4 percent of projected total coal production in 1985. Initial investment costs for the nine mines were pegged at almost $700 million.

Coal Research and Synthetics. Exxon and its affiliate, Exxon Research & Engineering Company, have had active coal research programs since 1966. The emphasis has been on removing sulfur and nitrogen oxides in coal-burning processes, and especially on processes for manufacturing synthetic gas and oil from coal. Exxon spent more than $55 million in coal synthetics research through 1976 and turned up some promising processes for gasifying and for liquefying coal, each of which had been tested in small pilot plants.

In 1977, synthetic fuels process testing was continuing under four contracts totaling $17.4 million and awarded by the Energy Research and Development Administration (ERDA) to Exxon Research and Engineering (ER&E). The largest contract was on a cost-sharing basis, with ERDA providing half of $12.74 million to finance continued development through mid-1977 of the Exxon Donor Solvent liquefaction process. Another contract was for the continuing development of a new catalytic coal gasification process and called for the expenditure of $2.4 million by the end of 1977. The third contract, for $1 million, was to study the feasibility of using an existing ERDA large pilot plant for scale-up of the catalytic coal gasification process. Under the fourth contract, ER&E received $1.3 million to evaluate the applicability of its proprietary coking technology to coal liquefaction residues; work on this project was scheduled to continue into early 1978. In addition, Exxon was evaluating potential coal liquefaction pilot plants, commercial coal gasification processes, plant locations, and markets. A considerable amount of Exxon's research into new coal technology stemmed from its expertise in the technology of petroleum processing and petroleum engineering.

In 1976, Exxon completed process design of a 250-ton per day liquefaction pilot plant. The total pilot plant program, including operations and associated research, was anticipated to cost up to $300 million through the end of the program in mid-1982. Management was attempting to secure major funding for this program from outside sources, including private industry and ERDA. Through October of 1976, 174 prospective sponsors had been contacted. Most of the companies declined to participate due to the lack of capital, or to the lack of certainty as to the time that a commercial-sized venture would become viable; only two expressed an intention to take part but it appeared that a Japanese consortium would fund a portion of the work. If the pilot plant program was successful in solving the technical problems, the next step was to be a commercial size "pioneer" plant—a first generation plant. Preliminary indications were that such a plant could cost over $1 billion in 1975 dollars for a plant capacity of 50,000 barrels per day.

Exxon was also working on two development programs utilizing fluid bed technology (a technique pioneered by Exxon in petroleum) for the clean combustion of coal in utility boilers and in major industrial fuel-burning units. These programs involved burning high-sulfur coal in fluid beds of coal and limestone. The limestone traps most of the objectionable sulfur compounds, and the coal is oxidized at a relatively low temperature, thus minimizing nitrogen oxides emissions.

The second program, sponsored by ERDA, was a fluid bed combustion system in which steam generating coils were immersed directly in a fluid bed of coal and limestone. Exxon operated a six-ton per day pressurized fluid bed pilot plant, and had demonstrated the feasibility of fluid bed combustion and simultaneous limestone regeneration.

From 1972 to 1975, Exxon's annual R&D expenditures in coal rose from $2.7 million to $17.1 million. About 90 percent of Exxon's 1974 and 1975 coal expenditures were company funded.

EXXON'S ENTRY INTO NUCLEAR ENERGY

Projections in the mid-1960s indicated that use of electricity was to grow about twice as fast as the demand for total energy, and nuclear power was expected to play an increasingly important role in meeting this future electric utility demand. The most recent nuclear power generation projections indicated that nuclear would grow from less than 10 percent of U.S. electric energy supply in 1976 to about 30 percent in 1990—an outcome which would greatly increase uranium demand and make diversification into uranium a profitable business opportunity.

The nuclear fuel cycle consists of several principal activities—uranium exploration, mining, and milling; uranium enrichment; fabrication of enriched uranium into nuclear fuel assemblies; chemical reprocessing of the spent fuel assemblies to recover uranium and plutonium for recycling into the fuel cycle, thus reducing requirements for new uranium supply and enrichment services; and, ultimately, safe storage and disposal of nuclear wastes.

Exploration, Mining, and Milling. Exxon initiated its uranium exploration program in the United States in 1966. By 1977, the company had made two uranium discoveries that had been brought into production and two others that were in varying stages of evaluation. The first commercial discovery was made in 1967 in south Texas, and was a relatively minor deposit. The second discovery was made in 1968 in eastern Wyoming, and was a much larger deposit having substantial proven commercial potential. Exxon's petroleum activities played a key role in both of these discoveries: the Texas discovery was located on a lease which was originally obtained as a petroleum prospect; the discovery in Wyoming resulted, in part, from information gained during geophysical exploration for hydrocarbons.

Initially, operation of the south Texas property was contracted to a third party. Production from this discovery began in 1970 and was temporarily halted in 1972 when the contractor terminated his agreement with Exxon. Present plans were to reopen the mine in 1978.

Mining feasibility studies on the Wyoming discovery were completed in 1969. Exxon decided this time to conduct its own operations; production from a surface mine and associated mill began late in 1972. In 1974 and 1975, uranium concentrate (yellow cake) production decreased as the company processed an increasing amount of lower grade ore yielding less uranium per ton of ore.

Development of an underground mine at the Wyoming site was started in late 1973. Production from this underground mine was scheduled to start in 1977.

Exxon's uranium concentrate production record (in millions of pounds of U_3O_8) was:

1970	1971	1972	1973	1974	1975
0.1	0.5	0.8	2.6	2.1	1.8

Exxon's uranium production of about 1.8 million pounds in 1975 was less than 8 percent of total U.S. output. Even so, during 1975 the Highland Mine was the most productive in Wyoming, averaging 1.76 tons of raw ore per man-hour versus an industry average of 0.76 per man-hour statewide.[8]

Exxon estimated that in 1977 it had about 5 percent of the uranium reserves in the United States. Those reserves that had been assessed as commercially viable were already committed under contract to the utility industry. With completion of the underground mine in Wyoming, total production was forecast to double. The company's uranium exploration program was believed by company officials to be among the more significant in the industry.

Other Nuclear Fuel Cycle Activities. Besides exploration, mining, and milling activities, Exxon was engaged in the marketing of uranium and in the design, fabrication and sale of nuclear fuel assemblies to utilities. The company also provided a range of fuel management and engineering services to that industry. Responsibility for these activities rested with Exxon Nuclear, Inc., a wholly owned and separately managed affiliate of Exxon Corporation.

Fuel Fabrication. About two years after start-up, a reactor is refueled just about annually over its 30 to 40 year life. At each such refueling, a portion of the fuel core is discharged and replaced with a batch of fresh

---

[8] Calculated from data in the Wyoming State Mine Inspectors Report for 1975, which reports man-hours and tons produced by individual companies.

"reload" fuel. Exxon Nuclear competed in this replacement fuel market, along with four other U.S. companies—Westinghouse, General Electric, Combustion Engineering, and Babcock and Wilcox. Exxon Nuclear was the only fuel fabricator not engaged in selling reactors and supplied about 6 percent of the domestic fuel fabrication market.

Fuel fabrication is technology intensive; quality requirements are of the highest order; and performance of reactors is directly dependent upon fuel assembly designs. An important objective of fuel assembly design, fabrication, and use management in the nuclear reactor is maintenance of mechanical integrity and reliability of operation of the nuclear power plant. Exxon Nuclear's research programs emphasized technologies to recycle plutonium and uranium into the fuel cycle, thus preserving valuable recovered products and conserving natural uranium. Exxon's capital investment in fuel fabrication and related facilities amounted to approximately $20 million.

Uranium Enrichment.   The processing of natural uranium into reactor fuel is complicated and expensive. Uranium as found in nature is composed of about 99.3 percent U-238 atoms and about 0.7 percent U-235 atoms. In order to use uranium as fuel in nuclear reactors commonly in commercial use today, it is necessary first to "enrich" the uranium; that is, to increase the percentage of U-235 atoms to approximately 2 to 3 percent, by decreasing the number of U-238 atoms.

ERDA owned and operated the only three plants in which uranium was enriched for use as fuel in nuclear power reactors. The ERDA (formerly the Atomic Energy Commission) enrichment plants were built during the 1941–55 period under government contract at a cost of more than $2 billion to produce enriched uranium for the nation's atomic weapons program. Although military needs for enriched uranium declined sharply, requirements for civilian use continued to increase. To keep pace with this demand, ERDA had underway a $1 billion improvement program (Cascade Improvement Program and Cascade Uprating Program, or so-called CIP/CUP) to increase the capacity of these plants, and also announced an add-on plant to the existing Portsmouth, Ohio, facility. These two expansions would, when finished, almost double existing enrichment capacity.

In Exxon's view, the primary challenge confronting would-be nuclear fuel suppliers was the improvement of processes and technology which would (1) reduce the requirements for massive capital investments, (2) conserve uranium as a vital energy fuel resource by achieving greater energy output per unit of new ore mined, and (3) demonstrate acceptable solutions to the nuclear waste management need. Exxon's research and development activities were aimed at meeting these perceived needs, and its programs concentrated on emerging, potentially more efficient technologies such as centrifuge enrichment and isotope separation by lasers.

Exxon's studies, which were undertaken at a cost of $10 million, indicated the centrifuge enrichment alternative required only 10 percent as much electric power as gaseous diffusion. The centrifuge approach lent itself to modular construction, which meant lead times for expansion of capacity in the two-to-four-year range rather than the eight-to-ten-years required for gaseous diffusion plants. Finally, for the centrifuge technology the economic "tails" assay range is reduced to 0.2 percent U-235 or less, which conserves new uranium ore.[9]

In addition to its work in the centrifuge area, Exxon Nuclear, through its subsidiary, Jersey Nuclear-Avco Isotopes, Inc., which was jointly owned with Avco Everett Research Laboratory, was developing a prospective new proprietary isotope separation process based on laser technologies. Some $29 million had been spent in developing this technical capability and had, in the company's opinion, resulted in it having a commanding lead over other companies conducting laser isotope separation (LIS) programs. Exxon believed that there were significant efficiencies in the LIS programs. The company regarded laser enrichment as the "next generation" technology which could contribute to its goals of (1) producing enriched uranium at lower costs, (2) more efficiently utilize U-235, and (3) enable the company to compete effectively in world markets (U.S. policy, taxes, and tariffs permitting).

Chemical Reprocessing of Spent Fuel. The chemical reprocessing of spent fuel is the last step in the nuclear fuel cycle and is the least developed. Very fundamental issues are posed at this step since the residual radioactive wastes must be properly and safely separated, packaged, and permanently stored. Exxon viewed escalating environmental protection requirements as dictating the development and demonstration of new, advanced, and drastically changed processes and technology.

Exxon Nuclear began its spent fuel reprocessing research and development programs in 1969, and its plant design and development studies in 1971. Exxon Nuclear's spent fuel reprocessing expenditures through 1976 totaled about $35 million.

In early 1977, however, planning work on a fuel reprocessing plant, spent fuel storage, and transportation facilities slowed down because needed government decisions had not been made. For instance, there were no decisions on whether and when to allow plutonium to be recycled; licensing criteria for plants had not been developed; and resolution of waste disposal issues was proceeding slowly. Moreover, given that reprocessing and its essential emphasis on safety, environmental protection, and waste management was difficult and demanding, that the commercial risks were high and the capital costs quite large, and that small changes in regulatory requirements often carried large financial implications, the company believed that the financial risks associated with the first plants would discourage broad industrial participation until the results of pioneering projects had shown the way.

---

[9] "Tails" are the uranium remaining after processing (mostly U-238, but some U-235). Lowering the content of U-235 in "tails" reduces the need for new uranium ore.

Nuclear R&D.   Although Exxon was increasing expenditures in absolute amounts in almost all phases of its total R&D budget, it was spending increasingly larger amounts both absolutely and relatively for nuclear R&D. Exxon spent about $130 million in nuclear research through 1976 for fundamental R&D, applied development, prototype testing, and pilot plant site operations; nuclear R&D expenditures for 1976 alone amounted to $30 million.

EXXON'S OTHER DIVERSIFICATION EFFORTS IN ENERGY

Exxon's diversification into other energy areas was motivated by some of the same factors that motivated its diversification into coal and the nuclear fuel cycle. As of 1977, Exxon's total expenditures on these other diversification efforts were small relative to coal and nuclear fuel cycle expenditures. The company's efforts were designed to learn about emerging technologies, to contribute to their development, and to position the company so that a competitive commercial contribution could be initiated when and if market demand led to profit opportunities that appeared to be commensurate with the risks involved.

Oil Shale.   Oil shale from deposits in Colorado, Utah, and Wyoming represents a potential source of supplemental liquid and gaseous fuels many times that of the proved domestic reserves of crude petroleum. While considerable shale lands are held by oil companies, the vast majority—about 80 percent—of potential reserves are federally controlled.

Exxon's oil shale activities were relatively limited.[10] During the early 1960s, Exxon acquired a number of small tracts of patented land and mining claims in the oil shale area of Colorado. These holdings, however, were widely scattered and would have to be consolidated to form minable blocks.

Exxon's expenditures on oil shale totaled more than $16 million as of 1977. Of this, $8.8 million went to acquire oil shale reserves in the early 1960s, $4.9 million was spent on research, and $2.8 million on core drilling, administrative expenses, and the like. Exxon believed that, in addition to the major environmental and cost problems, the lack of a government policy

---

[10] The same was true for most other companies. The large amount of federally controlled oil shale reserves were placed under a lease moratorium in 1930. It was not until 1968 that the Department of the Interior, in recognition of the possible need for future shale oil production, undertook to evaluate industry interest in federal lands by offering selected tracts for lease sale. Suitable offers were not received and no sales were made. In 1971, the government initiated a second leasing effort aimed at encouraging the development of commercial operations on a controlled basis to allow an assessment of the economic cost and environmental impact of shale oil production. This prototype lease sale culminated in early 1974 in the sale of four tracts—two in Colorado and two in Utah, each about 5,000 acres. Terms were designed to encourage purchasers to proceed with serious development of commercial facilities. Even then, there was a tremendous range of bids, demonstrating the asymmetry of oil company interests and the need to encourage these different assessments of potential energy sources in order to insure their most optimal development.

concerning this potentially significant energy source was an important factor in the delay of its commercial development.

Solar. The term "solar energy" covers a wide variety of activities. To simplify, there are currently under active development in the United States three methods for converting sunlight directly into energy: (1) the use of low-temperature thermal collectors for heating water and for space heating and cooling in low-rise buildings; (2) the use of high temperature collectors for generation of steam and electric power; and (3) the use of photovoltaic cells to convert sunlight directly to electric power—a process for which much of the R&D to date has been for the aerospace program.

Exxon had been investigating commercial uses of solar energy since 1970, when a research program was initiated to develop advanced low-cost photovoltaic devices. Exxon and other companies were beginning to develop terrestial applications for photovoltaic devices, such as for use in microwave transmitters and ocean buoys. However, in Exxon's view, mass production of low-cost solar photovoltaic cells would require major advances in technology. New manufacturing approaches and materials would have to be identified and developed to reduce costs by a necessary factor of 50. Exxon felt it was likely that firms with sophisticated technological resources and the financial capability to perform long-term R&D would be involved in photovoltaic cells. Exxon's R&D work had been augmented by a solar device assembly and marketing effort carried out by Solar Power Corporation (SPC), a subsidiary of Exxon Enterprises, the company's affiliate responsible for new venture activities outside of fossil fuel and chemicals.

Because the sun's radiation is only intermittently available, Exxon felt that solar energy growth would be limited in certain geographical areas, and would be restricted in all areas by the need to develop economical storage devices that would store solar energy and release it on a continuous basis. Other factors which Exxon thought would influence the pace of solar development included the high initial costs, government policies on property taxes, local codes on materials quality, and the legal status of "sun rights."[11]

Exxon had spent about $9 million on all solar-related activities through 1976.

Batteries and Fuel Cells. Recognizing the increasing electrification of energy and the need for efficiently storing solar-generated electricity, Exxon was carrying out research in electrochemistry. Fuel cells (devices that convert special fuels such as hydrogen to electricity) had been under study in Exxon Research and Engineering since 1960. In 1970, Exxon Enterprises entered a joint development effort with Alsthom, a division of CGE, a French electrical equipment manufacturer. The aim of the program was to develop a more efficient power supply for electric vehicles, and to replace

---

[11] For instance, does someone have the right to construct a building if it would shield a solar collector from the sun for part of the day?

generators driven by engines or gas turbines. Program costs through 1975 exceeded $15 million, but technical progress had not met expectations.

Although substantial effort in terms of time and money was being devoted to fuel cell and battery development by Exxon Enterprises in 1977, commercialization of either was not expected to occur before the 1980s, and even then only with major technical breakthroughs.

Laser Fusion. Exxon Research and Engineering Company was one of the sponsors of a program at the University of Rochester begun in 1972 to study the feasibility of laser-ignited fusion of light atoms (e.g., deuterium, tritium) for the economical generation of power. Out of an estimated program cost of $5.8 million through August 1975, Exxon Research and Engineering Company had contributed about $917,000. This included the cost of Exxon scientists on direct loan to the university.

Exxon's objectives in supporting this program included the development of technological expertise in lasers and laser fusion physics, and the identification of potential business opportunities in the fusion fuel cycle. However, at least 20 to 30 years of R&D were thought to be required before laser fusion could reach the pilot plant stage.

EXXON ENTERPRISES, INC.

Exxon Enterprises, officially known as the "new business development arm" of Exxon, as of 1976 had invested approximately $76 million in more than two dozen small new ventures, either by joining other investors in venture capital deals or by funding R&D projects and new businesses created and run by entrepreneurial researchers. Most of these fledgling firms were far removed from Exxon's traditional business. Only two involved the energy industry—Solar Power and Daystar, both of which made equipment for collecting solar energy. Scan-Tron sold scholastic tests that were automatically graded by its own machine; Environmental Data produced instruments for measuring air pollution; Graftek turned out graphite shafts for golf clubs and fishing rods; Delphi had developed a way to store voice messages in a computer; Zilog was working on a microprocessor to transmit and process data; Qume made high-speed printers; Vydec was involved in text-editing systems; and Periphonics made switching computers. Other companies that were a part of Exxon Enterprises included Amtek, Xentex, Qwip, Micro-Bit Corporation, and Intermagnetics General Corporation.

The corporate role of the Exxon Enterprises division was to develop options for Exxon's future, mainly in case Exxon's diversification into other energy sources was curtailed by political forces, and to take up the slack from the eventual decline of the oil business. Unlike other oil companies such as Mobil and Atlantic Richfield which chose to diversify by acquiring well-established companies, Exxon opted for buying ownership interests in small entrepreneurial companies which were just getting started and which appeared to have potential. The idea was to grow up with a new industry as opposed to entering an established industry where Exxon really didn't know the business.

Exxon Enterprises endeavored to avoid the mistakes made by other large corporations which got into venture capital activities and which failed because (1) they took too much time making decisions crucial to young companies, (2) they did not offer the kind of management assistance that the neophyte companies needed, and/or (3) they exerted so much control over the new business that they stifled the firm's entrepreneurial spirit. The chief executive of Exxon Enterprises, George T. Piercy, who was also a senior vice president and member of the board of Exxon, had the authority to approve decisions about new ventures where Exxon's ownership interest was less than $1.5 million without going to Exxon's corporate investment-advisory committee. On occasions, Exxon Enterprises' employees who found suitable companies were offered the opportunity to be Exxon's representative on the new company's board of directors. Exxon also tried to provide management assistance to the new companies by setting up accounting, planning, and control systems and by watching their financial conditions carefully to sound early warning if difficulties appeared. Nonfinancial problems were referred to an Exxon planning and research group of two dozen professionals. In extreme cases, Exxon even lent entrepreneurs its personnel; for example, one Exxon staff member served as the marketing vice president for Dialog while the company was trying to find the right man for the job. According to one top official of Exxon Enterprises, "we are sensitive to the nature and drives of the entrepreneur and we act as a kind of buffer between the entrepreneur and the [Exxon corporate] bureaucracy."[12] In so doing, Exxon sought to avoid "meddling" so much that the company's management became demoralized. Nonetheless, according to one of Exxon's experienced co-investors, "a decision of any consequence has to go up pretty high. When it comes back down from Piercy, it can have some unexpected twists. In the meantime, the henchmen are investigating and second guessing, and that builds up friction. And the delays have an effect—they have probably set back our venture a year."[13]

As of early 1977, several changes in the direction of Exxon Enterprises appeared to be in the making. One, the division was acquiring a majority position in many of the enterprises in which it had made investments. However, where this was the case, Exxon tried to avoid the appearance of domination by remaining in a minority position on the board. Two, Exxon was concentrating its investments, having cut its ten original areas of interest down to three—alternate energy systems, advanced materials, and information systems. Almost all of the $35 million invested in 1976 by Exxon Enterprises went to expand existing ventures rather than to launch new ones.

---

[12] As quoted in Bro Uttal, "Exxon Has Its Eye on More than Oil," *Fortune*, April 1977, p. 168.

[13] Ibid.

Three, the division appeared to be starting to concentrate on those ventures that had some degree of complementarity and synergism, although executives insisted that Exxon had no grand design for consolidation at the moment. It was speculated that this might have been because Exxon would not learn enough about how to market the products of these new companies effectively (if indeed such a market actually developed) until they grew large enough to prove themselves to be established competitors. It was clear, though, that Exxon had a longer time horizon, less aversion to risk, more money, and a greater determination to "stick with the winners" than many other venture capital firms.

OUTLOOK FOR THE FUTURE

Despite its diversification efforts, it was by no means clear whether and for how long Exxon could continue as the world's largest corporation. Barring major new oil and gas discoveries (which, even then, would only postpone the inevitable), its dominant lines of business seemed on the verge of long-term decline. Oil and gas reserves were being depleted at a rate exceeding new discoveries and this condition was held by many industry experts and government officials as unlikely to change. Environmental regulations and price controls were making exploration ventures either difficult or unattractive financially—at least according to industry officials.

Equally important was the fact that many members of Congress and a substantial portion of the general public were hostile to the major oil companies in general and in particular to oil companies like Exxon diversifying into other energy sources. In their view, allowing the giant oil companies to diversify and become "energy companies" was to risk the emergence of substantial monopoly control over energy on the part of these companies. According to Senator Tunney (Dem., California):

> The record shows an alarming degree of concentration within the energy industry. For example, three major oil companies control over 90 percent of the oil and gas reserves on the north slope of Alaska. Within District 5, which includes California, eight major oil companies account for 70 percent of crude oil production, 76 percent of refining capacity, 80 percent of marketing facilities, and 99 percent of crude oil transportation facilities.
>
> In terms of horizontal concentration, oil companies already own more than 35 percent of the existing coal reserves and five oil companies are among leaseholders who control 70 percent of the recoverable coal deposits on Federal lands.
>
> Oil companies already control more than 50 percent of the country's uranium reserves, and the key stages of uranium refining and processing are controlled by the oil companies.
>
> A classic example of how horizontal expansion by the oil giants can adversely affect the consumer is found in the geothermal fields of California, where the price for this potentially cheap source of energy is, strangely enough, under contract, tied automatically and directly to the prevailing price of oil.

The economic costs of excessive concentration have staggered. The Federal Trade Commission estimates that American consumers pay as much as $80 billion annually for this portrayal of the free enterprise principle.

Other economic costs that have been linked under concentration include inflation, recession, unemployment, environmental deterioration, periodic shortages, misallocated capital and other interferences with the operation of the free market.

Government regulation has failed to relieve the problems to any significant degree. Indeed, Government regulation seems to produce chiefly negative effects, the growth of unwieldly bureaucracies, an unholy alliance between the regulators and the regulatees, in which high profits and foreign bribes are tolerated, if not condoned.

The simple fact is that our largest multinational corporations, and particularly the oil giants, have become sovereign States accountable to their own self-serving interests.[14]

Senator John Durkin (Dem., New Hampshire) was equally explicit:

Three fundamental questions come to mind, Mr. Chairman. Who makes domestic energy policy and American foreign policy? Unfortunately the answer is "no one." Congress tries, through its powers to pass legislation and ratify treaties. But Congress was unaware until years later that the oil companies oversaw the coup d'état against the government of Iran in 1953. And they were unaware in 1969 that the oil companies orchestrated the rejection of a refinery proposed for Machiasport, Maine, which would have meant cheap oil for a northeast region now paying the highest heating bills in the country.

I cannot forget, Mr. Chairman, that it was the quiet but effective cooperation of the major oil companies which insured the success of the Arab oil embargo two years ago. I cannot forget that Exxon, the nation's largest oil company, refused to honor its commitment to supply fuel to our Sixth Fleet. I cannot forget that at the same time Gulf was saying it needed bigger profits to spur oil development, its officers were arranging for the purchase of a circus, and funneling thousands of dollars into the pockets of elected representatives.

This leads to the obvious second question—Who runs the oil companies? The equally apparent answer is once again, "no one." The very size of the oil octopus militates against the ability of any one man or one board of directors or regulatory agency to be aware of slush fund payments to politicians and pipeline pressure in Bahrain and tanker routes around the Cape of Good Hope. The oil companies themselves cannot even decide whose side they are on: OPEC's, America's, each other's. Perhaps it is every conglomerate for itself. There is no competitive structure to the industry. Cooperation among rivals has led to the blurring of traditional marketplace relationships of classical capitalism. As a result, the oil industry has lapsed into sluggish, profligate behavior.

This raises the third and final question facing the Subcommittee and the nation in our bicentennial year. "Who needs this situation anyway?" Once again, I submit the answer is a resounding "no one." Certainly the energy

---

[14] Hearings before the Subcommittee on Antitrust and Monopoly, Committee on the Judiciary, United States Senate, February 3, 1976.

consumer doesn't need to fork over $14 for a barrel of crude oil used in this country produced for a quarter of the price just because that is what the OPEC sheiks are asking for theirs. Certainly the stockholders of the oil conglomerates could use an increase in the value of their shares which could be brought about by a reorganized aggressive industrial structure. And certainly the industry could use a break from the oppressive and inept price controls of a federal bureaucracy and a respite from the constant threat of nationalization.

In 1871, reformer and railroad president Charles Francis Adams reported glumly that the large corporations of America "have declared war, negotiated peace, reduced courts, legislatures and sovereign states to unequalled obedience to their will." A century later, little has changed. Our economy continues to be dominated by combines. Twelve of our 25 largest corporations are oil firms.

Oil companies in 1974 spent $300 million to put a fine gloss on the fleecing they were giving the American consumer and to bemoan the fact that their profits were insufficient to generate enough capital to extract and deliver their precious commodity to an energy-starved nation. As if this was not contradiction enough, the financially hard-pressed oil industry was somehow able to muster enough money to play Medici with grants of some $60 million to the performing arts and to play Machievelli with contributions in the untold millions of dollars to politicians, all over the world.

We must act before this petroleum octopus violates and subverts any more of what is good, decent and fair in our political system, and before the price of fuel and gasoline eats away any more of the family budget. Millions of small, self-reliant, hard-working businessmen stand in jeopardy by our inaction.

What we need, Mr. Chairman, is legislation, swift and firm, to right our social and economic injustices. No one piece of legislation would accomplish more to that end, and restore confidence and faith in our government, than passage of legislation to break up the large oil companies.[15]

Exxon, of course, vigorously objected to the view that its entry into the coal and nuclear fuel businesses had decreased competition in the energy business as a whole. On the contrary, it argued that its diversification had increased competition through increased discoveries, increased production, and increased R&D. The company maintained that not only was there vigorous competition between the suppliers of individual fuels in each market and area of the United States but also that no one supplier or group of suppliers controlled any one energy source—see Exhibits 10–12.

In *coal,* the top four companies accounted for about 26 percent of total production and the top eight companies for about 36 percent in 1975. Of the top four coal producers, two were owned by companies engaged in petroleum activity, neither of which was listed among the top ten crude producers. The seven petroleum companies operating in coal accounted for about 20 percent of total coal production in 1975.

In *coal reserves,* the top four companies held about 21 percent of total

---

[15] Ibid.

EXHIBIT 10

A. Top 16 Companies in Each Energy Source (1975 production)

Crude Oil and Natural Gas	Coal	Uranium
1. Exxon	Peabody	Kerr-McGee
2. Texaco	Conoco	Utah International
3. Standard of Indiana	Amax	Anaconda
4. Shell	Occidental	Union Carbide
5. Gulf	Pittston	Exxon
6. Mobil	U.S. Steel	Un. Nuclear
7. Arco	Ashland/Hunt	Rio Algom
8. Standard of California	Bethlehem	Homestake
9. Union	Peter Kiewit	Conoco
10. Sun	North American	Cotter
11. Getty/Skelly	Sohio	Dawn
12. Phillips	American Electric Power Co.	Pioneer
13. Cities Service	Westmoreland	Atlas
14. Conoco	Eastern Association	Western Nuclear*
15. Tenneco	Gulf	Federal Resources/ American Nuclear*
16. Marathon	Freeman-United	Getty/Skelly*

* These three companies were ranked in the top 16 in 1974. However, the mills owned by Getty/Skelly and by Western Nuclear were shut down during 1975, and the Federal/American mill tolled for Utah International during 1975.

Sources: For crude oil and natural gas. *Annual Reports* and *Statistical Supplements*.

For coal, *Keystone News Bulletin*.

For uranium, Exxon estimate based upon ERDA mill production figures by state, annual reports, press releases, and mill capacities reported by ERDA.

B. Top 16 Energy Companies and Ranking in Individual Fuels (1975 production)

	Energy (BTU basis)	Crude Oil and Natural Gas	Coal	Uranium
Exxon	1	1	36	5
Texaco	2	2	—	—
Conoco	3	14	2	9
Standard of Indiana	4	3	—	—
Shell	5	4	—	—
Standard of California†	6	8	3	—
Gulf	7	5	15	—
Peabody	8	—	1	—
Mobil	9	6	—	—
Arco	10	7	—	—
Union	11	9	—	—
Sun	12	10	—	—
Getty/Skelly	13	11	—	—‡
Phillips	14	12	—	—
Kerr-McGee	15	*	—	1
Cities Service	16	13	—	—

Notes: Dash (—) indicates no production at all.

* Asterisk indicates some production, but not in top 16. Kerr-McGee ranks about 25th in oil and gas production. Exxon is 36th in coal.

† Standard of California acquired a 20 percent interest in AMAX in 1975.

‡ Getty/Skelly was 16th in uranium production in 1974, but did not operate its mill in 1975.

Sources: For crude oil and natural gas, *Annual Reports* and *Statistical Supplements*.

For coal, *Keystone News Bulletin*.

For uranium, Exxon estimate based upon ERDA mill production figures by state, annual reports, press releases, and mill capacities reported by ERDA. All statistics in Exhibit 10 were compiled and furnished by Exxon, U.S.A.

EXHIBIT 11
Oil Firm Coal Production* (millions of tons)

Coal Company	Parent Co.	1964	1965	1966	196⁊
Consolidation	Continental	45.4	48.6	51.4†	56.5
Island Creek	Occidental	21.2	20.6	23.7	25.9
Old Ben	Sohio	5.1	6.3	9.9	10.3
Pittsburgh & Midway	Gulf	7.1†	8.2	8.8	9.0
Arch Minerals	Ashland	2.3	5.1	6.8	7.5
Monterey Coal	Exxon	—	—	—	—
AMAX	SOCAL	8.2	8.3	8.5	8.6
Valley Camp‡	Quaker State	4.3	4.3	4.8	5.5
Eight company Total ...		93.6	101.4	113.9	123.3
Industry Total		487.0	512.1	533.9	552.6
Eight company output as percent of total		19.2%	19.8%	21.3%	22.3

* Includes only those companies with more than 1 million tons of coal production in 1975.
† Year acquired by oil company.
‡ Acquired in March 1976.
Source: Keystone Coal Industry Manual (McGraw-Hill), various years; Exxon U.S.A.

reserves in 1973, and the top eight held about 32 percent. Of the top four coal reserve owners, an oil company was the largest with 6 percent; the other three were all nonoil companies. Exxon was fifth largest with 3.7 percent. Petroleum companies accounted for only 20 percent of total coal reserves in 1973.

In *uranium mill output,* the top four companies accounted for about 54 percent of estimated mill output of U_3O_8 concentrate in 1975. Two of these companies, including Exxon, were also engaged in petroleum activity. Oil companies had about 28 percent of total estimated mill output in 1975, but excluding the largest uranium producer which produced little oil (less than 0.5 percent of total domestic production), oil companies had only about 11 percent. In 1973, the AEC reported that 84 companies conducted uranium exploration drilling.

In *uranium reserves,* the top four companies accounted for about 57 percent of total reserves in 1973. Two of the top four firms were also in oil and gas production. Petroleum companies accounted for 50–55 percent of total uranium reserves in 1973.

Nonetheless, the hostilities and suspicions toward the major oil companies, the uncertainties surrounding U.S. and world energy policies, and the lack of consensus about how much of what kinds of new and existing energy sources would be needed to meet domestic and international energy demands posed a major strategic dilemma to Exxon's top management.

1968	1969	1970	1971	1972	1973	1974	1975
59.9	60.9	64.1	54.8	64.9	60.5	51.8	54.9
25.9†	30.3	29.7	22.9	22.6	22.9	20.8	19.4
9.9†	12.0	11.7	20.5	11.2	10.8	9.5	9.3
9.2	7.6	7.8	7.1	7.7	8.1	7.5	7.3
7.0	6.8	6.3	7.2†	11.2	12.5	13.9	13.5
—	—	0.3	1.2	2.0	2.7	2.5	2.9
9.3	11.3	14.4	13.3	16.4	16.7	19.9	21.8†
5.2	5.3	5.5	4.2	4.8	4.1	3.3	3.4
6.4	134.2	139.8	121.2	140.8	138.3	129.2	132.5
5.2	560.5	602.9	552.2	595.4	591.7	601.0	646.0
3.2%	23.9%	23.2%	21.9%	23.6%	23.4%	21.5%	20.5%

EXHIBIT 12
1975 Concentration Ratios (percent)

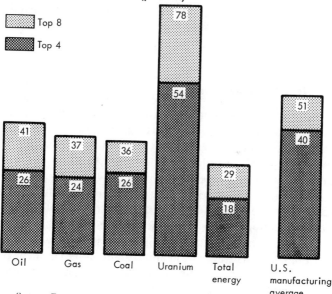

Source: Exxon, U.S.A.

28. Mobil Corporation*

"POOR IN OIL—but rich in business savvy" is how one commentator describes Mobil Corporation, the fifth largest industrial corporation in the United States and the sixth largest in the world. Mobil Corporation is the parent holding company of three operating units: Mobil Oil Corporation, Montgomery Ward, and Container Corporation of America. The Mobil Oil Division accounts for the major portion of revenues (almost 90 percent in 1976), but the nonenergy divisions are playing an increasingly important role in Mobil's total corporate strategy. In 1976, Mobil Corporation had business interests in more than 100 countries and employed in excess of 190,000 employees. Exhibit 1 is a financial summary for the years 1968–1976.

HISTORY AND BACKGROUND

In 1866, seven years after Drake found oil in Titusville, Pennsylvania, Matthew Ewing, a carpenter, persuaded Hiram Bond Everest, a grocer, to invest in a venture to produce kerosine by distilling crude oil in a vacuum. Ewing believed his method would produce higher kerosine yields than the conventional distillation at atmospheric pressure. The increased yields did not eventuate but an important difference did result; because of the lower temperatures used in the vacuum process, the residual undistilled oil proved to be of better lubricating quality than other oils on the market produced by the normal process. Ewing's method was patented in October 1866, and the Vacuum Oil Company was formed to capitalize upon it. The new company concentrated on lubricants for tanning leather, with its major product being Vacuum harness oils. Ewing soon lost interest in the company and was bought out, leaving Everest to pursue further development of oils and greases. In 1869, Everest patented a new oil—Gargoyle 600 W-Steam Cylinder Oil—for use in steam cylinders. Within a number of years, Vacuum Oil became a recognized leader in the industrial lubricant field.

The activities of the company attracted the interest of John D. Rockefeller, who purchased a controlling interest in 1879. Everest remained as presi-

---

* Prepared by Victor Gray, research assistant, and Professor Arthur A. Thompson, Jr., The University of Alabama.

dent, with his son, Charles M. Everest, as chief executive officer. In 1882, Rockefeller decided to consolidate his various interests under one central authority, and he set up the Standard Oil Trust in January of that year. In August, the Standard Oil Company of New York (Socony) was formed. When Rockefeller's Standard Oil empire was broken up in 1911, Socony emerged as one of the 34 individual companies, with Vacuum as another. From 1911 until 1931, Socony and Vacuum separately set about building, acquiring, and expanding their operations. Vacuum's interests were toward additional refining capacity, while Socony sought production interests— since the breakup left it devoid of production facilities. Vacuum was recognized worldwide for its industrial lubricants. Socony had marketing operations throughout the United States and the Far East, but mainly in the field of fuels. The interests, operation, and facilities of the two companies complemented each other, and a court-approved merger was consummated in July 1931, with a new name being chosen: Socony-Vacuum Corporation. In 1934, the company's name was changed to Socony-Vacuum Oil Company, Inc.

Socony-Vacuum had developed markets for its products in the Far East; these were supplied from the company's U.S. production. In contrast, Standard Oil (N.J.) had Far East production facilities but no strong marketing organization. The two companies saw the obvious advantages of combining their interests in *this market*, and a merger of their two interests in the Far East was agreed on in 1933. The merger resulted in the Standard-Vacuum Oil Company which operated only in the Far East as a separate company from its two parents, Standard Oil (N.J.) and Socony-Vacuum Oil. The new company prospered to such an extent that its integrated operations soon extended to 50 countries, from the East Coast of Africa to New Zealand.

By 1955, the brand name for Socony-Vacuum's gasoline and lubricants—Mobil—had become so well recognized that the company decided to include it in its corporate name. The firm's name was thus changed to Socony-Mobil Oil Company, Inc.

REORGANIZATION

When the Suez crisis of 1956 led to the closing of the canal, the traditional route of Middle East oil to its major markets in Europe had to be changed. The oil industry's reaction in developing alternative patterns of supply was such that in 1957, when the canal was reopened, the world market was oversupplied. The glut reduced prices and earnings of the major oil companies, and several were forced to revise their strategies. Socony-Mobil retrenched and reorganized, after posting combined earnings declines of nearly $100 million in 1957 and 1958. In 1959, its four U.S. subsidiaries were merged into two major divisions: Mobil Oil Company, which operated in the United States and Canada, and Mobil International Oil Company, which had

EXHIBIT 1
Financial Summary

	Year Ended on December 31			
	1976	*1975*	*1974*	*1973*
Revenues*	$28,046.5	$22,356.7	$20,491.0	$12,755.6
Operating and other expenses*	23,937.6	18,967.4	16,566.3	10,615.8
Interest and debt discount expenses*	295.2	216.2	150.2	96.9
Income taxes*	2,871.2	2,363.2	2,727.1	1,193.6
Total costs and expenses*	27,104.0	21,546.8	19,443.6	11,906.3
Net income*	$942.5	$809.9	$1,047.4	$849.3
United States*	62%	38%	35%	32%
Foreign*	38%	62%	65%	68%
Net income per share:				
United States	$5.66	$3.00	$3.60	$2.70
Foreign	3.42	4.95	6.68	5.64
Worldwide	9.08	7.95	10.28	8.34
Percent of net income (payout)	38.6%	42.8%	31.1%	33.6%
Cash dividends*	$363.6	$346.3	$325.9	$285.1
per share	$3.50	$3.40	$3.20	$2.80
Price range of common stock:				
High	65	48⅛	56½	75½
Low	47½	34¼	30⅝	43¼
At December 31:				
Shareholders' equity*	$7,651.8	$6,841.0	$6,436.4	$5,714.8
Per share (based on shares outstanding at end of year)	$72.30	$67.16	$63.19	$56.11
Total assets*	$18,767.5	$15,050.3	$14,074.3	$10,090.4
Number of shareholders	265,000	229,000	226,100	213,700
Number of shares outstanding	105,831,000	101,864,000	101,858,000	101,856,000
Number of employees	199,500	73,200	74,900	75,600

* In millions of dollars.

In the financial information above, the 54 percent voting interest in Marcor, Inc. (the parent company of Montgomery Ward and Container Corporation of America) has been accounted for on the equity method through July 1, 1976. On that date, Mobil became the owner of 100 percent of Marcor and began accounting for Marcor on a fully consolidated basis for Marcor's results.

Source: *1976 Annual Report.*

EXHIBIT 1 (continued)

		Year Ended on December 31		
1972	*1971*	*1970*	*1969*	*1968*
$10,295.1	$9,392.5	$8,310.3	$7,572.7	$7,092.7
8,832.6	8,152.5	7,370.6	6,729.9	6,333.9
85.6	81.2	74.2	65.3	63.0
802.7	618.0	383.0	321.0	265.0
9,720.9	8,851.7	7,827.8	7,116.2	6,661.9
$574.2	$540.8	$482.7	$465.5	$430.8
42%	43%	46%	55%	55%
58%	57%	54%	45%	45%
$2.35	$2.31	$2.44	$2.53	$2.34
3.30	3.02	2.33	1.97	1.90
5.65	5.33	4.77	4.50	4.24
46.9%	47.8%	50.3%	50.0%	48.3%
$269.3	$258.8	$243.1	$328.2	$207.6
$2.65	$2.55	$2.40	$2.55	$2.05
75⅞	60	58¼	69¾	64
49½	45¾	36	43¼	42⅛
$5,145.4	$4,831.9	$4,540.1	$4,309.1	$4,094.5
$50.57	$47.59	$44.81	$42.45	$40.44
$9,216.7	$8,552.3	$7,921.0	$7,163.1	$6,871.8
216,100	223,000	222,800	219,700	218,600
100,739,000	101,543,000	101,313,000	101,498,000	101,258,000
76,700	75,300	75,600	76,000	78,300

responsibility for operations throughout the rest of the world. In 1960, a new division was added: the Mobil Chemical Company.

A further name change was made in 1966, to Mobil Oil Corporation. In 1976, when Mobil merged with Montgomery Ward and Container Corporation of America, it was deemed desirable to form the Mobil Corporation as the holding company for all the various Mobil interests.

RECENT PERFORMANCE AND ORGANIZATION

In 1959, Mobil—under the leadership of Albert J. Nickerson, president and later chairman—reorganized its corporate structure. Divisions were organized as profit centers with an increase in authority for decision making. From 1959 to 1966, 11,000 U.S. employees were removed from the payroll, many through attrition or early retirement. Looking back at the reorganization, Nickerson commented:

> . . . the company had become non-competitive. Costs were too high. There was confusion as to accountability, and lines of communication were unclear.
>
> We created a new organization structure, centralized policy formulation, decentralized administration, and reduced expenses. . . .

Along with the organizational changes, management renewed its dedication to improving the ability of Mobil to "achieve planned profitable growth." Ten years later (1969), Nickerson, then chairman of the board, was able to report to the stockholders these improvements during the ten-year period: an increase in sales revenues from $3.5 billion to $7.1 billion, a gain in total assets from $3.3 billion to $6.9 billion, and an increase in dividend payments from $97 million to $207.5 million. Mobil's earnings per share rose 135 percent during the ten-year period, the largest increase of the five leading U.S.-based international oil companies. In addition, in 1969 Mobil alleged it had:

1. A lean, purposeful organization well structured to take on the problems of the 1970s and 1980s.
2. A management succession "pipeline" filled with high-potential individuals.
3. Heightened skill in planning and in seeking out and evaluating investment opportunities.

Mobil, in trying to manage change more effectively, claimed a strong commitment to long-range analysis and strategic planning. The company stated that its planning group was responsible for projecting and anticipating "technological, social, economic, governmental, and population factors that may affect Mobil's business as much as 30 years ahead."

In 1966, Mobil Oil realized substantial additions to its crude oil supplies, mainly in Canada and the Middle East. Gross output of crude oil was more than double the 1956 production levels. A new impetus in refining operations was also evident in 1966. Modernization of a number of plants was begun to allow production of additional higher value products and more efficient manpower utilization. It was anticipated that the modernization would reduce both maintenance and operating costs, as well as allow for the installation of antipollution equipment. Mobil Chemical achieved record sales during the year 1966. The year also saw new facilities and products, Hefty plastic bags for home food storage being one. The chemical interests at this time included industrial chemicals, plastics, paints, packaging material, agricultural products, and gases.

During 1958–69, Nickerson continued Mobil's long-standing policy of expanding reserves, production of crude oil, and natural gas liquids in an effort to relieve the long-standing shortage of internal crude production capability relative to refinery capacity. Mobil had, for many years, the lowest self-sufficiency ratio of the seven leading international oil companies. Production and refining interests ranged over every continent; no more than one fifth of the company's total crude production originated in any single country. In 1969, the company withdrew from the domestic retail fertilizer business, selling a major portion of its retail fertilizer assets and business to Swift and Company at a loss of $22 million or 22 cents per share. In explaining the company's move, Mobil's chairman observed, "We didn't do the proper analysis we should have. We didn't buy competent management, and when they left, we were oilmen running a business we didn't know much about."

MOBIL'S NEW MANAGEMENT TEAM

In 1969, Mobil got a new top-management team: Rawleigh Warner, Jr., chairman (Exhibit 2) and William P. Tavoulareas, president (Exhibit 3). Warner has been described as a man who appears to be a diplomat rather than a businessman. This urbane, trim, dapper executive is not the once-a-month chairman of a board meeting. As chairman of the executive committee, he is intricately involved in the day-to-day operations of the company.

EXHIBIT 2

Rawleigh Warner, Jr.:
1921 Born, Chicago. Father, chairman of Pure Oil Company.
1943 B.A. (cum laude), Princeton University.
1946 Secretary-treasurer: Warner-Bard Company.
1948 Continental Oil Company, various positions; left as assistant treasurer.
1953 Joined Mobil as assistant to the financial director of Socony-Vacuum overseas supply company.
1958 Manager of economics department.
1959 Regional vice president for Middle East.
1960 Executive vice president of Mobil International.
1963 President of Mobil International.
1964 Director, executive vice president, and member of executive committee, responsible for Mobil International and Mobil Petroleum Company, Inc.
1965 President of Mobil.
1969 Chairman of the board of directors and chief executive officer.

Director of Time, Inc., American Telephone and Telegraph Company, American Petroleum Institute, Caterpillar Tractor Company, Chemical New York Corporation and Chemical Bank, American Express Company. Republican.

EXHIBIT 3

William P. Tavoulareas:

  1919   Born, Brooklyn. Father a butcher.
  1941   B.B.A. St. John's University.
  1947   Joined Mobil as an accountant.
  1948   J.D., St. John's University.
  1957   Manager of Middle East accounting department of Middle East Affairs.
  1959   Manager of corporate planning and analysis department.
  1961   Vice president of plans and programs of Mobil's international petroleum division.
  1963   Vice president of supply and distribution and international sales.
  1965   Director, member of the executive committee and a senior vice president of Mobil.
  1967   President of North American Division.
  1969   President and vice chairman of executive committee of Mobil.

Director of Bankers Trust Company, General Foods Corporation.
Democrat.

The eight-man executive committee is comprised of the top senior officials within the company who are also directors of the company. In addition to his normal responsibilities as company chairman, Warner is also actively involved in the public relations of Mobil, particularly those dealing with government. Two other areas in which Warner has retained a special participation are corporate finance and legal affairs. Regarding Mobil's public relations, Warner explained the company's strategy: "Our posture of reacting when we were not properly treated has made our adversaries think a second time about zinging us. They may still zing us, but with facts and not emotions."

On becoming chairman and chief executive in 1969, Warner surprised many people in the oil world by appointing William P. Tavoulareas as president of the company. Unlike Warner, whose father was an oilman, Tavoulareas was the first in his family to enter the oil industry. One observer described Tavoulareas as "an irreverent, fast talking numbers man who has the crucial Rockefeller talent for lightning arithmetic." Another described him thusly:

> Tavoulareas is now widely regarded as the ablest of the major oilmen. He sits in shirt-sleeves, talking at top speed, blinking, twitching and staring, running to the telephone like an imp let loose; saying gimme and lemme, whadda ya want. In the Middle East, Tav was determined to increase Mobil's share, and was much more prepared to consider new partnership arrangements, which antagonized the other sisters, but also brought him closer to the producers; and he formed a close friendship with Yamani in Saudi Arabia.[1]

---

[1] Anthony D. Sampson, *The Seven Sisters* (New York: The Viking Press, 1975), p. 193.

Tavoulareas is well known in the industry for his negotiating skills. However, one Mobil official was quoted as saying:

> There are going to be problems with Tavoulareas. He's shown sheer genius with about 99 percent of the things he's touched. But it becomes more and more difficult to challenge him. If you were to take in a bad idea to Warner, he would tell you very diplomatically that your idea was bad. Tav would tell you the same thing in five seconds—and probably in four-letter language.[2]

Mobil is regarded as one of the best managed companies in the oil business, with much of Mobil's success being attributed to Warner. The company has been described as a financier's-lawyer's-businessman's company rather than an oilman-geologist company. The people Warner has chosen to work with him talk in terms of "managing assets" and "portfolios." A term used by Mobil to describe the Marcor acquisition was "risk aversion investment." Some suggest these terms are not the typical jargon of the oil industry. Warner has developed within the company a strong commitment to planning, and many analysts see planning as Mobil's strongest management characteristic. Tavoulareas said of planning:

> The real virtue of centralized planning is that it provides a person whose main responsibility is to question what the operator is doing. By his very nature, the person charged with day-to-day operations doesn't have time to worry about tomorrow's problems. The planner, on the other hand, can look over his shoulder and try to anticipate what kind of environment we will be operating in the future and how we can take advantage of it. In the end, his decisions will help the operator do his job better.[3]

Under Warner and Tavoulareas, Mobil continued the search for additional crude to try to bring production capability into better balance with refinery capacity. Geographical diversification of Mobil's crude reserve sources was a major objective. As a result of these efforts, crude production grew at an annual average of 16 percent between 1968 and 1971, compared to a 9.5 percent rate for the industry. The company's natural gas production increased at a rate of 136 percent greater than the industry's average for the same period. Exhibit 4 shows the U.S. crude oil reserves held by the various major petroleum companies for selected years. Exhibits 5 and 6 show the

---

[2] As quoted in *Business Week*, June 13, 1977, p. 84. Responding to this article via a letter to the editor of *Business Week*, Warner said in part: "The article [in *Business Week*] certainly could not have been intended to serve as a comprehensive examination of the managerial roles of Mobil executives—only three were interviewed. Nor was it a broad gauge review of the implementation of our diversification philosophy—as it had been represented it would be. . . . Especially unfair was the . . . inclusion of gratuitous and anonymous comments about Bill [Tavoulareas]. . . . It attributed to him a personality which his closest associates know to be an inaccurate characterization. . . . Had the reporter truly wished some personal insight into Mobil's management generally or Bill Tavoulareas in particular, he could easily have requested an opportunity to meet with him. . . ."

[3] As quoted in *Dun's*, December 1972, p. 38.

EXHIBIT 4
Sisters' Estimated Percentage Shares of Proved U.S. Crude Oil
Reserves for Selected Years

	1949	1969	1970	1976*
Exxon	11.0	9.76	9.92	12.6
Texaco	5.4	8.47	9.31	7.4
Gulf.......................	4.6	6.78	8.97	2.8
Socal	4.6	5.31	8.97	5.9
Royal Dutch/Shell	2.8	6.08	5.98	3.4
Mobil	5.0	3.94	4.87	3.1
British Petroleum	(has no reserves in United States)			

* U.S. reserves may include Canada for companies not reporting such reserves separately.
Sources:
For 1949, U.S. Federal Trade Commission, *The International Petroleum Cartel,* a staff report, 1952, p. 37.
For the years 1969 and 1970, U.S. Federal Trade Commission, *Preliminary Federal Trade Commission Staff Report on Its Investigation of the Petroleum Industry,* June 1973.
For 1976, John S. Herold, Inc., *Oil Industry Comparative Appraisals,* Greenwich, Conn., April 1976.

EXHIBIT 5
Capital and Exploration Expenditures of the World Petroleum Industry in
Selected Years, 1965–1974 (in millions of dollars)

Function	1965	1970	1972	1973	1974
Exploration	1,180	1,340	1,540	1,700	2,185
Production	5,785	7,230	10,105	12,925	19,535
Marine	1,215	2,575	3,775	6,550	8,900
Refining	1,865	4,000	4,955	4,865	7,720
Marketing	2,430	3,220	2,825	2,480	2,215

Source: The Chase Manhattan Bank, *Capital Investment,* Schedule 4, various annual issues.

EXHIBIT 6
Mobil's Capital Expenditures, 1965–1976 (in millions of dollars)

Function	1965	1966	1967	1968	1969	1970	1971	1972	1973	1974	1975	1976
Exploration*	95	96	100	110	117	124	127	150	148	189	243	208
Production	167	193	180	282	296	244	266	360	559	753	466	567
Marine	23	6	9	11	33	49	64	78	160	95	139	65
Refining	67	146	131	96	118	160	244	268	215	334	242	151
Marketing	116	130	176	174	187	226	256	252	190	113	114	102

Note: 1977 budgeted total expenditure $1,900,000,000.
* Includes nonproductive wells.
Source: Mobil's *Annual Reports, 1965–1976.*

EXHIBIT 7

Mobil's Gross Production of Crude Oil and Natural Gas Liquids by Areas, 1960–1970 (in thousands of barrels per day)

Country	1970	1969	1968	1967	1966	1965	1964	1963	1962	1961	1960
U.S. and Canada	565	527	521	475	413	372	346	330	316	302	288
Abu Dhabi	50	42	38	30	30	23	15	—	—	—	—
Indonesia	24	22	25	26	29	29	28	35	36	36	40
Iran	246	217	189	173	141	127	116	101	91	82	73
Iraq	185	181	178	145	164	155	148	137	119	118	114
Libya	165	172	154	136	128	76	34	2	—	—	—
Nigeria	54	—	—	—	—	—	—	—	—	—	—
Qatar	23	24	23	23	23	23	22	23	22	21	21
Saudi Arabia	360	303	287	262	240	203	173	162	152	139	125
Venezuela	114	106	120	132	140	144	140	131	117	113	117
West Germany	19	20	21	22	23	24	23	20	20	19	18
Other	22	34	33	35	37	36	32	30	28	31	27
Total	1,827	1,648	1,589	1,459	1,368	1,212	1,077	971	901	861	823
Total together with quantities received under long-term arrangements	2,083	1,960	1,835	1,663	1,527	1,387	1,251	1,146	1,078	1,005	938

* Less than 1,000 barrels per day.
Source: Mobil's *Annual Report, 1970.*

industry's and Mobil's capital expenditure by function for selected years. Exhibit 7 shows the geographical extent of Mobil's production activities from 1960 to 1970.

Since the early 1970s, Mobil (and other transnational oil companies) have found their operations in the major crude oil exporting countries increasingly subject to government control and/or nationalization. In Mobil's case, it has encountered diminishing control over its investments in a number of instances (Exhibit 8). Nationalization of Mobil interests has (or will) result in

EXHIBIT 8

Mobil's Loss of Holdings in Foreign Countries

Country	Mobil's Interest
Iraq	Nationalized 1972/73.
Libya	Nationalized 51 percent in 1973.
Nigeria	55 percent interest sought by national government.
Qatar	Mobil's 11.875 percent of Qatar Petroleum Coy Ltd. nationalized 1976.
Venezuela	Nationalized 1976.
Saudi Arabia	Arabian government will soon acquire 100 percent interest in Aramco. Mobil had an 11 percent interest in 1976.
Iran	20-year agreement of oil supplies whereby the participating companies acquire oil at prices that will substantially increase Iran's take from the operation. Mobil's share, 7 percent.

Source: Mobil's *Annual Report, 1976.*

compensation substantially less than the economic value of reserves given up although no accurate figure of the loss is as yet available. The loss of these overseas facilities triggered a very active response from Mobil. The outlay of capital for exploration during 1975 was $1.4 billion. Warner reported to the shareholders:

> We spent nearly half of our worldwide outlays during 1975 on exploration and producing. This maintained a momentum we achieved in 1974 when we responded to the Arabian embargo, increasing our exploration and producing outlays from the 1973 level. The main thrust of our capital investment program since the embargo has been to increase and diversify our worldwide supply of crude oil, natural gas and other energy sources.
>
> The largest segment of our investment area in 1975 went towards developing several significant oil and gas fields previously discovered by Mobil around the world.

Tavoulareas identified two major objectives for the company: (1) to increase crude supplies all around the world so as to bring Mobil closer to self-sufficiency in supplying its refineries with crude, and (2) to maximize the efficiency with which the supplies of crude oil were carried to refineries, and refined products to their marketing areas. To assist in achieving these objectives, Tavoulareas explained that Mobil's "exploration program around the world is proceeding above historical levels." Mobil concentrated a large proportion of its exploration capital in the United States. (See Exhibit 9.)

EXHIBIT 9
Mobil's Capital Expenditure for Petroleum,* Selected Years 1965–1976
(in millions of dollars)

Location	1965	1970	1973	1974	1975	1976
United States	246	494	530	711	615	774
Other countries	196	147	177	231	743†	470

* Expenditures are for exploration, production, refining, pipelines, and marketing.
† Substantial increase in drilling activity in the North Sea accounts for a major portion of this increase.
Source: Mobil, *Annual Reports, 1965–1976.*

During 1976, $495 million (approximately 65 percent of Mobil's total worldwide capital outlay for exploration and production) was expended in efforts to find and develop domestic U.S. sources of petroleum. This expenditure reflected management's continuing concern for a decrease in the company's net proven reserves of oil and gas in the United States. In 1973, Mobil had an estimated 12,000 million barrels of crude oil and natural gas liquids. Mobil's net proved reserves of natural gas were estimated at 8,300 billion cubic feet.

Mobil's exploration expenditures in the United States have produced mixed results. For example, wells in Prudhoe Bay in Alaska yielded an increase of some 200 million barrels of crude reserves to Mobil. (The company has a 5 percent ownership in the Trans-Alaska Pipeline System.) On the other hand, Destin Anticline, in the Gulf of Mexico, cost Mobil $227 million in lease bonuses; the increase to crude reserves: zero. No oil was found in the area. Although no public statistical record of Mobil's success rate in drilling is available, industry experts say that Mobil has, "after years of arriving in the oil patch too late with too little," considerably stepped up its expenditure in an effort to compete with the other majors.

Despite its record expenditures for exploration, Mobil's approach to exploration and development is one of the less adventurous in the industry. The company has employed a strategy of maximizing recovery of oil from fields already in production through expanded use of technology such as water-flooding and thermal recovery. About 70 percent of Mobil's U.S. production of crude oil in 1976 came from fields where improved recovery processes were used. Mobil's lack of bold effort is suggested by the number of exploratory wells it drilled in the United States in 1976 relative to other majors: Texaco 647, Gulf 629, Exxon 613, Mobil 377. When the companies which do not have interests in the Middle East are included in the comparison, Mobil's efforts fade even further (for example: Standard, Indiana, 781; Shell [U.S.], 715). On the list of companies drilling the "very risky" wildcat wells, Mobil was not among the top ten drillers. Mobil has, through its participation in federal lease sales, acquired 127 leases between 1970 and 1976. For the same period, it was involved in discovering 31 new commercial fields in the United States of various sizes.

In 1976, Mobil's U.S. gross crude oil and natural gas liquid production averaged 375,000 barrels a day. Gross production of natural gas averaged 2.3 billion cubic feet a day. At the end of 1976, Mobil had over 14,000 oil and gas wells in the United States. During the years 1970 to 1976, Mobil spent more than $1 billion on exploration in the Gulf of Mexico and over $2.5 billion throughout the United States.

Although Mobil's U.S. exploration is not as extensive as that of many other major companies, it has still managed to achieve success in regard to improving its crude reserves and supplies. In the Middle East it has active interests and related activities in Abu Dhabi, Iran, Iraq, Qatar and Saudi Arabia. Of the Sisters, only Royal Dutch/Shell is active in more Middle East countries than is Mobil. Mobil, which in 1974 held a 10 percent share of the Arabian American Oil Company (Aramco)—a joint venture of Mobil, Texaco, Exxon, Socal and Saudi Arabia—negotiated with its partners to increase its holding in the company to 15 percent; the increased share was to be accomplished in steps of 1 percent per year starting in 1975. Mobil viewed the increased share of Aramco as a way of gaining many billions of barrels of oil without the risk of exploration (albeit with the risk of loss due to "nationalization"). Moreover, Mobil felt that Saudi Arabia was the place for an oil company to be with by far the earth's largest petroleum resources, together with a business climate that favored American enterprise. Mobil's desire for increased ownership in Aramco reflected its view that Saudi Arabia would be an increasingly important source of crude in the future.

However, the strategy failed. A three-year period of negotiations—centered around the fact that the Saudis, who held a 60 percent in Aramco, wanted to increase their share to 100 percent—drew to a close in 1977. Industry experts were confidently predicting that by the end of 1977 a settlement would be reached which would give Saudi Arabia its 100 percent ownership. Despite the loss of its ownership interest in the total operations, Mobil's dollar return for its marketing services to the Saudis will remain similar to the pre-takeover levels. It is understood that the four previous partners will have continued long-range access to Aramco's production—but as buyers rather than as owners.

Although Mobil lost its ownership interest in Aramco, during the 1974–77 period, it continued efforts to foster a good business climate in which to ensure its access to the Arabian crude via joint ventures with Saudi Arabia on other projects including:

1. A one-million-barrel-a-year lube oil refinery, a 30–70 Mobil/Saudi venture.
2. A 75,000-barrel-a-year petrolube plant, a 29–71 Mobil/Saudi project.
3. A planned 250,000-barrel-a-day export refinery, a 50–50 Mobil/Saudi deal.
4. A 750-mile, 48-inch crude pipeline, designed and constructed by Mobil but 100 percent Saudi owned.
5. A petrochemical complex, a 50-50 Mobil/Saudi investment.
6. A dry cargo shipping company, a 60–40 Mobil/Saudi project.

Joint ventures have frequently been favored by Mobil in its exploratory programs. According to the company:

> Mobil has been an active participant in the offshore oil industry for many years. Mobil has participated in practically all general outer continental shelf sales held in the Federal offshore lease bids since the first sale in 1954 and has spent over $1.2 billion in bonus costs for 223 leases acquired at these sales. Mobil has bid alone and jointly with major companies, as well as with non-major companies.
>
> Mobil prefers to bid jointly with other companies both large and small because it believes it is prudent to hedge against the risk of failure by seeking a smaller interest in many tracts rather than a larger interest in a few, and limited capital is available for investment in exploration and producing because of the high risk nature of offshore investment.
>
> In selecting partners with whom to bid, primary consideration is given to the financial capabilities of the company as well as to the potential partners' technical expertise. With the initiation of leasing high cost frontier areas, it is increasingly important that a company be financially capable of providing its share not only of the lease bonus, but also of the subsequent expense for wildcat drilling and development if hydrocarbons are found. The ability of a

company to add data and expertise to the joint venture is very important given the risky nature of offshore exploration. The interpretation of data available at the surface as a means of predicting the state of nature many miles below the surface is not an exact science, and the interpretation by other qualified geologists and geophysicists is important.[4]

Exhibit 10 shows the companies with whom Mobil has entered into joint ventures. Exhibits 11 and 12 show Mobil's shares in U.S. and non-U.S. crude oil production.

EXHIBIT 10
Number of Mobil Joint Ventures in Exploration and Development with other Major U.S. Companies, 1960–1970

Amerada Hess	2
Atlantic Richfield	10
Continental Oil	29
Gulf Oil	9
Phillips Petroleum	2
Socal (Standard Oil, California)	14
Amoco (Standard Oil, Indiana)	10
Exxon	33
Sohio (Standard Oil, Ohio)	15
Shell Oil	23
Sun	5
Texaco	15
Union Oil California	2

Source: *Oil and Gas Journal.*

EXHIBIT 11
Sisters' Percentage Shares of Crude Oil Production Outside the United States, 1953 and 1972

Company	1953	1972
Exxon	24.9%	13.7%
British Petroleum	20.6	14.9
Royal Dutch/Shell	12.3	11.3
Gulf	11.2	8.1
Texaco	6.7	9.3
Socal	6.1	8.6
Mobil	5.3	5.0
Total—seven largest	87.1%	70.9%
Total—all others	12.9	29.1
Total Industry	100.0%	100.0%

Source: Neil Jacoby, *Multinational Oil* (New York: The Macmillan Company, 1974), p. 177.

[4] From a statement by Mobil to the House Subcommittee on Monopolies and Commercial Law, 1976. (Serial No. 48, Part 1, Joint Ventures, p. 235.)

EXHIBIT 12
U.S. Sisters' Percentage of U.S. Crude Production,
Selected Years, 1955–1974

Company	1955	1960	1969	1974
Exxon	6.1%	6.53%	9.76%	8.5%
Texaco	4.9	8.93	8.47	6.7
Gulf	3.4	5.13	6.78	3.8
Socal	3.6	4.75	5.31	4.0
Mobil	3.4	3.42	3.94	3.5

Sources: For 1955, U.S. Federal Trade Commission, *U.S. Concentration Levels and Trends in the Energy Sector of the U.S. Economy,* March 1974, p. 197.
For the years 1960 and 1969, Rice, Kerr & Co., Engineers. *Report on Crude Oil Gasoline Price Increases.*
For 1974, Paper delivered by L. C. Soileau III, Standard Oil Company of California, before the Subcommittee on Antitrust and Monopoly of the U.S. Senate Committee on the Judiciary, November 1975, Appendix, Exhibit 2.

UPSTREAM ACTIVITIES FROM CRUDE PRODUCTION

To complement its crude supplies, Mobil has, over the years, acquired a substantial fleet of tankers. The company has been able to reduce its transportation cost by the use of very large crude carriers (VLCCs) and a balance between owned and chartered vessels. The strategic acquisition of the vessels was planned so as to satisfy both the needs of the company and the supply position of the world tankers. In 1975, Mobil was sixth among the Seven Sisters in the percentage of free world tankers it owned or chartered. In 1976, because of a depressed world tanker market, Mobil was able to replace moderate and higher cost term charters with low-cost charters. A second advantage achieved by Mobil was the purchase of six tankers in 1976 at very favorable prices. In both 1975 and 1976, Mobil took delivery of two new tankers all of which were approximately 280,000 deadweight tons. Mobil had up to 1977 not ordered any ultra large crude carriers of the 400,000 plus deadweight ton class. During 1976, the Mobil fleet transported over 80 million tons of crude oil and product using 54 wholly owned tankers, plus 47 others on long-term charter.

As of mid-1977, the United States did not have a deepwater port facility (a port capable of accommodating vessels in excess of 160,000 deadweight tons). If the United States imported 4.5 million barrels of crude oil per day, the equivalent of thirteen 50,000 d.w.t. tankers would be needed to deliver the oil to present U.S. ports. If the United States located deepwater ports on the Atlantic and Gulf Coasts, the equivalent of only two 325,000 d.w.t. VLCCs would be needed to land the same amount of oil for a lower cost.

Realizing the advantages of such facilities, Mobil became one of nine companies to invest in Seadock, Inc. The Seadock project involved the development of an offshore Texas superport. Mobil quit the project in 1977 because of what the company claimed to be unacceptable provisions in the Department of Transportation's license. In so doing, Mobil forfeited the $2 million it had contributed to the project. Two other members of the project, Exxon and Gulf, followed Mobil's lead and withdrew in mid-1977. The other members of Seadock, Inc. were: Shell, Phillips, Continental Pipe Line Co., Cities Services Co., Crown-Seadock, and Dow Chemical. Later on in 1977, the entire Seadock project collapsed.

REFINING OPERATIONS

Mobil's last major new capital expenditure toward increasing U.S. refinery capacity was for its Joliet, Ill., refinery, which was put on line in 1973. Joliet, the largest U.S. refinery built from scratch, has a production capacity in excess of 160,000 barrels a day to service the U.S. north central states. The company's strategy has been one of modernization of existing plants. Exhibits 13 and 14 show Mobil's refining position in comparison to some other companies. On a worldwide basis, Mobil's degree of utilization of refinery capacity dropped 5 percent in 1975 from 1974. The U.S. operations dropped 7.2 percent. This drop was attributable to the recession and the impact of OPEC price increases. A further 3 percent drop in foreign refinery utilization occurred in 1976.

EXHIBIT 13
Sisters' Percentage of U.S. and World Refinery Capacity, Selected Years, 1920–1975

	1920		1950–1951		1975	
Company	United States	World	United States	World	United States	World
Exxon	9.5%	n.a.	11.1%	16.9%	7.8%	11.1%
Texaco	4.6	n.a.	7.3	6.6	6.8	5.4
Socal	7.6	n.a.	5.6	4.8	6.0	4.3
Gulf	4.6	n.a.	6.6	4.6	5.7	3.2
Mobil	3.1	n.a.	7.9	6.1	5.7	4.3
Royal Dutch/Shell	3.1	n.a.	5.5	11.6	7.3	9.6
British Petroleum	none	n.a.	none	6.6	none	5.0

n.a. = not available.
Sources: For 1920 for the U.S., John G. McLean and Robert W. Haigh, *The Growth of Integrated Oil Companies* (Boston: Harvard Business School, 1954), p. 528.
For the years 1950–1951 and 1975 for the U.S., Testimony of Donald C. O'Hara, President, National Petroleum Refineries Association, before the Subcommittee on Antitrust and Monopoly, November 1975.
For the world (all years), CIA Research Aid, *Free World Oil Refineries,* 1975.

EXHIBIT 14
Seven Companies Comparison—U.S. Crude Refining Capacity

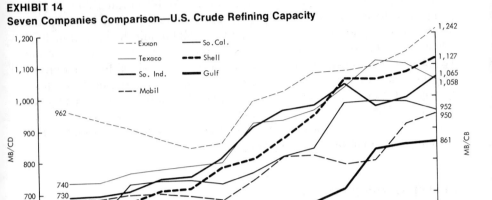

Source: Exxon Corporation.

In 1976, Mobil had seven U.S. refineries, along with 10 wholly owned and 21 partly owned foreign refineries located in 21 different countries. Mobil's involvement in pipelines ranks fifth behind the other four U.S. Sisters, with approximately a 6.8 percent share of the market. Mobil ranked fourth in 1951, with 8.4 percent of the total U.S. market in interstate oil pipeline movements. In 1976, the company had a complete or partial interest in 24,000 miles of crude oil, natural gas, natural gas liquids, and product pipelines in the United States and 17,500 miles in foreign countries.

After the 1911 split-up of Standard Oil, many of the "new companies" had concentrated marketing operations in clearly defined areas of the United States. Mobil's home ground and strong area for 20 years following the split was: Connecticut, Maine, Massachusetts, New Hampshire, Rhode Island, Vermont, and New York. Mobil's "claim" to these areas was through its Standard of New York (Socony) entity. Texas and Oklahoma were also major areas, through its wholly owned subsidiary Magnolia Petroleum Company. In 1926, within its area, Mobil had 46.1 percent of the gasoline market; other majors had 32.2 percent and nonmajors 21.7 percent. By 1932, Mobil was second to Texaco in the number of branded service stations (18,406 versus 23,459, respectively). Exhibit 15 shows Mobil's share of gasoline sales in recent years.

Mobil has always been an industry leader in lubricants, and this is a continuing goal. In April 1976, the company introduced into the U.S. market "Mobil 1," a synthesized engine lubricant. The sales of the lubricant were above projected figures for the product's first year on the market. Mobil's management feels that through the synthesized lubricant they have obtained

EXHIBIT 15

Top 20 U.S. Companies' Percentage of Gasoline Sales

Company	1970	1972	1973	1974*	1975
Texaco	8.12%	8.15%	8.09%	8.07%	7.89%
Shell	7.85	7.20	7.52	7.39	6.85
Exxon	7.41	6.86	7.62	7.38	7.32
Standard of Indiana	7.30	6.96	6.99	6.99	7.05
Gulf	7.12	6.50	6.73	6.55	6.22
Mobil	6.59	6.41	6.53	6.54	6.00
Socal	4.63	4.67	4.79	4.90	4.58
Arco	5.54	4.89	4.41	3.98	3.95
Phillips	3.96	4.07	4.05	3.81	3.90
Sun	4.14	3.84	3.72	3.72	3.48
Union	3.28	2.95	3.16	3.11	3.13
Continental	2.34	2.34	1.81	1.81	1.78
Cities Service	2.05	1.80	1.69	1.70	1.66
Marathon	1.73	1.58	1.52	1.49	1.49
Ashland	1.26	1.49	1.37	1.32	1.35
Standard (Ohio)	1.45	1.21	1.22	1.14	1.01
Clark	0.66	1.14	1.26	0.99	1.00
Amerada Hess	0.64	1.01	0.98	0.92	0.89
Tenneco	0.93	0.83	0.80	0.91	0.95
American Petrofina	0.64	0.63	0.80	0.85	0.99
British Petroleum Oil	1.40	1.12	0.66	0.54	0.63
Kerr-McGee	0.77	0.29	0.30	0.36	0.34
Murphy	0.75	0.66	0.62	0.67	0.64
Top Four	30.7	29.2	30.2	29.8	29.11
Top Eight	54.6	51.6	52.7	51.8	49.86
Top 20	80.0	76.7	77.5	75.9	71.49

* Ranked by 1974 sales.
Source: National Petroleum News, *Factbook Issues.*

an edge on the competition. In recent years, Mobil's overall marketing strategy has been to restrict marketing investment in new outlets to areas where significant growth would be likely and to close older, less-efficient outlets. Allied to this strategy is another of improving throughputs and profitability at service stations. Toward achieving these goals, the number of self-service stations has been increased (1,200 worldwide) and trials have been conducted to assess the effectiveness of snack shops and do-it-yourself repair bays. Sales areas were consolidated in 1976 by the wider use of centralized computerized order-taking and dispatching. In 1976 and 1977, steps were taken to bring computerized processing of all sales transactions and related inventory control together at one location.

At year-end, 1976, Mobil had 604 Mobil-operated gasoline retail outlets in the United States with an additional 20,088 independently owned Mobil retail outlets. Internationally, Mobil had a net reduction of 144 company-owned stations in 1976.

DIVERSIFICATION

Following the corporation's reorganization during the late 1950s and early 1960s, the top management of Mobil determined that one corporate objective should be "some kind of meaningful diversification." Mobil's performance had been questioned and criticized by some petroleum analysts for the small proportion of its earnings derived from domestic operations (see Exhibit 16).

EXHIBIT 16
Mobil's Geographical Distribution of Assets and Net Income
(in millions of dollars)

Location	1973	1974	1975	1976
Assets:				
United States	$ 4,893	$ 6,385	$ 6,296	$ 9,503
Foreign	5,797	7,689	8,754	9,264
Total	10,690	14,074	15,050	18,767
Net Income:				
United States	275	366	306	588
Foreign	574	681	504	355
Total	849	1,047	810	943*
Net Income from Petroleum Operations:				
United States	258	292	171	430
Foreign	558	654	510	342
Total	816	946	681	772

* Includes effective financing cost to Mobil Corporation of acquiring ownership of Marcor—a negative net income of $31 million.
Source: Mobil, *Annual Reports, 1973–1976.*

The officers of the company had frequently expressed goals and plans to create "the means of improving the U.S. earnings position."

Mobil, like many companies in the industry, fully realized that at some point the opportunity to productively spend dollars on petroleum exploration will diminish. When this situation arises, an oil company will continue to have a large cash flow, because it is cashing mineral reserves it had found earlier. The company will not, however, have the same opportunities to invest the large cash flow in its traditional business, raising the issue of where and how to expend its available capital. In addressing this issue, Mobil's chairman, Rawleigh Warner stated:

> . . . The oil industry in the past few years has been undergoing major changes in its relations with government in practically every country where it operates. Governments are interfering. The U.S. Government certainly is. The Federal Energy Administration tells us to whom we must sell our crude and what we can charge. They threaten us with a federal oil company that will be a yardstick to how effective we are. There are 3,000 bills before Congress, each of which will do something to the oil industry . . . an alert management doesn't ignore changes or challenges.

We concluded that there was a lot of wisdom in diversifying into a large business completely apart from the energy industry because we could see the government becoming more and more involved in energy activities . . . so we went out, picked an area in which we believed the government is not as interested as it is in the energy field.[5]

Mobil sought to acquire a company that was neither subject to the same business cycles and risks as the petroleum industry, nor seemed to attract as much government intervention. Mobil's executive vice president for planning and economics, Lawrence M. Woods, headed the team created in 1968 that searched for a company which would fit Mobil's diversification strategy. Wood attained his executive status through the financial arm of the company and was an accountant by training. During a five-year search, Mobil considered over 100 different firms in 25 industries. Eventually, Woods reported that Marcor, Inc. (the merged parent of Montgomery Ward and Container Corporation of America) appeared to satisfy the major criteria that Mobil had set: a low price/earnings multiple, a large share of earnings from U.S. operations, a large enough firm to impact Mobil's earnings, a management team whose track record (in this case turning the sagging business of Montgomery Ward around) was satisfactory.

In 1973, Warner obtained approval from Mobil's board to purchase 4.5 percent of Marcor's common stock. The purchase was to be made in a brokerage house's name in an effort to take a closer look at the company as a potential investment without revealing Mobil's interest. After having secretly bought 1,235,000 shares at an average price of $20 per share, Mobil approached the management of Marcor about increasing the investment to 51 percent. On June 14, 1974, Warner and Tavoulareas flew to Chicago to meet with the management of Marcor. Leo H. Schoenhofen, Marcor's chairman, had a previous engagement, but the company's president, Edward S. Donnell, and Gordon R. Worley, the vice president, met with the two Mobil executives. Commenting on the meeting, Warner said:

We told them we had one thing we wanted to tell them and one thing we wanted to propose to them. They were very surprised, just as I would be if someone walked into my office and told me they owned 10 million shares of Mobil. But it was all very cordial and businesslike . . . we told them we had financial resources that may be helpful to them, that we don't want to run their business, but we would be very interested as investors.[6]

Marcor's management was receptive and formal negotiations were initiated.

In an effort to get to know the company from the inside, four Mobil executives were appointed to the Marcor board. They reported no surprises, and in fact reported some strengths that had not previously been identified.

---

[5] As quoted by H. Lee Silberman, "Appeal to Reason," *Finance Magazine,* November 1975, pp. 9–13.

[6] As quoted in *Business Week,* June 29, 1974, p. 29.

The merger became effective July 1, 1976. Each outstanding share of Marcor common stock, other than shares held by Mobil Oil, was converted into and exchanged for 0.16 of one share of Mobil Corporation's common stock and $30 principal amount of Mobil Corporation's 8½ percent debentures due 2001. Cash was paid in lieu of fractions of shares of debentures in principal amounts less than $100. Each outstanding share of Marcor Series A preferred stock, other than shares held by Mobil Oil, received twice what was received for a share of Marcor common stock. As a result of the merger agreement, 3,577,970 shares of Mobil Corporation's common stock and $673 million principal amount of Mobil Corporation's 8½ percent debentures due 2001 were issued to Marcor shareholders. The total cost to Mobil of acquiring Marcor was $1.7 billion, approximately 13 times Marcor's 1975 earnings.

The merger had an appeal to both concerns. Short-term loans for working capital at that time were costing Marcor up to 16 percent and since part of Mobil's tender included $200 million for a new series of Marcor's voted preferred stock, this gave Marcor a cash inflow of $200 million at 7 percent. From Mobil's point of view, for the equivalent of one year's cash flow, Mobil had obtained two companies which in 1976 would add roughly $150 million to its net income from domestic operations.

Mobil made it plain from the beginning of the new operations that it had no plans to continually pump further working capital into Marcor. Mobil intended for the two major companies which comprised Marcor (Montgomery Ward and the Container Corporation of America) to stand on their own feet. Addressing the question of autonomy, Warner said,

> I don't see an operating role for Mobil in Ward for one fundamental reason. We are not retailers; we learned that a long time ago, that you can't anoint someone and expect him to do an effective job in a business that he doesn't know. You can question a commitment to autonomy if we took over another oil company, but retailing is a unique exercise. We have not been involved in it except for gas, which is totally different. . . .
>
> When our diversification quest finally led us to Ward, we told our board and management committee that we weren't deep enough to divert our energies to another business. We weren't broad-based in our management skills, so any acquisition had to have good management.[7]

Edward S. Donnell, the president of Marcor, said:

> [We] will check our management style against theirs. We will have financial counsel and advice, and a lot of good, hard pragmatic questions in planning areas. But there will be full freedom in operating areas. Mobil people aren't retailers and they don't have the people to run the business; we're people intensive and they are capital intensive.[8]

---

[7] As quoted by *Chain Store Age Executive*, September 1976.
[8] Ibid.

After the merger, Fredrick H. Veach, Ward's vice president for corporate planning, expressed it in a different way:

> We wondered if we would get the mushroom treatment. First, they [new owners] put you in the dark. Then they cover you with manure. Then they cultivate you. Then they let you steam for a while. Finally, they can you. We have been looking for evidence, but haven't found any of these steps. Maybe it's too early, but we can depend on everything they have said. I have faith and confidence, naïve as this may be.[9]

Formalized planning has been a strong feature at Mobil and Mobil's management quickly pressed Marcor's management to formalize its planning. "We want them to format what they have already been doing and what we have institutionalized since 1959. This will make things more understandable to us," said Woods. On the subject of long-range planning, Veach said:

> There's always resistance to formal planning. First, line managers see it as a threat to their authority. Second, they feel their business instincts will take care of problems better. Third, they don't really want to be as open as they think they have to be. Fourth, most incentive compensation plans are based on short-term results, so they couldn't care less about the future. And finally, managers aren't interested in long range because they get promoted or otherwide judged on the basis of what happens this year. These are generic obstacles.[10]

MARCOR, INC.

On October 31, 1968, when the stockholders of Montgomery Ward and Container Corporation of America voted to combine the assets and managements of the two companies, they created Marcor, Inc., a diversified, marketing-oriented, multibillion dollar company that brought together two leaders of the merchandising and packaging industries. Montgomery Ward, is a primary marketer of consumer goods and services and sells to one out of every five families in the United States. Container Corporation, serves more than 10,000 customers in the United States and abroad, providing packaging for $40 billion worth of consumer and industrial products.

After the merger, Marcor implemented no basic changes in the names, administration, or operation of its two subsidiaries. Montgomery Ward and Container continued to have their own boards of directors, officers, administrative staffs, and service functions. And each continued its own programs of growth and expansion in merchandising, marketing, and manufacturing.

The role of Marcor executives in the operation of Ward and Container was a blend of outside counselor and parent. While they expected to preserve what was best in each of the companies, they believed Marcor would introduce a new degree of objectivity and independent scrutiny, permitting a

---

[9] Ibid.
[10] Ibid.

EXHIBIT 17
Summary of Marcor Operations, 1973–1975 (prior to acquisition by Mobil)

Summary of Earnings (millions of dollars)

	1975	1974	1973
Net sales	$4,822.3	$4,667.5	$4,077.4
Costs and expenses:			
Cost of goods sold	$3,517.8	$3,379.9	$2,951.5
Operating, selling, administrative and research expenses	902.6	886.6	818.3
Interest expense	145.6	174.9	127.5
Provision for taxes on income†	121.1	105.7	83.4
Net earnings before change in accounting policy*,†	$ 135.2	$ 120.4	$ 96.7
Effect of change in accounting policy related to store pre-operating expense	—	4.7	—
Net earnings*,†	$ 135.2	$ 115.7	$ 96.7

Financial Data (millions of dollars except per share amounts)

	1975	1974	1973
Accounts receivable—parent and consolidated subsidiaries	$ 440.6	$ 339.2	$ 369.6
Accounts receivable—owned by credit subsidiary	2,075.7	1,880.1	1,512.7
Inventories	942.6	958.4	850.1
Net investment in properties and equipment	1,146.2	1,087.1	984.3
Additions to properties and equipment	179.9	214.8	202.6
Depreciation and amortization	87.7	80.0	75.9
Long-term debt	827.3	742.4	741.1
Stockholders' equity*,†	1,392.9	1,309.4	1,028.9
Book value per share‡	31.12	28.77	26.60
Primary earnings per share*,†	3.60	3.40	3.01
Fully diluted earnings per share*,†	2.85	2.63	2.32
Cash dividends per common share‡,§	1.00	0.97½	0.87½

Market History (calendar year basis)

	1975	1974	1973
Market price range of common shares (high–low)‡	29⅛–13⅞	28⅛–13¼	29⅝–17¾
Closing price year-end‡	28⅞	13⅞	20
Year-end price-earnings ratio (fully diluted earnings)	10	5	9

* Net earnings for 1974 includes a net loss of $4.5 from the sale of Pioneer Trust & Savings Bank. As of the beginning of 1974, the company adopted the Lifo method of determining inventory cost for a substantial portion of its domestic manufacturing inventories. This change in accounting had the effect of reducing net earnings for 1974 by $9.1.

† Amounts prior to November 1, 1968 have been reduced by the portions applicable to Container Corporation shares exchanged for debentures at that date.

‡ Adjusted for two-for-one stock split June 9, 1970.

§ Dividends prior to November 1, 1968 are those paid on common shares of Montgomery Ward & Co., Incorporated.

Source: Marcor's *Annual Reports, 1973–1975.*

fresh look at both operations. Marcor's management planned to remain small and "free form" so that it could respond quickly and effectively to new problems. It planned to draw freely on the management capabilities of both Ward and Container from time to time, assembling task forces to tackle particular projects, and disbanding or reshaping the force as each problem was solved or redefined. Marcor's officers expected the parent company to experience almost continuous restructuring and augmentation as its role evolved. Marcor's executives concentrated their effort and attention on developing and implementing broad corporate objectives.

One of the most direct and immediate benefits Marcor wanted to produce was the infusion of many of the specialized management skills and techniques of each company into the other's management force. Marcor executives would direct and channel the available management talent into critical areas first, while evaluating additional opportunities in all parts of both operations. Marcor also served as a focal point for determining what management resources of one company were available for the other.

Part of Marcor's task was to combine the development programs of each of the subsidiaries to provide "cross training" of the managements. Exhibit 17 shows financial highlights of Marcor prior to Mobil's acquisition.

MONTGOMERY WARD

Ward was founded in 1872, by Aaron Montgomery Ward and his brother-in-law, George R. Thorne. The company was exclusively a mail-order sales firm until 1926 when it opened the first of the chain of retail stores in Marysville, Kansas. Following World War II, when competitors undertook giant building and modernization programs, Ward—under the direction of Sewell Avery—refrained from store expansion for fear of impending return to the depressionary era of the 1930s. For 16 years, no new stores were opened—a strategic decision which has become one of the legendary mistakes in all of business history. In 1957, new management began the tremendous task of rebuilding what had become an outdated and outmoded chain and trying to regain the lost ground that Sears had easily captured.

From 1958 to 1969, Ward invested $500 million in modernizing and moving the thrust of its retail operations from the small town to the metropolitan suburb, while developing and installing computerized systems for reducing costs and improving efficiencies in handling catalog sales. The company's diversification program added new markets to its operations.

Presently, it is the third largest catalog and nonfood retail merchandiser in the United States, trailing Sears and J. C. Penney (see Exhibit 18). In 1976, the company sold through 2,300 retail and catalog outlets and employed approximately 100,000 employees. The company operated 439 retail stores having more than 58 million square feet of gross space, over half of which was in retail selling areas.

Ward semiannually published two large general merchandise catalogs, to-

EXHIBIT 18
Sales-Profit Comparisons of Top Three Leading Catalog Retailers, 1970–1976
(in millions of dollars)

Year	Sears Roebuck Sales	Sears Roebuck Net Income	J. C. Penney Sales	J. C. Penney Net Income	Montgomery Ward Sales	Montgomery Ward Net Income
1970	$ 9,262	$464.2	$4,150	$114.1	$2,227	$34.6
1971	10,006	550.9	4,812	135.7	2,376	36.8
1972	10,991	614.3	5,529	162.7	2,640	42.3
1973	12,306	679.9	6,243	185.8	3,231	54.9
1974	13,101	511.4	6,935	125.1	3,623	44.3
1975	13,639	522.6	7,678	189.6	3,779	67.7
1976	14,950	695.0	8,354	228.1	3,794	91.7*

* An 11-month period.
Source: Annual reports of the companies.

gether with a number of small seasonal catalogs. Catalog sales were made through direct mail, catalog order desks in retail stores, 550 catalog stores, and some 1,300 independently owned sale agencies. A support network of nine catalog distribution centers shipped some 100,000 items of merchandise to consumers throughout the country. Credit sales were a major portion of Ward's business, accounting for more than half of its sales in 1975. At many of its urban and suburban store locations, Ward offered customers such services as auto and appliance repairs, driver education, interior design

EXHIBIT 19
Comparative Statistics of Montgomery Ward, 1946–1976

Year	Sales (million $)	Net Earnings (million $)	Retail Stores	Catalog Stores	Catalog Sales Agencies	Average Number of Employees (000s)
1946	974.2	52.3	628	215	—	83
1950	1,170.4	74.2	614	250	—	65
1955	969.9	35.2	566	301	—	53
1960	1,248.9	15.0	529	627	—	67
1965	1,748.4	23.9	502	864	287	98
1966	1,894.1	16.5	493	793	569	105
1967	1,879.0	17.4	475	719	632	101
1968	1,985.6	33.3	468	695	804	100
1969	2,155.2	39.6	464	669	894	100*
1970	2,226.9	34.6	462	660	961	100*
1971	2,376.9	36.8	465	644	1,014	100*
1972	2,640.0	42.3	458	590	1,184	100*
1973	3,231.0	54.9	449	419	1,239	100*
1974	3,623.0	44.3	446	460	1,253	100*
1975	3,779.3	67.7	443	555	1,288	100*
1976	3,794.2	91.7	439	550	1,314	100*

* Estimated through to 1976.
Source: Montgomery Ward, *Annual Reports*, various years.

systems, kitchen planning, home cleaning and painting, pest control, key making, utility bill payment, postal services, tax return preparation, notary public service, ticket reservations for theatrical and sporting events, photocopying, and beauty, optical, and hearing aid shops. Exhibits 18 and 19 show details of Montogomery Ward's performance over the years.

CONTAINER CORPORATION OF AMERICA

The other company obtained in the acquisition, the Container Corporation of America, was founded in 1926 by Walter P. Paepcke who, for more than 30 years, was its chief executive officer. To form the company, Mr. Paepcke combined the paperboard packaging facilities of Chicago Mill and Lumber Company with the plants and facilities of several other paperboard-fabricating firms. The company grew through internal expansion and acquisition to become a major factor in the packaging industry. A corollary to its development of packaging products was Container Corporation's innovation in the application of marketing and packaging design services, where the company's influence extended far beyond its own industry.

In 1936, Container started a unique and comprehensive program of corporate design for the visual upgrading of everything from plant architecture to truck lettering. Its design and market research laboratories, established in the mid-1940s, were the industry's first to use programmed application of market research, design, and scientific testing in the development of more effective consumer packaging.

By 1976, Container Corporation was the nation's largest producer of paperboard packaging and the second largest manufacturer of paperboard. In 1975, it operated 90 facilities throughout the United States. Its overseas affiliations employed 8,000 employees in 56 different operations in Colombia, Mexico, Venezuela, Italy, Spain, and the Netherlands. Its total work force was more than 21,000.

Finished packaging products, which represented over 80 percent of container sales, included corrugated shipping containers, folding paper cartons, composite cans, fiberboard and drums, and industrial plastic containers. Production of paperboard in 1975 totaled almost 2 million tons, of which 1.5 million tons were produced by domestic mills. Allied to its paperboard packaging, the company offered packaging services including graphic design, structural design, market research, packaging testing, packaging machinery development, and manufacturing. To supply its operation in 1976, the corporation owned or controlled over 744,000 acres of timberlands and had a 49 percent interest in the T. R. Miller Lumber Company, Inc. This company owns almost 200,000 acres close to the company's Alabama paperboard mill. Container also had short-term cutting rights to timber on some 103,000 acres. The company had a continuing policy of increasing its holdings in timberlands.

Container Corporation had an operating characteristic similar to that of

EXHIBIT 20
Container Corporation's Financial Information for Ten-Year Period Ended December 31, 1967 (prior to becoming a subsidiary of Marcor)

	1967	1966	1965
Net Sales (000s)	$463,135	$460,365	$405,689
Earnings before income taxes (000s)	58,773	62,181	50,159
Provision for income taxes (000s)	25,867	27,950	22,858
Earnings for the year (000s)	$ 32,906*	$ 34,231	$ 27,301
Per share	2.95*	3.06	2.42
Percent return on shareholders' equity	14.7%	16.8%	14.2%
Total common stock dividends (000s)	$ 14,555	$ 13,996	$ 12,848
Per share	1.30	1.25	1.15
Property additions and improvements (000s)	$ 50,060	$ 44,032	$ 36,540
Depreciation and depletion (000s)	20,752	19,593	18,454
Current assets (000s)	$125,230	$133,214	$114,279
Current liabilities (000s)	53,725	67,971	48,583
Working capital (000s)	$ 71,505	$ 65,243	$ 65,696
Current ratio	2.33 to 1	1.96 to 1	2.35 to 1
Property, less reserves (000s)	$247,401	$236,251	$211,866
Deferred income taxes and other liabilities (000s)	19,660	17,421	12,850
Long-term debt (000s)	71,882	69,484	59,832
Shareholders' equity (000s)	241,105	223,417	203,717
Book value per share	21.64	19.95	18.19

* Excludes extraordinary earnings of $1,065,000 or 10 cents per share.
† Excludes extraordinary earnings of $1,894,000 or 18 cents per share.

EXHIBIT 21
Highlights of Container Corporation's Performance since Acquisition by Marcor (in millions of dollars)

Year	Sales	Earnings
1968	469	31.6
1969	510	27.7
1970	527	30.1
1971	559	24.1
1972	624	33.7
1973	755	50.0
1974	965	74.6
1975	953	64.0
1976*	995	53.9

* 11-month period. (See Exhibit 22 for explanation.)
Source: Container Corporation's *Annual Reports, 1968–1976.*

Mobil. They were timber shy, just as Mobil has been crude shy. Warner observed, "There is a kind of affinity between Container Corporation and ourselves . . . I suppose we were attracted to someone who has to live by their wits like we have had to do."

EXHIBIT 22 Recent Financial Performance of Container Corporation of America (and consolidated subsidiaries)

	11-Month Period* Ended December 31, 1976	11-Month Period† Ended December 31, 1975	Fiscal year Ended January 31, 1976
Financial Summary:	(dollars in millions)		
Sales:			
Shipping containers	$ 455.8	$410.6	$450.7
Paperboard cartons	236.1	200.8	221.0
Other packages	119.6	100.9	110.2
Paperboard and miscellaneous	183.4	157.0	171.4
Net Sales	994.9	869.3	953.3
Cost of products sold	792.5	668.4	734.9
Other costs and expenses	80.6	74.9	81.9
Income taxes on operations	58.1	62.7	67.9
Net income before effect of changes in accounting policies and Marcor interest charges‡	$ 63.7	$ 63.3	$ 68.6
Cumulative effect, less applicable taxes, on prior years of changes in accounting policies	5.6‡	—	—
Marcor interest charges less applicable taxes	4.2	4.2	4.5
Net Income	$ 53.9	$ 59.1	$ 64.1

	At December 31, 1976		At January 31, 1976
Current assets	$ 358.7		$335.9
Note receivable from affiliate	60.0		60.0
Investments and other assets	37.5		39.5
Properties, plants, and equipment, net	576.4		538.6
Total Assets	$1,032.6		$974.0
Current liabilities	$ 218.8		$203.1
Long-term debt	187.1		195.8
Deferred income taxes	47.3		45.4
Minority interest in consolidated subsidiary cos	22.4		23.7
Equity of Marcor Inc.	557.0		506.0
Total Liabilities and Shareholders' Equity	$1,032.6		$974.0

	11-Month Period Ended December 31, 1976		Fiscal Year Ended January 31, 1976
Operating Highlights:			
Paperboard produced (thousands of tons)	2,040		1,995
Recycled paperboard produced as a percentage of above	49%		47%
U.S. timberland owned or under long-term lease (thousands of acres) (at year-end)	744		716
Number of employees (at year-end)	21,400		21,200

Note: These income data do not represent Container's contribution to the net income of Mobil Corporation. For example, Container financial data shown above do not reflect the purchase accounting adjustments recorded in Mobil Corporation's consolidated financial statements for amortization of the exces of Mobil Corporation's investment in Container over Mobil Corporation's equity in the book value of Container's net assets.

* In 1976, Container changed from a fiscal year, ending on January 31, to a calendar year. Accordingly, 1976 financial data for Container are for the 11-month period ended December 31, 1976.

† To facilitate comparison, income data for the 11-month period ended December 31, 1975, have been developed.

‡ Container adopted the policy effective February 1, 1976, of not capitalizing either interest expense on construction in progress or preoperating expense of new facilities and charged earnings for these expenses capitalized in prior years.

Source: Mobil Corporation, *1976 Annual Report.*

Container Corporation in 1975 collected more than a million tons of waste paper for recycling. Approximately half of this collected material was used by its own domestic recycling mills, and the balance was sold to other countries. Exhibits 20–22 show financial information for Container Corporation for three years prior to becoming a subsidiary of Marcor, for selected years since acquisition by Marcor, and since acquisition by Mobil.

MOBIL'S CHEMICAL DIVISION

Mobil's diversification into the chemical industry in 1960 was a move that many other large petroleum companies also pursued. In 1976, the chemical division produced 8.3 percent of Mobil's net income on only 3.7 percent of the total revenues. In 1977, the Mobil Chemical Company had 49 plants in operation in eight countries. Although its chemical division was a part of Mobil Oil, had it been a separate entity its performance figures would have put it in the top half of the *Fortune 500* and among the 20 largest chemical companies in the United States. The company is the largest U.S. manufacturer of disposable plastic products. These products are of three major types: polyethylene, one use of which is the material for Mobil's Hefty bags; polystyrene, which is the base for foam containers; and polypropylene, which is the transparent packaging film used in many industries. The company in 1977 had a capacity to produce almost 3 billion pounds of petrochemicals per year. In addition, it ranked as the third largest producer in the United States of phosphate rock, sources of phosphorous chemicals, and fertilizer. The chemical division's profits for the years 1973 to 1976 were $36 million, $106 million, $89 million, and $78 million, respectively.

MOBIL: THE LAND DEVELOPER

A less obvious move was the company's involvement in land development. One such adventure was a 13,000 condominium apartment complex in Hong Kong. The complex, called Mei Foo New Village, consists of 99 separate 20-story towers which will house 65,000 people when completed in 1979. In 1970, Mobil created a real estate company, named Mobil Oil Estates Limited, which was involved in real estate development in California and Texas. Another major venture was a San Francisco Bay project at Redwood Shores, a residential community covering 1,300 acres.

In October 1974, Mobil reached an understanding with majority owners on a bid to purchase the Irvine Company, owner of 77,700 acres of land in Orange County, California, approximately 73,000 acres of which were undeveloped.

The Irvine Company was incorporated in 1894, and the land at that time was appraised at less than $1 per acre—the value at which it was presently shown on the company's balance sheet. Mobil's offer for the company in 1974 was approximately $200 million. A member of the company's board,

Mrs. Joan Irvine Smith, argued that the company was worth more than $200 million and at a board meeting in late 1974, Mrs. Irvine served notice that she had filed suit to enjoin the sale. In March 1975, an injunction was issued against the proposed sale to Mobil. In an effort to satisfy special tax considerations of minority shareholders, Mobil revised its offer—but never to the satisfaction of Mrs. Smith, who held 22 percent of the shares of the Irvine Company.

By May 1976, the majority of the minority shareholders had agreed to sell their shares to Mobil. It was anticipated that this would allow the injunction to be lifted, but it did not. The judge contended that alternative buyers, who may have been interested in the Irvine Company, had not been sought. Mrs. Smith was supported in her action by the attorney general of California. Other potential buyers came on the scene and bidding began in earnest.

The book value of the company was listed at $67 million, or approximately $8 per share. Lansing Eberling, Irvine's chief financial officer, estimated the value of undeveloped land at approximately $175 million based on a 40-year development period using discounted present value methods. The company's debt was less than $120 million. An estimate of its fair market book value was $248 million, equivalent to $29.50 per share.

By mid-October 1976, one of the three new contenders, Fluor Corporation, had left the race. The two remaining newcomers were a Canadian company, Cadillac Fairview Corporation, and a group of private investors led by Detroit developer A. Alfred Taubman. Cadillac Fairview entered a bid for $31.50 per share (or $265 million)—to be paid in ten-year notes totaling $120 million and $145 million in cash. Cadillac Fairview was heavily leveraged and the terms of its bid represented an attempt to purchase the Irvine interest with Irvine assets, however. Mobil countered with a new offer of $31.50 per share in cash. Two days later, Cadillac Fairview increased its bid to $32 per share. Mobil responded with $32.50, again in cash. Taubman's group upped the ante with a bid per share equivalent to $35.30. Mobil disputed the value of Taubman's bid and offered an alternative to its own bid, the alternative being almost a carbon copy of Cadillac Fairview's bid of $279.8 million but with $5 million more in cash and $5 million less in notes.

The bidding was continued with various parties offering sweeteners to improve their bids. Taubman's group offered minority shareholders the opportunity to buy back into the company. Taubman's group continued the bidding with Mobil through May 1977, at which time Mobil dropped out having bid more than $336 million for Irvine. The winning bid of Taubman's group was $337.4 million. Despite a request by the new owners to stay on, the three top executives of Irvine Company resigned.

MOBIL'S PUBLIC RELATIONS PROGRAM

Mobil had long been known, as Warner put it in 1976, "as a good gray Republican company. Some of us began to think around here that maybe there were two sides of the street to walk down and maybe we ought to walk down the other side of the street."

Herman J. Schmidt, vice chairman of Mobil, said in February 1977:

> Ten years ago, top management in a company such as Mobil could spend a minimal amount of its time communicating with the media, with legislators, and with the general public. Management in most companies could generally meet what seemed their public-affairs responsibilities by having the chief executive or some other senior officer go to Washington once in a while to talk with a few people or to testify before a Congressional Committee. He could grant an occasional interview to an essentially friendly reporter and make a speech now and then to an audience with which he felt comfortable.
>
> Today, however, large-scale communication has become a prime requirement of business—and not just big business. It is a major element in the time of even the most senior people in our company, and by that I mean our chief executive officer, our president, other of our employee directors and officers and managers below the directors' level.
>
> In retrospect we can see that our approach in the mid-1960s was a mistake. Those of us in top management should have paid greater attention to public opinion and to the media and to members of the Congress and of the state legislatures. We should have worked to establish greater credibility, which would have stood us in good stead when the going got tough. People seldom heard from us until we were in trouble, and by then it was usually too late.

Mobil in the 1950s and 1960s, like most petroleum companies, had few friends in the ranks of ardent Democrats, but did have some support in the House and Senate. As Warner put it:

> We had fellows like Lyndon Johnson, Sam Rayburn, and Bob Kerr, in the Senate and in the House who, coming out of that southwestern area, were very close to the oil industry. Every time the industry got in trouble, they would run to these four or five fellows. What we forgot as an industry was that those fellows weren't planning on living forever! The decision was made: Mobil crossed the line from a low profile to public.[11]

In a speech, Warner described the company's advertising practice:

> We published a quarter-page advertisement virtually every Thursday, year-round, on the page opposite the editorial page of *The New York Times*—called, as you might deduce, the Op-Ed page. This is the only space the *Times* will sell on those two pages. It therefore has pretty high visibility, which we try to enhance with an off-beat approach. The space gives enough room for essay-type ads similar in tone to other material appearing on those two pages.
>
> We try to surprise readers of the *Times* with our selection of subject matter, our headlines, and our brisk and often irreverent text. We try to be urbane but not pompous. We try not to talk to ourselves and we accept that we can never tell the whole story in any one ad.
>
> Our ads have ranged over a wide gamut—the energy crisis in its ramifica-

---

[11] As quoted by *Fortune*, September 1976, p. 109.

tions, the role of profits, earnings as expressed in rate of return, capital requirements and capital information, the need for national energy policies . . . why we support the New York Public Library, public television, the United Negro College Fund, the Better Business Bureau, . . . the need for economic growth, . . . the dangers of simplistic knee-jerk reactions, . . . the need to conserve energy, and ways to use less gasoline. The list is a long one.

We try to help people understand what options are open to them and what sort of costs are involved in the various trade-offs. The response has been strong and generally favorable, though in addressing ourselves to opinion leaders we deliberately opted for a rather thin cut of the total public. We believe we have had some impact and that we have been reaching people other than just those already wedded to the free market, but we realize we have not yet done enough to reach the public at large. In sum, we think the exercise has been useful, albeit somewhat expensive in toto, and sufficiently productive to continue.

Exhibits 23 to 25 present samples of Mobil's ads.

Heading Mobil's public relations since 1974 is Herman J. Schmidt, its vice chairman. Public affairs is Schmidt's sole corporate function. Schmidt who started in journalism in college but later turned to law was Mobil's general counsel before assuming line responsibilities. While Schmidt heads the overall public affairs program, however, it is Herbert Schmertz, Mobil's vice president, who has been the chief architect of Mobil's media campaign. According to one inside source,

> One of the things that Herb brought was an ability to talk to the Democratic side of the House and Senate and to know some of those people—particularly some of those people that we never, never would see before—the liberal element of the Democratic side.[12]

The op-eds were started on an infrequent basis in October 1970, but by mid-1971 it was determined that they would be a regular feature. It took Schmertz and his staff six months of experimentation and preparation to complete the 20 backup ads necessary to ensure that the most relevant topic would be included each week. In January 1972, Mobil was ready for a weekly column. It has been a regular feature since then.

The production of the op-ed ads involves considerable collective effort. The Schmertz staff and, on occasion, Warner and Tavoulareas are involved in the initial theme selection; the final draft always requires approval of either Warner or Tavoulareas.

To assist in keeping fully abreast of news and views, Mobil formed a "Secretariat." Among other things, the Secretariat has four news tickers, three TV-video recorders, a tap on the New York computerized information service, and an internal computerized index to Mobil's public statements issued since 1973. This level of backup service permits the corporation's public affairs arm to react promptly to adverse criticism with factual inform-

---

[12] Ibid., p. 108.

EXHIBIT 23
A Sample of a Mobil Ad

Musings of an oil person...

Wonder if oil company advertising isn't risking indecent overexposure these days. There's so much oil on the tube and in print. Gulf, Shell and Texaco all ran full-pagers on the same day last week in the Times. Mobil's on the Op-Ed page every Thursday. Why do we all do it? Some critics think the ads show the companies are conspiring to brainwash the public. Others think the advertising deluge proves we can't do anything right, not even conspire. But an oil company has to find some way of speaking its mind and letting the public know what's going on, especially now when oil companies are accused of being secretive. Have to take risk of moving Tom Wicker to nausea over the "...pious, self-serving, devious, mealy-mouthed, self-exculpating, holier-than-thou, positively sickening oil company advertisements in which these international behemoths depict themselves as poverty-stricken paragons of virtue embattled against a greedy and ignorant world." Tom turns a nice phrase, but doesn't he know we're frustrated in trying to get information to the public? Try to buy time on TV to say something substantive and the networks clobber you with the fairness doctrine. Same with radio. Several congressmen want the FTC to require a company to substantiate its idea advertising, just as if an idea were like a new toothpaste. Why don't they exhume Madison and make him substantiate the Bill of Rights? Sure, we can stick to print media to tell our story. But newspapers and magazines frequently don't understand the complexities of our industry. Only a few have oil specialists. And how many deadly news releases can we send them before they scream for mercy? Much better to use TV to try to reach the millions whose opinions about oil are swayed by what Cronkite, Chancellor and Reasoner say every evening. Briefly! In 30 seconds they can suggest enough wrongdoing that a year of full-page explanations by us won't set straight. Hate to be on the defensive all the time. Arm our top management people with facts and get them on TV panels and talk shows. They still look drab next to a politician making some wild allegation against us because he's running for something. Does he have to run on our backs? Sure he does--as long as there are gas lines. What do we tell the guy who's boiling mad at us--in our station or some other company's--after waiting two hours for the privilege of paying $1.10 for two gallons of gas? Are we going to tell him he's been wasting energy for years? No way. Tell him to lay off those jackrabbit starts? He'll find that out for himself. That Detroit's naughty for building big cars, that we shouldn't have built all those superhighways, that we're sorry we gave away all that glassware? Forget it. Should we remind him we've been warning for years that the energy crisis was coming? He'll mow down the pumps and who would blame him. No, have to focus on the positive things we can do. Tell him we're recycling the money he pays at the pump right back into oil-finding offshore, Alaska, anywhere. Into more refinery capacity. Into oil shale, synthetic fules from coal, tar sands, far-out processes in the lab. Dammit, we're a can-do company in a can-do country. Give us a few years and we'll make gas lines just a quaint recollection of the mid-70s. In the meantime, try to reason with Washington against counter-productive laws and regulations. Fight the two-times-two-equals-five logicians who think the same outfit that brings you the U.S. Mail can find oil three miles under the ocean bottom. Give people the facts. Give them genuine information. Speak out. Persuade them to listen. Never bore them. If at first we don't succeed, bust a gut trying again. No other way. Or we all end up working for the government.

EXHIBIT 24
A Sample of a Mobil Ad

can't tell the seven sisters apart?
we're the one with extra dimension

One of the seven largest international oil companies. But more than that.

The right diet of investments in recent years has filled us out. Made us a balanced, diversified energy company. With the flexibility to move ahead in the United States as well as abroad. In petroleum. Or in other businesses.

Our diversifications, begun in the '60s, are now rounded out. Container

Corporation of America, the nation's leading maker of paperboard packaging. Montgomery Ward. Mobil Chemical, grown to a billion dollar business. Among other virtues, it's America's largest manufacturer of disposable plastic products.

Sure, we're still big abroad. With substantial shares in the North Sea's largest oil field and the huge Arun gas

field in Indonesia. Both Mobil discoveries. And we're working closely with Saudi Arabia on a number of major projects.

But we're even stronger in the U.S. Where our diversifications are centered. Where our petroleum production in the Gulf of Mexico is growing. Especially natural gas.

So forgive us, sisters, if we think we're special.

Mobil®

EXHIBIT 25
A Sample of a Mobil Ad

On putting our money
where our mouth is

We've been saying all along that, given a go-ahead by federal and state governments and the courts, America's oil companies would work their tails off to help relieve our country's overdependence on foreign oil—now some 40 percent of the oil the United States uses annually.

After years of frustrating hearings and court battles, the Interior Department finally moved boldly on a key front. Two weeks ago, in an auction in New York City's Statler Hilton Hotel, it opened a portion of the Atlantic—50 to 90 miles off New Jersey—to bidding by the companies for drilling rights. The winning bidders can proceed to get drilling permits providing appellate courts agree that the environment will be properly protected. (As experience indicates it will be: In the Gulf of Mexico and off the California coast, there have been only four serious spills from the more than 20,000 wells drilled in the last quarter century. Each was promptly cleaned up, with no permanent ecological damage.)

No one knows for sure there's oil beneath the U.S. Atlantic (you never can be positive until you drill). But this is one of the few remaining areas where there can at least be real hope. The promising land areas of the United States where the industry could hope to find large reserves have been heavily explored. If this country is to find major new deposits of oil and gas, relieving our dependence on foreign petroleum, it will almost certainly have to be offshore.

The oil companies have been saying this repeatedly. Now the industry has put its money where its mouth is.

The Interior Department expected to realize some $600 million in lease bonuses at this auction.

The actual high bids which were accepted on 93 tracts totaled more than $1.1 billion.

And that's only the beginning of what will be needed to explore the tracts. All the lease bonuses really buy is the right of successful bidders to risk additional money on drilling. The companies will need to invest huge sums in exploratory wells, and then in producing wells if oil and gas in commercial quantities are found, and then in pipelines to the shore (again, with adequate protection for the environment.) Offshore costs are very high.

We at Mobil are proud to be leaders in the development of America's offshore oil and gas resources, including the latest sale. Yet, our critics have said that we diverted money from the search for energy when we acquired Marcor. They were wrong. Our diversification program, under way since 1968, includes Container Corporation and Montgomery Ward (from the Marcor acquisition), along with real estate development and expansion of our chemical ventures. These were prudent investments so portions of our company would be subject to different business cycles and a different climate of government regulation. But we never forget that our main business is petroleum.

And we repeatedly put our money where our mouth is. In the Gulf of Mexico, since 1970, Mobil has invested more money in lease bonuses—in excess of $1 billion—than any other oil company. And in this latest sale, a bidding group headed by Mobil made the largest single bid for a tract: nearly $108 million. All told, Mobil and its partners spent $274 million. Our company's own outlay on eight tracts came to more than $90 million.

We may be outspoken, especially on energy issues important to our country. But our actions speak even louder than our words.

©1976 Mobil Oil Corporation

This ad appeared in *The New York Times* of September 2, 1976.

tion. The Secretariat spends $400,000 annually on news-monitoring and information retrieval systems. Mobil has made it a policy to pay for advocacy ads from profits rather than expense them as operating costs.

The change from product advertising to idea advertising is one aspect that makes Mobil's policy ad unique in the petroleum industry. Warner recalls the matter of product advertising which was dropped when the gasoline shortage occurred in late 1973:

> I woke up one morning and suddenly realized all the industry was still going on with product advertising when we were fighting a shortage. I said to the fellows then, let's drop the product advertising because there's no sense telling people to go out and buy if you don't have it to give them.[13]

Considering all their media activity, it is perhaps their op-eds that have set Mobil apart. The measure of success that Mobil has enjoyed with the op-eds, however, has not been echoed in the TV media. In demonstrating the different attitudes, Schmertz quotes one example,

> In an ad we prepared to run on television, the camera would focus throughout on a beach and ocean waves while the announcer said:
>
> > "According to the U.S. Geological Survey, there may be 60 million barrels of oil or more beneath our continental shelves.
> > Some people say we should be drilling for that oil and gas. Others say we shouldn't because of the possible environmental risks. We'd like to know what you think.
> > Write Mobil Poll, Room 647, 150 East 42nd Street, New York 10007. We'd like to hear from you."

NBC accepted this ad without change. CBS turned it down in a letter, which read in part:

> "We regret that the subject matter of this commercial . . . deals with a controversial issue of public importance and does not fall within our 'goods and services' limitation for commercial acceptance."

ABC also turned down the ad in a letter which gave no explanation but merely said:

> "This will advise you that we have reviewed the above-captioned commercial and are unable to grant an approval for use over our facilities."

> We decided not to let this rebuff go unchallenged. We therefore took out a newspaper ad which reproduced the proposed visuals and text for our TV spot, together with the three networks' replies.
> We received over 2,000 replies to this newspaper ad, and the respondents overwhelmingly favored our right to express our viewpoint on the air.

Schmidt said in 1977:

> We have learned in the intervening years that unless we win our case with the

---

[13] John J. Connor, "Mobil's Rawleigh Warner Is Adman of the Year," *Advertising Age*, December 29, 1975.

general public, we stand little chance of winning it in the halls of Congress. Accordingly, we in Mobil have taken our case to the people, through the newspapers of the country and through local television and radio stations, as well as directly to Congressmen and Senators and others in Washington. This has required a sustained effort to the highest levels of management and throughout the organization but we are persuaded it has been worthwhile and may well represent the shape of the future for all business.

Mobil has put a number of executives through special training and sent them on media "blitzes" across the country during which they appear on numerous TV and radio programs, in addition to meeting newspaper editors. In all, we have had as many as half a dozen traveling around the country at one time. We also tape interviews for syndication.

In the last two years, Mobil representatives have appeared on a total of 365 television shows, 211 radio shows, and have had 18 newspaper interviews.

Schmertz also observed:

We know we have stiffened every employee's morale and that our people have been greatly pleased to see management stand up and fight for what they believe to be right. We have indications that many of our shareholders feel the same way.

In evaluating their new "public" policy, Warner said:

There is no way we can measure what we have accomplished with the program we have been following. If we hadn't done it, we would have left all of the media to our critics. And I have to assume we would be worse off today. Somebody had to answer, and thus, that's what we have tried to do.

RECENT TRENDS

In 1976, the U.S.-based petroleum industry could claim a year of recovery. Mobil, together with Gulf, led the big five U.S. international companies with earning gains of 16 percent over 1975. Petroleum earnings accounted for $772 million (82 percent of Mobil's total net income) in 1976. Of these petroleum earnings, those from the United States rose 152 percent to $430 million, with foreign earnings dropping 33 percent of $342 million. Much of the foreign drop represented the weakness of foreign currencies against the U.S. dollar.

A PERSPECTIVE VIEW

Since the Arab embargo, oil companies have repeatedly expressed a need for higher prices and higher profits to support the industry's efforts towards exploration and development of petroleum products and, more recently, toward development of alternative energy sources. Yet, Mobil's actions show distinct interest in areas outside of both oil and energy even though it remains primarily a petroleum company with comparatively small interests in other sources (Exhibit 26).

EXHIBIT 26
Mobil's Activities in Alternative Sources of Energy, 1977

Solar...........	$30 million interest in a joint venture with Tyco Laboratories to develop mass-produced solar cells to convert sunlight directly to electricity.
Coal	Mobil scientists had invented a process for converting methanol, which can be derived from coal, into high-octane gasoline. Mobil's estimated coal reserves in 1976 were over 3 billion tons. Mobil ranked 13th in U.S. coal reserves in 1974. Its share was 0.8 percent of total reserves.
Uranuim	Production plant in Texas due on line 1979. Drilling in New Mexico to establish potential of reserves there.
Oil Shale	Together with nine other companies Mobil was attempting to design in-place underground method of recovering oil from shale.

In December 1976, Warner summed up Mobil's strategic position as follows:

Mobil is one of the world's largest companies. Energy is and will remain our primary business, but a carefully balanced program begun in 1968 has broadened and strengthened our earnings base. . . .

For 16 consecutive years, Mobil has increased the size of its dividends. It is a record of which we are proud—one we are determined to improve. . . .

In the past, Mobil has been known primarily as an international oil company. Today, diversification has created an earnings mix which retains our ability to grow in the petroleum industry while offering attractive new earnings sources in fields that are subject to different economic cycles and less stringent government regulations. . . .

A result of this strategy has been to strengthen our U.S. earnings base. In 1976, more than half of Mobil's earnings are coming from domestic sources. And our diversification has been accomplished without weakening our position in energy. . . .

Mobil is beginning to benefit from the results of strategic petroleum exploration and production investments that were made overseas during the earlier years of the decade, improving the company's already strong position internationally with as diversified a base of oil and gas supply as possible. . . .

Nothing is more basic to Mobil's business than the search for energy.

Wherever energy is to be found—as oil, gas, coal, shale, shale oil, uranium, the sun—Mobil is prepared to lead in its development. . . .

Mobil Oil's exploration and production division was recently reorganized on a worldwide basis to provide effective response to energy opportunities so investment can be channeled to those that are most promising. . . .

Mobil Oil Corporation is totally integrated from the research laboratory to the gasoline pump. . . .

Mobil prides itself on having management in depth. We encourage our people to innovate, whether in the laboratories or refineries or in planning marketing or supply strategies.

We stress dynamic planning. Each year, managers of the Mobil group of companies at all levels, from domestic refineries to marketing operations in the South Pacific, develop assumptions about conditions likely to be encountered. They set objectives, not just for the year ahead but for the next five years. They develop a profit plan, then capital and operating budgets to implement these objectives.

At each level, this dynamic planning process is refined. Hard choices in investments and economies are made. Ultimately, top management has the information and the perspective necessary to make the broad decisions; to map not just year-by-year tactics, but long-term strategy. . . .

On Montgomery Ward:

"Large new retail stores—some 12 to 15 a year—are being added under its business development program. . . ."

On Container Corporation of America:

"Reflecting the broad diversity of its packaging applications, Container is a custom manufacturer, producing its packaging products only in response to specific orders. . . ."

With respect to Mobil's management philosophy:

Basic to the Mobil organization's management philosophy is the willingness to speak out on public policy affecting its business. Recognizing the critical necessity of a favorable climate for investment and operations, all levels of management are actively involved in public affairs. We give our views, repeatedly, and as wisely as we know how, on such issues as the need to develop additional sources of energy through encouragement of capital information. And we strive for the elimination of impediments to investment, such as counterproductive price controls and unrealistic environmental restrictions. . . .

The Mobil organization's strategy is conceived by a management that does not fear innovation or aggressiveness in the shareholders' interest.

We are not just aware of our customers' and shareholders' interests. We fight for them.

29. Alabama Power Company*

IN MID-1976, management officials of Alabama Power Company (APCo) were considering what strategic options they had following the Alabama Public Service Commission's decision to deny the company any of the $106.8 million increase in retail rates which had been requested. In flatly rejecting the entire $106.8 million rate increase (the largest rate increase ever requested by an Alabama utility), the PSC contended that Alabama Power Company's earnings and financial condition did not warrant a rate increase. The Commission said that the company could get along without a rate increase if it would:

1. Cut out all advertising programs—a saving to the company and to ratepayers of $920,000.
2. Eliminate $210,000 in charitable contributions.
3. Sell a 25 percent interest in the company's Farley nuclear plant in Dothan, Alabama, to rural electric cooperatives or to other subsidiaries of Alabama Power's parent the Southern Company, the revenues from which would result in some $200 million to Southern Co. and an actual savings to APCo's customers of $4.1 million.
4. Reduce the rate of return on common stock from nearly 20 percent (which two members of the PSC alleged the company was earning) to 13.2 percent. This reduction in the rate of return corresponded to some $80 million of the $106.8 million in rates that the Commission said APCo did not deserve.
5. Change one of the company's accounting practices to save $1.5 million.

APCo's president Joseph Farley in a press release criticized the PSC decision as "unrealistic and shortsighted" and said it would be appealed to the courts. Farley also said, "Without a doubt, future service to our customers is in serious question. Unless we can obtain a prompt reversal, the decision will have a devastating effect on our needed construction work."

The ruling marked the first time the PSC ever completely denied an Alabama Power rate increase request. Commissioners Chris C. Whatley and Jim Zeigler overrode recommendations of their own staff that the company be

---

* Prepared by Professor Arthur A. Thompson, Jr., The University of Alabama.

given at least an $8 million increase and also rejected the testimony of the PSC's own expert witness and special consultant, Dr. Matityahu Marcus, professor of economics at Rutgers University, that the company be allowed an increase of some $70 million of its $106.8 million request. In commenting to reporters after the decision was announced, Commissioner Whatley said he believed that the order would stand up in court, but conceded it depended on several unusual approaches to rate regulation. Commissioner Zeigler said of the decision, "It shows there is a solid majority for the consumer on the PSC now. The evidence clearly showed the rate increase was unnecessary. Alabama Power is in good financial condition."

Commissioner Juanita McDaniel, who defeated Zeigler in a runoff for the Democratic nomination for president of the Alabama PSC just one month earlier, dissented in the PSC decision but did not indicate how much of an increase she thought Alabama Power should have been granted. She said the other two PSC members ignored "historical rate-making practices" and that "The action taken, in my opinion, will not stand the legal test in court. I would be willing to bet the company is very pleased with that order."

GENERAL PROBLEMS OF THE ELECTRIC UTILITY INDUSTRY

During the 1970s, the electric utility industry experienced problems in a number of areas: (1) sharp increases in operating costs and construction costs owing to high inflation rates in the economy; (2) major increases in the cost of fuel for generating electric energy; (3) escalating interest rates on long-term securities; (4) difficulties in trying to raise exceptionally large amounts of both debt and equity capital to finance new construction programs; (5) difficulty in earning a sufficient rate of return on invested capital and in securing adequate and timely rate increases; (6) difficulty in meeting coverages on long-term bonds and preferred stock, as required in mortgage agreements and charters; (7) rising costs associated with complying with environmental regulations; (8) licensing and other delays affecting the construction of new facilities; (9) the effects of energy conservation and economic recession on the use of electric energy.

Alabama Power Company and the other operating affiliates of the Southern Company system experienced these problems in varying degrees, and in 1975 and 1976, announced substantial reductions in previously planned construction programs. The reductions were prompted by difficulties in financing, new estimates of increased construction costs, inadequate earnings coverages on securities, and an apparent shift in the projected rate of growth in the demand for electric energy.

COMPANY BACKGROUND AND GENERAL DESCRIPTION

Alabama Power Company is engaged in the generation, transmission, distribution, and sale of electricity in 56 of Alabama's 67 counties (parts or all of

11 counties in north Alabama are served by TVA). As of 1976, APCo distributed electric power at retail to customers in 639 communities, as well as in rural areas and at wholesale to 15 municipalities, 11 rural electric cooperatives, and one generating and transmitting cooperative. Total population in the company's service area was approximately 2.8 million persons. The company owned substantial coal reserves near its Gorgas steam-electric generating plant and used the output of coal from these reserves in its generating plants.

APCo also sold electric appliances through its own outlets—in addition to cooperating with dealers in selling electric appliances. The company's overall market share of the electric appliance business throughout its service territory was an estimated 5 percent.

As of 1976, Alabama Power owned and operated 13 hydroelectric and 6 steam-electric (coal-fired) generating plants. It was part owner of two other generating plants. The rated capacity of all of APCo's generating plants was 6,387,750 kilowatts. Through August 31, 1975, the all-time maximum demand from APCo's customers was 5,566,700 kilowatts (August 25, 1975).

ASPECTS OF POWER GENERATION AND POWER SUPPLY

An electric system consists of one or more generating plants interconnected by transmission lines which are connected to distribution lines through substations and other voltage transformation facilities. The distribution facilities, in turn, are connected to the electric facilities and equipment of various residential, commercial, and industrial customers. Unlike other enterprises, electric utilities are less able to regulate production rates and sales volumes. Users of electricity can change the demands upon a utility's electric system and utilize more or less electric energy by simply pushing a button, pulling a switch, or otherwise exercising their freedom to operate (or not to operate) a particular electrical device or series of equipment or machinery. Customers are also free to add new equipment and facilities activated by electric energy without prior notification. The degree to which customers place their electricity-using equipment in operation varies widely with the hour of the day, the day of the week, and the month of the year. Peak loads are typically encountered between 11:00 A.M. and 3:00 P.M. on a daily basis, during weekdays rather than on weekends, and in either summer or winter, depending on whether the utility is in a hot or cold climate. Alabama Power Company, along with its other affiliates in the Southern Company, experiences summer peaks due to the heavy use of air conditioning in its service area.

There is, of course, no way for an electric utility to store electric energy. It must be generated, transmitted, and distributed on an instantaneous basis in the precise amount required to meet the electric loads or demands being imposed by the aggregate utilization of all the utility's customers. Alabama Power Company, like other electric utilities, took the position that it *must* meet all the demands being imposed at any given time and thereby have available for instantaneous operation the necessary generating, transmission, and distribution facilities to meet the demand. This policy existed mainly out of a desire and responsibility to serve the full needs of customers and secondarily to protect the company's electric system from "brownouts" and damage that would necessitate extended and expensive repair work. Electric generators are constructed with characteristics which cause them to cease turning if the load or drag becomes greater than their capacity. Thus, if at any given time the total demand upon an electric system exceeds its capacity, the generating plants, unless otherwise disconnected from the load, will become overtaxed, cease operating, and discontinue supplying any electric energy to the system. The system can be reactivated only when a balanced relationship is restored between customer demand and supply capability. As a general rule of thumb, electric utilities seek to maintain a generating capability (nameplate-rated capacity) at least 15 percent greater than the maximum peak demand load they expect to encounter. This 15 percent margin provides not only a measure of safety against an unusually large peak load but also allows the firm to meet peak demands even if it should experience a breakdown in one of its generating units.

RELATIONSHIP WITH THE SOUTHERN COMPANY

Alabama Power Company is a wholly owned subsidiary of the Southern Company, the third largest electric utility firm in the nation. The Southern Company is a regulated public utility holding company and is the parent firm of Alabama Power Company, Georgia Power Company (serving almost all of Georgia), Gulf Power Company (serving the western part of the Florida Panhandle), and Mississippi Power Company (serving southeastern Mississippi). The Southern Company system also included Southern Services, Inc., which provided engineering, financial, R&D, statistical, technical, and management services, at cost, to Southern's four operating affiliates.

The Securities and Exchange Commission in 1947, after several years of investigation and analysis, concluded that Alabama Power, Georgia Power, Gulf Power, and Mississippi Power by reason of their location, physical interconnection, and history of coordinated operation constituted an appropriate holding company system in accordance with the Public Utility Holding Company Act of 1935.[1] In approving the formation of the Southern Company system, the SEC noted that the four operating companies "had a history of common planning, development and operation commencing in the middle 1920s and that since 1930 the central load dispatching office in Birmingham,

---

[1] The Public Utility Holding Company Act had as one of its principal objectives the restructuring of the electric utility industry to break up the large holding company systems which were then scattered across the nation. The Act was aimed at eliminating all holding company systems except those embracing operating companies which were physically interconnected and could be economically integrated in such a manner as to improve the reliability and economy of electric service.

Alabama, has closely coordinated the use of the generating capacity and the power interchange among the companies pursuant to contractual arrangements which exist among them." The SEC further observed that the affiliated companies would be operated in such a manner as to be responsive to local regulation and control, and that the customers of each of the operating companies would benefit from coordinated planning, diversity of loads, and other advantages which naturally flow from the interconnection and integration of electric utilities in position to give mutual assistance and aid to one another.

In the opinion of Alabama Power Company management, benefits that result from interconnected operation of the character engaged in by the operating affiliates of the Southern Company system include economies arising from (1) staggered construction of generating plants so that each of the four operating companies can take advantage of building the maximum optimum-size generating units; (2) differences in the timing of peak loads which occur among the four operating companies; (3) locating their respective hydroelectric operations so as to capitalize upon the diversity among various watersheds in the Southeast; (4) combining and programming their energy loads in such a manner as to fully utilize hydro-resources at a time of high water flows; (5) coordination of maintenance operations; and (6) the opportunity of the companies to implement a computerized, coordinated dispatch of power from all generating plants that takes into account the relative efficiencies of different generating units, the operative fuel costs at the respective plants, and the transmission line losses, all on an incremental (marginal cost) basis.

Each of the four operating affiliates has its own president and board of directors and issues first mortgage bonds and preferred stock in its own name. The Southern Company issues common stock in its name (traded on the NYSE), but does not issue any long-term debt securities.

FINANCIAL AND OPERATING HIGHLIGHTS OF THE SOUTHERN COMPANY

Summarized below are selected operating and financial statistics for the Southern Company system:

	1975	1974	1973	1970	1965
Operating statistics					
Operating revenues*	$1,998.9	$1,489.0	$1,165.8	$738.1	$446.8
Operating expenses*	1,601.2	1,216.1	896.6	566.3	338.9
Operating income*	397.7	272.9	269.2	171.8	108.0
Other income, net*	154.4	121.1	85.6	22.4	4.4
Interest charges*	273.3	233.4	176.2	79.4	39.0
Preferred dividends*	40.6	37.7	30.5	14.1	7.7
Net income (after pref. div.)* ..	238.2	122.9	148.2	100.7	65.7

Earnings per share	$2.26	$1.41	$2.07	$1.94	$1.38
Dividends per share	$1.40	$1.395	$1.34	$1.215	$0.915
Market price per share:					
High........................	15⅛	17¼	20⅞	28⅞	36⅛
Low	8¾	8⅝	14¾	19	31
Book value per share	$16.89	$16.58	$18.22	$16.33	$11.83
Average kwh use per					
residential customer	10,140	9,852	10,267	8,777	5,734
Average revenue per kwh.					
(total sales)	2.63 ¢	2.00 ¢	1.58 ¢	1.25 ¢	1.26 ¢
Average cost of fuel					
per kwh (mills)	11.08	8.69	4.94	3.21	2.58
Electric energy sales (in					
billions of kwh)					
Residential	20.28	19.40	19.59	15.47	8.84
Commercial	15.56	14.80	14.69	11.06	6.48
Industrial	25.96	26.72	26.57	22.01	14.88
Other	12.81	12.15	12.16	8.91	4.84

* In millions of dollars.

The very modest increases in kilowatt hour sales during the 1973–75 period were far below the Southern system's historical growth rate of nearly 10 percent per year. Southern attributed the reduced growth rate mainly to the effects of recession—particularly in the textile, automotive, chemical, and primary metal industries. But a portion was also due to mild weather and to increased efforts of some customers to conserve on electric energy—an effort precipitated both by publicity regarding the "energy crisis" and by comparatively sharp increases in electric rates. Even so, the average use per residential customer (10,140 kwh in 1975) was some 2,000 kwh greater than the national average for all investor-owned electric utilities. As of 1975, Southern's marketing activities were primarily aimed at informing customers of ways to use energy more efficiently and economically.

Southern's fuel expenses for 1975 consumed 38 percent of each revenue dollar. This compared with an average of 31 percent for the 1970–74 period. Virtually all of the energy sales made by Southern's four operating companies were covered by fuel cost adjustment clauses designed to adjust rates automatically to reflect increases and decreases in the cost of fuel and, in some cases, the increased cost of electric energy purchased from neighboring utilities. Total labor costs in 1975 rose 9.1 percent over 1974 and consumed 7.5 percent of 1975 revenues.

Two of Southern's major expenses were interest costs on long-term debt and dividend requirements on preferred stock. Interest and preferred stock dividend payments exceeded $313 million in 1975, up 16 percent over 1974. The interest and dividend rates on total outstanding preferred stock, first-mortgage bonds, and pollution control bonds rose from an *average* rate of 4.17 percent in 1965 to 7.56 percent in 1975.

The companies of the Southern System obtained more new capital in the stock and bond markets in 1975 ($690 million) than any other electric utility system in the United States. This included sales of $349 million in first-mortgage bonds, $105 million of preferred stock, $91 million of tax-exempt pollution-control revenue bonds, and 11 million shares of common stock at $12.50 per share with a total net yield to company of $130,790,000. Southern's common equity investments in its four operating affiliates in 1975 were as follows: Alabama Power—$67 million, Georgia Power—$35.1 million, Gulf Power—$1.8 million, and Mississippi Power—$8 million.

In January 1976, Alabama Power Company sold $50 million (500,000 shares) of preferred stock. In February 1976, Mississippi Power Company sold $25 million in first-mortgage bonds; that same month Alabama Power sold $12.9 million of pollution-control revenue bonds. In March 1976, the Southern Company raised approximately $285 million through the sale of 11 million shares of common stock at $15 per share and the sale to institutional investors of $125 million in notes due in 1980, 1981, and 1982. Also in March, Alabama Power sold $50 million in 30-year, 8.875 percent first-mortgage bonds at an annual interest cost to the company of 9.065 percent.

The Southern Company system's stated goal was a consolidated capital structure consisting of 55–57 percent long-term debt, 10–12 percent preferred stock, and 31–33 percent common equity.

The following retail rate applications were filed by or approved for the four operating companies in 1975:

			Test-Year Revenues	
Company	Date Filed	Date Granted	Amount Requested	Amount Granted
Alabama Power	6/14/74	1/14/75	$ 64,500,000	$ 54,200,000
	12/20/74	1/1/75		8,182,000*
	11/26/75		106,800,000	5,418,000*
Georgia Power	11/12/74	1/6/75	85,900,000	35,000,000†
		2/6/75		25,000,000†
	12/17/74	4/24/75	305,200,000	116,000,000
Gulf Power	6/2/74	5/7/75	22,400,000	20,200,000
Mississippi Power	11/7/75		14,300,000	

* Revisions in fuel clause adjustment resulted in test-year revenues of $8,182,000; a temporary surcharge January 1–March 31, 1975 produced $5,418,000.
† A temporary fuel clause surcharge.

In addition, the four companies had, at the end of 1975, wholesale rate increase requests of $49.5 million awaiting final approval by the Federal Power Commission.

Southern Company's total construction budget for 1976 called for expenditures of $1.1 billion, as compared to $992 million in 1975, and $1.2 billion in 1974. However, in 1974, Georgia Power suspended plans for construction of two units of a major nuclear plant (1,160,000 kilowatts each) in which $73,054,000 had already been invested; the company estimated that if the two units were ultimately cancelled, additional cancellation costs of $30 million would be incurred. In early 1976, Alabama Power announced the postponement for rescheduling of the first two units (1.2 million kilowatts each) of its Barton nuclear plant; construction costs already incurred for these two units totaled $18.7 million out of a total estimated cost of $1.98 billion. Further, APCo announced a one-year delay in the planned commercial operation dates of two steam units (660,000 kilowatts each) under construction; APCo attributed the delay to the company's inability to raise capital in adequate amounts to finance escalating construction costs.

REGULATION

In 1920, the Alabama legislature passed a bill creating the Alabama Public Service Commission and giving it the authority to regulate Alabama Power Company with respect to the issuance of securities, the extensions of its electric plant, the rates and charges for the service it provides, and related matters concerning the exercise of its public utility responsibility.

The Alabama PSC is responsible for seeing that every utility under its jurisdiction:

> . . . shall maintain its plant, facilities and equipment in good operating condition and shall set up and maintain proper reserves for renewals, replacements and reasonable contingencies. Every utility shall render adequate service to the public and shall make such reasonable improvements, extensions and enlargements of its plants, facilities, and equipment as may be necessary to meet the growth and demand of the territory which it is under the duty to serve.

Alabama Power is precluded from constructing any plant, property, or facility for production, transmission, delivery, or furnishing of electricity except ordinary extensions of its existing system in the usual course of business without first obtaining approval from the Commission and being issued a "certificate of convenience and necessity." A public hearing must be held before the Alabama PSC may issue such a certificate.

In addition, Alabama Power is prohibited from issuing securities (stocks and/or bonds) until application is made to the Commission and the Commission has determined that the securities issue is for some lawful object within the corporate purposes of the utility, is compatible with the public interest, and is necessary or consistent with the proper performance by the utility of its service to the public.

The section of the law governing the Public Service Commission's rate-fixing standards specifically provides the rates and charges for services rendered and required "shall be reasonable and just to both the utility and the public." This section further provides that every utility "shall be entitled to such just and reasonable rates as will enable it at all times to fully perform its duties to the public and will, under honest, efficient and economical management, earn a fair net return on the reasonable value of its property devoted to the public service." Moreover, the Commission "shall give due consideration, among other things, to the requirements of the business with respect to the utility under consideration, and the necessity, under honest, efficient and economical management of such utility, of enlarging plants, facilities and equipment of the utility under consideration, in order to provide that portion of the public served thereby with adequate service."

The Federal Power Commission has jurisdiction over the rates charged by Alabama Power Company in selling electric power at wholesale, such as sales to municipal and electric cooperative distribution systems, and where transactions involve the use of electric facilities interconnected with electric facilities located in other states.

Section 201 of the Federal Power Act declares "that the business of transmitting and selling electric energy for ultimate distribution to the public is affected with a public interest, and that Federal regulation of matters relating to generation . . . and . . . the transmission of electric energy in interstate commerce and the sale of such energy at wholesale in interstate commerce is necessary in the public interest." Section 202 confers specific powers upon the FPC "for the purpose of assuring an abundant supply of electric energy throughout the United States with the greatest possible economy and with regard to the proper utilization and conservation of natural resources."

Alabama Power must also obtain licenses from the FPC to build and operate hydroelectric facilities. When such licenses expire, the federal government, by an act of Congress, may take over the project or the FPC may relicense the project either to the original licensee or to a new licensee. In the event of takeover or relicensing to another, Alabama Power would be entitled to recover its net investment in the project (not in excess of the fair value of the property taken) plus reasonable damages to any other property directly associated with loss of the hydroelectric facilities. In 1976, APCo had pending before the FPC applications for relicensing and further development of its hydroelectric plants at Mitchell Dam (72,500 kilowatts), Martin Dam (154,200 kilowatts) and Jordan Dam (100,000 kilowatts).[2] The original expiration dates were 1971 for Mitchell Dam, 1973 for Martin Dam, and 1975 for Jordan Dam. Pending action on its relicensing applications, APCo had year-to-year licenses for these projects. The redevelopment plans included adding new generating capacity of 80,000 kilowatts at Mitchell Dam and 60,000 kilowatts at Martin Dam.

As with other corporations engaged in interstate commerce, the Securities

---

[2] Besides these projects, Alabama Power had pending before the FPC plans for reconstructing Walter Bouldin Dam which in February 1975 experienced a break that caused extensive damage and resulted in the loss of the dam's 225,000 kilowatt generating capacity. The company estimated that the major portion of the roughly $40 million–$50 million in repair costs was recoverable through insurance coverage.

and Exchange Commission maintains continuous surveillance over the financing activities of Alabama Power Company. APCo is required to register the sale of all of its securities with the SEC and it is prohibited from issuing or selling any bonds, preferred stock, or common stock that do not comply with SEC policies and regulations.

Alabama Power is required to comply with the regulations of the Energy Research and Development Administration in constructing and operating nuclear plants. ERDA has dominion over matters concerning the public health, safety, and environmental impact of a proposed nuclear plant; ERDA is also empowered to investigate the benefits of nuclear plants relative to other means of power generation as a basis for deciding whether to issue construction permits. Issuance of operating licenses by ERDA may be conditioned upon requiring changes in operating techniques or upon the installation of additional equipment to meet safety or environmental standards; moreover, opportunity is provided for interested parties to request a public hearing on health, safety, or environmental issues.

Alabama Power is also subject to regulation by the Corps of Engineers, the Alabama Water Improvement Commission, the Alabama Air Pollution Control Commission, and Alabama Public Health Department with respect to the construction and operation of plant facilities which could have an impact upon the environment.

RATE SCHEDULES OF ALABAMA POWER COMPANY

When Alabama Power requests permission to alter rate schedules, it is customary for the Public Service Commission to inquire into the factors which have influenced the company to seek changes in its rate schedules. The company must furnish whatever pertinent information is requested and, in particular, must present in public hearings justification for its request. This justification includes an analysis of all costs incurred in its electric service operations during a particular time frame, usually referred to as a *test year,* and a determination of what level of revenue would have been required during the test year to cover the company's costs and also provide a fair net return on the company's property devoted to its electric service operations.

In the early days of Alabama Power Company's operations, when its customers were scattered and fewer uses were made of the company's electric service, most residential customers utilized electric energy for lighting purposes only. The unit cost of electric service was relatively high. However, as electric service became more popular during the 1920s, 1930s, and 1940s, and the company's service became available on a broader scale, more and more people began to utilize electricity for a growing range of purposes. With the increased utilization and improvement in the density of electric consumers, along with improvements in the art and technology of providing electric service, definite economies were achieved, with the result that during the 1920s and continuing into the 1960s, Alabama Power Company fol-

EXHIBIT 1

**Summary of Actions Taken on Rate Increase Applications Filed
by Alabama Power Company***

Date Filed	Amount Requested	Amount Granted	Effective Date of Order	Commissioners For	Against
2-27-68	$ 7,396,981	$ 6,994,981*	4-18-69	Connor Owen	Pool
11-6-70	$19,946,600	$16,923,364	4-29-71	Connor Owen	McDaniel
6-9-72	$29,900,000	$26,900,000	12-13-72	Connor Owen	McDaniel
8-12-74	$64,484,144†	$7,577,955†	9-26-74	Owen McDaniel	Hammond
6-14-74	$64,484,144	$54,182,268	1-14-75	Owen McDaniel Hammond	

* Alabama Power Company filed no rate *increase* applications with the Alabama Public Service Commission prior to 1968.

† An emergency interim rate increase effective only from September 30, 1974 until January 14, 1975.

EXHIBIT 2

**How APCo's Average kwh Price for Industrial Electricity Compared
with the U.S. Average, 1960–1975**

Year	Average kwh Price of Industrial Electricity (in cents per kwh) APCo	United States	Amount APCo Average Was below U.S. Average	Percent APCo Price Was below (above) U.S. Average
1960	0.8654 ¢	0.9669 ¢	0.1015 ¢	10.5%
1961	0.8673	0.9701	0.1028	10.6
1962	0.8625	0.9604	0.0979	10.2
1963	0.8495	0.9258	0.0763	8.2
1964	0.8248	0.9118	0.0870	9.5
1965	0.8069	0.8964	0.0895	10.0
1966	0.8047	0.8891	0.0844	9.5
1967	0.8022	0.8981	0.0959	10.7
1968	0.7998	0.9005	0.1007	11.2
1969	0.8254	0.9054	0.0800	8.8
1970	0.8260	0.9485	0.1225	12.9
1971	0.9096	1.0349	0.1253	12.1
1972	1.0160	1.0921	0.0761	7.0
1973	1.1725	1.1749	0.0024	0.2
1974	1.5060	1.5482	0.0422	2.7
1975	1.9369	1.9208	+0.0161	(+0.8)

Sources: Alabama Power Company and Edison Electric Institute, *Statistical Year Book*, as reprinted in *EEI Pocketbook Statistics*, pp. 17–18.

EXHIBIT 3
How APCo's Average kwh Price for Commercial Electric Service Compared with the U.S. Average, 1960–1975

Year	Average kwh Price for Commercial Electric Service (in cents per kwh)		Amount APCo Average Was below the U.S. Average	Percent APCo's Price Was below the U.S. Average
	APCo	United States		
1960	1.9677 ¢	2.4634 ¢	0.4957 ¢	20.1%
1961	1.9680	2.3484	0.3804	16.2
1962	1.9309	2.3734	0.4425	18.6
1963	1.9183	2.2751	0.3568	15.7
1964	1.9023	2.1951	0.2928	13.3
1965	1.8585	2.1341	0.2756	12.9
1966	1.8417	2.0580	0.2163	10.5
1967	1.8301	2.0355	0.2054	10.1
1968	1.8142	2.0041	0.1899	9.5
1969	1.8136	1.9899	0.1763	8.9
1970	1.7336	2.0109	0.2773	13.8
1971	1.8718	2.1186	0.2468	11.6
1972	1.9685	2.2219	0.2534	11.4
1973	2.1963	2.3046	0.1083	4.7
1974	2.5528	2.8513	0.2985	10.5
1975	3.0480	3.2259	0.1779	5.5

Sources: Alabama Power Company and Edison Electric Institute, *Statistical Year Book,* as reprinted in *EEI Pocketbook Statistics,* pp. 17–18.

EXHIBIT 4
How APCo's Average kwh Price for Residential Electric Service Compared with the U.S. Average, 1960–1975

Year	Average kwh Price of Residential Electric Service (in cents per kwh)		Amount APCo Average Was below U.S. Average	Percent APCo Average Was below U.S. Average
	APCo	United States		
1960	1.8398 ¢	2.4725 ¢	0.6327 ¢	25.6%
1961	1.8354	2.4478	0.6124	25.0
1962	1.7854	2.4107	0.6253	25.9
1963	1.7686	2.3678	0.5992	25.3
1964	1.7328	2.3057	0.5729	24.8
1965	1.7172	2.2523	0.5351	23.8
1966	1.6963	2.1963	0.5000	22.8
1967	1.6884	2.1671	0.4787	22.1
1968	1.6926	2.1218	0.4292	20.2
1969	1.7716	2.0919	0.3203	15.3
1970	1.7020	2.1027	0.4007	19.1
1971	1.7964	2.1885	0.3921	17.9
1972	1.8982	2.2937	0.3955	17.2
1973	2.0788	2.3809	0.3021	12.7
1974	2.4442	2.8293	0.3851	13.6
1975	2.9723	3.2079	0.2356	7.3

Sources: Alabama Power Company and Edison Electric Institute, *Statistical Year Book,* as reprinted in *EEI Pocketbook Statistics,* p. 35.

EXHIBIT 5
Typical Residential Electric Bills, January 1976

Area and Company	250 kwh	750 kwh	1,000 kwh	2,000 kwh
New York City (Consolidated Edison)	$19.67	$53.77	$70.81	$139.0
Boston (Boston Edison Co.)	15.23	40.90	54.13	85.1
Portions of New Jersey (Public Service Electric & Gas)	16.79	39.96	51.26	96.4
Philadelphia (Philadelphia Electric Co.)	13.25	37.70	48.89	93.6
Long Island (Long Island Lighting Co.)	13.90	36.11	45.64	83.7
Manchester (Public Service Co. of N.H.)	15.17	33.93	44.75	80.4
Delaware (Delmarva Power & Light)	15.92	35.33	43.41	72.8
Virginia, East of Chesapeake Bay (Delmarva Power & Light)	16.15	34.65	42.96	74.4
St. Petersburg (Florida Power Corp.)	12.51	32.38	41.54	78.2
Maryland, East of Chesapeake Bay (Delmarva Power & Light)	15.32	33.49	41.17	70.27
Hartford (Connecticut Light & Power Co.)	15.24	33.04	41.03	73.0
Southern Portion of New Jersey (Atlantic City Electric Co.)	14.80	33.06	40.59	70.70
San Diego (San Diego Gas & Electric Co.)	11.94	30.86	40.26	77.85
Chicago and Northern Illinois (Commonwealth Edison)	11.67	30.57	40.01	77.81
Los Angeles (Dept. of Water & Power)	12.55	30.03	38.56	70.39
Jacksonville, Fla. (Jacksonville Electric Authority)	12.22	30.00	38.38	70.13
Connecticut (The Hartford Electric Light Co.)	14.27	28.21	37.14	72.86
San Antonio (City Public Service)	11.14	28.55	37.01	70.87
Baltimore (Baltimore Gas and Electric Co.)	13.75	30.06	37.01	64.81
Northeast Ohio (The Cleveland Electric Illum. Co.)	10.96	28.38	36.84	60.67
Orlando (Orlando Utilities Commission)	12.64	28.74	36.80	69.01
Northern West Virginia (Monongahela Power Co.)	13.16	29.22	36.65	62.94
Portions of Florida (Florida Power & Light Co.)	11.53	28.33	35.89	66.10
Portions of Southern California (So. California Edison)	12.18	27.82	35.19	63.02
Southeastern Michigan (The Detroit Edison Co.)	11.20	26.99	35.18	67.96
St. Louis (Union Electric Co.)	10.53	27.17	34.96	60.73
Arizona (Arizona Public Service Co.)	12.32	27.01	32.87	54.00
Raleigh (Carolina Power & Light Co.)	11.08	24.51	32.35	64.38
Eastern Maine (Bangor Hydro-Electric Co.)	11.64	25.64	31.85	56.70
Portions of Georgia (Georgia Power Co.)	9.33	23.35	30.01	52.27
Roanoke, Va. (Appalachian Power Co.)	10.31	22.48	28.02	49.50
Houston (Houston Lighting & Power Co.)	10.22	22.50	27.45	47.25
Portions of Alabama (Alabama Power Co.)	10.20	21.89	27.14	45.04
Dallas (Dallas Power & Light Co.)	9.70	21.85	27.12	48.20
San Francisco (Pacific Gas & Electric Co.)	7.99	20.24	26.33	50.68
Chattanooga (Electric Power Board of Chattanooga)	9.60	19.78	24.41	42.89
Memphis (Memphis Light, Gas & Water Division)	9.11	19.19	23.79	42.17

Source: Compiled by Jacksonville Electric Authority, Jacksonville, Florida.

lowed a general pattern of filing for and obtaining rate decrease after rate decrease.

It was not until 1968 that the company first filed an application for a general increase in its retail electric rates. While the Alabama Public Service Commission did not allow the company all of the increase it sought in 1968, it did allow rate increases averaging slightly more than 3 percent. The Commission also allowed the company to implement various fuel and tax adjustment provisions which enabled the company to recover reimbursement for increases in power costs and increases in certain taxes imposed upon the company's electric operations. By late 1970, the rates as revised in the 1968 case were deemed insufficient and the company sought rate increases averaging 8.5 percent; the Commission allowed an increase in retail rates amounting to approximately $16.9 million or an average 7.2 percent increase. Exhibit 1 summarizes APCo's rate increase requests and the amounts granted by the Alabama PSC.

Available data suggests that APCo's retail electric rates in 1976 were lower than those charged by many investor-owned utilities throughout the country. See the data shown in Exhibits 2, 3, 4, and 5.

APCO'S CONSTRUCTION PROGRAM

In 1975, Alabama Power spent $448 million on new construction; future plans called for plant additions and construction outlays of $491.1 million in 1976, $447.1 million in 1977, and $616 million in 1978. Exhibit 6 depicts the company's expenditures for generating facilities in 1975. Exhibits 7 and 8 present APCo's actual and planned construction outlays for the 1971–78 period and the sources of funds for plant additions during the 1971–76 period.

FINANCIAL CONSIDERATIONS

A key factor affecting the ability of Alabama Power to finance its construction program was the ratio of earnings to interest costs and to preferred stock dividends. These ratios are sometimes referred to in financial circles as "coverages." The mortgage indenture entered into by Alabama Power in 1942 (which the company has no authority to change without the consent of all bondholders) provided in effect that before the company could issue additional first-mortgage bonds, its before-tax operating income had to be great enough to cover pro forma annual interest charges on all such securities outstanding by at least two times. Hence APCo could not raise capital through first-mortgage bonds if a new issue would cause its coverage to fall below 2 times earnings (nor, of course, could it issue any new bonds if its coverage was already below the 2.0 level).

For the issuance of new preferred stock, APCo's charter required that the company have sufficient profits before interest charges, but after taxes, to cover pro forma annual interest charges on all debt plus preferred stock dividends (including any new issues) by at least one and one-half times. Hence, new preferred stock issues were forbidden if earnings were less than 1.5 times the total charges on indebtedness and on preferred stock dividend requirements. In both cases the coverage requirements had to be met for a period of 12 consecutive months within the 15 calendar months immediately preceding any proposed new issue.

EXHIBIT 6
Alabama Power Company's Estimated Expenditures for Generating Facilities, 1975

Plant and Location	Nameplate Capacity* (kilowatts)	Planned Commercial Operation Date	Type Fuel	Thousands of Dollars			Estimated Cost per Kilowatt
				Expenditures through 1974	1975 Estimated Expenditures	Total Estimated Cost	
Joseph M. Farley Nuclear Plant located near Dothan:							
Unit 1	860,000	1976	Nuclear	$385,797	$ 87,426	$ 494,911	$576
Unit 2	860,000	1977	Nuclear	146,847	109,148	378,605	441
Rother L. Harris Hydro Plant located in Randolph County.......	135,000	1979	Hydro	2,244	3,036	62,000	459
James H. Miller, Jr., Steam Plant located near Birmingham:							
Unit 1	660,000	1978	Coal	17,509	49,177	225,198	341
Unit 2	660,000	1979	Coal	132	2,655	161,733	245
Unit 3	660,000	1980	Coal	12	88	192,615	292
Alan R. Barton Nuclear Plant located in Chilton and Elmore counties:							
Unit 1	1,200,000	1984	Nuclear	10,488	8,000	1,061,042	884
Unit 2	1,200,000	1985	Nuclear	180	247	923,027	769
Other (including improvements of $37,171,000 to existing generating facilities)					48,368		
					$308,145		

* Nameplate ratings reflect turbine capability under certain conditions specified during manufacture and may vary from capacities originally announced.

EXHIBIT 7
Expenditures for Gross Plant Additions, 1971–1978 (in thousands of dollars)

	Estimated*			Actual				
	1978	1977	1976	1975	1974	1973	1972	1971
Electric:								
Production	$340,778	$279,433	$313,173	$317,400	$289,136	$275,861	$172,688	$137,235
Transmission	61,933	46,702	43,596	46,552	35,139	34,014	27,792	28,860
Distribution	88,576	66,368	59,125	50,921	60,051	53,736	49,788	41,129
General	42,104	17,725	19,193	19,310	24,229	8,876	5,394	4,051
Total Electric	$533,391	$410,228	$435,087	$434,183	$408,555	$372,487	$255,662	$211,275
Steam heat	363	381	347	126	429	1,671	1,605	866
Nuclear fuel	82,220	36,475	55,705	13,657	19,890	8,956	71	16
Total	$615,974	$447,084	$491,139	$447,966	$428,874	$383,114	$257,338	$212,157

Actual:
5-Year total (1971–75) .... $1,729,449   Represents 58 percent of gross plant at December 31, 1975
10-Year total (1966–75) .... $2,190,426   Represents 74 percent of gross plant at December 31, 1975

Estimated:
3-Year total (1976–78) .... $1,554,197   Will represent 35 percent of gross plant at December 31, 1978
13-Year total (1966–78) .... $3,744,623   Will represent 84 percent of gross plant at December 31, 1978

* Estimated as of October 1975.

EXHIBIT 8
Sources of Funds for Plant Additions, 1971–1976

	1976 Estimated		Five Years 1971–75 Inclusive		Actual				
	Amount	Percent	Amount	Percent	1975	1974	1973	1972	1971
Internal sources									
Depreciation and amortization	$ 58,591	11.9%	$ 213,139	12.3%	$ 52,217	$ 46,541	$ 41,859	$ 38,630	$ 33,892
Deferred income taxes, net	31,599	6.4	115,623	6.7	49,187	28,034	18,559	12,235	7,608
Investment tax credits	—	—	32,687	1.9	17,715	—	2,476	7,908	4,588
Reinvested earnings			53,059	3.0	17,782	2,194	19,289	5,145	8,649
Change in net current assets	(46,044)	(9.3)	(22,974)	(1.3)	2,428	(29,570)	11,630	296	(7,758)
Other internal sources, net	—		(184)	—	(6,830)	(2,000)	(1,063)	(1,269)	10,978
Total from Internal Sources	$ 44,146	9.0%	$ 391,350	22.6%	$132,499	$ 45,199	$ 92,750	$ 62,945	$ 57,957
External sources									
Bonds:									
First mortgage	$ 50,000	10.2%	$ 685,500	39.6%	$135,000	$100,000	$175,000	$190,500	$ 85,000
Refunded, retired, or reacquired	(10)	—	(86,225)	(5.0)	(10)	(7,021)	(8,373)	(70,696)	(125)
Pollution control obligations	24,400	4.9	71,606	4.2	40,405	31,201	—	—	—
Net issues	$ 74,390	15.1%	$ 670,881	38.8%	$175,395	$124,180	$166,627	$119,804	$ 84,875
Preferred stock	50,000	10.2	143,000	8.3	—	35,000	50,000	58,000	—
Paid-in capital	150,000	30.5	333,500	19.3	67,000	115,000	65,000	44,500	42,000
Interim indebtedness (net change)	172,603	35.2	190,718	11.0	73,072	109,495	8,737	(27,911)	27,325
Net external sources	$446,993	91.0%	$1,338,099	77.4%	$315,467	$383,675	$290,364	$194,393	$154,200
Total	$491,139	100.0%	$1,729,449	100.0%	$447,966	$428,874	$383,114	$257,338	$212,157

During the latter part of 1974 and the early part of 1975, APCo's earnings available for coverage requirements were insufficient to permit the issuance of either additional first-mortgage bonds or preferred stock. The company had to postpone a proposed first-mortgage bond issue in the amount of $80 million scheduled for late 1974 and had to structure pollution control revenue bond issues of $29,700,000 (December 1974) and $35 million (April 1975) without the benefit of collateralization with first-mortgage bonds, thereby incurring higher interest costs. However, coverages were sufficient to permit the issuance in May 1975, of $11,024,000 of first-mortgage bonds. The figures below show the coverage ratios which the company maintained in recent years:

Year Ended December 31	Coverage on First-Mortgage Bonds	Coverage on Preferred Stock
1958	5.11	2.63
1964	4.70	2.58
1969	4.26	2.41
1970	3.33	2.04
1971	2.73	1.87
1972	2.23	1.61
1973	2.50	1.71
1974	1.66	1.36
1975	2.29	1.57

The deterioration in the company's coverages stemmed from higher interest rates on new securities issues and on lagging earnings.

Alabama Power's capitalization ratios for selected years of the 1965–75 period were:

Year Ended December 31	Long-term Debt	Preferred Stock	Common Equity
1965	53.7%	10.6%	35.7%
1970	56.0	9.7	34.3
1971	56.9	8.5	34.6
1972	56.1	11.4	32.5
1973	56.0	12.4	31.6
1974	54.3	12.5	33.2
1975	55.9	10.9	33.2

Through 1975, the Southern Company had invested a total of $668 million in the common equity capital of APCo, of which $333 million had been invested since 1970.

Exhibit 8 shows the sources used by APCo to generate the funds for plant additions during 1971–76. The following table summarizes several other financial statistics of Alabama Power Company:

	1971	1972	1973	1974	1975
Net income available for common ($000s)	$39,950	$40,645	$65,089	$ 48,995	$77,782
Rate of return on average common equity (percent)	11.37%	10.12%	13.89%	8.61%	11.60%
Common dividends declared ($000s)	$31,300	$35,500	$45,800	$ 46,800	$60,000
Payout ratios (percent)	78.35%	87.34%	70.37%	95.52%	77.14%
Capital contributions from the Southern Company ($000s)	$42,000	$44,500	$65,000	$115,000	$67,000

At the hearings on its $106.8 million rate increase request, the expert witness for Alabama Power testified that the company needed a 16.5 percent return on common equity to be able to attract the needed capital for new construction and to give the stockholders a fair and reasonable return on their investment. Professor Marcus, the expert witness hired as a consultant to the Alabama PSC, recommended a rate structure commensurate with a 13.2 percent return on common equity.

Also of major concern to APCo's management was the ratings on its first mortgage bonds and preferred stock. Pending the decision by the Alabama PSC on the company's $106.8 million rate increase request, Moody's downgraded APCo's preferred stock from A to Baa in December 1975. Standard & Poor's rated both types of securities A-. However, following the PSC denial of the increase both agencies downgraded their ratings: Moody's to Baa (speculative grade) on both first-mortgage bonds and on seven pollution-control issues and S&P to BBB on first-mortgage bonds. The downgrading of the company's bonds from "investment grade" (an A rating) to "speculative" (Baa) not only meant higher interest rates on new bond issues but also the loss of a significant part of the market for the company's securities. A number of institutional investors (pension funds, insurance companies, savings banks) were precluded by law or by company policy from investing in securities below investment grade.

Testimony given by Mr. Walter Johnsey, executive vice president and chief financial officer, at the public hearings held by the Alabama PSC regarding the $106.8 million rate increase request revealed some additional aspects about the company's financial picture:

> The company's deteriorated financial position has been dramatically demonstrated by such developments as: The 8.62 percent return on average common equity experienced in December 1974—the lowest return on common equity since the wartime year 1944; the cancellation of a first mortgage bond sale in November 1974 of $80 million; cancellation of first mortgage bond and

preferred stock sales planned for April 1975 of $90 million and $30 million, respectively; the forced creation of an unprecedented and unwanted level of interim indebtedness of up to $290 million; and the sale for $11,161,000 and leaseback of five division office buildings which became necessary to ease a severe cash shortage. Insufficient earnings precluded the issuance of additional first mortgage bonds or preferred stock during the test period. Not until October 1975 could the Company issue first mortgage bonds. Even after the sales of $35 million in October and $100 million in December 1975 of first mortgage bonds, the Company ended 1975 with outstanding bank loans of $162,574,000.

To continue the financing of our corporate needs in 1975, the Company, together with Georgia Power Company and the Southern Company, entered into a revolving credit agreement with a consortium of the larger banks in New York and Chicago. Alabama Power Company is limited to a maximum outstanding borrowing under the agreement of $285 million. This revolving credit agreement expired December 31, 1975; however, the Company and the banks negotiated an extension of the agreement to March 31, 1976. The Company and the banks have under consideration a new agreement for bank credit, which would become effective for a two-year period following March 31, 1976. The total amount of credit available under this agreement has yet to be determined. . . . As negotiations move forward, the banks will be looking at what the Company is doing to improve its fixed charge coverage ratios and cash flow, as this will be the only way the banks can be assured that the Company will have cash to pay off the loan agreement.

MARKETING

After the appearance of the energy crisis in late 1973, Alabama Power's marketing efforts underwent significant change. When the Alabama PSC turned down the entire rate increase request in June 1976 and also refused to consider advertising costs as an allowable expense in assessing APCo's rate of return, company officials responded by announcing the cancellation of all media advertising, including ads which informed customers of ways to save on energy. But even before this, the company had stopped actively promoting greater usage of air-conditioning because of the uneven load balance it created on the generating system during summer and winter months. During the 1960s and early 1970s, sharp increases in the use of air-conditioning (both residential and commercial) caused the company to build new generating capacity to handle summer loads; however this capacity went largely unused during the remaining months. To counter this, Alabama Power aimed its marketing efforts at increasing "off-peak" loads so as to increase utilization of its facilities and to increase the revenues from its fixed investment. For example, APCo strived to promote electric heating to increase its wintertime load factor and dusk-to-dawn security lighting to increase its nighttime load factor.

The marketing significance of trying to balance the winter and summer peaks and to increase the overall load factor was that any resulting improvement in the utilization of existing facilities reduced fixed costs per kilowatt hour and paved the way for lower rates. At one point, APCo man-

EXHIBIT 9

Historical Appliance Saturation Rates among APCo's Residential Customers, 1955–1975

Customers Owning	1955	1957	1960	1962	1964	1966	1968	1970	1972	1975
Customer with:				(all figures in percent)						
2 Wire Service	—	—	—	21.3	19.6	14.3	12.4	12.5	9.0	5.6
3 Wire Service	—	—	—	78.2	79.9	84.9	87.2	86.8	90.7	94.1
Other Service	—	—	—	0.6	0.6	0.8	0.4	0.7	0.4	0.3
Natural gas available	—	—	—	66.5	72.6	72.8	73.6	77.4	76.7	76.7
Electric range	36.7	41.6	44.7	49.9	49.2	51.6	54.9	55.2	57.3	59.3
Gas range	—	—	38.4	38.4	40.6	39.4	39.4	42.3	40.9	40.2
Electric water heater	19.2	21.1	23.2	24.8	24.9	27.5	30.6	32.0	34.1	37.7
Standard	—	—	—	—	—	19.0	17.8	15.5	13.0	—
Quick Recovery	—	—	—	—	—	8.5	12.8	16.5	21.1	—
Gas water heater	—	—	51.9	51.9	53.7	54.3	57.7	56.6	59.0	57.3
Total Electric refrigerators	89.2	89.9	93.9	95.5	95.9	96.5	98.3	98.1	99.0	99.6
Frost free electric refrigerators	—	—	—	—	—	10.0	17.2	36.8	44.2	57.8
Gas refrigerators	—	—	2.5	2.5	2.1	1.7	1.5	1.4	0.6	0.2
Separate food freezer	8.8	12.9	16.8	19.7	21.4	23.6	27.6	33.6	39.5	48.5
Electric clothes dryer	1.2	3.5	6.4	8.0	11.7	15.5	22.6	28.9	35.0	44.3
Gas clothes dryer	—	—	1.4	1.4	1.5	1.9	3.0	3.2	3.2	4.5
Automatic clothes washer	21.0	30.5	40.4	44.8	47.2	52.3	55.7	62.5	66.3	72.1
Wringer type washer	35.6	31.5	28.7	25.3	20.1	18.5	15.6	12.4	8.6	4.2
Dishwasher	2.1	2.8	3.3	3.5	4.3	5.2	6.9	14.0	17.3	26.2
Garbage disposal	—	—	—	1.5	1.3	1.9	2.7	5.6	6.2	8.8
Electric compactor	—	—	—	—	—	—	—	—	—	1.5
Total electric air conditioning*	5.4	9.2	15.6	18.1	24.2	30.6	46.0	53.5	59.7	68.5*
Window air conditioning units	—	8.0	13.0	14.0	20.6	24.9	31.4	37.5	40.4	39.0
Total central air conditioning units	—	1.2	2.6	4.1	3.6	5.7	14.6	16.0	19.3	29.9
Central air conditioning units	—	1.1	2.5	3.9	3.1	4.7	12.3	13.5	15.6	24.9
Heat pump air conditioning units	—	0.1	0.1	0.2	0.5	1.0	2.3	2.5	3.7	5.0
Gas air conditioning	—	—	—	—	—	0.6	1.3	1.9	1.7	1.1
Total electric space heating	0.2	0.4	0.6	1.7	2.8	4.4	6.4	6.7	9.8	13.9
Heat pump—Space heating	—	0.1	0.1	0.2	0.3	1.0	2.3	2.5	3.7	5.0
Resistance space heating	0.2	0.3	0.5	1.5	2.5	3.4	4.1	4.2	6.1	8.9
Total gas space heating	—	—	—	—	—	—	75.0	80.8	81.3	80.4
Total television	—	—	—	—	—	—	—	95.2	96.3	97.4
Black and white TV	—	—	—	—	—	—	—	72.5	66.6	55.1
Color TV	—	—	—	—	—	—	—	30.9	46.2	60.7
Has both types	—	—	—	—	—	—	—	8.1	16.5	18.5
Electric post lantern	—	—	—	—	—	—	—	5.5	6.1	5.7
Gas post lantern	—	—	—	—	—	—	—	5.4	5.5	4.9

* Air conditioning subgroups will not add to total air-conditioning saturation since 0.4% of the residential customers own both window and central units.

Source: Alabama Power Company, *The '75 Residential Saturation Survey*, p. 19.

agement estimated that each 1 percent increase in the annual load factor was equivalent to a $2 million increase in rates. The company's load factor was 58.8 percent in 1973, 56.7 percent in 1974, and 56.1 percent in 1975.

Exhibit 9 shows appliance saturation rates among APCo's residential customers for the 1955–75 period. Exhibit 10 shows samples of ads which APCo and the Southern Company ran in various publications.

EXHIBIT 10
Samples of Media Advertising

Behind this simple device lies a profound solution.

The Electric Economy.

Electricity can't serve as an ingredient in medicines, asphalt, synthetic fabrics or fertilizers. For those applications we need oil and natural gas. Even the plastic in a light switch is a derivative of oil.

But that's where the switch to an Electric Economy provides a solution. The simple fact is that electricity can run cars, trucks, trains, entire factories, at the same time conserving gas and oil for jobs that only they can do. Electricity can be generated from a variety of sources. And that's simply more efficient than using up our scarce resources.

At The Southern Company we're concerned about other efficiencies too. The companies in our system are already using coal as fuel for generating more than 80 percent of their output. At our solvent refining research plant, we're studying a method that could raise the heat content of raw coal — more energy for every ounce of fuel. And what's more, the process removes pollutants from the coal even before it gets to the furnaces at the power plants.

In another area of research, the first mechanical draft cooling tower of its design in the U.S. is already in operation in our system. Its round configuration, unique to this type of cooling tower, saves both space and construction materials.

Efficiency — it can be increased also by balancing electric demand. We're working with systems that automatically schedule energy consuming industrial plant processes to off-peak hours. And we're experimenting with dual metering — a system that rewards consumers with lower rates if they use appliances during periods of low demands.

The switch is on, and at The Southern Company system we're preparing for the energy-efficient Electric Economy. If you'd like the details of what we're doing, just write Dept. 342 for our annual report.

The Southern Company:
Alabama Power Company,
Georgia Power Company,
Gulf Power Company,
Mississippi Power Company,
Southern Services, Inc.

The Southern Company

Perimeter Center East,
Atlanta, Georgia 30346

EXHIBIT 10 (*continued*)

One of a series of questions asked by customers of Alabama Power. This one is by Mr. Don Roberts of Birmingham.

Have Alabama Power's rates gone up?

Yes. Because of inflation, we've had to obtain increases in our rates for electricity. Inflation has hit us in the same way it has hit every other business and every family. The cost of nearly everything that's needed to provide electric service has risen very sharply in the past several years.

For example, the average wages paid our employees have jumped dramatically. A lineman in 1965 was earning an average of $3.55 per hour. Today, he is being paid $5.71 per hour. That's an increase of 61 percent. A truck driver's average hourly wage eight years ago was $2.73. Now, it's $4.33, an increase of 59 percent. And so it goes, in every classification. And, of course, we have more employees today; therefore, the total amount paid by the company in wages and salaries is considerably higher than in 1965.

The cost of materials and supplies used in our electric operations also has increased substantially in recent years. Operation and maintenance expenses in 1973 were 147 percent above 1965.

Equipment is more expensive to buy. Wooden utility poles cost 108 percent more than they did eight years ago; bucket trucks, comparably sized and equipped, cost 64 percent more than they did in 1965; and the unit cost of fuel used to generate electricity is up about 109 percent from what it was in January, 1966.

Another steep increase we face is what we must pay investors when we obtain money to construct new facilities. In 1965, for instance, we sold bonds at an interest cost of 4.9 percent. In August, 1973, we sold an issue of bonds at an interest cost of 8.9 percent. Which was the lowest received on competitive bids.

As another example, we sold preferred stock in 1965 at a dividend cost of 4.7 percent. In 1973, we sold an issue of preferred stock at a dividend cost of 8.2 percent. Again, the lowest offered our company on competitive bids.

And we can't put off these sales of securities, as can most other businesses, in the hope that the cost of money will go down. We have no choice under the law but to construct the new facilities necessary to serve our customers.

Even with these increases, however, our rates to you still rank among the lowest in the nation. For example, our average residential rate now is about 18 percent below the national average for investor-owned electric utilities. And did you know electricity per kilowatt-hour on our system is cheaper now than it was in 1942? We'll continue doing all we can to provide electricity at the lowest rates consistent with reliable service.

EXHIBIT 10 (continued)

Electricity.
How to use it better where you use it most.

Even if you're a gourmet cook, you probably don't know all the things electricity can do for you in the kitchen. Or how, at the same time, you can get the most out of the electricity you use.

Did you know, for instance, that vegetables should be cooked in very little water, and only until they're tender? The longer they cook, the shorter their vitamin supply will be. And the more electricity you'll be using.

Speaking of water, maybe you think a drippy faucet is no big thing. But, if your hot water faucet leaks one drop a second, you can lose 200 gallons a month. The electricity it took to heat that water is lost, too. Right down the drain.

Another thing. When you run your kitchen exhaust fan to take out food odors and excess heat, you shouldn't leave it on for more than fifteen minutes after you've finished cooking. If you do, you'll be taking out your heating or air conditioning.

Now. Clip the coupon, fill it in, and send it to us. We'll send you a free booklet that tells you how to use your electricity better. Because electricity is energy that's made from natural resources. And like all energy, it shouldn't be wasted. Knowing you're using energy wisely should make your life a little brighter.

Public Information and Advertising Dept.
Alabama Power
P.O. Box 2641
Birmingham, Alabama 35291
Please send me my free copy of "Electricity. How to use it for all it's worth."

Name_____
Address_____
City_____
State_____Zip_____

The People of Alabama Power

We've got to be there when you need us.

EXHIBIT 10 (continued)

ALABAMA POWER HAS A NEW ENERGY ADJUSTMENT ON ELECTRIC BILLS THAT'S FAIR AND EQUITABLE FOR EVERYBODY.

On January 1, 1975, Alabama Power began using a new energy adjustment factor in computing electric bills. The new factor modifies the old fuel adjustment provision that was in effect, with the approval of the Alabama Public Service Commission, for several years.

FUEL ADJUSTMENT PROVISIONS ARE COMMON IN THE U.S.

Fuel adjustment provisions are included in rates set by regulatory agencies in at least 46 other states and in rates set by the Federal Power Commission.

The new energy adjustment was approved unanimously in December by the Public Service Commission, with the concurrence of certain intervenors who opposed the company's then pending request for a retail electric rate increase, including representatives of the Governor and the State.

THE NEW ENERGY ADJUST- MENT PROVIDES NO PROFIT FOR ALABAMA POWER.

The new energy adjustment, like the old fuel adjustment, provides no profit for Alabama Power Company. It only recovers certain costs the company actually incurs in providing electric service.

Under the old provision, the fuel adjustment factor used in computing electric bills varied from month to month with the company's costs for fuel and with the amount of electricity generated by fossil fuels. The factor was chiefly affected by the cost of coal, which provides 80 percent of the electricity used by Alabama Power's customers. With the old method of determining the fuel adjustment factor, there was a lag of two months between the time the fuel costs were incurred by the company and the time the adjustments for those costs were made on customers' electric bills.

The new energy adjustment provision does not depend solely on the company's

IT INCLUDES ALABAMA POWER'S COSTS FOR, AND SAVINGS FROM, THE INTER- CHANGE OF ELECTRIC ENERGY WITH OTHER UTILITIES.

costs for fuel to generate electricity. It also takes into account Alabama Power's costs for, and savings from, the interchange of electric energy with other utilities. And the new provision will now reflect—on a current basis—the net effect of costs for both fuel and purchased electric energy, whether these costs are higher or lower.

If the price Alabama Power has to pay for fuel should drop, the energy adjustment factor used in computing electric bills would decrease, just as with the old fuel adjust-

ment. However, it should be noted that the cost of fuel to generate electricity has increased sharply in recent months, and a

CUSTOMERS' ELECTRIC BILLS WILL NOW REFLECT—ON A CURRENT BASIS—THE NET EFFECT OF COSTS FOR BOTH FUEL AND PURCHASED ELECTRIC ENERGY, WHETHER THESE COSTS ARE HIGHER OR LOWER.

price drop, particularly for coal, is not foreseeable right now. (In November 1973, we paid the equivalent of $11.47 per ton for coal as compared with $29.38 in November 1974.)

THE NEW ENERGY ADJUSTMENT WOULD ALLOW CUSTOMERS' BILLS TO REFLECT A PRICE DECREASE IN THE SAME MONTH IT OCCURRED.

But when the cost does go down, the current-billing basis of the new energy adjustment will allow customers' bills to reflect a price decrease in the same month it occurs, not several months later.

Alabama Power builds generating facilities to serve our own customers; we do not build plants dedicated to serving people outside Alabama. Any energy transactions we have with other utilities involve temporary surpluses and deficits of power. Our agreements with other utilities for the interchange of electric energy enable us and our neighboring utilities to assist one another in emergencies and thus help assure the reliability and economy of electric service.

NOW OUR CUSTOMERS CAN MORE DIRECTLY AND IMMEDIATELY SHARE IN THE BENEFITS OF OUR POLICY OF SEEKING THE MOST ECO- NOMICAL SOURCE OF ENERGY.

Now, with the new energy adjustment provision, anytime it's cheaper for Alabama Power to buy electric energy from other utilities than to burn coal in our own plants, then our customers can more directly and immediately share in the benefits of our policy of seeking the most economical source of energy.

The new provision also allows the immediate pass-along to our customers of the full benefits of increased efficiency in our newer fossil-fired generating plants.

THE NEW PROVISION IS FAIR TO ALL ALABAMA POWER CUSTOMERS.

The new provision is fair to all Alabama Power customers, including residential, commercial and industrial. When fuel costs

and purchased electric energy costs exceed the base (2.5 mills or one-fourth cent per kilowatt-hour) set by the Public Service Commission, each customer pays a share of the excess costs based on the amount of electricity used. By the same token, if the cost of either fuel or purchased energy, or both, should fall below the previous month's costs, then all customers would share proportionately in the decrease.

When the new energy adjustment went into effect, the company was about $6 million behind in recovering fuel costs which already had been incurred. It was behind because of the time lag in the old fuel adjustment provision. So that the company can recover these costs, the Public Service Commission has provided for a temporary surcharge of slightly more than one tenth of a cent per kilowatt-hour of electricity billed to you in January, February

AFTER MARCH 31, 1975, THE TEMPORARY SURCHARGE WILL BE DROPPED.

and March. After March 31, 1975, the surcharge will be dropped.

The old fuel adjustment would have added $7.48 per 1000 kilowatt-hours to your January electric bill. The new energy adjustment factor in January adds $7.40 per 1000 kilowatt-hours plus $1.02 for the temporary surcharge. In subsequent months the energy adjustment will decrease or increase depending on the cost of fuel and purchased energy.

YOU, OUR CUSTOMERS, WILL RECEIVE THE FULL EFFECT OF OUR CONTINUING EFFORTS BOTH TO PRODUCE AND TO OBTAIN ELECTRIC ENERGY AT THE LOWEST PRACTI- CABLE COST.

The new energy adjustment offers definite advantages both to Alabama Power and to our customers. In this time of increasing fuel costs, it enables the company to recover more promptly the excess costs we have to pay to be able to provide reliable service. At the same time, it assures that you, our customers, will receive the full effect of our continuing efforts both to produce and to obtain electric energy at the lowest practicable cost.

ALABAMA POWER COMPANY

EXHIBIT 10 (concluded)

Naturally, if I could have it my way, bad weather like this wouldn't happen. And your electricity would be there 100 percent of the time.

But it makes me feel good to know your electricity is there more than 99 percent of the time. A big part of that is the work I do every day—putting in new lines, transformers, poles, making normal repairs.

It's just that the forces of nature aren't always so friendly as we'd like. Power lines get damaged. And somebody's power goes off.

I don't like it to happen at my house, either. But if it happens to you, we linemen appreciate your patience and understanding while we try to do something about it.

Anytime things go wrong, we go to work. Right then. If you're sitting in your living room with no lights, we're out working on the power lines. If you miss the best part of the ball game, well, we miss it, too. And if you think it's dark where you are, just imagine how dark it can get where we have to be. Not to mention wet, and windy, and sometimes very cold.

But we'll be out there. No matter how much we'd rather be somewhere else. Because we don't like anybody being kept in the dark.

**At Alabama Power
somebody's working for you**

EXHIBIT 11

Alabama Power Company's Donations to Charitable Organizations, 12 Months Ending June 1975

Recipient	Amount
Alabama Association of Independent Colleges and Universities— Birmingham	$ 2,500
Alabama Heart Hospital-UAB—Birmingham	25,000
Alabama Christian College—Montgomery	1,000
Allied Arts Council—Mobile	1,750
American Cancer Society—Birmingham—Alabama Division, Inc.	2,525
Auburn University	15,000
Birmingham Festival of Arts Association	2,800
Birmingham Southern College	10,000
Birmingham Symphony Association Maintenance Fund	2,000
Boys Club of Etowah County, Inc.	1,025
Chauncey Sparks State Technical Trade School	1,238
Gorgas Scholarship Foundation, Inc.	1,000
Heart Association of Birmingham	1,000
Junior Achievement, Inc. (three cities)	5,500
Judson College—Marion	5,000
The Lighthouse—Montgomery	1,000
Miles College—Birmingham	5,000
Regan Memorial Museum of Natural History—Anniston	1,200
Salvation Army Capital Fund Drive—Anniston	3,500
Salvation Army Building Fund—Mobile	8,000
Samford University—Decisive Years Campaign—Birmingham	10,000
Sertoma International Center for Communicative Disorders—Birmingham	3,334
Southern Governors Conference—Point Clear—Prior year refund	(1,984)
Talladega College—Capital Funds Program	1,000
Thomas Alva Edison Foundation	1,500
United Appeal (seven cities)	109,171
University of Alabama in Birmingham	3,080
University of Alabama in Birmingham—School of Optometry	1,500
Walker College—Jasper Development Fund	3,500
Young Men's Christian Association—Enterprise—Building Fund	1,500
Young Men's Christian Association—Mobile—Building Fund	1,500
Young Women's Christian Association Development Program— Birmingham	6,000
Donations of less than $1,000 each:	
Agricultural organizations (6 items)	1,636
American Cancer Societies (11 items)	230
American Red Cross (6 items)	275
Boys Club (2 items)	100
Boy Scouts of America (14 items)	1,220
Community and national civic organizations (165 items)	11,582
Community or United Givers Fund (24 items)	4,785
Girl Scouts (4 items)	58
Heart Association (10 items)	220
March of Dimes (2 items)	22
Religious organizations (13 items)	1,691
Schools, colleges and universities (27 items)	1,081
Various health organizations (33 items)	2,822
	$261,861

Source: Report of Alabama Power Company to Federal Power Commission.

In July 1976, responding to the Alabama PSC'c cost-cutting suggestion, Alabama Power announced it was suspending all charitable contributions. The company said it was forced to do this because the PSC did not consider the company's charitable contributions to be an allowable expense in setting rates. A majority of the PSC took the position that APCo's charitable contributions should come from the stockholders' pockets (aftertax profits) rather than being financed by the ratepayers.

Following Alabama Power's decisions to cease all media advertising and to suspend corporate contributions to charity, a number of the state's newspapers printed editorials criticizing the PSC's ruling on both advertising and charitable contributions. Exhibit 11 presents a recent listing of APCo's charitable contributions.

APCO'S ATTEMPTS TO IMPROVE EFFICIENCY AND HOLD DOWN COSTS

In his testimony before the Alabama PSC in February 1976, APCo's president, Joseph M. Farley, stated:

> Although it is extremely expensive to build, maintain and operate an electric system as large and as complex as that of Alabama Power Company's, we were for many years able to avoid seeking rate increases, even though our expenses were going up. So long as our costs were increasing at a fairly moderate and stable pace, the Company managed to offset the increases by installing improved and more efficient generating units; by providing line crews with improved tools and equipment; by using computers for many functions; and by taking other measures to hold down expenses. We are continuing such efforts today, and, as a matter of fact, we are intensifying them.
>
> An example of such measures is an economic efficiency study of our supervision by the firm of Naus & Newlyn, Inc. Naus & Newlyn specializes in the design and implementation of quality, long-range, and long-lasting cost reduction programs. This management consultant firm has examined each activity in each of our various field offices in our Southern and Eastern Divisions. Personnel are now in our Western Division headquarters in Tuscaloosa. They review such activities as meter reading, customer accounting, engineering, and line construction. This firm has also completed a study of our Greene County Steam Plant and is now working at our Barry Steam Plant. In addition, we have engaged the firm of Williamson, Merrill, Taylor and Darling, Inc. to assist in a reorganization of several corporate departments so as to maximize effective management. Our corporate structure is now more functionally structured for greater operational ease and better communication.
>
> The Company has recently completed a General Services Complex which houses the general equipment and automotive shops, warehouses, test laboratory facilities, construction crew headquarters, and, in time, will house training facilities. The major purpose of the complex is to combine existing service operations to support more efficiently the Company's construction and operating activities.

The development of a computerized Materials Management System is under way, with planned implementation in mid-1976. This system will provide increased efficiency in general field operations and will reduce lost crew time due to material unavailability and provide improved forecast of delivery time of essential materials. The system should reduce the shifting of construction crews, with inherent costs caused by delay in material deliveries. The system will provide accurate, up-to-date information on the stock levels in all storerooms from the central warehouse down through the local storeroom level.

In April 1976, Alabama Power Company will begin operating a centralized salvage facility to provide a central clearing point for handling and processing all stores stock items and construction materials and equipment returned to the General Warehouse from job sites for possible re-use and for disposing of all unusable surplus, obsolete, damaged and scrap materials and equipment through those external channels providing the largest financial returns to the Company.

The Internal Auditing Department aids management in achievement of efficient operations by conducting financial and operational audits of various activities and departments. In addition, it audits records of contractors as required to verify costs billed. Audit findings are reported to the President, who ensures that any needed corrective action is taken to improve procedures, streamline methodology, and prevent recurrences of any inefficient practices noted.

Our first two customer service centers are another way we have improved efficiency, particularly in the handling of customer-oriented matters. These two centers, operating in our two largest metropolitan areas of Birmingham and Mobile, became operational on June 22, 1973, and December 9, 1974, respectively.

We are now economically re-using some equipment that some years ago we would have traded in. In November 1974, a program was implemented to seek out and re-use idle and underloaded transformers within the Company. As a result, transformer purchases were reduced by more than 8,000 units, and the Company's inventory of transformers was reduced by more than 2,800 units. We have been informed by transformer manufacturers that Alabama Power Company has the lowest, best managed transformer inventory in the United States.

In the area of personnel, the Company has made widespread efforts to reduce payroll expenditures since late 1974 where the level of work has declined, and in some instances where reliability of our service would not be adversely affected. At the end of 1974, the Company had 7,948 employees, and at the end of 1974, 7,870 employees, for a net reduction of 78 employees for last year. We were able to effect this reduction and serve more than 15,000 additional customers during 1975. In late 1974, stringent employment procedures were developed to cause my office to be appraised on new employments. All new employments since November 1974 must have the approval of a senior officer and myself.

The Company is searching for every possible way to economize—regardless of how small the economy might be.

COMPETITION

A portion of the area served by APCo adjoins the area served by TVA and its municipal and cooperative distributors. A 1959 act of Congress permits TVA to issue and sell up to $5 billion of revenue bonds to finance expansion of its electric utility system. The 1959 act limits the distribution of TVA power, unless otherwise authorized by Congress, to specified areas of customers being served on July 1, 1957.

The Rural Electrification Administration (REA) has authority to make loans to cooperative associations or corporations to provide electric service to persons in rural sections of the country. There are 15 REA-financed electric cooperative organizations operating in territory in which Alabama Power provides electric service at retail or wholesale. One of these, Alabama Electric Cooperative, Inc., is a generating and transmitting cooperative selling power to several distributing cooperatives, municipal systems, and other customers in south Alabama and northwest Florida and purchasing some of its power requirements from APCo. Alabama Electric Cooperative in 1969 completed an additional generating plant of 75,000 kilowatts with an REA loan secured by long-term contracts requiring distributing cooperatives to take their requirements from Alabama Electric Cooperative to the extent it has such power and energy available. REA, more recently, approved a guarantee of a loan to Alabama Electric Cooperative for additional generating capacity of 420,000 kilowatts and 135 miles of transmission lines. All 14 distributing cooperatives obtained some of their power requirements either directly or indirectly from Alabama Power.

In June 1972, APCo and Alabama Electric Cooperative, Inc., entered into a power supply arrangement, with an initial term of ten years, which provided for additional interconnections between the two systems and for the supply of emergency service, protective capacity and maintenance capacity to meet the deficiency power requirements of Alabama Electric Cooperative. The rates and charges for the services are subject to adjustment under varying circumstances during the term of the agreement and contain provisions for adjustments predicated upon changes in cost of fuel.

In the 12 months ended June 30, 1975, APCo sold 1.36 billion kwh of electric energy to cooperatives for which it received total revenues of $19,163,589. During the same period, APCo sold 1.18 billion kwh of electric energy to municipalities, for which it received total revenues of $17,098,766.

Aside from rivalry with neighboring electric utilities and rural cooperatives, Alabama Power was in direct competition with natural gas companies in its service area. Competition was keenest for heating of newly constructed commercial buildings and for space heating, water heating, and cooking in new residential homes and apartments. However, during 1974–76, the growing nationwide shortage of natural gas was beginning to result in APCo having some advantage in edging out natural gas companies for new business in several cities and counties.

THE DEMAND FOR ELECTRICITY

Like most other electric utilities, Alabama Power's sales of electric energy in 1974–75 shifted abruptly from the steady upward trend of previous years (see Exhibits 12 and 15). However, during the first half of 1976 as inflation slowed and the economy turned up strongly, the usage of electric energy appeared to be returning toward its former growth rate; kilowatt-hour sales were up in all three major customer groups—residential, commercial, and industrial.

Between 1965 and 1975, APCo expreienced a 6.6 percent annual rate of growth in total kilowatt-hour sales; the company's territorial peak-hour demand rose at a rate of 7.1 percent; and the number of customers served grew at the rate of 2.4 percent. Exhibits 12, 13, and 14 give more details on energy sales by customer category.

A comparison of APCo's kilowatt-hour sales and Alabama's gross state product (GSP) revealed that total electric energy usage rose an average of 3.64 billion kwh in additional energy sales for each $1 billion increase in Alabama's constant-dollar GSP during the 1960–75 period (see Exhibit 15). In the industrial sector of Alabama's economy, APCo's kilowatt-hour sales to industrial customers rose an average of 2.87 billion kwh for each $1 billion increase in constant-dollar output in mining and manufacturing. Residential consumption of electricity rose 533 kwh for each $100 increase in real personal income per capita during the 1960–75 period.

Exhibit 16 shows how the company's summer and winter peak loads have changed in conjunction with Alabama's gross state product.

The economic likelihood of further increases in the demand for electricity in Alabama Power's service area was outlined by a University of Alabama economist in testimony before the Alabama PSC:

> I would expect demand for electricity in Alabama Power's service area to increase. There are several reasons for this. First, Alabama's industry-recruiting successes of the past are likely to spill over into the future, at least for a foreseeable time, and this means a greater demand for electricity in the industrial sector. As I indicated earlier, Alabama needs new industry and more high-skill, high-wage jobs in manufacturing, both to provide jobs for new entrants into the labor force and for the unemployed and to open up better job opportunities for workers who have the skills and abilities to upgrade themselves. More and better manufacturing jobs are Alabama's key to closing the gap between the living standards and material well-being of its residents and those of other states. This means ensuring that the state has enough electric power to offer and to supply to new firms—otherwise their locating in Alabama is automatically foreclosed.
>
> Expansion in the industrial sector can be expected to stimulate expansion in the trade and service industries and, in turn, to expand commerical demand for electricity.
>
> As incomes rise in Alabama, there is ample reason to expect further increases in residential demand for electricity. To begin with, dwindling supplies

EXHIBIT 12
Kilowatt-Hour Sales of Electric Energy, 1965–1975

	Thousands of Kilowatt-Hours							Annual Percentage Rate of Growth		
	1975	1974	1973	1972	1971	1970	1965	1 Year 1974–1975	5 Year* 1970–1975	10 Year* 1965–1975
Territorial										
Residential	7,743,609	7,321,419	7,344,878	6,656,760	6,106,810	5,750,296	3,503,774	5.77%	6.13%	8.25%
Commercial	4,611,863	4,306,750	4,194,288	3,797,751	3,394,637	3,209,540	2,015,873	7.08	7.52	8.63
Industrial	10,742,325	10,992,118	10,867,180	10,278,181	9,725,873	9,434,059	6,929,359	(2.27)	2.63	4.48
Street lighting	109,687	103,681	95,418	92,235	87,412	81,203	76,463	5.79	6.20	3.67
Sales for resale	2,020,406	1,954,525	2,330,717	1,922,452	1,552,178	1,596,150	1,043,902	3.37	4.83	6.83
Other	1,626	1,308	1,679	1,258	1,529	1,428	1,906	24.31	2.63	(1.58)
Total territorial	25,229,516	24,679,801	24,834,160	22,748,637	20,868,439	20,072,676	13,571,277	2.23%	4.68%	6.40%
Nonterritorial										
Nonassociated companies	420,868	552,995	—	104,303	145,470	384,789	—	(23.89)	1.81	—
Total	25,650,384	25,232,796	24,834,160	22,852,940	21,013,909	20,457,465	13,571,277	1.65	4.63	6.57

Percent of Total Territorial Sales

	1975	1974	1973	1972	1971	1970	1965
Residential	30.69%	29.66%	29.58%	29.26%	29.26%	28.65%	25.82%
Commercial	18.28	17.45	16.89	16.69	16.27	15.99	14.85
Industrial	42.58	44.54	43.76	45.18	46.60	47.00	51.06
Street lighting	0.43	0.42	0.38	0.41	0.42	0.40	0.56
Sales for resale	8.01	7.92	9.38	8.45	7.44	7.95	7.69
Other	0.01	0.01	0.01	0.01	0.01	0.01	0.02
Total	100.00%	100.00%	100.00%	100.00%	100.00%	100.00%	100.00%

* Compound annual rate.

EXHIBIT 13
Revenues from Electric Energy Sales, 1965–1975

	Thousand of Dollars							Annual Percentage Rate of Growth		
	1975	1974	1973	1972	1971	1970	1965	1 Year 1974–1975	5 Year* 1970–1975	10 Year* 1965–1975
Territorial										
Residential	$230,161	$178,949	$152,689	$126,355	$109,703	$97,869	$60,167	28.62%	18.65%	14.36%
Commercial	140,568	109,944	92,121	74,758	63,541	55,640	37,464	27.85	20.36	14.14
Industrial	208,068	165,540	127,415	104,427	88,471	77,922	55,914	25.69	21.71	14.04
Street lighting	4,006	3,786	3,473	3,245	3,075	2,860	1,930	5.81	6.97	7.58
Sales for resale	38,229	21,362	17,434	11,784	9,351	9,758	6,420	78.96	31.40	19.53
Other	45	28	30	24	19	17	21	60.71	21.49	7.92
Total territorial	$621,077	$479,609	$393,162	$320,593	$274,160	$244,066	$161,916	29.50%	20.54%	14.39%
Nonterritorial										
Nonassociated companies	5,253	5,031	—	1,981	1,255	3,069	—	4.41	11.35	—
Total	$626,330	$484,640	$393,162	$322,574	$275,415	$247,135	$161,916	29.24%	20.44%	14.49%

Percent of Total Territorial Revenues

	1975	1974	1973	1972	1971	1970	1965
Residential	37.06%	37.31%	38.84%	39.41%	40.01%	40.10%	37.16%
Commercial	22.63	22.92	23.43	23.32	23.18	22.80	23.14
Industrial	33.50	34.52	32.41	32.57	32.27	31.93	34.53
Street lighting	0.65	0.79	0.88	1.01	1.12	1.17	1.19
Sales for resale	6.15	4.45	4.43	3.68	3.41	4.00	3.97
Other	0.01	0.01	0.01	0.01	0.01	—	0.01
Total	100.00%	100.00%	100.00%	100.00%	100.00%	100.00%	100.00%

* Compound annual rate.

EXHIBIT 14
Customer Data, 1965–1975

	1975	1974	1973	1972	1971	1970	1965	1 Year 1974–1975	5 Year* 1970–1975	10 Year* 1965–1975
								Annual Percentage Rate of Growth		
Number of Customers (Year-End)										
Residential	787,262	773,004	755,251	729,840	706,491	686,381	618,445	1.84	2.78	2.44
Commercial	107,440	105,887	104,307	101,613	97,903	94,665	90,415	1.47	2.56	1.74
Industrial	3,236	3,140	3,063	2,942	2,853	2,799	2,421	3.06	2.94	2.94
Other	720	675	651	622	615	573	529	6.67	4.67	3.13
Total	898,658	882,706	863,272	835,017	807,862	784,418	711,810	1.81	2.76	2.36
Average Annual Use per Customer (Kilowatt-Hours)										
Residential (1)	9,954	9,575	9,895	9,285	8,773	8,475	5,730	3.96	3.27	5.68
Commercial	43,398	40,936	40,574	38,053	35,191	34,262	22,591	6.01	4.84	6.75
Annual Revenue per Customer (Dollars)										
Residential (2)	295.85	234.02	205.70	176.25	157.60	144.24	98.39	26.42	15.45	11.64
Commercial	1,322.76	1,045.04	891.13	749.07	658.71	593.96	419.85	26.58	17.37	12.16
Revenue per Kilowatt-Hour (Cents)										
Residential (3)	2.97	2.44	2.08	1.90	1.80	1.70	1.72			
Commercial	3.05	2.55	2.20	1.97	1.87	1.73	1.86			
Industrial	1.94	1.51	1.17	1.02	0.91	0.83	0.81			
Total territorial	2.46	1.94	1.58	1.41	1.31	1.22	1.19			

Note: National averages (preliminary) for investor-owned utilities in 1975: (1) 7,865; (2) $278.42; (3) 3.54 cents.
* Compound annual rate.
Source: Edison Electric Institute.

EXHIBIT 15

APCo's Total Territorial Electric Energy Sales as Compared to Gross State Product (in constant 1958 dollars) in Alabama, 1960–1975, with Projections to 1976 and 1977

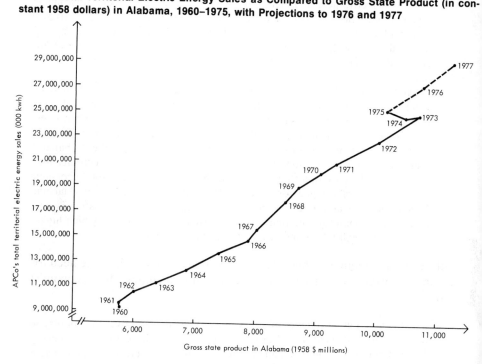

Gross state product in Alabama (1958 $ millions)

EXHIBIT 16

APCo's Territorial Peak Hour Loads, as Compared to Gross State Product in Alabama, 1960–1976, with Projections for 1977 and 1978

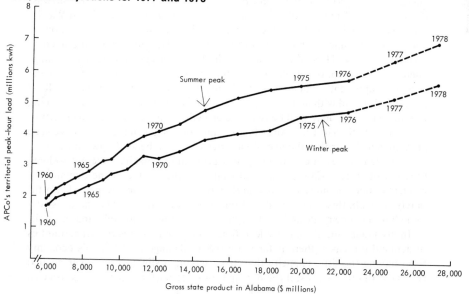

Gross state product in Alabama ($ millions)

of natural gas will likely influence growing numbers of builders and developers to install electric heat and electric appliances in new homes and apartments under construction. Shortage-induced shifts from natural gas to electricity will kindle additional residential electricity demand for home heating, water heating, and cooking. Second, there is certain to be more widespread use of air-conditioning and electrical appliances in Alabama households as incomes and purchasing power rise.

All three major components of electricity demand—residential, commercial, and industrial—have inherent built-in features to increase as the level of economy activity goes up and as the material well-being of the population improves. This is particularly true in states like Alabama where there is economic catching up to do. In other words, in a "less developed" economy like Alabama's, there are stronger "demand-pull" pressures being exerted for electricity than tends to be the case in a "mature" economy. Hence, there is solid economic reason to expect a higher demand for electricity to materialize in Alabama Power's service area over the next several years. The only question is how much the demand for electricity will increase and the extent to which higher electric rates will take some of the steam out of demand.

With regard to whether higher rates for electricity would reduce the need for Alabama Power to construct new generating facilities, the economist testified:

Although a great number of studies have been done all over the country to try to figure out what higher prices for electricity will do to electric energy demand both in the short run and in the long run, the results are not consistent and the answer remains quite uncertain. Such studies are necessarily based on historical or past data. The past may or may not be a reliable guide to the future. While it does appear that in 1974 and 1975 the demand for electric energy did not grow at the same pace of previous periods, the nation was, during this time, in the midst of its most serious recession since World War II; there was rampant inflation which struck hard at consumer purchasing power; and there was much publicity in the media and elsewhere about the need to conserve energy. These factors, along with higher prices for electricity, dampened the consumption of electricity. But, with economic recovery from the recession apparently under way, with inflation subsiding somewhat (at least temporarily), and with increases in the consumer's purchasing power beginning to reappear, there may well be renewed growth in the demand for electricity— if not in 1976, then in 1977. Already there are some signs in the data I have seen at Alabama Power that the use of electricity may be headed upward again.

If the lead times in constructing new generating capacity were not so long, then it would be a simple matter to wait until the course of the demand for electricity became more certain and then build capacity accordingly. Unfortunately, though, this is not feasible. Long lead times are a reality and construction plans must be made and work begun now to be ready for 1980 and beyond.

In my judgment, given these lead times and given the inherent uncertainties in demand forecasts, there is far more risk of damage to the state's economy from having too little capacity than from having a slight excess over needed reserves. In other words, if the demand for electricity materializes as forecast by the company, or is even a bit higher for whatever reason, and if ample generating capacity is not available, then the effect will be to choke off economic expansion that otherwise could have taken place. Some new industries that might have located in Alabama will go elsewhere. Expansions of existing operations may have to be delayed or else shifted to plant locations in other states. Construction of new homes and commercial buildings may be adversely affected. At the same time, consumers who are in a position to improve their living standards are thwarted from doing so. Of course, Alabama Power may be able to relieve its shortages partially by purchasing excess power from surrounding utilities if they should have extra generating capacity, but it is to be expected that the marginal costs of obtaining power in this manner will be higher and that such costs will have to be passed on to ratepayers in one way or another.

So, it is not clear to me that it is in the best interest of consumers or in the best interest of the state's economy to run the risk of not having an ample supply of energy. But let me hasten to add that it is equally unwise to overbuild and have too much capacity, thus incurring unneeded costs and causing an undue strain on the company's profitability. Given the degree of uncertainty now surrounding the rate of growth in the demand for electricity in Alabama, a posture of "maximum flexibility" in Alabama Power's construction plans seems especially appropriate. But it would seem more prudent to build in a safety margin that leans more to the side of "too much" rather than "too little" because an untimely electric energy shortage can choke off economic expansion and unnecessarily injure the state's economy.

OPPOSITION TO HIGHER ELECTRIC RATES

"While asking for increased revenues is an unpleasant task for us and our customers, the alternative is to jeopardize the economic future of the state, which must have an adequate and reliable supply of electricity both today and in the future." So said Joseph Farley in The Southern Company's *1975 Annual Report.* Yet, when Farley and other Alabama Power witnesses appeared at the Alabama PSC hearings to present the case for the $106.8 million rate increase, the company was confronted with "intervenors" representing the governor, a number of the state's largest industrial users of electricity (U.S. Steel, Kimberly-Clark, Olin Corp., Uniroyal, Diamond Shamrock, Ideal Basic Industries, the Alabama Textile Manufacturers Association, and others), the United Steelworker's Union, and several protesting consumers, including a prominent state senator. Newspaper reporters and TV newsmen regularly covered and reported on the hearings.

One of the issues raised related to the extent to which the proposed rate hike would be distributed among residential, commercial, and industrial customers. In this regard, a witness for Diamond Shamrock testified:

> Diamond Shamrock is willing to pay its fair share of any increase granted to Alabama Power Company by this Commission, provided the increase is applied against all three classes of customers on an equitable and fair basis. . . .

Diamond Shamrock would vigorously oppose any changing of the percentages as between residential, commercial and industrial customers. The percentages were changed to favor the residential customers by this Commission in two prior cases, and Diamond Shamrock is of the opinion that any such additional change would result in an unfair, inequitable, improper and discriminatory rate. . . .

The evidence is clear that industry is already paying more than its fair share, and there should not be placed on industry an even heavier share of the increase.

A spokesman for the Uniroyal plant in Opelika, Alabama, made the following remarks regarding how the proposed increases in industrial rates might affect the plant's costs and operations:

The Opelika Plant, unlike the older Uniroyal tire plants, was built with the concept to be highly automated, well ventilated, partially air conditioned and well lighted in order to improve the efficiency of the worker and to make the plant a safer and healthier place to work. Also, extensive use of cooling towers for process cooling water has minimized water usage and thermal pollution of this natural resource, together with air pollution control equipment making this manufacturing facility one of the cleanest. These features cause the Opelika Plant to use 33 percent more electrical energy than other Uniroyal plants.

Since the advent of the radial tire and the recent recession, all tire companies have suffered from reduced sales which in turn has caused reduced production. This means that because of overcapacity, top management is having the tires made at the plants which have the lowest operating cost. Therefore, if the Opelika Plant's operating cost is greater than its sister plants, Opelika's production would be shifted to one of its sister plants in another state.

The purchasing agent for the Cement Division of Ideal Basic Industries, which operates a cement plant in Mobile, explained why his company could not cost-justify generating its own electric energy requirements and why industrial rates ought to be lower than rates for other customers:

First, the utilities have historically designed their rates based on the true cost of serving their customer loads at various levels of usage. In this respect, you could say they supply a cost-plus product. Under this type cost-allocation and rate design condition, I do not feel that the potential benefits of generating our own electric energy [previously mentioned] could offset the savings of purchasing our power requirements from a utility. Secondly, steady high load factor users such as Ideal and the other industries represented here are an economic benefit to Alabama Power Company and its other customers, first because their consistent year round power usage prevents deep valleys of unused generating capacity from occurring during off-peak seasons of the year and, second, because we provide a volume of usage to the system that allows Alabama Power Company to buy and operate at lower production costs which are a benefit to every customer.

. . . industries such as Ideal, in purchasing electricity from Alabama

Power, cause other customers' bills to be lower than they would be if Alabama Power did not have industrial customers such as Ideal to level their load. Industrial customers are also very important to Alabama Power Company because of the basically low investment Alabama Power has in industrial customers, minimal expenses incurred by Alabama Power in servicing industrial customers, and the higher rate of return which Alabama Power receives from its industrial customers.

A representative of the Alabama Textile Manufacturers Association said:

> The company has proposed equal rate increases for each class. It is the position of the Alabama Textile Manufacturers Association that any increase which may be granted by the Commission should be spread so that each class of customer receives an equal percentage increase. This would be a fair, equitable and nondiscriminatory increase.

The director of manufacturing-industrial production for Olin Corporation's McIntosh plant testified that approximately 50 percent of the total costs of the plant were for electricity (Olin's plant at McIntosh was Alabama Power's third largest industrial customer) and further stated:

> Our basic position is that we are willing to pay our share of the Company's total cost of service. Of course, we would like to see our rate for electricity as low as possible. But we recognize that costs may be going up and we do not ask to be subsidized by any other users. In turn, we feel that the intense competition between our location and other locations in the Southeast and elsewhere in the country make it important that our rate be held as low as possible, consistent with recovering the cost of serving us.

Exhibits 12 and 13 contain the percentages of APCo's kilowatt-hour sales and revenues by customer category for the period 1960–75, thus providing one indication of differential rates between residential, commercial, and industrial users. The information in Exhibits 2, 3, and 4 provides yet another indication. At both the prevailing and the proposed rates, APCo was earning a substantially higher (3 percent–4 percent) return on investment from sales to industrial customers than it was on residential customer sales. This was true even though the average price per kwh paid by industrial users was considerably lower than for residential customers (see Exhibits 2 and 4)—an outcome which reflected sizably lower costs per kilowatt-hour in serving industrial customers.

The Residential Rate Structure.   At the public hearing on APCo's rate request, a number of people, including two commissioners, expressed concern over whether the proposed 20 percent rate hikes would place an undue burden upon retired persons, fixed-income groups, and low-income groups. In response to these concerns, the company presented data showing that social security recipients in Alabama were in a generally better income position to pay their electric bills in 1976 (given the proposed rate hikes) than they were in earlier years when rates were lower:

| Year | Percentage of Average Monthly Social Security Benefit for Retired Workers Required to Pay APCo's Bill for Electricity | | |
	400 kwh	*750 kwh*	*1,000 kwh*
1960	11.94%	18.60%	23.35%
1965	10.58	16.48	20.70
1970	8.44	12.65	15.65
1971	7.55	11.37	14.09
1972	6.90	10.32	12.76
1973	7.45	11.28	14.01
1974	7.29	11.32	14.18
1975	8.50	12.98	16.03
1976 (proposed rates)	8.19	14.56	18.97

The company presented additional figures showing that the above percentages were quite comparable to (and in some cases slightly less or roughly equal to) the same percentages computed for the United States as a whole. For example, the percentage of the average monthly social security benefit which the average retired U.S. worker would have had to pay for 400 kwh of electricity was 12.63 percent in 1960, 10.96 percent in 1965, 7.88 percent in 1970, and 7.41 percent in 1975. The company noted that the "burden" of APCo's residential rates upon social security recipients in Alabama compared quite favorably with the overall U.S. percentages despite the fact that the average monthly social security benefits in Alabama were $11–$24 below the U.S. average throughout the time period examined.

Alabama Power also demonstrated that while its residential rates steadily increased during the 1970s, the company's present and proposed bills for 400 kwh, 750 kwh and 1,000 kwh of service amounted to a smaller percentage of per capita personal income in Alabama than was the case in 1960 and 1965:

	1960	*1965*	*1975*	*1977 (projected)*
400 kwh.	5.94%	4.55%	4.29%	3.66%
750 kwh.	9.25	7.08	6.19	6.35
1,000 kwh.	11.61	8.90	7.70	8.27

Exhibits 17 and 18 present further information on APCo's residential rate structure and the sizes of customer bills.

EXHIBIT 17

APCo's Monthly Residential Electric Bills for 400 kwh, 750 kwh, and 1,000 kwh as a Percentage of Average Monthly Earnings of Employees in Selected Manufacturing Industries in Alabama, 1960, 1965, 1970, and 1975

Year	All Manu-facturing Employees	Primary Metals Employees	Textile Products Employees	Apparel Employees
1960:				
Number of employees	226,100	40,400	38,400	24,600
Average monthly earnings	$325.30	$440.53	$246.35	$197.21
Monthly residential bill for 400 kwh				
as a % of average monthly earnings	2.31%	1.71%	3.06%	3.82%
Monthly residential bill for 750 kwh				
as a % of average monthly earnings	3.61%	2.66%	4.76%	5.95%
Monthly residential bill for 1,000 kwh				
as a % of average monthly earnings	4.53%	3.34%	5.98%	7.47%
1965:				
Number of employees	279,600	43,900	38,900	37,100
Average monthly earnings	$412.01	$527.19	$347.10	$247.56
Monthly residential bill for 400 kwh				
as a % of average monthly earnings	1.83%	1.43%	2.17%	3.04%
Monthly residential bill for 750 kwh				
as a % of average monthly earnings	2.85%	2.23%	3.38%	4.74%
Monthly residential bill for 1,000 kwh				
as a % of average monthly earnings	3.58%	2.79%	4.24%	5.95%
1970:				
Number of employees	320,900	47,500	43,500	44,400
Average monthly earnings	$519.00	$679.34	$443.13	$336.18
Monthly residential bill for 400 kwh				
as a % of average monthly earnings	1.66%	1.26%	1.94%	2.56%
Monthly residential bill for 750 kwh				
as a % of average monthly earnings	2.48%	1.89%	2.90%	3.83%
Monthly residential bill for 1,000 kwh				
as a % of average monthly earnings	3.07%	2.34%	3.59%	4.74%
1975:				
Number of employees	327,500	39,200	47,000	48,600
Average monthly earnings	$760.41	$1114.79	$654.03	$479.01
Monthly residential bill for 400 kwh				
as a % of average monthly earnings	2.01%	1.37%	2.34%	3.20%
Monthly residential bill for 750 kwh				
as a % of average monthly earnings	3.05%	2.08%	3.55%	4.85%
Monthly residential bill for 1,000 kwh				
as a % of average monthly earnings	3.80%	2.59%	4.41%	6.03%

Sources: Employment and earnings data from: Alabama Department of Industrial Relations. *Alabama Labor Market*, January issues, 1962, 1967, 1972, 1973, 1974, 1975, 1976, and February issue, 1976. Earnings data are based on the December average weekly earnings of each year; this was then multiplied by 52 and divided by 12 to get average monthly earnings for each year.

EXHIBIT 18
Average Number of APCo's Residential Customer Bills at Selected kwh Intervals
Each Month, Summer and Winter, 12 Months Ending June 1975

	Average Number of Residential Customer Bills Each Month					
	Summer*		Winter†		Full-Year Average	
Kwh Range	Number	Percent of Total	Number	Percent of Total	Number	Percent of Total
0–250	122,619	16.7%	145,170	19.8%	133,895	18.2%
251–500	142,379	19.4	177,458	24.2	159,918	21.8
501–750	118,730	16.2	155,695	21.3	137,212	18.7
751–1,000	90,415	12.3	100,900	13.8	95,657	13.0
1,001–1,500	121,384	16.5	79,988	10.9	103,186	14.1
1,501–2,000	70,928	9.7	36,139	4.9	51,033	7.0
2,001–2,500	37,233	5.1	15,372	2.1	26,753	3.6
2,501–3,000	17,029	2.3	9,452	1.3	13,240	1.8
Over 3,001	13,420	1.8	12,193	1.7	12,807	1.7
Total	734,137	100.0%	732,367	100.0%	733,701	99.9%
Usage rate of median monthly residential bill	~725 kwh		~550 kwh		~630 kwh	
Average kwh usage	912 kwh		728 kwh		819 kwh	

* July, August, September, and October 1974; May and June 1975.
† January, February, March, and April 1975; November and December 1974.
Source: Alabama Power Company records.

EXHIBIT 19

ALABAMA POWER COMPANY
Income Statements, 1965, 1970, 1974, and 1975
(in thousands of dollars)

	1975	1974	1970	1965
Operating Revenues—Electric	$631,250	$489,455	$249,317	$163,77
Operating Expenses—Electric:				
Operation				
Fuel	$218,190	$156,085	$ 36,278	$ 20,07
Purchased and interchanged power, net......	33,018	43,210	27,233	14,76
Other	76,009	68,322	40,438	27,15
Maintenance	34,824	33,101	13,199	8,07
Depreciation and amortization	51,394	45,523	29,963	20,90
Taxes other than income taxes	38,147	34,370	15,755	12,62
Income taxes				
Federal	(5,088)	(8,157)	21,144	15,34
State	1,118	—	1,257	1,10
Deferred	50,548	37,155	5,526	3,28
Deferred in prior years, credit	(5,535)			
Investment tax credit	17,299	(2,572)	(1,508)	(92
		—	66	1,71
Total Income Taxes	$ 58,342	$ 26,426	$ 26,485	$ 20,52
Total Operating Expenses	$509,924	$407,037	$189,351	$124,12
Operating Income—Electric..................	$121,326	$ 82,418	$ 59,966	$ 39,654
Other Income and Deductions:				
Allowance for funds used during construction	54,151	40,328	4,472	2,123
Dividends from SEGCO	2,194	2,039	2,234	1,873
Other, net	18,667	13,016	402	1
Income Before Interest Charges	$196,338	$137,801	$ 67,074	$ 43,651
Interest Charges:				
Interest on long-term debt	$ 78,295	$ 67,729	$ 23,258	$ 13,188
Other interest expense	23,314	5,114	2,223	506
Total Interest Charges	$101,609	$ 72,843	$ 25,481	$ 13,694
Income before Extraordinary Item	$ 94,729	$ 64,958	$ 41,593	$ 29,957
Extraordinary Item:				
Dividends from SEGCO paid from earnings accumulated prior to January 1, 1963	—	—	—	1,300
Net Income	$ 94,729	$ 64,958	$ 41,593	$ 31,257
Dividends on Preferred Stock	16,947	15,964	3,979	2,956
Net Income after Dividends on Preferred Stock ...	$ 77,782	$ 48,994	$ 37,614	$ 28,301

* Commencing in 1973, the company began including in "Other Income" the income tax effect of the debt cos
portion of allowance for funds used during construction. This allocation decreases "Operating Income, Electric" an
increases "Other Income" in equal amounts, with the result that "Net Income" was not affected until the principle
involved received rate recognition in January 1975.

IBIT 20

ALABAMA POWER COMPANY
Balance Sheets, 1965, 1970, 1974, and 1975
At December 31
(thousands of dollars)

	1975	1974	1970	1965
Assets				
ity Plant:				
original cost	$2,971,681	$2,544,137	$1,321,152	$895,899
ess—Accumulated provision for depreciation	481,569	440,320	323,010	211,784
	$2,490,112	$2,103,817	$ 998,142	$684,115
er Property and Investments	$ 19,132	$ 19,110	$ 18,883	$ 22,574
rrent Assets:				
sh and temporary investments	$ 15,861	$ 12,376	$ 15,181	$ 5,461
ceivables—net	51,747	53,034	16,960	11,770
terials and supplies	82,990	62,617	18,324	15,573
payments	5,846	9,715	1,364	1,134
	$ 156,444	$ 137,742	$ 51,829	$ 33,938
ferred Charges	$ 14,252	$ 10,392	$ 3,399	$ 1,457
Total Assets	$2,679,940	$2,271,061	$1,072,253	$742,084
Liabilities				
pitalization:				
mmon stock and paid-in capital	$ 557,858	$ 490,858	$ 217,365	$169,365
emium on preferred stock	461	461	152	99
rnings retained in the business	154,878	137,096	108,812	67,979
Total common stock equity	$ 713,197	$ 628,415	$ 326,329	$237,443
eferred stock	235,400	235,400	92,400	70,400
st mortgage bonds	1,130,601	996,723	533,739	356,926
llution control obligations	69,686	30,259	—	—
	$2,148,884	$1,890,797	$ 952,468	$664,769
terim Indebtedness	$ 191,304	$ 118,232	$ 586	—
rrent Liabilities:				
counts payable	$ 78,814	$ 67,497	$ 23,027	$ 13,208
stomer deposits	10,872	9,120	4,488	903
xes accrued	10,376	8,969	13,604	13,306
terest accrued	23,927	20,966	5,201	2,558
scellaneous	5,766	2,075	1,796	693
	$ 129,755	$ 108,627	$ 48,116	$ 30,668
eferred Credit, etc.:				
cumulated deferred income taxes	$ 161,824	$ 128,706	$ 58,141	$ 41,073
cumulated deferred investment tax credits ...	39,676	22,946	12,205	4,790
scellaneous	8,497	1,753	737	784
	$ 209,997	$ 153,405	$ 71,083	$ 46,647
Total Liabilities	$2,679,940	$2,271,061	$1,072,253	$742,084

EXHIBIT 21

Disposition of Electric Operating Revenues, 1965, 1970, 1974, and 1975 (dollar figures in thousand

	1975	1974	1970	1965
Revenues from electric energy sales	$626,330	$484,640	$247,135	$161,916
Other operating revenues	4,920	4,815	2,182	1,862
Total electric operating revenues	$631,250	$489,455	$249,317	$163,778
Operation and maintenance expenses	$362,041	$300,718	$117,148	$ 70,068
Depreciation and amortization	51,394	45,523	29,963	20,903
Taxes other than income taxes	38,147	34,370	15,755	12,628
Income taxes (including deferred income taxes and investment tax credit)	58,342	26,426	26,485	20,525
Allowance for funds used during construction	(54,151)	(40,328)	(4,472)	(2,123)
Other income, net	(20,861)	(15,055)	(2,636)	(1,874)
Income before interest charges	$196,338	$137,801	$ 67,074	$ 43,651
Interest charges	101,609	72,843	25,481	13,694
Net income after interest charges	$ 94,729	$ 64,958	$ 41,593	$ 29,957
Extraordinary income item	—	—	—	(1,300)
Dividends on preferred stock	16,947	15,964	3,979	2,956
Net income after dividends on preferred stock	$ 77,782	$ 48,994	$ 37,614	$ 28,301

Percent of Electric Operating Revenues

	1975	1974	1970	1965
Operation and maintenance expenses	57.4%	61.4%	47.0%	42.8%
Depreciation and amortization	8.2	9.3	12.0	12.8
Taxes other than income taxes	6.0	7.0	6.3	7.7
Income taxes (including deferred income taxes and investment tax credit)	9.2	5.4	10.6	12.5
Allowance for funds used during construction	(8.6)	(8.2)	(1.8)	(1.3)
Other income, net	(3.3)	(3.1)	(1.0)	(1.2)
Income before interest charges	31.1	28.2	26.9	26.7
Interest charges	16.1	14.9	10.2	8.4
Net income after interest charges	15.0	13.3	16.7	18.3
Extraordinary income item	—	—	—	(0.8)
Dividends on preferred stock	2.7	3.3	1.6	1.8
Net income after dividends on preferred stock	12.3	10.0	15.1	17.3

EXHIBIT 22
General Organization as of November 1, 1975

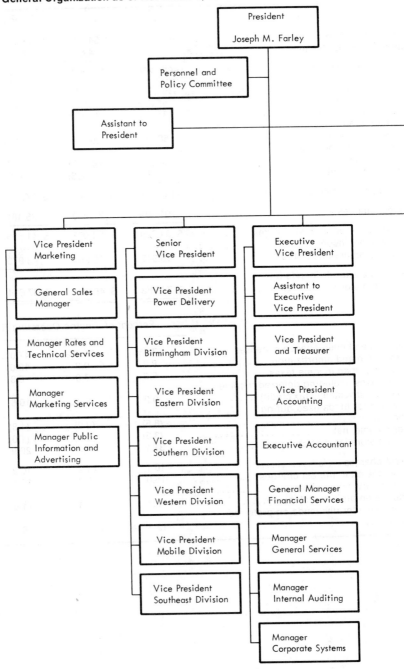

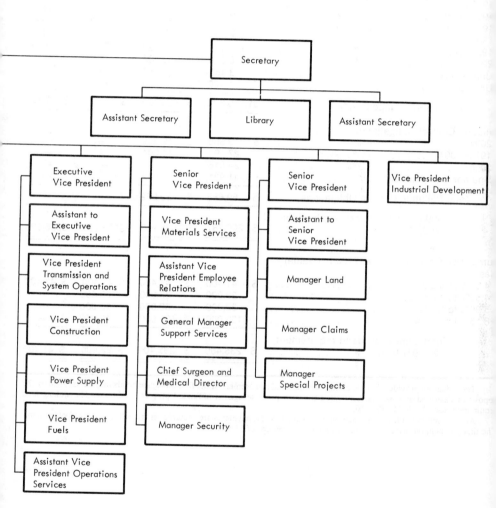

HIBIT 23

nior Security Issues Outstanding, Years ended December 31

Maturity	Interest Rates	1975	1974	1970	1965
			(in thousands of dollars)		
st-Mortgage Bonds*:					
1972 and 1974	3½% and 3%	—	—	$ 71,099	$ 71,610
1977 and 1978	3¼% and 3⅜%	$ 21,095	$ 21,105	21,145	21,195
1981–1985	3⅛%–4⅛%	70,939	70,939	70,939	70,939
1986–1990	3½%–5%	78,182	78,182	78,182	78,182
1991–1995	4⅜%–4⅞%	115,000	115,000	115,000	115,000
1996–2000	6¼%–9%	162,298	162,298	177,374	—
2001–2005	7½%–10⅞%	685,500	550,500	—	—
Unamortized discount		(3,483)	(2,457)	—	—
Unamortized premium		1,070	1,156	—	—
Total First-Mortgage Bonds		$1,130,601	$ 996,723	$533,739	$356,926
ollution Control Obligations†					
2004	6%	$ 19,600	$ 19,600	—	—
1979–2004	7¼%–9⅛%	27,191	11,601	—	—
2005	9½%	24,816	—	—	—
Unamortized discount		(1,921)	(942)	—	—
Total Pollution Control Obligations......		$ 69,686	$ 30,259	—	—
Total (annual interest requirement $92,494,000)		$1,200,287	$1,026,982	$533,739	$356,926
umulative Preferred Stock ($100 par value)					
lass					
4.20% to 4.52%		$ 41,400	$ 41,400	$ 41,400	$ 41,400
4.60% to 4.92%		29,000	29,000	29,000	—
5.96% to 8.04%		32,000	32,000	12,000	—
8.16% to 9.44%		133,000	133,000	10,000	—
Total (annual dividend requirement $16,947,000)....................		$ 235,400	$ 235,400	$ 92,400	$ 41,400

* The indenture provides that the annual sinking-fund requirement of the first-mortgage bonds may be satisfied by the eposit of cash and/or bonds authenticated for such purpose against unfunded property additions. The sinking-fund equirement for 1976 is $12,494,000.

† Annual amounts sufficient to meet principal and interest payments are required on the pollution control obligations. he first payment on principal is due in 1979 in the amount of $5 million.

E. Relating Corporate Strategy and Policy to External Environment

30. Consolidated Edison Company*

IN JULY 1972, the Appellate Division of the New York State Supreme Court handed down a decision giving Consolidated Edison Company the right to begin construction of its Storm King Mountain project; the decision came ten years after the company first began moving forward with plans for the project. The Court ruled that New York's Environmental Conservation Commission had provided no clear demonstration that the Storm King project would have any significant harmful effect upon water quality within the state of New York and that matters such as damage to the Catskill Aqueduct were unrelated to water quality and should be reconciled between New York City and the company.[1] With this favorable ruling in hand, Consolidated Edison Company began construction of its Storm King Mountain project in April 1974; the cost of Storm King was then estimated at $720 million, as compared to $115 million when first proposed in 1962.[2]

BACKGROUND

The Consolidated Edison Company (Con Ed) is in the business of providing electricity, steam, and natural gas to consumers in the New York City metropolitan area. It was established in 1936 as a result of two mergers of a number of smaller companies. The company gradually moved toward building an integrated utility system which could provide a total energy package to its customers. In 1975 it was the sixth largest company in the utility industry (ranked by assets) and the largest *electric* utility firm (ranked by sales revenues). Exhibits 1 and 2 present various operating statistics for the company during the period 1960 through 1976.

During the mid-1960s, at the time the Storm King controversy was just heating up, Con Ed's service area was concentrated in 660 square miles in and about New York City, with an average density of 5,000 customers per

---

* Prepared by Professors Robert J. Litschert, Virginia Polytechnic Institute and State University, and Arthur A. Thompson, Jr., The University of Alabama.

[1] David Bird, "Storm King Plant Backed by Court," *The New York Times,* July 1, 1972, p. 50.

[2] David A. Andluman, "Con Ed's Growth Plan Facing Big Obstacles," *The New York Times,* April 1, 1974, p. 1.

EXHIBIT 1
Sales Statistics, 1960–1976

	Sales			Meters (number at December 31)		
Year	Electric (000s of kilowatt-hours)	Gas (000s of cubic feet)	Steam (000s of pounds)	Electric	Gas	Steam
1976	32,206,901	75,025,554	35,571,453	2,995,746	1,200,752	4,701
1975	32,550,784	73,059,589	34,740,424	3,011,875	1,219,706	4,770
1974	32,648,897	72,758,378	35,085,934	3,027,757	1,241,616	4,802
1973	34,732,636	72,888,360	38,860,562	3,054,050	1,271,312	4,761
1972	33,144,326	73,968,215	39,313,999	3,063,328	1,288,432	4,728
1971	32,997,207	71,008,080	37,713,159	3,056,374	1,290,665	4,664
1970	32,399,483	68,891,652	36,938,726	3,054,453	1,291,857	4,616
1965	25,258,255	51,894,458	26.642,271	3,042,138	1,320,427	4,455
1960	18,899,691	43,140,040	19,712,000	2,904,624	1,343,634	4,100

Note: Population served, 1973—8,650,000
Service area—660 square miles.
Source: Company *Annual Reports.*

EXHIBIT 2
Generating Capacity, Peak Loads, and Residential Usage Statistics, 1963–1976

		Capability at Time of System Peak— Kilowatts					Residential	
Year	Generating Capacity December 31 (summer rating) (kilowatts)	Net Generating Capacity	Net Firm Pur-chases	Total Capacity Re-sources	System Summer Peak* Date	Kilowatts	Kilo-watt-hours per Cus-tomer	Rev-enue per Kilo-watt-hour
1976	9,880,000‡	10,030,000	437,000	10,467,000	June 24	7,579,000	3,314	9.0¢
1975	10,015,000	10,126,000	269,000	10,395,000	June 24	8,051,000	3,300	8.2
1974	10,383,000	9,931,000	428,000	10,359,000	July 9	7,973,000	3,248	7.6
1973	8,989,000	8,989,000	1,044,000	10,033,000	Sept. 4	8,220,000†	3,609	5.2
1972	8,947,000	9,173,000	778,000	9,951,000	July 19	7,872,000	3,367	4.6
1971	8,904,000	8,528,000	800,000	9,328,000	July 1	7,719,000	3,355	4.2
1970	9,077,000	8,957,000	520,000	9,477,000	Aug. 28	7,041,000	3,180	3.9
1969	8,144,000	8,143,000	260,000	8,403,000	July 17	7,266,000	2,950	3.9
1968	7,583,000	7,497,000	523,000	8,020,000	July 17	6,960,000	2,736	4.0
1967	7,473,000	7,512,000	20,000	7,532,000	July 24	6,147,000	2,522	4.0
1966	7,458,000	7,477,000	250,000	7,727,000	July 13	6,154,000	2,439	3.8
1965	7,491,000	7,527,000	260,000	7,787,000	June 23	5,710,000	2,277	3.9
1964	6,503,000	6,544,000	260,000	6,804,000	July 1	5,505,000	2,161	3.8
1963	6,559,000	6,605,000	260,000	6,865,000	July 29	5,105,000	2,050	3.9

* One hour net maximum load distributed locally.
† 1973 peak reduced by approximately 525,000 Kw by voltage reduction and customer appeals to conserve electricity.
‡ Excludes Indian Point No. 3.
Source: Company *Annual Reports.*

square mile—a density 300 times the industry average. Con Ed's average residential customer in 1975 used just 3,300 kwh of electricity as compared to 7,253 kwh for the United States as a whole and 4,957 kwh for the Middle Atlantic states. Con Ed's lower average annual kwh sales were partly due to the fact that 75 percent of the company's customers were apartment dwellers. Con Ed experienced roughly 3,000 interruptions in service to its customers each year because of failure in its distribution system. Since all of its transmission lines were underground (as required by city ordinances), Con Ed's 5,000 field workers made over 40,000 excavations per year. It had 66,000 miles of power lines underground, more than the rest of the United States combined.

In 1975, Con Ed's capital investment exceeded $3.1 billion and this grew at roughly 8.5 percent per year during the 1965–75 period. Internal pressure to maintain the company's stock as an "income stock" resulted in Con Ed paying out 75 percent of net income as dividends.

Management was widely viewed as inbred, conservative, and generally insensitive to its customers.[3] David Kosh, a Washington, D.C., utilities consultant, characterized Con Ed's public image thusly: "I've been in the utilities business for thirty-four years and I can't think of a company that goes out of its way to alienate customers the way Con Edison does. They're so stiff-backed . . ., they always think they are right."[4] Moreover, as the figures below suggest, the rates which the company charged for electric service in New York City were well above the average amounts charged by other electric utilities in the country:

	January 1, 1970		January 1, 1976	
	Con Ed	U.S. Average	Con Ed	U.S. Average
Residential rate (1,000 kwh)	$ 23.95	$ 18.31	$ 67.31	$ 34.85
Commercial rate (40 kw, 10,000 kwh)	$ 331.04	$ 239.37	$ 756.54	$ 431.69
Industrial rate (1,000 kw, 200,000 kwh)	$5,775.00	$3,492.00	$16,489.00	$7,395.00

In 1976 (as well as in several other years), Con Ed's rates were *the highest* of any electric utility company in almost every category of usage offered, according to statistics reported by the Federal Power Commission. Exhibit 3 reports the success of the company's special efforts to improve its admittedly bad record of customer service.

---

[3] Thomas O'Hanlon, "Con Edison: The Company You Love to Hate," *Fortune*, March 1966, p. 125.

[4] Ibid.

EXHIBIT 3
Results of Con Ed's Attempts to Improve Customer Service in 1975

	Performance Level Attained		
	End 1974	End 1975	Percentage of Improvement
Telephone Service			
One stop service	90%	97%	7.8%
Calls answered in 40 seconds	84%	99%	17.9%
District Office (interviews)			
Waiting time 10 minutes or less	83%	96%	15.7%
Waiting time 5 minutes or less	70%	90%	28.6%
Customer complaints (month of			
December)	18,687	12,424	33.5%
Customer complaints (annual)	319,589	190,889	40.3%
Customer complaints (backlog)			
Total	23,685	3,798	84%
Over 15 days old	18,306	1,382	92.5%
Over 30 days old	13,044	328	97.5%
Over 60 days old	8,017	22	99.7%
Wholesale meters read on schedule	81.0%	97.7%	20.6%
Nonwholesale meters read on schedule ..	89.9%	92.2%	2.6%
Customer Financial Data			
Accounts Receivable (from			
customers—at December 31)	$321 million	$302 million	5.9%
ENDRO (Accounts receivable			
expressed as equivalent number			
of days of revenue outstanding)	43.7 days	39.2 days	10.3%

Source: *1975 Annual Report*.

STORM KING MOUNTAIN PROJECT: THE EARLY CONTROVERSY

On September 27, 1962, *The New York Times* carried a story which created little concern at the time.[5] It described Con Ed's plan to build a 2,000 megawatt-unit hydroelectric power plant at Cornwall, New York, on the Hudson River. The project actually had been formally announced in January and was to be a reversible pumped-storage plant using water from the Hudson River. This system was designed so that during low kwh usage periods Con Ed could use its excess generating capacity to pump water up into the storage reservoir. During the day, the water from the reservoir would be released to flow back down the same pipe past large turbine generators, thereby producing electricity during peak usage periods. The idea was to allow Con Ed to use its generating facilities more efficiently throughout the day.

Mr. Harland C. Forbes, Con Ed's board chairman, explained that such a project had been studied for over 20 years but only now had become feasible

_____

[5] "Huge Power Plant Planned on Hudson," *The New York Times*, September 27, 1962, p. 1.

due to improved technology. He added that the pumped storage plant would give Con Ed the benefits "of a gigantic storage battery on our system." Particular features of the project included (1) a cost per installed kilowatt (kw) of capacity of $70 compared with $130–$150 per kw for very large steam plants, (2) no interference with river navigation, (3) use of a natural depression on top of Storm King Mountain for the reservoir, and (4) relative ease in negotiating for purchase of the land being sought since it belonged to just three or four private owners, including Harvard University.

No real controversy over the project emerged during 1962. It appeared then that the $115 million project would meet no public opposition and could be completed by 1967, as planned. Con Ed, thus went forward and submitted the proposal to the Federal Power Commission (FPC) for approval and licensing.

In May 1963, the New York–New Jersey Trail Conference announced its opposition to the plant.[6] The U.S. Army Corps of Engineers also expressed concern that canoeists might be sucked into the 40-foot tunnel required to pump water up the mountain, that large boats might be drawn off course during the periods of water intake and release, and that the level of the river would be raised or lowered when water was taken from or added to the river.

As criticism of the project continued to mount, the company found both a friend and advocate in Laurance S. Rockefeller, vice president of the Palisades Interstate Park Commission—as indicated by portions of a letter Rockefeller wrote to the editor of *The New York Times* and appearing in its June 26, 1963, edition:

> . . . electricity now is to be transmitted across the Hudson by underwater cables. The company elected to do this on its own so that the unspoiled character of the area would be maintained. . . . Other facts I think are important are as follows:
>
> The Consolidated Edison plant will be at the river level, facing north. Most of the plant will be below ground level and it has been designed to blend into the hillside. . . .
>
> Water will flow from the reservoir to the plant through a 40-foot-diameter, two-mile-long tunnel deep underground.
>
> The reservoir will be two miles east of the river, at 1,100 feet, which is about the top of the mountain. A native broken-rock-faced dam will be visible from the new Storm King highway, but this will be landscaped with bushes and trees.
>
> The site where the pump generating facilities are to be built . . . is not forest primeval. For the most part, the site is now occupied by houses in varying conditions of repair and an old hotel.

Nonetheless, opposition continued to build. Leo Rothschild, chairman of the New York–New Jersey Trail Conference, indicated that broad-based opposition to the Storm King project was needed. A new pressure group was

---

[6] John C. Devlin, "Power Plan Stirs Battle on Hudson," *The New York Times*, May 22, 1963, p. 43.

formed called the Scenic Hudson Preservation Conference (SHPC) and Rothschild was elected its president. The SHPC gathered support from a variety of individuals and groups, including nature lovers, environmentalists, and landowners who had voiced opposition to the project.

Con Ed was forced to constantly defend its position. Nature lovers charged that the project, if built, would "desecrate" the natural beauty of Storm King Mountain and the surrounding area. Con Ed replied that the plant would actually improve the area but did not elaborate. Environmentalists expressed concern that the project would set a precedent for future wilderness acquisitions. However, individuals owning property within the area thought to be Con Ed's proposed route for the overhead power transmission line were among the most vocal opponents. Most of these people owned land between Con Ed's Cornwall plant and its Millwood distribution station. Opposition was based primarily on the belief that overhead lines were unsightly, that land values would decline, and that safety of the area would be reduced. Con Ed stated that concern about the proposed route for the power lines was premature since no firm decision had been made. Con Ed officials said a study showed that the cost of placing cables underground would be 11 times greater than the cost of overhead lines and therefore would be prohibitive. Finally, despite Rockefeller's earlier support, the Palisades Interstate Park Commission indicated it opposed the project unless ". . . steps were taken to minimize scenic damage done by the generating plant and power lines."[7]

To try to quell the growing opposition and still start construction of the transmission lines by 1965, the company revealed that it hoped to use the right-of-way of the New York Central Railroad on the east bank of the Hudson River to avoid residential property. However, any additional land required would have to be condemned if property owners did not want to sell. Con Ed also announced that it would build a 4,000-foot riverfront park and give the park to the town of Cornwall. In addition, the company planned to replace the water system for the town because the present one would be partially taken over for part of the reservoir.

INITIAL FEDERAL POWER COMMISSION INVESTIGATION AND HEARINGS

Meanwhile, the FPC sent examiner Edward B. Marsh to evaluate the area and report on the environmental effect of the project. As a part of his report, Marsh pointed out that while the SHPC had had ample time to submit evidence on the project's negative impact, they had not done so. In addition, he stated, "The conclusion is inescapable [that the project] will have rela-

---

[7] Warren Weaver, Jr., "Hudson Power Project Upheld and Scored at Capital Hearing," *The New York Times,* February 26, 1964, p. 38.

tively little adverse effect upon the natural beauty of the area."[8] It was further revealed that Con Ed's proposed Storm King project was substantially more economical than the other alternative sources of new generation capacity (see Exhibit 4).

EXHIBIT 4
Alternatives to the Storm King Project

1. A 1,100 mw nuclear installation supplemented with 1,088 mw of kerosine-fueled gas turbines—the most economical alternative to Storm King but would cost $78.7 million more to operate over a 20-year period than Storm King.
2. A 2,000 mw facility powered by gas turbines. This alternative had a projected cost of $362.9 million over 20 years; its disadvantages included air and noise pollution, plus heavy natural gas requirements.
3. A 2,000 mw nuclear installation (cost not determined, but substantially higher than Storm King).
4. A 1,000 nuclear plant and a 1,000 fossil-fuel plant.
5. Several fossil-fuel peaking units having 2,000 mw of capacity.
6. Installing conventional fossil-fuel units of 2,000 mw capacity.
7. Purchase power from other utilities.

Source: *Electric World,* September 19, 1966, p. 60.

After the Marsh report was completed, Con Ed requested that the FPC reach a quick decision without further hearings. It was now 1964 and the company was becoming more and more concerned about its ability to adequately supply future power needs in the New York City area. However, just three days later, on March 20, 1964, *The New York Times* published an editorial calling for a slow FPC decision:

> . . . how much beauty of this storied land will be lost forever . . . ?
> . . . what path will the exposed overhead lines follow on the east bank . . .?
> Con Ed has asked the Federal Power Commission for a quick decision approving its application. We believe that this requires, instead, a slow decision. At the least, further investigation should be made into possibilities of concealing the reservoir, the plant and the lines if they can be concealed. And alternative sites may be found that would not deface even a small part of the Hudson's scenery forever.

Again, environmentalists came forward to challenge the Storm King project, this time questioning Con Ed's need for the plant. They argued that Con Ed was able to buy all necessary power very cheaply from Labrador and that neither Storm King nor any of its alternatives would be needed to supply the company's customers with electric power in the years ahead.

In May 1964, Con Ed announced that it was changing its plans regarding the 25 mile section of the overhead transmission line as a result of opposition by both homeowners and environmentalists. According to the company, this would increase the cost for this section from $6.5 million to $14.5 million.

---

[8] "FPC Report Blacks Hudson Power Plan," *The New York Times,* March 12, 1964, p. 16.

However, it was not clear whether the new plans called for underground cable or simply an alteration of the path for overhead lines. Later, it was announced that the first 1.7 miles of power lines would be placed underground along the river and, for the first time, the proposed route for the overhead transmission lines through Putnam and Westchester counties was made public. The citizens of Putnam Valley promptly responded to Con Ed's statement by passing a law requiring all transmission lines to be placed underground. Mr. Forbes, Con Ed's chairman, reacting to this ordinance, stated that rather than place the entire line underground at a cost of approximately $99.8 million, Con Ed would abandon the entire project.[9]

On May 12, 1964, the FPC ended its hearings and set June 15 as a deadline for further company briefs and June 30 as the final date for testimony by other interested parties. In the meantime, on May 20, *The New York Times* reported three significant events. First, the State Water Resources Commission approved the town of Cornwall's plans to sell its largest reservoir to Con Ed. In order to replace the lost portion of its water supply the town planned to dig wells and tap the Catskill Aqueduct. Second, Cornwall's mayor Michael J. Donahue, stated that the proposed power plant would add $50 million to assessed property values, thereby producing an additional $500,000 in tax revenue for the town. At that time, the town's total annual budget was $119,954. Donahue also said, "If the conservationists want to do something worthwhile, they should get after Newburgh and other cities upstream to build sewage-treatment plants. Not once at the hearings in Washington [D.C.] did they mention the needs of man. All they talked about was foliage. Charity means we should love our neighbors and help them."[10] Third, it was revealed that hilltop landowners planned to initiate legal action against Con Ed because of its decision to build 250-foot high dikes. The landowners believed the dikes were too flimsy and would not hold up. If the dikes broke apart, Mount Misery and White Horse Mountain would, they alleged, be flooded with "a billion gallons of sewage-polluted saline water pumped from the Hudson."[11] In another editorial (May 23, 1964), *The New York Times* said

> If the required power plant is not erected at Cornwall but at some other place of less notable scenic and historic interest, doubtless the consumers of New York will have to pay more than they would otherwise pay for their power. We think this choice should be faced frankly; and we also think that in the present instance, preservation is worth the price.

THE FPC STAFF'S RECOMMENDATION

Following the FPC hearings and the expiration of the deadline for further company beliefs, the FPC staff recommended that a license be granted to

---

[9] Warren Weaver, Jr., "Con Ed Eases Plans for Hudson," *The New York Times*, May 5, 1964, p. 45.

[10] Merrill Folsom, "Con Ed Project on Hudson Gains," *The New York Times*, May 20, 1964, p. 45.

[11] Ibid.

Con Ed to build and operate the Storm King project. The staff recommendation also included a proposal for an alternative route for the overhead lines. This route was 10 miles long, compared to the Con Ed route of 29 miles, and would cost $39,000 per mile. The FPC proposal entailed making use of existing Con Ed lines by converting the lines to higher voltage.

Con Ed agreed to the FPC's rerouting proposal and also suggested that the proposed Cornwall plant be increased in size to achieve even greater economies of scale. When these factors were made public, the SHPC reacted by vowing to increase its opposition. The SHPC was "particularly concerned over the apparent attitude of the Federal Power Commission staff which seems to feel that if Con Ed is going to destroy the natural beauty of the area, it might as well wring every possible drop of power out of the project."[12] The Hudson River Conservation Society had only partially opposed the project but, in the wake of Con Ed and FPC moves to build a larger plant at Cornwall, it joined forces with the SHPC in totally opposing Storm King.

Opposition increased generally in the months that followed. The president of Harvard University, Dr. Nathan M. Pusey, wrote a letter to the editor of *The New York Times* which appeared on June 19, 1964:

> As President of the Board of Trustees of the Harvard Black Rock Forest Corporation, I wish to applaud the position taken by *The New York Times* in its strong opposition to the plans of the Consolidated Edison Company to build hydroelectric facilities in the Storm King Mountain area near Cornwall, N.Y.
>
> This proposal threatens a significant portion of the Black Rock Forest, a tract of about 3,700 acres, bequeathed to Harvard University in 1949, remarkable for its hardwoods characteristic of the middle Appalachian region and important for the study of silviculture and conservation practices. . . .
>
> For this reason, unless Consolidated Edison Company can demonstrate that there is no alternative to this radical proposal for altering the scenic beauty and scientific value of a largely unspoiled section of the Hudson River Valley, we wish to ally ourselves with *The Times* and with the individuals and organizations who are protesting the plans of the Consolidated Edison Company. It is our hope that an acceptable alternative can be found.

The town of Yorktown, N.Y., objected to the new transmission line route because the 100-foot towers would require razing at least 30 houses and other buildings in the community. As a part of the protest, the residents of Yorktown petitioned the FPC to reopen the hearings. The FPC rejected the motion as premature, and indicated it would submit the motion at later hearings set for November 17, 1964.

A WIDENING OF THE CONTROVERSY

As publicity about the project increased, both state and national political figures entered the controversy. State Assemblyman R. Watson Pomeroy,

---

[12] "Hudson Group Plans Con Ed Opposition," *The New York Times*, June 24, 1964, p. 37.

chairman of the Joint Legislative Committee on Natural Resources, proposed a delay in the Storm King project until the state legislature could formulate a policy regarding areas of great natural beauty and historical significance. Mr. Pomeroy argued, "We believe that the State of New York should have the opportunity to determine what policy it wishes to establish for the control and determination of the most effective and beneficial use of its natural resources."[13] In another politically related move, Congressman-elect Richard L. Ottinger pledged to support the SHPC in its bid to stop the Storm King project. As the political opposition increased, Con Ed offered to sit down with opponents and work to solve the differences, as long as the FPC was allowed to act as the mediator and conservationists did not use the meetings to simply delay the project.

Up to this point, Governor Nelson Rockefeller had successfully avoided taking a position on the project despite attempts by both proponents and opponents to draw him into the controversy. However, on December 11, 1964, Governor Rockefeller, feeling that he could no longer avoid the issue, stated, ". . . in my judgment, the values of the project . . . outweigh the objections which have been raised to it."[14] In response, Mr. Rothschild, president of the SHPC, commented to the press:

> Nelson A. Rockefeller has a truly bad habit of deeply disappointing his real friends and supporters. . . . Now, alas, he has done it again. Incomprehensible is the only word truly descriptive of the Governor's flat-footed failure to use his influence to help enable the citizens of this state to make their own decision regarding the future uses of the Hudson River and its great valley.[15]

THE VIEWS OF LOCAL RESIDENTS

At various times in 1964, several local officials and individuals living in the towns directly affected by construction began to express their sentiments about the Storm King project. The mayor of the town of Cornwall, Michael J. Donahue, was probably the most vocal advocate for the project; *The New York Times* quoted him as saying:

> The project will improve the waterfront, since Consolidated Edison will give us a mile of park on the water where only shacks, rotted piers and dirty shoreline now exist. The rock taken from the tunnel will be used to fill in along the shore. The tunnel will be so far underground that nobody will even know it is there.
>
> We have five reservoirs on the mountain and Consolidated Edison is taking only one. . . .[16]

---

[13] "Assemblyman Urges Power Plant Delay," *The New York Times,* October 1, 1964, p. 26.

[14] "Governor Backs Storm King Plant," *The New York Times,* December 12, 1964.

[15] Ibid.

[16] Merrill Folsom, "Storm King Plant Moves Step Nearer," *The New York Times,* December 17, 1964, p. 43.

And in a typical reply to environmentalists' charges that faults existed under Storm King Mountain which made it likely that the dams would collapse, Donahue argued, "Storm King has been there 100,000 years and I think it will stay put."[17]

A local businessman who supported the project commented:

> The power plant will be in a ravine on the waterfront where hardly anyone will see it. It will replace a ramshackle boarding house that paid low taxes and caused continuous annoyances. The tunnel will be underground and the reservoir will not be unsightly. And Con Ed has even agreed to paint its power lines green. Building lots that we couldn't sell for $2,000 now bring $15,000.[18]

However, several residents expressed disapproval of the project. Mrs. Siegler, a long-time resident of Cornwall stated, "Hundreds of people here are opposed to Consolidated Edison's plan, but are too afraid of intimidation, reprisal, and loss of jobs to speak out."[19]

Despite the role played by other groups and individuals involved, the controversy surrounding the Storm King project shaped up as a major clash between Con Ed and the environmentalists. In order to advance their position and gain the support of influential officials, each side started utilizing the testimony of experts. For instance, several national and regional environmentalist groups, such as the Sierra Club, aligned themselves with the SHPC. Fishermen groups, both sport and commercial, also sided with the environmentalists after hearing reports that the project was a threat to many types of aquatic life, including striped bass. The Hudson River had traditionally been the spawning grounds of many kinds of fish and was a popular fishing spot; sport fishing along the Hudson was estimated to be a $45 million industry.[20]

EVENTS ON THE NATIONAL SCENE

As the controversy over the project heightened, it moved to the national political arena. Congressman Ottinger introduced a bill in the U.S. House of Representatives which would preclude "destructive intrusions" along the Hudson River. On the Senate side of the U.S. Congress, Senators Jacob Javits and Robert Kennedy entered the controversy for the first time in early 1965 following introduction of the Ottinger bill. Neither initially favored stopping the project, although Kennedy reportedly planned to introduce a bill similar to Ottinger's to prevent such actions in the future. Kennedy commented, "I do not believe that the Consolidated Edison project by itself will destroy the breathtaking beauty of the lower Hudson River, but it is

---

[17] Ibid.

[18] Ibid.

[19] Ibid.

[20] McCandlish Phillips, "Fishermen Score Storm King Plan," *The New York Times,* January 8, 1965, p. 10.

quite clear that a few more encroachments on the river could make the situation irretrievable."[21]

President Lyndon Johnson, in his State of the Union Address in 1965, noted that the development and control of rivers should be left to state and local governments, if optimum control was to be achieved. Johnson used the controversy over the Storm King project as a specific example, and thus greatly diminished the possibility of enacting the Ottinger or Kennedy bills into law, should they reach the president for his signature.

At the state level, a special committee named The Hudson River Valley Commission was formed by the State Council of Parks to preserve the natural beauty of the lower Hudson Valley. Laurance Rockefeller, chairman of the new committee, remarked that "the need for the panel had been 'dramatized' by the plan of Consolidated Edison" to build a plant at Storm King Mountain.[22] During the same period, Governor Nelson Rockefeller reinforced his position but noted ". . . if so many people want to block Consolidated Edison's hydroelectric project . . . they ought to band together and buy the land."[23]

FEDERAL POWER COMMISSION RULING

In early 1965, the FPC voted 3 to 1 in favor in granting Con Ed a license for the Storm King project and refused to order the company to place all transmission lines underground. The majority opinion stated in part:

> We find that the impact of the project upon scenic resources will be minimal, that it will create additional recreational opportunities, and that its advantages for power-supply purposes far outweigh any negative considerations.
>
> In these circumstances and viewing sympathetically the case made by the Scenic Hudson Preservation Conference, we cannot conclude that the Cornwall powerhouse substantially impairs the scenic, historic, or recreational values in the area.

The FPC report also cited the following positive factors associated with the project: (1) there would be savings of $12 million to $15.6 million per year over a conventional steam plant in New York City; (2) the 240-acre reservoir would be visible from the air only; (3) there would be a net increase in land available to the public of 80 acres; (4) the total plant height would be 110 feet, 80 feet of which would be below ground and the remainder would be shielded by foliage; (5) there would be no air pollution or gas seepage as would very likely be the case with other alternatives; and (6) the Storm King project was superior to other alternatives. The FPC also noted that the

---

[21] Warren Weaver, Jr., "FPC 3-1 Grants Con Ed a License for Hudson Plant," *The New York Times,* March 10, 1965, p. 1.

[22] "New Group Meets on Hudson Valley," *The New York Times,* January 23, 1965, p. 11.

[23] "Governor Bids Project Foes Buy Land at Storm King," *The New York Times,* January 13, 1965, p. 30.

impact on the town of Cornwall included: a tripling of assessed property value, possible reductions in taxes to one-half the present level, 1,200 jobs during the three-year construction period, new schools, an expanded water system, a new firehouse, a new town hall, and an increased police force.

Following the FPC ruling, the environmentalists and other individuals opposed to the project expressed dismay. An American flag was flown from a tree on the top of Storm King Mountain as a symbol of protest. A *New York Times* reporter wrote "By licensing a power plant in the Hudson Highlands before the controversy over it has been resolved, the Federal Power Commission has indicated the value it attaches in public opinion. It regards public opinion as a nuisance and a bore."[24] The towns of Cortland, Putnam Valley, and Yorktown joined the SHPC in requesting the FPC to reopen the case. The FPC politely denied the request.

A suit was filed in the U.S. Court of Appeals asking for an order forcing the FPC to reopen the case. On December 30, 1965, the Court ruled that the FPC had not looked closely enough at the alternatives. "In this case, as in many others, the commission claimed to be the representative of the public interest. This role does not permit it to act as an umpire, blandly calling balls and strikes for adversaries appearing before it; the right of the public must receive active and affirmative protection at the hands of the commission."[25] The successful suit led Rod Vandivert, head of the SHPC, to remark:

> This proves one thing: that a citizen's fight for right can be pursued and can be upheld. We now hope that Con Ed will review the information which has been developed since the hearings regarding the problems and will change their minds. This is truly a breakthrough in saving the Hudson River.[26]

During this same period, Con Ed sought to dispel some of the opposition by offering to build a $1.5 million barrier to protect the fish in the river by keeping them from being sucked into the intake of the reservoir. Also, Con Ed and New York City jointly announced that the reservoir would be used as an alternative source of water for the city. The proposal received immediate opposition.

THE COMPANY'S POSITION

The foregoing events prompted the following commentary in Con Ed's *1965 Annual Report:*

> Delay in construction of the Cornwall project is unfortunate because it will postpone the time when this added reliability to New York City's power supply

---

[24] Brooks Atkinson, "The FPC Action on Storm King Mountain Disregards Strong Public Opinion," *The New York Times,* March 19, 1965, p. 32.

[25] Edward Ranzal, "Storm King Plant Blocked by Court," *The New York Times,* December 30, 1965, p. 1.

[26] Ibid.

can be provided. No city in the world is more dependent on electricity than New York and it needs the utmost in reliability of service. One of the basic reasons for proposing this project was to provide protection against the type of disturbance that resulted in the November 9 power interruption. Hydroelectric generating equipment such as that proposed for Cornwall represents the ultimate in reliability and in ability to pick up load quickly in an emergency.

Furthermore, the Cornwall project will enable the Company to cut down air pollution in the city by reducing the amount of fuels burned there and by eliminating much of the daily starting up and shutting down of steam units, an operation that often causes undesirable stack emissions. It will also permit retirement of several hundred thousand kilowatts of older capacity and this too should help to reduce air pollution further.

Great care has been taken in the design of the Cornwall plant to blend it in with its surroundings and to improve the shoreline of the Hudson. Plans for the project include clearing out abandoned unsightly buildings, sunken barges, a burned out pier and other blighted waterfront structures on the Hudson River shoreline, and constructing a mile-long 55-acre waterfront recreational park in their place. The great majority of those who live in the area favor the project as one that offers economic, scenic and recreational benefits, as well as an improved local water supply.

While the further delay of this project is regrettable, the Company welcomes the renewed opportunity to give authorities and the public the fullest possible information of the Company's desire to serve the public interest by improving the scenic beauty and recreational aspects of the area while making best possible use of one of the great natural resources available to our country.

The benefits the Cornwall project promises for millions of people should be realized and the Company will make every effort to see the project through to completion.

THE CONTROVERSY CONTINUES INTO ITS FOURTH YEAR

At the beginning of 1966, Governor Rockefeller proposed that a 15-man commission be jointly created by New York, New Jersey, and the federal government. The commission would attempt to achieve a cooperative approach to achieving a solution to the controversy over the Hudson River Valley. Rockefeller also switched from his straight endorsement of the project, to one which recommended that "if another solution can be found, then it should be."[27]

At the same time, the Hudson River Valley Commission published a report detailing its recommendations. Among the proposals was a recommendation that the state of New York acquire Storm King Mountain and search for another site for Con Ed. The report continued:

> The growing pressures are mounting. The State's population will reach 30 million by the end of the century, and the great bulk of this growth will take

---

[27] McCandlish Phillips, "Rockefeller Seeks Start of New Era in Hudson Valley," *The New York Times*, February 1, 1966, p. 1.

place in the valley. . . . There will be many more industrial plants, new highways, new subdivisions—indeed, whole towns. This growth is vital. The question is whether it can be shaped to enhance the beauty of this great valley, rather than destroy it.[28]

However, the residents of Cornwall still strongly favored the construction of the generating plant. Gordon Carnerson, town supervisor, emphasized "God knows no one up here wants to abuse our area's natural beauty, but we've got to eat. An area's industrial, commercial, and scenic potential should all be developed together, but the commission is oriented only to scenery and recreation."[29]

In the meantime, Con Ed's request for a hearing before the Supreme Court was denied. This meant the FPC had to reopen the hearings in accordance with the District Court's earlier decision. Con Ed offered to put the entire project underground so that no part of the plant would be exposed to mar the scenery. However, despite the offer, the entire project and all the alternatives were placed before the FPC for another hearing. At the time of this review in 1966, the minimum cost of the Storm King project had increased to $162 million—up from $115 million in 1962.

Environmentalists then came up with a new attack upon the Storm King plant, alleging it would be a potential source of air pollution; this was because the electricity required to pump the water into the reservoir would be produced at coal-burning plants in New York City. At this time, these plants did not burn coal 24 hours a day. Con Ed countered this argument by stating that it would purchase the necessary power from the cheapest source available and this would probably be a hydroelectric plant upstate.

Other arguments used to oppose the project included the killing of fish, alternative uses of the land, marring the scenic area, projected demand for electricity, changing property values, and the cost of the alternatives. As pressure against the project gathered momentum, Con Ed relied more heavily on the argument that the plant was needed to avoid potential blackouts. If this were to occur during rush hour, the company argued, New York City would be paralyzed.

Dr. Teller, a nuclear physicist, testified in support of the project saying,

> I appear solely on my own initiative; my motivation for appearing stems from my conviction that the Cornwall project can make significant contributions both to the prevention of future power failures and to the reduction of sulphur oxide and particulate concentrations in New York City.
>
> I would also like to mention that the premature deaths of scores of people during periods of prolonged inversion or the thought of many thousands of people trapped below the ground in the subway system during a massive power failure, weighs heavily on my mind.[30]

---

[28] Ibid.

[29] "7 Towns on Hudson Fighting Park Plan," *The New York Times*, February 23, 1966, p. 32.

[30] Maurice Carroll, "Teller Supports Storm King Plant," *The New York Times*, March 21, 1967, p. 53.

EXHIBIT 5
Features of the Agreement between New York City and Consolidated Edison,
May 1966

Con Edison agrees to:

1. Recognize that its air pollution control program is a basic and vital part of the planning for its total operation.
2. Undertake or participate in research programs designed to reduce sulfur content in coal and fuel oil.
3. Accept the principle that, to the fullest extent possible, power from fossil-fuel plants will be generated outside the city.
4. Present to the mayor, within six months, a plan for shutting down its power-generating stations at Sherman Creek, Hell Gate, and Kent Avenue, and for retiring older units at its Hudson Avenue station.
5. Reduce to an absolute minimum the soot, smoke, and sulfur oxides caused by burning fossil fuels, pending shutdown of units specified.
6. Seek federal authorization to increase use of natural gas for boiler fuel pending the shift of generating capacity outside the city.
7. Assign the use of natural gas on the basis of reducing air pollution from the more inefficient units and in the areas of dense population.

New York City agrees to:

1. Support Con Edison's effort to obtain additional supplies of natural gas for boiler fuel.
2. Support Con Edison's plan to build a 2,000 mw pumped storage project at Cornwall, N.Y., provided the utility is able to overcome objections relative to destruction of marine life and natural beauty.
3. Cooperate with Con Edison in devising a long-range plan for substantial development of nuclear generation outside the city.
4. Assist Con Edison in obtaining rights-of-way into the city for transmission lines from outside power sources.

Source: *Electric World,* May 30, 1966, p. 45.

In an effort to secure political support for the Storm King project, Con Ed and New York City established a formal agreement in May 1966; the substance of the agreement is presented in Exhibit 5.

FURTHER OPPOSITION TO THE PROJECT

When the controversy returned to the FPC for further hearings, Con Ed charged, "This latest delaying tactic of the Scenic Hudson Preservation Conference makes it clear that it intends to attempt to kill by delay and attrition of a project which it apparently no longer hopes to defeat on the merits."[31]

However, opponents were not quieted by the verbal attack. Congressman Ottinger questioned the propriety of Con Ed's payment of $2.7 million to

---

[31] "Experts Defend the Hudson River Power Project," *The New York Times,* November 19, 1966, p. 29.

the town of Cornwall. These payments were for engineering and legal services and construction costs related to the town's new water supply. Con Ed defended the payments on the grounds that the Storm King project was the direct cause of why the town incurred the expenses. The state controller stated that he saw no violation associated with the company's payments.

Ottinger also focused attention on Con Ed's expenses related to pursuit of the license for the project. He stated, "If it isn't against the law for a company to spend $15 million for a license that hasn't even been granted yet, then it should be."[32] The company acknowledged that it had spent a considerable sum of money trying to get the license, but felt that the benefits derived from the project justified the expense.

In a separate move, the Jackson Hole Corporation, also headed by Laurance Rockefeller, planned to purchase land at Breakneck Ridge, opposite Storm King Mountain and across the Hudson River. This land was to be used to construct a state park. Opponents hoped that once the land was designated as a park, then the Strom King project could be successfully blocked as an indirect intrusion on a state park area.

Despite these attempts to block or influence Con Ed, the company insisted that the Storm King project was vital to operations and superior to the alternatives which had been suggested. Thus, Con Ed officials continued their pursuit of licenses from the FPC and necessary State agencies.

FEDERAL POWER COMMISSION REASSESSMENT

The FPC held hearings during a three-year period between 1966 and 1969. As a part of the reassessment, Ewing G. Simpson, a FPC examiner, again reviewed and evaluated the impact of the proposed plant on the area surrounding the site. This evaluation took place during the first eight months of 1968. After completing his study, Simpson stated, ". . . There was no evidentiary support that these installments would scar and change scenic values associated with the mountain."[33] He also noted that there were no real suitable alternatives or any evidence that the plant was a threat to fish life. After further examination of Storm King Mountain based on several boat trips up the Hudson River, Simpson stated,

> . . . the gorge is not an area of untouched natural beauty. For approaching from the south, one sees along the west shore a continuing vista of railroad tracks, . . . highways, bridges and trestles, docks and river shore pilings, barges, stand pipes, sewage disposal plants and boat houses . . . particularly noticeable in certain situations are the highway and railroad embankments . . . which disfigure Crow's Nest and Storm King, the most devastating single

---

[32] Peter Millones, "Ottinger Decries Con Ed Payment," *The New York Times,* August 25, 1967, p. 24.

[33] Eileen Shanahan, "Storm King Plan by Con Ed Gains in FPC Report," *The New York Times,* August 7, 1968, p. 1.

impression being that of the cut of the scenic Old Storm King Highway that rips high up and half around the face of Storm King.[34]

Simpson also noted in his report that the parks and recreation facilities to be built by Con Ed would actually improve the attractiveness of the area. As a final recommendation, he suggested that Con Ed operate a hatchery to replace any fish lost due to the operation of the plant.

Con Ed praised the evaluation and continued to press the FPC for a license while it defended itself to the public. Charles Luce, president of Con Ed, said, "There's no reason why we can't have power and not louse up the environment." On the other side, the SHPC said that they would wait for the final FPC ruling, but would take the issue to court if the license was granted.

SOME EFFECTS OF THE CONTROVERSY ON CON ED

The controversy swirling about Con Ed's Storm King project was only one of many such problems. Con Ed faced public opposition of one kind or another with most of its projects. The results of such continual conflict were felt by the company in several ways.

Con Ed's bond rating fell from Aa in the early 60s to BB in the late 60s; in 1974 the company's bonds were downgraded even further. In 1965, the company attempted a $100 million bond issue; yet it was able to place only $40 million at 4.85 percent, when the going rate for other utility companies ranged between 4.64 percent and 4.75 percent. Subsequently, the company was able to sell the entire $100 million at a cost to the company of 4.99 percent.

The company was frequently involved in requests for rate increases. During the period 1970 through 1976, Con Ed was granted 13 rate increases totaling almost $600 million. Nonetheless the rate increases granted the company tended to lag behind increasing costs, making it difficult for the company to raise the financial capital to continue its expansion plans and renovation program.

Con Ed's ability to provide reliable electric service also suffered. Because of opposition to nearly all of Con Ed's proposed projects during the 1960s and early 1970s, its generating capacity tended to remain relatively static. However, the peak kilowatt demand placed on the company's system by its customers continued to grow, with the result that the company's reserve margin over peak was reduced (see Exhibit 2). As a result, New York City suffered several blackouts during the summer months of the late 1960s. The company's *1965 Annual Report* described the blackout which interrupted power service throughout the Northeast on November 9, 1965:

> . . . the widespread power interruption in the Northeast on November 9 affected an area of some 80,000 square miles which included New York State, most of New England, parts of Canada and small areas in Pennsylvania and

---

[34] Ibid.

New Jersey. The disturbance originated at 5:16 P.M. on the Ontario Hydro-Electric Power Commission system just north of Niagara Falls. This initiated a cascading loss of generating capacity in upstate New York that threw a sudden huge load on New England and downstate utilities, including Con Edison. The unprecedented magnitude and nature of this load was such that the generating facilities in New England and downstate New York could not pick it up. By 5:28 P.M. the balance of the interconnected system, including nearly all of Con Edison's, had shut down.

The enormously complicated process of restoring electric service to our customers began immediately and continued through the night. By 1 A.M., service had been restored to 25 percent of our customers; by 3:30 A.M., 50 percent; and by 7 A.M., 99 percent. By evening of November 10 service was essentially normal.

It took longer for service to be restored in New York City than in other areas because of the nature of the system. There is no other electric system as immense, complex and concentrated as that serving New York City. Furthermore, the Company had no quick starting hydroelectric capacity to assist in the process as did most other utilities in the affected area. This is a handicap that the Cornwall plant would remedy.

As a result of the shutdown, generating units on our system with a combined capacity of 1.5 million kilowatts sustained mechanical damage. These units have all been returned to service.

As a result of the power interruption, questions have been raised as to the desirability of interconnection with neighboring utilities. The Company has continually placed maximum dependability foremost in its system planning, and interconnections play an important role in this. They have demonstrated their great value in protecting utility systems from interruptions time and time again, and are fundamental to reliability of electric service. A return to the operation of numerous, relatively small, completely isolated systems would certainly be a step backward that would result in more, rather than less, trouble.

Con Edison continued to have periodic blackouts attributable to power supply shortages. Shortages during the summer of 1969 were particularly acute and prompted a study by the New York PSC; the study placed the blame for insufficient capacity on delays in constructing new generating capacity stemming from the opposition of environmentalists and from strikes and labor disputes at construction sites. The study prompted the FPC to recommend that Con Ed line up potential sources of power because "potential power shortages, similar to those that occurred a number of times this past summer, may possibly recur during the 1970 summer peak load season."[35] It was these periods of peak demand that had initially motivated Con Ed to begin the Storm King project.

One resident in a letter to *The New York Times* observed:

---

[35] Richard Madden, "U.S. Urges Con Ed to Prepare," *The New York Times*, December 13, 1969, p. 37.

If all the conservationists and their followers, who always are so free to advance obstacles, would only now voluntarily do without or cut down on their use of electricity, there would be no crisis. . . . But they and so many others want it all ways—nothing to disturb our ecology, low prices for power, and yet sufficient reserve electric capacity to take care of all breakdowns.[36]

FEDERAL POWER COMMISSION GRANTS LICENSE—AGAIN

On August 19, 1970, the FPC granted another license to Con Ed to build the hydroelectric plant at Storm King Mountain. The cost estimate for the project now stood at $234 million, more than double the original estimate of $115 million. Also by this time, Con Ed had spent more than $17.6 million on the project without beginning construction. In its decision the FPC said that no alternative could

> . . . so well meet the requirements with lesser detriment to our environment. . . . The balancing and weighing of conflicting values is our task. It is not a preoccupation with more and more electric power which moves us. It is not a preoccupation with cheap power which moves us. It is not sympathy for New Yorkers nor lack of it for the Hudson highlanders which moves us. Yet we cannot avoid these charges.[37]

The SHPC and the Sierra Club filed an application with the FPC for a rehearing, saying that the FPC had failed to comply with the 1965 court ruling. The FPC denied the requests for a rehearing. A spokesman for the SHPC remarked, "The FPC ruling was an automatic formality. Now we'll go ahead with our plans to file a complaint with the Court of Appeals."[38]

The following year, in August 1971, Con Ed received certification from the New York Commission of Environmental Conservation to proceed with the Storm King plant; the Commission stated that its view was the facility would not violate water quality standards. Environmentalists had contended that the plant would draw so much water out of the Hudson River that salt water from the ocean would be drawn up into the river and ruin freshwater supplies. In response to this possibility the Commission stipulated that the certification was good only if construction would be halted "immediately in the event of contravention of water quality standards." The SHPC questioned the viability of the arrangement noting that once the plant was completed, it would be used regardless of the impact upon the environment.

At this stage, the cost of building the project had ballooned to $400 million with a construction time of six years.

---

[36] Letter to the Editor—Walter G. Steinbrucker, "Power Crisis," *The New York Times,* August 7, 1970, p. 32.

[37] Richard L. Madden, "FPC Authorizes Con Ed to Build Storm King Plant," *The New York Times,* August 20, 1970, p. 1.

[38] Francis X. Clwes, "Ottinger Backed by Construction Workers Group," *The New York Times,* October 8, 1970, p. 39.

RETURN TO THE COURTS

Following the FPC denial of a rehearing and the issuance of the water quality certificate by the state of New York, the SHPC decided to shift the forum of the battle back to the courts. The FPC license was challenged in the U.S. District Court of Appeals; a second motion was filed in the State Supreme Court against the water quality certificate, charging that no independent studies had been conducted and that Con Ed should not be allowed to monitor its own pollution.

When U.S. Court of Appeals upheld the FPC license, Alexander Saunders, the new president of the SHPC, commented, "We are certain there are grounds which finally will require the word of the Supreme Court."[39] Nevertheless, in June 1972, by a vote of 8 to 1, the U.S. Supreme Court rejected the motion of the SHPC to review the case.

However, at the state level, things did not go as smoothly for Con Ed. In March 1972, the New York Supreme Court ruled that the Commissioner of Environmental Conservation, Henry Diamond, had overstepped his bounds and had not shown "reasonable assurance" that the project would not violate the water quality standards. The Court also called attention to the restriction he placed on the license, branding it, "impractical to the point of being ridiculous. . . ."[40] An official of the SHPC, rejoicing at the State Court's ruling, stated, "They'll get more electricity out of a hand crank than they'll get out of Storm King in the next 20 years.[41]

Con Ed appealed to the Appellate Division of the New York State Supreme Court, asking for a reversal of the earlier voiding of the water quality certification. In July 1972, the Appellate Division handed down a decision validating the commissioner's certification, thus reversing the State Supreme Court's ruling. Commenting on the Appellate Court ruling and his own responsibilities, Mr. Diamond pointed out that he was limited to rule only on the quality of the water, a rather narrow issue. Yet, in spite of his earlier decision and the court ruling, Diamond stated, "I'm still not persuaded that this project is environmentally desirable."[42]

AFTERMATH AND NEW BEGINNING

Following the favorable court rulings, Con Ed started construction of the plant in March 1974, having spent over $25 million during the 12-year controversy to obtain the licenses necessary simply to begin construction. The cost of the Storm King project had risen to an estimated $720 million and was

---

[39] "Appeals Court Approves Con Ed Storm King Plant," *The New York Times*, December 24, 1971, p. 1.

[40] John Darnton, "Water Certificate Voided for Con Ed Power Plant," *The New York Times*, March 16, 1972, p. 94.

[41] Ibid.

[42] David Bird, "Court Backs Con Ed on Storm King," *The New York Times*, March 16, 1972, p. 94.

scheduled for completion in the summer of 1980, 18 years after its initial proposal.

Yet, events quickly showed the issue was not settled. In May 1974, the U.S. Court of Appeals directed the FPC to once again reopen licensing hearings initially on the issue of fish protection but with the possibility of later extending to other issues. The Court ruled that since the plant was in a tidal estuary, there was greater danger to aquatic life than had been recognized earlier. John Adams, director of the National Resources Defense Council, stated, "Let them [Con Ed] make any studies they want, they just can't win on the fish kill issue because the evidence is so damning."[43]

In 1974, for the first time since 1885, Con Ed failed to pay its regular quarterly dividend. The second quarter dividend of 45 cents was omitted entirely and the third and fourth quarter dividends were limited to 20 cents each. Management stated the action was necessitated by a combination of (1) sharply increased fuel oil costs resulting from the Arab oil embargo and its aftermath, (2) a reduction in sales as a consequence of energy conservation, and (3) inadequate cash flow to finance both operations and construction programs.

When Con Ed's board of directors voted to pass the second quarter dividend, the action sent shock waves not only through the company's stockholders but also through Wall Street and utility stockholders in general. Con Ed's stock price fell almost immediately from the $17–$19 range to the $6–$7 range (see Exhibit 6). The prices of many other utility stocks and bonds fell

EXHIBIT 6
Market Price Range on New York Stock Exchange and Dividends Paid on Voting Stock

	1976			1975			1974		
	High	*Low*	*Dividends Paid*	*High*	*Low*	*Dividends Paid*	*High*	*Low*	*Dividends Paid*
Common:									
1st quarter	$18	$15	$0.40	$12⅜	$ 7½	$0.30	$21½	$18⅞	$0.45
2d quarter	18⅛	16⅜	0.40	14½	11	0.30	19⅝	6	—
3d quarter	20	17⅝	0.40	13⅞	11¾	0.30	9	6	0.20
4th quarter	21	19⅜	0.40	15	12	0.30	8½	6¼	0.20

also—though less drastically. Con Ed's bonds were downgraded severely. One of the two leading bond rating agencies suspended the rating on the company's bonds and the other lowered the rating to below investment grade. The company was unable to issue the common stock which it had planned to issue in May 1974 or the bonds which it had planned to issue in October 1974. Cutbacks in construction spending were implemented and two

---

[43] David Bird, "New Storm King Hearings Ordered: Aid for Con Ed Stalled in Albany," *The New York Times,* May 9, 1974, p. 1.

of the generating plants which the company had under construction were sold to the Power Authority of the State of New York to provide an emergency source of funds.

It was in this environment that Con Ed announced in July 1974 that it was suspending all work on its Storm King project, pending settlement of the fish protection issue and any other issues that might arise. In making the announcement, Con Ed's chairman, Charles F. Luce, remarked "There comes a point when human environment must prevail over fish habitat. I think in New York we've reached it."[44] Exhibit 7 details the amounts which the company spent for environmental protection in 1975.

EXHIBIT 7
Expenditures Related to Environmental Protection, 1975

	$ Millions
1. Plants—operations and maintenance of environmental protection devices	$ 9.7
2. Plants—annual depreciation and taxes on environmental features	12.5
3. Incremental cost, including taxes, of very low sulfur oil compared to coal and high sulfur oil	135.0
4. Extra costs of going underground—annual depreciation and taxes	102.8
5. Transmission and distribution—including right-of-way maintenance	5.9
6. Substations—aesthetic enhancement and annual depreciation and taxes on environmental features	0.9
7. Environmental planning—including Hudson River Studies	6.1
8. Energy conservation programs	0.9
Total	$273.8

Source: *1975 Annual Report.*

Shortly thereafter, the New York Public Service Commission ordered six major power companies in New York to cooperate with Con Ed to determine if the Storm King project was needed. Con Ed hoped to have both its fish kill study and the Storm King review completed by March 1, 1977. However, in August 1975, another lawsuit against the Storm King project was being prepared, this one on grounds that the project was economically unsound. The basis for this view was the fact that when originally planned the plant would use oil priced at approximately $1.97 per barrel, whereas the current price of oil was now in excess of $13.

In its *1976 Annual Report* Consolidated Edison made the following comment about the status of the Storm King Mountain project at Cornwall:

> The Company had an investment in the Cornwall pumped-storage project at December 31, 1976 amounting to approximately $35 million, excluding $1.7 million for the cost of the land. Construction of this project has been delayed,

---

[44] Reginald Stuart, "Con Ed Chief at Meeting Scores Taxes and Ecologists," *The New York Times,* May 20, 1975, p. 53.

EXHIBIT 8

CONSOLIDATED EDISON COMPANY
Comparative Income Accounts
Years Ending December 31, 1962–1976

	1976	1975
Operating Revenues:		
Electric operating revenues	$2,361,754,000	$2,256,855,635
Gas operating revenues	268,991,000	204,706,830
Steam operating revenues	226,898,000	194,409,999
Miscellaneous operating revenues[6]	22.659.000	11,965,642
Gross Revenues[6]	$2,880,302,000	$2,667,938,106
Operating expenses[6]	1,436,316,000	1,372,744,830
Maintenance	189,641,000	182,918,490
Federal income tax	6,890,000	50,000
Provision for deferred income tax[3]	30,480,000	49,500,000
Investment tax credit[1]	70,842,000	4,360,000
Other taxes	525,904,000	476,134,657
Depreciation[2]	164,865,000	155,269,164
Operating Income	$ 455,364,000	$ 426,960,965
Interest charged to construction[7]	9,314,000	36,558,681
Other income	—	2,318,841
Total Income	$ 482,188,000	$ 465,838,487
Interest	180,777,000	189,526,653
Miscellaneous deductions[4]	—	1,578,232
Income before extraordinary items	$ 301,411,000	$ 274,733,602
Other items[8]	—	—
Extraordinary items[5]	—	(23,350,000)
Net Income	$ 301,411,000	$ 251,383,602

[1] See footnote 3 under Comparative Balance Sheet.
[2] Estimated deduction for depreciation for federal income tax purposes:

	Total (000s)
1974	$245,600
1973	200,700
1972	186,500
1971	202,400
1970	195,800
1969	186,700
1968	166,200
1967	160,000
1966	153,900
1965	142,700
1964	130,100
1963	124,817
1962	108,700

[3] Adjusted for 2-for-1 split in February 1965.
[4] 1968–67: Other income included with amortization of debt, and so forth, 1966 and prior years not restated.
[5] See footnote 2 under Comparative Balance Sheets taken from reports to stockholders.
[6] Excludes interdepartment rents.
[7] See footnote 2 (above) under comparative income accounts taken from reports to Federal Power Commission.
[8] Represents cumulative effect on prior years of change in accounting for fuel costs.

1974	1973	1970	1965	1962
$2,096,877,222	$1,483,362,013	$ 951,962,810	$693,591,000	$583,667,363
169,825,051	152,716,414	117,779,012	104,291,577	103,618,248
162,720,193	95,730,565	55,780,971	38,424,671	34,177,953
10,048,895	4,430,137	2,956,818	3,933,026	3,689,756
$2,439,471,361	$1,736,239,129	$1,128,479,611	$840,240,274	$725,153,320
1,306,461,898	809,628,983	484,132,646	328,411,568	290,260,377
170,451,731	161,594,756	104,622,621	78,866,385	72,535,061
100,000	(744,000)	(19,930,000)	8,200,000	75,650,000
30,720,000	(3,643,000)	(900,000)	(900,000)	(925,227)
—	—	2,430,000	9,500,000	4,150,000
424,531,959	360,403,394	246,791,546	160,102,186	129,292,050
144,407,904	124,041,612	100,728,686	83,560,592	68,832,281
$ 362,797,869	$ 284,957,384	$ 210,604,112	$172,499,543	$135,358,778
45,398,885	47,769,775	23,453,850	(6,096,129)	(9,676,326)
1,401,119	5,367,314	551,852	227,015	976,211
$ 409,597,873	$ 338,094,473	$ 234,609,814	$178,822,687	$146,011,315
194,620,687	155,133,062	105,523,003	62,704,768	52,570,681
6,039,095	1,398,403	659,559	4,340,424	2,805,016
$ 208,938,091	$ 181,563,008	$ 128,427,252	$111,777,495	$ 90,635,618
5,120,644	(26,143,476)	—	—	—
(19,554,000)	—	—	—	—
$ 194,504,735	$ 207,706,754	$ 128,427,252	$111,777,495	$ 90,635,618

and is presently suspended, as a result of protracted licensing and environmental proceedings. It remains the Company's conviction that Cornwall is the most advantageous and reliable source of peaking power for the Company's service area and New York State as a whole, and is as economic as the cheapest alternatives. If the Company is unable, because of financial considerations, legal difficulties or otherwise, to construct or operate the plant either alone or in combination with others, the Company would incure substantial losses and would apply to the PSC for permission to treat the unrecovered investment for accounting and rate purposes as an extraordinary property loss chargeable to operations over a number of years.

HIBIT 9

CONSOLIDATED EDISON COMPANY
Comparative Balance Sheet
As of December 31, 1962–1976

	1976	1975	1974
sets:			
ility plant[2]	$6,900,961,000	$6,645,081,415	$6,728,865,271
preciation reserve balance	1,407,345,000	1,340,295,206	1,225,175,099
	5,493,616,000	5,340,786,209	5,503,690,172
clear fuel assemblies, net[5]	26,536,000	18,419,227	57,624,092
Net Plant	$5,520,152,000	$5,359,205,436	$5,561,314,264
apital stock expense[3]	—	—	—
vestments, special deposits and other physical property, at cost or less	8,447,000	13,081,136	15,089,130
rrent Assets:			
ash	27,805,000	33,355,412	49,632,023
mporary cash investment	376,644,000	45,000,000	—
nds held by trustee for retirement of series B bonds	87,745,000	—	—
tes and accounts receivable (net)	280,210,000	575,520,518	350,865,882
ock and bond subscriptions	—	—	—
aterial and supplies (cost or less)[5]	163,318,000	141,067,206	164,729,890
her current assets	17,027,000	30,349,429	17,671,116
deral income tax recoverable	—	—	—
namortized debt discount and expense	25,613,000	26,994,131	25,110,840
eferred debits[4]	81,702,000	90,835,775	101,016,997
Total Assets	$6,588,663,000	$6,315,409,043	$6,285,430,142
abilities:			
referred stock[1]	$ 750,894,000	$ 750,901,810	$ 750,907,410
apital stock	—	—	—
ommon stock[1]	1,338,264,000	1,338,256,533	1,338,250,933
etained earnings	995,122,000	836,481,924	703,250,781
apital stock expense	(34,164,000)	(34,164,211)	(34,164,211)
Total Stockholders' Equity	3,050,116,000	2,891,476,056	2,758,244,913
ong-term debt	2,826,366,000	2,988,630,439	2,992,911,338
uclear fuel assemblies and comp. leased	—	—	42,959,857
ccumulated deferred inc. tax	148,300,000	112,486,866	62,986,866
urrent and Accrued Liabilities:			
lotes payable to bank	88,786,000	9,093,264	114,000,000
ccounts payable, etc.	125,911,000	88,632,141	115,620,065
ustomers' deposits	49,495,000	41,605,999	33,878,661
ccrued taxes	61,578,000	23,973,004	22,098,120
ividends payable	11,074,000	11,073,615	11,072,911
nterest accrued, etc.[5]	112,080,000	104,244,294	115,953,358
eferred credits and reserves	22,271,000	19,483,365	13,547,655
namortized premium (net)	—	n.a.	2,156,198
ccumulated deferred investment tax credits	92,730,000	24 710,000	—
Total Liabilities and Stockholders' Equity	6,588,663,000	$6,315,409,043	$6,285,430,142

1973	1970	1965	1962
$6,537,375,811	$5,075,809,476	$3,875,594,043	$3,191,007,069
1,153,881,620	985,015,991	706,056,472	591,211,151
5,383,494,191	4,090,793,485	3,169,537,571	2,599,795,918
21,208,087	16,004,327	—	—
$5,404,702,278	$4,106,797,812	$3,169,537,571	$2,599,795,918
—	—	10,029,117	6,031,571
14,572,934	14,742,164	6,297,226	5,726,833
19,120,335	16,409,215	23,601,613	36,216,792
—	—	—	—
305,566,742	188,575,888	85,754,560	72,588,534
—	—	—	—
101,933,825	68,058,793	62,583,444	60,178,000
13,196,206	8,321,792	6,489,631	12,260,800
—	17,500,000	—	—
22,925,670	11,724,087	3,250,500	—
86,156,702	16,788,557	19,462,838	37,816,232
$5,968,174,692	$4,448,918,308	$3,387,006,500	$2,830,614,680
$ 750,911,410	$ 626,537,210	$ 444,999,927	$ 404,451,327
—	—	—	—
1,338,246,933	798,494,799	750,469,455	548,386,595
605,356,716	433,957,782	321,662,209	261,496,212
(34,114,111)	(14,361,621)	—	—
2,660,400,948	1,844,628,170	1,517,131,591	1,214,334,134
2,842,990,854	2,256,639,500	1,710,972,500	1,439,111,400
—	—	—	—
12,365,627	12,803,627	17,303,627	20,017,974
64,000,000	—	10,000,000	20,000,000
106,594,708	67,248,737	38,418,801	40,528,982
30,364,254	31,689,540	28,454,849	21,648,302
22,219,768	16,304,426	27,377,139	41,353,970
11,072,971	9,025,568	5,810,399	5,213,873
203,710,795	55,878,677	19,987,028	21,684,450
12,090,916	10,913,143	7,428,528	4,632,099
2,363,851	3,008,218	4,122,038	2,089,496
—	—	—	—
$5,968,174,692	$4,448,918,308	$3,387,006,500	$2,830,614,680

EXHIBIT 9 (*continued*)

n.a. = not available.

[1] 1,915,319 no par shares of $5 preferred; $100 par shares; 600,000 5¾ percent A, 750,000 5¼ percent B, 600,000 4.65 percent C, 750,000 4.65 percent D, 500,000 5¾ percent E, 400,000 6.20 percent series F preferred; cumulative preference; $100 per shares: 919,812 6 percent convertible series B.

Common stock: 1968, 37,290,409; 1967–65, 37,257,292 $10 par shares. 1964–62, no par shares: 1964, 18,628,646; 1963, 17,488,976; 1962, 16,094,044.

[2] Uniform systems of accounts prescribed by Public Service Commission of New York shall be recorded at "original cost" and that "difference between book cost as of December 31, 1937, and original cost" (as defined) be included in account "electric (gas or steam) plant acquisition adjustments." Pursuant to foregoing, net amount of $66,769,368 (for company, separately, $52,356,632) was transferred to "plant acquisition adjustments," to December 31, 1937.

In connection with the July 31, 1945, merger, the companies charged to surplus the balance in plant acquisition adjustments accounts on the books of the three companies aggregating $52,356.632.

[3] Represents charges to fixed capital account "organization" prior to January 1, 1938, of $5,305,153 reclassified to account "capital stock expense" pursuant to new uniform system of accounts plus additions of $121,648 in 1938. Further additions were made in 1939 and 1940. In 1945, $1,363,354 applicable to the two merged companies was written off to surplus.

In 1967 and subsequent presented as a deduction from capital stock and surplus, 1966 and prior years, not restated, total stockholders equity, if restated, would be: 1966, $1,575,251,963; 1965, $1,507,102,474; 1964, $1,410,611,204; 1963, $1,330,567,653; 1962, $1,208,302,563; 1961, $1,117,505,394.

[4] Include unamortized expenses of converting to natural gas: 1965, $260,644; 1964, $1,606,733; 1963, $3,871,554; 1962, $6,136,375; 1961, $8,401,196; extraordinary property losses: 1968, $1,093,956; 1967, $2,187,924; 1966, $3,281,892; 1965, $6,382,892; 1964, $9,483,892; 1963, $12,458,366; 1962, $16,522,902; nuclear research and development cost: 1968, $6,282,938; 1967, $7,000,987; 1966, $7,719,038; 1965, $8,437,088; 1964, $9,155,138; 1963, $9,873,188; 1962, $10,591,238.

[5] Restated for nuclear fuel assemblies beginning 1969.

31. Champions of Competition versus the Breakfast of Champions: The Case of Ready-to-Eat Cereals*

ON JANUARY 24, 1972, the Federal Trade Commission charged the four largest manufacturers of ready-to-eat (RTE) breakfast cereals with illegally monopolizing the market for breakfast cereals and threatened to break them up into smaller, more competitive companies.

The four companies were Kellogg's, General Mills, General Foods, and Quaker Oats. The case was considered unusual in that no conspiracy was charged as being the cause of the alleged monopoly. The allegedly illegal acts, in the form of anticompetitive practices, were maintained to be in violation of Section 5 of the Federal Trade Commission Act which prohibits unfair and deceptive trade practices, including the restraint of competition. These practices involved the introduction of a proliferation of cereal brands that are trademarked but that the FTC says differ only "artificially," asserted unfair methods of promotion, acquisition of competitors, and interference with the marketing efforts of other producers of RTE cereals by adherence to a restrictive program for controlling retailer's shelf space.

The case was considered important because of its potentially precedent-setting nature. In addition to being attacked because of allegedly unfair methods of competition—such as false advertising claims—the RTE cereal industry was being attacked because of its specific structure—a differentiated oligopoly; the four defendents are alleged to comprise a "shared monopoly." With quite a number of major U.S. industries falling into the category of "differentiated oligopoly," many economists, antitrust practitioners, and businessmen consider that, if the FTC complaints succeeds against the breakfast cereal manufacturers, the "writing will be on the wall" for many other major industry leaders.

The importance of the complaint was immediately recognized by the "defendants." Following the initial January 24, 1972, announcement by the

---

* This case was prepared by Anthony Hourihan, research assistant, under the supervision of Professor Jesse W. Markham, Harvard Business School.

885

FTC, Kellogg quickly accused the FTC of being against bigness. The company said the FTC's action means "it's a crime to be big, to be efficient." General Mills issued a statement denying any wrong doing and retorting that the government brought "a test case which seeks to write new law." General Foods and Quaker Oats both asserted the industry was "extremely competitive."[1]

Following the announcement of its intention to take legal action against the industry's leaders, the FTC waited the normal 90-day period before issuing a formal complaint. This 90-day period serves the purpose of affording the "defendants" and the FTC the opportunity of reaching a settlement without going through the process of litigation.

However, no such settlement ensued and on April 26, 1972, the FTC lodged a formal complaint against the four companies. The contents of this complaint are contained in Exhibit 1.

HISTORY AND NATURE OF THE RTE CEREAL INDUSTRY

Size

Ready-to-eat cereal producers form the major part of the "cereal preparations" industry. During the period 1947 to 1970, the dollar value of industry shipments rose from $284.3 million to $953.1 million. By 1970, approximately 12,000 people were employed by the industry, earning an annual payroll of $115.1 million. The amount of "value added" by the industry rose from $243.1 million in 1958 to $592.9 million in 1970 with annual capital expenditures rising from $17.1 million to $30.9 million over the same period.[2]

Although the breakfast cereals requiring cooking still constitute an important part of the breakfast cereal industry, nearly all of the growth in the industry has occurred in the ready-to-eat breakfast cereal sector. In 1957, "hot" cereals accounted for sales of $70 million. By 1966, this figure had only climbed to $89 million. In contrast, during the same period sales of "cold" (that is, RTE) breakfast cereals had risen from $329 million to $574 million.[3]

Structure of the Industry

In terms of structure, the RTE cereal industry is a classic case of "differentiated oligopoly." The three most important elements of market structure are seller concentration, barriers-to-entry, and product differentiation. The RTE cereal industry rates a high score with respect to each of these three dimensions of structure. As one economist has aptly stated, "If the workabil-

---

[1] *The Wall Street Journal*, January 24, 1972, p. 11.
[2] U.S. Department of Commerce, Bureau of the Census, *Annual Survey of Manufacturers*, 1970, p. 16.
[3] *Food Topics*, February 1968, p. 27.

ity of competition were to be questioned purely on the basis of structured indexes, by far the most likely candidate of all industries is the ready-to-eat cereal industry."[4]

In terms of concentration the industry ranks as one of the most concentrated in the U.S. manufacturing sector. In 1970, the largest four companies in the industry (the four defendants in the FTC complaint) accounted for 90 percent of all industry sales. This four-firm concentration ratios had risen from a level of 68 percent in 1935. A complete set of concentration ratios for the industry appears in Table 1 below.

TABLE 1

Percent of Value of Shipments Accounted for by the Largest Cereal Manufacturing Companies, 1935–1970

			Percent of Shipments Accounted for by:			
Year	Number of Companies	Total ($ millions)	4 Largest Companies	8 Largest Companies	20 Largest Companies	50 Largest Companies
1970	n.a.	$953.1	90%	—	n.a.	n.a.
1967	30	793.0	88	97%	99+%	100%
1966	n.a.	742.9	87	—	n.a.	n.a.
1963	35	625.1	86	96	99+	100
1958	34	433.0	83	95	99+	100
1954	37	345.8	88	95	99+	100
1947	55	294.3	79	91	98	n.a.
1935	n.a.	n.a.	68	82	n.a.	n.a.

n.a. = not available.

Source: U.S. Department of Commerce, Bureau of the Census, *Annual Survey of Manufactures, 1970* (AS)–9, p. 6.

Table 1 illustrates the fact that not only has the level of concentration increased over the last three decades but that, in addition, the absolute number of competitors has declined substantially.

Early Storm Signals

This trend of increasing concentration and reduction in the absolute number of cereal producers had been noted well in advance of the 1972 FTC complaint. A joint Senate-House commission, the National Commission on Food Marketing, as far back as 1966 had contrasted the increasing degree of concentration and reduction in the number of producers of breakfast cereals with the fairly stable level of concentration and constant number of producers in the "crackers and cookies" industry.[5]

---

[4] Jesse W. Markham and Charles C. Slater, "Standards of Competition and Food Industries," *American Marketing Association Proceedings of the 1966 World Congress*, p. 28.

[5] "Food from Farmer to Consumer," Report of the National Commission on Food Marketing, June 1966, p. 65.

Another important dimension of the structure of the industry has been the alleged high barriers-to-entry that have protected existing firms from potential competitors. Barriers-to-entry refer to the advantages possessed by existing industry members over potential entrants. Such advantages may arise out of a variety of factors.

Barriers-to-entry may exist because of substantial economies of scale in production. To the extent that economies of scale are substantial the minimum efficient scale of a production plant will be large. The minimum efficient scale refers to the smallest possible plant size at which the lowest possible production costs will be achieved. Obviously, if large economies of scale exist in an industry potential entrants will have to be confident of securing a sufficiently large share of the market—large enough to secure production economies of scale—before entering the industry. In other words, large economies of scale mean that a firm cannot enter the new market on a small scale and "grow up" over a period of time. Breakfast cereal producers do not appear to gain significant economies from very large production. Differences in labor productivity appear relatively minor among various sizes of plants.[6]

A second form of barriers-to-entry is lack of access to essential factors of production. In other words, potential entrants may not have access to patents on essential production processes or to essential raw material sources. For example, Alcoa managed to maintain its monopolistic control over the U.S. aluminum market during the latter part of the 19th and earlier years of the 20th century due in large part to the fact that it controlled nearly all of the bauxite mines and was thus capable of excluding domestic potential competitors from producing virgin aluminum ingots.

Also, absolute cost barriers-to-entry may exist simply because of the sheer size of capital required for entry into an industry. The larger the capital requirements for entry, the more difficult the task facing the potential entrant.

The breakfast cereal industry is said to owe its fairly high barriers-to-entry to the absolute cost facing potential entrants in the form of the substantial amount of funds required for advertising new products. As indicated in the complaint in Part IV, the four largest producers of RTE cereals alone spent $81 million on advertising their products in 1970. As will be indicated below, advertising—in massive doses—along with frequent introductions of new brands and types of cereals (criticized by some as "brand proliferation") represent the major forms of competition in the RTE cereal industry. Any potential entrant would have to raise a substantial amount of capital for investment in advertising alone in order to launch and promote its products in a manner competitive with existing firms. Added to the large size of the required investment in advertising is the problem of raising any substantial amount of capital in order to invest it in an asset of such intangibility as

---

[6] Report of the National Commission on Food Marketing, p. 66.

"expected returns from advertising outlays." Obviously lending institutions would impose a substantial risk premium on any funds invested in a company whose first major task in a new industry would be to launch a massive advertising campaign.

Finally, it is contended that product differentiation—itself a significant dimension of market structure—is a barrier-to-entry in the cereal industry. To the extent that product differentiation is prevalent in an industry, potential entrants face an additional hurdle in attempting to break into the industry. By differentiating its products a firm may achieve a "quasi-monopolistic" degree of control over its segment of the market. With very high levels of product differentiation an industry is, in effect, divided into a number of "subindustries"; in each "subindustry" a single firm produces and sells its highly differentiated product without fear of intense competition from rivals who produce highly imperfect substitutes for its product. A high degree of production differentiation establishes for each product a high degree of brand loyalty. Such extremely high levels of product differentiation are probably very rare; in most instances a variety of "less perfect but acceptable" substitutes are available to the consumer. However, product differentiation and its attendant brand loyalty are usually considered a barrier-to-entry and a key concept in understanding the nature of competition in certain consumer goods' industries.

Sources of Product Differentiation

There are many sources of product differentiation. Differences among products may be based on such "real" factors as physical dissimilarity, differences in quality, differences in services attached to the purchase of a product, and differences in the type or number of locations where it can be purchased. Another type of product differentiation—and one which the FTC has labeled artificial in its complaint against the cereal producers—is that known as "image differentiation." Image differentiation refers to the attempts by producers to "create" product differences in the minds of consumers where no "real" differences exist. Image differentiation is usually affected by advertising, specifically by that type of advertising labeled "persuasive" as opposed to "informative." One economist has aptly summarized the problem of product differentiation as follows:

> The relevant question for economic analysis is not . . . whether product differentiation is a good thing, but rather, how much product differentiation there should be, and whether certain market conditions may lead to excessive or inadequate differentiation. Unfortunately, there are no hard-and-fast answers, partly because we lack data on the costs and benefits of diversity but even more because economic theory has provided no operational calculus for comparing the benefits of diversity with its social costs. There is general agreement that more diversity is preferable to less if the cost is the same; and that consumers are better off if they can choose freely between high-service (or quality or convenience), high-price consumption bundles and low-service (or

quality or convenience), low-price bundles than when they face only one possibility. By such weak rules alone, much of all product differentiation is apt to pass the test of social desirability. Thus, if the typical consumer can choose between several well-stocked, price-competitive supermarkets within 15 minutes driving distance of home and a friendly but high-priced Mom-and-Pop grocery store within five blocks walking distance, the state of consumer welfare can hardly be said to be seriously amiss. Our task . . . is to identify circumstances in which product differentiation efforts lead to outcomes less clearly in harmony with the public interest. . . .

. . . . Product differentiation activities most often singled out for a vote of public disapproval include image differentiation and those aspects of physical differentiation which entail the most superficial, transitory variations in product style or design. Was the American economy better off for having spent $17 billion on advertising in 1968, or was an appreciable fraction of this sum wasteful or even counterproductive? Were the users of deodorants, pain remedies, hair bleach and similar products benefited because Bristol-Myers devoted 28 percent of its 1966 sales revenues to advertising? What are the consequences of the American automobile industry's annual model change cycle, which rapidly renders aging vehicles stylistically obsolete?[7]

With reference to the RTE cereal industry it is alleged that product differentiation, alongside and interrelated with large advertising expenditures, is mainly of the "image" or "artificial" type. Vast amounts of money are expended on highlighting the "superiority" of the respective producers' brands whereas in fact most differences are slight—involving minor variations in taste and content and some differences in packaging and shape.

Nature of Competition in the Industry

These structural dimensions of the RTE cereal industry are said to account for the prevalent form of competition among cereal manufacturers. Almost 92 percent of breakfast cereals are sold through the manufacturers' own salesmen, with the remainder going through food brokers.[8] Virtually all (99 percent) cereals are sold under the producer's own brand name or trademark; apparently the high level of advertising has made consumers sufficiently brand conscious so that private labels have never been successful, even when priced a few cents less per package.[9] However, private label cereals have never been in open competition with the manufacturers' own advertised brands on sufficient scale to offer most of the consuming public a genuine viable alternative. In fact, one official of the FTC is said to have stated off-the-record that this was one of the factors that influenced the FTC in initiating the case. Consumers have generally not had the option of buying RTE cereals with advertising and *without* advertising.

[7] F. M. Scherer, *Industrial Market Structure and Economic Performance* (Chicago: Rand McNally & Co., 1970), p. 325.

[8] Report of the National Commission on Food Marketing, p. 66.

[9] Ibid.

The main forms of competition between RTE cereal producers therefore involve product "innovation" and advertising campaigns. Although the trend has been toward introducing more items with real product differences, most new brands are not substantially different from those already available.

Product "innovation"—or brand proliferation as the FTC prefers to call it—bears significantly upon the "product life cycle" in the cereal industry. RTE cereal producers have managed to avoid the saturation and decline stages of the cycle by maintaining for their products a stage in the cycle known as "innovative maturity."[10] This involves periodical "enhancement" of the product line by introducing new brands and new ideas which forestall deterioration of the sales trend by attracting new customers, winning back "lost" customers or increasing the per capita consumption of existing customers. The RTE cereal producers have managed to maintain this stage of "innovative maturity" by introducing new presweetened cereals in the late 40s and "nutritional" cereals in the early 50s. They have subsequently attempted to increase sales by suggesting a variety of times and places for eating cereals other than at the morning breakfast table. Most recently "natural" cereals have been introduced and heavily promoted.

It should be noted that this policy of maintaining "innovative maturity" by RTE cereal manufacturers is not unlike the so-called life extension or market stretching policies followed by such companies as Du Pont who often forestall the maturity stage of their products' life cycles and maintain them in the rapid growth stage by identifying new users of, and new uses for, many of their products.

One result of this continuous introduction of new brands in the RTE cereal industry is high advertising expenditures relative to sales. The National Commission on Food Marketing estimated that the cost of marketing a group of new RTE cereals in 1964 amounted to 66 percent of sales during the first year of regular distribution, and 30 percent of sales during the second year.[11] Other studies have reached similar conclusions. Overall, the percentage of advertising to sales has been in the 13 percent to 15 percent category over the last decade. Packaging costs are also rather high—as much as 17 percent of sales in 1964—with a portion of these costs being incurred primarily for promotional reasons.

CRITICISMS OF ADVERTISING EXPENDITURES IN THE RTE CEREAL INDUSTRY

Several critics of the industry have alleged that not only has the level of advertising been exceedingly high, but its very nature has restrained the

---

[10] Robert D. Buzzell and Robert L. M. Nourse, "The Product Life-Cycle," in S. Marple and H. Wissman, *Grocery Manufacturing in the United States* (New York: Frederick A. Praeger, 1968), chap. 4, pp. 58–61.

[11] National Commission on Food Marketing, p. 66.

degree of competition in the industry—for basically two reasons. First, they say, apart from the "pure" contribution of advertising as an absolute cost barrier-to-entry—which has been discussed earlier—these large advertising outlays used to promote product differentiation, and consequent brand loyalty, result in the market being "hardened" to potential entrants. In other words, in order to get consumers to switch from brands to which they have become loyal, new entrants may have to spend considerably more on advertising "per customer" than existing firms. This factor further increases the absolute advantage of existing cereal producers. Second, the existence of significant economies of advertising scale—in the form of the ability to launch national campaigns and to take advantage of "quantity discounts"— favors the larger producers and is a significant handicap to smaller competitors. Approximately 80 percent of media advertising by cereal producers goes to television. An FTC staff report of June 1966 reported the effects of quantity television discounts in the following manner:

> Professor Harlan Blake, co-author of "Network Television Discounts," 74 *Yale Law Journal* 1339 (June 1965), testified before the Senate Antitrust and Monopoly Subcommittee that discounts to the largest advertisers went up to an extreme of 75 percent on rate cards. Gerald Arthur, former advertising executive and owner of radio and TV properties, testified that the largest advertisers, such as General Foods, would get their TV advertising at a rate of $2.50 per thousand households (audience estimated by Nielsen Ratings), whereas a smaller advertiser would have to pay $3.50–$4 for the same audience. This means that smaller advertisers would have to pay 40 to 60 percent more for the coverage.
>
> The economic effect of these discounts on network TV advertising time is to foreclose smaller manufacturers from this very productive sales-producing media.[12]

From the above-mentioned FTC staff report in 1966, the National Commission on Food Marketing Report of the same year, and a variety of other evidence, it is clear that some of the questionable aspects and consequences of the market structure and nature of competition in the RTE cereal industry were being closely scrutinized by both economic analysts and government agencies long before the current FTC complaint was issued.

The Nutrition Debate

Consumer advocates have also attacked the cereal industry for not paying greater attention to the nutritional value of some of their products. Allegedly false advertising claims have frequently been attributed to the industry. Furthermore, the fact that so much advertising has specifically been aimed at children, with the use of such cartoon characters as "Tony the Tiger" for Kellogg and "Cap'n Crunch" for Quaker Oats, has annoyed certain sectors

---

[12] Report of the Staff of the FTC published as Technical Study No. 8, "The Structure of Food Manufacturing," National Commission on Food Marketing, June 1966, p. 70.

of the public and been duly noted by the FTC—as indicated in the formal complaint.

The question of the nutritional content of breakfast cereals is one which has by no means been settled. Nutritionists are far from unanimous in their assessment of cereals. Testimony before a Senate consumer subcommittee in the summer of 1970 shows that experts in this area differ considerably in their evaluation of the nutritional value of ready-to-eat cereals. Exhibits 2, 3, and 4 illustrate the various shades of expert opinion as presented in the newspapers of July and August 1970. Exhibit 5, provided by a spokesman for the industry, favorably compares the "cumulative nutrient content" of dry breakfast cereals with that of other popular breakfast foods such as eggs, bacon, fruit, and so on. Exhibit 6 refers to the state of affairs in the dispute as of March 1972.

The Industry Responds

The industry has vigorously defended the nature of product innovation prevalent in the RTE cereal industry. Although the FTC may regard minor variations in taste and content and some differences in packaging and shape to be indications of "brand proliferation" rather than "true" product innovation, the industry viewpoint is the complete opposite. In order to get children to eat cereals—or any breakfast food—it is essential to maintain their interest in the product. The "novelty" of breakfast cereals is maintained through minor variations in taste, shape, packaging, and so on. Without these variations children would grow bored with their breakfast cereals and cease to eat them or substantially reduce their consumption. For this reason, continuous new brand introduction is entirely justifiable, according to the industry's viewpoint, even though new brands may only differ slightly from the old brands they replace.

TABLE 2
Sales and Advertising Expenditure Indexes, 1959–1964

Year	Sales Index*	Volume Index (millions of pounds)		Advertising Expenditure Index	
		Actual	Adjusted†	Actual	Adjusted‡
1959	100.0	100.0	100.0	100.0	100.0
1960	103.9	102.5	99.7	98.1	94.8
1961	108.2	106.9	103.0	102.2	98.0
1962	111.5	109.3	103.0	106.3	98.6
1963	120.0	116.3	108.6	117.0	108.0
1964	124.8	122.0	112.8	124.1	111.1

* Computed from Nielson estimates of average price and volume in pounds.
† Data adjusted for changes in the number of households.
‡ Taken from Table 34 of Robert S. Headen and James W. McKie, *The Structure, Conduct, and Performance of the Breakfast Cereal Industry: 1954–1964.*
Source: Jesse W. Markham and Charles C. Slater, "Standards of Competition and the Food Industries," *New Ideas for Successful Marketing* (Chicago: American Marketing Association, 1966), Table 3, p. 30.

TABLE 3
Changes in the Market Position of Individual Firms as It Is Related to the Degree of Successful Product Innovation

Year	Kellogg		General Mills		General Foods		Nabisco		Quaker		Ralston	
	Market Share	Percent in New Products*	Market Share	Percent in New Products*	Market Share	Percent in New Products*	Market Share	Percent in New Products*	Market Share	Percent in New Products*	Market Share	Percent in New Products*
1954	39.6	—	19.6	—	24.4	—	7.7	—	3.1	—	2.6	—
1955	41.3	—	19.4	3.3%	23.7	—	7.4	—	2.8	—	2.8	—
1956	42.2	7.0%	19.4	8.7	22.4	0.5%	7.9	6.0%	2.7	—	2.8	—
1957	42.0	9.0	19.0	7.4	22.8	2.0	7.6	6.0	2.6	—	3.4	—
1958	40.9	9.6	19.1	10.0	24.3	11.5	7.1	6.5	2.4	—	3.6	—
1959	40.9	12.2	18.9	14.5	23.9	12.0	7.1	6.0	2.4	—	4.3	13.0%
1960	42.3	15.5	18.5	19.0	22.2	11.5	7.0	7.5	2.4	—	5.1	21.0
1961	42.5	16.0	18.1	20.0	21.9	13.0	6.8	7.7	3.3	33.0%	5.1	22.0
1962	43.5	17.5	18.8	25.0	21.2	17.0	6.2	8.0	3.5	49.0	5.0	22.0
1963	43.6	18.3	19.7	30.0	20.3	17.5	6.1	7.5	3.5	52.0	4.9	21.0
1964	43.5	22.0	20.5	34.0	19.6	19.0	6.0	9.0	3.9	58.0	4.8	22.0

* Data from A. C. Nielsen Co. These data indicate the share of the company's cereal sales attributable to new products introduced into the market since 1954.
Source: Jesse W. Markham and Charles C. Slater, "Standards of Competition and the Food Industries," *New Ideas for Successful Marketing* (Chicago: American Marketing Association, 1966), Table 5, p. 32.

Critics of the high level of advertising in the RTE cereal industry have also provoked a strong industry response. First of all, it has been suggested that the growth of advertising expenditures has been substantially exaggerated. When adjustments are made for rising media costs and changes in market size, the rate of advertising growth is no greater than the rate of growth of volume in sales per household. Table 2 clearly illustrates this fact. Second, as has already been pointed out, the heaviest advertising costs are incurred during the first year of a new product's life. Data presented in Table 3 show that successful efforts to gain business through new product development is strongly associated with rising market share. Between 1954 and 1964, four of the largest six firms increased their market shares. These four also had the largest share of business in new products. Two firms showed losses in market share and they also had the lowest share in new products.

Profits

A final point to note in connection with the RTE cereal industry is that profits have generally been higher than in the food industry as a whole. Table 4 shows the 1964 profit rates of the industry in relation to other foods industries for a variety of firm sizes. Table 5 presents a breakdown of costs and profits in 1964 for the breakfast cereal industry in contrast to the same figures for the less concentrated cookies and crackers industry.

TABLE 4
Profits of Food Manufacturers, 1964

Net Income after Taxes	Breakfast Cereals	Crackers and Cookies	Food and Kindred Products
As a percent of sales:			
Largest four companies	7.8%	5.1	—
Next four companies	4.2	4.5	—
All other companies	2.6	1.8	—
All companies	7.3*	4.2†	2.7
As a percent of net worth:			
Largest four companies	19.4	13.3	—
Next four companies	11.3	16.4	—
All other companies	1.6	8.5	—
All companies	18.0‡	12.7§	9.8

* 13 companies.
† 99 companies.
‡ 11 companies.
§ 86 companies.
Source: National Commission on Food Marketing Survey.

ECONOMIC THEORY AND ANTITRUST POLICY

Briefly stated, the main attribute of oligopolistic market structures is the high degree of seller interdependence. In other words, the higher the degree of concentration in an industry the more likely are the major firms to recog-

TABLE 5
Manufacturers' Consolidated Operating Statements, 1964

Operating Item	Breakfast Cereals (percent)	Crackers and Cookies (percent)
Total net sales	100.0%	100.0%
Production costs:		
Ingredients	20.7%	29.4%
Containers and other materials	14.4	14.2
Manufacturing payroll	10.8	15.2
Other manufacturing expense	6.8	4.2
Total	52.7%	63.0%
Salesmen and brokers	2.4%	7.6%
Advertising and sales promotion:		
Media advertising	15.2%	1.7%
Sales promotion	2.3	1.8
Marketing research	0.5	0.1
Other advertising expense	1.7	0.1
Total	19.7%	3.7%
Physical distribution and delivery	6.8%	12.9%
Administrative and general	4.3	4.8
Net income (before other income and federal income taxes)	14.1%	8.0%
Other income	0.4	0.1
Net income (before federal income taxes)	14.5%	8.1%
Federal income taxes	7.2%	3.9%
Net income (after taxes)	7.3	4.2

Source: National Commission on Food Marketing Survey.

nize that each firm's actions have immediate impact on the profits and sales of all other firms. This recognition of interdependence pressures firms toward what is known as "oligopolistic coordination," a condition which can arise from a variety of means such as price leadership, use of common pricing rules of thumb, use of focal points, and covert or overt agreements. Whatever form oligopolistic coordination may take, when effective its net result is to foster a "shared monopoly" which affords the oligopolists the opportunity of enjoying profits in excess of those found in more price competitive circumstances. The smaller the number of sellers (i.e., the higher the degree of concentration) the easier it is for oligopolists to reach some agreement or arrangement which is agreeable to all industry participants. These considerations have led to two key oligopolistic theoretic tenets which have been deeply imbedded in U.S. antitrust policy:

1. A firm's market power is roughly proportional to its share of the market.
2. When the entire market is in the hands of a very few firms, each of them is less likely vigorously to use price as a competitive weapon against its rivals than it would be inclined to do if competitors were more numerous and none had a significant share of the market.[13]

The effect of this latter factor—the reluctance of firms to compete on a price basis lest they provoke price retaliations and consequent price deterioration—is to pressure firms to adapt various forms of nonprice competition, such as product differentiation and advertising. Thus we see that the RTE cereal industry, both in structure and type of competition, appears to conform to the model of a classic "differentiated oligopoly."

Economic theory has, moreover, frequently implied that price competition, resulting in the lowest possible prices, is the "best" form of competition for efficient resource allocation and social welfare optimization. Clearly, to the extent that economic theory has universally favored price competition, it has oversimplified the problem of efficient resource allocation. The more restrained statement by Scherer cited earlier more accurately reflects the real value of product differentiation, and the same arguments can be made for other forms of nonprice competition.

Antitrust policy reflects to a large degree the economists' mistrust of nonprice competition—and, therefore, highly concentrated industries, and specifically differentiated oligopolies, have long been suspect. Antitrust philosophy basically states that high rewards (in the form of high profits) should be earned only as a result of above-average effort and efficiency. Specifically, super-normal profits should not accrue to firms due to the inherent structure of their industry. If oligopolies (i.e., shared monopolies) earn higher than average profits the general public suffers by having to accept high prices and a misallocation of society's resources.

Studies in industrial organization have, on the whole, tended to support the theoretical assertions of oligopoly theory—namely, that firms in highly concentrated industries with high barriers-to-entry earn above normal profits. F. M. Scherer has summarized some of the empirical evidence as follows:

> There have been many empirical studies relating profitability (which reflects success in holding prices above cost) to the number of sellers or (more frequently) seller concentration. It is not easy to obtain appropriate measures of profitability and concentration, and different analysts have used widely divergent measures and statistical techniques. Yet with only one significant exception, they have reached the same conclusion: that profitability rises with concentration.
>
> In a pioneering study of 42 meaningfully defined four-digit manufacturing industries, Bain found that producers specializing in lines whose leading eight

---

[13] Summarized from Markham and Slater, "Standards of Competition and Food Industries," pp. 23–24.

firms accounted for 70 percent or more of total industry shipments had 1936–1940 after-tax profits as a percentage of stockholders' equity averaging 11.8 percent, while profits in industries with eight-firm concentration ratios below 70 percent averaged only 7.5 percent.

Using different techniques, Weiss reached similar conclusions for the period following World War II. By computing weighted average four-firm concentration ratios for 22 broad two-digit industry groups, he was able to cover the whole of U.S. manufacturing industry. For the 1949–1958 period, he found average after-tax profits as a percentage of stockholders' equity to be strongly and positively correlated with concentration, with a correlation coefficient of 0.73. Industry groups with average four-firm concentration ratios above 40 percent achieved average profits of 12.7 percent, while those with ratios below 30 percent averaged only 8.8 percent. . . .

. . . Collins and Preston found moderate to strong positive correlations between their price-cost margin index and four-firm concentration ratios for the four-digit industries in six groups: food products; stone, clay and glass products; primary metals; fabricated metal products; electrical machinery; and miscellaneous manufacturing. In four other groups (textile mill products, apparel, chemicals, and nonelectrical machinery), the correlations were more often positive than negative, but all were statistically insignificant.

Although doubts remain and more research with better data is needed, the bulk of the evidence supports the hypothesis that profits increase with the degree to which market power is concentrated in the hands of a few sellers. Nevertheless, none of the analyses reveals a perfect correlation between profitability and concentration. A considerable fraction of the inter-industry variance in profitability cannot be explained by simple differences in concentration. For a fuller explanation, we must look to other structural and behavioral variables. . . .[14]

Other studies have incorporated elements other than seller concentration alone; Mann[15] has studied the relationship between seller concentration, barriers-to-entry, and rates of return in 30 industries over the period 1950–1960. Tables 6 and 7 summarize his findings.

Given this relation of profits to structural dimensions, antitrust laws have sought to "preserve" a certain degree of competition in industries by such methods as breaking up monopolies, preventing mergers between major rivals, and proscribing "unfair methods of competition." One of the most potent weapons in the hands of the FTC is Section 5 of the Federal Trade Commission Act. This section prohibits unfair methods of competition. "Unfair" need not entail lack of fairness in the usual moral sense of the word; anything which restrains competition may be challenged as unfair under Section 5, and it is up to the courts to decide what is unfair or anti-

---

[14] Scherer, *Industrial Market Structure and Economic Performance,* pp. 184–86.

[15] H. Michael Mann. "Seller Concentration, Barriers to Entry, and Rates of Return in 30 Industries, 1950–1960," *Review of Economics and Statistics,* August 1966, pp. 299–300.

TABLE 6
Average Profit Rates for 30 Industries, 1950–1960*

Industry*	Average Profit Rates
Above 70 Percent:	
Automobiles	15.5%
Chewing gum	17.5
Cigarettes	11.6
Ethical drugs	17.9
Flat glass	18.8
Liquor	9.0
Nickel	18.9
Shoe machinery	7.4
Sulfur	21.6
Aluminum reduction	10.2
Biscuits	11.4
Steel	10.8
Soap	13.3
Farm machinery and tractors	8.8
Copper	11.5
Glass containers	13.3
Tires and tubes	13.2
Rayon	8.5
Gypsum products	14.4
Metal containers	9.9
Cement	15.7
Average	13.3
Below 70 Percent:	
Petroleum refining	12.2
Shoes (diversified)	9.6
Canned fruits and vegetables	7.7
Meat packing	5.3
Flour	8.6
Beer	10.9
Baking	11.0
Bituminous coal	8.8
Textile mill products	6.9
Average	9.0

* The industries are classified into two groups: those industries with a concentration ratio equal to or above 70 percent for the top eight firms and those with a concentration ratio below 70 percent for the top eight firms.

Source: H. Michael Mann, "Seller Concentration, Barriers to Entry, and Rates of Return in 30 Industries, 1950–1960," *Review of Economics and Statistics*, August 1966, pp. 299–300.

competitive. Up until the present complaint, the FTC had never attacked "differentiated oligopoly" per se. (It was for this reason that the General Mills' spokesman quoted in the beginning of the case referred to the FTC complaint as "a test case which seeks to write new law.")

TABLE 7
Average Profit Rates for 30 Industries 1950–1960,
Classified by Barriers-to-Entry

Industry	Average Profit Rates
Very High Barriers:	
Automobiles	15.5%
Chewing gum	17.5
Cigarettes	11.6
Ethical drugs	17.9
Flat glass	18.8
Liquor	9.0
Nickel	18.9
Sulfur	21.6
Class Average	16.4
Substantial Barriers:	
Aluminum reduction	10.2
Biscuits	11.4
Petroleum refining	12.2
Steel	10.8
Soap	13.3
Farm machinery and tractors	8.8
Copper	11.5
Cement	15.7
Shoe machinery	7.4
Class Average	11.3
Moderate-to-low-Barriers:	
Glass containers	13.3
Tires and tubes	13.2
Shoes (diversified)	9.6
Rayon	8.5
Gypsum products	14.4
Canned fruits and vegetables	7.7
Meat packing	5.3
Flour	8.6
Metal containers	9.9
Beer	10.9
Baking	11.0
Bituminous coal	8.8
Textile mill products	6.9
Class Average	9.9

Source: H. Michael Mann, "Seller Concentration, Barriers to Entry, and Rates of Return in 30 Industries, 1950–1960," *Review of Economics and Statistics,* August 1966, pp. 299–300.

EXHIBIT 1
The FTC Complaint

UNITED STATES OF AMERICA
BEFORE FEDERAL TRADE COMMISSION

DOCKET NO. 8883

In the Matter of	)
KELLOGG COMPANY,	)
a corporation;	)
GENERAL MILLS, INC.,	)
a corporation;	)
GENERAL FOODS CORPORATION,	)
a corporation; and	)
THE QUAKER OATS COMPANY,	)
a corporation.	)

COMPLAINT

The Federal Trade Commission has reason to believe that the party respondents named in the caption hereof, and herinafter more particularly designated and described, have violated and are now violating the provisions of Section 5 of the Federal Trade Commission Act (Title 15, U.S.C. # 45). Accordingly, the Commission hereby issues this Complaint stating its charges with respect thereto as follows:

1. Respondents have been and are now engaged in, among other business activities, the manufacture and sale of ready-to-eat (RTE) cereals. RTE cereals are food products made from barley, corn, oats, rice or wheat and various combinations of such grains which are flaked, granulated, puffed, shredded or processed in other ways. RTE cereals are eaten primarily as a breakfast food requiring no cooking or heating preparation by the consumer.

All of the respondents have been engaged in the cereal business for over 40 years, and in the RTE cereal business for over 30 years. Since 1950 respondents have consistently accounted for over 84 percent of the sales of RTE cereals.

2. A. Respondent Kellogg Company (Kellogg) was founded in 1906. It is a corporation organized and doing business under the laws of the State of Delaware, with its principal office and place of business located at 235 Porter Street, Battle Creek, Michigan 49016. Kellogg manufactures and sells, among other things, RTE cereals, tea, soup, gelatin, and pudding.

In 1970 Kellogg had assets of $347 million and sales of $614 million. In 1970 Kellogg ranked 191st in sales among the nation's 500 largest industrial corporations.

In 1969 Kellogg's domestic sales of RTE cereals were $300 million and advertising expenditures for RTE cereals were over $36 million. Kellogg is the largest producer of RTE cereals in the United States.

B. Respondent General Mills, Inc. (General Mills) was incorporated in 1928. It is a corporation organized and doing business under the laws of the State of Delaware with its principal office and place of business located at 9200 Wavzata Boulevard, Minneapolis, Minnesota 55440. General Mills manufactures and sells, among other things, RTE cereals, flour, toys, chemicals, clothes, and jewelry.

In 1970 General Mills had assets over $655 million, and sales were over $1 billion. In 1970 General Mills ranked 116th in sales among the nation's 500 largest industrial corporations.

In 1970, General Mills' domestic RTE cereal sales amounted to $141 million and advertising expenditures for RTE cereal were $19 million. General Mills is the second largest producer of RTE cereals in the United States.

EXHIBIT 1 (continued)

C. Respondent General Foods Corporation (General Foods) was incorporated in 1922. It is a corporation organized and doing business under the laws of the State of Delaware with its principal office and place of business located at 250 North Street, White Plains, New York 10602. As the nation's largest food manufacturer, General Foods produces and sells, among other things, RTE cereals, coffee, beverages, frozen foods, pet foods, and desserts.

In 1970 the total assets of General Foods were over $1.3 billion and sales were over $2 billion. In 1970 General Foods ranked 45th in sales among the nation's 500 largest industrial corporations.

In 1970, General Foods' domestic sales of RTE cereals were over $92 million and advertising expenditures for RTE cereals were over $9 million. General Foods is the third largest producer of RTE cereals in the United States.

D. Respondent The Quaker Oats Company (Quaker) was incorporated in 1901. It is a corporation organized and doing business under the laws of the State of New Jersey with its principal office and place of business located at Merchandise Mart Plaza, Chicago, Illinois 60654. Quaker manufacturers and sells, among other things, RTE cereals, frozen food, cookies, pet foods, and chemicals.

In 1970, Quaker had assets over $391 million and sales of $597 million. In 1970 Quaker ranked 195th in sales among the nation's 500 largest industrial corporations.

In 1970 Quaker's domestic sales of RTE cereal were $56 million. Approximately $9 million was spent in 1970 to advertise Quaker RTE cereals. Quaker is the fourth largest producer of RTE cereals in the United States.

E. Nabisco, Inc. (Nabisco) is not a respondent herein. It has, however, participated in some of the acts and practices alleged herein and has contributed by acquiescence to the noncompetitive structure of the RTE cereal market, as alleged herein. Nabisco was incorporated in 1898. It is a corporation organized and doing business under the laws of the State of New Jersey with its principal office and place of business located at 425 Park Avenue, New York, New York 10022. Nabisco manufactures and sells, among other things, RTE cereals, cookies, candy, and snack foods.

In 1970 Nabisco's total assets were over $503 million and sales were over $868 million. In 1970 Nabisco ranked 140th in sales among the nation's 500 largest industrial corporations.

Nabisco's domestic sales of RTE cereals were $26 million in 1969 and advertising expenditures for RTE cereals were $3 million. Nabisco is the fifth largest producer of RTE cereal in the United States.

F. Ralston Purina Company (Ralston) is not a respondent herein. It has, however, participated in some of the acts and practices alleged herein and has contributed by acquiescence to the noncompetitive structure of the RTE cereal market, as alleged herein. Ralston was incorporated in 1894. It is a corporation organized and doing business under the laws of the State of Missouri with its principal office and place of business located at Checkerboard Square, St. Louis, Missouri 63199. Ralston manufactures and sells, among other things, RTE cereals, pet foods, animal feed, snack foods, and frozen food.

In 1970, Ralston's total assets were over $775 million and sales were over $1.5 billion. In 1970 Ralston ranked 71st in sales among the nation's 500 largest industrial corporations.

In 1969 Ralston's domestic RTE cereal sales were over $20 million and advertising expenditures were over $4 million. Ralston is the sixth largest producer of RTE cereal in the United States.

3. In the course and conduct of their business, respondents now ship, and for

EXHIBIT 1 *(continued)*

some time past have shipped, their RTE cereals from their respective production facilities in various states to locations in various other states of the United States, and maintain and at all times mentioned herein have maintained, a substantial course of trade in RTE cereals in commerce, as "commerce" is defined in the Federal Trade Commission Act.

4. Each of the respondents is in substantial competition with each and all of the other respondents and with other cereal producers in the manufacture and sale of RTE cereals in interstate commerce, except to the extent that competition has been hindered, lessened and eliminated as hereinafter set forth.

5. During the past 20 years the RTE cereal industry has experienced substantial growth. In 1940, 453 million pounds of RTE cereal were produced; 900 million pounds were produced in 1960; and in 1970 over 1 billion pounds of RTE cereal were produced. The value of RTE cereal increased from $163 million in 1950 to over $650 million in 1970.

In 1940 respondents' sales accounted for approximately 68 percent of the RTE cereal market; in 1950, for 84 percent; and in 1970, for 90 percent. In 1969 respondents controlled the following approximate shares of the RTE cereal market: Kellogg, 45 percent; General Mills, 21 percent; General Foods, 16 percent; and Quaker, 9 percent. In 1969 Nabisco and Ralston each had an approximate share of four percent of the RTE cereal market.

6. For at least the past 30 years, and continuing to the present, respondents, and each of them, have engaged in acts or have practiced forbearance with respect to the acts of other respondents, the effect of which has been to maintain a highly concentrated, noncompetitive market structure in the production and sale of RTE cereal.

During this period respondents, in maintaining the aforesaid market structure, have been, and are now engaged in, among others, the following acts and practices:

A. *Brand Proliferation, Product Differentiation and Trademark Promotion*

Respondents have introduced to the market a profusion of RTE cereal brands. During the period 1950 through 1970 approximately 150 brands, mostly trademarked, were marketed by respondents. Over half of these brands were introduced after 1960. In introducing and promoting these new brands respondents have employed intensive advertising directed particularly to children. Respondents have used advertising to promote trademarks that conceal the true nature of the product.

Respondents artificially differentiate their RTE cereals. Respondents produce basically similar RTE cereals, and then emphasize and exaggerate trivial variations such as color and shape. Respondents employ trademarks to conceal such basic similarities and to differentiate cereal brands. Respondents also use premiums to induce purchases of RTE cereals.

Respondents have steadily increased the level of advertising expenditures for RTE cereals. During the period 1950 through 1970, respondents' aggregate annual advertising expenditures for RTE cereals tripled from $26 million to $81 million. In 1970, respondents' advertising to sales ratio for RTE cereals averaged 13 percent.

These practices of proliferating brands, differentiating similar products and promoting trademarks through intensive advertising result in high barriers to entry into the RTE cereal market.

B. *Unfair Methods of Competition in Advertising and Product Promotion*

(1) By means of statements and representations contained in their advertisements, respondents:

In advertisements aimed at children, represent directly or by implication, that their RTE cereals without any other foods enable children to perform the physical activities represented or implied in their advertisements.

EXHIBIT 1 *(continued)*

In truth and in fact:

Respondents' RTE cereals do not enable children to perform the physical activities represented or implied in their advertisements. A child's ability to perform such physical activities depends on many other factors, including but not limited to general body build, exercise, rest, a balanced diet and age.

(2) By means of statements and representations contained in their advertisements respondents Kellogg, General Mills, and General Foods represent, directly or by implication, that consuming RTE cereal at breakfast:

(a) Will result in loss of body weight without vigorous adherence to a reduced calorie diet,

(b) Will result in maintenance of present body weight even if total caloric intake increases, or

(c) Will result in loss or maintenance of body weight without adherence to regular exercise.

In truth and in fact:

(a) Consuming RTE cereal at breakfast will not result in loss of body weight without vigorous adherence to a reduced calorie diet.

(b) Consuming RTE cereal at breakfast will not result in maintenance of body weight even if total caloric intake increases.

(c) Consuming RTE cereal at breakfast will not result in loss or maintenance of body weight without adherence to regular physical exercise.

(3) By means of statements and representations contained in their advertisements respondents General Mills and Kellogg:

(a) Represent, directly or by implication, that failure to eat one of their RTE cereals results in the failure of athletes or others to perform to their full capabilities.

(b) Represent, directly or by implication, that the ingestion of one of their RTE cereals by athletes or others enables them to perform better in their respective activities.

In truth and in fact:

(a) Failure to eat one of the RTE cereals of such respondents will not result in the failure of athletes or others to perform to their full capabilities.

(b) The ingestion of one of the RTE cereals of such respondents will not enable athletes or others to perform better in their respective activities.

(4) The use by respondents of the aforesaid unfair methods of competition in advertising and product promotion has the capacity and tendency to mislead consumers, particularly children, into the mistaken belief that respondents' RTE cereals are different from other RTE cereals, thereby facilitating artificial differentiation and brand proliferation. These unfair methods of competition have contributed to and enhanced respondents' ability to obtain and maintain monopoly prices and to exclude competitors from the manufacture and sale of RTE cereal.

C. *Control of Shelf Space*

Kellogg is the principal supplier of shelf space services for the RTE cereal sections of retail grocery outlets. Such services include the selection, placement and removal of RTE cereals and allocation of shelf space for RTE cereals to each respondent and to other RTE cereal producers.

Through such services respondents have interfered with and now interfere with the marketing efforts of other producers of RTE and other breakfast cereals and producers of other breakfast foods. Through such services respondents restrict the shelf positions and the number of facings for Nabisco and Ralston RTE cereals, and remove the RTE cereals of small regional producers.

All respondents acquiesce in and benefit from the Kellogg shelf space program which protects and perpetuates their respective market shares through the

EXHIBIT 1 (continued)

removal or controlled exposure of other breakfast food products including, but not limited to, RTE cereal products.

D. *Acquisition of Competitors*

During the past 70 years numerous acquisitions have occurred in the breakfast cereal industry. One of the effects of these acquisitions was the elimination of significant sources of private label RTE cereal. Among them are the following.

In 1943, General Foods acquired Jersey Cereal Company, a Pennsylvania Corporation. Before acquisition by General Foods, Jersey Cereal Company was a substantial competitor in the sale of private label and other RTE cereal.

In 1943, Kellogg leased and controlled the manufacturing facilities of Miller Cereal Company, Omaha, Nebraska, a substantial competitor in the sale of private label and other RTE cereal. In 1958, upon termination of the said leasing agreement, Kellogg purchased the assets of Miller.

In 1946, General Foods acquired the RTE manufacturing facilities of Campbell Cereal Company, Minneapolis, Minnesota, a substantial competitor in the sale of RTE cereal. Following this acquisition, General Foods dismantled the RTE facilities of Campbell and shipped said facilities to South Africa.

The aforesaid acquisitions have enhanced the shared monopoly structure of the RTE cereal industry.

7. Respondents, and each of them, have exercised monopoly power in the RTE cereal market by engaging in the following price and sales promotion practices, among others:

(a) Refrained from challenging each other's decisions to increase prices for RTE cereals, and, in general, acquiesced in or followed the price increases of each of them;

(b) Restricted the use of trade deals and trade-directed promotions for RTE cereals;

(c) Limited the use of consumer-directed promotions for RTE cereals, such as coupons, cents-off deals, and premiums.

8. Respondents' acts and practices aforesaid have had the following effects, among others:

(a) Respondents have, individually and collectively, established and maintained artificially inflated prices for RTE cereals.

(b) Respondents have obtained profits and returns on investment substantially in excess of those that they would have obtained in a competitively structured market.

(c) Actual and potential competition in the manufacture and sale of RTE cereals has been hindered, lessened, eliminated and foreclosed.

(d) Significant entry in the RTE cereal market has been blockaded for over thirty years.

(e) Meaningful price competition does not exist in the RTE cereal market.

(f) American consumers have been forced to pay substantially higher prices for RTE cereals than they would have had to pay in a competitively structured market.

9. Through the aforesaid acts and practices:

(a) Respondents individually and in combination have maintained, and now maintain, a highly concentrated, noncompetitive market structure in the production and sale of RTE cereal, in violation of Section 5 of the Federal Trade Commission Act.

(b) Respondents, individually and collectively, have obtained, shared and exercised, and now share and exercise, monopoly power in, and have monopolized, the production and sale of RTE cereal, in violation of Section 5 of the Federal Trade Commission Act.

EXHIBIT 1 (concluded)

(c) Respondents, and each of them, have erected, maintained and raised barriers to entry to the RTE cereal market through unfair methods of competition, in violation of Section 5 of the Federal Trade Commission Act.

WHEREFORE, THE PREMISES CONSIDERED, The Federal Trade Commission on this 26th day of April, A.D., 1972, issues its complaint against said respondents.

EXHIBIT 2
Dry Cereals' Nutrient Content Criticized by Food Expert

On July 23, 1970, Mr. Robert Choate gave testimony to the Senate Subcommittee on Consumers. Mr. Choate, a civil engineer by training, had been active in the malnutrition field for several years. He had served as a special consultant for the White House Conference on Food, Nutrition and Health and had assisted the Senate Select Committee on Nutrition and Human Resources. He had also served as a consultant for the Department of Health, Education, and Welfare when that agency studied its role in eliminating domestic poverty-induced hunger and malnutrition.

In his testimony to the subcommittee, Mr. Choate charged that "our children are deliberately being sold the sponsor's less nutritious products over television, . . . [and] are being programmed to demand sugar and sweetness in every food, . . . [and] are being counter-educated away from nutrition knowledge."

Mr. Choate also presented a variety of charts showing the nutritional merits of 60 dry cereals. In tabulating the 60 cereals by nutritional content, showing cumulative nutritional merits, he used the cereal companies' own figures. Although there were three cereals possessing high nutritional content (Kellogg's Product 19, General Mills' Kaboom and General Mills' Total) the "bottom 40" in Mr. Choate's opinion were "empty calories." "For a budget-conscious family, they are a bad nutrient investment for the dollar. They have calories and little else."

In his testimony, Mr. Choate pointed out that cereals with less nutritive content did not cost less. He stated, "I think it is fascinating to note that the average price for the top 20 cereals is 3.8 cents per ounce, 4.5 cents for the middle 20, and 4.4 cents for the bottom 20."

Mr. Choate continued by pointing out that many of the less nutritional cereals had the highest advertising expenditures. Cheerios, he said, was the nation's most advertised cereal, had a television budget of $5.4 million out of General Mills' total TV budget of $29.4 million. Cheerios, however, ranked 25th out of the 60 in cumulative nutrient merits.

The lowest 40 brands, of which Mr. Choate was most critical, included the five best sellers. These were Kellogg's Corn Flakes, Kellogg's Rice Krispies, Kellogg's Sugar Frosted Flakes, General Mills' Cheerios, and General Mills' Wheaties.

Mr. Choate presented evidence, including monitored television commercials, indicating the nature and extent of cereal promotion to children, especially on Saturday mornings. He pointed out that in one Saturday morning 100 minute segments of TV programming on CBS and NBC 11 Kellogg's and 9 other breakfast cereals were "touted."

The major cereal companies did not take long to respond to these charges. Both the Kellogg Company and General Foods Corp. released announcements the same morning, the Kellogg announcement being handed out in the subcommittee hearing room. Both companies defended the nutritional contents of their products. Kellogg quoted Dr. Frederick J. Stare, Chairman of the Nutrition Department of the School of Public Health, Harvard University, as saying that "Cereals are excellent foods. In fact, I think more Americans would be in better health if they would con-

EXHIBIT 2 *(continued)*

sume more cereal, primarily because they are essentially devoid of fat and choles-
terol. Cereal has always been the backbone of the diets of most of the peoples of the
world. "I don't know of any other place where one can get more nutrition, for less
money, Washington or Timbuktu."

General Foods was equally vehement in its denial of Mr. Choate's charges. In
their statement, they asserted that he had "totally ignored the very important factor
of taste preferences. You cannot force a youngster to eat a breakfast food he does
not like no matter how loaded it might be with nutrients." Their statement concluded that "the total of the nutrients" (of RTE cereals) "is exceptionally well balanced for efficient nutrition."

Source: Hearings before the Consumer Subcommittee of the Committee on Commerce, U.S.
Senate, 91st Cong., 2d sess. on Dry Cereals, July 23, August 4 and 5, 1970.

Cumulative Nutrient Content of Dry Breakfast Cereals

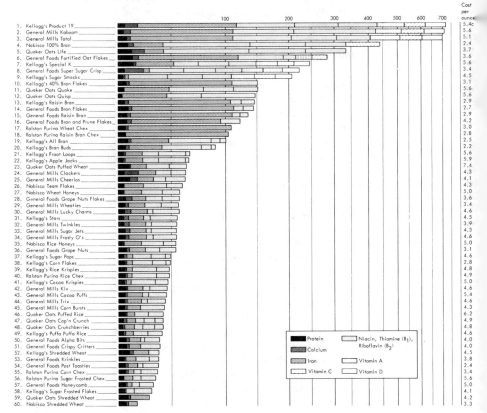

Source: Hearings before the Consumer Subcommittee of the Committee on Commerce, U.S. Senate, 91st Cong.,
2d sess. on Dry Cereals, July 23, August 4 and 5, 1970, p. 41. (Chart prepared by Robert Choate & Associates.)

EXHIBIT 3

Cereal's Value Defended by Dr. Stare

by RICHARD H. STEWART*

The cereal producers of the nation, championed by several of the nation's leading nutritionists, yesterday disputed testimony given a Senate subcommittee last week that characterized many breakfast cereals as mostly "empty calories."

One of the key witnesses for the cereal manufacturers was Dr. Frederick J. Stare, head of the Department of Nutrition at Harvard, who told the Senate Consumers Subcommittee he was testifying at the request of the Kellogg Co. and the National Biscuit Co.

Dr. Stare, who writes a syndicated newspaper column on nutrition and health, said he was "shocked" by the testimony condemning breakfast cereals.

He called the testimony of Robert Choate, the earlier witness, "grossly misleading."

Choate, a civil engineer by training and for three years one of the prime movers in the battle to end hunger and poverty in America, graded 60 cereals on the basis of their nutritional value and classified 40 of them as "empty calories."

He also criticized the cereal manufacturers for spending the bulk of their advertising budgets to market through children's television programs the cereals with the least amount of nutrients.

Stare told the subcommittee that a breakfast of cereal with milk along with fruit and toast with polyunsaturated margarine is more nutritious than the bacon and eggs with toast because the cereal breakfast has less saturated fat and cholestorol.

He said Choate's scale of judging dry cereals was "absolutely meaningless" because it ignored the fact that 95 percent of those who eat cereal use milk on it, which completes the nutritional value of the cereal.

Stare and the other nutritionists agreed that no breakfast cereal should be expected to be a complete meal in itself. They insisted that even those cereals that were listed on the bottom of Choate's scale had some nutritional value, especially with the addition of milk.

Stare and the other experts also took issue with Choate's

* Source: *The Boston Globe*, Wednesday, August 5, 1970.

EXHIBIT 3 *(continued)*

contention that each cereal ought to have 100 percent of the vitamin content needed in the daily diet.

They argued that this might prove dangerous, since other foods consumed during the day probably contain additional amounts of the same vitamins, which would produce an imbalance of a particular vitamin in the system. They mentioned Vitamin D as of particular concern.

Stare also insisted that adding sugar to cereal to get a child to eat it is not objectionable.

"If a child won't eat breakfast but will if you put sugar on it I don't see anything wrong with that," Stare said.

"For the information of Mr. Choate and associates, Popeye's spinach doesn't begin to compare with the over-all nutritional worth of breakfast cereal—any cereal," said Dr. Stare.

Stare, under questioning, said that 4.1 percent of his department's research budget is contributed by the cereal firms but added, "We don't accept a nickel if they tell us what to do with it.

"The only people who give you money and tell you what to do with it is the Federal government and I don't like it."

Stare said he does get funds from the cereal firms for acting as a consultant. He characterized this money as "considerably less than my salary from Harvard."

There were no witnesses to refute Choate's testimony concerning the imbalances in the industry's advertising budget or their use of children's television programs to promote less nutritional cereals.

A spokesman for the Cereal Institute supported by all of the companies to do research, conceded that they had not produced witnesses to refute those charges preferring to concentrate on the nutritional value of their product.

Stare said he had not watched the Saturday morning children's programs on which the cereals are advertised adding, "I don't get paid to review TV ads."

Choate issued a statement later in which he contended that from the testimony from industry witnesses one would gather that cereals were identically good, that television advertising had no role in shaping food patterns and that eggs and bacon were the All-American breakfast threat.

Choate declared, "The witnesses today I am afraid, represent less of a solution to our nutritional woes; they are part of the problem"

Sen. Frank Moss (D., Utah), subcommittee chairman, said Choate's claims about TV advertising "stand unrefuted. In fact testimony today confirms my own worst fears about the way in which food advertising policies are set."

EXHIBIT 3 *(continued)*

"Sugar frosted flakes may be less nutritious than some product, but given present advertising practices you can bet Tony will never be a paper tiger to the millions of children plopped in front of their television sets on Saturday morning."

Choate added that the industry's response to his findings, he said, "exemplifies the worry (I) expressed over the independence and forthrightness of the nation's leading nutritionists."

Choate's rating of 60 popular cereals placed Kellog's Shredded Wheat at the bottom of the list in nutritional value. Stare, who testified for Kellogg, said Shredded Wheat "is one of the best and because it is made from whole wheat and includes the wheat germ, it even ought to satisfy my many food faddist friends."

EXHIBIT 4

Cereal Could be Better, Panel Told

(United Press International)*

Harvard Professor Jean Mayer, a White House nutrition adviser, said today many breakfast cereals could be nutritionally "upgraded" and their advertising should be monitored by government health and nutrition experts.

Another nutritionist, Prof. Michael C. Latham of Cornell University, said the housewife gets less nutrition for her dollar from cereals than from bread, hominy grits, spaghetti, baked beans or pizza.

"Breakfast cereals are no more the food of champions than are bread and corn and rice," Latham said in prepared testimony. ". . . We have been brainwashed by big business through the medium of advertising."

Mayer and Latham presented their comments to the Senate Commerce Committee's consumer subcommittee in a third day of hearings on breakfast cereal nutrition.

Mayer and Latham generally appeared to steer a middle road between Robert B. Choate, who testified last week that most cold cereals offered little but "empty calories," and three nutritionists who testified yesterday that cereal and milk make a healthier breakfast entree than bacon and eggs.

Mayer chaired last December's White House Council on Food, Nutrition and Health, and serves on President Nixon's Consumer Advisory Council.

* From the *Boston Evening Globe,* Wednesday, August 5, 1970.

EXHIBIT 4 *(continued)*

"Because of the place of cereals in the national diet, it is obviously important that they be as nutritious as possible," Mayer said in a letter to the subcommittee. He did not appear in person but Sen. Frank E. Moss (D., Utah), subcommittee chairman, read the letter aloud.

"There are wide differences in nutritional value between various types of breakfast cereals," Mayer said. "With present technology and using modern knowledge of nutrition, such differences could easily be avoided and many products upgraded. Big food companies have the resources and the expertise necessary to do this."

Mayer did not say which brands or types of cereal are more nutritious than others.

". . . When advertising is directed at children and pertains to their health and their nutrition, it should be closely monitored by the FCC (Federal Communications Commission) either through a special committee where nutritionists, physicians and educators constitute a majority, or through delegation to the Food and Drug Administration or other appropriate . . . body," Mayer said.

In a statement submitted to the subcommittee, the Antitrust Law and Economics Review, a professional journal, said cereal prices are probably at least 25 percent higher than they would be "under a competitive industry structure."

The Review said about 85 percent of the nation's cereal sales, estimated at $1 billion a year, are shared by the Kellogg Co., General Foods Corp. and General Mills.

The statement said the three firms spend about 15 percent of each sales dollar on advertising, maintain profits at "supracompetitive levels," and keep cereal quality "at a very low level."

The Federal Trade Commission is investigating whether the dominant position of the big cereal companies has resulted in artificially high prices or other anticompetitive effects.

EXHIBIT 5
"Cumulative Nutrient Content" of Dry Breakfast Cereals and Other Foods*

	Product (One Standard Serving)†	Total "Points"‡
1–4.	Kellogg's Product 19 } General Mills Kaboom } General Mills Total } Quaker Oats King Vitaman } all approximately	700
5.	Nabisco 100% Bran	440
6.	Quaker Oats Life	330
7.	General Foods Fortified Oat Flakes	270
8.	Kellogg's Special K	240
9.	General Foods Special Sugar Crisp	220
10.	Kellogg's Sugar Smacks	205
11.	Milk, whole (8 oz.)	146
12.	Quaker Oats Quake	145
13.	Ground beef (4 oz.)	143
14.	Quaker Oats Quisp	140
15.	Egg, 1 large	71
16.	Bacon, 3 slices	45
17.	Apple	39
18.	Sweet roll, one commercial	30
19.	Doughnut, one cake-type, frosted	29
20.	Whole wheat bread, one slice, toasted	24

* Twenty products (19 typical breakfast foods plus ground beef) ranked by "points" on the basis of the percentage they contribute toward 60 grams of protein per day and Minimum Daily Adult Requirements for calcium, iron, vitamin A, vitamin C, vitamin D, niacin, thiamine, riboflavin. This is the ranking system used for 60 cereal products of Mr. Robert B. Choate in his testimony before the Senate Commerce Subcommittee on July 23, 1970.

† No milk included for any of the cereals.

‡ Point value for all cereals are as read from Mr. Choate's exhibit of 60 cereals, July 23, 1970.

Source: Assembled by the staff of one of the leading cereal manufacturers.

EXHIBIT 6
Testimony before the Senate Committee on Commerce, Consumer Subcommittee, March 2, 1972

On March 2, 1972, Mr. Choate returned to the Consumer Subcommittee to give evidence on the current state of nutritive content in dry cereals. He stated that, of the 40 dry RTE cereals which he condemned in 1970 more than 26 had been so reformulated as to "now represent a different food product on the shelves." He presented the accompanying chart to illustrate this point but added that the fortification of cereals, however, applied mainly to vitamins and minerals and did not result in any "real improvement of protein quantity, or protein quality."

Mr. Choate introduced Mrs. J. Gussow, nutrition educator, of Columbia University, who presented testimony highly critical of the current nutritive content of cereals.

In addition, it should be noted that in March 1973, in testimony before the Senate Select Committee on Nutrition and Human Needs, nutrition and dental experts urged that children-oriented television ads for sugary breakfast cereals be banned. The food makers in question reacted by boycotting the Senate hearings. During the

EXHIBIT 5 *(continued)*

hearing, the committee chairman, Senator George McGovern, announced that eight leading executives of food producers and their advertising agencies, who had been scheduled to testify . . . had declined to appear as witnesses.

Improved Nutrient Content of Dry Breakfast Cereals

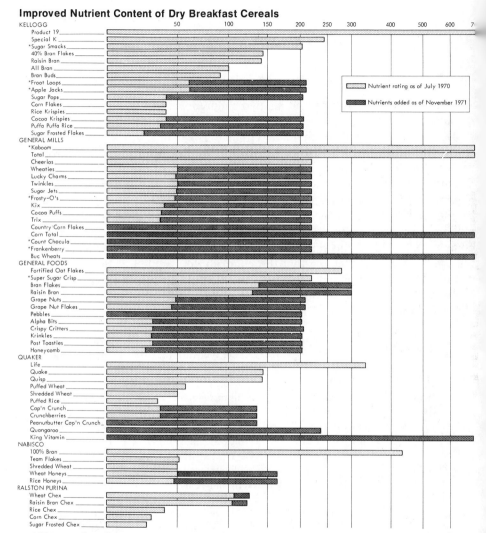

* These products have sugar listed first in the list of ingredients. This means they contain more sugar than any other ingredient.

Source: Hearing before the Consumer Subcommittee of the Committee on Commerce, U.S. Senate, 92d Cong., 2d sess., Nutritional Content and Advertising for Dry Breakfast Cereals, p. 56. Chart prepared by Robert Choate and Associates.

32. A. H. Robins Company*

A KEY WEST, Florida, man and his two children were awarded a $425,000 damage settlement in May 1975, as a result of legal action brought against the A. H. Robins Company, Richmond, Virginia. The man's wife had died due to complications from the use of a Dalkon intrauterine shield birth control device produced by the company. This was only 1 of the 226 cases the Robins Company stated it was defending at that time.[1] By spring 1976, the number had grown to some 533 pending civil actions alleging injuries caused by the Dalkon Shield. Customers were seeking punitive damages of $233 million and compensatory damages of $211 million. Mr. William Zimmer, the company's president and chief executive officer, informed stockholders during the 1976 annual meeting that the company had settled or disposed of another 117 cases originally seeking $75 million in damages, but which had been settled for about $2 million.[2] The company's "Message to Stockholders" in its *1975 Annual Report* stated in part:

> Consolidated net sales for the year totaled $241,060,000, an increase of 14.4 percent over the 1974 total of $210,713,000. Net earnings from 1975 operations increased 9.1 percent to $29,373,000, or $1.12 per share, before deducting after-tax charges of $2,739,000 (equal to 10 cents per share) for the settlement during 1975 of litigation, legal fees, recall of customers' inventories and other expenses related to the Dalkon Shield, an intrauterine contraceptive device which the Company marketed in prior years. Charging Dalkon Shield expenses to 1975 operations reduces the net earnings to $26,634,000, or $1.02 per share.
>
> We believe these charges should be treated under generally accepted accounting principles as a prior period adjustment in 1974, since the problem from which the charges stem originated in that year and had no relation to 1975 operations.
>
> Under this treatment, earnings for 1974 would be restated from $26,917,000, or $1.03 per share, to $24,178,000, or $0.93 per share. However, the staff of the Securities and Exchange Commission has insisted that the charges be absorbed

---

* Prepared by Professor Robert J. Litschert, Virginia Polytechnic Institute and State University.

    [1] "Settlement of $425,000 Is Awarded in Case over Dalkon Shield," *The Wall Street Journal*, May 22, 1975, p. 12.

    [2] "A. H. Robins Co. Faces 533 Pending Civil Suits on Birth-Control Item," *The Wall Street Journal*, April 28, 1976, p. 10.

in 1975 operations, and as of the printing of this report the matter has not been finally resolved.

The product which allegedly caused these problems was voluntarily removed from the market in June 1974 by the Robins Company following reports of septic abortions, some of which were fatal to women wearing the intrauterine device.

COMPANY HISTORY AND BACKGROUND

The A. H. Robins Company was incorporated in Virginia in 1878. Mr. Albert Hartley Robins, the Company's founder, was a typical pharmacist in the tradition of the Old South. Upon discharge from the Confederate Army he opened, with great expectations, his drugstore in downtown Richmond. The business grew and prospered and when Mr. Robins' son, Claiborne Robins, became a registered pharmicist, he was handed the manufacturing end of the business and given a free rein to do what he could with it. The younger Robins' first decision was to establish a separate firm to differentiate this operation from the drugstore. At this time, the company was given the name A. H. Robins Company. After several years of just modest success, Claiborne Robins met with an untimely death and his wife, Martha Robins, elected to continue the business.

The company barely managed to survive the depression years of the 1930s under the control of Mrs. Robins. In 1933, the company employed only three people and had gross sales of $4,800. During this year, Mr. Robins' son, E. C. Robins, graduated from the Medical College of Virginia and became a registered pharmacist. He immediately borrowed $2,000 in an attempt to get the company back on its feet.

As a result of the loan and improved economic conditions, the company began to experience significant growth. By 1942, sales volume had reached $100,000. At this time, E. C. Robins began to think seriously of changing the organization from a completely salesminded operation to one which combined both research and sales. Initially, the company struggled along with a small research staff turning out only an occasional new or improved product, but with moderate success built for the future.

In 1952, the company moved into what is now a very small part of its present plant. Acquisition of the new building provided additional space for the research group. By 1955, a program of clinical research was under way and the company's first original product, Robaxin, was marketed in 1957. In 1958, a pharmacology program was initiated, and in 1960 the ground was laid for the company's current research and development group which now occupies the research center constructed in 1963. By 1965, the Robins Company was doing business in 50 states and about 55 foreign countries, with gross sales of more than $65 million.[3]

---

[3] E. C. Robins, *The Story of A. H. Robins Company* (Princeton, N.J.: Princeton University Press, 1966).

During the last decade the company has continued to expand, especially through the acquisition of other firms. For the year ending December 31, 1975, consolidated net sales were approximately $241 million, with net earnings after taxes of $26.6 million (see Exhibits 1 and 2). At the time, the company was still principally engaged in the manufacture and sale of pharmaceutical specialities promoted ethically through activities directed at physicians, dentists, and pharmacists. The principal ethical products were drugs for cough and cold ailments, antispasmodic drugs for gastrointestinal disorders, and skeletal muscle relaxants. The company distributed pharmaceutical products throughout the United States and through subsidiaries or branches, in West Germany, France, Canada, Mexico, Colombia, the United Kingdom, South Africa, Venezuela, Brazil, Australia, the Philippines, Japan, Greece, and Kenya, and through independent agents in various other countries in Latin America, Europe, the Far East, Middle East, and Africa. Sales of these ethical products accounted for 73 percent of net sales and approximately 84 percent of earnings in 1975.

Robins also manufactured through subsidiaries several brand name consumer products including Sergeant's pet care products, Chapstick lip balm, and Caron perfumes and other fragrance products. These products accounted for the remaining 27 percent of the company's net sales and 16 percent of net earnings in 1975. In the pharmaceutical industry, 105 firms had sales of over $1 million in the ethical pharmaceutical market. From this group, A. H. Robins ranked approximately 18th in sales volume.[4] Based on new prescriptions written, the company ranked fifth among U.S. pharmaceutical manufacturers and 11 of the company's products were among the most widely prescribed in the world.

Robins concentrated its basic research and development in areas in which it felt it had its greatest expertise—therapeutic agents for use in nervous system and gastrointestinal, cardiovascular, and rheumatic illnesses. Emphasis was placed on the development of new synthetic medicinal compounds and new formulations. Approximately 300 employees with fields in chemistry, pharmacology, statistics, and medicine were engaged in research and development activities. In 1975, total research and development expenditures amounted to $10.7 million, an increase of $1.1 million over 1974. The company employed approximately 4,450 people, of which 2,300 were in facilities outside the United States.[5]

While the pharmaceutical industry has been described as a growth industry and the Robins Company has experienced substantial growth during the last two decades, it has also been plagued with problems during the 1970s. During 1973 and a portion of 1974, Robins' stock dropped from $40 to $12 per share and its price/earnings ratio dropped from 42 to 12. There were

---

[4] A. H. Robins Company, *Form 10-K, Annual Report Pursuant to Section 13 or 15 (D) of the Securities Exchange Act of 1934,* Fiscal year ending December 31, 1974.

[5] A. H. Robins Company, *Annual Report 1975* (Richmond, Va.:, February 18, 1976).

several factors which apparently contributed to the negative reaction of the public and the company's declining financial performance. Sales of a promising appetite suppressant, Pondimin, were disappointing. The Food and Drug Administration challenged the claims of a number of the company's ethical drug products. Its 90–day flea collar for pets, made from a substance akin to Nazi nerve gas, allegedly killed pets as well as fleas. But the most disastrous setback was the Dalkon Shield®, an intrauterine birth control device. The bad publicity came as a shock to management, who, as a result of their ability to develop marketing strengths, had always successfully maintained positive company and product images.[6]

BIRTH CONTROL DEVICES

According to Dr. Sheldon Segal, medical director of the Population Council, "there is no such thing as absolute safety when it comes to contraception—you get nothing for nothing. It is not enough to look at just the risks, you must consider the benefits—the hazards that the contraceptive is protecting you from, as well as other advantages, such as convenience."[7] However, the question of the safety of modern contraceptives remains paramount in the minds of many. Family planning specialists also add that decisions as to which birth control method to use are often based on incomplete information about risks and benefits of the various methods, and are reached without taking into account factors other than safety that should influence the choice of a contraceptive.

An analysis of medical statistics suggested that although oral contraceptives and intrauterine devices could sometimes cause serious, even fatal, side effects, they nonetheless tended to be the surest methods of birth control available. While other contraceptive methods, such as the condom and the diaphragm, caused few, if any, adverse side effects, these traditional methods were more likely to result in an unwanted pregnancy than the pill or IUD. Statistics also showed that even for women receiving the best of medical care, the nine months of pregnancy, childbirth, and the postpartum period were far more dangerous to life and health than any existing contraceptive method. Family planning specialists who had analyzed the relative risks and benefits of the various birth control techniques concluded that when the hazards of the various methods of birth control were weighed against the hazards of the unwanted pregnancies, the average couple was better off relying upon the pill or IUDs than upon the diaphragm, condom, foam, or rhythm methods.

Another dimension influencing relative safety was the quality of medical care a woman received. Those in the upper socioeconomic brackets had a

---

[6] "A Plague of Problems," *Forbes,* August 15, 1974, p. 35.

[7] Jane E. Brody, "Birth Control Devices: What Studies Show about Side Effects," *The New York Times,* March 4, 1975, p. 28.

much lower pregnancy-related death rate—approximately two thirds less than the national average of 20 per 100,000 live births. These same women were also likely to receive better medical care for contraceptive side effects.[8]

Table 1 summarizes a portion of the data prepared by the Rockefeller Foundation involving 1 million women over a span of one year. The table identifies the effectiveness of the device and deaths per million women result-

TABLE 1
Results of Use of Contraceptive Devices among 1 Million Women 20 to 34 Years Old over a One-Year Period of Time

	Percent Effective Preventing Pregnancy	No. of Deaths per Million by Method	No. of Deaths per Million by Pregnancy
Pill	99.5%	13	1
IUD	97	2	7
Diaphragm	88	0	27

Source: Jane Brody, "Birth Control Devices: What Studies Show about Side Effects," *The New York Times*, March 4, 1975, p. 28.

ing both from use of the device itself and from pregnancies which in turn had resulted from the ineffectiveness of the device. On the average, the pill was found to be the most effective device for preventing unwanted pregnancies, but the study further showed that the pill's use was directly tied to the largest number of deaths. The IUD was less effective than the pill but was associated with fewer deaths overall. The diaphragm was the least effective of the three devices used, and while no deaths resulted directly from its use, a relatively large number of deaths resulted from pregnancies associated with ineffectiveness of the device. Researchers indicated that the relative safety of the diaphragm would have been higher had it been used exactly as prescribed. Correctly used, the diaphragm was thought to be about 98 percent effective; studies showed five pregnancy-related deaths per million women per year.

THE INTRAUTERINE DEVICE

Intrauterine devices, or IUDs, are little pieces of metal or plastic in various shapes and sizes that are inserted into a woman's uterus to prevent pregnancy. Surprisingly little is known about IUDs despite the fact the device is by no means new. It is mentioned in the writings of Hippocrates and in the Jewish Talmud. One reason for the lack of knowledge may be that IUDs cannot be effectively tested on nonhuman subjects. Most drugs can be successfully tested on animals but an IUD can only be tested on women.

---

[8] Ibid.

However, two widely accepted theories as to why the device works have emerged. The first is that an IUD irritates and inflames the uterine wall, making it unreceptive to the implantation of an egg should it become fertilized. The second theory is that the continual effort of the uterus to expel the foreign object by contracting forces the egg out of the fallopian tubes before it is sufficiently developed to implant itself.

Like the pill, annoying but minor side effects are common complications of the IUD; nonetheless, as of 1975, it was used by 3 million to 5 million women. Most frequent complaints were heavy and prolonged menstrual bleeding and menstrual cramps, causing up to 20 percent of IUD users to request removal of the device within a year. More serious side effects were relatively rare. The most common serious complication associated with the use of the IUD was infection. One study revealed that pelvic infection necessitated the removal of an average of two IUDs among 100 users within two years of use. However, evidence indicated that the IUD was not so much a cause of pelvic infection as a contributor to an increase in the severity once infection arose. If treatment was delayed or inadequate, infertility could result. Another potentially dangerous side effect associated with the IUD was piercing of the uterine wall, usually at the time of insertion. Perforations occurred in about 4 in 10,000 insertions, with the risk lowest when the inserter was an experienced physician. Most perforations were of minor consequence, yet if undetected, it could mean that the IUD was not properly situated and therefore ineffective. Regardless of the type of IUD used, a pregnancy that occurred with the device in place was more likely to end in miscarriage.[9]

THE ROBINS COMPANY ENTERS THE BIRTH CONTROL MARKET

The Robins Company introduced its own version of the intrauterine device, the "Dalkon Shield," in late 1970. Its initial success was believed to be related to this country's ongoing "sexual revolution." It was advertised as the first device that could effectively be worn by a young woman who had never borne a child. The device, shaped like a crab with prongs, was difficult to expel, thereby reducing the problem of expulsion so common among young women. By the end of 1973, the shield was being used by approximately 2.2 million of the estimated 5 million American IUD users. Another 1 million shields were sold abroad.[10]

During 1973, however, the Robins Company became aware of some disquieting facts. The accidental pregnancy rate for users of the Dalkon Shield appeared to be substantially higher than earlier estimated. In addition, the company learned of 36 septic abortions among women who became pregnant

---

[9] Ibid.

[10] "A Plague of Problems," p. 35.

while wearing the shield. Of these 36 women, 4 had died.[11] Septic abortions, which can also occur without the use of an IUD, are spontaneous abortions that cause an infection of the uterus lining which can lead to septicemia, a widespread infection of the blood system; this had been identified as the cause of death of all four women.

A spokesman for the Robins Company stated that various studies put the failure rate of the device at between 0.5 to 5.0 pregnancies for every 100 users—a figure comparable to other IUDs on the market. The spokesman also noted that the company changed the Dalkon Shield's labeling in October 1973, to add a warning about "severe sepsis with fatal outcome" associated with pregnancies that occur while the device is in place. The company also alerted the Food and Drug Administration in June 1973, to the rumors about side effects associated with the shield, and gave complete tabulated data to the agency in December. Dr. Fletcher Owen, Robins' director of medical services, reported that the company had put internal and external medical experts to work evaluating the data and was "confident" that the problem wasn't unique to the Dalkon Shield.[12]

However, as a result of the four deaths, on May 8, 1974, Robins Company sent letters to 125,000 (one third) of the physicians in the United States warning them that severe complications, including death, could occur in a small number of women becoming pregnant while wearing the company's Dalkon Shield. The letter urged doctors to remove the IUD immediately if the patient should become pregnant and if that was impossible to give "serious consideration . . . to offering the patient a therapeutic abortion."[13] The letter added that if the patient elected to continue the pregnancy, whether or not the IUD had been removed, the patient should be watched closely. The letter continued, "Furthermore, we suggest that any patient for whom you consider inserting a Dalkon Shield be advised prior to the procedure that a therapeutic abortion may be recommended in the event of an accidental pregnancy."[14]

Based on the information provided in the letter, the Planned Parenthood Federation of America instructed its 700 affiliated birth control clinics to cease prescribing the Dalkon Shield. In Washington, D.C., a Food and Drug Administration spokesman said the agency was attempting to gather data to present along with the Robins' data to two advisory panels. The panels would then recommend alternative courses of action. The spokesman stated "we're trying to see if the problems are peculiar to the Dalkon Shield, or to all IUDs. We'll make a decision as soon as possible, but we've get to get the facts first."[15]

---

[11] Ibid.

[12] Barry Kramer, "Robins Warns That Its IUD May Cause Severe Complications, Including Death," *The Wall Street Journal*, May 29, 1974, p. 8.

[13] Ibid.

[14] Ibid.

[15] Ibid.

ACTION BY THE FOOD AND DRUG ADMINISTRATION

Although the Food and Drug Administration (FDA) was directly involved in the control of IUD devices once marketed, the Robins Company did not have to obtain FDA clearance before marketing its Dalkon Shield. This was because it was a medical device, not a drug, and such devices do not require FDA clearance. However, legislation had been introduced in Congress in late 1971 to require premarket approval, but it had not been passed.

On June 28, 1974, the Robins Company voluntarily removed the Dalkon Shield from the market until questions of safety could be resolved. Seven maternal deaths and ten septic abortions had then been associated with the use of the shield. Still, at this time, the FDA insisted that there was no immediate concern among women using the product, and did not recommend that it be removed as a precautionary step. A few weeks later, the agency issued a bulletin similar to Robins' original letter to physicians. However, the FDA bulletin had a far wider distribution and more emphatically stressed the need for pregnancy testing. The agency also continued to gather data about the extent of use and adverse reactions to all forms of IUDs. In addition, the bulletin asked physicians to report their experience with patient use of IUDs.[16]

On July 5, 1974, it was reported that a 1973 survey by the Health, Education, and Welfare Department's Center of Disease Control of all types of IUDs showed that the Dalkon Shield was linked to a significantly higher number of complications of pregnancy than other forms of IUDs. The study tied the Dalkon Shield to 54 percent of pregnancy complications compared to 46 percent for IUDs known as the Lippes Loop and the Saf-T-Coil. Nonetheless, Dr. Alexander Schmidt, FDA commissioner, stressed that a final decision on banning Robins' Dalkon Shield would not be made until after a review of new evidence that was being gathered from all manufacturers and sought from approximately 300,000 physicians. Several weeks prior to this statement, the two advisory panels mentioned above, after reviewing current evidence, recommended that Dr. Schmidt ban the Dalkon Shield from the market. It was speculated that this would be a serious blow to Robins since the shield was the leading seller in the field and had been adopted for use in most birth control clinics.[17]

In August 1974, after evaluating more recent data, the FDA reported a sharp increase in the number of deaths and uterine infections among women using the Dalkon Shield. An audience of 200 scientists, physicians, and industry representatives were told that the number of deaths and septic abortions associated with the use of the shield had risen to 11 and 209, respectively. The updated information gathered by the FDA's Bureau of

---

[16] "A. H. Robins Will Stop Sale of Dalkon Shield, Pending Safety Study," *The Wall Street Journal*, June 28, 1974, p. 11.

[17] "Ban on Robins' IUD Becomes More Likely after New U.S. Study," *The Wall Street Journal*, July 5, 1974, p. 15.

Medical Devices, also showed that another intrauterine device, the Lippes Loop, was associated with five deaths and 21 septic abortions and another, the Saf-T-Coil, with one death and eight miscarriages, following uterine infection. The findings also revealed that between 1966 and 1974, 8.8 million IUDs had been marketed.[18]

After further investigation, in October 1974, an FDA advisory panel concluded that the Dalkon Shield didn't pose any greater risk to women than other types of IUD contraceptives. An eight-member subcommittee of the Agency's Obstetrics and Gynecology Advisory Committee, which recommends regulatory policy for IUDs, reported that it hadn't found any increased hazard from the use of the shield. "It isn't apparent from the available information that the safety and efficiency of the Dalkon Shield is significantly different from other IUDs," stated the subcommittee.[19] The panel also noted that difficulties associated with the use of IUDs appeared to be higher when they first entered the market, and then decreased with time. The Dalkon Shield was the most recent device to have been introduced, going into use in 1970. In addition, the panel noted that the liberalized abortion laws of recent years had brought more women with contraceptive problems to the attention of physicians at a time when the Dalkon Shield came into widespread use. Two thirds of the women fitted with IUDs during this period were fitted with the shield. At this point, however, the FDA didn't appear to be in any rush to recommend that the shield be placed back on the market. The FDA also planned to require that new cautionary labeling be provided with all IUDs.[20]

In December 1974, in a surprise move, the FDA ended a six-month moratorium on prescription by physicians of the Dalkon Shield. This action, however, was contrary to the recommendations of its Obstetrics and Gynecology Advisory Committee. The 18-member panel believed the moratorium should have remained in effect pending accumulation of definitive data. At a news conference, Dr. Schmidt stated that the agency's actions did not constitute an overruling of the committee's recommendations. The FDA had arranged with Robins to keep a registry of all patients using the device. The company agreed to report the number and kinds of adverse reactions, the rate at which the device was expelled by women, along with other details. Dr. Schmidt stated that the arrangement would allow for collection of the definitive data the committee called for and that he hoped manufacturers of competing devices would also agree to participate in a registry. The FDA arranged with Robins to limit distribution of Dalkon IUDs to doctors who agreed to register each patient at the time of insertion and to keep a detailed record of each patients' experience with the device in order

---

[18] "FDA Links Rise in Deaths to Birth Device," *The New York Times*, August 22, 1974, p. 17.

[19] "Robins' Dalkon Shield Found No More Risky Than Other IUDs," *The Wall Street Journal*, October 14, 1974, p. 2.

[20] Ibid.

to ensure the necessary data. At this time a joint study of the effects of IUDs was initiated by the FDA and the National Institute of Child Health and Human Development.[21]

However, after the FDA action was made public, the Planned Parenthood Association of America announced that it would continue its ban on the current model of the Shield. The ban prohibited the use of the device by its own doctors and clinics. By this time the associated deaths had increased to 14 and septic abortions had grown to 219.[22]

At least one member of the FDA advisory committee disagreed with Dr. Schmidt's explanation of the lifting of the moratorium. Protesting the FDA's action, Dr. Richard Dickey of the Louisiana State University Medical Center argued that the agency action circumvented the recommendations of the committee and might needlessly endanger many women. He believed the moratorium should remain in effect until additional data were obtained. He also felt the majority of the panel agreed with him on this issue.[23]

REACTION BY THE ROBINS COMPANY

After clearance by the FDA, the Robins Company intended to resume marketing of the Dalkon Shield. However, a spokesman for the company stated that as a practical matter resumption probably would not occur until late 1975 so as to allow the FDA to develop new labeling guides for the product.[24] In his message to the stockholders for the year 1974, E. C. Robins, chairman of the board, summarized the company's position, "the company is of the opinion that when appropriately used with proper techniques, the shield's performance has been satisfactory."[25]

In January 1975, the company announced it would collect all unused IUDs in the United States, and fully refund its customers for the unused inventory. The announcement also indicated the company would modify the new shields. The modification would be a change in the "tail" of the Dalkon Shield. All IUDs have a tail consisting of a cord or string which facilitates their removal from the uterus. The old shield had a tail made of a woven, or multifilament string. Some medical scientists argued that it was possible for woven filament to act as a reservoir for bacteria that could infect the uterus when it swells during pregnancy and the tail is drawn into the uterus. Other IUDs, which had a nonwoven, or nonfilament tail, presumably did not harbor bacteria. Robins contended that the multifilament tail was not any more

---

[21] Harold M. Schmeck, "Moratorium Is Ended by FDA on IUD Challenged over Safety," *The New York Times,* December 21, 1974, p. 25.

[22] Ibid.

[23] Harold M. Schmeck, "End of IUD Ban Viewed as Peril," *The New York Times,* January 7, 1975, p. 16.

[24] "A. H. Robins Wins Clearance from FDA to Resume IUD Sales," *The Wall Street Journal,* December 23, 1974, p. 7.

[25] E. C. Robins, *Annual Report 1974* (Richmond, Va.: February 10, 1975), p. 1.

dangerous than the nonfilament tails on other IUDs, but agreed to replace the woven tail when it resumed marketing the Dalkon Shield.

Despite FDA approval to resume marketing, the U.S. Agency for International Development (AID), announced that it did not plan on continuing to supply the Dalkon Shield abroad. About 200,000 of the devices were returned to Robins by AID. A spokesman for AID also stated that due to the medical follow-ups required on the new shield, they had no plans to resume the use of the device. At this same time, the Planned Parenthood Federation of America also announced it intended to return all of its Dalkon Shields to Robins, including 96,000 meant for distribution overseas. Like AID, the Federation did not plan to use the new shield.[26]

LAWSUITS

In late 1974 and early 1975, the Robins Company was inundated with lawsuits brought by customers and relatives of those using the shield. In the company's *1974 Annual Report,* E. C. Robins stated, "unfortunately, the emotionally charged atmosphere of the IUD investigation, stimulated by much publicity, which in many cases was misleading, had led to a large number of lawsuits involving the Dalkon Shield being filed against A. H. Robins."[27] The report noted that as of February 10, 1975, the company had been named defendant in 148 product liability cases which alleged various injuries due to use of the shield. The complaints, in many of the suits, sought punitive as well as compensatory damages. The report further stated the company was insured for potential liability resulting from compensatory damage awards which might be granted. However, exposure to punitive damages was not insurable in most jurisdictions.[28]

On February 6, 1975, a judgment was entered for the plaintiff in a suit filed in Sedgewick County, Kansas. The plaintiff was awarded $10,000 in compensatory damages and $75,000 in punitive damages for injuries allegedly resulting from a uterine perforation caused by a Dalkon Shield. The company planned to appeal the Kansas verdict and denied liability in the remaining liability cases.[29]

As of March 18, 1975, the company had been named defendant in 186 product liability cases involving the shield. The alleged injuries included perforations of the uterus, deaths related to septic abortions, pregnancies followed by therapeutic or spontaneous abortions, and pelvic inflammatory diseases. In its *Annual Report* to the Securities and Exchange Commission, the company stated that suits were pending in approximately 85 courts,

---

[26] "1.5 Million Is Paid to Settle Contraceptive Device Cases," *The New York Times,* October 21, 1975, p. 53.

[27] Robins, Annual Report 1974, p. 3.

[28] Ibid., p. 34.

[29] Ibid.

which in the aggregate sought $110 million in compensatory and $70 million in punitive damages. Robins added that it believed the amounts claimed in many of the cases were inflated and disproportionate to the injuries alleged. The company also noted that beginning March 1, 1975, the aggregate deductible amount for insurance coverage for Dalkon Shield related actions had been increased to $4 million for alleged injuries occurring after that date. Since it was not possible to predict the outcome of the pending suits, the company made no provisions for contingent liabilities in its balance sheet (see Exhibit 1).[30]

By the time Robins filed its Interim Report for the first three months of 1975, another 40 cases had been instituted against the company. In the report, E. C. Robins stated, "given the emotionally charged atmosphere of the FDA's IUD investigation, we anticipate that there will be still more, but it is impossible to predict with any degree of accuracy the number of additional cases, the outcome of any of these cases, or the eventual aggregate financial impact on the company."[31] Still, the company denied liability in all of the cases. The report added that the company continued to believe that when appropriately used with the proper technique, the device was a useful IUD. At that time, Robins still intended to place the shield back on the market. It was estimated that the continued suspension of sales, due to working with the FDA on the development of a registry system, would adversely affect 1975 earnings by about two cents per share.[32]

In July 1975, the company announced the adoption of an accounting procedure that would minimize the effects on current earnings of the potentially heavy expenses that might be incurred from litigation involving the Dalkon Shield. A Robins official said that they had decided to recognize the expenses arising from the lawsuits as a retroactive charge against the earnings of the quarter in which the alleged injury occurred.[33] The earnings for the first half of 1975 did not include charges for settlement of litigation, legal fees, and other expenses involving the intrauterine device. In the Interim Report for the first six months of 1975, E. C. Robins reported that legal charges had reached a total of $1,022,000 after taxes.[34]

DALKON SHIELD REMOVED FROM PRODUCT LINE

Finally, in its Interim Report for the first nine months of 1975, the company announced that in August it had decided to delete the Dalkon Shield from its product line. In the report E. C. Robins verified the decision: "we

---

[30] A. H. Robins Company, *Form 10-K, Annual Report,* December 31, 1974, pp. 20–21.

[31] E. C. Robins, *Interim Report/First 3 Months 1975,* April 25, 1975, pp. 2–3.

[32] Ibid.

[33] "A. H. Robins Uses Plan to Ease Effect on Net From IUD Litigation," *The Wall Street Journal,* July 18, 1975, p. 24.

[34] E. C. Robins, *Interim Report/First 6 Months 1975,* July 24, 1975, p. 2.

had anticipated re-marketing the intrauterine contraceptive device under a patient registry system being developed by the Food and Drug Administration, but with the passing of time we couldn't foresee a date for completion of the design of such a system. The additional delay which thus could have been expected, coupled with the interruption in marketing which had already extended for more than a year and the adverse publicity which had already eroded physician and patient confidence, would have made the successful reentry of the device into the market difficult, if not impossible. We concluded that this unfavorable market prospect for the Dalkon Shield did not warrant further expenditure of company funds and personnel time even though we remain firm in our belief that the device, when properly used, is a safe and effective IUD."[35] Within another month, Robins reported that it had paid $1,548,000 for the settlement of litigation, legal fees, and other expenses involved in the controversy.[36]

The Wall Street Journal in February 1976, reported that the number of civil actions alleging death and injuries had grown to 547. One hundred sixty-seven of these were pending in 48 U.S. District Courts in 28 states, with another 276 pending in state courts. The other 104 cases had been settled, presumably with payment by the company in some, if not all, of the cases. The company did not state the size of its total settlement payments, but it did reveal in 1976 that the company had incurred an aftertax charge of $2.7 million resulting from settlements and costs resulting from the IUD problem.

---

[35] E. C. Robins, *Interim Report/First 9 Months 1975*, October 27, 1975, pp. 2–3.

[36] "1.5 Million Is Paid to Settle Contraceptive Device Cases," p. 53.

EXHIBIT 1

A. H. ROBINS COMPANY
Comparative Balance Sheets
December 31, 1970, 1974, and 1975

	1970	1974	1975
Current Assets:			
Cash	$ 6,770,105	$ 5,004,000	$ 10,872,000
Certificates of deposit	—	10,346,000	16,497,000
Marketable securities—at cost which approximates market	3,813,924	13,878,000	14,394,000
Accounts receivable—less allowance for doubtful accounts	23,413,846	33,011,000	44,104,000
Inventories	21,767,094	49,061,000	49,906,000
Prepaid expenses	3,100,091	4,010,000	4,133,000
Total Current Assets	$ 58,865,060	$115,310,000	$139,906,000
Property, Plant, and Equipment—Net	$ 21,924,959	$ 30,418,000	$ 34,640,000
Intangible and Other Assets:			
Excess of cost over net assets of subsidiaries acquired	25,253,876	36,315,000	42,343,000
Patents, trademarks, goodwill	2,109,164	4,586,000	3,927,000
Deferred charges	938,008	2,696,000	1,580,000
Other assets	361,804	938,000	1,148,000
Total Intangible and Other Assets	$ 28,662,852	$ 44,535,000	$ 48,998,000
Total Assets	$109,452,871	$190,263,000	$223,544,000
Current Liabilities:			
Notes payable	$ 3,152,807	$ 1,784,000	$ 2,681,000
Accounts payable	5,081,687	12,096,000	21,126,000
Long-term debt payable within one year	4,119,590	750,000	750,000
Federal, foreign, and other income taxes	3,565,854	5,145,000	6,752,000
Accrued liabilities	2,415,387	6,076,000	8,210,000
Total Current Liabilities	$ 18,335,325	$ 25,851,000	$ 39,519,000
Long-term debt	11,600,000	5,250,000	4,500,000
Deferred income taxes	—	341,000	794,000
Deferred foreign currency exchange gains	—	1,097,000	10,000
Minority interest in foreign subsidiaries	241,300	29,000	1,446,000
Stockholders' Equity:			
Capital Stock:			
Preferred $1 par—authorized 10,000 shares, none issued	—	—	—
Common $1 par—authorized 40,000 shares	12,712,253	26,127,000	26,127,000
Capital Surplus	347,868	693,000	693,000
Retained Earnings	66,216,125	130,875,000	150,455,000
Total Stockholders' Equity	$ 79,276,246	$157,695,000	$177,275,000
Total Liabilities and Stockholders' Equity	$109,452,871	$190,263,000	$223,544,000

EXHIBIT 2

A. H. ROBINS COMPANY
Statement of Consolidated Earnings
December 31, 1970–1975

	1970	1974	1975
Income:			
Net sales	$132,551,922	$210,713,000	$241,060,000
Interest and other income	551,449	3,143,000	2,279,000
Total Income	$133,103,371	$213,856,000	$243,339,000
Costs and Expenses:			
Cost of sales	41,047,042	71,233,000	89,304,000
Research and development	5,881,875	9,568,000	10,690,000
Marketing, administrative and general	52,663,269	79,209,000	87,362,000
Interest	1,752,838	1,134,000	1,189,000
Litigation settlement and related expenses ...	—	—	5,065,000
Total Costs and Expenses	$101,345,024	$161,144,000	$193,610,000
Earnings before income taxes and extraordinary items	$ 31,758,347	$ 52,906,000	$ 49,729,000
Provision for income taxes	16,030,349	25,989,000	23,895,000
Earnings before extraordinary items	$ 15,727,998	$ 26,917,000	$ 25,834,000
Discontinued operations and loss on disposal	—	—	—
Net earnings	$ 15,727,998	$ 26,917,000	$ 25,834,000
Earnings per Common Share:			
Continuing operations	$ 1.24	$ 1.03	$ 1.02
Discontinued operations and loss on disposal	(0.05)	—	—
Net earnings	$ 1.19	$ 1.03	$ 1.02
Cash dividends	$ 0.40	$ 0.208	$ 0.20
Weighted average number of common shares outstanding	n.a.	26,126,000	26,127,000

n.a. = not available.

EXHIBIT 3
Selected Notes to Financial Statements, 1975

Litigation

A private action which was filed by the Portland Retail Druggists Association on August 6, 1971, as assignee of certain community pharmacies, against the company and several other pharmaceutical manufacturers, is pending in the United States District Court for the District of Oregon. The complaint demands damages for alleged violations of the antitrust laws with respect to the sale of pharmaceutical products in the Portland area. Although the outcome of this case cannot be predicted with certainty, the company does not anticipate that the ultimate disposition of the action will have a material effect on its financial position or operating results.

EXHIBIT 3 *(continued)*

Another antitrust action filed by Medcor, Incorporated seeks damages in the sum of $1,000,000, plus attorneys' fees, from the company and seven other defendant pharmaceutical manufacturers. The complaint which was filed on December 8, 1975, in the United States District Court for the District of South Dakota, Western Division, alleges that the defendants conspired to prevent Medcor from competing with the defendants and to force the plaintiff out of business. Although the factual basis of the plaintiff's claim has not yet been fully developed, the company has denied liability and is not aware of any facts which might result in liability being imposed against it.

As of February 18, 1976, there were pending in various state and federal courts 467 product liability cases, in which the company has been named as a defendant and which allege various injuries arising from use of the Dalkon Shield®, an intrauterine contraceptive device formerly marketed by the company. Approximately 97 other cases involving the Dalkon Shield have been dismissed with prejudice, in most cases following settlement by the company and its insurer. As of February 18, 1976 approximately 200 Dalkon Shield claims which have not resulted in litigation were being evaluated by the company's insurer, and approximately 96 other claims have been settled or withdrawn. The pending cases (as did those dismissed) seek in some instances substantial compensatory damages and in others substantial compensatory and punitive damages. As of February 18, 1976, the company and its insurer have paid the sum of $2,014,000 in full settlement of the 97 cases and 96 claims referred to above. The major portion of the amount paid by the company was charged against the deductibles under its insurance coverage. The company believes that its potential liability for compensatory damages in the remaining cases pending as of that date and claims then under evaluation is covered by insurance except for the unused portion of the deductibles, which is relatively insignificant for policy periods before March 31, 1975 and is approximately $4,000,000 for the policy period April 1, 1975 through February 29, 1976. Exposure to punitive damages is not insurable in most jurisdictions. On February 6, 1975, in a suit originally filed in the District Court of Sedgwick County, Kansas, judgment was entered for the plaintiff for the sum of $10,000 as compensatory damages and $75,000 as punitive damages for injuries allegedly resulting from uterine perforation associated with the Dalkon Shield. This case is presently on appeal to the Supreme Court of the State of Kansas. The company has denied liability in the remaining Dalkon Shield product liability cases and claims. No provision has been made for contingent liabilities which may arise from these actions and claims, since it is not possible to predict their outcome.

Accounting for Litigation Settlements and Related Expenses

During the year 1975, the company incurred a charge of $5,065,000 ($2,739,000 after income tax benefit) resulting from settlement of litigation, legal fees, recall of customers' inventories and other expenses related to the Dalkon Shield. The company believes it would have been preferable under generally accepted accounting principles to accord prior period adjustment treatment to this charge which would have increased 1975 net earnings and decreased 1974 net earnings by $2,739,000 ($.10 per share). However, at the insistence of the staff of the Securities and Exchange Commission, the charge was included in earnings for the year 1975.

EXHIBIT 4

Report of Independent Certified Public Accountants

To the Stockholders and Board of Directors
A. H. Robins Company, Incorporated
Richmond, Virginia

We have examined the consolidated balance sheet of A. H. Robins Company, Incorporated and subsidiaries as of December 31, 1975 and 1974 and the related statements of consolidated earnings, stockholders' equity and changes in financial position for the years then ended. Our examinations were made in accordance with generally accepted auditing standards, and accordingly included such tests of the accounting records and such other auditing procedures as we considered necessary in the circumstances.

Included in the statement of consolidated earnings for the year ended December 31, 1975 is a charge of $5,065,000 resulting from litigation settlements and related expenses (as more fully explained under Accounting for Litigation Settlements and Related Expenses in Notes to Financial Statements), which the management of A. H. Robins Company, Incorporated believes should have been recorded as a prior period adjustment. It is our opinion that it would have been preferable to accord this charge prior period adjustment treatment, which would have increased 1975 net earnings and decreased 1974 net earnings by $2,739,000 ($.10 per share).

As discussed under Litigation in Notes to Financial Statements, the company is defendant in lawsuits alleging various injuries arising from use of the company's products and claiming general and punitive damages. The ultimate outcome of the lawsuits cannot presently be determined, and no provision for any liability that may result has been made in the financial statements.

In our opinion, subject to the effects, if any, on the financial statements of the ultimate resolution of the litigation discussed in the immediately preceding paragraph, the financial statements referred to above present fairly the consolidated financial position of A. H. Robins Company, Incorporated and subsidiaries at December 31, 1975 and 1974 and the results of their operations and the changes in their financial position for the years then ended, in conformity with generally accepted accounting principles applied on a consistent basis.

A. M. Pullen & Company

Richmond, Virginia
February 18, 1976

33. *The Wall Street Journal* versus Combustion Engineering*

On Tuesday, May 7, 1974, *The Wall Street Journal* carried a story written by one of its reporters which stated that Combustion Engineering, Inc., accepted a series of orders for nuclear-power plants involving *"contractual risks unusual for both the company and the industry:* allowing power utilities considerable freedom to back out of deals they had made with Combustion, and extending broad warranties that even cover equipment changes that may be required by future revisions in Atomic Energy Commission rules." Trading in Combustion Engineering stock was halted by New York Stock Exchange officials that same day, but was allowed to resume on Wednesday, at which time trading in C-E common reopened on a block of 120,000 shares at 48, down 27⅛ from its Monday close of 75⅛. Throughout Wednesday's session C-E common traded in a range of 45 to 49½, finally closing on a volume of 332,000 shares at 46½, down 28⅝ from the Monday closing.

Following Duke Power Company's statement on Thursday, May 9, that its 1973 order placed with Combustion Engineering for six nuclear steam supply systems in close competitive bidding had contained no unusual terms or conditions, the per share price of Combustion Engineering common rallied to 55⅛ on Friday, May 10. However, the rally was short lived and Combustion's stock price fell even further during succeeding weeks. As of August 1974, C-E common was trading in the low to mid-30's—a price far below its 1974 high of 106¼.

Exhibit 1 depicts the weekly price range and trading volume of C-E common for months both preceding and following *The Wall Street Journal's* article.

COMPANY HISTORY AND BACKGROUND

Combustion Engineering, Inc., founded in 1912 and headquartered in Stamford, Connecticut, is a leading U.S. producer of fossil fuel steam supply systems and nuclear-powered steam supply systems. In addition to its power

---

* This case was prepared by Arthur A. Thompson, Jr., and A. J. Strickland, III, both of The University of Alabama.

EXHIBIT 1
Weekly Price Range and Trading Volume of C-E Common Stock, March–August 1974

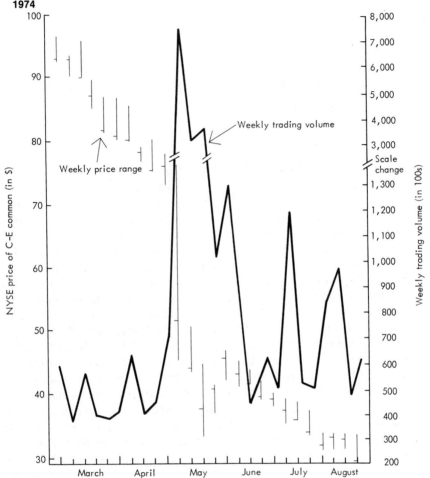

supply system's business, C-E manufactures industrial equipment, heat exchangers, equipment related to oil and gas production, industrial and marine boilers, chemical recovery systems, building products, screening equipment, wire cloth, flat and tempered glass, and metal casting equipment. The company also has an engineering group offering design, engineering, and construction supervision services to a variety of industrial customers.

However, the mainstay of C-E's sales and earnings is derived from power supply systems. In 1973, the steam generating segment of C-E's activities accounted for 44 percent of sales and for 48 percent of earnings; all told, C-E had an estimated 35 percent share of the steam-generating market. C-E's major competitors in the market for these products are General Electric, Westinghouse, and Babcock and Wilcox.

As of 1973, a typical 800 megawatt coal-fired steam generating unit sold for approximately $30 million and had a lead order time of four to five years ahead of initial start-up; a representative 1,300 megawatt nuclear system had a price of about $55 million and required a lead time of eight to ten years. At year-end 1973, C-E had placed three nuclear systems into commercial operation; the industry as a whole had placed 36 nuclear plants into operation, accounting for 5 percent of total U.S. generating capacity. The most recent major development in the industry was the attempt to promote the standardization of nuclear steam supply systems.

RECORD NUCLEAR ORDERS IN 1973

In 1973, electric utility firms in the United States ordered a total of 39 nuclear steam supply systems with an overall generating capacity of approximately 45,000 megawatts, the highest for any year to date. Combustion Engineering received contracts for 11 of these systems, bringing its total awards for nuclear steam supply systems to 25. Orders for the remaining 28 nuclear units were placed with C-E's three principal competitors—General Electric, Westinghouse, and Babcock and Wilcox.

Of the 11 nuclear units ordered from C-E during 1973, 10 were for Combustion's newly announced System 80s. The System 80 is referred to by C-E as "a standardized nuclear steam supply system." Six of the System 80s were ordered by Duke Power Company of Charlotte, North Carolina, an award announced in April 1973 and valued at over $260 million. In July 1973, Combustion Engineering announced it had received a $55 million contract to supply a System 80 nuclear steam supply unit and associated fuel to Washington Public Power System of Richland, Washington. In October 1973, C-E announced the receipt of an award for three 1,300-megawatt System 80s from the Arizona Nuclear Power Project group of southwestern utilities. Combustion's 11th unit was a $50 million contract award from Gulf States Utilities, Beaumont, Texas, for a 950 megawatt nuclear system, announced in February 1973.

The orders which Combustion Engineering received for nuclear units, together with orders received for fossil fuel steam generating units, raised the company's reported backlog of unfilled orders by $995 million during the year to a record $2.6 billion by year-end 1973.

Exhibit 2 shows the weekly pattern of change in Combustion Engineering's stock price and trading volume during 1973 along with the dates of Combustion's announcements of its new contracts on the nuclear units. At year-end 1973, Combustion's stock was selling at an all-time peak of 105, up from a low of 47 earlier in the year; during the same time span, however, the Dow Jones Industrial Average closed the year at 851, down from its January

EXHIBIT 2
Weekly Price Range and Trading Volume of C-E Common Stock, 1973

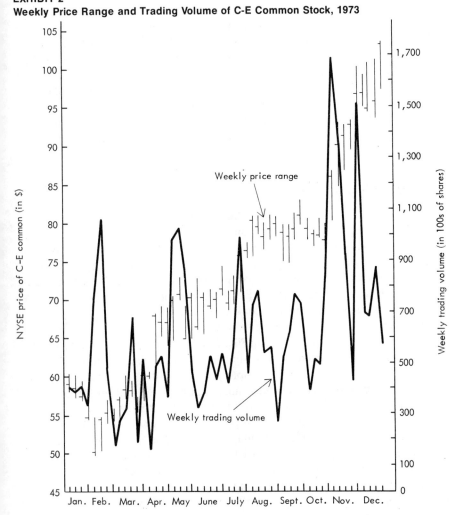

1973 all-time high of 1051. C-E's price/earnings ratio increased during 1973 from around 15 to well-above 20.

C-E'S OPERATING RECORD IN NUCLEAR POWER

For a number of years, Combustion had little experience with nuclear facilities and was hard put to show utility firms that it could build a reliable commercial nuclear system. C-E's first nuclear system, the Palisades plant of Consumers Power Company in Michigan, went on stream in 1972 and began operating within a year of its original schedule. In 1973, two more C-E nuclear systems started operation: one built for the Omaha Public Power

District and a larger unit for the Maine Yankee Atomic Power Company in Wiscasset. The Maine Yankee plant set an industry record by commencing operation just 70 months after the contract was signed.

According to a report in *Business Week's* January 12, 1974 issue, it was the Palisades plant which caused the utility firms to have faith in C-E's nuclear capabilities. Palisades had been running for more than a year when Duke Power placed its unprecedented "six-pack" order with C-E.

However, in August 1973, a minuscule leak of radioactive water was found at the Palisades plant. This led to discovery of erosion in the steel tubes of the two steam generators, a problem which subsequently was traced to a chemical and water reaction rather than to a chemical and nuclear reaction—the former being labeled as much less serious. There was also another discovery at the Palisades plant: evidence of vibration that had damaged the reactor vessel. While this difficulty was also nonnuclear it did result in a plant shutdown of several months.

General Electric and Westinghouse both are reputed to have turned the corner on profits in the nuclear business, after having lost several hundred millions getting started. But, according to estimates of one analyst, Combustion lost $3 million in its commercial reactor activities in 1971, $5 million in 1972, and over $5 million in 1973.[1] Combustion management disagreed with the observation that such losses indicated the company was trying to buy its way into the nuclear market by bidding below costs. On the contrary, C-E's vice president of the power systems group, H. M. Winterton, claimed that "all our plants are sold at adequate profit margins," and attributed the lack of profitability to extended delivery times brought on by environmental hassles and licensing delays at the Atomic Energy Commission.[2] Winterton indicated that public opposition to nuclear sites, fears of thermal pollution, concern over a disposal of spent reactor fuel, and closer AEC surveillance of safety measures was stretching the period between the contract signing and commercial start-up from five-six years to nine-ten years.

The January 12, 1974 article in *Business Week* also reported that Baltimore Gas & Electric Company, which once had intended to purchase four C-E nuclear units, had canceled its orders for two units, blaming AEC licensing delays, rising construction costs, and environmentalist opposition as the causes. In addition, in late 1973, the California Coastal Conservation Commission in a 6-5 vote refused to approve two San Onofre units to be purchased from C-E, even though the units were licensed by the AEC. The two nuclear units canceled by Baltimore Gas & Electric and the two units at San Onofre that could be killed represented about $200 million in Combustion's 1972 order backlog.[3]

---

[1] See *Business Week,* January 12, 1974, p. 49.

[2] Ibid.

[3] Difficulties with the San Onofre project have apparently since been resolved. The October 25, 1974 issue of "Regulatory Operations, Status Summary Report" published by the Atomic Energy Commission reported that the project is proceeding.

COMBUSTION ENGINEERING'S NO PENALTY CLAUSES

In its article of Tuesday, May 7, *The Wall Street Journal* called attention to several provisions in C-E's announced agreements to furnish the 11 units contracted for during 1973. In part, the article said:

> What Combustion didn't announce was that the "orders"—which were actually letters of intent—provided that:
>
>> Gulf States can cancel without cost until the contract is signed. This was supposed to happen last spring, but the contract still is hanging fire.
>>
>> Duke had rights, later maintained in the contract, to cancel all six units for a penalty of $50,000 a month through one year, or four units at no charge through two years, or three units at no charge through three years, or two units at no charge through four years, making four units tantamount to options.
>>
>> Washington Public Power could cancel at no charge through March 1974, making its contract in effect a temporary option.

The Wall Street Journal article acknowledged that because beginning costs are relatively small it has become the custom in the nuclear power-plant industry for manufacturers to grant utilities the right to cancel their orders for new facilities at a very low initial penalty up until the final contract is signed. The cancellation charges usually are set at a level no higher than just necessary to cover the manufacturer's actual expenses. Typically, the penalty is stated in terms of so many dollars per month, with the monthly rate increasing at specified points in order to cover the gradually increasing costs incurred by the manufacturer.

What was apparently unusual in Combustion Engineering's case was that it offered Duke Power and Washington Public Power the right to cancel their orders for a period of several months at no charge after the contracts were signed. In response to *The Wall Street Journal*'s queries about the propriety of such arrangements, Combustion's management pointed out that they knew of no utility which had canceled a nuclear order with one company and placed it with another; hence, they felt that this indicated that any risks associated with no-cost cancellation were minimal. Combustion officials offered *The Wall Street Journal* no explanation as to why the rights of the utilities to cancel their orders at no cost were not mentioned by Combustion when it made its announcements of the new contracts to the public. Nor was any mention made of the perhaps "unusual" and "risky" provisions in C-E's *1973 Annual Report.*

The January 1974 *Business Week* article did give some hint, however, of C-E's cancellation policies. In this regard, *Business Week* reported:

> Combustion Engineering does write some protection into its orders. "None of the contracts we write contains an indefinite cancellation privilege," notes Financial Vice President Lambert J. Gross. Thus, the company, at least collects on work already done, even if the contract is terminated. "Let's say we're

two years into contract with a customer," Gross explains, "and he says, 'Please stop work. We want to cancel.' There are not so many utilities in the country that we can say, 'Get lost, pay up.' " Instead, they negotiate payment on the work completed.

That procedure, Gross adds, is rare. "There is great incentive for the customer to follow through because he won't get anything for the work in progress," he says.

The Wall Street Journal claimed that CE's experience with Washington Public Power gave some indication of the extent of Combustion's exposure to no cost cancellation. According to *The Wall Street Journal*, during the no cost cancellation period Combustion's expenses totaled $300,000 for engineering and unspecified amount for materials needing long lead times. The company's contract administrator allegedly wrote an officer and corporate director an internal memo saying "due to the exposure indicated above, I respectfully request your approval to release this contract for engineering and ordering of basic materials."

COMBUSTION'S WARRANTY AGREEMENTS

In addition to the no-cost cancellation clauses, *The Wall Street Journal* article reported that Combustion agreed to assume the costs for certain major safety and license-requirement changes which the Atomic Energy Commission might impose. Both concessions were allegedly used to help Combustion win its four major nuclear orders in 1973.

According to knowledgeable sources, nuclear contractors and their utility customers have long been wary of the probability that between the time a contract is signed and the agreed-upon facility is licensed for operation, the Atomic Energy Commission could institute new safety requirements costing tens of millions of dollars. To provide for this contingency, it is common industry practice for contracts to call for any AEC-caused cost overruns to be shared between the utility and the manufacturer, with the utility paying at least two thirds of the extra costs. The most far-reaching of the AEC-related clauses pertained to Combustion's contract with Arizona Power where it was agreed that Combustion would pay for any changes to equipment the AEC might require until Arizona received its final operating license from the AEC, a period of as much as six to eight years into the future.

Other warranties which Combustion Engineering granted and which, according to *The Wall Street Journal*, were unprecedented or had not been granted before in combination included the following:

> Agreeing to five-year guarantees on the steam generators installed at Duke Power Company. (Combustion's warranties on generating units sold to other utilities were for only one year or two years at most.)
>
> Agreeing to a $17,000-a-day penalty for late delivery even if the delay was caused by circumstances beyond Combustion's control such as inability to secure necessary materials because of a steel strike or a commodity

shortage. (Construction contracts in the industry usually free manufacturers from responsibility for circumstances beyond their control.)

Agreeing to assume a maximum liability for failure to demonstrate or meet warranties on the Duke Power contract equal to the price of equipment, systems and services furnished—an amount which allegedly could run close to $300 million with overruns. (Industry sources indicated that this was one of the largest express warranties ever granted.)

Combustion's other contract awards also contained substantial dollar penalties for equipment failures and malfunctions. However, the company's *1973 Annual Report* made no reference to the new warranty policies reflected in the contracts the company negotiated during 1973, nor were these policies made public prior to *The Wall Street Journal*'s May 7 article.

In response to *The Wall Street Journal* article, Combustion Engineering executives insisted that company profits were not unduly endangered by the warranty risks. Yet, when told of Combustion's contractual obligations, a number of knowledgeable industry sources expressed skepticism about the wisdom behind such liberal provisions on C-E's part. One industry consultant compared Combustion's warranties to a car dealer promising to install free any safety equipment, such as air bags, that might be required in the next few years. Spokesmen from Babcock and Wilcox, when informed of the warranties with Combustion's name concealed, said that the warranties were unprecedented in the industry to their knowledge. Further investigation revealed that General Electric's published terms of sale were considerably less generous in regards to warranties.

Although acknowledging that Combustion's agreement to assume the entire cost for certain major AEC licenses-requirement changes was unusual, Combustion management said that it gained advance indication of some of the AEC safety criteria under consideration by sending staff members to meet with the AEC's staff. C-E management, therefore, expressed confidence that any new criteria which the AEC might require in the future would be of a nature which would not impair Combustion's profitability on the contracts.

INSIDER SALES OF COMBUSTION STOCK

During the period over which Combustion Engineering was announcing its new contracts, insider-trading reports at the Securities and Exchange Commission showed that a number of the company's officers and directors sold shares of C-E stock. Eight directors or officers sold from one-third to all of their common stock holdings; four others sold more than 1,000 shares net. Only one was a net buyer, and this was in the amount of only 778 shares. Of 24 other insiders who reported trades, including employees, subsidiary officers and their children, all were sellers.

COMBUSTION'S REACTION TO *THE WALL STREET JOURNAL* ARTICLE

On Friday, May 10, 1974, Combustion Engineering wrote its shareholders alleging nine major inaccuracies in the Tuesday article published by *The Wall Street Journal*. The company's letter is reproduced below as Exhibit 3. Also, on Friday, May 10, *The Wall Street Journal* carried a story acknowledging that it had used an incorrect name for one utility company (using Arizona Power and Light Company instead of the correct name of Arizona Public Service Company), and one other possible error (regarding whether or not Washington Public Power's no-cost cancellation clause was controversial within the company). But, otherwise, the *Journal* said it "stood by the gist of its story."

EXHIBIT 3
C-E's Letter to Stockholders

COMBUSTION ENGINEERING, INC.
900 Long Ridge Road, Stamford, Connecticut 06902

May 10, 1974

DEAR FELLOW STOCKHOLDERS:

On Tuesday, May 7, an article appeared in *The Wall Street Journal* concerning your company's nuclear steam supply system business. The article alleged that your company had been awarded large nuclear orders in 1973 following "a decision by its management to take contractual risks unusual for both the company and the industry." The article also implied that there was heavy insider selling of company stock last year which was related to these alleged contractual risks. We want you to know the following:

The *Journal* states on page one: "Combustion Engineering has won a series of nuclear power plant contracts after a four-year lull, a turnaround that now appears to have followed a management decision to take unusual contractual risks."

That statement is not true. Management did not make a decision to take unusual contractual risks. We believe our contract provisions are not unusual in the industry and our customers have confirmed our belief. See the enclosed press releases. Moreover, there was not a "four-year lull". In the four years preceding 1973, C-E was awarded orders for nuclear steam supply systems having a value of over $300 million (exclusive of fuel); in 1970 C-E received approximately 26 percent of the orders placed for such systems in the United States.

The article mentions 1973 contracts with four utilities: Gulf States Utilities, Duke Power Company, Washington Public Power Supply System and Arizona Power & Light Co. (which we believe is a reference to Arizona Public Service Company).

In response to the article, three of the utilities named have issued press releases, copies of which are enclosed. The releases speak for themselves. Since the article appeared, the other named utility, Gulf States, has advised us that the terms of our proposal were essentially the same as those proposed by the other nuclear steam supply manufacturers.

The article states that the "debate over these risks has grown so hot that a contracting executive" went to the *Journal* with documents "describing the new contracts."

EXHIBIT 3 *(continued)*

The facts are that an employee took memos from the company's files and delivered them to the *Journal. We do not know the identity of this employee,* nor are we aware of any hot debate within Combustion over the alleged risks. Each set of bid specifications received from a customer for a nuclear steam supply system is carefully reviewed by various departments and ultimately evaluated by a committee in the Power Systems Group in accordance with our long-standing practice. After full discussion by members of the committee in which any differences in views are expressed, a responsible decision is made.

The *Journal* states that "Gulf States can cancel without cost until the contract is signed" and that the contract is still "hanging fire."

That statement is not true. Your company advised the *Journal* on May 3, prior to the article, that "we are proceeding under various *letter agreements* with the customer" and that a formal document incorporating the terms agreed to has been completed and we expect it will be signed shortly. Since the article we have been in touch with responsible officials of Gulf States. They have advised us that, to their knowledge, no one in a responsible position in Gulf States was contacted by the *Journal* prior to the article. They have also told us the following:

"Gulf States has complete confidence in C-E and has and has had a viable contract with C-E. Also, C-E will be totally and fully paid in accordance with the contract for any work performed and further we are exercising a letter of commitment for the second unit today. Any other details regarding our contracts are confidential; however, the terms of C-E's contract were essentially no different than those of B&W, GE or Westinghouse."

The article states that "Combustion's no-cost deal with Washington Public Power last year was so controversial inside the company that the contract administrator wrote for special approval from a corporate director before releasing the contract for ordering."

The facts are that this award was not controversial within the company, that the request for approval was in accordance with our operating procedures, and that the request was properly made to the officer in charge of the Power Systems Group, who also happens to be a director. Contracts with limited no-charge cancellation provisions, such as the Washington Public Power agreement, are not unusual within the industry.

The article states that C-E "promised to pay for any changes to equipment the AEC might require until it issued the final operating license for Arizona Power & Light, which likely would take six or eight years."

That statement is inaccurate. In the enclosed press release, Arizona Public Service confirms our understanding that "C-E's contractual responsibility for making changes required by the AEC at its own expense is substantially less than that indicated in the May 7 article." The contract provisions referred to are complex and, while C-E does have obligations to make certain changes at its expense should they be required by the AEC, it is not so obligated as to all changes required by the AEC. Management believes these obligations are reasonable and they were taken into account in the pricing of the contract. Indicating that these provisions were not unusual, Arizona Public Service said ". . . evaluation of these proposals showed that, in the aggregate, including price, technical capability, warranties, termination provisions, and all other terms and conditions, all of the proposals were closely competitive and generally responsive to [its] requests for bids."

Various other contract provisions and warranties are characterized in the article as "unprecedented" or "unusually risky".

EXHIBIT 3 *(continued)*

C-E's nuclear proposals are developed in response to detailed bid specifications from its customers, as are the proposals of the other nuclear steam system suppliers. In its release Duke said:

"The terms and conditions of Duke's contract with Combustion are not substantively different from the offerings made by the other vendors at the time this decision was reached . . ."

C-E does have no-charge cancellation provisions for specified periods in some of its contracts. So do other suppliers. The negotiation and award of a nuclear steam supply order is a complex, lengthy process usually involving many months. A utility does not place an order until its studies show that it will require the plant to satisfy its system's needs for electricity. It may want a no-charge cancellation privilege for a limited period, but its requirements do not disappear. Experience has shown that cancellation during the no-charge period is unusual; we know of no utility that has cancelled a nuclear order with one company and placed it with another.

In view of the industry's experience, it has become customary practice for the utility and the nuclear supplier to announce an order when it is awarded, whether or not the definitive contract has been signed and without describing cancellation privileges or other contract details. It should be noted our reported backlog does not include options or amounts attributable to those portions of contracts which are subject to cancellation without charge to the customer.

Insider Selling

The implication that there was improper insider selling is particularly serious and deserves a detailed answer. The facts with respect to sales of stock, which were made known to the *Journal* prior to publication of the article, indicated that the reasons for the sales were not in any way related to C-E's nuclear steam supply business. The *Journal* was also advised that your company is not aware of any developments concerning its business or prospects which would have influenced sales by its officers or directors during 1973.

The article states that your company's officers and directors "were heavy sellers of the Company's stock last year after the good news started to flow . . . Eight directors or officers unloaded from one-third to all of their common stock holdings; four others sold more than 1,000 shares net."

The facts are these:

Six of these "eight directors or officers" sold to liquidate bank loans incurred in 1972 in order to exercise stock options which otherwise would have expired. A seventh was preparing for retirement and sold for personal income tax reasons on the advice of his tax advisers. The total shares sold by the seven amounted to 22,050 shares; the total shares retained by these seven amounted to 20,808. The only person who sold all of his shares sold 500.

The eighth person is a trustee of a trust which sold 17,852 shares in 1973 in order to diversify its holdings. This individual sold 580 shares of his personal holdings because he wanted cash for gifts to his family. At the end of 1973, his personal holdings were in excess of 9,500 shares.

The "four others" who "sold more than 1,000 shares net" sold a total of 7,250 shares. Three sold to liquidate bank loans; the fourth is retired and his personal situation required cash. The combined holdings of the four at year-end amounted to 53,291 shares.

EXHIBIT 3 *(concluded)*

The president of C-E sold no shares during 1973 and holds more than 41,000 shares. The vice president in charge of the Power Systems Group (which manufactures and sells nuclear steam supply systems) sold only 500 shares in 1973 out of total holdings of more than 10,000 shares.

Officers and directors as a group presently hold more than 145,000 shares of your company's stock.

Every officer or director who sold any shares of your company's stock has advised us that his sales were in no way related to C-E's nuclear steam supply business or contracts and that when he made his sales he knew of no material non-public information concerning C-E.

The article states "Of 24 other insiders who reported trades, including employees, subsidiary officers and their children, all were sellers—many, heavy sellers."

This statement refers to sales by persons other than officers or directors who hold restricted stock which they acquired in connection with acquisitions in prior years. For many, C-E stock was the sole or major asset in their investment portfolios; for some, 1973 was the first year in which sales could be made under the securities laws. None of these people was involved in the company's nuclear steam supply business.

In short, these people were *not* "insiders" with respect to C-E's nuclear steam supply business. Some were not even the company's "employees, subsidiary officers or their children." Although we have not been able to verify the remaining holdings of all of these people, the ones we have been able to contact have told us that they continue to hold in excess of 300,000 shares of your company's common stock.

―――――――――――――――

Combustion Engineering has been serving the electric utility industry for over 50 years. We have furnished hundreds of steam supply systems to the industry, and have an established reputation for the quality of our products and their performance. In those five decades we have had a great deal of experience in contracts and business procedures. We have presently operating in the United States three nuclear steam supply systems. One, Maine Yankee, established an industry record of 70 months from the time of award to commercial operation. We have delivered more than 65 nuclear reactor vessels and nuclear steam generators, all of them on the required date.

We regret the loss in stock value that followed publication of *The Wall Street Journal* article. I and my associates in management continue to expect a good year for the company in 1974 and trust that the value of C-E's common stock will reflect these expectations. The record of accomplishment compiled by your company is impressive. Our faith in Combustion Engineering's prospects for continuing growth and success remains strong.

I wish to thank our loyal employees, stockholders and customers for their strong support during this difficult period.

Sincerely yours,

Arthur J. Santry, Jr.
President

STOCKHOLDER ACTIONS

On Thursday, May 16, 1974, a Combustion Engineering shareholder filed a class action suit in Federal District Court in Philadelphia seeking unspecified damages from the company, the New York Stock Exchange, Arthur Andersen and Company, and Wagner, Stott and Company. The shareholder, an owner of 20 common shares, charged that Combustion Engineering and 21 officers and directors, also named as defendants, violated disclosure requirements of the Securities and Exchange Act and engaged in insider-trading violations that enabled them to sell stock at "grossly excessive" prices.

The complaint further alleged that the terms and conditions of many of Combustion Engineering's contracts for the construction of nuclear and fossil power systems were falsely represented, especially terms relating to the warranties and cancellation privileges which Combustion Engineering granted to its customers.

The suit further alleged that the New York Stock Exchange and Wagner, Stott (the NYSE's specialist in Combustion stock) failed to maintain an orderly market in Combustion Engineering shares. (A specialist is charged by the NYSE with maintaining orderly markets in assigned stocks, using his own money to do so when necessary.) On May 8, the first day of trading in C-E stock after the story in *The Wall Street Journal,* the price of C-E's common closed down 28½ points from its previous close on Monday, May 6.

EXHIBIT 4
Auditor's Report to Combustion Engineering in C-E's *1973 Annual Report*

To the Board of Directors and
Stockholders of Combustion
Engineering, Inc.:
    We have examined the consolidated balance sheet of Combustion Engineering, Inc. (a Delaware corporation) and consolidated subsidiaries as of December 31, 1973, and December 31, 1972, and the related consolidated statements of income, retained earnings and changes in financial position for the years then ended. Our examination was made in accordance with generally accepted auditing standards, and accordingly included such tests of the accounting records and such other auditing procedures as we considered necessary in the circumstances.
    In our opinion, the accompanying consolidated balance sheet and consolidated statements of income, retained earnings and changes in financial position present fairly the financial position of Combustion Engineering, Inc. and consolidated subsidiaries as of December 31, 1973, and December 31, 1972, and the results of their operations and the changes in financial position for the years then ended, in conformity with generally accepted accounting principles consistently applied during the periods.

Arthur Andersen & Co.

Stamford, Connecticut
February 15, 1974

Arthur Andersen and Company, Combustion Engineering's auditing firm, was charged with acquiescing in the filing of false and misleading financial and other statements with the SEC. Arthur Andersen's report of its audit of Combustion Engineering's 1973 financial statements and annual report to shareholders is shown in Exhibit 4. Exhibit 5 is a copy of Arthur Andersen and Co.'s letter to C-E following the May 7 *Wall Street Journal* article.

EXHIBIT 5
Arthur Andersen & Co.'s Letter to C-E Following the *WSJ* Article

---

May 14, 1974

Combustion Engineering, Inc.
900 Long Ridge Road
Stamford, Connecticut 06902

Dear Sirs:
You have advised us that the New York Stock Exchange has requested a letter from your independent public accountants with respect to the article published in *The Wall Street Journal* on May 7, relating to certain orders for nuclear power plants that your company received during 1973. This letter is written in response to your request.

We examined the December 31, 1973, financial statements of Combustion Engineering, Inc. and our report thereon dated February 15, 1974, is included in the company's annual report to stockholders. The scope of our examination was set forth in our report which stated that, "Our examination was made in accordance with generally accepted auditing standards and accordingly included such tests of the accounting records and such other auditing procedures as we considered necessary in the circumstances."

Our opinion paragraph included in that same report stated, in effect, that the various financial statements included in the annual report presented fairly the financial position, results of operations and changes in financial position for 1972 and 1973 in accordance with generally accepted accounting principles consistently applied.

We have read the above-mentioned article in *The Wall Street Journal* and have reviewed the terms, conditions and other related financial data with respect to the nuclear orders referred to in such article. There was no information included in the article or arising out of our review which would cause us to change the scope of our examination or our opinion on the consolidated financial statements of Combustion Engineering, Inc. as of December 31, 1973.

We have not examined and do not express any opinion with respect to the company's financial statements for any period subsequent to December 31, 1973.

Very truly yours,

ARTHUR ANDERSEN & CO.

By _____
Edward J. Collins

INDEXES

INDEX OF CASES

A. H. Robins Company 915
Alabama Power Company 809
Alpha Electronic Systems Corporation 403

Better Burgers, Inc. 616
Bright Coop Company, Inc. 281

Champions of Competition versus the Breakfast of Champions:
The Case of Ready-to-Eat Cereals 885
Citizens State Bank and Trust Company (A) 575
Citizens State Bank and Trust Company (B) 587
Consolidated Edison Company 857
Coral Industries, Inc. 599
Cottage Gardens, Inc. 340

Exxon Corporation 722

Fourwinds Marina 250

Hewlett-Packard Company—A Time for Strategy Reappraisal? 191

Ivie Electronics, Inc. (A) 322
Ivie Electronics, Inc. (B) 331

Jackson Brewing Company (C) 362

Kramer Carton Company 510

Mobil Corporation 770
Morgan Hospital 453

Narragansett Bay Shipbuilding and Drydock Company (A) 414
Northern Scrap Processors, Inc. (A) 668
Note on the Petroleum Industry 686

Public Assistance (A) 530
Public Assistance (B) 552

Riverview Apartments 237

Small City (B) 472

Small City (D) 485
Small City (E) 501
Spring Thing, The 440
Steadman Realty Company 264

The Devil's Own Wine Shoppe 641
Triangle Construction Company 657

United Products, Inc... 209
University of Arkansas Athletic Department, The (A) 224
University of Arkansas Athletic Department, The (B) 230

Village Inn 426

Wall Drug Store... 303
Wall Street Journal, The versus Combustion Engineering 931

SUBJECT INDEX

A

Ackerman, R. W., 52 n, 94 n
Acquisition, 77
  horizontal integration, 64
Administrative role of management, 17
Aguilar, Francis, 94 n
Alaskan pipeline, 78
American Biltrite Rubber Company, 71
Andrews, Kenneth R., 5 n, 17 n, 18 n, 19 n,
  29, 30 n, 31 n
Ansoff, H. Igor, 25 n, 38 n, 67 n, 107 n, 109
Argyris, Chris, 144 n
Attiyeh, Robert S., 83 n
Avon Company, 63
Avots, Ivor, 141 n

B

Barnard, Chester I., 17 n, 125 n
Baruch, Bernard M., 91
Beatrice Foods, 12–13
Becton, Dickinson Company, 71
Berg, Norman A., 11 n, 86 n
Blackwell, Roger D., 39 n, 49 n
Boise Cascade Company, 32–33
Booz, Allen & Hamilton, Inc., 80
Bower, Joseph L., 5 n, 17 n, 18 n, 19 n
Boyle, Stanley E., 74 n
Bryant, Paul W., 149–50
Buchele, Robert B., 178 n
Bucyrus-Erie Company, 71
Burroughs Corporation, 106
Business Week, 102
Buskirk, Richard H., 23 n

C

Cannon, J. Thomas, 58 n, 123 n
Carroll, Lewis, 3
Case analysis
  classroom experience, 179–81
  company evaluation, 175–79
  education for management, 170–88

Case analysis—*Cont.*
  objectives, 172–73
  preparing, 173, 181–87
Chandler, Alfred D., 19 n, 24 n, 117, 119, 121
Christensen, C. Roland, 5 n, 11 n, 17 n, 18 n,
  19 n, 31 n, 86 n
Cicero, J. P., 141 n
Clayton Act, 64
Colt, Samuel B., 121
Common thread concept, 38–41, 44
Company evaluation checklist, 175–78
Competition, 97–101
  reaction to, 109–10
Concentration strategy, 86
  horizontal integration, 64
Conglomerate, 39–41
  diversification, 44
Consortium, 78
Control Data Corporation, 106
Cooper Industries, 75–77
Cordtz, Dan, 44 n
Corey, E. Raymond, 119, 120 n, 121, 122 n,
  125 n, 132 n, 138, 143 n
Coun, Robert L., 74 n
Curran, Joseph R., 49 n

D

Dalton, Gene W., 145 n
Dennison, H. S., 125 n
Dirks, Laura M., 97 n, 141
Diversification, 61, 67–78, 86–88
  acquisition, 77
  concentric, 69–70
  conglomerate, 72–74, 87
  internalized growth, 77
  technological, 70
Divestiture, 61, 81–83, 87
Dow Chemical Company, 71
Drucker, Peter, 6–7, 17, 35, 37–38, 60, 64 n,
  67 n, 68, 70, 73 n, 74 n, 78 n, 79 n, 82 n,
  83 n, 116, 122 n, 141, 145, 150 n, 151 n,
  152, 154 n, 155 n, 157 n
Du Pont Company, 117, 121–22

E

Eastman Kodak Company, 71
Economic environment, 101
Entrepreneurship, 17
Environmental threats to organization strategy, 50–53
Ethyl Corporation, 78
Evaluation of company, checklist for, 175–78
Exxon, 78

F

Fayol, Henri, 125 n, 144 n
Fine-tuning strategy, 88–89
Flavin, Joseph, 43
Florsheim Shoe Company, 23 n
Ford, Henry, II, 151
Freeman, R. E., 119 n
Friden, Inc., 42–44

G

Galbraith, Jay R., 125 n, 141 n
Geneen, Harold, 40
General Electric Company, divestiture, 105–7
General Foods Corporation, Post Division, 132–38
General Motors Company, 14, 71
  joint venture, 78
General Precision Equipment Company, 42
Geographical market expansion, 48
Goals of organization; *see* Organization goals
Goldner, C. R., 97 n
Goodman, R. A., 141 n
Goodrich, B. F. Company, 71
Gragg, Charles I., 171, 187 n
Granger, Charles H., 7 n
Grant, W. T. Company, 37–38
Greene, Harold, 148
Gulick, 144 n
Gustafson, Philip, 158, 159 n
Guth, William D., 31 n, 53 n

H

Hall, Jay, 153 n
Hamilton, James L., 57 n
Hamm Brewing Company, 31
Henderson, Bruce D., 49 n
Heublein Company, 31
Honeywell, Inc., 105–7
Horizontal integration, 61, 64, 87
  merger, 87

I

IBM, 105
Innovation strategies, 61, 79
  channel-based, 80
  technologically oriented, 80

Integrated company, 35
International Nickel Company (INCO), 102
International Telephone and Telegraph Company (ITT), 40

J–K

Johnson and Johnson Company, 71
Joint venture, 61, 78–79, 87–88
  foreign companies, 79

Kami, Michael, 29, 86 n
Kipling, Rudyard, 169
Kircher, Donald, 41–43
Kollat, David T., 39 n, 49 n
Koontz, Harold, 153 n, 157 n
Kotler, Philip, 47 n, 79 n, 80 n, 86 n, 143 n

L

Lamont, Lansing, 102 n
Lawrence, Paul, 145 n
Leadership, 153–56
  autocratic, 154
  "great person" concept, 154
  instrumental, 154
  participative, 154
  Theory Y, 154 n
Learned, Edmund P., 31 n, 115, 155 n
Likert, Rensis, 144 n
Ling-Temco-Vought, 81
Liquidation strategies, 83, 87–88
Litton Industries, 41
Lockheed Aircraft Corporation, 5–6
Lorange, Peter, 35 n
Lorsch, Jay W., 144 n, 145 n
Loving, Rush, Jr., 36 n
Lowell, Abbott L., 125 n

M

McCarthy, Daniel J., 49 n
McGregor, 144 n, 154 n
Machiavelli, Niccolo, 21 n, 147, 162
McNair, M. P., 171 n, 182 n
Management; *see also* Manager
  administration, 17
  case analysis, 170–88
  education, 170–88
  entrepreneurship, 17
  leadership, 20–21
  organization building, 18–20
  strategy and policy, 15–18, 22–25
Management controls, 156
  communication, 159
  personnel, 159–61
  reward-punishment structure, 158
Management fit, 39

Manager; *see also* Management
  job demands, 21–22
  leadership, 20–21
  middle level, 161–62
  organization builder, 18–20
  personal values, 53–54
  politics, 161–62
Mansinghka, S. F., 67 n
Market segment, 34
Marshall, George C., 151
Martin, Linda Grant, 13 n
Mee, John F., 141 n
Melicher, Ronald W., 67 n, 75 n
Meman, Lewis, 41 n
Merger, 87
Middleton, C. J., 141 n
Miller, Johnny, 169
Minichiello, Robert J., 49 n
Minnesota Mining and Manufacturing Company, 71
Mission of organization; *see* Organization purpose
Mitchell, David, 63
Mobil Oil Company, 55–56
Monsanto Chemical Company, 130
Mooney, J. D., 125 n, 144 n
Morale, 150, 152
Motivation, 147–50
  positive or negative incentives, 147–48
  tension, 148

N

National Biscuit Company, 72
National Cash Register Corporation, 106
Newman, William H., 4 n
Nicklaus, Jack, 169
North American Phillips Company, 72

O

Objectives of organization; *see* Organization objectives
O'Donnell, Cyril, 153 n
OPEC, 53
Operating fit, 39
Operating strategy, 45–46
Organization concept
  broad based, 34
  integrated, 35
  market segment, 34
  specialized, 35
Organization goals, 10–11
  definition, 15
Organization objectives
  definition, 15
  efficiency, 18
  marketing, 7
  operational, 7
  profitability, 7

Organization objectives—*Cont.*
  resource supply, 8
  social responsibility, 8
  technology, 7
Organization policy, 13–14
  definition, 15
  responsibility for, 15
Organization purpose or mission, 4, 15, 32, 35, 38
Organization strategy, 12–14
  completeness, 58–59
  concepts of, 29–50
  definition, 15
  determinants, 46–59
  environmental threats, 50–53
  explicit, 30–32
  implementation, 115
  managers' values, 53–54
  operating, 45–46
  opportunities, 47–48
  responsibility for, 15
  root, 45–46
  social constraints, 54
  supporting, 45–46
Organization structure
  adequacy, 122
  contingency approach, 145
  cross-functional teams (task force), 141
  customer departmentation, 129, 131
  free-form approach, 144–45
  functional, 127–28
  geographic, 127–28
  matrix, 141–42
  process departmentation, 129, 131
  product group (divisionalized) departmentation, 130, 138–40
  project manager (staff) concept, 140–41
  tight-ship approach, 144–45
  venture team concept, 143
Organizational
  adequacy, 122–23
  diagnosis, 123–25
  competence, 48–49
  development, stages of, 117–22
  personality, 57
  politics, 161–64
  power games, 161–63
  principles, 125–26
Owens-Illinois Company, 72

P

Palmer, Arnold, 169
Performance targets, 10
Personnel management problems, 159–61
Player, Gary, 169
Policy of organization; *see* Organization policy
Power game, 161–64
Price, Raymond, 121

Prince, The, 162
Product-market fit, 39
Product-market opportunities
  company, 47
  environmental, 48
  geographical expansion, 48
  vertical integration, 48
Purex Corporation, 130
Purpose of organization; *see* Organization
  purpose or mission

R

Raymond, Thomas J., 182 n
RCA Corporation, 106
Reeser, C., 141 n
Reilley, A. C., 125 n
Retrenchment Strategy, 61, 81, 87–88
Robeson, James F., 39 n, 49 n
Rogers, David C. D., 5
Root strategy, 45–46
Rosenblum, John W., 52 n, 94 n
Ross, Joel, 29, 86 n
Ruch, David F., 74 n
Rumelt, Richard P., 72
Rush, David F., 67 n
Ryan, William G., 141 n

S

Salter, Malcolm S., 11 n, 86 n, 117 n, 121 n
Sampson, Anthony, 148
Scheuing, Arthur A., 64 n, 79 n, 80 n
Schmidt, Warren H., 156 n
Schoen, D. R., 172 n, 174 n
Scott, Bruce R., 117 n
Sears, Roebuck & Company, 65–66, 121
Selznick, Philip, 49 n
Sheldon, O., 125 n
Sihler, William H., 157 n
Singer Sewing Machine Company, 41–44
Single business, concentration on, 61–64; *see
  also* Specialized company
Smith, George A., Jr., 11 n
Smith, R. A., 24 n
Social responsibility, 54
Socony Mobil Company, 122
Specialized company, 35, 61–64, 70–72
Spirit of performance, 150–53
  reward-punishment structure, 152
Sprague, Philip A., 173 n, 174 n
Sproat, A. T., 155 n
Standard Oil of New Jersey, 78
Star, Steven H., 119, 120 n, 121, 122 n, 125 n,
  132 n, 138, 143 n
Steiner, George A., 5, 6 n, 67 n, 68 n
Strategic
  alternatives, 60–89
  choice, 91, 108–10

Strategic—*Cont.*
  competitive reactions, 109–10
  risk/reward trade-off, 108
  timing strategic move, 108–9
  clusters, 86, 88
  evaluation, 91–108
  fit, 39
  forecast, 94–97
  profile of industry, 91–94
Strategy
  formulation of process, 110–12
  implementation, 115
  of organization; *see* Organization strategy
  options, catalogue of, 84–86
  supporting, 45–46
St. Regis Paper Company, 72

T

Tagiuri, Renato, 53 n
Tannenbaum, Robert, 156 n
Taylor, Frederick W., 125 n, 144 n
Temperamental fit, 82
Textron, 39–40, 82
Thain, Donald H., 117 n
Theory Y style of management, 144 n, 154 n,
  155 n
Thompson. Arthur A., 64 n
Tilles, Seymour, 30 n, 109 n
Timex Company, 50–53
Tracey, Eleanor J., 102 n

U

Underwood, John, 150
United Airlines, Management control, 158–59
United Fund, 130
United States Rubber Company, 121
United States Steel Corporation, 72
Urwick, L., 125 n, 144 n
Uyterhoeven, H., 52 n, 94 n

V–W

Vancil, Richard F., 35 n
Vertical integration, 48, 61, 64–67, 86–87
  backward, 65
  forward, 66

Walker, Arthur H., 144 n
Wall, Jerry, 99 n
Webber, Ross A., 162 n
Weber, Max, 66, 144 n
Westinghouse Electric Corporation, 5
Weston, J. F., 67 n, 74 n
Weyerhauser Company, 72
Wilemon, D. L., 141 n
Wilson Company, 83 n
Wrapp, H. Edward, 22 n

This book has been set in 10 and 9 point Times Roman, leaded 2 points. Part numbers and titles are in 24 point Times Roman; chapter numbers are in 72 point Caslon; and chapter titles are in 18 point Times Roman. The size of the type page is 28 x 46½ picas.